P9-CSH-881

Current Biography Yearbook 2000

THE H. W. WILSON COMPANY
NEW YORK DUBLIN

SIXTY-FIRST ANNUAL CUMULATION—2000

PRINTED IN THE UNITED STATES OF AMERICA

International Standard Serial No. (0084-9499)

International Standard Book No. (0-8242-1004-2)

Library of Congress Catalog Card No. (40-27432)

Table of Contents

Preface v

List of Biographical Sketches vii

Biographical Sketches.......................1

Obituaries...............................611

Classification by Profession—2000 651

Cumulated Index—1991–2000.................655

PREFACE

The aim of *Current Biography Yearbook 2000*, like that of the preceding volumes in this series of annual dictionaries of contemporary biography, now in its seventh decade of publication, is to provide reference librarians, students, and researchers with objective, accurate, and well-documented biographical articles about living leaders in all fields of human accomplishment the world over. Whenever feasible, obituary notices appear for persons whose biographies have been published in *Current Biography.*

Current Biography Yearbook 2000 carries on the policy of including new and updated biographical profiles that supersede earlier articles. Profiles have been made as accurate and objective as possible through careful researching of newspapers, magazines, the World Wide Web, authoritative reference books, and news releases of both government and private agencies. Immediately after they are published in the 11 monthly issues, articles are submitted to biographees to give them an opportunity to suggest additions and corrections in time for publication of the *Current Biography Yearbook.* To take account of major changes in the careers of biographees, articles are revised before they are included in the yearbook.

Classification by Profession and *Cumulated Index—1991–2000* are at the end of this volume. *Current Biography Cumulated Index 1940–1995* cumulates and supersedes all previous indexes.

For their assistance in preparing *Current Biography Yearbook 2000,* I thank the staff of *Current Biography* and other members of The H. W. Wilson Company's General Reference Department, and also the staffs of the company's Computer and Manufacturing departments. In addition, I thank Denise M. Bonilla, a former member of the General Reference Department.

Current Biography welcomes comments and suggestions. Please send your comments to: The Editor, *Current Biography,* The H. W. Wilson Company, 950 University Ave., Bronx, NY 10452; fax: 718-590-4566; e-mail: cthompson@hwwilson.com.

Clifford Thompson

List of Biographical Sketches

Abdullah bin Hussein, *King of Jordan* 1

Christina Aguilera, *Pop singer* 4

Madeleine Korbel Albright, *United States Secretary of State* 7

Tadao Ando, *Architect* 11

Kofi Annan, *Secretary-General of the United Nations* 15

Michael Apted, *Filmmaker and television director* 19

Backstreet Boys, *Pop-music group* 23

Jeff Bagwell, *First baseman with the Houston Astros* 25

John N. Bahcall, *Astrophysicist* 27

Ann Bancroft, *Outdoor adventurer and teacher* 30

Jillian Banfield, *Geologist and educator* 33

Roy Barnes, *Governor of Georgia* 35

John Barry, *Composer for films.* 38

Charlene Barshefsky, *U.S. trade representative* 41

George Bass, *Underwater archaeologist* 45

Kelsey Begaye, *President of the Navajo Nation* 48

Art Bell, *Former radio talk-show host* 51

Joshua Bell, *Violinist* 54

R. Michael Blaese, *Chief scientific officer of Kimeragen Inc. and investigator for the National Human Genome Research Institute* 57

Michael L. Blakey, *Biological anthropologist* 60

St. Clair Bourne, *Documentary filmmaker and social activist* 64

Toni Braxton, *Pop singer* 67

Charles H. Brenner, *Forensic mathematician* 70

Connie Briscoe, *Novelist* 72

E. Margaret Burbidge, *Astronomer* 74

LeVar Burton, *Film and television actor* 77

John Byrne, *Comic-book artist and writer* 81

Don Byron, *Clarinetist* 84

Marcus Camby, *Power forward for the New York Knicks* 87

Bebe Moore Campbell, *Writer* 90

Neve Campbell, *Film and television actress* 93

Alexa Canady, *Neurosurgeon* 96

John Carmack, *Computer executive and software engineer* 98

Rubin Carter, *Human-rights activist and former boxer* 101

Hugo Chávez, *President of Venezuela* 105
Linda Chavez-Thompson, *Executive vice president of the AFL-CIO* 108
Chen Shui-bian, *President of Taiwan* 111
Margaret Cho, *Actress and comedian* 113
Helen Clark, *Prime Minister of New Zealand* 116
Kevin Clash, *Puppeteer for* Sesame Street*'s Elmo* 119
Eva McPherson Clayton, *U.S. Representative from North Carolina* 121
Jackie Collins, *Novelist* 124
Susan Collins, *U.S. Senator from Maine* 127
Ward Connerly, *Chairman of the American Civil Rights Institute* 130
Russell Crowe, *Actor* 134
Clive Cussler, *Author of the "Dirk Pitt" novels and founder of the National Underwater and Marine Agency* 137
Raymond V. Damadian, *Developer of magnetic resonance imaging (MRI)* 140
Clive Davis, *Businessperson, recording-industry executive, and record producer* 142
Rosa DeLauro, *U.S. Representative from Connecticut* 145
Felix Dennis, *Publisher of the magazine* Maxim 147
Daljit Dhaliwal, *Journalist and television news anchor* 150
Ernest Dickerson, *Cinematographer, screenwriter, and film director* 153
Dixie Chicks, *Country-music group* 157
David C. Driskell, *Painter, educator, art historian, art collector, and curator* 159
Michael Clarke Duncan, *Actor* 163
Charles S. Dutton, *Actor and director* 165
Dave Eggers, *Editor of* McSweeney's, *writer, and graphic artist* 169
Ruth Ellis, *Gay-rights activist* 172
Roland Emmerich, *Film director, producer, and screenwriter* 175
Joseph Estrada, *President of the Philippines* 178
Nancy Evans, *Co-founder, president, and editor in chief of iVillage.com: The Women's Network* 181
John Eyler, *President and CEO of Toys R Us Inc.* 183
Shawn Fanning, *Founder of Napster* 185
Gloria Feldt, *President of Planned Parenthood Federation of America* 189
David Fincher, *Filmmaker and music-video director* 191
Carleton Fiorina, *CEO of Hewlett-Packard* 193
Ric Flair, *Professional wrestler* 196
Tom Fontana, *Television producer and writer* 199

Norman Foster, *Architect* 202

Kirk Franklin, *Gospel singer, songwriter, and record producer* 205

Lenora Fulani, *Political activist* 208

Bonnie Fuller, *Editor of* Glamour *magazine* 212

James Gandolfini, *Star of the HBO series* The Sopranos 215

Martin Garbus, *Lawyer* 217

Nomar Garciaparra, *Shortstop for the Boston Red Sox* 220

Jane F. Garvey, *Director of the Federal Aviation Administration* 223

Andrei Gavrilov, *Pianist* 226

Elizabeth George, *Mystery writer* 229

Andy Goldsworthy, *Sculptor and photographer* 232

Jeff Gordon, *Professional stock-car racer* 234

Tipper Gore, *Social activist, photographer, and writer* 238

Macy Gray, *Singer* 241

Tim Green, *Writer and former professional football player* 243

Maurice R. Greenberg, *Chairman and CEO of American International Group Inc.* 246

Brian Greene, *Physicist* 249

Robert Guillaume, *Film and television actor* 252

Buddy Guy, *Blues musician* 255

Carol Guzy, *Photojournalist* 258

Conrad L. Hall, *Cinematographer* 260

Roy Hargrove, *Jazz trumpeter* 263

Mary Harron, *Film and television director* 266

Zahi Hawass, *Archaeologist, Egypt's undersecretary of state for the Giza Monuments, and director of the Pyramids* 269

Tony Hawk, *Skateboarder and entrepreneur* 273

April Heinrichs, *Head coach of the U.S. Women's National Soccer Team* 275

Orlando Hernandez, *Pitcher for the New York Yankees* 277

Paloma Herrera, *Principal dancer with American Ballet Theatre* 281

Marshall Herskovitz, *Television and film producer and director* 284

James Hetfield, *Lead singer and rhythm guitarist for Metallica* 286

Homer H. Hickam Jr., *Aerospace engineer and writer* 290

Julia "Butterfly" Hill, *Environmental activist* 293

Mike Holmgren, *General manager, head coach, and executive vice president of football operations for the Seattle Seahawks* 296

Sarah Blaffer Hrdy, *Primatologist and anthropologist* 300

Cathy Hughes, *Founder and chair of Radio One network* 303

D.L. Hughley, *Comedian and television actor* 306

Steve Irwin, *Herpetologist and wildlife conservationist* 308
Molly Ivins, *Journalist and political commentator* 310
John Paul II, *Supreme Pontiff of the Roman Catholic Church* 313
Dwayne "The Rock" Johnson, *Professional wrestler* 318
Randy Johnson, *Pitcher for the Arizona Diamondbacks* 321
Angelina Jolie, *Actress* 324
Lionel Robert Jospin, *Prime Minister of France* 326
Ashley Judd, *Actress* 330
Andrea Jung, *President and CEO of Avon Products Inc.* 333
Roger Kahn, *Writer* 336
Janusz Kaminski, *Cinematographer and film director* 339
Mel Karmazin, *President and CEO of CBS Corp.* 341
Ben Katchor, *Cartoonist* 343
Claudia J. Kennedy, *Retired three-star general in the U.S. Army and former army deputy chief of staff for intelligence* 347
Thomas Kinkade, *Artist and entrepreneur* 349
Kim Komando, *Radio host and journalist* 351
Tim Koogle, *President and CEO of Yahoo!* 354
Rem Koolhaas, *Architect* 356
Michael Kors, *Fashion designer* 359
Diana Krall, *Jazz pianist and vocalist* 363
David Lang, *Composer* 365
Liz Lerman, *Founder and artistic director of the Liz Lerman Dance Exchange* 368
Lil' Kim, *Rap singer and record-company executive* 371
Liza Lou, *Artist* 373
Rob Lowe, *Actor* 377
Laurie Marker, *Co-founder and director of the Cheetah Conservation Fund* 380
Ellis Marsalis, *Jazz musician and teacher* 383
Steve Martin, *Actor, comedian, and writer* 385
Christian McBride, *Jazz bassist* 389
Tim McCarver, *Baseball commentator* 392
James McDaniel, *Actor* 395
Gerald W. McEntee, *President of the American Federation of State, County, and Municipal Employees* 396
Kevin McKenzie, *Artistic director of American Ballet Theatre* 399
Vashti Murphy McKenzie, *African Methodist Episcopal bishop* 403
Kate Michelman, *President of the National Abortion and Reproductive Rights Action League* 405
Arnon Milchan, *Film producer and entrepreneur* 408

Ennio Morricone, *Film composer and arranger* 411
Michael Moschen, *Juggler* 414
Walter Murch, *Film editor, sound designer, writer, and director* 417
Dikembe Mutombo, *Center for the Atlanta Hawks* 419
'N Sync, *Pop-music group* 422
Nursultan Nazarbayev, *President of Kazakhstan* 425
Edward Norton, *Actor, director, and screenwriter* 428
Lynda Obst, *Film producer and writer* 431
Michael Palin, *Writer, actor, and founding member of* Monty Python's Flying Circus 434
Francine Patterson, *Zoologist and animal-rights activist* 437
Penn & Teller, *Magicians and comedians* 439
Robert Pittman, *President and COO of America Online* 442
Sidney Poitier, *Actor and director* 447
Sandy Powell, *Costume designer* 451
Vladimir Putin, *President of Russia* 453
Franklin D. Raines, *Chairman and CEO of the Federal National Mortgage Association (Fannie Mae)* 456
Steven Redgrave, *Rower* 459
Judith Regan, *President of ReganBooks* 462
Willy T. Ribbs, *Race-car driver* 465
Richard Riordan, *Mayor of Los Angeles* 468
Eloy Rodriguez, *Plant chemist and educator* 472
Ileana Ros-Lehtinen, *U.S. Representative from Florida* 475
Karl Rove, *Political consultant* 478
J. K. Rowling, *Author of the "Harry Potter" series of children's books* 481
Ann Rule, *True-crime writer* 484
Matthew Rushing, *Dancer* 488
Scott Sassa, *President of NBC West Coast* 490
Michael Saylor, *Co-founder and CEO of MicroStrategy, Inc.* 493
Marjorie Scardino, *CEO of Pearson PLC* 496
Miriam Schapiro, *Artist* 499
André Schiffrin, *Co-founder, director, and editor in chief of the New Press* 502
Chloë Sevigny, *Actress and model* 505
Jenny Shipley, *Leader of the National Party of New Zealand* 508
Alvaro Siza, *Architect* 511
Theda Skocpol, *Social scientist and educator* 514
Frederick W. Smith, *Founder and head of Federal Express* 517

Robert Smith, *U.S. Senator from New Hampshire* 520
Zadie Smith, *Writer* 523
Aaron Sorkin, *Screenwriter, playwright, and television producer* 525
Britney Spears, *Pop singer* 528
Brent Staples, *Editorial writer for the* New York Times 530
Robert A. M. Stern, *Architect, architectural historian, and dean of the Yale School of Architecture* 532
Alice Stewart, *Epidemiologist* 536
George Strait, *Country-and-western singer* 540
Hilary Swank, *Actress* 543
Richard L. Tafel, *Executive director of the Log Cabin Republicans* 545
Strobe Talbott, *Deputy Secretary of State* 548
Pamela Thomas-Graham, *CEO of CNBC.com and mystery writer* 552
Rupert Thomson, *Novelist* 555
Tom Tomorrow, *Political cartoonist* 558
David Trimble, *First Minister of Northern Ireland and leader of Ulster Unionist Party* 561
Felix Trinidad, *Boxer* 564
Neil de Grasse Tyson, *Director of the Hayden Planetarium* 567
Atal Behari Vajpayee, *Prime Minister of India* 570
Patricia M. Wald, *International War Crimes Tribunal judge and former U.S. Federal Appeals Court judge* 573
Jay Walker, *Founder and vice chairman of Priceline.com* 576
Kara Walker, *Artist* 579
Diane Warren, *Songwriter* 583
Meg Whitman, *CEO of eBay* 585
Jeffrey Wigand, *Educator, founder of Smoke-Free Kids, and former executive with the Brown & Williamson tobacco company* 588
Kevin Williamson, *Film director, producer, and screenwriter* 591
James Lee Witt, *Director of the Federal Emergency Management Agency* 594
James D. Wolfensohn, *President of the World Bank* 597
Yohji Yamamoto, *Fashion designer* 601
Dwight Yoakam, *Country-and-western singer, actor, and director* 604
Dolora Zajick, *Opera singer* 607

Current Biography Yearbook 2000

Current Biography Yearbook 2000

Courtesy of the Embassy of Jordan

Abdullah bin Hussein

Jan. 30, 1962– King of Jordan. Address: Royal Palace, Amman, Jordan; c/o Embassy of Jordan, 3504 International Drive N.W., Washington, DC 20090

On February 7, 1999, within hours of the death of King Hussein, the Parliament of Jordan installed Abdullah, the oldest of Hussein's sons, as the nation's new king. Formally, Abdullah is known as King Abdullah II of the Hashemite Kingdom of Jordan. King Hussein, who ruled Jordan for 46 years, "was a father to every one of you, as he was my father," Abdullah said during a televised address after he became monarch. "Today you are my brothers and sisters and you are dear to me. We will preserve the course that Hussein set." Educated mostly in the West, Abdullah made his career in the military; he was serving as commander of Jordan's Special Forces when, on January 25, 1999, in an action that took Jordan and the rest of the world greatly by surprise, the gravely ill Hussein removed the title of crown prince from his brother Hassan, who had held it for 34 years, and conferred it on Abdullah. Its unexpectedness notwithstanding, the transfer of power from Hussein to Abdullah caused only mild anxiety within Jordan or elsewhere.

One week after Abdullah became king, he seemed to Scott MacLeod, writing for *Time* (February 15, 1999), to look "almost too young for the job"; nevertheless, MacLeod continued, "outwardly at least he is unmistakably Hussein's son. Like his father, he leaned forward on the edge of his seat as he chatted informally last week with half a dozen journalists, displaying the same self-confidence, modesty, and British-accented speech. He parried questions as if he had been doing so all his life, instead of literally for the first time. He has stepped smartly into his new role." "I have my own areas of interest, the economy, things I'd like to concentrate on as things settle down," Abdullah told MacLeod and the other interviewers. "But you are not going to see anything different. His Majesty [King Hussein] has given me a mission, and I will carry it out to the letter."

Abdullah bin Hussein was born on January 30, 1962 in Amman, Jordan. He is descended from the Hashemite clan, which traces its ancestors to the prophet Muhammad, the founder of Islam, who lived from about 570 to 632 A.D. Abdullah and his brother, Prince Faisal, and sisters, Princess Zein and Princess Aisha, are their father's children by his second wife, Princess Muna, who was born Antoinette ("Toni") Gardiner in Great Britain; Hussein and Muna, who married in 1961, divorced in 1972. Abdullah also has a half-sister, Princess Alia, from his father's first marriage, which also ended in divorce; a half-sister, Princess Haya, a half-brother, Prince Ali, and an adopted sibling from his father's third marriage, which ended in 1977 with the queen's death in a helicopter crash; and two half-brothers, the princes Hamzah and Hashim, and two half-sisters, the princesses Iman and Raiyah, from his father's union with the former Lisa Halaby, an American citizen of Arab descent, who became Queen Noor after marrying Hussein, in 1978.

Abdullah's paternal great-grandfather, Abdullah I, was the first leader of what is now Jordan. From 1516 until 1920, the land was part of the Ottoman Empire, which was ruled by the Turks. Turkey, which sided with Germany and the other Axis powers during World War I, lost control of the area following the victory of Great Britain and its allies in the war; the League of Nations, which grew out of the peace treaties that ended the war, made Transjordan, as the land was called, a protectorate of Great Britain. In 1923 Britain formally recognized Transjordan as a state, with Abdullah I—then known as Emir Abdullah—as its head. The country gained full independence, as a constitutional monarchy, in early 1946, and two months later the Parliament of the newly named Hashemite Kingdom of Jordan proclaimed Abdullah king. In 1951 Abdullah was assassinated by a Palestinian nationalist during a visit to a mosque in Jerusalem. His successor, his son Talal, suffered from schizophrenia, and within a year of his being crowned king, the Parliament forced him to abdicate. According to the Jordanian constitution, the crown prince, Talal's son Hussein, was too young to become king, so a regency council appointed by Parliament governed Jordan until Hussein's 18th birthday (according to the Muslim calendar), in 1953, when he ascended to the throne. Hussein's son Abdullah was named Jordan's crown prince when he was a year old. After the boy turned three, Hussein decided that, in light of the many attempts on his own life, he should rule out the possibility that his successor would be a small child, and he chose his brother Hassan, who was then 18 years old, to be next in line to the throne. (This appointment required a change in the Jordanian constitution, such that a brother of a king as well as a son can be an heir to the throne.)

Abdullah started his schooling as a toddler, at the Islamic Educational College. Beginning at age four he attended St. Edmund's School, in Surrey, England. He later entered the Eaglebrook School, a Massachusetts prep school, where he was often bullied and even beaten by other students. At the beginning of his 10th-grade year, he transferred to the Deerfield Academy, another residential prep school in Massachusetts, where he became expert in wrestling. According to Kim Hubbard in *People* (February 22, 1999), he was reluctant to reveal his royal pedigree to other students, and for some time he pretended that his father owned a telephone company. In a conversation with Jeffrey Goldberg, who profiled him for the *New York Times Magazine* (February 6, 2000), Abdullah described the time he spent at Deerfield as "the three best years of my life."

After earning his high-school diploma, in 1980, Abdullah enrolled at the Royal Military Academy at Sandhurst, England. (Hussein had taken an accelerated, six-month course there in 1952, after learning that the Jordanian Parliament had proclaimed him Talal's successor.) He took classes at the academy for three years and then enrolled at Oxford University, in England, where he studied international affairs for a year. Abdullah is fluent in English; his knowledge of Arabic is weaker.

Upon his return to Jordan, in 1984, Abdullah became a first lieutenant in the Jordanian army, serving as a platoon commander and company second-in-command in the 40th Armored Brigade. During the following years, according to the Jordan Travel Exchange (on-line), he interrupted his military service to take courses at three institutions overseas: the School of Foreign Service at Georgetown University, in Washington, D.C., where he was a fellow, and two military colleges in Great Britain. Back in Jordan he eventually achieved the rank of general and became commander of the Special Forces, an offshoot of the army that helps to maintain order within the country. Abdullah inspired strong loyalty among his officers, and according to the Jordan Travel Exchange, in 1998 many Jordanians speculated that Hussein intended someday to name Abdullah chief of land forces.

In 1992 King Hussein underwent surgery to remove malignant tumors from his ureter and kidney. During the next six years, he seemed to be cancer-free. Then, in August 1998, he revealed that he had again been diagnosed with cancer. (This time it was non-Hodgkin's lymphoma, a cancer of the lymphatic system.) Hussein made the disclosure to his subjects via a satellite transmission from the Mayo Clinic, in Rochester, Minnesota, where he had begun getting chemotherapy treatments. He remained at the clinic for the next six months. During his absence from Jordan, Crown Prince Hassan took charge of the government and reported back to Hussein on his activities. Aides of Hussein's also kept him apprised of what Hassan was doing, and according to various sources, the king learned that Hassan—who at that point had been crown prince for over three decades—was approaching his duties not like someone who knew he was filling in temporarily but rather like a person who was trying to put his own stamp on the kingship, and who even acted as if the throne would soon be his. Moreover, it was public knowledge that Hassan's wife was making plans to redecorate parts of the palace, under the assumption that she would soon be living there as queen. In addition, Hassan refused to promise Hussein that if he became king, he would name one of Hussein's sons, rather than his own son, Prince Rashid, as the heir to the throne.

On January 19, 1999 Hussein returned to Jordan and announced to his subjects that his treatment had succeeded in destroying his cancer. At the same time he sent a 14-page, handwritten letter to Hassan (the whole of which was later read aloud on Jordanian television) in which he accused Hassan of needlessly interfering in the affairs of the army and navy and of instigating the spread of lies about Queen Noor and his and Noor's children with the aim of sullying their reputations. Days later Hussein's doctors discovered a resurgence of his cancer, and it became plain that the king was gravely ill. Only a week after arriving back in Jordan, he returned to the Mayo Clinic to undergo what proved to be an unsuccessful bone-marrow transplant. Before doing so, he stripped Hassan of the title of crown prince and bestowed it on Abdullah. The king's choice of successor was unexpected, because it had been widely believed that Prince Hamzah was his favorite son and that he had hoped Hamzah would someday succeed him. He reportedly turned to Abdullah because he feared that Hamzah, who was still in his teens, lacked sufficient maturity to take on the burdens of the throne. "I feel sorry for Abdullah," a friend of the royal family told an interviewer for *Newsweek* (February 8, 1999). "He's got his father's common touch, but none of his charisma." "By most accounts," *Newsweek* reported, "Hamzah outshines his half-brother in character and personality and in his command of Arabic." On a more complimentary note, *Newsweek* also quoted a senior official in the administration of President Bill Clinton as saying, "Everybody who has met Abdullah thinks he's a savvy guy who's got a lot of leadership skills."

On February 6 King Hussein was flown back to Amman, where he died the next day. As many commentators pointed out, the vast majority of Jordanians had known no other king than Hussein, and he had maintained what *Newsweek* described as "a close, almost fatherly relationship" with his subjects. His death triggered a massive outpouring of grief on the streets of Amman. Outside of Jordan, too, Hussein was mourned, as a major force for peace and stability in the volatile Middle East. As the ruler of a small but strategic country that shares a long border with Israel and that has sheltered a huge Palestinian refugee community, he had steered a precarious course with bravery, agility, and finesse. He had played a vital role in negotiating a peaceful resolution of the Palestinian question; in 1994, along with Prime Minister Yitzhak Rabin of Israel, he had signed a peace treaty bringing to an end the tacit state of war that had existed between the two countries since the Arab-Israeli War of 1948. Thus when Abdullah, a few hours after his father's death, placed his right hand on the Koran, Islam's holy book, declared his loyalty to Jordan and its constitution before a joint session of the country's two houses of Parliament, and became the new king of Jordan, he was filling the place of a man beloved among his people and highly respected as a senior world statesman.

Abdullah was also accepting a degree of responsibility for an array of serious domestic problems. With an area of 34,442 square miles (slightly more than the state of Maine), most of which is desert, Jordan must support a population currently estimated at more than five million people, well over half of whom are of Palestinian descent. The past half century has seen an influx of hundreds of thousands of Palestinians, as a result of armed conflicts between the Arab states and Israel and among the Arab states—for example, more than 300,000 Palestinians flocked into Jordan after Iraq invaded Kuwait in 1991; this has greatly strained the economy, as has the country's high birth rate. (Currently, the population is increasing by 2.9 percent annually.) Natural resources, including water, are scarce, and great quantities of food have to be imported. The nation's foreign debt amounts to some $7 billion. According to the *Political Handbook of the World: 1998*, the unemployment rate is officially 15 percent but may be as high as 25 percent; at least a third of the population lives below the poverty line, and the gap between rich and poor has been widening. About 16 percent of Jordanian men and more than half the women are illiterate. Abdullah must also deal with continuing unhappiness among Jordanians with the 1994 peace treaty between their country and Israel. In addition, he must grapple with rivalries and simmering resentments within the Hashemite dynasty. In the area of foreign affairs, Abdullah faces the ongoing task of maintaining friendly relations with Jordan's Arab neighbors—prominent among them Syria, Iraq, and Saudi Arabia, with each of which it shares a border—as well as with Israel. Fred Halliday, a professor of international relations at the London School of Economics and Political Science, observed to Barry Came for *Maclean's* (February 15, 1999) that King Hussein "was forever walking the tightrope" in dealing with Jordan's neighbors. "The big question now," he said, "is whether Hussein's son, Abdullah, is going to be as good a tightrope walker as his father."

Eager to "reassure our nationals, many of whom had worried that Jordan might have severed too many Arab bonds" under King Hussein, as he told Douglas Jehl for the *New York Times* (May 7, 1999), Abdullah visited Jordan's Arab neighbors before making his first official visit to Israel, on April 23, 2000. During his stay in Israel, which lasted only four hours, the king met with the nation's prime minister, Ehud Barak, and members of the Israeli cabinet. Their talks focused on the possibilities of increasing trade between Israel and Jordan, as one means of bolstering Jordan's sluggish economy. Although Hussein had hoped that his nation's 1994 peace treaty with Israel would lead to an expansion of trade and greater Israeli investment in Jordan, as of mid-2000, as William A. Orme Jr. reported in the *New York Times* (April 24, 2000), "commerce between the two countries still constitute[d] barely 5 percent of Jordan's total foreign trade and less than 1 percent of Israel's." According to Orme, Abdullah "is also actively courting Israeli high-tech entrepreneurs." The king has called upon Jordan's major creditors—Japan, France, and Germany—to forgive a large portion of the nation's approximately $7 billion foreign debt. (In 1998 the United States erased $700 million of Jordan's debt to the American government.) In April 2000 Jordan joined the World Trade Organization. On another front, King Abdullah was instrumental in engineering the peace talks held in Washington, D.C., in December 1999 between Farouk al-Shara, the foreign minister of Syria, and Prime Minister Barak; the goal of the talks was to end the state of war that has existed between Israel and Syria for half a century. (As of the fall of 2000, that goal remained unrealized.)

As one means of displaying his concern with domestic problems, on several occasions Abdullah has gone out in public in disguise, to get a firsthand glimpse of everyday life for ordinary Jordanians. Traveling incognito, he has thus far visited, among other places, a local office of the finance ministry and a hospital; at both sites, he found service to the public seriously wanting, and he promised to attack the kinds of problems he had witnessed. When William A. Orme Jr., interviewing him for the *New York Times* (February 6, 1999, on-line), asked him if "under his reign," the Hashemite dynasty would "subordinate its near-feudal power to a constitutionally protected parliament," Abdullah answered, "Democracy is not something that can be done overnight. It is a learning experience. It is also a discipline. Because we have a democracy, it doesn't mean that people can take things into their own hands."

King Abdullah and his Palestinian-born wife, Rania, who was given the title of queen on March 21, 1999, were married in 1993. The couple have a son, Hussein, born in 1994, and a daughter, Iman, born in 1996. Abdullah has many friends among the members of other Arabic royal families. "We went to the same schools," he explained to William A. Orme Jr. "We ate in the same restaurants. We like the same movies. We have a lot in common." His recreational interests include racing cars, collecting antique weapons, and engaging in water sports. During a conversation recorded for ABC News (May 18, 1999, on-line), Peter Jennings noted that Abdullah had referred to his father "on more than one occasion" as "first and foremost a teacher," and he asked the new king what his father had taught him that was "most important" to him now. "He showed me his heart . . . ," Abdullah answered. "I think his humanity, his . . . caring about people, that was the secret to my father. He didn't put himself above the law. He didn't put himself above other people, and that was a great example for us to be brought up with." — M.H.

Suggested Reading: *ABCNews.com* (on-line) May 18, 1999; CNN (on-line), Feb. 7, 1999, with photos; Jordan Travel Exchange (on-line); *Maclean's* p37 Feb. 15, 1999, with photo; *New York Times* A p4 May 7, 1999, with photo, A p1+ Aug. 9, 1999, with photos; *New York Times* (on-line), Jan. 24, 1999, Jan. 26, 1999, Feb. 1, 1999, Feb. 6, 1999; *New York Times Magazine* p42+ Feb. 6. 2000, with photos; *Newsweek* p38+ Aug. 10, 1998, with photos, p40+ Feb. 8, 1999, with photos; *Time* p35 Feb. 8, 1999, with photo, p23+ Feb. 15, 1999, with photo

---

Aguilera, Christina

(ah-gwih-LAIR-uh)

Dec. 18, 1980– Pop singer. Address: c/o BMG Entertainment, 1540 Broadway, New York, NY 10036-4039

Albert Sanchez/Courtesy of RCA Records

"Pop is actually my least favorite kind of music, because I think it lacks real depth," the singer Christina Aguilera told a reporter for the MTV Radio Network, as quoted on an MTV Web site. That revelation notwithstanding, Aguilera's singles "Genie in a Bottle" and "What a Girl Wants" each remained in the number-one spot on the pop charts for weeks, and her self-titled debut album has sold almost seven million copies since its release, in August 1999. Many music critics agree that, unlike a majority of the teen singing sensations currently popular with young audiences, Aguilera shows real talent and promise. In *Time* (August 16, 1999), for example, David E. Thigpen wrote that she has "a crystalline voice full of wonderful shadings and with a soulful ring that sets her apart in the over-hyped teen market." The *Washington Post* staff writer Richard Harrington, in an article dated February 13, 2000 and posted on Aguilera's official Web site, declared, "Aguilera separates herself from the pack the moment she opens her mouth. She's blessed with a true powerhouse voice, one that belies both her small frame and her youth." Frequently referred to in the media as the next Mariah Carey or Whitney Houston, Aguilera won the 2000 Grammy Award for best new artist of the year. While her midriff-baring outfits and catchy dance tunes have captured the attention of adolescents, industry observers predict that Aguilera's vocal range and power will eventually win her older fans and ensure her continued success.

Christina Aguilera was born on December 18, 1980 on Staten Island—officially, the New York City borough of Richmond—to Fausto Aguilera, a U.S. Army sergeant born in Ecuador, and his Irish-American wife, Shelly. Her father's military career often forced the family to move, and at various times they lived in Texas, New Jersey, and Japan. Aguilera always loved music, and as a toddler she would sing out loud while riding a public bus or walking down the street. "When she was two, I knew what Christina was going to do," her mother told Anthony Bozza for *Rolling Stone* (October 28, 1999). "She'd line up all her stuffed animals and sing to them with my little majorette baton [as her microphone]. I've never seen anybody so focused." By the time she was five years old, Christina had taught herself all the songs from *The Sound of Music.* When she was seven, her parents divorced, and she and her younger sister, Rachel, moved with their mother to Wexford, a middle-class suburb near Pittsburgh, Pennsylvania, to live with Shelly's mother, Delcie Fidler. Shelly eventually married James Kearns, a paramedic, who already had two children of his own, Stephanie and Casey. In about 1996 the couple had a son together; sometimes fans of Aguilera's mistakenly assume that the boy, named Michael, is her child.

As a youngster Aguilera often entertained at neighborhood block parties and competed in local talent shows. As word of her singing abilities spread, she was invited to perform the national anthem at Pittsburgh-area sporting events, including Pirates and Steelers games. When she was eight years old, she appeared as a contestant on the national television talent show *Star Search*, singing Whitney Houston's "I Wanna Dance with Somebody." Her defeat in the competition, she has recalled, devastated her. When her mother insisted that she shake hands with the 12-year-old boy who had won, she did so with tears streaming down her cheeks. Her classmates, whom Aguilera has frequently described as resentful and jealous of her growing fame, did nothing to soften the blow; indeed, they teased her mercilessly. Such experiences strengthened her resolve to succeed. She told Harrington, "I always envied people who had childhood friends and memories of growing up together because I never really had that. Then the divorce and the hard times at school, all those things combined to mold me, to make me grow up quicker. And it gave me the drive to pursue my dreams that I wouldn't necessarily have had otherwise." When she was 10, Aguilera attended an open audition in Pittsburgh for the *New Mickey Mouse Club* TV show, but its producers decided that she was too young. They remembered her, though, and two years later asked her to try again. This time she won a spot on the show, as a singer, dancer, and actress. Her fellow cast members included Keri Russell, now an accomplished actress; Justin Timberlake and J. C. Chasez, both of whom later joined the popular singing group 'N Sync; and Britney Spears, who has since become a celebrated teen singer. Speaking of her two-year association with the *New Mickey Mouse Club*, Aguilera told Anthony Bozza, "It was great to be around other kids who were as passionate about their careers as I was." The media have suggested that a rivalry developed between Aguilera and Spears, but each singer professes to be happy about the other's success and to consider her a friend.

While on the *New Mickey Mouse Club*, Aguilera came to the attention of the talent manager Steve Kurtz, who signed her as a client. When her stint on the show was finished, she traveled overseas under his direction to develop her skills further. (Her formal schooling ended with eighth grade; subsequently, she received instruction from her mother and from "an occasional math tutor," according to Luisita Lopez Torregrosa in the *New York Times* [September 6, 1999].) She toured Japan, where she recorded a well-received duet with the Japanese pop star Keizo Nakanishi, and she later performed before a crowd of 10,000 at a festival in Romania, on a bill that also included Diana Ross.

In early 1998 Kurtz commissioned the production of a demo tape for Aguilera and sent it to Ron Fair of RCA Records. Fair was equally impressed by her voice and burgeoning beauty; confident that with his help, she could be molded into a major performer, he offered the 17-year-old Aguilera a recording contract. In the middle of contract negotiations, Fair received word from a friend at Disney that the company was searching for a young female vocalist to sing the lead song on the soundtrack to Disney's upcoming animated feature, *Mulan* (1998). A ballad called "Reflection," it required a singer capable of hitting a high E—two octaves above middle C—and Fair thought instantly of Aguilera. To prove that she could handle the high note, he sent Disney executives a rough demo that Aguilera had made using a tape recorder in her living room. The Disney representatives immediately summoned Aguilera to Los Angeles to audition, and within two days, she had gotten the job. It took about a week to record the song, during which Disney arranged for Aguilera to receive her first vocal lessons ever, in order to help her cope with the demands of singing for extended periods of time in the recording studio. Shortly afterward, her contract with RCA was finalized. Aguilera then embarked on a promotional tour for *Mulan*, singing "Reflection" live on *CBS This Morning* and the *Donnie and Marie Show.* "Reflection" was nominated for a 1998 Golden Globe Award for best original song in a motion picture, and the video version played frequently on MTV. Aguilera now refers to the high E as the "note that changed my life."

Meanwhile, the singer had begun work on her debut RCA recording. Over the course of a year, the company reportedly spent almost a million dollars on songs for the album (the songwriters David Frank and Diane Warren were among those commissioned), voice lessons for Aguilera, and marketing. (RCA executives refused to confirm the figure, saying only that the amount was no more than would have been budgeted for any promising new artist.) Aguilera was especially appreciative of the voice lessons, having realized while working on the *Mulan* soundtrack how valuable such instruction could be. "I was never trained enough to know when is too much, what's going to blow my voice out," she told Harrington. "Since [the lessons], I fell in love with technique, how to make your range go even farther, how to place notes, all these things I never knew about, rather than just singing and listening to my favorite vocalists and going on instinct." She admitted, "I never would have been able to hit the notes I'm hitting now a couple years ago." Fair chose with great care the songs for Aguilera's RCA debut. "When I met her she was a world-class singer but hadn't really formed opinions about what style she wanted to sing or what her direction should be," he told Harrington. "She was very much a raw talent, so building a collection of songs that would become her first album was a time-consuming process. We wanted to find the ones that could knock the door down and put her up there." The frothy pop tune "Genie in a Bottle" was chosen to be the first single, despite Aguilera's objection that the song didn't showcase her voice to advantage. Fair explained his decision to Harrington, saying, "Christina was just 18 and she needed to connect with her audience and there was never any question that this was the way to do it. In our business it's more important to start off with a number one record on a debut act than it is to start off with a great song."

Besides topping *Billboard*'s "Hot 100" list for weeks after its release, in June 1999, "Genie in a Bottle" became a constant feature of the MTV program *Total Request Live*, a show on which callers to the station request their favorite songs. "What a Girl Wants," Aguilera's second single, released soon after "Genie in a Bottle," did equally well. When Aguilera made a guest appearance on *Total Request Live* in August, the show's host, Carson Daley, had a difficult time keeping the studio audience under control, so excited were they about seeing the singer in person. Daley himself claimed to be almost as impressed as Aguilera's enthusiastic fans. "She can really sing," he told Anthony Bozza. "Her range is amazing. She can do gospel and R&B if she wants to, and can really perform. The hook in most teen pop is in the dancing and the imaging, while the voices are only good to fair. But she's really talented. . . . I think she's got a long career ahead of her." Aguilera, who had often watched *Total Request Live* and wondered if she would ever appear there, was gratified by the audience's response. "It gives me a feeling that's different from any other feeling in the world," she told Luisita Lopez Torregrosa. "When I see all these people screaming and chanting and holding those signs they made just for me, my eyes light up, and my whole body just lifts, and I just feel in another state. I feel like I'm floating on air. It's the most incredible feeling, and I've always wanted it." More adulation soon came her way. Her album, which was released on August 24, 1999, quickly climbed the charts, thanks in part to Aguilera's presence on MTV, carefully orchestrated appearances on several late-night talk shows for the general public, and live performances staged specifically for radio and retail representatives, with the aim of ensuring air play and store space for the record. Within six months, more than six million copies of *Christina Aguilera* had been sold.

In November 1999 RCA released Aguilera's version of "The Christmas Song," which had last been a hit when Nat King Cole recorded it, in 1961. It reached number 18 on the charts, becoming Aguilera's third single to reach the Top 20 within three months. *Mi Reflejo*, the Spanish-language version of her eponymous album, was released in September 2000. Although some industry observers have noted that Aguilera seems to be taking advantage of the current popularity of such Latino stars as Carlos Santana and Ricky Martin, she has defended *Mi Reflejo* as being a tribute to her father (whom she has "lost track of," according to Lopez Torregrosa). When dates were announced for Aguilera's first North American tour, which took place in mid-2000, some venues sold out within hours. Besides concert tickets, her fans have been buying an assortment of Aguilera-related merchandise, including trading cards, hats, and a fashion doll that sings "Genie in a Bottle" when her navel is pressed. Plans are also underway for a clothing line bearing her name.

Aguilera, who often sings a blues number by Etta James when she performs live, has expressed the hope that her next English-language album will include a wider variety of songs. She has begun to write some of her own material and intends to branch out into producing someday. "Right now, whenever I go to the recording studio, I'm always soaking in everything," she said during her interview with MTV Radio Network. "I'm absorbing, I'm learning, I'm getting more familiar with the technical aspect of it. But I have a great ear; I definitely have an ear for it, and one day I will be producing." She envisions a future for herself beyond the record industry as well. "I plan to take this to the absolute fullest, venturing off into all sorts of different areas of this business, all aspects of creativity," she told Lopez Torregrosa. "I look up to people like Madonna, who has been able to just completely reinvent herself over and over and over again."

"Right now my whole persona is that of a pop star . . . ," Aguilera said to Lopez Torregrosa. "I think if I became this serious, appeared to be this deep thinker all the time, people would almost be scared. They want to see the very bubbly, perky, outgoing personality." She also declared, "I am fearless. I'm more afraid of the little things than of the bigger things." For Aguilera, the "bigger things" include "wanting to conquer something, to make an impact on the world," perhaps by working in behalf of battered women and children. — M.R.

Suggested Reading: *Entertainment Weekly* (online) Mar. 23, 2000, Mar. 31, 2000; *Interview* p112+ Apr. 2000, with photos; *New York Times* E p1 Sep. 6, 1999; Official Christina Aguilera Web site; *People* p75+ Sep. 27, 1999, with photos; *Rolling Stone* p52+ Oct. 28, 1999, with photos; *Seventeen* p120+ July 2000, with photos; *Time* p70+ Mar. 6, 2000, with photo; *TV Guide* p20+ Aug. 21–27, 1999, with photo; *Washington Post* C p1 Sep. 8, 1999

Selected Recordings: *Christina Aguilera*, 1999; *Mi Reflejo*, 2000

Courtesy of the U.S. State Department

Albright, Madeleine Korbel

(AHL-brite, MAD-eh-lin KOR-bel)

May 15, 1937– United States Secretary of State. Address: U.S. State Department, 2201 C St. N.W., Washington, DC 20520

NOTE: An earlier article on Madeleine Albright appeared in *Current Biography* in 1995.

A naturalized American citizen who was born in Czechoslovakia and came to the United States at age 11, Madeleine Korbel Albright served as the country's permanent representative to the United Nations for four years before becoming the 64th U.S. secretary of state, in 1997. During her tenure at the U.N., Albright acted not merely as a spokesperson for the executive arm of the U.S. government but as a key behind-the-scenes strategist and policy-maker. Now, as the first woman to be appointed secretary of state and the highest-ranking woman in government in U.S. history, Albright has broken into one of the nation's last male bastions of power. Though staunchly Democratic in ideology, she has won nearly unanimous support from all political corners, because of her strong pro-American stance toward foreign policy and her direct, almost confrontational style. Her conviction, clear perspectives, and common touch have helped to make American foreign policy relevant again to U.S. citizens.

The daughter of Josef Korbel, a Czechoslovakian diplomat, and the former Anna Spiegelová, Albright was born on May 15, 1937 in Prague. She has a younger sister, Anna Katherine Korbel Silva, and a younger brother, John Joseph Korbel. At birth she was named Marie Jana Körbelová; the name "Madeleine" evolved from "Madlenka," a childhood nickname. A loyal member of the Czech government as well as a secular Jew, Josef Korbel was forced to flee his native land with his family after the dismemberment and occupation of Czechoslovakia by Germany in 1939. They lived for two weeks in Belgrade, Yugoslavia, and then settled in London, where Madeleine became fluent in English. After World War II ended, in 1945, Korbel worked briefly in Prague before accepting a three-year assignment in Belgrade as ambassador to Yugoslavia. Being uprooted time and again apparently did not faze young Madeleine. "I made friends very easily," she told Molly Sinclair for the *Washington Post* (January 6, 1991). "I think it has to do with the fact that I lived in a lot of different countries, went to a lot of different schools, and was always being put into situations where I had to relate to the people around me." Beginning when she was seven or eight, she was tutored by governesses for a year or two, because her father, who staunchly opposed totalitarianism, wanted to avoid exposing her to the influence of communism in Yugoslavian schools. At age 10 she was sent away to the Prealpina School in Chexbres, Switzerland, where she learned French.

In 1948 Josef Korbel became Czechoslovakia's representative to the U.N. Commission for India and Pakistan. At about the time he began working on the Indian subcontinent, the Czech government was overthrown in a Communist coup. Realizing that his family was in danger, primarily because of his well-known advocacy of democracy, he instructed his wife to seek refuge in London with the children; he himself was safe as long as he remained beyond Czechoslovakia's borders. In early November 1948 Anna Korbel and her children traveled to New York; one month later Josef was dismissed from Czechoslovakia's foreign ministry, and he rejoined his family in the U.S., which granted the Korbels political asylum. In 1949 the family settled in Colorado, where Josef Korbel had secured a position as a professor of international relations at the University of Denver.

As a scholarship student at Denver's prestigious Kent School, Madeleine set about Americanizing herself by ridding herself of her foreign accent, and she enjoyed success as president of the international relations club. She entered Wellesley College, in Massachusetts, in 1955, also on a scholarship. While in college she "indulged her twin passions"—journalism and politics—both inside and outside the classroom, Jacob Heilbrunn reported for the *New Republic* (August 22 and 29, 1994). A political-science major, she campaigned for Adlai Stevenson in the 1956 presidential race and for at least one year edited the campus newspaper. She earned a B.A. degree, with honors, in 1959.

Three days after her graduation, Madeleine Korbel married Joseph Albright, a scion of the Robert R. McCormick–Alicia Patterson newspaper dynasty, whom she had met during the summer of 1957 while both were interning at the *Denver Post*. The couple settled in Chicago, where Joseph Albright had begun working as a *Chicago Sun-Times* reporter. Madeleine Albright abandoned her own journalistic ambitions soon after their move, as the result of an interview she had with a *Sun-Times* editor. Addressing her as "Honey," the editor told her that neither the *Sun-Times* nor its competitors would hire a spouse of a *Sun-Times* reporter, and he advised her to pursue another career. For a brief period in 1960, she held a job in public relations in the Chicago offices of *Encyclopedia Britannica*.

In 1961 the Albrights moved to Long Island, New York, where Joseph had taken a job with *Newsday*. Between 1961 and 1967 Madeleine Albright gave birth to three daughters, including a set of twins. During that period, she enrolled in the graduate program in public law and government at Columbia University, in New York City. She studied under, among others, Zbigniew Brzezinski, who at that time directed Columbia's Institute on Communist Affairs. In 1968 she earned both an M.A. degree and a certificate in Russian studies from Columbia. She then began doing research for her doctoral dissertation, about the part played by the press in Czech dissidents' abortive attempt in 1968 to loosen the grip of communism in their country through democratic reforms. In the course of her research, she interviewed many of the dissidents who had participated in those events. Albright has said that in order to write the dissertation—which she described as "the hardest thing I ever did"—she had to arise every morning at 4:30.

Meanwhile, in 1968, with Joseph Albright's promotion to Washington bureau chief of *Newsday*, Albright and her family had moved to the nation's capital. She served on the board of directors of the Beauvoir School, a private school that her twins attended. In the early 1970s, at the suggestion of a parent who had noted her skill at soliciting donations to the school, Albright helped to raise funds for Edmund S. Muskie's ultimately unsuccessful bid for the 1972 Democratic presidential nomination. (Several sources identified Muskie as an Albright family friend.) In 1976 Muskie, a senator from Maine, put Albright on his payroll as his chief legislative assistant. "I had just received my Ph.D.," she told Molly Sinclair. "That made it possible for Senator Muskie to introduce me as Dr. Albright, instead of Madeleine Albright, little housewife." Muskie was a member of the Senate Foreign Relations Committee, and Albright spent a lot of time dealing with foreign affairs.

In 1978 Albright joined the staff of the National Security Council, where, working under Zbigniew Brzezinski, who was then President Jimmy Carter's national security adviser, she served as a congressional liaison, with a focus on foreign policy legislation. After Ronald Reagan became president, in 1981, she temporarily left government service. From 1981 to 1982 she was a senior fellow in Soviet and Eastern European affairs at the Center for Strategic and International Studies. Also in 1981 she was awarded a fellowship at the Smithsonian Institution's Woodrow Wilson Center for Scholars. As a fellow at the center until 1982, she wrote *Poland: The Role of the Press in Political Change* (1983).

In 1982 the School of Foreign Service at Georgetown University, in Washington, D.C., appointed Albright to the dual positions of research professor of international affairs and director of the Women in Foreign Service Program. By 1993, when she left Georgetown, she had won four "teacher of the year" awards—a record number for that university, according to Jacob Heilbrunn, who attributed her success to her "approachability and knack for presenting complicated issues in plain language." Meanwhile, she had begun hosting in her home what has been referred to as a high-powered foreign-policy salon, at which she and her guests—who through the years included hundreds of politicians, professors, and theoreticians aligned with the Democratic Party, among them Bill Clinton when he was the governor of Arkansas—analyzed and debated current issues over dinner. "These were not mere social gatherings, but sessions aimed at laying the groundwork for a Democratic return to power," Jacob Heilbrunn reported.

During the 1984 presidential race, Albright served as the foreign policy coordinator for Walter F. Mondale, the Democratic candidate, as well as for Mondale's running mate, Geraldine A. Ferraro. Also in that year she was named vice-chairman of the National Democratic Institute for International Affairs, a nonprofit corporation that conducts nonpartisan international programs to help promote and strengthen democratic institutions. In 1987 she became Michael S. Dukakis's senior foreign-policy adviser (without pay) in the then-Massachusetts governor's campaign for the presidency. "I have a lot of contacts of my own," she explained to Elaine Sciolino for the *New York Times* (July 26, 1988) a few days after Dukakis's nomination, in 1988, "and a lot of people, once they read my name in the paper, started sending me their papers. There's a whole network of people in think tanks and academia who like to give their ideas to presidential candidates." Albright reportedly wrote many of Dukakis's speeches, and she apparently became so important to him that, according to Molly Sinclair, "virtually anyone who wanted to see him about a foreign policy issue had to go through her."

In 1989 Albright took over as president of the Center for National Policy, a nonprofit Democratic interdisciplinary research institute, and her prominence in Democratic circles grew significantly. Her influence on Capitol Hill was also increasing. A spokesperson for the Senate Foreign Relations Committee told Molly Sinclair in 1991 that Albright was "one of the people we turn to for advice and perspective" and that she conducted meetings at the Capitol at which leaders of Eastern European countries and other nations met with members of Congress and their senior aides. One of those leaders, the Czech playwright and human-rights campaigner Václav Havel, recruited her to serve as his interpreter and adviser during his first state visit to the United States, which he made in early 1990, shortly after being elected president of Czechoslovakia by his nation's Parliament.

Albright helped the Democratic National Committee formulate the party's platform in 1992, and, in collaboration with Warren Christopher, Anthony Lake, and Samuel R. Berger, she developed foreign policy position papers for Bill Clinton after Clinton won the Democratic nomination for president that summer. At a press conference held on December 22, 1992, after his election, Clinton introduced Albright as his choice for delegate to the U.N. Commenting on that announcement for the *Washington Post* (December 29, 1992), the columnist Mary McGrory described Albright as "an intellectual . . . with a heart" and added, "She is precisely the kind of woman everyone wished could have been in the room when the men were making their disastrous decisions about Vietnam." The Senate unanimously confirmed Albright's nomination on January 27, 1993, and the next day she was sworn into office, with the ranks of Cabinet officer and ambassador extraordinary and plenipotentiary. A member of the National Security Council and a key presidential adviser on foreign policy, she attended a biweekly conclave known as the "principals meeting," along with the director of the CIA, secretaries of defense and state, and national security adviser. During her ambassadorship Albright shuttled between U.N. headquarters in New York City and Washington as often as five times weekly. "The people I work with appreciate the fact that I'm plugged into Washington," Kevin Fedarko quoted her as saying in *Time* (October 31, 1994). "I'm in the inner circle. I'm involved in everything."

The duties of the post required that Albright inspect peacekeeping operations and other U.N. initiatives in more than a dozen countries overseas, including the former Yugoslav republics of Bosnia, Croatia, and Slovenia; the former Soviet republics of Moldova, Georgia, Armenia, and Azerbaijan; Somalia, Ethiopia, Mozambique, and the Sudan, in Africa; Cambodia, in Asia; El Salvador, in Central America; and Haiti, in the Caribbean. Matters that required her attention included the ethnic conflicts in the former Yugoslavia; the civil wars in Somalia and Rwanda; the reinstallation of the democratically elected government of Jean-Bertrand Aristide in Haiti; and the continuing use of economic sanctions as a means of pressuring Iraq to abandon its terrorist activities, aggressive actions toward Kuwait, and other behavior deemed unacceptable by the United States. She also strived to build support and enthusiasm among Americans for the activities of the U.N. "We have a responsibility now to convey the fact that in today's world, domestic policy and foreign policy are no longer separable things," she declared in a 1993 speech. "Yes, it costs money to help keep peace around the world. But by any measure, the most expensive peacekeeping mission is a bargain compared to the least expensive war—not just because it costs fewer dollars, but because it costs fewer lives [and] creates fewer refugees and orphans, and because it plants the seeds of future reconciliation, not future revenge."

In time Albright retreated somewhat from her emphasis on the superiority of "assertive multilateralism" over unilateral responses in thwarting the ambitions of what she has called "petty tyrants and defiant warlords." In a 1994 address to State Department employees, she said that "in seeking to further the full range of our interests, we will need—and we should use—every available foreign policy tool. . . . We should not be boxed into rigid choices between force and diplomacy, economic and political, unilateral and multilateral. Nor should we be lured by what [Ralph Waldo] Emerson called 'foolish consistencies'—a foreign policy that responds in the same way regardless of circumstance will be consistent only in its failure. Foreign policy is not auto mechanics; it is an art. The tools we select must be weighed against a matrix of past commitments, present capabilities, future hopes, and constant values. In each instance, we should seek to combine principle with pragmatism—to do the right thing and to do the thing right. . . . American military power and the credibility of its possible use remains the most potent force for international order in the world today."

On December 5, 1996 President Clinton announced his selection of Albright for secretary of state. Shortly after she was sworn in, on January 23, 1997, Michael Dobbs, a veteran *Washington Post* reporter and eventual Albright biographer, broke the story that her parents had been born Jewish and that three of her grandparents had died in Nazi concentration camps. Albright, who was raised a Roman Catholic and became an Episcopalian after her marriage, claimed—dubiously, some thought—to have had virtually no knowledge of her heritage. Eventually Albright made a trip to the Pinkas Synagogue in Prague, where names of some of her relatives appear on a memorial to Holocaust victims. During the trip she also visited Terezín (once known by its German name, Theresienstadt), the site of the concentration camp where her grandparents died, and Letohrad, her paternal grandfather's native town. Albright has never publicly expressed curiosity about her parents' motives for keeping her past from her. As she said to Michael Dobbs for the *Washington Post* (February 4, 1997), "I believe my parents did wonderful things for us."

Aside from the media scrutiny regarding her personal history, Albright's first 100 days as secretary of state were distinguished by solid achievements. On the first stop of a world tour that began in Europe and extended throughout Asia, she met with the prime minister of Italy, Romano Prodi, whom she knew favored restructuring and expanding NATO, an item high on her agenda. Meeting in Russia with then–President Boris Yeltsin and his foreign minister, Yevgeny Primakov, she set the stage for a summit meeting between Yeltsin and Clinton, to be held on March 21, 1997, regarding Russia and NATO. From there Albright visited Seoul, South Korea, and Beijing, China, where she conferred with Chinese leaders about the nuclear armament of Communist North Korea and the future of Hong Kong, which was to be transferred on July 1, 1997 from the rule of Great Britain, which cultivated a free-market economy on the island, to the governance of Communist China.

Domestically, Albright helped to end the decades-long debate within the halls of government as to which agency is responsible for carrying out American foreign policy. Spurred by Albright, on April 17, 1997 President Clinton authorized a major redistribution of power within the State Department. Under the new plan, the Arms Control and Disarmament Agency and the U.S. Information Agency, which previously had operated independently of the State Department, were made subsidiaries of it; the Agency for International Development was left independent but was made answerable to the State Department. The increased authority of the State Department has led to a more unified and streamlined approach to American foreign policy.

Albright pushed successfully for the Senate's ratification of the International Chemical Weapons Treaty. Conceived in the 1980s during President Ronald Reagan's administration and signed by his successor, George Bush, the treaty sought to outlaw the purchase or manufacture of chemical weapons by any nation. By 1997 160 nations had signed the treaty. Libya and Iraq had not approved it, and neither had the U.S. Indeed, many conservatives in the Senate justified their opposition by pointing to Libya and Iraq's histories of terrorism and rogue behavior. They reasoned that if chemical weapons were to be used on the U.S. during warfare, the U.S. should be free to respond in kind. North Carolina Republican Jesse Helms, the staunchly conservative chair of the Senate Foreign Relations Committee, had serious reservations about the treaty, but he had a high regard for Albright; indeed, he had helped to ensure the Senate's unanimous confirmations of her two appointments. Albright, in turn, persuaded the Clinton administration to accede to some of Helms's demands, such as providing the U.S. with a way to circumvent the treaty's obligations if another nation fails to comply with them. On April 29, 1997 the Senate ratified the chemical weapons ban, and President Clinton signed it into law.

Less than a year later Serbian police, under the orders of the president of Serbia, Slobodan Milosevic, invaded the province of Kosovo as part of a campaign to rid the region of ethnic Albanians. In September 1998 Albright and Foreign Minister Igor Ivanov of Russia called on Milosevic to end the offensive and engage in negotiations with the Kosovars, who were seeking political independence from Serbia. Unable to resolve the conflict, the United States, in collaboration with other NATO members, levied air strikes against Milosevic's troops. Responding to criticism of her call for military retaliation, Albright explained to Michael Dobbs for his biography *Madeleine Albright: A Twentieth Century Odyssey* (1999), "My mindset is Munich. Most of my generation's is Vietnam. I saw what happened when a dictator was allowed to take over a piece of a country and the country went down the tubes."

According to Mary McGrory, Madeleine Albright is kind and hospitable, has a "strong strain of maternal solicitude," and is "universally known as a good soul." "What I've always found striking about Madeleine is her humanity, her true concern for individuals and their welfare," Kirk O'Donnell, a former president of the Center for National Policy, told Dan Balz for the *Washington Post* (December 23, 1992). A diplomat interviewed by Barbara Crossette for the *New York Times* (November 25, 1994) described her as "a person of passionate temper." Renowned for her outspokenness and for "her willingness to wield the big stick whenever the president needs to make a point," as Kevin Fedarko put it, she is also "a quintessential team player who hates to improvise and rarely says anything that isn't thoroughly vetted first in Washington," Julia Preston wrote for the *Washington Post* (October 14, 1994). Preston quoted a senior delegate from a developing nation as saying of Albright, "There's no pussyfooting around with her; you know exactly where you stand. She's tough—so what?"

Throughout 2000 Albright focused much of her energy on the Middle East. On March 17, 2000 she announced that the Clinton administration was easing sanctions on the import of non-energy products from Iran, as a way of showing the Iranian people that the U.S. government sympathized with their economic problems. At the same time, she reiterated that the U.S. would not resume full diplomatic relations with Iran until the country ended its efforts to build nuclear weapons. In June 2000 Albright met separately in the Middle East with the Palestinian president, Yasir Arafat, and the Israeli prime minister, Ehud Barak, to help advance the peace negotiations. "There is no higher foreign policy priority for the Clinton administration than an Israeli- Palestinian peace," she declared, as quoted in *Facts on File* (June 15, 2000).

Albright also continued to try to ease tensions in Kosovo. "History teaches us that America cannot be secure if Europe is not secure," she wrote in an op-ed piece for the *New York Times* (March 28, 2000), "and events have reminded us repeatedly that Europe cannot be secure when conflict engulfs the Balkans." Along with General Wesley K. Clark, the supreme commander of NATO, she warned Albanians not to start an insurgency in southern Serbia; to back up that warning, NATO kept peacekeeping troops stationed on the border between Croatia and Serbia. Albright has promised that even after President Clinton leaves office, the Balkans will remain high on her list of priorities: "No matter where I am, we're not going to forget them," she told Jane Perlez for the *New York Times* (July 3, 2000).

At a talk Albright gave for a group of Georgetown University women students in 1991, she recalled that as a staff member of the National Security Council in the late 1970s, she "had to learn to speak out" for herself. "I would be in a White House meeting, and I would think of something and not say anything because I wasn't sure that it would add to the discussion. Then some man would say what I had been thinking, and it would be hailed as a great idea." During her time with the U.N., Albright worked to forge closer ties among the few women (then numbering seven) among the organization's 185 permanent representatives and expressed her determination to try to increase their numbers. She has since sought, using her significantly higher profile as the first woman secretary of state, to encourage young women to consider careers in politics and international relations.

In addition to three books, among them *The Soviet Diplomatic Service: Profile of an Elite* (1968), Albright has written many book chapters and articles for professional journals. Her activities have included service as a trustee of the Black Student Fund, the Democratic Forum, and Wellesley College and as a member of the boards of directors of the Washington Urban League and the Atlantic Council. She is a member of the Council on Foreign Relations, the Czechoslovak Society for Arts and Sciences, the American Association for the Advancement of Slavic Studies, the executive committee of D.C. Citizens for Better Public Education, and several other groups. In addition to English, French, and Czech, she speaks and reads Russian and Polish. Albright lives in a townhouse in the Georgetown section of Washington and owns a farm in Virginia. Her daughters Anne and Alice were born in 1961; her daughter Katharine, called Katie, was born in 1967. Her marriage to Joseph Albright ended in divorce in 1983. — J.K.B.

Suggested Reading: *Biography* p61+ Mar. 1998, with photos; *Harper's Bazaar* p156+ Aug. 1997, with photos; *New Republic* p19+ Aug. 22–29, 1994; *New York Times* A p16 July 26, 1988, with photo, A p1+ Nov. 25, 1994, with photos, A p10 May 14, 1997, with photo; *New Yorker* p40+ Oct. 13, 1997, p50+ Mar. 29, 1999; *U.S. News & World Report* p60+ Feb. 13, 1995, with photo, p46+ Jan. 19, 1998; *Washington Post* F p1+ Jan. 6, 1991, with photos, A p10 Dec. 23, 1992; Blackman, Ann. *Seasons of Her Life: A Biography of Madeleine Korbel Albright*, 1998; Blood, Thomas. *Madam Secretary: A Biography of Madeleine Albright*, 1997; Dobbs, Michael. *Madeleine Albright: A Twentieth Century Odyssey*, 1999; *Who's Who in America, 2000*

Selected Books: *The Soviet Diplomatic Service: Profile of an Elite*, 1968; *The Role of the Press in Political Change: Czechoslovakia 1968*, 1976; *Poland: The Role of the Press in Political Change*, 1983

Courtesy of the Pritzker Architecture Prize

Ando, Tadao

(ahn-doh, tah-day-oh)

Sep. 13, 1941– Architect. Address: Tadao Ando and Associates, 5–23 Toyosaki, 2–chome, Kita-ku, Osaka 531, Japan

For a short while before he became a full-time architect, Tadao Ando was a professional boxer in Japan, and occasionally his pugilistic instincts have resurfaced in his present work life. In one instance, a construction worker unthinkingly threw a cigarette butt into a concrete mix for one of Ando's buildings, and the architect became so enraged that he got into a fistfight with the worker. "It's happened more than once," he admitted to Cheryl Kent for *Progressive Architecture* (June 1993). "If you were caring for your son and someone abused him it would be natural to get upset." "I'll quit architecture when I lose that emotion," he added. "You've got to really fight."

Ando's passionate nature is reflected in his more than 80 buildings. Though many of his creations incorporate simple geometric shapes and are constructed of such mundane materials as steel, glass, and concrete, they are a far cry from the monotonous glass and steel boxes that dominate urban architecture. Most architectural critics have been struck by the expressiveness of his works, particularly his designs for places of worship. One, a Christian church, features a cross cut into a wall so as to allow light to pour through it. Entrants to another, a Buddhist temple, must descend steps that bisect an elliptical lotus pond on the roof. Ando has also designed many residences, museums, and commercial spaces; noteworthy buildings include Rokko Housing, which from afar looks like cubes gently spilling down a hillside.

Ando has often been praised for his subtle use of concrete—so often, in fact, that he once proclaimed, "I am not in the concrete business!" By having the concrete poured into wooden molds that are varnished to ensure exceptional smoothness, Ando has succeeded in producing what have been referred to as "smooth-as-silk" surfaces. Describing the effect in Ando's buildings, the architectural critic Paul Goldberger wrote for the *New York Times* (April 23, 1995), "For Mr. Ando, hardness does not equal harshness. He has somehow found a way to turn hardness into grace, and for eyes accustomed to thinking of graceful buildings as always being in some way soft, his architecture is a revelation."

The designs of Ando's buildings do not fit easily within deconstructivism or postmodernism, the most fashionable architectural trends of the past two decades; but they are not modernist throwbacks, either. Perhaps not surprisingly, in light of Ando's maverick background and the fact that he studied architecture almost entirely on his own, his buildings seem to embody a unique architectural vocabulary. "With Modernism's technology came this utopian ideal that every man's life would improve," Ando observed to Cheryl Kent. "But what was built were simple boxes that didn't fulfill the manifestoes. That wasn't utopia, and there was a revolt. Post-Modernists looked to the decorative aspects of historicism. Basically, they made the same simple Modern box and added appliqué. My architecture is about making the box rich in its own way, by restructuring it with my own methodology." This methodology, Ando explained, involves creating strong contrasts of shadow and light; it also entails embracing natural phenomena, so that the experience of light, wind, rain, and snow is heightened. "My intention is to create a spiritual world," he has said, as quoted by Benjamin Forgey in the *Washington Post* (July 19, 1986), "to make a space which is so strong and deep it will penetrate to the people who contact that space." He has also said, "I do not believe architecture should speak too much. It should remain silent and let nature in the guise of sunlight and wind speak." In 1995 Ando won the Pritzker Architecture Prize, which is widely considered the discipline's highest honor.

The older of twin boys, Tadao Ando was born on September 13, 1941 in Osaka, Japan. After he reached the age of two, according to *pritzkerprize.com* (on-line), his maternal grandmother raised him. Ando grew up in a working-class neighborhood known for its skilled carpenters and artisans. From early on he had a strong interest in trees and lumber. As an adolescent and teenager, he enjoyed making wooden models of planes and ships. He first became attracted to architecture as a discipline at the age of 13, during a major renovation of his family's home. After watching the renovators remove the roof and seeing how the sun lit up the once-dark lower level of the house, he knew he had found his calling. "I was fascinated by the transformation of the environment," he recalled to Merrill Goozner for the *Chicago Tribune* (April 21, 1995).

Bored in his classes and unhappy about what he viewed as the excessive rigidity of his schools, Ando never received any formal education in architecture. Instead, he read books on architecture on his own and apprenticed himself briefly to a carpenter. He also went to see traditional tea houses, shrines, and other buildings in Japan. Over a span of about nine years beginning in 1962, he visited the most famous buildings in Asia, Europe, the United States, and Africa, studying first-hand, by himself, what others learned about second-hand. He made drawings in a little sketchbook of what he saw, a practice he has maintained to this day. During his period of self-education, he supported himself by driving a truck and boxing professionally. He had taken up boxing when he was 17, and he fought well enough to win most of his matches.

In 1970 he opened his office, Tadao Ando & Associates. It was a brash move. He had not yet constructed any buildings; moreover, he set up shop in Osaka rather than Tokyo, where most talented architects maintained an address if they hoped to get noticed in Japanese architectural circles. For about eight years Ando labored in relative obscurity, designing mostly residential homes. One of his earliest buildings was the Tomishima House (1971–73), which he bought for himself and enlarged 10 years later. Renamed the Atelier in Oyodo I, it now serves as one of his studios.

The design that first brought Ando notice was the Azuma House in Osaka, which he completed in 1976 and which won the top prize from the Architectural Institute of Japan in 1979. The house is a simple, two-story, rectangular structure made of concrete, steel, and glass. Most strikingly, the smooth concrete façade completely lacks windows. Light enters the house through an interior courtyard. The design of the house, Ando once said, was an "attempt to generate a microcosm," as if the house were turning inwards away from the urban chaos that surrounded it. Since the occupants could get to and from certain rooms only by crossing the courtyard, they had to use umbrellas to do so when it rained or snowed. This inconvenience, Ando felt, was offset by the contacts with the natural world that his design afforded. "I have the somewhat arrogant belief that the way people lead [their] lives can be directed, even if by a little, by means of architecture," he has said.

In the Azuma House and in his other buildings, Ando went beyond the modernist tenet that form follows function. "I like to see how far architecture can pursue function and then, after the pursuit has been made, to see how far architecture can be removed from function," he told Christopher Andreae for the *Christian Science Monitor* (October 18, 1994). "The significance of architecture is found in the distance between it and function." In a brief essay in *Tadao Ando* (1991), the catalogue that accompanied *Beyond Horizons in Architecture*, a retrospective of his work mounted by the Museum of Modern Art in New York City, he explained that in designing the Azuma House, his "chief concern was the degree of austerity of geometric form that could be fused with human life. . . . Geometric abstraction collides with human concreteness." He added that the same tension predominates in several of his other works, including the Koshino House (1979–81), in Ashiya, and the Kidosaki House (1982–86), in Tokyo.

Ando's creative use of geometry is strikingly evident in Rokko Housing (1978–83), in Hyogo Prefecture, one of his more famous designs. Named after the mountain on which it sits, the 70-unit complex is built on a 60-degree slope. Choosing a cube as the basic motif, Ando varied the placement of terraces, steps, and open spaces so that each of the 70 units appears unique. Seen from afar Rokko Housing looks like a cluster of concrete cubes nestled in the mountainside. "Underlying its design was the idea of sinking the building in along the slope, governing its projection above the ground in order to merge it into the surrounding cover of dense forest," Ando wrote for the *Beyond Horizons in Architecture* catalogue. "This affords each dwelling unit an optimal view of the ocean from a terrace provided by its neighbor's roof."

Ando's designs have been compared to early modernist design in the West and traditional Japanese architecture. He has said that he has been influenced by such modernist architects as Louis Kahn, Frank Lloyd Wright, and Le Corbusier. A book about Le Corbusier that he found in a used-books store excited him tremendously. "I traced the drawings of his early period so many times that all the pages turned black," he recalled, as recorded on the Pritzker Prize Web site. "In my mind, I quite often wonder how Le Corbusier would have thought about this project or that [of mine]." Ando has named no specific Japanese architects as influences; instead, he has said, certain Japanese attitudes toward nature have affected his sense of design. "The Japanese tradition embraces a different sensibility about nature than that found in the West," he explained in his *Beyond Horizons in Architecture* essay. "Human life is not intended to oppose nature and endeavor to control it, but rather to draw nature into an intimate association in order to find union with it. One can go so far as to say that, in Japan, all forms of spiritual exercise are traditionally carried out within the context of the human interrelationship with nature. This kind of sensibility has formed a culture that deemphasizes the physical boundary between residence and surrounding nature and establishes instead a spiritual threshold."

An example of how Ando has incorporated nature into a design is the Hata House (1983–84), in Nishinomiya. The southern section of the house, which provides views of a nearby national forest, represents the "open" relationship to nature. A bedroom on the ground floor that faces a sunken court represents the "closed" relationship to nature: the landscape is shut out, so that the occupant focuses on such natural phenomena as sunlight, rain, and wind. "When water, wind, light, rain, and other elements of nature are abstracted within architecture, the architecture becomes a place where people and nature confront each other under a sustained sense of tension," he wrote in his *Beyond Horizons in Architecture* essay. "I believe it is this feeling of tension that will awaken the spiritual sensibilities latent in contemporary humanity."

The integration of nature and spirituality is prominent in Ando's most admired structures, his houses of worship. The Chapel on Mt. Rokko (1985–86), in Kobe, features a long, light-filled corridor that leads to a dark, meditative chapel lit on one side. In the Church of the Light (1987–89), in Ibaraki, a cut in the altar wall allows sunlight to flow into the church in the shape of a cross. In the Church on the Water (1985–88), on Awaji Island, the pews face a cross rising majestically from the middle of an artificial lake. The Water Temple (1989–91), in Hyogo Prefecture, is a Buddhist shrine whose roof supports an elliptical pool in which lotus flowers and lily pads float. The pool is part of the entrance to the inner sanctum of the temple.

In a sign of his growing prominence in Japanese architecture, Ando has designed at least seven museums, including the Children's Museum (1987–89), in Himeji; the Museum of Literature (1988–91), in Himeji; the Chikatsu-Asuka Historical Museum (1989–91), in the Osaka area; the Forest of Tombs Museum (1989–91), in Kumamoto; the Nariwa Museum (1992–94), in Nariwa; the Naoshima Contemporary Art Annexe, (1993–95), in Naoshima; and the Suntory Museum (1995), in the Osaka area. As in his other works, he has tried to integrate nature, culture, history, and landscape in his museum designs. The Nariwa Museum fits snugly between a hillside and the old stone wall of a traditional house; the Chikatsu-Asuka Historical Museum and the Forest of Tombs Museum, both of which enable the public to view burial mounds, were built partially underground, to minimize intrusion on the sites. Dramatic walkways integrate the various elements of the designs. "One approaches the Chikatsu-Asuka museum via a curved walkway defined on one side by a concrete wall and on the other by a meandering pond," Benjamin Forgey wrote for the *Washington Post* (October 5, 1991). "The wall hides the steps; as one approaches its end they reveal themselves as a daunting but somehow an inevitable surprise. One climbs them in a ceremony akin to, say, mounting the steps of the pyramid at Tenochtitlan; then one goes down the appropriately shadowy depths of the museum, or up to the startling tower platform [to view the burial mounds]."

In the past decade Ando has designed several works outside his native country. These include the Vitra Seminar House (1989–93), in Weil-am-Rhein, Germany; Gallery 109 (1992), an 1,800-square-foot exhibition space punctuated by 16 oak columns at the Art Institute of Chicago, in Illinois; the Japan Pavilion, a four-story, all-timber structure assembled at Expo 1992, in Seville, Spain; FABRICA (1992–96), a center for the study of photography, graphics, and textiles, located in Treviso, Italy, and built around and under a 17th-century Palladian villa; and the Meditation Space UNESCO (1994–95), constructed next to the UNESCO headquarters in Paris to celebrate the 50th anniversary of the organization. The last-named building, a small cylindrical structure, is meant to be a place where people will pray for eternal peace. The floor is made of granite that was exposed to radiation when the United States dropped an atomic bomb on the Japanese city of Hiroshima in 1945, shortly before the end of World War II. In 1997 Ando won a commission to design a new building for the Modern Art Museum of Fort Worth, Texas.

Ando has designed some projects before actually securing a commission to build them. "When one stands on a site which is still empty, one can sometimes hear the land voice a need for a building," he has written, as quoted in Forgey's 1991 *Washington Post* article. The Chapel on the Water began with such a "message"; so did his proposed design for the restoration of Nakanoshima, an island in central Osaka. Ando's project calls for the construction of a large egg-shaped auditorium in a still-standing Meiji-era building, as well as a "row of immense, mysterious, partially buried geometric forms—spheres, pyramids, cubes—for as yet undesignated cultural and commercial facilities," as Forgey described it in 1991. According to Forgey, Ando is optimistic that his Nakanoshima proposal will someday become a reality.

Ando has held visiting professorships at three American universities: Harvard, Yale, and Columbia. Among his many honors are the Finnish Association of Architects Alvar Aalto Medal (1985), the French Academy of Architecture Gold Medal (1989), the Carlsberg Architectural Prize (1992), the Japan Art Academy Award (1993), and the Asahi Prize (1995). In 1995 he also won the Pritzker Architecture Prize, which was established in 1979. The third Japanese national to receive the prize, Ando donated the $100,000 award to a scholarship fund for children who lost parents as a result of the January 17, 1995 Kobe earthquake, which killed about 5,000 people. (The quake did not damage any of Ando's structures.)

Ando has been married since 1970 to Yumiko Ando, who manages his architecture office and serves as his translator. — W.G.

Suggested Reading: *Chicago Tribune* V p2 Apr. 21, 1995, with photo, XIII p13+ May 28, 1995, with photo; *Christian Science Monitor* p12 Oct. 18, 1994; *Far Eastern Economic Review* p78, May 27, 1993; *Harper's Bazaar* p388+ Mar. 1999, with photo; *House Beautiful* p33 July 1995, with photo; *Japan Quarterly* p426+ Oct./Dec. 1993; *New York Times* II p38 Apr. 23, 1995, with photo, C p1+ Sep. 21, 1995, with photo, II p1+ May 18, 1997, with photo; *pritkerprize.com* (on-line); *Progressive Architecture* p112+ June 1993; *Washington Post* G p1+ July 19, 1986, with photo, D p1 Oct. 5, 1991, with photo; Johnson, Donald Leslie, and Donald Langmead. *Makers of 20th Century Modern Architecture: A Bio-Critical Sourcebook*, 1997

Selected Buildings (in Japan, unless otherwise noted): Atelier in Oyodo I (formerly Tomishima House), 1971–73; Azuma House, Osaka, 1976; Koshino House, Ashiya, 1979–81; Rokko Housing, Hyogo Prefecture, 1978–83; Kidosaki House, Tokyo, 1982–86; Hata House, Nishinomiya, 1983–84; Chapel on Mt. Rokko, Kobe, 1985–86; Galleria Akka, Osaka, 1985–87; Church of the Light, Ibaraki, 1987–89; Church on the Water, Awaji Island, 1985–88; Children's Museum and Seminar House, Himeji, 1987–89; Museum of Literature, Himeji, 1988–91; Water Temple, Hyogo Prefecture, 1989–91; Chikatsu-Asuka Historical Museum, Osaka, 1989–91; Vitra Seminar House, Weil-am-Rhein, Germany, 1989–93; Nariwa Museum, Nariwa, 1992–94; Gallery 109 at the Art Institute of Chicago, Illinois, 1992; Japan Pavilion at Expo 1992, Seville, Spain, 1992; FABRICA, Treviso, Italy, 1992–96; Naoshima Contemporary Art Annexe, Naoshima, 1993–95; Meditation Space UNESCO, Paris, France, 1994–95; Suntory Museum, Osaka 1995

Archive Photos

Annan, Kofi

(AN-nan, KOH-fee)

Apr. 8, 1938– Secretary-General of the United Nations. Address: United Nations Headquarters, Room S-3800, New York, NY 10017

"The peace we seek, in Iraq as everywhere, is one that reflects the lessons of our terrible century: that peace is not true or lasting if bought at any cost; that only peace with justice can honor the victims of war and violence; that without democracy, tolerance, and human rights for all, no peace is truly safe," Kofi Annan, the secretary-general of the United Nations, declared in an op-ed article for the *New York Times* (January 19, 1999). A Ghanaian diplomat, Annan began his five-year term as secretary-general on January 1, 1997. He is the seventh person and the first from a sub-Saharan African nation to reach the U.N.'s highest post. He is also the first to have arrived there after rising through U.N. ranks. Building his career almost entirely within the organization and primarily in a variety of behind-the-scenes, unpublicized bureaucratic jobs, he has acquired unusually broad expertise in peacekeeping and refugee issues as well as in management, administration, budgeting, and finance. Considered an honest, straightforward manager and negotiator with a singular ability to remain cool and good-humored under fire, Annan has, in almost four decades with the United Nations, gained the respect of diplomats and national leaders alike. He is known for his kindness and politesse among people at the grassroots level as well as among high-ranking diplomats, and he is said to command unusual loyalty from lower-echelon U.N. staffers.

Annan began to attract public attention in the early 1990s, when he negotiated the release of Western hostages from Iraq following that country's invasion of Kuwait in 1990. He made headlines again in 1994, when he oversaw the withdrawal of U.N. forces from Somalia, and he drew further notice as the special representative for the U.N. peacekeeping operations in the former Yugoslavia, where, between November 1995 and March 1996, he supervised the transfer of peacekeeping duties from U.N. to NATO-led forces. People with whom he worked in Yugoslavia applauded Annan for his negotiating skills, which he demonstrated in his frequent discussions with the U.N. ambassadors from the U.S., Great Britain, France, and Russia. As one American official commented to a reporter for *Newsweek* (December 23, 1996), "To come out of that, with all four [ambassadors] feeling that they had never been misled, is what's called diplomacy." Annan has expressed a strong commitment to economic development and the pursuit of social justice everywhere. "Intolerance, injustice, and oppression—and their consequences—respect no national frontiers," he declared in an address to the U.N. General Assembly shortly after his appointment as secretary-general, as quoted by the Council for a Livable World (January 10, 1997, on-line). He also said, "We now know more than ever that sustainable economic development is not merely a matter of projects and statistics. It is, above all, a matter of people—real people with basic needs: food, clothing, shelter, and medical care."

In April 2000 Annan issued what the U.N. referred to as a millennium report, entitled *We the Peoples: The Role of the United Nations in the 21st Century.* According to a U.N. press release, the report was "the most comprehensive presentation of the UN's mission in its 55-year history." In particular, it set forth an ambitious agenda that included reducing by 50 percent, by the year 2015, the number of people living in extreme poverty and lacking safe water; ensuring, also by 2015, that all children complete the primary grades and that females and males have equal access to education; decreasing by 25 percent HIV infection rates among people 15 through 24 years old within the next decade; improving the living conditions of some 100 million slum dwellers in the next 20 years; expanding the access of poor nations to the markets of industrialized countries by phasing out duties and quotas; instituting debt-forgiveness measures for poor countries; taking steps to increase world security, "through firmer enforcement of international humanitarian and human rights law" and programs to encourage disarmament; and ensuring the health of the planet for future generations. "We must put people at the centre of everything we do," Annan declared. "No calling is more noble, and no responsibility greater, than that of enabling men, women and children, in cities and villages around the world, to make their lives better. Only when that begins to happen will we know that globalization is indeed becoming inclusive, allowing everyone to share its opportunities."

The secretary-general has now completed four-fifths of his term, and during that time he has emerged as "one of the most provocative leaders the United Nations has known," Barbara Crossette reported for the *New York Times* (December 31, 1999). He surprised many observers, for example, when, in 1998, he said publicly that the U.N. had not done enough to stop the genocide that occurred during the civil war in Rwanda in 1994, and when he expressed regret for what he identified as a bias in the U.N. against Israel. In 1999 he again startled many people, by urging the members of the U.N. to intervene faster and more aggressively in national humanitarian crises like those that had occurred in Rwanda and Bosnia. "Nothing in the Charter precludes a recognition that there are rights beyond borders," he declared in a speech to the General Assembly on September 20, 1999. Sir Brian Urquhart, a former U.N. under-secretary-general for political affairs who has written biographies of past U.N. officials Dag Hammarskjöld and Ralph Bunche, told Crossette that Annan "seems to feel that he's in a position to say, in a perfectly civil way, things that other people really might not have found the courage to say."

A member of an upper-class merchant family descended from tribal chiefs of the Fante group, Kofi Atta Annan was born in Kumasi, Ghana, on April 8, 1938. His penchant for activism and leadership skills became apparent early on: friends have recalled a successful hunger strike that he organized at the Ghanaian boarding school he attended in the 1950s, during which he and fellow students demanded—and got—better food. After attending the University of Science and Technology at Kumasi, he enrolled at Macalester College, in St. Paul, Minnesota, where he completed his bachelor's degree in economics, in 1961. In the following year he continued his education, at the Institut des Hautes Études Internationales, in Geneva, Switzerland.

In 1962 Annan accepted a position as an administrative and budget officer at the World Health Organization (WHO), a branch of the U.N. with headquarters in Geneva. After serving in various other U.N. posts in Geneva, New York City, and Addis Ababa, the capital of Ethiopia, he was named Alfred P. Sloan fellow for the 1971–72 academic year at the Massachusetts Institute of Technology, in Cambridge, where he received a master's degree in management. Except for a two-year stint between 1974 and 1976, when he served as managing director of the Ghana Tourist Development Co., Annan has been on the U.N.'s staff since 1972. Between 1976 and 1983 he worked in the personnel department at the Office of the U.N. High Commissioner for Refugees, eventually rising to deputy director of administration and head of personnel. He was then reassigned to the U.N. headquarters, in New York City, where he held an array of managerial positions, including director of budget in the Office of Financial Services (1984–87), assistant secretary-general in the Office of Human Resources Management, security coordinator for the U.N. (1987–90), and assistant secretary-general for program planning and controller of budget and finance (1990–92).

In 1992 Annan advanced to the U.N.'s high-profile peacekeeping division. Early in the post–Cold War period, when regional conflict and ethnic strife seemed the order of the day, he quickly distinguished himself, first as assistant secretary-general of peacekeeping operations and then, from March 1993 until his appointment as secretary-general, under-secretary-general of peacekeeping operations. In that last, highly sensitive position, Annan oversaw 17 military operations and a $3.5 billion budget, more than 15 times the size of the 1988 budget. Although he was noted for his smooth diplomacy regarding U.N. involvement in the civil wars that erupted in Somalia and Bosnia, Annan expressed clear frustration at governments—chief among them that of the U.S.—that were unwilling to throw military and financial support behind the Security Council's peacekeeping resolutions. "Peacekeeping is always cheaper than war," he said at a press conference in March 1994.

By the fall of 1996, it had become clear that the U.S., alone among the members of the Security Council, was firmly opposed to Boutros Boutros-Ghali's reelection as U.N. secretary-general, and the council, which makes that appointment, began considering other candidates—specifically, African diplomats, primarily because no African diplomats had yet served as secretary-general. (Boutros-Ghali is from Egypt, but, like other people from North Africa, he is often not considered African; that designation applies chiefly to the black peoples who live in nations south of the Sahara Desert. Boutros-Ghali's predecessors—Trygve Lie, Dag Hammarskjöld, U Thant, Kurt Waldheim, and Javier Pérez de Cuéllar—hailed from Norway, Sweden, Burma, Austria, and Peru, respectively.) Most countries came out in support of Annan, who enjoyed an international reservoir of good will and was frequently touted as the only candidate who could successfully extinguish the widespread resentment triggered by the U.S.'s refusal to consent to Boutros-Ghali's reappointment. The French government stated its preference for a leader from a francophone country, but in late December, when all three African nations on the Security Council—including Egypt—threw their support behind Annan, France withdrew its dissent.

Soon after his appointment, on December 17, 1996, Annan remarked, as quoted in *Newsweek* (December 23, 1996), "I have 185 masters," referring to the U.N.'s 185 member nations and thus indicating his keen appreciation of the U.N. as a truly international organization. (The number of member nations has since risen to 189.) His dedication to consensus-building became clear when he announced that a comprehensive U.N. reform package—upon which the U.S. Congress had predicated the payment of its massive debt to the organization—would not be announced until at least midsummer 1997, after all U.N. members had been consulted. "A good leader must also be a good follower," he was quoted as saying by Elaine Sciolino in the *New York Times* (February 9, 1997). Earlier, an editorial in the *Chicago Tribune* (December 18, 1996) had expressed optimism about his chances of successfully instigating organizational reform because of his "insider's ability to read between the lines of the U.N. organization chart and [to see] . . . where the skeletons are buried—so they can be dug up and exposed." But others expressed doubt about whether a career U.N. civil servant like Annan could summon the political will to change the very bureaucracy that had nurtured his advancement.

In July 1997 Annan unveiled a plan for streamlining the U.N.'s bureaucracy, which at the time supported 50,000 employees in 30 agencies worldwide. His proposal included the consolidation and regrouping of 24 agencies that reported to the secretary-general into five divisions—peace and security, humanitarian affairs, economic and social welfare, development programs, and human rights—that would report to the secretary-general and also to a deputy secretary-general, with the creation of the latter position being part of the plan. (On January 12, 1998 Louise Frechette, Canada's deputy minister of national defense, was appointed to the post.) While some viewed this effort as an important step toward saving money, others contended that the plan "simply reshuffles the deck at a time when the number of cards needs to be reduced," as Minnesota senator Rod Grams, the Republican chairman of the Senate Foreign Relations Committee, expressed it. Despite such objections, in November 1997 the General Assembly approved the first package of proposed reforms, which were designed to save the U.N. $123 million. (Even after it was approved, the United States remained intransigent regarding its refusal to clear its debt. Failure to pay a specified percentage of the arrears by January 1, 2000 would have resulted in the loss of the United States' seat in the General Assembly. Finally, in November 1999, Congress passed budget legislation earmarking $819 million for repayment of the back dues, which by then totaled some $1 billion.)

The year 1998 opened with the threat of a violent confrontation between Iraq and the United States over the issue of weapons inspections. Saddam Hussein, the president of Iraq, insisted that unless the U.N. lifted the economic sanctions that it had imposed in 1990, after Iraq's invasion of Kuwait, his country would continue to bar inspectors from sites (including what were labeled presidential palaces) where, it was believed, Iraq had stockpiled biological and chemical weapons, long-range ballistic missiles, and other weapons of mass destruction. The United States, meanwhile, had warned Hussein that the U.S. was prepared to unleash air strikes on Iraq if he did not cooperate with the inspectors; indeed, in anticipation of such an attack, the U.S. had deployed an armada of warships in the Persian Gulf. Determined to end the deadlock by means of diplomacy rather than force—"I kept asking, 'After the bombing, then what?'" he explained to Crossette—Annan met face-to-face with Hussein in Iraq. "I had to deal with him to avoid a tragedy and to save lives . . . ," Annan said during an interview for *Time* (March 9, 1998). "Once I got through to him and explained what was at stake, and what he could do for his nation and his people, and what he would face if he did not agree, he got focused. . . . When he said, 'I know you are a courageous man,' I realized he was probably warming to me, but otherwise I saw no sign. It was at that point that I moved into the critical issues. . . . [The Iraqis] are very keen to get rid of the sanctions. I made it very clear to him that the only way to do that is to cooperate with [the U.N. Special Commission, which was set up in 1991 to ensure the elimination of Iraq's weapons of mass destruction]." During their meeting, Annan spoke English and Hussein spoke Arabic. "He had an interpreter," Annan told the *Time* interviewer. "Unfortunately, I made a mistake. I should have had my interpreter, too. But, anyway, we did get the result."

That result was the so-called Memo of Understanding, dated February 22, 1998, whereby Iraq, by accepting all previous Security Council resolutions pertaining to the issue, agreed to "unconditional and unrestricted" inspections and the eradication of various weapons. The Security Council approved the pact on March 2; at the same time, the council raised from $4 billion to $7.4 billion the annual limit on Iraq's sales of oil, the money from which was to be used to buy food and medicine and pay for repairs of the country's crumbling infrastructure. In some quarters, Annan was regarded as a hero for securing the agreement; others expressed doubt that Iraq would abide by the agreement for long. The skeptics were right: On August 5, 1998 Hussein again halted inspections, claiming that Iraq had fulfilled its end of the deal and demanding that the sanctions be removed. Annan's renewed efforts to resolve the issue came to naught, and on December 16, 1998—in what Annan described as a "sad day" for the world and himself—the U.S., with support from Great Britain, bombed targets in Iraq. But Saddam Hussein refused to budge, and no inspections of suspected Iraqi storage sites took place in 1999. "Yes, [the Iraqis] didn't live up to the undertaking," Annan acknowledged to Barbara Crossette. "But does that mean we should not try diplomacy? I know some people have accused me of using diplomacy. That's my job. That's what I'm paid for."

In March 1998 Annan visited the Middle East. In a speech to the Palestinian Legislative Council in Gaza City, he urged patience regarding the Arab-Israeli peace process and nonviolence. Later, addressing the Israeli Foreign Relations Council in

West Jerusalem, he said that the U.N. had sometimes acted unfairly toward Israel. But he also accused Israel of purposely undermining the good will of its neighbors by establishing settlements in Palestinian areas and imposing hardships on Palestinians, and he called upon Israeli officials to soften their attitude toward Palestinians. Two months later he went to Africa, where he made stops in eight countries. In what he termed a "healing mission" to Rwanda, he appeared before the Rwandan Parliament. Following a vehement denunciation by Anastase Gasana, the country's foreign minister, of the U.N.'s actions in Rwanda in 1994, Annan—who had then been under-secretary-general for peacekeeping operations—acknowledged the inadequacy of the organization's response to the widespread massacre of Tutsi civilians by Hutu militants. His failure, in that speech, to apologize for the U.N.'s dismal performance or to assume part of the blame himself angered many Rwandan lawmakers, among them the nation's president, Pasteur Bizimungu, and deputy president, Paul Kagame, who refused to attend a reception held in Annan's honor.

At the opening session of the General Assembly in September 1998, Annan urged the organization to intervene in the growing conflict between Serb forces and ethnic Albanians in the Serbian province of Kosovo. That intervention started to materialize in June 1999, when the Security Council voted to send a NATO-led peacekeeping force of 50,000 troops into Kosovo and to assign temporary responsibility for administering the province to the U.N. The newly created U.N. Mission in Kosovo (UNMIK), headed by the French minister of health, Bernard Koucher (a co-founder of Doctors without Borders), was given the formidable task of forming a 3,000-member multinational police force, setting up a judicial system, dealing with human-rights abuses, tackling the problems anticipated with the return of hundreds of thousands of ethnic Albanian refugees, and rebuilding homes and infrastructure. The continuing presence of the Kosovo Liberation Army (a guerrilla group composed of ethnic Albanians) and still-intense animosity between Serbs and ethnic Albanians compounded the difficulties UNMIK faced. As of late November 1999, Steven Erlanger reported in the *New York Times* (November 22, 1999), intolerance and the widespread desire for revenge were thwarting progress toward the creation of a peaceful, multiethnic, democratic, self-governing province.

In June 1998, in what Annan referred to, in an interview with Afsané Bassir Pour for *Le Monde* (on-line), as "a giant step that we have taken for future generations," the U.N. created the International Criminal Court, in Rome, to bring to justice "those who commit crimes against humanity." Describing what he termed the "completely unjust situation" that had existed "because the necessary international framework did not exist," he noted that someone who kills an individual would, "in all likelihood, be tried and punished, but someone who kills a hundred thousand will not be brought to justice; that is unacceptable. We have seen that criminals like the former chief of the Khmer Rouge [in Cambodia], Pol Pot, have never been punished." Other matters that required Annan's attention included reported misconduct of U.N. peacekeeping troops (who are citizens of various member nations). In August 1999 Annan issued a directive stipulating that all troops under U.N. command must follow international laws—prominent among them the Geneva Conventions—governing behavior of soldiers during wartime, with the aim of safeguarding civilians and prisoners of war. Signed to date by 188 nations (but not the United States), the Geneva Conventions prohibit the use of land mines, booby traps, and other weapons of indiscriminate destruction.

Several challenges faced Annan in 2000. Peacekeeping missions in East Timor, Sierra Leone, Kosovo, and the Democratic Republic of Congo, among others, severely strained the resources of the United Nations peacekeeping department, which, with approximately 400 employees, is only half the size of the organization's public-information staff. In March 2000 Annan appointed an international panel to come up with ways in which peacekeeping missions could be handled more effectively. "Partly it is a question of being clearer about what [the missions] are trying to do. And partly it is a question of getting the nuts and bolts right," Annan explained, as quoted by Barbara Crossette in the *New York Times* (March 8, 2000). Backed up by the panel, Annan called for strengthening and reorganizing the peacekeeping department and enlarging the U.N. Security Council.

Annan also asked member states to respond more generously to the U.N.'s requests for help. His plea came on the heels of a United States offer of military aircraft to transport needed personnel from various nations to Sierra Leone during a crisis there in which 500 U.N. soldiers were taken hostage; the Pentagon's charter rates for the job were higher than those of commercial airlines or private charter companies. In another case, U.N. operations in Congo were jeopardized because of insufficient aid from the member states. "One country which had undertaken to provide four airfield crash-rescue units subsequently withdrew the offer and proposed only one unit instead," Annan declared in a report to the Security Council, according to Barbara Crossette in the *New York Times* (June 14, 2000). "Another, which was supposed to provide an infantry battalion, ha[d] none of the 20 armored personnel carriers required and lack[ed] significant amounts of other materiel, including generators, engineering equipment, and radio-equipped jeeps."

In late September 2000 violence broke out between Israelis and Palestinians, following a visit by the Israeli politician Ariel Sharon, the leader of the right-wing Likud Party, to a site in Israel considered holy by both Jews and Muslims (the Temple

Mount, known to Arabs as Haram al-Sharif). In an effort to defuse the crisis, Annan flew to Paris to talk with the Israeli prime minister, Ehud Barak, the Palestinian leader, Yasir Arafat, and the U.S. secretary of state, Madeleine Albright. On October 16 he flew to the Middle East to attend a summit with President Hosni Mubarak of Egypt and President Clinton. As of November 1, the results of his diplomatic missions remained unclear.

According to Barbara Crossette in the *New York Times* (September 13, 2000), U.N. diplomats were "nearly unanimous in praising [Annan's] steady hand over the last year, in opening the United Nations to strong criticism of peacekeeping operations for the sake of salvaging its credibility, in moving into new activities to defend human rights, and in working in tandem with a global economic and technological revolution."

From his first marriage, to a Nigerian woman, which ended in divorce, Kofi Annan has a daughter, Ama, and a son, Kojo. His second wife, Nane Lagergren, who is Swedish, has a daughter, Nina, from her previous marriage. A prominent lawyer in Sweden, Lagergren formerly served as a legal officer for the U.N. High Commissioner for Refugees; she is now an artist. Annan and Lagergren live in the official residence of the U.N. secretary-general, on the East Side of Manhattan, in New York City.

Asked during a 1998 visit to the Commonwealth Club of California what he hoped his legacy to the U.N. would be, Annan replied, as reported on the club's Web site, "I think I will be very pleased if by the time I leave, the U.N. is considered as an organization that has renewed itself, and is responsive to the needs of the world, and it is seen as an organization that is doing what it was established to do. In other words, a United Nations that is focused, that is effective, and that is responsive. If by the time I leave, we are there, I will be very happy." — M.R.

Suggested Reading: Commonwealth Club of California (on-line); *Ebony* p136+ Oct. 1998, with photos; *Newsweek* p30+ Dec. 23, 1996, with photo; *New York Times* I p7 Dec. 14, 1996, with photo, A p6 Dec. 28, 1998, with photo, A p1+ Dec. 31, 1999, with photo; *New York Times Magazine* p44+ Mar. 29, 1998, with photos; *Time* p54+ Mar. 9, 1998, with photos ; Toronto *Globe & Mail* A p1 Dec. 14, 1996, with photo; *Washington Post* A p1+ Dec. 14, 1996, with photo, A p22+ Dec. 14, 1996, with photo

---

Apted, Michael

Feb. 10, 1941– Filmmaker; television director.
Address: c/o Osiris Films, Bldg. 137, 300 S. Lorimar, Burbank, CA 90067

Although Michael Apted has had a distinguished stay in Hollywood, guiding Jodie Foster to an Oscar nomination in *Nell* (1994) and directing *Coal Miner's Daughter* (1980), *Gorillas in the Mist* (1988), and the 19th James Bond feature, *The World Is Not Enough* (1999), his lifeblood remains the 14 British children who started his career. Every seven years, the director returns to his native country to catch up with the stars of the acclaimed documentary *7 Up* (1964), the first in the series of films that would follow its subjects' lives. To date, the original installment has spawned five sequels (the most recent entry, *42 Up*, was released in 1999) and inspired similar projects in countries around the world. Discussing the *Up* films, as the series has come to be known, Vincent Canby wrote for the *New York Times* (February 16, 1992), "There have been a number of notable documentaries in recent years. . . . Yet none of these has the narrative, emotional, and even esthetic impact of the enchanting, singular *7 Up* films." While Apted has acknowledged that the film series has affected his life profoundly, he is unsure of how the *Up* participants perceive him. In an interview with Georgia Dullea for the *New York Times* (October 13, 1985), he mused, "To them, I'm probably some exotic bird who lives in Hollywood and makes movies and flies in every seven years to catch up on their lives."

Deidre Davidson/Archive Photos

A self-described "English tourist," Michael Apted was born on February 10, 1941 in Aylesbury, Buckinghamshire, England. The son of an insurance inspector, Apted was a quiet, bashful child who enjoyed listening to the radio and going to soccer games with his father. At age 14 he received a scholarship to a private school in London. While there, he was exposed to the theater and cinema of the city's trendy West End. He became fascinated with the world of theater, but he remained too shy to perform in school plays.

In 1959 Apted entered Cambridge University, in England, and began studying law. Still, his interest in theater was very much alive, and it finally became all-consuming. At Cambridge Apted starred in plays with many people who would go on to stardom, among them Trevor Nunn, Stephen Frears, Jonathan Lynn, and Monty Python's John Cleese. Although he realized that he had discovered his passion, Apted felt that a career as an actor was still little more than a pipe dream. After he graduated from Cambridge, in 1963, he went to work for Granada Television in Manchester, in northern England. "I learned the television business in Manchester," Apted told Nan Robertson for the *New York Times* (May 20, 1984), noting that he worked on "current affairs, documentaries, music, drama." In addition, he directed several episodes of the long-running British soap *Coronation Street.* Apted stayed with Granada for seven years. It was during this time that he became involved in the film that would change his life.

Although *7 Up* was initially inspired by the Jesuit maxim "Give me a child until he is seven and I will give you the man," as Apted wrote for the *New York Times* (January 12, 1992), "our underlying concept was political." The idea was to examine the ways that conditions in 1960s England, which was arguably the pop-culture capital of the world then, would affect the lives of the country's youth. As Apted wrote in his *Times* article, the situation presented several unknowns: "Did everybody have a fair chance, or did the accident of birth bring power, wealth, and success? Were children made into winners and losers by class divisions, or was the old order changing forever?" Although Apted is often credited as the director of *7 Up*, in reality he was a researcher on the project; the directorial credit went to Paul Almond. Apted did, however, have an active role in the production of the documentary. Various British departments of education recommended children to the crew; the 14 children who were chosen, based on their on-camera presence, were asked questions on such topics as love, work, money, and class and race relations. The film was shot in a very straightforward style, with hand-held equipment, and almost instantly after it debuted on British television, in 1964, it was hailed as a classic. Audiences in the United States first saw *7 Up* in 1985, at the New York Film Festival, and like their counterparts in Great Britain, they were captivated by the young children and their precocious, idealistic view of life in modern England.

The demand for a sequel was overwhelming. It resulted, seven years later, in *Seven Plus Seven* (1971), which Apted himself directed and which caught up with the original film's stars, now well into adolescence. Like its predecessor, *Seven Plus Seven* was a blockbuster. In the late 1990s *7 Up*'s subjects turned 42; some have achieved the dreams they outlined in the earlier films, while others have fallen short. Two have refused to be a part of the project any longer, regarding it an intrusion. Despite the changes the years have wrought, one constant remains: the rapt attention the world pays these 14 people and the impact the films have on viewers. Apted plans to continue the project for as long as his subjects will cooperate. In his 1992 piece for the *New York Times*, he explained the importance of the series to him: "I remember sitting with Mike Scott, then Granada's head of programming, in Los Angeles, and saying wasn't it about time for *28 Up*, and him responding that it would never happen because I wouldn't leave Hollywood. He couldn't guess the power the films have in my life and how I doubt whether I'll ever have the chance to do anything as original as this again."

In the meantime Apted had made a string of other successful features in the United Kingdom, including *Triple Echo* (1973), *The Squeeze* (1977), and *Agatha* (1979), starring Dustin Hoffman. With the success of the *Up* films, Hollywood came knocking. Apted made his American film debut with *Coal Miner's Daughter* (1980). Based on the life of country-music icon Loretta Lynn, it was a smash hit, earning $80 million at the box office and netting Sissy Spacek a best-actress Oscar for her portrayal of the singer. The movie was also honored with a Golden Globe Award for best picture and a nomination for Tommy Lee Jones as best actor. Perhaps the most surprising thing about *Coal Miner's Daughter* was how well Apted, a native Englishman, captured the feeling and tone of Appalachian mining towns. He was so successful in that regard, in fact, that most of the cast and crew assumed that he had grown up in the coal-mining country of northern England. George Vecsey, who wrote the book on which the film was based, recalled to Nan Robertson his reaction to the picture. "I went to a screening prepared to be embarrassed about what an English director would do in a Hollywood film about this subject," he said. "Within 10 minutes I wanted to poke somebody in the screening room and say, 'Hey, that's my book up there.'" Indeed, the film's stars credited the flair of *Coal Miner's Daughter* to Apted's directing style. "Actually, Michael was the key to it all," Sissy Spacek remarked to Nan Robertson. "I shudder to think what the film would have been without him."

Apted followed up his successful Hollywood debut with *Continental Divide* (1981), a road-trip comedy starring John Belushi. The film, which favored slapstick gags—such as repeated shots of Belushi falling down while carrying heavy camping gear—was a departure for Apted; it signaled the eclecticism that would come to characterize his career. *Continental Divide* received mixed critical reviews, but most called attention to the light touch Apted had brought to otherwise tepid material. In the *Christian Science Monitor* (October 8, 1981), David Sterritt wrote about the film, "On the down side, it moves rather slowly, its laughs are intermittent, and its rhythms are a bit slack. On the up side, however, it has the virtues of its maker—Michael Apted." *Continental Divide* has since become something of a cult favorite.

As the 1980s progressed, Apted worked steadily, making at least one movie a year. These included the Cold War crime drama *Gorky Park* (1983); *Firstborn* (1984), a drama about suburban teens faced with an abusive stepfather; and the Richard Pryor bomb *Critical Condition* (1987). During this period he also made two documentaries: *Bring on the Night* (1985), which chronicled the formation of the rocker Sting's first post-Police band, and *28 Up* (1984), the fourth film in the *Up* series. Of the latter picture, Apted noted in his *New York Times* essay, "I doubt that *28 Up* achieved the magical quality of the original—maybe that's the prerogative of seven-year-old children—but according to the critics, it had power and resonance." In 1988 he directed *Gorillas in the Mist*, which starred Sigourney Weaver in the story of the primatologist Dian Fossey's quest to save endangered mountain gorillas. The film was another feather in Apted's cap, drawing rave reviews and several award nominations for the film and Weaver.

Apted began the 1990s with a proverbial bang. By 1991 he had completed *35 Up*, shot the legal thriller *Class Action*, with Gene Hackman and Mary Elizabeth Mastrantonio, and started work on two films on the plight of Native Americans—*Incident at Oglala* (1992) and *Thunderheart* (1992)—which put Apted's name in the forefront of the public consciousness once again. *Incident at Oglala* was a documentary on the famous case of Leonard Peltier, who is often considered America's only political prisoner. Peltier, an American Indian Movement activist, was convicted under questionable circumstances for the 1975 murders of two FBI agents on the Pine Ridge Reservation, in South Dakota. While Apted felt strongly that the conviction was a miscarriage of justice, he made a point of portraying the story from a neutral position. "The point was to create some action, get people to think for themselves," he told Paul Evans for the *Washington Post* (April 5, 1992). "If only nine people see this film and are moved to seek justice, I've succeeded." *Incident at Oglala* was praised by critics for its sensitive treatment of the subject matter. Stanley Kauffmann commented in the *New Republic* (June 8, 1992) that the "film is further evidence of our country's ability to ignore miseries—well-known miseries—among our own people."

Released concurrently with *Incident at Oglala* was the crime drama *Thunderheart*, which was loosely based on the same story. Apted found this to be a trickier film to shoot, as he was faced with delicate issues that he had to compress into a Hollywood format. He worked very closely with Native Americans on the Pine Ridge Reservation, making sure that everything in the film was portrayed with accuracy. On the whole, Native American spokespersons responded positively to the film, though some took issue with its content. Glenn Morris, a member of the Shawnee tribe and a professor at the University of Colorado at Denver, told M. S. Mason for the *Christian Science Monitor* (May 12, 1992), "There are a few positive roles in the film. . . . But the problem I had with it is that, while it wasn't supposed to be historically accurate, it did try to represent what happened at Pine Ridge between 1972 and 1976. And like *Mississippi Burning* [a film about the murder of three civil-rights workers in 1964], it presented a severely revisionist history."

After completing *Thunderheart* and *Incident at Oglala*, Apted went on to direct the documentary *Moving the Mountain* (1994), a look at events that took place before and during the uprising of students in Tiananmen Square, in Beijing, China, in 1989. Also in 1994 two of his feature films premiered. The first, *Blink*, is an eerie thriller in which a blind woman becomes the target of a serial killer. In a review of *Blink* for *People* (January 24, 1994), Leah Rozen wrote, "Michael Apted directs with a sure hand, keeping the movie hurtling along with the speed of the Chicago [elevated train]." The second, released in December, remains one of Apted's best-known Hollywood films. *Nell*, the story of a woman raised in the woods of North Carolina who speaks a language of her own, was a tour de force for its star, Jodie Foster, and ultimately landed her an Oscar nomination. Apted earned high marks as well, for his direction. Roger Ebert remarked in the *Chicago Sun-Times* (December 23, 1994), "In real life, a wild child might not be quite so inspiring or pleasant to know. But in *Nell*, the result is a quiet poem to the more natural side of our natures."

After *Nell*, Apted moved on to the medical thriller *Extreme Measures* (1996), starring Hugh Grant and Gene Hackman. The highly anticipated film boasted solid reviews, with Janet Maslin of the *New York Times* (September 27, 1996), for example, writing that it "remains stylish and taut with a taste for macabre little surprises." Glowing praise could not save *Extreme Measures* at the box office, however; the film grossed only $17 million, a far cry from its $38 million budget.

Apted bounced back the following year with *Inspirations* (1997), a documentary that explored the creative process through the eyes of seven artists, including the rock star David Bowie and the Pop artist Roy Lichtenstein. The success of the film, according to Apted, hinged on avoiding as many details of the subjects' lives as possible. As he explained on the *Indie Network* Web site, "I didn't want the film to be biographical. . . . I felt the film would only get going once you started to deal with issues and could counterpoint the various answers that people had." Apted followed *Inspirations* with the television drama *Always Outnumbered* (1998), based on a book by Walter Mosley and starring Laurence Fishburne as an ex-con who conveys life lessons to the residents of an L.A. suburb. That same year Apted made *42 Up* (which was released in 1999); by then he had recognized just how connected with the *Up* subjects he had become. "Without being nauseating about it, they are very much like a family," he remarked in the *New York Times* (June 24, 1998), "and our lives are interwoven whether we like it or not."

By the late 1990s Apted had begun to notice certain similarities in the feature-film scripts he was being shown. While he had always tried to have a varied career, tackling dramas, comedies, and romances in rapid succession, he felt that studios had a preconceived notion about him. "I get pegged if a movie has a certain documentary slant," he told the *Indie Network*'s Web site, "whether it's *Gorillas in the Mist* or someone wants a piece of material to have a documentary tone to it like *Nell.* I don't get pegged in documentaries, but I certainly get pegged in feature films. I don't get offered big-budget science fiction films or action films or comedy films."

That changed in early 1999, when Apted was given the chance to direct *The World Is Not Enough* (1999), the next film in the James Bond series. The offer surprised many, as Apted was certainly not known for the sorts of big-budget spectacles that characterize the Bond films. Even Apted himself was initially puzzled. "I did hesitate in accepting the offer," he remarked to Alan Jones for *Cinefantastique* (December 1999). "All I kept thinking was, 'What the hell do they want me for?' Then I found out they wanted a better story to go between all the action and someone well versed in drama to make it pay the dividends."

The film finds British master spy James Bond (Pierce Brosnan) battling a terrorist who seeks to control the world's oil supply. Apted was drawn by the timeliness of the subject matter, which appealed to his documentarian instincts. "The story we have in Bond is playing out in front of us at the moment . . . ," he explained to Jones. "This time last year the papers were full of who was going to have what oil pipelines going through which country in the Caspian area to the West. We are the first film to be dealing with the whole issue and it's great to be doing a Bond that's ahead of the game for a change rather than dealing with old hat intrigues about Russians." Apted's background also played a key role in his choices of exotic locales, sites that typify a Bond picture. "For the reality of our story I managed to persuade them to take Bond to Azerbaijan. That perked my interest a great deal and appealed to my documentary roots." In addition to his stylistic touches, Apted decided to take a fresh approach to the series by doing away with Bond's womanizing. "Women are central to the film but in a completely different way," he told Alison Boshoff for the *Age* (October 21, 1998, online). "We want to bring Bond into the 21st century with a different attitude to women and different women in the film."

The World Is Not Enough received largely positive critical notices. It grossed $30.5 million in its first weekend, setting an opening-weekend record for a James Bond film. The picture eventually pulled in over $100 million in the U.S. and millions more overseas. As of late October 2000, reports that Apted has been asked to direct the 20th Bond film could not be substantiated. (In the past 10 years, no one has directed two consecutive Bond films.)

Apted currently lives in Los Angeles with his wife, Jo. He has two grown sons, Paul and James. He continues to seek out new challenges in films, balancing his eclectic résumé by taking on documentaries, TV commercials, and feature films in no discernible order. Apted has said that he feels a need to inject each of his films with some small measure of social importance. "I do feel movies and television are very powerful," he commented to M. S. Mason. "I do believe in their power to influence and inform. So I do want my films to have that quality of good citizenship: Without turning everybody into a goody-goody, you do take notice of other people, you do treat people decently." Although he has strived to incorporate that common thread in his films, Apted otherwise tries to avoid putting his personal stamp on them. "I don't make material out of my own life," he told Nan Robertson. "I use other people's material. I enter new ground with every film I do. I love new adventures, new pressures, new stimulation." — J.K.B.

Suggested Reading: *Chicago Tribune* XIII p18+ Feb. 9, 1992, with photos; *Christian Science Monitor* p11 May 12, 1992, with photos; *New Republic* p32+ June 8, 1992; *New York Times* H p27 May 29, 1984, with photos, II p13+ Oct. 13, 1985, with photos, II p11+ Jan. 12, 1992, with photos, C p11+ Apr. 26, 1995, with photos, E p1+ June 24, 1998, with photos; *Washington Post* G p1+ Apr. 5, 1992

Selected Films: *Triple Echo*, 1973; *Stardust*, 1974; *Agatha*, 1979; *Coal Miner's Daughter*, 1980; *Continental Divide*, 1981; *Gorky Park*, 1983; *Firstborn*, 1984; *Bring on the Night*, 1985; *28 Up*, 1985; *Gorillas in the Mist*, 1988; *Class Action*, 1991; *35 Up*, 1991; *Incident at Oglala*, 1992; *Thunderheart*, 1992; *Moving the Mountain*, 1994; *Blink*, 1994; *Nell*, 1994; *Extreme Measures*, 1996; *Inspirations*, 1997; *42 Up*, 1999; *The World Is Not Enough*, 1999

Selected Television Shows: *7 Up*, 1964; *Seven Plus Seven*, 1970; *The Collection*, 1975; *21 Up*, 1977; *Stronger than the Sun*, 1977; *P'tang Yang Kipperbang*, 1982; *The Long Way Home*, 1989; *Always Outnumbered*, 1998

Backstreet Boys

Pop-music group

Carter, Nick
Jan. 28, 1980–

Dorough, Howie D.
Aug. 22, 1973–

Littrell, Brian
Feb. 20, 1975–

McLean, A.J.
Jan. 9, 1978–

Richardson, Kevin
Oct. 3, 1972–

Address: c/o Mitch Schneider Organization, 14724 Ventura Blvd., Suite 410, Sherman Oaks, CA 91403

"There's a sound that looms large in rock mythology from Elvis and Beatles documentaries yet it is seldom heard live," Robert Christgau wrote for *Rolling Stone* (September 3, 1998). "It's the sound of thousands of barely pubescent females screaming for their heroes, their white knights, their dreamboats. The finest thing one can say about the Backstreet Boys is that—unlike their forerunners, New Kids on the Block—they are worthy of this ecstatic, not-quite-knowing, supernaturally high sound." Comprising Nickolas Carter, Howard "Howie D." Dorough, Brian Littrell, Alexander "A.J." McLean, and Kevin Richardson, the Backstreet Boys are among the most successful of the current crop of young male singing groups. Their self-titled debut album sold almost 30 million copies, stayed on *Billboard*'s Top 20 album chart for two years, and generated five Top 10 singles. Their follow-up record sold 1,134,000 copies in its first week of release alone, and when a 39-city arena tour was announced in August 1999, almost 765,000 tickets were sold within one hour. The Backstreet Boys have been featured in teen magazines on a regular basis, and their devoted preadolescent and adolescent female fans maintain several Web sites detailing nearly every facet of the singers' lives, including favorite foods, pets, and pastimes. Unlike most other teen idols, however, the Backstreet Boys are occasionally taken seriously by rock critics, who have praised the members' tightly controlled vocal harmonies and maturing musicianship.

The group was formed in 1993 in Orlando, Florida, a magnet for young actors and singers hoping to land jobs as performers at Disney World and other theme parks in the area. At the time four of the five Backstreet Boys were among such aspiring entertainers. Alexander James McLean, born on January 9, 1978 in West Palm Beach, Florida, grew up with his divorced mother in Kissimmee, Florida, and moved to Orlando when he was in the seventh grade. He immediately landed a part in a Nickelodeon show and later appeared in about 70 plays. Howard Dwaine Dorough was born in Orlando on August 22, 1973 to a Puerto Rican mother and an Irish-American father; his parents raised him in the Catholic faith. Like McLean, he was involved in show business as a child, acting in commercials for theme parks and local theater productions. Nickolas Gene Carter was born on January 28, 1980 in Jamestown, New York. Migrating to Orlando in search of show-business opportunities, he often ran into McLean and Dorough while auditioning for parts. The three became friends, and, inspired by the music of Boyz II Men and Color Me Badd, two popular all-male singing groups, they passed time between auditions by singing a capella.

The trio caught the attention of Lou Pearlman, head of Trans Continental, an Orlando-based conglomerate that owned, among other businesses, a travel agency and charter planes and managed the Chippendale dancers. Pearlman had taken note of the commercial success of New Kids on the Block a few years before and hoped to find a similar singing group. He recruited McLean, Dorough, and Carter and added Kevin Richardson, who was then portraying Aladdin at Disney World. Born on October 3, 1972 in Lexington, Kentucky, and raised on a farm, Kevin Scott Richardson had sung in a church choir and played in a band called Paradise before heading out to Orlando at the suggestion of his father (who died of cancer before Richardson was accepted into the Backstreet Boys). For the group's fifth member, Richardson suggested his cousin Brian Thomas Littrell, with whom he had performed while growing up in Kentucky. Born on February 20, 1975, Littrell abandoned his plan to attend Cincinnati Bible College after he flew to Florida and successfully auditioned for the group.

Taking their name from the Backstreet Market, a popular teen hangout in Orlando, the quintet played in high-school auditoriums and at other local venues, including Sea World. Their stage personas developed quickly. Carter, the youngest and blondest, was the heartthrob of the group and often elicited the biggest sighs from female fans; Dorough, the sweetest and most soulful of the members, was cast as the Latin lover; McLean was the rebel, sporting several tattoos and outrageously dyed hair; Littrell, who bears an uncanny resemblance to singer-turned-actor Mark Wahlberg, had the most boyish charm; and Richardson, with his swarthy complexion, heavy brows, and carefully sculpted goatee, looked exotic, at least by Middle-American standards. Playing in venues of a modest size, the group consistently drew positive responses from their young audiences, who applauded the boys' dance moves and trendy outfits with as much enthusiasm as they did the group's music, which was made up predominantly of cover versions of Top 40 tunes by more established all-male groups. The Backstreet Boys eventually began opening for bigger acts, among them the Village People and Brandi.

Courtesy of Mitch Schneider Organization

The Backstreet Boys (left to right): A.J. McLean, Brian Littrell, Kevin Richardson, Nick Carter, and Howie D. Dorough

During one concert a Backstreet Boys manager instructed Dorough to ask the audience to scream. The resulting din was recorded by the answering machine of a Mercury Records executive whom the manager had telephoned, with the aim of giving him a sample of audience reaction to the Boys. The next day Bobby Ducket and David McPherson, both from Mercury Records, came to hear the group perform. Although their company declined to sign the group, McPherson engineered a contract for the quintet after he moved to Jive Records, in 1994. The following year the Backstreet Boys released a single, "We've Got It Going On," which was cowritten by Max Martin, the composer of catchy pop tunes for many of the leading teen acts of the 1990s. On U.S. charts the song peaked at an unimpressive number 69; in Europe, the group met with much greater success. They won a 1995 Smash Hits Award in London (for best new tour act) and were invited to perform on the British TV show *Top of the Pops.* Their second single, "I'll Never Break Your Heart," was a big hit in Germany, Austria, and Quebec, Canada, and in early 1996 German television viewers voted the performers the number-one international group. In April 1996 their first, self-titled album was released in Europe and Canada, and in the summer of that year, they mounted a sold-out 57-performance European tour. They then embarked on a 32-performance Canadian tour that sold out in the first 20 minutes after tickets went on sale. By the end of the year, they had won the 1996 MTV Europe Viewers Choice Award, sold almost 10 million albums, and seen their popularity spread to Asia and Australia. Only the U.S. market remained indifferent to them; whenever they returned to the States, they were forced to play in smaller, less prestigious venues, such as a Wal-Mart parking lot.

In 1997 the group recorded several new songs in Florida. These songs, along with their European hits, made up their first U.S. album, *The Backstreet Boys*, which was released on August 12, 1997. At about that time, American taste finally caught up with the group's R&B–tinged brand of pop. According to the Recording Industry Association of America, the album ranked third in sales in 1998, topped only by the soundtrack to the blockbuster film *Titanic* and Celine Dion's *Let's Talk About Love.* A writer for *Billboard* (December 5, 1998) reported, "With the massive commercial success of the Backstreet Boys' self-titled debut, the Jive Records vocal group has achieved nothing short of global domination and, in the process, helped usher in a new era of youthful pop music." The songs "Quit Playing Games (With My Heart)," "As Long As You Love Me," "Everybody (Backstreet's Back)," and "I'll Never Break Your Heart" each received extensive airplay on the radio, and when the fifth single, "All I Have to Give," was released, the *Billboard* (December 5, 1998) writer commented, "It's hard to believe that we're still being offered new singles from Backstreet Boys' only U.S. album release, given what seems like growing maturity with each successive single. . . . By the time this one's good and saturated in the next couple months, a lot of folks are going to drop that 'boy band' label and start treating the Backstreet Boys like the talented and serious ensemble of men they've become."

Although 1998 was a triumphant year for the Backstreet Boys in terms of sales and critical recognition, the year had its low points as well. In May Littrell underwent open-heart surgery to correct a heart defect that he had had since birth. He took eight weeks to recover; after he resumed touring, paramedics with oxygen tanks stayed on the alert backstage, to help him if the need arose. The group also ran into problems with Pearlman, whom they accused of keeping an unfair share of their profits, and they initiated a lawsuit to negotiate a new contract. The conflict worsened when the musicians discovered that Pearlman was also managing 'N Sync, a rival all-male vocal group. "That hurt our feelings," Richardson told Jancee Dunn for *Rolling Stone* (May 27, 1999). "Because for a while it was like, 'We're a family.' Then all of a sudden, 'It's business, guys, sorry.' We have nothing against . . . that group, personally. It was [Pearlman's] not being honest." The Backstreet Boys' legal suit was settled in October 1998, and at the start of 1999, they acquired new management. Shortly afterward 'N Sync announced that they would be moving from RCA Records to Jive that year. The Backstreet Boys reacted by threatening to abandon Jive if their rivals were signed. They eventually agreed to remain, even though 'N Sync began recording on the Jive label.

Despite the problems that plagued the Backstreet Boys during 1998, they continued to tour, sometimes causing near riots in the 10,000-seat arenas where they played. They were listed among *Entertainment Weekly*'s "Best Entertainers of 1998" and among *People*'s "25 Most Intriguing People of the Year." Their follow-up album, *Millennium*, was released on June 5, 1999 and entered the *Billboard* album chart at number one, having sold more than one million copies in the first week alone. The record also dominated the foreign charts in Canada, Mexico, Austria, Belgium, Denmark, Germany, South Korea, and several other countries. *Millennium*, for which the boys had co-written four of the album's 12 songs, was nominated for Grammy Awards for best pop album and best overall album, and the first single, "I Want It That Way," was nominated for best single record and best song. *Black and Blue*, their latest Jive album, was scheduled to be released in late November 2000.

Each Backstreet Boy still calls Orlando home; most now live in gated communities to escape the sometimes intrusive attention of fans. In June 2000 Richardson married Kristin Willits, whom he had met while performing at the Disney-MGM studios. In September 2000 Littrell married the actress Leighanne Wallace, who had a small role in a 1997 Backstreet Boys video. Anticipating the eventual waning of the group's popularity, McLean is developing condos on the east coast of Florida as an investment. The musicians have no plans to stop performing, though. They hope to gain tighter control over the merchandising rights to their name and image and to expand their fan base to include men and older women. (They already have a small gay following, thanks to their early opening performances for the Village People.) "We hope to be old people onstage together," Carter told Jeffrey Zaslow for *USA Weekend* (January 10, 1999), "as old as the Rolling Stones." *Backstreet Boys: The Official Book*, a photographic scrapbook by Andre, Anore, and Andrea Csillag, was published in 2000. —M.R.

Suggested Reading: *Entertainment Weekly* p25+ Sep. 4, 1998, with photos; *People* p238+ Sep. 14, 1998, with photos; *Rolling Stone* p38 Sep. 3, 1998, with photo, p44+ May 27, 1999, with photos; *Village Voice* p71+ May 25, 1999, with photo

Selected Recordings: *Backstreet Boys*, 1997; *Millennium*, 1999

Bagwell, Jeff

May 27, 1968– First baseman with the Houston Astros. Address: Houston Astros, P.O. Box 288, Houston, TX 77001-0288

Houston Astros first baseman Jeff Bagwell is known to baseball fans for two things: being the most talented player since Babe Ruth to be traded away by the Boston Red Sox organization, and having the most peculiar batting stance in the major leagues. Crouching low, with his legs spread wide and his hands head-high, Bagwell, as he swings, takes a step back from the ball with his lead foot, rather than the conventional stride toward the pitch. The stance has confounded the many pitchers he has faced, and even he is puzzled by his quirky backward step. "That is not . . . planned. Not planned at all. Nobody else does it, and I don't know why it happens. It just does," Bagwell remarked to Will Kuhns for the *Washington Post* (June 23, 1997). "When I'm hitting well, I do it. When I'm not, I tend to lean forward a little bit, instead of standing back." Though unconventional, his stance and swing have served him well. In the 10 seasons since the Red Sox traded him to the Houston Astros, Bagwell has amassed a total of 263 home runs and a batting average of .304. In five of those years, he hit more than 30 home runs, thus becoming the only Houston player to achieve that feat.

Gary Caskey/Archive Photos

Because Bagwell was traded in 1990, when he was a third baseman for Boston's double-A farm club—the New Britain (Connecticut) Red Sox—Beantown fans never got the chance to see him play in Fenway Park. Moreover, in giving up this future All-Star player, Boston took in a 37-year-old relief pitcher who left the Red Sox the following season for a bigger free-agent salary with the San Diego Padres. Many among the Red Sox faithful think of the Bagwell trade as the biggest error in judgment in Red Sox history since 1919, when team executives sold the rights to Babe Ruth to the New York Yankees for $125,000 (the equivalent of about $1.35 million in 1999) and a promise of an additional $300,000 loan to the Red Sox franchise. (The Yankees have since become one of professional sports' winningest teams, and the Red Sox—suffering from what has been dubbed the "Curse of the Bambino"—have endured one of the longest championship droughts in baseball history.) Bagwell, who grew up an avid Red Sox fan, was initially crushed by the trade, but later he said that it had turned out well for him. "The worst moment of my life turned out to be the best moment of my life," he told Leigh Montville for *Sports Illustrated* (July 26, 1993). "Isn't it strange how these things happen? If I'd stayed with the Red Sox, who knows where I'd be? I have to think something would have happened and I'd be in the major leagues somewhere, but who knows. I might be playing in Triple A in Pawtucket [Rhode Island]. I might be sitting on the bench in Boston. Who knows?"

Jeffrey Robert Bagwell was born on May 27, 1968 in Boston, Massachusetts. When he was a year old, his family moved to Connecticut, which, like its neighboring state, is considered "Red Sox country." "Our house was one of those places where you couldn't mention the word *Yankees* when you came inside the front door. Every weekend the television would be tuned to channel six. The Red Sox. No other games," Bagwell recalled for Montville. "My grandmother Alice Hare, she's 81 years old, she still lives in Newton, and she can tell you anything you want to know about the Red Sox."

As a baby, Bagwell demonstrated a preternatural ability in athletics. "He could throw a ball before he could walk," his mother, Jan, told Bill Ryan for the *New York Times* (August 28, 1994). "When he was six months old, we'd throw a ball to him and he would throw it back." Bagwell's father, Robert, a former semi-pro pitcher, coached his son in Little League baseball when he was six. Both of his parents encouraged his interest in baseball, continuing to do so even after their divorce, when Jeff was 11. In addition, they both stressed hard work and discipline as the keys to success. "My mother and father pushed me very hard," Bagwell told Jim Molony for the *Houston Post* (July 3, 1994). "If there was one thing they stressed, it was to never quit."

At Xavier High School, in Middletown, Connecticut, Bagwell "played shortstop but was better known as a crack soccer player," Bill Ryan wrote. After graduating from high school, Bagwell attended the University of Hartford on a baseball scholarship; it was the only college that had offered him one. Hartford coach Bill Denehy put him at third base, where he flourished and became the team's star player. Bagwell enjoyed three stellar years at Hartford, capping his college career with a season in which he batted .413. He supplemented his collegiate training by playing summer ball in the Cape Cod Baseball League, which has historically featured some of the best young talent in the game. In June 1989 Bagwell was drafted in the fourth round by the Boston Red Sox. "It was a dream come true," he told Molony. "Everybody [back home] is a Red Sox fan and I was on cloud nine."

That year Bagwell started in Florida's Gulf Coast Rookie League, where he hit .316 in five games. He then moved on to Winter Haven, a single-A club once affiliated with the Red Sox; playing out the remaining 64 games in their season, he hit two home runs and compiled a batting average of .308. For the 1990 season he was promoted to Boston's double-A affiliate in New Britain, Connecticut, where he averaged .333 and earned the Eastern League's MVP award. All the while Bagwell was developing his signature stroke. "Some people didn't like his stance," the current Red Sox manager, Butch Hobson, who coached Bagwell in New Britain, told Molony. "But all the guy did was hit line drives. There was no question he was going to be a major leaguer. The only question we had was whether he would have much power—and he didn't show us much back then." As a result, the Red Sox, eager to win the American League East Division Championship, traded Bagwell to the Houston Astros in exchange for relief pitcher Larry Anderson. The trade was devastating for Bagwell, who still harbored dreams of playing in Fenway Park. "I was one of the saddest guys you'll ever see," he told Leigh Montville. "I had to go back into the clubhouse, take off the uniform, and watch the game from the stands."

The Houston Astros invited Bagwell to the team's 1991 spring training, hoping that he would provide some healthy competition for their young but established third baseman Ken Caminiti. Both Bagwell and Caminiti had hot bats that spring, and the Astros kept both players, moving Bagwell to first base. Although he had hit only six home runs in his two years in the minors, Bagwell displayed a powerful swing throughout his rookie season, leading the team in home runs. "I had hit some long balls in batting practice, so I knew I could hit it out," he told Montville. "I just never thought about it much. Then I made some adjustments in my swing. I've always lifted weights anyway. The ball started going out. Now, sometimes, that's all I think about, and it gets me in trouble." Bagwell also led the team in RBIs and earned 23 of 24 votes to be named the National League's Rookie of the Year. The Astros selected him the team's most valuable player. "I got lucky," Bagwell said of his successful year, as quoted in the *New York Times* (November 7, 1991). "I got a chance to play and that was the main thing."

During the next few seasons, Bagwell continued hitting well, leading the league in RBIs and ranking consistently among the league's top 10 in drawing intentional walks. Indicative of his newfound power, Bagwell, in his second season, became only the seventh person to hit a home run that reached the press boxes in Atlanta-Fulton County Stadium. In 1993 he was in sixth place in National League batting with a .320 average, before an errant pitch from Ben Rivera of the Philadelphia Phillies fractured a bone in his left hand 20 games before the end of the regular season. At the time of his injury, Bagwell had played 304 consecutive games, more than any other player in the history of the franchise.

Bagwell enjoyed one of his best years to date in 1994: he swatted 39 home runs, a club record. "A few years ago, I would have told you that I thought I'd hit 39 homers—in my career, maybe," he told a reporter for the *Sporting News* (October 31, 1994). "I think a couple of things happened, but the biggest one was that the stance I was using allowed me to get my legs and whole body in my swing." He also led the National League in runs scored, RBIs, and total bases, and ranked second in batting average, with .368, when—with about 50 games left to play in the regular season—the players' association voted to strike. The remainder of the season passed without a settlement, and baseball commissioner Bud Selig announced that there would be no World Series. Meanwhile, a few days before the walkout, Bagwell's left hand was broken by a pitch, this time thrown by San Diego's Andy Benes.

In April and May of the 1995 season, Bagwell batted under .200. "You get to the point when you're in a slump where you're just trying to find answers," he told Claire Smith for the *New York Times* (June 19, 1995). "You go back and look at tapes where you've done well and you try and get back to that. I've done all that—and more. The situation now, is that I have to get comfortable in the batter's box." In June he bounced back, going on to hit at a .336 pace and amassing 16 home runs and 70 RBIs by July 30. On that date he was struck by a pitch from the Padres' Brian Williams and again suffered a broken bone in his left hand. Consequently, he missed four weeks of play. "I can't tell you how sad I am about this right now," he commented to a reporter for the Associated Press (July 31, 1995), "because we're three-and-a-half games behind the Reds, and we're playing great baseball. We've still got a great team and everything, but I know that my production was helping, at least." Bagwell returned to play on September 1, 1995 and finished the season with a .290 average. The slump and injury limited his home run total to 21. He has since worn a protective pad on his batting glove.

In the 1995 off-season, Bagwell hired a bodybuilder to train him. He adhered to a strict high-protein diet and a vigorous workout program—adding 20 pounds of muscle to his frame—and returned the following season to hit 31 home runs and steal 21 bases, making him only the sixth "20–20" player in Astro history. Bagwell continued his upswing in 1997, by breaking Jimmy Wynn's 24-year-old record (93) for most home runs hit in Houston's Astrodome. (Bagwell hit 22 homers in the arena that year, bringing his total to 95.) In 1997 he also became the sixth player in baseball history to hit 40 or more home runs and steal 30 or more bases in a single year, and the first member of the Astros ever to reach the "30–30" mark. By the conclusion of the 1999 season, Bagwell set several additional Houston franchise records in career home runs, RBIs, extra-base hits, and walks. Furthermore, in 1999 he reached the "40–30" mark for the second time in his career, becoming only the second player ever to do so. In the 2000 season Bagwell hit 47 home runs and accumulated 132 RBIs. He was pleased with his overall performance but disappointed that his team did not have a shot at the championship. "I put up some good numbers, but the thing you want more than anything is to go to the World Series," he remarked on the Web site *athletesdirect.com*. "That's what everybody looks at, that's what people remember and that's what I want to do."

Jeff Bagwell lives in Houston with his wife, Shaune. Known for his modesty, he refrains from bragging about his success on the field or about his lucrative contracts. "Everyone sees what you've done, so why talk about it?" he told Rick Weinberg for *Sport* (May 1995). "I think success and money should make someone more humble." In spite of the great success he has enjoyed in Houston, Bagwell has admitted that he still dreams of playing for the Red Sox. "I've thought about it a thousand times," he told Weinberg. "Don't get me wrong, I love Houston, I love playing for the Astros. But in today's market, it's definitely feasible I might move on. . . . I've wondered what it would be like to put on that uniform, to play in Fenway, to play where Yaz [Carl Yastrzemski] played. It'd be a wonderful feeling." — J.K.B.

Suggested Reading: *Houston Post* (on-line) July 3, 1994; *New York Times* XIII p1+ Aug. 28, 1994, with photos, B p23 Nov. 7, 1991, with photos; *Sport* p18+ May 1995, with photos; *Sports Illustrated* p44+ July 26, 1993, with photos, p56+ July 19, 1999, with photos; *Washington Post* C p6+ June 23, 1997, with photos

---

Bahcall, John N.

Dec. 30, 1934– Astrophysicist; educator. Address: School of Natural Sciences, Institute for Advanced Study, Olden Lane, Princeton, NJ 08540

Thanks in part to the research of John N. Bahcall, scientists have gone far toward puzzling out how stars create energy and have gained more of what they need to know to foretell the future of the universe. While investigating quasars, sound waves in the sun, and many other areas of astrophysics in a

Courtesy of the Institute for Advanced Study
John N. Bahcall

career that has spanned four decades, Bahcall has focused on the study of neutrinos. Mysterious subatomic particles that have no charge, neutrinos, unlike most other atomic and subatomic particles, can zip from the sun or other stars straight through Earth and emerge unscathed. In an article for *Astronomy* (March 1990), Bahcall listed questions that, as he put it, "motivate the study of neutrino astronomy": "How does the sun shine? Does the neutrino have a mass? Can solar neutrinos be used to test the theory of stellar evolution? Can solar neutrinos be used to explore the unification of the strong, weak, and electromagnetic forces?" A professor of natural sciences at the Institute for Advanced Study, in Princeton, New Jersey, since 1971, Bahcall was awarded the 1992 NASA Distinguished Public Service Medal for his contributions to the planning and development of the Hubble Space Telescope, the largest space-based observatory ever built for long-term scrutiny of the heavens. In 1998 he earned the National Medal of Science, the most prestigious of U.S. science honors, for both his work on the telescope and his pioneering research in neutrino astrophysics.

John Norris Bahcall was born on December 30, 1934 in Shreveport, Louisiana. He attended the University of California at Berkeley, from which he graduated with a B.A. degree in physics, in 1956. The following year he received a master's degree from the University of Chicago. In 1961 he earned a Ph.D. in physics from Harvard University, in Cambridge, Massachusetts, where he was supervised by the astrophysicist and cosmologist David Layzer.

Upon completing his graduate work, Bahcall took a postdoctoral position as a research fellow in physics at Indiana University. Lectures by Emil Kanapenski on the theory of weak nuclear interactions led him to read widely about beta decay, a process in which the weak nuclear force causes changes in nuclei, among them the emission of neutrinos. What he learned inspired him to begin an in-depth investigation of the neutrino. While reading a paper by four scientists—the astrophysicists Eleanor Margaret Burbidge, Geoffrey Burbidge, and William A. Fowler and the astronomer Fred Hoyle—about the creation of new nuclei (and therefore different chemical elements) within stars, Bahcall noticed that in calculating beta decay in stellar interiors, the four had used reaction rates determined from phenomena observed in the laboratory—rates that were far different from those he himself had calculated for beta decay. Acting on that observation, Bahcall recalled in an interview with Simon Mitton for *Science Watch* (September 1995), "I wrote a short paper saying that the weak interaction rates being used by astrophysicists could not be correct because the laboratory rates would be changed in stars: ionization [the loss or gain of electrons] and the Pauli principle [which states that no two particles in an atom can have precisely the same characteristics] would play an effect at the high densities inside stars."

In 1962 Bahcall joined the staff of the Kellogg Radiation Laboratory, at the California Institute of Technology (Caltech), in Pasadena, where he continued his work on weak interactions. About three years later the astrophysicist Raymond Davis (often referred to as Ray Davis), of the Brookhaven National Laboratory, on Long Island, New York, and the University of Pennsylvania, suggested using Bahcall's calculations on solar nuclear reactions to deduce the presence of neutrinos in the sun. Davis's idea bore fruit: with that approach, it was proved that energy indistinguishable from stellar energy is produced in nuclear reactions. That finding ended a debate about nuclear reactions that had been ongoing since the mid-19th century.

Upon further examination, the discovery led to the recognition of one of the greatest mysteries in modern physics: the "solar neutrino deficit." Bahcall described the enigma in his article for *Astronomy*: "The solar neutrino problem can be stated simply. The number of solar neutrinos detected on Earth is less than one-third as many as expected based on the most accurate theoretical calculations of how the Sun generates energy." In 1986 two Soviet scientists, S. P. Mikheyev and A. Y. Smirnov, announced that they had come up with a possible explanation for the deficit: stellar neutrinos from electrons might change into higher-energy neutrinos as they passed through the sun. Such differences among neutrinos would not have been recognized because scientists had not been looking for them.

This theory, in turn, raised new questions: for example, if neutrinos could gain energy, some of the higher-energy types might have a small mass, and that could account for some of the dark matter that many scientists believe exists throughout the universe. Dark matter has never been detected; the theory about its existence is based on the fact that the quantity of detectable matter in the universe is not sufficiently large to account for the gravitational pulls that hold the universe together. Without dark matter, the universe would, over the course of billions of years, be reduced to clouds of dust drifting ever further apart. The presence of dark matter would insure that the universe would eventually stop expanding and then, because of gravitational forces, start contracting.

In February 1987, for the first time since 1604, a supernova—the explosion of a giant star—suddenly became visible in the night sky. Dubbed Supernova 1987A, it was located in the Large Magellanic Cloud, a small satellite galaxy of the Milky Way, the galaxy of which Earth and the rest of the solar system are a part. And for the very first time, because of SN1987A's relative nearness, detectors on Earth—one in Japan and one in the U.S.—succeeded in recording neutrinos that had come from a stellar explosion. Those recordings, Ronald A. Schorn wrote for *Sky and Telescope* (May 1987), transformed neutrino astronomy "from a theoretical pursuit to a genuine observational science." (Schorn also noted that because of the extreme difficulty of detecting the presence of the elusive neutrino, the small number of neutrinos detected—just 19—suggested that "some 10 billion of these particles passed through every square centimeter of Earth during a period of a few seconds.") The recordings made it possible for Bahcall to determine whether certain types of neutrinos really do have mass. Along with the Nobel Prize–winning physicist Sheldon L. Glashow, of Harvard University, he noted the exact time of each neutrino's arrival on Earth and calculated its energy level. Theoretically, arrival times would correspond with energy levels, with neutrinos having greater energy reaching the planet before those with less. But as Bahcall and Glashow discovered, arrival times and energy levels did not correspond. That finding indicated that neutrinos do not have significant mass: according to Bahcall and Glashow, their mass cannot be more than 11 electron-volts, which is 13 electron-volts less than the amount needed to positively identify neutrinos as the dark matter of the universe. While Bahcall and Glashow's finding did not prove that whatever constitutes dark matter would never be found, it indicated that scientists would have to look elsewhere in their search for it. Recently it has been theorized that at least half of this mass is present in white dwarf stars.

"These neutrino observations are so exciting and significant," Bahcall told Malcolm W. Browne for the *New York Times* (April 3, 1987), "that I think we're about to see the birth of an entirely new branch of astronomy: neutrino astronomy. Supernova explosions that are invisible to us because of dust clouds may occur in our galaxy as often as once every 10 years, and neutrino bursts could give us a way to study them." Bahcall was also prominent in calling for the construction of new, larger and more sensitive neutrino detectors. "With somewhat more sensitive detectors," Bahcall told Browne in another interview for the *New York Times* (April 7, 1987), "and by knowing what to look for, we can really begin systematic study of neutrino sources throughout the universe." More-sophisticated neutrino detectors would enable scientists to study neutron stars in the process of formation and to investigate black holes in greater detail. In the late 1990s state-of-the-art neutrino detectors were being built in Japan, Canada, and Italy. Recently, Bahcall's calculations on neutrinos have been used to support the theory that if, as happens every 100 million years or so, a nearby giant star were to collapse, enough neutrinos would hit Earth to damage DNA and increase cancer rates. A similar event may explain the mass extinction of the dinosaurs about 65 million years ago.

On another front, Bahcall was a principal lobbyist for the development of the Hubble Space Telescope, and from 1973 to 1992 he served as an interdisciplinary scientist on the Hubble Telescope Working Group. In an article for *Scientific American* (July 1977) in which he pushed for its construction, he explained, "The earth's atmosphere is an imperfect window on the universe. Electromagnetic waves in the optical part of the spectrum (that is, waves longer than X rays and shorter than radio waves) penetrate to the surface of the earth only in a few narrow spectral bands. The widest of the transmitted bands corresponds roughly to the colors of visible light; waves in the flanking ultraviolet and infrared regions of the optical spectrum are almost totally absorbed by the atmosphere. In addition, atmospheric turbulence blurs the images of celestial objects, even when they are viewed through the most powerful ground-based telescopes." The designing of the bus-sized Hubble telescope began in 1979, and in April 1990 it was launched into orbit 330 miles above Earth. Operated cooperatively by the European Space Agency and the National Aeronautics and Space Administration (NASA), the telescope has dozens of handholds and other features that enable astronauts to service it from space shuttles. Capable of detecting stars more than 14 billion light years distant from Earth, the telescope has generated an incredible wealth of data and sent back to Earth spectacular images 100 times more revealing than those obtainable by land-based telescopes. Bahcall has been using the Hubble telescope to study quasars, immensely bright quasi-stellar objects that are found in galaxies extremely far from Earth.

Bahcall has been a leader in the field of helioseismology, the study of sound waves in the sun, and he played a part in proving that dark matter was not present in a type of star known as red dwarfs. Among other activities, from 1989 to 1991 he chaired the 15-member Astronomy and Astrophysics Survey Committee, which was commissioned by the National Research Council to recommend new areas of research in astronomy. Since 1997 he has held the title of Richard Black Professor of Natural Sciences at the Institute for Advanced Study. He is also a visiting lecturer with the rank of professor at Princeton University.

Bahcall is the author of *Neutrino Astrophysics* (1989) and the co-author of *The Redshift Controversy* (1973), *The Decade of Discovery in Astronomy and Astrophysics* (1991), and *Time for the Stars: Astronomy in the 1990s* (1994). He co-edited the books *The Galaxy and the Solar System* (1987), *Solar Neutrinos: The First Thirty Years* (1995), and *Unsolved Problems in Astrophysics* (1997). Bahcall's honors include the 1970 Warner Prize, from the American Astronomical Society; the 1994 Heineman Prize from the American Astronomical Society and the American Institute of Physics; and the 1998 Hans Bethe Prize, from the American Physical Society. Bahcall's wife, the Israeli-born Neta Assaf Bahcall, whom he married in 1966, is a professor of astrophysics at Princeton University; her research interests include properties of galaxies, the structure of the universe, dark matter, and cosmology. The couple have three children—Safi, Dan, and Orli. Commenting on his field of study in an interview for *Sky and Telescope* (January 1990), John Bahcall said, "We should do astronomy because it is beautiful and because it is fun. We should do it because people want to know. We want to know our place in the universe and how things happen." — G.O.

Suggested Reading: *Astronomy* p40+ Mar. 1990; *Christian Science Monitor* p12 Apr. 25, 1995; *John Bahcall Homepage* (on-line); *New York Times* A p16 Apr. 3, 1987, III p7 Apr. 7, 1987; *Scientific American* p40+ July 1982; *Sky and Telescope* p19+ Jan. 1990

Selected Books: as author—*Neutrino Astrophysics*, 1989; as co-author—*The Redshift Controversy*, 1973; as co-editor—*The Galaxy and the Solar System*, 1986; *Dark Matter in the Universe*, 1987; *Solar Neutrinos: The First Thirty Years*, 1994; *Solar Modeling*, 1995; *Unsolved Problems in Astrophysics*, 1997

Bancroft, Ann

1955– Outdoor adventurer; teacher. Address: Base Camp Promotions, 119 N. Fourth St., Suite 406, Minneapolis, MN 55401

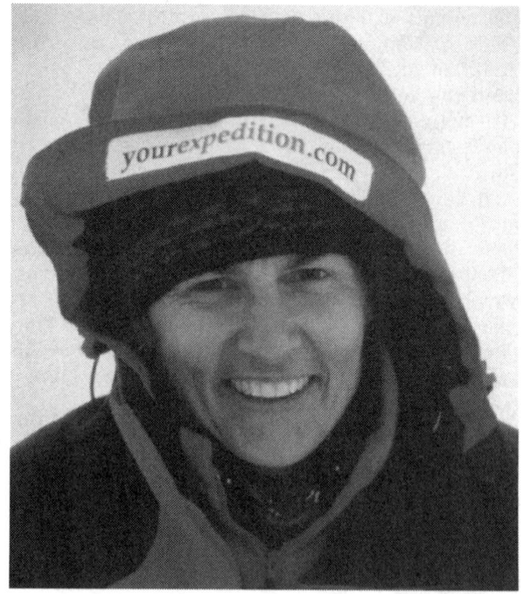

Courtesy of yourexpedition.com

On January 14, 1993, when Ann Bancroft realized her longtime dream of reaching the South Pole, she became the first woman in history to have journeyed over the ice to both of Earth's poles. It was the latest in a series of achievements for this outdoor adventurer and teacher, who had also climbed Mount McKinley, the highest peak in the United States, and led the first American women's team to cross Greenland east to west. In accomplishing these feats, Bancroft has had to contend with frigid temperatures, daunting physical trials, inadequate funds, and sexism. "People think I'm sick," Bancroft told Erika Dillman for *Runner's World* (January 1994), "but I'm in love with these cold, faraway places." Hoping that young people and others will come to appreciate those parts of the globe, she has developed ways for anyone interested to track her expeditions, and she has designed school curricula based on them. "If people don't have experience with the wilderness in some way—whether it's through visuals or stories or personal experience—they're not going to feel impassioned about it," she explained to Martha Irvine for *Ms.* (January/February 1993). One of Bancroft's goals is to convince the public that women have "what it takes" to endure the toughest physical challenges. "We need to keep breaking down myths about what women can't do," she told Erika Dillman. "It hasn't been that long since women were first allowed to run the marathon in the Olympics. It's important to keep expressing ourselves physically." Bancroft plans to participate in the first women-only crossing of the continent of Antarctica, in late 2000.

Ann Bancroft was born in Mendota Heights, Minnesota, in 1955, the second of the five children of Richard Bancroft, an insurance agent, and Debbie Bancroft, a homemaker. She grew up in Minnesota except for the years when she was in fifth and sixth grades, which she spent with her family in East Africa; inspired by President John F. Kennedy's calls for public service, her parents worked there as volunteers under the auspices of the Presbyterian Church of East Africa. After the family returned to the States, her father often took her on camping and canoeing trips in the million-acre Boundary Waters Canoe Area, which borders the Superior National Forest, in the northern part of Minnesota, and as she grew older, she began to go on such outings by herself. As a child she was diagnosed with a form of dyslexia. At age 12 she read with fascination about Sir Ernest Shackleton's arduous and ultimately unsuccessful attempt, beginning in 1914, to traverse Antarctica for the second time, during which he trekked hundreds of miles in search of help after his ship was crushed by ice. In high school Bancroft started running; she has continued to run ever since, for many years as part of her physical training for expeditions, and has participated in four marathons, with a best time of three hours and 42 minutes. After graduating from high school, in 1974, Bancroft attended the University of Oregon, where she played field hockey and earned a bachelor's degree in physical education. She began her post-college career by teaching physical and special education at the St. James Elementary School, in St. Paul, Minnesota; after two years there she left to teach at the Clara Barton Open School, a public primary school in Minneapolis.

When she was 28, in her first major outdoor venture, Bancroft scaled Mount McKinley, Alaska, with a friend. About two years later, in 1985, Will Steger and Paul Schurke, who were planning an expedition to the North Pole, chose her as the only female member of their team. Bancroft quit her job in order to prepare for the trek, which *National Geographic* was sponsoring. In addition to physical workouts, she polished her camera skills, because *National Geographic* had picked her to serve as the team's back-up photographer and cinematographer. Traveling 1,000 miles on sleds pulled by dogs, the group arrived at their destination after 55 days, and Bancroft became the first woman to reach the North Pole over the ice. She and her fellow trekkers were widely celebrated after they returned to the States; their honors included an invitation to the White House extended by President Ronald Reagan and the First Lady. Bancroft also earned compliments for the expressiveness and honesty of the diary she had kept during the expedition, excerpts from which were published in *National Geographic.* In one nerve-jangling sequence, she described her near-drowning after she fell through an ice shelf into the frigid Arctic Ocean. Although Bancroft found the trip rewarding, she reported that she had had difficulty in dealing with what struck her as sexist behavior on the part of her seven teammates. "I was doing the same things all the guys were doing," she told Stephan Herrera for *Mpls. St. Paul* (May 1994), "and still at the end of the day someone would come up and ask me if I was OK, or if there were any problems. It might be well intended, but after [38 days] on the ice, it got real old and irritating."

During the next few years, Bancroft received many offers for jobs, among them TV network anchor positions, and for roles in various projects, including a place on a team that intended to climb Mount Everest, but she rejected all of them. In 1989 she established the American Women's Expedition (AWE), with the goal of planning the first all-woman crossing of Antarctica. Bancroft tirelessly sought corporate funding for the undertaking, which she estimated would cost $1 million, but she was consistently rebuffed. Most corporate representatives were uninterested; others told her outright that they would consider backing the team only if it included a man. Bancroft noted that her being a lesbian made matters worse. "I know for a fact, in my heart, regardless of what answers we get [from the corporations], whether it's hard times or whatever, that [my sexuality] is a factor," she told Herrera. "They don't know what to do with that. That's certainly not an image they want to portray." She rejected suggestions that she not reveal her sexuality. "I can't lie for anybody," she declared to Herrera. "I can't lie to get corporate money."

Because of her strongly held stands regarding the environment and education, Bancroft refused to accept offers of sponsorship from Marlboro, Coors, and Exxon. Instead, she raised money through donations, many of them from friends, family members, and even schoolchildren who had held fund-raisers in her behalf. The money she collected quickly disappeared into the coffers of Adventure Network Co., which she had hired for round-trip transit from South America to Antarctica; without steady payments, the firm warned, it would not arrange transportation. The shortfall in funds forced Bancroft to postpone the expedition for a year and to cut costs by $200,000. Nevertheless, she continued to train two to three hours a day. In addition to her usual six-mile runs six days a week, she increased her endurance by lifting weights, cycling, swimming, and skiing. In 1992, as part of their training, Bancroft led her team across Greenland east to west on skis; they thus became the first American women's team to negotiate that route.

Bancroft launched the antarctic expedition in October 1992, when she arrived in Punta Arenas, Chile, with her teammates—Anne Dal Vera, a wilderness-school instructor; Sue Giller, a computer programmer; and Sunniva Sorby, a travel-store manager—but without the money still owed Adventure Network. "Here I am in South America," Bancroft told Rhonda Hillbery for the *Chicago Tribune* (April 4, 1993), "saying, 'Take us. We'll pay you later.' I remember sitting there in an office with these people, looking down into a yard full of all our gear. And the other three [members of the team] are packing madly for this flight onto the continent, if we got the go-ahead. And the flight company people said to me, 'Do you think you can do it? Do you women have what it takes?'" Eventually, Adventure Network agreed to fly them to Antarctica, but bad weather and airplane problems delayed their flight until November 9, nine days later than scheduled.

After they arrived on Antarctica, the team skied from eight to 10 hours a day at a speed rarely exceeding one and a half miles an hour. Although it was the Antarctic summer, when the sun never sets, they faced wind chills of up to minus 70 degrees Fahrenheit. The women traveled single-file most of the way, each pulling a 200-pound sled. Bancroft's sled included an additional 30 pounds—the weight of a special radio, which she used to keep her sister informed of the team's progress. Bancroft's sister, who was staying in Chile, would relay Ann's reports to an answering machine, which people could call for updates.

An estimated 250,000 U.S. students who followed the team via updates and curricula based on the expedition learned that Bancroft and her colleagues ate high-calorie and high-fat foods to alleviate the effects of the bitter cold. To protect themselves against the harsh winds at night, the women would cut blocks of snow and arrange them around their tents. Despite that tactic, on mornings after overnight snowstorms, they sometimes had to shovel their way out of the tents. The students also learned that the widely held image of the antarctic landscape as desolate and uninteresting is not accurate. "We saw the snow make beautiful patterns, in some places six to 10 feet high," Dal Vera told Hillbery. "Other times we saw beautiful rainbows around the sun."

The final weeks of the trek were particularly arduous. One member of the team sprained her ankle and then contracted bronchitis. Another began to suffer serious emotional problems, apparently because of the hardships of the trip, the extreme cold, and the punishing winds. All but one of the women suffered from frostbitten thighs, and all had scabs from windburn on their faces. As the group edged closer to their goal, they faced increasingly difficult conditions. "It was a climb for us the whole way," Bancroft recalled to Dillman. "We gained almost 10,000 feet. We were literally leaning over our ski tips trying to make the sleds go." She also told Dillman, "I kept having these vivid deja vu feelings about the last few miles, the gradual uphill of the Twin Cities Marathon. It's not a massive hill, but it's long, and you're at the end of your line and you're hurting the most. But knowing that I'd been through it—that I'd been able to pull myself through when I was completely beat—helped me get through the expedition." On January 14, 1993, 67 days after starting on their 660-mile trek, the women reached the South Pole. They had planned to ski another 900 miles, to McMurdo Bay, on the Ross Ice Shelf, and be picked up by a cruise ship, without charge, on February 17, but problems had lengthened their trip by many days, making it impossible for them to arrive at the bay on time. If they were to arrive after February 17, they would have to arrange a costly emergency pickup. Not wanting to fall further into debt, Bancroft reluctantly put aside her dream of crossing Antarctica and arranged to be picked up by a plane that had already been scheduled to deliver food to the team.

Back in the U.S., the women underwent tests to see how the extreme temperatures and exertion had affected their mental and physical health. The results showed that although each had lost between five and 15 pounds, all were fine. Gloria Leon, a University of Minnesota psychology professor who interviewed the women, told Hillbery, "The group did seem to interact in a different way than all-male groups interact, or even mixed groups of men and women." Leon said that the women had supported one another emotionally and had cooperated when making group decisions. Bancroft told Erika Dillman, "The goal was not so much reaching the pole itself, it was a bit more universal. Why do we all take on struggles? Why run a marathon? I think we're all striving to push ourselves, and in the process of overcoming struggles and challenges, we get to know ourselves better."

After resuming her life in Minnesota, Bancroft suffered from restlessness and financial problems. The article she wrote about the antarctic trip for *National Geographic* was killed because the magazine's editor, William Graves, thought that the quality of her photos was wanting. "I hate not running that story," Graves told Herrera. "It's a great story, it's unique, it has many, many marvelous features, but when the pictures aren't there, it's awfully hard for us to run the story." Graves's decision shocked Bancroft. "*Geographic* is my magazine, my dream," she told Herrera. "I was devastated. I couldn't tell the team for two weeks. I couldn't even talk about it without bursting into tears." In addition, she struggled to raise money, through fund-raising and talks, to pay off the team's debt—more than $200,000. She also filmed public-service announcements for government agencies and nonprofit organizations while working on a documentary film about the trip. All the while, she missed Antarctica. "[There] I knew what my job was," Bancroft told Hillbery. "In a way it was very simple. Now I'm back in this world. Where's the ice? I want it back."

After clearing the debts Bancroft began planning another expedition: what she hopes will be the first women-only crossing of Antarctica. This time she teamed up with Liv Arnesen, a Norwegian teacher and cross-country skier who was the first woman to ski solo to the South Pole. The two plan to leave Queen Maud Land in November 2000 and arrive at the Ross Ice Shelf in February 2001, after skiing a distance of 2,400 miles. They hope to travel one mile an hour and cover 15 miles pulling, or 25 miles sailing, their 250-pound supply sleds along the ice. After they reach the South Pole, an air drop will resupply them for the second half of their journey. To raise the minimum $1.5 million needed for the expedition, Bancroft set up Base Camp Promotions, a marketing group that has been pitching the project to corporations and trying to persuade them that the expedition's Web site is a high-profile place to advertise. "I didn't want to return to Antarctica poorly funded," Bancroft told *Expedition News* (on-line). "I knew it was important to approach a potential sponsor as a marketing opportunity. We're selling a sponsorship this time, not asking for a charitable donation. With the Base Camp team in place, I think we're changing the model of how expeditions are funded." Base Camp plans to provide educational coverage of the trip to some 30,000 classrooms through the Internet. After promoting the expedition until its completion, the group will consider marketing other such expeditions.

In 1994 Bancroft lived with her two dogs and two cats in Sunfish Lake, Minnesota, in a small house that had no source of heat except a stove. Bancroft rented the house from her parents, who were living nearby. She has since bought land near the St. Croix River north of Minneapolis. "I'm really an introvert," she told Herrera; "my life doesn't have much room anymore for anything else but AWE, so when I can, I escape [to the St. Croix] to recharge. That doesn't leave much room for anything or anyone." Bancroft's activities include volunteer work connected with research on women's health, the Special Olympics, and organizations that seek to help victims of cerebral palsy, multiple sclerosis, and learning disabilities. She has served as an instructor at Wilderness Inquiry, a Minneapolis-based program that helps both disabled and able-bodied people experience outdoor adventures. She has also helped to develop curricula for teachers at the grade-school through college levels in areas ranging from mathematics to the environment to women in nontraditional roles. "I have an opportunity now, with some of the projects I've done, i.e. the North Pole and the South Pole, to speak to larger audiences and talk about things that have nothing to do with physical education or special ed," she told Hillbery.

Four to the Pole!: The American Women's Expedition to Antarctica, 1992–1993, which Bancroft wrote with Nancy Loewen, was published in October 2000. Bancroft is the subject of *On Top of the World* (1990), a biography for young people by Dorothy Wenzel. In 1987 Bancroft was among *Ms.* magazine's 12 Women of the Year, and in 1988 the U.S. Jaycees named her one of 10 Outstanding Young Americans. She was inducted into the National Girls and Women in Sport Hall of Fame in 1992 and the National Women's Hall of Fame in 1995. She earned the Distinguished Minnesotan Award in 1997.

The AWE Foundation, now known as the Ann Bancroft Foundation, awards grants and scholarships to recognize the potential and achievements of girls and women. Each year, at a corporate-sponsored event called the Ann Bancroft Awards, the foundation gives four $1,000 prizes to organizations and accomplished individuals who have helped or inspired girls and women. "I'm not a politician," Bancroft remarked to Herrera. "I'm not a doctor who can go over to Somalia—I wish I could. I'm a teacher and [an] outdoor adventurer, and this is a way I can give back something to society, by raising awareness of the environment, by shrinking the globe for kids and teaching them about success, failure, and risk." — G.O.

Suggested Reading: *Chicago Tribune* B p1+ Apr. 4, 1993; *Mpls.St.Paul* p38+ May 1994; *Ms.* p82+ Jan./Feb. 1993; *Runner's World* p37+ Jan. 1994; *yourexpedition.com*

Selected Books: *Four to the Pole!: The American Women's Expedition to Antarctica, 1992–1993* (with Nancy Loewen), 2000

Courtesy of Jillian Banfield

Banfield, Jillian

Aug. 18, 1959– Geologist; educator. Address: University of Wisconsin, 315 Lewis G. Weeks Hall for Geological Science, 1215 W. Dayton St., Madison, WI 53706

When an earthquake strikes, a volcano erupts, or the discovery of a significant deposit of oil, coal, a precious metal, or a gemstone is announced, geologists make the news, in their roles as expert commentators. Geologists study phenomena linked to Earth's history and makeup and the physical, chemical, and biological changes taking place on the planet, and though their work rarely makes headlines, some of it may dramatically affect the environment—and thus people's lives. Jillian Banfield, a geologist who is a full professor at the University of Wisconsin at Madison, has conducted just such studies. In 1998, for example, she and an interdisciplinary team of chemists and biologists as well as geologists investigated a heavily polluted, abandoned iron mine in a mountainous region of California, from which tons of acidic wastes drained daily. It was very hot at the site—the temperature was 40 degrees Centigrade, or 104 degrees Fahrenheit—and extremely dark, and the water in the mine was bright green, because of all the particles of metal in it. In this inhospitable environment, Banfield and her fellow team members discovered microorganisms unrelated to any known species. The interactions of these microorganisms with air, water, and minerals contribute to the acidic wastes draining from the mine; thus, determining the extent to which the microorganisms contribute to the acidification and the extent to which inorganic processes are responsible will enable scientists to devise cost-effective ways to clean up the site—and many other similarly tainted sites as well.

Banfield is a pioneer in the field of molecular geomicrobiology—the study of the role that microorganisms play in geologic processes. Scientists know that bacteria and other microorganisms are vital participants in those processes, but precisely what they do is unknown. Banfield and her colleagues are confident that discovering more about the role of microorganisms will help in developing valuable new biological and environmental technologies. In collaboration with others at the University of Wisconsin and the University of Tokyo, in Japan, she is trying to elucidate, on an atomic level, the chemistry and physical structure of minerals, the mechanisms and products of mineral reactions, and the molecular-level pathways that are central to biological survival and metabolism. In 1998 the University of Wisconsin honored her with its H. I. Romnes faculty fellowship, which is awarded to professors who are considered "rising stars," and the following year the John D. and Catherine T. MacArthur Foundation named her a MacArthur Fellow. That prestigious fellowship, commonly called a "genius grant," provides her with $290,000 over the course of five years, to use in any way she wants. "We look everywhere for the most exciting among us and give them a chance to follow their best instincts over an extended period of time," Daniel J. Socolow, the director of the MacArthur program, explained to Ron Seely for the *Wall Street Journal* (June 23, 1999). In announcing the award, the MacArthur Foundation cited Banfield's valuable insights into the chemical and physical forces that shape the Earth's surface and noted that her observations are not only leading to a greater understanding of the factors that affect water quality and various environmental processes but are also providing clues to the origins of life.

Often called Jill, Jillian Fiona Banfield was born on August 18, 1959 in Armidale, a town midway between Sydney and Brisbane, in Australia. Once, while Jill was growing up, her mother, a chemistry teacher, took a course in geology that entailed field trips, and the instructor allowed Jill to accompany the class. By her own account, Banfield's fascination with geology took root during those excursions. She majored in that subject at the Australian National University, in Canberra, the nation's capital, from which she earned a B.S. degree, with first-class honors, in 1981. By that time she had already won several awards, including the Geological Society of Australia Prize, in 1978; the W. B. Clark Prize in Geology, in 1979; and the Ampol Prize for undergraduate geology, in 1980. After she graduated she got a job as a research geologist with the Western Mining Corp., one of Australia's multinational mining giants. She worked in the Snowy Mountains, south of Canberra, mapping rock distributions and searching for ore. In 1983 she returned to the Australian National University and entered a graduate program in geology. With her thesis on the mineralogical and geochemical aspects of the weathering of granite, she received an M.S. degree in 1985.

In 1986 Banfield began working toward a doctorate at Johns Hopkins University, in Baltimore, Maryland, having won a Fulbright Scholarship to study in the U.S. and a special three-year grant from the university. At Johns Hopkins she served as both a research assistant and a teaching assistant. Under the supervision of the mineralogist David R. Veblen, she completed a dissertation on high-resolution electron-microscopy studies of weathering and diagenesis. (Diagenesis is a process of transformation in which a substance changes chemically or physically into a very different substance. A common example in geology is the transformation of sediments into rock.) She later cowrote several research papers with Veblen, for such professional journals as *American Mineralogist, Contributions to Mineralogy and Petrology, Geochimica et Cosmochimica Acta*, and *Science*. In mid-1999 her curriculum vitae listed 64 published articles or book chapters (a dozen in 1999 alone), 21 articles and chapters submitted for publication or in preparation, and close to 100 abstracts of papers presented at scientific meetings held between 1992 and 1999. In addition to Veblen, her research collaborators include William W. Barker, K. J. Edwards, Robert J. Hamers, Tetsuo Kogure, R. Lee Penn, and Hengzhong Zhang.

After she received a Ph.D. degree from Johns Hopkins, in 1990, the University of Wisconsin at Madison hired Banfield as an assistant professor in the Department of Geology and Geophysics, which began offering courses in 1854. The department is in Weeks Hall, which contains laboratories, teaching facilities, a science museum, a library, and an auditorium. Banfield works in a geomicrobiology facility, where she has access to such state-of-the-art equipment as a high-resolution transmission electron microscope, which enables the user to study bits of materials as tiny as a few nanometers (billionths of a meter) in diameter, and an X-ray diffractometer, which aims X-rays at substances (most commonly crystals) and thereby reveals distinctive patterns that aid in the identification of minerals. Banfield's research includes a study of weathering, the products of which affect the chemistry of water near the Earth's surface and form the basic constituents of soils and sediments. Because the products of biomineralization and weathering are typically minuscule crystals, she is trying to determine the fundamental nature of finely crystalline materials.

Banfield has taught courses in mineralogy, crystal chemistry, analytical techniques, and gemology, on both the undergraduate and graduate levels. In 1995 the University of Wisconsin promoted her to associate professor. That same year she taught the university's first almost totally on-line class. Called "Gems and Precious Stones," it covered a subject that she had taught to about 100 nonscience majors every semester. Supported by a grant designed to encourage teachers to use technology in the classroom, she spent two days at a jewelry studio in Madison, taking hundreds of photos of gems. She then scanned the images into her computer and posted the syllabus, and later the exams, on the World Wide Web. Immediately after taking an on-line exam, students could learn their test results and access explanations of each answer.

Eager to show female students that one can successfully combine marriage and a career, Banfield has also posted personal material on the Web, including photos of her husband and children and her favorite places (Red Man Camp Ground, Rhymney Ridge, and a site near Numeralla, all of which are in Australia). "It gives me a more three-dimensional character instead of being somebody who walks in and gives a semi-authoritative lecture and walks out again," she told Dave Newbart for the Madison, Wisconsin *Capital Times* (October 26, 1995, on-line). "It makes me more approachable." She added that many students were more willing to use E-mail than talk to a professor face-to-face, so that—contrary to critics' fears that an on-line course would be too impersonal—the new technology had actually increased her interactions with students.

In 1996 Banfield took a leave of absence from the University of Wisconsin and moved with her family to Tokyo, Japan, to accept a position as an associate professor at the Mineralogical Institute at the University of Tokyo. In 1997 she was promoted to full professor, thus becoming the first female science instructor to hold that rank at the university. One Tokyo newspaper, the *Asahi Evening News*, published a piece about her husband's role as a stay-at-home father.

After returning to the University of Wisconsin, in 1998, Banfield became involved with the Why Files, an award-winning Web site (funded by the university's graduate school) that seeks to explain "the science behind the news." The site focuses on the scientific aspects of events, issues, and phenomena that affect people's everyday lives. Using colorful graphics and current lingo, the site aims to engage people who have previously felt intimidated by such subject matter. Banfield has helped to prepare a course based on materials from the Why Files; repackaged into modules that form a coherent syllabus, it began with the spring 2000 semester and is offered primarily to nonscience majors.

Banfield became a full professor at the University of Wisconsin in 1999. During a sabbatical leave from the school in 2000, she worked at the Department of Microbiology and Parasitology at the University of Queensland, in Australia. Her honors include an award for outstanding research from the U.S. Department of Energy, in 1995; the D. A. Brown Medal, from Australian National University, in 1999; and the Faculty Achievement Award in geology and geophysics from the University of Wisconsin at Madison, also in 1999. In 2000 she is slated to receive the Marion L. and Christie M. Jackson Mid-Career Clay Scientist Award, from the Clay Minerals Society.

Banfield lives with her husband and three children in Madison. She sometimes takes her children along on field trips with her students. Unlike their mother as a child, she told *Current Biography*, they enjoy camping and hanging out with the undergraduates a lot more than they do anything related to geology. — M.R.

Suggested Reading: (Madison, Wisconsin) *Capital Times* (on-line) Oct. 26, 1995; *Tedtick.com* (on-line); *Wall Street Journal* (on-line) June 23, 1999, with photo

---

Barnes, Roy

Mar. 11, 1948– Governor of Georgia. Address: State Capitol, Room 203, Atlanta, GA 30334

According to his family legend, a particularly bad heat wave was responsible for the decision of Roy Barnes, the governor of Georgia, to enter into law and then politics. The story goes that on a warm summer day, when Barnes was just a teenager, he helped unload a boxcar of horse feed onto a truck. "There were bumblebees floating around the size of silver dollars," Barnes recalled, according to the *Access Atlanta* Web site. After all the feed was loaded, he headed back to the general store owned by his parents. On the way, he passed a law office, and in a window adjacent to the lawyer's shingle, he saw an air conditioner. It occurred to the tired, sweaty teen that some people didn't have to labor

Courtesy of the Governor's Office

Roy Barnes

in the heat to earn a living, and a seed was planted in his mind.

Still, in following a white-collar path to the governor's office, Barnes never lost touch with his working-class roots. Considered a savvy and persuasive politician by state insiders, he is lauded by much of the Georgian public as a populist who has his constituents' best interests at heart. During the 1999 legislative session, his first as governor, he pushed through popular legislation to strengthen state laws pertaining to open meetings and open records, with fines imposed on officials who don't make records available to the public; to reduce unemployment taxes by about $1 billion and raise unemployment benefits; to provide $83 million in tax credits and approximately double the state homestead exemption; to allow patients to go outside their managed health-care systems to choose doctors; to appoint a state insurance-consumers' advocate, who would help settle disputes between patients and HMOs; and to give teachers more power to eject disruptive students from their classrooms.

Roy Barnes was born on March 11, 1948 to Agnes and W. C. Barnes in Mableton, Georgia, a small town in Cobb County, across the Chattahoochee River from Atlanta. His parents ran a store, nestled between the highway and the railroad tracks, which carried merchandise as varied as work boots, produce, hardware, and shotguns. As soon as he was old enough, Barnes began to work in the store. Balmy days found him outside, where he would sell fruits and vegetables to travelers waiting for the bus to Atlanta. People congregated in the store to socialize and swap stories, and often the talk turned to politics. Young Roy listened avidly to these discussions. He also spent time next door to the store, in the small office of the justice of the peace, where voting took place and where Barnes's father presided over Magistrate Court. Such activities sparked Barnes's curiosity enough that by the age of 12, he was routinely traveling to the state capitol to watch the legislators in action. Barnes's interest in law was also spurred by Harold Glore, a law clerk for a justice on the Georgia Supreme Court, who lived across the railroad track from Barnes's parents' store and who became a mentor to the young man. "He had me reading law books by the time I was in high school," Barnes said, according to the *Access Atlanta* Web site. "He's the one that really pushed me to go to college and law school."

Barnes graduated from South Cobb High School, with honors, in 1966, then enrolled at the University of Georgia. Unlike many students at that school and elsewhere during the politically turbulent 1960s, Barnes did not engage in overt antiestablishment protests. Indeed, he appeared to take the opposite course, joining the Young Republicans and the Army Reserve Officers Training Corps. (ROTC classes were frequently targeted by student protestors, but Barnes crossed their picket lines to attend.) Still, Barnes has explained his brief affiliation with the Republican Party as a rebellion of another sort—against the administration of Georgia's governor at the time, the Democrat Lester Maddox, a staunch segregationist. By the end of his undergraduate years, however, having become disenchanted with the presidency of Richard Nixon, a Republican, he abandoned the GOP.

In his senior year Barnes met Marie Dobbs, an education major from Marietta, Georgia; in 1970, the year after Barnes began attending the University of Georgia Law School, the couple married. Barnes received his J.D. degree, cum laude, in 1972, having been elected outstanding senior. (He had also served on the law school's board of governors and as president of the student bar association.) Right after graduating he began a four-month stint in the U.S. Army Reserve. On his return he took a job as prosecutor in the Cobb County district attorney's office.

In 1974, just two years out of law school, Barnes ran successfully for the state Senate, becoming, at age 26, the youngest legislator elected in Georgia since Reconstruction. Within a few years he had been appointed to chair the Judiciary Committee, and in 1983 he was tapped by then-governor Joe Frank Harris as his floor leader in the chamber. During his tenure in the Senate, where he served eight two-year terms, Barnes also served on the governor's Growth Strategies Commission and was Senate chairman of the Constitutional Revision Committee. He initiated and took part in numerous studies on topics such as transportation; workers' compensation; child abuse and domestic violence; and problems of the aged, the homeless, and the mentally disabled. He gained a reputation as a champion of the underdog and sponsored several bills aimed at combating domestic violence, increasing and enforcing child-support orders, and promoting affordable day care.

While he was establishing himself in the Senate, Barnes was also building a private law practice in Marietta with fellow attorney Tom Browning. The firm handled a lot of criminal cases—at first they were the only ones the fledgling practice could attract. The nature of his practice later left Barnes open to attack from his opponents, who charged that he should not have been representing criminals. But Barnes has been steadfast in his beliefs that even criminals deserve a competent defense and that sometimes being a lawyer means representing an unpopular cause.

Barnes made a run for governor in 1990, finishing third in the Democratic primary behind Zell Miller, who eventually won election, and Andrew Young. Recovering from the disappointment, he visited the family store. His brother Ray told the *Atlanta Journal-Constitution*, as quoted on the Atlanta Access Web site, "He came down [to the store] and worked a day or two. The first thing you know is he's talking to people. They said, 'Roy, we're still behind you.' It wasn't but a few days [before] he was back up and going."

Barnes returned to the state legislature in 1993, with his election to the House of Representatives. He served on the Banks and Banking Committee and the Rules Committee and, according to some observers, began planning another run for governor almost immediately—methodically forging alliances with fellow House members and local officials.

In 1998 Barnes announced that he was making another bid for the office of governor and entered the race against Republican opponent Guy Millner, a successful entrepreneur who had never held an elective position, despite repeated attempts. The race was seen by the media as having national significance, since Georgia remained the only state that had not elected a Republican governor since Reconstruction—and since it seemed possible that Millner might prevail during this run. Millner, with personal wealth estimated at $167 million, was able to spend freely on his campaign. Barnes was able to rally only by raising almost $10 million from private contributors, many of whom had never before contributed to a political cause.

The campaign was marked by negative ads from both sides, with each party accusing the other of lying and distorting his opponent's history. Millner fumbled when asked to explain how the state's revenue estimates were determined, and Barnes pounced upon the misstatement as proof of his opponent's lack of experience. Millner countered by suggesting that as a political outsider, he could bring needed changes to the state. He conceded that Barnes "can tell you every bill number line by line," but then asked, according to the *New York Times* (October 26, 1998, on-line), "Is that what is needed?"

Indeed, Barnes's experience was, in some ways, a detriment to his campaign. Millner, who had no public record, was able to attack Barnes's extensive voting record without fear of reprisal. When Millner charged that Barnes was a bleeding-heart liberal who voted for the early release of convicts during his time in the legislature, Barnes countered with the explanation that the federal courts at the time had been threatening to take over Georgia's prisons because of severe overcrowding. When Millner reminded voters that Barnes had opposed the immensely popular state lottery implemented by then-governor Zell Miller, Barnes responded that since the proceeds from the lottery were being used for educational purposes, he would continue the program and make sure that it was well administered. Millner brought up racially charged issues; he accused Barnes of opposing racial "quotas" when speaking to white voters and then championing affirmative action in the presence of black voters, and he pointed to Barnes's vote years earlier against a holiday in honor of Martin Luther King Jr. Barnes readily conceded that the vote was the worst he had cast in his years as a lawmaker and that it had since caused him deep regret. He charged that Millner was purposely using racially divisive tactics to separate the state along color lines.

Both candidates realized that the black vote was critical. Blacks made up a quarter of Georgia's 3.9 million registered voters, and in the previous four elections, Democratic candidates for office had gotten between 83 and 92 percent of their votes. The Sunday before the election, Barnes and his wife made stops at churches in predominantly black Atlanta. Kevin Sack, writing for the *New York Times* (November 2, 1998, on-line), noted that this type of pilgrimage has become a ritual for white Democratic candidates, since the church has been seen for generations as both a spiritual refuge and a political staging ground for the traditionally Democratic African-American community. The day, by any measure, was a resounding success for Barnes; in a representative endorsement, Reverend Cynthia Hale of Ray of Hope Christian Church told her congregants that Barnes's "attendance demonstrated his concern for the community, just as God had demonstrated his by sending Jesus to Earth," as Kevin Sack reported.

Besides the support of much of the black community, Barnes also enjoyed the endorsement of many of the area's major newspapers. The *Augusta Chronicle* (November 1, 1998, on-line) called him "the very best practitioner of government the Peach State has to offer" and pointed out that just as Guy Millner wouldn't expect to hand over the reins of his company to an unproven outsider, neither should the governing of Georgia be left to someone with no governmental experience. As quoted on the *Barnes for Governor* Web site, the *Albany Herald* ran an editorial on October 18, 1998 that read, "Gov. Zell Miller will leave mighty big shoes to fill in January, but Georgians are fortunate

Roy Barnes is prepared for the job." The editorial conceded that "the job could be done by someone with much less first-hand knowledge of how government works," but concluded, "there is no reason Nov. 3 to cast aside this valuable resource being offered to the state."

On November 3 Barnes won the election with 53 percent of the vote. In his inaugural address, on January 11, 1999, he commented on the relationship between himself and the state's chief justice, Robert Benham, who had sworn him in—and what the relationship signified for Georgia. "The greatest change in Georgia is exemplified by two who share this stage today," he said, as quoted on the State of Georgia's Web site. "Both, are the first in their family to attend college. Both, came to know each other in an integrated University of Georgia. And both were, and continue to be, friends. One is white, and one is black. One is the chief Justice of the Supreme Court of Georgia who today administered the oath to the other, as the new Governor of this state. This act, which would have been impossible 100 years ago, shows Georgia at its best, as a place where neither race, gender, nor geography will ever divide us."

The transition from Zell Miller's administration to that of Barnes went smoothly. Barnes made his staff appointments slowly and carefully. If the press hoped for sweeping legislative change to fuel their headlines, they were disappointed. Governor Barnes deliberately and methodically set out to implement the campaign promises he had made, and even his seemingly radical proposal for a transportation agency with broad power to regulate traffic and urban sprawl passed both houses of the legislature with hardly any dissent. His first act after being sworn in won applause: with the goal of increasing the public's trust in its elected officials, he issued an order prohibiting conflicts of interest and banning all gifts from lobbyists and corporations to executive-branch personnel. As promised, he continued to administrate the lottery in the manner that Miller had established. The *Savannah Morning News* (March 28, 1999, on-line) went so far as to call the 1999 legislative session "The Roy Barnes Show," for the ease with which the governor handled the General Assembly. Once the session was over, Barnes turned his attention to education, a major component of his campaign platform. Appointing a committee to study education reform, he vowed to overhaul the ineffective 1985 Quality Basic Education Act, increase school funding, and hold school officials accountable for their students' poor performance—plans that meet with the approval of most of his constituents.

In March 2000, amid much dissension from teachers' professional organizations in Georgia, a far-reaching overhaul of the state educational system was overwhelmingly approved by the state legislature. The plan, which Barnes engineered, called for the elimination of tenure (or job security) for Georgia's teachers. Once dismissed, a teacher would have no right to a hearing. "Good teachers don't need tenure," Barnes said in his State of the State Address on February 3, 2000, as quoted on his official Web site, "and bad teachers don't deserve it." Less contentious provisions in the bill, which was signed into law on April 25, 2000, called for smaller classes and bonuses for teachers at schools in which students performed well on annual tests in reading, writing, math, science, and social studies.

Barnes and his wife have three children. Those who know Barnes personally have said that he has an engaging personality and a biting wit. After getting the governor to admit to being a bit of a prankster in his youth, Dick Pettys of the Associated Press commented that Barnes was "a little bit like Tom Sawyer and a little bit like Clarence Darrow. But mostly, he's like the garrulous neighbor who swaps stories over the backyard fence—only funnier." The *Marietta Daily Journal* ran an editorial that read, "After they made Roy Barnes they broke the mold. There just aren't many politicians and public servants with his populist touch any more. There aren't many who embody the Jeffersonian principle that government officials are the public's servants, not its masters." — M.R.

Suggested Reading: *Augusta Chronicle* (on-line) Nov. 1, 1998; *Governing* p20+ May 1999; *New York Times* A p18 Oct. 26, 1998, A p20 Mar. 25, 1999; *state.ga.us/governor* (on-line)

Barry, John

Nov. 3, 1933– Composer for films. Address: c/o Decca Records, 60 Music Sq. E., Nashville, TN 37203-4325.

Film music affects audiences in many ways. It may startle moviegoers, with blaring brass and pounding percussion; uplift them, by means of orchestral majesty; pull at their heartstrings, through the plaintive voices of violins; make their spines tingle, with the eerie tones of a Theramin. Some film scores linger in listeners' minds, transcending the works for which they were written and becoming part of the everyday soundscape. In his 40-year career as a composer for film and television, John Barry has affected audiences in all those ways, displaying such versatility that he defies rigid classification; indeed, Barry, a self-described "musical dramatist," has been compared to such masters of the genre as Erich Korngold, Max Steiner, and Henry Mancini, whose styles were distinctly different from one another. Probably best known for the theme that accompanies the pre-title sequences of the James Bond films, the British-born, classically trained Barry has written music for more than 100 motion pictures, among them *Seance on a Wet Afternoon*, *The Lion in Winter*, *Midnight Cowboy*, *The Cotton Club*, *Out of Africa*, *Jagged Edge*, *Peggy*

Michael Putland/Retna Ltd.

John Barry

Sue Got Married, Dances with Wolves, Chaplin, Cry, the Beloved Country, The Scarlet Letter, and a dozen Bond films, among them *From Russia with Love, Goldfinger*, and *The World Is Not Enough.* A conductor, arranger, and songwriter as well, Barry has won five Oscars and four Grammy Awards and is the subject of two full-length biographies: *John Barry: A Life in Music* (1998), by Gareth Bramley, Geoff Leonard, and Pete Walker, and *John Barry: The Sound of the Sixties* (1998), by Eddi Fiegel.

One of three children, John Barry was born Jonathan Barry Prendergast on November 3, 1933 in York, England. His father, Jack, owned several local cinemas, and as a child Barry became an avid moviegoer; by his early teens, he had learned to operate a projector. In a March 7, 1996 interview conducted at a film-music conference and transcribed for *Film Score Monthly* (November 1996, on-line), he cited as particularly influential in his musical development "the great adventure scores," such as Korngold's for *Robin Hood* and Steiner's for *The Treasure of the Sierra Madre*, and "all" the film music of Bernard Hermann and Alfred Newman; the work of the prolific Miklós Rózsa also impressed him. Produced in large part during the so-called Golden Age of Hollywood, such scores were written for the studios' in-house orchestras, and Barry would pay careful attention to the sound, "appreciating what was being done," as he explained in the *Film Score Monthly* interview. Beginning at age nine, he studied piano, and in his mid-teens he received instruction in composition from Francis Jackson, a composer, conductor, and long-time organist at York Minster, the largest Gothic cathedral in northern Europe. He also learned to play the trumpet, and he took a two-year correspondence course given by Bill Russo, an arranger for the composer and bandleader Stan Kenton. "I was a big, big fan of Stan Kenton's," *Film Score Monthly* quoted him as saying.

Drafted into military service in the 1950s, Barry was stationed in Egypt and Cypress, among other places, where he played in an army regimental band. After resuming his civilian life in York, he formed his own jazz group, the John Barry Seven, with which he played trumpet. "I wanted to be a professional musician, but I also wanted to be my own boss," he said, according to *Film Score Monthly.* The group, which remained together for four years, landed a recording contract with EMI Records, and several of their singles became hits, among them "Hit and Miss" and a cover version of the Ventures' surf-guitar classic "Walk Don't Run." Having gained notice through such exposure, Barry became an arranger for the popular British teen crooner Adam Faith, and he wrote the score for Faith's movie *Beat Girl* (1960). That same year he composed the music for the film *Never Let Go*, which starred Peter Sellers.

Dr. No (1962), the first of the 19 films that have been made so far about the suave, resourceful spy James Bond, was scored by Monty Norman, but Barry was tapped to create its theme. Referring to what he described as Stan Kenton's high and low brass sounds, he recalled, as quoted by *Film Score Monthly*, "I think the genesis of the Bond sound was most certainly that Kenton-esque sharp attack; extreme ranges, top C's and beyond, and on the low end you'd go right down to the low F's and below, so you'd have a wall of sound. The typical thing, that Bond thing, is very much this brass sound." The *Dr. No* theme reached the Top 20 on charts in the United Kingdom. Barry later wrote the complete scores for 12 James Bond films: *From Russia with Love* (1963), *Goldfinger* (1964), *Thunderball* (1965), *You Only Live Twice* (1967), *On Her Majesty's Secret Service* (1969), *Diamonds Are Forever* (1971), *The Man with the Golden Gun* (1974), *Moonraker* (1979), *Octopussy* (1983), *A View to Kill* (1985), *The Living Daylights* (1987), and *The World Is Not Enough* (1999). The title singles for *From Russia with Love, Goldfinger*, and *You Only Live Twice*, sung by Matt Monro, Shirley Bassey, and Nancy Sinatra, respectively, became hits.

Among the 27 non-Bond films for which Barry wrote scores in the 1960s are his first Hollywood picture, Bryan Forbes's *King Rat* (1965), a prisoner-of-war story set in Singapore during World War II; *The Ipcress File* (1965); *The Knack . . . and How to Get It* (1965); *Born Free* (1966); *The Lion in Winter* (1968); and *Midnight Cowboy* (1969). For "A Man Alone," the theme of *The Ipcress File*, a spy thriller based on a Len Deighton novel, Barry used a cymbalom, a type of dulcimer capable of emanating a creepy, foreboding sound. "With Bond I concentrated on the action and adventure, whereas with *Ipcress* I built the score around the hero or antihero Harry Palmer," he explained, according to excerpts adapted from *John Barry: A Life in Music* that appear on the Play It Again Records Web site. He chose an organ, cellos, and an all-female choir for *The Knack . . . and How to Get It*, a tale, directed by Richard Lester, about a pair of naïve would-be seducers and a brash but innocent young woman who has just arrived in the big city. *Born Free*, based on Joy Adamson's true story about a lioness that she and her husband rescued in Africa and ultimately released, brought Barry two Academy Awards, for best score and best song (the latter shared with lyricist Don Black). He had only three weeks to complete the writing and recording of the music for *The Lion in Winter*, a powerful family drama, set in 12th-century England, that starred Peter O'Toole as King Henry II and Katharine Hepburn as his wife, Eleanor of Aquitaine. Because of the time pressure, he forwent his usual practice of orchestrating the score himself; that task went to Bobby Richards. Their collaboration was eminently successful: the score, in which choral music predominated, earned Barry another Oscar as well as the Anthony Asquith Award, from the British Film Academy. In his *Film Score Monthly* interview, Barry reported that he had incorporated passages for synthesizer in the music for *The Lion in Winter*. In the dark urban drama *Midnight Cowboy*, directed by John Schlesinger and co-starring Dustin Hoffman and Jon Voight, he again used a synthesizer, in a fantasy sequence set on Miami Beach. "I had this flute on the melody, and I had this synthesizer playing off to give a sense of humor that the flute didn't have," he explained in *Film Score Monthly*.

In 1971 Barry picked up another Oscar nomination, for *Mary, Queen of Scots*, one of the five movies with his scores that premiered that year. During the rest of that decade, he wrote the music for 18 more films, among them an adaptation of Henrik Ibsen's play *A Doll's House*, starring Claire Bloom, Anthony Hopkins, Denholm Elliott, and Dame Edith Evans. One melody from *A Doll's House* was recorded for the 1977 compilation *Very Best of John Barry*. The rendition by the disco diva Donna Summer of "Down Deep Inside," Barry's theme for the underwater thriller *The Deep* (1977), reached number five on the charts in Great Britain. Earlier, in 1971, Barry's own recording of the theme music that he wrote for the television series *The Persuaders*, which featured Roger Moore and Tony Curtis, reached number 13 on British charts. He later composed the music for other TV series (*The Adventurer*, in 1972, and *Orson Welles' Great Mysteries*, in 1973, for example) and a dozen made-for-TV films. Prominent among the latter are *Eleanor and Franklin* (1976) and its sequel, *Eleanor and Franklin: The White House Years* (1977), which were based on a Pulitzer Prize–winning biography of the Roosevelts by Joseph P. Lash. According to *John Barry: A Life in Music*, the Hollywood biographer and film historian Tony Thomas described Barry's Emmy Award–nominated theme for the sequel as "simple yet wistful . . . essentially American in character and yet one that has universal regret for the past as it fades into memory. It is a prime example of the eloquence of music when written as an extra dimension to visual experience."

Also during the 1970s, Barry achieved success as a composer for the stage. He had first tried his hand at theater in the mid-1960s, when he wrote the music for *Passion Flower Hotel*, for which Trevor Peacock supplied the lyrics. Despite a few scathing reviews among the generally mixed assessments, the musical ran for six months, in 1965–66, at the Prince of Wales Theatre, in London. Barry's next theatrical effort, *Lolita My Love*, a collaboration with Alan Jay Lerner, closed soon after its opening. *Billy* (1974), which he created with Don Black, ran for some two years at another London venue, the Theatre Royal. Based on Keith Waterhouse's 1959 novel *Billy Liar* and the play and movie that Waterhouse and Willis Hall adapted from the book, *Billy* starred Michael Crawford as an undertaker's clerk who takes refuge from his real life by creating a fantasy world and becoming an obsessive liar. According to Bramley, Leonard, and Walker, Crawford's departure from the show triggered its demise, and except for a two-week run at the 1992 Edinburgh Festival, in a production mounted by the National Youth Music Theatre of Great Britain, Barry's plans to revive it have come to naught.

In the 1980s Barry composed the scores for 27 feature films. They include Lawrence Kasdan's *Body Heat* (1981), which starred William Hurt and Kathleen Turner in a sinister tale of sex and murder reminiscent of Billy Wilder's 1944 melodrama *Double Indemnity*; *Frances* (1982), in which Jessica Lange starred as the real-life Frances Farmer, who spent many years in mental institutions after a brief career as an actress; the legal thriller *Jagged Edge* (1985), for which Barry chose solo flute and solo piano for the main theme but relied mostly on a synthesizer; and Sydney Pollack's *Out of Africa* (1985), for which he earned his fourth Academy Award, for best score. (*Out of Africa*, which is based on the experiences of the Danish writer who called herself Isak Dinesen, also captured the Oscars for best picture, director, cinematography, art direction, sound, and adapted screenplay.) Although at first Pollack had wanted the music to recreate traditional African sounds, Barry came up with a sweepingly romantic score, having persuaded Pollack that, as he put it in his *Film Score Monthly* interview, the screenplay was "not about Africa" but about "two people who are madly in love with Africa and with each other." The one "African" sound that he incorporated (that of a drum), in his opinion, "did not work."

Barry's creative life came to an abrupt halt in 1988, after he swallowed a "health-food drink" that "proved to be unbelievably toxic," as he told Jon Burlingame for *Premiere* (December 1990). The concoction caused his esophagus to rupture. "Unable to eat normally for 14 months," Burlingame wrote, "Barry underwent four major surgeries and, he reports, twice nearly died." "George Bernard

Shaw said that any artist in his 50s should take a sabbatical—18 months to two years off," Barry told Burlingame. "I did it involuntarily, but I wouldn't recommend this method to anybody else."

After his recovery Barry wrote the music for *Dances with Wolves* (1990), Kevin Costner's directorial debut, in which Costner starred as John Dunbar, a Civil War soldier who finds fulfillment by joining the Sioux Indian tribe. A 91-piece orchestra and a choir performed the music, which contains 15 distinct themes. "Though it's a big score, in a strange way it had to be very simple," Barry told Burlingame. "Dunbar is a simple, decent man, and the story has a kind of purity to it." According to Burlingame, Barry carried out his assignment "intuitively" and did not research Indian music or music of the Civil War period. "I approached the whole score from John Dunbar's point of view—his observations of the Sioux tribe. As he says in the movie, 'All of the things I've ever heard and ever been told about these people are totally wrong.' And so, musically, it's his assessment of the dignity and graciousness of these people." According to *Variety Movie Guide '96*, Barry's music "makes a major contribution" to the film, "varying from the elegiac tone of the main theme to the heart-racing primal rhythms of the buffalo and scalp dances."

In the last decade Barry has worked at a far more leisurely pace than he did before his illness. His score for *Chaplin* (1992), Richard Attenborough's epic biopic of the comic genius Charlie Chaplin, garnered him his seventh Oscar nomination. Among other movies, he also wrote the music for Bruce Joel Rubin's *My Life* (1993), starring Michael Keaton as a terminally ill man who is making a video of his life for his unborn child; Adrian Lyne's *Indecent Proposal* (1993), about a married couple (Demi Moore and Woody Harrelson) who are offered $1 million by a billionaire (Robert Redford) for a one-night-stand with the wife; the South African–made *Cry, the Beloved Country* (1995), based on Alan Paton's classic novel about apartheid, with James Earl Jones and Richard Harris; the universally trashed *The Scarlet Letter* (1995), which reviewers agreed had little resemblance to Nathaniel Hawthorne's same-named novel; and, most recently, *The World Is Not Enough* (1999), for which the British director Michael Apted guided Pierce Brosnan as James Bond.

In 1998 Barry received a standing ovation after conducting the English Chamber Orchestra at the Royal Albert Hall, in London, in a performance of a "musical autobiography," a dozen compositions that Decca has released as the album *The Beyondness of Things*—his first nonsoundtrack album in 25 years. The many Barry soundtrack albums and compilations of his music still being sold include the album *Moviola* (1992), a collection of romantic themes that was accompanied by a promotional documentary.

In the 1960s Barry was prominent among London swingers, and his many affairs, friendships with celebrities, and fancy sports car attracted a lot of media attention. A past resident of London and Majorca, he currently lives with his fourth wife, Laurie, and their son, Jonpatrick, in Oyster Bay, New York. He has at least one other child—a daughter, Kate, from his second marriage, to the British actress Jane Birkin. Barry received Grammy Awards in 1969, for *Midnight Cowboy*; 1985 (with Bob Willis), for *The Cotton Club*; 1986, for *Out of Africa*; and 1991, for *Dances with Wolves*. — M.C.

Suggested Reading: *Film Score Monthly* (on-line); *Premiere* p65+ Dec. 1990, with photo; Bramley, Gareth, Geoff Leonard, and Pete Walker. *John Barry: A Life in Music*, 1998; Fiegel, Eddi. *John Barry: The Sound of the Sixties*, 1998; *Motion Picture Almanac, 1999*

Selected Films: *Beat Girl*, 1960; *Dr. No*, 1962; *From Russia with Love*, 1963; *The L-Shaped Room*, 1963; *Goldfinger*, 1964; *Seance on a Wet Afternoon*, 1964; *Zulu*, 1964; *King Rat*, 1965; *The Ipcress File*, 1965; *The Knack . . . and How to Get It*, 1965; *Thunderball*, 1965; *Born Free*, 1966; *You Only Live Twice*, 1967; *The Lion in Winter*, 1968; *Petulia*, 1968; *Midnight Cowboy*, 1969; *On Her Majesty's Secret Service*, 1969; *Mary, Queen of Scots*, 1971; *Diamonds Are Forever*, 1971; *Alice's Adventures in Wonderland*, 1972; *A Doll's House*, 1973; *The Man with the Golden Gun*, 1974; *The Tamarind Seed*, 1974; *The Day of the Locust*, 1975; *Robin and Marian*, 1976; *The Deep*, 1977; *The Black Hole*, 1979; *Moonraker*, 1979; *Body Heat*, 1981; *Frances*, 1982; *Octopussy*, 1983; *The Cotton Club*, 1984; *Out of Africa*, 1985; *Jagged Edge*, 1985; *Peggy Sue Got Married*, 1986; *Howard the Duck*, 1986; *Dances with Wolves*, 1990; *Chaplin*, 1992; *My Life*, 1993; *Indecent Proposal*, 1993; *The Scarlet Letter*, 1995; *Cry, the Beloved Country*, 1995; *Playing By Heart*, 1998; *Mercury Rising*, 1998; *The World Is Not Enough*, 1999

Barshefsky, Charlene

1951(?)– U.S. trade representative. Address: Office of the U.S. Trade Representative, 600 17th St. N.W., Washington, DC 20508

Charlene Barshefsky, the United States trade representative (USTR), once compared a senior European trade official to the pompous character Owl in the Winnie-the-Pooh stories. "I've learned a lot of negotiating strategies reading stories to my daughters," David Sanger quoted her as saying in the *New York Times* (December 14, 1996). The Office of the U.S. Trade Representative, originally called the Office of the Special Trade Representative, was established in 1962. Its mission is to develop and coordinate international trade and investment policy and to negotiate with other countries about those

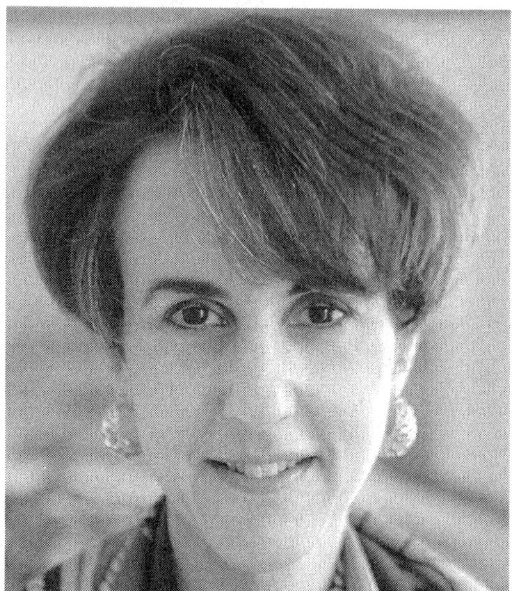

Courtesy of the Office of the USTR
Charlene Barshefsky

issues. The USTR, who serves a four-year term, is a member of the president's Cabinet and has the rank of ambassador, with direct responsibility to the president and Congress. Barshefsky believes that successful trade agreements can greatly strengthen international relationships. Trade "takes the place of Cold War alliances, which were based largely on fear or a grudging acceptance of foreign aid," she told Elsa Walsh for a *New Yorker* (March 18, 1996) profile of her. "Today, trade is necessary not only to ensure our domestic growth but also to ensure that our alliances become vehicles for the spread of democracy and American values." She elaborated on that theme in a 1996 interview with David Sanger: "You have to make countries understand that this is an age in which they will define their relationships with America largely in their economic interactions with America."

The daughter of immigrants from Eastern Europe, Charlene Barshefsky was born in about 1951 in Illinois. Each of her parents had come to the United States as a teenager, with little command of English but with a firm belief in the importance of education. Barshefsky's father studied for the rabbinate before becoming a chemical engineer in Chicago. Her mother taught school, and her two older siblings pursued doctorates in academic fields. Barshefsky attended the University of Wisconsin, from which she received a B.A. degree, with honors, in 1972. She then enrolled at the Columbus School of Law at the Catholic University, in Washington, D.C.; when she graduated, in 1975, she ranked seventh in her class. Her decision to study law had distressed her family, which considered law to be a trade, unworthy of anyone with as great an intellect as Charlene's; only her maternal grandmother had supported her, reasoning that a job in law would allow for self-sufficiency. That instinct proved correct: after earning her law degree, Barshefsky immediately found a job in the trade division at Steptoe & Johnson, one of the District of Columbia's most prestigious law firms. Trade was a relatively new area for the firm, and unlike most legal specialties at that time, it was not dominated by men. Barshefsky rose through the ranks quickly; by 1993 she had been promoted to co-chair of Steptoe & Johnson's international division and was earning about $500,000 a year.

That year Mickey Kantor, then the newly appointed U.S. trade representative, asked Barshefsky to become his deputy in charge of Asian and Latin American trade. Barshefsky had never held a political post and had never negotiated professionally, but she had always been a fast learner, and she felt up to the challenge. The job paid only about a quarter of her salary from Steptoe & Johnson, but the family was financially able to absorb the loss. The largest area of concern for Barshefsky was the effect that her work, which involves long hours and a good deal of travel, would have on her family. "The dilemma in this job is that her kids will only be this age once," her husband, Edward B. Cohen, explained to Elsa Walsh. "And yet she has this professional opportunity only once. And can you say no to either of them? The answer is very difficult. She's chosen not to, and I think appropriately. But the cost of that is being constantly torn. It is an overriding emotion that she lives with." Cohen, a solicitor at the Department of the Interior, encouraged Barshefsky to take the job: his family had always been enthusiastic about politics, and he felt that everyone should have a stint in public service. Barshefsky's young daughters, Mari and Devra, were excited by the idea that she might get to know the president of the United States. With the encouragement of her family—and some trepidation—she accepted the appointment.

Almost immediately after being sworn in, on May 28, 1993, Barshefsky went to Japan to try to establish a framework for future trade talks there. While Japanese products were freely admitted into the United States, the government of Japan had a history of erecting formidable barriers to American products, and Barshefsky intended to correct the inequity. While she was in Japan, her tough negotiating style quickly earned her the nickname "Stonewall" among her colleagues. That style angered the Japanese, and the talks initially broke down, resuming at the behest of Japan's prime minister. Barshefsky chose to negotiate with the Japanese on a product-by-product basis, rather than engaging in broad multiple-issue agreements (such as the Structural Impediments Initiative favored during the administration of President George Bush), which had not proved successful. Her strategy resulted in several agreements that opened the Japanese market to American computers, semiconductors, paper, glass, wood, and agricultural products. She also spearheaded agreements for government procurement of medical equipment and technology, telecommunications services and equipment, insurance, and cellular telephones. In *Business Week* (July 21, 1997), Barshefsky detailed some of her achievements. "The number of U.S. [sawmills] allowed to ship to Japan has gone from 80 to 1,000. For the first time in, say, 3,000 years, foreign tomatoes can now be shipped to Japan because of one of these agreements. And Japan's National Police Agency, which has decided to buy $200 million to $300 million worth of radios, has agreed to redo its procurement process [which excluded U.S. manufacturers]." Barshefsky pointed out that she was being vigilant in enforcing the agreements, bringing Japan before the World Trade Organization (WTO, which monitors global trade) when it failed to comply with agreements. This was a diplomatic move, she explained, because "any win in the WTO is a multilateral win, which is to say, not simply viewed as a product of [U.S.] bashing of [Japan], but a multilateral decision."

Barshefsky drew a a great deal of media attention as a result of her negotiations with the Chinese—a significant accomplishment, given that traditionally, the American press has barely covered trade issues, perhaps assuming that the topic would bore most people. Although U.S. foreign policy called for China to honor U.S. copyrights on intellectual property such as computer software, music CDs, and movies, Chinese companies were openly manufacturing and selling illegal copies of these products. This piracy was costing American industries as much as $2 billion a year and had become so rampant by 1995 that a trade war was brewing, with the U.S. threatening to impose $1 billion in sanctions on Chinese goods. Barshefsky explained the gravity of the situation to Elsa Walsh: "These are our potential markets. These are the fastest-growing markets in the world. These are the markets to which we're going to have to be able to sell to remain competitive. If our goods are pirated, if our trademarks are stolen, if our patents are violated, to whom do we sell?" With the deadline for the sanctions looming, Barshefsky and Wu Yi, China's foreign-trade minister, hammered out and signed the 22-page U.S.-China Intellectual Property Rights Agreement on February 26, 1995. (In Asia, Wu Yi, Barshefsky, and the Malaysian government official Rafidah Aziz are known as the "Three Iron Ladies.") The agreement called for China to implement an enforcement policy over the next three to five years, to set up task forces to control violators, to raid factories engaged in manufacturing the pirated goods and retailers selling them, and to give customs officials greater authority to halt their export. The agreement also called for China to open its markets to American software and audiovisual products and to allow American manufacturers of these products to enter joint ventures to produce their goods in China. Her colleagues were not surprised that Barshefsky, who has claimed never to tire, had reached a last-minute accord with Wu Yi. One of her top aides told David Sanger in December 1996, "Sometimes I think countries sign trade deals with Charlene simply so their negotiators can get some sleep."

After the agreement was signed, China's president, Jiang Zemin, invited Barshefsky to have tea at his home. While some observers viewed the invitation as a sign of China's willingness to improve relations with the U.S., others warned that enforcing the agreement would be difficult. The skeptics were right. When Barshefsky returned to China in November 1995, she found that factories were still pirating American products. She diplomatically reminded Chinese officials that the nation's admittance into the WTO, a long-held goal of the Chinese government, was largely dependent on compliance with global trade rules. In addition, as she has in all her negotiations with the Chinese, she brought up the country's dismal human-rights record, which has repeatedly led Congress to consider revoking China's most-favored-nation status. In May 1996 Barshefsky threatened to impose $3 billion in sanctions on Chinese goods, noting that Chinese officials had stamped out pornography in Guangdong Province virtually overnight, evidence that their failure to do the same for intellectual-property piracy was a question of "national will" rather than ability. Thanks to a breakthrough agreement in November 1999 that further opened China's markets to U.S. goods, the country's entry into the WTO is expected to become a reality in the near future.

On September 19, 2000 the U.S. Senate voted to grant China permanent normal trading privileges. Some commentators felt that by granting the country permanent rights, rather than renewing them yearly, as had been done in the past, the U.S. would weaken its leverage in China, thus making it difficult to address China's abuses of human rights and the environment. Despite such reservations, the bill, which includes a provision barring excessive import of Chinese goods into the U.S., passed with a vote of 83 to 15, making it the biggest foreign-policy victory for President Bill Clinton since the passage of the North American Free Trade Agreement, in 1993.

Although Chinese-American relations remain unpredictable, President Clinton has remained pleased with Barshefsky's performance. When Mickey Kantor became secretary of commerce, in April 1996, the president, citing her ability to "bring tears to the eyes" of other world leaders, named Barshefsky acting U.S. trade representative and announced that the position would become permanent when Kantor's term officially ended, in 1997. (Barshefsky has claimed that she learned of her appointment after persuading hockey fans in an airport lounge to change the TV channel from a hockey game to the president's news conference; she noted wryly that the rowdy group didn't even buy her a drink afterwards.) Clinton's announcement provoked a mixed response. Her critics said that Barshefsky lacked Kantor's long political experience and insider connections—a charge she readily admitted; her admirers countered that her abilities more than made up for any lack in political savvy. "She may be the most intuitive negotiator I've ever seen," Joan Spero, the undersecretary of state for economic and agricultural affairs, said, as quoted in the *New York Times* (May 17, 1996). Spero added, "She has this incredible ability to pick up the body language of the negotiator on the other side of the table. She reads them brilliantly." But before she could be sworn in, Barshefsky had to face more than mere criticism: by law, the position of trade representative is out of bounds to people who have acted on behalf of a foreign government in a trade dispute, and while with Steptoe & Johnson, Barshefsky had represented the Canadian lumber industry and served as a consultant to the Canadian Embassy. Republican senator Phil Gramm of Texas, among many others, considered the law unfair; he told *Congressional Quarterly* (February 1, 1997), "This takes the naïve approach that if anybody has ever worked for a foreign interest they are tainted. I hope we have people who are qualified enough that everyone in the world would want their services." The Senate approved a waiver of the law, and on March 17, 1997 Barshefsky was sworn in.

Earlier, as acting trade representative, Barshefsky had had to grapple with a longstanding problem involving the vast U.S. telecommunications market. For many years other countries had demanded access to that market, while claiming that their own were not developed enough to reciprocate. Barshefsky felt that, in trying to engineer a global agreement, the office of the USTR had offered too many concessions. "Twenty years ago we were willing to enter nonreciprocal agreements," she told David Sanger in May 1996. "We were a fully developed nation, compared to others, and we had economic leeway and political leeway to place other priorities ahead of trade. And there was the cold war, which drove our agenda. Now, we expect foreign countries to provide the same level of access to us that we have provided the world." With characteristic bluntness, she concluded, "You get what you give. It's that simple. No free rides." While she ended negotiations on the pending deal, Barshefsky invited other nations to try again when they had more to offer. Her approach paid off: eventually 64 WTO member nations agreed to more-open telecommunications markets. Barshefsky trumpeted the agreement as a foundation for the global information economy of the next century. Later, during her first year as permanent USTR, Barshefsky developed global agreements expanding trade on information technology and financial services. Despite such achievements, in 1997 Barshefsky was unable to persuade the House of Representatives to vote for the "fast-track" trade authority requested by President Clinton. Under a fast-track policy, Congress would be allowed only yes or no votes on trade agreements, with no amendments permissible, thereby speeding up negotiations with foreign countries. Barshefsky felt that fast-track authority would encourage other nations to negotiate freely with the U.S., since they would not be unduly hampered by congressional demands. But the measure was defeated, because many members of Congress wanted to maintain the prerogative of adding child-labor or working-condition stipulations to trade agreements.

Meanwhile, Barshefsky was busy on other fronts, scoring several triumphs, for example, in her dealings with Latin America. U.S.–Latin American trade was growing fast, and Barshefsky negotiated agreements with Brazil, Argentina, and Caribbean and Central American nations. President Clinton has credited her with helping to push forward the Free Trade Area of the Americas (which aims to unite the economies of all Western Hemisphere countries). Her negotiations with the European Union (E.U.)—particularly regarding bananas and beef—have been more troubled. The United States has contended that the E.U. has favored bananas from former European colonies in Africa, the Caribbean, and the Pacific and has refused exports from Latin America, where many banana producers, such as Chiquita, are American-owned. Although the E.U. offered to modify its policy in 2000, Barshefsky derided the changes as inconsequential and predicted that the E.U. would not end trade discrimination. Accordingly, she imposed enormous duties on a range of E.U. exports, including whiskey, cheese, and cashmere, effectively doubling the prices of those products. She calmly explained to a stunned European press that she had nothing against those industries but that retaliatory actions, permissible by international law, were necessary.

In 1989 the E.U. had banned import of beef from animals that had received hormones. In 1998 the WTO had ruled the ban illegal, on the grounds that there was little evidence that hormone-treated meat caused health problems, but the E.U. refused to rescind it. In April 1999 the E.U. announced plans to ban *all* beef from the U.S., after traces of hormones were found in 12 percent of 258 random samples of American beef. European officials rejected Barshefsky's proposal to have all hormone-treated beef labeled as such before its export. Later in April the E.U. agreed to accept imports of meat from non-hormone-treated animals.

In anticipation of the third WTO Ministerial Conference, scheduled to be held November 30 to December 3, 1999 in Seattle, Washington, Barshefsky, who was to chair the event, declared on the WTO Web site, "This will be the largest trade event ever held in the United States, and it will inaugurate global negotiations which will shape world trade as we move to the next century." But the talks collapsed; the E.U. pulled out, accusing Barshefsky of demanding too many concessions, particularly in the area of agricultural subsidies. Many countries felt that the conference was ill-timed, since the upcoming presidential election was certain to influence the U.S. negotiators. (In effect, the U.S.

negotiators were acting as representatives of the president, and in an election year, the foreign negotiators believed, the president would not want to appear weak by allowing the U.S. to bow to other countries' wishes.) Moreover, several developing countries expressed dissatisfaction with the way the talks were conducted, accusing the larger, industrialized nations of excluding them. While Barshefsky acknowledged that there had been room for improvement, she attributed the failure of the conference to the novelty and complexity of the issues on the table. Further marring the event were the large protests against the WTO conducted on Seattle streets by environmental, human-rights, and union groups. The violence of some demonstrators led Seattle to impose its first public curfew since World War II. Despite the problems in Seattle, during 2000 Barshefsky negotiated significant trade agreements with several countries, among them India, Jordan, and Vietnam.

Barshefsky, whose long, narrow face and delicate features have reminded some journalists of portraits by Modigliani, has written and lectured extensively on trade policy and law. As USTR, she chairs the Trade Policy Review Group, which helps the president formulate overall trade policy. On the frequent trips that her job requires, she maintains close contact with her husband and children and has sometimes supervised the girls' homework long-distance. When out of town or overseas, she never sightsees; instead, she returns to her home, in Washington, D.C., as soon as she can, to be with her family. — M.R.

Suggested Reading: *BBC Online*; *New York Times* D p1 May 17, 1996, with photo, A p1+ Feb. 27, 1995, with photo; *New Yorker* p86+ Mar. 18, 1996; Office of the U.S. Trade Representative (on-line); *USA Today* A p2 Nov. 7, 1997; *Working Woman* p17 June 1999, with photo; World Trade Organization (on-line)

Courtesy of Institute of Nautical Archaeology

Bass, George

Dec. 9, 1932– Underwater archaeologist.
Address: Institute of Nautical Archaeology, P.O. Box 2310, College Station, TX 77841-9932

At first, George Bass thought of underwater archaeology as a lark. The University of Pennsylvania, where he was pursuing a Ph.D. in classical archaeology, held the permit for the archaeological excavation of a Bronze Age shipwreck off the coast of Turkey, and needed someone to direct the project. Until then, no scientifically organized dig had ever been conducted underwater, and Bass himself had never even led one on land. Nevertheless, he took six diving lessons at the local YMCA and, in the summer of 1960, accompanied by his bride of a few months, went to Cape Gelidonya, in Turkey, where, he later wrote, he "had the good fortune to direct the first complete excavation of an ancient shipwreck on the seabed." When he and his crew started the dig, the accepted wisdom was that only the Myceneans (who entered what is now Greece from the north in about 2000 B.C.) had plied the waters of the eastern Mediterranean during the Bronze Age (which extended from between 4000 and 3000 B.C. to about 1000 B.C.). Bass was astonished to discover many artifacts indicating that the ship's builders had probably been Near Easterners—perhaps Canaanites (the ancestors of the seagoing Phoenicians). Despite the hardships he and his wife experienced at their Cape Gelidonya camp—in *Johns Hopkins Magazine* (April 1997, on-line), Dale Keiger reported that "expedition members lost an average of 30 pounds over the summer due to insufficient nutrition"—Bass returned to the area the next year, to excavate the remains of a Byzantine ship. "I just kept coming back year after year after year, until that's what I was doing with my life," he told Robert Locke for *Discovering Archaeology* (May/June 1999).

Now recognized as the father of underwater archaeology, Bass has devoted the past four decades to "the development of nautical archaeology as a serious scholarly pursuit," in his words. In 1973 he founded the Institute of Nautical Archaeology (INA), which has sponsored the excavations of shipwrecks that represent dozens of cultures from three continents and date from as long ago as 1,600 B.C. The discoveries of Bass and his co-workers have shed new light on the histories of the Old and New Worlds. "The hair-stands-up-on-the-back-of-my-neck excitement comes in the library at, say, three A.M. . . . ," he told John Stein for *Omni* (November 1991). "I enjoy the feeling of being underwater, the freedom. But diving is not where the excitement comes. We don't understand the significance of something when we find it." "It's not the physical act of discovery that counts most," he said to Robert Ostermann for the *National Observer* (February 8, 1965). "It's the new facts that you find." In a cover article for *National Geographic* (December 1987) about the oldest known shipwreck, he explained, "On the average we devote two years to conservation and research for every month of diving on site." He declared at the conclusion of the article, "We are salvaging the greatest of all treasures—the treasure of knowledge."

A son of Robert D. Bass and Virginia (Wauchope) Bass, George Fletcher Bass was born in Columbia, South Carolina, on December 9, 1932. "I had a fascination with diving ever since I was a very small child," he told Robert Locke. "My brother and I, when I was about seven and he was about nine, used to draw plans for these submarines we were going to build. But I never dreamed I would dive myself—I just liked to read about it." Although he did not lack for a role model in his eventual field (one of his uncles was an archaeologist), he entered Johns Hopkins University, in Baltimore, Maryland, in 1950, with the intention of becoming a professor of English, like his father and grandfather. He spent his sophomore year overseas, taking courses in English literature at the University College of the Southwest of England (now called the University of Exeter). But after seeing Roman ruins in Italy that year, he "sort of forgot about Virginia [Woolf] and Shakespeare," as he recalled to Locke, and when he returned to Johns Hopkins he changed his major to archaeology. In 1955 he earned an M.A. degree in Near Eastern archaeology (without first getting a bachelor's degree).

Bass spent the next two years at the American School of Classical Studies, in Athens, Greece. During that time he assisted at digs in Greece and Turkey. After returning to the United States, in 1957, he began a two-year stint with the U.S. Army Security Agency; when he completed his service, he held the rank of first lieutenant. In 1959 he enrolled at the University of Pennsylvania (UPenn), in Philadelphia, where, while preparing for his doctoral degree, he worked in the university's museum (now known as the University of Pennsylvania Museum of Archaeology and Anthropology), first as an assistant in the Mediterranean section (1959–60) and then as a special assistant for underwater archaeology (1962–64). In 1964 he was awarded a Ph.D. in classical archaeology, with a specialty in the Bronze Age. That year he began teaching at UPenn as an assistant professor of classical archaeology. He also became an assistant curator in the University Museum. From 1968 to 1973 he held the titles of associate professor and associate curator.

In 1969, after almost a decade of seafloor explorations off the coasts of Turkey and Greece, Bass decided to end his fieldwork. He came to that decision after watching a worker die from the bends (also known as decompression sickness), a disorder that occurs when a diver rises to the surface too quickly. "I'd never seen a dead person," Bass told Dale Keiger. "This fisherman died in our [decompression] chamber. I didn't want to pull another dead person, one of our people, out of the water." Later that year he accepted a position as a visiting scholar at St. John's College, a division of Cambridge University, in England. In 1971 he headed a terrestrial excavation of a Neolithic and Bronze Age settlement in Italy.

The pull of the sea proved to be greater than the strength of his resolution to stay away from it, however. Eager to return to underwater activities, in 1973 Bass founded the Institute of Nautical Archaeology (INA), to train students in the work of underwater archaeology, develop exploratory techniques, and provide opportunities for researchers. Referring to his experiences at the land dig in Italy, he explained to John Stein, "I missed the excitement of finding whole objects rather than bits and pieces. We were trying to find out about the introduction of certain types of pottery and domestic animals into the region. I thought, If [whoever made the objects] came across the Adriatic from present-day Yugoslavia, there must be one shipwreck out there that's going to tell us as much as digging here year after year." Moreover, as he told Robert Locke, "you can excavate far, far more carefully underwater than you can on land. Literally, with one finger, you can fan away the sand and dig down one grain of sand at a time. If you're properly weighted, your feet are up above your head and you're hanging there, not touching anything. You don't need picks and shovels, or even paintbrushes." After failing to work out an agreement with UPenn as to how the new organization would be administered, Bass struck out on his own (while maintaining a teaching position at UPenn, as an adjunct professor, until 1976). "My wife, Ann, and I sold everything except my library and her baby grand piano to set up headquarters on Cyprus," he told a writer for *National Geographic* (December 1987). Armed conflict on Cyprus forced them to leave, and after two years with no address, the INA moved to landlocked Texas A&M University, in College Station. (For some years the INA has also maintained an annex in Turkey.) At the same time, Bass joined Texas A&M's faculty, as a professor of anthropology. He has held the title of distinguished professor of anthropology there since 1980. Between 1986 and 1993 he also headed the school's nautical-archaeology program.

Some land-based archaeologists and other academics have questioned the validity of underwater archaeology, even likening its practitioners to treasure seekers whose primary goal is to turn a profit from discovered objects. But, as Bass has explained, seabed exploration as he and his colleagues conduct it is a true science. "Those of us who pioneered [underwater archaeology] had all worked on land before we began to dive, without exception, so we were simply doing the same archaeology with the same careful records," he told Robert Locke. "Archaeology is a destructive process. When you dissect a site by excavation, you have destroyed it forever, so it is immoral if you don't have extremely accurate records and plans. That is the philosophy we brought to the seafloor." Bass and other pioneers in the field introduced such research techniques as mapping, in which a grid is created, sectioning the site of a wreck into labeled areas, as lines of latitude and longitude do on land maps; making color-coded diagrams that show the precise locations of the objects before excavation; and photographing every stage of the excavation (using a camera mounted high enough to record "aerial" views). Bass has also devoted much effort to ensuring the safety of divers—who, to avoid decompression sickness, are limited to two 20-minute descents each day—while, at the same time, maximizing their efficiency. Toward those ends, he has helped to develop such tools as a balloon lift, which brings heavy objects to the surface; a decompression chamber that sits four people, who, during their slow ascent to the surface, can read or talk among themselves or with their shipboard mates; side-scan sonars, which help to detect the presence of telltale debris; and an air lift, which, functioning like a vacuum cleaner, removes sand grains from buried objects. His thousands of dives and years of research have led to many historical revelations. With evidence, for example, that many centuries ago seafaring men repaired fishing nets by using spindles, he has cast doubt on the widely held assumption that ships' rosters must have included women to do such chores.

In 1984 Bass began working on what he has called "an archaeologist's dream." Two years earlier a Turkish sponge diver had discovered cargo from an ancient shipwreck, and his captain had notified the INA. "I felt no emotion as I scanned the cargo for the first time that summer of 1984," Bass recalled in his 1987 *National Geographic* article. "I was standing upright, my diving fins resting on a rock outcrop 150 feet below the surface of the Mediterranean. The world's oldest known shipwreck lay before me—the shapes of jars and copper ingots dated back to the 14th or early 13th century B.C. But I had no more than five minutes to plan its excavation. Five minutes to estimate the lie of the ship's hull beneath its cover of sand and cargo. Five minutes to decide where to place our air-filled Plexiglas dome—dubbed the 'phone booth'—in which our divers might take refuge in an emergency or telephone the surface. Five minutes to decide what mapping techniques we would use. Five minutes spent fighting nitrogen narcosis caused by breathing at such depth." He spent the next five years as the director of the excavation and an additional six as its co-director. During that time (although, for health reasons, he stopped diving professionally in 1985), he oversaw the discovery of more than 1,200 artifacts, among them the oldest known "book" (two wooden "leaves," recessed to hold a message written in beeswax [the beeswax was gone] and joined with ivory hinges); a ton of tin ingots; a gold chalice; and a gold, hieroglyphic-inscribed scarab that is the first such amulet found in Asia Minor to bear the name of the Egyptian queen Nefertiti. "Even more important," Bass wrote in his 1987 *National Geographic* article, "the form in which Nefertiti's name is written on the scarab strengthens the theory that she ruled alongside her husband [the pharaoh Akhenaten]. What Egyptologist, enduring a cruel sun in pith helmet and desert boots, could have imagined such a discovery coming from the cool blue sea?" Such treasures and the volume of raw materials at the site of the wreck led Bass to conclude that the sunken vessel was, in his words, "no tramp steamer." Indeed, he found archival resources that supported his theory that the ship was Canaanite in origin and its cargo was intended as tribute to the Egyptian pharaohs.

Among Bass's many honors are two awards from the National Geographic Society (the John Oliver La Gorce gold medal, in 1979, and the Centennial Award, in 1988); two from Texas A&M University (the Faculty Distinguished Achievement Award in Research, in 1984, and the President's Award of Honor, in 1989); the Lowell Thomas Award of the Explorers Club, in 1986; and the Gold Medal for Distinguished Archaeological Achievement from the Archaeological Institute of America, also in 1986.

Bass and his wife, Ann Singletary, who was a piano teacher, married on March 19, 1960. Their children, Gordon and Alan, work in fields unrelated to archaeology. Recalling his sons' early years, Bass acknowledged to Robert Locke, "There are times when I think I never took them fishing or camping or a lot of other things that fathers do. On the other hand, for good or ill, they lived in Cyprus and Greece and Turkey and England and places like that. But my career came so high on my list of priorities that I regret that fact, that I might have let them down." Bass has written half a dozen books, the most recent of which is *Ships and Shipwrecks of the Americas* (1988); he has also edited several books and written many articles for professional and popular periodicals and books edited by others. "I'm pleased that I not only started this field by being the first archaeologist to learn to dive and excavate and publish [papers on] an ancient shipwreck," he told Gary D. Ford for *Southern Living* (April 1995), "but I also turned it into an academic discipline where students are now teaching courses in ancient seafaring, which has never been done." — K.S.

Suggested Reading: *Christian Science Monitor* p13 Nov. 14, 1968, with photos; *Discovering Archaeology* p32+ May/June 1999, with photos; *Johns Hopkins Magazine* (on-line) Apr. 1997, with photos; *National Geographic* p693+ Dec. 1987, with photos; *Omni* p71 Nov. 1991, with photos; *Contemporary Authors* new revision series vol. 48, 1995

Selected Books: *Archaeology Under Water*, 1966; *Cape Gelidonya: A Bronze Age Shipwreck*, 1967; *Archaeology Beneath the Sea*, 1975; *Yassi Ada, Vol. I., A Seventh-Century Byzantine Shipwreck* (with F. H. van Doorninck Jr.), 1982; *Shipwrecks in the Bodrum Museum of Underwater Archaeology*, 1996; as editor—*A History of Seafaring Based on Underwater Archaeology*, 1972; *Ships and Shipwrecks of the Americas*, 1988

Courtesy of the Navajo Nation

Begaye, Kelsey
(bih-GAY)

1951– President of the Navajo Nation. Address: Office of the President, Navajo Nation, P.O. Box 9000, Window Rock, AZ 86515

On January 12, 1999 Kelsey Begaye was sworn in as president of the Navajo Nation, North America's most populous Native American tribe. A Vietnam veteran and former drug and alcoholism counselor who had earlier surmounted his own alcoholism, Begaye served in the Navajo legislature for eight years before assuming the office of president. He is reportedly the first Christian to head the Diné—meaning "The People," as Navajos call themselves in their native language—since the tribe established elective government, in 1923. "Navajos who have accepted Jesus Christ into their lives have not rejected all that is Navajo," Begaye said during his inaugural speech, as transcribed on *navajo.org* (online). "It is the role of both Christian and Traditional Navajo alike to respect each other's views, and to value and preserve the history, language, cultures, and traditions of the Diné. It is essential to our future that our young children learn their history, their language, their cultures, and their traditions. I am proud to be a Navajo and that same pride must be paramount in every home throughout our land."

The Navajo Reservation covers about 25,000 square miles in the Four Corners area of the United States (where Utah, Colorado, Arizona, and New Mexico meet); approximately the size of West Virginia, it is larger than 10 states. By far the biggest portion of Dinetah, as the Navajos call their land, lies in Arizona, with another section in New Mexico and a tiny part in Utah. (The much smaller Hopi Indian Reservation lies wholly within the Navajo Reservation.) Dinetah encompasses Monument Valley, Canyon de Chelly National Park, Rainbow Bridge National Monument, Petrified Forest National Park, and a dozen other national monuments, tribal parks, and historic sites.

Anthropologists believe that ancestors of the people who became known as the Navajos probably crossed into North America from Asia via the Bering Strait land bridge between 800 and 1,000 years ago. After arriving in what is now the American Southwest, they began practicing rudimentary agriculture; they became sheepherders after contact with the Spanish in the 16th century. During the Mexican War (1846–48), United States troops wrested control of what is now New Mexico from Mexico, and for years afterward Navajos and white Americans clashed violently. Then, in 1863–64, Kit Carson, a colonel in the U.S. Army, instituted what is widely viewed as a scorched-earth policy against the Navajos; by burning their homes and crops and stealing or killing their sheep and other livestock, the U.S. troops "starv[ed] the Navajos into submission," to quote *navajoland.com* (online). In the spring of 1864, in what the Navajos refer to as "The Long Walk," Carson forced an estimated 8,000 Navajo men, women, and children to trek about 300 miles to Fort Sumner, New Mexico. Those who survived this ordeal were imprisoned at the fort for the next four years. In 1868, after signing a treaty with the United States, the Navajos returned to Dinetah with a small number of sheep provided by the federal government and began their lives anew. In the 1930s severe erosion on Navajo land prompted the federal government to reduce by half the Navajos' stocks of sheep, cattle, and horses, and many tribespeople were forced to seek their livelihoods outside the reservation. Earlier in the century the discovery of oil, natural gas, and valuable minerals on Navajo territory spurred the Navajos to establish a tribal legislature as a mechanism for dealing with American oil companies and other corporations seeking to lease Navajo land. In 1991 their government was reorganized into executive, legislative, and judicial branches.

In 1999 the number of Navajos living on the Navajo Reservation was estimated to be 165,000; more than 100,000 other members of the tribe live elsewhere. According to the 1990 census, in that year the median family income among Navajos was less than $12,000 (in all of the U.S., the corresponding figure was more than $35,000), and more than 56 percent of the people were living below the poverty line. Also as of 1990, more than a third of adult Navajos had less than a ninth-grade education; fewer than 25 percent had graduated from high school. Currently, 60 percent of Navajos are less than 24 years old; in the U.S. as a whole, the corresponding figure is 35 percent. In *Population Today* (November 1996), C. Matthew Snipp reported that among Native Americans throughout the U.S., the mortality rate was 22.9 deaths per 1,000 people in 1990, compared to nine deaths per 1,000 whites; deaths due to alcoholism were 630 percent higher among Native Americans than among whites in the years 1989–91; and the death rate of American Indians ages 15 to 24 was 133 percent higher than the rate among whites between those ages, with 85 percent of Indian deaths resulting from accidents, suicide, and homicide. Moreover, Snipp wrote, "there is evidence that all American Indian deaths . . . may be under-reported." In November 1998, when Begaye was elected head of the Navajo Nation, unemployment in the United States, according to federal statisticians, stood at 4.4 percent, while unemployment among Navajos was 43 percent—almost 10 times greater. More than three-quarters of Navajo homes do not have telephones, many lack running water and electricity (and thus refrigeration), and many are inadequately insulated and heated. "In a land of plenty, too many Navajo children go to bed hungry at night . . . [and] lack decent clothes and toys," Begaye said during his inaugural speech. He also said, "Too many Navajo children live lives of hopelessness, poverty, delinquency, and despair." Like African-Americans and members of other minority groups, many Navajos have experienced racism both directly and indirectly in personal and business matters.

In his "State of the Nation Address," presented to the Navajo Nation Council in April 1999, Begaye described his administration's "guiding principles" as including "preservation of the Navajo culture" and "the preservation, protection, and enhancement of Navajo sovereignty." He listed his administration's priorities as economic progress; infrastructure development; environmental protection and better management of land and water resources; and improvements in education, health and social services, government operations, and the justice system, including increasing public safety. In creating his agenda, Begaye has said, he is guided by words penned by the British writer George Bernard Shaw: "Some men see things as they are and say 'Why?' I dream things that never were and say 'Why not?'"

The son of sheepherders, Kelsey Begaye was born in 1951 in Kaibeto, Arizona. According to the *OCB Tracker* (December 1998/January 1999, online), he "traces his lineage through his maternal clan (Todichiinii or Bitter Water) and his paternal clan (Tabaha or Edgewater)." He was raised on the desert plateau of the Navajo Nation's northwestern corner. One of his parents was an alcoholic, and Begaye has traced the roots of his own alcoholism to his experiences at home during his childhood. As a 13-year-old, Begaye has recalled, he once stowed away on a bus headed for the Albuquerque Indian School, a boarding school, in the vain hope of escaping his troubled home life. While still in his teens, he joined the army, and in 1969–70 he served a one-year tour of duty as a radio operator in Vietnam, during the Vietnam War. "Marijuana was a daily thing there," he told Leslie Linthicum for the *Albuquerque Journal* (October 18, 1998, online). "I used to think you had to be crazy to go into the jungle sober." By the time he returned to the United States, Begaye had become a full-fledged alcoholic.

Begaye's struggle with alcoholism continued for six years. Then, in January 1976, the 25-year-old Begaye checked himself into an alcohol treatment center in Page, Arizona, and shortly afterward, he gave up drinking for good. He also became a Christian. "A miracle took place" the day he accepted Christ as his savior, he told Linthicum. "It was like a brand new stage, a brand new show. I made a turnaround." He began counseling other addicts, and eventually worked his way up to the position of residential director of a regional treatment center (now called the Rainbow Bridge residential Treatment Center).

After years of sobriety Begaye entertained thoughts of becoming a Christian evangelist, but his popularity among friends and clients led him into politics, instead. In 1990 he won election as the delegate from the Kaibeto community to the Navajo Nation's tribal council, which is equivalent to a state legislature. In 1994 he was elected to the powerful position of speaker of the council, which currently consists of 88 members. As speaker, according to an official bio of him, he made programs for young people his top priority.

In late 1994 the wife of Albert Hale, the president of the Navajo Nation, accused the chief executive of having an extramarital affair with a staff member. During the course of an investigation into her accusation, accountants discovered thousands of dollars in personal purchases for Hale charged to the tribe's credit card. Despite his damaged reputation and the controversy that surrounded him, Hale remained in office until February 1998, when it was discovered that he had violated tribal ethics laws by accepting corporate gifts. To avoid prosecution, Hale resigned. He was replaced by his vice president, Thomas Atcitty, a former New Mexico state legislator. But in July 1998 Atcitty, too, resigned, after revelations that he, too, had broken ethics rules, by accepting housing, meals, and expense-paid golf junkets from American companies that were doing business with the reservation. His successor was Milton Bluehouse, who had served as vice president under Atcitty.

The next presidential election was scheduled to take place in November 1998. Early that year Begaye, who had developed a reputation as an honest, no-nonsense public servant, threw his hat into the ring. "The president's office is an honorable position," he told Linthicum. "I looked in the mirror and said, yes, I can do that." In a primary election held in August 1998, Begaye and Joe Shirley Jr., a Navajo Council delegate, captured the top two spots in a field of eight candidates. Meanwhile, Bluehouse had missed the application deadline for presidential aspirants (he was still vice president on that date and apparently had not intended to seek the presidency at that time), and he joined the race as a write-in candidate. Mindful of the Navajo people's impatience with dirty politics, the three competitors avoided mudslinging and name-calling. On November 3, 1998 Begaye won the election, with 28,415 votes; Shirley finished second, with just over 21,000, while Bluehouse earned about 7,000 write-in votes.

Begaye's decision to make his inauguration an alcohol-free event made it possible for the ceremony to be held on Navajo ground. (It is illegal to bring alcoholic beverages onto the Navajo Reservation.) Unlike some of his recent predecessors, who arrived at their inaugural ceremonies in traditional tribal attire, surrounded by supporters, and with rock music blaring, Begaye came unescorted and dressed in a conservative business suit. In his inaugural speech he exhorted his fellow Navajos to "value our children, our parents, our spouses, our grandparents, and our clans. We must teach and demonstrate ethical relationships, honesty, and integrity . . . ," he continued. "We must find the time to raise, nurture, and endow our children with the qualities of good and decent people, with a desire to help others, and a passion for living." He asked tribal employees to "daily recommit yourself to the great cause of serving others" and to "treat all people fairly, promptly, and courteously." Addressing young people, he said, "You must work hard in your studies, play hard in your sports, and show leadership in your communities."

After declaring that the guiding principle of his government would be "Doing for ourselves," Begaye said that he planned to introduce legislation to charter a Navajo Nation National Bank, based in Window Rock, the Navajo capital, and to set up branches throughout Dinetah, to enable the Navajo Nation "to earn interest off its own money, to insure fairness in lending and interest rates to our people, and to provide access for funds for new enterprises and other economic initiatives." "Navajo money has created great wealth for many non-Navajos," he said; "indeed, the border towns [towns adjacent to the reservation] would be ghost towns without Navajo business. It is time for some of that wealth to be returned to the Diné, to meet the critical and urgent needs of our people." In addition, he announced that he intended to create a nonprofit organization, to be called the Fund for the Development of the Navajo People, for which he would solicit contributions from "affluent Americans, corporations, foundations, churches, and other philanthropic organizations." Others among his proposals were reforming the welfare system; exploring the possibility of building a plant along the California coast that would desalinize water for transport to the reservation; and creating a department of housing and urban development, an urban development board, an agricultural development program, and what he called a "division of Youth and Navajo Nation Youth Council," which would be devoted to combating drug and alcohol use among youths. "In a land where there are so few of us, we cannot afford to lose a single Native American life to drug and alcohol abuse and the alienation, delinquency, suicide, and despair they lead to," he told supporters soon after his term began, according to *penchang.net* (on-line). "The core of drug and alcohol abuse is the oppression and suppression of our people and our lack of self-esteem and self-worth. We must change the way our Navajo sees himself or herself. We must restore our sense of self."

Since taking office Begaye has helped to breathe new life into the nearly moribund Navajo People's Tourism Association. Among other matters requiring his attention are two lawsuits that the Navajo Nation has brought against the federal government. The lawsuits were triggered by a 1985 decision by Donald P. Hodel, then secretary of the Interior, to block a ruling by John W. Fritz, another Interior Department official, that would have sharply increased the fees paid to the Navajos by companies mining coal on Navajo land. "It was the first time we had ever been specifically instructed not to go ahead with the decision-making process," Fritz, who currently works as a consultant to Native American tribes, told Barry Meier for the *New York Times* (July 18, 1999). The Navajos recently learned that while Fritz's decision was under review, the Peabody Coal Co. had lobbied Hodel to put Fritz's ruling on hold, and that Peabody lawyers had drafted the memo in which Hodel had told Fritz to do so. The Navajo Nation contends that because the coal-mining fees were not increased, the reservation lost $600 million in income. One lawsuit, which names two utilities, the Southern California Edison Co. and the Salt River Project, in addition to Peabody, "accuses the Interior Department and the Bureau of Indian Affairs of failing to fulfill their mandate to act as trustees to get tribes the best possible return on valuable assets like natural resources and land leases," Meier reported. Robert A. Williams, a professor of law at the University of Arizona at Tucson, observed, as paraphrased by Meier, that "lawsuits like the one brought by the Navajos against Peabody Coal reflect a belief by tribes that the Government allowed companies to harvest their natural resources at rock-bottom rates."

Kelsey Begaye and his wife, Marie, have six children. Their family also includes more than a half-dozen children whom Begaye has helped to raise. — M.B.

Suggested Reading: *Albuquerque Journal* (on-line) Oct. 18, 1998, Nov. 4, 1998, Jan. 18, 1999; *navajo.org* (on-line); *navajoland.com* (on-line)

Courtesy of Premiere Radio Networks

Bell, Art

June 17, 1945– Former radio talk-show host. Address: P.O. Box 4755, Pahrump, NV 89041-4755

For some 15 years, seven hours every night of the week but one, the voice of the radio talk-show host Art Bell, emanating from the Nevada desert, told "tales of the supernatural, the paranormal, and the just plain weird," as *Who 2?* (on-line) put it, and warned of government cover-ups and the impending global apocalypse. Bell's syndicated programs *Coast to Coast AM*, which debuted in 1984, and his Sunday show, *Dreamland*, which was broadcast for several years in the late 1990s, captured the imaginations of those who believe in the omnipresence of things sinister and mysterious in the universe. In 1999 *Coast to Coast AM* was carried by more than 420 stations nationwide and, with some 20 million listeners, had become the nation's highest-rated late-night radio talk show. Taking unscreened calls from people in all walks of life, Bell offered discussions on topics ranging from underground bases supposedly populated by reptilian aliens to the existence of photos allegedly showing dinosaurs when they roamed the Earth. "I try to be a source of information you can't get elsewhere," he said in an interview with Justin Cord Hayes for *Las Vegas Weekly* (October 14, 1998, on-line). "I let *you* be the judge. I don't tell you what to think." "People are always fascinated by the big questions," Bell observed to Hayes. "Are we alone in the universe? Is there life after death? Issues like these are more important than who the president may or may not be sleeping with." The disdain with which many critics regarded his shows apparently did not bother him. "All we glorify really is the possibility that we as humans are more than we appear to be," he told James Willwerth for *Time* (April 14, 1997). "I have an opportunity to push in that direction, and I do. I have an open mind. I'll listen to anybody."

Art Bell was born on June 17, 1945 in Pahrump, Nevada, the same desert town from which he broadcasts his show. His father was a colonel in the marines, and Bell spent his childhood traveling the country. He developed an interest in radio early on. With a seven-transistor radio tucked under his pillow, he would listen to popular talk-radio hosts of the period. Bell received his first ham license at 12, and by 13 he had earned a radio technician's license from the Federal Communications Commission (FCC). When Bell was 15 he got his first job in radio, reading the news for a religious station in Franklin, New Jersey. The station was at the top of a mountain, which, by his own account, he had to climb on foot during the winter, when the road was too icy for driving. For a short time he studied engineering at the University of Maryland. He quit to join the air force, and, at their base in Amarillo, Texas, he and a buddy set up a pirate radio station and broadcast rock music. "The idiots on the base, not knowing it was illegal, provided me with a barracks for the radio station," Bell told a reporter for the *San Diego Union Tribune* in December 1996, as quoted by *CNI News* (on-line). (*CNI News* disseminates reports of UFO sightings and contacts with extraterrestrials.) "After a year on the air, a survey on the Amarillo Arbitron [a media research firm] had me in the ratings, and the real stations called and complained to the general, who called us into his office, told us to stop and we said, 'Yes, sir!'"

After leaving the air force, Bell worked for a series of more than two dozen radio stations. In the 1970s he set a record (as cited in the *Guinness Book of World Records*) for continuous hours of broadcasting by the same individual—116, which he accomplished at station KENI in Anchorage, Alaska, along with the legendary radio personality Wolfman Jack. Also in the 1970s Bell raised money to charter a DC-8, which he himself flew to Vietnam to rescue children orphaned as a result of the Vietnam War. (According to his Web page, he brought 130 children back to the U.S., and they were eventually adopted by Americans.) For some years he lived in Okinawa, in the Ryukyu Islands of Japan, working for radio station KSBK. He also spent time in San Diego, California, from which he commuted to Tijuana, Mexico, to broadcast on XTRA. "For a lot of years I starved," he told the *San Diego Union Tribune* reporter. "A lot of people in this business do, and I did. So it's kind of nice that doing what I love decided to feed me." His background in engineering, albeit skimpy, enabled him to serve as a "combo man," working simultaneously as KSBK's board operator and chief engineer.

After a short stint in television, Bell accepted an offer from radio station KDWN in Las Vegas, Nevada, to broadcast at night to 13 western states. At first the content of his show focused on political matters, with a conservative slant. After a while, much to the consternation of the station's management, he began shifting more and more toward the paranormal. "It drove [my station manager] up a tree," he recalled to Joshua Hammer for *Newsweek* (July 13, 1998). "She called me on the hotline and said, 'What the hell are you doing?' But the audience loved it." Indeed, the ratings for Bell's show rapidly spiked, thanks to detailed on-air discussions of such topics as the alleged 1947 crash of a UFO in Roswell, New Mexico, reported sightings of a huge, hairy primate known as Bigfoot or Sasquatch, and what were described as mysterious goings-on at the military outpost code-named Area 51, in Nevada. After realizing that he was reaching listeners ignored by other talk shows, Bell began to cover paranormal topics exclusively. He theorized that because his show aired at night, the otherworldly material he presented seemed much more palpable to many people than it might have during daylight hours. "There's a difference in what people are willing to consider, daytime versus nighttime," he told Marc Fisher for the *Washington Post* (March 29, 1998). "It's dark and you don't know what's out there. And the way things are now, there may be something." Bell has said that he will never broadcast before sundown, and, while he has made guest appearances on the television shows *Dark Skies* (1996) and *Millennium* (1996), he has insisted that he will never bring his own act to TV. "I talk about weird stuff," he explained to Fisher. "What I do works at night, only on the radio."

When Bell was offered syndication of his radio program, in 1984, he jumped at the opportunity. The result was *Coast to Coast AM*. Before long Bell began including a panel of guests on his show, to add to *Coast to Coast AM*'s distinctive atmosphere. The guests—usually scientists, physicians, and engineers—would offer strange theories about topics dear to listeners. One of the most popular subjects was Bell's theory of "millennium madness," which he called the "quickening." According the Bell, every aspect of our lives is, in his words, "accelerating and changing" so fast that we can no longer keep up, and, as various signs make clear to him, the acceleration and change are carrying the world headlong toward its doom. Among the many signs are the emergence of a drug-resistant form of malaria, rampant crime and immorality, acts of political terrorism, out-of-control consumerism, global warming, and the use of inexpensive overseas labor and other effects of the global economy. Bell's book *The Quickening: Today's Trends, Tomorrow's World* (1997), which credits Jennifer L. Osborn as editor, discusses signs of the coming apocalypse and what human beings might do to prevent it.

Bell changed *Coast to Coast AM* further when he began taking unscreened calls during the broadcast. This added an element of spontaneity absent from most other talk shows. "If you're a half-decent talent you can take any call and make it humorous or interesting," Bell told Andrea Adelson for the *New York Times* (May 18, 1998). "I take them all on. Screeners take the edge off." Bell's callers have made unusual claims: one, for example, said that a bottomless hole existed on his property; another declared that a 1957 Chevy had fallen from the sky into a Los Angeles neighborhood; a third said that he had created a time machine from a CD player and sent a screw into the future. Among the most notable calls were those that dealt with Area 51, a military facility housed at Nellis Air Force Base, which is separated from Bell's studio by a single mountain range. Rumors have abounded about Area 51 for more than a half-century. According to one, the remnants of a UFO that crashed in the New Mexico desert in 1947 are housed there; as another has it, the air force—with the help of technology stolen from aliens—is creating ultra-sophisticated aircraft capable of evading even the most advanced radar systems. Bell himself has claimed that he spotted one such aircraft hovering near his home. "I used to commute between Las Vegas and Pahrump," he told Hayes. "One night, a mile from the house, my wife said, 'What the hell's that?' We pulled over and got out. There was a full moon, and here comes this giant triangular object that couldn't have been more than 150 feet in the air. . . . We just watched it float toward Area 51 for five minutes." When he asked air-force employees about what he had seen, he continued, "Nellis's response was that there'd been a secret mission flown by a C-130 aircraft. Now I've flown those, and I can tell you with certainty that that wasn't what we saw." Inspired by this sighting and those of several other people, Bell established a telephone line devoted exclusively to calls about Area 51. Once he accepted a call from a man who claimed to be a former Area 51 employee. Speaking in an agitated voice, the man described a vast conspiracy involving the U.S. government and an alien race, and he warned that the government and the aliens were planning an orchestrated Armageddon as a way of keeping the human population under control. Suddenly, while the man was talking, Bell's show went off the air. It was later determined, according to Joshua Hammer, that the satellite that carries Bell's signal had momentarily "shifted away from Earth." "Weird," Bell said to Hammer. "Truly weird."

In November 1995 an amateur astronomer named Chuck Shramek called Bell's program to say that he had spotted what he characterized as a "Saturn-like object" in the tail of the Hale-Bopp comet, which was then passing close to Earth. Soon afterward Shramek's report was corroborated by Courtney Brown, a professor of political science at Emory University, in Atlanta, Georgia, who—independently of his university work—runs the Farsight Institute. That organization spreads news about a psychic phenomenon called "remote viewing," through which, according to Brown and others, a person can leave his or her body and travel in both space and time. Brown said that he and a team of other "remote viewers" had determined that the object was a spacecraft piloted by aliens and that it was emitting radio signals, a sure sign of intelligent life. Brown subsequently sent Bell a photograph of the Hale-Bopp comet, along with a message about an unidentified astronomer who would be holding a press conference to talk about the photo. After waiting in vain for the press conference to take place, Bell posted the picture on his Web site. Almost immediately two astronomers demonstrated that the photo was a hoax. Nevertheless, in March 1997 Marshall Applewhite, the leader of a cult called Heaven's Gate, and 38 Heaven's Gate members committed suicide in San Diego, after claiming that they would be making a rendezvous with a spaceship traveling in the tail of the Hale-Bopp comet. Instantly, the press targeted Bell as the instigator of the tragedy. "I started getting a lot of messages saying, 'Art Bell, you killed 39 people,'" he told James Willwerth. "It's important to understand that the only person who ever said there was a spacecraft following Hale-Bopp was Courtney Brown." While he denied any connection with the deaths, Bell banned Brown from any further appearances on his show.

On October 13, 1998 Bell closed his show by saying, as quoted by Angie Wagner for the Associated Press (October 14, 1998, on-line), "I told you there was an event, a threatening, terrible event occurred to my family, which I could not tell you about. Because of that event, and a succession of other events, what you're listening to right now is my final broadcast on the air." Alarmed listeners, fearing for Bell's safety, immediately phoned the sheriff's office in Pahrump, and in the following days, speculation about his departure abounded on the Internet. According to one theory, his exit—on October 13, or 10/13—was linked to the popular paranormal-themed television show *The X-Files*, which is produced by a company called Ten Thirteen. For the remainder of that week, the station re-aired previous Bell shows, and the next week the broadcaster Hilly Rose sat in for Bell. On October 23 the station played a recording in which Bell announced that he planned to return to work on October 28. "This has been the worst ten days of my life," he commented in a posting on his Web site, *artbell.com*. True to his word, Bell returned to his show, but he revealed nothing about his absence, other than to tell Robert Macy for the Associated Press (October 24, 1998, on-line), "This was not any kind of a hoax or stunt. It was not a contract ploy. This was and is a family crisis."

The nature of the crisis came to light in May 1999, when Bell's son, Art Bell IV, then 18, filed an amended federal lawsuit against the Nye County School District that charged the district with careless hiring procedures. (The original suit, filed in 1998, listed John and Jane Doe and Peter Doe as the complainants.) The suit charged that when Art Bell IV was 16, a substitute teacher named Brian Lepley had plied him with alcohol and marijuana and then engaged in sexual acts with him, and that Lepley had had a history of improper behavior when the district hired him. (Lepley, who is HIV-positive, was convicted in 1998 of sexual assault and attempted transmission of the AIDS virus, among other crimes, and is currently serving a life sentence in prison.) Although Bell's son has so far tested negative for HIV, "psychologically," his father told Richard Corliss for *Time* (August 9, 1999), "it slammed him into the ground. He sat in his empty room and wrote poems about death. He failed in school and dropped out. I got him a job, but he couldn't hold it. He's not doing well."

Earlier, in 1998, despite the Bell family's attempt to hide their identities in the original lawsuit, two men living in Nashville, Tennessee, had discovered that a person named Art Bell had been involved in a molestation case; according to Richard Corliss, the men spread the story (via an international shortwave signal) that Art Bell had molested children and had been indicted for it. "My own son had been molested," Bell told Corliss, "and then I was accused of molestation. I couldn't open my mouth because that would reveal my son's situation. The impact on me was profound. I couldn't sleep; sometimes I couldn't breathe. I had fits of alternating anger and depression. My private life was falling apart while I was going on the air every night. It was a living hell." By early 2000 Art Bell IV's lawsuit had not come to trial or otherwise been resolved, and, to attend to matters pertaining to it, he reduced his on-air time to three nights a week. On March 31, 2000 he officially announced his retirement from radio. He attributed his decision to end his career on radio to emotional turmoil stemming from his son's situation. In a statement quoted in the *Las Vegas Review-Journal* (April 13, 2000, on-line), Premiere Radio Networks, which carries *Coast to Coast AM*, reported that Bell hoped to adopt an "anonymous lifestyle" and planned to quit not only radio "but also all other forms of media including book publishing [and] television." On April 27, 2000 the Seattle-based talk-show personality Mike Siegel replaced Bell as host of *Coast to Coast AM*. As of November 1, 2000 *Dreamland* was not on the air.

His public persona notwithstanding, Bell lives quietly in a modest house in Pahrump with his wife, Ramona. The couple have a cat, Giza, and a dog, Shadow. For some years he published a monthly newsletter, *After Dark*, which was available through subscription. Bell's books include an autobiography, *The Art of Talk* (1998); *The Source* (1999), written with Brad Steiger and Jennifer L. Osborn, about various unexplained phenomena; and *The Coming Global Superstorm* (2000), written with Whitley Streiber, about the potentially catastrophic effects of global warming. — J.K.B.

Suggested Reading: Associated Press (on-line) Oct. 24, 1998, Oct. 29, 1998; *Las Vegas Weekly* (on-line) Oct. 14, 1998, with photo; *New York Times* D p7+ May 18, 1998, with photo, C p8+ Oct. 26, 1998; *Newsweek*, p62+ July 13, 1998, with photo; *San Diego Union Tribune* (on-line) Dec. 1, 1996; *Time* p46 Apr. 14, 1997, with photo, p64+ Aug. 9, 1999, with photo; *Washington Post* F p1+ Mar. 29, 1998, with photo

Selected Radio Shows: *Coast to Coast AM*, 1984–2000; *Dreamland*, 1997(?)–2000

Selected Books: *The Quickening: Today's Trends, Tomorrow's World* (with Jennifer L. Osborne), 1997; *The Art of Talk*, 1998; *The Source* (with Brad Steiger and Jennifer L. Osborne), 1999; *The Coming Global Superstorm* (with Whitley Strieber), 1999

Frank Ockenfels, courtesy of Sony Classical

Bell, Joshua

Dec. 9, 1967– Violinist. Address: c/o Kirshbaum Demler & Associates, Inc., 711 West End Ave., #5KN, New York, NY 10025; c/o Sony Music Entertainment, 550 Madison Ave., 16th Fl., New York, NY 10022

"Everything about Joshua is special—his charm, his brains, his naturalness," the renowned Russian-born violinist Josef Gingold said of one of his most famous and accomplished students, the violinist Joshua Bell, during a talk with Charles Michener for *New York* (July 16, 1990) when Bell was 22. "He's very distinctive; you know his playing at once. Certainly he's one of the greatest violin talents I've heard in 70 years—he was born to play the instrument. He has what I call radar fingers—they instinctively find the right place. And he has tremendous powers of concentration: As fast as I could give him the repertoire, he absorbed it. Just as important, he's levelheaded. . . . What sets him apart? Well, there's that unusual beauty of tone. And there's his great dedication to his calling. But you can't say exactly what it is that makes him so remarkable. I like to say, 'When I hold my fiddle, it's close to my heart.' In the final analysis, you play who you are. With Joshua, I can't find a single negative thing to say about him."

After he made his professional debut, at the age of 14, Bell became known not only for his technical skill and rare expressiveness but also for his appearance and manner: in the Australian Broadcasting Corp. publication *24 Hours* (August 1999, on-line), for example, Shirley Apthorp wrote that as a teenager he resembled "the good, clean-cut, corn-fed all-American boy," a "polite wunderkind" who "looked like a model." "Every teenage girl who had ever taken a violin lesson was in love with him," Apthorp wrote. Overcoming his image as a pinup boy for classical-music aficionados, Bell has taken his place among the first rank of international classical artists. Widely described as a "brilliant" and "superb" musician and as having a flawless technique, Bell, who made his name as an interpreter of 18th- and 19th-century romantic standards, has expanded his repertoire to include such works as violin arrangements of pieces by George Gershwin; film scores, including the soundtrack to the 1999 movie *The Red Violin*; music by the eclectic contemporary bassist and composer Edgar Meyer; and Nicholas Maw's Concerto for Violin (1993), which was written for Bell. "Josh has a huge career, and he deserves it," the conductor, pianist, and composer André Previn told Richard Jerome for *People* (April 28, 1997). "He plays with a great deal of commitment, but he doesn't grandstand. That's remarkable in a young virtuoso."

The middle child of three and an only son, Joshua Bell was born on December 9, 1967 in Bloomington, Indiana. His father, Alan Bell, is a psychologist who teaches at Indiana University; earlier, he was an Episcopal priest. Alan Bell has played the violin avocationally. Bell's mother, who is Jewish, is an educational counselor; at one time she studied piano. From an early age Joshua Bell displayed extraordinary musical ability. As a little boy, he would stretch rubber bands between the knobs of his dresser and pluck out nursery tunes and other melodies. "By opening the drawers to different degrees, I could make them play at different pitches," he explained to Jerome. When he was five, his parents gave him a violin—"mostly, I guess, because my father liked the instrument," as Bell told Michener—but they did not try to push their son into a career in music. "And never did I feel I was doing it to please *them*," he said to Michener. His mother told Jerome, "Whether it was Rubik's Cube, chess, computers, the violin, there was a need to master his environment." Bell described his younger self to Michener as "just a kid in school who loved sports." As a 10-year-old he won a state tennis competition in his age group and took fourth place in the national finals that year.

At age eight Bell began violin lessons with a local teacher, Mimi Zweig, who, he told a reporter for *Strad* (May 1996, on-line), helped him correct some of the bad habits he had developed in his technique. By the time he was 11, Bell's interest in playing the violin had deepened considerably. During the summer of 1979 he attended the Meadowmount School of Music, in New York State, founded in 1944 by the influential violinist and teacher Ivan Galamian. "There were 150 students there, and I was the second-youngest—I'd never been surrounded by so much talent," Bell told Michener. "I was very, very shy—in school I was terrified to get up in class and talk—and basically all I did was stay by myself and practice. Eight hours a day for four weeks. Before Meadowmount, I'd never practiced more than an hour a day." While at Meadowmount Bell met Josef Gingold, who by then was among "the last living links to the elegant, masterly 19th-century school of violin playing," as Alex Ross wrote for the *New York Times* (January 13, 1995). Gingold—who had studied with the Belgian virtuoso Eugene Ysaye and had served as first violinist in the NBC Orchestra, under the legendary conductor Arturo Toscanini, and as concertmaster in the Cleveland Orchestra, under the equally revered conductor George Szell—was recognized as one of the most influential teachers of the instrument in the United States. Impressed by Bell's talent, Gingold invited the boy to study at the University of Indiana's School of Music. That fall Bell began a new regimen, which he continued through 12th grade: after a truncated session at his regular school, he would spend half a day at the music school. A year later Gingold became his teacher.

Bell told Michener that Gingold was "warm, embracing, very Old World, and very funny." "The main thing he taught me was to love the music and not be intimidated by it," he said. Gingold recalled to Michener that the young Bell "always loved it when I talked about the grand tradition of violinists. I gave him many of the old masters on 78 [rpm] records, which he still plays on an old Victrola." Bell told K. Robert Schwarz for the *New York Times* (October 8, 1995) that Gingold passed down to him "his use of rubato, the kind of freedom one gets from playing around the beat but still keeping a very strict pulse. And some of the fingerings that I do I would never have thought of if not for Gingold. There are some incredibly slurpy slides that Gingold learned from Ysaye, things I wouldn't dare do. But there are many things I would do that are rather old-fashioned." Gingold served as a mentor to Bell until his death, in 1995, at age 85. "He was like a grandfather to me," Bell told Jerome.

During his teens, while keeping up his study of the violin, Bell remained active in sports. "Music was, and is, the most important thing in my life," he told Michener, "but it wasn't *everything*. In school I goofed off a lot. My mother would drop me off at the music school and I'd go right out the back door to a video arcade, where I'd play four hours at a time." (Years later a young Bloomington resident who recognized him on the street told him, "Your name is on every video game in the arcade as the highest scorer.")

In March 1982, at 14, Bell won the *Seventeen* Magazine/General Motors National Concerto Competition, with his rendition of Mozart's Third Violin Concerto. According to Nancy Malitz in *USA Today* (September 27, 1982), "He was the youngest finalist and the overwhelming favorite of the judges," and the "*New York Times* cultural correspondent compared him to the young Yehudi Menuhin [who as an 11-year-old electrified a Carnegie Hall audience]." Soon afterward, thanks to his victory, he performed the same concerto, to great critical acclaim, at a matinee concert given by the Philadelphia Orchestra, under Riccardo Muti. According to Malitz, the musicians in the orchestra "gave him an enormous 'bravo'" when the concerto ended. In the next few years the media almost invariably referred to Bell as a prodigy or even a genius. "It was annoying to be labeled a prodigy," Bell told Jerome. "Everything was 'the young Joshua Bell.' It becomes a circus act."

In 1985 Bell made his debut at Carnegie Hall, performing with the Saint Louis Symphony led by Leonard Slatkin. In the next year he earned the prestigious Avery Fisher Career Grant, and in 1987, at age 19, he signed an exclusive contract with London/Decca Records. In 1988 London released four albums featuring Bell, two of which have both been described as his debut recording. On one of those, he played the Mendelssohn Violin Concerto and Max Bruch's Violin Concerto No. 1, accompanied by the Academy of St. Martin in the Fields, under Sir Neville Marriner; reviewing that effort for *High Fidelity* (August 1988), K. Robert Schwarz declared that Bell "display[ed] astonishing maturity as an interpreter" of the Mendelssohn work and, in the Bruch, "show[ed] that he has a real concept of musical style." On the other "debut" disk, *Presenting Joshua Bell*, the violinist performed shorter pieces, by Schumann, Wieniawski, Paganini, Sibelius, and others, along with the pianist Samuel Sanders, a veteran accompanist. His two other 1988 recordings were of the Tchaikovsky Violin Concerto and Wieniawski's Violin Concerto No. 2 (on one album), with the Cleveland Orchestra under Vladimir Ashkenazy, and violin and piano sonatas by Fauré, Debussy, and Franck, accompanied by Jean-Yves Thibaudet.

In hopes of appealing to a broad audience, London presented Bell as an All-American hunk, and with such items as a video and pinup-style album covers, the company succeeded in creating a slew of preteen and teenage Bell fans. But such tactics harmed the violinist's credibility among older members of the classical community. "It took several years to get people over the thought that I was a promotional flash in the pan and earn their respect," Bell told Richard Jerome. Indeed, various profiles of him have mentioned his smooth transition from "authentic child prodigy" to outstanding mature performer and have pointed out that unlike many other young instrumentalists, he has lived up to his early promise.

The 13 albums that Bell made for London/Decca also include recordings of, among other works, Lalo's *Symphonie Espagnole* (with the Montreal Symphony Orchestra under Charles Dutoit, 1989) and violin concertos by Mozart (with the English Chamber Orchestra under Peter Maag, 1991); Prokofiev (with the Montreal Symphony under Dutoit, 1993); Brahms and Schumann (with the Cleveland Orchestra under Christoph von Dohnanyi, 1996); and Barber and Walton (with the Baltimore Symphony Orchestra under David Zinman, 1997). The last-named disk, which also contains Ernest Bloch's *Baal Shem Suite for Violin and Piano*, was nominated for a Grammy Award and was named concerto album of the year in 1998. In a review of it for Amazon.com, the music critic Edith Eisler wrote that Bell's performances displayed "unlimited virtuosity always used in the service of the music, a flawlessly beautiful, intense tone with a warm glow in the low register and a shimmering radiance in the stratospheric passages, and a genuine, heartfelt expressiveness." Eisler and others expressed similar enthusiasm for *The Kreisler Album* (1996), on which Bell, with the pianist Paul Coker, gave his interpretations of a bevy of pieces composed by the violin virtuoso Fritz Kreisler. "Bell's love of the music suffuses every note," Eisler declared in an assessment for Amazon.com; "he captures mood, character, and expression with flair and impeccable style. His playing, technically brilliant and tonally ravishing, has humor, wit, grace, elegance, and irresistible charm."

Bell's second Grammy-nominated record was *Gershwin Fantasy* (1998), with the London Symphony Orchestra under John Williams. That album presents more than a dozen George Gershwin songs arranged for violin and orchestra, among them, from Gershwin's folk opera *Porgy and Bess*, "It Ain't Necessarily So," "I Got Plenty o' Nuttin'," "Summertime," and "Oh, Bess, Oh, Where's My Bess" (for the last of which Bell composed an original cadenza) and, from various Gershwin scores for the musical theater, "I Got Rhythm," "Embraceable You," and "Sweet and Low-Down." *Gershwin Fantasy* was Bell's first album on the Sony label, to which he had switched in mid-1996, with the goal of exploring new musical avenues while continuing to expand his classical repertoire. "I've always loved Gershwin, and I've always felt that there was never enough Gershwin to play, for violinists," he told James R. Oestreich in the *New York Times* (August 31, 1998).

In 1999 Bell collaborated with Edgar Meyer and the string players Sam Bush and Mike Marshall to make *Short Trip Home*, which offers compositions by Meyer that blend elements of bluegrass and classical music. In *Billboard* (August 21, 1999), Timothy White wrote that *Short Trip Home* "is one of the most inspired and beautiful listening experiences of our era." For *Listen to the Storyteller: A Trio of Musical Tales from Around the World* (1999), which won a Grammy Award for best spoken-word album for children, Bell accompanied the Orchestra of St. Luke's in "The Fiddler and the Dancin' Witch," written and narrated by the jazz musician Wynton Marsalis.

Also in 1999 Bell appeared in *Music of the Heart*; directed by Wes Craven and starring Meryl Streep, the movie is about a real violin teacher, Roberta Guaspari, who in the 1980s started a program at three Harlem schools that offered students instruction in the violin. When funding cuts threatened to end the program, Guaspari organized a benefit concert, held at Carnegie Hall in 1992, at which a dozen world-class violinists performed. The concert, in which Bell played, was re-created in the film. Bell made a far larger contribution to *The Red Violin* (1999), about the fictional history of a mysterious fiddle over a span of four centuries. He performed all the solos on the soundtrack, which was composed by John Corigliano, who won an Oscar for his score. At the request of François Girard, who directed the film, Bell also served as musical adviser and as a stand-in for one of the characters. "I was like a stunt man, with complete body shots, but from behind, playing," he told Andréa C. Basora for *Newsweek* (June 18, 1999, online). "And then there were shots where [the actor] would hold the violin, and my arms were around him, and someone else, a third guy, his arms are playing the bow. So I'm doing the left hand, someone else is doing the right hand—I couldn't do both because I would be reaching around him—so we got his head with the two real violinists playing." In 1997 Bell played at the premiere of Corigliano's concert piece *The Red Violin: Chaconne for Violin and Orchestra*, accompanied by the San Francisco Symphony under Robert Spano. In a review for the *San Francisco Chronicle* (November 28, 1997), Joshua Kosman wrote, "It was Bell . . . who gave the work most of its vitality. Here is a performer who makes his instrument sing so beautifully and so precisely that the music seems to emerge directly from his own soul."

Bell's recording and film work constitute only a small part of his professional activity; for years he has spent far more of his time concertizing. "Recording, frankly, is not my favorite thing to do, and I'm never particularly happy with the results," Bell told James Oestreich. "It's the way records are done, it's the permanence. . . . You do it over and over again. I like just shooting for it in a performance. I really love the performance atmosphere, the risk taking." In 1987 Bell gave a recital in Tokyo, Japan, that was aired on Japanese television nationwide. Three years later he toured throughout the United States, Europe, and the then–Soviet Union with the American-Soviet Youth Orchestra, with whom he was a featured soloist. In addition to appearances with the world's major orchestras, he has performed repeatedly at the Mostly Mozart Festival, at Lincoln Center, in New York City, and at many other music festivals, among them Tanglewood, in Lenox, Massachusetts; Ravinia, in Highland Park, Illinois; Wolf Trap Farm Park, in Vienna, Virginia; Caramooor, in Katonah, New York; Marlboro, in Vermont; Spoleto, in Italy; and Tivoli, in Helsingborg, Sweden.

The Marlboro Music Festival focuses on chamber music, which a 1994 Mostly Mozart *Stagebill* described as a "special passion" of Bell's. With the cellist Steven Isserlis and the pianist Olli Mustonen, he recorded Shostakovich's Piano Trio No. 2, on an album (1997) that also contains Olivier Messiaen's *Quartet for the End of Time*, for which the clarinetist Michael Collins joined the trio. Speaking of his collaboration with Mustonen and Isserlis, Bell told the *Strad* interviewer, "We all became friends before we started to play together, so it was a bit scary as to whether it was going to work. But we all share certain musical ideals. . . . We've had horrible arguments. We're all pretty strong-willed, so it can be very difficult when we don't agree. Often there's no room for compromise. It happened with Olli and me once—we had completely opposite ideas of the tempo of a Beethoven sonata and there was just no way we could compromise. . . . So we just . . . played something else." Bell plays a Stradivari violin that was made in 1732; it is known as the Tom Taylor, for one of its 19th-century owners.

During the 1997–98 academic year, Bell taught as a visiting professor at the Royal Academy of Music, in London, and since then he has taught there when in that city. He holds an artist diploma from Indiana University. At times, by his own account, his schedule of some 110 concerts a year has felt arduous. Even though his career is a demanding one, he knows, as he told K. Robert Schwarz in 1995, "how to have a good time. That's never been a problem. In the past I've been willing to sell out, either because of money or because something will bring me more fame. As I get older, other things matter more. I would like to look at my life and feel that I'm living it with integrity, that I'm being true to myself. Integrity is the most important thing, even more than happiness." — J.K.B.

Suggested Reading: *Billboard* p5 Aug. 21, 1999; *New York* p36+ July 16, 1990, with photos; *New York Times* II p31+ Oct. 8, 1995, with photos, E p1+ Aug. 31, 1998, with photos; *Newsweek* (on-line), June 18, 1999; *People* p111+ Apr. 28, 1997, with photos; *Strad* (on-line) May 1996

Selected Recordings: *Presenting Joshua Bell*, 1988; Tchaikovsky: Violin Concerto, 1988; Mendelssohn: Violin Concerto, 1988; Wieniawski: Violin Concerto no. 2, 1988; Bruch: Violin Concerto no. 1, 1988; Lalo: *Symphonie Espagnole*, 1989; Chausson: *Poeme*, 1992; *The Kreisler Album*, 1996; Bloch: *Baal Shem Suite for Violin and Piano*, 1998; *Gershwin Fantasy*, 1998; Goldmark: Violin Concerto, 2000; Maw: Violin Concerto, 2000; Sibelius: Violin Concerto, 2000

Courtesy of R. Michael Blaese

Blaese, R. Michael

(blayz)

Feb. 16, 1939– Medical researcher; chief scientific officer of Kimeragen Inc.; adjunct investigator at the National Human Genome Research Institute. Address: Kimeragen Inc., 300 Pheasant Run, Newtown, PA 18940

The medical researcher R. Michael Blaese is a trailblazer in the field of gene therapy. As chief of the Clinical Gene Therapy Branch of the National Center for Human Genome Research, he developed a way of treating disease by delivering copies of normal genes into patients' cells. The first tests of his technique on humans suffering from severe combined immune deficiency disease made front-page headlines in 1990, and with reports of his patients' improvement, gene therapy was hailed as heralding a new era in medicine. In early 1999, after more than three decades at the National Institutes of Health, Blaese began working full-time for Kimeragen, a private research firm, where, as chief scientific officer, he is exploring the potential of chimeraplasty, a revolutionary technique for repairing damaged genes that makes use of a naturally occurring DNA repair mechanism. The winner of many awards for his achievements, Blaese has also been recognized for his unusual dedication to his patients.

Born on February 16, 1939 in Minneapolis, Minnesota, Robert Michael Blaese attended Gustavus Adolphus College, in St. Peter, about 55 miles southwest of his hometown. He had an interest in science and decided to try his hand at engineering, but he found that it bored him. Thinking that he would enjoy working in a field that would allow him human contact while engaging his interest in science, he changed his career goal to general-practice medicine. After graduating from college, magna cum laude, he entered the University of Minnesota's medical school.

Eager to save enough money to marry his college sweetheart, Julianne Johnson, Blaese, as a first-year medical student, landed a job in the laboratory of Robert A. Good, where he was to work during all four years at med school. Good is considered the father of clinical immunology and a pioneer in the field of bone-marrow transplantation, and the projects Blaese pursued while under Good's tutelage led him to abandon the idea of becoming a general practitioner and to devote himself instead to research. But as the time to choose an internship approached, he decided that he should have as broad a background as possible. In 1964 he secured an internship in internal medicine at the Parkland Memorial Hospital, in Dallas, Texas. He returned to his home state the next year, to complete a one-year residency in the Department of Pediatrics at the University of Minnesota Hospital, in 1966.

After his residency Blaese accepted a two-year position with the Metabolism Branch of the National Cancer Institute, in Bethesda, Maryland. The National Cancer Institute is one of 25 institutes and centers that comprise the National Institutes of Health (NIH), which sprawls over a modern 300-acre campus. The NIH began in 1887 as the one-room Laboratory of Hygiene, with a budget of about $300 (equal to approximately $5,400 in 1999), and has since grown into one of the world's foremost biomedical research centers, with annual funding in the $15 billion range. Blaese's two-year stint at the NIH as a clinical associate and immunology fellow would eventually stretch into a distinguished 33-year career there.

From 1968 until 1973 Blaese was a senior investigator in the Immunophysiology Section of the Metabolism Branch. In 1973 he was appointed chief of Cellular Immunology, a position he held until 1993; concurrently, from 1985 to 1993, he served as deputy chief of the entire Metabolism Branch. Much of Blaese's work during this time focused on primary immune-deficiency diseases, a group of more than 70 distinct and rare conditions in which the body's immune system is either missing or functioning improperly. Children born without effective immune systems often die very young from infections or cancers. One such disorder, severe combined immune deficiency (SCID), was brought to public attention by the 1976 film *Boy in the Plastic Bubble*, which starred John Travolta. Popularly known as the "bubble-boy disease," SCID is most commonly identified with the sterile plastic enclosure patients must live in to avoid contaminants. Blaese's mentor, Robert Good, was the first to use bone-marrow transplants in the 1960s to treat children with this affliction. If no matching donor was found, however, doctors had few other options, making treatment of such patients a frustrating—and heartbreaking—exercise.

By the 1980s advancements in molecular biology had led Blaese to believe that he could develop techniques for treating disease in an entirely new way. For decades doctors had been treating illness on the cellular level, that is, trying to kill the viruses and bacteria that invade cells and cause illness. Blaese reasoned that there must be a way to use scientists' better understanding of the genetic code, or DNA, in devising treatments.

Blaese teamed up with French Anderson, a scientist working at the National Heart, Lung, and Blood Institute (a division of the NIH), to develop a strategy through which specially engineered viruses would deliver copies of normal genes into a patient's abnormal cells to correct abnormal cellular behavior. He and French decided to concentrate on patients with adenosine deaminase (ADA) deficiency. This devastating form of SCID is so rare that at one point there were more researchers studying it than patients suffering from it. Children with this condition lack the gene that makes ADA, a crucial enzyme needed to transform metabolic by-products that would otherwise destroy the body's immune cells. Children lacking ADA have virtually no protection against viral or bacterial infections.

Initially Blaese and his colleagues assumed that the best strategy would be to insert the gene into the bone marrow stem cells, which produce white blood cells. The soldiers of the immune system, white cells attack infections that invade the human body. Blaese and his co-workers theorized that, armed with the ADA protein they lacked, the stem cells would produce new immune cells with ample ADA. Two unforeseen difficulties arose: stem cells proved hard to harvest in the needed quantities, and the gene insertion was difficult. Forced to formulate a different strategy, the team decided to insert ADA directly into lymphocytes, a type of white blood cell, and then transfuse them into a patient.

The next step was to choose a suitable patient. Of the 20 children known to have the deficiency at the time, the team chose five potential candidates. Ultimately, a four-year-old girl, Ashanti DeSilva, was chosen, mainly because she was in stable condition and because her blood cells grew well in the laboratory. Blaese and his colleagues planned to remove some of the child's blood cells and separate out the T cells, which are a class of lymphocyte. Next they would insert a copy of the ADA gene into a virus engineered to be harmless. The doctors would then infect the girl's separated T cells with the benign virus and grow large quantities of the cells, which would be transfused back to her.

The research team now needed approval from the director of the NIH and from the Food and Drug Administration (FDA). On July 31, 1990 the Recombinant DNA Advisory Committee, which counsels the NIH director on all genetic-engineering projects, approved the gene-therapy proposal by a vote of 16 to 1. The director of the NIH, William H. Raub, granted his approval on September 12 of that year. Then, within 48 hours, with a degree of speed that amazed everyone involved, the FDA gave its OK to the project. The doctors, hoping that permission was imminent, had already advised the DeSilva family to come to Bethesda, so that by the time Anderson received the FDA's blessing, the team and patient were ready.

When it became clear that Ashanti was responding well to the innovative therapy, a second child, eight-year-old Cindy Cutschall, was selected for treatment. Both girls made frequent return visits to the institute for fresh infusions of ADA-enriched cells. (Ashanti had 11 infusions over a two-year period, and Cindy received 12 over the course of 18 months.) The doctors felt hopeful that eventually the treated T cells would prove so hardy that they would survive for several months or even years. The girls were monitored for antibody levels and other signs of immune function. As a therapeutic backup, both girls continued to get enzyme-replacement injections of a synthetic form of ADA called PEG-ADA, which they had received from the time their condition had been diagnosed.

On October 19, 1995 preliminary results of the first human gene therapy trial were published in *Science*. The paper reported that Ashanti's health had improved significantly. She was maintaining a normal white-blood-cell count, as well as significant levels of the ADA enzyme. Cindy's response was somewhat less encouraging: her levels of ADA had not increased, and only about 1 percent of her T cells appeared to have functioning ADA genes. Still, four years after they had begun treatment, both girls were in good health and showed some improved immune reactions. The results indicated that replacement genes would remain stable in white blood cells over extended periods of time and, furthermore, that the disabled virus used to transfer the replacement gene into the cell would not pose health risks.

Although critics charged that PEG-ADA, not the gene therapy, was responsible for the girls' improvement, Blaese and his co-workers felt encouraged. "The results of the study are very gratifying and will help to forward the field of gene therapy," Blaese said, according to an October 19, 1995 press release posted on the National Human Genome Research Institute's Web site. "But, as a physician, I'm most pleased that the girls are doing so well four years later. It's been really remarkable to observe." In spite of their excitement over the results, the doctors cautioned against unrealistic expectations, because gene therapy was still considered experimental.

During the period between Ashanti's first treatment and the release of the preliminary results, Blaese and his associates began treating three newborns suffering from ADA deficiency. Working with Donald Kohn, Blaese isolated cells from the infants' umbilical blood and transferred the ADA gene to them using harmless viral cells. He also began to apply the gene-transfer technology to other diseases, among them cancer and AIDS. Along with Kenneth Culver, he devised a strategy for treating cancer in situ—meaning where it existed in the body—by inserting "suicide genes," such as herpes thymidine kinase, that he theorized would make the cancer cells susceptible to otherwise ineffective chemotherapy treatments. Working in collaboration with doctors from the National Institute of Neurological Disorders and Stroke, Blaese and Culver tested this method on 15 patients with brain tumors and produced measurable encouraging results in one-third of them. Blaese also undertook a long-term project to develop gene therapy for AIDS sufferers, testing various gene modifications in the T cells of sets of identical twins who differed in that one twin of each set was infected by HIV and the other was not.

From 1994 to 1999 Blaese was chief of the Clinical Gene Therapy Branch of the NIH's National Center for Human Genome Research, which was later renamed the National Human Genome Research Institute. He also acted as the clinical director for several years. The center's mission was to head the Human Genome Project, an ambitious international research project to map each human gene and to completely sequence human DNA. Blaese also accepted a consulting post as chief scientific officer for Kimeragen, a small biotechnology firm based near Philadelphia that was researching a process called chimeraplasty.

While in previous methods of gene therapy, a normal copy of a patient's defective gene was used in an effort to reverse disease, in chimeraplasty an attempt is made to repair the defective gene. Kimeragen had formulated a way to use a small molecule designed especially to correct a genetic defect in an individual or family. Called a chimeraplast, the molecule is a combination of both RNA and

DNA sequences that can bind selectively to the portions of the patient's DNA that need correcting. The chimeraplast then activates the body's own repair mechanism without affecting the rest of the genome or altering cell function. Although Blaese was excited by the research, ethical standards of practice prevented him from using methods developed by Kimeragen, a private-sector lab, in his publicly funded, NIH lab.

In January 1999 Blaese committed himself full-time to Kimeragen, by becoming its chief scientific officer and president of its molecular pharmaceuticals arm; he also agreed to continue as an adjunct investigator at the National Human Genome Research Institute. "I'm tremendously excited to become part of a team developing gene repair solutions that are, in my estimation, elegant and highly promising, with profound application in all forms of life," Blaese said, as quoted in a January 14, 1999 press release posted on Kimeragen's Web site. "The technology platform, called chimeraplasty, is a theoretically solid approach and has shown great potential in preclinical models with direct relevance to human therapy. In important ways, chimeraplasty represents a major next step in the development of genetic therapies for human disease." Blaese's primary responsibility at Kimeragen is to guide chimeraplasty from the preclinical to the clinical stage.

In June 1999 Blaese and other Kimeragen researchers were drawn to Amish and Mennonite communities in Lancaster County, Pennsylvania. The residents of those communities descended from a small number of Swiss or German Anabaptists who settled in Lancaster County in the 18th century. Forbidden to marry outside of their faith, members marry within their religious community. Generations of marriage within the same community have limited the gene pool, which increases the odds that parents will carry recessive hereditary genes, for conditions that don't affect them but may affect their children. As a result, the communities suffer from unusually high rates of genetic disorders, such as Crigler-Najjar syndrome.

Crigler-Najjar syndrome is a disorder in which bilirubin, a waste product from the disposal of old red-blood cells, builds up in the liver. Bilirubin is normally broken down by an enzyme in the liver and excreted through the intestines, but in people with the syndrome, the enzyme is either scarce or missing altogether. Toxic to the nervous system, excess bilirubin causes jaundice, which is a yellowing of the skin and whites of the eyes, and it can lead to brain damage. Children suffering from Crigler-Najjar must spend 10 to 18 hours daily under special lights that break down the bilirubin. The lights keep their bilirubin levels in check, but just barely; a routine childhood illness can cause the bilirubin to surge out of control, sometimes fatally. As a child reaches adolescence, the light therapy becomes less effective. The chances of a Crigler-Najjar child living into adulthood without a liver transplant are slim.

Blaese and his colleagues at Kimeragen believe that chimeraplasty will help Crigler-Najjar patients. The disease is also a good choice for clinical trials because the results will be easy to monitor—if the treatment is effective, the children will become less jaundiced and their bilirubin levels will drop. Blaese told Denise Grady for the *New York Times* (June 29, 1999, on-line), "I left what I thought was the best job in the world to do this because I believe so strongly in it and believe we'll be successful. I think it will really fundamentally change the way we practice medicine." As of late 2000 he was awaiting FDA approval to start the chimeraplasty trials.

R. Michael Blaese has written more than 300 research reports, articles, and textbook chapters. He is the recipient of some 19 awards and honors, most recently the Federal Laboratory Consortium's Award for Excellence, in 1997, and the American Association of Blood Banks' 1997 Tibor Greenwalt Award. He and his wife, the former Julianne Johnson, were married in 1962. One of their two daughters is a NASA scientist; the other is a commercial pilot and air-traffic controller.

Although technically a researcher, and thus often relegated to the lab, Blaese actively seeks interaction with his young patients; indeed, colleagues of his have said that his compassion is as far-reaching as his contributions to medicine. According to Denise Grady, the plight of the families who rely upon his research became even more real to Blaese during a visit to Lancaster County in June 1999. One evening, after a meeting with the parents of his young patients, he walked outside the inn where he and the families were staying, and he noticed a purplish light emanating from several rooms. The light was coming from bilirubin lamps. "I saw five rooms with that eerie blue glow, and it really hit me," he told Grady. "I'll never forget it."
— M.R.

Suggested Reading: Kimeragen Inc. (on-line); *New York Times* A p1+ Aug. 1, 1990, p1+ Sep. 15, 1990, D p17 June 12, 1992, A p22 Oct. 20, 1995; *New York Times* (on-line) June 29, 1999; Organic Acidemia Association (on-line); *Science* p1287 Mar. 16, 1990

Blakey, Michael L.

Feb. 23, 1953– Biological anthropologist.
Address: W. Montague Cobb Biological Anthropology Laboratory, Dept. of Sociology and Anthropology, Howard University, Washington, DC 20059

Michael L. Blakey, a biological anthropologist, came to national attention as director of the African Burial Ground Project in New York City. The African Burial Ground (ABG), one of the most

Courtesy of Michael Blakey

Michael L. Blakey

important archaeological finds in the U.S. during the 20th century, was in use from before 1712 until 1794 and captured the imagination of millions when it was rediscovered in 1991. Then–mayor David N. Dinkins, an African-American, declared, as quoted by Blakey and Cheryl J. La Roche in *Historical Archaeology* (Volume 31, 1997), "Millions of Americans celebrate Ellis Island. . . . Others celebrate Plymouth Rock. . . . There was no place which said, we were here, we contributed . . . right from the beginning." The ABG changed that. The final resting place for many slaves brought from West and Central Africa and possibly the Caribbean, the ABG holds cultural artifacts as well as human remains. As director of research at the burial ground, Blakey guides the scientists who analyze the bones and artifacts and serves as a spokesperson for the project. In addition to his ABG work, Blakey is a Howard University professor of anatomy and biological anthropology, the latter of which concerns the biology of human populations rather than individuals.

Michael L. Blakey was born on February 23, 1953. His great-uncle, Kermit Moseley, introduced him to his favorite childhood hobby: hunting for spears, axes, knives, arrowheads, and stone ornaments of the Algonquins (his mother's Native American ancestors), in rural Delaware. As a boy, he also collected small fossilized animals, reading about them in books that fed his imagination with their pictures of artifacts, fossils, and insects. For three consecutive years, in junior high school, he prepared an exhibit of Native American artifacts and fossils from the cliffs of Chesapeake Bay, in Maryland, for the school's annual science fair. The first two years he won honorable mention, and the third year he took the grand prize. When he was in ninth grade, his father helped him find a summer job studying Native American skeletons with the anthropologist Donald J. Ortner at the Smithsonian Institution, in Washington, D.C. He studied 50 ancient skulls and made many discoveries—finding, for example, that Pueblo people had developed many cavities from eating corn, while the Suroque people, whose diet consisted largely of oysters, had far less dental decay. That summer he also met his hero, the anthropologist Louis Leakey. One of his science teachers encouraged him to join an amateur archaeologists' club, and on weekends he helped to dig at a local site.

In high school Blakey dedicated less time to science and more to playing the guitar and learning about African and African-American cultures. He went on to enroll at Howard University, in Washington, D.C., initially planning to study guitar and become a composer; his first college archaeology course, however, reignited his old passion. During his junior year he went on a dig in the forests of Belize, in Central America, where he mapped Mayan villages. In his senior year he studied population biology and decided to become a biological anthropologist.

Blakey received a bachelor's degree in anthropology from Howard in 1978. He continued his studies at the University of Massachusetts at Amherst, earning a master's degree in 1980. Next, he went to England to do research on the biology of contemporary Londoners at the University of London and Oxford University. In 1985 he received a Ph.D. in anthropology from the University of Massachusetts and began teaching at Howard University. He has worked as a research associate in physical anthropology at the National Museum of Natural History, part of the Smithsonian Institution; a visiting associate professor at Spelman College, in Atlanta, and at the Università di Roma, in Italy; a distinguished visiting scholar at Columbia University, in New York City; and president of the Association of Black Anthropologists, from 1987 to 1989.

Blakey is curator of the W. Montague Cobb Biological Anthropology Laboratory at Howard University, which has the third-largest collection of skeletons in the U.S. While other large collections for the most part feature the remains of people of European descent, three-quarters of the skeletons at Howard are those of African-Americans, born as far back as 1850 and ranging from 17 to 106 years old at the time of death. The collection was assembled by W. Montague Cobb, a Howard professor of anatomy, who saved the bones of cadavers dissected by his medical students. The skeletons are used to establish standards of height, weight, and bone development among a sampling of African-Americans, so that scientists can learn how social and economic conditions affected their growth, diet, and health. (The cadavers have come mainly from coroners' offices, with permission from family members to use them for scientific purposes. At the beginning of his tenure, Blakey established a procedure for those who want to claim the remains of relatives who have willed their bodies to science.) Blakey has published numerous articles, on subjects ranging from the dentition of contemporary and ancient peoples to the politics involved in passing on knowledge in the fields of anthropology and archaeology from one generation to the next. He is particularly concerned with these disciplines as they regard African and African-diaspora populations.

In the summer of 1991, the excavation of a 34-story, $500 million General Services Administration (GSA) office building, in the Wall Street area of New York City, disrupted graves as deep as 28 feet below street level—graves that were discovered to be part of the ABG, which was then known as the "Negroes' Burying Ground." Since the Historic Preservation Act of 1966, it had been routine for archaeologists to evaluate the sites of excavations before construction began; but although the ABG was represented on a map of the area dating from 1755, archaeologists estimated that there were at most a few dozen bodies in it, and that public interest in the burial ground would not be sufficient to warrant calling off the excavation. As the excavation proceeded, however, bones and artifacts continued to turn up. According to Blakey, the GSA's main objective was to "contain" the inconvenience that the discovery represented to them and to remove the skeletons from the site. The anthropologists they hired from the New York Metropolitan Forensic Anthropology Team (MFAT), none of whom had a background in African-American studies, were ill-equipped to study the find: their 12-page report dedicated only two pages to African or African-American bioarchaeology and offered no serious discussion of black history in New York. (This was to be expected, Blakey wrote, because the fields of archaeology and African-American studies had been kept separate. African-Americans, along with other minority groups, had historically been excluded from the study of archaeology. After 125 years of American archaeology, there were fewer than a half-dozen African-Americans with doctoral degrees in the field.) The MFAT proposed that the study of the bones focus on "racing," a forensic approach based on strictly racial categories—and one that Blakey later criticized as being dissociated from culture and history and as having a great potential for stereotyping.

Meanwhile, in New York, members of the media and civic groups were voicing concerns over the excavations, demanding to know whether or not the removal was being performed with respect, and who had the rights to the bones and artifacts. The issue brought together "scholars, academicians, researchers, cultural resource managers, politicians, religious leaders, community activists, school children, and the general public . . . in a complex and often contentious . . . relationship," Blakey wrote.

Then–congressman Gus Savage, chairperson of the Subcommittee on Public Buildings and Grounds, challenged the GSA approach to the find. Mayor Dinkins joined Savage and New York state senator David Paterson to form the Task Force for the Oversight of the ABG. The U.S. Congress intervened in October 1992, finding the GSA to be in violation of its own rules requiring an adequate research design and responsiveness to public input. By March 1993, 427 skeletons had been collected, and that fall construction was indefinitely postponed. The Subcommittee on Public Buildings and Grounds opened the burial-ground research contract to bidders.

Before deciding to take on a project, Blakey asks himself three questions: Does the project interest him? Does it require work he is good at? Does it study an issue that is key to resolving a serious problem? The answers to those questions were all positive for him when it came to directing the research at the ABG. Blakey submitted a 130-page research design, proposing to marshal the fields of molecular genetics, bone chemistry, skeletal biology, American and African history and archaeology, ethnology, conservation, and African art history in studying the bones and artifacts. The disciplines would be used to examine the "historical interactions of biology and culture," Blakey and La Roche wrote. Having recently worked on the First African Baptist Church Cemetery project in Philadelphia, a project that involved the reburial of 140 skeletons, Blakey had an experienced team of scholars in African and African-American studies ready.

Since 1986 Blakey, along with Native American advocates and others, had been working on the issue of reburying and repatriating the remains of indigenous people from around the world. The struggle to do so is an ongoing one, as anthropologists need to "relinquish presumption of authority over other peoples' ancestral remains," he wrote in a chapter of the book *Building a New Biocultural Synthesis* (1998), edited by A. H. Goodman and T. L. Leatherman. He had contributed to position papers on the issue for the American Anthropological Association (AAA) and the World Archaeological Congress (WAC) and developed the concept of an anthropology of "public engagement." That term refrs to the policy of taking into consideration the effects of anthropological practices on communities not officially connected with such projects. In an illustration of public engagement, the GSA was an example of a "business client," while the "ethical client" in the case of the ABG was the "descendant community"—that is, present-day African-Americans. Following the AAA Statement on Ethics and Professional Responsibility and the WAC's First Code of Ethics, Blakey's ABG proposal recognized the rights of the descendant community to modify or reject the research design.

Blakey's proposal raised four main questions: Where did the people buried at the site come from? What was their physical quality of life? What biological and cultural transformations took place as

Africans adjusted to life in the U.S.? And how did they resist slavery? His plan was rooted, he wrote, in the "vindicationist" position of African-American activist scholars, initiated by Carter G. Woodson in 1915. Vindicationist studies attempt to correct the distortions of previous research used "either to systematically victimize or alternately ignore" the population studied, Blakey wrote. That the public history of New York was Eurocentric and had distorted the contribution of Africans was not accidental, according to Blakey. "By omission, northern slavery and racism were denied," he wrote. Blakey's approach to history would involve assessing the breeding population by combining historical and archaeological data (including radioactive dating of bones and other objects) of culturally affiliated populations: the Ashanti, Yoruba, Dutch, and Lenape. Blakey's bid for the contract was accepted.

Anthropological interpretation is only as accurate as the observer's knowledge of the culture studied. In the case of the forensic anthropologists, for example, a pattern of nail heads on a coffin at the ABG had been thought to represent a heart and was not considered further. A Ghanaian historian of African art and associate of Blakey's, however, recognized in the same design an African symbol that represented the tie of "the past with the present . . . to prepare for the future," as Blakey and La Roche wrote. The first initiative of Blakey's team was to change the name of the site from the "Negroes' Burying Ground" to the "African Burial Ground," which reflected the terminology preferred by 18th-century blacks—as reflected in the names of such organizations as the African Mutual Relief Society, the African Free School, and the African Methodist Episcopal Church. For the purposes of the project, the team also replaced the terms of ahistorical condition such as "master" and "slave" with such terms as "slave holder" and "enslaved African."

Blakey's work has turned up information about the quality of colonial life for African-Americans in the urban North. While free blacks had farmed under the Dutch in 15th-century New York, by 1716 the British had passed laws prohibiting blacks' owning land, and churches refused them burial, necessitating a separate cemetery. Poverty was apparent from the fact that people were not buried in their clothes. About half of colonial New York Africans, Blakey's team estimated, died by age 12. Between 30 and 40 percent of the youth died in infancy; another 40 percent of the skeletons are those of preadolescent children, many with thickened skulls indicating anemia and osteomalacia—a weakening of the bones due to poor diet and nutrition. Enlarged muscle attachments on the skeletons are attributed to heavy stress loads, while signs of arthritis in the neck are linked to the practice of carrying heavy items on the head. Lesions on the thigh bones indicate muscle and ligament tears. The people represented "were obviously working at the very margins of human endurance and capacity. Arguably a few were worked to death in a time when it was considered cost-effective to work slaves to death," Blakey observed, as quoted by Carla Garnett on the National Institutes of Health Web site.

Blakey's laboratory has been visited by scholars from Japan, Germany, South Korea, the Caribbean, Canada, England, Ireland, and many African nations. Media coverage of the ABG has included three film and video productions; more than 500 newspaper articles; and two historical reference books. On the diplomatic front, a Royal Ghanaian delegation visited the site and Howard University in 1995. The Ghanaian chiefs came to affirm cultural and spiritual ties between Africans and African-Americans, and in a ceremony held at Howard University, Nana Oduro Numapau II, the president of the Ghana National House of Chiefs, symbolically asked forgiveness for past rulers' collaboration in the trans-Atlantic slave trade. In 1996 a briefing on the ABG research was held for the United Nations Human Rights Commission, in Geneva. The remains from the site are scheduled to be reburied when research is concluded. A portion of the original site will be preserved in order to memorialize those buried there.

Blakey has served on many boards of the American Anthropological Association and published more than 40 articles on the history and philosophy of science, paleopathology, historical demography, medical psychophysiology, and racism, in journals including the *American Journal of Physical Anthropology*, *American Anthropologist*, the *International Journal of Anthropology*, and *Critique of Anthropology*. He received an honorary doctor of science degree in 1995 from York College of the City University of New York.

Blakey's wife, Cecelie Counts Blakey, is a lawyer with a long career in political activism. The couple's son, Tariq, is named for the African conqueror who invaded Spain in 711 A.D. — V.K.

Suggested Reading: *Historical Archaeology* Vol. 31 p84+ 1997; *New York Times* p41 Aug. 9, 1992; *Washington Post* B p1 Aug. 3, 1995; Cummings, D. and L. Cummings, eds. *Talking with Adventurers*, 1998; Goodman, A. H. and T. L. Leatherman, eds. *Building a New Biocultural Synthesis*, 1998

Courtesy of St. Clair Bourne

Bourne, St. Clair

(born)

Feb. 16, 1943– Documentary filmmaker; film producer; social activist; founder of Chamba Mediaworks Inc. Address: Chamba Mediaworks, 580 Broadway, Suite 501, New York, NY 10012

The filmmaker St. Clair Bourne "has made a career out of bringing African-American legends to life," Ann Brown wrote for *American Visions* (February/March 1999). The founder of Chamba Mediaworks, which produces documentary films aimed at encouraging social change, Bourne has directed more than 40 documentaries, among them *In Motion: Amiri Baraka, John Henrik Clarke: A Great and Mighty Walk*, and *Paul Robeson: Here I Stand*. Making his mark in television as well, he was one of the youngest producers of *Black Journal*, the first nationally televised public-affairs program that focused on issues of special concern to black Americans. He directed "America: Black and White," an episode of the award-winning *NBC White Paper* on the subject of race relations, and he produced two of the six episodes of *The Will to Win*, a BBC series on the political effect that black athletes have had on sports internationally. He has also ventured into fiction filmmaking, as the co-producer of *The Long Night* (1972), and he directed *On the Boulevard*, a short film for PBS that dramatized the economic difficulties many people suffered during the presidency of Ronald Reagan. Bourne has been honored with retrospectives at the Whitney Museum of American Art, in New York, the Kennedy Center, in Washington, D.C., and the Cineclube Estacao, in Rio de Janeiro, Brazil.

In *Struggles for Representation: African American Documentary Film and Video* (1999), edited by Phyllis R. Klotman and Janet K. Cutler, Cutler described Bourne's style of filmmaking: "He links materials in inventive ways, creating elegant transitions. . . . He mixes edgy *cinéma vérité* footage—utilizing hand-held cameras, zooming in and out, and rapid editing—with more conventional voice-over narration and talking head interviews." In a conversation with Klotman and Cutler, Bourne said that he "came to documentary film through political work. I saw the representation, misrepresentation, and confusion of the civil rights movement in the major media by white male spokespeople who attempted to tell white America what 'those people' were doing, and usually what they said was wrong, or distorted, for their own psychic needs. And I knew that I had a better handle on that."

According to Janet Cutler, "St. Clair Bourne and others have turned their cameras on black artists not only to praise their accomplishments but to make two related political points: blacks have been systematically stripped of their African heritage, and their cultural production in America has too often been co-opted by the mainstream entertainment industry." Bourne told Klotman and Cutler that he learned from the filmmaker William Greaves that by targeting his films at an African-American audience, he is not necessarily preventing others from appreciating his work. "In fact, the purer the African American taste, the more interesting it is to other people," he said. "Because the more specific the better—the purer—so people can lock into it. . . . If somebody [says] 'I didn't know that,' and doesn't feel threatened, then I know I've done it. Even if they feel threatened, that's still alright. But they have to really be given the purest version of the person or the subject matter. That's the job of the documentarian. The whole issue of universality is basically something concocted to prevent people of color from getting access to the tools of self-definition."

Born on February 16, 1943 in Harlem, in New York City, St. Clair Bourne grew up in the Bedford-Stuyvesant section of the borough of Brooklyn. His father, St. Clair Thomas Bourne, worked as a reporter for the *Amsterdam News*, New York City's oldest and largest African-American newspaper, and then as the managing editor for the *People's Voice*, a national black weekly; he later worked for the city's housing department in the area of community relations. Bourne's mother moved from a career in nursing to become an administrator in the city's social-services agency. Bourne's mother had immigrated to the United States from the West Indies to make a better life for herself, and she and her husband had high hopes for their son, attempting to groom him as a future diplomat.

Bourne attended a Catholic grammar school and then Xavier High, a Jesuit military day school in Manhattan. In 1960 he enrolled at the Georgetown University School of Foreign Service, in Washington, D.C., where he majored in international affairs. As an undergraduate he joined the Air Force ROTC; he quickly rose through the ranks to cadet lieutenant and qualified for the pilot course. While taking part in an historic sit-in in Arlington, Virginia, in February 1963, Bourne was arrested along with 14 other Georgetown students for refusing to leave the Gateway Diner, which had a policy of serving only white customers. Consequently, Georgetown expelled Bourne, who was then a junior.

For two years beginning in 1964, Bourne served in the Peace Corps, which sent him to Lima, Peru, to edit a community newspaper. That experience led to his realization that "communications could be used for social good," as he told Clyde Taylor for *Artist and Influence* (January 21, 1996). "People [in Lima] couldn't read, so we had to put three or four pictures in sequence in the newspaper and have very basic captions. So in a sense [I was] making a movie, and I could see how people would actually look at the pictures, and I could see the thinking process in their heads."

After leaving the Peace Corps, Bourne entered Syracuse University, in upstate New York, where he pursued a dual major, in journalism and political science. While fulfilling the requirements of a work-study scholarship, he instructed Peace Corps volunteers. He received a bachelor's degree in 1967 and then, with another scholarship, enrolled in the film program at the Columbia University School of the Arts, in New York City. Once again he was expelled, this time for his participation in the 1968 student takeover of the Columbia campus, which led to his arrest. Meanwhile, one of his professors, the filmmaker Arthur Barron, having recognized Bourne's skills, recommended him to the producers of a recently launched television news program entitled *Black Journal.* "Literally three days after I got out of jail," Bourne told Richard Baimbridge for the *Independent* (March 1999), "I was [an] associate producer of a national black television show." The first national public-affairs program of its kind, *Black Journal,* which aired on PBS from 1968 until 1976, provided an arena from which hosts and guests—often appearing in African dress—gave voice to a pan-African perspective never before offered on American television. Its producers sought to address the frustrations of young black people whose concerns were being ignored by the mainstream press. "Whenever the media dealt with black people they always had a white person that was the interpreter," Bourne recalled to Lisa Jones for the *Village Voice* (February 23, 1988). "He would assume that the audience was white. He would take the position of 'don't be activist,' of course, and it always ended up sounding like 'what are these strange people doing throwing rocks?'"

Bourne believes that what made *Black Journal* possible was the establishment's fear of black rage and self-determination in the wake of the urban riots that had erupted earlier in the 1960s. "Black Power was still happening . . . and the mainstream institutions had to relate to that," he told Clyde Taylor. "They could no longer just treat us like victims, because we could always threaten to burn down the city. . . . I believe to this day that *Black Journal* came into existence because too many brothers threw too many bricks at some rich white people's house, and they said, 'Okay, let's cool them out somehow.'" Bourne and his colleagues at *Black Journal* organized a strike in a successful effort to replace the show's white producer with an African-American. William Greaves took over, and he gave the 12 young black filmmakers on the staff full creative freedom to prepare stories that they felt needed to be told. *Black Journal* won an Emmy Award in its second season.

"It's hard to imagine what an impact *Black Journal* had," Bourne told Richard Baimbridge. "Even though we only had an hour a month on public television, I think we really made a difference in people's lives, as well as in television. The news magazine format, for example—I think we set the standard for that." Bourne himself, however, who was promoted to producer within five months of his arrival, soon found *Black Journal*'s format limiting and sought to make films on his own terms. "The difference between documentary and news to me is that you don't really have rules in documentary," he explained to Baimbridge. "It's fiction under the guise of objectivity. . . . I realized that I couldn't live under the so-called 'rules' of journalistic TV. . . . I wanted to combine analysis and style, and in a traditional [news] doc, you can't do that too much. Then I found out where you *could* combine analysis and style, and it was called 'independent film.'"

After leaving *Black Journal*, in 1971, Bourne created Chamba Mediaworks, a filmmaker's collective. He chose its name, which means "house" or "home" in Swahili, because he wanted the collective to be a home "for positive, afrocentric media thought," he told Victoria Valentine for *Emerge* (November 1994). Chamba's early productions were industrial and educational films for such organizations as the Children's Television Workshop.

In 1973 a group of black ministers who had seen his work on *Black Journal* commissioned Bourne to make a documentary about them. "It was really a grass-roots Black effort," he told Clyde Taylor. "These middle-class church people wanted to reach the working-class. They were getting left behind politically, because in the '60s a preacher was a symbol of the status quo, of the less progressive element." Bourne told Taylor that the resulting work, *Let the Church Say Amen!* (1973), fulfilled his "desire to make a narrative film using real people" while providing an inside look at the role of religion in the black community. The film followed a young minister who had joined the seminary to avoid being drafted to serve in the Vietnam War; eventually, he became a devoted cleric with a decidedly progressive agenda. *Let the Church*

Say Amen! was one of the first films produced by an African-American to be recognized by the independent film circuit. It was shown as part of the New American Filmmakers series at the Whitney Museum of American Art and at the Museum of Modern Art (both in New York City), two of the most important venues for independent film at that time.

As the impact of the Black Power movement began to diminish, Bourne found it more difficult to secure funding for his projects. He turned to teaching for a time, but he felt frustrated because his schedule left little time for film work. In 1975 he taught at Cornell University, in New York State, and then as a guest lecturer at the film school of the University of California at Los Angeles (UCLA). He also served as the North American film coordinator for the Festival of African Arts and Culture, held in Lagos, Nigeria. Between 1975 and 1980, while living in Los Angeles, Bourne made three documentaries for public television. He also received a $20,000 grant from the National Endowment for the Arts to publish *Chamba Notes*, a newsletter for filmmakers of African descent that he distributed worldwide for 10 years.

In 1980 Bourne resettled in New York City, and in the following years his films became more political. In the next year he began working on a profile of the controversial poet, playwright, and activist Amiri Baraka (formerly LeRoi Jones). Entitled *In Motion: Amiri Baraka*, the film centers on the two weeks leading up to the writer's sentencing in federal court, in 1981, on charges of beating his wife and resisting arrest. Bourne used what impressed him as musical patterns in the speech of Baraka as a guide to creating what he intended to be a rhythmic structure in the film. Although the documentary, which premiered in 1983 on television, earned praise in the media, many critics wrote harshly of its subject, Baraka.

On the last day of shooting *In Motion*, Baraka spoke before a group of Irish- and African-Americans at a rally protesting apartheid in South Africa. At that event Bourne met members of the H-Block Armagh Committee, an American-based group that supported Catholics who had been jailed in Northern Ireland for activities related to the Irish Republicans' fight to end British rule in Northern Ireland. The committee later invited a number of African-American activists and ministers to Belfast, the capital of Northern Ireland, to see for themselves the similarities between the struggle of blacks in the U.S. and that of the Catholic minority in Ulster, as Northern Ireland is sometimes colloquially called. Bourne was invited to accompany the travelers and document the historic visit. Through making *The Black and the Green* (1983), he learned that the Irish Republicans had been greatly influenced by the civil-rights movement in the U.S. but had concluded that nonviolent resistance was futile.

In an example of the similarities he detected between the situation of African-Americans in the U.S. and Catholics in Northern Ireland, Bourne told Richard Harrington for the *Washington Post* (April 12, 1983) about his attempt to interview a British army officer "who was half-English, half-Irish. To hear him talk about the Irish, you could have thought he was an old Southern sheriff talking about blacks." At one point Bourne and his crew were surrounded by British soldiers. "It's the only time in my film career when being black and American helped," he remarked to Harrington. The experience showed him that "black perspective is not just American," Bourne told Clyde Taylor. "Here were Irish people in the film saying 'We Shall Overcome,' because they saw . . . what we did on television. They would come up to me and say, 'The British treat us worse than the white people there treat you.' They saw us as the definitive role model for strugglers, and they were so happy when we got there." *The Black and the Green* was banned in Great Britain, and to this day has seldom been seen either there or in the United States. "If you up the ante on political work, or if you chose a subject who [was] really on it in terms of political analysis, you run the risk of getting it censored," Bourne told Clyde Taylor. "With Baraka in New York there were cultural allies . . . so it got on. But the film about Northern Ireland made direct connections with the African American struggle and the Irish struggle, and it didn't condemn armed struggle, it explored it. The [Irish] said, 'We don't really like to shoot people, but the British are here in our land, and as you know, if there is oppression you must resist.' And he was saying this to a brother, so you imagine the white people here seeing this!"

Although Bourne was busy professionally during the 1980s, the conservative political climate made it more difficult to secure funding for documentaries; the number of venues available for presenting such films also decreased. Pointing to the era as one that was repressive generally, he cited the frequent instances of police brutality and such racially motivated incidents as the one in 1986 in the Howard Beach section of Queens, New York, in which a black man was killed by a car while trying to escape a white mob. In this climate, "the documentary itself was under attack," Bourne told Clyde Taylor. "The documentary exposes wrongs. It catches the politicians in statements, and you go find out what the real deal was, put it on the air and embarrass people. Well, Reagan didn't want that, and he had a press secretary who called the news directors of the networks and said, 'Don't do that. If you do that, we're going to restrict your access to information.' That's on record. At the same time they started cutting NEA [National Endowment for the Arts] and NEH [National Endowment for the Humanities] money so that places where the few independent documentary filmmakers would go to get research money was less. Then they started cutting back PBS money."

For the PBS series *Voices and Visions*, Bourne directed *Langston Hughes: The Dream Keeper* (1988), for which he employed such techniques as animation and dramatization to illuminate aspects of the writer's life. In that same year Bourne's work was the subject of a 20-year retrospective at the Whitney Museum of American Art. The event drew the attention of the producers of National Geographic's *Explorer* television series, and at their invitation, Bourne directed three films for the series: *The Gullah Connection* (1990), about the effects of tourism in South Carolina on the Gullahs, a group of African-Americans who live in coastal parts of that state, Georgia, and northeastern Florida; *New Orleans Brass Bands* (1994); and *Heritage of the Black West* (1995), a history of African-American cowboys and cowgirls.

Earlier, the filmmaker Spike Lee, having been impressed by *Langston Hughes: The Dream Keeper*, had invited Bourne to shoot a documentary chronicling the making of Lee's *Do the Right Thing* (1989), a widely debated film about race relations set in Bedford-Stuyvesant, about 10 blocks from where Bourne grew up. After starting the project, Bourne fired his director of photography, who was white, having concluded that the man's prejudices were compromising the documentary. "All the footage he shot in Bed-Stuy was of kids playing in the gutter . . . ," Bourne told Richard Baimbridge. "That's not what it's like." *Making 'Do the Right Thing'* (1989) focused primarily on the impact of Lee's enormous undertaking on residents of the neighborhood that he had chosen as the story's locale. Bourne focused his attention on people who had become extras in Lee's film.

Among Bourne's films from the 1990s is *John Henrik Clarke: A Great and Mighty Walk* (1996); produced and narrated by the actor Wesley Snipes, the picture profiles Clarke (1915–98), an African-American historian, Pan-African activist, and black-studies advocate, who endeavored to debunk many myths about African peoples while uncovering more than 5,000 years of African history. The film was named best documentary at the 1997 Urban World Film Festival. Bourne's two-hour *Paul Robeson: Here I Stand*, broadcast on PBS in February 1999, is a comprehensive study of the pioneering black actor, singer, and champion of civil rights. Enriching the film was material that Bourne gleaned from Robeson's personal papers, which his family had released for the first time. In 2000 the film earned the International Documentary Association's Distinguished Achievement Award in the Strand category, which recognizes films that are part of an ongoing series—in this case, *American Masters*. *Halfpast Autumn: The Life and Works of Gordon Parks*, Bourne's documentary (which he also produced) about the photographer, filmmaker, writer, composer, and painter, was scheduled to be broadcast on HBO in November 2000. Bourne has served as the executive producer for three documentary films: *A Question of Color*, *Opposite Camps*, and *Innocent Until Proven Guilty*. In 2000 he was working on a film about the civil-rights activist Kwame Ture (1941–98), known earlier as Stokely Carmichael, and developing the feature film *Exiles*.

Bourne has received fellowships from the National Endowment for the Arts, the Rockefeller Foundation, the American Film Institute, the Charles H. Revson Foundation, Columbia University, and the MacDowell Colony, a retreat for writers, artists, and musicians. His honors include the John Russwurm Citation for excellence in broadcasting, the Liberty Bell Achievement Award, and, most recently, the Connecticut Filmmaker Award 2000, which he received from the Connecticut Film Commission. Somini Sengupta reported in the *New York Times* (June 17, 2000) that Bourne lives in Connecticut with the former Black Panther member and activist Kathleen Cleaver. — C.L.

Suggested Reading: *Artist and Influence 1996* vol. 15, Jan. 21, 1996; *Emerge* p12 Nov. 1994, with photo; *Independent* p34+ Mar. 1999, with photos; *New York Times* II p21+ May 29, 1983, with photos; *Village Voice* p46 Feb. 23, 1988, with photos; *Washington Post* D p3 Apr. 12, 1983, with photo; Klotman, Phyllis R., and Janet K. Cutler, eds. *Struggles for Representation: African American Documentary Film and Video*, 1999

Selected Films: *Let the Church Say Amen!* 1973; *The Black and the Green*, 1983; *In Motion: Amiri Baraka*, 1983; *Making 'Do the Right Thing'*, 1989; *New Orleans Brass Bands*, 1994; *Langston Hughes: The Dream Keeper*, 1988; *Heritage of the Black West*, 1995; *John Henrik Clarke: A Great and Mighty Walk*, 1996; *Paul Robeson: Here I Stand*, 1999

Braxton, Toni

Oct. 7, 1967– Pop singer. Address: c/o LaFace Records, 3350 Peach Tree Rd., #1500, Atlanta, GA 30326

The singer Toni Braxton first attracted widespread notice with "Give U My Heart" and "Love Shoulda Brought You Home," which she recorded for the soundtrack to the film *Boomerang* in 1992, when she was 24 years old. Her self-titled debut album, released in the following year, went multi-platinum; it earned her three Grammy Awards and comparisons to such celebrated vocalists as Aretha Franklin, Whitney Houston, Anita Baker, and Roberta Flack. *Secrets* (1996), her second disc, brought her two more Grammys and much publicity that focused on her newly revealed, unabashed sexiness. During the next four years, she made no records, in part because she became embroiled in a legal action against her record label, LaFace, and

Archive Photos

Toni Braxton

filed for bankruptcy. After the release of *The Heat*, in the spring of this year, Braxton told an interviewer for *Jet* (July 17, 2000), "I've been taking control of my life and I'm being responsible for what happens in my career. This third album shows the positive direction I'm feeling in my life. I'm not worried like I once was about how things would turn out when I put out a record. I'm just anxious to have my music out there so people can hear me again!" A crossover success who is popular among aficionados of rhythm and blues as well as fans of pop, Braxton has specialized in songs about heartbreak and unrequited love. With her unusually deep, lush contralto, she "is able to infuse every song with an emotional intensity that can transform the banal into true confessions," as Stephen Holden wrote for the *New York Times* (July 17, 1996). In *Time* (July 15, 1996), Christopher John Farley called Braxton "one of the sultriest singers around."

Toni Braxton was born on October 7, 1967 in Severn, Maryland, near Baltimore, to Michael and Evelyn Braxton. At the time of her birth, her father was a power-company worker and part-time minister in an Apostolic church; her mother was a cosmetology instructor. The eldest of six children, Toni has four sisters—Towanda, Trina, Tamar, and Traci—and a brother, Michael Jr. The Braxtons maintained a strict Apostolic household, in which secular music was forbidden. Evelyn Braxton, however, who had sung with a doo-wop group when she was younger, belonged to an amateur opera society, because she believed that opera was a form of gospel, and she gave her daughters singing lessons. Toni Braxton began singing in the church choir when she was six years old. Her parents' rules notwithstanding, from an early age she was drawn to popular music. On Saturdays, after her parents would leave the house to do their weekly grocery shopping, she would listen to pop music on the radio; sometimes she would go to a neighbor's house and watch Stevie Wonder, Chaka Khan, Quincy Jones, and others perform on *Soul Train*, the first national black dance and entertainment television show. One day while viewing the sitcom *Good Times* when she was about 10, she saw Janet Jackson—who was about the same age—sing "You Don't Have to Be a Star to Be in My Show" to the character J.J. (played by Jimmie Walker). "I went, 'Oh, I'm going to learn that song so *I* can sing it to J.J. too," Braxton told Richard Harrington for the *Washington Post* (November 21, 1993). "And it was because of my crush on J.J.—and Huggy Bear [a character, played by Antonio Fargas, on the TV crime series *Starsky and Hutch*]—that I knew I wanted to be a secular singer. I didn't want to sing gospel." When Braxton was 11 her parents changed their religious affiliation, joining the United Methodist Church, and for the first time Toni was allowed to wear pants and nail polish (in subdued hues). Her parents also permitted her to sing in local talent shows, where her voice was sometimes criticized as too husky or deep.

Braxton attended Glen Burnie High School, where she was a member of the glee club, and then enrolled at Anne Arundel Community College, in Maryland, where she studied social work before switching her major to music. Eventually, she transferred to Bowie State College, also in Maryland, but did not earn a degree. Once, as an undergraduate, she tried out, unsuccessfully, for the Miss Black America pageant, singing Anita Baker tunes for the talent portion of the contest. After leaving school she reportedly worked briefly as a secretary and a court reporter. She continued to enter talent shows and often performed with three of her sisters as the Braxtons. One day while at a gas station in Annapolis, she struck up a conversation with the attendant, Bill Pettaway, and learned that he had seen her group shortly before. Pettaway was an aspiring songwriter who had his own small studio; he had already co-written "Girl, You Know It's True," which would become a hit for the duo Milli Vanilli in 1989. Pettaway introduced Braxton and her sisters to Ernesto Phillips, a producer, who in turn arranged for them to sign a contract with Arista Records. In 1990 they released a single called "The Good Life."

Despite its dismal sales, "The Good Life" caught the attention of two young producers, Antonio "L.A." Reid and Kenny "Babyface" Edmonds. The pair had launched their own record label, named LaFace, and had already signed TLC, a promising three-woman group. Seeking a female soloist, they approached Braxton and asked her to perform without her sisters. Hesitant to do so, she consulted with her siblings and parents. "Go do your thing, make a name for yourself and then you can bring us up," they told her, as she recalled to Harrington. (Later, her sisters sang back-up vocals for her; currently, only one of them—Tamar—is singing professionally.) Her mother, who sometimes regretted not having pursued a singing career herself, was especially enthusiastic about LaFace's offer, and she persuaded Toni to grab the opportunity.

In her first work for LaFace, Braxton contributed two songs to the soundtrack of the 1992 Eddie Murphy film *Boomerang*. One of them—"Give U My Heart," a duet that she sang with Babyface—reached number 29 on the pop charts; her second track on the album, "Love Shoulda Brought You Home," which was released shortly afterward, performed almost as well. (Anita Baker, a singer whom Braxton admired, had been scheduled to perform those tunes for the soundtrack but had backed out after discovering that she was pregnant.) In August 1993 Reid and Babyface, who were by then referring to Braxton as "the first lady of LaFace," released Braxton's debut album. Called *Toni Braxton*, it includes the singles "Another Sad Love Song" and "Breathe Again," both of which reached the Top 20 on *Billboard*'s pop and R&B charts. Mitchell May, reviewing the album for the *Chicago Tribune* (October 7, 1993), wrote, "The market is flooded with singers who try to knock each and every song out of the park with over-the-top vocals. Braxton wisely lets the mood of a tune dictate her approach, allowing her to supply an emotional depth that perhaps even the songwriters didn't know was there." He added that she "conveys a sense of despair and longing that is rare." Other critics compared her to Whitney Houston, Roberta Flack, or Anita Baker, but Braxton modestly deflected such praise. "I don't think of myself as a diva at all," she told Amy Linden for *Essence* (December 1993). "I'm just a new singer who has been blessed to work with renowned producers. Whitney, Roberta, all those other women . . . they're the divas. Not me." The comparisons to other female singers intensified, however, when she beat out several of them, including Aretha Franklin, Janet Jackson, and Patti LaBelle, to win two Soul Train Music Awards, three American Music Awards, and two 1993 Grammys—for the best female R&B vocal performance, for "Another Sad Love Song," and as best new artist. The album eventually sold more than seven million copies. (According to one source, sales have topped 10 million internationally.) Braxton won a third Grammy Award, again for best female R&B vocal performance, in 1994, for "Breathe Again," another cut from the recording.

In 1995 Braxton recorded "Let It Flow" for the film *Waiting to Exhale*. A year later she released her sophomore album, *Secrets*, whose contributors include the singer R. Kelly and the saxophonist Kenny G. Its highly erotic single "You're Makin' Me High," which deals with masturbation, quickly reached number one on the *Billboard* pop chart. (Braxton has joked that her father's only comment about the song was that it had a nice beat.) The album also contained the single "Un-break My Heart," written by Diane Warren, which received heavy radio airplay and has been credited with helping Braxton to gain recognition as the Female Rhythm & Blues Artist of the Year at the 1997 *Billboard* Music Awards ceremony. Her rendition of "Un-break My Heart" also earned her the 1996 Grammy Award for best female pop vocal performance; with "You're Makin' Me High," she captured the 1996 Grammy for best female R&B vocal performance. After the release of *Secrets*, Braxton toured with Kenny G, whose albums many critics have disparaged as "elevator music" and who has been accused of watering down jazz to appeal to mainstream audiences. Her association with Kenny G, who is white, led some people to accuse her of "selling out." Such criticism "upset me more than a lot," she acknowledged, as quoted on the Smith/McIver Entertainment Web site. "They [the faultfinders] would ask me 'Do you consider yourself a black artist?' Yeah, I look at myself every day. This color ain't coming off."

Braxton received nearly as much attention in the media for her appearance as for her music. Observers often commented on the incongruity of such a big voice emanating from such a tiny frame. Standing just five feet, two inches, Braxton wore size-two clothing, which she chose by perusing magazines and frequenting designers' fashion shows. For two years in a row in the mid-1990s, *People* magazine listed her among the 50 most beautiful people of the year. By the time *Secrets* came out, she had begun to cultivate a sexy, seductive look. In the following year she caused a minor uproar, by posing almost nude for the June/July 1997 cover of *Vibe* magazine—a move that some saw as detrimental to the image of black women. According to an unsigned article in *Jet* (October 26, 1998), she herself came to consider her decision a mistake. But currently, she seems to view it with equanimity: in an interview with Jim Farber for the New York *Daily News* (April 23, 2000), she said, "I was embarrassed at first. I didn't know they were going to show [my nipples]. But it's just a nipple. We all have them. And they did a great job of making me look beautiful, for which I am grateful."

On December 7, 1997, citing a California statute that restricts the length of personal-service contracts to seven years, Braxton filed a lawsuit against LaFace and its parent company, Arista, claiming that her agreement with them had been invalid as of August 1996. The move was widely seen as a tactic to force LaFace to pay her more; although her recordings had reportedly brought Arista and LaFace an estimated $170 million, she told reporters she had received only 35 cents for each album sold—about a third of what other artists of her stature were getting. Eight weeks after filing the suit, Braxton declared bankruptcy, having accumulated more than $1 million in debts—another attempt, according to some observers, to get an increase in royalties. (The group TLC had instituted similar actions against LaFace in 1995.) The media pilloried Braxton for her behavior, charging her with disloyalty to the company that had provided her with her big break and wagging fingers at her extravagance and financial naiveté. When she appeared, by invitation, on the *Oprah Winfrey Show*, Winfrey delivered a scathing lecture on fiscal responsibility. "I guess I expected her to give me a hug and a kiss and tell me it was going to be all right," Braxton admitted to Allison Samuels for *Newsweek* (May 1, 2000). "But she took a different approach. Sitting there, though, made me know that I was never going to let this happen again." She also told Samuels, to explain how she had racked up such large debts, "I wasn't making the money I should have, but it's hard not to live the lifestyle." Braxton remained friendly with Reid and Babyface, however, and the dispute was ultimately settled amicably. In the midst of the legal actions, Braxton appeared on Broadway as Belle for an eight-month stint in Disney's long-running musical *Beauty and the Beast*. Coached by the veteran actress Ella Joyce, she received favorable reviews for her portrayal. "I've seen the other Belles perform in the play," Braxton told a reporter for *Jet* (October 26, 1998). "You could say her character was like a big old glass of punch, and I had to spike her a little bit."

In the spring of 2000, LaFace released Braxton's third album, *The Heat*, the cover of which shows a scantily clad Braxton with long, straight hair. A mix of love ballads and R&B, the recording includes two songs written by Diane Warren—"Spanish Guitar" and "I'm Still Breathing"—and, among other tunes, "Fairy Tale," written by Babyface; "Just Be a Man About It," a duo with Dr. Dre; and "He Wasn't Man Enough," written and produced by Rodney Jerkins. In a cover story for *Jet* (July 17, 2000), Braxton labeled two other cuts—"The Art of Love" and "Speaking in Tongues"—"official Toni Braxton baby-making songs!" "I don't know how often people have told me that they became parents off of one of my records, so this time I made a conscious effort to create a couple of songs with that in mind," she explained. In a review of *The Heat* for the *All-Music Guide* Web site, Stephen Thomas Erlewine called the album "stylish, sultry, seductive, appealing urban contemporary soul" and described it as a "confident, assured, sexy effort that reaffirms Braxton's status as one of the finest contemporary mainstream soul singers."

Commenting on her reputation as "pop's poster girl for romantic misery," as Jim Farber put it in the New York *Daily News* (April 23, 2000), Braxton told Farber, "I consider myself to be the musical equivalent of the Lifetime Channel for women. I do sing a lot of sad, 'I'm going to kill myself' songs. But I always try to have a sense of resurrection in my music." — M.R.

Suggested Reading: *Ebony* p134+ May 1994, with photos; *Jet* p32+ Jan. 26, 1998, with photos, p32+ Oct. 26, 1998, with photos, p56+ July 17, 2000, with photos; New York *Daily News* (on-line) Apr. 23, 2000, with photo; *Newsweek* p72 May 1, 2000, with photo; *Time* p67 July 15, 1996, with photos; *USA Today* D p6 Feb. 24, 1997, with photo; *Washington Post* G p1+ Nov. 21, 1993, with photos

Selected Recordings: *Toni Braxton*, 1993; *Secrets*, 1996; *The Heat*, 2000

Courtesy of Charles H. Brenner

Brenner, Charles H.

Mar. 18, 1945– Forensic mathematician.
Address: 6568 Sobrante Rd., Oakland, CA 94611-1123

DNA-View software, developed by the mathematician Charles H. Brenner, has helped to change the way scientists and judicial systems around the world analyze evidence. The software assists scientists in determining the statistical chances that two DNA samples match. The tool makes it possible to determine with far greater accuracy than before whether an individual is related to legal immigrants and to establish paternity in cases in which the identity of a child's father is in doubt. Brenner, a former professional bridge player and one of the world's first freelance mathematicians, has labeled himself a forensic mathematician. He currently helps scientists all over the world to interpret the data they retrieve from his software and occasionally takes on clients himself.

Charles Hallam Brenner was born on March 18, 1945 in Princeton, New Jersey. His mother, Frances Hallam Brenner, was an artist, and after the family moved to California, she became a city councilwoman and a member of the Palo Alto planning committee. She also served as president of the Palo Alto League of Women Voters for a time. Brenner's father, Joel Lee Brenner, was a mathematician at the Stanford Research Institute. By the age of five, Charles Brenner had already developed an interest in math. His father's colleagues would test the boy's abilities with various puzzles, such as one that required him to determine which of several seemingly identical coins weighed less or more than the others, by weighing pairs of the coins on a balance beam a minimum number of times. Mathematics that had practical applications, such as statistics, however, was "frowned on" by his family, he told Claudia Dreifus for the *New York Times* (August 8, 2000). "Statisticians, we didn't even talk of them. I find it rather amusing that I now do very practical mathematics," he added. As a student at Palo Alto High School, Brenner used computers for the first time, when he learned to operate the IBM 650, an early model housed at nearby Stanford University. He also played tic-tac-toe against the computer, using a Bell Labs program, and thus helped to hone his skills in mathematical competition. After graduating from high school—where he won prizes in math—in 1961, Brenner enrolled at Stanford, continuing to work with computers while pursuing a bachelor of science degree. There, he twice won honorable mention in the Putnam Mathematics Competition, administered by the Mathematical Association of America.

In 1967—"somewhat belatedly,"as he told *Current Biography*—Brenner graduated from Stanford and joined the IBM research staff at the T. J. Watson Research Center in Yorktown Heights, New York; he was involved in the development of the APL computer-programming language. In April 1968 he left his job and moved to London, England, to do graduate work and to avoid being drafted into the military during the Vietnam War. Before long, Brenner lost interest in his mathematics studies and was able to stay in England only by taking violin lessons, which allowed him to retain his student papers. Unable to get work legally in England, he earned his living by playing bridge. His knowledge of math served him well at the card table, and for six years he supported himself as a bridge player, winning between £100 and £300 a month, occasionally saving enough to take month-long vacations in such places as Mexico and South Africa.

In 1974 Brenner returned to the United States to get his doctorate in number theory from the University of California at Los Angeles. In addition, he started to work as a software consultant. Brenner completed his degree in 1984 and found through his consulting business that DNA identification work, or the use of people's DNA samples to establish kinship (in cases involving paternity questions or immigration status) or guilt or innocence (in criminal cases) engaged his interest in both mathematics and computers. His work led to the development of the DNA analyzation software called DNA-View, which is now used by some 50 laboratories around the world and is serviced by Brenner himself. "We are always reading about people who are very critical about the justice system," Brenner told Dreifus. "With this kind of work, at least you have something you can hold on to. It's a tool that can make the system more just." Brenner is now one of the world's few fully employed freelance mathematicians and calls his field forensic mathematics. "It's a term that I invented," he explained to Dreifus. "It has to do with the application of mathematics in the courts. Virtually all I do is DNA identification. The most obvious example is I work out probabilities." To elaborate, Brenner or other mathematicians or scientists use his software to analyze DNA samples—most often in paternity or inheritance cases. If there are similarities in samples from two people, the next step is to try to measure the probability that the similarity is simply coincidence. If the probability is low, then one is looking at almost irrefutable evidence. Although mathematicians cannot determine beyond a doubt whether DNA samples match exactly, they can come extremely close. "If you prove it to one chance in a million or one chance in a hundred thousand," Brenner explained to Gina Kolata for the *New York Times* (August 9, 1998), "that's better proof than most of us ever see." Immigration services of several countries have bought his software.

Although Brenner mostly advises other scientists on DNA data, he sometimes takes on clients and cases himself. Among other projects, he helped reunite family members who were separated in the "dirty war" in Argentina in the 1970s, when parents were massacred by the military and their children given to childless military couples. He also helped to establish which children were the illegitimate offspring of the late American millionaire Larry Hillblom and were thus entitled to inheritance money, as they had not been specifically disinherited in Hillblom's will. In 1998 Brenner became a visiting scholar at the Department of Public Health at the University of California, Berkeley, a position he still holds. He has held similar posts throughout his career. "I like teaching as an academic exercise," he told Dreifus. "But in many places, the academic environment can be stultifying. So [traveling and advising scientists] is a wonderful alternative. I get to travel the world, encounter different cultures, rub shoulders with some great scientists, and I get to look at vexing human problems." In addition to bridge, his hobbies include bicycling up steep hills and traveling, by his own admission using business as an excuse to indulge in the latter. — G.O.

Suggested Reading: *New York Times* (on-line) Aug. 8, 2000

Welton B. Doby II/Courtesy of HarperCollins

Briscoe, Connie

Dec. 31, 1952– Novelist. Address: c/o HarperCollins Publishers, 10 E. 53d St., New York, NY 10022-5299

Like Terry McMillan, Connie Briscoe is an African-American writer whose best-selling novels—beginning with her first, *Sisters and Lovers* (1994)—deal with the romantic ups and downs of black women. But unlike McMillan's books, Briscoe's work has also taken on such themes as political action and personal responsibility, in *Big Girls Don't Cry* (1996), and slavery, in *A Long Way from Home* (1999). In a piece about her third novel, she wrote for *Essence* (July 1999): "Our ancestors used their wits and intelligence to carve out a tolerable existence. . . . If they could do so much back then, I have no excuse on Earth for not getting ahead now. This is the message we ought to be handing down to our children."

The older of two daughters, Connie Briscoe was born on December 31, 1952 in Washington, D.C. "I had a happy, normal childhood in every way," Briscoe wrote for the Author Biographies section of the Public Library of Charlotte & Mecklenburg County (PLCMC) Web site. "Although shy and quiet in my early years, I began to get a little rebellious in my teens—but nothing far out of the ordinary." She graduated from Hampton University, in Virginia, then enrolled in a graduate program in urban affairs at American University, in Washington. "The only thing unusual about my life," Briscoe wrote, is the hearing loss that runs in her father's family. By her late 20s, she had gone from a 20 percent hearing loss to an 80 percent loss. "First, you can't hear things on the phone. Then you can't hear it ring," Briscoe explained to Felicia R. Lee in an interview for the *New York Times* (September 2, 1999, on-line). "You make excuses for what's happening. Then you get to the point you can't ignore it anymore. I went through the period of the doctors, the emotional adjustment, but I'm lucky I have a supportive family."

After college and graduate studies, Briscoe did research for a time at a computer firm, then got an editorial job at the Joint Center for Political Studies in Washington, where she did not advance as quickly as she would have liked. "My career wasn't progressing the way I wanted it to because I couldn't use the telephone," she told *Essence* (July 1994) in an interview. She later joined the editorial staff at Gallaudet University, in Washington, the nation's only university for the deaf, eventually becoming managing editor of the Gallaudet publication *American Annals of the Deaf*. As she told an interviewer for the *Quarterly Black Review* (on-line), her career as an editor is tied to her fiction writing: "I can remember thinking about wanting to be a writer way back when I was a young girl, but back then during the 60s and 70s it was something I thought black people did not aspire to do. . . . So I pursued other things career-wise." But she finally entered the world of publishing, "because the need to work with the written word was so strong. In some ways I believe I was preparing myself slowly, making the transition. I can see how I was inching towards that novel. Working as an editor was part of that process, and it worked to make me a better writer." She told *Essence* that during "the period between losing my hearing and learning to cope with it," she started writing a mystery novel, which she never completed.

Briscoe married at the age of 28; the union ended after a few years. "Maybe I lowered my standards too far," she explained to David Streitfeld in an interview for the *Washington Post* (July 23, 1994). "Now I'd rather wait until I find the almost-perfect person." It was the ongoing search for the "almost-perfect person," and the difficulties faced by other African-American women during that process, that inspired her first published novel, *Sisters and Lovers* (1994). The story of three sisters, Beverly, Evelyn, and Charmaine, and the men in their lives, it became a best-seller and enabled Briscoe to pursue a full-time career as a writer.

The character most closely identified with Briscoe herself is the unmarried Beverly, who endures many terrible dates in her search for a mate—an experience similar to the author's, according to Streitfeld. Beverly's sisters are married but have problems at home. Charmaine's husband is unfaithful, and Evelyn, a psychologist who has married a successful lawyer, fears the consequences—including the effect on her expensive lifestyle—if her husband quits his job and starts his own firm. Beverly's travails include clashes with her family over her choice to date a white man when she is unable to find a suitable black mate. Beverly is "almost 30, with not a thing to show for it except a halfway decent paycheck. No man, no kids, no house. Nothing that really mattered," Briscoe wrote.

Sisters and Lovers was for Stephanie B. Goldberg, the reviewer for the *Chicago Tribune* (July 31, 1984), "the perfect commentary on postmodern romance." Goldberg noted that in today's world, "the object isn't to be rescued by a handsome prince but merely to meet one's equal." A number of other reviewers echoed Goldberg's favorable assessment. Angela Washington-Blair, writing for the *Library Journal* (April 1, 1994), termed the novel "at once humorous, poignant, realistic, and romantic," with "witty but realistic dialog" that refreshingly portrays "black women in a positive light." Comparing Briscoe with Terry McMillan, Roz Spafford, who reviewed the novel for the *Washington Post Book World* (May 1, 1994), found that in contrast to McMillan, "Briscoe trusts plot and dialogue to carry her meaning." Although she wished for "more complexity in her characters' evolution as well as in the structure of the book itself," she deemed "Briscoe's message . . . a warm one and the novel . . . entirely readable."

A dissenting voice came from Karen Ray, who, writing for the *New York Times Book Review* (September 18, 1994), found the male characters "thinly portrayed" and called the novel "commercial fiction at its most commercial—a little preachy, a lot contrived." Reacting to such charges, Briscoe told Streitfeld, who called her "unabashedly a commercial writer," that reviewers were misguided when they compared her with "more literary women," such as Alice Walker or Toni Morrison. "I shouldn't be compared to them any more than you would compare, say, Judith Krantz to Edith Wharton," she declared.

That comment notwithstanding, Briscoe's second novel, *Big Girls Don't Cry* (1996), deals with themes more weighty than those addressed in most commercial fare—namely, political issues facing the African-American community. The main character, Naomi Jefferson, growing up in Washington in the 1960s, has to confront racism. Her father advocates patience, but her older brother is a radical. When her brother dies in an accident on the way to a civil rights demonstration, she picks up the torch of action, organizing a demonstration in response to her college statistics teacher's statement that African-American women are incapable of excelling at mathematics. "The prejudice against women and minorities in technological fields is one of Briscoe's main themes," Emily Listfield observed in the *Washington Post Book World* (April 28, 1996). "Briscoe, a talented writer, is not afraid to take on serious concerns: racism, the glass ceiling, the importance of personal responsibility." Naomi's first moves toward taking on responsibility are unsuccessful; the demonstration achieves nothing. Her disappointment is compounded when she discovers that her boyfriend is cheating on her, and she descends into drugs and promiscuity before recovering her bearings and going on to a successful career in a high-tech company. "The obstacles that Naomi faces are genuine, but they are drawn here with a sketchiness that undermines their impact," Listfield wrote. "Riddled with stock characters and pat answers, *Big Girls Don't Cry* never truly engages us the way Briscoe's wonderful first novel, *Sisters and Lovers*, did. Instead, it reads more like an inspirational allegory than a compelling tale."

After the publication of *Big Girls Don't Cry*, Briscoe entered a period of intensive historical research into her own family origins that was to culminate in her third novel, *A Long Way from Home* (1999), a story of Founding Father James Madison's slaves. Susan, who was Briscoe's great-great-grandmother, and Ellen are sisters born on the plantation owned by Madison; the identity of their father is unclear. In the novel Susan marries a former slave, Oliver, who has been able to buy his freedom. "While researching my slave ancestors . . . ," Briscoe wrote in a piece for *Essence* (July 1999), "I came across the usual grim tales of whippings, sales, and miscegenation. But I also uncovered stories of love and hope. One of the most heartwarming was the story my Grandma Corine told me about how my great-great-grandparents met in a park in Richmond, Virginia. Oliver would walk through the park on his way to the store, and Susan would take her master's children there to play. Oliver could write and had bought his freedom, and Susan was a slave. I don't know if Susan was literate, but she was clever enough to snag a smart, industrious brother like Oliver. I love that story. It shows, despite the bleakness of slavery, moments of tenderness and triumph."

In the novel, Oliver's plea for Susan's freedom is preempted by the fall of Richmond in the Civil War. As Susan flees, the master to whom she has been sold tries to give her a bag of coins to help her on her way. "But just like back then, he wasn't prepared to give her what he'd denied her all these years, what she wanted most. An identity. A real family. So she wanted nothing else from him," Briscoe explained, as quoted by Felicia R. Lee. Although her family lore places Briscoe in the Madison family, no real proof exists, as she told Lee. "It's a side of slavery and that era we don't talk about, but it's an open secret. There are a lot of us walking around who don't know who our great-grandfather was or hear stories about white ancestors."

Kim McLarin, who reviewed *A Long Way from Home* for *Emerge* (August 1997), praised the novel as being "lively, enjoyable, and original. . . . Briscoe effectively illuminates the dehumanizing and demeaning effects of slavery, even under 'good' masters." She concluded, however, that a defect in the novel was Briscoe's failure to make the history come alive. "Briscoe seems constrained by the history behind the narrative. There's not enough room for fictionalization to invigorate the book's more predictable elements. . . . By the book's end, the characters' stories don't haunt you the way the corrupt institution that inspired them continues to haunt our national imagination."

According to Felicia R. Lee, Briscoe, who is "thin and sandy-haired," communicates by reading lips and employing a sign-language interpreter; she can speak, "although her diction is somewhat muffled." Lee wrote that Briscoe "spends no time feeling sorry for herself or other black people and says that awareness of the wrenching abuses that black people historically endured can put steel in the spine of African-Americans today." Briscoe told Lee that by "not looking into our history and our past in a realistic way, we are depriving our young people. We are too accepting of the history of ourselves that has been handed down and written about." As she wrote in *Essence*, "One of the things that kept me going is best expressed by the Ghanaian word *sankofa*, which means 'in order to move forward we must understand the past.'" — S.Y.

Suggested Reading: *Chicago Tribune* XIV p5 July 31, 1994; *Emerge* p80 Aug. 1997; *Essence* p32 July 1994, p95+ July 1999, with photo; *Library Journal* p130 Apr. 1, 1994; *New York Times* (online) Sep. 2, 1999; *New York Times Book Review* p20 Sep. 18, 1994; *Washington Post* C p1 July 23, 1994; *Washington Post Book World* p11 May 1, 1994

Selected Books: *Sisters and Lovers*, 1994; *Big Girls Don't Cry*, 1996; *A Long Way from Home*, 1999

Courtesy of Center for Astrophysics and Space Sciences, UCSD, 1978

Burbidge, E. Margaret

Aug. 12, 1919– Astronomer; college professor. Address: Center for Astrophysics and Space Sciences, University of California, San Diego, CA 92093

"I believe that the picture of the universe we have now is much too simplistic," the astronomer and astrophysicist E. Margaret Burbidge told Yvonne Baskin for the *San Diego Union* (February 28, 1985). "I believe the real thing is much more complicated." A native of Great Britain, Burbidge has devoted the past six decades to increasing our understanding of the universe. Overcoming sexual discrimination in what has traditionally been a male-dominated field, she is ranked among the leaders of her discipline and has earned many prestigious awards for her achievements, among them the National Medal of Science and the American Astronomical Society's Warner Prize. In collaboration with her husband, Geoffrey Burbidge, who is also a distinguished astronomer, she has investigated the composition and evolution of stars, the nature of quasars, and the properties of galaxies, among other astronomical phenomena. "Geoff has the ideas," she told Timothy Green for *Smithsonian* (January 1974), "I do the observing."

Burbidge began teaching at the University of California at San Diego in 1962; she directed the university's Center for Astrophysics and Space Sciences for nearly a decade, and in 1984 she was named a university professor, an honor bestowed upon only a handful of the university's scholars. During her long career she has also worked at the University of London Observatory; the Cavendish Laboratory, at Cambridge University; the California Institute of Technology; and the University of Chicago, and she has viewed the heavens through a bevy of world-class telescopes. She was the first woman to serve as the director of the Royal Greenwich Observatory, in England, and has served as president of both the American Astronomical Society and the American Association for the Advancement of Science (AAAS). She also helped design and interpret data from instruments carried on the Hubble Space Telescope. In a statement written for *Science* (February 27, 1981) after Burbidge had been elected president of the AAAS, the astronomer Vera C. Rubin described her as "a leader in the drive to observe from space, a spokesperson for the astronomical community, and a strong supporter of women and minorities in science." She also wrote, "Her leadership capabilities, obvious in all phases of her career, are combined with a warm and friendly personality, and have made for her a wide circle of friends and colleagues throughout the world."

Burbidge was born Eleanor Margaret Peachey on August 12, 1919 to Stanley Peachey, a research chemist and teacher, and Marjorie Peachey. Marjorie had studied chemistry under Stanley at the Manchester School of Technology, but she did not pursue a career in the field. Their daughter first became aware of the beauty of celestial bodies at the age of four, while crossing the English Channel. "We slept in bunks on the boat and I felt seasick," Burbidge told Timothy Green for *Smithsonian* (January 1974), "so my mother took me into her upper berth, and to distract me, showed me the stars through a porthole." As a young girl she enjoyed reading books on astronomy for children by the British astronomer and physicist James Jeans, a distant relative of her family's. At age 12, Lisa Yount reported in *A to Z of Women in Science and Math* (1999), Margaret "was delighted to learn that astronomy involved not only stars but her other favorite thing, large numbers." "I decided then and there that the occupation I most wanted to engage in 'when I was grown up' was to determine the distances of stars," Yount quoted her as saying.

Burbidge graduated from the Francis Holland School, a private primary and secondary school for girls in central London. She then enrolled at University College, London (part of the University of London), which—unlike most other colleges at the time—offered a major in astronomy, so that, contrary to her long-held assumption, she did not have to specialize in physics or math. She was one of only four University College students, and the only woman, who majored in astronomy. In 1939, after earning a B.S. degree, with first-class honors, she enrolled in the graduate program of the University of London Observatory. Thanks to the blackouts enforced in London during World War II, the sky was dark enough for stargazing, and she became skilled at operating the observatory's one functional telescope. She was awarded a Ph.D. degree in 1943. Her curriculum vitae does not indicate what she did during the next two years. In 1945 she took a course in higher physics at University College, where she met Geoffrey Burbidge, who was then working toward a Ph.D. degree in physics; the two married in 1948. Earlier, in 1946, on the strength of her facility with the telescope, she had secured a job as an assistant to the director of the University of London Observatory. By the time she left, in 1951, she had become the observatory's acting director.

In Great Britain, frequent cloudiness and other climatic conditions often make it difficult to view any heavenly bodies. "I began to realize that if I really wanted to do observational astronomy, I'd have to leave the country," Burbidge told Timothy Green. The ideal setting for a telescope, she explained to him, is a "clear climate, far from pollution, and at an altitude of between 5,000 and 9,000 feet. Then you need a steady atmosphere, because hot and cold ascents and descents can blur the image . . . an empty place away from civilization, where the prevailing wind comes off the ocean." In 1947 Burbidge applied for a Carnegie Fellowship to study at the Mount Wilson Observatory, outside Pasadena, California, in the San Gabriel Mountains; in response, she received a letter informing her that the facility had only one toilet and that only men could work there. The next year she got permission to use the telescope at the Haute-Provence Observatory, in southeastern France, where conditions are excellent for astronomical observations about 170 nights a year. The month that she spent at Haute-Provence, she told Timothy Green, "was a revelation. After England the sky was so *clear*."

Beginning in 1951, having won a fellowship from the International Astronomical Union, Burbidge did research for two years at the Yerkes Observatory; located in Williams Bay, Wisconsin, the observatory is a research branch of the University of Chicago's Department of Astronomy and Astrophysics. Her husband also spent a year as a research fellow at the university, after working for a year at Harvard University, in Cambridge, Massachusetts, as an Agassiz Fellow. (By that time—thanks to his marriage to an astronomer, as he has said—he had become interested in astronomy as well as physics.) In 1953 the couple returned to England, to work at the Cavendish Laboratory, as the Department of Physics at Cambridge University is known; Margaret Burbidge served as a volunteer research associate. At the Cavendish Laboratory the Burbidges formed an association with the British astronomer and cosmologist Fred Hoyle and the American nuclear physicist William A. Fowler, the latter of whom worked at the California Institute of Technology (Caltech) but often visited Cambridge. The four began to collaborate on an investigation of the creation of chemical elements within stars—specifically, the transformation of hydrogen to helium and the transformation of helium to a form of carbon and other heavier elements—and the hypothesis that all chemical elements might originate in stars.

In 1955 Geoffrey Burbidge, despite his scant experience with telescopes, was awarded a Carnegie Fellowship to work at the Mount Wilson Observatory (the same fellowship for which Margaret had been turned down). At the same time, Margaret won a research fellowship from Caltech, in Pasadena. Barred from the all-male dormitory at the Mount Wilson Observatory, the Burbidges stayed in a nearby cottage, which had neither hot water nor a shower and where a small wood-burning stove served for both cooking and heating in the cold, snowy winter. Although women were not permitted to use any of the telescopes, Margaret actually spent far more time than her husband at telescopic observation. (Geoffrey told administrators that she was his "assistant.") Seated in the unheated dome of a Mount Wilson telescope, Margaret (who was then pregnant) photographed stars—or, rather, the light emanating from stars; later, through what is known as spectral analysis, she, Geoffrey, Hoyle, and Fowler determined which elements were present in the stars. (Although several members of the Mount Wilson Observatory staff protested the administrators' policy of excluding women, nearly a decade passed before women gained the right to use the facility's telescopes.)

In 1957 the Burbidges returned to the University of Chicago, where, because of a policy against nepotism, Margaret suffered further discrimination: while her husband earned a full salary as an assistant professor of astronomy, she had to settle for a research fellowship, while teaching astronomy as an associate professor. (Such rules against favoritism based on kinship "are always used against the wife," Margaret Burbidge has said, as quoted by Yount.) That same year Margaret and Geoffrey Burbidge, Fowler, and Hoyle published an 89-page paper entitled "Synthesis of the Elements of Stars" in *Reviews of Modern Physics*, the scholarly journal of the American Physical Society; now considered a seminal contribution to the then–new field of nuclear astrophysics, the paper shed light on the evolution of stars and the way in which nuclear reactions within stars produce chemical elements of increasingly great atomic weights. The ideas it presented became known as the B^2FH theory (read as "B squared F H"), in honor of the first letters of its originators' surnames. "Ultimately," Vera C. Rubin wrote in 1981, "B^2FH brought eight nuclear processes into recognition: hydrogen burning, helium burning, the alpha-, e-, s-, r-, and p-processes, and the x-processes, x for an unknown but necessary process to produce the especially difficult isotope of deuterium, and also lithium, beryllium, and boron." It is now possible, because of those findings, to reconstruct the way in which the production of heavy elements proceeds in stars "and in successive generations of stars in our galaxy," Rubin wrote. In 1959 the American Astronomical Society recognized the importance of the B^2FH theory and the Burbidges' role in its development by naming them co-winners of the Helen B. Warner Prize for Astronomy.

In 1962 the University of California at San Diego (UCSD) hired Geoffrey Burbidge to teach in the Department of Physics. (The university does not have a separate department of astronomy; the Center for Astrophysics and Space Sciences is part of the Department of Physics.) Because of a school policy designed to avoid nepotism, Margaret was accepted as a member of the Department of Chemistry, while holding the title of associate research physicist. In 1964 UCSD abolished its antinepotism rule, and Margaret joined her husband as a full professor in the physics department. Earlier in the decade, she had begun conducting some of the earliest research into the nature of quasars—formally known as quasi-stellar radio sources. ("Radio" refers to electromagnetic waves with radio frequencies, that is, frequencies within a specified range; the frequencies used in radio and television transmission lie within that range.) Quasars are believed to be as bright as a trillion suns or a thousand galaxies, but because they are so distant from Earth—many billions of light-years away, making them among the most distant objects yet detected by astronomers—they cannot be seen with the naked eye and are much more easily perceived by means of radio telescopes (which capture radio waves) than optical telescopes (which gather light). Burbidge showed that quasars were distinguished by significant red shifts. "Red" indicates the red end of the visible spectrum of light, where the wavelengths of light are longest; "red shifts" are changes toward ever-longer wavelengths. The increasing wavelengths of light emitted by quasars indicated that the distances between these mysterious objects and Earth were increasing at incredibly rapid rates; at least some quasars may have been traveling at speeds as great as 95 percent of the speed of light. (Light is believed to travel faster than anything else in the universe; in a vacuum, its speed is 186,000 miles per second.)

In 1967 Margaret and Geoffrey Burbidge published a book, *Quasi-Stellar Objects*; the first comprehensive work on quasars, it is considered a classic in its field. In the preface to their book *Quasars and Active Galactic Nuclei* (1999), Ajit K. Kembhavi and Jayant V. Narlikar wrote, "*Quasi-Stellar Objects* . . . captured the excitement generated by the early research on quasars" that Geoffrey and Margaret Burbidge and others had done "and posed the numerous challenges of quasar astronomy very succinctly." They added, "Now, three decades later, we have the benefits of vast progress in the techniques of observational extragalactic astronomy and the intricate sophistication of ideas in high energy astrophysics. Yet it is fair to say that the understanding of quasars and the related field of active galactic nuclei . . . has not reached the same level of success that stellar studies had attained 30 years ago."

During this time Margaret Burbidge also began research concerning the dynamics and masses of galaxies, which are huge assemblages of stars, gas, dust, and other matter—the other matter including Earth, its moons, and other planets and their moons in the case of the Milky Way, the galaxy of which our solar system is a part. Galaxies intrigued her because, as she told Timothy Green, they are "the building blocks of the universe." At the McDonald Observatory, a facility operated by the University of Texas at Austin, she recorded the spectra of spiral galaxies, from which she determined the velocities of clouds of ionized gas. Later, with the help of both her husband and Kevin Prendergast (now a professor of astronomy at Columbia University, in New York City), she measured the rotational properties and masses of more than 50 spiral galaxies; by 1970, her research and work linked to it accounted for most of what was then known about galaxy dynamics.

In 1972 Margaret Burbidge returned to England to take the post of director of the Royal Greenwich Observatory; founded in 1675, it was the oldest scientific institution in Great Britain. When Timothy Green asked her why she had agreed to work in "cloudy Britain" again, she said, "For years I've been a user of telescopes that others have put hard work into producing, so I felt it was time I did some of the organizing myself. And it is decades since there was anything reasonable here for optical astronomers to work with, so I wanted to try to provide good facilities for the young British astronomers." In what many charged was an act of sex discrimination, Burbidge did not receive the title "astronomer royal," an honor bestowed upon all of the observatory's previous directors; instead, the title was given to Martin Ryle, a leader in the development of radio astronomy. Undaunted, Burbidge concentrated on reviving Britain's sagging reputation for optical astronomy. She sought to complete two tasks—to hasten the construction of a 150-inch telescope in Siding Spring, Australia, and to create the Northern Hemisphere Observatory, which would be based in England but would make use of telescopes in more suitable climates. But before long she began to feel stymied; moreover, she missed her husband, who had remained in California, having failed to find satisfactory employment in Great Britain. In October 1973 she announced her resignation from the post, effective in early 1974. (The observatory closed in 1998.)

Burbidge then returned to UCSD, where she later served (1979–88) as the director of the university's Center for Astrophysics and Space Sciences. As the first female president of the American Astronomical Society (1976–78), she persuaded the organization to refuse to hold meetings in states that had not ratified the Equal Rights Amendment to the Constitution. In 1978 she became the first female astronomer elected to the National Academy of Sciences. In 1982 she served as president of the American Association for the Advancement of Science (an elective office) and in 1983 as chairwoman of its board of directors.

Burbidge helped to design the Faint Object Spectrograph (FOS), one of the instruments installed on the Hubble Space Telescope. The most sophisticated device of its kind, the FOS is 350 times more powerful than comparable instruments on Earth, in terms of the clarity and abundance of spectra it records. From 1990 until 1996 Burbidge was the co-principal investigator for the team that worked with data emanating from the FOS, which have provided additional clues into the nature of both black holes and quasars. According to Margaret Burbidge's home page on the World Wide Web, "Among the important results from the FOS team was conclusive evidence for the presence of a massive black hole in the nucleus of the nearby elliptical galaxy, M87."

In 1972 Burbidge was awarded the Annie J. Cannon Prize from the American Astronomical Society, but she refused to accept it, on the ground that since that honor was awarded only to women, its existence represented just the sort of discrimination she had long worked so hard to eliminate. "Because of the small number of women in the field," she told the society, as quoted by *Time* (March 20, 1972), she would not be surprised "if we all in our turn are selected for the prize." In 1982 she became the first woman in the 84-year history of the Astronomy Society of the Pacific to receive its Catherine Wolfe Bruce Medal; one of the highest honors in astronomy, the prize is awarded for a lifetime of achievement and distinguished service in the field. In 1985 President Ronald Reagan presented Burbidge with the National Medal of Science, pointing to her work as "proof that there are no limits to discovery and human progress when men and women are free to follow their dreams," as Yvonne Baskin reported. Burbidge's other honors include the 1988 Albert Einstein World Award of Science, from the World Cultural Council. From 1979 until 1981 she served on the Committee on Science and Public Policy of the National Academy of Sciences, a position in which she continued her career-long practice of communicating the importance of science to the public. Since 1990 she has held the title university professor emeritus at UCSD; she is a research professor there as well. Burbidge and her husband live in La Jolla, California. Their only child, Sarah, studied law. — C.L.

Suggested Reading: *New York Times* D p5 Feb. 15, 2000, with photos; *San Diego Union* B p1+ Feb. 3, 1980, with photos; *Smithsonian* p34+ Jan. 1974, with photos; *Time* p38 Mar. 20, 1972, with photos; Overbye, Dennis. *Lonely Hearts of the Cosmos: The Scientific Quest for the Secret of the Universe*, 1991; Yount, Lisa. *A to Z of Women in Science and Math*, 1999

Selected Works: *Quasi-Stellar Objects* (with Geoffrey Burbidge), 1967

Burton, LeVar

Feb. 16, 1957– Film and television actor.
Address: c/o Reading Rainbow, Lancit Media Productions, 601 W. 50th St., New York, NY 10019

From his explosive debut as the African slave Kunta Kinte in the television miniseries *Roots* (1977), to his nearly 20-year run as host of PBS's *Reading Rainbow*, to his turn as the blind engineer Geordi LaForge on the TV series *Star Trek: The Next Generation*, the actor LeVar Burton has defied stereotyping. An effervescent, spiritual man who often refers to himself in the third person, Burton has strived to give his work meaning and depth, selecting roles for their emotional weight as well as their entertainment value. "I'm really lucky," he told Scott Moore for the *Washington Post* (July 31, 1993). "I've been in some of the finest productions since the medium [of television] was created. I can't think of a better career, a better job."

Laura Luongo/Outline Press

LeVar Burton

Levardis Robert Martyn Burton Jr. was born on February 16, 1957 in Landstuhl, West Germany. His father, Levardis Sr., an army sergeant, was stationed in Germany as a photographer. His parents separated when LeVar Jr. was three, and his mother, Erma Christian, a teacher, took him and his two sisters to live in Sacramento, California. Today all he remembers of his father are some photos that his father took. His childhood, Burton recalled to Louie Robinson for *Ebony* (October 1977), "was very comfortable. We never hurt for anything. . . . Ma always saw to it that her kids had the best of education." She also encouraged recreational reading. "Reading was like breathing in the house where I grew up," Burton told Jackie Hyman for the *Chicago Tribune* (July 13, 1993).

The Roman Catholic religion was also prominent in Burton's upbringing. By age seven he felt called to the priesthood, and at 13 he entered a seminary. "I used to dream that when I preached my first sermon, I would knock them dead, have them roaring in the aisles," he recalled to Stephen Godfrey for the Toronto *Globe and Mail* (July 22, 1980). "I had a tremendous need for public expression and communication, and it seemed like the best means to do that." By age 15, however, he felt differently. "I just realized . . . that there were a lot of things I didn't know about the world," he told Robinson, "a lot of things I still didn't know about myself, and it was just too early to make that kind of life commitment: celibacy and the whole trip."

After giving up thoughts of the priesthood, Burton made acting his goal. He left the seminary and successfully applied for an acting scholarship to the University of California (UC). In 1976 he played a leading role in *Almos' a Man*, a 38-minute film, directed by Stan Lathan, that was based on a short story by Richard Wright. While rehearsals were underway for a UC production of *Oklahoma*, in which Burton had a major part, the casting director Lynn Stallmaster asked the UC drama department to recommend a young black student for the television miniseries *Roots*. Based on Alex Haley's Pulitzer Prize–winning book *Roots: The Saga of an American Family* (1976), the miniseries traced the painful journey of Haley's ancestors from Africa to the U.S. and enslavement, and then their fight for freedom and equality. Burton auditioned for the role of Kunta Kinte, a young Mandinka warrior who is taken in chains from Africa and forced into slavery. "They told me that I looked right for the part . . . ," Burton told Robinson. "They were looking for somebody 18 or 19 who could look 15 or 16, somebody with the maturity and intelligence to understand the subject matter, but who also could come off as a young kid." After several meetings and screen tests, Burton won the part.

Filming the series, on location in Savannah, Georgia, proved to be very trying for Burton. "The scenes in the hold of the ship were the toughest to recreate for the film," he told Robinson. "There's something I like to think of as 'sense memory': even though I have personally never undergone any experience like being captured, put in chains, and living in the dark hold of a ship in my own waste and that of others around me for weeks or months, it all came back to me, just like the memory of voyages of my ancestors; in fact, the voyage of Kunta Kinte that I was living. And it hurt. It was the psychological effect, not to mention the physical anguish and discomfort that we experienced." The hard work paid off. *Roots*, which debuted on ABC-TV on January 23, 1977, was an enormous success. Attracting an average of 130 million viewers with each installment, it became the most-watched television show in the history of television till then. "The movie made us begin to look at each other differently," Burton told Alan Carter for the New York *Daily News* (January 18, 1987). "It changed the perception of how black people saw themselves and how others saw us." That change was illustrated by an anecdote that Haley related to Carter: "A young white boy came up to me yesterday in Texas and said that his father always hated my people. But after seeing *Roots* the boy said he watched his father cry for the first time in his life."

With the success of *Roots*, Burton became an instant star. He left college, moved into a spacious apartment in trendy Marina Del Rey, California, and bought his first car. Wherever he went, people recognized him. "I make it a point to get time to myself to keep a good part of my life still private just to keep my sanity," he told Robinson. "But I do like the public side of being a celebrity. I enjoy it an awful lot." Still, he did not escape the less positive aspects of sudden fame. "I was moving at a very fast pace," he confessed to Chris Pritchard for the *National Enquirer* (August 22, 1978). "I could have inadvertently committed suicide. I didn't have the same kind of self-destructive attitude that Freddie Prinze had. . . . But there were times when, in a very excited state, I might have driven off the edge of a cliff!" Before long the frequent displays of his quick temper and swelled head took their toll. One major casualty was his engagement to Winter Chapman. Burton eventually turned to psychotherapy. "I feel very stable right now," he said during his conversation with Pritchard, which took place a year and a half after his first appearance on TV, "and it's all the result of making a conscious effort to move through my problems." A decade later he told Elaine Warren for *TV Guide* (August 13, 1988), "The most worthwhile endeavor I have ever undertaken is responsibility for my own life. It's hard, and it's worth it."

In his next acting jobs after *Roots*, Burton had a bit part in the film *Looking for Mr. Goodbar* (1977) and starred in the television movies *One in a Million: The Ron LeFlore Story* and *Battered*, both in 1978. In 1979 he played the title character in *Dummy*, a made-for-TV film based on the murder trial of Donald Lang, who was deaf, mute, and illiterate. "To play a two-hour drama without speaking one word presents obvious obstacles for an actor," he told Bob Thomas for *TV Radio Week* (May 27, 1979). "There was not much I could do except just resort to being an actor." Burton next accepted a small role in the film *The Hunter* (1980), with Steve McQueen, thinking it would be a stepping stone to parts in feature films. "I can't say I would have chased after [the *Hunter* assignment]," he told Godfrey in 1980. "But this is a career choice. McQueen likes my work and is definitely helping to push me into films." But offers from Hollywood failed to come his way, and he returned to television, where, in the summer of 1983, he debuted as the host of the educational children's program *Reading Rainbow*. He has served in that capacity ever since.

"I am a lover of words," Burton told Arthur Unger for the *Christian Science Monitor* (July 8, 1983). "The written word is something we can't afford to let go of. We've already butchered the English language to the point of unrecognizability in spoken slang. So losing books in which proper English is used would be a disaster." For each episode of *Reading Rainbow*, Burton or a guest actor reads aloud the text of a selected book; then, with the aim of bringing the subject matter to life, he demonstrates an aspect of the book or is shown in an environment inspired by it. "I get to do great things," Burton told Carol Mauro for *Dial* (July 1984). "Like riding on horseback. And I get to exercise a lot of my fantasies, like dancing with eight professionals. I get to go [to] great places—the New England Aquarium, in Boston, the Dinosaur National Monument, in Utah. . . . It may sound corny, but this show has also been hours of growth and experience for L.B." Thanks in large part to Burton, in its first season *Reading Rainbow* attracted 6.5 million viewers. "LeVar is someone kids relate to," Tony Buttino, the program's executive producer, remarked to Mauro. "He instills in children a total feeling of trust." The show has earned a slew of Emmy Awards, and Burton garnered a 1994 Image Award for outstanding performance in a children's series.

Burton flirted briefly with the idea of leaving *Reading Rainbow* to give himself greater flexibility in the shooting of *Star Trek: The Next Generation* (the first of several series inspired by the original *Star Trek*, which had a three-year run in the 1960s). He decided to stick with the children's series because he felt that it was "important work," as he told Elaine Warren. "I really feel that with this show I'm able to contribute significantly to the lives of a pretty important group of people on the planet. I meditated on it, and it just felt like the right thing to do." In a 1998 interview with Christopher Brandon for *TNT Rough Cut* (on-line), Burton said that he planned to continue with the series indefinitely.

At about the same time that he starting working on *Reading Rainbow*, Burton learned that he had fathered a son. Then three years old, the child was the product of Burton's brief relationship with a woman who has not been publicly identified. After blood tests confirmed his paternity, he obtained joint custody of the boy. Deciding to do so was easy for Burton, according to his lawyer, Gloria Allred. "He has a saying, 'A tree is only as strong as its roots'—and that's why, for LeVar, this goes much deeper than monetary support. He wants the boy to have a sense of family," Allred explained to a *New York Post* (July 1, 1983) reporter.

In 1987 Burton debuted on *Star Trek: The Next Generation* (*TNG*) as Lieutenant Commander Geordi LaForge, the blind chief engineer on the exploration starship *Enterprise*. To prepare for the role, he took a self-help course designed to teach reliance on senses other than sight. As part of the final assignment, he climbed a 30-foot pole blindfolded and then hurled himself into the air to grab a trapeze eight feet away. "I couldn't believe what I'd done," he later told Lois Armstrong for *People* (March 7, 1988). "It was the most alive I have ever felt." Burton detested the wraparound visor that his character wore, because it drastically reduced his vision. By the second *TNG* feature film, *Star Trek: First Contact* (1996), the character had been fitted with prosthetic eyes and had discarded the visor.

In 1988 the made-for-TV sequel *Roots: The Gift* premiered on ABC, to much acclaim. "I wouldn't have been able to do this even a few years ago," Burton, who reprised the role of Kunta Kinte in the film, told Nancy Mills for the New York *Daily News* (June 19, 1988), "because I would have felt I was forever and [in]extricably linking myself with Kunta for the rest of my career." *Roots: The Gift* is a tender story in which Kunta and his friend Fiddler, played by Louis Gossett Jr., lead a group of slaves to freedom on Christmas Eve. "I grew up in this country, and every year we'd sit around and watch *A Christmas Carol*," Burton told Mills. "Now my children will be able to see a black Christmas story, and white children can see what Christmas was like for blacks in this part of history."

On May 29, 1993 Burton made his debut as a director, with an episode of *TNG* in which Commander Riker, played by Jonathan Frakes, comes face-to-face with his alter ego. Others who had served as *TNG* directors gave him pointers. "I got . . . different advice from each," Burton told Ian Spelling for the *Chicago Tribune* (May 21, 1993). "They were pretty helpful; especially Jonathan [Frakes]. I couldn't have done it without him." Well-received by critics, the episode, entitled "Second Chances," featured a guest appearance by Mae Jemison, the first African-American female astronaut. Burton later directed other *TNG* installments.

In the spring of 1994, Paramount canceled *TNG*. Its termination angered many people, but, by his own account, Burton was not among them. "This has been a very fulfilling seven-year cycle in my life," he told a reporter for the *Vancouver Sun* (May 9, 1994), as quoted in *Contemporary Black Biography* (1995), "but I feel in my very being that it's time to move on." That fall he and his *TNG* castmates appeared in the film *Star Trek: Generations* (1994). An ambitious movie that pairs the original *Star Trek* series' Captain Kirk (William Shatner) with the new series' Captain Picard (Patrick Stewart), it drew pans from critics; nevertheless, fans attended in droves. Burton reprised the role of LaForge in *Star Trek: First Contact*, a full-throttle action film that pits the *Enterprise* crew against a race of cyborgs bent on dominating the universe. A smash hit, the film earned over $90 million at the box office; it was one of the few *Star Trek* films to appeal even to those not enamored of the TV series. Burton returned two years later in *Star Trek: Insurrection* (1998), in which marauding aliens threaten the peace on a fountain-of-youth planet. *Insurrection* gave Burton a chance to stretch his character a bit, notably in the scene in which LaForge regains his sight through the planet's curative powers. "I think it was important for him to have that experience," Burton told Brandon, "because it was one aspect of his character that always kept him from his friends. And the way they wrote the [scene], Geordi said, 'I've never seen a sunrise.' And that was it. And I said, 'No, no, no. That's not it. Geordi sees sunrises all the time. He had never seen a sunrise the way other human beings see it.'" Burton has since appeared in several *Star Trek* video games as well as an episode of *Star Trek: Voyager*.

In late 1994 or early 1995, Burton joined the cast of *Christy*, a family-oriented television series that chronicled the trials of a young teacher in a backwoods community in 1912; the show was canceled shortly after he signed on. He made a guest appearance on the TV series *Deadly Games* (1995), which Leonard Nimoy produced. The next year he played a villain in *Yesterday's Target* (1996), Barry Samson's R-rated science-fiction thriller for the silver screen.

Lately, Burton has branched out as a director. In addition to episodes of *Star Trek: Voyager* and *Star Trek: Deep Space Nine*, he directed the Showtime original movie *The Tiger Woods Story* (1998). An unauthorized profile of the golf prodigy, the film touched vicariously on some of Burton's own experiences. As he told Ann Oldenburg for *USA Today* (April 3, 1998), "It is a very difficult thing to be 21 years old and feel like you are the center of the universe." Burton's most recent directorial effort was the family comedy *Smart House* (1999), for the Disney Channel. On other fronts, he has provided the voice for the character Kwame, an African superhero who fights to protect the environment, on the long-running animated TBS series *Captain Planet and the Planeteers*. He runs a production company, Eagle Nation films, and has written a science-fiction novel, *Aftermath* (1997), about life in the U.S. in the wake of an earthquake, a race war, and other cataclysms.

Burton lives in Los Angeles with his wife, the makeup artist Stephanie Cozart Burton. Married since 1992, the couple have a daughter, Michaela, whose birth, in 1994, resulted from in vitro fertilization. In recent years Burton and his wife have spoken publicly about their problems with infertility. "In this culture, there is still the traditional stigma, especially among men, against seeking help," he told Nadine Brozan for the *New York Times* (October 15, 1996). "Technology has advanced to the point where you owe it to yourself to honor the desire that exists to bring children into the world. There are miracles available." — J.K.B.

Suggested Reading: *Dial* p21+ July 1984, with photos; *Ebony* p146+ Oct. 1977, with photos; New York *Daily News* C p28 June 19, 1980, with photos, p23 Jan. 18, 1987, with photos; *People* p27+ Feb. 21, 1977, with photos, p65+ Mar. 7, 1988, with photos; *TV Guide* p13+ Aug. 13, 1988, with photos

Selected Films: *Almos' a Man*, 1976; *Looking for Mr. Goodbar*, 1977; *The Hunter*, 1980; *Star Trek: Generations*, 1994; *Star Trek: First Contact*, 1996; *Trekkies*, 1997; *Star Trek: Insurrection*, 1998

Selected Television Shows: *Rebop*, 1976; *Roots*, 1977; *Billy: Portrait of a Street Kid*, 1977; *One in a Million: The Ron LeFlore Story*, 1978; *Battered*, 1978; *Dummy*, 1979; *Guyana Tragedy: The Story of Jim Jones*, 1980; *The Acorn People*, 1981; *Reading Rainbow*, 1983– ; *The Jesse Owens Story*, 1984; *And the Children Shall Lead*, 1985; *Star Trek: The Next Generation*, 1987–94; *Roots: The Gift*, 1988; *Captain Planet and the Planeteers*, 1990; *Firestorm: 72 Hours in Oakland*, 1993; *Christy*, 1994; *Yesterday's Target*, 1996; as director—*The Tiger Woods Story*, 1998; *Smart House*, 1999

Courtesy of John Byrne

Byrne, John

1950– Comic-book artist and writer. Address: Marvel Entertainment Group, 387 Park Ave., New York, NY 10016

Writer and artist John Byrne, one of the major figures in comic books, has drawn or written stories for virtually every superhero in the Marvel Comics and DC Comics stables. As a young boy he was a great admirer of the legendary work of writer Stan Lee and artist Jack Kirby, who in the early 1960s established the "Marvel Age" of comics. Lee and Kirby's very human superheroes, who battled all manner of angst and dealt with everyday problems when not fighting villains and saving the world, inspired Byrne to become a comic-book artist. Employed first by the now-defunct publisher Charlton Comics, Byrne gained a reputation for a crisp, detailed drawing style and soon found himself working on Marvel's most popular magazine, the *X-Men*, which he took to new heights in the late 1970s and early 1980s. From 1981 to 1986 he was the chief writer and artist for the *Fantastic Four*, bringing that series a popularity it had not known since its inception under Lee and Kirby. In 1986 DC Comics offered him the challenge of a lifetime—to revamp and modernize Superman, the grandfather of all superheroes. Byrne responded with a hugely successful limited series of stories that simplified the legend, at once harkening back to the character's origins and contemporizing his new adventures. Since then, Byrne has received many offers from both DC and Marvel not only to work on new characters but also to revamp old ones. For DC he pumped new life into Wonder Woman; for Marvel he reinvented Spider-Man and fleshed out some of the X-Men's history. Having recently completed his run of Spider-Man titles, he is hard at work developing stories for the *X-Men: The Hidden Years* and *Marvel: The Lost Generation*.

John Byrne was born in 1950 in the town of West Bromwich, near Birmingham, England, and immigrated with his parents to Canada when he was eight. The family moved often throughout Canada, and young John attended nine different schools in 11 years. His first exposure to a comic-book character came through the 1950s television show *The Adventures of Superman*, starring George Reeves; afterward he began reading *Superman* comic books. At 12 he was introduced to the publications of the Marvel Comics Group through their fifth issue of the *Fantastic Four*. Unlike Superman, which by the early 1960s had been around for decades, the Fantastic Four had just been created, by Stan Lee and Jack Kirby. Bombarded by cosmic rays during an experimental rocket flight, the characters crash-landed on Earth to discover that each of them now had an extraordinary ability: Reed Richards, the leader of the group, discovered he could stretch his body to virtually any length or shape; Sue Storm, his fiancée, could become invisible at will; her brother, Johnny, had the power to burst into flame; and their friend and pilot Ben Grimm had transformed himself into a hideous, rock-like creature with tremendous strength. Realizing that they were now something more than human, they dedicated their lives to helping humanity—though that didn't prevent them from bickering like mere mortals and having everyday problems. Young Byrne was instantly captivated. "It blew me away," he told Mark Lerer for *Marvel Age* (May 1984). "First of all, the artwork was like nothing I had ever seen. It was more exciting, more alive—not necessarily more realistic, but more alive—than other comics. Second, it was a full-length story—not three little eight pagers! That bowled me over. And to top it all off, the action took place in New York! I knew that there was no such place as Metropolis [where Superman lives], but I knew that there was a New York—I had been there! . . . It made me wonder if it could be real."

In high school Byrne developed an interest in science fiction. "During that time I wrote about 15 novels, and it must be over 500 short stories. My parents' closet is full of them!" he told Mark Lerer. "The good ones eventually got turned into comic book stories, by the way—for example the Galactus story in *Fantastic Four* number 262 is based on one of those old stories I wrote then." But Marvel comics remained special to him. He was an ardent admirer of the art of Jack Kirby, who drew the Fantastic Four, the Avengers, and the X-Men, among others, and Steve Ditko, who drew such heroes as Spider-Man and Doctor Strange. He bought as many Marvel magazines as his parents would allow. He collected comic books until he was 15, when his attention was diverted by other interests. At 22 he began collecting again, tracking down all of the back issues he had missed.

Byrne attended the Alberta College of Art, in Calgary, but completed only two and a half years of their four-year program; he and his instructors agreed that there was little the school could offer someone who wanted to be a cartoonist—a label that belies how seriously Byrne pursues his art. In a column for *John Byrne's Next Men* (January 1993), Byrne complained about types of comic-book artists he termed "stylists," by which he meant those who can draw stylized figures in skin-tight outfits but who know little about the basics of art and visual composition. "An instructor of mine, back in Art College days, said it best (actually one of the few solid bits of usable information that came out of my Art College experience): to paint an abstraction, you must know what it is you're leaving out," he wrote. "[The artist Pablo] Picasso did not start with 'Guernica.' He started with perfectly defined, realistic renderings of the world around him. . . . Brother, if you can't draw the real world, you can't draw *nothing!*"

Beginning in the early 1970s, Byrne shopped his portfolio around to comic-book publishers. Some drawings were accepted by a comic-book fan magazine, also known as a fanzine, called *CPL*, which also published the work of such notables as Roger Stern and Bob Layton. Byrne was eventually hired by Charlton Comics to work on their low-end books, including *Wheelie and the Chopper Bunch* and *Doomsday + 1*. He also dabbled in writing story lines. Marvel took notice of his early work and asked him to pencil their fifth issue of *Giant-Size Dracula*, which was published in 1975. That year he also worked on an issue of *Marvel Chillers*, a book devoted to stories about monsters, and an issue of *Marvel Premiere*, which spotlighted lesser-known Marvel superheroes. His first regular Marvel series was *Iron Fist*, which described the adventures of a superhero who used Asian martial and mystic arts to fight crime. Receiving steady work from Marvel, Byrne ended his relationship with Charlton Comics with the sixth issue of *Doomsday +1* (1976).

While working regularly on *Iron Fist*, Byrne also did a great deal of filler work on several small-circulation Marvel titles through 1977, including *Daredevil*, about a blind superhero whose other senses are extraordinarily acute; *Ghost Rider*, whose main character is a flame-headed, motorcycle-driving demon; and *The Champions*, which featured a short-lived superhero team comprised of the demi-god Hercules, Ghost Rider, an ex-Soviet agent called the Black Widow, and two former X-Men named Iceman and Angel. Between 1977 and 1978 Byrne had a steady run penciling *Marvel Team-Up*, which featured Spider-Man, Marvel's most popular hero, paired up with a different hero from the Marvel universe each month. Byrne's first great success would come in 1978, when he took over the artistic chores on *X-Men*.

The X-Men were created in 1963 by Lee and Kirby. The premise of their story is that human evolution has produced a new species, known as mutants or "homo superior," that look like humans but have extraordinary powers. The powers become apparent with the onset of puberty, adding to the characters' already troubled adolescent state. The original X-Men were a group of such teenagers who fell under the tutelage of Professor Charles Xavier—a mutant with the ability to read and control minds—who taught his charges to harness their powers for the benefit of humanity. The series was a success during its early years but fell on hard times in the early 1970s and subsequently went into reprints for more than two years. In 1975 the creative team of writer Chris Claremont and artist Dave Cockrum revived the book with new X-Men adventures, starring an almost completely different cast of characters. The stories were edgier and dealt more directly with the fear and prejudice the mutants encountered. When Byrne took over the drawing chores, with *X-Men* number 108, he defined the X-Men style for future generations of artists and raised the bar for graphic storytelling.

At some point during his X-Men tenure, Byrne began co-plotting adventures with Claremont. One of their most notable story lines involved the death of the Phoenix, a telepathic and telekinetic character who was an original member of the X-Men (once called Marvel Girl) and had grown so powerful that she could tap a star's energy to increase her own power. Driven mad by her own power, she drained the star's radiance, resulting in the deaths of billions of people on a planet that orbited it. Phoenix was eventually subdued by the X-Men, and measures were taken to control her power; however, an alien civilization wanted her destroyed. Though the X-Men fought to defend their friend—with great reservation, since she had wantonly killed billions—Phoenix decided to take her own life to prevent future mass destruction. This bold and daring plot, ending in the death of a major character, brought Claremont and Byrne sacksful of fan mail whose contents ranged from praise to condemnation.

In 1980 Byrne began a short run drawing for *Captain America* and drew several issues of the *Fantastic Four*. He did not become the regular writer and artist for the *Fantastic Four*, however, until issue 232, in 1981; he subsequently worked on the series for more than 60 issues before leaving, in 1986. This run, one of Byrne's longest stints with any comic, was warmly received by fans who believed that his scripts and art had restored the Four to their former glory. The book's sales, sluggish for many years, soared during the Byrne era, and the magazine again became one of Marvel's best-sellers. Byrne's scripts made full use of every character created by Lee and Kirby, and his artistic rendering of the Four struck a balance between retro and modern. "Turn the clock back," he told Mark Lerer about his method. "Get back and see fresh what it was that made the book great at its inception."

During the early and mid-1980s, Byrne's star was on the rise at Marvel Comics, not only for his work on *X-Men* and *Fantastic Four*, but also for his creation of the Canadian supergroup Alpha Flight and the launch of a successful book focusing on the Thing, a character from the Fantastic Four. Until that point he had done almost no work for Marvel's biggest competitor, DC Comics, publisher of such comic icons as Superman, Batman, and Wonder Woman. In 1986 DC's editors approached Byrne about revamping and modernizing Superman, who, by the 1980s, had been almost submerged in his own vast mythology. As he had during his run with the Fantastic Four, Byrne returned to the beginnings of Superman's history and pared away most of the story elements that had been added over the years. Gone was Superman's incarnation as Superboy in his hometown of Smallville; gone was his cousin, Supergirl; gone was Krypto, the Superdog. What remained of the legend was what had been there at the beginning: Superman had traveled to Earth as a child in a spaceship from the doomed planet Krypton and was raised by adoptive parents, the Kents, who taught him to use his powers for good. Byrne's Superman was not invincible, as the Superman of the 1960s, 1970s, and early 1980s had been; he could no longer break the time barrier in flight or move planets. He was still supernaturally fast and powerful but was weak enough that villains posed a legitimate threat. Byrne also added subtly to the Superman myth: the Kents lived to see their adopted child become an adult; Clark Kent, Superman's alter ego, wasn't as weak or goofy as he had been portrayed in the past; and his archenemy, Lex Luthor, changed from a power-mad scientist in a purple and green leotard to a business-suited billionaire determined to destroy Superman because he feared Superman's influence on the citizens of Metropolis. While some longtime fans hated the changes Byrne made in the legend, others felt that Byrne had helped to restore the spirit of the character. His two-year run on the Superman titles *Superman* and *Action Comics*, as well as the six-issue miniseries *Man of Steel*, proved highly successful. In addition, Byrne wrote and drew the *World of Krypton*, the *World of Metropolis*, and the *World of Smallville* miniseries, which fleshed out the Superman universe. Byrne's work during this period also appeared in DC's *Legends* miniseries and selected issues of *Batman*.

Byrne returned to Marvel Comics in 1989 to write and draw *West Coast Avengers*, a spin-off of the popular *Avengers* comic, and the *Sensational She-Hulk*, cousin to the Incredible Hulk. Byrne broke new ground with *She-Hulk* by allowing the character to talk directly to both the reader and Byrne, her creator. In 1990 Byrne reintroduced comic fans to Namor the Sub-Mariner, Marvel's first superhero, who had been created in 1939. Byrne left Marvel in 1992, when he and fellow comic-creators Frank Miller and Art Adams took their talents to the creator-owned Dark Horse Comics' Legend imprint. In a growing trend in the industry at the time, many writers and artists fled the major houses to start their own imprints, so that they could own and control the rights to their material. Byrne's Dark Horse series, *John Byrne's Next Men*, failed to make a profit and lasted only two years, from 1992 to 1994. In 1995 Byrne worked again with DC Comics, contributing to the *Wonder Woman* and *Jack Kirby's Fourth World* series. His work at DC resulted in several changes to Wonder Woman, the legendary Amazonian princess who came to a "man's world" to fight for justice: he modernized her, extended her bullet-proof bracelets to cover her forearms, and clad her in armor with Grecian flourishes. He also put greater emphasis on her incredible strength, placing it on par with Superman's. For *Jack Kirby's Fourth World*, he reintroduced the fictional planet New Gods, which Kirby had originated in the 1970s but which had proved too far ahead of its time and did not succeed. Byrne also contributed to DC's *Genesis* miniseries in 1997 and wrote several issues of *New Gods*.

In 1998 Byrne was lured back to Marvel Comics by the opportunity to revamp *Spider-Man*, which in recent years had seen declining sales due to poor writing. Created by Stan Lee and Steve Ditko in the early 1960s, Spider-Man was the alter ego of the teenage Peter Parker, who had been bitten by a radioactive spider during a science experiment and consequently developed the proportionate strength, speed, and agility of a spider, as well as the creature's ability to walk on walls. Parker, who at first wanted nothing more than to profit from his newfound powers, had the chance to stop a burglary in progress but chose to watch idly as the thief escaped. In a cruel twist of fate, that same thief murdered Parker's beloved Uncle Ben during a later burglary. Learning that "with great power comes great responsibility," Parker dedicated himself to fighting crime, while maintaining the façade of a normal life. Byrne's formula for retooling Spider-Man was similar to the one he had used for Superman: bringing the character back to his roots while keeping the story contemporary. "It's been a number of years since I really paid that much attention to [Spider-Man], and I confess that I sort of lost interest in the character when he got married," he told Polly Watson in an interview for *Marvel* (number 4, 1998). "I felt that down through the years, the character had sort of drifted away from the things that made him interesting." Before his turn as writer and artist for Spider-Man, the character had four monthly titles; when Byrne took the creative reins, Marvel scaled their Spider-Man output down to two monthly titles, *The Amazing Spider-Man* and *Peter Parker: Spider-Man*, and started them from issue one. Byrne was also given a 13-issue miniseries, *Spider-Man: Chapter One*, to retell and update the character's beginnings. Never one to turn away work, he also wrote several issues of *Incredible Hulk* and launched a new title, *Spider-Girl*, about Peter Parker's daughter.

Byrne's latest project is a return, of sorts, to the X-Men. His new series, *X-Men: The Hidden Years*, fills in the adventures of the original team during the more than two years in the early 1970s when the title went into reprints. He is also completing work with Roger Stern on the 12-issue miniseries *Marvel: The Lost Generation*, which features the generation of superheroes that Marvel published between World War II and the first appearance of the Fantastic Four.

John Byrne, who is divorced, currently lives in Connecticut; earlier, he lived in Evanston, Illinois, and Brooklyn, New York. In addition to his comic-book work, he has written several novels, including *Fear* (1988), *Whipping Boy* (1992), and *Wonder Woman: Gods and Goddesses* (1997). — C.M.

Suggested Reading: *Danger Unlimited* no. 3 Apr. 1994; *Incredible Hulk* no. 314 Dec. 1985; *John Byrne's Next Men* no. 2 Mar. 1992, no. 4 May 1992, no. 11 Jan. 1993, no. 12 Feb. 1993, no. 28 Sep. 1994; *Marvel Age* no. 14 May 1984, no. 70 1988; *Superman* no. 1 Jan. 1987

Courtesy of Blue Note Records

Byron, Don

Nov. 8, 1958– Jazz musician; clarinetist; saxophonist; bandleader. Address: c/o Blue Note Records, 304 Park Ave. S., New York, NY 10010

Don Byron is "easily the most interesting and technically accomplished clarinetist to come along in a very long time . . . ," Francis Davis, jazz critic for the *Atlantic Monthly*, once declared, as quoted by Stephen Sherrill in the *New York Times Magazine* (January 16, 1994). "He's also among the most open-minded, which is rare in jazz." Byron has studied and performed many genres of music, among them classical, klezmer, and avant-garde jazz. An important player in New York's downtown experimental music scene since 1985, he has collaborated with other avant-garde musicians, such as John Zorn, David Murray, Hamiet Bluiett, and Craig Harris. He counts among his influences composers as diverse as Sonny Rollins and Igor Stravinsky, and his recordings have brought renewed attention to the music of such jazz greats as Duke Ellington and Ornette Coleman as well as to the work of lesser-known artists. Among Byron's albums are *The Tuskegee Experiments* (1990); *Don Byron Plays the Music of Mickey Katz* (1993); *Music for Six Musicians* (1995); *Bug Musik* (1996); *Nu Blaxploitation* (1998); and *Romance with the Unseen* (1999). His most recent recording, *A Fine Line: Arias and Lieder* (2000), offers music by such classical composers as Gustav Mahler, Giacomo Puccini, and Robert Schumann as well as pop favorites by Stevie Wonder, Roy Orbison, Henry Mancini, and Stephen Sondheim, among others.

Don Byron was born on November 8, 1958 and raised in the New York City borough of the Bronx. His father was a postman who had formerly played bass in calypso bands; his mother worked for a telephone company. Byron told Francis Davis for the *Village Voice* (July 17, 1990) that although his parents "were almost militant about me checking out all different kinds of music," he developed a love for classical music at an early age. When his allergic reaction to the family dog developed into asthma, the doctor recommended that Byron take up either swimming or a wind instrument as therapy. "I have a phobia about going into the water," he told Davis, "so I inherited a clarinet from the family pool of instruments." Byron attended New York's High School of Music and Art (a public school that accepts students on the basis of an exam), before enrolling in the New England Conservatory of Music (NEC), in Boston.

Byron soon became aware of some people's racist and/or classist preconceptions about classical music. "Nobody wanted to believe that I was capable of the classical stuff," he told Stephen Sherrill. "I'd show up and they'd say, 'You want to play jazz.' In the classical pedagogy, I had teachers telling me my lips were too big." Whether or not he found such comments offensive, Byron discovered and developed a love for jazz while studying at the NEC. He played the music of Scott Joplin with Gunther Schuller's NEC Ragtime Ensemble. Later, in the late 1980s and early 1990s, he would play in the Duke Ellington Orchestra under the jazz great's son, Mercer.

Professor Hankus Netsky's decision to recruit Byron to play three klezmer songs at an NEC faculty concert would prove to have a significant impact on the young musician's career. "Klezmer" is a Yiddish word, meaning "instrument or vessel of music," which came to describe a secularized form of Yiddish folk music brought to the U.S. by Jewish immigrants in the 1880s. Netsky chose Byron not only because of his virtuosity but because the clarinet is traditionally the lead instrument in klezmer music. "I responded immediately to the *mischief* in that music—the place on each of the old records where the clarinetist would play the most *out* thing he could think of," Byron told Francis Davis. "It's not like in jazz, where a guy gets hot and takes another chorus. There might be just one exciting trill, but that's where the creativity is. . . . Those guys on the records were taking risks. That's what I think I brought to klezmer that excited the rest of the band. Maybe some of the stuff I played was inappropriate, especially in the beginning. But at least I was doing something new. And as time went by, I developed my own voice in that language."

The 14-member Klezmer Conservatory Band, started by Byron, facilitated a nationwide klezmer revival. The clarinetist was the only African-American in the group and one of the few members of the band who was not Jewish. "The first year or two was terrifying," Byron told Peter Watrous for the *New York Times* (January 19, 1990). "This is a community not used to having deep cultural stuff examined by outsiders, and most of our performances were in [synagogues]. . . . I was one of the two people who fronted the band, and the reception I got wasn't always pleasant."

Jazz and klezmer music have several elements in common; both employ intricate rhythmic patterns, complex harmonies, and improvisation. Byron was affected by the emotional power of klezmer music. "When a klezmer piece bursts with joy, there's also a bittersweet undertone, and when it wails with pain, there's still a hint of joy," he told Ron Grossman for the *Chicago Tribune* (October 26, 1990). "It's the music of people living where happiness and suffering are never far apart. I had no trouble relating to that." The Klezmer Conservatory Band also touched the lives of people who had not heard the music since they were children. "We'd play a gig in a senior citizens center and people would come over to say thanks and I'd see the concentration camp number on their wrist," Byron recalled to Grossman, referring to the identification numbers that the Nazis tattooed on people imprisoned in such camps before and during World War II.

Byron left the Klezmer Conservatory Band in 1986. In the meantime he had begun collaborating with avant-garde musicians, contributing to Hamiet Bluiett's *Live in Berlin with the Clarinet Family* (1984) and Craig Harris's *Shelter* (1986), among other records. In 1990 he released his solo debut album, entitled *The Tuskegee Experiments,* which featured Bill Frisell on guitar, Ralph Peterson Jr. on drums, and Lonnie Plaxico on bass. The album included "In Memoriam: Uncle Dan," a largely improvised duet with bassist Reggie Workman (known for his work with John Coltrane, Art Blakey, and Wayne Shorter), as well as interpretations of tunes by Duke Ellington ("Mainstem") and the 19th-century German composer Robert Schumann ("Auf einer Burg," meaning "In a Castle"). The album's title track featured the poet Sadiq and referred to two infamous experiments conducted at the Tuskegee Institute in Alabama. In the first, the United States Public Health Service chose to observe the effects of syphilis on a group of African-American men, rather than treat them; as part of the second, African-American pilots who wished to fly military aircraft during World War II were humiliated in order to discourage them from continuing their training. "To me, these experiments are metaphors for African-American life," Byron told Peter Watrous for the *New York Times* (February 23, 1992). "In one, we see again that black life is cheap. . . . The aviation experiment reflects the struggle black people constantly face: having to be smarter, better, more qualified simply to justify being given any opportunity."

Byron maintained his love for klezmer music, and for a time he played at weddings with former members of the Klezmer Conservatory Band. Eventually he discovered the music of Mickey Katz, a klezmer bandleader who had become famous for recording Yiddish parodies of popular songs. Believing that Katz's work had been wrongly overlooked because he used comedy (a similar bias had affected the career of Louis Armstrong), Byron put together a band that played Katz's music in small clubs. When Katz's son, the Broadway entertainer Joel Grey, learned that his father's music had found a new audience, he sneaked into one of Byron's performances. "I was staggered, bewildered, touched, and moved," Grey told Ron Grossman. "It was like my father, who died [in 1985], was inside of him." Grey was so impressed that he helped Byron's group get a gig at Michael's Pub, the largest New York nightclub Byron had played up to that time.

In 1993 the clarinetist released *Don Byron Plays the Music of Mickey Katz.* He vehemently disagreed with critics who argued that he had championed a novelty act who was not closely connected with klezmer music or, by extension, with Jewish culture. "None of those klezmer cats [criticizing me] are doing what they're doing any more authentically than I am. Some of the same type of cats said this stuff about Mickey, too: 'No, this isn't really klezmer,'" Byron explained to Stephen Sherrill. "As if klezmer is just one thing. Well, this is really Mickey Katz, and if they want to make a value judgment about that, that's their business. But to say it's not real—it's really what it is." Byron pointed out the irony of the debate, given that many Jewish musicians of the 1920s had rejected klezmer music. "They wanted to play jazz, or symphony," he told Sherrill, "anything to avoid being stereotyped by klezmer."

Byron saw klezmer as fitting comfortably into the category of world music. "It's hard, though, because I'm expected, because I'm black, to only play jazz," he told Peter Watrous for the *New York Times* (January 19, 1990). "It's not very easy for me, as a black person, to exercise a world music option. A white musician can just say he's a blues musician, and nobody will challenge him and deny an ethnic connection. But it's not so easy to see the other way around—you don't see a lot of black musicians saying they play Bulgarian music." He noted that the authenticity of world-music explorations by white musicians such as Ry Cooder are seldom questioned. "When Itzhak Perlman made his jazz record, it was filed in both jazz and classical [sections of record stores]," Byron told Peter Margasak for the *Chicago Reader* (January 23, 1998, on-line). "No one's going to tell Perlman that his Paganini sounds kind of Jewish. . . . I resent that because when I play a specific kind of music, I play it as seriously as someone who plays that kind of music exclusively."

On *Music for Six Musicians,* released in 1995, Byron revisited the Afro-Cuban jazz to which his father had introduced him. The album blended various compositional styles and reflected Byron's continuing desire to express political concerns. Many of the pieces were inspired by modern events; for example, the titles of the cuts include "SEX/WORK (Clarence/Anita)" and "(The Press Made) Rodney King (Responsible for the L.A. Riots)."

Byron's *Bug Musik* (1996) featured his versions of songs written by John Kirby, Duke Ellington, and Raymond Scott, the last-named of whom composed music for many classic Warner Bros. cartoons. Byron also appeared on *Mistaken Identity,* a solo album by former Living Colour guitarist Vernon Reid. "The thing that's interesting about Don's playing is that his approach to the horn is very unsentimental," Reid told Jim Macnie for *Down Beat* (November 1996). "So there's real tension there. He can play the classics, all the things associated with the clarinet. But he's a modernist, too. . . . We have a real sympatico; I don't have to tell him what I want. He knows."

Byron created a soundtrack for the silent film *Scar of Shame* (1927) in 1998. The film and its new score were presented at the American Museum of the Moving Image, in the Astoria section of New York City, and at the Museum of Contemporary Art in Chicago. Byron chose the film because it dealt with intraracial tensions, a subject seldom portrayed on screen before or since *Scar of Shame*'s original release. Racial politics also played a role in *Nu Exploitation,* an album Byron made the same year, with the band Existential Dread. The record, which featured Sadiq as well as rap legend Biz Markie, included the songs "Fuhrman" (the surname of a police officer who testified in the O. J. Simpson murder trial) and "Blinky," which commented upon a recent case in which officers in the New York City borough of Brooklyn beat and sodomized a Haitian immigrant. Outrage over this and other instances of mistreatment inspired the creators of *Nu Exploitation.* "This record is about the way I experience things day to day, and I'm sensitive," Byron told David Yaffe for the *New York Times* (October 25, 1998). He elaborated on that theme in an interview with Fred Jung for *All About Jazz* (October 1999, on-line). "Every black man I know has been harassed by the police in his car. Every black man I know has some story about the police harassing him."

Romance with the Unseen (1999) featured Bill Frisell on guitar, Drew Gess on bass, and Jack DeJohnette on drums. The album contained new versions of songs by the Beatles ("I'll Follow the Sun") and Herbie Hancock ("One Finger Snap") as well as tunes about the artist Jean-Michel Basquiat and the New York subway vigilante Bernhard Goetz. Byron once again looked to Duke Ellington for inspiration, covering "A Mural from two Perspectives" and "Perdido" in commemoration of the late composer's 100th birthday.

Byron places himself in the lineage of such eclectic artists as Duke Ellington. "Ellington, along with Stevie Wonder and Prince, has that gift to lay really out stuff on audiences and they don't always notice that it's weird," he told David Yaffe. "Ellington will sneak in something really subversive, but still make the average person like it. He makes these funny, awful choices. Someone like Sun Ra lets you feel the struggle because there's a roughness there that let's you feel that things don't go so smooth for him. Ellington doesn't really do that. His music is so subversive, he might as well have been a Bolshevik. But Ellington is more like a secret agent."

Byron has tried through his work to bring exposure to often neglected artists such as Mickey Katz and the Mexican painter Diego Rivera. Although his music reflects his ideological perspective, he told *Blue Note* (1999, on-line) that rather than reiterate a particular theme, "I've tried to represent a level of composition, not a style." Byron told Frank J. Oteri and Nathan Michel for *New Music Box* (January 2000, on-line) that an artist's role "is to define the smallest space possible. . . . Because to make real art . . . you have to be looking inwards . . . defining small places in yourself, at different times, different places."

Byron has appeared in two films: Robert Altman's *Kansas City* (1996) and Paul Auster's *Lulu on the Bridge* (1998). A curator at the Brooklyn Academy of Music, he divides his time between New York and Boston. He has been named *Down Beat*'s Jazz Artist of the Year several times, and the magazine's readers and critics voted him their favorite clarinet player in 1993. — C.L.

Suggested Reading: *Chicago Reader* (on-line) Jan. 23, 1998, with photo; *Chicago Tribune* V p1+ Oct. 26,1990, with photos, V p11 June 15, 1995, with photo; *Down Beat* p24+ Nov. 1996, with photos; *New Music Box* (on-line) Jan. 2000; *New York Times* C p1+ Jan. 19, 1990, with photo, H p32 Feb. 23, 1992, with photo, VI p19+ Jan. 16, 1994, with photos, II p38+ Oct. 25, 1998, with photos; *Village Voice* p18+ July 17, 1990, with photo

Selected Recordings: *The Tuskegee Experiments,* 1990; *Don Byron Plays the Music of Mickey Katz,* 1993; *Music for Six Musicians,* 1995; *Bug Musik,* 1996; *Nu Blaxploitation,* 1998; *Romance with the Unseen,* 1999; *A Fine Line: Arias and Lieder,* 2000

Jonathan Daniel/Allsport

Camby, Marcus

Mar. 22, 1974– Basketball player. Address: New York Knickerbockers, Madison Square Garden, 2 Penn Plaza, New York, NY 10121

During the 1998–99 National Basketball Association (NBA) play-offs, the first in the post–Michael Jordan era of the game, Marcus Camby, the six-foot 11-inch power forward for the New York Knicks, emerged as one of the most agile "big men"—the term for forwards and centers—in the game. With well-developed rebounding skills and magnificent dunks, he helped the Knicks capture dramatic upset victories over the Miami Heat, the Atlanta Hawks, and the Indiana Pacers in the first three rounds of the play-offs. Although he and the Knicks eventually came up short against the powerful San Antonio Spurs, who were led by All-Stars Tim Duncan and David Robinson, Camby proved himself to be among the most exciting players in basketball. Even after a disappointing 1999–2000 season, characterized by his injuries and his resulting inability to recapture the glory of the previous year, Camby is seen as a force to reckon with in the NBA. At 225 pounds, routinely described by sportswriters as "wafer-thin," "spindly," and "threadlike" and as having an "exclamation-point physique," Camby is nonetheless a key weapon in the Knicks' arsenal.

Born on March 22, 1974 in Hartford, Connecticut, Marcus Camby faced hardships from a young age. He and his two younger sisters were raised by his mother, Janice Camby, a social worker, and his grandmother in the Bellevue Square housing projects of Hartford's North End, a notorious slum. His biological father, Ames Mandeville, did not play a major role in his life. Camby began playing basketball when he was about five years old. Throughout much of his youth, he played guard; he did not fill the forward and center positions until high school, when he began to grow at a remarkable rate. He led the Hartford Public High School team to two state championship titles, and in his senior year he averaged 25 points, 12 rebounds, and five blocks per game. Despite those impressive figures and his imposing height—as a senior he measured his full six feet 11 inches—he did not draw an unusual amount of attention from top U.S. colleges and was known primarily for his shot-blocking ability and defensive skills.

In the autumn of 1993, Camby entered the University of Massachusetts at Amherst. Although its basketball program is not considered outstanding, the school is the alma mater of the legendary Julius Erving, commonly referred to as Dr. J., who played for the University of Massachusetts Minutemen from 1969 to 1971. Dr. J's career averages of 26.3 points and 20.2 rebounds per game during two seasons at U. Mass. set school records for scoring and rebounding. Following in Dr. J's footsteps, Camby shone on the U. Mass court. He won recognition for possessing phenomenal athletic ability for someone so tall. Indeed, unlike most people his size, Camby possessed fine coordination, agility, and speed.

With those skills, Camby quickly emerged as a formidable college center, and he helped his team capture an Atlantic-10 Conference championship title at the end of the 1993–94 season. He did so despite serious problems during workouts. "That first year the conditioning was pure misery for him," John Calipari, the head coach of the Minutemen at the time, recalled to Tim Crothers for *Sports Illustrated* (December 18, 1995). "He'd be running sprints with the other guys, and all of a sudden he'd drop to the floor like he'd been shot in the back. He wasn't used to dealing with adversity, because everything had always come so easy to him. I had to literally drag him, push him, prod him along while he kept telling me, 'Coach, I can't do it.'"

With improved conditioning, Camby finished the 1994–95 season averaging 14.5 points, 6.6 rebounds, 3.4 blocks, and one assist per game, while playing only 23 minutes per contest, on average. (A National Collegiate Athletic Association [NCAA] basketball game consists of two 20-minute segments.) Camby's relatively limited playing time was a result of Calipari's penchant for making use of his bench and Camby's tendency to make fouls.

During his sophomore year Camby helped his team to another Atlantic-10 Conference championship title. He also helped the Minutemen reach the Sweet-16 round, the regional final round of the NCAA Division I postseason tournament—often referred to as "March Madness"—in which 64 top college teams compete for the national title. The Minutemen lost in the East Regional Final to the Oklahoma State University Cowboys, the team that featured the seven-foot, 300-pound Bryant Reeves.

By the end of that season, there was much speculation that Camby would leave college for the NBA. Such a move would no doubt have been immensely lucrative for Camby, since big men are generally the most prized draftees. Indeed, the 1995 NBA draft featured several young big men who had been Camby's rivals in the college ranks. Among them were Rasheed Wallace, a University of North Carolina power forward/center, who was drafted fourth overall by the Washington Bullets after his sophomore year, and Joe Smith, a University of Maryland center, who was drafted first overall by the Golden State Warriors after his sophomore year.

Camby, by contrast, remained in college for another year. By doing so, he faced the small risk that he might suffer an injury that year and thus lose out on future earnings of millions of dollars. On the other hand, he gave himself the opportunity to further develop his basketball skills and mature personally. And he used this time profitably: he increased his strength, improved his competence at passing, and established himself as the leader of his team. Thanks in no small part to Camby, the Minutemen were ranked number one in the nation for much of the 1995–96 season. Then, in January 1996, Camby suffered a minor setback. Before a routine game against St. Bonaventure University in Olean, New York, he collapsed and lost consciousness for 10 minutes. He was rushed to a hospital, where doctors tried in vain to pinpoint the reason for his collapse. "I know that they'll probably never find out what was wrong," Camby said soon after his release from the hospital, as quoted by Malcolm Moran for the *New York Times* (January 28, 1996). "I still have doubts in my mind. I just have to be strong about it, I guess." Camby missed four games as a result of that episode, but he soon returned to form and, with an average of 21.4 points, 8.2 rebounds, and 3.9 blocks per game, helped the Minutemen to achieve a remarkable regular-season record of 28 wins and one loss and to capture the Atlantic-10 Conference championship title for the fifth consecutive time. Then, in the 1996 NCAA Tournament, Camby put together a string of dazzling performances and led the Minutemen to the first Final Four appearance in the team's history. But the team was not to enjoy a glorious finish to a magnificent season: in the Final Four, the Minutemen lost to the eventual champions, the University of Kentucky Wildcats, 83–63. Camby, meanwhile, had been named Atlantic-10 player of the year. He also won every other major national college-basketball player-of-the-year honor, including the award named for James A. Naismith, the winner of which is selected by a panel of leading basketball coaches, journalists, and administrators; the John R. Wooden Award; and the Adolph Rupp Trophy, which is bestowed by the Associated Press.

After the 1995–96 season, Camby made himself eligible for the 1996 NBA draft. Making the decision to leave college for the NBA before earning a degree had been difficult for him. "I looked into the mirror every day," Camby explained to Malcolm Moran for the *New York Times* (April 30, 1996), "and I said, 'Marcus, are you ready to do this?' And I was like, 'Yeah.' That was probably the best advice that I got." Having blocked 336 shots during his three years at the University of Massachusetts, Camby had set the all-time Atlantic-10 Conference and University of Massachusetts records for most career blocked shots.

In June 1996 Camby was selected by the Toronto Raptors, a struggling expansion team, becoming the second overall pick of that year's NBA draft. (Allen Iverson, a guard out of Georgetown University, was first overall, selected by the Philadelphia 76ers.) Soon afterward Camby signed a three-year contract with the Raptors; reportedly, it was worth a little more than $8.4 million.

Camby's transition to the NBA did not go smoothly, because soon after the 1996 draft, he became immersed in a scandal. Two sports agents revealed that starting before Camby's junior year at the University of Massachusetts, they had regularly showered him and his friends with money and extravagant gifts in violation of NCAA regulations, in order to win Camby as a client when the promising star turned professional. The agents had become angry after Camby signed with another agency, and one of them had even tried to extort money from him before the two made their disclosure. Commenting on the improper payments, Camby told Phil Taylor for *Sports Illustrated* (September 15, 1997), "It was a crazy time. People were coming up to me, offering me things, trying to get close to me. The phone was always ringing. Everything was happening so fast my head was spinning, and I did some things I'm not proud of. I did some things I shouldn't have done." As a result of those violations, in June 1997 the NCAA stripped U. Mass. of its 1996 NCAA regional championship title and forced the school to return the $151,000 it had earned as a bonus for reaching the Final Four. Camby reimbursed the full amount to his alma mater, but the controversy surrounding the episode tainted people's memories of his college career and turned many journalists and fans against him. For instance, although Camby had long been extremely popular in the Massachusetts area, as a Raptor he was booed whenever the team played against the Boston Celtics on the Celtics' home court.

Meanwhile, during the 1996–97 season, Camby averaged 14.8 points, 6.3 rebounds, and 2.06 blocks per game and emerged as a key component of the Raptors' offense. He was named to the NBA's All-Rookie First Team and played in the All-Rookie Game during All-Star Weekend. He also won rookie-of-the-month honors in March 1997. On the down side, he had missed 11 games due to illness and injuries, and many basketball aficionados expressed disappointment at his relatively good but unspectacular play. Moreover, he was dogged by questions concerning his drive and work ethic. These doubts remained during the 1997–98 season, even though Camby led the NBA in blocked shots, with an average of 3.65 per game, and averaged 12.1 points and 7.4 rebounds per game. Indeed, many critics and disenchanted fans dubbed him "Cotton Camby."

In June 1998 the Raptors traded Camby to the New York Knicks in exchange for both the 34-year-old Charles Oakley, a 10-year Knicks veteran who was a favorite among fans, and the rights to the University of California forward Sean Marks, whom the Knicks had acquired in the second round of the 1998 NBA draft. Although front-office Knicks representatives explained that Camby's youth and athleticism would strengthen the Knicks, particularly in contests with the Indiana Pacers, a conference rival that had eliminated the Knicks in the 1998 play-offs, many Knicks fans and journalists criticized the trade. Unhappy about Oakley's departure from New York, they expressed skepticism about Camby's ability to fill Oakley's shoes; Camby's finesse and speed, they suggested, were not sufficient to compensate for the absence of Oakley, who was known for his aggressive playing style.

Camby did not see much playing time during the 1998–99 season, which was abbreviated because of a dispute between NBA team owners and players concerning salaries and pensions. (The regular season started in February 1999 and extended for only 50 games.) He functioned as a reserve and became a member of the Knicks' highly talented second unit, which included Chris Childs and Latrell Sprewell and thrived by means of a fast-tempo game. Despite the boost from this second unit, the Knicks finished the regular season with a less-than-spectacular record of 27 wins and 23 losses and just barely earned the eighth and last play-off spot in the Eastern Conference.

The first round of the 1999 NBA play-offs pitted the Knicks against the Miami Heat, who were seeded number one in the Eastern Conference. Coming off the bench to support Allan Houston, Larry Johnson, and Patrick Ewing, Camby helped the Knicks upset the Heat 3–2 in a best-of-five-game series. Camby surprised his critics by playing aggressively and using his considerable speed to rebound and score over bulkier opponents. His talents were particularly apparent against the Atlanta Hawks, whom the Knicks swept 4–0 in a best-of-seven-game series.

Camby was even more impressive in the Eastern Conference Finals, which pitted the Knicks against the Indiana Pacers, conference rivals long known for their physical style of play. As the series progressed, Camby became a dominating force, scooping rebounds seemingly from out of nowhere, to the dismay of such Pacers as Antonio Davis, Chris Mullin, and Dale Davis. Camby's contributions became even more valuable after Patrick Ewing, the Knicks' captain, was sidelined with a partially torn left Achilles tendon after game two. Camby filled the void; with increased playing time and the encouragement of his teammates, he proved too quick and athletic for the Pacers as he captured one rebound after another and turned them into thundering slams. Fueled in large part by Camby's superb play and the offensive output of guards Allan Houston and Latrell Sprewell, the Knicks eliminated the Pacers 4–2 and thus became the first eighth-seeded team in the play-offs ever to reach the NBA Finals. "If Marcus hadn't been sensational, we could not have won this series," New York point guard Chris Childs said after game six of the Eastern Conference Finals, as quoted by Phil Taylor in *Sports Illustrated* (June 21, 1999). "It's as simple as that."

In the NBA Finals, the Knicks faced the San Antonio Spurs, a formidable team that had enjoyed a remarkable play-off run. The Spurs had the best regular-season record, 37–13, and had dominated the competition. They had eliminated the Minnesota Timberwolves 3–1, then swept the Los Angeles Lakers and the Portland Trailblazers. As the finals unfolded, it quickly became apparent that even with Camby's improved play, the Knicks were seriously overmatched. Whereas the Spurs featured the seven-foot All-Stars Tim Duncan and David Robinson in their front court, the Knicks, in the absence of Ewing, relied on their guards, Allan Houston and Latrell Sprewell, for the bulk of their offense. Although Camby played a strong series, he was unable to neutralize the Spurs' powerful front line, and the Spurs prevailed, 4–1. Robinson won his first NBA championship ring, and Duncan—whom Camby had outplayed during the 1995–96 season when the Minutemen faced off against the Wake Forest Demon Deacons—was named the most valuable player (MVP) of the NBA Finals.

Camby began the 1999–2000 season with an ailing right knee that was thought at first to be caused by tendinitis. During a game against Miami in February 2000, he suffered what appeared to be a torn anterior cruciate ligament in his knee; exploratory surgery revealed the injury to be a strain rather than a tear, but he nonetheless missed five weeks of play. Afterward, Camby—who also suffered from elbow trouble, a cut eyelid, and a sprained right knee over the course of the season—was unable to match his performance of the previous year. The Knicks swept the Toronto Raptors, 3–0, in the Eastern Conference Quarterfinals, then defeated Miami 4–3 in a hard-fought best-of-seven series; in the Finals, however, the Indiana Pacers proved to be too much for the Knicks, besting them 4–2. Throughout the play-offs, Camby posted comparatively unimpressive statistics, averaging 6.7 points and 7.7 rebounds against Toronto, 5.3 points and 7.1 rebounds against Miami, and 3.3 points and 6.5 rebounds against Indiana, after suffering knee trouble in game three of that series. Still, the extent to which the Knicks continue to depend on Camby—especially after the trading of Patrick Ewing to the Seattle Supersonics, in September—was evident in a *New York Times* (October 5, 2000) article about the power forward. "Camby could make a big impact this season," Chris Broussard wrote. "If he is healthy . . . Camby could help catapult the Knicks toward a long postseason run."

During the NBA season, Camby lives on a rented estate near Purchase, New York. In 1996 he founded the CambyLand Youth Foundation, which aims, according to its Web site, "to provide positive recreational and educational opportunities" for young people, through, among other things, college scholarships, a computer-literacy program, and workshops for young parents. Camby enjoys watching movies, surfing the Internet, and playing video games. He has two dogs, named Stone Cold and Goldberg. Camby, who studied education at the University of Massachusetts, has expressed an interest in becoming a high-school principal someday. He signed a six-year, $39 million extension with the Knicks in March 1999. — Y.P.

Suggested Reading: *New York Times* D p1+ Nov. 2, 1998, with photos, D p1 May 27, 1999, with photo; *Sports Illustrated* p46+ Dec. 18, 1995, with photos, p66+ Sep. 15, 1997, with photos, p38+ June 21, 1999, with photos

---

Barbara DuMetz/Courtesy of G. P. Putnam's Sons

Campbell, Bebe Moore

(BEE-bee)

Feb. 18, 1950– Writer. Address: c/o Beth Swofford, William Morris Agency, 151 El Camino Dr., Beverly Hills, CA 90212

"A keen and candid social critic, and a masterful storyteller," as Donna Seaman described her for *Booklist* (June 1–15, 1994), Bebe Moore Campbell has plumbed the complexities of race relations in three novels that—like those of Terry McMillan, Connie Briscoe, and a growing number of other female African-American writers—have impressed black and white readers alike. The crossover appeal of *Your Blues Ain't Like Mine, Brothers and Sisters*, and *Singing in the Comeback Choir* has been attributed to Campbell's unusual skill at articulating the thoughts and feelings of people of different races and of men as well as women. "I appreciate the fact that white people are not monolithic; neither are Asians or Latinos," Campbell said to DeNeen L. Brown for the *Washington Post* (January 27, 1998). In an enthusiastic review of *Brothers and Sisters* for *Time* (October 17, 1994) that echoed and prefigured observations by others about her writerly strengths, Christopher John Farley reported that Campbell had presented her story not only from the perspective of the main character, a young black professional woman, but "through the eyes of her other characters as well. We see sexual harassment from both sides; we experience the exultation of a black man who is promoted and the bitterness of the white man who is replaced; and we are given both views as two women, one black, one white, warily become friends. Writing with wit and grace, Campbell shows how all our stories—white, black, male, female—ultimately intertwine." Campbell, whose journalism and essays have appeared in many newspapers and popular magazines, has also written two books of nonfiction: *Successful Women, Angry Men: Backlash in the Two-Career Marriage* and the autobiographical *Sweet Summer: Growing Up With and Without My Dad*.

Campbell was born Bebe Moore on February 18, 1950, 19 years to the day after the birth of her favorite writer, Toni Morrison. Her mother, Doris Moore, a social worker, and father, George Moore, divorced when she was very small. Starting in childhood Campbell lived during the school year with her upwardly mobile mother, maternal grandmother, and an aunt in North Philadelphia. Their community, she said during a conversation with Joyce Carol Oates (moderated by Veronica Chambers) for the *New York Times Magazine* (December 25, 1994), "consisted of middle-class people, blue-collar people, teachers, doctors, lawyers, factory workers. . . . Everybody was just fresh up from the South, post World War II, and the schools by that time were all black." Nevertheless, as an adolescent and teenager, Campbell had both black and white friends. Discussing her use, since childhood, of both standard English and African-American dialect (commonly called black English), she wrote in an essay for the *Washington Post* (July 16, 1980), "Proper English met my outside world needs, but . . . wasn't trying to get no good grades or fast service from my friends." As an adult, she reported, "I likes to slip out of standard English like I slips out of stiff, starchy business suits, crisp with ambition and high-collared superiority."

Campbell spent summers in North Carolina with her father, who had lost the use of his legs after a car accident when she was 10 months old. "Despite my father's handicap and despite the great distance which separated us, he was a good father," she told Lisa See for *Publishers Weekly* (June 30, 1989). "Other men, my uncles, my neighbors rallied around and were paternal without being asked." Campbell wrote *Sweet Summer: Growing Up With and Without My Dad* (1989) partly in response to what she viewed as the media's unfair portrayals of black fathers. "There's a stereotype that black fathers are deserters, but it's not because they're bred to walk away," she said to See. As a youngster Campbell had idolized her father and regarded him as a hero who could do no wrong. After learning that he had been speeding when he had the car crash, and that a boy had been killed as a result of it, she had to grapple with the new knowledge that her father was not flawless. Writing *Sweet Summer*, she explained to See, was a way of "fac[ing] whatever remaining demons were chasing me in regards to my father." In an essay for *Essence* (June 1989), she lamented the absence of old men from her life after her father's death in another car accident, in 1977.

After she graduated from high school, Campbell attended the University of Pittsburgh, where she majored in elementary education. She earned a B.S. degree, with highest honors, in about 1972. For the next five years she worked as a schoolteacher, first in Atlanta, Georgia, and then in Washington, D.C. After the birth of her daughter, Maia, in about 1976, she decided to write as a freelancer, with the goal of becoming a novelist. Acting on the suggestion of an editor at *Essence* magazine, she successfully sought assignments for such magazines and newspapers as *Black Enterprise, Ebony, Lear's, Ms.*, the *New York Times Book Review, Publishers Weekly, Seventeen*, the *Washington Post*, and *Working Mother.* Her topics ranged from household budgeting and her daughter's obsession with name-brand jeans to interracial dating, affirmative action, and the power of the black vote. In 1980 Campbell received a literary grant from the National Endowment for the Arts to develop her nonfiction coming-of-age account, "Old Lady Shoes," into a work of fiction. She later converted the story into a radio play, which won the first-place award in the Midwestern Radio Theater Workshop Competition.

An article Campbell wrote for *Savvy* magazine led to her first book, *Successful Women, Angry Men: Backlash in the Two-Career Marriage* (1986), which examines the effects that the struggle for career advancement has on marriages and families—mostly within the upper-middle class—in which wife and husband both work. In offering ways of dealing with conflict-laden situations, Campbell included accounts related to her by many individuals. The book has appeared on reading lists for courses in women's studies at various colleges.

Campbell's first book of fiction was *Your Blues Ain't Like Mine* (1992). The story was inspired by the murder of Emmett Till, which occurred in the summer of 1955, when he was 14. (Campbell, who was five years old then, has recalled that the crime dominated the conversations of people in the church her family attended.) An African-American from Chicago, Till had been visiting relatives in Mississippi, where he had little understanding of the local mores regarding black–white interactions. After he allegedly made a pass at a white woman, the woman's husband and the husband's half-brother maimed Till and then killed him. The men later admitted their guilt, but only after an all-white jury had acquitted them of the crime, so they were never punished. While the plot of *Your Blues Ain't Like Mine* echoes events surrounding the Till tragedy, it goes further, by looking at several generations of blacks and whites and following the murdered boy's brother, who becomes a gang leader years after the killing. "Thus Campbell's ultimate question," Mae Ghalwash wrote for the *Washington Post* (October 10, 1992): "'Is it going to hurt [the boys' mother] more to have [one son] hurt by a white man or to have [the other son] shot by a black gang member?'"

Your Blues Ain't Like Mine also incorporates such themes as "the fear of being ostracized that kept whites who could not stomach the abuse of blacks from speaking out, the platonic relationships between white men and black women, the impregnation of black women by white men, and the mulattoes they left behind," Ghalwash reported. In a review for the *School Library Journal* (January 1993), Judy Sokoll wrote that the novel "exposes family, race, and class divisions in America from the 1950s to the present, and the rich characterization explores the base, the noble, and the ordinary in all of us." Clyde Edgerton, who assessed *Your Blues Ain't Like Mine* for the *New York Times Book Review* (September 20, 1992), observed, "Much of the power of this novel results from Ms. Campbell's subtle and seamless shifting of point of view. She wears the skin and holds in her chest the heart of each of her characters, one after another, regardless of the character's race or sex, response to fear and hate, or need for pity, grace, punishment, or peace."

Campbell's next book, *Brothers and Sisters* (1994), became a best-seller. It is set in Los Angeles a few months after the 1992 riots in that city, which were sparked by the acquittals by an all-white jury of four white police officers on trial for beating Rodney King, an unemployed black construction worker. The main character is Esther Jackson, a black bank manager, who strives to develop a friendship with a white co-worker, Mallory Post. A crisis ensues after Humphrey Boone, an African-American who becomes the women's supervisor, is accused of sexually harassing Mallory. According to Pamela Newkirk, who interviewed Campbell for the *New York Times* (November 15, 1995), the writer viewed *Brothers and Sisters* as "a blueprint for overcoming racial differences, because any progress will result not from legislation, [Campbell] said, but from one-on-one interracial relationships, which most often occur in the workplace." "It's the only place we gather," Campbell observed to Newkirk. "We don't live in the same neighborhoods or go to the same churches. Our schools are still segregated, de facto. But many of us meet day to day at the job. That's where we can make the inroads." She also told Newkirk that *Brothers and Sisters* was her "attempt to bridge a racial gap. That's the story that never gets told: how many of us [blacks and whites] really like each other, really respect each other."

"Racism isn't the overriding factor governing what happens to the characters, black or white," Sheryl Hilliard Tucker wrote in a review of *Brothers and Sisters* for *Black Enterprise* (February 1995). "Ambition, greed, vulnerability, and lack of moral fiber fuels sexual harassment, embezzlement, and wrongful dismissals. Another interesting observation: The black characters feel . . . happy to make big corporate bucks, but conflicted about the relationship of the haves and have-nots in the black community." In *Booklist*, Donna Seaman wrote that in unfolding her story, Campbell had succeeded in "illuminat[ing] a host of issues connected to race, culture, romance and finance" and had also "brilliantly interpret[ed] all the shades of meaning inherent in the concept of 'brothers and sisters.'"

In a dissenting view, Kari J. Winter complained in the *African American Review* (Summer 1997) that "in imagery, character, dialogue, and ideology [the novel] is a marriage of *The Cosby Show*, *L.A. Law*, and *Waiting to Exhale*." Campbell's style, Winter wrote, "is crisp but cliché-ridden, and her use of 'realistic' details (designer labels, street names, food brands) is unrelenting. Despite the novel's purported attack on racism and sexism, *Brothers and Sisters* replicates many of the objectifying spiritually bankrupt attitudes of American capitalism. Campbell . . . enthusiastically commodifies her characters." In a mixed assessment for the *New York Times Book Review* (October 16, 1994), Elizabeth Gleick expressed the view that "too often Ms. Campbell's good intentions" had led her "to create caricatures. No white character appears able to express unequivocal outrage over the Rodney King beating. . . . The black characters, at least, span a broader range of humanity . . . but even they seem to exist to make specific points." "For readers who wish to see some of the same themes treated in an infinitely more sophisticated and haunting manner, I suggest they find . . . *Your Blues Ain't Like Mine*," Gleick declared.

Campbell's most recent book, *Singing in the Comeback Choir* (1998), was a main selection of the Book-of-the-Month Club. The story focuses on Maxine, the executive producer of a popular talk show, who travels from Los Angeles to Philadelphia after an urgent call about her grandmother, Lindy, who raised her. Like Lindy, a one-time jazz singer who had become a nurse, the neighborhood where Maxine grew up has suffered a steep decline, and Maxine's encounters with childhood acquaintances who now hustle to support their drug habits leave her stunned. But within a few days she finds, as *Kirkus Reviews* (January 1, 1998, on-line) put it, that although "drugs and crime have infiltrated [her] block, the sense of community has remained intact." While grappling with concerns about her husband's fidelity, her impending motherhood, and the value of her work, she "discovers the redeeming quality of community involvement and the healing that comes from a sense of purpose," in the words of the *Kirkus* reviewer. According to a synopsis for Amazon.com, after "realiz[ing] that Lindy and [Lindy's street] itself have been the source of her own strength and success, . . . [Maxine] is moved to help both reclaim their glory." "By the end of *Singing in the Comeback Choir*," Betsy Groban wrote for the *New York Times Book Review* (April 12, 1998), "we have come to care deeply about Maxine and Lindy, which makes the novel's inventive solution even more gratifying." Patricia Elam had a different reaction; in an evaluation for the *Washington Post* (February 5, 1998), she wrote, "Although all the characters reveal their various purposes by the book's end, Campbell tries too hard to ensure that everyone is authentic in terms of culture, class, and experience. Much of the dialogue consists of sound bites rather than conversation, and Campbell leaves out the distinctive motivations for the characters' behavior and emotions. The effect is that they sometimes become caricatures instead of real people."

Campbell is a contributing editor at *Essence* and a commentator on National Public Radio. She has often been a guest on radio and television talk shows, and she has done many readings on her book tours. Through such face-to-face encounters, she has recognized that some African-Americans among her readers find her sympathetic treatment of whites off-putting. "You want your enemy to be a monster . . . ," Campbell explained to Karen Brailsford for *Emerge* (October 1994). "You don't want to know about her problems. You don't want to think she's suffered as much as you have." In an interview with Barbranda Lumpkins for *USA To-*

day (September 2, 1994), she said, "I get some resistance from black people who say, 'Don't humanize my enemies for me.'" From white people, she continued, she gets "universal amazement and gratitude that I'm not coming after them in rage. I know where they're coming from. I'm glad I'm getting [reactions from] both sides." During her 12-city tour to promote the appearance of *Brothers and Sisters* in paperback, she told Pamela Newkirk that being asked to comment on racial issues was "nerve-racking": "Am I saying the right thing? Am I being understood? I'm not an expert on race, but on making up stories. I wish I could write it and never have to talk about it. I don't have solutions; I have ideas."

Campbell's honors include the Body of Work Award from the National Association of Negro Business and Professional Women and the NAACP Image Award for outstanding literary work. Her daughter, Maia Campbell (who was born during her marriage to Tiko F. Campbell, which ended in divorce), is an actress and model. The writer and her second husband, Ellis Gordon Jr., a banker, to whom she has been married since 1984, live in the View Park section of Los Angeles. Her stepson, Ellis Gordon III, is about 29. "Like a lot of American families, ours is no Norman Rockwell painting . . . ," she acknowledged in an essay for *USA Today* (November 30, 1997). "The mistakes my husband and I have made with our children and with each other glare like a midday sun. . . . I wrote books instead of baking casseroles, and squeezed mothering in between the pages. . . . But in a world of flawed, fragile human beings, the connection of family is the closest thing to grace I know." — V.K.

Suggested Reading: *African American Review* p369+ Summer 1997; *Emerge* p65+ Oct. 1994, with photo; *New York Times* C p1+ Nov. 15, 1995, with photo; *New York Times Magazine* p16+ Dec. 25, 1994, with photos; *Publishers Weekly* p82+ June 30, 1989; *Washington Post* D p1+ Oct. 10, 1992, with photos

Selected Books: *Successful Women, Angry Men: Backlash in the Two-Career Marriage*, 1986; *Sweet Summer: Growing Up With and Without My Dad*, 1989; *Your Blues Ain't Like Mine*, 1992; *Brothers and Sisters*, 1994; *Singing in the Comeback Choir*, 1998

Campbell, Neve

(nev)

Oct. 3, 1973– Film and television actress. Address: c/o Creative Artists Agency, 9830 Wilshire Blvd., Beverly Hills, CA 90212-1825

Fans of the acclaimed Fox television series *Party of Five* are familiar with the trials San Francisco orphan Julia Salinger experienced during the show's run. In five seasons she went through a miscarriage, a divorce, an abusive relationship, the alcoholism of one sibling, and the cancer of another. "If I were Julia, I'd probably have had a nervous breakdown by now," Neve Campbell, the 26-year-old actress who portrayed the troubled teen, joked to David Kronke in December 1997 for the *Los Angeles Times* (on-line). While many actors have tried to parlay small-screen success into careers in film, Campbell is one of relatively few to have succeeded. To date she has appeared in the blockbuster horror/comedy *Scream* series as well as in *The Craft* (1996), *Wild Things* (1998), and *Three to Tango* (1999).

Paul Smith/Retna Ltd.

Neve Adrianne Campbell was born on October 3, 1973 in Toronto, Ontario, Canada, and grew up in the nearby town of Guelph. "Neve," which means "snow" in Italian, is the maiden name of her mother, Marnie. An immigrant to Canada from the Netherlands, her mother owned a dinner theater before becoming a psychologist; currently, she teaches yoga. Campbell's father, Gerry Campbell, a native of Scotland, is a high-school drama teacher who also directs a Scottish theater group. Campbell's parents divorced when she was a baby, and she and her brother Christian, who is a year and a half older than she is, went to live with their father. Because she grew up in an all-male household, "girlie things were never my thing. My style was what my dad threw me in—corduroys and a shirt, and I mucked them up a lot," she recalled to Josh Rottenberg in *Australian TV Week* (September 20, 1997). Despite the divorce, Campbell's mother remained a presence in her life. From her mother she learned "spirituality, and how to be nonjudgmental toward others," she told an interviewer for *Jane* magazine (May 1999). "She taught me how to do yoga, and if you have any difficulties in life, remember to breathe." Campbell has two half-brothers, Damian McDonald and Alex McDonald.

From an early age Neve Campbell knew that she wanted to be in show business, as her brother Christian discovered when he was performing in a high-school production of the Gilbert and Sullivan operetta *H.M.S. Pinafore* that her father was directing. "I came into the living room all dressed up in my little costume," Christian Campbell told Daniel Howard Cerone for *TV Guide* (February 8, 1997). "Neve broke into tears because she felt so left out." When she was six her father took her to see the ballet *The Nutcracker*. That day, she told Dan Jewel for *People* (May 27, 1996), becoming a ballerina "became my dream." Soon afterward she enrolled at Toronto's prestigious National Ballet School, where she danced in productions of *Sleeping Beauty* and *The Nutcracker*. She felt somewhat like a misfit at the school. "I was definitely the loser of my class . . . ," she recalled to a reporter for *Sassy* (1997, on-line). "We had this awful thing at school where we had cookies on Valentine's Day, and every student could buy them and send them to other class members," she told Cerone. "They would call up each student every time their name came out of the box. I was called up once because the *teacher* gave me a cookie. No one would spend five cents to send me a cookie." She made valiant efforts to make friends, but to no avail. "Oh I would try," she recalled to Jancee Dunn for *Rolling Stone* (September 8, 1997). "Like any kid, desperately, every moment thinking, 'Oh, they smiled at me. Wait, maybe they do like me!'"

Campbell also felt pressure to succeed at the competitive ballet school. "I basically had problems dealing with the backstabbing mentality that's a big part of the ballet world," she told Bernard Weinraub for *Cosmopolitan* (January 1997). Of 150 students in the beginners' class, only 20 students were expected to graduate. "The best dancers in the world come out of there—and the most messed up people sometimes come out of there," she told Jamie Portman for the *Ottawa Citizen* (December 11, 1997). "I mean, they're wonderful and try to take care of you, but they have many, many psychologists on staff so that kind of tells you something about it." At the age of 14, after a bout of soul-searching, Campbell realized that staying at the school would take too heavy an emotional toll on her, and she decided to leave. Reflecting on her time there, Campbell told Portman, "I definitely believe that the school is the reason I'm able to stay in the business, both psychologically and physically. It wasn't just the discipline, it was understanding the need to take care of yourself and realizing that if you want to be successful you must be prepared to do the work."

After leaving the National Ballet School, Campbell attended a public high school. She found it much easier to fit in there. "I think, because I was so happy, that people felt that energy," she told Dunn. Not long after starting the 10th grade, however, Campbell found that she missed performing. She immediately enrolled at Interact, an alternative school that offered a flexible schedule tailored to the needs of young actors, artists, and athletes. At 15 she won a role as one of the ballet-dancing girls in the Toronto production of the musical *The Phantom of the Opera*. The role gave her a chance to use skills she had honed at the National Ballet School. "I still think of that as the best experience of my life," she told Weinraub. "I was so young and extremely enthusiastic. Everyone in the cast was older and they all looked after me and showed me the ropes. I did 800 shows in two years and I loved it!" Campbell's experience working on *Phantom of the Opera* led her to make two major decisions. The first was to drop out of high school. In her interview with Cerone, she recalled, "I was working so much during school that I wasn't happy. I've been training since I was six, and all of a sudden I'm 15, and the member of a fantastic company. So it didn't make a lot of sense to say, 'Oh, I'm not going to [stay with] *The Phantom of the Opera* because I need to learn more about history.'" Campbell's second big decision was to move out of her father's house and live with her brother Christian. "I was doing *Phantom*, working with people who were my father's age and older, and being treated on an equal basis with them," she explained to Jamie Diamond for *Mademoiselle* (September 1998). "You grow up very quickly, and it doesn't make much sense to [answer to] someone whom you could consider a peer." After seeing a performance of *The Phantom of the Opera*, a theatrical agent, believing that Campbell had potential, signed her on. One result was that she won a role in the short-lived Canadian television series *Catwalk*, about a young rock band in search of fame and fortune. After only a year on the show, Campbell quit, feeling that her character, Daisy, was becoming too much of "a sex symbol sleeping with everyone in the band," as she told Jewel. "All my fan mail was from prisoners," she explained. After *Catwalk* Campbell starred in TV commercials, a handful of made-for-TV movies, and a Canadian feature film, *Paint Cans*. In 1994 U.S. audiences got their first look at Campbell, when MTV began airing episodes of *Catwalk*. That same year she appeared in the NBC-TV movie *I Know My Son Is Alive*, alongside television veterans Corbin Bernsen and Amanda Pays.

NBC producers persuaded Campbell to move to Los Angeles and explore opportunities in the U.S. market. Within weeks of her arrival in Hollywood, she auditioned for the role that would send her career into high gear: the part of Julia in *Party of Five*, an ensemble drama about five orphaned siblings in San Francisco. The series debuted on the Fox TV network in 1994 to much critical acclaim, but it attracted few viewers. Hoping to boost the show's ratings, Campbell and her castmates set off on a barnstorming promotional tour of U.S. malls. Looking back on that period, Campbell said to Kronke, "I've been to so many states in this country, and I can't even tell you which ones they are. When I travel, people ask, 'Have you been here before?' and I say, 'I think I may have. I recognize the airport, I've seen that mall before.' But you don't see anything else! You fly out that day and fly back at night, and all you see are thousands of people who want your autograph." The tour not only raised the visibility of the cast but also helped to bring all the players together. Campbell told Dunn that during the series' first season, "we'd cook dinner at each other's houses every weekend. We really were like a family." This feeling came through on the show, making the story believable and accessible to viewers. Nevertheless, the program's ratings remained mediocre. In 1995, just when the show appeared to be down for the count, thousands of letters from devoted *Party of Five* fans arrived at Fox's offices, leading studio executives to order another season's worth of episodes. The following year *Party of Five* shocked the industry by winning the Golden Globe Award for best drama series, beating out such top-rated shows as *ER* and *NYPD Blue*. After that its ratings began to rise steadily, and the show became a hit at last. As it aged, it tackled such weighty issues as drug use, alcoholism, and cancer. Its most controversial plotline came when Campbell's character, Julia Salinger, became pregnant and chose to have an abortion. Although the producers gave in to studio pressure and changed the script so that Julia miscarried on the way to the abortion clinic, the episode brought the series its highest ratings up to that point. While Campbell disagreed with the script change—"Miscarriage was an easy way out. It was just silly," she commented to Weinraub—she regarded her role as a base from which to address a broad audience about common issues that affect teens. "It's a wonderful position to be in," she told a reporter for *Us* magazine (on-line). "It's wonderful that people look up to me and that they can learn things from Julia." Campbell made no apologies for the occasionally morose tone of *Party of Five*. "The show has always been a tear-jerker," she told Ian Spelling for the *Chicago Tribune* (June 30, 1998). "People come back to *Party* with a box of Kleenex so they can cry for an hour, which they may not get to do in the rest of their lives. It's hard at times to constantly play such heavy stuff, but I'd rather play heavy stuff than light fluff." The Fox network canceled *Party of Five* in May 2000.

The series was still doing well in the ratings when, in 1996, Campbell made the move to feature films. She began with the supernatural thriller *The Craft*, about four teenage girls who discover how to perform witchcraft on their tormenting classmates. *The Craft* proved to be a sleeper hit. That fall Campbell starred in horror master Wes Craven's teen-slasher film *Scream*, playing Sidney Prescott, a young woman who becomes the target of a serial killer who is obsessed with horror films. A relatively small-budgeted and unheralded film, *Scream* went on to become a smash hit, grossing over $100 million and drawing a lot of attention to both Campbell and screenwriter Kevin Williamson. For Campbell, working on the film proved to be a very positive experience. "I loved the fact that it makes fun of the horror genre within the film," she told *Australian TV Week* (May 1997). "People have been saying that they love the fact that it's just as funny as it is scary. So, people that wouldn't normally get to a horror film are surprised and enjoyed it. And I love the character also, Sidney, who has a big transition in the film. She goes from lost soul to someone who fights back."

In December 1997 Campbell returned to the horror world, reprising her role as Sydney in *Scream 2*. Campbell confessed to Portman, "I had apprehensions because the only reason any sequel is ever made is because the first one was so good. You think—who are we to try and outdo ourselves? But I was incredibly happy with Kevin's script." A bigger, funnier, and bloodier excursion than its predecessor, *Scream 2* was another blockbuster, breaking the $100 million mark at the box office.

With her place on the list of Hollywood's most bankable ingenues thus assured, Campbell decided to try a role unlike anything on her résumé—the part of Suzie Toller, the drug-addicted, bisexual ex-con in the erotic thriller *Wild Things* (1998). "Suzie's very different from anything I've done before. I don't think it's what people expect of me, but that's sort of the reason I did it. I didn't want to be typecast in any one kind of thing," she said in an interview for *Entertainment Tonight Online* in 1998. While not as popular as the *Scream* films, *Wild Things* drew a respectable profit and has become a cult favorite on video and cable.

Campbell next joined the cast of *54*, one of the most eagerly anticipated films of 1998. A story of the drug-filled heyday of Studio 54, New York's famous disco club, *54* had enviable buzz and a star-studded cast, which included Ryan Phillipe, Salma Hyek, and Mike Myers as club owner Steve Rubell. The film opened to scathing reviews, however, many of which attacked Campbell's acting. A major flop, the picture barely recouped its costs and disappeared from theaters almost immediately.

Meanwhile, Campbell was continuing to work on *Party of Five*, which was still going strong after almost five years on the air. She also served as the producer for *Hair Shirt* (1998), a small Canadian film in which she starred alongside her brother Christian. In 1999 she appeared with Matthew Perry and Dylan McDermott in the romantic comedy *Three to Tango* and filmed *Panic*, with William H. Macy and Donald Sutherland. She returned to the horror genre with *Scream 3*, released in February 2000. Many critics agreed that Campbell was the film's strongest asset. In the *New York Times* (February 4, 2000), Elvis Mitchell wrote that she "shows real ability, no longer just the cupcake about to [be] hacked with the phallic carving knife. She has developed as an actress; when her eyes go dark with concern and fear, she is nerve-racked and tormented, not play-acting." Later in 2000 Campbell appeared in the black comedy *Drowning Mona*. She will play a leading role in the comedy *Investigating Sex*, slated for release in 2001.

In 1995 Campbell married her longtime boyfriend, Canadian actor Jeff Colt, whom she had met while appearing in *Phantom* in Canada. Her sudden decision to marry him came after the realization that Colt could not stay in Los Angeles without a green card. The couple have since divorced.

By her own account, Campbell is ambivalent regarding the trappings of fame. "I think my greatest insecurity would just be standing in the middle of a room and having everyone watching me and think that's what I want," she told Cerone. "If I am interesting to you because of who I am, then that's incredible. But if I'm interesting to you only because of what I am, then let's not bother, you know?" — J.K.B.

Suggested Reading: *Rolling Stone* p57+ Sep. 18, 1997, with photos; *People* p79+ Mar. 3, 1997, with photos; *Mademoiselle* p149+ Sep. 1998, with photos; *TV Guide* p24+ Feb. 8, 1997, with photos; *Time* p78+ Mar. 23, 1998, with photos

Selected Films: *The Craft* 1996; *Scream* 1996; *Scream 2* 1997; *Wild Things* 1998; *The Lion King II: Simba's Pride* 1998; *Hair Shirt*, 1998; *Three to Tango* 1999; *Scream 3*, 2000; *Drowning Mona*, 2000

Selected Television Shows: *I Know My Son Is Alive*, 1994; *Party of Five*, 1994–2000; *The Canterville Ghost*, 1996

Courtesy of Children's Hospital of Michigan

Canady, Alexa

Nov. 7, 1950– Director of neurosurgery at Children's Hospital of Michigan. Address: Children's Hospital of Michigan, 3901 Beaubien Blvd., Detroit, MI 48201

"I can't watch people get shot and cut up in the movies," the neurosurgeon Alexa Canady told Brian Lanker for his book *I Dream a World: Portraits of Black Women Who Changed America* (1989). "It freaks me out. You're being a voyeur. You can't intervene, you can't help. This is a very different quality than going to the emergency room where somebody's got blood and gore all over the place and you can do something. . . . You get to be a part of people's families in a very intimate way. You get to see the strengths of the human spirit that can survive terrible, devastating things. . . . You can't make it not painful, but you can certainly make it much easier in terms of their understanding of what's happening." As the chief of pediatric neurosurgery at the Children's Hospital of Michigan since 1987, Canady has helped thousands of children suffering from traumatic brain injuries, brain tumors, epilepsy, or other neurological problems. And as the first female African-American neurosurgeon in the United States, she has also inspired many young members of minority groups to pursue professions once closed to people of color in the U.S. "Those of us in small, highly specialized fields have an opportunity to reaffirm the equality of black people in the entire gamut of study," she has said, as quoted in *Notable Black American Women* (1992).

The second of four children and an only daughter, Alexa Irene Canady was born on November 7, 1950 in Lansing, Michigan. Her father, Clinton Canady Jr., was a dentist; he became well-known in Lansing for his activities as a member, at various times, of the city's police, fire, parks, and recreation boards. Her mother, Hortense Golden Canady, a Fisk University graduate, was the first black person to be elected to the Lansing Board of Education. After her children grew up, she became a college administrator; a longtime member of various organizational and corporate boards, she served from 1983 to 1988 as the national president of Delta Sigma Theta, an international sorority whose mission is "to provide services and programs to promote human welfare"; currently, she is the director of the Lansing Community College Foundation. Alexa Canady, who is also a Delta Sigma Theta sister, has said that her mother fostered a love of learning in her children and encouraged them to be goal-oriented. Her maternal grandmother, too, was a role model for her, she told Brian Lanker. Born in 1903, her grandmother graduated from college and eventually became a professor at Lane College, in Tennessee, an almost unheard-of achievement for a black woman at the time. "She always treated me like I was a person who was worth listening to even when I was a little person and not worth listening to," Canady told Lanker. As a youngster, Canady pressured her parents to give her and her brothers—Clinton III, Alan, and Mark, all of whom became lawyers—equal treatment. Forced to wash the dishes—a chore she so disliked that her father has joked that she broke plates on purpose, rather than washing them—she talked her parents into requiring her brothers to take turns at the task, too.

In the predominantly white area on the outskirts of Lansing where she grew up, Canady felt "very much aware of being in the minority," as she was quoted as saying in a series on African-American scientists on the Albion College, Michigan, Web site. "On the other hand," she said, "in terms of [the] general society, it makes you very comfortable living in that world, which is certainly in many ways representative of the world." At the local elementary school, Canady and her younger brother Mark were the only two black pupils. In the second grade, in an incident of racism that Canady remembers well, her teacher switched the high score that Alexa had achieved on a statewide reading test with the lower score of a white boy. (After the deception was discovered, the teacher was fired.) Except for two years during junior high, when she was bused to an integrated school, Canady attended schools in which all but a few of the students were white. An excellent student, she earned a National Achievement Scholarship as a high-school senior. (Funded by colleges and universities, the scholarships are awarded to outstanding black students by the National Merit Scholarship Corp.)

After graduating from high school, in 1967, Canady enrolled at the University of Michigan at Ann Arbor, where she began studying for a degree in mathematics. Although she got good grades in her math courses, she came to realize that she felt little of the passion for the discipline that many of the men in her classes displayed, and she decided against pursuing a career as a mathematician. Unsure of what new path to choose, she "had a crisis of confidence," she admitted to Patricia Anstett for the *Detroit Free Press* (March 8, 1999, on-line). During the summer after her sophomore year, she worked evenings as an editor at the *Michigan Daily*, the university's campus newspaper, with the aim of honing her writing skills. Then one of her brothers told her about a daytime health-careers program at the university, targeted at minority students, who were paid for their participation. Eager to save enough money to buy a car, she gained a place in the program. She worked with Art Bloom, a geneticist and pediatrician, and felt "an instant connection" with medicine, as she told Patricia Anstett. The next term she began concentrating in science courses, to prepare for medical school, and in 1971 she earned a B.S. degree. Despite a mediocre grade-point average, Anstett reported, she gained admission to the University of Michigan Medical School, thanks to "good test scores, her journalism experience, and two years of debating prowess" as a member of the university team.

Canady entered medical school with the intention of becoming an internist, but after becoming fascinated with the nervous system—"it's so neat and logical and precise," she was quoted as saying on the Albion College Web site—she decided to focus on neurology instead. While at med school she was elected to the Alpha Omega Alpha Honorary Medical Society and earned a citation from the American Medical Women's Association. She received an M.D. degree, cum laude, in 1975. Ready for a change of scene, she accepted an internship at the Yale-New Haven Hospital, in Connecticut, soon finding that she preferred what she perceived as the less status-conscious atmosphere of the Midwest. The next year she gained admission to the residency training program of the Department of Neurosurgery at the University of Minnesota, thus becoming the first black as well as the first female neurosurgical resident at that institution.

On the first day of her five-year residency at Yale, an administrator callously remarked to Canady that she must be the school's new "equal-opportunity package." Although she was stung by his words, Canady has readily conceded that affirmative action and other strides made during the civil-rights movement have directly benefitted her. "When I got a residency in neurosurgery, I got it not because I'm smarter than somebody 40 years ago, but because the politics were such that they needed a black woman and I was there and qualified," she told Brian Lanker. "I had impeccable credentials coming out of medical school, but there was an undercurrent of, 'How can you, a black woman, have the audacity to want to do this? Don't you know that you've got a double whammy?' Well, I came along at a time when it offered them a double positive. They could fulfill the quotas and say, 'I finished woman, I finished blacks, and all it took was one person instead of two.' So that became a positive for me."

From 1981 to 1982 Canady continued her training, as a resident in pediatric neurosurgery under Luis Schut at the University of Pennsylvania and the Children's Hospital of Philadelphia. She regarded Schut as "a father figure," she told Anstett, who would "share with you how it really worked" and "was a person who I knew was on my side." Schut told Anstett that when he met Canady, "she had a giant chip on her shoulder" and acted defensive, because "she thought people would pick on her." After he had a heart-to-heart talk with her, he said, "she changed overnight." By the end of the year, her peers voted her one of the top residents. "She's unforgettable," Schut declared. "She's one of the best trainees I've ever had. The others complain because Alexa always was my favorite. She's got guts." During her year in Pennsylvania, Canady taught neurosurgery at the University of Pennsylvania College of Medicine.

In 1982 Canady returned to Michigan, to accept a combined teaching-surgical post in neurosurgery at the Henry Ford Hospital in Detroit. In 1983 she moved to the neurosurgery department at the Children's Hospital of Michigan, where she was named Teacher of the Year in 1984. In 1985 she began teaching at the Wayne State University School of Medicine, in Detroit. She was promoted to clinical associate professor in 1987 and associate professor of neurosurgery, in 1990; since 1991 she has served as vice chairman of the Department of Neurosurgery. Meanwhile, in 1986 she was named assistant director of neurosurgery at the hospital, and the next year she was named the facility's chief of neurosurgery. "If you get to be where I am and you're black, [people] figure you must be really damn good . . . ," she told Brian Lanker. "When I, a black neurosurgeon and director of the department, walk in and see a family, I must be a messiah. They perceive me as being more powerful than a white physician in the same role. It's just racism in a more benign form."

Canady has been widely credited with making the Children's Hospital of Michigan Department of Neurosurgery one of the best such specialty providers in the country. Nearly every week she performs more than a dozen surgical procedures. These include the removal of brain or spinal tumors and the insertion of shunts in the heads of infants suffering from hydrocephalus—a potentially fatal condition in which excess fluid builds up in the skull. Her areas of expertise also include treatment of epilepsy, craniofacial abnormalities, and head trauma, and she has helped to develop neuroendoscopic equipment, which is used to examine the brain's interior. Canady views her job as more multifaceted than many people might imagine. "One of the things I think surgeons have to do is shift emphasis," she told Brian Lanker. "My job is really not to cut. My job is to help people, which often includes cutting, and that's a very different focus." Canady is known at the Children's Hospital of Michigan for her warmth: she always remembers the names of her current and recent patients and, when she senses a hug would be welcome, gives one along with medical treatment. An avid Nintendo fan, she often impresses young patients with her prowess at hockey and snowboarding video games.

During a 1995 speech at Harvard University, according to the *Harvard Medical Web* (on-line), Canady warned black medical students that they would face more pressure than their white counterparts to be active on committees, attend official functions, and mentor minority youths. She herself considers mentoring young people to be a vital part of her life. Nevertheless, she is realistic about the obstacles that face anyone whose goal is a career in neurosurgery. "You do a disservice to children if you paint it as too rosy," she told Patricia Anstett. "They hit a bump and feel like a failure. Well, everybody fails at some time or another. But no one talks about it."

In 1986 Canady was named Woman of the Year by the National Association of Negro Business and Professional Women's Clubs. That same year she won the Candace Award from the National Coalition of 100 Black Women. She received an honorary degree from Marygrove College, in Detroit, in 1994 and has been inducted into the Michigan Women's Hall of Fame. She has also been honored with the Wayne State University Distinguished Service Award, the Starlight Foundation's Shining Star Award, the Roeper School's Golden Apple Award, and the University of Michigan Alumnae Council's Athena Award, for public excellence and public service.

In June 1988 Canady married George Davis, a retired navy recruiter. Her marriage, she told Anstett, is "the best thing I did with my life." "Everything else is relatively conditional," she explained. "But with my marriage, I don't have to be anything different than who I am." Davis often delivers lunch to the hospital so the two can eat together. They spend free time quietly at home or taking drives around West Bloomfield, where they currently live. Although Canady told Anstett that she looks forward to retiring within seven years or so, she also said, "I love working at this hospital. It's been joyous. I'll work until it's no longer fun." — M.R.

Suggested Reading: *Detroit Free Press* (on-line) Mar. 8, 1999, with photos; *U.S. News & World Report* p55 Feb. 13, 1989, with photo; Lanker, Brian. *I Dream a World: Portraits of Black Women Who Changed the World*, 1989; *Notable Black American Women*, 1992; *Notable Twentieth-Century Scientists*, 1995

Carmack, John

1971(?)– Owner of and head programmer at id Software. Address: id Software, Town East Tower, Suite 615, 18601 LBJ Freeway, Mesquite, TX 75150

"If hard-core gaming ever had a god, John Carmack is it," Paul Keegan wrote for the *New York Times Magazine*, quoting the Gamespot Web site (May 23, 1999, on-line). In the past, computer games were most often two-dimensional affairs, in which the characters moved jerkily from one side of the screen to the other. Carmack, a software engineer and co-founder of id Software, envisioned a game in which the player would control a character who seemingly entered the computer and roamed through three dimensions. In the early 1990s he pi-

Reid Horn

John Carmack

oneered the technology that allows computer-game aficionados to interact with this virtual environment in a startlingly realistic manner. The media scrambled for the term that would most accurately describe the player/characters in the resulting games, and most settled on "first-person shooter," because the characters were generally equipped with high-tech weaponry with which to fight heavily armed 3-D opponents. Carmack's games began attracting cult followings, and they were so realistic that the United States Marine Corps eventually began to use them in training sessions. While fans raved about the games' copious amounts of blood and flying "gibs"—slang for "giblets," or body parts—critics worried that young people, who were the most avid players, were receiving dangerously high doses of violent imagery. Carmack, along with others in the industry, was blamed for a rash of high-school shootings, most notably those in Columbine, Colorado, and West Paducah, Kentucky, when it was discovered that the culprits were devotees of first-person shooter games. Carmack felt that he was being made a scapegoat by parents unwilling to accept responsibility for their children's actions. Defending his games to Keegan, he explained, "It's just like playing Cowboys and Indians like little kids do, except with visual effects."

An intensely private person, Carmack grants few interviews, and he told Keegan, "I wish the world would pretty much leave me alone." Little is known, therefore, about his personal life. Sources often describe him as shy and soft-spoken, and photos reveal him to be a pale, gangly man, with wire-rimmed glasses and a ponytail. According to Keegan, he is originally from Kansas City, Missouri. Most sources agree that he was born in about 1971 and that he taught himself computer programming when he was a teenager. Articles about Carmack typically begin with the fact that he was working at Softdisk Publishing, a Shreveport, Louisiana, firm, in 1990, when he developed a two-dimensional, arcade-style game called Invasion of the Vorticons, along with fellow Softdisk employees John Romero and Adrian Carmack (no relation). John Carmack was already experimenting with new software engines that would bring about an unprecedented level of realism, and the trio decided to leave their jobs and form their own company to make use of the engines. On February 1, 1991 they founded id Software in partnership with Apogee, a firm that was exploring the distribution of software through the Internet rather than on store-bought floppy disks.

Based in Dallas, Texas, id released its first game, Wolfenstein 3-D, on May 5, 1992. Romero, who has been described as the Quentin Tarantino of computer games for the stylized depictions of violence in his work, had designed an eerie, Nazi-filled castle. The player, armed with a virtual machine gun, moved about the three-dimensional environment killing German guards and attack dogs before being confronted in the final level by a Gatling-wielding Adolf Hitler. Players had never seen anything like it, and the game became an immediate sensation, at one point bringing in about $120,000 in monthly sales.

Apogee's marketing strategy was as revolutionary as Carmack's software. Wolfenstein 3-D was unavailable in stores; players instead loaded the first installment, free of charge, from computer services such as Compuserve or from the Internet, which at the time was not in widespread use by the general public. The rest of the game could then be ordered by phone for $45. An estimated one million people downloaded the free version, and approximately 10 percent went on to buy the complete version.

Computer-game fans eagerly awaited the team's next effort, and in 1993 Doom was released. Set in a futuristic military compound on Mars, the game required the player, in the guise of a marine, to stalk the halls of the base, blasting away at evil-looking aliens. Carmack has explained that the name Doom referred to a line in the film *The Color of Money*, in which Tom Cruise's character arrives at a pool hall and is asked about the case holding his customized pool cue. He replies that the case contains doom—and then proceeds to decimate his opponents. Carmack envisioned his new creation as having much the same effect on the computer-game industry. In a marketing move similar to that used with Wolfenstein 3-D, the first three episodes of Doom were loaded onto a server for free downloading, and then the entire package could be purchased by phone using a credit card. So many people downloaded the free episodes that the computer system at the University of Wisconsin, where they were posted, crashed.

Carmack had further perfected the software engine, making possible a never-before-seen level of graphic detail. He had intentionally released a portion of the source code so that hackers could add their own touches to the game, and they responded by imaginatively incorporating Disney characters or various television figures (Barney the purple dinosaur was particularly popular) in place of the aliens. Romero's design took full advantage of Carmack's improved technology, and fans hailed the bleak and gritty atmosphere of the base's seemingly endless corridors. Industry insiders were no less laudatory, and computer-gaming magazines called the game's visual effects "seismic" and "inestimable." Doom was named "Game of the Year" in 1994 by both *PC Gamer* and *Computer Gaming World* and garnered an award for technical excellence from *PC Magazine* in the same year. From then on, any new computer game would be measured against the standards set by Doom, and Carmack and Romero began to be thought of as the John Lennon and Paul McCartney of the gaming world. An estimated 15 million to 20 million copies of the game's opening levels have been downloaded since its introduction. As of early 2000 Doom (and its somewhat less popular spin-off, Doom II) had sold four million copies worldwide and earned approximately $100 million in sales. Doom is considered one of the best-selling computer games of all time, second only to Myst, a role-playing game set on a mysterious island.

The eagerly anticipated follow-up to Doom took two years to develop. In late June 1996 the free first episode of Quake, as the game was called, was released. Within a few days, tens of thousands of fans had downloaded it. Since Carmack had designed the game with the capacity to be played on the Internet by several people at once, many of the most dedicated enthusiasts established Quake servers, on which they hosted multiplayer "death matches." Encouraged by id, Quake "clans" formed, with their own logos and colorful names—such as PMS, an all-female clan. Quake's story line was sketchy—the emphasis was on simply annihilating as many enemies as possible, rather than on following an intricate plot—but Carmack's newest graphics engine made possible an amazing array of minute detail, and players were even able to aim their view up or down, as well as side to side, while maintaining the proper perspective. Romero had designed more violent and gory scenarios, and the game quickly became a phenomenal success, spawning huge conventions (or "Quakecons") at which thousands of fans would gather to play. Quake won numerous awards in 1996 and 1997 from almost every major gaming publication, including *Computer Gaming World*, *PC Games*, and *PC Computing*. Part of the game's success undoubtedly resulted from a new sales strategy devised by Mike Wilson, id's head of marketing and distribution. Wilson reasoned that if Quake was released on a disk costing just $10, instead of the $50 or so that most software cost in conventional outlets, the product could be placed in venues such as convenience stores, which had never before sold computer products because of their high prices. The disks would include the first episode (also available via the Internet), which could be played immediately, but would also have the complete version encrypted. The buyer could then use a credit card to get a code word allowing him or her to access the encrypted material. Wilson envisioned teenage customers thumbing through gaming publications on magazine racks and then buying the disks on impulse. Southland Corp., the owners of 7-Eleven stores, agreed to his proposal, and Quake was sold at many outlets of the 5,000-store chain.

With the success of the company came increasing tension between Carmack and Romero, who was adopting what Carmack considered "rock star" habits—wearing all-black designer clothing and growing his hair long—and cultivating media attention rather than concentrating on work. The basic disagreement centered on which of the pair's contributions was more important—Carmack's programming prowess or Romero's design ability. Romero resigned at the height of Quake's popularity, in 1996, and started his own company, Ion Storm, which would focus less on new technology and more on imaginative (and increasingly bloody) story lines. Without him, id developed two highly successful and award-winning sequels, Quake II and Quake III. The latter was designed to be played almost entirely on the World Wide Web by large groups rather than individuals—a phenomenon that observers are calling "social computing." Carmack explained the appeal of this group play to Christopher Palmeri for *Forbes* (October 18, 1999): "I may not be seven feet tall and weigh 300 pounds, but I can be a champion."

Although Carmack believed that his games had a healthy equalizing effect on players, many of his critics disagreed. In 1998 Michael Carneal, a 14-year-old Doom fan, went on a shooting rampage in West Paducah, Kentucky, that killed three members of his high school's prayer group and injured five others. Media attention immediately focused on the teen's love of violent computer games, and many commentators posited a direct connection between the games and a propensity for real-life violence. One expert on the psychology of killing, David Grossman, a retired army lieutenant colonel, has explained to the press that although an inexperienced killer's natural instinct is to shoot repeatedly at one target, Carneal had used the much more effective technique of moving quickly from one victim to the next, aiming at the head of each. This technique is often used in computer games, and Carneal, being adept at the games, had shot eight people in the head or torso with just eight bullets, despite never having fired an actual gun before. The families of the victims named id Software, along with several other entertainment companies, in a $130 million lawsuit, for which Grossman was to be an expert witness. Negative press attention intensified when a rumor began circulating that Doom fans Eric Harris and Dylan Klebold, the teenage shooters at the April 1999 massacre at Columbine High in Colorado, had used Carmack's source code to design a computer replica of the school's hallways, on which to play one level of the game. The tale received wide circulation but later proved to be false.

Bad press and outspoken critics do not seem to have had much of an effect on the financial success of id Software. The 13-person company is said to bring in close to $20 million a year. Carmack, who works seven days a week, often in 14-hour stretches, continually receives offers from financiers interested in investing in or purchasing the company, but he has so far turned down all of them. "I make several million dollars a year. I own several Ferraris," he told Palmeri. "I don't need $40 million in the bank if it means I have someone else telling me what to do." The sports cars to which he refers are reported to be Carmack's only indulgence. His collection is often written about in automotive magazines, and he has been known to award a Ferrari to the grand-prize winner at a Quake convention. — M.R.

Suggested Reading: *Forbes* p157+ Oct. 18, 1999, with photos; *Gentlemen's Quarterly* p96+ Oct. 1996, with photos; id Software (on-line); *New York Times Magazine* p36+ May 23, 1999, with photos

---

Courtesy of Speakers' Spotlight

Carter, Rubin

May 6, 1937– Human-rights activist; former boxer. Address: Association in Defense of the Wrongly Convicted, 438 University Ave., 19th Fl., Toronto, Ontario, Canada M5G 2K8

When he was a boxer, Rubin Carter stalked the ring like a panther, instinctively sizing up his opponents before raining blows on them so fiercely that New Jersey fight promoter Jimmy Colotto dubbed him "The Hurricane." The fight of his life occurred not in a crowded arena, however, but in a cell measuring four and a half by seven and a half feet. In 1967 Rubin "Hurricane" Carter was convicted of triple homicide and given three consecutive life sentences. Throughout the years that followed, he maintained his innocence, despite a second conviction a decade after the first. After many appeals were denied, Carter was freed, in 1985, through the efforts of a dedicated team of lawyers and a group of Canadian entrepreneurs. His struggle has come to symbolize for many the flaws in the American legal system as well as the ability of an individual to triumph over injustice. No fewer than three books have been written about Carter's experience, and his life's story is the subject of the acclaimed feature film *The Hurricane* (1999), which stars Denzel Washington. Although his time in prison accounts for decades of his life and cost him his marriage, his family, and the use of his right eye, Carter has insisted that he holds no grudges. "There is no bitterness," he told Frank Houston in an interview for *Salon* (December 24, 1999, on-line). "If I was bitter, that would mean they won."

The fourth of Lloyd and Bertha Carter's seven children, Rubin Carter was born on May 6, 1937 in Clifton, New Jersey, and raised in the nearby city of Paterson. As a boy he "never wanted for anything," he told Milton Gross in a 1964 interview for the *Saturday Evening Post*, as cited on *graphicwitness.com* (on-line). "We had good food and clothes. We were the first in our neighborhood to have a television set." Nevertheless, Carter was often in trouble; afflicted with a stammer, which made him the butt of ridicule, he was often forced to defend himself physically and was prone to lash out unpredictably. Carter's early years were peppered with incidents of petty theft, street fights, and trouble in school. At 14 he was sent to New Jersey's Jamesburg reformatory for attacking a man with a broken bottle and taking his watch. Carter's stay at the reformatory was extended because of continued misbehavior. "I was contumacious," he told Gross. "I just kept getting into more trouble, . . . and they just kept adding time. I was past 16 when I began realizing about girls, clothes, and music. I said, 'What am I doing here?'" He then made a largely successful effort to reform. Thirty days before he was due to be released, however, he received a disciplinary report informing him of the reformatory board's recommendation that he be shipped to Annandale, another New Jersey reformatory. Determined not to go, he broke out of the reformatory that same night.

Upon his return to Paterson, Carter's mother sent him to Philadelphia to live with an aunt. Shortly thereafter, in 1954, he joined the army, in which he served as a paratrooper. In the authorized biography *Hurricane: The Miraculous Journey of Rubin Carter* (2000) by James S. Hirsch, Carter recalled jump school as comprising "three torturous weeks of 24 hour days of corrosive annoyance." The rigors of jump school were insignificant, however, when compared with the racial inequality he faced in the army. During Carter's tenure black soldiers were crammed into the last two cars of troop trains, while white soldiers had the run of the remaining 20. In addition, during road trips from Fort Jackson, South Carolina, to Fort Campbell, Kentucky, white soldiers ate in restaurants "while blacks stayed on the bus and ate cold bologna sandwiches," as Carter recalled to Houston.

Carter discovered boxing while stationed in Germany. In the ring he proved to be a devastating force, pummeling opponents with swiftness and fury. His boxing prowess won him the army's European light-welterweight championship on two occasions. In time Carter felt ready to make boxing his career. "I loved prize fighting, but I wasn't about to prolong my Army career in order to compete in nothing," he wrote in his book *The Sixteenth Round: From Number 1 Contender to #45472* (1974), as quoted by Houston. "Shucks! I wanted to go home." In June 1956 he returned to Paterson, where he was promptly picked up by the local police for his escape from Jamesburg. He was sent to Annandale, where he served out nine months of a 13-month sentence. "When I got out I didn't care for nothing or nobody," he told Gross. "I'd lost my car, lost my job, lost my GI bill. I was just mad at life and mad at the world. I wanted to hit out at anything. Before I got home I stopped in a store and got me a bottle and started drinking, and I didn't stop for three, four weeks until I got picked up again." Carter resumed his wild living with a vengeance, carrying a gun wherever he went and taking part in numerous muggings and robberies. Eventually he was arrested and sentenced to six years, on two counts of robbery and one count of assault with intent to commit robbery. He served three years and four months in a New Jersey state prison and emerged a changed man.

In 1961 Carter began boxing professionally, amassing a four-fight winning streak in the fall of that year. Circling the ring like a predator before unloading a reported 80 punches per minute, Carter took on the nickname "Hurricane." Over the next three years, he continued to overwhelm his opponents, losing only three fights out of 20 between 1961 and 1964 and scoring knockouts in more than half of his victories. On December 14, 1964 Carter fought a legendary bout against middleweight champion Joey Giardello, losing the punishing 15-round match in a controversial split decision. "I lost because I didn't knock him out," Carter told Ira Berkow for the *New York Times* (January 24, 1993).

By this time Carter had begun attracting attention as much for his outspokenness as for his boxing ability. Milton Gross's *Saturday Evening Post* article caused a stir by quoting Carter as saying to a friend, regarding riots by police in Harlem that April, "Let's get guns and go up there and get us some of those police. I know I can get four or five of them before they get me. How many can you get?" Carter has maintained that the quote was taken out of context and that the conversation was off the record. In a 1975 interview with *Penthouse* (online), Carter noted, "My real problems began when the *Saturday Evening Post* printed what I said . . . that the black people ought to protect themselves against the invasions of white cops in black neighborhoods—cops who were beating little children down in the streets—and that black people ought to have died in the streets right there if it was necessary to protect their children. . . . Well, when that came out, the police throughout the world thought I had declared war on them . . . and when war is declared, truth is always the first casualty." Indeed, as Carter's profile began to rise, so did the number of his run-ins with the police. "I had a few friends who were Secret Service men and Federal Marshals, and they told me about the file they had on me," he told the *Penthouse* reporter. "They were following me around. Each state that I went in to fight, the moment I got into town the police rode down on me, fingerprinted me, and mugged me, and I would have to carry this card attesting to the fact that I was an ex-convict. The harassment was steady . . . constant." Death threats prevented Carter from attending the 1965 civil rights march in Selma, Alabama, led by Martin Luther King Jr., and he was forced to fight in other countries in order to avoid confrontations with the police.

At 2:30 a.m. on June 17, 1966, two black men walked into the Lafayette Grill, a quiet establishment in the predominantly white Riverside section of Paterson. Almost instantly they opened fire on the four patrons with a shotgun and .32 caliber revolver. Two people, James Oliver and Fred Nauyoks, were killed instantly, while Hazel Tanis and Willie Marins were severely wounded. (Tanis died a month later.) The gunmen then walked casually out into the street, where they were seen by Alfred Bello. A man with a long criminal record, Bello was acting as a lookout for Arthur Bradley, who was breaking into a nearby factory. Bello walked into the bar and, although shocked at the sight that greeted him, took $62 from the cash register. He then called the police, telling them that he had seen the killers drive away in a white car. This claim was corroborated by Patty Valentine, a woman who lived upstairs from the bar.

Across town, Carter was driving home from the Nite Spot, a local hangout. With him were his friend John Royster and 19-year-old, college-bound John Artis. Paterson police stopped the car but then, having been told to look for two—not three—men, let Carter and the others go. Later, the car was spotted in the vicinity of the Lafayette Grill, with only Carter and Artis inside. This time, the police took them to the crime scene, where no one could identify either of the men as one of the killers. Carter and Artis were then taken to Paterson General Hospital, where neither Tanis nor Marins could identify them, and were given lie-detector tests, which they both passed. Carter and Artis were released at about 7:00 p.m. on June 17; the following month they testified before a grand jury, which exonerated them. Almost four months later, on October 14, 1966, they were arrested again, in light of testimony given by Bello. That morning Bello had signed a statement claiming that Carter and Artis were the Lafayette gunmen. He, as well as Bradley, testified to that effect in Carter and Artis's trial, held the following May. An all-white jury convicted Carter and Artis on May 27, 1967. The prosecutors sought the death penalty, but the jury recommended mercy. Carter and Artis thus received three life terms each.

When Carter arrived at Trenton State Prison, he was told to wear the standard prison uniform. He refused, saying that he would not wear the clothes of a guilty man. As he explained to Hirsch, if he were to keep his dignity in prison, he would have to fight the system. "Why should I be a good prisoner when I haven't been a bad civilian?" he explained. "That's the depth of insanity." His defiance landed him in solitary confinement ("the hole," in prison vernacular) for three months, throughout which he wore the suit and jewelry he had had on when he arrived. During this period, at a routine checkup by the prison doctor, Carter was told that the retina in his right eye was detached, and that without surgery, he would certainly lose sight in that eye. Such a loss would end his boxing career, which he intended to continue upon his release. Fearing that he would attempt to flee, prison officials refused to allow Carter to undergo surgery outside the prison. Instead, the operation was performed at the penitentiary. The surgeon, who claimed to have lacked proper equipment, failed to save his sight. While he could never prove it, Carter believed that the entire scenario was devised to handicap him and leave him vulnerable to attack.

When Carter joined the prison's general population, he was sent to the wing designated for "incorrigibles." He abstained from work, ate his meals alone, and refused to cooperate with the prison psychiatrists. As time wore on, he began a detailed study of the technical aspects of his case and started writing about his experience. He hoped that through these efforts he could publicize his story and thereby turn the wheels of justice in his favor.

On the night of April 30, 1974, a phalanx of armed guards, clad in riot gear and carrying Mace and shackles, aligned themselves outside Carter's cell in Rahway State Prison, to which he had been transferred in 1971. They had come to take him to the readjustment unit at Trenton State Psychiatric Hospital. Carter, fearing that they would take his manuscript, barricaded the door and decided to meet his jailers on the terms with which he was most comfortable: as a fighter. In an interview with William Nack for *Sports Illustrated* (April 4, 1992), he recalled that he had challenged the guards, practically daring them to come in and get him. "I mean this," he told them. "I ain't going with you. If anybody comes in here to get me, God forbid. You'll need 20 men! First come, first served." Bobby Martin, a sergeant of the guards whom Carter considered a friend, persuaded Carter to leave his cell, promising that nothing would happen to his manuscript and that Martin himself would take him to Trenton. Carter agreed, and he left Rahway with the document tucked inside his pants. "If they had stripped me naked," he told Nack, "I would have taken that manuscript. It was a little thread of hope. The hope that somebody, someday, would read it and understand what had happened to me. What *was* happening to me. It was my lifeline—my message beyond the walls."

In July 1974 Carter filed a federal suit against the state for inflicting cruel and unusual punishment, and as a result he was released from the readjustment unit. That September his book, *The Sixteenth Round*, was published by Viking Press, to much critical acclaim. At about the same time, both Bello and Bradley recanted their testimony for a *New York Times* article, stating that they had been pressured by Paterson detectives to identify Carter and Artis as the Lafayette gunmen—and that they had been offered $10,000 in reward money as well as leniency in pending criminal charges in exchange for false testimony. "I was 23 years old and facing 80 to 90 years in jail [for robbery]," Bradley told Selwyn Raab for the article. "There's no doubt Carter was framed. . . . I lied to save myself." In spite of this, Judge Samuel Larner denied the request of the state public defender's office for a new trial. Carter began a lengthy appeal process, which would ultimately take him to the New Jersey Supreme Court.

During this period Carter's struggle became a cause célèbre, thanks largely to folk singer Bob Dylan's recording "Hurricane," an eight-minute song that chronicled Carter's arrest and conviction. In March 1976 the New Jersey Supreme Court overturned Carter and Artis's convictions, stating that evidence favorable to the defense had been withheld. A new trial was ordered, and Carter and Artis were released on bail. During the second trial, Bello renounced his recantation, returning instead to his original statement from the 1967 trial. On the stand, Bello made confusing and contradictory statements. At one point, asked to draw a diagram of a boxing ring where he claimed to have seen Carter fight, Bello simply scribbled a crude rectangle and then sat down. Not willing to rely on such shaky testimony, the state suggested racial revenge as Carter and Artis's motive, citing the Lafayette as an establishment that catered only to whites and pointing to the nationwide racial tension that was prevalent in 1966 to support that argument. The strategy worked, and Carter and Artis were once again found guilty. After his second conviction Carter spiraled into despair. "I had closed down emotionally," he told John Kalish for the *Chicago Tribune* (February 3, 1992). "I had closed down to anything from the outside."

In 1980 a black teenager named Lesra Martin bought a used copy of *The Sixteenth Round* at a Toronto book fair. Martin had, in effect, been adopted by a group of eight Canadian entrepreneurs, who had plucked him from Brooklyn and had been home-schooling him in Toronto. The book engrossed Martin, who felt that much of Carter's troubled youth paralleled his own. He read passages from *The Sixteenth Round* out loud to his housemates, who also became caught up in the story. Martin wrote to Carter, praising his courage and asking him to write back. The letter moved the former boxer, who had begun studying Eastern religions and was undergoing something of a spiritual transformation. "I was leaving me, and I didn't even know it," he told Nack. "I was opening up. And suddenly this letter came. How could I not respond? His letter had so much energy! There was a feeling there. . . . I typed a reply." Thus began an exchange between the two that culminated in Martin's visiting Carter in prison. Carter felt an instant connection with the young man, as he recalled to Nack. "Lesra was in a state of joy," he remarked. "You could feel it. It was like a son coming to see me. He was just so effervescent, and I loved the way he spoke, so precisely, and the way he laughed, even in this death house." It wasn't long before Martin's housemates were also visiting Carter. They, too, formed a bond with him and became interested in working toward his exoneration. "The way Lesra was gave a lot of credibility to the Canadian family," Carter said. "I knew then this was not a hoax. These people were not playing with our lives. It made me listen to them, and at the time I wasn't listening to anybody."

In the fall of 1983, the Canadians sold their home in Toronto. Three of the eight—Sam Chaiton, Lisa Peters, and Terry Swinton—moved to New Jersey to devote themselves fully to Carter's case. (By this point, Martin was a straight-A student who had enrolled at the University of Toronto.) With all of Carter's appeals having been exhausted, his lawyers, who had been working on the case since his imprisonment, felt that the best course of action was to file a petition for the writ of habeas corpus. Latin for "release the body," habeas corpus is a controversial writ that allows a federal court to overturn a state conviction on constitutional grounds. While some feel that the writ strips the state courts of their power, making the federal courts something of a deus ex machina for criminals, others regard it as the last defense of an individual's basic freedoms. In preparation for the filing of the motion, Carter's lawyers handled the legal facets of the case, while Carter and the Canadians pored over the facts. Carter did, however, involve himself in the writing of the documents, pushing for straightforward language rather than legal jargon. "There is a traditional style of legal writing, an objective statement of facts, but Rubin didn't accept that," Ed Graves, one of Carter's lawyers, told Hirsch. "He would edit word by word, sentence by sentence, and he wanted to advocate in every sentence of every filing."

After almost 20 years behind bars, Carter was set free, on November 7, 1985, when Judge H. Lee Sarokin approved his release. In his statement to the courtroom, as quoted by Hirsch, Sarokin observed, "If my ruling is correct, Mr. Carter's past imprisonment may have been a travesty. To continue it would even be a greater one." Prosecutors attempted to appeal the decision, saying that Carter was a dangerous man, but they were met with denials each time. On February 19, 1988 the state officially dropped all charges against Carter and Artis.

Upon his release Carter went to live with the Canadians, feeling indebted to them. For a while, life in Canada was idyllic for him. He lived in a six-bedroom house on 10 acres of land and helped his housemates build a two-stall barn behind the house, where he kept his horse, Red Cloud. He would ride Red Cloud for hours along the miles of trails that wound along the property. In 1989 he married Lisa Peters. Eventually, however, Carter came to feel constrained by the group's communal lifestyle, which dictated that the members of the group do things together or not at all. For Carter, who had been denied his freedom for nearly half his life, the situation proved intolerable. In 1992 he and Peters separated (they remain legally married), and he left the commune. While he is no longer in contact with the group, he bears them no ill will. Chaiton and Swinton chronicled their experiences with Carter and Martin (who is now a prosecutor in Kamloop, British Columbia) in *Lazarus and the Hurricane* (1991), which, along with *The Sixteenth Round*, provided the inspiration for Norman Jewison's film *The Hurricane*.

Rubin Carter currently lives in Canada, where he works as executive director of the Association in Defense of the Wrongly Convicted, based in Toronto. In addition, he is a member of the board of directors of the Southern Center for Human Rights, in Atlanta, and the Alliance for Prison Justice, in Boston. In great demand on the lecture circuit, Carter speaks at high schools, universities, and corporate conferences. Although he no longer boxes, the World Boxing Council awarded him an honorary championship belt on December 16, 1993. He and his first wife were divorced in 1977, and he rarely sees his grown children, Raheem Rubin and Theadora. Nevertheless, his daughter maintains a great deal of respect for Carter. "No matter what he does, I love him," she told Hirsch. "Sometimes I'd like to be more in contact, but mentally we're together. We have a bond that cannot be broken."

Although his days of boxing with unbridled fury are behind him, Carter is no less a fighter today. The intensity that drove him in the ring now serves to see him through life's everyday challenges. "Keep on pushing and keep on dreaming," he told Paul Fruitman for the University of Western Ontario *Gazette* (March 14, 1997, on-line). "If you see an obstacle in front of you, it's not there to stop you. It's there to make you stronger for the next obstacle that comes around." — J.K.B.

Suggested Reading: *Chicago Tribune* V p1+ Feb. 3, 1992, with photos; *Entertainment Weekly* p40+ Feb. 4, 2000, with photos; *New York Times* VIII p2 Jan. 24, 1993, with photo; *Sports Illustrated* (on-line) Apr. 4, 1992; *Washington Post* B p3 Oct. 3, 1993, with photo; Hirsch, James S. *Hurricane: The Miraculous Journey of Rubin Carter*, 2000

Courtesy of the Venezuelan Embassy

Chávez, Hugo

July 28, 1954– President of Venezuela. Address: Oficina del Presidente, Palacio de Miraflores, Av. Urdaneta, Caracas, Venezuela; c/o Embassy of the Republic of Venezuela, 1099 30th St. N.W., Washington, DC 20007

"They ask me if I am a revolutionary," Hugo Chávez, the president of Venezuela, said to Gabriel Escobar for the *Washington Post* (July 24, 1994). "Well, I'm not afraid of the word." A fiery political figure, Chávez has been on the forefront of governmental change in Venezuela. The leader of a failed coup attempt, in 1992, Chávez rode a wave of public discontent that carried him to victory in the presidential election of December 1998, and he easily won reelection in July 2000, this time for a six-year term. He has since supervised the writing of a new constitution and guided his country through one of its worst natural disasters ever. The people's choice in the struggle to eradicate political corruption and introduce fiscal reform, Chávez has been the bane of Venezuela's traditional governing elite, who bristle at his dictatorial style and have expressed both uneasiness about his amorphous political philosophy and alarm about his apparent lack of a unified economic strategy. "If you try to assess me by traditional canons of analysis, you'll never emerge from confusion," he told Larry Rohter for the *New York Times* (April 10, 1999). "If you are attempting to determine whether Chávez is of the left, right, or center, if he is a socialist, Communist, or capitalist, well I am none of those, but I have a bit of all of those."

Hugo Chávez Frías was born on July 28, 1954 in Sabaneta, Venezuela, the second of the six children of two elementary-school teachers. His father, Hugo de los Reyes Chávez, also worked as a grassroots political organizer, and following a 40-year teaching career, he was elected governor of the state of Barinas. Raised in a small riverside house with a palm roof and mud floors, Chávez grew up very poor. As a boy he sold fruit and ices to soldiers outside a military barracks every afternoon after school and before baseball practice. Although he was an avid reader and gifted student, his first love was baseball. Eustoquio Duque Castro, a retired Venezuelan military officer, told Rohter that Chávez "could do it all, hit, field, run, and pitch, but couldn't afford the equipment he needed."

After completing high school, from which he graduated near the top of his class, Chávez was accepted into the Venezuelan Military Academy, a tuition-free institution known for its strong academics and fine baseball team. He spent the next four years studying military sciences—and honing his curveball. "The army for me was the only way to the major leagues . . . and to Caracas [the nation's capital]," he told Serge F. Kovaleski for the *Washington Post* (February 13, 1999). "My father could not pay for my studies anywhere else." After he was sidelined because of an arm injury, he abandoned his dreams of a big-league career and immersed himself in the military. He graduated from the academy in 1975 and went on to distinguish himself as a member of an elite paratroop unit, advancing to the rank of lieutenant colonel. Along the way, he grew disenchanted with his country's government.

Since 1958 Venezuela had been governed under the Punto Fijo system. Put in place after the fall of the dictator Marcos Pérez Jiménez, the system resulted from a pact, signed in the city of Punto Fijo, among the Democratic Action Party (A.D.), the Social Christian Party (COPEI), and the Democratic Republican Union (URD). According to the agreement, the three political parties would share power regardless of which one held the majority of seats in the National Congress. This form of democracy made Venezuela's government one of the most stable in South America for decades. Eventually, A.D. and COPEI became dominant and gained control of the income generated by sales of oil from the country's vast reserves. Both parties steered Venezuela's government and economy toward a heavy reliance on oil revenues while increasing state subsidization for civil programs. As a result, subsidies were increasingly directed to A.D.'s and COPEI's constituents, and political office became a means to profit from oil. When oil prices fell drastically in the 1980s, Venezuela's economy foundered, swelling the ranks of the lower class and depleting the national treasury.

Social unrest over Venezuela's limping economy came to a head in February 1989, when—incited by widespread shortages of basic foodstuffs and government-imposed increases in gasoline and public-transportation prices—riots broke out in Caracas. An estimated 300 people were killed before order was restored. The administration of then-President Carlos Andrés Pérez Rodríguez, who had taken office in February of that year, became wildly unpopular. Over the next few years, the public's discontent was fueled further by a series of scandals involving advisers close to Pérez. Pérez himself was often criticized for spending too much time on international trips and diplomacy and too little on the problems facing his people. While his program of slashing import tariffs and ending subsidies of foods and other commodities was well received internationally, the income of most Venezuelans had dropped more than 30 percent in the previous three years. In January 1992 a Caracas newspaper published a poll in which 81 percent of the 1,000 respondents declared that they had no faith in the government.

Earlier, in 1982, Chávez, who then held the rank of captain, and several other mid-ranking officers had formed the Bolívarian Revolutionary Movement–200. Born of their growing distaste for the Venezuelan government and named in recognition of the 200th anniversary of the birth of Simón Bolívar, who led much of South America to independence from Spanish rule in the 1820s, the group convened to protest the fiscal and social effects of the government's economic policies. For years the organization operated clandestinely. In 1989 Chávez and his colleagues began plotting against Pérez. On February 4, 1992 Chávez, backed by more than 1,000 rebel soldiers clad in fatigues and red berets, stormed the presidential palace in an attempt to overthrow the government. Simultaneously, troops led by Chávez's co-conspirators launched similar attacks at key government positions throughout the country. A brief but bloody battle between the rebels and loyalist forces ensued. The coup attempt ended within hours, largely because the rebels had no means of communication—a private supplier had never delivered the cell phones they had ordered. Chávez was captured at the military museum in Caracas, where he had been bunkered. He later appeared on television, urging rebels in other districts to surrender to avoid further bloodshed.

Chávez was put in prison, where he remained for two years. "The first days were like being in a grave; it was cold and we were kept in a basement," he told Serge F. Kovaleski. "I felt as if I had been buried alive." During his time behind bars, Chávez underwent something of a spiritual and intellectual rebirth. He and nine other imprisoned coup leaders began reading widely, from works ranging from the Bible to the political and philosophical writings of Karl Marx, Plato, Jean-Paul Sartre, and Albert Camus. "We started studying things like political doctrines . . . and I was also maintaining my physical and moral strength," he recalled to Kovaleski. "We were opening ourselves to many new ideas." Meanwhile, Venezuelans had come to regard Chávez as a folk hero, a champion of the people who lived in abject poverty in a land rich with oil. Word about their support eventually reached Chávez in prison.

In March 1993, just months after a second major coup attempt, Carlos Pérez was brought before the Venezuelan Supreme Court on charges of embezzlement, based on $17 million of state funds that he had allegedly used for nonofficial purposes. He was found guilty, and the Venezuelan Senate appointed Senator Ramón José Velasquez to complete the last eight months of Pérez's term. In December 1993 Rafael Caldera Rodríguez was elected president; he had held the office once before, from 1969 to 1974. Caldera pardoned Chávez in March 1994 in an effort to stem the steady growth of the dissident's popularity. He failed to take into account that, although Chávez had been in jail for two years, the coup leader had never been officially sentenced for his actions, leaving him eligible to run for public office.

Chávez immediately set about building grassroots support for his movement. He curried favor among the poor and disenfranchised and preached revolution, all but demanding the dissolution of the National Congress on the grounds that its members had become hopelessly corrupt and inefficient. "The crisis is so deep. The gangrene is so profound, as Bolívar used to say, that it can't be cured by palliatives," he said at one rally, as quoted by James Brooke in the *New York Times* (May 19, 1994). "The only way is revolution." While he made politically charged speeches, Chávez insisted that he was not seeking office. He frequently noted, however, that if he were in a position of power, he would impose a "war economy" and would appropriate resources, including privately owned land, in an effort to fight corruption and poverty. Public response to his rhetoric was immediate and affirmative. Graffiti proclaiming "Bolívar

Lives Again" was sprayed liberally on walls across Venezuela. "We appeal to the 70 percent of the population who don't vote," Chávez told Brooke, referring to the political apathy and poor voter turnout that had plagued recent Venezuelan elections. Among power brokers, however, the response to Chávez's orations was less positive. Media barons called for a press blackout, and President Caldera placed his son-in-law in charge of a heavily armed presidential security unit. Being branded a revolutionary by his adversaries pleased Chávez. "I think Latin America has to return to the revolution," he told Gabriel Escobar. Despite his repeated denials that he would run for office, his actions indicated that he might politicize his movement. In April 1997 his backers polled several thousand Venezuelan citizens, asking them if they thought Chávez should run for the presidency and if they would vote for him. The overwhelmingly positive response encouraged Chávez to seek the office in earnest.

Campaigning under the banner of his newly formed party, the Fifth Republic Movement (MVR)—so named to signal his intention of establishing a new constitutional period, the fifth in Venezuela's history—Chávez predictably created a stir. His platform called for sweeping governmental reform that included eliminating the traditional party-ruled system, dissolving the National Congress, and rewriting the constitution—all of which raised the hackles of old-guard politicos, who derided him as a dictator-in-waiting and warned against his unorthodox proposals. The United States, too, showed disapproval of Chávez's rhetoric and past, denying him a visa to visit the country during his campaign. Such opposition actually helped Chávez, a skilled polemicist who thrives on resistance, and on December 6, 1998 he won the election, with 56 percent of the vote. Demonstrating the people's desire for change, another independent reform candidate, the Yale-educated businessman Henrique Salas Römer, placed second, with 40 percent, while the candidates from Venezuela's most entrenched parties, A.D. and COPEI, captured a total of only 3 percent of the vote.

When he was sworn into office, on February 2, 1999, just two days shy of the seventh anniversary of his failed coup attempt, Hugo Chávez inherited an ailing economy: Venezuela was suffering from high unemployment, an inflation rate that fluctuated between 25 and 45 percent, and a fiscal deficit of 9 percent of its gross domestic product. Chávez wanted to reduce the deficit while increasing social spending for the poor and honoring foreign-debt commitments. With the support of Congress, which allowed him to pass emergency economic policies by decree—thus centralizing the making of fiscal decisions at the executive level of government—Chávez initiated a set of tax measures. He also followed through on an agreement made with Norway, Mexico, and the Organization of Petroleum Exporting Countries (OPEC) during Caldera's administration to cut oil production and raise prices. By the middle of 1999, the prices had doubled, and as a result, Venezuela's deficit shrank to about 5 percent. In addition, the president launched an aggressive public-works project, dubbed Plan Bolívar 2000, through which he deployed 45,000 soldiers to purchase food in the countryside for resale at cost in public markets and to repair roads, schools, hospitals, and government buildings. Further emphasizing his commitment to his country's fiscal health, he refused his presidential salary, choosing instead to subsist on his military pension. (The money he would have been paid is being given to charities.) He has also rejected such trappings of political power as living in the presidential palace and traveling by limousine.

At the same time that he pushed for fiscal and social reform, Chávez made good on his promise of solid political change. Within two weeks of taking his oath of office, he ordered the scheduling of a public referendum to approve the writing of a new constitution. Although opposition was strong among Chávez's critics, who feared that he aimed to acquire dictatorial powers, most Venezuelans approved his decree, which also survived a legal challenge in the Supreme Court. The referendum took place on April 25, 1999, and of the 39 percent of the registered voters who cast ballots, 92 percent favored the proposal. Three months later Venezuelans elected 131 delegates to the National Constituent Assembly, which convened in August to begin rewriting the constitution. Submitting to pressure from Chávez, the delegates completed the job by November 19, 1999, more than two months before the original deadline. In another public referendum, held on December 15, 1999, to approve the document, only 45 percent of all registered voters came to the polls; of those, 72 percent approved the new consitution, thus ending 40 years of rule under the Punto Fijo system and beginning Venezuela's fifth republic.

The major political changes introduced by the new constitution affect the executive branch of government. The presidency was awarded more centralized control, and the holder of the office gained longer term limits and the right to run for reelection while in his or her last term, rather than having to wait 10 years, as the old constitution had stipulated. The new constitution also reduced public control over the military and transformed the bicameral National Congress, composed of the Senate and the Chamber of Deputies, into a unicameral body.

The unveiling of the constitution was overshadowed by torrential rains that unleashed havoc on Venezuela. Beginning the same day as the constitutional referendum, a deluge struck the coast, causing massive flooding and mudslides. As many as 30,000 people were killed and 300,000 left homeless in the worst natural disaster to hit Venezuela in decades.

On the eighth anniversary of their abortive 1992 coup, three of Chávez's co-conspirators in the uprising—Jesus Urdaneta, Francisco Arias Cardenas, and Yoel Acosta Chirinos—issued a public warning in which they accused his administration of the same sorts of corruption that tainted previous regimes. The allegations sparked an internal probe, but the investigators were appointed by Chávez aides, so their impartiality was questioned.

Calling attention to logical and legal inconsistencies in the new constitution, Chávez's opponents attacked the speed with which the document was drawn up and accused Chávez's administration of using state funds to support the campaign to win voter approval of the changes. They also rebuked the president for his friendships with the Cuban dictator Fidel Castro and the Argentinean political writer Norberto Ceresole, who has been widely derided for his fascist beliefs and his claim that the Holocaust never occurred. In addition, they criticized him for corresponding with Ilich Ramirez Sanchez, a Venezuelan better known as Carlos the Jackal, who is serving a life sentence in a Paris prison for fatal bombings and other terrorist acts.

On March 15, 2000 Francisco Arias Cardenas entered the race for the presidency. After the 1992 coup Arias had entered mainstream politics, eventually winning the governorship of Zulia, a northwestern coastal state that contributes significantly to the nation's production of oil. He presented a distinct challenge to Chávez, who many thought would run unopposed; Arias's renegade background and anticorruption stance were thought to have as much appeal among the electorate as Chávez's revolutionary rhetoric, and he garnered the support of A.D. and COPEI. The elections, delayed by the allegations of corruption and the disastrous storms, were finally held on July 30, 2000. Chávez won easily, with 59 percent of the vote, and his supporters captured 60 percent of the 165 parliamentary seats—a few short of the two-thirds majority that Chávez needed in the National Assembly to implement his reforms unimpeded.

Chávez angered U.S. officials many times before his reelection, and he has continued to do so. He refused the help of hundreds of American military engineers during the 1999 floods, on the grounds that to accept would be to perpetuate U.S. domination of the world. (Chávez did allow 120 American soldiers to help purify drinking water for survivors.) His refusal to permit Venezuelan airspace to be used for American surveillance and pursuit of suspected drug-cartel planes has undoubtedly weakened the effectiveness of regional drug interdiction. Chávez reignited a dormant border dispute with Guyana after that country allowed an American company to build a satellite-launching facility near Venezuela's eastern flank; he charged that its presence would threaten his nation's security. In August 2000, during a tour of petroleum-producing countries in the Middle East, Chávez became the first head of state to visit Iraq since 1991. Much to the disapproval of U.S. and British officials, Chávez met with Iraq's president, Saddam Hussein, and called for an end to the strict trade sanctions that were imposed on Iraq after the Persian Gulf War and have been maintained because of Hussein's refusal to stop stockpiling weapons of mass destruction.

"Hurricane Hugo," as Chávez has been nicknamed for his style of governing, is married to Maria Isabel Rodriguez. The couple have five children: Rosa-Virginia, Maria, Hugo, Raul, and Rosa-Ines. In addition to baseball, Chávez enjoys writing and painting. — J.K.B.

Suggested Reading: *Current History* p66+ Feb. 2000; *Economist* p38+ Feb. 19, 2000; *New York Times* A p4+ May 19, 1994, with photos, A p12+ Mar. 16, 1995, A p3+ Apr. 10, 1999, with photo; *New York Times* (on-line) Dec. 6, 1998, with photo, Apr. 9, 1999; Public Figure Web site; Stratfor Intelligence Services Web site; *Washington Post* A p21+ Feb. 5, 1992, with photos, A p28+ July 24, 1994, with photo, A p27+ Sep. 20, 1998, A p21 Feb. 13, 1999, with photo

---

Courtesy of the AFL-CIO

Chavez-Thompson, Linda

Aug. 1, 1944– Executive vice president of the AFL-CIO. Address: AFL-CIO, 815 16th St. N.W., Washington, DC 20006

The American Federation of Labor–Congress of Industrial Organizations (AFL-CIO), a voluntary federation of labor unions, represents more than

13 million working men and women of every race and profession. Beginning in the early 1990s, the media often derided the group's leadership as being too "pale, stale, and male" to serve as advocates for its broad base of members. That changed in 1995, when Linda Chavez-Thompson was elected executive vice president of the organization. The first person of color ever to serve on the AFL-CIO's executive board and the highest-ranking woman in organized labor, Chavez-Thompson has noted that the face of labor is changing—and that her election is proof. During the many speeches she has been called upon to make, Chavez-Thompson—who brought three decades of experience to her position—has often stated emphatically, "We are not your father's union."

One of eight children of sharecroppers, the labor official was born Lydia Chavez on August 1, 1944 in Lubbock, Texas. She began calling herself Linda when a first-grade teacher complained that her given name was too hard to pronounce. In the summers, beginning when she was 10 years old, Chavez-Thompson joined her parents in the fields to pick cotton. Working 10 hours a day, six days a week, in often brutally hot conditions, the entire family could earn 30 cents an hour. "That's when I did my first 'negotiating,' convincing my father that it would be better for all of us if my mother stayed home and took care of the house rather than working the cotton fields during the day and then having to come home and cook the meals and clean house," she told Herb Kaye in a 1996 interview for *People's Weekly World*, as quoted on the World History Archives Web site. Like her negotiating skills, her compassion for the disenfranchised exhibited itself early on. Chavez-Thompson saw that the migrant workers and their children who seasonally passed through her town were treated poorly by others. "They were U.S. citizens, but [they were] treated like third-class [citizens], and their living conditions were horrible," she told Valerie Menard for *Hispanic* magazine (September 1998). "I felt powerless to do anything other than to befriend them and have lunch with them when others in the school would not." Although things were always difficult for her family financially, they went through a particularly hard time when Chavez-Thompson was in ninth grade, and she dropped out of school to work in the fields full-time. A few years later, at the age of 19, she married Robert Thompson and began cleaning houses to supplement the wages her husband earned as a city employee.

In 1967, when the laborers' union in Lubbock, of which her father was a member, needed a bilingual secretary, Chavez-Thompson applied for and won the job. Although a majority of the union members were Latino, no one else in the local spoke Spanish, so Chavez-Thompson soon found herself drafting letters of grievance for the workers and representing them during their hearings. With no knowledge at first of how unions worked, Chavez-Thompson spent hours studying various handbooks, and she took courses in organization. She soon became a staunch supporter of unions, and within a few years, she had been recruited for the staff of the American Federation of State, County and Municipal Employees (AFSCME) in Austin, Texas. Following a brief stint there, Chavez-Thompson decided to take a less demanding position at the AFSCME branch in San Antonio, so that she could spend more time with her daughter, who had been born in 1965. (A son followed 11 years later.)

The job was not less demanding for long, as Chavez-Thompson moved rapidly through the union's ranks. From 1971 to 1973 she acted as what AFSCME calls an international representative in San Antonio, addressing the membership's needs throughout a seven-state region encompassing Arizona, Colorado, Nevada, New Mexico, Oklahoma, Texas, and Utah. She became assistant business manager for AFSCME Local 2399, in San Antonio, in 1973 and was later awarded the post of business manager. In 1977 she was named executive director of the local, a position she held until 1995. Concurrently, in 1986, Chavez-Thompson was chosen by the Labor Council for Latin American Advancement, an arm of the AFL-CIO, to be its national vice president, a post she still holds. In 1988 her career took another leap, when she was elected AFSCME vice president and took charge of all union efforts in her area. The seven-state region in which she worked was known to be generally hostile to attempts at unionization. "Trying to defend the rights of government workers in Texas was a difficult proposition, because Texas law didn't allow for unions of government workers to be recognized as such," Chavez-Thompson told Herb Kaye. "You had to maneuver and 'persuade' state officials that workers' grievances needed to be satisfied, and we had to be creative to make headway against unfriendly politicians."

Her regional AFSCME activities provided Chavez-Thompson with a valuable education in dealing with politicians, and she has remained steadfast in her belief that union members should vote for those office seekers who understand the concerns of working people. Explaining to Kaye how important it is for labor to mobilize the votes of its members, she said, "We've got to put a stop to the loss of jobs through outsourcing, contracting out, export of jobs—all of which hurt communities as well as workers and devastate the infrastructure." She continued, "Changing Congress can also give us the means to improve the welfare system, to legislate new protections for children, low income people and those in need of proper health care." Chavez-Thompson not only urges union members to be informed and careful voters: she would like to see more of them become candidates themselves. "We're training many of our own people in political action classes across the country in how to campaign and run for office, and we need more of that," she told Kaye.

Despite working in a part of the country traditionally unfriendly to labor, Chavez-Thompson oversaw the recruitment of approximately 5,000 new AFSCME members during 1988. Her background made it easy for her to relate to the workers. Once, during a meeting of garbage collectors in San Antonio, she was taunted by one man who charged that she did not know what it was like to haul smelly garbage in a hot truck. While admitting that she had never collected garbage, Chavez-Thompson explained to the gathering that she was no stranger to hard work, describing for them her backbreaking days of picking cotton. The heckler immediately asked for and signed a union card and got his fellow workers to do the same. Just as her common touch served her well during that exchange, Chavez-Thompson's political savvy has been an asset at other times. An avid early supporter of former Texas governor Ann W. Richards, she aggressively brought labor issues to Richards's attention. For example, in 1992, Chavez-Thompson enlisted the governor's support to kill a proposal to weaken the penalty for attacks on prison guards—who were members of AFSCME. She won victories in other states in the region too, and she was particularly proud when New Mexico passed a law allowing for wage bargaining by public employees. In addition, she had a knack for inspiring loyalty and confidence in her own employees. Terri Ramos, a clerk with the San Antonio local at the time, explained to Herb Kaye what it was like to work with Chavez-Thompson: "I watched her in action—it was amazing the way she could encourage people on one hand and stand her ground with management types the next minute," Ramos said. "She always encouraged me to take on new responsibilities and to make decisions. All she asked for in return was loyalty to the union. It would be better to say that she demanded loyalty to the union."

While Chavez-Thompson's region was gaining union members, other parts of the country were not faring as well. By 1995 AFL-CIO membership had shrunk to just 15.5 percent of the workforce, compared with 35 percent during the 1950s. The only segments of the union that were growing were those composed of women, who then made up about 40 percent of the total membership, and those with primarily people of color, who accounted for about 23 percent. The union's leadership realized that in order for the organization to flourish, women and minorities—the so-called "growth markets"—had to be targeted. John Sweeney, the AFL-CIO president, pushed for increasing the number of executive council members and for including a minority woman on the council. He and secretary-treasurer Richard Trumka approached Chavez-Thompson, who readily agreed to run for the newly created post of executive vice president. The announcement of her candidacy set off a maelstrom of controversy. Critics, ignoring her three decades of service to the union, charged that she was merely a token and that she lacked the experience to hold the post. Sweeney defended his candidate, explaining to Mary Beth Regan for *Business Week* (November 13, 1995), "I wanted someone for my executive vice president who lived and worked outside of Washington. Someone who knew what it was like to go door-to-door organizing and to come home at night dead-tired and footsore." For the same article, Chavez-Thompson herself dismissed the criticism: "I've walked, talked, and done everything a labor leader has needed to do to protect her workers." The federation also came under fire from those who said that the $165,000-a-year vice-presidential position was a waste of funds, but many felt that the money would be well spent if Chavez-Thompson proved able to provide a link between organized labor and women and minorities. After a bitterly contested battle, Chavez-Thompson won the election. She set about her new job with characteristic zeal, speaking at conventions, picket lines, college lecture halls, and even before Congress. Her mission was to increase membership, particularly among women and minorities, and to serve as a liaison between union and government officials—tasks for which she had a proven talent.

One of the accomplishments of which she was proudest during the early part of her tenure was her role in organizing a program called Union Summer, which first took place in 1996 and has been held every year since then. Participants in the program include students, community activists, and union members drawn from all over the world, who spend four weeks talking to unaffiliated workers, organizing actions against abusive employers, and walking picket lines. The participants are paid a small stipend; in addition to their hands-on work, they attend classes in labor history, organizing skills, and political economy. "[Union Summer] has injected powerful new energy into all aspects of labor's struggles and at the same time given new hope to young people across the country," Chavez-Thompson was quoted as saying on the Hispanic Resource Center Web site, adding that she expected the project to generate new ideas and new union supporters for years to come.

In 1997 Chavez-Thompson was reelected to her post with much less dissension than she had faced two years earlier. She pledged to continue her efforts at grassroots organizing and was instrumental in getting the rest of the executive council to agree to devote 30 percent of their yearly budget to recruitment efforts—a larger percentage than had ever been earmarked for that purpose. That year the AFL-CIO brought in 400,000 new members. Large numbers of strawberry workers in California, poultry processors in the South, and casino workers in Las Vegas organized for the first time thanks to Chavez-Thompson's efforts.

In addition to currently serving on President Clinton's Committee on Employment of People with Disabilities, Chavez-Thompson is the only Hispanic member of the president's Race Advisory Board, and she has been widely praised for bringing the concerns of Latinos to his attention. She is also on the boards of the United Way, the Democratic National Committee, the Council on Competitiveness, the Labor Heritage Foundation, and the Institute for Woman's Policy Research, as well as several other respected organizations. In 1999 she won the Gold Medal from the National Policy Association for her "exceptional leadership in promoting a more productive and just society." To Chavez-Thompson, the concerns of a just society are closely tied to the concerns of labor. In a speech at the opening session of the President's Committee on Employment of People with Disabilities, she recalled that Martin Luther King Jr. believed in strong unions, because, as he expressed it, "What good is it to be allowed to eat in a restaurant if you can't afford a hamburger?" She is quoted on the committee's Web site as saying, "In the past, some people used to suggest that there was one struggle of the union movement for economic justice . . . and a separate struggle of people with disabilities, people of color, women, immigrants, and lesbians and gays for dignity. But the truth is they are not separate. They are one struggle and one dream. The core ideals of labor and the core ideals of civil rights are both economic justice and social justice. They happen together or else they don't happen at all."

Chavez-Thompson's current battles for justice include ensuring that women, who currently earn, on average, 74 cents to every dollar earned by men, obtain equal pay. She is also engaged in a movement to increase the minimum wage, so that the lowest-paid workers will be able to maintain a basic standard of living. She recently spoke out, without success, against granting China permanent trading rights with the U.S., on the ground that doing so would take jobs from Americans. She also opposed the passage of the Agricultural Opportunities Act of 2000, which requires migrant workers to register with the U.S. Department of Labor. Earlier, with an eye on the future of the American worker, in November 1999 Chavez-Thompson presented Vice President Al Gore with a plan to strengthen the nation's educational system, with the aim of ensuring that future workers will have the skills needed to thrive in a new economy. In a speech that she gave in March 2000, as quoted on the AFL-CIO Web site, she described Gore as "one of the best friends that working women have had in public life in this generation." — M.R.

Suggested Reading: AFL-CIO Web site; *Business Week* p46 Nov. 13, 1995, with photo; *Hispanic* p70+ Sep. 1998, with photos; *U.S. News & World Report* p95+ Dec. 25, 1995–Jan. 1, 1996, with photo; World History Archives (on-line)

Chen Shui-bian

(CHEN shwee-BEE-an)

1950– President of Taiwan. Address: Office of the President, 122 Chungking S. Row, Section 1, Taipei, Taiwan; Embassy of Taiwan, 4201 Wisconsin Ave. N.W., Washington, DC 20016

"We firmly believe that in any time or any corner of the world, the meaning and values of freedom, democracy and human rights cannot be ignored or changed," Taiwan's newly elected president, Chen Shui-bian, told supporters in his inaugural address, as reprinted in the *Taipei Times* (May 21, 2000, on-line). Chen is a member of Taiwan's Democratic Progressive Party (DPP), which favors the permanent establishment of the nation's independence from the People's Republic of China, and his election ended the half-century reign of Taiwan's Nationalist Party. Chen worked his way out of poverty to become a staunch advocate of freedom, first as a legal representative for political dissidents during the 1980s and later as the mayor of Taipei. Since he became president, Chen has struggled to bring democratic reforms to Taiwan. He has also encouraged negotiations with the mainland government as well as a strengthening of economic ties between China and the U.S.

Archive Photos

The roots of Taiwan's contemporary problems can be traced back to the 1920s, when civil war on the Chinese mainland broke out between the Chinese Communist Party, led by Mao Zedong, and the Chinese Nationalist Party, the Kuomintang (KMT), founded in 1912 by Sung Chiao-Jen and Sun Yat-sen and led by Chiang Kai-shek after Sun's death, in 1925. Communist victory in 1949 led to the establishment of the People's Republic of China. Defeated, Chiang led two million refugees to the island of Taiwan, where they settled permanently. Under Chiang's rule, Taiwan was a capitalist dictatorship. He initiated a land redistribution program that eventually facilitated Taiwan's transformation from an agriculture-based economy to an industrial model, but he also repressed civil liberties. In keeping with the notion that the Taiwanese were a Chinese people, children were forced to speak Mandarin Chinese rather than their native tongues, and the teaching of local history was forbidden, because it wasn't Chinese history. Meanwhile, Communist China maintained that it had sovereignty over Taiwan and viewed the nation as a renegade province, over the objection of many Taiwanese, who pointed to the "principle of self-determination," contained in the Charter of the United Nations, as the precedent for their call for independence.

Chiang Kai-shek, who died in 1975, was succeeded by C. K. Yen. Chiang's son Chiang Ching-kuo took over as the country's president in 1978 and served in that post until his death, in 1988. Chiang Ching-kuo began to restore political freedom to the nation; in 1987 he suspended martial law, which the KMT had imposed in 1948. In 1996, as Taiwan and China appeared to be on the brink of military conflict, Lee Teng-hui became the first native Taiwanese to be elected president, and his pragmatism went a long way toward easing hostilities between the two nations. Lee included members of the native Taiwanese majority in his government, an action that paved the way for democratic reform, and he permitted the formation of the opposition party, the DPP, whose calls for independence would have been illegal under martial law. Eventually Lee's popularity waned, as he began to be perceived by some as corrupt and incompetent. The KMT's power declined considerably after its decision to allow free elections; the party was viewed as both inefficient and unethical, not least because of the continued existence of huge traffic jams and pollution, in spite of the considerable sums spent to repair a desperately inadequate infrastructure. Additionally, the party's ties to organized crime cast doubt on its commitment to reform. It was into this scenario that Chen Shui-bian stepped in the spring of 2000.

Chen Shui-bian was born in 1950, and immediately afterward he became so ill that his parents did not expect him to live; Chen's mother and father waited several months to document his birth, and so his birthdate is listed in official biographies as February 18, 1951. His parents were illiterate day laborers who lived in a sparsely furnished mud house and were often forced to send their son to school without lunch. But Chen overcame those disadvantages, applying himself to his studies and finishing high school as one of Taiwan's top students. In 1969, on a scholarship, he enrolled at the National Taiwan University, from which he graduated with a law degree in 1975. The following year he married Wu Shu-jen, the daughter of a successful doctor. Chen joined a maritime law firm and soon became wealthy.

In 1980 Chen was called upon to defend one of eight opposition leaders charged with sedition for their role in organizing a pro-independence rally in Kaohsiung that had turned violent. Although Chen lost the case, the defense team was successful in saving its clients from the death penalty (all eight defendants were sentenced to long prison terms). In an official biography published in 1988 and quoted by Mark Landler in the *New York Times* (March 19, 2000), Chen commented that by the time the case had concluded, he had come "to accept the defendants' political arguments and ideals. I became a believer. We should have two separate countries across the Taiwan [Strait, which separates the island from the mainland]—one country on each side of the straits." Politicized by his contact with the dissidents, Chen campaigned for and won a seat on the Taipei city council. In 1985, one day after Chen's defeat in a race for county chief of Tainan, Wu Shu-jen was hit by a truck in what many saw as an assassination attempt against Chen by supporters of the KMT. The truck narrowly missed Chen, who watched in horror as the vehicle backed up and struck his wife again, hitting her a total of three times. Wu Shu-jen was left permanently unable to walk; no one was ever charged in connection with the incident. The act only strengthened Chen's resolve to effect political change, and he soon developed a reputation as a fighter.

In the year following his wife's injury, Chen was sentenced to an eight-month prison term for committing libel against a high-ranking member of the KMT; he had accused the official of plagiarizing a doctoral thesis. Upon his release from prison, Chen joined the DPP. Sympathy for the sacrifices he and his wife had made for the cause of democracy assisted him in winning a seat in Taiwan's legislature in 1989. Five years later Chen delivered a major upset when he defeated the KMT candidate in an election for the mayoralty of Taipei. (Taiwan's capital, Taipei contains the largest concentration of families who arrived from the mainland in 1949.) As mayor he worked to clear traffic gridlock, reduce bureaucracy, and improve sanitation; Chen also waged a battle to eradicate brothels, massage parlors, and gambling dens in the city, forcing many gangsters out of business. He initiated projects such as the construction of a subway and the creation of small parks throughout the city. Chen's popularity was boosted by his frequent attendance at street parties and youth concerts, where he was often seen adorned in bright costume.

In 1998 Chen campaigned for reelection on a strong pro-independence platform, stating that a nationwide referendum was the only solution to the issue. His opponent was Ma Ying-jeon, a Harvard Law School graduate and popular former justice minister whose family had followed Chiang Kai-shek into exile in Taiwan. Ma's accomplishments included successfully battling organized crime and corrupt election practices, and his supporters hoped that his clean-cut persona would help repair the KMT's damaged credibility. Narrowly defeated by Ma, Chen set his sights on becoming the next president of Taiwan.

Throughout the 2000 campaign for the presidency, Chen and his running mate, Annette Lu, downplayed the independence issue in favor of a "contract with the people" that promised to bring peace and stability to the nation. But at a rally at his campaign headquarters, Chen revealed that his previous position had not changed, telling supporters, "That Taiwan is an independent and sovereign state is a historical fact, as well as the consensus of all the people," according to a *China Post* article reprinted in *Taiwan Headlines* (January 18, 2000, on-line). Chen also called for a repeal of the ban on direct cross-strait transportation, communication, and commerce, known as "the three links." If approved, the policy change would allow China and Taiwan to open trade offices in each other's country, and all transactions would be insured by an investment protection agreement.

When it came time to decide who would run as the KMT candidate in Taiwan's 2000 presidential election, President Lee Teng-hui chose Lien Chan over James Soong, the popular governor of Taiwan, thus forcing Soong to run as an independent candidate. Lee's bitter feud with Soong led many to believe that the incumbent president had deliberately sabotaged his party's chances for reelection. Soong also dropped in the polls when it was discovered that he had deposited $7.6 million of the KMT's funds into bank accounts held by his son and sister-in-law. Political infighting among members of the KMT ultimately worked to Chen's advantage; he won the election with 39.3 percent of the vote, while James Soong gathered 36.85 percent of the ballots, and the Kuomintang candidate, Lien Chan, took 23.1 percent. Chen's election ended more than 50 years of rule by the KMT; the youth of Taiwan, who by and large do not share their parents' allegiance to the Nationalist Party, were instrumental in bringing Chen to office. (In all, more than 82 percent of eligible voters turned out for the 2000 election, surpassing participation in the 1996 campaign.) Speaking to supporters, Chen emphasized that his success was "not a victory for the Democratic Progressive Party—it is a victory for democracy," Erik Eckholm reported for the *New York Times* (March 19, 2000).

The new president promised to bring "permanent peace" to Taiwan. Soon after winning the election, he invited China's president, Jiang Zemin, and its premier, Zhu Rongii, to visit Taiwan. Chen appeared to be softening his earlier stance on independence for Taiwan. "We do advocate self-determination, but that is not the same as advocating independence," he told Lally Weymouth for *Newsweek* (April 17, 2000). "Unless China invades or uses force, we will not declare Taiwan independence unilaterally." The Chinese government has been calling for acceptance of a "one China" resolution; recently officials in the mainland agreed to abide by the 1992 Shanghai accords, which would allow each country to define separately what "one China" means. Despite China's poor human-rights record, the United States recently loosened restrictions on trade with the nation; although the U.S. provides military support to Taiwan, the administration of President Bill Clinton publicly opposed the establishment of an independent Taiwan. Chen has been criticized by the mainland government for his earlier statements in favor of independence and by members of his own party for statements that seemed more conciliatory toward China. In a September 1, 2000 interview with Mark Landler for the *New York Times* (September 2, 2000), Chen took a strong position against unification. "Since he came to power . . . ," Landler wrote, "Chen Shui-bian has labored to convince China that he is not a wild-eyed separatist, driven by dreams of Taiwanese independence. But Mr. Chen's charm offensive has come to an abrupt end."

"When I lost the 1998 mayoral election, I was very sad," Chen told Weymouth. "But as my wife has said, maybe it was God's will to let me lose the mayoral election to give me this opportunity to lead Taiwan into the next century. This is just another of Taiwan's miracles." — C.L.

Suggested Reading: *Asiaweek* (on-line) May 24, 2000; *New York Times* p1+ Mar. 19, 2000, with photos, p1+ Mar. 20, 2000, with photos; *Newsweek* p37 Apr. 17, 2000, with photo; *Taipei Times* (on-line) May 21, 2000, with illustration; *Time* (on-line) Mar. 27, 2000, with photos

---

Cho, Margaret

Dec. 5, 1968– Comedian; actress. Address: P.O. Box 252081, Los Angeles, CA 90025; c/o Richard De La Font Agency, 4845 S. Sheridan Rd., Suite 505, Tulsa, OK 74145-5719

In her most recent stand-up routine, as reported by the NBC Internet publication *xoom.com*, the Korean-American comedian Margaret Cho recalls a late-night phone call she received from a television executive shortly before work began on her 1994 television sitcom *All-American Girl.* "The producer called me one day after a rehearsal and said, 'Margaret, we had a meeting and we thought it would be a really good idea if you lost 10 lbs. before we

John Spellman/Retna Ltd.

Margaret Cho

started shooting.' Now, the fact that they said this is no big deal, but just the idea that these people had a meeting to discuss my big fat ass. Unrolled a picture, 'these are the problem areas we need to target.'" One might expect Cho to harbor a great deal of bitterness: determined to keep her role, she lost 30 pounds in two weeks and ended up in the hospital with kidney failure, all because—as she later told Esther Pan for *Newsweek* (August 2, 1999)—the network officials "were used to seeing a certain kind of Asian woman: meek, quiet and slim. I was none of that." Yet she is also able to joke about the experience, and while her sense of humor possesses an undeniable edge, there is a cathartic and even liberating aspect to it as well. By rendering the effects of racial and sexual discrimination absurd and laughable, Cho transforms prejudice into something less malignant and in the process becomes, as the essayist and novelist Ralph Ellison wrote in a different context, "both the source and master of an outrageous and untenable situation."

The older of two children, Margaret Cho was born Moran Cho on December 5, 1968 in San Francisco, following a difficult pregnancy during which her survival was uncertain. The name Moran (pronounced "moo-RAN") refers to a Korean poem about a peony that will flower under any conditions. "My father named me that because I almost died several times," Cho explained to Martha Southgate for the *New York Times Magazine* (October 30, 1994). "No matter what happens to this flower it will always bloom. It's a total hippie name too, like being named Leaf, or Sunshine, or Summer." At age 10, she chose for herself the name Margaret.

Cho's parents had come to the United States from Seoul, South Korea, five years before her birth. Her mother, Young Hie, came from a fairly prominent family. Cho's maternal grandfather was a Methodist minister who ran an orphanage in Seoul during the Korean War and who later, in 1960, was a presidential candidate. In the U.S., Cho's mother worked as a teacher. Cho's father, Seung Hoon Cho, found employment in his new country as a janitor and as an auditor for an insurance company. Something of an amateur comedian himself, he has published a book of jokes in Korean. Apparently, though, Cho doesn't share her father's sense of humor: "Well, not really jokes," she commented to Susan Schindehette for *People* (October 10, 1994) about her father's book. "They're more like Aesop's fables. Very *in* humor in Korea. I don't get it at all." Later, Cho's parents were to open a general-interest bookstore in San Francisco.

San Francisco in the 1970s was a vibrant city. The flower children, or hippies, who in the late 1960s had migrated to the Haight-Ashbury neighborhood in droves, had left their mark, and the gay scene in the Castro district—before the AIDS epidemic, which began in the 1980s—was in its heyday. In an interview with Tim Ryan for the *Honolulu Star-Bulletin* (January 17, 2000), Cho fondly recalled the carnivalesque atmosphere of the time: "I grew up and went to grammar school on Haight Street during the '70s. There were old hippies, ex-druggies, burnouts from the '60s, drag queens, and Chinese people. To say it was a melting pot—that's the least of it. It was a really confusing, enlightening, wonderful time." On a separate occasion, speaking with Esther Pan, she joked that "some people were raised by wolves. I was raised by drag queens." The open environment in which she grew up continues to exert an influence on Cho's work, most visibly in her choice of material, which is often sexually frank and is frequently drawn from her own experience. Indeed, while Cho's act appeals to a wide range of people, she recognizes a special affinity with the gay community, and with gay men in particular. As she recently told the Web site *PlanetOut*, "Gay men are my true audience."

A second formative influence on Cho was popular culture. Growing up, she enjoyed such classic television pabulum as *Charlie's Angels*, *Wonder Woman*, *Solid Gold*, and *The Brady Bunch*. As she told Jeff Hayward for the *Chicago Tribune* (October 16, 1994), "In my experience the pull of American culture was very strong, and my American experience came from television. It was a constant presence in our household, and I was very influenced by it. Television seems to permeate every aspect of my life. It was overload sometimes." Beyond providing entertainment, though, TV gave Cho a way to connect with her father, who seemed to her most relaxed when laughing at comedy programs. Nowadays, mordant references to the popular shows of the 1970s constitute a staple of Cho's stand-up act. As she once quipped in a performance, quoted in *People* (October 10, 1994), "Growing up, I always thought that *Kung Fu*, with David Carradine, should have been called *That Guy's Not Chinese*!" Somewhat later, in her early adolescence, Cho was the self-proclaimed "biggest-fan" of the English pop phenomenon Duran Duran; to this day, she remains a staunch and unapologetic "Duranie," as fans of the group are wont to call themselves.

While attending San Francisco's High School of Performing Arts, Cho began to develop her own stand-up routine. At 16 she delivered her first performance—an improv act—at the Rose and Thistle, a San Francisco comedy club located just above her parents' bookstore. On her break from her duties at the bookstore, "I would go upstairs and do a set," she told Jeff Hayward. "My parents were less than thrilled." Thereafter, she began to appear at other local clubs, such as the Improv, the Punchline, and the Holy City Zoo. After a brief stint in the theater arts program at San Francisco State University, Cho came out on top in the West Coast division of the College Comedy Competition and was invited to participate in the competition finals in Daytona Beach, Florida, moderated by the comedian Jerry Seinfeld. Cho ultimately placed second, but after the performance, as she told Malissa Thompson for *Seventeen* (October 1994), "Jerry came up and urged me to continue. He was, like, the king of stand-up to me. Besides, he was really cute."

In 1991 Cho moved to Los Angeles, in order to devote herself fully to stand-up. For the next three years she worked the college campus circuit and made a number of television appearances with such well-known figures as Bob Hope and Arsenio Hall. After she won the 1994 American Comedy Award for female comedian, ABC invited Cho to appear in her own network sitcom. Among the more dubious titles suggested by ABC executives were "East Meets West" and "Wok on the Wild Side"; Cho favored the more straightforward "The Margaret Cho Show." Eventually, producers settled on *All-American Girl*.

Based loosely on Cho's own experiences, *All-American Girl* aimed to depict a young Korean-American caught between the values of her traditional family and those of American popular culture. Since *All-American Girl* was the first network series to feature a predominantly Asian-American cast, it set a precedent of sorts and was held up to correspondingly high expectations; before it even went on the air, it was heralded in some quarters as an Asian-American version of *The Cosby Show*, the highly popular sitcom starring the black comedian Bill Cosby. None of this was lost on Cho, who embraced the challenge: "The whole point of the show is to take away the foreignness that Asian-Americans have, to demystify us," she told Susan Schindehette. "What I want in 25 years is for people to see *Girl* in syndication and be like, 'Remember when they didn't have Asians on TV all the time?'" She appears to have been quite sanguine at the outset of the project about the degree of artistic input the producers would grant her. As Cho told Schindehette, she could "pretty much at any time stop everything and tell them what I want and what I don't want. I can change lines of dialogue. I have a lot of freedom."

All-American Girl elicited mixed reactions from critics and viewers. While the debut episode posted an impressive number five in the ratings, many attributed this strong performance to the show's propitious time slot, immediately following the top-rated *Home Improvement*. Indeed, when *All-American Girl* migrated to its regular Wednesday time slot, only modest numbers of viewers made the trek with it, and after the initial buzz had quieted down, ratings settled into a respectable (if not exactly enviable) position in the mid-30s. Network officials didn't immediately reach for the ax, but they didn't celebrate, either. Some critics were less than charitable, particularly those who purported to speak for the Korean-American community. John H. Lee, writing for the *L.A. Weekly*, as quoted in Martha Southgate's *New York Times Magazine* article, slammed *All-American Girl* for its "butchered Korean language and pseudotraditions" and added that the show "seems about as Korean-American as the dry, puff-job thing the prop people tried to pass off as *pap*, sticky short grain rice." Even sympathetic critics, such as Southgate, were less than impressed with *All-American Girl*, whose "trouble spots are obvious." Southgate, however, attributed the show's shortcomings to its prime-time sitcom format, as well as to the infelicitous interventions of network officials. For Cho herself, the writer had nothing but praise: "People who are uproariously funny in stand-up are often muzzled by flat sitcom writing, grim network censors and the dulling influence of the laugh track. Thus, Cho's biting, sardonic wit . . . is turned into that of a bland, 'all American' girl." Liam Lacey, writing for the Toronto *Globe and Mail* (June 21, 1995), agreed, noting that "the Margaret Cho who appeared on *All-American Girl* was a pale, bland echo of her stage performance. . . . Cho's graphic humor was replaced with coy sexual innuendo."

Despite its moderately successful ratings—the show never dropped out of the top 40—ABC cancelled *All-American Girl* after a single season. The decision proved difficult for Cho to accept. "I took the cancellation personally," she told Tim Ryan. "I was devastated. I wanted it to work so badly. . . . After the cancellation, my life took a very bad turn. I did a lot of self-destructive things. I did things that made my situation worse. I had no self-confidence; the esteem was shot." While she continued to perform her stand-up act in clubs across the country, she also began to abuse drugs and alcohol and to diet obsessively. While Cho is uncharacteristically reticent on the subject of this difficult period ("I really haven't talked about it, and I certainly haven't been able to laugh about it," she told Jesse McKinley for the *New York Times* [May 14, 1999]), at some point she appears to have made a turnaround.

These days she is sober and is channeling her energy into writing and performing. Her disciplined approach to her work seems to be paying off: Cho's one-woman Off-Broadway show, *I'm the One That I Want*, has won critical acclaim and a number of awards, including *New York* magazine's Performance of the Year award and a MAC (Manhattan Association of Cabarets and Clubs) award for outstanding female comedy. It has also been designated one of *Entertainment Weekly*'s Great Performances of the Year. A movie version of Cho's show was released in August 2000. "How funny is *I'm the One That I Want*?" Stephen Holden wrote in his review of the film for the *New York Times* (August 4, 2000). "Several times . . . I laughed until the tears were running down my face."

Cho has also received a Golden Gate Award from the Gay and Lesbian Alliance Against Defamation (GLAAD), an honor bestowed upon entertainers who have made "a significant difference in promoting equal rights for all, regardless of sexual orientation," as stated on the Richard De La Font Agency Web site. While Cho now receives no shortage of television and movie offers, and has appeared in the films *Attack of the 5'2" Woman* and *Face/Off*, she prefers to concentrate on solo projects. She is currently working on a book about her experiences on *All-American Girl*, scheduled for publication in 2001. — P.K.

Suggested Reading: *New York Times* E p22 Aug. 4, 2000, with photo; *New York Times Magazine* p52+ Oct. 30, 1994; *People*, p91+ Oct. 10, 1994; (Toronto) *Globe and Mail*, A p9 June 21, 1995

Selected Films: *Attack of the 5'2" Woman*, 1994; *Face/Off*, 1997; *I'm the One That I Want*, 2000

Selected Television Shows: *All-American Girl*, 1994

Courtesy of the Ministry of Foreign Affairs, New Zealand

Clark, Helen

Feb. 26, 1950– Prime minister of New Zealand. Address: Parliament House, Wellington, New Zealand

The election of Helen Clark as prime minister of New Zealand, on November 27, 1999, capped her 30-year career in the Labour Party. A former university political-science instructor, Clark is the longest-serving woman in the New Zealand Parliament, having first won her seat, as a representative of an Auckland constituency, in 1981. She became the leader of the Labour Party in 1993. During the previous Labour government, in the 1980s, she served simultaneously as minister of housing and conservation and then, also concurrently, of labor and health. In 1989–90 she held the position of deputy prime minister. An avid theatergoer and opera lover, she currently serves as minister for arts, culture, and heritage as well as prime minister. Widely described as center-left in ideology, Clark, like President Bill Clinton and Prime Minister Tony Blair of Great Britain, is a proponent of what has been dubbed "third way politics"; an alternative to traditionally leftist, or liberal, and traditionally rightist, or conservative, politics that lies somewhere between the two, the third way, or "new middle," calls for fiscal conservatism, economic growth, and individual responsibility, on the one hand, and, on the other, the provision of the educational training and other social programs necessary to promote financial independence in the rapidly changing global economy.

In a profile of her for the New Zealand *Dominion* (November 29, 1999), Helen Bain wrote that in her maiden speech as a member of Parliament, delivered in April 1982, Clark expressed a political philosophy and goals virtually identical to those that she presented to New Zealanders during her latest electoral campaign, nearly 18 years later. In her first speech Clark said, "My objectives for, and the demands of, the Government are relatively simple. They centre on the right to work and to be adequately housed, the need for better living standards, for access to health care at a price everyone can afford, for free and quality public education, for recognition of the rights of minorities, and for tolerance and social peace within the community." She also said, "If Labour's objectives are to be met, a strong economy is required. That strong economy is not an end in itself; it is a means to an end. A strong economy produces the wealth to fund our social objectives, to employ our people, to house them and to give them the means to live in dignity. A strong economy must enable us to do those things, or else it has failed in its central purpose."

Helen Elizabeth Clark was born on February 26, 1950 in Hamilton, New Zealand, to George Clark and his wife, Margaret. She and her three sisters grew up on the family's sheep and cattle farm in Te Pahu, west of Hamilton, which is on the North Island, one of the two main islands that comprise New Zealand. A shy bookworm, she suffered from asthma and other maladies during her childhood and was often absent from school. "I was the weak one who stayed at home while others rode horses," she told Virginia Myers for her book *Head and Shoulders* (1986), as quoted by Helen Bain. She attended the Te Pahu Primary School and then spent five years at Epsom Girls' Grammar School, a large, state-run secondary school in Auckland. Along with a small percentage of Epsom students, she boarded at the school, which was about 100 miles north of her home.

After she graduated from Epsom, Clark enrolled at the University of Auckland, where she majored in political science and history. During her undergraduate years she became active in various political and social causes, including opposition to the Vietnam War; the policy of apartheid in South Africa; the testing of nuclear weapons over the South Pacific by France and other foreign nations; and the then-rampant discrimination in New Zealand against Maori, the descendants of the nation's aboriginal inhabitants. In connection with the last-named issue, she contributed to the efforts of such organizations as HALT (Halt All Racist Tours), which fought against the exclusion of Maori in overseas sporting events in which New Zealand teams participated. She earned a B.A. degree in 1971 and an M.A. degree, also in political science, with honors, in 1974. A year earlier she had begun lecturing in that subject at the university, and she continued to do so until 1975. In 1976, with a university grant, she did research as a postgraduate scholar. She worked as a lecturer in the Political Studies Department at the University of Auckland for four years beginning in 1977. In 1981, the year she gave up that job, she married Peter Byard Davis, who later became a professor of public health.

A decade earlier, in 1971, Clark had joined the Labour Party. Founded in 1916, the Labour Party first won control of the government in 1935, in the midst of the Great Depression, and stayed in power for the next 14 years. During that time, a system of social security and other national social-welfare programs were introduced, as were price and trade regulations, compulsory unionism, and the limited nationalization of broadcasting and banking. New Zealand became, in essence, a welfare state whose economy was largely regulated by the government, and it remained so for the next half century, even during non-Labour administrations. Since 1950 the Parliament has been composed of a single legislative body, officially known as the House of Representatives.

Clark soon took on positions of responsibility within her party. She served as president of the Labour Youth Council (1973–75), member of the Auckland Labour Regional Council (1973–75), secretary of the Labour Women's Council (1977), and Labour Party executive (1978–88). In 1975 Clark made her first run for Parliament, in the Piako district, near Auckland—universally acknowledged to be a safe seat for the conservative National Party (NP). That year the NP assumed the leadership of the government, after about three years of Labour Party rule, and, to no one's surprise, Clark lost the election to the NP candidate. When she next ran, in 1981, this time in Mount Albert, an Auckland suburb, voter support nationally for the NP had dwindled significantly. The NP retained power—by a margin of a single seat—and Clark emerged victorious. (Between 1996 and 1999 the Mount Albert district was known as Owairaka.)

With the 1984 elections, leadership of the government returned to the Labour Party, under David Lange. Although he was labeled a moderate social democrat, Lange took steps to shrink the role of government in the marketplace, by, for example, deregulating the financial system and decreasing various government subsidies. His free-market policies, developed with the help of his finance minister, Roger Douglas, came to be known as Rogernomics. During Lange's administration Clark became increasingly prominent. Between 1984 and 1987 she chaired the Foreign Affairs and Defense Select Committee—a high-profile appointment, because the government's policy of excluding from New Zealand waters all nuclear-powered and nuclear-armed ships met with strong disapproval from the administration of the U.S. president, Ronald Reagan. In 1986 the Danish Peace Foundation awarded Clark its Peace Prize for her work in promoting peace and disarmament.

After the 1987 elections, in which Labour held onto its majority in Parliament by a comfortable margin, Clark joined Lange's Cabinet, with an appointment as minister of both housing and conservation. She gave up those portfolios in 1989 to become minister of both labor and health. As health minister she sponsored the legislation that prohibits smoking in the workplace and public areas and bans the advertising of tobacco products at sporting events and tobacco-company sponsorship of such events. In August 1989 she was named deputy prime minister; she was the first woman in New Zealand to hold that post. She remained in that position after Lange resigned, in September 1989, and Michael Kenneth ("Mike") Moore took his place. Then, in October 1990, the Labour government fell to the NP in national elections, and James B. ("Jim") Bolger became prime minister.

From 1990 to 1993 Clark served as the deputy leader of the Labour Party. In countrywide elections held in November 1993, the NP again captured a majority of the seats in Parliament. Soon afterward, following what Terry Hall, writing for the *Financial Times* (December 2, 1993), described as a "grueling and bitter battle," a Labour caucus—"led by activist women party workers," according to Hall—ejected Moore and chose Clark to succeed him as head of the Opposition. (In New Zealand, as in many other countries, the out-of-power parties are known collectively as the opposition; the leader of the biggest of those parties becomes the leader of the opposition.) She thus became the first woman to lead a major political party in New Zealand. Recalling Clark's behavior during the events that led to Moore's ouster, Judith Tizard, a Labour Party parliamentarian who is currently minister of state, told Bain that Clark had proceeded "in a very one-foot-in-front-of-the-other way. When heads were being lost all around her, she just said, 'Oh well, that's politics.'" Hall wrote that Clark hoped "to turn Labour back to its socialist roots" and had expressed "the need to raise taxes to help the underprivileged."

New Zealand's first female prime minister, Jenny Shipley, took office in December 1997, after masterminding an NP coup in which party officials removed Bolger as NP leader and installed Shipley in his place. During the next 15 months, Shipley was subjected to two significant votes of confidence. The first took place after her coalition government (formed with the New Zealand First Party) disintegrated; the second was carried out at the request of the Labour Party, after Shipley refused to answer questions in Parliament regarding a multimillion-dollar contract awarded by the Ministry of Tourism that, according to members of the Labour Party, benefited the NP. Although she surmounted those tests, her authority was weakened.

In the weeks preceding the next general election, scheduled for November 27, 1999, Clark and Shipley campaigned vigorously as the respective heads of their parties. (New Zealanders cast their ballots not only for the people whom they want to represent them but also for their preferred political parties; each party that captures at least 5 percent of the latter vote earns at least one seat in the 120-seat Parliament.) While Shipley promised to cut personal taxes and decrease interest rates, Clark told New Zealanders that she intended to raise taxes, in order to make improvements in the health-care system and other social services. "Never a charismatic leader" and widely perceived as "straight-laced," according to Helen Bain, Clark acquitted herself well in televised debates against Shipley, "despite rarely showing much sparkle," as Bain wrote. On the day of the election—in what *Facts on File* (December 2, 1999) characterized as "a desire for change rather than a strong personal preference for either candidate" and John Braddock, writing for the *World Socialist Web Site* (December 2, 1999), identified as "hostility to the impact of a decade and a half of 'market reform' policies"—some 90 percent of New Zealand's registered voters cast their ballots for 52 Labour candidates and only 41 NP aspirants, thus transferring the reins of power from the NP to Labour. Two weeks later, on December 10, Clark took the oath of office as prime minister. Since Labour lacked a majority in the legislature, she formed a center-left coalition government along with the left-leaning Alliance Party, which had captured 11 seats in Parliament; Jim Anderton, the leader and co-founder of Alliance, became the deputy prime minister. Clark also put together what she described as the "most diverse [Cabinet] in New Zealand's history," by including in it 11 women, four ethnic Maori, and a descendant of Pacific Islanders. She named herself minister in charge of the New Zealand Security Intelligence Service and also minister for arts, culture, and heritage. "I believe that arts and culture have been undervalued in our political culture—and that one way to demonstrate how important and indeed how crucial their role is was to throw the weight of the Prime Minister's position behind the portfolio," she explained, as quoted on the Labour Party Web site (May 18, 2000).

When Clark took office, New Zealand was still suffering the effects of the severe recession that had crippled many Asian economies in the late 1990s. But not all New Zealanders had suffered equally; indeed, the gap between rich and poor had widened significantly, to the point where it was greater than in any other country in the developed world. In a joint statement on the first 100 days of the Clark government, as quoted on the Labour Party's Web site (March 14, 2000), Prime Minister Clark and Deputy Prime Minister Anderton noted the steps they had already taken to "create a stronger economy and a fairer society." "We are . . . moving to boost the level of economic development, to close the gaps between Maori and Pacific people, and other New Zealanders, to make the public service more responsive and fiscally responsible, to reduce disparities in our health system and to help the arts and cultural sector flourish," they declared. Among their first actions was the introduction of legislation to restore a single public fund for workers' compensation. The government increased the minimum wage and presented to Parliament the Employment Relations Bill, "aimed at a fairer balance of power in the workplace." They established a new ministry, that of economic development and industry; moved to set up district health boards; advanced plans to restore a system through which public-housing rents are based on income; formed a "closing the gaps" committee, charged with finding ways to improve the lives of Maori and Pacific Islanders, who trail far behind other New Zealanders in income, education, and other areas; stopped the sale of the government-owned Waikaremoana power station, and abandoned the Shipley government's plans to "corporatise" roads.

In an address dated June 15, 2000 and quoted on the Labour Party Web site, Clark talked about her government's first budget. "It reconciles the need for fiscal prudence with the need for investment in the economy and in our social areas," she said. "It provides for the non-material parts of our national life, for our environment, our arts, our culture and our heritage." She noted that her predecessor's government had not allocated adequate funds for the operations of such entities as the Children, Young Persons and Family Service; Te Papa (New Zealand's national museum); or the New Zealand Symphony Orchestra, a situation that her government's cultural recovery package was designed to correct. She also announced large increases in the financing of scientific and technological research and development, the allocation of $140 million for Maori and Pacific peoples' organizations, and the institution of a "fairer loan system" for college students. "This budget is not about cutting and slashing public services and spending," Clark declared. "It is a budget that is about building and it is about making investments for the long term, starting right now."

According to Helen Bain, Clark "can be tough on under-performers, but she is just as quick to praise good work." "She never demands more from others than she does of herself," Judith Tizard told Bain. Tizard also said, "She never makes a fuss. It is that country outlook on life—you just get on with the task. She's a very calm person. I have never seen Helen get over-excited." In her leisure time Clark enjoys traveling, reading, and going to the theater, concerts, and operas. She works out regularly in a gym and is a serious hiker and cross-country skier. In January 1999 she climbed Africa's highest peak, Mount Kilimanjaro. By choice, she and her husband have no children—a preference that some of her opponents have criticized during the course of her political career, according to Helen Bain. —V.K.

Suggested Reading: (New Zealand) *Dominion* p14 Nov. 29, 1999, with photo; New Zealand Labour Party Web site; *Socialist Affairs* p54 Vol. 48, Issue 3–4, 2000, with photo

---

Courtesy of Children's Television Workshop

Clash, Kevin

1961(?)– Puppeteer; the voice of Sesame Street*'s Elmo. Address: Muppets, P.O. Box 20726, New York, NY 10023-1488*

"I'm Elmo, damn it! I'd like to use that line to get into a restaurant," Kevin Clash joked to a reporter for *People* (January 13, 1997). A six-foot-tall, 185-pound African-American who has been described as matinee-idol handsome, and whose natural voice is a mellow baritone, Clash is indeed Elmo, the fuzzy, cherry-red puppet with a bulbous nose and ping-pong-ball eyes, who is one of the most endearing and popular characters on the long-running Children's Television Workshop series *Sesame Street.* More precisely, Clash is the talent behind Elmo: he created the character's persona—that of a sweet, innocent toddler—and he provides its high-pitched voice. Clash, whose career in puppetry began when he was in his mid-teens, has worked for *Sesame Street* since the 1980s; known as a principal puppeteer, he also produces and directs performances and scouts for new talent all over the United States. In 1990 he won a Daytime Emmy Award as outstanding performer in a children's series, and he has been nominated for three Emmys. In an interview with Scott Moore for the *Washington Post* (December 1, 1996), Brian Henson, the chairman of the Jim Henson Co., which created Elmo and his fellow Muppets, said that Clash had "shown probably the widest range of any performer" with whom he had worked. "He's got a gut instinct, that little something extra that makes him a genius as a performer."

Kevin Clash was born into a loving and creative family in about 1961 in Maryland and grew up in Baltimore County. "My parents never put a negative twist on this [interest in puppets]," he told Scott Moore. "They never persuaded me to go out and play sports if I chose not to." Indeed, Clash's father, a steelworker, and his mother, who ran a day-care center in the family's two-bedroom home, encouraged him in his pastime—even after he cut part of the lining out of his father's coat to supplement the supplies he had purloined from his mother's sewing basket. He made his first puppet when he was 10 years old, transforming an old stuffed toy into a hand puppet as a way of comforting himself after his dog died. The third of four children, he often entertained his siblings and the children enrolled in his mother's day-care center with puppet shows inspired by *Sesame Street*, which he watched regularly. (He was eight or nine when the series debuted on public television, in 1969.) Although his peers in his predominantly black neighborhood sometimes teased him for his interest in what they called his "dolls," his enthusiasm for puppetry did not diminish. Encouraged by a high-school history teacher to apply his natural talents to his course work, Clash designed a troupe of puppets for a unit about Russia. He recruited a classmate to interview the characters about their homeland, and with Clash providing the puppets' voices, the pair presented the skit for their class. Later, at the principal's behest, they repeated the performance in the auditorium for the whole school. A local newspaper piece about their act led to invitations to Clash to put on shows at Baltimore's restored Inner Harbor, where street musicians and other performers entertain patrons.

Thanks to those gigs, Clash met Stu Kerr, a local weatherman, who recruited him to collaborate on a children's television show he was developing. Called *Caboose*, the show aired on a local CBS affiliate and featured puppets that Clash designed and manipulated. Then in 10th grade, he earned $200 a week for his efforts. Kerr had served in the military with Bob Keeshan, who for three decades played the title character on *Captain Kangaroo*, and at Kerr's urging, Keeshan's producers selected several of Clash's puppets to use on the show. After Clash graduated from high school, he began working full-time for *Captain Kangaroo*, commuting between his home in Baltimore and his job in New York City. He was paid about $3,000 a week for the 13-week television season, plus another $1,200 for each puppet he constructed. Word about his skills spread, and after the first season, he took on a second job, playing the life-size animal figure Goriddle Gorilla on *The Great Space Coaster*, a syndicated series consisting of songs and stories for children.

During this period Clash met Kermit Love, an associate of Jim Henson, the originator of the Muppets—the whimsical puppets that appear along with live actors on *Sesame Street*. In 1981, thanks to Love's influence, Clash began working irregularly for *Sesame Street*, which was based in the New York City borough of Queens. In 1985, just as his longstanding commitments to the other shows were coming to an end, Henson asked him to join *Sesame Street* as a full-fledged member of the cast. Clash was thrilled at the chance to work full-time with the puppeteers he had idolized since his youth. "I got to work with the best, and I never take that for granted," he told Caroline Veronica Clark for *Black Enterprise* (February 1995). "When they were here, I sat with my butt as close as I could to them so that I could learn and learn and learn." Many people who have watched Clash at work have marveled at the fact that he seems to disappear behind his puppets—even when he is in plain sight. "When a good puppeteer puts a puppet on the hand, they live and breathe—you believe in them," Lisa Simon, a *Sesame Street* director, told Scott Moore. "From the minute we saw Kevin work, we saw he was very very talented. . . . He can do things with Elmo and other puppets that are always surprising and believable."

For a while after he joined *Sesame Street* full-time, Clash played various minor characters—mainly chickens and pigs. His assignment changed after Brian Meehl, the puppeteer who had first performed Elmo, left the show. Meehl had performed with the hand puppet only three or four times, and he had just begun to develop the character's personality. Elmo, who was supposed to represent a two- or three-year-old child, was next delegated to the *Sesame Street* veteran Richard Hunt. Turned off by what he regarded as the creature's insipidness, Hunt passed the puppet along to Clash. "He handed him to me like a piece of trash and said 'Here, come up with a voice,'" Clash recalled to Jacques Steinberg for the *New York Times* (December 22, 1999). Drawing on memories of his mother's day-care kids, Clash developed the puppet's falsetto squeal, which has been described as resembling what the actress Carol Channing might sound like in a cloud of helium. Elmo's lovable persona, too, grew out of Clash's recollections of his day-care acquaintances. Elmo's popularity increased rapidly, and the character soon joined Big Bird, Kermit, Bert, and Ernie among *Sesame Street*'s most prominent Muppets.

Clash has played Elmo not only on *Sesame Street* but in videos, television specials, and feature films as well. When he won the 1993 Daytime Emmy Award as outstanding performer in a children's series for his work on *Sesame Street*, he beat out such formidable competitors as Fred Rogers, LeVar Burton, and PeeWee Herman. In addition to Elmo, Clash has performed the roles of Kingston Livingston III, Baby Natasha, Benny the Bunny, and Hoots the Owl on *Sesame Street*. He has worked on non–*Sesame Street* projects as well. He operated puppets in the fantasy film *Labyrinth* (1986) and performed the role of the wise rat Splinter in the movie *Teenage Mutant Ninja Turtles* (1990) and its 1991 successor. (Industry observers have noted that operating Splinter required a degree of dexterity that only a small number of the world's puppeteers have.) Clash also contributed to other television shows, notably the Henson series *Dinosaurs* (which aired from April 1991 to September 1993 and for two months in 1994), on which he played the spoiled but charming Baby Sinclair, and *Muppets Tonight!* (broadcast since 1996), for which he developed the jazz-loving, dreadlocked host, Clifford.

During the mid-1990s, evidence began to mount that Elmo's fans included people of all ages. Teenage girls, for example, wore Elmo T-shirts and carried Elmo backpacks, and the television personality Bryant Gumbel was photographed holding an Elmo toy. "Every adult I've put Elmo or Clifford in front of, they turn into kids," Clash said to Moore. "They want to believe it." Elmo's popularity skyrocketed after Rosie O'Donnell displayed a Tickle Me Elmo on her show in October 1996. The plush toy, which spoke in Clash's voice and giggled and vibrated when tickled, sold in the hundreds of thousands before Christmas of that year, and when supplies threatened to run out, some would-be purchasers became desperate. *People* reported that a Wal-Mart clerk holding the store's last Tickle Me Elmo suffered a concussion, a broken rib, and injuries to the jaw, back, and knee when a mob of about 300 stampeded him. Elsewhere, shoppers paid up to $1,000 to scalpers to obtain one of the toys.

According to Clash, a large part of Elmo's appeal is his naïveté and positive attitude. "Elmo brings [adults] back to why we're here . . . the excitement of living and learning," he told Donna Britt for the *Washington Post* (February 14, 1997). Rosie O'Donnell was quoted in *People* (January 13, 1997) as saying, "Elmo has all the innocence of a two-year-old. He wants to take love and give love with that purity." Clash told Scott Moore, "Elmo helps me find that positive, important side of life. . . . When I come in [to work] and have some serious problems to deal with, it's very hard to find him and bring him to life. I begin to think about the things I'm going through so I can perform him. He helps me in that way. It's kind of therapeutic." He also said that it "humbles" him when he hears about Elmo's importance to some people, such as one adult cancer patient who had clutched her Elmo doll through every session of her chemotherapy and was later buried with it. "It's wonderful to be a part of these people's lives in a positive way," he told Moore. "I can go away from here saying that I've definitely helped in making people's lives happier." In a mid-1990s poll of children and parents by the magazine *Sesame Street Parents*, Elmo was voted the favorite Muppet. In 1999 the puppet starred in a feature film, *The Adventures of Elmo in Grouchland* (the soundtrack of which won a Grammy Award for best children's recording of that year). A further sign of the character's popularity is that a lengthy segment of *Sesame Street* is now devoted to "Elmo's World."

"No one knows what a puppeteer is," Clash commented to Jacques Steinberg. Unlike many of his colleagues, who he said have resigned themselves to working in anonymity, Clash is trying to gain more recognition for people in his profession. "We express what we do in a different way, but it's acting," he explained to Scott Moore. Presumably referring to the entertainment industry and the media, he said, "I think this industry should look at this as a very important art form." He is especially troubled by the lack of coverage of people like himself in publications aimed at black audiences. "I like that Elmo's a household word—and that I am African American and perform that character. And I want my people to know it," he declared to Donna Britt. Clash, who was earning about $1 million a year in the mid-1990s, wants young people to be aware that sports and music are not the only lucrative fields open to them.

Because of his workload, Clash is often away from his daughter, Shannon, who lives with her mother in the Baltimore area. "Shannon thinks of Elmo as a friend of mine who happens to be with me all the time," Clash told P. J. Tanz for an undated interview posted on the Children's Television Workshop Web site. "She doesn't think about the fact that I make the puppet come to life. Like all children, she uses her imagination, and then the magic is there."

Clash told Scott Moore, "It still gives me chills to see Big Bird coming out through those doors on *Sesame Street.* The most joyous thing—that I'll never forget as long as I live—is seeing Big Bird walking down that church aisle in New York singing 'It's Not Easy Being Green' at Jim Henson's memorial service [at the Cathedral of St. John the Divine, in 1990]. It was the most beautiful thing I've ever seen, besides Shannon being born." — M.R.

Suggested Reading: *Black Enterprise* p95+ Feb. 1995, with photos; Children's Television Workshop Web site; *Emerge* p17 Sep. 1997, with photos; *New York Times* B p2 Dec. 22, 1999; *People* p144+ Jan. 13, 1997, with photos; *Washington Post* C p1 Feb. 14, 1997, Y p6 Dec. 1, 1996, with photo

Selected Films: *Labyrinth*, 1986; *Teenage Mutant Ninja Turtles*, 1990; *The Adventures of Elmo in Grouchland*, 1999

Selected Television Shows: *Sesame Street*, 1981– ; *Dinosaurs*, 1991; *Muppets Tonight!*, 1996–

Clayton, Eva McPherson

Sep. 16, 1934– U.S. Representative from North Carolina. Address: 2440 Rayburn House Office Bldg., Washington, DC 20515; District Office, 400 Martin Luther King Jr. Dr., Suite 106, Greenville, NC 27834

On November 3, 1992 Eva McPherson Clayton made history by becoming the first African-American woman to represent North Carolina in the United States House of Representatives. (She was also only the second African-American to win a seat in Congress from the state since 1901; her colleague Melvin Watt was the first.) She took office weeks earlier than the day that members of Congress traditionally begin their terms, in January, because she was replacing a representative who had died in office. Since then she has made her presence known on Capitol Hill by fighting for

Mike Theiler/Archive Photos

Eva McPherson Clayton

the rights of North Carolina's peanut and tobacco farmers, pushing for increased funding for education, housing, and health care, and seeking ways to prevent teenage pregnancy. Known for her friendliness, Clayton, who represents her state's First Congressional District, quickly won the respect of her colleagues in the House. While she shares many views with her fellow Democrats, she has sometimes taken stands associated with more conservative political ideologies. In particular, she has differed with many urban Democrats on agricultural issues. Her positions have made her popular among her constituents: in 1994, 1996, and 1998, she won reelection with at least 60 percent of the popular vote.

Eva McPherson Clayton was born on September 16, 1934 in Savannah, Georgia. An excellent student, she attended Johnson C. Smith University, in Charlotte, North Carolina, from which she graduated in 1956 with a bachelor's degree in biology. Shortly after her graduation, she married Theaoseus T. Clayton Sr., who is a lawyer in Warrenton, North Carolina. She went on to receive a master's degree in biology and general science, in 1962, from North Carolina Central University, in Durham. Clayton next entered the law school of the University of North Carolina, in Chapel Hill. While studying law, in 1968, she sought the Democratic nomination to run for the congressional seat occupied by Democratic representative L. H. Fountain. She launched a grassroots door-to-door campaign to gain the support of blacks living in the Second Congressional District of North Carolina, many of whom felt ignored by Fountain. But her bid failed, and she lost the election to the incumbent, by a margin of more than three to one.

Clayton dropped out of law school after her fourth child was born. She later became involved in several public- and private-sector projects in the state. In the early 1970s she directed the North Carolina Health Manpower Development Program at the University of North Carolina, Chapel Hill, which sought to recruit and train minority students for careers in health care. In 1974 Clayton cofounded the Soul City Foundation, an antipoverty group that renovated abandoned buildings for use as day-care centers and homeless shelters; she acted as its executive director from its inception until 1976. From 1977 to 1981 she served as North Carolina's assistant secretary for community development, overseeing the state's policies on welfare reform, rural housing development, and community assistance. Next, in 1981, she founded Technical Resources International, a management and consulting firm that specialized in economic development. In 1982 she won election to the Warren County Board of Commissioners, ascending immediately to the post of chairperson, which she held until 1990. During her 10 years on the board, Clayton helped to create a rural health-care facility, secure 900 new jobs, and attract $555 million in investments. She was also instrumental in the successful passage of a bond issue for school construction. For her efforts, her fellow board members voted her Outstanding North Carolina Commissioner in 1990. In 1991 Clayton, who was by then an elder in the Presbyterian Church, took part in an ecumenical conference on the environment, held in Switzerland.

With the help of the contacts she had made through her community work and the financial support of various women's groups, in 1992 Clayton made another bid for a seat in Congress. In the Democratic primary election, held on June 2, her strongest opponent was Walter B. Jones Jr.—the son of the 13-term incumbent, who was retiring. Although Jones won the primary, with 38 percent of the vote—Clayton came in second, with 31 percent—he failed to secure the 40 percent minimum required by North Carolina law for a party nomination. In the subsequent two-candidate runoff, Clayton, armed with the endorsements of the candidates excluded from the runoff, won by 10 percentage points. Clayton then went on to defeat Republican Ted Tyler, first in a special election to finish the term of Walter B. Jones Sr., who had died in September, and then in the general election, which determined the next full-term representative. In addition to making history in her state, as its first African-American congresswoman, she made congressional history, by becoming the first woman to be elected president of a freshman Democratic class.

As she had with the Warren County Board of Commissioners, Clayton gained immediate seniority in Congress, primarily because she had arrived to fill Walter B. Jones Sr.'s unexpired term. During her first full term she proved loyal to the Democratic Party on most votes brought before the House. In an unusual move by any representative—whether Democrat or Republican—from a rural district, she voted for gun-control measures that required a five-day waiting period for handgun purchases and banned semiautomatic assault weapons. Yet her greatest loyalty was ultimately reserved for her constituents. Breaking from the Clinton administration's stand on the North America Free Trade Agreement (NAFTA), she voted against the accord, because she felt that competitive pricing in an open North American market would hurt small farmers from her district and would result in the loss of low-wage jobs. Clayton also focused much of her energy on legislation aimed at saving Section 515 of the Department of Agriculture's affordable-housing program, which arranges loans for projects that provide multiunit housing for low-income families in rural areas. Her work earned her an award from the Housing Assistance Council, a national nonprofit corporation whose mission, according to its Web page, is "to increase the availability of decent and affordable housing for low-income people in rural areas throughout the United States."

In the 104th Congress Clayton served as a senior member on the House Committee on Agriculture and the House Committee on Small Business. She played a significant role in passing the Agriculture Research Bill, which allocated federal funds for research and crop insurance. In the 105th Congress Clayton won approval from the Committee on Agriculture to arrange the distribution of unused Department of Agriculture funds to disadvantaged farmers and African-American farmers who had no access to credit, and she successfully pushed for ending the statute of limitations on suits brought by farmers in cases of alleged racial discrimination. Clayton successfully opposed the Republican Party's "Freedom to Farm" legislation of 1996, which proposed replacing the half-century-old federal system of farm subsidies with progressively smaller payments meted out over seven years. Although costly, the farm subsidies help to ensure the survival of smaller, poorer farms. Clayton was dismayed to find that these grants were being targeted not only by the GOP, but also by Democrats who represented urban areas. In *Politics in America* (1998), she was quoted as saying during a debate with Representative Nina M. Lowey of New York, "You may not know who these farmers are, but I do know, and many of them are minority farms, many of them are low-income farms." Not all of her efforts were successful, however. In 1998 her proposed amendment to a bill designed to ease credit restrictions for farmers was rebuffed. The amendment would have provided federally backed loans to farmers who were unable to repay loans on their own.

In 1996 Clayton joined ranks with representatives from other tobacco regions to lobby against federal legislation seeking to end crop insurances and other government support for tobacco growers. Clayton argued that the loss of federal funding would force tobacco farmers to convert to other crops—a costly and time-consuming process. "This is not about smoking," she was quoted as saying in *Politics in America* (2000). "This is about discriminating against the poorest of the poor in that industry. Our colleagues are not attacking the big boy [giant tobacco corporations]. They are attacking the small farmer." For her efforts on this issue, Clayton received numerous accolades, including an award from the Food Research Action Committee.

On other fronts, Clayton has been an ardent supporter of education, welfare benefits, and health care. During the 105th Congress she backed the Clinton administration's proposal to provide funding for 100,000 additional public-school teachers and to distribute voter registration forms to college students when they register for classes. In addition, she has fought for funding for the repair and refurbishment of public schools and has supported efforts by local police to curb youth violence and drug abuse in schools. In 1996, when Congress refused to enact legislation for a summer-job program for young people, Clayton and Representative Sheila Jackson Lee of Texas voiced their disapproval on the floor of Congress. "If some members have their way, 615,000 youth will not have a work experience nor will they have educational assistance in some 650 communities across the United States," Clayton explained to a reporter for *Jet* (April 15, 1996). "This is the first opportunity many of these young people have to get a job." In August of that same year, Clayton opposed legislation, ultimately signed by President Clinton, that cut funds in the food-stamp program and denied food stamps to able-bodied adults who are out of work.

Clayton has supported efforts to expand health-care benefits for children and to provide medical coverage for adults who lack insurance and are not yet eligible for Medicare. She has firmly expressed her belief that health-care decisions should be made by physicians, not employees of insurance companies. In 1998 Clayton joined the battle to reduce teen pregnancy, thus acting on her belief that people are not capable of assuming the responsibilities of parenthood until they are adults. She has served as co-vice chair of the House Congressional Advisory Board to the National Campaign to Prevent Teenage Pregnancy.

In an indication of the Democratic leadership's confidence in her and her growing clout within the party, Clayton was asked to sit on House minority leader Richard Gephardt's Democratic Advisory Committee, in 1995. The mission of the committee, which was created after the Democrats lost the House majority to the Republicans in the 1994 elections, was to formulate strategies to counter the Republican Party's agenda. In 1997 Clayton agreed to join the Budget Committee, giving up her place on the Small Business Committee to do so. She currently also serves as a member of the Social Security Task Force; ranking minority-party member of the Department Operations, Oversight, Nutrition, and Forestry Subcommittee of the Agriculture Committee; co-chair of the Democratic Task Force on Health; and chairperson of the Congressional Black Caucus Foundation.

The affable and garrulous Clayton holds regular public forums in her district, covering a wide range of topics, among them school safety, Social Security, and matters of concern to women entrepreneurs. She believes that such meetings are especially important in light of the redrawing of district lines in North Carolina in 1997. The changes, which received final judicial approval in June 1998, added 165,000 new constituents to the First Congressional District.

Eva Clayton lives in Littleton, North Carolina, with her husband. The couple have four grown children—Theaoseus Jr., Martin, Reuben, and Joanne—and five grandchildren. — J.K.B.

Suggested Reading: *Congressional Quarterly Weekly Report* p118 Jan.16, 1993 supplement; *Jet* p39 Apr. 15, 1996, with photo; *Almanac of American Politics*, 2000; Foerstel, Karen. *Biographical Dictionary of Congressional Women*, 1999; Gill, LaVerne McCain. *African American Women in Congress*, 1997; *Politics in America*, 2000

Greg Gorman, courtesy of Simon & Schuster

Collins, Jackie

Oct. 4, 1941(?)– Novelist. Address: c/o Simon & Schuster, Inc., 1230 Ave. of the Americas, New York, NY 10020

The novelist Jackie Collins has been called "the grande dame of trash," "the queen of trash-and-flash romance," "the Margaret Mead of Hollywood," and a "gleaner of great celebrity rubbish." She has been widely criticized for including steamy sexual scenes in her sagas of the rich and famous—criticism that she attributes to her being a woman. "They don't say the same things about Sidney Sheldon . . . ," she told Paul Galloway for the *Chicago Tribune* (October 1, 1990), referring to a popular male novelist known for his graphic depictions of sex. "I think some people are bothered by the language. It's strong, but that's the kind of language the people I write about use. . . . But there's no violence in my books. If there is, it happens off screen. I think we're too steeped in violence these days. But sex seems to upset people more than violence does." Paradoxically, Collins considers herself a staunch moralist, despite the charges that her writing borders on the pornographic. "Some of my characters may be raunchy, but my books have an underlying morality," she explained to Galloway. "If you do drugs, you're going to come to a bad end. If you screw around on your spouse, you're going to get caught. I often attack the double standard. I stand up for women's rights."

Many who are not bothered by Collins's frequent descriptions of sexual acts still find much to criticize in her novels. In a review typical of those Collins often receives in the mainstream press, James Wolcott wrote for *Vanity Fair* (February 1986) that prose "is not a precision instrument in Collins's hand; her paper-doll characters are cut with dull, bent scissors, and she shows a . . . disdain for correct usage." He also pointed out that she "at least three times uses the verb *husk* in the absence of corn," apparently intending it to mean that a character spoke in a husky voice, as in the line "'My game,' husked Francesca." Collins has said that while such comments sometimes sting, she has learned to take them in stride for the most part. "You just know that the reviewer has a manuscript novel in the drawer that nobody will buy, and here's a way to let off resentment," she told Leslie Hanscom for *Newsday* (October 20, 1985). "Would you send an out-of-work actress to review a movie with Jessica Lange? For me, they handpick them that way."

Over the last three decades, the two dozen novels Collins has written have been translated into 40 languages and have collectively sold an estimated 200 million copies worldwide, making her name an almost constant presence on best-seller lists. Although Wolcott wrote that Collins could have done her research by merely perusing the tabloid papers at a supermarket checkout line, her fans feel that they are getting an inside look at Hollywood decadence—in the form of alcoholism, seedy affairs, and secret face lifts. Collins, who currently lives in Beverly Hills and maintains several highly publicized friendships with celebrities, has trumpeted the fact that most of the scenarios in her books are based on actual incidents that she has learned about firsthand. For example, Alana Hamilton Stewart, the ex-wife of both the actor George Hamilton and the rock star Rod Stewart, admitted to Nikki Finke for *New York Newsday* (September 12, 1987) that she confided many intimate details of her marriages to Collins. "I trust her completely to change the names so I'll be safe," she said. The actress Angie Dickinson, also a friend of Collins's, explained to Finke, "I love her but that doesn't mean I trust her. I mean, she'll take notes right in front of me." Collins is careful to make her characters composites of several well-known figures rather than easily recognizable versions of particular stars. She is not worried about offending those in her social circle, pointing out that many people are actually pleased to recognize themselves in her characters. "A lot of them *want* to be in my books," she told Hilton Als for *Interview* (November 1990). Besides, she laughingly told Als, "People in Hollywood don't read. They have people who do it for them. They page through *Vanity Fair* every month and think they're well-read."

The novelist was born Jacqueline Jill Collins on or about October 4, 1941 in London, England. (According to some sources, she may have been born during the late 1930s.) She has a younger brother, Bill, now a businessman, and an older sister, Joan, who is a well-known film and television actress. Their father was a theatrical agent, and their mother had been a professional dancer before the children were born. Collins remembers her father as being somewhat cool and chauvinistic; after she became a successful writer, he criticized her novels as too provocative. She remembers her mother, who died in 1962, as being "extremely feminine" and protective of, as well as totally devoted to, her children. Collins was always a voracious reader and knew at a young age that she wanted to write. She would think up clever, naughty limericks, which she then sold to classmates for pocket money. "It was instinctive with me; I just knew I was born to be a writer," she told Richard Christiansen for the *Chicago Tribune* (September 23, 1979). "I practically memorized the Mickey Spillane detective books when I was young; then I graduated to Raymond Chandler and Harold Robbins and all the others. I still read F. Scott Fitzgerald's *The Great Gatsby* every year, because I think it's the most beautiful novel ever written." She has admitted, however, that she was not a good student and was frequently in trouble for her antics, such as sneaking away from home or school to go to the movies. When she was 15 years old, she was expelled. "I was thrown out for smoking, being truant, and waving at the resident flasher," she recalled to Eve Babitz for *Los Angeles* magazine (September 1994).

Upon her expulsion, Collins's parents sent her on an extended visit with Joan, who by that time was living in California and working as a contract player for the Twentieth Century-Fox movie studio. When Jackie Collins arrived, in 1956, Joan was just leaving to film a picture on location overseas. Her only advice to her younger sister was that in order to survive in Los Angeles, one had to drive. Left on her own, Collins learned to drive and, living in Joan's apartment, threw herself into Hollywood life. She met Joan's circle of glamorous friends and spent much of her time attending parties and movie premieres. She considers this unsupervised period, during which she had an affair with the actor Marlon Brando, to have provided invaluable fodder for some of her future novels. After a two-year stay in the U.S., she moved back to England, where at 18 she married Wallace Austin (some sources list his first name as Richard), a businessman and inveterate gambler. "He was in his 30s, and we would do wild things like go for dinner in London and end up on a plane to the south of France, where we would gamble for 24 hours," Collins told Babitz. During their first year of marriage, the couple had a daughter, Tracy, and Austin became addicted to prescription drugs. "I had a little child, a maniac husband who hid his drugs from me, and a dying mother—it was a very traumatic time for me," Collins explained to Babitz, noting that when she writes about a drug-addicted character, she is drawing on painful personal experience. She eventually divorced Austin; a year later he was found in his car, dead of a drug overdose. Collins had by that time embarked on a short-lived acting career that included small roles on the British action-adventure TV shows *The Saint* and *The Avengers*, as well as a few largely forgotten films. At a time when the pert, light-haired actress Julie Andrews was thought of as the English feminine ideal, Collins was often cast as an exotic or foreign character, owing to her dark, striking features.

Collins had not forgotten her ambition to write, however. She had begun working on her first novel, *The World Is Full of Married Men*, which was inspired by her disgust at the frequency with which she had been propositioned by supposedly happily married acquaintances. It took her several years to complete the story, which she wrote sporadically in notebooks, in longhand. She had married Oscar Lerman, a successful nightclub owner, in 1966, and with his encouragement she finished the manuscript and sent it, unsolicited, to a publisher whose stable of authors she admired. The book was accepted two months later, and within a week of its publication, in 1968, it was on the British best-seller lists. Explaining the novel's unexpected success, Collins told Hilton Als, "I think one of the reasons was that I was one of the first women to write about a strong, sexual female. . . . People were outraged. The English papers ran these half-page editorials saying, 'This is the most disgusting book we've ever read.' Naturally, it zoomed up to number one." Collins had discovered a successful formula, one that she would repeat several times over the next three decades. She followed up *The World Is Full of Married Men* with *The Stud* (1969), the tale of a gigolo who becomes the manager of a discotheque. She researched the book by going to Lerman's club, which was then a popular spot among London's jet set, once a week. The novel was made into a high-grossing 1978 film, which starred Collins's sister, Joan, and was produced by Lerman. (Joan also starred in the 1979 sequel, *The Bitch*, based on Collins's novel of the same name.)

In 1981 Collins and her husband moved to the U.S.—where her books had enjoyed moderate success—settling in Los Angeles with their two daughters, Tiffany and Rory; Tracy, Collins's daughter from her first marriage, elected to remain in England. In Los Angeles Lerman opened Tramp, a branch of his London club, which would prove just as popular as its British counterpart, and Collins often went there to watch the celebrities who frequented the spot. In 1981 she introduced a character who would prove to be one of her most popular heroines, Lucky Santangelo, in the novel *Chances*. Many observers have commented that Lucky, with her long, dark hair and penchant for leather clothing, closely resembles Collins herself. Collins has denied that the physical similarity is intentional but has admitted that the character exhibits a streak of independence and strength that mirrors her own. Several sequels featuring Lucky, a former mob princess turned movie mogul, have been among Collins's highest-selling books; the heroine was even featured in a widely watched 1990 television miniseries.

But as popular as *Chances* and its sequels—*Lucky* (1985), *Lady Boss* (1990), and *Dangerous Kiss* (1999)—remain today, many publishing-industry observers feel that Collins's 1983 novel, *Hollywood Wives*, was the one that cemented her reputation. "All I did was to write the truth about certain women—right down to their tummy tucks, designer panties, $5,000 'little' dresses and important jewels!" Collins wrote for *USA Weekend* (October 10–12, 1986). "I don't think I was unkind, merely accurate. And let's face it—though my book was fiction, everyone thought they recognized absolutely *everyone*!" Many of Beverly Hills's socially prominent residents thought they had been portrayed unfairly in the book, and reviewer Kay Gardella wrote for the New York *Daily News* (August 12, 1983) that "Hollywood, as seedy as it can be, doesn't deserve *Hollywood Wives*," citing the book's frequent references to prostitution and cocaine addiction. But Collins defended the novel in her *USA Weekend* article: "Let me set the record straight. There are some terrific Hollywood wives. Lively, interesting women, who don't take the power game or themselves too seriously, and manage to lead fairly normal lives. I don't write about them, because by page 20 you would probably be wondering where all the action is!" The hardcover version of the novel remained on the *New York Times* best-seller list for 28 weeks and eventually sold 10 million copies; the paperback edition enjoyed similar success, hitting number one the week after its release. The book was made into a miniseries starring Angie Dickinson, Suzanne Somers, and Candice Bergen, and Collins followed up with *Hollywood Husbands* (1986) and *Hollywood Kids* (1994).

Collins became so closely identified with the trendy California lifestyle depicted in her books that in 1998 she was hired to host *Jackie Collins' Hollywood*, a half-hour television program featuring celebrity interviews, fashion coverage, and movie news. The show was not a commercial success and was quickly canceled; Collins, apparently unfazed, simply continued her disciplined schedule of writing. She reportedly writes for 12 hours a day, turning out an average of 20 pages. It takes her approximately a year to finish one novel, and she is proud of the fact that most of her books are published with few revisions. Her editors, critics have theorized, understand that grammar and character development matter little to her loyal fans. Her latest book, which was published in July 2000, is *Lethal Seduction*.

Although Collins briefly defected to ReganBooks, an imprint of HarperCollins, in 1996, her U.S. publisher has been mainly Simon & Schuster, where she works with the legendary editor Michael Korda and commands multimillion-dollar advances. Of a deal he once made with Collins, Korda told Dominick Dunne for *Vanity Fair* (March 1988), "If this isn't the largest amount of money in American book publishing, it sure ought to be. It's about the same size as the Brazilian national debt."

The novelist has maintained that despite her high-profile friendships and glamorous reputation, she lives a relatively simple life in a white-stucco Beverly Hills home built for her by Lerman before his death, from cancer, in 1992. The house is decorated with her collection of panther and tiger statuettes: Collins loves big cats and has made wild-animal-print clothing one of her trademarks. Although the media have occasionally reported tension between Collins and her sister—particularly after Joan published two novels of her own, in 1989 and 1991—the pair contend that they get along well and that they share much of the same social circle. Collins prefers to stay at home in the evenings when her schedule permits, to read or entertain quietly. She prides herself on her domestic abilities and loves to cook. She has admitted that this surprises and disappoints many of her fans, who expect her to lead a more exciting life. "If I were living the kind of frenetic life now that my characters are living," she told Nikki Finke, "then I would be too exhausted to write about them." —M.R.

Suggested Reading: *Chicago Tribune* XII p1+ Sep. 23, 1979, with photos, V p1+ Oct. 1, 1990, with photos; *Interview* p153 Nov. 1990; *Los*

Angeles p96+ Sep. 1994, with photos; *New York Newsday* II p2+ Sep. 12, 1987, with photos; *Newsday* p18 Oct. 20, 1985, with photo; *People* p55+ Nov. 12, 1984, with photos; *USA Weekend* p4+ Oct. 10-12, 1986, with photos; *Vanity Fair* p38+ Feb. 1986, p120+ Mar. 1988, with photos

Selected Books: *The World is Full of Married Men*, 1968; *Hollywood Wives*, 1983; *Lucky*, 1985; *Hollywood Husbands*, 1986; *Rock Star*, 1988; *Lady Boss*, 1990; *American Star*, 1993; *Dangerous Kiss*, 1999; *Lethal Seduction*, 2000

Courtesy of U.S. Senate

Collins, Susan

Dec. 7, 1952– United States Senator from Maine. Address: 172 Russell Senate Office Bldg., Washington, DC 22204

Susan Collins was elected United States senator from Maine in 1996, making her the 15th woman in U.S. history to win a seat in the upper house of Congress. In keeping with Maine's tradition for independent thinking, Collins is a moderate Republican who takes liberal stances on certain social issues, such as abortion and gay rights, while remaining a fiscal conservative who fights hard for small businesses. A Senate deputy whip since she entered the Senate, she currently serves on the Committee on Health, Education, Labor, and Pensions; the Special Committee on Aging; and the Committee on Governmental Affairs, where she became the first freshman senator to chair the Permanent Subcommittee on Investigations, which handles consumer issues—including Medicare and telephone billing fraud—as well as food safety. She has also actively pushed for campaign-finance reform and student loans for higher education.

One of Collins's first accomplishments as a member of the 105th Congress was her successful repeal of a $50 billion tax break for the tobacco industry, a measure she worked on with Illinois senator Richard Durbin. She was also appointed by Senate majority leader Trent Lott to serve on task forces concerning Social Security, education, and health-care policy. According to *Politics in America 2000: The 106th Congress*, Collins's presence in the Senate acts as "something of a tonic" in a government body continually stifled by partisan conflict. The publication described her as "a Republican who values bipartisanship and focuses on such traditional Democratic values as education and consumer protection. . . . The unassuming Collins operates in a low-key manner and likes to move cautiously, studying an issue before proposing a remedy."

One of six children, Susan M. Collins was born on December 7, 1952 in Caribou, a small city in northern Maine, where both her father and mother have served as mayor. As a child she studied piano and dance and worked as an aide at the local library. "We had trouble with some of the girls," Margaret Butterfield, the librarian who hired Collins, recalled in an interview with Michael Winerip for the *New York Times* (July 20, 1997). "They'd wear those sun dresses that showed too much and were not . . . permitted by the library trustees. I never had a problem with Susan Collins. She was so calm for a young girl." Collins's younger brothers, Sam and Gregg, are the fifth-generation operators of the lumber business founded by their ancestors, in 1844.

Collins remembers her mother's strength as one source of the self-confidence she developed as a young woman. As a high-school senior, Collins participated in the William Randolph Hearst Foundation's Senate Youth Program, where she met Margaret Chase Smith, the Republican senator from Maine known for her bold opposition to the destructive anti-Communist hysteria stirred up by Senator Joseph McCarthy in the 1950s. She recalled the meeting for *Women's Wire* (June 18, 1997, on-line): "I remember leaving her office thinking that women can do anything, and that women can get to the highest level of government and make a difference."

In 1974 Collins completed a summer internship with Senator William S. Cohen, who was beginning to make his reputation in the investigation of the Watergate conspiracy, named for the Washington office-apartment complex that became the site of a break-in at the Democratic National Committee's headquarters by White House operatives. (As a junior member of the House Judiciary Committee, Cohen voted to impeach President Richard Nixon; he currently serves as President Bill Clinton's secretary of defense.) After graduating with a B.A. in government, magna cum laude, from St.

Lawrence University, in Canton, New York, in 1975, Collins went to work for Senator Cohen. For six of her 12 years on his team, she served as the staff director of the Senate Subcommittee on Oversight of Government Management. From 1987 until 1992 Collins served under Maine governor John McKernan Jr. as a cabinet member and commissioner of professional and financial regulations. She then spent a year as the New England administrator of the Small Business Administration.

During her campaign for governor in 1993, Collins became the first woman in her state's history to win a major-party nomination for the office. Although she won an eight-candidate primary in June 1994, she came in third in the fall general election, behind the Independent candidate, Angus King (who won the governorship), and Democrat Joseph Brennan—both millionaires who had outspent her.

Another factor that may have contributed to her loss was her support of abortion rights and gay rights, which met with the disapproval of many of her fellow Republicans. Members of the Christian Right were outraged when, before the election, she attended a fund-raising event at the Underground, a gay bar in Portland, Maine. After the election Collins turned down an award from the Maine Lesbian–Gay Political Alliance, telling reporters that she didn't agree with the group's advocacy of gay marriage. B. J. Broder, an activist who attended the fund-raiser and who had hoped to present her with the award, speculated to Winerip that Collins had rejected the honor to avoid controversy while she waited to hear about an important job at Husson College, in Bangor, Maine. In December she accepted the position, as the executive director of the Center for Family Business at Husson.

Collins resigned from her post in 1996, when Senator Cohen announced that he would be vacating his Senate seat. During her primary campaign, Collins promised that if elected senator she would reduce estate taxes in order to make it easier for family businesses to survive and would push for such measures as a constitutional amendment to balance the federal budget and a supermajority vote requirement (that is, approval by two-thirds of the members of Congress) for any increase in taxes. She also pledged her support for a seven-year expiration date on federal regulations. Collins, who believes in congressional term limits, promised to serve no more than two terms if elected. She won the Republican primary as well as the four-way general election later that year. Also in 1996, Maine voters chose Olympia J. Snowe to represent them, making theirs the first state in history to elect two female Republicans to the Senate. Collins's victory was seen as an indication of the voters' disgust with the hardball politics of her rivals, Senator John Hathaway and A. G. Monks, a wealthy businessman.

After the election the Senate counted nine women (of whom two were newly elected) among its ranks. Many of the other new members of Congress were, like Collins, moderates—perhaps reflecting voters' disdain for the partisan acrimony that had characterized the government for some time. As a freshman senator Collins found that her moderate viewpoint put her in high demand as a legislator. "I'm consistently sought out for co-sponsorship of bills," she told Winerip. "I have a lot of power—I like that."

Collins had been elected by a constituency who agreed with her position on campaign-finance reform (her campaign cost a relatively low $1.6 million). In Maine voters had approved an uncommon method of supporting campaigns, one that awarded public funds to candidates who limited their spending. "People are angry about the system," Collins told Francis X. Clines for the *New York Times* (March 7, 1997). "They don't necessarily know what they want to do to change it. But they know that the system stinks, and they know the root of the problem is too much money. . . . It's not a coincidence that the Senate is over a third multimillionaires now." Although Collins has never suffered from financial hardship, she still had to make sacrifices in order to get elected. "When I ran for the Senate, I seriously debated whether I could afford to keep my $160-a-month health insurance," she told Winerip. "I considered borrowing from my parents, but I was 43 and didn't want to unless I was desperate."

Republican leaders Trent Lott and Mitch McConnell personally requested that she not cosponsor the campaign-finance reform bill, but Collins defied them, joining Republican senator John McCain of Arizona and Democrat Russell Feingold of Wisconsin in calling for wide-ranging hearings on fund-raising practices. As a result she soon received national exposure in the news media. In 1997 Collins served on the 16-member Governmental Affairs Committee, which investigated illegal campaign donations made to the Democratic Party during the previous year's election. In her section of the committee's final report (March 10, 1998), Collins stated, "The pressure for money is so great that we may have no choice but to recognize that there will be a recurring need to amend our campaign finance laws to deal with the latest abuses. . . . If we fail to aggressively enforce our current laws, and amend them when necessary to close loopholes, we risk a democracy driven not by the quality of one's ideas or the level of one's integrity but rather by the thickness of one's wallet."

Collins's record in the Senate reflects her ability to follow her own beliefs rather than those that are politically expedient. The senator has often gone against the Republican Party line. She opposes the death penalty and continues to support abortion rights. In 1997 Collins was one of only four Republicans in the Senate to hold a pro-choice view regarding the ban of so-called "partial birth" abortions. She also publicly favors gay rights, although she opposes federal gay-rights legislation. Collins believes that her constituents in Maine support her decision to follow her heart. "There will be people who will be very unhappy no matter what I do," she told Guy Gugliotta and Lorraine Adams for the *Washington Post* (January 27, 1999). "But one thing I do know. When I'm in Maine, people tell me what they think—but then they tell me to do what I think is right."

On other fronts, in 1996 she opposed a 90-cent minimum-wage increase (although she spoke in favor of a 50-cent increase) on the grounds that it was more than small businesses could afford. Although Collins has worked hard to make student loans more readily available, she also follows the GOP's agenda in supporting the elimination of the Department of Education. Her friendly relationship with the American Forest and Paper Association, which contributed $80,000 to her Senate campaign, did not make her popular with environmentalists. She has expressed her desire to repeal the ban on certain semiautomatic assault rifles and has campaigned to put an end to the five-day waiting period to buy handguns established by the Brady Law. (In Maine, where there are many hunters and supporters of the Second Amendment to the Constitution, which concerns the right to bear arms, gun-control measures anger a substantial portion of the electorate.)

Collins became a sought-after talk-show guest in 1999 during the impeachment trial of President Clinton, who stood accused of obstructing justice in his efforts to hide his relationship with the former White House intern Monica Lewinsky. She proposed that the Senate adopt a policy known as "findings of fact," a compromise that would allow members of Congress to express their disapproval of the president's actions without voting to remove him from office. But some of her colleagues, including Democratic senator Charles E. Schumer of New York, questioned the constitutionality of her proposal, on the grounds that it denied the president his right to due process under the law. Although conflicted over the impeachment, Collins concluded that the president had indeed obstructed justice. Nevertheless, she was one of only five Republican senators to vote against the president's impeachment. During the trial she read accounts of past impeachments and kept a diary of the hearings, so that, as she told Lorraine Adams for the *Washington Post* (January 29, 1999), students of history could "read about what the Senate did, how we conducted ourselves, and find it ennobling."

Collins has recently supported important bills in the areas of health and education. In 1999 she co-sponsored the Teacher Empowerment Act (TEA), which gives state and local schools more flexibility in spending federal grant money. The TEA consolidated three preexisting programs, providing an additional $2 billion to be spent annually over a period of five years. The act aims to put spending power back into the hands of local district officials, who are more aware than federal organizations of what is needed in their schools. "At the same time that we are giving states and local districts this added flexibility, we are also asking them to take greater responsibility," Collins explained in an official press release dated August 2, 1999. "States would have to describe how the funds would be used to improve student academic achievement, close academic achievement gaps, and increase the percentage of core classes taught by fully qualified teachers." Under the TEA local districts are required to have set performance standards. The money may also be used to hire new teachers.

Collins also supported the reauthorization of the Higher Education Act, which promises lower student-loan rates as well as more-flexible loan options. "I have been concerned for some time that Congressional efforts to increase student aid may have been undermined by continued tuition increases far above the level of inflation and far exceeding the growth of family income," Collins stated in a press release dated February 9, 2000. "At the very least, the increasing availability of aid has made it easier for colleges to raise tuition without experiencing signs of consumer resistance. The suggestion that federal assistance is not a factor is, according to a report by the Council for Aid to Education, 'akin to arguing that the ready availability of home mortgages has no impact on the price of housing.'"

In January 2000 Collins delivered the Republican response to President Clinton's State of the Union address. In her speech, she outlined a GOP plan aimed at providing enhanced educational opportunities for all children. The senator has continued to be involved in debates over health-care issues, including measures to curb Medicare fraud. In 1998 and 1999 the Senate approved measures to increase funding for biomedical research by 15 percent per year. Collins supported these measures and hopes to double this funding by the year 2005. In 2000 she has worked with the Senate Rural Health Caucus to urge the Senate Appropriations Committee on Labor, Health, Human Services and Education to continue or increase funding for a number of rural health programs.

In February 2000 Collins joined Republican senator Ben Nighthorse Campbell of Colorado in calling for a temporary suspension of the 24.4-cents-per-gallon federal excise tax on diesel fuel, a measure aimed at assisting truck drivers adversely affected by the current increase in crude-oil costs. "It's very important for women to be able to speak authoritatively on economic issues—what I call the hard issues, as opposed to the social issues—because those are what is most on the minds of citizens now," Collins told *Women's Wire*. She has fought to eliminate the stereotype of women as "being less able to deal with economic and defense issues."

Former senator William S. Cohen has commented that Collins possesses strong political skills as well as an understanding of the need to compromise in order to achieve a consensus. "You'd have to go back to her roots in Caribou, see her family, see how public-minded they are, how open to ideas, how intellectually engaged, to understand just how open-minded, tough-minded, and fair-minded she is," Cohen told Lorraine Adams. "She has a very orderly mind and she is extremely smart and well-organized. She has a unique blend of capabilities. She has a real keen grasp of substance combined with a sophisticated appreciation of the political process."

Collins holds honorary degrees from Husson College and St. Lawrence University. She has received many awards, including the 1998 Advocate for Higher Education Award from the College Board; the Uncommon Service Award from Maine Common Cause, a group that advocates campaign-finance reform; the 1999 Legislator of the Year Award from the Visiting Nurses Association of America; the Golden Carrot Award from Public Voice, for her efforts to improve food safety; and the Friend of the Farm Bureau Award from the Maine Farm Bureau. As of the first week of March 2000, Collins had a perfect record for roll-call votes, having been present at each of the 1,000 roll calls since she began her term as a senator, in 1997. — C.L.

Suggested Reading: *Congressional Quarterly* p3399+ Dec. 14, 1996, with photos; *New York Times* B p12 Mar. 27, 1997, with photo, VI p18+ July 20, 1997; *Washington Post* A p11 Jan. 27, 1999, with photos, A p1 Jan. 29, 1999, with photos; *Politics in America 2000*

Courtesy of American Civil Rights Institute

Connerly, Ward

June 15, 1939– Businessman; chairman of the American Civil Rights Institute. Address: P.O. Box 188350, Sacramento, CA 95818

"There is no public policy which has greater potential to rip the fabric of American democracy than affirmative action," the businessman Ward Connerly told B. Drummond Ayres Jr. for the *New York Times* (January 16, 1997), referring to efforts to help members of historically disadvantaged groups obtain educational and employment opportunities. "Every citizen should have an equal chance at the starting line of life's race. But there should not be a guaranteed outcome in the race. If you discriminate for someone, you discriminate against someone else." Connerly is the co-founder and CEO of Connerly and Associates Inc., a land-development consulting firm, and is considered to be an expert in housing and development issues. As a member of the University of California Board of Regents, he brought attention to what he refers to as the institution's use of "race preferences" in the admissions process; following Connerly's suggestion, the University of California (UC), in a landmark decision, voted to end the race-based system. In his role as chairman of the California Civil Rights Initiative, he contributed to the passage of Proposition 209, a 1996 ballot initiative that put an end to affirmative action with regard to education and employment in the state of California. Connerly is the chairman of the American Civil Rights Institute, a nonprofit organization whose goal is to end affirmative action throughout the United States. His memoir, *Creating Equal: My Fight Against Race Preferences*, was published in 2000.

Connerly's critics point out that college admissions departments must take many factors into account when making their selections, and that these decisions are never based on one factor alone. Wade Henderson, executive director of the Leadership Conference on Civil Rights, told Trevor W. Coleman for *Emerge* (March 1998) that Connerly's "passion seems false and one dimensional. It's especially disingenuous to attack affirmative action in education while largely ignoring the underlying discrimination and disparity in resources that continue to make these programs necessary."

Although Connerly himself once supported affirmative action, he points out that it was originally meant as a temporary solution to the problem of discrimination, and he no longer sees it as necessary. "I think there were compelling reasons in 1960 to change the culture of our country," he told William H. Honan for the *New York Times* (July 19, 1995), "but today we're not in an institutionally racist society as we were in 1965." Connerly told Honan that such policies send a message to minority youth that they are expected only "to do enough to get by" and, furthermore, devalue "the black person who gets up every morning and works and excels." The focus of Connerly's efforts has been the elimination of race-based preferences in college admissions. In his view, those who support such preferences "don't want to believe that the American dream is realizable for black people," he told Michael W. Lynch for *Reason* (February 1998, on-line). "It contradicts their whole value system. Their arguments rest on the notions that Americans are bad, that white people cannot be trusted, that you have to have this gun to their head to make them do the right thing, and that black people need this system to navigate the daily transactions of American life. That we can't make it without it—not because we're not talented, but because we won't get a fair deal. It's really hard to defend affirmative-action preferences. The only arguments you can use are either that we need diversity just for the sake of diversity, or that America is still racist." Although he has benefitted from his business and political connections throughout his career, Connerly insists that it is possible for other members of minority groups to be successful without affirmative action. "If I could make it, anybody can," he told B. Drummond Ayres Jr. for the *New York Times* (April 18, 1996), "because the playing field is a lot closer to level now. The truth is that preferences at this point are not just reverse discrimination, they're degrading to people who accept them."

Ward Connerly was born in Leesville, Louisiana, on June 15, 1939. His parents divorced when he was two. His mother died two years later, and he was placed in the custody of his maternal grandmother, Mary Soniea, who was reportedly part Irish and part Choctaw Indian. Soniea told Connerly that his father, who was fighting to regain custody of the boy, had abandoned him; she sent Ward to Sacramento, California, to live with her daughter Bertha and son-in-law James Louis. Connerly's uncle made his living in the lumber industry and provided a positive role model for his nephew, encouraging him to take pride in himself. Mary Soniea followed the rest of her children to California and resumed taking care of Ward when he was 12 years old. Although Connerly has frequently referred to his childhood as an impoverished one—during which he sometimes had nothing to eat but sweet potatoes and once repaired the sole of his shoe with a piece of cardboard—several members of his family and others have disputed this account. The newspaper publisher William Lee, a childhood friend of Connerly's, told Barry Bearak for the *New York Times* (July 27, 1997) that Connerly's "portrayal of his childhood is highly exaggerated." (Bearak's article became a source of controversy for other reasons as well: the reporter quoted both neighbors and family members who claimed that Connerly's grandmother had been a bigoted woman who instilled in her grandson racist notions concerning African-Americans.) Connerly has pointed to several acts of kindness on the part of white people, including a bus driver who always waited for him when he was en route to his after-school job as a janitor, as the basis for his belief that people can behave fairly when left to their own devices.

After attending American River Junior College, in Sacramento, Connerly studied political science at Sacramento State University, where he was elected student-body president. He was a member of the Young Democrats and also led a group that sent black "testers" into white neighborhoods to provide evidence of housing-discrimination practices. Two months after graduating, in 1962, he married Ilene Crews, a Sacramento State classmate whom he had been dating for a year. After a brief stint as a part-time trainee in urban renewal at the Sacramento Redevelopment Agency, Connerly became a manager for the California Department of Housing and Community Development. He and a partner soon acquired a number of single-person homes as well as an apartment complex, the latter of which he renovated and leased to Sacramento's housing authority. (In 1972 Connerly was investigated on charges of conflict of interest; he was later cleared.)

In 1968 Connerly became friends with then–California assemblyman Pete Wilson, who had recently been elected chairman of the Assembly Housing Committee. Under pressure to diversify the committee, he brought aboard Connerly, who soon became one of Wilson's most generous campaign supporters. In 1971 Connerly returned to the Department of Housing, where he served as deputy director for the next two years. Connerly and his wife co-founded Connerly and Associates Inc., a land-use consulting firm, in 1973.

When Wilson was elected governor of California in 1990, he offered his friend the post of secretary of state, but Connerly declined. In 1994, however, he accepted Wilson's offer of a 12-year term as an unpaid member of the UC Board of Regents. Connerly soon became concerned with what he saw as a "culture of self-imposed segregation" at the university, as he told Marc Fisher for the *Washington Post* (October 29, 1996). He eventually concluded that academia had suffered from its blind acceptance of the notion "that groups ought to be represented, that there ought to be parity," he explained to the *Chronicle of Higher Education* (July 28, 1995), a view that was "fundamentally different from the one I grew up with, of individuals working hard to succeed and working hard to move up that ladder on the basis of individual effort."

Also in 1994 Connerly met Jerry and Ellen Cook. The Cooks informed him that their son James, a white Phi Beta Kappa graduate of UC San Diego, had been accepted to doctoral programs at the California Institute of Technology (or Caltech), the Massachusetts Institute of Technology (MIT), and Harvard University, three of the nation's most competitive schools, but rejected by each of the University of California's five medical schools.

Connerly investigated the situation and learned of a quota system that awarded 20 percent of the available slots at UC to minorities, even though they made up only 10 percent of the applicants. He also learned that at the San Diego campus, prospective students who identified themselves as American Indian, African-American, Chicano, or Latino automatically received 300 bonus points in a system the university used in its admissions decisions. "The significance of a 300-point preference is huge," he explained to Michael W. Lynch. "In many cases, *five* points can be decisive. At Berkeley, a middle-to-upper-income black student with a 3.0 grade point average who was not a California resident had a better chance of being admitted than a 4.0, low-income, California resident who was Asian or white." Due largely to Connerly's efforts, on July 20, 1995, with Pete Wilson present, the UC Board of Regents voted 14–10 to end their race-based admissions system, eradicating 30 years of affirmative action at the university.

Earlier, in 1994, the California Civil Rights Initiative was launched, to eliminate affirmative action through the passage of Proposition 209. When the initiative began losing money, the authors of Proposition 209, Glynn Custred and Tom Woods, invited Connerly to chair the campaign to pass the ballot initiative. After resisting for several months, he accepted the position in November 1995. In part through his connections with wealthy conservatives, including the publisher Rupert Murdoch, Connerly was successful in gathering more signatures than necessary to qualify the proposition for inclusion on the 1996 ballot. Opposition to Connerly's efforts came from many corners. Members of the Campaign to Defeat 209, for example, explained their stance by stating that efforts to end affirmative-action programs adversely affect women, who constitute a worldwide majority. Connerly's opponents regularly referred to him as an "Uncle Tom," or a black person who tries to please whites, in the wake of his success with Proposition 209, and he received so many threats on his life that he was forced to hire bodyguards.

Perhaps the most vehement attacks came from prominent African-Americans, such as Jesse Jackson, who referred to Connerly as a "house slave" and a "puppet of the white man," according to Barry Bearak, and Diane Watson, a Democrat who represents Los Angeles in the California State Senate, who considers Connerly's marriage to a white woman to be evidence of his lack of loyalty to his race. "He wants to be white," she told the *Los Angeles Times*, in an article quoted by Marc Fisher. "He wants a colorless society. He has no ethnic pride." For his part, Connerly rejected the notion that he should be characterized as an African-American. "I'm a black man," he told Fisher. "I have Indian in me, I have French, some Irish. The choice of what I am should be mine. Yet I've had reporters call me African American! What does that mean?"

Critics have also pointed out that in California, 15 percent of state housing contracts are set aside for minority-owned businesses such as Connerly's. Although it was widely reported that Connerly benefitted from this policy, he has claimed to oppose the practice and denied that he took advantage of it. (He has also denied claims that he used his minority status to obtain a $1.3 million contract with the California Energy Commission in 1989, before California's policy took effect.) The pundit Adolph Reed commented that Connerly did not provide a list of his major clients, which all potential UC Regents members are required to file with California's Fair Political Practices Commission. "Like all government contractors who were formerly employed by the state, he enjoys personal and informal contacts that give this enemy of 'preference' a competitive advantage, just as his friendship with Wilson helped him win the Regents appointment," Reed wrote for the *Village Voice* (August 15, 1995). "He has consistently profited from precisely that sort of old-boy network that operates to exclude minorities and women in pursuit of contracts, employment, and even university admissions. Affirmative action arose in part to compensate for the discrimination perpetuated by this kind of cronyism."

In California, ballot propositions have brought about sweeping changes in areas including property-tax reform, term limits, and the discontinuation of bilingual education. "The California legislature for the past 20 years has been totally indifferent to the will of the majority," Connerly told *American Experiment Quarterly* (Fall 1998). "People change when they're elected and walk into those hallowed halls—even my fellow Republicans. When that happens, there has to be some escape valve for the people. No state should be without the initiative process." In 1996 California voters passed Proposition 209 by a margin of 55 to 45 percent. Admissions of African-Americans at the University of California dropped by 81 percent the following year, while admissions of Hispanics at UC Berkeley's Boalt Hall Law School fell by 50 percent. Connerly claimed that the drop was accompanied by an increase in admissions of minorities at less competitive schools, where those students have a better chance of graduating. In an article defending Proposition 209 in the *New York Times* (June 15, 1997), co-authored by then–House Speaker Newt Gingrich, Connerly stated that the decrease in admissions at the University of California "shamefully underscores how much race and race alone has been used instead of merit in our halls of higher education."

Connerly has emphasized that he is not opposed to all forms of affirmative action. He pointed out to *Intellectual Capital* (March 27, 1997, on-line) the importance of outreach programs that "prepare young kids of every race who happen to be low income, to prepare and compete for a college education." He also supports "advertising as broadly as we can availability of jobs . . . [and] the availability of public contracts." In 1997 he expressed his approval for a plan by the University of California to reach out to California's 50 lowest-performing schools, although he objected to language in the proposal that stated that the program was designed to help members of particular ethnic groups. Connerly appeared unconcerned that this decision might be seen as inconsistent with his previous stances. "Too many people take hardline positions for fear of being accused of waffling," he told Ethan Watters for *Mother Jones* (November/December 1997, on-line). "I've never said I've had all the answers. I'm just trying to do the right thing."

Connerly angered many Americans when he chose January 15, 1997, the 68th anniversary of Martin Luther King Jr.'s birth, as the occasion to launch the American Civil Rights Institute, his nationwide organization whose purpose is to end affirmative action. "Ward Connerly has crossed the line, by spitting on the grave of Dr. Martin Luther King Jr., by announcing that he's going to end the programs that [King] died for," Reverend Timothy Malone, a minister affiliated with UC Davis, told the Associated Press, in an interview quoted by *about . . . time* (November/December 1997, on-line). Connerly has often referred to King's famous "I Have a Dream" speech, in which the civil rights leader spoke of his longing for a day when black children would be judged "not by the color of their skin but by the content of their character," as being in line with his own views, while, in fact, King was one of the first proponents of affirmative action: in 1968 his Poor People's Campaign sought to expand the government's role in aiding the impoverished. Michael Eric Dyson, author of books including *Race Rules* and *The True Martin Luther King Jr.*, told Trevor W. Coleman that Connerly and others on the far right have co-opted "the language of civil rights quests for freedom, equality and justice" in an attempt to destroy many of the advances made by the civil rights movement. King's son Martin Luther King III is among those who have opposed Connerly's anti–affirmative action campaign.

When Connerly attempted to reevaluate UC's internationally renowned ethnic-studies programs, students attempted to have him removed from the Board of Regents; a group known as Citizens Working Against Connerly initiated a letter-writing campaign toward that end. In an interview with Frank Bruni for the *New York Times* (June 18, 1998), Connerly questioned whether the programs had "academic value or whether they were created largely because of political pressures that came about in the 1970's and 1980's, when black nationalism was taking hold." By contrast, Connerly surprised conservatives and liberals alike when he joined the American Civil Liberties Union in a class-action lawsuit against the state of California, accusing the state of failing to provide free and equal education for black and Latino children by not enforcing a state law that requires that advanced-placement classes be taught in all public schools. Connerly told Brent Staples for the *New York Times* (August 23, 1999) that poor school districts do not offer the courses "because they feel the students wouldn't take them and succeed academically. It becomes a self-fulfilling prophecy."

So far, Connerly's state-by-state campaign to end affirmative action has drawn mixed results. Fifty-eight percent of the voters in Washington State approved the ban, in spite of their state's liberal reputation. Connerly's anti–affirmative action initiative in Texas, Proposition A, was rejected by its citizens. Efforts to introduce a similar initiative in Florida have met with widespread opposition. "The issue for this state is really simple: Either you are going to face your diversity and work with it and help everybody move forward, or you are going to be in a perpetual state of confusion and conflict," Florida NAACP president Leon Russell told Tim Nickens for *Intellectual Capital* (May 6, 1999, on-line). "We don't need Ward Connerly in Florida." Florida governor Jeb Bush derided Connerly's campaign as too divisive, although some commentators suggested that his response was colored by his concern for the presidential campaign of his brother, Texas governor George W. Bush, which had emphasized the governor's "compassionate conservatism."

Connerly is a lifetime member of the California Building Industry Hall of Fame and serves on the board of directors of the California Chamber of Commerce. His honors include the Courage in Leadership Award from Black America's Political Action Committee (1997), the Thomas Jefferson Award from the Council for National Policy (1998), and the Ronald Reagan Award from the California Republican Party (1998). In 1998 the Log Cabin Republicans presented Connerly with its Spirit of Lincoln Award for his support of domestic-partnership benefits. Connerly and his wife have one son and one daughter and reside in Sacramento. — C.L.

Suggested Reading: *American Experiment Quarterly* p49+ Fall 1998; *Chronicle of Higher Education* A p27+ July 28, 1995, with photo; *Emerge* p30+ Mar. 1998, with photos; *New York Times* A p1 Apr. 18, 1996, with photo, IV p15 Jun. 15, 1997, with photos, p1+ July 27, 1997, with photos; *Reason* (on-line) Feb. 1998; *Village Voice* p17 Aug. 15, 1995; *Washington Post* E p1 Oct. 29, 1996, with photos; Connerly, Ward. *Creating Equal: My Fight Against Race Preferences*, 2000

Fred Prouser/Archive Photos

Crowe, Russell

Apr. 7, 1964– Actor. Address: c/o International Creative Management, 8942 Wilshire Blvd., Beverly Hills, CA 90211

From his portrayal of the neo-Nazi Hando in *Romper Stomper* (1992), to his turn as the avenging-angel cop Bud White in *L.A. Confidential* (1997), to his total immersion in the persona of tobacco-industry whistle-blower Jeffrey Wigand in *The Insider* (1999), which won him an Oscar nomination, Russell Crowe has made a name for himself playing characters of ferocious intensity. His role in the 2000 film *Gladiator* only contributed to that reputation. "There's a fire in him," the actor Burt Reynolds told Trish Deitch Rohrer for *Gentlemen's Quarterly* (March 1999), "that burns all night long, all day long, all the time." Indeed, Crowe, whom *Insider* director Michael Mann described to Rohrer as "a young Marlon Brando," has earned a reputation for being as fiery and temperamental offscreen as he is on. The actor makes no apologies for this, nor does he express a desire to fit into any mold Hollywood may have in mind for him. "People talk . . . as if an actor who could do one thing in one kind of movie couldn't do another thing in the other," he told Terry Lawson for the *Detroit Free Press* (November 4, 1999). "They can impose those limitations. It doesn't mean I have to mind them."

The younger of two boys, Russell Ira Crowe was born on April 7, 1964 in Auckland, New Zealand. His parents, Alex and Jocelyn Crowe, were film-set caterers, and the family moved around often. "We lived in about 14 different places in the first 10 years," Crowe told Chris Copas for the *Sunday Examiner* (November 2, 1997). When Crowe was four, the family moved to Australia, where they continued their nomadic existence. Crowe has recalled spending most of his school holidays on the sets of movies and television shows. The experience gave him an unusual perspective on both the magic and reality of moviemaking. "I loved going to the sets and opening doors and seeing if there was anything behind them," Jamie Diamond quoted him as saying in the *New York Times* (March 26, 1995). "It took the fear out. All acting was, was putting on a costume and playing." As a child, Crowe displayed a gift for imitating people. "I was an embarrassment to my parents," he told Ivor Davis for the Australian magazine *Woman's Day* (November 1, 1999, on-line). "I'd mimic their friends when they came to the house, and my mum used to say, 'Don't worry about Russell. He's a bit mental.'" When he was six years old, Crowe decided to try acting himself. "It became apparent to me that acting was a really fun thing to do," he explained to Jil Derryberry for a profile in *Interview* (August 1995). "And when you're six years old and three feet tall, that's a good enough damn reason."

Crowe's first role was as one of a group of orphans rescued by the character played by Jack Thompson in the World War II series *Spyforce*. After that he found a lot of work as an extra, but he yearned for bigger things. "Even at six," he said to Chuck Arnold for *People* (October 6, 1997), "I would look at the 28-year-old guy playing the war veteran in a film and tell my parents, 'I don't know why the director doesn't see me in that role. I might be a little short, but I can do it.'"

When he was 14, Crowe and his family returned to New Zealand, where his father became the manager of a hotel called the Potter's Wheel. As Crowe recalled to Jessica Sully for *Air New Zealand* (May 1998), "The nickname for the hotel was 'The Flying Jug'—this place was famous for fights." Around this time Crowe became interested in a career in music. He adopted the stage name Russ Le Roq, and he and fellow musician Dean Cochran formed the band Roman Antix, which produced a series of singles, including the eerily prophetic "I Want to Be Like Marlon Brando." Crowe admitted to Sully that those songs "went rocketing straight to the bottom of the charts. I actually have two or three of the worst recordings in the history of the New Zealand music industry. I've got that whole bottom end covered." As bad as his initial foray into music may have been, it gave him the inspiration to try his hand at musical theater. Throughout his early 20s, in between stints as a waiter, street musician, deejay, insurance salesman, and fruit picker, among other occupations, Crowe starred in such musicals as *Grease* and *Blood Brothers*. He also played the cross-dressing Dr. Frank N. Furter in the quintessentially camp *Rocky Horror Picture Show*. "Yeah, I did around 415 performances of that from '86 to '88," Crowe told Kim Basinger for *Interview* (September, 1997). "It's the only show that kept my interest, and that's because it changed every night because of the audience interaction. My favorite screen villain is Tim Curry as Frank N. Furter, although I was pretty good in high heels myself."

At 25, Crowe, fitting auditions and casting calls among his myriad other pursuits and experiencing frequent rejection, took steps that he hoped would improve his marketability. "I got my tooth kicked out in a football game when I was 10," he told Diamond. "I was 25 when I got it replaced, and that's when I started getting work. It's pathetic to find out how much people are tuned in to the visual thing." Soon after he got the tooth replaced, Crowe was picked by director George Ogilvie for *The Crossing* (1990), a film about a love triangle. He followed this role with one in the World War II POW drama *Prisoners of the Sun* (1990) and a turn as a dishwasher who becomes the pawn of a blind man in *Proof* (1991). The Australian Film Institute (AFI) recognized Crowe for his work in those films, nominating him for best actor for *The Crossing* and naming him best supporting actor for *Proof.* These roles put Crowe on the map and gave him the opening he needed for the role that would make him famous.

Romper Stomper (1992), Geoffrey Wright's brutal portrayal of neo-Nazi gang life, was hailed by many as a modern-day version of Stanley Kubrick's seminal film *A Clockwork Orange* (1971), while others chastised it for its apparent glorification of gang violence and hate crimes. Even Crowe, who won raves—and an AFI Award for best actor—for his seething performance as Hando, the hateful leader of the gang, admitted to being taken aback initially. He told a reporter for *Juice* (May 1993) that, after reading the script, "I rang Geoff Wright, the director/writer, and asked him if he was a Nazi." To prepare for the role prior to filming, Crowe took on the physical appearance of a skinhead, complete with shaved head, tattoos, and Doc Marten boots. The result had a visible effect on strangers, who would move out of the way whenever Crowe walked by. "I wanted to see why people did these things, what the buzz was like," the actor told Amruta Slee for the *New York Times* (June 6, 1993). "It's certainly heady stuff. You can understand why, if there's nothing else for you, why adrenaline becomes addictive." *Romper Stomper* was released to decidedly mixed reviews but performed well at the box office. One byproduct of the film's success was some people's glorification of Hando as a symbol of white supremacy. To combat this trend, Crowe chose for his next role a character who was not conventionally masculine—a gay plumber, in *The Sum of Us* (1994). "There are very elemental, testosterone-driven rules for life as a male in Australia," he told Sully, "but I have a twisted sense of humor and thought it would be funny for people who have loved *Romper Stomper* to line up on the first day and see *The Sum of Us.*"

Crowe's performance in *Romper Stomper* caught the attention of Hollywood. The actress Sharon Stone was so taken with the young actor that she lobbied strenuously to have him cast in her next film, the Sergio Leone–inspired Western *The Quick and the Dead* (1995). Working on the film was a sobering experience for Crowe, who arrived in Hollywood to discover that most of his lines had been removed from the script. "I was scared," Crowe told a reporter for *Elle* (October 1995). "Because that changed my influence level dramatically. If your dialogue's taken out, you've got no ammunition. You've got no status." Things did not improve for Crowe when he arrived on the set to begin shooting. Almost instantly he found himself at odds with the film's co-stars, Gene Hackman and Leonardo DiCaprio. "Here's this young Australian guy coming in to play what is, on paper, the third lead in a $35 million film," he explained to Howard Feinstein for *Detour* (October 1997). "And nobody's ever heard of him—except for Sharon. So I wouldn't say it was easy for any of these guys to accept that they should give over any kind of respect or consideration at all." *The Quick and the Dead* opened to mediocre reviews.

Crowe followed that film with *Virtuosity* (1995), a cyber-thriller in which he played a computer-generated sociopath who locks horns with a rogue cop, played by Denzel Washington. The film's director, Brett Leonard, knew right away that he wanted Crowe for the role of Sid 6.7, who embodies the personalities of 183 of history's most evil characters, including Adolf Hitler and Charles Manson. "I could tell he wanted to have fun with this role," Leonard commented for *Elle* (October, 1995). "He saw a way of *liking* this guy! That isn't easy, because Sid's a *very* bad man. . . . Russell's ability to remain menacing, while at the same time being funny and charming, is a very rare amalgam. Very few screen actors have true menace. Russell has." Crowe's take on his character was that he is "pretty far out," as he remarked to Bruce Kirkland for the *Toronto Sun* (August 2, 1995). "As is revealed in the movie, Sid is totally interactive, so he's just playing with what he's got. He's come out of the machine, he's looked around, he's examined humanity in the one half of the millisecond it takes him to work it out, and he realizes that human beings couldn't possibly go around doing what they do if they didn't want to die. He's just trying to help them out. He's a very generous guy." *Virtuosity* was savaged by critics, with Mike Clark writing for *USA Today* (August 4, 1995), "Director Brett Leonard dresses this with . . . techno-dazzle . . . but it can't camouflage the overriding ugliness here." Still, most agreed that Crowe's acting was a bright point in the film. Mick LaSalle noted for the *San Francisco Chronicle* (August 4, 1995) that "Crowe . . . eerily inhabits the nonsoul of this character and turns in what may be a star-making performance." Despite such praise for Crowe, *Virtuosity* died rather quickly at the box office. Crowe followed up his performance in *Virtuosity* with a series of roles in such smaller, independent films as *Rough Magic* (1995), *No Way Back* (1996), and *Breaking Up* (1997), in the last of which he starred alongside Salma Hayek.

He next joined the ensemble cast of the crime drama *L.A. Confidential* (1997). Based on the novel by James Ellroy, the film, a stylish look at the sordid underbelly of post–World War II Los Angeles, proved to be a critical darling, earning raves for its noirish feel and intricate plot. The director, Curtis Hanson, considered Crowe the perfect choice for the role of Bud White, the hard-bitten cop who has a tendency to use his fists in place of words—and who also has a good heart. "I saw Russell in *Romper Stomper* and thought 'Wow! Who is this guy?'" he told Sully. "I knew from seeing the picture that he had the stuff to hold the screen and that he was able to play violence and still keep a character interesting." Crowe recalled to Adam Smith for *UK Empire* (December 1997, on-line) what drew him to the role. "It had a lot to do with the journey of the character," he explained. "I'd read Ellroy's *The Black Dahlia* but I hadn't read *L.A. Confidential.* What struck me when I read it was that this guy was on a self-righteous moral crusade. I mean, if you're stopped by him he's kind of a nightmare policeman, but then you have to try and find a heart in this guy which makes it a very interesting journey for an actor."

Crowe has continued to work steadily since *L.A. Confidential.* In *Mystery, Alaska* (1999) he played the sheriff of a small Alaskan town whose amateur hockey team accepts a challenge to play the New York Rangers. "The major point of *Mystery, Alaska* for me was the physical challenge of learning how to ice skate from zero, from scratch," he told Francesca Dinglasan for *Box Office* (on-line). "Starting in November, shooting in January, learning how to ice skate. And I failed dismally."

Crowe earned high praise from critics for his portrayal in *The Insider* (1999) of Jeffrey Wigand, the tobacco-industry executive who confirmed that his bosses had knowingly lied to Congress about the addictiveness of nicotine. Crowe admitted that he felt he was a strange choice to play the 53-year-old, Bronx-born Wigand, and that he was surprised to hear that the director, Michael Mann, wanted him for the part. "I loved the script and I liked Michael Mann's movies," he told Lawson. "I figured I'd meet with him and tell him how silly it would be for me to do this, and maybe he'd remember me for something else down the line." Nonetheless, Crowe landed the role, and then embarked on a diet of cheeseburgers and bourbon in order to replicate Wigand's well-fed physique. He also shaved his head, so that the requisite gray wig would fit better, and changed the way he walked. More challenging than imitating Wigand's appearance and mannerisms was figuring out what made him tick. "He's not a convenient pop hero," Crowe said to Terry Lawson. "His motivations aren't easily dissected and dismissed. So then it became less about how old he was and what color his hair was, and more about what he was." Boasting a stellar cast that included Al Pacino and Christopher Plummer, *The Insider* was a favorite with critics, many of whom championed Crowe's acting. Wesley Morris wrote for the *San Francisco Examiner* (November 5, 1999), "[Crowe's] performance is an unraveling knockout. . . . [His] sullen, trenchant, beleaguered demeanor makes you grateful that it's Wigand and not you." Crowe won an Academy Award nomination for best actor for his work in *The Insider*, which made the short list for best picture.

Crowe starred in the highly anticipated *Gladiator* (2000), a sprawling epic, directed by Ridley Scott, that chronicles the heyday of Rome's bloodiest spectator sport. Many reviewers cited Crowe, who played a disgraced soldier turned arena champion, as the movie's breakout star. In the *San Francisco Chronicle* (May 4, 2000, on-line), for example, Mick LaSalle wrote, "Watching him here, it's clear that Crowe has that thing that [Clark] Gable had and Sean Connery has—that assured, undiluted, 100 percent guy-ness that makes any man standing next to him look, by comparison, like Quentin Crisp in lounging pajamas." (The homosexual Crisp, a British-born writer and actor, was widely described as "dapper.") In its opening weekend *Gladiator* earned $34 million, thus breaking box-office records; it eventually collected more than $180 million in receipts. The film's success raised Crowe's profile considerably, leading many industry pundits to label him the "new Mel Gibson." Indeed, in the half-year since its release, Crowe has found himself competing with Gibson for roles, notably for the lead in Wolfgang Peterson's forthcoming film *Endurance*, which will chronicle the British explorer Ernest Shackleton's disaster-plagued attempt to reach the South Pole early in the 20th century.

Crowe will next star in *Proof of Life*, as a hostage negotiator who falls in love with the wife (played by Meg Ryan) of the man he is trying to save. During filming, Crowe and Ryan became romantically involved. Ryan was still married to the actor Dennis Quaid, and her association with Crowe has received a great deal of publicity in supermarket tabloids and on the Internet.

Offscreen, Crowe leads a life no less rugged than those of some of his characters. An avid motorcycle rider, he recently logged a three-week trip from one end of New Zealand to the other. In addition, he enjoys writing and performing songs with his band, 30 Odd Foot of Grunts, which concertizes in Australia, where Crowe makes his home. He owns and runs a working farm in the Australian bush. "Where I live used to be a rain forest," he explained to Feinstein. "Half of my place is cleared pasture, and the other half is tall trees. It's the bush. It's not really that isolated if you want to commute every day to the shops, but it's totally isolated if you want it that way. I'm actually living in the middle of a valley, so from where my shack is, it stretches away on both sides of me, and I have a range of mountains in front of 48 cows, a horse, three dogs, and five chickens. It's a simple existence, but it's also extremely time consuming." With regard to his acting career, Crowe has made it clear that he will pursue success only on his own terms. "I'm not a student for anybody else's agenda. I go out and find the answers to the questions that become apparent to me in life, not from somebody else's list." — J.K.B.

Suggested Reading: Australian *Woman's Day* (on-line) p18+ Nov. 1, 1999; *Detroit Free Press* (on-line) Nov. 4, 1999; *Gentlemen's Quarterly* p238+ Mar. 1999, with photos; *Interview* p26 Aug. 26, 1995, with photo; *New York Times* H p24+ Mar. 26, 1995, with photos, II p26 June 6, 1993, with photo

Selected Films: *Prisoners of the Sun*, 1990; *The Crossing*, 1990; *Hammers Over the Anvil*, 1991; *Proof*, 1991; *Romper Stomper*, 1992; *The Sum of Us*, 1994; *The Quick and the Dead*, 1994; *Virtuosity*, 1995; *Rough Magic*, 1995; *No Way Back*, 1996; *L.A. Confidential*, 1997; *Breaking Up*, 1997; *Mystery, Alaska*, 1999; *The Insider*, 1999; *Gladiator*, 2000

Associated Press

Cussler, Clive

July 15, 1931– Writer; founder and chairman of the National Underwater and Marine Agency. Address: c/o Peter Lampack, Lampack Agency, 551 Fifth Ave., New York, NY 10017

While it is a truism that works of fiction reflect their writers' experiences, the channels through which life passes into fiction often remain a mystery, even to the authors themselves. For the most part, that is not the case for the action-adventure writer Clive Cussler, 16 of whose books have spent time on the *New York Times* best-seller list. Cussler bears a striking resemblance to his fictional alter ego, Dirk Pitt, who has been featured in more than a dozen of his creator's 19 books, among them *Raise the Titanic*, *Pacific Vortex*, *Deep Six*, *Treasure*, *Sahara Gold*, *Inca Gold*, *Flood Tide*, and *Atlantis Found*. Like Pitt, Cussler is an avid underwater explorer: working with others connected with the National Underwater Marine Agency (NUMA), which he founded (and which employs Pitt), he has located the remains of more than 60 "historically significant wreck sites," as he reported on the NUMA Web site. Thanks to creative license, Pitt has certain advantages over Cussler: in 25 years, for example, Pitt has barely aged. Moreover, Pitt is dazzlingly charming, and his capacity for hair-breadth escape often beggars belief. But such discrepancies between life and fiction merely underscore the fact that Pitt is an idealized self-portrait; as Cussler declared to Harry Thomas for the *San Antonio Express-News* (October 5, 1997, on-line), "Pitt is me, of course."

Before launching his career as a novelist, Cussler worked for 18 years in the field of advertising. In a 1987 interview with Jean W. Ross for *Contemporary Authors*, he said that having to write "short, snappy ad copy" for so long prepared him "to write easy, understandable prose, and also to look at writing and publishing from a marketing angle. So I predetermined what I wanted to write—in fact, I spent months researching it—before I actually sat down and punched out the first chapter." Since the publication of *Raise the Titanic*, in 1976, Cussler has produced a Dirk Pitt novel every two to three years, on average. By and large the books offer the author's proven mix of derring-do, carefully researched historical detail, and exuberantly convoluted plotting. In total, the "Dirk Pitt" novels have sold more than 100 million copies worldwide; they have been translated into some 40 languages, and many have been published in large-print editions. "The old man of adventure," as Cussler has been called, has also written two novels with Paul Kemprecos, *Serpent* (1999) and *Blue Gold* (2000); each subtitled "A Novel from the NUMA Files," they feature the NUMA field operatives Kurt Austin and Joe Zavala. Cussler's two books of nonfiction are *The Sea Hunters* (1996), in which he and his co-author, Craig Dirgo, describe some of the shipwrecks he has researched (that book had a first printing of 400,000 copies); and *Dirk Pitt Revealed* (1998), written with Dirgo and Arnold Stern, which includes Cussler's account of the evolution of Pitt, synopses of all of the Pitt novels' plots, and a concordance that contains, among other things, the names of every major character and car model mentioned in the books.

The only child of a homemaker and an accountant, Clive Cussler was born in Aurora, Illinois, on July 15, 1931. He spent much of his youth in Alhambra, California, outside Los Angeles. In interviews he has recalled avidly reading adventure stories as a boy. Partly because of his fascination with such tales, he was never much of a student; as he told Walt Jayroe for *Publishers Weekly* (July 11, 1994), "I detested school. I was always the kid who was staring out the window. While the teacher was lecturing on algebra, I was on the deck of a pirate ship or in an airplane shooting down the Red Baron." After attending Pasadena City College, in California, for a short time, Cussler turned his back on formal schooling. In 1950, at the outbreak of the Korean War, he enlisted in the air force, motivated to some extent by a desire for adventure. During four years of service as a mechanic, he flew supply missions for the Military Air Transport Service throughout the Pacific but never saw combat. One of his fellow mechanics, Al Giordino, later materialized in Cussler's novels as the loyal sidekick of Dirk Pitt. Cussler has traced his longtime interest in sunken ships to his military experiences: while stationed in Hawaii he learned to scuba dive and explored underwater wrecks in his free time.

After his discharge from the air force, Cussler returned to California. He operated a gas station with a friend for a time and then landed a job as an advertising copywriter. From 1961 to 1965 he co-owned Bestgen & Cussler Advertising. During the next three years he worked as creative director at the D'Arcy Advertising Co., in Los Angeles (now part of D'Arcy Masius Benton & Bowles). His D'Arcy credits include the memorable slogan for Ajax detergent, "It's stronger than dirt," which he thought up with the help of friends. During his tenure at D'Arcy, he garnered several Clio Awards, an industry honor that recognizes creative excellence and has been called the Oscar of advertising. From 1967 to 1969 he was the advertising director at Aquatic Marine Corp., in Newport Beach, California. His last stint in the field (1970–75) was with Mefford Advertising, in Denver, Colorado, where he held the titles of vice president and creative director.

In spite of his successes at work, Cussler became restless, and by the late 1960s he had resolved to try his hand at writing. "When I decided to write, my wife was working nights at the local police department," he recalled to Lewis Frumkes for the *Writer* (September 1996). "I'd put the kids to bed and have nothing to do. What was I going to write? I didn't have the 'Great American Novel' burning inside me. So, I decided on a series. I was working in advertising then, and I looked at writing from a marketing angle. I went out and researched all the series' heroes, beginning with Edgar Allen Poe's Inspector Dupont, who was really the first one. Then, of course, Doyle's Sherlock Holmes, Ian Fleming's James Bond, and [Mickey Spillane's] Mike Hammer."

The first book that Cussler wrote, *Pacific Vortex*, features a diabolical hero-villain, a kind of combination of Fu Manchu and Aquaman whom Cussler described to Lewis Frumkes as an "old, evil guy with yellow eyes who lived under water with a gill system." Cussler told Frumkes that he had originally planned to reintroduce this amphibious scoundrel in his second novel, *The Mediterranean Caper*, but Dirk Pitt, who had been scripted for a minor role, "just took the book over." His two manuscripts interested neither literary agents nor publishers. As Cussler recalled to Pam Lambert for *People* (September 21, 1992), "People in publishing would say, 'Don't waste your time. Nobody buys adventure.' " Eager to prove them wrong, Cussler resorted to a desperate measure: using his father's Laguna Hills, California, address, he ordered business stationery bearing the letterhead of a fictitious writers' agency. Posing as "Charles Winthrop," he wrote to the literary agent Peter Lampack. Cussler recalled the text of the letter for Walt Jayroe: "Dear Peter, As you know, I primarily handle motion pictures, television and screenplays. I ran across a couple of book-length manuscripts that have a great deal of potential. I'd like to pursue them, but as I mentioned, I'm retiring." Lampack replied promptly: "Dear Charlie, I didn't like the first one [*Vortex*], but the second [*Mediterranean Caper*] is pretty good. Where can I sign Clive Cussler?" Four years later, in 1973, Lampack found a publisher (Pyramid Publications) for *Mediterranean Caper*, which sold fairly well.

Cussler's next book, *Iceberg* (1975), was published by Dodd. His breakthrough came in 1976, with the publication (this time by Viking) of *Raise the Titanic*. In *Titanic*, the tangled plot structure with which Cussler had experimented in *Iceberg*—and which he himself, speaking with Pam Lambert, called "horribly convoluted"—reached an even greater level of complexity. Indeed, dizzyingly baroque plots are a hallmark of the mature Cusslerian style. As *Titanic* opens, U.S. government scientists, covertly funded by a lame-duck president, have concocted a top-secret plan to erect an impregnable missile defense system, which would incorporate a device that concentrates sound waves. The scientists lack one crucial ingredient: byzanium, a rare (fictional) radioactive element. The only known specimen of byzanium, discovered on an island in Russia in Czarist times, sank with the *Titanic*, in 1912, along with the reckless band of Colorado miners who had stolen the entire stockpile of the precious substance. The task of recovering the byzanium has been delegated to Dirk Pitt, who, outfitted with an inflatable apparatus, must raise the sunken luxury liner from its frigid grave. But the Russians, in what was then the Soviet Union, learn of Pitt's plan, and will stop at nothing to retrieve the byzanium for themselves. Additional complications include a wayward hurricane, mysterious sabotage, a cadre of Soviet marines, a madman's dying words, a puzzling murder aboard a submarine, and an insane physicist unhappily married to an oversexed marine archaeologist.

Improbable as the plot may seem, *Raise the Titanic* sold more than 150,000 copies and remained on the *New York Times* best-seller list for 26 weeks. The critical response to *Raise the Titanic* was less enthusiastic. Evan Connell, for example, writing for *Harper's* (as quoted in the *New York Post* on January 15, 1977), declared that "if good books were rewarded with flowers and bad books with skunks, on a scale of one to five, *Raise the Titanic* would deserve four skunks." Opinions on whether the book succeeded on its own terms, as an action thriller, were divided. In the *National Observer* (October 16, 1976), Lee Ewing wrote, "Every story must meet some minimum standard of credibility, and the language, while it need not be elegant, at least should not hinder the telling of the tale. Judged by these less-than-lofty criteria, *Raise the Titanic* . . . scrapes over the shoal of credibility only to run aground on a reef of dead language." While Ewing conceded that Cussler's plot had engaged his curiosity in spite of its "preposterous" aspects, he found that he had been "distracted by the lack of craftsmanship in the writing, by awkward exposition, by abundant clichés and contrived dialog." He cited as an example a remark about a salvaged cornet; the instrument had been so well preserved, one character said, that "it shined up like a newborn baby's ass."

By contrast, Edmund Fuller, in the *Wall Street Journal* (November 8, 1976), mentioned the cornet, which Pitt and his investigators find before locating the wreck, as evidence of the "persuasive detail" that Cussler had used to flesh out the narrative. According to Fuller, the novelist had "spun skillfully a plot for the nuclear age." "Cussler resorts to dramatic overkill before he has finished, [but] he also fires, and thoroughly satisfies, our imaginations," Fuller wrote. While Fuller noted the novel's stylistic flaws—he described Pitt, for example, as a man "whose technical skills and daring are superior to his grammar"—he found that such blemishes did not significantly detract from the book, which he judged to be "a boldly conceived, well executed thriller."

Titanic's mixed reviews are fairly representative of critical opinion regarding Cussler's other novels. Positive assessments tend to emphasize the entertainment value of the books; they generally advise readers, in the words of Joe Collins, who reviewed *Inca Gold* (1994) for *Booklist* (April 1, 1994), to take Cussler's "breathless approach with a grain of salt and just relax and enjoy the adventures of Pitt and company." Many negative assessments contain the argument that the clichés and tangles of Cussler's prose interfere with the story. In a typical instance, the pseudonymous Newgate Callendar, critiquing *Inca Gold* for the *New York Times Book Review* (May 22, 1994), complained, "There is the germ of a story here. . . . But the writing! Mr. Cussler has revived the cliché and batters his reader with choice specimens: 'the cold touch of fear'; 'a set look of determination in the deep green eyes'; 'before death swept over him'; 'narrow brush with death.' In the Cussler style, virtually every noun has to have a modifier: 'morbid waters'; 'piercing eyes'; 'furtive dark eyes'; 'you thieving scum.' There are also unhissable hisses: '"We have no radio," he hissed.'"" Cussler himself admitted to Pam Lambert, "There's no literary merit in my books," and he told her that he is happy if his readers "reach the end and feel they got their money's worth." If sales are an accurate gauge of reader satisfaction, Cussler has ample reason to be happy. His books sell well abroad as well as in the United States; according to Walt Jayroe, "at least 40 percent of his sales are international and, like clockwork, he always hits No. 1 in Japan."

Cussler's financial success has provided him with the means to indulge two passions that he shares with Dirk Pitt: restoring vintage automobiles and exploring undersea shipwrecks. His automobile collection includes more than 80 vehicles, including a 1930 L-29 Cord, the same model that Pitt drives. Since 1979, when he founded the National Underwater and Marine Agency, NUMA engineers and scientists have conducted dozens of underwater archaeological expeditions; among the wrecks they have either located or surveyed are the Confederate submarine *Hunley*, the German submarine *U-20* (which sank the British luxury liner *Lusitania* on May 17, 1915, an event often said to have precipitated the United States' entrance into World War I), and the Allied troop transport *Leopoldville* (which sank off the coast of Cherbourg, France, in 1944, during World War II). "We're dedicated to preserving our maritime heritage, and we do this by locating the lost ships of historical significance," Cussler, who chairs NUMA, told Jean W. Ross. "When we are lucky enough, after research and time and diving, to find and identify them, we turn over all the information to the state or federal government, or to museums, libraries, universities, and in some cases the navy, in the hope that someday the finds will attract the necessary funding and technology from either individuals, corporations, or the government to salvage and conserve the artifacts for public display, or perhaps raise the old shipwrecks themselves." Many NUMA expeditions have furnished material for Pitt's fictional exploits.

Cussler and his wife, the former Barbara Knight, married in 1955. They divide their time between Colorado and Paradise Valley, Arizona, an affluent suburb of Phoenix, where they own a winter home. The couple have three children—Teri, Dirk, and Dana—and two grandchildren. Cussler has repeatedly intimated that he plans to retire Dirk Pitt, but as of December 1999, his hero was as busy as ever. That month saw the publication of *Atlantis Found*, the latest installment in the Pitt series. — P.K.

Suggested Reading: *National Observer* p19 Oct. 16, 1976 ; *People* p93+ Sept. 21, 1992; *Publishers Weekly* p58+ July 11, 1994; *Writer* p15+ Sep. 1996; *Contemporary Authors* New Revision Series Vol. 21, 1987; Cussler, Clive, Craig Dirgo, and Arnold Stern. *Dirk Pitt Revealed*, 1998

Selected Books: *The Mediterranean Caper*, 1973; *Iceberg*, 1975; *Raise the Titanic*, 1976; *Cyclops*, 1986; *Vixen 03*, 1978; *Pacific Vortex!*, 1983;

Deep Six, 1984; *Cyclops*, 1986; *Treasure*, 1988; *Dragon*, 1990; *Night Probe!*, 1992; *Sahara*, 1992; *Inca Gold*, 1994; *Shock Wave*, 1996; *The Sea Hunters: True Adventures with Famous Shipwrecks*, 1996; *Flood Tide*, 1997; *Atlantis Found*, 1999

Courtesy of Fonar Corp.

Damadian, Raymond V.

Mar. 16, 1936– Developer of magnetic resonance imaging (MRI); physician. Address: FONAR Corp., 110 Marcus Dr., Melville, NY 11747

In the summer of 1977, Raymond V. Damadian saw the culmination of years of tireless research when one of his graduate students, Larry Minkoff, stepped inside *Indomitable*, the ungainly metal creation that had long been the focus of nearly all of Damadian's creative, scientific, and financial resources. When Minkoff stepped out of the machine, he did so as the first person in history to have his torso explored by a magnetic resonance scan. Defying the doubts of his peers and the media, Damadian had proven that passing a strong magnetic field through the body could aid scientists and researchers in detecting tumors and other abnormalities in a painless and noninvasive manner. Today, magnetic resonance imaging (MRI) is the chief method for such detection and represents a $2 billion a year industry, with almost every major city in the world having at least one imaging center where the machines are used. Despite his achievement, it was not until the late 1990s that Damadian, through legal battles with technology companies, was able to reap the financial rewards from his invention. He has used the settlements to further the use of the MRI procedure.

The son of Vahan and Odette (Yazedijian) Damadian, Raymond Vahan Damadian was born on March 16, 1936 in the Forest Hills section of Queens, a borough of New York City. As a child and adolescent, he studied violin at the Juilliard School of Music, in New York, for eight years. In 1952 he won a scholarship from the Ford Foundation and entered the University of Wisconsin as a 16-year-old freshman. After graduating in 1956, with a B.S. degree in mathematics, he opted to attend medical school. "The one thing I found appealing about medicine was that it didn't seal your options," he told David Schneider for *Scientific American* (June 1997). Damadian earned an M.D. degree from the Albert Einstein College of Medicine, in the New York City borough of the Bronx, in 1960. After a string of postgraduate stints, including fellowships in nephrology at the Washington University School of Medicine, in St. Louis, Missouri, and biophysics at Harvard University, in Cambridge, Massachusetts, as well as a hitch in the U.S. Air Force, Damadian joined the faculty of the State University of New York Downstate Medical Center, in the New York City borough of Brooklyn, in 1967. There he studied the balance of electrolytes in the human body, eventually using his training in medicine and physics to develop a new theory of the living cell, known as the ion exchanger resin theory.

For some time Damadian was hesitant to make laboratory research his career. "I lacked confidence," he told David Schneider. "I was always one of those guys who dropped the crucible." Nevertheless, in 1969, Damadian's investigations of sodium and potassium in living cells led him to begin using the school's equipment in experiments with nuclear magnetic resonance (NMR). This phenomenon was discovered in 1938 by the physicist Isidor Rabi, who won the 1944 Nobel Prize in physics for developing a method of measuring magnetic properties of atoms, molecules, and nuclei. After World War II several other scientists, prominent among them Edward Purcell and Felix Bloch, made further discoveries concerning nuclear resonance, using such substances as paraffin and water. In 1947 Nicolaas Bloembergen showed for the first time that the decay times (relaxation times) of the nuclear response signal varied with the freedom of the molecules (viscosity). Damadian picked up on that notion and applied it to the human body, a connection no other scientist had made up to that point. Damadian was intrigued by the difference between the signals emitted by cancerous tissues in mice, as opposed to those sent by the rodents' healthy tissues. Damadian's tests, which were run with a makeshift NMR scanner that created a magnetic field by using liquid helium to super-cool magnets in a cylindrical chamber, proved that the NMR signals took longer to decay in cancerous cells than they did in healthy ones. These results were described in his now-famous paper,

"Tumor Detection by Nuclear Magnetic Resonance," which appeared in the March 9, 1971 issue of *Science* magazine.

In the following year Damadian filed the patent application for his invention and set about the task of procuring funds to build a human-sized scanner. This turned out to be a more daunting task than he had anticipated, in part because of his unrelenting insistence on the importance of his discovery to his colleagues. "Damadian is a little too quick to tell people they are idiots, and that doesn't go down well in academia," Benjamin M. Stein, president of Brunswick Hospital, in Amityville, New York, who purchased one of the earliest MRI machines, told Claudia H. Deutsch for the *New York Times* (July 12, 1997). Indeed, Damadian's manner alienated many of his peers and hampered his efforts to advance his research. "I was an outsider in a field run by chemists," he said to Deutsch, "and they treated me that way." (While he still feels hurt by the reactions of some other scientists, he recognizes what occurred as part of the give-and-take that often accompanies scientific innovation.) In an act of desperation, Damadian fired off a letter directly to then-president Richard Nixon, in which he asked for a research grant. "I was young and not understanding of the way things worked," he admitted to David Schneider. Surprisingly, his plea reached sympathetic ears, and he received a modest grant. Throughout the 1970s Damadian would continue to find unconventional methods to secure funds to keep his research going.

That all changed in 1977, after Damadian and his colleagues created the prototype NMR scanner, which they dubbed *Indomitable*. On July 3 of that year, in his small Brooklyn laboratory, Damadian stepped into the machine to run a test on himself. His attempt failed, for the simple—if somewhat embarrassing—reason that his girth was far too ample to fit within the radio coils that Michael Goldsmith, one of his graduate students, had made. Still, the initial test was not a total failure: it proved that a person could sit for hours under the constant bombardment of the magnetic fields and experience no apparent ill effects. This discovery prompted Damadian's graduate student Larry Minkoff to become a part of medical history by placing his slimmer frame inside *Indomitable*. Although the image of Minkoff's chest was crude, especially when viewed against today's standards, his heart, lungs, and chest wall were clearly visible. Despite all his naysayers' claims, Damadian had been proved right. As a testament to Damadian's achievement, *Indomitable* now sits in the Smithsonian Institution, in Washington, D.C.

The success of his experiments did not immediately bring Damadian prosperity or acceptance in either public or academic circles. Although his initial experiments were successful, many people still expressed disbelief at the idea that a magnetic field could be used to locate tumors with precision. As a result, Damadian found it difficult to commercialize his invention. Determined to do so nonetheless, in 1978 he formed his own company, Field Focused Nuclear Magnetic Resonance (FONAR), to manufacture NMR scanners—later called MRI scanners—himself. In 1980 FONAR introduced the world's first commercial MRI, and the company went public in 1981. The Food and Drug Administration (FDA) approved the MRI technology in 1984, and the process began its slow but sure evolution. With the aid of researchers from around the world, MRI technology grew to a point where doctors could use it to detect abnormalities ranging from tumors to slipped disks.

In 1988, after a decade of receiving little or no recognition from his peers, Damadian was honored by then-president Ronald Reagan with the National Medal of Technology for his contribution to MRI technology, which by then had become common. Less than a year later, he was inducted into the National Inventors Hall of Fame, where he joined such celebrated Americans as the Wright brothers, Henry Ford, Thomas A. Edison, and Alexander Graham Bell.

In addition to his pioneering achievements in the field of MRI research, Damadian has championed the rights of other inventors all over the world. Although he has been honored repeatedly for his invention, he has had extraordinary difficulties in collecting royalties from others within the MRI industry. The problem stems from the fact that, in his original patent, Damadian was not entirely clear on how the technology would work; he thereby created a legal loophole through which many industry giants have slipped. "No sooner did we invent than the big guys took it away," he told Claudia Deutsch. In the late 1980s Damadian began to wage a battle against these companies, which included Hitachi, Johnson & Johnson, and General Electric (GE). For years he met with one defeat after another, until a similar case, involving a dispute between Honeywell Inc. and the Minolta Camera Co. over patents on auto-focus cameras, resulted in the payment of $200 million in back royalties to Honeywell. "The Minolta case had a big impact on us," Damadian told Edmund L. Andrews for the *New York Times* (September 5, 1992). "It showed us that the courts are now aware that there is a hidden asset in America, which is the patent."

One by one, the companies began to pay Damadian undisclosed sums as settlements. GE was the last holdout. In 1995 that company's executives were issued a court injunction that prohibited them from selling FONAR-patented technology on their new scanners. "A crucial message has been sent by the court to inventors and entrepreneurs across the nation," Damadian stated in a FONAR press release (October 6, 1995). "Their pioneering work will, in fact, be protected. The patent system in the United States, created two centuries ago by George Washington and Thomas Jefferson, is alive and well, and America remains committed to protect the little guy in his bid to create new inventions." Finally, on June 30, 1997, the other shoe dropped, when GE paid FONAR $128.7 million.

Damadian has used the money to create the Health Management Corp. of America (HCMA). A wholly owned subsidiary of FONAR, HCMA is headed by Damadian's son Timothy. Its primary purpose is to acquire and manage medical practices, ultimately getting them to use MRI technology.

After over two decades in the industry, Damadian still works ceaselessly to improve the technology he created. FONAR has continued to extend and advance MRI systems, by introducing such innovations as a room-size MRI and "stand-up" MRI. Damadian is also heavily active in the expansion of FONAR's mammography scanners. As he explained in the FONAR press release, "FONAR expects the superior images of the MRI to overcome many of the shortcomings of the X-ray mammography machines, provide a superior diagnosis, and permanently eliminate the indignities suffered by women patients including the disrobing and painful breast compression typical of current day X-ray mammography."

Damadian and the former Elizabeth Donna Terry were married in 1960. In addition to Timothy, their children are Jevan and Kiera. *A Machine Called Indomitable* (1985), by the former *New York Times* business reporter Sonny Kleinfield, offers a profile of Damadian and an account of the development of MRI technology. — J.K.B.

Suggested Reading: *Business Week* p32 Dec. 16, 1985; *New York Times* p32 Sep. 5, 1992, p33 July 12, 1997, with photos; *Scientific American* June 1997; *Smithsonian* p22+ June 2000, with photo; *U.S. News & World Report* p66 Jan. 26, 1987; Kleinfield, Sonny. *A Machine Called Indomitable*, 1985; *Who's Who in America, 2000*

Courtesy of Arista Records

Davis, Clive

Apr. 4, 1933– Businessperson; record producer; recording industry executive. Address: Arista Records Inc., 6 W. 57th St., New York, NY 10019

Until his contract ran out, in June 2000, Clive Davis was the president of Arista Records, a label with a relatively small roster of artists that nonetheless saw $425 million in profits in 1999. Taking a hands-on approach to the business, Davis made a personal investment in the careers of the artists on his label, sometimes co-producing their releases. As president of Columbia Records, from 1966 to 1973, he helped guide (and in some cases launch) the careers of many of the most successful recording artists of the 1960s and 1970s, including Lou Reed; Bruce Springsteen; Chicago; Barbara Streisand; Pink Floyd; Johnny Winter; Neil Diamond; Miles Davis; Taj Mahal; Leonard Cohen; and Johnny Cash. While president of Arista, Davis worked with such artists as Annie Lennox; Pam Tillis; Aretha Franklin; Patti Smith; the Grateful Dead; Carlos Santana; Melissa Manchester; Dionne Warwick; Gil Scott–Heron; A Flock of Seagulls; the Kinks; Alan Parsons Project; Earth, Wind, and Fire; Monty Python; the Headhunters; Outkast; and Puff Daddy. Davis is known for his uncanny ability to spot a potential hit song and, when necessary, to find the right person or group to perform it. Universal Music Group chairman Doug Morris told Robert Sam Anson for *Vanity Fair* (February 2000) that he considers Davis to be "one of the finest and most talented executives in the history of the record business."

Many of the biggest names in the music industry publicly defended Davis when, in November 1999, BMG, which owns Arista, announced its plan to replace Davis with LaFace Records co-owner Antonio "L.A." Reid, explaining that Davis was well beyond retirement age and that it was in BMG's best interest to have someone lined up to succeed him. One of Davis's champions was Sony Music Entertainment CEO Tommy Mottola: "Everybody in this business looks up to him," Mottola told Anson. "I never knew that age had anything to do with hearing a hit or identifying a star." For his part, Davis announced that he had no plans to retire anytime in the near future. He saw his fight to remain a presence in the industry as a struggle between corporate and individual interests. "With right on one's side, the voice is eventually heard," Davis told Doreen Carvajal for the *New York Times* (November 27, 1999). "Cheers for the reasoned vigilantes in society who prevent those in power from overwhelming the rights of the individual." Recently, Davis signed a deal with BMG that gives him partial control of the newly created J Records.

Clive Jay Davis was born to Herman and Florence (Brooks) Davis in the New York City borough of Brooklyn on April 4, 1933. As a child he followed the Brooklyn Dodgers and enjoyed playing stickball; he also discovered that he had perfect pitch. After graduating from Erasmus Hall High School, where he was an honors student, Davis attended New York University, in New York City, on a full tuition scholarship. When he was a freshman, he lost both his parents; within a year, his mother died of a cerebral hemorrhage and his father of a heart attack. Nonetheless, Davis went on to graduate magna cum laude, in 1953. He married Helen Cohen, a social worker, and entered Harvard Law School, in Cambridge, Massachusetts, on a full scholarship, graduating with honors in 1956. In the following year Davis was hired by Rosenman, Colin, Kaye, Petschek, and Freund, a law firm whose clients included both the CBS television network and its then-chairman, William S. Paley. In 1960 Davis joined Columbia Records as a corporate lawyer. By 1966 he was the label's general manager, and in 1967 he became its president. When he took over at Columbia, he was the single father of two small children, having divorced sometime earlier. He later married the opera singer Janet Adelberg.

In an interview with Ethan Smith for *New York* magazine (April 6, 1998), Davis described the moment that, in his view, marks the beginning of his career as a record executive: "I had never signed any artist, and I found myself in December '67 at the Monterey Pop Festival. I saw a group that was incredibly charismatic, with a lead singer who was breathtaking and soulful and just the best white soul singer imaginable, but with a rock edge. And she of course turned out to be Janis Joplin, and the group was Big Brother and the Holding Company. That event proved to be a catalyst for my awareness that a tremendous change was taking place in society, certainly among youth." Not long afterward, in New York City, he saw the then-unknown group Blood, Sweat, and Tears, whom he was instrumental in signing. "Then I signed Billy Joel, Aerosmith, and Bruce Springsteen in '72," he recalled. Davis quickly increased rock and roll from 15 percent to 50 percent of Columbia Records' output, thus contributing to the success of Bob Dylan and Carlos Santana, among other artists.

Davis's tenure with Columbia Records came to an abrupt end in 1973, when he was unceremoniously fired for alleged misuse of funds. He was accused of using $54,000 to redecorate his New York City apartment, $20,000 to pay for his son's bar mitzvah, and $13,000 to rent a summer house in Beverly Hills. The case soon became the subject of a larger, Newark, New Jersey–based grand-jury investigation into payola and drugs in the record industry. The name of David Wynshaw, Davis's right-hand man, was found among the papers of Pasquale Falcone, a former manager of the rock/soul group Sly and the Family Stone who had been convicted of smuggling heroin. Falcone, who was reported to have ties to the organized-crime family headed by Vito Genovese, was eventually indicted for defrauding CBS of up to $2 million. The story scandalized the music industry and introduced the term "drugola" to the public consciousness. Davis, who was later exonerated, maintained that he had been fired because Columbia Records had panicked and decided to use him as a scapegoat. There was also speculation in the press at the time that CBS executives were offended by Davis's perceived arrogance and image-consciousness.

After Davis's firing, Columbia artists were prohibited from mentioning his name in their liner notes, and all footage of Davis was edited out of *A Week to Remember* (1975), the promotional film for a 1973 concert he had hosted that had featured Bruce Springsteen and Miles Davis. The singer Patti Smith said of the producer, for an article by Chet Flippo in *Rolling Stone* (December 18, 1975), "He's always dealt with outlaws—not outlaws—let's say pirates. He dealt with Sly Stone, with Janis Joplin; *he likes it.* He's an independent businessman but he loves art." While unemployed Davis worked with former *Time* magazine writer James Willwerth on a book entitled *Clive: Inside the Record Business*, which chronicled his rise in the industry and presented his side of the payola scandal. His unapologetic memoir, published in 1974, became a best-seller.

Also in 1974 Davis became a consultant for Bell Records, a failing subsidiary of Columbia Pictures International (CPI, which is not affiliated with Columbia Records). In November of that year, at the suggestion of CPI president Al Hirschfield, Davis assumed the presidency of the label, which was renamed Arista, receiving $10 million in seed money as well as a 20 percent equity in—and complete control of—the company. Davis retained only two of the artists under contract with Bell: Melissa Manchester and Barry Manilow. The first successful single to be released by Arista Records was Manilow's "Mandy," which became a number-one hit on January 18, 1975. Manilow was one of the first artists at Arista whom Davis took under his wing, and the singer-songwriter has acknowledged Davis's role in his stardom. In an interview with Wayne Robins for *New York Newsday* (March 14, 1990), Manilow recalled Davis's involvement in another of his hit songs: "I didn't want to do 'I Write the Songs.' . . . I kept turning it down, and he wouldn't budge. Clive believed it would be a number one record for me, that it would be a signature song. And he was right." By the end of Davis's first year as president, the label's profits had gone up 600 percent. In 1980 Arista Records was bought by BMG, which is owned by the German company Bertelsmann AG.

Davis spoke with Ethan Smith about his time-tested ability to bring about highly successful matches between singers and songs: "You gotta find artists who are unique, you gotta find material that could become standards. Yes, there's always the one-hit wonder. Yes, there's always the one that appears more artificial or manufactured. But you're really looking for the unique talent, whether or not they can write their own material. . . . Ultimately, it's no fun to be in this business if you don't have hits." Davis has worked with songwriters as well as singers able to interpret material written by others. "If it's someone who can write, like Springsteen or Patti Smith, they have to have a point of view and something to say that's special," he explained to Sheila Rule for the *New York Times* (December 2, 1992). "If it's a performing artist that doesn't write—look at the genius of Aretha [Franklin], Dionne [Warwick]—they have to bring songs to life in a manner never thought of." In February 1983 Davis saw a 19-year-old model and former gospel singer perform at a New York supper club. "I was stunned by her talent," he recalled for Robert Sam Anson. "I wanted to sign her immediately." Whitney Houston went on to become one of Arista's greatest successes, and even Davis, who worked hard to promote her talent, was surprised by the scope of her impact on the entertainment industry. "When I signed Whitney Houston, I did herald her, I took her on the *Merv Griffin Show,* and I did say that she'd be a combination of Lena Horne and Aretha Franklin, and that would be her uniqueness," he told Wayne Robins. "But I never dreamt that this artist would sell nine million copies in America, and nine million copies abroad, of each of her first two albums." The 1992 song "I Will Always Love You," featured on the soundtrack to the film *The Bodyguard* (in which Houston starred with Kevin Costner), was the fastest-selling single of both Houston's career and Arista's then–17-year history.

Davis has had a hand in the success of many "crossover" songs—in his case, those that were hits with black listeners before achieving mainstream popularity. His approach is usually to market them first to black radio stations, then wait for the Top 40 stations to pick them up once they are established as hits. Examples include the cuts on the soul superstar Aretha Franklin's recording for Arista, *Who's Zoomin' Who* (1985), which was the first platinum-selling album of her long career. "I listen for the songs. . . . That's why Aretha was able to [make a comeback]," Davis told Jonathan Taylor for the *Chicago Tribune* (July 24, 1983). "Her talent never diminished, but some people make artistic decisions based on image or style instead of the quality of the material. . . . Pop entertainers need songs. They need material and producers, and I think that this company has made a major mark in that area." The singer Taylor Dayne spoke to Wayne Robins about Davis's relationship with artists: "What you see is his commitment and devotion to an artist. . . . Sometimes Clive gets down and dirty, really involved, and sometimes it's appreciated. Sometimes it's not. It's criticism, and you either take it correctly, or get insulted. He gets so involved, he really likes to listen and give his input. He cares enough to say, 'I want to like everything on there, I want to know everything on there.'"

The year 1999 was a successful one for Davis; Arista Records' revenues exceeded $425 million. Recently Prince signed with the label, in his first record deal since 1996; that move surprised many, since the artist had spent years bemoaning the treatment he had received at the hands of Warner Brothers Records, even painting the word "Slave" on his face during his battle to get out of his contract. Carlos Santana's "comeback" album, *Supernatural,* his first for Arista Records, received nine Grammy Awards in February 2000, including best rock album and album of the year. Although Santana had maintained a steady following over the course of his 30-year career, guest appearances by hot young artists such as Lauryn Hill, Wyclef Jean, and Rob Thomas (of Matchbox 20) on the album helped the rock veteran to find a new audience. At the Grammy Awards, Davis, who had served as *Supernatural*'s executive producer, and Santana thanked one another enthusiastically before an international audience. In March Patti Smith paid tribute to Davis during his induction into the Rock and Roll Hall of Fame; the following month Davis hosted an all-star celebration for Arista's 25th Anniversary, which was televised in May.

On May 2, 2000 BMG officially announced that Antonio Reid had been named the new chief executive of Arista Records, replacing Davis; the company bought the half of LaFace Records that it did not already own, effectively consolidating it with BMG. This development struck some as bitterly ironic, considering that in 1989 Davis had provided Reid and Kenneth "Babyface" Edmonds with the money to start LaFace. Although acknowledging the successes of the past year, Reid told Doreen Carvajal for the *New York Times* (May 3, 2000) that he intended "to make Arista the home for many Latin artists, record producers, and Latin superstars." For an article in *Entertainment Weekly* (December 3, 1999), Strauss Zelnick, the president and CEO of BMG Entertainment, told Tom Sinclair about the company's decision: "I have a responsibility to make decisions based on what's right for the company, and that includes making sure we have an appropriate succession plan in place at Arista."

Many artists with whom Davis had worked criticized BMG's decision. "Clive and I are family, and it hurts me to think that he is being treated with disrespect," Whitney Houston told Robert Sam Anson. Barry Manilow protested to Doreen Carvajal, "It seems that corporations are taking over a lot of the decisions that were once made by individuals. It may make sense to them as a corporation, but . . . when you have someone as brilliant as Clive, you push those corporate rules away and you just let him do his own thing." In the same article the singer Carly Simon described her reaction to the news: "You don't fix something if it's not broken.

Not only is it not broken, but it's one of the prides of the record business. I feel so emotional about this. It feels like my home is being destroyed." In August 2000 BMG and Davis announced the creation of J Records, a label controlled by both Davis and BMG. The deal, which was reported to be worth as much as $150 million, allowed Davis to retain only a few Arista artists and a number of Arista's top executives.

Davis has received many awards from the music industry. He was named the Record Company President of the Year at five annual Poe Broadcasting and Music Conventions for the Radio and Record Industry, and he has been the keynote speaker three times at the annual National Association of Record Merchandisers Convention. Davis's other honors include a Lifetime Achievement Award from the National Academy of Recording Arts and Sciences and the Martin Luther King Humanitarian of the Year Award, presented to the producer by the Congress for Racial Equality in 1985.

When Davis's children were young, his schedule often left him little time to spend with them. Twenty-four years ago, Davis told Stanley Mieses for the New York *Daily News* (August 31, 1976), "When you begin your day in the office at 9 a.m. . . . and end it at the office at 8:30 and 9 p.m., and then maybe have to rush downtown to hear someone, or out of town, or even home with stacks of records and tapes to listen to and contracts and memoranda to read, it's hard I suppose to stay in touch with your family. I always try to keep Sundays open, but during the week, it's dinners only." All four of his children now work in the entertainment industry. — C.L.

Suggested Reading: *Chicago Tribune* XII p18+ July 24, 1983, with photo; *Entertainment Weekly* p98 Dec. 3, 1999, with illustration; *New York* p83 Apr. 6, 1998, with photo; New York *Daily News* p29 Aug. 31, 1976, with photo; *New York Newsday* II p3+ Mar. 14, 1990, with photo; *New York Times* C p17 Dec. 2, 1992, E p3 May 3, 2000, with photo; *Rolling Stone* Dec. 18, 1975, with photos; *Time* June 11, 1973, with photo; *Vanity Fair* p120+ Feb. 2000, with photos

---

DeLauro, Rosa

Mar. 2, 1943– U.S. Representative from Connecticut. Address: 436 Cannon House Office Bldg., Washington, DC 20515

Courtesy of the House of Representatives

It was only a matter of time before Rosa DeLauro would be one of "the most powerful people in Congress," the *Washington Post* (May 10, 1992) predicted early in the 1990s. Bearing out that forecast, in 1999 DeLauro became the highest-ranking female Democrat in the United States House of Representatives, with her election as assistant to the House Democratic leader, Richard Gephardt. DeLauro first went to Congress in 1990, representing Connecticut's Third District as a progressive activist seeking to cut defense spending, win universal health care, and defend women's right to seek abortions. She represents a new breed of women who have actively chosen political careers, rather than inheriting them from deceased husbands or coming to them indirectly from school and civic organizations. As the executive director of various political campaigns, she established a reputation as a valuable fund-raiser long before running for office herself.

Rosa L. DeLauro was born on March 2, 1943 in New Haven, Connecticut, the only child of Luisa and Theodore DeLauro. Her father was an Italian immigrant who worked as an insurance salesman. DeLauro grew up in an atmosphere of community service, her home acting as a magnet for Italian immigrants and others who needed help finding places to live or work. So active was her father in this regard that he became known as the "mayor" of the neighborhood. But it is a letter written by her mother in 1933, urging women to get involved in politics, that DeLauro keeps for inspiration. Still active in her 80s, Luisa DeLauro is the longest-serving member of the New Haven Board of Aldermen. A sweatshop seamstress during Rosa DeLauro's youth, she held firm in her belief that only education would allow her daughter to work elsewhere; DeLauro heeded the lesson, studying at the London School of Economics in 1962 and 1963 and graduating cum laude from Marymount College, in Tarrytown, New York, in 1964. She received a master's degree in international politics from Columbia University, in New York City, in 1966.

DeLauro began her activism as a community organizer in President Lyndon B. Johnson's War on Poverty. In the National Urban Fellows program, she helped to create employment opportunities for women and minorities. She became the first woman executive assistant to the mayor of New Haven, managing Frank Logue's mayoral campaign in 1978. Next she was executive assistant to New Haven's development administrator, working to attract jobs and federal assistance. Christopher J. Dodd of Connecticut noticed DeLauro and hired her to run his 1980 U.S. Senate campaign. After his victory she became his chief of staff, working with him on comprehensive child-care legislation that was passed by Congress. During one Senate campaign she found out that she had ovarian cancer. This encounter with mortality persuaded her to run for office herself, after she overcame the disease.

In 1987 DeLauro left Senator Dodd's staff to become the executive director of Countdown '87, a national coalition formed to end U.S. military aid to the Contras in Nicaragua. The group raised $1 million for TV commercials that drew analogies between the Contras' activities and the U.S. experience in Vietnam. The coalition asserted, moreover, that government money would be better spent on domestic programs. Their campaign was successful, and DeLauro went on to become executive director of Emily's List, a national fund-raising organization that seeks to increase the number of women in elective office.

When Democratic representative Bruce A. Morrison, of Connecticut's Third Congressional District, left his seat to run for governor of the state, DeLauro saw her chance to pursue elective office. The district had been badly hit by recession and layoffs, and she ran on a platform that called for a highway jobs bill. By now she had the contacts to raise money and to discourage intra-party competition. Her rival was state senator Thomas Scott, a conservative Republican who opposed gun control and abortion rights. Scott accused DeLauro of being a far-left radical, but her campaign, emphasizing her working-class roots and political connections to Democratic labor leaders, belied his accusations. Raising less than half the money that DeLauro secured, Scott decried her as a Washington insider dependent on Political Action Committee (PAC) money, citing the fact that $300,000 of the $1 million she had raised came from PACs. Despite that charge, DeLauro won the election, going to Congress in 1990.

DeLauro's congressional career has focused on improving economic and health conditions for her middle-class constituents. The first legislation she introduced in Congress was the Middle Class Tax Relief Act of 1991, which sought tax cuts for middle-income taxpayers; the measure was vetoed by President George Bush. During the 102d Congress she helped write a transportation bill, which succeeded in bringing jobs to her state. She was also able to effect the passage of the "DeLauro amendment," which saved Connecticut taxpayers $400 million in bridge-repair funds. She introduced legislation to create jobs nationwide through infrastructure development, and she continues to organize an annual Connecticut Jobs Fair. In the 106th Congress she supported an increase in the minimum wage, and she has written legislation aimed at bringing men and women equal pay for equal work. DeLauro supported a $500-per-child tax credit as well as tax cuts for children's health care, college education, and child care. She obtained a tax refund for Connecticut police officers and firefighters whose disability payments had been taxed. She supports legislation to reduce class size and modernize public schools.

In 1992 DeLauro focused on health-care reform, working to guarantee comprehensive private health insurance and to stop health-care billing fraud. Her tenure on the Subcommittee on Labor, Health and Human Services, and Education reflects her experience as a cancer survivor. She won funding for the National Institutes for Health (NIH) to establish the Office of Women's Health Research; wrote legislation ensuring minimum hospital stays for women undergoing breast-cancer surgery; promoted research leading to the discovery of a major cause of cervical cancer; and secured research funds for a drug to treat ovarian cancer. She has continued to promote the expansion of preventive-care health services. In 1993 she worked on legislation to create a cancer screening program for women with limited access to health care. DeLauro has sat on the Select Committee on Aging and has supported a tax cut for families providing long-term care to a parent or relative. In addition, she has co-sponsored legislation lowering prescription-drug costs for senior citizens. In 1999 she organized an Internet petition to overhaul the managed-care system and to pass a Patients' Bill of Rights. Her legislation, supporting the right of patients to sue their health-care providers, was opposed by the Republican Party and the medical industry.

Beginning in the late 1990s, both the left and the right decried government as the servant of plutocrats, and politicians' fund-raising came under scrutiny. In this climate, DeLauro was asked by Jeff Shear of the Center for Public Integrity whether her political significance rested primarily on her ability to raise funds. "People need to know that you come here and you represent their interests and that you're not here only in your self-interest or in [that of] those who can help to finance your campaign," she responded, as quoted in the center's publication *Investigative Reports* (November 6, 1997, on-line). "Now, don't get me wrong. . . . You have to be able to raise money because of the way the system is structured," she said. Criticized for redirecting contributions from her own campaign funds to those of other Democratic Party members, she admitted that the amount she has had to raise for each election is less than that for the previous campaign, allowing her to contribute to other party members. But, as she explained in 1997, "The fact of the matter is that I had the opportunity to support good candidates, solid candidates, and I took that opportunity and will continue to take that opportunity if my circumstances are such." At the same time, DeLauro has said that she supports campaign reform, believing that independent expenditure "cuts off free speech. . . . I'm a supporter of banning soft money. . . . I support the strongest and toughest legislation" on campaign finance reform.

DeLauro participated in the sweeping anticrime legislation of the 1990s, which funded the hiring of 100,000 new police officers nationwide and required tough sentences for repeat violent offenders. She also helped lead the campaigns for the assault-weapons ban and the Brady Bill, which mandated a criminal-background check and a waiting period for unlicensed gun purchasers. During the 104th Congress she was named to the House National Security Committee. She was instrumental in writing an amendment to the Defense Reauthorization Bill that protected the interests of small-business subcontractors. DeLauro has also been a member of the Agriculture Subcommittee; in that capacity she has written legislation, supported by environmental, business, and labor organizations, to upgrade the infrastructure for handling water pollution and to finance the cleanup of the nation's estuaries. During her fifth term in the House of Representatives, she was the chief deputy House minority whip, and she has continued to sit on the House Appropriations Committee.

DeLauro is considered a pragmatic politician. For example, she supported an antiabortion colleague—David E. Bonior, a Michigan Democrat—for House whip in 1991, because she did not believe that he would allow his views to influence the House. "I am not a one-issue person," she explained. On the other hand, she has also been praised for having "the courage of her convictions," having campaigned even amid the pro-military climate sparked by the Persian Gulf War to cut defense costs and to channel money toward domestic programs and the retraining of defense workers. In 1998 DeLauro was named the House of Representatives' top "workhorse" by *Washingtonian* magazine and was called a "hero for working families" by national columnist Tom Oliphant. When she lost her bid for chair of the Democratic Caucus in 1998, no women were left in party leadership, provoking complaints by women in Congress. But the new post of assistant to the Democratic congressional leader was reported to be "tailored to fit" DeLauro by *Roll Call*, even before she was elected to the position, in January 1999. She is regarded as an effective communicator, and House Minority Leader Richard Gephardt said that her election as his assistant would strengthen the "coordination of policy, communication, and research" for the 2000 elections.

In 1978 DeLauro married Stanley Greenberg, who is now president of Greenberg Quinlan Research, a public-issue and political research and polling firm. Their three children—Anna, Kathryn, and Jonathan Greenberg—are adults pursuing college degrees and careers. During the week the couple live in Washington; most of their weekends are spent in New Haven, with DeLauro holding neighborhood office hours on Saturdays. Speaking as the natural heir to her parents' community politics, she told Jeff Shear, "I live and breathe this stuff." — V.K.

Suggested Reading: (American Cancer Society) *Capitol Focus* May 1999, with photo; (Center for Public Integrity) *Investigative Reports* (on-line) Nov. 6, 1997; *Congressional Quarterly Weekly Report* p93 Jan. 12, 1991; *National Journal* (on-line) Jan. 30, 1993; *New Haven Register* (on-line) Apr. 7, 1999; *New York Times* (on-line) May 8, 1994, with photo, Aug. 29, 1996; Foerstel, Karen. *Biographical Dictionary of Congressional Women*, 1999

Dennis, Felix

1947– Publisher of the magazine Maxim.
Address: Maxim, *1040 Ave. of the Americas, 14th Fl., New York, NY 10018*

The British magazine tycoon Felix Dennis believes American men want above all else three things: sex, beer, and ways to procure ample amounts of both. His successful Stateside launch of *Maxim* in the spring of 1997 may have reinforced that idea. A hardened veteran of England's so-called "laddie mag" industry, which openly panders to the pubescent side of an otherwise adult male audience, Dennis introduced *Maxim* to what he had concluded was an untested market in the United States. In comparison with his publication's testosterone-charged mix of images of scantily clad models, bathroom humor, and service-oriented articles about such topics as sex gadgets, American magazines struck him as downright boring. "That's capital B-O-R-I-N-G," Dennis said, as quoted in *Fortune* (April 14, 1997). "They all take themselves so seriously. *GQ* is for men who like socks better than sex."

A long-standing tenet of the American magazine industry has been that men prefer publications devoted to a single subject, be it cars, sports, busi-

Courtesy of Four Corners Communications

Felix Dennis

ness, woodworking, or nude women. Another was the belief that men would resist any magazine that offered advice in certain areas; hence, certain topics—marital problems, hair loss, and impotence, for example—were never addressed. Men's magazines that were classified as general interest—notably, the venerable titles *Gentlemen's Quarterly* (*GQ*) and *Esquire*—aimed to offer sophistication and style; they eschewed service journalism in favor of literary journalism and fashion. *Men's Health*, launched in 1986 by Rodale Press, redefined the category by introducing the type of service articles formerly found only in women's magazines. Reformulated for male consumption, features about health, fitness, and relationships helped propel *Men's Health* to a circulation of 1.6 million by 1999, which forced *GQ*, *Esquire*, *Details*, and *Men's Journal* to expand their contents with similar offerings. To Dennis's mind, however, *Men's Health* did not go far enough.

Based on the assumption that all grown men inherently possess an adolescent side, *Maxim* serves its advice spiced with pictures of busty models, scatological humor, and an overriding tone of goofiness. The February 2000 issue, for instance, includes advice on how to avoid being pushed around by your co-workers, mother, or girlfriend; a list of the 50 all-time greatest B movies; a graphic report on quack surgery; and a survey of what women find most and least appealing in porn films. Although he has been the target of numerous attacks for promoting a beer-guzzling mentality over a champaign-sipping one, Dennis has gone a long way toward proving that lowbrow sells.

Published 10 times per year, *Maxim* reached a circulation of 350,000 by its fourth issue, placing it on par with *Esquire* and *GQ*. After only 15 issues its rate base (or readership, as compiled by the Audit Bureau of Circulations) had grown to 800,000, passing that of every competitor other than *Men's Health* and making it the most successful launch since *Martha Stewart Living*. For the first half of 2000, only three years after its debut, *Maxim* promised its advertisers a monthly readership of 1.5 million, putting it ahead of *Men's Health*. In light of the publication's extraordinary growth, that figure was revised upward to two million in the second half of the year, making *Maxim* the fastest-growing magazine in American history. "I think a circulation of five million by [2005] is not out of the question," a *Maxim* staffer told Charles Pappas for *Advertising Age* (April 26, 2000). Especially notable is the demographic (marketing jargon for reader profile, or characteristics of a typical buyer) of *Maxim*'s subscribers. Rather than what many might expect—a quintessential modern-day caveman—*Maxim*'s average reader is 30 years old and earns approximately $62,000 per year, according to market research. Furthermore, 51 percent of its readers are college graduates and 86 percent hold down full-time jobs.

"I have one talent," Dennis has remarked, according to *Fortune*, "and that's figuring out what people want about two minutes before they know it themselves." Largely an autodidact and self-made man, Felix Dennis was born in 1947 in Kingston-upon-Thames, an industrial town south of London. He and his younger brother, Julian, were raised by their mother, Dorothy Sawyer, after their father abandoned the family, in 1949. Living with her boys in her mother's house, which lacked electricity and an indoor bathroom, Sawyer worked as an accountant by day and attended classes at night. At 15 Dennis dropped out of school and left home to make a go of it as a drummer and singer. He migrated to Harrow-on-the-Hill, a London suburb legendary in rock annals as a one-time haven for Elton John, Eric Clapton, Jeff Beck, and Rod Stewart before they became famous. His days were spent on street corners hawking *Oz*, an underground magazine he helped publish; in the evening he jammed with future music luminaries. Dennis's day job led him to his true calling. "The underground press was a part of a broad social movement, and there were a lot of people who were involved in it just to sort of *hang out*," Roger Hutchinson, a Scottish journalist who was involved with *Oz*, told Alex Williams for *New York* (July 26, 1999). "They weren't in the 'publishing business.' Felix was. Felix was one of those rare people who could have brought out a magazine all by himself. He could have written it, laid it out, sold advertising, balanced the books." *Oz* proved a little too subversive, however, for British authorities. In 1971 Dennis and his co-editors, Richard Neville and Jim Anderson, were charged with obscenity after publishing an issue that featured smutty jokes and cartoons. The subsequent court battle became the longest obscenity trial in British legal history. The jury found the *Oz* trio guilty, and the judge sentenced Dennis to 11 days in jail—a lighter penalty than that imposed on Neville and Anderson—because, as several sources quoted him as saying, he found Dennis "very much less intelligent" than his comrades. The verdict was overturned on appeal.

Dennis first displayed his talent for chronicling popular trends in the 1970s, with the hit magazine *Kung Fu Monthly*, which capitalized on the growing interest in the martial arts generated by Bruce Lee's movies. Later in the decade and into the 1980s, he made a small fortune publishing collectors' magazines that capitalized on industries spawned by such films as *Star Wars* and *E.T.* Then, in 1985, just as the Apple Macintosh personal computer became popular, Dennis launched *MacUser*; a year later he sold the U.S. edition of the title to computer-publishing giant Ziff-Davis for the then-unprecedented sum of $25 million. (Dennis still publishes a magazine under the same title in England, but the two have no affiliation.) Having found a growing market for computer publications, Dennis continued to produce a sheaf of best-selling consumer and trade computer periodicals. By the mid-1990s his self-named, privately owned company had become the fourth largest publishing firm in Britain, and Dennis had entered into computer retail as a co-founder of Micro Warehouse, which is based in Connecticut. He sold his shares in that successful mail-order company for $83 million in 1995, just before the value of its stock peaked.

Flush with cash, Dennis launched the British edition of *Maxim* in April 1995. The concept for the publication came to Dennis from Mat Snow and Lloyd Bradley, two veteran magazine editors who had failed to interest other publishers in it. Snow and Bradley's proposed periodical resembled the British magazine *Loaded*, which had debuted earlier in the decade. Dubbed a "laddie mag" for its machismo-rich perspective on life and love, *Loaded* sought to inform men in much the way that a chat with the lads down at the neighborhood pub might enlighten them. The format appealed to Dennis, who was seeking a new challenge. "We own the computer market," he told Maggie Brown for the London *Independent* (April 4, 1995), "now we'll steal someone else's lollipop. It's a growing market." He agreed to work with Snow and Bradley to put together a dummy issue (a prototype intended not for sale but to spark interest among potential advertisers). Having deemed the dummy issue a success, Dennis recruited Gil Hudson, an editor and seasoned veteran of the women's magazine market, to guide the launch of *Maxim*. An editorial amalgam of Hudson's specialty, service journalism, and the sort of offbeat humor that Dennis favored, *Maxim* provided further proof of Dennis's uncanny ability to judge popular trends. While most magazines operate in the red for four to eight years, *Maxim* began turning a profit only two years after its premiere. Dennis soon had sufficient resources to launch an edition of the magazine in the United States.

In the U.S., general-interest men's magazines had never been notably popular. With the exception of latecomer *Men's Health*, their readerships hovered at about a half million—a small figure given that there are more than 89 million men in the U.S. between the ages of 15 and 64. Although these magazines portrayed an ideal of male sophistication and refinement the editors believed the average man would aspire to, Dennis felt that their content attracted primarily gay men and various elite minorities rather than a broad male readership. "Anyone who reads *GQ* next to *Maxim* cannot help but come away with feeling that these two magazines are aimed at the same men. And they are," Dennis told Tony Silber for *Folio:* (June 1999). "The difference for me is that one is witty, funny, amusing, very relevant, and highly entertaining. The other is self-important and pompous, and makes you feel inadequate because you're not going to spend $2,300 on a suit."

Less raunchy than its British cousin, the U.S. edition of *Maxim*, launched in the spring of 1997, relies more on adolescent double entendre and gonzo journalism for its punch. Furthermore, pornography laws in the U.S. prevent the magazine from showing women clothed in anything less than a bikini if it is made available to people under age 18, a market Dennis readily, if obliquely, admits to coveting. "*Maxim* has no 15-year-old readers," he quipped to Alex Williams. "And there is no drug problem in America, and the president would never tell a lie."

To ensure the success of his Stateside effort, Dennis raided the ranks of American publisher Condé Nast's top sales executives, recruiting Lance Ford, the former associate publisher of *Bon Appétit* magazine, as his U.S. publisher. Ford persuaded *Bon Appétit*'s ad director, Carolyn Kremins, to jump ship with him to become associate publisher. Dennis selected a woman, Clare McHugh, to be his first American editor, perhaps, it has been suggested, as a preemptive move in anticipation of feminist backlash against *Maxim*'s content. After McHugh's departure, a year later, he hired a man, former *Prevention* and *Cosmopolitan* editor Mark Golin. Condé Nast struck back in 1999 by hiring Golin as editor of *Details*. Dennis reacted by refusing to release Golin from his contract for several months, thereby leaving *Details* without an editor. Said to be a shameless as well as a skilled self-promoter, Dennis then let it be known that he had decided to give Golin his freedom out of the goodness of his heart. Finally, he named Sammy, the office's pet hamster, as Golin's interim replacement, to suggest that Golin had nothing to do with *Maxim*'s growing success. Dennis eventually replaced Golin by stealing Mike Souter from the staff of the competing British laddie-mag *FHM*.

Many media critics in the United States have bristled at *Maxim*'s off-color content and condemned as vulgar such recurring features as the "sports injury of the month," which highlights grotesque injuries. On the other hand, Dennis's periodical seems to have struck a chord with American male readers. One *Maxim* reader, identified only as an Ivy-League graduate and investment banker, described the magazine to Alex Williams for *New York* (July 26, 1999): "You know how in college there's always a sorority that has this certain attitude like they're untouchable, they have this image they have to exude? And then there's this other one—they're just as cute, but you can always jump their bones if you want to? Well, *Maxim* is the *other* sorority. They think like you think—they just want to party."

Some critics predicted that corporate advertisers, who represent the lion's share of revenue for most magazines, would reject *Maxim* as a forum for their messages because of its raciness; American corporations, particularly giants like AT&T, GM, Ford, and American Express, they noted, are traditionally very conservative in their choice of advertising venue. Yet their ads have consistently run in *Maxim*, undoubtedly because of its steadily growing audience. Due in part to *Maxim*'s remarkable success, Dennis launched *Stuff* in 1999. Similar in tone and format to its brother publication, *Stuff* focuses more of its content on gadgets that appeal to men.

A lifelong bachelor, Dennis has been subjected to criticism of his personal as well as his professional life. Although Dennis professes that he no longer practices penetrative sex, he boasts that he regularly dates at least 10 women concurrently. "Most of the women I see, I've been seeing for a very long time—some of them for more than 10 years," he explained to Alex Williams. "I encourage them to have boyfriends and to get married. I even go to their weddings." Since the late 1980s Marie-France Demolis, a native of France, has been his main companion. "She spends a lot of time with me in various homes," Dennis explained to Williams. "And if I do turn up with somebody Marie-France doesn't like much, she won't hesitate to let me know. So to that extent, there is compromise." "It's quite unusual, but it's not hard to live with. And it has its rewards," Demolis told Williams. "Felix is a very generous, very compassionate man."

One of the 100 wealthiest people in England, Dennis divides his time among his five homes: apartments in London and New York; a country estate in Warwickshire, England; a home on the Caribbean island of Mustique; and a waterfront house located on Candlewood Lake, in Connecticut. A decade ago he purchased 700 acres in Warwickshire, on which he planted shrubbery and trees and constructed footpaths for local public access. He reportedly hopes to plant, also in Warwickshire, some 30,000 acres of hardwood trees native to the district; that land, too, would be open to the public. He has estimated the cost of carrying out this project to be about £1 billion, of which he will contribute £200 million out of his own pocket. "I have no children and have already put out trust funds for the loved ones in my life," he told Geoffrey Lean for the London *Independent* (November 7, 1999). "So, I have this mad idea this is the best thing I could do with [my money]."

By turns sincere, bombastic, affable, and imperious, Dennis clearly relishes the role of the larger-than-life buffoon. "It's been my job for many years to play the fool, because fools are always let off," he said to Alex Williams. "The Brits love the underdog. We despise success here in Britain—just despise it." — T.J.F.

Suggested Reading: *Folio:* p38+ June 1999, with photos; London *Independent* p22 Apr. 4, 1995; *New York* p30+ July 26, 1999, with photos; *New York Times* C p4 Oct. 19, 1998; *Newsweek* (online) Feb 1, 1999

Christopher Kolk/Outline Press

Dhaliwal, Daljit

(DAL-ih-wahl, DAL-jeet)

1962(?)– Journalist; anchor of ITN World News for Public Television. *Address: ITN, 200 Gray's Inn Rd., London WC1X 8XZ, England*

Daljit Dhaliwal never anticipated becoming a celebrity when she launched her career in journalism, with a job at the BBC, in 1990, and her chances of becoming a media star did not seem to increase when she began to anchor *ITN World News for Public Television*, in 1995. "The thinking viewer's alternative to the blow-dried coverage offered by America's anchormen," as the London *Times* (August 8, 1998) put it, *ITN World News* tends to eschew the sensationalistic gimmicks that most U.S. news shows use to enliven their content, and Dhaliwal maintains a reserved and professional demeanor throughout each broadcast. Nevertheless, the London-born Dhaliwal has recently become the object of much attention—and even veneration—in the United States. In the last two years, she has been featured in such trendy magazines as *Vogue*, *Esquire*, *Rolling Stone*, and *George*, and in 1999 *People* included her name in its reader-generated list of the world's 50 most beautiful people. She has even gained something of a cult following in the U.S., with an increasing number of Internet fan sites devoted to her. "Cool Britannia's evening Muse," as Reggie Nadelson dubbed her in *Vogue* (September 1999), Dhaliwal has downplayed her role on *ITN World News*. "Anchors do have a personal following and a lot of people out there like the English accent . . . ," she said to Mark McClelland for the *Week* (August 1, 1999, online), an Indian news magazine. "I'm not personally looking to be recognised, I just do my job. Everyone is integral to the show's success."

Daljit Dhaliwal was born and raised in London's Southall district in late 1962 or early 1963. Her parents immigrated to Great Britain from India—her father, a factory worker, in the 1950s, and her mother, a caterer, in the 1960s. Dhaliwal told a *People* (May 10, 1999) reporter that her parents, who had had an arranged marriage, were so conservative that they were "horrified" when, at 16, she plucked her eyebrows for the first time. But she also recalled, in an interview with Patricia Brennan for the *Washington Post* (August 6, 2000), that she and her siblings—one younger sister and two younger brothers—were "basically left . . . to our own devices." In a conversation with Mark McClelland, she said that her parents "emphasised education but let me make my own decisions about my career." The independent cast of mind she developed while growing up, she has said, figured prominently in her choice of career.

After earning a bachelor's degree in philosophy and history from Polytechnic of East London (now the University of East London), Dhaliwal completed a master's degree in politics, history, and economics from the University of London. She planned to make either teaching or journalism her profession, she told Patricia Brennan, explaining that she "was always interested in doing something involving public service." Ultimately, she chose journalism, because she thought it would be "more exciting and fun." "And I'm right," she added, "because some of my friends who went into teaching are so depressed."

Responding to a newspaper ad, in 1990 Dhaliwal joined the BBC (the British Broadcasting Corp., Great Britain's oldest and largest television and radio network), lured by the chance to attend the network's journalist training program. In her talk with Mark McClelland, she characterized the program as "the best training course in the country," and added that "because of it you get opportunities that might not be available to other journalists." Dhaliwal has emphasized the importance of hands-on experience for aspiring journalists. She told Patricia Brennan, "The best way to learn your craft is to be in the business. I don't think you can learn journalism sitting in a classroom. If you want to be a reporter, and you want to sharpen your instincts, you can only do that on the road."

Upon completing her training, Dhaliwal was assigned to various BBC newsrooms in England, Scotland, and Northern Ireland (sometimes called Ulster). She was based in Belfast, the capital of Northern Ireland, for a year and a half and reported for *Inside Ulster*, a 30-minute regional news program. Northern Ireland, she told Brennan, "is basically where I cut my teeth as a journalist." At that time, Belfast was the scene of repeated outbreaks of violence, connected with the longstanding conflict between Northern Ireland's Protestant majority and its Catholic minority. Once, she recalled to Brennan, after learning that a bomb had just exploded in Belfast not far from the newsroom, "I grabbed the walkie-talkie and my editor sent me down with a camera crew. The IRA [Irish Republican Army, a Catholic paramilitary group] had thrown a coffee-jar bomb at a police station, so we went down to get some pictures, and about 20 minutes into filming, another bomb went off. The secondary bomb would have been planted to catch the security services while they were cordoning off the area. I fell to the floor, while the debris rained down. My editor came across the walkie-talkie and said, 'Are you alright?' and I said, 'I'm fine.' And he said, 'Okay, Daljit, get to a phone—you've got to file a piece for the lunchtime news in about 20 minutes.' I went into a Chinese restaurant and borrowed a phone and filed a report. You have to be resourceful."

In 1995 Dhaliwal left the BBC to work for its London-based rival, ITN (Independent Television Network), which provides news for Britain's three commercial channels—ITV, Channel 4, and Channel 5. Before stepping in as anchor—or "news reader," to use Britain's preferred term—for *ITN World News*, later in 1995, Dhaliwal co-hosted a regional ITN newscast (on which she still appears from time to time) and reported for *First Edition*, an ITN news program aimed at schoolchildren. Defending her switch from field reporter to anchor, Dhaliwal said to Littlefield, "Just because you're reading a script, you don't suddenly become someone with an inactive mind. I'll come in, look at the rundown that Jeff [Henderson, an *ITN World News* producer] has decided, look at the wires, at what other programs are presenting, do my research for interviews. I'll look through the scripts, sometimes put them into a style that I'm comfortable delivering." She observed to a *Rolling Stone* (August 20, 1998) reporter, "In international news, you're invariably dealing with gruesome stories: earthquakes, coups, genocide. You keep your objectivity, but at the same time you're a human being and you've got to be compassionate."

Although ITN was well-known and highly regarded in Britain, and *ITN World News* had aired sporadically in the U.S. since 1987, few Americans seemed to take notice of either the network or its international news program before Dhaliwal began appearing on U.S. broadcasts, in November 1996. Within a few months of that date, distribution of *ITN World News* had jumped from 19 PBS affiliates to more than 40. Many viewers became staunchly loyal fans: in 1998, when a number of stations dropped *ITN World News* in favor of a BBC rival, there was a deluge of demands for the show's reinstatement. The outcry prompted some of the stations to retain *ITN World News* and even led stations that had not previously carried the program to pick it up. As of August 2000 the show was regularly broadcast on 72 PBS affiliates throughout the U.S., potentially reaching some 55 percent of the nation's population. In most cities *ITN World News* airs five nights a week in the early evening, placing Dhaliwal in direct competition with such national network heavyweights as ABC's Peter Jennings, NBC's Tom Brokaw, and CBS's Dan Rather. "We have a loyal following in the States because people know they'll get very serious news without editorializing," Dhaliwal told the *Rolling Stone* interviewer.

While the U.S. version of *ITN World News* is modified to accommodate American audiences—for example, there are no mentions of cricket scores, and the role of the U.S. in world affairs receives added emphasis—the program remains vigorously international in outlook. In late 1998, for instance, at a time when the focus of most American newscasts was the stained blue dress connected with the President Bill Clinton–Monica Lewinsky sex scandal, *ITN World News* devoted a substantial portion of its air time to the escalating crisis in Kosovo, in western Croatia. More than anything else, Dhaliwal feels, it is this wider coverage that sets the program apart from its chief rivals, the major network newscasts. Of course, some have attributed the show's popularity to Dhaliwal's good looks. London's Channel Four News anchorman Jon Snow, for example, remarked to *People* (May 10, 1999), "The camera either loves you or it hates you, and it does appear to definitely love her." Dhaliwal, however, maintains that her looks are merely incidental: as she told Brennan, "In Britain we don't have the tradition of picking somebody because they look and sound good. I'm very, very opposed to that." Instead, she emphasizes the program's international outlook. "It makes me wonder," Dhaliwal told James Barron for the *New York Times* (May 2, 1999). "People always say there's no desire for international news. That's what the focus groups always say. Yet they say they like the program. It covers stories they wouldn't see on other news programs. So you feel like you're providing a really crucial service. It reminds me of what it was like in the Soviet Union. People were deprived of what was going on. I feel that way about Americans. They've got to get their fix of international news."

Indeed, the program's format is rather spare by American standards: Dhaliwal reads brief introductions to prerecorded segments, while seated alone before a hazy, blue-toned backdrop featuring an empty newsroom. (The intended effect, she told Kinney Littlefield for the California newspaper the *Orange County Register* [May 13, 1999], is, "It's late at night and I'm all alone here, but I've got to get the story out.") "We do tell it as it is," Dhaliwal said to Littlefield. "There is none of that banter between co-hosts. I think viewers actually find it quite refreshing." On the other hand, she is quick to point out, the producers of *ITN World News* do make concessions to the medium of television, primarily by striving to create a measure of visual appeal. "We make sure the program is not too heavy with infomercial politics," *ITN World News* producer Jeff Henderson told Littlefield. "Say, a very dull picture digest of men going in and out of doors and giving sound bites in Brussels [NATO headquarters]. The pictures are a very important part of the show." Nevertheless, *ITN World News* is rather sparing when it comes to flashy graphics and other visual fireworks, and the show's producers uphold fairly rigorous standards regarding content. "A light story might be something on the Oscars," Dhaliwal told Littlefield. "We did cover them, as well as the Golden Globes. We are a serious, hard-hitting, half-hour international news program. Of course, sometimes it's nice to leave viewers with smiles on their faces. But we don't do skateboarding ducks—at least at the moment we don't do skateboarding ducks."

In an interview with Murali Krishnan for *Rediff* (September 18, 1998, on-line), Dhaliwal described *ITN World News* as a program that proceeds by "talking to audiences rather than talking at them." A number of media critics have agreed with Dhaliwal's claim that *ITN World News* is a sober and generally fair news source. William Hoynes, for example, in "The Cost of Survival: Political Discourse and the 'New PBS,'" an independent report on the state of public television reproduced on the FAIR (Fairness and Accuracy in Reporting) Web site, determined through the statistical analysis of a two-week sample that *ITN World News* "generally employed a reportorial approach that focused on the voices of participants in events, eschewing the expert-oriented analysis and punditry that is so common on public television." Hoynes found that members of the general public appeared as news sources on *ITN World News* four times as often as they did on other U.S. public-television programs. *ITN World News* thus avoided the bias of much television news, which according to Hoynes "generally highlights the views of a narrow set of elite voices, often to the exclusion of those who lack government or corporate status or 'expert' credentials." His primary concern regarding *ITN World*

News was that airing a program that originates in Britain suggests that public-television leadership is looking abroad for fresh perspectives, a tendency that "does not bode well for those voices in the United States that are consistently underrepresented." Another critic who found *ITN World News* praiseworthy was Walter Goodman, who, in the *New York Times* (November 5, 1998), pronounced it "well produced, relatively uncluttered with promotional graphics and not committed to medical wonders" and described Dhaliwal as "as businesslike an anchor as anyone could ask for." In comparison with the BBC's *World News* program, he wrote, the ITN offering made "slightly more of an effort at luring the American market."

According to the writer for *Rolling Stone*, Dhaliwal "radiates cool intelligence and quaint English good-neighborliness," and her "elusive combination of gravity and humanity" makes her "worth keeping an eye on." Dhaliwal is single and currently resides in London's Notting Hill district, where she owns an apartment. When Barbara McMahon interviewed her for *LondonLife* (May 18, 1998, on-line), Dhaliwal refused to answer a question about whether she had a boyfriend. "I think it's nice to keep a private side, don't you?" she said. Although *ITN World News* is recorded and produced in ITN's London studios, Dhaliwal frequently travels to New York City, where she has moderated three conferences for the United Nations; her most recent trip was sponsored by the *Late Show with David Letterman*, on which she appeared as a guest. — P.K.

Suggested Reading: *Chicago Tribune* (on-line), Apr. 12, 2000; *New York Times* 13 p55 May 2, 1999; *Orange County Register* (on-line) May 13, 1999; *Washington Post* Y p6 Aug. 6, 2000, with photo

Selected Television Shows: *ITN World News for Public Television*, 1995–

Outline Press

Dickerson, Ernest

1952– Cinematographer; screenwriter; film director. Address: c/o Gersh Agency, 232 N. Canon Dr., Beverly Hills, CA 90210

"For me, photography visualizes feelings," the cinematographer and film director Ernest Dickerson explained to Bernard Weinraub for the *New York Times* (January 30, 1998). "Films are an experience; it's not a neutral but a visceral medium. That's what I try to convey." Dickerson began his career in film as a cameraman. Working with Spike Lee, in what David Mills, writing for the *Washington Post* (January 17, 1992), called "one of the most productive film collaborations of the 1980s," he shot Lee's widely praised student movie, *Joe's Bed-Stuy Barbershop: We Cut Heads.* After his first foray into feature filmmaking, in which he photographed John Sayles's soulful sci-fi comedy *The Brother from Another Planet*, he worked on six Spike Lee films: *She's Gotta Have It*, *School Daze*, *Do the Right Thing*, *Mo' Better Blues*, *Jungle Fever*, and *Malcolm X.* In 1992, the year *Malcolm X* was released, Dickerson appeared in the documentary *Visions of Light: The Art of Cinematography*, among some two dozen of the world's most respected cinematographers. "To my mind, the camera placement and lighting can help to tell as much of the story as the script," he told Weinraub. "Photography is, after all, writing with light, telling the story with pictures."

Dickerson made his debut as a director in 1992, with the PBS television film *Spike and Company: Do It A Capella* and his full-length feature-film *Juice.* He has since directed *Surviving the Game*, *Ambushed*, and *Blind Faith*, among other movies for the big screen, and for television, most notably *Strange Justice.* "I like being able to plug into all the facets of filmmaking," Dickerson said to Chuck Walton for *Hollywood.com* (1998, on-line). "[The filmmaker] Orson Welles was right. A film studio is the best train set a kid ever had."

An only child, Ernest R. Dickerson was born in 1952 in Newark, New Jersey, where his family lived in a housing project. His mother was a librarian; his father, who managed a supermarket, died when he was eight. As a child Dickerson saw many movies. David Lean's celebrated epic *Lawrence of Arabia* (1962) impressed him greatly, as did Lean's

1948 screen adaptation of the Charles Dickens novel *Oliver Twist*; filmed by Guy Green, the picture has been lauded for the high quality of its camerawork. "That was the first film that made me realize that films are photography," Dickerson told Nick Ravo for the *New York Times* (April 18, 1993). Later, Stanley Kubrick's horrifying futuristic satire *A Clockwork Orange* (1972) resonated with him.

As a student at Howard University, in Washington, D.C., Dickerson majored in architecture, believing that he ought to pursue a more practical career than one in cinema. But he also took courses in films and filmmaking, taught by Haile Gerima, an acclaimed Ethiopian filmmaker whose credits include *Child of Resistance* (1972), *Bush Mama* (1975), and *Sankofa* (1993), and Roland Mitchell, an African-American cinematographer who later contributed to such documentaries as *When We Were Kings* (1996), about the 1974 Muhammad Ali–George Foreman prize fight in Africa. "Roland was the first man to put a movie camera in my hands," Dickerson told David Mills. In his free time Dickerson frequented Washington's many art-house cinemas and the National Film Theater, run by the American Film Institute, which offered classic foreign films.

After graduating from Howard, in the mid-1970s, Dickerson worked for several years as an archival and medical photographer in the Washington area. One of his assignments entailed photographing surgical operations, including amputations, at the Howard University Medical School—work that he eventually found intolerably gruesome. Seeking a change of scene, he enrolled at New York University (NYU), in Manhattan, as a graduate student in the renowned Institute of Film and Television at the Tisch School of the Arts. Spike Lee, too, was studying there, and he tapped Dickerson to shoot his second-year film, *Sarah*, about a Harlem family on Thanksgiving Day. The two worked together again in their final year at NYU, when Dickerson shot Lee's hour-long thesis film, *Joe's Bed-Stuy Barbershop: We Cut Heads*. Produced, written, and directed by Lee and featuring an original jazz score by Lee's father, Bill Lee, the film offered a realistic, wry look at ghetto life through the story of a Brooklyn barber whose shop serves as a front for the neighborhood numbers racket. *Joe's Bed-Stuy Barbershop* earned a student Academy Award from the Academy of Motion Picture Arts and Sciences, became the first student production to be picked for Lincoln Center's prestigious "New Directors/New Films" series, and aired to general critical acclaim on the public television series *Independent Focus*. It went on to be shown at film festivals in San Francisco; Los Angeles; Atlanta, Georgia; and Locarno, Switzerland.

Dickerson's work on *Joe's Bed-Stuy Barbershop* impressed the maverick independent filmmaker John Sayles, and after Dickerson earned his master of fine arts degree, in 1982, he agreed to shoot Sayles's fantasy *The Brother from Another Planet* (1984). "Brilliant science-fiction with a social conscience," as Rita Kempley called it in the *Washington Post* (November 16, 1984), the film stars Joe Morton as a dark-skinned extraterrestrial who finds himself in Harlem. "Through the Brother's eyes we see what we look at every day and really never see," Sayles explained to Kempley for the November 30, 1984 issue of the *Post*. Dickerson, who before making the film had worked only with 16-millimeter film, confessed to Nick Ravo, "I lied when [Sayles] asked me if I had ever shot 35-millimeter before. I figured a camera is a camera. All the camera is is a recording device. You have got to see it first in your mind's eye, manipulate the image to make it look like it does in your head." Although some critics thought that the film looked crude by Hollywood standards, most gave it thumbs-up reviews.

Dickerson filmed *Krush Groove* (1985), Michael Shultz's movie about rap artists, before rejoining Spike Lee to serve as cinematographer on *She's Gotta Have It* (1986), a low-budget comedy about a woman who juggles three male lovers. Shot in black and white, the movie offered poignant and entertaining observations about sex and relationships. It turned into an art-house hit, and its earnings topped $7 million—more than 40 times the $175,000 that it had cost to produce. The success of *She's Gotta Have It* gave the reputations of both Lee and Dickerson a powerful boost. The two worked together again to make *School Daze* (1988), which is set at a fictitious black college and depicts enmity between light- and dark-skinned students, among other issues rarely examined in the mainstream media. *School Daze* received less friendly critical assessments than its predecessor, and it stirred much controversy, particularly among African-Americans.

Lee and Dickerson's next collaboration, *Do the Right Thing* (1989), sparked even more debate, among whites as well as blacks—as Lee had hoped it would. Reactions to the movie diverged widely: many viewed it as a humanely realistic, remarkably insightful and informed examination of racism, as an excellent prod to thinking and action on racial problems, and as an example of brilliant filmmaking, while many others criticized it as overly cynical and as condoning violence. Set on a blisteringly hot summer day in the Bedford-Stuyvesant section of Brooklyn, the film portrays events that transpire when rising tensions among whites and blacks—stemming from long-simmering prejudices, conflicting allegiances, and irritating personal quirks, all exacerbated by the brutal heat—erupt violently, leaving one black man dead from a police officer's stranglehold and the neighborhood Italian-American-owned pizzeria destroyed by fire. In planning how to photograph the action, Dickerson told an interviewer for *Millimeter* (June 1990), as transcribed on *members.aol.com*, that he and Lee had an "overriding" concern "with heat and the sun"; a shot of the sun-bleached sky, and another of rays glinting off metal, set the mood at the start. In the *New York Times*

(June 30, 1989), Vincent Canby wrote that "in its look," the movie "has the heightened reality of theater." For his accomplished use of light and color to enhance the story of *Do the Right Thing,* Dickerson won a New York Film Critics Award for cinematography.

In the ensuing years Dickerson and Lee teamed up to make four more films. For *Mo' Better Blues* (1990), a film about jazz, Dickerson told the *Millimeter* interviewer that he and Lee had "wanted to really get the feeling of jazz, and so Spike and I developed a jazz approach to shooting film. Usually we go into a film ultra-prepared in terms of storyboards, extensive shot lists. [Here] we had shot lists which gave us a structure, but we used that structure to improvise. We just felt that that would be more in keeping with the music and the feeling, kind of let the music inspire us to do what we did. . . . It seemed like it worked. I think especially in the club sequences, the camera moves we did to really give the feeling of the movement of the music, I think that pretty much worked. We were able to work out some pretty complex moves along the way." To convey tension between the main character and some of his band members, Dickerson chose a hand-held camera, which is impossible to operate with a perfectly steady hand. "The movement adds a nervousness . . . to the frame," Dickerson told *Millimeter.* Also in 1990 Dickerson shot *The Laserman,* a screwball thriller written and directed by Peter Wang.

Dickerson and Spike Lee's next collaboration, *Jungle Fever* (1991), is about a white-black romantic relationship and the intolerant response it elicits in the families of the protagonists. For *Sex, Drugs, Rock & Roll* (1991), Dickerson's next effort, he photographed Eric Bogosian's solo stage show of that title, in which the performer portrayed 10 distinctive urban characters. That film was followed by *Malcolm X* (1992), whose screenplay, co-written by Spike Lee and Arnold Perl, is based on *The Autobiography of Malcolm X* (as told to Alex Haley). In depicting the life of the black religious leader, who was assassinated in 1965, Dickerson married light and texture to narrative in various ways. He used diffused light and filters when photographing Malcolm X's early years, to add warmth to the scenes. After Malcolm is imprisoned, "we went the opposite—stark, cold," he explained to Nick Ravo. "No warmth is allowed to seep in until he sees the image of Elijah Muhammad. Then, out of prison, it's all very straightforward, no gimmicks. Then, in Mecca, it's softened. It was an attempt to put the journey of a man's life in light. I didn't want the audience to see the changes, but I wanted them to feel them." *Malcolm X* marked the last time that Dickerson served as Lee's cinematographer. "I knew there would come a day where he would not be able to shoot my films," Lee told Sally Weltman for *Premiere* (February 1992). "'Cause I always knew he would end up directing. In school, Ernest had the best films. This is what he's wanted to do all along."

Dickerson told Weltman that in the course of their partnership, he and Lee had "developed sort of a shorthand where a lot of times we know exactly what the other is thinking." The collaborative nature of filmmaking comes across clearly in *Visions of Light: The Art of Cinematography* (1992), a 90-minute documentary directed by the film scholar Stuart Samuels, the film editor Arnold Glassman, and the film critic Todd McCarthy; demonstrating Dickerson's status among Hollywood's most accomplished cinematographers, it includes an interview with Dickerson, among such other masters of the craft as Néstor Almendros, William Fraken, Conrad L. Hall, Sven Nykvist, Vittorio Storaro, Gordon Willis, and Vilmos Zsigmond. When *Visions of Light* was made, Dickerson was the only prominent African-American cinematographer in Hollywood, and as of mid-1993 he was the only black member of the American Society of Cinematographers, which admitted him in 1989.

In 1990 Dickerson had directed *Spike & Company: Do It A Capella,* for the PBS television series *Great Performances.* Co-hosted by Spike Lee and the actress, choreographer, and director Debbie Allen, the musical featured prominent a capella groups worldwide, among them the all-male South African group Ladysmith Black Mambazo and the all-female British singers Mint Juleps. Discussing his transition to directing, Dickerson told Lawrence Van Gelder for the *New York Times* (May 24, 1991), "A lot of the directors that I worked with also worked in front of the camera as actors: Spike Lee, John Sayles, Peter Wang. And so I had a chance to really find out what directing is like. Directors also entrusted me with designing entire sequences of their movie in terms of shot structure, and I think seeing how these sequences worked in the final films taught me I should trust my instincts."

Juice, the first feature film that Dickerson directed, premiered in 1992, eight years after he had embarked on writing the script. (The credits list Gerard Brown as co-writer.) Starring Omar Epps, Khalil Kain, Jermaine Hopkins, and Tupac Shakur, the film is about four frustrated, inner-city youths who rob a store as a means of acquiring "juice," a slang term for power and respect. "I wrote this story for me to debut as a director," Dickerson told Lawrence Van Gelder. "That was my reason for writing." Dickerson turned down four major studios' offers to buy the screenplay after learning that each intended to change the script. "I didn't want my name put on anything like that," he explained to David Mills. "That's when you start getting rewritten by people who write black characters and don't even know any black people." *Juice* drew mixed reviews, among them those of Peter Travers, who, in *Rolling Stone* (February 6, 1992), described it as an "exciting, disturbing film that pulses with feeling," and Leah Rozen, who, in *People* (January 27, 1992), labeled it "well-crafted but bleak."

Juice became a subject for news reporters as well as reviewers when violence broke out among moviegoers at several theaters upon its release. To prevent further incidents, Paramount Pictures, which produced the film, hired extra security guards for theaters where it was being shown. Those events led some critics and members of the mainstream press to fault the film and others in its genre for glorifying and encouraging violence. Others pointed out that while "*Juice* sends a mixed message just by illustrating the dangers it deplores," as Janet Maslin wrote for the *New York Times* (January 22, 1992), Dickerson had condemned the "bad-boy character" by the end of the story and in other ways had "[left] no question as to where [the film's] values lie." "At a time when black American film makers have achieved new prominence, and when an important creative boom is under way among them," Maslin declared, "they can't be faulted for matching white Hollywood's standards of violence. None of these films makes crime any more alluring than it has long been in movies about the Mafia, and none is any more violent than a vehicle for Bruce Willis or Arnold Schwarzenegger." *Juice*, which cost about $3 million to make, eventually grossed more than $30 million.

The release of *Juice* was followed several months later by that of *Cousin Bobby* (1992), a documentary directed by Jonathan Demme and shot by Dickerson. The film focused on Robert Castle, an Episcopal priest who was a second cousin of Demme's; a social activist, Castle had a congregation in Harlem. Dickerson next directed *Surviving the Game* (1994), about a homeless man who is made the object of a sadistic hunt in the wilderness; *Demon Knight*, also called *Tales from the Crypts Presents Demon Knight* (1995), a gory horror film; *Bulletproof* (1996), starring Damon Wayans and Adam Sandler, which Stephen Holden, in a review for the *New York Times* (September 6, 1996), called "a screwball love story disguised as an action film"; *Ambushed* (1998), an action film that addressed racial problems; and *Blind Faith* (1998). The last-named film, written by Frank Military, is about three African-American brothers: a policeman, played by Charles S. Dutton; a lawyer, portrayed by Courtney B. Vance; and a jazz musician (Kadeem Hardison). Their family is ripped apart after Dutton's son is charged with the murder of a white man, and Vance takes on his defense. Set in 1950s Harlem, the story involves homophobia as well as racism—an unexpected twist that appealed to Dickerson. "Unlike the other 110 scripts lying around, I couldn't tell where this was going," he explained to Chuck Walton. "It was a story of a family heading in a lot of directions." He also told Walton that all the actors in *Blind Faith* were his first choices for their roles. "It was great because I could concentrate on these actors and use the visuals to supplement their performances," he said. "The old saying about directing is really true. Eighty-five percent of directing is casting." He also said, "In my films, the thing I'm most proud of is the acting." *Blind Faith* received an enthusiastic reception at the 1998 Sundance Film Festival, and it was later shown at the Pan-African Film and Arts Festival, the National Black Arts Film Festival, the Nantucket Film Festival, and the San Francisco and Human Rights Watch International Film Festivals. Nevertheless, it generated no interest among distributors, because, according to Dickerson, they feared that a film about blacks that did not have a happy ending would not fare well at the box office. The picture aired on the Showtime cable-television channel in early 1998.

In the next year Showtime broadcast another of Dickerson's directorial efforts: *Strange Justice*, a re-enactment of the 1991 Senate Judiciary Committee hearings that resulted in the confirmation of Clarence Thomas as a justice of the Supreme Court. The made-for-TV film examined events surrounding the testimony by Anita Hill (played by Regina Taylor), a law professor who accused Thomas (portrayed by Delroy Lindo) of sexually harassing her in the early 1980s, when the two worked together at the U.S. Department of Education. The picture also starred Mandy Patinkin as the White House consultant Kenneth Duberstein, who was seen behind-the-scenes coaching Thomas on what to say to at his confirmation hearings. Adapted by Jacob Epstein from committee transcripts and from the book *Strange Justice* (1994), by Jane Mayer and Jill Abramson, the drama accused neither Thomas nor Hill of lying; rather, it indicted the political system and politicians who, it suggested, ignore truth and ethics in their determination to get their way. In the *New York Times* (September 6, 1999), Margo Jefferson termed Dickerson's rendition "terrific" and "fresh and powerful because it use[d] television to intensify but also to abstract the melodrama" that characterized the historic hearings.

In addition to films, Dickerson has shot a Nike commercial and several music videos, among them Bruce Springsteen's "Born in the U.S.A," Patti LaBelle's "Stir It Up," Miles Davis's "Tutu," and Branford Marsalis's "Royal Garden Blues." According to Chuck Walton, his "quiet honesty" and "humanity" are "easily recognized." — M.H.

Suggested Reading: *Hollywood.com*, 1998; *members.aol.com*, 1997; *New York Times* C p8 May 24, 1991, H p14+ Apr. 18, 1993, with photos, E p10 Jan. 30, 1998, with photo; *Premiere* p40+ Feb. 1992, with photo; *Washington Post* C p1 Jan. 17, 1992, with photos; *International Motion Picture Almanac, 2000*

Selected Films: as cinematographer—*Joe's Bed-Stuy Barbershop: We Cut Heads*, 1982; *The Brother from Another Planet*, 1984; *Krush Groove*, 1985; *She's Gotta Have It*, 1986; *School Daze*, 1988; *Do the Right Thing*, 1989; *Laser Man*, 1990; *Mo' Better Blues*, 1990; *Jungle Fever*, 1991; *Sex, Drugs, Rock & Roll*, 1991; *Malcolm X*, 1992; *Cousin Bobby*, 1992; as director—*Surviving the Game*, 1994; *Demon Knight*, 1995;

Bulletproof, 1996; *Ambushed*, 1998; *Blind Faith*, 1998; *Strange Justice*, 1999 (for television); as director and co-writer—*Juice*, 1992

Dixie Chicks

Country-music group

Maines, Natalie
Oct. 14, 1974–

Robison, Emily
Aug. 16, 1972–

Seidel, Martie
Oct. 12, 1969–

Address: c/o Sony Music Entertainment, Inc., 550 Madison Ave., New York, NY 10022-3211

"People have asked us how it feels to be an overnight success. I tell them it feels great, but it took us eight-and-a-half years to do it," the singer-songwriter Martie Seidel told Michael McCall for *launch.com* (on-line), speaking of Emily Robison, Natalie Maines, and herself. With fashion-model looks as well as musical talent, the Dixie Chicks, as the group is called, have become one of the most powerful forces in country music. Their major-label debut, *Wide Open Spaces* (1998), which followed three albums released independently earlier in the 1990s, thrust them into the limelight and brought the catchphrase "Chicks rule" into the public consciousness. *Wide Open Spaces* set records: it went platinum faster than any other recording by a country group and any other album in the history of Sony Music, and as of late 2000, its sales exceeded 10 million copies, making the Dixie Chicks the first group to have an album reach diamond status. In addition, the Dixie Chicks are the only country group whose first two albums went double platinum. "Half the people come up and tell us that they're glad we're staying with traditional country music," Robison told Michael McCall for *TV Guide* (February 20, 1999). "And the other half say, 'Y'all are so different. It's great to hear someone taking country music in a new direction.' For us, it's not about definitions. We don't worry about whether it's too country or too out there. We just know when it's right."

The Dixie Chicks' road to fame began in Dallas, Texas, where Martie was born Martha Elenor Erwin on October 12, 1969 and Emily Robison was born Emily Erwin on August 16, 1972. When the sisters were young, their parents, Barbara and Paul Erwin (both private-school teachers), would take them to symphony-orchestra concerts, and they encouraged the girls to learn a variety of instruments. Martie began playing the fiddle when she was five, and Emily was playing banjo, Dobro, and guitar by age 10. Their mother would monitor their daily practice sessions with an egg timer. "I'd hear kids outside playing kick ball, and I hated that I was inside," Robison told Jeremy Helligar for *People* (September 28, 1998). "Now, of course, I'm grateful for it."

By 1984, according to the undated article "Ruling the Country Roost," on *geocities.com*, the pair were touring the country in a teen bluegrass group known as Blue Night Express. They were with the group for five years before it disbanded. Then, uniting with bassist Laura Lynch and guitarist Robin Lynn Macy, they formed the Dixie Chickens, the name taken from the title of a song by the blues/rock/country band Little Feat. (Fans later shortened the name to Dixie Chicks.) Adopting a full-blown "cowgirl" image, complete with Dale Evans–style outfits and oversized hairdos, the women began playing at bars and clubs and even on Dallas street corners. In 1990 they independently released their first album, *Thank Heavens for Dale Evans*, an amiable collection of folk and country songs. Their next recording, *Home on the Radar Range* (1991), contained only two songs and could be ordered only via their newsletter, *The Chick Chat.*

By this time, the Dixie Chicks had attracted a loyal following, and they soon found themselves opening for such major country acts as Garth Brooks, George Strait, and Emmylou Harris. Shortly after they released their acclaimed second album, *Little Ol' Cowgirl* (1992), Macy left the band, and Lynch took over the lead vocal duties. The band performed at one of President Bill Clinton's inaugural balls in 1993, and that same year their last independently produced album, *Shouldn't A Told You That*, came out. "Those first five or six years as Dixie Chicks happened so fast," Seidel recalled, as quoted on *geocities.com*. "It was really growing time for the band. We went from street corners to dance halls, from jeans and boots to tailor-made cowgirl get-ups with rhinestones."

In 1995 Lynch quit the group in order to spend more time with her daughter. At about the same time, Martie married a pharmaceutical sales rep, Ted Seidel. Intent on keeping the Chicks together, she and her sister, neither of whom wanted to sing lead, let it be known that they were seeking a vocalist. Their search came to the attention of the Texas steel-guitar legend Lloyd Maines, who had played on two of the Chicks' albums, and he passed them his daughter Natalie's demo tape. Born on October 14, 1974 in Lubbock, Texas, Natalie Maines had learned piano and guitar by age 12 and had won a scholarship to the Berklee College of Music, in Boston, as a voice student. "We were both secretly listening to [the demo tape]," Seidel told Laura Jamison for *Seventeen* (April, 1999). "I had to call [Lloyd Maines] and ask for another because I thought I lost it. It turned out that Emily was hoarding it." Maines accepted their invitation to join them, but with one proviso: "The only thing I knew for sure was that I wasn't going to wear those cowgirl clothes," she recalled to Jeremy Helligar. Feel-

Rose Prouser/Archive Photos

The Dixie Chicks (left to right): Emily Robison, Natalie Maines, and Martie Seidel

ing ready for a change, Seidel and Robison set about remaking the Chicks' image. "When Natalie joined, that's when the wheels really started to turn for us," Seidel told Michael McCall. "A whole new kind of excitement seemed to be brewing around us. There was a different kind of energy that really caught people's attention."

In about 1997, reportedly entranced by the energy and spirit of the Chicks' music, Sony executives signed the trio to a contract on the Monument Records label. Shortly after, the Chicks began work on *Wide Open Spaces* (1998). Intent on reaching a wider audience, the band worked on fine-tuning their sound while retaining their country roots. Drawing from such wide-ranging influences as James Taylor, the Indigo Girls, Bonnie Raitt, and Dolly Parton, they mixed country rhythms with catchy folk-pop hooks. "The day Natalie was laying down the tracks for the tune 'Wide Open Spaces,' our producer said, 'Man, she sounds like [the pop singer] Alanis Morissette,'" Seidel recalled to Jamison. "'We gotta make her sound more country.' He was freaked out thinking nobody would relate to this chick country singer who has such an edgy sound." The Chicks, however, felt certain that they had hit upon a formula for success, and they made a pact to get tattooed with the image of a tiny chicken's foot each time they produced a hit single or a record went gold.

The Chicks soon had to limit their pact to career milestones only. Released in January 1998, *Wide Open Spaces* went platinum seven times over and became the best-selling album ever by a country duo or group. The record also spawned five singles that reached the country-charts Top 10, among them "There's Your Trouble," "You Were Mine," and the title track. To the surprise of Sony executives, the Dixie Chicks' appeal extended past country audiences to mainstream listeners, thanks in part to their "girl-power" ethos, which had led them to sell T-shirts reading "The rooster crows but the hen delivers" and to adopt the slogan "Chicks rule." Offering reasons for the group's success, their manager told Chris Willman for *Entertainment Weekly* (September 3, 1999), "They *are* their audience. They like to shop, do makeup together . . . it's like a [expletive] slumber party on the bus. I'll go on and they've got their pajamas and their blankets and some girlie movie going."

In 1998 the Chicks gave 160 shows worldwide, in many of which they joined the bill on the tremendously successful George Strait tour. That same year they collected a half-dozen awards, including a Country Music Award for vocal group of the year; Country Music List's rising group award and album of the year, and two of the three Grammy Awards for which they were nominated, for best country performance (for "There's Your Trouble") and best country album. In 1999 they won an American Music Award for favorite new country artist, became the first country act to perform in the Lilith Fair, an all-female concert tour, and found themselves fielding, and rejecting, silly scripts from Hollywood. Disregarding the warnings of industry pundits that overexposure could lead to a commercial backlash, they also returned to the studio to cut their second album. "It's been a year and a half since the release of our [last] album," Maines told a interviewer for *Entertainment Weekly* (June 11, 1999), "and with all that's happened this year, it seems like ages ago. We aren't the kind of gals to sit on our butts and admire our trophies."

Working on their second effort for a major label, the group had a definite game plan. "We didn't want to remake *Wide Open Spaces*," Robison explained on the Web site *countrystars.com*, "so we had to go back to that nothing-to-lose feeling. I definitely think we've grown. . . . We're not as scared to let the harmonies come through or take extra time to have an awesome solo. The only rule this time around was that there were 'No rules.'" When they felt ready to start writing, the band went into a self-imposed seclusion. "We don't have time to just block free time, because there are so many demands on our time," Seidel said to Chet Flippo for *Billboard* (July 31, 1999). "So we started going on these retreats, where we rented cabins out in the country. I think we were wise to go on these retreats, because it was the only way to really get time to write. I think that gave us a head start, and the writing flowed more freely." The recording of the album proved to be a more personal experience than the band had perhaps intended. Natalie was in the process of divorcing her husband, the musician Michael Tarabay, while Emily was preparing to wed the songwriter Charlie Robison. These events "shed a new light on the whole project," Seidel recalled to Willman. "There'd be a phrase in almost every song where I'd get choked up and have a hard time singing because I'd be thinking of Natalie about to go through that. And then there are songs like 'Cowboy Take Me Away' where I was thinking about Emily about to get married."

Released on August 31, 1999, the Dixie Chicks' second album, *Fly*, got an even better reception than its predecessor, debuting at number one on the *Billboard* pop and country charts and earning high praise from critics. Richard Corliss, for example, wrote for *Time* (September 20, 1999), "*Fly* lives up to the virtuosity of its members." A free-spirited endeavor, *Fly* is chockablock with songs about female empowerment and women defining themselves. Some of these, such as the ribald "Sin Wagon," with its references to "mattress dancin'," and the *Thelma and Louise*–inspired "Goodbye Earl," in which an abused wife gleefully dispatches her husband with the help of her best friend, raised some eyebrows. But the band felt that the album, including its title, accurately reflected their state of mind. "It's the whole Chicks thing. We've kind of earned our wings," Seidel noted, as quoted on *countrystars.com*. "The first album was like the mama bird, the record company, pushing us towards the edge so we could learn to fly. And now we're doing it on our own. We've always stood up for what we believe in. But now we have more confidence and ability to soar and fly. Our career has really taken off. Natalie was flying from a situation she didn't want to be in. Emily's flying to a better place with someone she loves, and I'm experiencing the musical flight that I've waited so long to take. When I said to the girls, 'What about *Fly* for the title of our album?' we started to see how many references there were to flight, birds, or wings in the songs. There are so many meanings to it. It was like a sign."

Fly generated two *Billboard* Top10 singles—"Ready to Run," which was also prominently featured in the film *Runaway Bride* (1999), and the emotional ballad "Cowboy Take Me Away," which reached number one. A second single, "Goodbye Earl," also charted well, boosted by the success of its video, which features Dennis Franz, from the television series *NYPD Blue*, as the title character. Moreover, *Fly* has gone quadruple platinum, and with that album, the Dixie Chicks have added to their trophies three Country Music Association Awards, including vocal group of the year, and two Grammy Awards, including best country album. In October 2000 the Dixie Chicks again scored on the Country Music Association awards night, collecting four of the biggest honors, including entertainers of the year. To date, they have earned nine awards from the Country Music Association in two years.

In the media, the Dixie Chicks have often been portrayed as giddy, frenzied sprites who do everything in tandem; on fan sites, they come across as being similar to sorority sisters. In reality, Seidel, who is divorced, currently lives in Dallas, and Robison and her husband live in San Antonio, Texas. In July 2000 Maines, who had been living in Nashville, Tennessee, married the actor Adrian Pasdar. The trio embarked on a worldwide tour in the summer of 2000. "I feel like right now is the good old days," Seidel told Helliger. "I think right now is the proving stage, to prove that we're for real." —J.K.B.

Suggested Reading: *Billboard* p1+ July 31, 1999, with photo; *Entertainment Weekly* p30+ Sep. 3, 1999, with photos; *Ladies Home Journal* p90+ Sep. 1999, with photos; *People* p167+ Sep. 28, 1998, with photos; *Time* p80 Sep. 20, 1999, with photo; *TV Guide* p21+ Feb. 20, 1999, with photos

Selected Albums: *Thank Heavens for Dale Evans*, 1990; *Home on the Radar Range*, 1991; *Little Ol' Cowgirl*, 1992; *Shouldn't A Told You That*, 1993; *Wide Open Spaces*, 1998; *Fly*, 1999

Courtesy of University of Maryland at College Park

Driskell, David C.

(DRIS-kel)

June 7, 1931– Painter; educator; art historian; art collector; curator. Address: 42065 Decatur St., Hyattsville, MD 20781

"Art is a priestly calling," David C. Driskell, the Distinguished University Professor of Art Emeritus at the University of Maryland, told Pamela Newkirk for *Art News* (May 2000). "It's the kind of visual mobility that shows us life can be so beautiful. I've been blessed to have that happen to me."

Driskell is an accomplished painter, teacher, and art historian who has curated more than 35 exhibitions featuring works by such black masters as Jacob Lawrence, Romare Bearden, and Elizabeth Catlett. Public figures including Bill Cosby, Oprah Winfrey, and President Bill Clinton and his wife, Hillary Clinton, have consulted with Driskell on purchases of art. He has been instrumental in providing an historical context for African-American art and is known for his extensive knowledge of a wide range of work. "He has probably had more to do with the seriousness of the way African American art is treated than has any other single person," Harry C. Parker, the director of the Fine Arts Museums of California, told Newkirk.

Driskell's own painting incorporates elements of nature, collage, African art, and Christian iconography and has been exhibited in the United States, Africa, and Europe. His early paintings, such as *Pines at Falmouth* (1961), were influenced by the work of the French artists Paul Cézanne and Henri Matisse; for more recent pieces he has drawn on childhood memories. "I am led by ideas, by experiences," he told Alan Bostick for the *Tennessean* (November 28, 1999, on-line). "Those ideas and experiences move me around in various directions, so I kind of follow."

David C. Driskell was born into a family of sharecroppers in Eatonton, Georgia, on June 7, 1931. When he was five years old, his family moved to a stone house deep in the woods of North Carolina's Appalachian Mountains. From the beginning, art was an integral part of his daily life. One of Driskell's grandfathers fashioned African figures out of tree bark; his father, a Baptist minister and blacksmith, painted and constructed furniture; and his mother made baskets from bulrushes and pine needles and quilts colored with dyes made from berries, onion peel, and black walnuts. Driskell excelled in school and maintained a close relationship with his two older sisters. In 1949, when he became the first member of his family to go to college, the local newspaper announced his departure. He left for Howard University, in Washington, D.C., with money he had earned by working in the fields, and arrived unannounced at his sister Jean's apartment on Capitol Hill.

His appearance was also unexpected at Howard, where he showed up with his high-school report card, believing this was all that was required for admittance. After first being chided for his naiveté, he was given an application and was eventually accepted for the following quarter, in 1952, as a scholarship student of painting and history. He received a good deal of encouragement from his teachers. Professor James A. Porter introduced him to the work of the black artists Aaron Douglas and Henry Ossawa Tanner, and Professor William H. Johnson suggested that he switch to art history, encouraging him to engage in the work of establishing a place for African-American artists in the discipline. "My teachers impressed upon me that collecting art was an affirmation of one's own participation in his or her own culture," Driskell told Janet Kutner for the *Dallas Morning News* (June 6, 1999, on-line). As an apprentice at the university's Gallery of Art, Driskell was instructed by the gallery's founder, James V. Herring, in the collection and cataloging of art. Herring suggested that he collect art by European-American and Japanese artists as well as work by African-Americans. Initially, Driskell could afford only pieces priced at $10 or less.

During this period Driskell befriended and often traded work with such artists as Romare Bearden, Sam Gilliam, and Jacob Lawrence. At the time—in the early and mid-1950s—it was very difficult for African-American artists to get access to commercial galleries, and few had teaching positions. As the civil rights movement was gathering steam, Charles White, Elizabeth Catlett, Driskell, and other artists began to incorporate social commentary in their work. "I don't think the artists cared about social acceptance anymore," Driskell told Pamela Newkirk. "We were impatient—disillusioned with integration. We wanted to be left alone. Some of us severed relations with majority culture." In 1955 Driskell painted *Behold Thy Son*, a response to the murder of Emmett Till, a black teenager who was lynched that year by a white mob in Mississippi, allegedly for whistling at a white woman; the artist portrayed Till's mother holding her son in a manner that recalled the crucifixion of Christ.

Driskell graduated from Howard University in 1955 with a bachelor's degree in fine art. Although he possessed only a bachelor's degree, he was hired as an assistant professor at Talladega College, in Alabama, by Arthur D. Gray, the school's first black president. "Going to Talladega brought me face to face with the harshest form of segregation one could imagine," Driskell wrote for the *International Review of African-American Art* (Volume 15, No. 1, 1998). "Ku Klux Klan marches and occasional drive-by shootings from Klan members were commonplace on some black colleges in those days. Somehow we learned to live with all of the uncertainties of life that we encountered in the 1950s without losing sight of the 'brighter day a-coming' that was anticipated in the Negro spiritual." Talladega was also the site of Driskell's first one-person show, at the Savery Art Gallery in 1956. After receiving a master of fine arts degree from the Catholic University of America, in Washington, D.C., in 1962, he returned to Howard University as an associate professor of art. A fellowship enabled Driskell to continue his postgraduate study at the Netherlands Institute for the History of Art in the Hague in the summer of 1964.

From 1966 until 1977 Driskell served as the chair of the art department at Fisk University, in Nashville, Tennessee; it was here that he "matured as an artist," he recalled for Alan Bostick: "I was handed a mantle there to define and redefine my own work as an artist and an art historian." Driskell's scholarly work was first recognized when he curated shows featuring work by such artists as

William T. Williams and Ellis Wilson. He also presided over the university's Alfred Stieglitz collection, donated to Fisk by the artist Georgia O'Keeffe in memory of Stieglitz, her late husband. The collection included work of Cezanne and another French master, Pierre-Auguste Renoir, as well as that of Stieglitz and O'Keeffe. Driskell got to know O'Keeffe well, and she educated him further in how to choose carefully and document valuable works of art.

Following a trip to Africa in 1969, Driskell's own work began to incorporate traditional African forms such as ritual masks and textiles. He later experimented with expressionism in a series of portraits of black women. Upon the recommendation of Mary Beattie Brady, an arts patron who ran the Harmon Foundation—an organization that had collected and preserved more than 4,000 works by African-American artists—Driskell was chosen to organize a retrospective of the work of William H. Johnson for the Smithsonian Institution's National Museum of American Art in Washington, D.C., in 1972.

Four years later Driskell curated a traveling exhibition entitled *Two Centuries of Black American Art* for the Los Angeles County Museum of Art, the most ambitious show of its kind up to that time. Driskell also wrote the exhibit's catalog, which has become widely used as a reference source for scholars of African-American art. Whitney Museum of American Art curator Thelma Golden told Esther Iverem for the *Washington Post* (November 23, 1998) that she had discovered the catalog as an undergraduate and found that it contained "a whole range of literature—primarily from historically black colleges—that was relatively unknown. The bibliography alone is a critical contribution to the field."

Driskell's selections for *Two Centuries* included the work of black craftsmen from colonial days to the modern era—in all, more than 200 pieces by artists ranging from anonymous slaves to acknowledged masters. He included many works by African-American women, among them Loïs Mailou Jones; Selma Burke; Alma Thomas; Minnie Evans; Laura Waring; Clementine Hunter; and Elizabeth Catlett. The exhibit also featured previously unseen works by David Butler and Clementine Hunter as well as a daguerrotype by Jules Lion of the naturalist and illustrator John J. Audubon.

"I was looking for a body of work which showed first of all that blacks had been stable participants in American visual culture for more than 200 years, and by stable participants I simply mean that they had been the backbone," Driskell told C. Gerald Fraser for the *New York Times* (June 29, 1977). "Secondly, I wanted quality work which reflected the kind of cultural emancipation that blacks subscribed to in the 18th and 19th centuries, which, contrary to popular opinion, was not social emancipation as we are experiencing now." He also hoped to combat preconceived notions of African-American art as being limited to "primitivism" and social protest; as he reminded Fraser, early black artists "were not caught up in subject matter that reflected ethnic themes." Work by such painters as Joshua Johnston, Edward Mitchell Bannister, and Henry Ossawa Tanner were collected by both Europeans and Americans and had many white patrons, securing their inclusion in the history of mainstream art. In 1866 a critic for the London *Times* referred to the painter Robert Duncanson, an artist in the tradition of the Hudson River School, as "the best landscape painter in the Western world," Driskell told Fraser.

Conservative art critic Hilton Kramer savagely attacked the show in the *New York Times* (June 26, 1977), dismissing Driskell's accomplishments on the grounds that his choices were "often more interesting as social history than for its esthetic revelations. We do not feel the presence in this exhibition of any stringent esthetic criteria in its selection." Driskell responded to the criticism a few weeks later on NBC's *Today Show*; claiming not to know who Kramer was, he told Tom Brokaw, then the *Today* anchor, that the critic's attack revealed a lack of knowledge of black art as well as racism.

In 1977 Driskell was commissioned by CBS television to write the script for a documentary on African-American art entitled *Hidden Heritage*; he also narrated the program, which won a CBS award. Driskell was the chairman of the art department at the University of Maryland from 1978 until 1983 and continued to teach at the university until his retirement, in 1998. Recently he has served as an adviser to art historians, among them Deborah Willis Kennedy, curator at the Smithsonian Center for African-American History and Culture, and Richard Powell, chairman of the Department of Art and Art History at Duke University, in Durham, North Carolina.

In 1996 Driskell advised President Bill Clinton and the First Lady on the first purchase of work by an African-American artist for permanent display in the White House. Tanner's *Sand Dunes At Sunset: Atlantic City* (1885) was installed in the Garden Room of the White House during a ceremony on October 29, 1996. Driskell has also acted as a personal curator for entertainer Bill Cosby and his wife, Camille, since 1977, assisting them in gathering one of the world's largest personal collections of African-American art. In 1981 he bid $250,000 on their behalf at an auction at Sotheby's to acquire Tanner's *Thankful Poor*, the largest amount ever paid for a work by a black artist. Driskell also selected artworks that appeared on *The Cosby Show*. In the spring of 2001, Pomegranate Publications will publish his book on the couple's collection, tentatively entitled "The Other Side of Color: The African-American Collection of Camille O. and William H. Cosby, Jr."

In 1996 Talladega College installed 65 stained-glass windows, designed and created by Driskell, in the campus's DeForest Chapel. From October 2000 until February 23, 2001, a traveling exhibition entitled *Echoes: The Art of David Driskell* will be on display at the Aljira Gallery, in Newark, New Jersey. The show will feature 34 works, including paintings, collages, prints, and drawings. *Narratives of African-American Art & Identity: the David Driskell Collection*, an exhibit of more than 100 works from Driskell's personal collection, will be on view at the High Museum of Art, in Atlanta, through September 10, 2000.

While studying as an undergraduate at Howard, Driskell met Thelma G. Deloatch. They were married in 1952 and eventually had two daughters, Daviryne and Daphne. Thelma shared her husband's passion for art, and together the couple began to acquire a modest collection. "Sometimes my wife and I say that we took a little milk out of our two daughters' mouths to buy art," Driskell told Owen Findsden for the *Cincinnati Enquirer* (March 19, 2000, on-line). "But we are delighted that we did, because now they have a framework for culture that they would not have had otherwise." Over the years Driskell and his wife have collected art both through purchase and exchange. Driskell told Pamela Newkirk that the collection reflects the collective struggle of African-American artists "to break free of the confines of race in America, while embracing a common cultural heritage." The artists represented "had the same training as mainstream artists. But as good as they are, they are still viewed as black artists." The exhibit includes the work of Driskell's former teacher Loïs Mailou Jones, whom he remembers as being particularly pained by this unfair separation. "Her question was, 'Will I ever live to be just an artist?'" he told Newkirk.

The collection contains works painted during the Harlem Renaissance—a period, beginning in the 1920s, when black artists endeavored to combat stereotyped images of African-Americans with portrayals that humanized them—as well as protest art of the 1950s and 1960s. During the Harlem Renaissance, particularly, black artists' work enjoyed acceptance in the larger society, especially the upper classes. "Whites elevated themselves through black culture," Driskell explained to C. Gerald Fraser. "The Harlem Renaissance wasn't the glorification of black culture so much as it was to glorify whites in the process of patronizing black culture."

Because members of the art world have persisted in propagating "the notion that blacks are not a part of the system," as he explained to C. Gerald Fraser, Driskell continues to present exhibitions that concentrate exclusively on African-American art. Although he understands the reasoning behind the use of the term "black art," he does not believe that such labels reflect the variety of stylistic choices represented in African-American art. "I think it's a sociological concept," he told Fraser. "I don't think it's anything stylistic. We don't go around saying white art, but I think it's very important for us to keep saying black art until it becomes recognized as American art."

Driskell is the author of more than 40 exhibition catalogs. In 1989 the Arts Council of Great Britain funded a one-hour documentary on the artist entitled *Hidden Heritage: The Roots of Black American Painting*, produced by CUE films of London for British television. He has been a visiting professor at Bowdoin College, in Brunswick, Maine; Bates College, in Lewiston, Maine; Queens College, in New York City, and the University of Ife-Ife in Nigeria, Africa. In 1995 Driskell was named Distinguished University Professor of Art, Emeritus, by the University of Maryland at College Park. His many honors include 10 honorary degrees, from the Maine College of the Arts, the State University of New York at Old Westbury, and Tougaloo College, in Tougaloo, Mississippi, among other institutions; the President's Medal from the University of Maryland in College Park (1997); three Rockefeller Foundation Fellowships; a Danforth Foundation Fellowship; and a Harmon Foundation Fellowship. Both Howard University, in 1981, and the Catholic University of America, in 1996, have named him a distinguished alumnus.

Driskell and his wife live in a 112-year-old Victorian house in Hyattsville, Maryland. They spend summers in their second home, in Falmouth, Maine, purchased in 1961 with the money he earned from the sale of a print by Vassily Kandinsky. They also have a home in New York City. Driskell works in a small, wood-frame studio in Hyattsville; when he is not painting, he tends the garden, goes to church, and makes quilts. — C.L.

Suggested Reading: *Art News* p198+ May 2000, with photos; *Cincinnati Enquirer* (on-line) Mar. 19, 2000, with photos; *Dallas Morning News* (on-line) June 6, 1999; *International Review of African-American Art* p5+ vol. 15 no. 1 1998; *New York Times* II p25 June 26, 1977, with photos, C p18 June 29, 1977, with photo; *Tennessean* (on-line) Nov. 28, 1999; *Washington Post* D p1 Nov. 23, 1998, with photos

Selected Books: as author—*Two Centuries of Black American Art* (exhibition catalog), 1976; *Hidden Heritage: Afro-American Art, 1800–1950*, 1985; *Contemporary Visual Expressons: The Art of Sam Gilliam, Martha Jackson-Jarvis, Keith Morrison, William T. Williams*, 1987; *Astonishment and Power*, 1993; as co-author: *Afro-American Collection, Fisk University* (with Earl J. Hooks), 1976; *Harlem Renaissance: Art of Black America* (with David Levering Lewis and Deborah Willis Ryan), 1987; *Against the Odds: African-American Artists and the Harmon Foundation* (with Gary A. Reynolds and others), 1989; as editor—*Amistad II, Afro-American Art*, 1975; *African American Visual Aesthetics: A Postmodernist View*, 1995

Armando Gallo/Retna Ltd.

Duncan, Michael Clarke

Dec. 10, 1957– Actor. Address: c/o Dolores Robinson Entertainment, 112 S. Almont Dr., Los Angeles, CA 90048

"So big he's like a ZIP code with a pulse," as Elvis Mitchell described him in the *New York Times* (February 18, 2000), Michael Clarke Duncan wowed moviegoers—and won an Oscar nomination—with his performance as John Coffey, an inarticulate, seemingly simpleminded convicted murderer, in *The Green Mile* (1999), an adaptation for the screen of a novel by Stephen King. Standing six feet, five inches and weighing more than 300 pounds, Duncan had previously found himself relegated to roles of bouncers or bodyguards. But portraying the childlike Coffey, who has a supernatural gift for healing, was not as much of a stretch for the powerfully built Duncan as it may have seemed. "The minute I read [King's novel], I said nobody can bring passion to this guy but me," he told Christopher Brandon in an interview for the TNT network Web publication *Rough Cut* (December 1999). "It was like looking at myself. I felt sorry for him. I cried when he was crying because I felt it. I could really visualize this going on. And then I visualized me as him." According to Brandon, "Duncan is just as gentle, just as giving, just as warm and friendly as the character he so passionately brought to life on screen."

Michael Clarke Duncan was born on the South Side of Chicago on December 10, 1957. Surprisingly, given his present size, as a child he was often subjected to physical attacks by his sister and others. "My sister used to say I had a frail chest and she'd beat me up all the time," he told Christopher Brandon in an interview for *drdrew.com* (December 1999). "She was shorter but stockier, so she pummeled me around for years." Neighborhood kids, too, targeted him for abuse during his youth. "Back then I was like an oddity," he told Christopher Brandon during their conversation for *Rough Cut*. "Kids used to pick on me because I was different. My mother made sure I wore blue-jeans, Momma had creases in my jeans. I had on a white shirt every day. Back then, little black kids weren't wearing nice white shirts and nice pants to school. So kids were like, 'He's the odd one.'" Duncan described his neighborhood to Brandon as "a war zone." "There was always something happening that you had to watch out for," he said. "My mother raised us to be out there and just be careful and watch yourself and don't get caught up in all this craziness. I never did. If everybody sat on the corner, Momma always taught me, 'You get off the corner.' And people would throw rocks at me. 'He's a big sissy, he's always leaving.' Hey, I'm here today." As a teenager Duncan longed to play football, and various faculty members at the schools he attended encouraged him to do so. But his mother ruled against it. "My mama said, 'My baby is not going to play football,'" he told Joanna Connors for the Newhouse News Service (December 9, 1999, on-line). "And that was the big joke at my college. People would say, 'See that big guy there? His mama said he can't play football.'"

Duncan briefly attended Alcorn State University, in Lorman, Mississippi, but returned to Chicago when his mother fell ill. He later transferred to Kankakee Community College, to which he commuted from Chicago; he played basketball there. After earning an associate's degree, in the late 1980s, Duncan went to work digging ditches for the People's Gas Co. in Chicago. He became the butt of constant teasing from his co-workers after revealing to them that he had become interested in pursuing a career in acting. (Duncan told Brandon for *drdrew.com* that his "becoming an actor was actually my mother's dream.") Having dubbed him "Hollywood," his co-workers would joke, "'Oh Hollywood. Show 'em that Hollywood walk. Show 'em how you're going to walk for the producers when you get to Hollywood.' They thought it was so funny," he recalled to Brandon. During this period Duncan began lifting weights. "I had a girlfriend a long time ago in Chicago, and she took me to the gym, and those guys were so humongous," he recalled to Brandon, "I was so intimidated and bewildered in this gym. But I kinda liked it. I started lifting weights. I remember I bought a 40-pound dumbbell set with only one little bar. I started working out, and I could not lift that 40-pound weight one time. Finally I got it one good time, and that started it right there."

After six years with the gas company, Duncan quit his job and headed for Los Angeles, intent on making it as an actor. (In a different account of his move to Los Angeles, he told T. W. Siebert for *well-rounded.com* [December 1999] that he had toured "for about a year" as a cast member of a play called *Beauty Shop, Part II* and had decided to remain in the city after the production ended its run there.) Lacking both contacts and experience, he failed to get work. Before long he found himself down to his last $20. With nothing to do in the cheap motel room he had rented, "I was actually talking to the roaches," he told Connors. After flirting with the idea of joining the Los Angeles police department, Duncan called his mother to ask for a plane ticket back to Chicago. "Pull up your bootstraps and get tough," she told him, as he recalled to Connors. Heeding her advice, he landed a job with a security firm, which sometimes assigned him as a bodyguard. Those under his protection included the actors Martin Lawrence and Will Smith. Duncan became friendly with Smith, who was then the title character of the television sitcom *The Fresh Prince of Bel Air*, and Smith eventually helped to open a door for Duncan, by getting him a part on one episode of the show. "He only gave it to me because I worked security over there," Duncan told Brandon for *Rough Cut*. "I kept saying, 'Man, Will, put me in. Let me show you what I can do.'" Duncan later got bit parts on the sitcom *The Jamie Foxx Show* and on the daytime soap *The Bold and the Beautiful*.

Duncan segued from television to movies in 1995, when he appeared, without a credit, in the Ice Cube comedy *Friday*. His screen time was extremely brief; as he told T. W. Siebert, "If you blink, you'll miss me. I'm the guy who, when the guy comes to get his bike, I hold the money. That's my big scene. But it was the very first movie I'd done." Duncan's next roles were in the films *Back in Business* (1997), directed by Philippe Mora, Darin Scott's *Caught Up* (1998), Ice Cube's *The Player's Club* (1998), and Warren Beatty's *Bulworth* (1998), in the latter two of which he played a bouncer. His first substantial role was that of the roughneck oil driller Joyotis "Bear" Kurleenbear in Michael Bay's action epic *Armageddon* (1998); acting alongside Bruce Willis, Steve Buscemi, Ben Affleck, and Billy Bob Thornton, he played a member of a crew conscripted to save the world from a giant asteroid. With a deft blend of physical prowess and comedic timing, Duncan won over audiences with his characterization of Bear. In one notable scene, Bear bursts into tears in a psychiatrist's office, saying, "I'm feeling a little emotional right now!" *Armageddon* was a smash hit, becoming the highest-grossing movie of 1998.

Thanks to his being cast in *Armageddon*, Duncan developed a friendship with Bruce Willis. Before filming began, the prospect of working with Willis had made him nervous. "A lot of people told me when Bruce Willis gets in character you can't look at him," he told Chuck Arnold for *People* (August 17, 1998). Eager to avoid a confrontation, Duncan spent the first half of the *Armageddon* shoot avoiding eye contact with Willis and keeping his head down when the actor walked by. Finally, Willis approached him and broke the ice. "He said, 'What's wrong? You never speak to me, you always avoid me,'" Duncan recalled to Connors. "I said, 'Well, personally, man, people told me you're not the greatest actor to work with.' He said, 'Really? Do I treat you that way?' I said, 'No, you never have.' He said, 'Well, all right, can we be friends?' He stuck his hand out, and I shook it, and ever since then we've been the best of friends." Duncan tried to console Willis during his breakup with his wife, the actress Demi Moore. "I told him I didn't want him to feel down, no matter what he was going through," he told Arnold. "I knew he could pull through it because he pulled me through a lot of times when I was feeling down on the [*Armageddon*] set."

It was Willis who alerted Duncan to "the role of a lifetime," as Willis called it—that of John Coffey. "He said, 'I'm going to call Frank Darabont [the director of *The Green Mile*] when we get back to L.A.," Duncan recalled to Connors. "'After that, I'm through. But you are this guy. Go to a bookstore, get the novel, read it, so by the time you get back you'll have some insight into this character and you can go to the audition and knock it out.'" The novel to which Willis referred was Stephen King's *The Green Mile*, which was first published as a serial in 1996. Before his audition, Duncan read the book twice. His conviction that he was right for the part of Coffey proved to be well-founded. "There was something about [Duncan] that I just couldn't ignore," Darabont recalled to Connors. "After his first reading, he kept haunting me." Meanwhile, Duncan had returned to his security job. He was in his apartment in South Central Los Angeles when his agent called him to let him know the result of his tryout. "I didn't have any furniture . . . ," Duncan told Andrew L. Urban during an undated interview for *urbancinefile.com*. "My agent said, are you sitting down, and at that point I was on my knees. . . . When my agent said, yes, you got the part, I screamed YESSSSS! And hung up and called my mother right away. I said maaam, I'm gonna be working with Tom Haaaanks!' And we was crying, and then I called my sister."

Duncan now faced the task of portraying a frightened child in a man's body. "I wasn't used to doing that," he told Urban. "I used to be one of the boys. Big Mike . . . yeah! I lift all the weights, I don't show any emotion. Then, you come to John Coffey who's a little kid at heart, afraid of the dark. Big Mike could never have done that. I had to drop all that and start all over as a five-year-old kid." To prepare for his role, Duncan worked with the acting coach Larry Moss. "We put the script away and just talked," Duncan told Connors. "We talked about childhood, we talked about the things that I want in life, and the next thing I know, me and Larry, we're sitting there crying. I don't know where it came from, the emotions just came up in me."

The Green Mile was released on December 10, 1999, Duncan's 37th birthday. Critics and audiences alike embraced the movie and described Duncan's performance as spellbinding. Lawrence

Toppman wrote for the *Charlotte Observer* (December 10, 1999) that Duncan played his "breakthrough role with pathos and dignity"; Desson Howe observed in the *Washington Post* (December 10, 1999) that Duncan's "presence is literally the biggest thing in the movie." *The Green Mile* earned more than $130 million at the box office and collected four Academy Award nominations, including those for best picture, best adapted screenplay, best sound, and best supporting actor—Duncan. "Every night I get down on my knees and pray, 'Please, please let me win that golden trophy!'" Duncan admitted to Connors. (The prize went to Michael Caine, for his work in *The Cider House Rules.*) Duncan also earned Golden Globe and Image Award nominations and won a Broadcast Film Critics Award for best supporting actor.

Duncan followed his star-making turn in *The Green Mile* by playing Frankie Figs, a mob enforcer, in the black comedy *The Whole Nine Yards* (2000). The movie was a modest hit at the box office, and critics applauded Duncan for his comedic as well as dramatic skills. In *Entertainment Weekly* (February 18, 2000), after panning the picture, Owen Gleiberman wrote, "Duncan, sporting a Mr. Clean earring, gets to loosen up and show a bit more personality than he did as the simpleton savior of *The Green Mile*. He turns out to be as fast and light-fingered as he is large of scale."

Duncan is slated to appear in several films in 2001, including the comedy *See Spot Run* and *Like Cats and Dogs*, in which he will star opposite Alec Baldwin. In addition, he will be seen as an ape warrior in Tim Burton's highly touted remake of *Planet of the Apes* (1968). Speaking of his preparation for the role, Duncan told William Keck for *Entertainment Weekly* (October 20, 2000), "You have to learn to roll your shoulders forward, hunch your back, and round out your arms the way apes do. I'm also learning how to pick things up with a curved arm."

In late 1999 Duncan was living alone in a one-bedroom apartment in Los Angeles. He has been known to give $5 bills to strangers on the street who recognize him and know his full name, rather than—as is more often the case—mistaking him for the actor Ving Rhames. He is also an avid animal lover. In his interview with Brandon for *Rough Cut*, Duncan expressed the hope that someday he will be cast in a love story. "You wouldn't think about me being romantic, and you wouldn't think about me being a romantic lead. So I would love to do a love story. . . . You want to be different. It would be different for me, this big ol' guy, he's in love. People think that guys like us don't fall in love, but we fall in love too. So that's a twist, anything that's different from what I look like, I think that's what I would like to entertain." As he explained to Urban, he realizes that his large size may hold him back. "It's a double-edged sword," he said. "It's boosted my stock in Hollywood but it also has made people look at me and say, the acting's great. . . but he's biiiig! What else is he going to play? He can't play a journalist, he's too big. He can't play a doctor . . . so I've started to try and shave down." Along with his higher profile, he believes, comes a greater responsibility. "We, as actors, have to choose our roles carefully," he told Brandon for *Rough Cut*. "If you see me on a big screen shooting some guys up, I'm still going to let kids know I'm an actor, I'm an entertainer. That's my job. If you want to be an actor and do that, that's cool. But don't go out on the streets and do it." —J.K.B.

Suggested Reading: *Entertainment Weekly* p71 Mar. 2000 (with photo); *Jet* p58+ Dec. 20, 1999, with photo; Newhouse News Service (on-line) Dec. 9, 1999, with photos; *People* p110 Aug. 17, 1999, with photo

Selected Films: *Friday*, 1995; *Back in Business*, 1997; *Caught Up*, 1998; *The Players Club*, 1998; *Bulworth*, 1998; *Armageddon*, 1998; *A Night at the Roxbury*, 1998; *The Green Mile*, 1999; *The Whole Nine Yards*, 2000

Selected Television Shows: *The Fresh Prince of Bel-Air*, 1990; *The Jamie Foxx Show*, 1996; *Sparks*, 1996

Dutton, Charles S.

Jan. 30, 1951– Actor; director. Address: c/o Tavel Entertainment, 9171 Wilshire Blvd., Suite 406, Beverly Hills, CA 90210

While many actors talk about the monumental impact that theater has had on their lives, perhaps no one has felt that impact more than the veteran actor Charles S. Dutton, who read his first play and began acting during the seven and a half years he spent behind bars for manslaughter. "Without the theater," Dutton said, as quoted by Ross Wetzsteon for *New York* (May 7, 1990), "I'd be dead." Dutton has overcome desperate circumstances and the stigma of having been incarcerated to emerge as an accomplished actor on stage and screen. Since he rose to prominence, in the mid-1980s, by giving life to the haunting characters created by Pulitzer Prize–winning playwright August Wilson, Dutton has—among other projects—starred in the television sitcom *Roc* and recently won an Emmy Award as the director of the HBO miniseries *The Corner*, which deals with everyday life in an inner-city Baltimore neighborhood, much like the one where he grew up. "When I stand on that corner [in Baltimore]," Dutton told Wetzsteon, "I remember all my friends who were killed there. I think of all the times I went down to hang out and my mother expected to get a phone call asking her to come down to the morgue to identify my body. And when I look up at that prison where I spent seven and a

Steve Granitz/Retna Ltd.

Charles S. Dutton

half years of my life, I have a certain anger, sure, but I know that if I hadn't found something to believe in while I was there, I wouldn't be alive today. Prison? Bitter? Prison was my *blessing*."

Charles S. Dutton was born on January 30, 1951 in Baltimore, Maryland, the second of three children. His mother, who cleaned houses, and his father, a truck driver, separated when he was three, and Charles was raised by his mother in a Baltimore public housing project near the Maryland Correctional Institution. He would see his father, who died when Dutton was 15, only when the elder Dutton came into Baltimore to load trucks. Surrounded by poverty and bored by school, Dutton dropped out at age 13, preferring the excitement of the street, where he constantly got into fights. "My mom would still like to think that I was being influenced by the older guys, but I blame nobody but me," he told Michael Kuchwara of the Associated Press, as quoted in *Newsday* (November 11, 1984). "No society stuff. I wasn't a poor, hungry kid. I always had food on the table. I could get anything."

By the time he was a teenager, Dutton had already gained the nickname that would follow him for the rest of his life. "When I was a kid, we had rock fights," Dutton told Kenneth R. Clark for the *Chicago Tribune* (August 25, 1991). "My gang would line up on one side of the street and another gang would line up on the other side and we'd let fly. I was always out front, leading the charge, and I got my head busted about twice a month. As a result, the guys started calling me 'Rockhead.' Somewhere along the line, the 'k' and the 'head' got dropped and it's been 'Roc' ever since." His constant involvement in gang activity meant that like many youths in his neighborhood, Dutton spent much of his adolescence in reform school. "The only thing reform school prepares you for is prison," Dutton told Ross Wetzsteon. "But actually it was fun. You got to go to a rural area, you got to do things you could never do in the city, and most of your friends were already there anyway. So you'd even plan when you wanted to go—spring and summer especially—and you'd make sure you got sent by cursing out the principal or acting defiant with the probation officer."

In 1968 Dutton got into a fight involving a friend of his, the friend's girlfriend, and another man. The latter man knifed Dutton; in self-defense, Dutton grabbed the weapon and stabbed the man, who later died in a hospital. Dutton's lawyers set up a deal that would have saved him from serving jail time, but, as the actor told Michael Ryan for *Parade* (October 14, 1990), "I went into the courtroom with such a swagger and such a disdain for the proceedings that all of a sudden the prosecutor and the judge changed their minds about whatever they had in mind. I had no remorse." Dutton received a five-year prison sentence for manslaughter but was released on parole after 18 months. Soon afterward, he returned to prison to serve a three-year term for possession of a deadly weapon. He then took part in a prison riot and went one-on-one with a prison guard, which increased his sentence by eight years. "[In prison] you have to harden yourself to deal with all the stuff you see," Dutton told Martha Southgate for the New York *Daily News* (April 29, 1990). "It's commonplace to be sitting at breakfast talking to someone and all of a sudden somebody walks in and cuts his throat. And blood flies from his neck into your face, into your tray of food, everywhere. Or to see someone get his head bashed in by a baseball bat. That's commonplace. Every day something's gonna happen. That's the world of prison."

Behind bars, Dutton maintained his reputation as a troublemaker while also becoming involved with the Black Panthers and embracing the ideas of other segments of the radical left. During his seven and a half years in prison, Dutton spent 120 days in solitary confinement, which he passed in a five-foot-by-seven-foot room; there, the only light came from the crack under the door, and Dutton received one meal every three days. Sometimes the guards would flood the room with Dutton's urine and excrement. Allowed to bring one book with him for each turn in solitary, one day Dutton accidentally took with him a book of plays sent to him by his girlfriend, instead of his usual volume of writings by the Russian revolutionary Vladimir Ilich Lenin. Reading by the light that came under the door, he made it through *A Day of Absence*, by the African-American playwright Douglas Turner Ward. The satirical play tells the story of African-Americans in a southern town who stop working until the whites who live there realize how much they need them. That play led him to seek out the works of other dramatists, from the ancient Greeks, to Shakespeare, to modern playwrights. Soon, Dutton formed a theater group with fellow inmates and began producing theatrical productions inside the prison. The first time he performed, he was hooked. "Doing the play before a sea of very hard men," Roc told the *San Francisco Examiner*, as quoted in *Contemporary Black Biography*, Volume 4, "I felt this eerie kind of power. I could make them quiet, I could make them think. It was the only thing positive I had at that time in my life, the only immediate remedy for prison life. I suddenly knew what I was born to do."

Dutton's transformation was cemented after a fellow inmate stabbed him in the neck with an ice pick. Upon recovering from the near-fatal injury, Dutton chose not to retaliate against his attacker, hoping that the other man would be transferred or decide not to repeat his act. "It was the greatest pressure of my life," Dutton told Ross Wetzsteon. "In a way I felt it was a kind of divine retribution, me getting stabbed and nearly killed for having stabbed and killed a man myself. But then I started looking at the older guys I'd idolized. Fifty years old and they were in the same prison as me. Why should I follow these guys to hell? The whole vernacular of prison life suddenly seemed prehistoric. Forget this stupidity. My life was bigger than my cell." Dutton was soon transferred by a sympathetic warden to a different prison, where he became a model inmate. While there, he earned his high-school equivalency diploma and an associate of arts degree from nearby Hagerstown Junior College.

After being released on parole, on August 22, 1976, Dutton enrolled at Towson State University, in Towson, Maryland, and studied acting, graduating from the theater program in 1978 with a bachelor of arts degree. For the next several years, he performed a comedy act with a friend. Then, in 1980, he applied and was admitted to the acting program at the Yale School of Drama, in New Haven, Connecticut. "I was shocked when I got in," he recalled to Martha Southgate. "Shocked. I didn't go out of the house for three or four days. I thought I'd get hit by a bus or run into some old enemies or something would happen to me and I'd blow it. Sometimes I still don't believe I ever went." He excelled in the program, appearing in the title roles in Shakespeare's *Othello* and Bertolt Brecht's *Baal*, among other parts, before graduating in 1983 with a master of arts degree.

It was while he was at Yale that Dutton began working with the playwright August Wilson, who was undertaking an epic cycle of plays about the African-American experience in the United States. In 1982 Dutton participated in a staged reading of Wilson's play *Ma Rainey's Black Bottom*, about a group of jazz musicians in the 1920s. The play is set at a recording studio where the band and Gertrude "Ma" Rainey, an actual blues singer of that period, have been called to cut a disc for white record producers. The following year, when the play was produced at the Yale Repertory Theater, Dutton performed as Levee, an angry trumpet player who is frustrated by Ma Rainey's style of singing. When the play moved to Broadway, in 1984, Dutton, who had learned to play the trumpet for his role, electrified audiences and went on to win a Drama Desk Award and a Theater World Award and was nominated for a Tony Award. "I relate to Levee," Dutton told *People* (November 26, 1984). "He's a guy waving a knife at God, calling everyone a fool but himself. When I was younger I thought I was real slick, that I knew it all."

Dutton then starred in *The Piano Lesson*, Wilson's play about a family in Pittsburgh in the 1930s and their struggle to deal with the legacy of slavery. Wilson later stated that he wrote the play with Dutton in mind. When *The Piano Lesson* was produced at the Yale Repertory Theater, in 1987, Dutton won raves for his portrayal of Boy Willie, a hard-working and extremely talkative young man who wants to sell an old piano, a family heirloom, in order to buy farmland in the South. After winning acclaim at regional theaters across the country, the play opened on Broadway in 1990 and won a Pulitzer Prize, while Dutton came away with his second Tony Award nomination. "What [being a part of *The Piano Lesson*] means to me is simply and purely history," Dutton told Paula Span for the *Washington Post* (June 12, 1990). "One hundred years from now, some little boy will be trying to do Boy Willie in high school. When August Wilson finishes his cycle, black people in America will have their own theatrical history."

Dutton worked again with Wilson on *Joe Turner's Come and Gone*, after the play arrived on Broadway, in 1988. In that play, set in a Pittsburgh boardinghouse in 1911, he played Herold Loomis, who has come from the South in search of his estranged wife. The pathos of the characters stems in large part from the specter of slavery.

Meanwhile, Dutton appeared in several other plays, on and off Broadway, and began staking his claim on the silver screen. He appeared in supporting roles in a slew of films, including *Crocodile Dundee II* (1988), *Jacknife* (1989), *Q & A* (1990), *Mississippi Masala* (1991), *Alien III* (1992), *Menace II Society* (1993), *Rudy* (1993), *Nick of Time* (1995), *Get on the Bus* (1996), and *Random Hearts* (1999). His role as Charles Williams in the courtroom drama *Blind Faith* (1998) brought him accolades, although the movie did not do well at the box office. He also produced and played the title role in the television sitcom *Roc*, about a hard-working garbage collector who lives with his family in Baltimore's inner city. During its run on the Fox network, from 1991 to 1994, *Roc* received much critical acclaim for its talented ensemble cast, which included several members of the cast of *The Piano Lesson*, and for its willingness to address serious issues while realistically portraying a struggling African-American family. Dutton won an NAACP Image Award for his role in the show. For Dutton, the experience of producing *Roc* was a mixed bag, since Fox executives had on several occasions interfered with the more issue-oriented scripts and nixed guest spots by such prominent African-Americans as Jesse Jackson. "On one hand," Dutton told Kristal Brent Zook for the *Village Voice* (June 28, 1994), "I have to praise Fox for allowing me to do the kind of television I wanted to do for those three seasons. On the other hand, I have to criticize them for an uphill battle in basically trying to do the kind of show I did." Later in the same interview, he noted, "It's indicative of the industry period: whenever you do a show that has more to say and more to do than just the mindless, senseless television that we've known . . . when you go beyond that, it seems historically to have always been a problem with white Hollywood."

After the cancellation of *Roc*, Dutton found time to act in various television and movie roles. Among other projects, he starred in the acclaimed television movie version of *The Piano Lesson* (1995). "To actually get to do it for posterity, with several members of the original cast coming back for it, is a joy to behold," Dutton told Michael E. Hill for the *Washington Post* (February 5, 1995). "The play never left my system. I wanted to take one more shot at doing it before I got too old." For his role, Dutton was nominated for an Emmy Award and a Golden Globe Award.

Dutton had his directing debut with *First-Time Felon* (1997), a movie made for cable television. In 1999 he starred as Willis, a man who is falsely accused of murder, in Robert Altman's *Cookie's Fortune* (1999), a comedy-drama set in a small Mississippi town and written with Dutton in mind. "What was attractive to me," Dutton told Bernard Weinraub for the *New York Times* (April 8, 1999), "was that although this was set in the South, in the state of Mississippi and all that entails, it was about a black man totally devoid of anger and rage and bitterness. It's one of the first times in film I've gotten to play a complete human being, with a range of emotions and nuances, and not just somebody's partner."

In 2000 Dutton directed the acclaimed HBO miniseries *The Corner*. Based on the Baltimore crime reporter David Simon's book *The Corner: A Year in the Life of an Inner-City Neighborhood*, which focuses on an area blocks away from where Dutton grew up, the miniseries differed from other movies about inner-city life in that it concentrated on families instead of drug dealers. It was this aspect of the film that piqued Dutton's interest. The filming of *The Corner* was a trying process for Dutton and the crew. Upon arriving at the set (*The Corner* was filmed on location in Baltimore), Dutton was angry to note that the majority of the crew who were to shoot the movie in this inner-city neighborhood were white. Although more African-Americans were added to the crew, Dutton was never fully satisfied with the ratio of blacks to whites on the set. Furthermore, he eyed Simon, who was often on the set, with a degree of suspicion. Dutton felt that no matter how earnest Simon—who is white—may have been, he was, as Dutton told Janny Scott for the *New York Times* (June 11, 2000), "taking somebody else's misery and making a dollar off of it. Which can't be denied, whether he's the most sincere goddamn white man in the world." By the end of the filming, however, the two men had grown to understand each other somewhat better, and Dutton, as quoted by Eric Deggans of the *St. Petersburg Times* (April 16, 2000, on-line), praised Simon: "Finally, something was written that was not from the perspective of drug dealers, but from the point of view of addicts . . . people who struggle with addiction every day. It would have been easy for somebody else to screw this up . . . make it look like your typical 'in da hood' movie. My challenge was, how do you bring out the humanity of these people?" *The Corner* captured four Emmy Awards, including one each for Dutton and Simon.

Charles S. Dutton is stockily built and has a shaved head. He possesses a booming voice and is known for his strong presence, on stage and off. He currently divides his time between Los Angeles and New York. He divorced his wife, the actress Debbi Morgan, in 1993. Members of his family, who live in Baltimore, have been plagued by drugs. His brother, a heroin addict for nearly 25 years, died in 1993 at age 44 from an AIDS-related illness. His sister recently won her battle against cocaine addiction. Dutton has said that during his visits to Baltimore, he has found himself handing out money to old friends who are hooked on drugs or alcohol. "When you change [in your mind]," he told Enid Nemy for the *New York Times* (October 15, 1984), "and you go back and your friends talk about dope, it's not even a question of communication, it's like dealing with dinosaurs. It's very painful when it's somebody you used to love. But I have a few friends who also changed and I stay in touch with them." Dutton has traveled the country at times, visiting prisons to perform monologues or to talk to the inmates. Currently, he is slated to star in *The Arturo Sandoval Story* with Andy Garcia and in *Eye See You* alongside Sylvester Stallone. He has voiced interest over the years in making a film based on his life. "It's an old cliché, but I'm never satisfied with a performance," Dutton told Enid Nemy. "I always need to go deeper and do more. It's self-gratification. I act for me. That need is what makes me forget about those seven and a half years." — G.O., Y.P.

Suggested Reading: *Chicago Tribune* XI p5+ Aug. 25, 1991, with photo; *New York* p48+ May 7, 1990, with photos; *New York Times* C p13 Oct. 15, 1984, with photo, C p17+ Apr. 19, 1990, with photos, p1+ June 11, 2000, with photos; *People* p133+ Nov. 26, 1984, with photos; *Village Voice* p51+ June 28, 1994; *Washington Post* E p1+ June 12, 1990, with photos

Selected Films: as actor—*Crocodile Dundee II*, 1988; *Jacknife*, 1989; *Q & A*, 1990; *Mississippi Masala*, 1991; *Alien III*, 1992; *Menace II Society*, 1993; *Rudy*, 1993; *Nick of Time*, 1994; *A Time to*

Kill, 1996; *Get on the Bus*, 1996; *Blind Faith*, 1998; *Cookie's Fortune*, 1999; *Random Hearts*, 1999

Selected Television Shows: as actor—*Roc*, 1991–94; *The Piano Lesson*, 1995; as director—*First-Time Felon*, 1997; *The Corner*, 2000

Eduardo de la Manzana, Courtesy of Simon & Schuster

Eggers, Dave

1970– Editor of McSweeney's*; writer; graphic artist. Address:* McSweeney's*, 394A Ninth St., Brooklyn, NY 11215*

A reader encountering a book called *A Heartbreaking Work of Staggering Genius* might assume that the author either suffers from an inflated ego or is painfully self-aware. In the case of Dave Eggers, whose first, autobiographical book bears that very name, the latter is true. "Like most titles, it was a place-marker for a long time, and it kind of became too late to change it," Eggers told Sarah Lyall for the *New York Times* (February 10, 2000). "And it made me laugh." A partly fictionalized account of how Eggers dealt with the loss of his parents to cancer and accepted the responsibility for raising his younger brother, Toph (short for Christopher), the book has succeeded critically and commercially and inspired pronouncements that its 30-ish author is the voice of his generation. Publishing rights to the book have been purchased around the globe, and there have been rumors that several film studios are interested in the story. The book's boastful, attention-grabbing title notwithstanding, Eggers seemed unprepared for the reception it received upon its publication, in early 2000. "I didn't write the thing to have it read by a lot of people. That's not the sort of audience I've ever sought," he told Nadine Ekrek for the *Washington Post* (February 11, 2000). "It's nice when people say they enjoyed it. But I had no idea when I finished it that anyone would like it at all. It seemed to me like a very strange and ugly book. But either I was very wrong, or strange and ugly books are now very popular."

With such modest protestations Eggers has risked sounding disingenuous, mainly because he spent the latter half of the 1990s as a rising star in the publishing world. Beginning with *Might*, the doomed but celebrated satire magazine he founded in San Francisco in 1994, and continuing with his cheeky and influential literary journal *McSweeney's*, Eggers has made a career of criticizing—from the sidelines—the mainstream media's affinity for hype. The success of *A Heartbreaking Work of Staggering Genius*, however, has launched him from the periphery of the media into the midst.

At the root of all the attention—and the best evidence that Eggers is sincere in his response to it—is his particular vision. Like *Might* before it, *McSweeney's* is defiantly uncommercial and reflects its founder's tastes and sensibilities. *A Heartbreaking Work of Staggering Genius*, by turns funny, tender, sad, and maddeningly self-aware, is no less a product of Eggers's artistry, insecurity, and integrity. His book, Michiko Kakutani wrote for the *New York Times* (April 22, 2000), "uses all the latest postmodern hardware: his account of his parents' deaths and his rearing of his eight-year-old brother is prefaced with a coy discussion of the major themes of the book, 'Rules and Suggestions for Enjoyment of This Book,' and an emotional flow chart; it demonstrates, however, that such devices can enhance, rather than undermine, the emotional power of his story."

The third of four siblings, David Eggers was born in Boston in 1970 and raised in Lake Forest, Illinois, a tony suburb of Chicago most famous for being the setting for the 1980 film *Ordinary People*. His father practiced law, and his mother taught in an elementary school. Eggers led a seemingly unremarkable childhood. "I never rebelled. Not in any conventional way. I wanted to please my parents," he told Amy Benfer for *Salon* (February 22, 2000, on-line). "When I liked an album, I wanted them to like it too. I was desperate to make connections with them, and I really liked doing that. So I don't ever identify with the idea that you try to upset your parents in some deliberate way." Despite his father's chronic drinking problem, which he described in *A Heartbreaking Work of Staggering Genius*, Eggers has characterized his mother and father as good parents, both loving and supportive. In particular, he has praised his mother's ability to interact with children. "She was a parenting genius. I'm not the only one who would say that," he told Benfer. "She taught for many years and had hundreds of kids and I think almost all of them would say that."

The relative quietude of his early life ended during his third year at the University of Illinois at Urbana-Champaign, where Eggers was studying painting and journalism. That year his mother endured drastic surgery for stomach cancer, and shortly thereafter doctors found tumors in his father's brain and lung. In 1991, about six months after his father's diagnosis, Eggers's parents died, within 32 days of each other. "On the one hand you are so completely bewildered that something so surreal and incomprehensible could happen," Eggers told Sarah Lyall, describing his reaction to his parents' deaths. "At the same time, suddenly the limitations or hesitations that you might have imposed on yourself fall away. There's a weird, optimistic recklessness that could easily be construed as nihilism but is really the opposite. You see that there is a beginning and an end and that you have only a certain amount of time to act. And you want to get started."

In the wake of the family's tragedy, Eggers dropped out of college, assumed the lion's share of responsibility of raising Toph, and moved with his younger brother to the San Francisco Bay area to be closer to his sister, Beth, who was pursuing a law degree at the University of California at Berkeley. "People said, 'That's so nice of you to do that,'" Eggers told Lyall about raising his younger brother. "But I would rather have had Toph as a roommate than anybody else, and the alternative was much worse. What were we going to do, break up the family and send Toph to a salt mine?"

The unconventional situation and Eggers's age led some to question his ability to care for an adolescent. In his book Eggers wrote at length about acquaintances and neighbors who would never have questioned the judgment of a 40-year-old mother yet didn't think twice about challenging his own parental decisions. "I think a lot of parents assumed that our house was a young bachelor pad, chaotic sort of thing," he recalled for Amy Benfer. Contrary to the expectations of such people, Eggers filled the parental void for Toph, mingling a brotherly playfulness with the protectiveness of a more conservative parenting philosophy. "I think there is a strange American Puritanism, of course, that's always there, right below the surface, that favors incredible simplicity and austerity for the raising of a child. And I did too in a way," he said to Benfer. "I really believe strongly that kids should be spared the runoff of their parents' lives and problems."

As for the effects of becoming a guardian so unexpectedly at a time when most young adults are looking to ease into responsibility and pursue an active social life, Eggers has said that living with a youngster did not really hinder his lifestyle. "I never went out a whole lot. Never more than once a week, usually. I always attributed that fact to the conviction I had that something horrible would happen to my brother if I left, obviously, and that I would pay for it the rest of my life," Eggers explained to Benfer. "But a lot of it had to do with work. I like working. I like staying home and working on things and pretending to work on things. And half the time I prefer hanging out with Toph at home to just going to a bar. We had real fun. We had pingpong."

As he and Toph got used to the new familial roles and responsibilities thrust upon them, Eggers took a job as a graphic designer with *SF Weekly*, an alternative news and arts paper, and reunited with his high-school friend David Moodie, who was also living in the area. Media junkies both, Moodie and Eggers decided to take over *Cups*, an arts publication that was circulated free of charge and served as an accroutrement to San Francisco's pervasive café culture. They published the periodical in their spare time. "At first we thought it would be fun to have a place where we could run our own stuff," Eggers told Joel Selvin for the *San Francisco Chronicle* (January 27, 1994). "But soon it was, like, when we were done with all our other work, we'd go and spend a week without sleep." Having decided that running *Cups* was no longer worth the effort and having failed to secure a buyer, they gave the publication away. The duo then began working on a concept for a new publication, this time with another high-school friend, Marny Requa, who had moved to California. The result, *Might*, was launched in January 1994.

Might's title, taken from a literary journal the three had worked on at Lake Forest High School, was intended to evoke the word's two primary but separate connotations: ambiguity and power. Its first issue was a fairly straightforward celebration of 20-something achievement, far different from the bitingly satiric bimonthly into which it quickly evolved. "After the second issue we stopped preaching," Eggers told Laurie Sandell for *Shift* (January/February 2000, on-line). "It's sort of that the people we attracted were, like, a little too earnest for us." With a puny budget that rarely allowed the editors to pay contributors, *Might* lacked the polish of typical newsstand glossies but offered funny and often trenchant commentary on rampant consumerism and the ways of the media. One oft-cited example was a cover story reporting the alleged murder of former child actor Adam Rich, who portrayed Nicholas on the TV show *Eight Is Enough*. The hoax, perpetrated with the actor's knowledge and cooperation, lampooned the media's willingness to capitalize on the misfortunes of even minor celebrities and ultimately proved its point: it prompted the *National Enquirer* and television's *Hard Copy* to contact *Might* for follow-up stories they were planning.

Although several of the publication's essays—a selection of which was published by the editors in the anthology *Shiny Adidas Tracksuits and the Death of Camp* (1998)—are considered contemporary classics of the genre, the magazine was best known for its asides and marginalia. Fake footnotes and retractions would pop up on random pages; one example read: "On page 111, in our 'Religious News Round-up,' we reported that Jesus Christ was a deranged, filthy protohippy. In fact, Jesus Christ was the son of God. We regret the error." Another favorite was the magazine's bogus contents page, which promised nonexistent articles with outrageous and sardonic titles. In typical David-versus-Goliath fashion, *Might* often used this page to take on such media giants as the *New York Times*. For instance, one issue's contents page announced the piece "Harrummph harrummph harrummph," by conservative *Times* editorial columnist and word maven William Safire, and another by *Times* theater critic cum political commentator Frank Rich, called "Politics! Entertainment! Can't Tell the Difference!"

Such editorial fearlessness won *Might* and its editors a rabid cult following and frequent requests for their services. Microsoft tapped the editors for freelance submissions for its Generation X magazine *Mint*, and *New York* asked them to contribute an article to its Academy Awards coverage. But with circulation figures that never broke the 30,000 mark, the publication was bound for failure. In an effort to prolong the magazine's life, and maybe even earn a living from it, Eggers, Moodie, and Requa approached several publishers for financial backing. (They later mocked their own actions, by reprinting a rejection letter from Hearst Magazines.) "We didn't do anything that we were supposed to do to appeal to the people that give money to magazines," Eggers acknowledged to Nadine Ekrek. "We probably could have shaped it in such a way as to be solvent, but, you know, I just didn't give a [expletive] about any of that." Their best prospect for solvency came from the magazine *Wired*, but when that deal fell through, *Might*'s editors closed shop, in 1997, after their 16th issue.

Throughout the life of *Might*, Eggers had supplemented his income with freelance design work from the graphics studio he and Moodie had started. For a time he also edited the "Media Circus" section of the on-line magazine *Salon*. After *Might* folded, *GQ* and *Esquire* each approached Eggers about a plum staff position; he accepted *Esquire's* and moved with Toph to New York. At first, being an editor at large for a magazine that he had revered for years seemed to him a great opportunity. Eggers quickly grew disdainful, however, of the mainstream tone *Esquire* was increasingly adopting to compete in a men's-magazine market dominated by such titles as *Maxim* and *Details*, which feature scantily clad models and puerile humor alongside service journalism. "It was a learning experience, the first real job I'd ever had," Eggers told Laurie Sandell. "I learned that I could never have a regular job. It's good to know that early on." Eggers often voiced his distaste for *Esquire*'s new direction. "After a few months, no one listened to me. I was always complaining about misogyny and stupidity," he said to Michael Colton. "I was a lunatic screaming from the woods." Before leaving the magazine, in 1998, Eggers used his numerous contacts to solicit contributions for a literary and humor publication he planned to launch, titled *Timothy McSweeney's Quarterly Concern*.

Indicative of Eggers's imagination and sense of humor, *McSweeney's* (as the quarterly and its accompanying Web site, *Timothy McSweeney's Internet Tendency*, are commonly called) is named after a mentally ill man who once claimed to be a relative of Eggers's. An idiosyncratic hodgepodge of literary fiction and nonfiction, Eggers's own artwork and designs, and overtly silly, made-up tales about the lives of buttoned-down public figures, particularly the political pundit David Gergen, *McSweeney's* allows its contributors to pursue virtually any topic, however eccentric, they choose. "*McSweeney's* is an effort to experiment with form," he explained to Sarah Lyall. "It's an effort to tell the same story, in a different way, without taking it too seriously."

As with *Might*, what sets *McSweeney's* apart from other publications are its digressions and marginalia: fine-printed footnotes dot the perimeter and simultaneously add to and divert attention from the main text. The journal's structure changes from issue to issue (one recent issue was sent to subscribers in the form of 14 slender, individually bound volumes wrapped in a custom-made carton); but its basic design concept gives it the look and feel of a 19th-century periodical. "We'll keep upping the ante," Eggers declared to Mark Horowitz for *New York* (January 31, 2000). "Whether doing them in hardcover, or putting in every bell and whistle we can: die cuts, vellum, different paper stocks. That stuff interests me as much as—sometimes even more than—the words on the page." Also unique to *McSweeney's* is its quixotic, self-conscious tone, often described as postmodern.

Although contributors are not paid for their submissions, Eggers has attracted notable contemporary writers, including David Foster Wallace and Rick Moody, thus acquiring cultural cachet for his journal. In addition to longtime Eggers fans and admirers of postmodern writing, the journal has become a "must read" among book and magazine editors looking for fresh new voices. Within its first four issues, the press runs of *McSweeney's* have jumped from about 2,000 to 12,000.

Further boosting the journal's appeal was the launch, in February 2000, of Eggers's much-anticipated book, *A Heartbreaking Work of Staggering Genius*. *A.H.W.O.S.G.*, which is said to be Eggers's preferred acronym for the book, chronicles Eggers's life from the onset of his parents' illnesses to his and Toph's move from California. The bulk of the memoir (a word Eggers prefers not to use to describe the book, because he changed some names, conflated some incidents, and fabricated most of the book's dialogue) recalls Eggers and Toph's years in California. Interspersing the core story with contrived conversations and interviews, which act almost as Socratic dialogues that expose his internal conflicts, Eggers painted a vivid picture of the turmoil that for a time marked his and Toph's lives.

In spite of the sobering events Eggers wrote about in the book, he incorporated many of the same peripheral elements familiar to readers of *Might* and *McSweeney's*. On the copyright page, normally reserved for legal disclaimers, Library of Congress information, and the like, the reader learns, among other things, that the author is five feet 11 inches tall, weighs 170 pounds, and rates a three "on the sexual-orientation scale, with one being perfectly straight, and 10 being perfectly gay." There are 32 pages of prefatory notes and acknowledgments that comment on the major themes of the book and anticipate reader reaction: "[The author] would also like to acknowledge that no, he is not the only person to ever lose his parents, and that he is also not the only person ever to lose his parents and inherit a youngster. But he would like to point out that he is currently the only such person with a book contract. . . . And that he too is well aware of all the book's flaws and shortcomings, whatever you consider them to be, and that he tips his hat to you for noticing them." The acknowledgments section also gave Eggers the opportunity to indulge his affinity for marginalia, including charts further inventorying the book's themes and metaphors, a breakdown of how he has spent the $100,000 advance he received from his publisher, Simon & Schuster, and a drawing of a stapler.

Predictably, the physical form the book would eventually take proved to be an important element of the writing process for Eggers, who wrote his memoir late at night on a computer program that allowed him to see the text as it would appear on a page. "I had to see it right in front of me. I had to see how the paragraph breaks looked, with the margins a certain way," Eggers told Fred Kaplan. "I'm really reluctant to write for something where I don't control the design." He insisted on being involved in the book's final design, choosing the artwork for its dust jacket and urging that the word "memoir" be stricken from the title. "I bullied my way," he joked to Anne Fulenwider for *Vanity Fair* (March 2000). "I'm a pain in the ass."

A.H.W.O.S.G. spent nine weeks on *Publishers Weekly*'s best-seller list and earned Eggers a largely laudatory critical response. "To call this book brazen is like calling a blizzard white—it's true, but it leaves out most of the story," the *Boston Globe* (February 27, 2000) chief book critic, Gail Caldwell, wrote in her review. "Dave Eggers's memoir-maybe is a defiantly Not Tragic soliloquy; it's also hip, funny, wildly intelligent, and as flushed with narrative energy as anything I've read in some time." She concluded, "It's a carnival ride of insights from a writer who can be breathtakingly articulate, and who (it must be said) comes off sounding like a really cool guy." Sara Mosle, in her appraisal of *A.H.W.O.S.G.* for the *New York Times Book Review* (February 20, 2000), found "Eggers's book, which goes a surprisingly long way toward delivering on its self-satirizing, hyperbolic title," to be "a profoundly moving, occasionally angry, and often hilarious account of those odd and silly things, usually done in the name of Toph." Above all, in Mosle's estimation, "Eggers's real achievement is to provide a counterweight to what Ian Frazier once called 'the encroaching Hefty bag of death,' and to write about it, in our age of irony, with genuine, unsentimental poignancy."

In light of his recent celebrity, Eggers does not allow journalists to interview Toph, now in his teens, and has conceded only that his brother has read the book and liked it. Despite *A.H.W.O.S.G.*'s popularity, Eggers has claimed that he has not read it since it was written and doesn't even own a copy of it. He told Fred Kaplan, "There are five or six parts of the book—the rough ones to write, the raw, more emotional parts—I don't know what's on those pages." Eggers, who has said that he will not write another memoir, admitted that he is working on his first novel and on an art book with Russian artists Vitaly Komar and Aleksandr Melamid, who provided the dust-jacket artwork for Eggers's first book. — T.J.F.

Suggested Reading: *Boston Globe* F p1 Feb. 22, 2000, with photo; *Brill's Content* (on-line) Mar. 1999; *Salon* (on-line) Feb. 22, 2000; *Shift* (on-line) Jan./Feb. 2000; *New York* p31+ Jan. 31, 2000, with photo; *New York Times* E p1 Feb. 10, 2000; *Newsweek* p71 June 19, 1995, with photo; *Washington Post* C p1 Feb. 11, 2000

Selected Works: *A Heartbreaking Work of Staggering Genius*, 2000; as editor—*Might*, 1994–97; *Shiny Adidas Tracksuits and the Death of Camp*, 1998; *Timothy McSweeney's Quarterly Concern*, 1998–

Ellis, Ruth

July 23, 1899– Gay-rights activist. Address: P.O. Box 76, Okemos, MI 48805-0076

At the age of 101, Ruth Ellis is said to be the oldest acknowledged African-American lesbian in the United States. When Ellis became aware of her sexual orientation, in about 1914, homosexuality was considered taboo, both as a lifestyle and as a subject of discussion, and homosexual acts—even between consenting adults—were illegal in every state of the union. (In some two dozen states, laws against homosexuality still remain on the books.) Hollywood's Motion Picture Production Code would later, and for many years, prohibit references to homosexuality in films, and a law banning lesbian and gay citizens of other countries from entering the U.S. remained in force from 1952 to 1990. For decades, both the American Medical Association and the American Psychiatric Association categorized homosexuality as a sickness. In

Courtesy of Sisters in the Life

Ruth Ellis

1981 the U.S. Department of Defense barred gays and lesbians from serving in the military; now, they are permitted to serve, but only if they keep their homosexuality hidden. In 1997, more than 80 years after Ruth Ellis recognized her homosexuality, the decision by the comedian Ellen DeGeneres to have her TV sitcom character "come out" (as she herself had done) was treated as big news. "I was always out of the closet," Ruth Ellis has said. "I didn't have to come out." A printer by trade, Ellis opened her home to African-American female and male homosexuals after she moved to Detroit in the early 1940s, at a time when there were few nightclubs or other public places where black lesbians and gays could socialize freely without fear of reprisals. Her parties attracted people from a wide swath of the Midwest, and she became a mentor to many of them. "Ruth . . . always [took] care of younger gays," the filmmaker Yvonne Welbon told Ted Shen for the *Chicago Tribune* (August 26, 1999). Speaking of Ellis with Rhonda Smith for the *Washington Blade* (May 28, 1999, on-line), Kofi Adoma, a gay civil-rights organizer in Detroit, said, "In the African American community, elders are held in high esteem, and she's one of our elders. She's able to bring our history to us and is such a symbol and a reminder that if she can live openly as a Lesbian, we can, too." Ellis, who has spoken before many groups throughout the U.S. on the rights of the elderly as well as homosexuals, is the subject of Yvonne Welbon's documentary film *Living with Pride: Ruth Ellis @ 100* (1999).

The youngest child and only daughter of Charles Ellis Sr. and Carrie Ellis, Ruth Ellis was born on July 23, 1899 in Springfield, Illinois. Her twin sibling died as a baby. Her mother was a homemaker. A slave at birth, her father was self-educated; he kept a small home library that contained an encyclopedia, the works of Shakespeare, and history books. One of the first African-Americans hired by the U.S. Postal Service in Springfield, Charles Ellis Sr. worked as a mail carrier before losing his job after a confrontation with someone who had insulted him. "He never got a good job after that," Ruth Ellis told Rochella Thorpe for *Inventing Lesbian Cultures in America* (1996), as reprinted in the *Lesbian News* (February 1999). Ellis's brothers—Charles Jr., who became a physician; Harry; and Wellington—each played an instrument, and all three served in World War I (in segregated units: the U.S. military was not integrated until 1946, half a year after World War II ended). Charles Jr. and Harry served overseas. Only Wellington ever got married; Ellis believes that Charles Jr. was probably gay.

The Ellis family lived in an integrated section of Springfield, where their neighbors included miners, factory workers, and state employees. As a small child Ruth had a white friend, but after the girls started school, they "couldn't play together anymore," as Ellis told Terri Jewell for an interview published in *Piece of My Heart: A Lesbian of Colour Anthology* (1991). "When children are left alone, they don't care about all the foolishness that the parents worry over," she added. "Children get all that hate from their parents." Despite the peaceful relations that blacks and whites in Ellis's and other integrated neighborhoods enjoyed, Springfield laws prevented black people from eating in city restaurants or going to the local Y. "We had to go to the river to learn how to swim," Ellis told Rochella Thorpe. In movie theaters and the opera house, blacks had to sit in the balcony, and some shows were barred to them. Although the public schools that Ellis attended were integrated, nonacademic school activities were usually segregated.

An influx of both blacks and whites to Springfield at the turn of the 20th century swelled the town's population and led to increasing competition for jobs and, consequently, increasing racial tensions. During the sweltering summer of 1908, two black residents of Springfield were jailed, one accused of the murder of a white man following a break-in of the man's home, and the other charged with the rape of a white woman. (Long afterward, the woman admitted that she had lied about the rape.) Incensed whites—their anger inflamed by lurid newspaper accounts in which the foiled robber was labeled a would-be or actual attacker of the homeowner's daughter—threatened to lynch the two prisoners. After law-enforcement officers moved the suspects to a distant jail, white mobs took to the streets and set fire to many black people's homes. By the time the state militia and National Guard restored order, large parts of Springfield's black neighborhoods had been destroyed, at least two blacks had been killed, and many people had been injured. (The 1908 Springfield race riot spurred the formation of the National Association for the Advancement of Colored People [NAACP] by a small group of whites and blacks, in 1909.)

Ellis, who was nine when the riot occurred, has recalled that although many blacks took refuge in a state armory, where the National Guard offered protection, her family did not leave their home. "My father didn't have a gun, but he was a 32nd degree Mason and he had a sword," Ellis told Doug Pokorski for the Springfield *State Journal-Register* (February 23, 1997). "He lay down in the front room with that sword, and my brothers had brickbats upstairs." But he and his sons did not have to use their weapons, because the rioters never reached the Ellises' house. Years later, when Ellis was living in Detroit, she witnessed the race riots that erupted there in 1943 and 1967.

By her own account, Ellis was a "slow learner," and she received a poor education in the series of primary schools that she attended. "[Teachers] didn't pay attention to colored kids then," she told Terri Jewell. As quoted on the Web site of the Gay and Lesbian Association of Decatur (September 1999), she said that her teachers "just passed me to get me out of their class."

At Springfield High School, she told Terri Jewell, she was a "loner"; she told Doug Pokorski, however, that she belonged to a club for black girls. When she was in her mid-teens, she fell in love with her gym teacher, a Portuguese woman who treated blacks and whites equally. At that time she knew nothing about homosexuality, and what she knew about sex had come from a book that she read sometime after the death of her mother from a massive stroke, when Ruth was about 12. Her father had left the book on his desk, knowing, as Ellis recalled to Kathleen Wilkinson for *Curve* (November 1999), that "I'd be meddlesome and look in to read it." Although she and her father never talked about her homosexuality, she believes that her father knew that she was gay, and that he was secretly "glad," as she put it to Wilkinson, because it freed him from the worry that she might get pregnant and leave home. "He wouldn't let me go with boys," she told Rhonda Smith. "He would say, 'Books and boys don't go together.'" Later, she gained some understanding of homosexuality by reading a book on psychology as well as *The Well of Loneliness* (1928), by the British writer Radclyffe Hall (the pen name of Marguerite Radclyffe-Hall), a semi-autobiographical novel about two lesbians. (The book was banned in Great Britain and was published in the U.S. only after a court battle.)

For years after she graduated from high school, in 1919, Ellis worked for families as a nursemaid, earning $3.50 a week—a salary considered low even then. (In 1999 dollars, $3.50 was equivalent to less than $38.) But her pay went far, as she recalled to Terri Jewell: "You could buy two cents worth of potatoes, a steak for 15 cents, a loaf of bread for a nickel. You could buy a penny's worth of candy, your [life] insurance would be five cents a week . . . " Eventually she got a job with a printer, who taught her how to set type and run a printing press.

Ellis was past 35 when she met the woman who became her first, and only, real "girlfriend," as Ellis has referred to her: Ceciline "Babe" Franklin, a restaurant cook. In the early 1940s Franklin followed her to Detroit, where Ellis had moved at the suggestion of her brother Charles, who had told her that she would earn more there. She found work with a printer, and in 1942 she bought a two-family house in Detroit, in which she and Babe lived together for nearly three decades. In the early 1950s she purchased her own linotype machine and opened the Neighborhood Print Shop, in the front room of the bottom floor of the house. The Ellis and Franklin Printing Co., as it was formally known, was the first woman-owned printing business in Detroit. Since she worked alone, Ellis accepted only small jobs, such as church bulletins and wedding invitations, and relied mainly on walk-in business. Franklin's income and the rent from the gay couple to whom they leased the remainder of the bottom floor supplemented what Ellis earned from her shop.

Until the 1970s or so, black lesbians were not welcomed in the few Detroit nightspots that catered to white lesbians, so private homes became their meeting sites of choice. The house on Oakland Avenue that Ellis and her partner shared became one of the most prominent of those gathering places, for both male and female homosexuals. According to Rochella Thorpe, lesbians and gays knew that at Ellis's house, they could "relax, have fun, and eat good food." In addition to music and large pots of spaghetti or other easy-to-prepare fare, Thorpe reported, Ellis and Franklin provided an "open and friendly atmosphere" where people felt comfortable enough to identify themselves by their real names and talk about their jobs—something homosexuals virtually never did in heterosexual company then, for fear of being fired or other reprisals. Ellis's parties also gave them an opportunity to expand their network of friends. "One of the most important activities at Ruth's parties was dancing," Thorpe wrote. "Dancing, as important to courtship for lesbians as it was for heterosexuals, was something that African-American lesbians could hope to do only in private or at lesbian and gay parties." Ellis's gatherings became so well known that people from far-flung parts of Detroit and other cities in Michigan, and even from other states, would come to them. Sometimes a visitor would become a temporary houseguest.

In the 1960s the Detroit city government tore down Ellis's house as part of an urban renewal program. With the loss of their home, Ellis and Franklin ended their joint living arrangement. Franklin, who owned a car, moved to a Detroit suburb, near to her job; she died in the mid-1970s. Ellis moved into a housing complex for senior citizens in downtown Detroit. After she retired, at about age 65, she joined various senior citizens' clubs in Detroit. In the 1980s, through a white lesbian who taught a class in self-defense in which Ellis had enrolled, she began to make many new friends among

Detroit's younger generation of white and black homosexuals. "I keep meetin' the women . . . oh, I just know a gang of them now . . . ," Ellis told Nancy Andrews for her book *Family: A Portrait of Gay and Lesbian America* (1994). "Everyone wants to meet this old lesbian. They just take me around here, there, and yonder. I specialize in women. I love women. . . . I get most of my joy from women. Since I met all these women, that's what's keepin' me alive." Thanks to the devoted attention of her friends, Ellis maintains an active social life and still goes to lectures, plays, concerts, and other such events. For many years she attended the annual Michigan Womyn's Music Festival, held near Grand Rapids, and, as an advocate for the elderly as well as for homosexuals, she has spoken before numerous women's groups and school groups nationwide. In 1999 she was honored at the San Francisco Dyke March, during which thousands of attendees sang "Happy Birthday" to her. The city of Detroit gave her a certificate of appreciation in 1997, and her 100th birthday was declared "Ruth Ellis Day" there.

Yvonne Welbon's film *Living with Pride: Ruth Ellis @ 100* (1999), an hour-long documentary, is based in part on 50 hours of conversations with Ellis and people who know her. The movie premiered at the Gay and Lesbian Film Festival in San Francisco; it was also shown during the 1999 Black Harvest Festival at the Film Center of the Art Institute of Chicago and at that year's Toronto Film Festival, among other venues. Welbon first saw Ellis at the National Women's Music Festival in Bloomington, Indiana, in 1997. "I saw this woman dancing and I was wondering how old she was," Welbon told Lesley Rogers for the Springfield *State Journal-Register* (May 12, 1998). "I got tired and sat down, and she was still dancing. I got some water, and she was still dancing. Then I found out she was 97." — V.K.

Suggested Reading: *Chicago Tribune* V p1+ Aug. 26, 1999, with photos; *Curve* p18+ Nov. 1999, with photos; *Lesbian News* p56 Feb. 1999, with photos; Springfield, Illinois *State Journal-Register* p1+ Feb. 23, 1997; *Utne Reader* p26+ Jan./Feb. 2000, with photo; *Washington Blade* (on-line) May 28, 1999; Lewin, Ellen, ed. *Inventing Lesbian Cultures in America*, 1996; Silvera, Makeda, ed. *Piece of My Heart: A Lesbian of Colour Anthology*, 1992

Emmerich, Roland

(EM-mer-ik)

Nov. 10, 1955– Film director; producer; screenwriter. Address: Centropolis Effects, 10950 Washington Blvd., Studio B, Culver City, CA 90232

Armando Gallo/Retna Ltd.

Summer has long been thought of as the season when film studios bring out their "event" movies—vehicles with epic-scale special effects, thundering action, and audience-pleasing heroes and villains. Few contemporary Hollywood directors have made as big a name for themselves with event movies as Roland Emmerich. In 1996 Emmerich's alien-invasion film *Independence Day* made the Fourth of July *the* hot-button movie weekend of the summer and toppled box-office records. His two follow-up films, *Godzilla* (1998) and *The Patriot* (2000), have also earned solid receipts. Emmerich's skill as a filmmaker lies not in creating something never before seen but rather in remixing others' approaches to an established genre and providing fresh takes on old ideas. *Independence Day* features references to *The Day the Earth Stood Still*, *War of the Worlds*, and *The X-Files*, while his 1994 film *Stargate* has been described as a modernized mix of *Star Wars* and the *Indiana Jones* films. His ability to reinvent the so-called "popcorn movie" with great success has earned Emmerich the nickname "The Spielberg of Sindelfingen," which links him to the director Steven Spielberg and the Stuttgart suburb, in Germany, where Emmerich grew up. It has also occasionally earned him the castigation of critics, who have derided his films as mindless and plotless. Referring to Dean Devlin, his filmmaking partner, he told Tom Russo for *Premiere* (June 1998), "It's the tragedy of what Dean and I do. Maybe in 10 years they'll say, 'Oh they're stupid movies.' Or perhaps they'll say, 'Look, these guys very cleverly reworked something which keeps getting reworked every decade.'"

Roland Emmerich was born on November 10, 1955 in Stuttgart, in what was then West Germany. As a child he was fascinated by American science-fiction films and television shows. "I remember being most impressed at the time by *2001: A Space Odyssey* (1968)," he wrote for the Web site *box-off.com*. "We had moved from Stuttgart . . . to the suburbs where there was only one theatre, a first-run theatre that almost never played German movies. Because Germany has very strict laws on how old you have to be to get into the movies, I wasn't allowed to go in. But my older brothers, who went to the movies constantly, always managed to sneak me in with them." Emmerich has at least one sister, Ute Emmerich, a producer who has worked with him on several of his films.

After graduating from Sindelfingen's high school, Emmerich worked briefly in advertising before moving to Munich, in southern Germany, to study cinema. At film school he made such pictures as *Frog* (1979) and *The Noah's Ark Principle* (officially released in1984), the latter of which was the most expensive student movie produced in Germany up to that time. Focusing on a crisis aboard a European-American space station, *The Noah's Ark Principle* opened the 1983 Berlin Film Festival, in Germany, and brought Emmerich notice as an up-and-coming director. Thanks to its success, he got the wherewithal to form his own production company, Centropolis Entertainment, and make bigger-budgeted studio films. Mindful of the world market, Emmerich, who was working in Germany, opted to shoot his films in English beginning with the science-fiction fantasy *Joey* (1985). Also known as *Making Contact*, *Joey* is the story of a boy who can communicate with his deceased father via a toy telephone. The picture earned an International Fantasy Film Award nomination for best film at the Fantasporto film festival, in Portugal. Emmerich next made the horror-comedy *Ghost Chase* (1987), which failed to generate much interest.

While working on *Moon 44* (1990), about a group of prisoners who battle to protect a mining colony in outer space, Emmerich met Dean Devlin, a cast member who had a small role, that of a computer genius. Devlin rewrote his dialogue, and Emmerich was impressed with the results. During their first conversation, Devlin recalled to Louis B. Hobson for the *Edmonton [Canada] Sun* (June 30, 1996, on-line), they discovered that they both "loved the same kinds of science fiction." "I pitched Roland a few of my ideas," Devlin said. "He liked them and we've been working together ever since."

One of Devlin's ideas involved a pair of technologically enhanced soldiers and longtime rivals who fight each other in the not-too-distant future. The concept materialized as the film *Universal Soldier* (1992); co-written by Devlin, Richard Rothstein, and Christopher Leitch and directed by Emmerich, it stars Jean-Claude Van Damme and Dolph Lundgren. Although it was universally panned—in a typical review, Ralph Novak, writing for *People* (July 20, 1992), described it as "crass, imbecilic, confused and easily predictable from start to finish"—action and science-fiction fans turned out in droves to see *Universal Soldier*, and the film earned $100 million worldwide. It also spawned three sequels, none of which Emmerich worked on.

Emmerich and Devlin next made *Stargate* (1994), with Kurt Russell, James Spader, and Jaye Davidson in the lead roles. Based on an idea Emmerich had had in film school, *Stargate* chronicles the exploits of a group of soldiers who learn the origins of life on Earth after traveling through an interdimensional gate. Critics savaged the film. "The movie *Ed Wood*, about the worst director of all time, was made to prepare us for *Stargate*," Roger Ebert wrote for the *Chicago Sun-Times* (October 28, 1994). In spite of critical drubbing, the film earned $200 million worldwide, making it the highest-grossing science-fiction film of 1994. Emmerich's hopes of continuing the story in a series of films were dashed when a spin-off TV series was produced instead; airing on the cable station Showtime in 1997, it was called *Stargate SG1*.

The unexpected success of the film *Stargate* boosted Emmerich's profile, and studio executives at Twentieth Century Fox gave him free rein over his next project. The idea for that movie, *Independence Day*, came to him during the press tour for *Stargate*, during which Emmerich repeatedly found himself fielding questions about the possibility of extraterrestrial life. "The 15th time somebody asked me that question," Emmerich recalled to Steve Pond for *Premiere* (August 1996), "I started to tell what I think is fascinating about it: What would you do if one morning you woke up and there's a loud rumble and [a spacecraft is] there? And driving home, I said, 'Gosh, why is nobody doing that? Why has everybody always done secret-invasion scenarios, where aliens disguise themselves as humans or as little worms crawling on the backs of people, when they would have the technology to blast us away? Why isn't somebody doing a new *War of the Worlds*? Two days later, I decided to do it." (Howard Koch's radio adaptation of H.G. Wells's 1898 novel *War of the Worlds* was broadcast on Orson Welles's *Mercury Theater on the Air* in 1938. The program caused widespread panic among listeners, thousands of whom thought an invasion by Martians was actually taking place.)

Written by Devlin and Emmerich, *Independence Day* is about Earth's near destruction by an army of aliens one Fourth of July weekend and the planet's salvation by a small cadre of Americans. The film was a throwback to the disaster movies of the 1970s, in which an all-star cast tries to vanquish a seemingly insurmountable threat. The cast of *Independence Day* features such diverse talent as Jeff Goldblum, Bill Pullman, Mary McDonnell, and Will Smith. Although the film boasted impressive special-effects sequences (most notably when the aliens wipe out all of the world's major cities with all-consuming fireballs), Emmerich worked hard to keep the budget down, by using models rather than more costly digital technology for some scenes, for example. Released on July 3, 1996, *Independence Day* rocketed to the top of the box-office charts, setting a record by pulling in $100 million in its first six days. By the end of the year, *Independence Day* had grossed almost $800 million worldwide. Although the response of most critics to the film was lukewarm, many hailed it as the official return of the summer blockbuster. "If *Star Wars* was the high-water mark of the comic-book space adventure movie almost 20 years ago, *Independence Day* is its apotheosis," Mick LaSalle declared in the *San Francisco Chronicle* (July 2, 1996).

After *Independence Day*, Emmerich found himself flooded with offers to direct films, many of which were knockoffs of the "alien invasion" scenario he and Devlin had devised. During this period he and Devlin created and produced the television series *The Visitor*, about a World War II pilot who disappears over the Bermuda Triangle and reappears a half-century later, in the present-day U.S., with enhanced physical skills. Although *The Visitor* attracted a loyal following, it was canceled by the Fox network after a brief run, in 1997–98. The show was ultimately picked up by the Sci-Fi Channel, where it plays in reruns.

In the meantime, Emmerich had received the script for an updated version of the monster movie *Godzilla*. Since 1955, when the first *Godzilla* film was released, the Japanese *Godzilla* franchise has been a consistent moneymaker, giving rise to more than two dozen sequels and spin-offs, and for several years Hollywood studio heads had been eager to create an American version. The latest script did not appeal to Emmerich, because, as he explained to David Poland for the Web site *roughcut.com*, there wasn't enough human interest. But he accepted the assignment nevertheless. "For me, it was always very simple," he told Howard G. Chua-Eoan for *Time* (May 25, 1998). "Godzilla was one of the last concepts of the '50s that had never been done in modern form—that idea of the giant monster as in *Tarantula* or *The Beast from 20,000 Fathoms*. Why not do them again?" However, he added, he and Devlin "were really concerned about the cheese factor." The pair commissioned a new design for the monster and reworked the *Godzilla* script, placing the creature in and around New York City. (Emmerich, Devlin, Ted Elliot, and Terry Russio got credit for the final screenplay.) "Godzilla can outrun any taxi, and that was the core idea for the movie," Emmerich told Chua-Eoan. "No one can catch it. Dean and I realized we could make a different Godzilla, a movie about a hunt, about hide-and-seek."

To promote *Godzilla*, Sony Pictures mounted a tremendous—and tremendously expensive—marketing campaign, much of which aimed to build anticipation about Godzilla's appearance, which was kept secret. In various cities, buses were outfitted with signs reading, "His foot is as long as this bus," while skyscrapers in New York City and elsewhere were adorned with signs reading, "He's as tall as this building." *Godzilla* opened in several thousand theaters on May 19, 1998 and took a beating from critics. Mick LaSalle, writing in the *San Francisco Chronicle* (May 20, 1998), called the film "an overblown action monstrosity with no surprises, no exhilaration and no thrills." While it fell far short of *Independence Day*'s phenomenal earnings, *Godzilla* still raked in over $100 million in domestic receipts and collected a further $200 million overseas. In addition, the film was spun off into a successful animated series, for which Emmerich serves as producer.

Eager to distance himself from his reputation as an "event movie" maker, Emmerich chose his next project with care. He settled on the Revolutionary War epic *The Patriot* (2000). Written by Robert Rodat, who produced the script for *Saving Private Ryan* (1998), *The Patriot* is about Benjamin Martin, a farmer who is reluctantly drawn into the fight for American independence. Emmerich believed that the film's weighty subject matter and tense battle scenes would elevate his status in Hollywood's eyes, and he was excited about the prospect of directing a script that he had neither written nor co-written. "It definitely freed me as a director to have a certain distance from the material," he explained to a reporter for the Web site *empireonline.co.uk*. "There's things you'd never change because they inspired you to do the movie but there's other things you can correct because you're on the outside."

Starring Mel Gibson and the up-and-coming Australian actor Heath Ledger, *The Patriot* opened on June 30, 2000 to mixed reviews. Those who reacted most favorably included David Denby, who, in his assessment for the *New Yorker* (July 3, 2000), described the film as "an intelligent and frightening drama about the essence of war" and "a very able and stirring piece of cinema." Most of those who expressed reservations about *The Patriot* found something to praise as well. In *Newsweek* (June 26, 2000), for example, David Ansen wrote that the movie is "a handsome and sometimes gripping production" but "ultimately appears to have been written by a committee of studio executives and contains a 21st-century sensibility that undermines its historical accuracy"; in *People* (July 3, 2000), Leah Rozen wrote, "The movie's first half succeeds remarkably well in portraying the causes and costs behind the birth of America, but things ultimately turn clichéd and obvious." To date, *The Patriot* has grossed $100 million at the box office.

Roland Emmerich makes his home in Puerto Vallarta, Mexico. He is an avid collector of books and films. His current projects include *Cellular*, the directorial debut of Dean Devlin, and *Arac Attack*, a horror film in which mutated spiders invade a small Nevada town. The latter picture adds to abundant evidence of Emmerich's ongoing love affair with the science-fiction genre. "For me," he explained to Richard Corliss for *Time* (July 8, 1996), "going on a science-fiction movie set is like visiting toyland. You see, my brother trashed all my toys when I was a kid. It's very Freudian. For my movies you can blame my brother Andy." — J.K.B.

Suggested Reading: *Calgary Sun* (on-line) July 3, 2000; *Newsweek* p49 May 25, 1998, with photos; *Premiere* p64+ Aug. 1996, with photos; *Time* p58+ July 8, 1996, with photos, p 74+ May 25, 1998, with photos

Selected Films: as director—*The Noah's Ark Principle*, 1984; *Moon 44*, 1990; *Universal Soldier*, 1992; *Stargate*, 1994; *Independence Day*, 1996; *Godzilla*, 1998; *The Patriot*, 2000; as producer—*Eye of the Storm*, 1991; *The High Crusade*, 1994; *The Thirteenth Floor*, 1999

Selected Television Shows: as producer—*The Visitor*, 1997

Erik de Castro/Archive Photos

Estrada, Joseph

Apr. 19, 1937– President of the Philippines. Address: Office of the President, Manila, Philippines

Sporting a jet-black pompadour and ample belly, with a reputation as a drinker and womanizer, Joseph Estrada appears at first glance more likely to be a hard-living Lothario than to be the president of the Philippines. But supporters of the swaggering former B-movie idol, known affectionately as "Erap," maintain that such earthiness accounts in large part for his popularity among Filipinos. The star of more than 100 action films in which he portrayed variations on the common man who champions the poor and oppressed, Estrada deftly parlayed his big-screen image into a political career. Beginning as mayor of San Juan in 1969, he climbed the political ladder with a swiftness that astounded many of his detractors, who see him as little more than a bungler with limited political savvy and even less intelligence. Two and a half years into his presidency, questions about his ability gathered force, in the face of an economic downturn, a surge in corruption and cronyism among government officials, and a wave of violence among Muslim separatists. "Estrada has increasingly become the subject of jokes, gossip and that old Philippine staple, coup rumors," Seth Mydans reported in the *New York Times* (August 20, 2000). Mydans also wrote, "Unlike his American hero [President Ronald Reagan], he has little philosophy in government and is not leading the nation in any direction." In the fall of 2000, Estrada was accused of accepting bribes from illegal gambling rings, and as of the beginning of November, he faced impeachment. Nevertheless, his ascension to the presidency has proven that a seemingly ordinary person can rise to extraordinary heights.

Joseph Estrada was born Joseph Ejercito on April 19, 1937 in one of the toughest ghettos of Manila, the capital of the Philippines. His father, Emilio Ejercito, worked for the government as an engineer. His mother, Maria Marcelo, who had studied music at the College of Santa Rosa, near Manila, was a homemaker. Estrada was the ninth of 10 children—and the only one not to finish college. Today, his siblings include doctors, lawyers, pharmacists, and teachers. "But now," Estrada observed to Seth Mydans for the *New York Times* (October 3, 1997), "they are all the brothers and sisters of Erap." Estrada attended St. John Academy in his elementary-school years and was a student at Ateneo de Manila as a teenager. Never a model student, in 1952 Estrada was kicked out of high school for fighting in a restroom. ("I was praying that somebody would open the door," he told William Branigin for the *Washington Post* [November 12, 1994], "because the guy was beating the [expletive] out of me.") Despite that episode, he eventually finished high school and entered the Mapua Institute of Technology, with the intention of following in his father's footsteps by studying engineering. By his third year, however, he had concluded that his talents lay elsewhere, and he dropped out. When he announced that he was forsaking engineering in favor of a career in movies, his parents became irate and forbade him to use the family name in his acting pursuits. As a result, he chose "Estrada," which is Spanish for "street," as his surname, and adopted the nickname "Erap," which is "pare" (meaning "friend" in Tagalog, the principal language of the Philippines) spelled backward.

Estrada made his film debut in *Kandilerong Pilak* (1954). He then went on to star in more than 100 other movies, including *Sumpa at Pangako* (1959), *True Confessions* (1960), *Deadly Brothers* (1964), and *Alex Big Shot* (1967). His films were wildly popular with the public, portraying Estrada as a lone crusader, championing the rights of the poor and downtrodden. Many of his characters held ordinary jobs—ice cream vendor, street sweeper, taxi driver—that the average Filipino audience could identify with. Through the course of his career, Estrada captured five best-actor prizes in the Philippine equivalent of the Academy Awards, and five films in which he appeared won awards for best picture. In addition, many lauded Estrada's screen efforts for their social relevance as well as for the high-octane entertainment they provided. A prime example of this is *Under the Claws of the Eagle* (1989), in which Estrada played a labor leader and blue-collar truck driver who fights American soldiers who are abusing women. The film was a comment on the United States' post-colonial dominance of the Philippines. "As long as there were U.S. military bases, we would always be in a predicament in this country," Estrada told Don Kirk in an interview for the *International Herald Tribune* (May 25, 1998, on-line), "and we would never be self-reliant." In 1981 Estrada was entered into the Filipino Academy of Movie Arts and Sciences (FAMAS) as best actor, the first person to be so honored. In 1983 the organization recognized him for his efforts as a producer.

Estrada's first foray into politics came in 1968, when he ran successfully for mayor of San Juan; he took office in 1969. As mayor, Estrada blurred the line between his movie characters and his real self, adopting a tough-guy persona against corrupt members of the local police department. "I was walking tall in San Juan," he recalled to Seth Mydans for the *New York Times* (February 25, 1989). "I used to punch the police, the hoodlums in uniform. It was the only language they understood. I knocked them down, just like in the movies. I had my gun in its holster." During his 16-year stay in office, Estrada was named one of the Ten Outstanding Young Men in Public Administration. He was also named Most Outstanding Mayor and Foremost Nationalist as well as Most Outstanding Metro Manila Mayor, both in 1972. In 1986 the new government of President Corazon C. Aquino put an end to his mayoral position, forcing him out along with all other local officials who had taken office under the repressive administration of the previous president, Ferdinand E. Marcos. Although Estrada barricaded himself in his office for several days, defending his action by pointing out that he had won in free elections, he was eventually replaced by an officer-in-charge as part of the reorganization of local governments. Of all the Metro Manila Mayors replaced, Estrada was the only one to leave any savings behind in the municipal treasury.

The year after he left the office of mayor, Estrada ran for the Senate. Defying many people's expectations, he won and held the office for five years. Some observers attributed his unexpected victory to his being in touch with the needs of Filipinos. "I think actors have a feel for the pulse of the people," he told Mydans. "I have always played the role of the oppressed and downtrodden, which I believe my colleagues in the Senate have no experience of being with through the years." Estrada has used this "common-man" persona to his advantage throughout his political career. He takes great pleasure in being the college drop-out in a roomful of lawyers and polished politicians. Addressing the Senate, he once asked rhetorically, "Why do we pass all these laws when nobody follows them?" As he noted in his interview with Mydans, "We're like school children in there. Roll call: Senator Estrada—Present! They all know my favorite time is when the Senate president bangs his gavel and says, 'Recess.'"

As a senator, Estrada was vehemently pro-poor and pro-Philippines. He worked feverishly to protect the interests and traditions of the various cultural communities in his country, and he co-sponsored the law that allowed low-income or indigent litigants to receive free court transcripts. He also chaired the Senate Committee on Rural Development, which provided accelerated programs for the construction of irrigation apparatuses. He became the nation's most outspoken advocate of population control, all but unheard of in the heavily Roman Catholic nation. In addition, Estrada, a staunch nationalist, opposed the 1991 renewal of an agreement that would extend the presence of the U.S. military in the Philippines. He maintained that he was not anti-American but simply wanted to see the Philippines reclaim its full sovereignty. "If I love America less, it is because I love the Philippines more," he told Uli Schmetzer for the *Chicago Tribune* (September 6, 1992). The renewal was not approved, and American military occupation ended in the Philippines after almost a century. Today, Estrada recognizes the importance of strong relations with the U.S., provided the freedom of the Philippines is not compromised. Currently, the U.S. is permitted port visits and military exercises in the Philippines. "Military visits will prove beneficial to our country, especially to our armed forces." he told Kirk. "I welcome visits and war games. Our armed forces will learn many things from the Americans."

In 1992 Estrada ran for vice president and won by a large margin. His victory was not initially of great concern to his opponents, who predicted that he would have no important role in the government, especially since he did not belong to the same political party as the president. As it turned out, however, President Fidel V. Ramos offered Estrada the chance to head the Presidential Anti-Crime Commission, which targeted organized crime and police corruption. One month after accepting the position, Estrada found himself wearing a bulletproof vest and carrying a concealed nine-millimeter pistol as he invited Chief Inspector José Pring, a suspect in five kidnap-for-ransom cases, to his home for a supposed joint press conference. When Pring arrived, Estrada produced a fugitive police officer who fingered Pring as the head of a gang of kidnappers who targeted rich Chinese businessmen in downtown Manila. The incident was eerily reminiscent of Estrada's screen efforts, as he recalled to Schmetzer. "All the time I told myself this was no longer a film, this was more dangerous than the scripts, and I could get myself killed here," he said. Many claimed that Estrada had designed the drama of the arrest as a publicity stunt, but Estrada vehemently denied the charge. "It was the only way I could trap them because I'm fighting the enemy within the police organization," he told Schmetzer. Overall, he noted in the same interview, the episode was a sad commentary on the state of political affairs in the Philippines. "Where else in the world but in the Philippines can you find the chief of an anti-kidnapping task force turn out to be the king of kidnappers?" he lamented. Estrada's skull-cracking approach to crime fighting earned him the nickname "Wyatt Erap" from his followers. However, when one bloody shootout resulted in the death of six suspects, two of whom turned out to be police officers, Estrada was removed from the Anti-Crime Commission.

As his vice presidency continued, Estrada began to be highly touted as a candidate for the presidency. The public responded to Estrada the politician even more enthusiastically than they had to Estrada the movie star, and this fact was not lost on Erap. He cleverly turned what might have been reputation-harming foibles—his gambling, womanizing, and tendency to utter malapropisms—into parts of his overall image as an appealingly earthy, blue-collar Joe. For example, when the Miss Universe contest was held in Manila, in 1994, Estrada was so smitten with one of the contestants that he joked, "If Miss Colombia will have me, I'll leave my wife for her, or even have her assassinated." He also displayed a softer side, tearily explaining his painful separation from his wife and the affairs it had driven him to. "I was an actor surrounded by temptations with no wife at home," he was quoted as saying in the *Economist* (November 8, 1997). "I was in the prime of my life. I dated a lot. I had numerous relationships."

Estrada was also capable of poking fun at himself, even going so far as to authorize the book *ERAPtion: How to Speak English Without Really Trial.* A collection of some of his more famous flubs (when asked why he frequented a restaurant, for example, he replied, "I like the ambulance"), the book was a best-seller in the Philippines, topping the charts for several weeks and bringing the "Erap-joke" into the public forum with full force. Estrada welcomed this attention, feeling that it would keep his name in the minds of voters. By 1997 he had begun his campaign in earnest and was drawing a great deal of support. On September 21, 1997 a throng of Filipinos took part in the country's largest political rally in almost a decade to oppose President Ramos's attempt to amend the Constitution and make a bid for a second term in office. Eventually, Ramos agreed not to pursue another term, and the road was left open for Estrada, whose average-guy persona again worked to his advantage. "I feel sorry for our people," he told Keith B. Richburg for the *Washington Post* (May 12, 1998). "They get gypped by these so-called intellectuals every election year because they all promise to be pro-poor."

Estrada's election campaign proved to be a colorful one, with attacks on his character on one side and Estrada's branding of his opponents as "intellectual snobs" on the other. Typical of the barbs from his opponents was a political cartoon that depicted Estrada on a television talk show on which the host asked, "If you become president, what will you do about the abortion bill?" In reply, Estrada blurted, "I'll pay it!" "He doesn't engage with visions and thought," the political analyst Cristina Montiel remarked to Berton Woodward for *Maclean's* (May 11, 1998). "That's a mild way of putting it—he's just not very bright." Estrada took all the flak in stride, comparing himself to another famous actor who went on to become president: Ronald Reagan. "The most powerful nation in the world can elect a movie actor," he told Woodward. "I don't see why the Philippines can't." On May 11, 1998, running against José de Venecia, the House Speaker, and Mayor Alfredo Lim of Manila, Estrada was elected president of the Philippines in a landslide victory. "It is revenge of the masses," the noted Estrada advocate Joel Rocamora said to Seth Mydans for the *New York Times* (May 12, 1998). "They are tired of being led by smart people."

Once he took office, the Filipino people were treated to a new, improved Joseph Estrada. He lost weight, quit smoking, curtailed his drinking, and hired a media coach. However, many feared that Estrada's reign as president would have echoes of that of Ferdinand Marcos, a sentiment that Estrada emphatically dismissed. "My goal is to unite the Filipino people," he told Kirk. "We will forgo this labeling in favor of honest-to-goodness reconciliation. I am identified with Marcos because I was a mayor during the period of martial law under Marcos, but I was detained twice because I didn't like Marcos." As a gesture toward reconciliation, Estrada informed Kirk that he had agreed to allow Imelda Marcos to bury her husband's body in Heroes' Cemetery in Manila. "I am a Christian. Let us bury the past with his body and start life with a new beginning," he said.

Shortly after his term began, Estrada once again found himself the target of heavy criticism, when Philippine Airlines workers went on strike following failed negotiations for a 10-year suspension of collective bargaining in return for shares in the company and seats on the board. Estrada tried to keep both sides talking but was portrayed as siding with big business over oppressed workers, a sharp contrast to the image he had cultivated during his campaign. Those close to him, however, maintain that his support of the poor does not mean giving handouts or pandering. "His concept of fighting poverty is not the Robin Hood type," presidential adviser Roberto Aventajado told Tanzer. "He has shown everybody he embraces the open market." Estrada effectively settled the dispute when he contracted Cathay Pacific, based in Hong Kong, to fly Philippine Airlines' domestic routes, a move that prompted both sides to return to negotiations and agree to the deal they had previously rejected. Estrada's quick and decisive actions served to silence his critics, if only for a while. "They are underestimating me," he remarked in the *Economist* (October 3, 1998). "So I'll give them the surprise of their lives."

For some time after Estrada became president, the Philippines enjoyed relative prosperity. An estimated $8 billion a year in remittances from the more than four million Filipinos working overseas helped the economy. But evidence of widespread corruption at all levels of government, along with favoritism in the awarding of both political appointments and business contracts, led to increasing criticism of Estrada. Even many of his supporters grew disenchanted in the face of the president's habit of arriving late to work and leaving early, his penchant for drinking whiskey, and his practice of carousing with his friends until dawn in so-called midnight Cabinet meetings. Rumors abounded that Estrada even made policy decisions in the midst of such revelries. Eventually, in an effort to quell expressions of dissatisfaction about his behavior, the president stopped his late-night partying and began coming to work early.

Estrada also tried to stop the escalating violence by Muslim rebels, who seek to create an independent Islamic nation in the southern Philippines. After declaring an all-out war against the two main rebel groups, he backed down and attempted to negotiate with them instead. In exchange for money from Libya that was supposed to be used for "development," the rebels agreed to release some hostages. But, as Joshua Kurlantzick reported in the *New Republic* (September 25, 2000), the insurgents used the money to buy more weapons and promptly took more people hostage.

In October 2000 Estrada was accused of receiving millions of dollars in bribes from illegal gambling syndicates. He has vehemently denied the charges, but he has also said, as quoted on the BBC Web site, "If it is proven that I accepted a single centavo from illegal gambling or took it from the national coffers, I shall not stay a minute longer in my position as your president." Among other signs that the scandal was hurting the already struggling economy, the value of the peso dropped significantly. Gloria Macapagal-Arroyo, the nation's vice president, was among "tens of thousands" of Filipinos who urged Estrada to resign, "to spare the country further economic turmoil," the Associated Press reported (November 6, 2000, on-line). According to that Associated Press article, impeachment of the president appeared certain. — J.K.B.

Suggested Reading: *Chicago Tribune* I p10 Sep. 6, 1992, with photo; *Economist* p45 Nov. 8, 1997, with photo; *Forbes* p170+ May 31, 1999, with photos; *Maclean's* p31 May 11, 1998, with photos; *New Republic* p16+ Sep. 25, 2000; *New York Times* I p4 Feb. 25, 1989, with photo, A p6+ Oct. 3, 1997, with photo, A p3+ May 12, 1998, with photos, C p4+ May 12, 1999, with photos, p12 Aug. 20, 2000, with photo; *Washington Post* H p1 Nov. 12, 1994, with photos, A p16 May 12, 1998, with photos

---

Outline Press

Evans, Nancy

Apr. 12, 1950– Co-founder, president, and editor in chief of iVillage.com: The Women's Network. Address: iVillage.com, 212 Fifth Ave., New York, NY 10010

When most people think of a village, they envision a small municipality with an idyllic name, like Bedford Falls or Pleasantville. Perhaps the typical imagined village has tree-lined neighborhoods, a Main Street bordered by storefronts, and a few hundred residents. To some five million Internet-savvy women, however, the word "village" has taken on a new meaning. Begun in 1995 by Nancy Evans and Candice Carpenter, iVillage.com: The Women's Network has grown into one of the Web's most frequently visited properties. It offers a network, or "virtual village," of more than 20 specialized sites, all targeted to women. By offering advice and a place to congregate on-line to discuss such topics as child rearing, career development, personal finance, and health issues, iVillage has attracted a growing population whose purchasing power many marketers believe will change the face of on-line retailing. As the company's president and editor in chief, Nancy Evans has received most of the credit for shaping iVillage's content and turning the site into a desirable destination for Web surfers.

A key to Evans's success in so-called "new media" has much to do with her training in traditional print media. Evans, who was born on April 12, 1950 in Philadelphia, earned a B.A. degree from Columbia University, in New York City, in 1972. While pursuing a master's degree, which she would receive from Columbia in 1974, Evans worked as a copy editor in nearby Middletown, Connecticut. She parlayed that experience into an associate editorship at *Harper's Weekly* when it was launched, in 1974. After a two-year stint with the magazine, she turned to freelance journalism. An avid reader, Evans got steady work from *Glamour*, managing the fashion journal's book serialization before becoming its book columnist. In addition, her work frequently appeared in a number of other publications, including the *New York Times Book Review*, *Ms.*, and *Family Circle*. She coauthored with Judith Applebaum *How to Get Happily Published* (1978), a writer's guide to the publishing industry, and from 1983 to 1985 she cohosted the weekly PBS author-interview and book program *First Edition*, which was underwritten by the Book-of-the-Month Club.

Evans's love of books and her high-profile association with the Book-of-the-Month Club paid dividends in 1985, when she was named the club's editor in chief. Evans displayed a keen sense of readership trends despite her lack of experience in book publishing. "She came to us without any real editorial background," Al Silverman, Evans's former boss at the Book-of-the-Month Club, told Edwin McDowell for the *New York Times* (August 8, 1987). "But before she set foot in our door she knew the tradition and culture of the club. And she found ways to adapt the past to the present with very smart ideas for marketing books." Evans's two successful years at the helm of the club persuaded Alberto Vitale, who was CEO of the Bantam Doubleday Dell Publishing Group, to appoint her president and publisher of Doubleday in January 1987.

At the time Doubleday was undergoing major change. The industry had begun one of its most competitive intervals, with such publishing houses as Simon & Schuster and Random House experiencing significant growth in a relatively short period. A stalwart in the industry for decades, Doubleday had begun to slide. Capitalizing on its established name and falling market share, the German publishing group Bertelsmann had bought Doubleday in 1986 and committed resources to the revitalization of the house. Evans soon became the talk of the book world. To some, her appointment seemed risky, because she had no direct experience in a publishing house; to others, Evans came to symbolize the infusion of new life into a once-robust company grown stale. "My feeling is you need new blood in this industry to foster innovation and to keep us fresh and competitive," Vitale said to McDowell. "Nancy brings both those qualities, as well as boundless energy."

Under Evans, Doubleday regained some of its prominence. She emphasized new author and title acquisitions, which resulted in the signing of a number of commercially viable properties. In turn, the house's presence on best-seller lists across the country increased. She also sought to make Doubleday books physically more attractive, and thus more marketable, by improving design and production quality. Her alliances with literary agents and authors made her well-liked within the book publishing world, and before long she was looked upon as the glamour girl of the industry. Two years after her appointment she was awarded the 1989 Women in Communications Matrix Award for excellence in book publishing. Despite Evans's best efforts, Doubleday reportedly lost approximately $6 million in 1989, prompting rumors that she would resign. She did so in January 1990.

Evans bounced back the following year with a concept for a new monthly parenting magazine called *Family Life*. In 1991, with the backing of *Rolling Stone* publisher Jann Wenner, she successfully launched the publication. Focusing on such lifestyle topics as family vacations and children's fashions, rather than such core parenting issues as child safety, *Family Life* was targeted to baby-boomers with children ranging from toddler to preteen. Because the magazine was more likely to feature ads for BMW and Ralph Lauren than for diapers, some media critics charged it with being frivolous and pandering to upper-middle-class consumerism. Despite such criticism and a parental-magazine market already glutted with high-circulation slicks, *Family Life* sold well under Evans's direction. Her reputation for good editorial ideas and high standards grew with the magazine's circulation during her four-year reign. Nevertheless, Wenner sold the publication in 1995 to Hachette Filipacchi, leaving Evans jobless.

That spring Evans received a call from a friend, Candice Carpenter. At the time Carpenter, a well-known media executive, was working as a consultant for America Online (AOL). Aware of Evans's editorial talents, Carpenter asked Evans to help her advise AOL on content for an on-line magazine that would teach their subscribers how to use the Web. Also part of the consulting team was a young entrepreneur named Robert Levitan, who specialized in start-up business models. Evans, Carpenter, and Levitan saw the Internet's potential for business and began to exchange ideas about a new on-line venture. By the autumn of that year, the three had formed a partnership, rented offices in Manhattan, and chosen iVillage as their corporate name.

The Internet was first created in the early 1970s as an improved method of communication and data exchange among government researchers. By 1990 forward-thinking retail marketers were using it as a new outlet for merchandising, spurring an explosion of Web start-ups. It is a widely held tenet among marketers that women account for approximately 70 percent of all purchases. Yet until recently, women have not been a major force in Internet commerce. According to estimates from the mid-1990s, women comprised only 20 percent of the total Internet audience. Estimates from the end of the decade, however, suggest that the Web's female audience has more than doubled and that women are responsible for about 50 percent of all purchases over the Internet. As the Internet continues to move into the mainstream, it is probable that Web purchases by women will approach the 70 percent mark, thus reasserting women's market primacy.

In many ways iVillage is an amalgam of the two primary uses of the Internet: communication and commerce. By combining the strengths of several Web sites, iVillage has created a virtual community where women can gather information and interact. Guest experts and chat-room moderators facilitate discussion on a number of topics that concern women. Through its content iVillage draws a desirable marketing target—women—which in turn makes iVillage a desirable medium for advertisers. On-line specialty stores, such as iBaby, which offers items to expecting parents, are also part of the network, and iVillage siphons a percentage of sales made through the network.

Each year iVillage has lost approximately $40 million. It has remained solvent thanks to three rounds of private financing and an initial public offering in March 1999, which infused the company with millions of dollars. While Candice Carpenter is known as the company's "rainmaker," or the one responsible for bringing in sponsors and financiers, Evans has gotten most of the credit for iVillage's popular content. Evans closely monitors the issues her audience wants discussed most, and in that way she has allowed the iVillage audience to drive content. Furthermore, she has initiated several creative, integrated sponsorships, in which advertisers contribute to the site and interact directly with the Web audience. "We did not want our members just clicking on a banner and going out into cyberspace. . . . We wanted the advertiser to be the good-guy store on the block who you could count on, who was a part of that community and not just trying to sell you something," Evans explained to John Flinn and Laura Rich for *Adweek* (September 23, 1996). "For instance, Nissan is the sponsor of the American Youth Soccer Organization, which I happen to know because I'm a soccer coach. We mentioned to the Nissan agency, it would be great if they would come in and talk to parents about soccer and be a sponsor of our sports area, and that's what they did with us. In each case, it was to link them in to a particular part of our community." Long-term plans for iVillage include establishing the site's own on-line shops to increase profitability.

At the 2000 Democratic National Convention, Evans moderated a panel called "From Soccer Moms to Webwise Women: Women, The Internet, and the 2000 Elections." Since April 1999 she has written a monthly advice column for *Redbook* magazine.

Nancy Evans lives with her husband, Seymour Wishman, and their daughter, Samantha, in Manhattan. Jann Wenner characterized Evans to Erik Larson for the *New Yorker* (October 11, 1999) as a hands-on perfectionist and taskmaster, but she is also known for her candor and ability to teach younger colleagues. For instance, Evans helped Macdara MacColl mature as a businessperson. MacColl began her career as a producer for iVillage and had a reputation as an intelligent worker who lacked interpersonal skills, as she discovered when she asked Evans for a promotion. "Nancy told me, 'People don't like working with you, and I think that will keep you from succeeding,'" MacColl recalled to Pamela Kruger and Katharine Mieszkowski for *Fast Company* (September 1998). "That was one of the most painful moments of my life." During the following months Evans helped MacColl change her behavior. Since then, MacColl has been named iVillage's vice president of member services and marketing. — T.J.F.

Suggested Reading: *Adweek* p22+ Sep. 23, 1996, with photos; *Fast Company* p93+ Sep. 1998; *New Yorker* p76+ Oct. 11, 1999, with photo; *Wired* (on-line) Feb. 8, 1999; *Who's Who in America, 1992–93*

Eyler, John

(EYE-ler)

1948(?)– President and CEO of Toys R Us Inc.
Address: Toys R Us Inc., 461 From Rd., Paramus, NJ 07652

In 1992, when John Eyler became president and CEO of FAO Schwarz, one of the most prestigious and well-known toy-store chains in the world, Stephanie Strom wrote for the *New York Times* (May 14, 1992) that the appointment was "something akin to being crowned king of Toyland." After an almost eight-year reign there, Eyler accepted a position as president and CEO of the industry giant Toys R Us Inc. Although it is less upscale than FAO Schwarz, Toys R Us, with almost 1,500 stores, is acknowledged to be the world's largest retailer of toys, clothing, baby items, and other children's products.

Little is known about the early years of John Eyler, who was born in about 1948. He graduated from the University of Washington, in Seattle, with

Courtesy of Toys R Us

John Eyler

a bachelor's degree and then received a master's of business administration from the Harvard University School of Business, in Cambridge, Massachusetts. He began his career in retailing at the May Department Stores Co., which had been founded in 1877 with one store in the silver-mining town of Leadville, Colorado. By the time Eyler joined the company, in 1979, it had developed into a large conglomerate with several affiliates, including Hecht's and Kaufmann's. In 1980, at the age of 32, Eyler became the president and CEO of the Denver-area May D & F division, which had been named in the late 1950s following the acquisition of the Colorado-based Daniels & Fischer Stores Co. He oversaw May D & F's stores until 1983, when he left the company to become the chairman and CEO of Main Street, the family-apparel branch of Federated Department Stores. During his six-year tenure Main Street expanded to 27 stores with 4,000 employees and $250 million in annual sales, but the division later disbanded.

Eyler next joined the Hartmarx Corp., a clothing manufacturer that also operated 27 small retail chains, which sold a mixture of brand-name and private-label apparel and accessories. He was appointed chairman and CEO of the company's specialty-stores division. The entire firm had been suffering badly when he arrived, due to a drop in the market for men's tailored suits—a significant segment of its sales—and Eyler set out to revitalize the retail stores. In 1991, instead of mailing a conventional holiday catalog to all the customers on Hartmax's mailing list, he had a specially made video sent to the 150,000 consumers who had purchased the most merchandise during the past year. Titled "A Picture Perfect Christmas," the 12-minute video depicted a photogenic family and their guests, all wearing clothing from Hartmarx stores. Eyler's move was considered fairly innovative at the time, and though that holiday season was not very profitable for most of the nation's retailers, industry analysts applauded Eyler's fresh approach to slumping sales. Eyler stayed with the ailing firm for three years, until Hartmarx merged the specialty-store business with Kuppenheimer, its retail division for men's discount clothing.

On May 13, 1992 Eyler was appointed president and CEO of FAO Schwarz. "I think it's going to be sort of like a second childhood," he told Stephanie Strom. "When you look at the store environment, these are the most exciting, most playful, most fun places to shop you can find anywhere in the world." FAO Schwarz, named for its founder Frederick August Otto Schwarz, had been in business since 1870 and had established itself as one of the all-time leading retailers of specialty toys. Its flagship shop on New York City's Fifth Avenue is visited yearly by more tourists than either the Statue of Liberty or the Empire State Building. The store has been the setting for several movie scenes—perhaps most memorably in the film *Big*, when Tom Hanks's character dances on a giant piano keyboard. But it appeared to analysts as though Eyler had jumped from one floundering company to another. FAO Schwarz had been purchased by the Dutch retail group Koninklijke Bijenkorf Beheer (KBB) in 1990, and in the year before Eyler's arrival, the toy store's losses were greater than they had ever been before. Eyler blamed the poor performance on the series of owners before KBB, who had lacked sufficient capital to keep the chain competitive.

With the support of the Dutch conglomerate, Eyler began implementing what he has called a "back to the future" policy. "It was a matter of looking at what had made FAO Schwarz great in the past—its capacity to create 'magic' for people," he told Marguerite Rigoglioso for a profile on the Harvard Business School Web site, "and restoring it to its former glory." To that end, Eyler initiated renovations of many of the chain's stores, including the one on Fifth Avenue, to which he added an elevator shaped like a huge robot. He changed the stock so that almost 70 percent of the toys were either totally exclusive to FAO Schwarz—such as the FAO Schwarz Barbie, who wears a sweatshirt bearing the store's logo—or hard to find. He decreed that rather than stock any toys on high shelves, all toys had to be displayed so that they could be readily demonstrated by specially trained sales associates or tried by customers. "The whole environment of FAO Schwarz encourages people to interact with the merchandise, not just take it off the shelf and pay for it and be out the door in 10 minutes," Eyler told Strom. "We beg our customers to play." He also announced plans to open several new stores overseas, explaining to Strom, "Around the world, everyone likes fantasy. And entering an FAO Schwarz store is making fantasy a reality."

Although Eyler kept close watch on trends in the toy industry, even FAO Schwarz was caught unaware by the popularity of the Tickle Me Elmo doll in 1996. The next year, in anticipation of a similar phenomenon, Eyler was careful to stock the New York store with 15,000 Sing and Snore Ernie dolls. He made frequent appearances at store functions, working the crowd at the opening of a new *Star Wars* boutique, for example, and showing up at the launch of a new line of dolls. Although FAO Schwarz's instantly recognizable name and carefully crafted image made it an undisputed marketing success, during his tenure the store posted several quarters of operating losses and diminishing profits.

When the retail giant Toys R Us asked Eyler to take the place of president and CEO Robert Nakasone, who had resigned unexpectedly amid dissension about the company's future direction and problems with its fledgling Web site, Eyler agreed. The company, founded in 1948, also operated a chain of children's-clothing stores, called Kids R Us, and a separate chain of stores for baby items, called Babies R Us. Eyler assumed his new responsibilities on January 17, 2000. At the time Toys R Us was facing stiff competition from the retailing behemoth Wal-Mart, and in the previous 12 months its stock prices, which had been weak for a decade, had fallen more than 25 percent. They fell even further after Eyler's appointment was announced. Some industry analysts believed that the drop stemmed from Eyler's reputation of working with losing companies. Others blamed the fact that he had been working for the most part with specialty toys rather than the mass-market items that Toys R Us carried.

In a statement quoted on *TheStreet.com* (January 11, 2000), Eyler said, "I look forward to working with the Toys R Us family to help the company reach its potential of being the premier retailer for toys and children's products." Industry insiders agreed that Eyler's task was formidable. In addition to falling stock prices (which would plummet another 27 percent during his first quarter at the company), problems with the Web site, and increased competition from other retailers, Toys R Us had experienced shortages of many of the 1999 holiday season's most popular toys, such as Pokémon and Game Boy systems. Eyler immediately announced plans to expand and diversify the stores' inventory, remodel aging stores, and repair the Web site. He also initiated an IPO in Japan of shares of Toys R Us–Japan; with 93 stores, Toys R Us–Japan accounted for 10 percent of the parent company's worldwide sales. Believing Toys R Us stock to be undervalued given the relative strength of its brand name, Eyler also instituted a new $1 billion share-repurchase plan to buy back shares of common stock in open-market or private transactions. By March 20, 2000 Anne Newman had written for *Business Week* that the company's last earnings announcement had exceeded all estimates, and she theorized that a turnaround for the company, while not assured, was at least a possibility. She quoted the investment analyst John Taylor as saying, "[Toys R Us] is not in damage-control mode any more." In May 2000 the chain's earnings rose for the first time in two years, a gain that Eyler attributed to better customer service and inventory control.

In August 2000 Toys R Us and Amazon.com merged their on-line toy-sales operations, acknowledging that marketing toys on the Internet had been too difficult for either of them acting individually. Standing alongside Jeff Bezos, the CEO of Amazon.com, Eyler was photographed smiling broadly and hugging a stuffed toy. On *Fortune* magazine's "Global 500" list of the world's largest corporations in 2000, Toys R Us ranked 416th. With revenues of $1.1682 billion, the company placed 148th on the "Fortune 500" list of the highest-grossing U.S. firms that year.

Eyler lives with his wife, Dolores, in Rye, New York; the couple have three sons. He is on the boards of directors of Toys R Us and Donna Karan International. In *Worth Magazine* (January 1994, on-line), James Kaplan described him as "gray-haired but boyish, smooth-faced, and cool-eyed, . . . the very model of the modern young chief executive." Kaplan noted that Eyler did not "bear any resemblance to some avuncular—or even flinty with a heart of mush—ideal of a toy-store boss." —M.R.

Suggested Reading: FAO Schwarz Web site; Harvard Business School Web site; *New York Times* D p1 Oct. 9, 1991, with photo, D p6 May 14, 1992; *Worth Magazine* (on-line) Jan. 1994

Fanning, Shawn

1981– Internet software developer; founder of Napster. Address: Napster, Inc., 4 W. 4th Ave., Suite 401, San Mateo, CA 94402

Clad in his typical attire—a baseball cap and jeans—Shawn Fanning may not seem like a young revolutionary. Yet, after he created the software for Napster, in 1999, Fanning became a central figure in one of the most far-reaching controversies that has erupted so far regarding the power of the Internet. Bearing the name that was his high-school alias, Napster is an openly available "shareware" program that users download onto their computers and then use to trade MP3 audio files with other users. (MP3, which is the acronym for MPEG layer3, is a program that compresses digitally recorded music into files that are one-11th their normal, uncompressed size; the condensed size of MP3 files makes sending and downloading music on the Internet, as well as storing and playing CD-quality audio files on desktop machines, faster and easier.) Napster, acting as the electronic conduit

Thomas Engstrom

Shawn Fanning

for MP3 files, thus makes it possible to disseminate music, in a highly efficient and relatively easy manner, for free. What began as underground software traded mostly by college students, who are the music industry's core market and who often have access to high-speed Internet connections, has since become the start-up company Napster, Inc. Located in the heart of Silicon Valley and nurtured by venture capital, the company and the controversy surrounding its product have been making headlines countrywide. "Napster is the nail in the coffin if you're in the business of selling digits on a disc," the music-industry consultant Jim Griffin told Karl Taro Greenfeld for *Time* (March 27, 2000, on-line). This kind of doomsday rhetoric has made record executives tremble, prompting the Recording Industry Association of America (RIAA) to file a lawsuit against Napster on behalf of 18 record companies. The conflict between Napster supporters and the RIAA is cast along familiar lines: on one side are mostly young, tech-savvy individuals who want free access to the music they love, even if it means circumventing copyright laws, and on the other are large corporations protecting their traditional base of money and power. If Napster and its users are not the perpetrators of a true social revolution, their cause has at least the air of one, having the potential, according to many experts, to affect profoundly the way many forms of media are controlled and disseminated in the near future.

Shawn Fanning was born in 1981 in Brockton, Massachusetts, into a household that already included eight children, one of whom was his mother, Colleen. When, at age 17, she became pregnant with Shawn, her father lent his support; Shawn's biological father did not. Colleen later married an ex-Marine who drove a delivery truck for a local bakery, and together they had four more children. "Money was always a pretty big issue," Fanning told Spencer Ante for *Business Week* (May 1, 2000, on-line). "There was a lot of tension around that." Fanning's uncle John, Colleen's younger brother, became a mentor to Shawn, giving him $100 for each "A" he earned in school and nurturing his interest in computers. When Fanning was a sophomore in high school, his uncle bought him his first computer, eventually adding an Internet connection and paying for a new phone line. "I saw this as a way for him to work his way out of his situation," John Fanning told Ante. "He absorbed the stuff faster than anyone I've ever known." Shawn soon discovered Internet Relay Chat (IRC), an application that enabled him to talk to people all over the world and trade knowledge about the Internet. At about the same time, Fanning's mother and her husband had a falling out, and Shawn and his siblings were placed in a foster home temporarily; despite the turmoil, he maintained his interest in computers.

During summer vacations in high school, Fanning worked as an intern at his uncle John's computer-games company, NetGames, and learned about programming from Carnegie Mellon University students who worked alongside him. After he graduated from high school, Fanning, having failed to gain admittance to the computer-science program at Carnegie Mellon, enrolled at Northeastern University, in Boston, where he was placed in junior- and senior-level courses as a freshman. Even so, he felt bored and looked elsewhere for stimulation. His roommates introduced him to MP3s, and soon he was downloading and collecting music files. Fanning's only previous programming experience had been in designing programs for the UNIX platform, but with the encouragement of his uncle and the help of a Windows programming book, he began designing his own music application for the Internet. After working 16-hour days for several weeks, Fanning had the prototype for Napster. On June 1, 1999 he tested the software by giving it to 30 friends, asking them not to tell anyone about it; they broke their promise, and within days it was on the Internet and had been downloaded by perhaps as many as 15,000 people. "I think the point at which I realized it had serious potential was when download.com put us in the download spotlight," Fanning told Giancarlo Varanini for the on-line magazine *ZDNet* (March 1, 2000). "It was very early . . . and we started receiving a ton of download. The server became overloaded, and that's when I realized that this had a huge market." Fanning's uncle also recognized the software's potential, and he incorporated Napster, Inc. on behalf of his nephew and quickly began to search for investors to develop the project. Later that summer, a fledgling company was in place in San Mateo, California, led by Eileen Richardson, a venture capitalist with 10 years of experience in the technology industry. Fanning left college to devote himself to Napster, Inc., becoming part of an expanding group of young people who leave or opt out of college in favor of joining Internet companies, as Shelley Donald Coolidge noted in the *Christian Science Monitor* (June 6, 2000). "That's why I ended up leaving school—because [refining the program] required so much time," Fanning told Varanini. "I figured I would regret not going full force with this idea. It seemed we could make something of it."

Fanning's concept for the software is elegant and surprisingly simple—what Bob Brand referred to in the *Newtown Bee* (March 10, 2000, on-line) as "a pure cyber-insight." The idea arose, Fanning has said, out of hearing his roommates complain about the difficulty of accessing MP3 files through the search engines available then, such as MP3.com and Scour.net. Napster software takes advantage of MP3 technology by serving as a forum through which users can search a database of songs and artists, chat about their favorite music, and trade audio files—the Internet generation's version of making bootlegged cassette tapes. Rather than using a centralized warehouse server, the program allows users to share the music files using their own computers, which often means fewer broken links and faster downloading time. Imagine this scenario: someone hears a song on the radio, and likes it so much that she wants to hear more music by the same artist. After downloading the Napster software to her computer, she searches for the music she wants in its large, evolving database of songs and artists. If another current Napster user has copied the music she's looking for into MP3 format and placed it on a designated file on his or her hard drive, the searcher can access it and download it onto her own computer. With the benefit of a fairly fast Internet connection, she can listen to music she wants in a matter of minutes, by using headphones or speakers on her computer, or on an MP3 player, or by copying, or "burning," the music onto a CD. The Napster software operates on the share-and-share-alike principle; each time a user turns on Napster, it will automatically post to its database a list of the files the user has designated to be shared, making them available to all other users. With a user base that is growing exponentially—at the rate of 5 percent to 25 percent a day, according to Greenfeld—the technology has found many fans. And, as a model of how people can use the Internet to share information and media, it has vast implications for the future. Napster and the forum it has created for music fans and musicians are a reminder that the "information superhighway" is truly a two-way street; its users can publish and sell as well as consume, borrow—and steal.

It is potential thievery that has caused so much acrimony in the music industry. Napster's technology has made it much easier to distribute music electronically and thereby circumvent the need to purchase CDs, greatly magnifying the threat to record companies posed by the Internet. Though some of the files traded through Napster's software are shared legally, much of what is available and being traded are copyrighted versions of the latest hits from big-name stars. The "fair use" doctrine of copyright law gives consumers the right to make copies of CDs for their personal use, but Napster makes copying on a much greater scale possible. A recent RIAA press release, quoted by Janelle Brown in the on-line magazine *Salon* (February 3, 2000), said as much: "Napster is similar to a giant online pirate bazaar: Users log onto Napster servers and make their previously personal MP3 collections available for download by other Napster users who are logged on at the same time. Napster provides its users with all the facilities and means to engage in massive copyright infringement." The company's position is that it is not guilty of wrongdoing since it does not keep any of the illegal files on its servers. Eileen Richardson, Napster's interim CEO, told Brown: "Napster is like an ISP [Internet Service Provider], protected under the 1998 Digital Millennium Copyright Act. It isn't the company's fault that people use its service to exchange illegal files, just as it wouldn't be AOL's legal responsibility if terrorists used one of its private chat rooms to plan a bombing." The RIAA, for its part, claims that, in providing an area for people to trade files illegally, Napster is liable.

Fanning, himself an amateur musician (he plays the guitar), originally conceived of the Napster software as a way to create a virtual network among the many niche groups of music listeners. In testimony before the Senate Judiciary Committee on October 9, 2000, as quoted on the Napster Web site, Fanning said that he hoped to create "genuine opportunity for participation, interaction, and individual involvement by the [Napster] members sharing files." The company runs a "New Artist Program" that gives serious music fans opportunities to find independent music that they would not typically encounter on FM radio play-lists or MTV and that, in turn, offers independent artists a chance to share their music and tap into a community of listeners. Richardson told Brown that Napster works as a music cooperative: "People are naturally passionate about music, naturally want to share it; artists naturally want to create and share their music and find their fans: That's what music is all about. Now we have the Internet—why can't we do some of that there?" The response from the music industry has been skeptical. "We love the idea of using technology to build artist communities, but that's not what Napster is all about," Cary Sherman, RIAA's senior executive vice president and general counsel, told Varanini. Sherman told Amy Harmon for the *New York Times* (March 7, 2000, on-line),"There's an incredible disconnect out there between what is normal behavior in the physical world versus the on-line world. There are people who think nothing of downloading entire CD collections on Napster who wouldn't dream of shoplifting from Tower Records. There's just a massive education program that's needed here for people to understand what goes into the creation of music."

Some intellectual-property lawyers have said that the existing laws favor Napster. Since the company doesn't actually control the music, which runs through the users' own computers, it would be very hard to prove that Napster is inducing illegal activity. Moreover, the RIAA will have to prove that Napster is used almost exclusively for illegal activity, which may be difficult, since the company also provides access to unsigned artists and has plans to allow users to trade other items, such as photographs, using its software. In early May, however, a federal judge decided not to dismiss the RIAA's lawsuit against Napster. Another judge recently found that MP3.com's vast on-line database of music constituted copyright infringement, and the company later reached a settlement with two labels involved in the suit, BMG Entertainment and Warner Music Group, agreeing to pay $20 million to each.

In an injunction issued on July 26, 2000 by Marilyn Hall Patel, a Federal District Court judge, Napster was ordered to remove all links to music copyrighted by major record labels by midnight July 28, which would have effectively shut down its business. In the two-day interval between the injunction and the deadline, Napster users flooded the site to make use of what they thought would be their final days of swapping music over the Internet; it was estimated that Napster logged on an average of 600,000 individual visitors each day. Then, on July 28, at Napster's request, the U.S. Court of Appeals for the Ninth Circuit granted a stay on the injunction. The federal appeals panel found, as expressed on its written order, that there were "substantial questions" concerning Patel's decision and issued a six-week formal appeals schedule. In October the RIAA and Napster made their arguments before a panel of judges from the Ninth Circuit Court of Appeals. As of early November, Napster was still awaiting the federal appeals court ruling on whether it can continue operating, pending trial in the lawsuit filed on behalf of RIAA.

Reactions to this controversy among the artistic community have been mixed. "I couldn't believe it when I found out that this Napster was linking thousands of people to the new Notorious BIG album, 'Born Again,' a week before it even hit the streets," the rap artist Sean Combs, also known as Puff Daddy, told Varanini. "This album is a labor of love from Notorious BIG's friends to the man, his kids, the rest of his family. . . . BIG and every other artist Napster abuses deserve respect for what they give us." In the *New York Times* (May 4, 2000, on-line), Barnaby J. Feder reported that representatives of the heavy-metal band Metallica brought to Napster headquarters a list of 300,000 names of people who had downloaded Metallica's music without the band's permission. Other artists seem to welcome the chance to be distributed to wider audiences through the Internet. The group They Might Be Giants released their latest recording in MP3 format only, and Courtney Love and her band, Hole, are in a legal fight to end their recording deal with Geffen Records. "Love is among the musicians raising the revolutionary notion that the Internet may offer them a better shake than the labels, which they accuse of imposing burdensome contracts," Alec Foege wrote for the *New York Times* (June 11, 2000, on-line). Foege pointed out that most artists get only pennies from the sale of each of their CDs; the rest of the money goes into production, marketing, promotion, and the record company's coffers. Napster's supporters also include the investors who so far have contributed $15 million in venture capital to the company. One venture capitalist, Stewart Alsop, said to Harmon, "Who's to say that because the music business is structured the way it is structured, that's the way it should always be structured? If I believe that the new model is a better way for artists to operate, that is a moral justification for feeling good about investing in Napster, even though technically what they're doing is facilitating illegal behavior."

The scale of copyright violation by Napster users, and the impossibility of enforcing the copyright law under such circumstances, may indicate that the law is lagging behind reality. Napster employees compare the controversy to the early days of the VCR, when the movie industry tried to prevent Sony from selling its Betamax machine because it could be used to make illegal copies of videocassettes. Eventually the Supreme Court ruled in favor of Sony, arguing that, though the machines could be used for illegal copying, they could also be used for a legitimate purpose. In the end, the spread of VCRs resulted in enormous extra profits for the movie industry. As with most Internet startups, Napster has yet to post a profit, but potentially it could thrive as a subscriber-based site, a marketing vehicle for record labels, or an e-commerce outlet for CDs and other merchandise. At a hearing before the House of Representatives' Small Business Committee in Washington, D.C., one digital entertainment analyst declared that it is "rash to assume that every time someone downloads an illegal music file, the recording industry has lost a sale," as Jeri Clausing quoted him as saying in the *New York Times* (May 25, 2000, on-line). "When music is free, people will try a lot they wouldn't have otherwise. And while Napster may have enabled the worst climate for casual piracy ever, the music industry is growing. Total revenue is up, CD shipments are up. It's worth wondering whether free music and MP3 swapping have stimulated sales."

On October 31, 2000 there was yet another development in the Napster legal saga. According to Matt Richtel and David D. Kirkpatrick in the *New York Times* (November 1, 2000, on-line), Napster and the German media giant Bertelsmann—whose subsidiary BMG is one of the five major record companies suing Napster—struck a deal to pursue a joint business strategy. Although details of the deal had not yet been hammered out, Bertelsmann agreed to lend Napster money to help Napster revamp its business plan. In essence, Napster will change course and charge a fee for its service, and then distribute part of that fee as royalties to record companies. As part of the deal, Bertelsmann received an option to buy a controlling stake in Napster. "This is a call for the industry to wake up," Thomas Middelhoff, chairman and chief executive of Bertelsmann, told Richtel and Kirkpatrick. "It is not enough to fight file sharing in the courtroom." The deal came as no surprise to the many industry observers who had predicted that rather than alienate their best customers by trying to shut down Napster and similar enterprises, record companies would ultimately join forces with them and explore ways to profit from on-line music distribution. The bare outlines for such a business model already exist. Some Web sites, such as *Emusic* and *Musicmaker.com*, provide secure music downloads for a fee. But there are other sites that mimic Napster's software, offering music for free with no central server, and some industry analysts speculate that Napster users will simply migrate to those sites rather than pay even a nominal fee for subscription services. The court case was still pending as the deal was being pursued.

In *Salon* (February 3, 2000), Scott Rosenberg argued that the CD will gradually vanish, just as the vinyl record and the shellac 78 did before it. "At some point, I think we will all wake up and accept that storing this stuff as discrete physical objects rather than data no longer makes any sense, except for collectors," he wrote. "Along with many new ways to catalog and access the music we love, we'll all gain a lot more shelf space. Meanwhile, the waves of change that are roiling the music world today will crash into the movie and TV industries next, as bandwidth improvements make the loose electronic redistribution of video as easy as audio has become today. No wonder the media behemoths are worried." Fanning himself foresees his company developing in many directions. "Napster is not media specific," he told Varanini. "I could see a system like Napster evolving into something that allows users to locate and retrieve different types of data other than just MP3s or audio files."

Currently, Fanning is hard at work in Silicon Valley, trying to improve Napster software. Two years ago his uncle John tracked down Shawn's biological father and facilitated a meeting between the two. "It was pretty strange," Shawn told Spencer Ante for *Business Week* in 2000; he learned, he said, that his father runs a software company. —M.A.H.

Suggested Reading: *Business Week* (on-line) May 1, 2000; *Fortune* p129+ Mar. 20, 2000; *New York Times* (on-line) Mar. 7, 2000; *Newsweek* (on-line) Mar. 27, 2000; *Salon* (on-line) Feb. 3, 2000, Feb. 4, 2000; *Time* (on-line) Mar. 27, 2000

Feldt, Gloria

Apr. 13, 1942– President of Planned Parenthood Federation of America. Address: Planned Parenthood Federation of America, 810 Seventh Ave., New York, NY 10019-5818

"Battles energize me," Gloria Feldt, president of the Planned Parenthood Federation of America (PPFA), told Sharon Lerner for *Ms.* (July/August 1996). If that is true, then Feldt should have plenty of energy: the PPFA is under constant attack from political conservatives and religious fundamentalists, whom she has accused of deliberately misrepresenting the nature of the services provided by the organization in order to further their anti–sex education and antiabortion agenda. Although abortion rights form an important aspect of PPFA's mission, Feldt emphasizes that the group's primary role is to improve education and health care for women. The fight she wages daily "isn't about abortion," she told Helen Thorpe for *Texas Monthly* (September 1996). "It's about women's role in society. It's about whether we're going to be a nation that embraces knowledge and education about responsible sex, as opposed to trying to keep people ignorant about it. I think the abortion debate is not about abortion at all. I really think it's much more about the future of women and children and families in this country."

© Bachrach, courtesy of Planned Parenthood Federation of America

Although Feldt had been a teenage mother, it was not until she was in her 30s that she began to realize how limited women's reproductive choices were, and to reflect on the number of women whose lives had been forever circumscribed because of their lack of education and resources. Her political awakening eventually led to her leadership of Planned Parenthood, the women's health and education service established by Margaret Sanger in 1916 in the New York City borough of Brooklyn. Under Feldt's guidance the organization has seen its influence expand significantly, both in the United States and around the world.

Gloria Feldt was born on April 13, 1942 in Temple, Texas. Her grandparents were among the wave of immigrants who arrived in the U.S. from Eastern Europe during World War I. Feldt's parents met in Temple and, after marrying, opened a clothing store. In 1955 Feldt's family moved to the town of Stamford, Texas. "I just wanted to be a blonde, all-American, normal girl," she told Michael Neill and Lynda Wright for *People* (June 24, 1996). "That meant all I was thinking about was who I was going to marry." When she was 15 Feldt married Wallace Bosse, a college football player from a local family of farmers. (The couple divorced in 1975.) By the time she was 20 years old, she was the mother of three children. Nonetheless, she found the time to earn her high-school diploma through a correspondence course and to attend the University of Texas, from which she graduated in 1974, at age 32, with a B.A. in sociology and speech.

Feldt's long career in activism began during her college years, with her involvement in the local Parent Teacher Association, the League of Women Voters, and the civil rights movement. She was also one of only five members of the National Organization of Women in the entire state of Texas. After getting a job as a teacher in a Head Start program, Feldt began to realize that in most young people's lives, lessons in family planning were virtually nonexistent. Her class was held in the parish hall of a Catholic church, whose independent-minded priest also happened to be on the board of Planned Parenthood in Odessa, Texas.

It was in this way that Feldt's association with PPFA began. In 1974 she was hired as the executive director of the Planned Parenthood office in Odessa. Planned Parenthood provides reproductive-health services and educational programs to women, men, and children nationwide. Its primary medical service is contraception, along with related health care and counseling. Although Planned Parenthood does provide abortions, most of the women who come to the organization seeking abortions are referred elsewhere. Feldt joined the staff of the Odessa office one year after the Supreme Court legalized abortion in the landmark *Roe v. Wade* decision and nine years after *Griswold v. Connecticut*, in which the court ended a ban on the use of contraception by married couples. In the four years that she served as the director of the affiliate, Feldt expanded Planned Parenthood's influence in the area considerably, increasing the number of clinics in Odessa from five to 11. In 1978 she became the executive director of the organization's Phoenix, Arizona, affiliate. Two years later she married Alex Barbanell, an insurance broker who had served on the committee that hired her. Feldt supervised Planned Parenthood's services in Phoenix for the next 18 years. In her tenure there she increased fund-raising 2,000 percent, expanded the annual budget six-fold, to $8 million, and increased the number of health centers from three to 16.

Feldt also received an education in political warfare, tangling with legislators and antiabortion activists over issues including family planning and sex education. In an address to the National Press Club in Washington, D.C., reprinted on PPFA's Web site (June 18, 1999), Feldt spoke about the necessity of the free exchange of ideas. "I love what [the political columnist] Molly Ivins calls 'the cacophony of democracy.' Democracy cannot survive unless we embrace controversy, learn from our differing perspectives, and thereby clarify the issues. We need more argument, not less. People should have the courage, the skills, and the opportunity to air their beliefs. That's how society makes progress." Doug Scott, now the head of the pro-life watchdog group Life Decisions International, was one of Feldt's primary adversaries in his position as the executive director of Arizona Right to Life. He described her as a "go-for-the-throat kind of person," Joe Maxwell wrote for the *World* (July 20/27, 1996, on-line). "She can be very personable. But if she decides she wants to take you on, she can just be vicious about it. She's smart."

In 1984 the pro-life congressman Jim Skelly persuaded the chairman of the board at Phoenix Memorial Hospital to deny Planned Parenthood the renewal of its lease at the institution. Feldt rose to the challenge, galvanizing supporters of family planning; gaining PPFA's approval for a major capital drive; organizing a letter-writing campaign; and conducting a public-opinion poll to prove that she had the support of members of the community. Soon the Phoenix affiliate had moved into a new location, and six additional clinics were opened. Feldt's enthusiasm also helped to attract new donors.

When Faye Wattleton, the president of Planned Parenthood Federation of America, resigned in 1993, Feldt was urged to succeed her, but for personal reasons, she did not believe that the timing was right. Planned Parenthood's next president, Pam Maraldo, hoped to move the organization toward a broader approach to women's health care that would forge a closer relationship with health management organizations, or HMOs. That strategy proved controversial, because of the widespread complaint that HMOs take decision-making from the hands of doctors and give that power to bureaucrats, whose primary concern is the bottom line rather than patients' well-being. The controversy provoked by this strategy led to Maraldo's resignation, and Feldt was promoted to the position in April 1996. Under Feldt's supervision Planned Parenthood continued to expand its services. Still, as Feldt explained to Sharon Lerner for *Ms.* (July/August 1996), "The manner in which we provide services may change over time, but the fundamental vision does not."

PPFA now has close to 1,000 health-care clinics as well as 152 affiliates in the United States. The organization successfully campaigned to prevent the 104th Congress from repealing Title X of the Public Health Service, which provides the organization with a budget of $41 million annually. "The moment [Title X] passed I realized that the whole thing was absurd," Feldt told Evan Smith for *Mother Jones* (March/April 1997). "We used so many resources to just hang on by our fingernails to a tiny program that doesn't begin to address the real family planning needs of American women." Feldt hopes to build a pro-choice majority in the Republican Party, and toward that end she has lobbied for passage of the Equity in Prescription Insurance and Coverage bill, which, if successful, will increase insurance coverage to include contraception.

Many young people were mobilized through *Vox: Voices for Planned Parenthood,* a national program aimed at educating 18-to-30-year-olds about family planning and reproductive freedom. "Over the last 30 or 40 years, America's university student community has constantly raised its voice to further freedom's cause," Feldt told students at New York's Barnard University, in a speech excerpted for Planned Parenthood's Web site (January 31, 2000). "But no one is truly free who cannot control her own body. That truth is what connects reproductive choice to every freedom movement that's ever been or ever will be."

Planned Parenthood's plans include the licensing of merchandise such as condoms and home pregnancy tests. The organization also produces many educational resources, including *Planned Parenthood Women's Health Encyclopedia,* recently published by Crown Books, and its award-winning video for families, *Talking about Sex.* PPFA has initiated a powerful political-action committee and increased its efforts to reach out to women of various cultural backgrounds. This initiative includes Global Partnerships, a program that will attempt to build relationships between Planned Parenthood and family-planning programs around the world. According to Feldt, Planned Parenthood's mission cannot be reduced to a single issue. "It's about unwanted children," she told Michael Neill and Lynda Wright. "It's about whether we're going to be able to live on this planet and survive."

Feldt maintains a busy lecture schedule, and her commentary is published regularly in the *New York Times*, the *Washington Post*, *USA Today*, and *Time*. She also appears frequently on many major television news and public-affairs programs. She has been recognized with numerous honors, including the Ruth Green Award, presented to her by PPFA's National Executive Directors Council in 1990, and the Martin Luther King Jr. Living the Dream Award, which she accepted from the Phoenix Human Relations Commission in 1996. In November 1998 *Vanity Fair* included her in its list of America's Top 200 Women Leaders, Legends, and Trailblazers.

Since she became Planned Parenthood's president, Feldt has divided her time between an apartment in New York and her family's home in Phoenix. She now has six children and nine grandchildren. Feldt's life has been threatened many times, so she avoids working alone after hours and maintains a home-security system. Although she believes that her opponents are often unfair in their misrepresentations of her organization, she defends their right to express their opinions. "It would be nice if there were a fairness doctrine, but the reality is, if somebody else is putting out ideas that you object to, you can't fault them for using the democratic process," she told Evan Smith. "What you have a responsibility to do is use the democratic process more and better. You need to call that talk show. You need to write that letter to the editor. That's the only antidote, because democracy is not about restraining people." — C.L.

Suggested Reading: *Mother Jones* p67+ Mar./Apr. 1997, with photo; *Ms.* p17 July/Aug. 1996, with photo; *People* p67+ June 24, 1996, with photos; *Texas Monthly* (on-line) 1996; *World* (on-line) July 20/27, 1996

Fincher, David

Aug. 28, 1963– Filmmaker; music-video director. Address: c/o Creative Artists Agency, 9830 Wilshire Blvd., Beverly Hills, CA 90212-1825

David Fincher's dark and cynical films combine an updated noir sensibility with meticulously crafted cinematography to create, in the opinion of many critics and moviegoers, hypnotic viewing experiences. Fincher's strong visual sense and clarity of purpose aid him in creating compelling tales of the complexity of human nature. *Seven*, for example, examines the essence of evil and its kinship with religious fundamentalism, while the controversial *Fight Club* explores the link between man's brutality and his sense of his own value, questioning whether the hunger for violence can ever be completely satiated. The filmmaker's other credits include *Alien 3* and *The Game.*

David Fincher was born on August 28, 1963 in Marin County, California. His father was a *Life* magazine reporter, and his mother worked in a clinic that sought to rehabilitate drug addicts. Inspired by *The Empire Strikes Back* and other films, many of which he saw with his father, Fincher dreamed of being a filmmaker from the time he was eight years old. "When I was younger," Fincher told Stephen Farber for the *New York Times* (August 31, 1997), "I studied painting, photography,

Armando Gallo/Retna Ltd.
David Fincher

and sculpture, but movies incorporated everything I loved. And I also liked the idea of being in control."

Unlike many of today's young directors, Fincher never attended film school or pursued a college degree. His first job was as a camera loader for Korty Films, an animation studio. Then, at the age of 18, he joined the staff at George Lucas's special-effects studio, Industrial Light and Magic (I.L.M.), where he worked on *Return of the Jedi* (1983) and *Indiana Jones and the Temple of Doom* (1984), among other pictures. Although he was able to learn much about filmmaking in a short time, Fincher left the company after a few years, feeling that his creative impulses were being stifled. As he explained to Stephen Farber, "I was not cut out for technical subservience. . . . I have problems with authority, and I'm definitely not a team player. I.L.M. was very team-oriented. But it was a good place to try things out." After leaving Industrial Light and Magic, Fincher worked for the American Cancer Society, where he directed a well-remembered public-service announcement that featured a fetus smoking a cigarette.

In 1986 Fincher and the producer Steven Golin founded Propaganda Films, a company that soon collected a roster of hot young directors. The Propaganda team today includes Michael Bay, the director of *The Rock* and *Armageddon*; Dominic Sena, whose credits include *Kalifornia*; Simon West, who made *Con Air* and *The General's Daughter*; and Antoine Fuqua, known for *The Replacement Killers*. Fincher has also directed many music videos and television commercials. The latter include advertisements for Coca-Cola, Nike, and Levi's, and among his videos are those for Madonna's "Vogue" and "Express Yourself," Aerosmith's "Janie's Got a Gun," George Michael's "Freedom 90," the Wallflowers' "Sixth Avenue Heartbreak," and the Rolling Stones' "Love Is Strong" (in which the band towers above Manhattan skyscrapers). In making his video for Don Henley's "The End of the Innocence," his ability to imitate the visual styles of other artists worked against him: the photographer Robert Frank sued Fincher, claiming that certain shots in the video too closely resembled images in Frank's book *The Americans.* He and Frank settled out of court.

Fincher won the assignment to direct *Alien 3*, one of a series of popular science-fiction films starring Sigourney Weaver, after a protracted process that saw the firing of the film's first director, Vincent Ward, as well as the hiring and sacking of several writers, including William Gibson, author of the prototypical cyberpunk novel *Neuromancer.* Although reports regarding the cost of *Alien 3* (1992) varied from $40 million to $60 million, the budget was certainly one of the largest ever entrusted to a director for his debut. Fincher, a fan of the *Alien* series, was characteristically single-minded regarding his choices. In an interview with John H. Richardson for *Premiere* (May 1992), he boldly stated, "I'm not making this movie for 50 million people. I'm making it for eight people, my friends, people who know cameras and lighting." Fincher's unconventional entry in the series, featuring a bald Weaver and an outer-space prison colony, proved less popular than the original film or its first sequel.

Seven (1995) brought Fincher into American moviegoers' consciousness, with its gruesomely detailed scenes and strong performances by Morgan Freeman, Brad Pitt, Gwyneth Paltrow, and Kevin Spacey—whose character, a deranged killer, disposes of his victims through a series of creative renderings of the seven deadly sins. (The fact that Spacey's name was left out of the opening credits added to the mystery of the film.) Fincher's widely praised visuals perfectly complemented Andrew Kevin Walker's script (his first), and the film was a success with critics and fans.

Fincher's next film was *The Game* (1997), a cautionary tale that stars Michael Douglas as Nicholas Van Orton, a rich and powerful man who finds his life dull and unfulfilling. On his 48th birthday, Nicholas's brother gives him a most unusual present: a gift certificate from Consumer Recreation Services, a mysterious entity that purports to provide thrills for its customers but wreaks havoc in Nicholas's life. The film effectively evokes the protagonist's growing paranoia and sense of helplessness as his identity is systematically stripped away and he must fight for his very survival; in this way it owes a debt to post-Watergate films of the 1970s, such as Francis Ford Coppola's *The Conversation* (1974) and Alan J. Pakula's *The Parallax View* (1974). "I like to subvert expectations," Fincher said to Stephen Farber about the film, adding, "I hope *The Game* is entertaining, but it's also a little prurient, a little sadistic, because you enjoy the suffering and anxiety of the central character. You want to see him learn a lesson. And nobody embraces that quite as eagerly as Michael Douglas."

Fincher outlined his approach to filmmaking in an interview with Fred Schruers for *Rolling Stone* (April 3, 1997): "My attitude is: Take the camera out of the box and work as hard as you can to tell your story as simply as possible. . . . You know, the best analogy for moviemaking is you're doing a watercolor from three blocks away through a telescope, with 40 people holding the brush, and you have a walkie talkie." In the same interview, Fincher recalled some advice he had received from filmmaker Martin Scorsese: "He said, 'Remember the mistakes that you make are as important a part of your style as the things you do well.' At a certain point you've just got to commit to something." Michael Douglas told Stephen Farber, "David is a stubborn guy, but it comes out of vision. I loved the extent to which he would go to re-create the picture he had in his mind." Douglas said to Fred Schruers, "David lives and breathes movies. He doesn't have any hobbies. He is consumed by film."

Fincher's latest film is *Fight Club* (1999), a daring adaptation of Chuck Palahniuk's novel about disenchanted men who find that fighting is the only way to break through the malaise they experience as participants in the consumer culture. The film stars Edward Norton as the Narrator, an average drudge whose life has lost so much of its meaning that he must attend support groups for the sick and dying in order to feel any emotion. At one of these meetings he spots Marla (Helena Bonham Carter), another "tourist," with whom he strikes up a contentious friendship. The arrival of Tyler Durden (Brad Pitt), a charming but dangerous instigator, leads the Narrator down the road toward liberation through anarchy. *Fight Club* is a satire that targets both capitalism and the New Age trends that buffer its effects. In an interview with Gavin Smith for *Film Comment* (September/October 1999), Fincher referred to the film as "a stylized version of our Ikea present. It is talking about very simple concepts. We're designed to be hunters and we're in a society of shopping. There's nothing to kill anymore, there's nothing to fight, nothing to overcome, nothing to explore. In that societal emasculation this everyman is created." The men in *Fight Club* attempt to combat this emasculation by beating each other and, finally, by planning acts of terrorism designed to cripple big business.

Discussing the film, Norton explained to Johanna Schneller for *Premiere* (August 1997), "*Fight Club* has a generational energy to it, a protest energy. . . . So much of what's been represented about my generation has been done by the baby boomers. They dismiss us: the word slacker, the oversimplification of the Gen-X mentality as one of hesitancy or negativity. It isn't just aimlessness we feel; it's deep skepticism. It's not slackerdom; it's profound cynicism, even despair, even paralysis, in the face of an onslaught of information and technology."

Fight Club employs many different cinematic devices to lead the viewer inside the mind of a narrator who may be losing his sanity. The film begins, for example, in the fear center of the Narrator's brain; the protagonist's hopes, anxieties, and suspicions are represented visually, and time is rendered in a decidedly nonlinear fashion. All of this points toward a new film language, one that attempts to portray the inner workings of the human mind.

Fincher's firm grasp of the technical aspects of filmmaking, coupled with a willingness to explore the dark recesses of the human condition, contributes to his growing reputation as a postmodern commentator and observer of the harsh realities of contemporary society. — C.L.

Suggested Reading: *Film Comment* p58+ Sep./Oct. 1999, with photos; *New York Times* II p9+ Aug. 31, 1997, with photo; *Premiere* p62+ May 1992, with photos, p68+ Aug. 1999; *Rolling Stone* p52+ Apr. 3, 1997

Selected Films: *Alien 3*, 1992; *Seven*, 1995; *The Game*, 1997; *Fight Club*, 1999

Courtesy of Hewlett-Packard Corp.

Fiorina, Carleton

Sep. 6, 1954– CEO of Hewlett-Packard. Address: Hewlett-Packard, 3000 Hanover St., Palo Alto, CA 94304-1185

"I hope that we are at a point that everyone has figured out that there is not a glass ceiling," Carleton Fiorina said at a press conference announcing her appointment as chief executive officer of Hewlett-Packard, the world's second-largest computer company, as quoted by John Markoff in the *New York Times* (July 20, 1999). "My gender is interesting but not really the subject of the story here." Her remark did not stop most of the reporters present from making her gender the focus of their articles. That wasn't surprising, in light of the fact that Fiorina is currently the only woman to hold the post of CEO at a Dow 30 company (that is, one of the 30 "blue-chip" companies chosen for calculating the stock-market barometer known as the Dow Jones industrial average), and one of only three—the others are Jill E. Barad of Mattel and Marion O. Sandler of Golden West Financial—to head a *Fortune* 500 firm (one of the nation's top 500 companies, as ranked in terms of revenue by *Fortune* magazine). None of the journalists suggested that Fiorina won the position *because* she is female, however; her managerial savvy and other outstanding abilities are too well documented for anyone to even hint such a thing. For two years before taking the helm at Hewlett-Packard, Fiorina had headed a $20 billion division of Lucent Technologies; a year before that, she had planned and directed the phenomenally successful initial public offering of Lucent and the company's subsequent spinoff from AT&T, where she began her career in the telecommunications industry in 1980. "No woman [before Fiorina] has achieved leadership at this level of American business," Sheila W. Wellington, the president of Catalyst, an advocacy organization for the advancement of women in the corporate world, told Karl Taro Greenfeld for *Time* (August 2, 1999) after Fiorina's appointment at Hewlett-Packard was made public. What Fiorina has accomplished, Wellington declared, is "going to give young women, girls, a powerful message." Fiorina herself believes, as quoted by Patricia Sellers in *Fortune* (October 12, 1998), that "anytime you have a fiercely competitive, change-oriented growth business where results count and merit matters, women will rise to the top."

Fiorina was born Cara Carleton Sneed to Joseph and Madelon Sneed on September 6, 1954 in Austin, Texas. During the American Civil War, all her Sneed ancestors with the given name Carleton were killed. To honor them, each of their descendants have named a son Carleton or a daughter Cara Carleton. Carly Fiorina, as she is universally known, is the ninth Cara Carleton to be born in her family since the Civil War ended, 135 years ago. Fiorina's father was a federal court judge and law professor; her mother, who died in 1998, was a painter. In another era, Fiorina believes, her mother would have become a fine businesswoman. "She was the strongest person I've ever known," Fiorina told Peter Burrows and Peter Elstrom for *Business Week* (August 2, 1999). "She had an unquenchable zest for life. She worked incredibly hard to make me the best person I could be." Fiorina has credited her parents for teaching her to think positively and never to limit her dreams.

The Fiorina family moved several times during Carly's childhood and adolescence; as a result, Fiorina attended five different high schools, including one in Ghana. She got her undergraduate education at Stanford University, in California, where she earned a bachelor's degree in medieval history and philosophy, with honors, in 1976. For a brief period during her college years, she worked at Hewlett-Packard as a secretary. Although she had once entertained the thought of becoming a classical pianist, Fiorina decided to follow in her father's footsteps and attend law school. She persevered for one year at the University of California at Los Angeles (UCLA) law school, but she disliked it so intensely that she decided to drop out. She has said that telling her father about her decision was one of the hardest things she has ever done.

During much of the following year or two, Fiorina seemed to lack direction. For a while she taught English in Italy; she was also married briefly, in California. "Had anyone told me that I was going to have a career in business, I would have said, 'No way,'" she recalled to Patricia Sellers. Nevertheless, in about 1979 she entered a graduate program at the Robert H. Smith School of Business at the University of Maryland in College Park to study marketing, and she was awarded an M.B.A. degree there in 1980. She then got a job as an account executive for AT&T Long Lines, AT&T's core long-distance division. When she was invited to participate in the company's savings plan, she refused, because she thought that she would not find corporate work satisfying and would not remain with AT&T long enough to reap the benefits of the plan. But she was wrong. Not only did she enjoy her job, she was an almost immediate success, making her mark by selling phone services to large federal agencies.

Fiorina next took a step that puzzled many of her colleagues: she transferred to Network Systems, AT&T's decidedly unglamorous equipment-manufacturing division. "The rap on Network Systems was that it was all guys with 20-inch necks and pea-sized brains. You know, heavy metal bending," Fiorina told Patricia Sellers. "I went because it was a huge challenge, completely male dominated, and outside everything I'd experienced." Fiorina is "comfortable in uncomfortable situations," Daniel C. Stanzione, who at that time was the president of the Network Systems' Global Public Networks, observed to Burrows and Elstrom. Fiorina's ability to adapt to unusual situations and her willingness to participate in typically male bonding rituals gained her acceptance in the male-oriented business worlds of South Korea, Japan, and Taiwan, where she often traveled for her job. And it helped make her a standout at AT&T, too: at 35 she became the company's first female officer, and by age 40, she was heading its North American operations.

Fiorina's marketing and sales prowess became legendary within the company. When AT&T's subsidiary Bell Atlantic wanted to diminish the time it took to fill orders for phone equipment, Fiorina decreased the wait from nine months to three. When a large telecommunications company requested a certain type of switch for its wireless business, she provided a switch that could handle not only wireless but long-distance traffic as well, at a cost no higher than that of a single-function switch. "She never just tries to sell the customer a box," Nina Aversano, who in 1995 was president of the Global Commercial Markets division of AT&T Network Systems, told Burrows and Elstrom. "I remember we were talking with the chairman of a major Internet company and [Fiorina] asked, 'What keeps you up at night?' That's the attitude she has."

When At&T decided to combine Western Electric and Bell Labs, in 1996, Fiorina was chosen, from a large pool of qualified senior personnel, to orchestrate the initial public offering (IPO) of the new company and help develop a corporate image for it. The IPO for Lucent Technologies, as the company was named, turned out to be the biggest ($3 billion) in business history, and most of the credit for its success went to Fiorina. "Carly is wickedly smart," Rich McGinn, Lucent's CEO, who had handpicked her for the undertaking, told Patricia Sellers. "I told her that given her knowledge of the outside world and her ability to synthesize disparate flows of information, no one could do the job better." Fiorina subsequently handled Lucent's spinoff from AT&T. It was she who chose Lucent's logo—a roughly rendered, bright red "O"; the design appealed to her because it reminded her of one of her mother's abstract paintings.

After Fiorina was appointed president of Lucent's consumer-products division, she reached the conclusion that selling such merchandise was not in Lucent's best interest. She therefore sold much of the business to the large Dutch firm Philips Electronics. By doing so, she eliminated her own position. Commenting on her action, Harry Schact, who had recently retired as Lucent's chairman, told Patricia Sellers, "Remember, this is the company that invented the telephone, so the idea of giving up that business wasn't obvious to any of us at the time. Carly made an absolutely correct decision. And she did it without knowing what her next job would be." That next job, which Fiorina took in 1997, was group president of the arm of Lucent Technologies known as the Global Service Provider business. Under her leadership the division grew dramatically, gaining shares in every part of the U.S. and expanding its international market. With more than $20 billion in annual receipts as of July 1999, it accounted for 60 percent of Lucent's total revenues.

In its October 1998 issue, *Fortune* magazine ranked Fiorina at the top among the 50 most powerful women in American business. "Fiorina is a star in nothing less than the hottest, most important industry in American business: telecommunications," the editors of *Fortune* declared. "Without it, or the products her company produces, few of us could do our jobs. . . . Fiorina, as president of Lucent's core Global Service Provider division, sells no less than 'the things that make communications work'—big-ticket networking systems and software for telephone, Internet, and wireless-service operators around the globe. In short, she's at the center of the ongoing technology revolution that's changing how we live and work."

On July 19, 1999 Hewlett-Packard, which is based in Palo Alto, California, and is often referred to in the media as HP, announced the appointment of Fiorina as the company's new president and CEO. Fiorina succeeded Lewis Platt, who had decided to retire a year early and who remained as chairman of HP until the end of 1999. "Leaving Lucent was a very difficult decision, but this is a once-in-a-lifetime opportunity for me," she said, as quoted by *Silicon Valley Daily* (on-line). "Hewlett-Packard is a company of great accomplishment and even greater potential. HP has a proud history, a powerful brand, superb technology, talented employees, strong partner and customer relationships, and an innovative new e-services strategy. . . . I will strive to strike the right balance between reinforcing HP's values and working to reinvent its business."

According to many industry analysts, striking that balance will probably be Fiorina's greatest challenge. Founded in 1938 by William R. Hewlett and David Packard, who, with combined capital of $538, built their first product, an electronic test instrument, in a Palo Alto garage, the firm became renowned for its engineering proficiency. In recent years it was reputed to have a stodgy corporate culture, with marketing and sales low on the agenda, and to be slow to take bold steps in new directions—a real disadvantage in today's fast-paced, Web-driven world. For example, at the time of Fiorina's appointment, Hewlett-Packard had not introduced a breakthrough product since the inkjet printer, in 1984. According to Lewis Platt, Hewlett-Packard's board expected Fiorina to change all that. "We are convinced she has the talent and toughness to reinvent our businesses without losing sight of HP's core values," he told Jennifer Hagendorf for *Computer Reseller News* (on-line). In the end the board decided that now was the time for fresh leadership. Carly Fiorina was the first choice of the search committee and the only candidate presented to the full board.

Ranked 13th on the *Fortune* 500 list in 2000 and 43d on the magazine's list of the best companies to work for in the U.S., Hewlett-Packard earned $48.2 billion in net revenues in its 1999–2000 fiscal year. With more than half of its business coming from outside the U.S., it is one of the nation's top exporters. In mid-2000 HP split into two companies. One, which retained the HP name, has continued the firm's computing and imaging businesses, which accounted for about $40 billion of HP's fiscal 1998 revenue; as the president and CEO of this company, Fiorina has 87,000 employees under her. The other company, called Agilent Technologies, is headed by Edward W. ("Ned") Barnholt; it handles HP's measurement business (which includes the production of medical electronic equipment and instruments for chemical analysis) and semiconductor products.

On November 15, 1999 Fiorina gave the keynote speech at Comdex/Fall '99, a computer trade show. "I believe an absolute mandate is that companies need to build a culture of radical ideas," she said in her address, as transcribed on the Hewlett-Packard Web site. "Take a look at your company culture, and ask yourself: Is this a place where unorthodox ideas are allowed to flourish? Is it a place that encourages creativity? In an economy of ideas, your worth depends almost exclusively on you building that kind of culture." Later that day Fiorina announced that Hewlett-Packard was introducing a new logo as part of a $200 million global brand campaign. "Our brand is the strongest expression of who we are," she said. "We are a company founded by inventors, fueled by invention, and adept at reinventing ourselves to track with new market opportunities. Our new brand will give us a clearer, stronger voice in the marketplace, and the world will get a picture of us that reflects our true inventiveness."

Fiorina's management style is said to inspire fierce loyalty among her staff. She has often given employees flowers or balloons to celebrate their achievements and is said to try to make sure that they receive proper medical advice and emotional support when they are ill. She has been known to stay with people who are working late on a project and to call workers who she knows are struggling with a problem. Offering an example of her managerial astuteness, Michael Meyer reported in *Newsweek* (August 2, 1999) that at a gathering of Lucent executives to celebrate a year of record profits, she asked, "So where do we go from here? I know you won't want to rest on your laurels." According to an employee present at the meeting, her words illustrated her knack for gentle encouragement. "The boss didn't say, 'Great job, but I'm not satisfied.' Instead, it was, 'You're wonderful, and I know you want to do even better,'" the person pointed out.

Fiorina holds a master of science degree from the Sloan School of Management at the Massachusetts Institute of Technology, in Cambridge. She is a member of the board of directors of Merck & Co. and the Kellogg Co. Earlier she served on the boards of Goldstar Information & Communications, Inc., of Seoul, Korea, AT&T Taiwan Telecommunications, of Taipei, Taiwan, and the United States–Republic of China Economic Council. Recently, she was elected to the United States–China Board of Trade. Fiorina's husband, Frank Fiorina, was a vice president at AT&T when he took early retirement, in 1998, at the age of 49. The couple have two grown daughters from Frank's first marriage and a granddaughter, named Carly. — M.R.

Suggested Reading: *Business Week* p76+ Aug. 2, 1999, with photos; *Fortune* p76+ Oct. 12, 1998, with photos; Hewlett-Packard Web site; *New York Times* C p8 Sep. 29, 1999, with photo; *Newsweek* p56 Aug. 2, 1999, with photos; *Time* p72 Aug. 2, 1999, with photo; *U.S. News & World Report* p44+ Aug. 2, 1999, with photo; *Wall Street Journal* B p1+ July 20, 1999

Joseph Marzullo/Retna Ltd.

Flair, Ric

Feb. 25, 1949– Wrestler. Address: c/o World Championship Wrestling, 1 CNN Center, Box 105366, Atlanta, GA 30348-5366

Stalking the ring like a mad dictator, taunting his opponents with cocksure brashness, and letting loose with his trademark rallying cry of "Whooo!," the wrestler Ric Flair has sparked the ire and adulation of fans with equal measure. A self-proclaimed "stylin', profilin', limousine ridin' son of a gun," with his shock of electric-white hair, dazzlingly gaudy robes, theatrical entrances, and formidable ring skills, Flair has been a major figure in the sport for over a quarter-century. "No one has mastered [the] peculiar blend of Flairsport and theater like Ric Flair," Mike Mooneyham noted for the *Charleston Post & Courier* (February 20, 1997). "He has been to wrestling what Muhammad Ali was to boxing." A master of high drama, Flair has been at the center of some of the most notorious scenarios the circus-like world of pro wrestling has ever seen. Recently, for example, his son David—also a wrestler—had him committed to a mental institution; after escaping, Flair repaid his son's treachery by secretly orchestrating a match that ended with David's being taken out of the ring on a stretcher. While Flair's status as an icon has many regarding him with reverence, he much prefers playing the villain. "I like being a heel," he told Mary Elizabeth Deangelis for the *Charlotte Observer* (May 9, 1999). "I'm good at it."

The wrestler was born Richard Morgan Fliehr into a wealthy family on February 25, 1949 in Memphis, Tennessee. When he was young his family moved to Edina, Minnesota, where he spent the remainder of his childhood. His father, Dick Fliehr, was an obstetrician; his mother, Kay Fliehr, worked as a marketing executive for the Guthrie Theater in Minneapolis. Feeling that school was a waste of time that kept him from playing sports and hanging out with friends, Flair brought home poor grades. Eventually, his parents sent him to Wayland Academy, a military prep school in Wisconsin. "I had to either go to a military school or boarding school," he told Mooneyham. "I wasn't a bad kid, just a little wild. No trouble with the police or anything like that. . . . They knew that I was under-achieving." During his junior year at Wayland, he won the Wisconsin state wrestling championship.

In his senior year Flair was offered football scholarships from colleges in Wisconsin, Illinois, Nebraska, Arizona, and Michigan. He signed a letter of intent with Michigan State, but his academic counselor refused to write a letter that would have enabled him to attend the school. "I had already made three trips to Michigan and made up my mind," he told Mooneyham. "I loved it there. But he [the counselor at Wayland] wouldn't do it. All he had to do was write a letter. And I haven't given a dime to the school ever since. They write me every year, asking for appearances. That was a major thing to do to me." Flair returned home to Minnesota, where he attended the state university on a football scholarship. He played offensive and defensive guard for a year before losing his academic eligibility and leaving school. "I guess I could still be playing football now, but I realized a college education wasn't going to make me any money," he told Bob Heller for the *Charlotte Observer* (1976, on-line).

After selling life insurance for a year, Flair enrolled in the training camp run by the midwestern wrestling star Verne Gagne. At first he found the regimen there too grueling, and he dropped out; he returned before long, however, and ultimately finished the program. He was living with Ken Patera, who had wrestled in the 1972 Olympics and who "had pretty much decided to be a pro wrestler," as Flair said in an interview with Shannon Stanfield for the *Knoxville News-Sentinel* (August 22, 1997, on-line). "I seized the opportunity to follow him . . . and was lucky enough to be with the right people at the right time, and it worked out real well." Flair had put off telling his parents about his new pursuit. "I don't know what they thought," he told Mooneyham. "They knew I liked [wrestling] and that I watched it on TV, but they had no idea." In time, his parents came to respect his decision.

Flair's first professional match took place on December 10, 1972 in Rice Lake, Wisconsin, where he grappled with George "Scrapiron" Gadaski to a 10-minute draw. "That first match was phenomenal," Flair noted in the *Ric Flair Record Book*, as quoted by Coveh Solaimani in the *Richmond Times Dispatch* (June 10, 1999, on-line). "I was really confident in what I had learned." Once Flair stepped into the ring, it became apparent to those who knew him that he had found his calling. "He struck me as having a complete personality change," his mother told Deangelis. "It was an eye-opener—this kid was serious. There wasn't anything that was going to stop him." Shortly after starting his career, Flair headed south to Charlotte, North Carolina, and soon he began collecting titles in both tag-team and solo matches in the Mid-Atlantic League. While his career seemed to be taking off, the money had yet to start rolling in. Flair has recalled sleeping in a $9-a-night motel room, eating on a tab at a local restaurant, and hitchhiking to the Charlotte coliseum to compete. He used his first paycheck, in the amount of $1,000, to buy a used Cadillac. "That's terrible, isn't it?" he remarked to Mooneyham. "I wanted to be somebody and all the big guys had Cadillacs."

Things were on the upswing for Flair when his career was almost ended by a plane crash on October 4, 1975. "When we got up to 4,000 feet, 18 miles out of Wilmington, we ran out of gas . . . ," he recalled for *prowrestling.com*. "When a plane runs out of gas, the propellers do not go 'put, put, put.' . . . You go straight down, and we actually hit the ground after going through a mass of trees. . . . We stopped at a railroad bank at about 300 miles per hour." Flair broke his back in three places, and doctors told him that he would never walk again. Refusing to accept the diagnosis, he threw himself into an intensive rehabilitation regimen. Within six months he was back in the ring. "I was apprehensive at first," he recalled to Solaimani. "I was very nervous. I called the doctor 10 times that day making sure it was OK."

After returning to wrestling, Flair began cultivating the "black hat" personality that would become his trademark. To start, he adopted "Nature Boy" as a nickname. "The promoter I was working for at that time kinda came up with that handle for me," Flair told Stanfield. "He thought I resembled Buddy Rogers, who was the original 'Nature Boy.'" Flair began storming through the Carolinas and Virginia, wrestling more than 300 nights a year. His over-the-top histrionics, blended with his natural charisma, endeared him to fans, and he became a sensation almost overnight. His bone-crunching matches with such heavyweights as Ricky Steamboat, Wahoo McDaniel, Jimmy Snuka, and Roddy Piper remain some of the best-remembered in the region. In the ring, Flair combined skill and stamina, creating such signature moves as the figure four leglock and the flying knee drop and spilling more than his share of his own blood on the mat. "So much goes into our business to be successful," Flair told Kevin Eck for the *Baltimore Sun* (online), "from being a great in-ring performer to being able to convey your real-life enthusiasm for what you do and send it through the television monitor. I knew that every time I got in the ring, beyond a shadow of a doubt, that there was no one that was remotely close to me." During the remainder of the 1970s, Flair collected numerous titles, alternating between the heavyweight title and the tag-team championship, which he shared with his longtime partner, Greg Valentine.

By the start of the 1980s, Flair had emerged as one of the most dynamic performers in the business. Traveling the world to defend his title against some of the most notorious opponents available, he struck promoters for the National Wrestling Alliance (NWA) as having the makings of a national icon. "When he was on," David Meltzer told Solaimani, "nobody could do a better angle or interview than Flair." Flair took the world championship for the first time on September 17, 1981, in a thunderous match with Dusty Rhodes. Critics initially dismissed the win as a fluke and predicted that Flair would be unable to repeat it. But the wrestler had other ideas. He went on to win the title 14 more times in the 1980s. In addition to crushing all comers on the world-title circuit, in 1986 Flair formed an alliance with fellow wrestlers Ole and Arn Anderson and Tully Blanchard to create the Four Horsemen, a name inspired by the biblical figures whose arrival signals the apocalypse. The Four Horsemen proceeded to storm wrestling rings the world over, leaving a slew of crushed opponents in their wake. With the advent of cable television, the crusades of the Four Horsemen were beamed into homes everywhere. Soon fans from all over were holding up four fingers in homage to the Horsemen. "It was the greatest array of talent ever assembled in one limousine, one hotel room, one dressing room, and one bar of all time," Flair told Solaimani.

Entering the 1990s, Flair found himself somewhat disillusioned with the wrestling business. The World Championship Wrestling league (WCW) had relegated Flair and the NWA to a backseat position. WCW head Jim Herd, feeling that Flair was past his prime, asked him to reduce his role and salary when his contract was up, in the summer of 1991. Flair refused and took his act to the rival World Wrestling Federation (WWF). There, he felt revitalized, working with WWF president Vince McMahon and clashing with such WWF mainstays as Hulk Hogan and Randy Savage. "It was a great time for me," Flair told Solaimani. "It was probably as much fun as I've had except for the late 80s with the Horsemen."

In 1993, following an amicable split with McMahon, who wanted to move him down to midcard status, Flair—believing he still was in the running for the world title—decided to return to the WCW. Shortly thereafter, he was again the WCW's champion. As the decade progressed, Flair's persona developed even further. He staged a retirement match in 1994, only to return in glory a year later. In addition, he has now claimed the title of "on-air" president of the WCW. That position has allowed him to adopt the role of Machiavellian taskmaster in a series of ever-twisting story lines that have become the staple of the TNT cable network's *Nitro*, a two-hour wrestling blitz that dominates its time slot on cable. It wasn't long after Flair's return that old rivalries began to resurface; within six months the WCW had also signed Hulk Hogan, Flair's arch-nemesis from the WWF. Hogan and Flair met in what was billed as "The Match of the Century." Hogan's higher profile with fans made the conclusion of the match rather predictable, and Flair lost his title. (Although it is now common knowledge that the outcomes of professional wrestling matches are often predetermined, Flair's prowess as an athlete has served him well in executing countless falls, leaps, and opponent-tossings over the years. Also, while pro wrestling has always been theatrical, many of the victories Flair has amassed—particularly in the early part of his career—have been genuine.) Flair and Hogan were to clash several more times, the most recent match occurring in June 1999, in which Flair claimed his 14th championship title.

In 1998 Flair was sued for breach of contract by WCW president Eric Bischoff, who claimed that the wrestler had missed a scheduled TV appearance in April of that year. Flair instantly countersued, insisting that he had been granted permission to miss the performance so that he could watch his 10-year-old son, Reid, compete in a wrestling tournament. "It was time to take a stand," Flair told Solaimani. "I wasn't going to let my son down." The suit dragged on for several months, during which Flair did not wrestle at all. "It's just been really hard for me to make an adjustment," he said in a 1998 interview with Bruce Mitchell on WKEW, in Greensboro, North Carolina. "I'm so used to being gone and being on the end of that lightning bolt that revolves around that telephone ringing with someone saying you have to be somewhere. . . . I've just had to re-educate myself to being home; it's not too bad actually." The actions of the WCW served to galvanize Flair's fans, who inundated the company's offices with angry phone calls and E-mail, boycotted events, and passed out strongly worded pamphlets protesting the WCW's actions. Eventually, the suit was settled out of court, and Flair returned to the ring on September 14, 1998, to the roar of adoring fans. The standing ovation he received was so overwhelming that it moved him to uncharacteristic tears. "It was the most emotional moment and the highlight of my career," Flair told Solaimani.

After 25 years of blazing around the world, Flair has lately forsaken all-night parties and year-long blitzes on the road in favor of spending time with Beth, his wife of 16 years, and their children—Reid, now 11, and Ashley, 13. Flair has two children from a previous marriage: David, 20, who has followed his father's footsteps into the world of professional wrestling, and Megan, 25, who recently graduated from nursing school. In addition to his work with the WCW, Flair is a partner in nine Gold's Gyms in and around North Carolina. While there are many theories regarding Flair's longevity in a rather unforgiving business, promoter Larry Matysik believes that the explanation is simple. "Ric is a very dynamic performer and wrestler," he told Keith Schildroth for the *St. Louis Post-Dispatch* (December 19, 1998, on-line). "He understands the crowd and doesn't need the music, face paint, or fireworks to win his audience over. He's never needed that stuff. He knows what people want." — J.K.B.

Suggested Reading: *Charleston Post & Courier* (on-line) Feb. 20, 1997; *Charlotte Observer* (on-line) May 9, 1999; *Entertainment Weekly* p17+ Apr. 16, 1999, with photos; *Knoxville News-Sentinel* (on-line) Aug. 22, 1997; *Richmond Times-Dispatch* (on-line) June 10, 1999

Courtesy of Levinson Fontana Co.

Fontana, Tom

Sep. 12, 1951– Television producer and writer. Address: Levinson Fontana Co., 448 W. 16th St., Sixth Fl., New York, NY 10011

Tom Fontana, who has penned some of television's most intelligent series, has distinguished himself from other TV writers and producers by his refusal to kowtow to network executives and the Nielsen ratings. Though Fontana's shows have not proven to be network cash cows on the level of, say, *The Cosby Show* or *Seinfeld*, he has built a reputation in the industry among actors, critics, and other dramatists as one of the most prolific and profound writers for the small screen. Beginning with his work on NBC's *St. Elsewhere*, an hour-long medical drama set at a fictional, maligned municipal hospital in Boston, and continuing with *Homicide: Life on the Street*, also on NBC, which took an intimate look at the workings of a Baltimore police precinct's homicide division, Fontana made his name by finding the extraordinary in the quotidian. Since 1997 he has brought audiences into the bowels of a fictional state penitentiary with his one-hour drama series *Oz*. In *Oz*, which is broadcast weekly on the HBO cable network, where shows are not subject to the censorship rules that govern over-the-air networks, Fontana has the freedom to use his particular brand of gritty realism to its fullest, most brutal effect. "He's like a late 20th-century American version of [the 19th-century British novelist Charles] Dickens," the actor Austin Pendleton, who starred in a Fontana play in the early 1980s and has had roles on *Homicide* and *Oz*, said of the writer to Diane Snyder for *APBNews* (July 13, 1999, on-line). "More than anybody who's writing now, he really heads right into all the darkest things that are going on today in America, and that's so exciting to actors. You really feel that you're right at the heart of it when you work on his shows."

The son of Charles Louis and Marie Angelica (Internicola) Fontana, Thomas Michael Fontana was born on September 12, 1951 in Buffalo, New York. After he graduated from Canisius High School, where he got a rigorous Jesuit education, Fontana attended Buffalo State College. In 1973 he earned a bachelor's degree in theater. Within two years he had accepted a position with the Writers Theatre in New York City as a playwright in residence, a title he held until 1993. He got his first big break in television in 1982, from producer Bruce Paltrow—the father of the actress Gwyneth Paltrow—who hired him as a writer for the drama series *St. Elsewhere*.

Compared favorably by critics to the groundbreaking police drama *Hill Street Blues*, which rewrote the rules for prime-time television by featuring a large cast and a true-to-life mix of drama and comedy, *St. Elsewhere* debuted in October 1982. The series used continuing story lines and a large ensemble cast to build a universe around the fictional St. Eligius Hospital. Although the program was greeted with critical acclaim when it debuted, *St. Elsewhere* finished its first season near the bottom of the ratings. Nonetheless, NBC decided to renew the show, which eventually gained a small but avid following and ran until May 1988. The show's writers were lauded by critics for their imaginative plots, which kept the show fresh, and the frequent pop-culture references they embedded in their scripts. For instance, *St. Elsewhere* was among the first series in which characters mentioned other television shows as well as movies, a practice now commonplace on television. Having stretched its genre beyond traditional parameters, *St. Elsewhere* is generally credited with blazing a trail for such medical dramas as *Chicago Hope* and *ER*.

The *St. Elsewhere* writing and production team of Fontana, Paltrow, and John Tinker stayed together after the show's final episode to work on a new hour-long NBC program. Called *Tattinger's*, it centered on a successful restaurateur, his former wife, and their two daughters. Like *St. Elsewhere*, *Tattinger's* used an ensemble cast, was set in a single location, and blended comedy and drama—but far less successfully. Following a nine-episode run from October 1988 to January 1989, during which the show flagged in the ratings, *Tattinger's* went on hiatus for some repair. After extensive doctoring of its concept, the series returned three months later under the name *Nick and Hillary*. But in its new incarnation, it proved even less popular, and it was pulled from the air after two episodes, in April 1989.

In 1991 Fontana rejoined Paltrow and Tinker again, this time to produce NBC's *Home Fires*. At first considered a mid-season replacement, *Home Fires* had a short run in the summer of 1992. The promising series starred Kate Burton, daughter of the late Welsh stage and screen legend Richard Burton. As they had in their previous efforts, the producers attempted to blur the line between sitcom and drama, but the formula failed, and the show was canceled after six episodes.

For his next television project, Fontana teamed with Oscar-winning director Barry Levinson, who had begun his career in the 1970s in television before switching to film. For his return to television, Levinson wanted "a show about thinking cops with no car chases and no gun battles," Fontana told Mike Flaherty for *Entertainment Weekly* (December 25, 1998). "I thought, This man is completely insane—so I guess I have to go do it with him." The result of their collaboration was *Homicide: Life on the Street*. A one-hour crime drama, the series was inspired by the reporter David Simon's acclaimed book *Homicide: A Year in the Killing Streets* (1991), a true account of a year in the lives of 19 Baltimore homicide detectives. The concept fed Fontana's fondness for gritty realism and large ensemble casts. Fontana headed a team of writers—including three women, a rarity among the creators of police dramas who based many of their story lines on events that were still fresh in the newspapers; they also collaborated with the writers of the successful NBC legal drama *Law & Order* to produce tales that crossed from one series to the other. Adding to the difficulty of this feat, the complexities of the future syndication of both series dictated that each crossover story, while flowing through and enhancing both shows, had to be able to stand alone in each series. "I have to put challenges down for myself," Fontana told Flaherty, "because God knows the medium doesn't expect you to challenge yourself. It *asks you* not to."

In *Homicide*, Fontana and Levinson, working with the writer Paul Attanasio, created a dark universe with quirky characters. Stretching the boundaries of conventional television drama, the show was filmed on location in Baltimore, largely with harsh lights and handheld cameras that did not flatter the actors' facial features. The series, which debuted in 1993, succeeded in stirring a feeling of intimacy in viewers, and the show's following, though small, was almost cultish in its devotion. Critics were also responsive to the show's high level of writing, imagination, and acting. Offering an impressive array of talent, the cast included the esteemed stage and screen veterans Yaphet Kotto and Ned Beatty; actor cum comedian Richard Belzer; Daniel Baldwin, one of four brothers in a family of performers; and Andre Braugher, whom many considered the finest actor to have graced television screens in the 1990s. Critical praise notwithstanding, the show's ratings were moderate at best; coupled with the demands it placed on NBC's resources, its small viewership made *Homicide* the network's embattled stepchild. "I would call up [network executives] and go, 'OK, it's Tuesday night. I just saw an ad for *Law & Order* and then one for *ER* and then one for *Profiler*. We're on Fridays, *Profiler's* on Saturday—how come we didn't get a promo,'" Fontana griped to Diane Snyder. "They would say, 'You're getting promos,' and I would never see them. *That* was frustrating." In the spring of 1999, after staying afloat for six years, *Homicide* was pulled from the air, just shy of its planned season finale.

"I always want—especially when doing an episodic television drama—to go to a place, an environment, where ordinary, everyday people live and work," Fontana said to Gabrielle deGroot and Gabriella Daley for the criminology journal *Corrections Today* (February 1998). "And yet, the environment itself has to have an energy or an urgency to it, a life-and-death aspect that enhances the characters' point of view about life."

Perhaps no setting for a Tom Fontana drama series is charged with more life-and-death energy than the penitentiary that provides the backdrop for the writer's latest ongoing television effort, *Oz*, which he co-produces with Barry Levinson. Debuting on the HBO cable network in 1997, *Oz* (whose name was inspired by that of the magical place created by L. Frank Baum in *The Wonderful Wizard of Oz* and other novels) depicts life within the fictional Oswald State Penitentiary's segregated experimental unit, Emerald City. Despite its pretensions to being a model cell block, "Em City" is more brutal than the section that houses the prison's general population. The series is filmed in a full-size jailhouse set that has been built inside a warehouse in Manhattan's meat-packing district, in New York City. Because the show is broadcast by a cable network, Fontana is free to expose as much of the underbelly of his prison universe as he wants. He has included extreme violence, male frontal nudity, and copious amounts of cursing in his scripts. "The things I'm getting away with, I should be arrested for," Fontana quipped to Bruce Fretts for *Entertainment Weekly* (July 11, 1997). "I've told my 75-year-old Italian-American mother she can't watch the show. She's going to be the oldest person on the planet with a V-chip." Comparing his network experiences with his freedom on cable, Fontana said, "Instead of getting calls saying 'Can't they hug each other at the end?' I'm getting 'Just go a little further, a little edgier.' I feel so *unleashed*."

Some viewers have praised *Oz* as being the best deterrent to crime since the 1978 prison documentary *Scared Straight*; others have condemned it for its foul language, depictions of sexual abuse, and what they consider gratuitous violence. In light of the shootings at Colorado's Columbine High School in 1999, during which two students killed 13 of their peers and teachers, many have questioned the wisdom of portraying the kind of violence Fontana routinely writes into *Oz*. In defense of his work, Fontana said to Diane Snyder, "I've never done anything that wasn't to me the logical thing that would happen in the story. I think television is guilty of encouraging violence when it makes violence palatable. When you see somebody on TV shoot somebody and they don't bleed . . . that's when you create an image for children that I think is wrong. But if you take violence and say, 'This is what violence really costs,' then I think you are doing something that is worthwhile." "I would say my first responsibility is to entertain, and my second responsibility, very close, is to enlighten," he told the interviewers from *Corrections Today*. "My responsibility is to raise questions and not look down on my audience and preach to them. I have such respect for the people who watch my shows that I don't want to look down at them."

Fontana has attempted to present as balanced a point of view as possible in each episode of *Oz*. "I don't have an agenda regarding prison reform," he told Justine Elias for the *New York Times* (July 6, 1997). "I always come at these stories asking, 'What is the basic human truth here, and how does this setting twist it?' My job is to cast a light on a dark place and make people talk about it." Apparently, he has succeeded: *Oz* has taken its place in the pantheon of television's "water-cooler" shows—that is, the show is frequently discussed around water coolers by office workers on breaks. Critics who have praised the program have noted its unrelenting intensity and strange ability to both attract and repulse. Perhaps the finest homage paid to Fontana and *Oz* has been that of actors, who have clamored to work on the show in spite of its meager payroll. The budget for each episode is about $1 million, which is average for a one-hour drama series. However, the large cast and substantial production costs leave little for actors' salaries. Nevertheless, the series has attracted a high caliber of talent that credits Fontana's writing as the primary draw. "I'm not exactly going to buy a house with what I'm getting. Forget that—I'm not going to buy a designer suit," Rita Moreno (the only performer who has won all four major awards in the entertainment industry: Oscar, Emmy, Grammy, and Tony) said to Bruce Fretts. "But you do it because you don't have the opportunity—particularly in TV—to work with such a high-quality writer."

In an essay for the *New York Times Magazine* (September 20, 1998), the critic Stanley Crouch named *Oz* as his favorite show: "To my delight, it had a fully integrated cast, with a range of characters who 'looked like America' and were conceived with impressively realistic ethnic nuances. . . . In every respect, *Oz* went beyond the vast majority of our celebrated contemporary fiction, where the idea of trying to achieve expression across lines of race, class, and religion is truly a minority effort. . . . Remarkably, the imprisoned characters, no matter how human and complex, are never depicted as though they should be anywhere other than prison. No small feat, because clichéd popular entertainment usually projects the naive idea that the prisons are chock-full of endlessly brilliant types who, but for the unfairness of fate, race, and class, would be out in the big, wide world doing great things." Crouch ended his essay with the statement, "If only for the consistently brilliant acting—some of the best in the history of television—*Oz* is a landmark for the medium. It's something we should celebrate, even as we realize that it is, without a doubt, not for everyone."

For the 1999 season of *Oz*, Fontana hired Bradford Winters to help write episodes, while he and Levinson pursued other projects. In July 1999 *Hoop Life*, another drama series from the team, premiered on the Showtime cable network. A hard-edged look at the lives of a group of professional basketball players, *Hoop Life*, like *Oz*, deals openly with sexual situations and drugs. Fontana and Levinson also prepared for the March 21, 2000 premiere of *The Beat*, another police drama series, which they created for the UPN network. They structured the series around the true-to-life, minute-by-minute existences of New York City officers. "This is much more about the bits and pieces of lives," Fontana told Lucy Kaylin for *Gentlemen's Quarterly* (April 2000). "They don't pursue a case; they don't solve a murder. They're New York cops—they don't give a s—t. They want to get away from the job as fast as possible and get home to their families." After only seven episodes had aired, UPN announced that *The Beat* was being placed on hiatus; several sources, however, have reported that the network has canceled the series.

Among his numerous honors, Tom Fontana has earned four Peabody Awards, three Emmys, a CableACE Award, and three Writers Guild of America awards. He owns the New York City bistros Match and La Nonna and lives in Manhattan. — T.J.F.

Suggested Reading: *APBNews* (on-line) July 13, 1999, with photo; *Corrections Today* p50+ Feb. 1998, with photo; *Entertainment Weekly* p36+ July 11, 1997, with photo; *Who's Who in America, 1999*

Selected Television Shows: *St. Elsewhere*, 1982–88; *Tattinger's*, 1988–89; *Nick and Hillary*, 1989; *Home Fires*, 1992; *Homicide: Life on the Street*, 1993–99; *Oz*, 1997– ; *The Beat*, 2000

Courtesy of Pritzker Architecture Prize

Foster, Norman

June 1, 1935– Architect. Address: Foster and Partners, Riverside Three, 22 Hester Rd., London SW11 4AN, England

To walk into Norman Foster's huge London studio is to enter a space that embodies all that this renowned British architect has stood for in his nearly four decades of innovative design work. The studio, which Foster designed himself and which looks out on the Thames River, glows with natural light that pours in through glass walls. The lack of internal subdivisions creates an open atmosphere for the employees at Foster and Partners, his architectural firm, and encourages communication among them. Foster's reverence for natural light, his preference for designs that enhance people's quality of life, his determination to maintain both the health of the planet and the integrity of urban environments, and his insistence that form follow function have secured him a place among the preeminent architects of our time. In 1999 he was awarded the Pritzker Architecture Prize, the most prestigious award in the field; as the winner, who is chosen by a jury of seven experts from more than 500 nominees from dozens of countries, he received $100,000 and a bronze medallion. That honor followed a long string of others, among them more than 130 architectural awards, some four dozen international and national design competition victories, and a knighthood from Queen Elizabeth II of England, in 1990. On the Pritzker Prize Web site in 1999, Bill Lacey, the executive director of the group that awards the prize, said, "Sir Norman Foster's buildings set a standard for design excellence in the use of modern technology pushed to its artistic limits. His buildings represent the highest attainment of contemporary architecture in the 20th century and will undoubtably be the design standard for much of the architecture of the next century."

The son of Robert Foster and the former Lilian Smith, Norman Robert Foster was born on June 1, 1935 in Redditch, England, and grew up in a working-class suburb of Manchester. His father managed a pawnshop before World War II and later worked in a factory as a painter. As a child Foster built model airplanes. He did well in his studies at the local high school, but it was understood that his education would stop there. "The idea that anyone in the neighborhood where I grew up would go to a university was like saying I'd be the next Pope," Foster commented to one of the Pritzker Prize jurors in 1999. One of his first jobs was in the Treasury Department of the Manchester Town Hall, a beautifully ornamented Victorian-era building. Before his arrival there, Foster had begun reading books by such architects as Frank Lloyd Wright and Le Corbusier, and to this day he is able to describe in detail the handrail fittings at the town hall.

After two years with the Treasury Department, Foster served for eighteen months as a radar engineer in the Royal Air Force. The turf-covered hangar in which he spent much of his time would later influence his designs. He next found a position in the contracts department at John Beardshaw & Partners, an architectural firm in Manchester. By that time he had set his sights on becoming an architect and had begun drafting on his own, but he was so embarrassed about his humble origins and inferior education that he was loath to converse with the young architects at the firm. When he finally summoned up the courage to discuss the work of Frank Lloyd Wright with one of them, he discovered that the designer knew nothing about this eminent architect. His confidence bolstered by that encounter, he showed some of his many architectural drawings to his supervisor. He was immediately promoted to the drawing office. Soon afterward, in 1956, the 21-year-old Foster enrolled at the Manchester University School of Architecture. To pay his way, he worked as an ice-cream vendor, a baker, and a nightclub bouncer.

At Manchester University Foster won nearly every architectural award. He graduated in 1961, with a diploma in architecture and a certificate in town planning. He spent the next year as a Henry Fellow at the Yale School of Architecture, in New Haven, Connecticut. After he left Yale, he and Richard Rogers, a British student whom he had met at Yale, along with Wendy and Georgie Cheesman, who were sisters, formed a partnership called Team 4. (Wendy Cheesman and Foster married in 1964.) Team 4's innovative projects included, most notably, the design of the Reliance Controls electronics factory, in Swindon, England, in 1966, in which a steel frame enclosed 32,000 square feet without any supporting columns, so that all partitions were nonstructural and could be rearranged at will. The unusual flexibility of its design and the ease and rapidity with which it was constructed earned it the *Financial Times* Award in 1967. Soon after this success Team 4 broke up. (Rogers later became, along with Foster, a leading purveyor of the "high-tech" style of architecture, characterized by the use of glass, steel, and exposed frames.)

In 1967 Wendy Cheesman and Foster formed Foster Associates. During the next year Foster met the American architect and engineer Buckminster Fuller, who became one of his major influences. The two collaborated on the design of the Samuel Beckett Theatre, at St. Peters College, Oxford University, in England, in 1969, and on several others before Fuller's death, in 1983. "The thing about Bucky was that he made you believe anything is possible," Foster has said, as quoted in a Pritzker Prize profile of him (April 12, 1999).

Perhaps it was the inventive Fuller who influenced Foster's next major project, the world's first inflatable building. Built in 1970 and designed to shelter the 70 employees of Computer Technology Ltd., in Hemel Hempstead, near London, the nylon and polyvinyl chloride (PVC) structure was 200 feet by 40 feet and could be inflated in 55 minutes. The building had full access to electrical and telephone cables and was anchored to beams driven into the company parking lot.

In 1971 IBM hired Foster to design a structure for approximately 1,000 employees, to be built on marshy ground in Hampshire, England, within 18 months, at a price comparable to that of the cheapest temporary structures. The project was completed within the specified cost and time, and the offices are still in use today. In keeping with his tendency to break down barriers and unify spaces, Foster included both offices and space for the computers in the same building—an unorthodox arrangement at that time. "The computer had never been inside the office; it had always been in a hallowed shrine," Foster explained to Robert Ivy for the *Architectural Record* (July 1999). "To demystify that and bring it onto the office floor was a radical departure."

Foster is famous for handling each of his commissions with obsessive thoroughness. To come up with the best design, his company examines dozens of approaches to the various aspects of every project. With the goal of using products that best suit his purposes, Foster even visits factories to influence product designs and testing procedures. Also notable is his concern for the well-being of the people who will work in buildings that he designs, and his determination to make their environments cheerful. Foster has received much of the credit for the trend toward worker-friendly commercial space in recent decades. One of the first applications of this new design objective was the Willis Faber & Dumas headquarters, in Ipswich, England, completed by Foster in 1974. The building contains a central atrium, a rooftop restaurant and garden, and a ground-floor swimming pool. To ensure that the building would blend in with the medieval buildings that surround it, Foster kept the structure relatively low (three stories), and he hung reflective-glass exterior panels along a steel frame that parallels the curvature of the narrow streets at the site. In daytime, the building presents a smooth, curving surface of silver glass. At night, the spacious interior of the building is clearly visible, lit by green and orange lights.

The Carré d'Art in Nimes, France, represents another example of Foster's concern for maintaining the flavor of an urban environment. A complex containing a contemporary art museum and a library, it is situated opposite the Maison Carrée, a beautiful Roman temple still in good repair. Foster's design echoes the Maison Carrée without imitating it. While the temple's portico is dominated by thick, imposing columns, Foster's complex is fronted by widely spaced, thin white pillars. So that the complex would not tower over nearby buildings, half of the Carré d'Art's stories are located underground. David Cohn described the building for *Architectural Record* (October 1993): "A vertiginous, six-story atrium admits daylight into the lowest public levels. It is criss-crossed by open, cantilevered glass-treaded stairs, which soar in dizzying spans from one end of the void to the other, while glass-enclosed elevators rise and fall from various levels." The project, finished in 1993, earned Foster a Gold Medal from the American Institute of Architects in 1994.

When asked by Soren Larson for the *Architectural Record* (May 1999) to define his main design themes, Foster said, "There's always been an interest in the humanizing quality of natural light." Foster's use of light is well illustrated in the Sainsbury Center for the Visual Arts, at the University of East Anglia, in Norwich, England, which was completed in 1977 and had a wing added in 1991. Describing the addition for *Art News* (September 1993), Paula Dietz wrote, "At dusk, when the time comes to leave the new galleries, the visitor begins to see that Foster is a modern alchemist. For as day fades on this ordinary London rooftop, the foyer becomes a deep reservoir of silvery blue light."

In 1979 Foster won the commission to design the Hongkong and Shanghai Banking Corp. headquarters, in Hong Kong. Completed in 1986, the building is a prominent symbol of the high-tech movement in architecture; it is also widely viewed as Foster's masterpiece and as one of the great buildings of the 20th century. Stretching nearly 50 stories, the structure resembles a series of giant steel ladders of varying heights. Previously, skyscrapers had a solid central core for structural support; in a sharp break with that tradition, Foster opened the core by means of a skylight, thus allowing sunlight to bathe the interior; the structural integrity of the building was maintained by other means. The building has become a popular gathering place, thanks to the large square, overlooking the waterfront, on which it is located—the only significant open space in the central business district—and a pedestrian course that runs beneath the building. This skyscraper, Robert Hughes wrote for *Time* (October 23, 1996), "has probably done more to change the way people think about what Foster calls 'the culture of office buildings' and the relation of the corporate to the public domain in a city's matrix than any other 20th century structure."

Although he has often made brilliant use of the aesthetic possibilities of technological innovations, Foster does not believe in using technology merely as an aesthetic tool. "High technology is not an end in itself, but rather a means to social goals and wider possibilities," he told Mark Alden Branch for *Progressive Architecture* (March 1986). That philosophy underlies Foster's design of the ultramodern terminal building for the Stansted Airport, near London (1991). In contrast to other airport terminals, in which the duct work is in the ceilings, Foster placed it in the floors; reducing the weight of the ceiling eliminated the need for the usual heavy supports and made it possible to use light from outdoors. Moreover, with far less artificial lighting than usual, the facility also uses much less electricity than similar buildings; and with fewer lights emitting heat, the savings extends into the realm of air conditioning as well. The terminal in Hong Kong's new international airport, at Chek Lap Kok, another Foster project, is the biggest such building in the world. Completed in 1998, it is shaped somewhat like a mammoth skeleton key and employs many of the design principles embodied in the Stansted Airport, carried out on a grander scale. The baggage hall alone is the size of New York's Yankee Stadium—a space big enough to contain five Boeing 747s, wingtip to wingtip.

Foster's abiding concern for the health of Earth's environment is evident in his design for the Micro Electronic Centre, an office building in Duisberg, Germany (1988–97), which makes use of solar energy and actually generates more electricity than it needs. The Commerzbank headquarters, in Frankfurt am Main, Germany, a Foster project that was completed in 1997, is among the world's first ecologically designed high-rise towers. The three main structural towers of the building, which is the tallest skyscraper in Europe, support a central triangular core; nine greenhouses, each four stories high, spiral around the core, so that greenery is visible to every office. The windows that open onto the greenhouses create natural ventilation.

For his remodeling of the Reichstag (1992–99), the building that houses the German Parliament, in Berlin, Foster was charged with coming up with a design that would represent the nation's democratic government. Two transparent spiral staircases that rise into the dome capping the main parliamentary hall enable visitors to watch their elected officials in action. As Foster told jurors of the 1999 Pritzker Architecture award, "Both literally and symbolically, the public stands above the members of parliament who represent them. They can look in on them, down on them, and see the process of democracy at work." The reconstruction is also meant to demonstrate the government's determination to continue to grapple with Germany's actions during World War II and the years leading up to the war. While renovating the building, workers uncovered bomb damage and anti-Nazi graffiti left by Russian soldiers who stormed the building at the end of the war. The damaged areas, repaired just enough to prevent collapse, were left in place, and some of the graffiti was kept as well, to serve as a reminder of the past. In addition, to illustrate Germany's desire to lead the world in environmentally sustainable practices, the building is heated by clean-burning vegetable oil, and excess heat is stored in underground aquifers and rerouted to provide energy for nearby government buildings. Thanks to Foster's design, the carbon dioxide emissions of the Reichstag have been reduced by 96 percent.

Foster's recent projects include the Millennium Bridge, a pedestrian walkway over the Thames in London; stretching between St. Paul's Cathedral and the new Tate Gallery, it has been described as a slender "blade of light." Shortly after its highly publicized opening, on June 10, 2000, while thousands of people traversed it for the first time, the bridge began to sway noticeably. According to Maev Kennedy, writing for the London *Guardian* (June 29, 2000, on-line), "When pedestrians felt the natural movement of the bridge, they fell instinctively into step, and their own movements alarmingly increased the vibration and caused the swaying." On June 12 the bridge was closed; to prevent the build-up of vibrations, Kennedy reported, "the equivalent of car shock absorbers" will be constructed, a job expected to take several months. While members of the British press began to refer to Foster as "Lord Wobbly," the architect expressed no regret about his radical design of the bridge. "Can you ever be over-ambitious? I would rather be accused of being over-ambitious than of being lily-livered and retreating into a nostalgic past that never existed," he said to Kennedy.

Foster's other recent, continuing, or upcoming works include the new Citibank European headquarters in England; the new headquarters for the Greater London Authority government building; offices for Slough Estates at Ascot and Slough in

England; and the new Social Studies Faculty Centre and Library at Oxford University, in Oxford, England. Foster and Partners' Web site also lists dozens of "unbuilt projects."

Foster's many honors include the Royal Academy of Arts Royal Gold Medal for Architecture (1983); the Yale Arts Award for Outstanding Achievement (1985); the Japan Design Foundation Award (1987); the Chicago Architecture Award (1991); the Gold Medal of France's Academy of Architecture (1991); and the Architecture and Urbanism Award, given by the city of Barcelona (1993). He and his third wife, Elena Ochoa, live in London with their baby daughter, Paola, and Jay, the youngest of Foster's sons from his first marriage, which ended with Wendy Cheesman's death, in 1989. (His second marriage ended in divorce.) The family's apartment, designed by Foster, is on the top floor of the building that houses his studio. "We're at the magical level where you are most aware of the skyline, of the constant changes of the light and seasons," Foster told Michael Webb for *Architectural Digest* (August 1995). "This house is about us, and it's totally malleable, like a lump of clay. It's in the nature of a house to evolve. People change and develop, and a house can adapt to that." — P.G.H.

Suggested Reading: *Architectural Record* p95 May 1999, p94+ July 1999, p94+ July 1999; *Architecture* p139+ May 1994; *Art News* p148+ Sep. 1993; *Time* p70+ April 19, 1999; Treiber, Daniel. *Norman Foster*, 1995; Williams, Stephanie. *Hongkong Bank: The Building of Norman Foster's Masterpiece*, 1989; *Who's Who 1999*

Selected Buildings: Willis Faber and Dumas Insurances Head Office, Ipswitch, England, 1975; Sainsbury Center at the University of East Anglia, Norwich, England, 1978; Technical Park for IBM, Greenford, England, 1979; Renault Distribution Center, Swindon, England, 1983; Hong Kong and Shanghai Bank tower, Hong Kong, 1986; Century Tower, Tokyo, Japan, 1987; project for the Millennium Tower, 1989; ITN Headquarters, London, England, 1988–90; terminal for Stansted Airport, England, 1981–91; Carrée d'Art, Nimes, France, 1985–93; Torre de Collserola for telecommunications, Barcelona, Spain, 1988–92; Commerzbank headquarters, Frankfurt, Germany, 1997; Reichstag reconstruction, Berlin, Germany, 1992–99

Franklin, Kirk

Jan. 26, 1970(?)– Gospel singer; songwriter; record producer. Address: c/o Gerald Wright, Wright Group, 5609 S. Archbridge Ct., Arlington, TX 76017; c/o Nu Nation Fan Club, P. O. Box 8160, Inglewood, CA 90308-8160

Marsh Starks/Archive Photos

Not since Edwin Hawkins, with his hit 1969 song, "Oh Happy Day," has a gospel musician experienced as much crossover success as Kirk Franklin is currently enjoying. Perhaps the best-selling gospel singer of all time, the stylishly attired, bejeweled Franklin has aroused such fervor among fans that some of them have tried to rip off his clothes during concerts. Smoothly fusing a spiritual message and a danceable groove, he praises Jesus over beats reminiscent of the music of James Brown, Parliament Funkadelic, and KRS-One. In response to traditionalists who have complained that his songs are a perversion of gospel music, Franklin has pointed out that he has never watered down the Christian message of love and humility in his songs. Unlike gospel musicians who, with the aim of appealing to crossover audiences, include no specific antecedents when they use the pronoun "He," Franklin sings forthrightly about Jesus and God. "Jesus is da bomb," he has said, and God is leading a "Holy Ghost party." Moreover, Franklin believes that dancing is an eminently suitable way to praise the Almighty, and that if singing songs that inspire boogying brings more people to religion, all the better. As Carol Cooper wrote for the *Village Voice* (August 26, 1997), "He is constructing a subliminal Trojan horse for spiritual pedagogy. . . . If Kirk Franklin keeps reclaiming and transforming pop-chart fodder into sanctified boogie, the Devil soon won't have any tunes at all."

Franklin was born Kirk Smith on January 26 in about 1970 in Fort Worth, Texas. His teenage parents abandoned him when he was very young; he has since met his biological parents only a handful of times. Immediately after their departure, his great-aunt Gertrude Franklin took responsibility for him. Although she was then 64 years old, she adopted him, and he came to consider her his mother. A religious woman who lived in the Riverside neighborhood of Fort Worth, Gertrude Franklin attended a Baptist church, and by the age of four, Kirk was singing with the church choir. At four he was also taking piano lessons, which Gertrude paid for by collecting aluminum cans. (She died when Franklin was about 20.)

Franklin's musical talent became evident early on. Beginning at age seven, he would rewrite the lyrics to pop tunes such as Elton John's "Bennie and the Jets," to transform the song into a tribute to God. When he was seven, he was offered a record deal, which his great-aunt rejected. At 11 the precocious youth was chosen to lead the choir of Mount Rose Baptist Church, in Fort Worth, which paid him $100 a month for his services. "There were a few people who didn't like the idea of a little kid telling them how to sing," Franklin recalled to *People* (July 8, 1996).

Franklin did not want to come across as an angelic choir boy, however, because he was eager to gain the acceptance of the kids in his neighborhood. Toward that end, he got into fights, hung around poolrooms, smoked marijuana, and made friends with gang members. "The guys in church were considered gay, sissies," he told Alan Light for *Vibe* (October 1997). "So whatever it took for me to prove that I wasn't that, that's what I did. From trying to sleep around, drink, go to clubs, smoke. Man, when I was in high school, I was called gay so much that I used to wake up in the morning crying and begging my mother not to send me to school."

Franklin became motivated to clean up his act after one of his friends, Eric Pounds, was killed in a freak accident in the summer of 1985. While rummaging in a closet, Pounds had been struck by a bullet when his parents' gun fell from its storage place and discharged. Suddenly aware of his own mortality, Franklin gave up smoking and drinking and returned to religion. The straight and narrow path wasn't easy for him to follow, however. His girlfriend at the time became pregnant, and their son, Kerrion, was born when Franklin was 18.

Fortunately, Franklin could rely upon his musical talent for inspiration and income. At the Greater Strangers Rest Baptist Church, in the Lake Como section of Fort Worth, he met Reverend R. E. West, "the closest thing I had to a father," as he told Alan Light. West selected the 18-year-old Franklin as choir director, and immediately, Franklin began blending gospel music with the pop tunes he heard on the streets. To the dismay of some church members and the delight of others, he played the piano with jazzy gusto and often bobbed and danced in the pulpit. "The older people were horrified," West recalled to Light. "But the majority of the younger people loved it. It gave them a chance to free themselves in worship, to cast off their cares and stand up for the first time and dance and praise."

To supplement his income from the church, Franklin took a series of menial jobs, but he could never keep them. "My focus was on music," he told *Ebony* (October 1995). "Instead of mopping the floor, I was in the back humming a tune." He put together a demo tape, a copy of which wound up in the hands of Milton Biggham, the president of Savoy Music Group. Biggham hired Franklin, with the titles associate songwriter and assistant director, to work with the Dallas–Fort Worth Mass Choir on their albums *I Will Not Let Nothing Separate Me* (1991) and *Another Chance* (1993). Franklin soon assembled his own choir, recruiting 17 of the best voices he knew in the Fort Worth area. "I wanted to create something as wild, as abstract, as me," he told Alan Light.

Courted by major record labels, Franklin and his group, the Family, made the risky decision to sign with Gospo Centric, a fledgling gospel record company founded by Vicki Mack Lataillade with $6,000 she had borrowed from her father's retirement fund. Their first album, *Kirk Franklin and the Family* (1992), was only the second disc to bear the Gospo Centric label. It was recorded live in 1992 at the Grace Temple Church in Fort Worth and released in 1993. Sales remained modest until the following year, when Franklin made his first television appearance on the *Arsenio Hall Show.* Louis Farrakhan, the controversial head of the Nation of Islam, was featured that night, and, having failed to persuade anyone else to share the stage with him, Farrakhan had invited Franklin to come as the musical guest. This exposure on national television immediately boosted sales of Franklin's record. Meanwhile, the first cut on the album, "Why We Sing," a modern version of "His Eye Is on the Sparrow," began to receive a lot of play on R&B radio stations. *Kirk Franklin and the Family* ultimately sold more than a million copies and became the first gospel album since Aretha Franklin's *Amazing Grace* (1972) to break the Top 10 on the R&B charts. According to *Texas Monthly* (September 1996), *Kirk Franklin and the Family* was the first album by a gospel artist to go platinum.

Franklin's first album was not distinguished by the hip-hop and funk beats that would characterize his later work, but it was not traditional gospel, either. As Carol Cooper wrote, "Tunes like the hit 'Why We Sing' sounded more like a Diane Warren power ballad than like soul or hip-hop. Yet as an instrumentalist and vocal arranger, Kirk has the dapper flamboyance of a swing-era bandleader, orchestrating classical interludes and jazzy breaks so seamlessly one has to admire the sheer artistry of it." In his subsequent albums, elements of urban contemporary music figure more prominently in the gospel songs. For instance, his second album with the Family, *Christmas* (1995), contained a funk-inspired "O Come All Ye Faithful." Although Franklin was certainly not the first singer to mix gospel with nightclub music, he was fast becoming the most successful. His third collaboration with the Family, *Watcha Lookin' 4* (1996), recorded live at Calvary Temple, in Dallas, in 1994, went platinum and won the 1997 Grammy Award for best contemporary soul gospel album.

Predictably, some gospel traditionalists found Franklin's brand of sacred music too secular for their tastes, but Franklin has called attention to the distinction between the beat and the message. "Gospel music is not a sound; gospel music is a message," he explained to *Jet* (February 2, 1998). "Gospel music means good news. It's good-news music. As long as the message is still the good news about Jesus loves you and He died for you. He's coming again for you. You're His child. He went through a lot for you. So no matter how radical my music might seem, does the music say Jesus or does it not say Jesus? It does say Jesus." (Franklin has not denied that he listens to profanity-laden contemporary music. "I have to monitor how much I listen to because my wife can tell when I've been riding around listening to a hip hop CD all day," he explained to Alan Light. "She says I walk different.")

In November 1996, just two days after starting the national "Tour of Life," his third such venture, Franklin took a wrong step onstage at the Memphis Cook Convention Center, in Tennessee, and plunged nine feet into the orchestra pit. He suffered brain injuries and slipped in and out of consciousness in the hospital. Despite predictions that he might die or suffer permanent damage, Franklin recovered, with no apparent long-term problems. Six weeks after the accident, he went onstage in Nashville, Tennessee, for the 12th Annual Stellar Awards Show. The day after Christmas he resumed the Tour of Life. By his own account, he viewed the accident as a message from God. "There were some things in my life that had to fall," he told *Ebony* (April 1997). "So, when I fell, some things in my life fell, such as my temper, low self-esteem, and other old habits and insecurities that God couldn't take to the next level."

For his fourth album, Franklin signed with the B-Rite label, which is distributed through Interscope Records (one of whose divisions is the now infamous Death Row Records), and collaborated with God's Property, a 50-member choir of people aged 16 through 27 that was organized by Linda Searight in 1992. The album, *God's Property from Kirk Franklin's Nu Nation*, was released in 1997 and yielded the hit "Stomp." Presented on the album in two versions—one featuring Cheryl James, the "Salt" of the female rap duo Salt-N-Pepa—and containing melodic samples from George Clinton's album *One Nation Under a Groove*, "Stomp" was a huge crossover hit, and it reached number one on *Billboard*'s R&B chart. The video of the song is said to be the first gospel video that MTV has scheduled on heavy rotation. The album sold more than two million units and won the 1998 Grammy Award for best gospel album by a choir or chorus. In addition, "Stomp" was nominated for the Grammys for best R&B song and best R&B performance by a duo or group with vocal, and Franklin was nominated for producer of the year.

Franklin's next album was *The Nu Nation Project* (1998), another collaboration with God's Property. The record, which has sold 1.5 million copies, produced the hit single "Lean on Me"—an original composition, not a remake of the Bill Withers classic. Such music stars as Bono from U2, R. Kelly, and Mary J. Blige participated in the creation of "Lean on Me." At the 1999 Grammy Awards, *The Nu Nation Project* was nominated for best-engineered nonclassical album and won in the category of best contemporary soul gospel album; "Lean on Me" was nominated for song of the year, best R&B song, and best R&B performance by a duo or group with vocal.

In 1998 Franklin formed One Nation Crew (also referred to as 1NC), a multiethnic group of nine male and female vocalists. Along with the Family, CeCe Winans, Trin-Ni-Tee 5:7, and the Steps of Praise dancers, One Nation Crew accompanied Franklin on the 1999 national Nu Nation Tour. Highlights from the tour were shown on HBO, as a pay-per-view offering, and were made into a video. One Nation Crew was featured on Franklin's most recent album, *Kirk Franklin Presents One Nation Crew* (2000). He himself wrote all but one of the 13 songs on the record, which include "Movin' On," "Unconditional," "Be Like Him," "Could've Been Me," "I Can't Live without You," "Nobody," "In Your Grace," and "When You Fall." Five tracks were spoken-word interludes.

In a $1 million lawsuit filed in the spring of 2000, members of the Family charged Franklin, his manager, Gerald Wright, and Gospo Centric Records with fraud and conflict of interest. Specifically, several of the singers claimed that they had been tricked into signing a contract according to which they were paid a one-time fee but no royalties for music ostensibly recorded only for Steven Spielberg's film *Amistad* but later used on *The Nu Nation Project* (and not on the *Amistad* soundtrack). As reported in *Jet* (May 29, 2000), the suers also charged that, without getting their permission, Franklin had used the Family's name to promote Church's Chicken, a fast-food franchise that he owns in Dallas, and then had never compensated the singers. In response to the suit, Franklin released a statement in which he declared, as quoted by *Jet* (June 19, 2000), "I regret that gospel music has to face this type of tragedy. But I trust that God will use it for His glory."

In addition to producing and recording his own albums, Franklin has contributed to film soundtracks: he recorded the song "My Life Is in Your Hands" for Spike Lee's *Get on the Bus* (1996) and "Joy" for *The Preacher's Wife* (1996). His autobiography, *Church Boy: My Music and My Life*, was published in 1998. He is producing local gospel acts for his company, Fo Yo Soul, and reportedly hopes to launch a clothing line, Praise Joint. A few years ago he was slated to star as a pastor in a United Paramount Network (UPN) sitcom, but he withdrew from the cast, in part because in one episode the pastor gives his stamp of approval to homosexuality after a choir member admits to being gay. "Let me stress to you that I'm not homophobic," Franklin told Alan Light. "I have very good friends who are gay. They know that I don't agree with that lifestyle, but I don't beat them, I don't cuss them out. . . . My own personal belief is that I don't believe that a person is born gay. . . . That don't give me the right to condemn you, but I do believe there is a better way." Franklin has recently been exploring another possible deal with Universal Television.

The five-foot four-inch gospel singer told *Jet* (February 2, 1998), "Success is when I go home and I'm tired and I know I'm tired, but my kids want to play or my kids want to go to the park. And for me not to get selfish and say, 'Oh, come on, Daddy's tired' and then give the long speech on 'This is how Daddy makes his living, so you've got to give him time.' No, I have to get up and spend time with my kids; that's what success is for me." His wife is the former Tammy Renee Collins, a makeup artist who used to sing with the R&B group Ashanti. The couple, who were wed on January 20, 1996, have two daughters: Carrington, Tammy's child from a previous relationship, whom Franklin has adopted, and Kennedy. Their home is in Arlington, Texas. Franklin's memoir, *Church Boy: My Music & My Life*, written with Jim Nelson Black, was published in 1998. — W.G.

Suggested Reading: *Ebony* p64+ Oct. 1995, with photos, p124+ Apr. 1997, with photos; *Interview* p146 Sep. 1997, with photo; *Jet* p58+ Feb. 2, 1998, with photos; *People* p56+ July 8, 1996, with photo; *Texas Monthly* p104+ Sep. 1996, with photo; *USA Today* Life p7 Oct. 2, 1998, with photo; *Vibe* p91+ Oct. 1997, with photos; *Washington Post* N p15 May 19, 1995, with photo, G p2 Jan. 7, 1996, with photo, N p12 Dec. 27, 1996, with photo; Franklin, Kirk, and Jim Nelson Black. *Church Boy: My Music & My Life*, 1998

Selected Recordings: *Kirk Franklin and the Family*, 1993; *Christmas*, 1995; *Watcha Lookin' 4*, 1996; *God's Property from Kirk Franklin's Nu Nation*, 1997; *The Nu Nation Project*, 1998; *Kirk Franklin Presents One Nation Crew*, 2000

Fulani, Lenora

1950(?)– Political activist. Address: c/o Reform Party, P.O. Box 203, Cedar Key, FL 32625

The surprise at Patrick J. Buchanan's press conference on November 11, 1999 was not his announcement that he was departing the Republican Party for the Reform Party. Rather, what shocked political observers and the media alike was the endorsement of the conservative columnist's presidential campaign by the only African-American in the room, Lenora Fulani, the controversial leftist and perennial presidential candidate of the New Alliance Party. In explaining her support for Buchanan, Fulani said that they were both anti-establishment candidates who stood up for the ordinary American. As early as 1996, in "Black Empowerment," an article by Fulani posted on-line by the Committee for a Unified Independent Party, she had acknowledged her respect for what Buchanan was trying to accomplish, saying, "I do not agree with many of Mr. Buchanan's positions. However, I do not believe it is in the interests of the American people to demonize him or his candidacy. I think it is important that we understand it. . . . He has tapped into the anti-government, anti-big business, pro-people sentiments of a significant portion of the American people." In a 1999 column, "We're Ending the Hate," she declared, "Pat Buchanan and the Reform Party offer the black

George Dabrowsky/Archive Photos

community the opportunity to join in new alliances. In particular, in an alliance with white blue collar Americans. With so many black Americans unemployed or underemployed, you might call it a blue collar/no collar coalition. And if we break the 'collar barrier,' by bringing these two populations together, we will have also broken the color barrier that divides the American people to this day." To those who have criticized Fulani for being little more than a spokesperson for a "smoke and mirrors" organization, her endorsement of Buchanan seemed to be merely an attempt by her and the New Alliance Party's founder, Fred Newman, to gain power and political credibility. Others might argue that Fulani already has a claim to legitimacy, having become, in 1988, the first female and first African-American presidential candidate to win a place on the ballot in all 50 states and Washington, D.C. Whatever one's viewpoint, Fulani and Newman now wield considerable power in the Reform Party organization, thanks to tactics several observers have called into question.

The youngest of five children, Lenora Fulani was born Lenora Branch in about 1950 in Chester, Pennsylvania. Her mother, Pearl Branch, was a registered nurse; her father was a baggage handler for the Pennsylvania Railroad. When Lenora was 12 her father became seriously ill with pneumonia and needed to be taken to the hospital. Despite repeated calls for an ambulance, the family waited five hours without a response, because no ambulance would come to the black part of town. Eventually a neighbor drove them to the hospital, but Fulani's father died as he was being transferred from a stretcher to a hospital bed. "I realized then he did not have to die," Fulani told the London *Observer* (July 26, 1987), "and I will never forget or forgive that casual approach to a black man's living or dying." "I grew up in about two hours," Fulani recalled later for the *New York Times* (September 11, 1994). "I didn't even know the word racism." Fulani's philosophy would develop over the next few years. Perceiving that whites' failure to understand blacks had led to much of the conflict between the two groups, she resolved to help foster a more harmonious relationship between the races.

In high school Fulani won what the *New York Times* (September 11, 1994) identified as several "local scholarships." After her graduation, in 1968, she enrolled at Hofstra University, in Long Island, New York, becoming the first member of her family to attend college. As quoted in *Ms.* (May/June 1992), Fulani later compared the experience to "going to Hollywood, it was such a major step." As a means to resolving differences between the races, Fulani decided to study psychology. She also became a member of the Hofstra black student union, and she participated in student takeovers of campus buildings. After graduating, in 1971, she married a college boyfriend. She and her husband changed their surnames to that of a West African tribe: Fulani. In 1972 Fulani received a master's degree from Columbia University Teachers College, in New York City.

"There was a lot of devastation, poverty, pain, and craziness in my family," Fulani told *Ms.* "I was looking for a psychology that had some relevance to the black community and to poor people, and I just hated Freud." For that reason she attended a lecture by Fred Newman, who had developed a social-therapy program loosely based on the work of Soviet psychologist Lev Vygotsky and built around the idea that mental illness results solely from negative influences in society—such as racism, sexism, or homophobia. One could overcome these influences and become a stable, productive person, so the theory went, by transferring control of one's life to a therapist and working with—and recruiting for—the New Alliance Party, a leftist organization run by Newman. "Other identifications—whether with feminism, the gay community, independent activist organizations," Bruce Shapiro noted in the *Nation* (May 4, 1992), "are derided as bourgeois and self-limiting" by the party. The New Alliance Party (NAP) had grown out of the International Workers Party (IWP), which had been associated briefly with Lyndon LaRouche, a fringe candidate in several presidential elections. Fulani joined the NAP in 1980 and started group therapy at its main institute. She was soon trained as a social therapist and became director of community clinics at the Institute for Social Therapy and Research in the Harlem section of New York. Meanwhile, in 1984, she earned a doctorate from the City University of New York. In an article for the New York *Daily News* (October 27, 1986), Fulani described the NAP as "a black-led, multiracial, independent, progressive, third party." The party touted itself as especially active in the fight for the rights of women, gays, and minorities.

In 1984 the NAP began running its own candidates for high office. Fulani made an unsuccessful run for lieutenant governor of New York State under the campaign slogan "A chance to choose progress." In the same year the New Alliance Party ran the former Socialist Dennis Serrette for president. He received 35,000 votes nationwide, less than a 10th of 1 percent of the total number of ballots cast. The following year Fulani ran unsuccessfully for mayor of New York City against Edward I. Koch.

In 1986 Fulani set her sights on the governorship of New York. Despite a controversial campaign in which she was denounced for supporting the leader of the Nation of Islam, Minister Louis Farrakhan, she ended up receiving 25,000 votes, more than any independent candidate had won in the state since the 1930s. Two years later, when asked to comment on Farrakhan's reputed anti-Semitism, she told the *New York Times* (October 26, 1988), "I think everybody is racist or anti-Semitic. People in this country are constantly being taught filth about each other and saying it all the time. You have to ask what is going on when black leaders are identified as haters of Jews." Fulani also came under attack for traveling to Libya in 1987 in the company of other leftists at the invitation of Colonel Muammar al-Qaddafi.

In 1988 Fulani ran for president on the New Alliance Party ticket. She was the first black—and first female—presidential candidate whose name appeared on ballots in every state and the District of Columbia. More than 1.5 million signatures were required to achieve that feat. Recognizing that her chances of winning were slim, she said that she was running primarily to make more Americans aware of the viability of a third party, to impress upon minorities how the Democratic Party had "sold them out," and to press the agenda of the NAP's Rainbow Movement coalition. "If I end up with a million votes, people will have to take us seriously," she had told the London *Observer* in 1987. At the same time that she was running, she also supported Jesse Jackson's ultimately unsuccessful second attempt for the Democratic Party's presidential nomination. Certain that Jackson had been denied the nomination by the party elite, she blasted the Democratic Party. "It bluntly rejects . . . the black agenda," Fulani told the *Christian Science Monitor* (July 7, 1988). "It bluntly rejects the just demands of the Palestinian people for an independent state. It bluntly ignores the peace movement's call for massive cuts in the military budget.

Fulani received $905,000 that year in federal matching funds, becoming only the second third-party candidate ever to receive such a large amount. Her platform called for cutting the military budget in half, raising taxes on large corporations, and offering free or low-cost health care to all American citizens. Many of her proposals were phrased in general terms, with few details. Fulani was more thorough in her efforts to win other third-party candidates more air time and media attention. She filed two suits to stop the presidential debates, claiming that they granted an unfair advantage to the dominant parties. When that failed, she attempted to get 45 minutes of free air time in compensation; that request, too, was denied. Controversy dogged the campaign because of the party's connections to Farrakhan and another controversial African-American figure, the Reverend Al Sharpton. Many commentators also questioned the party's strategy of attempting to siphon votes away from Michael Dukakis, the Democratic nominee, to force the Democratic Party to take notice of NAP issues. Fulani stated, as quoted in the *Wall Street Journal* (November 4, 1988), that the NAP was going to "teach that party to never ever take the black vote for granted again." Other statements Fulani made, such as, "We should follow the lead of the people of Cuba, and throw all the rich, white males out of the government," quoted in the same article, drew charges of hypocrisy, since the NAP was itself largely white and run by a white male—Fred Newman. Fulani received 240,000 votes on Election Day, a large number for a fringe candidate.

In 1992 Fulani, identifying herself as a Democrat, entered the Democratic New Hampshire primary. She energetically attempted to gain media attention, traveling around the state in the style of the leading candidates, despite the lack of support for her campaign. The previous year she had won notice for her attempts to get Senator Paul Tsongas removed from the Democratic primary ballot in New York for what she claimed was his failure to get the requisite number of signatures. Although Fulani was not treated as a major candidate by the press and was barred from the debates, she remained aggressive. She earned the ire of many in the media by interrupting Democratic debates and press conferences with shouted criticisms of the way the party was run. Fulani received only 402 votes in New Hampshire and afterward endorsed the protest candidate Larry Agran. She continued her attacks at events organized by other candidates, demanding that they debate Agran.

When the primary season ended, Fulani began her candidacy for president with the New Alliance Party, which could now legitimately claim to be the fourth-largest party in the U.S. This time Fulani received about $1.45 million in federal matching funds. Meanwhile, the party now owned or had connections to a publishing house, a law firm, an art center, and other business ventures. However, with the New Alliance Party subject to increased scrutiny, observers noticed some reportedly shady aspects of the organization. Former NAP members claimed that the group operated as a near cult, forcing patients at their social-therapy centers to work for next to nothing or even to abandon their families. Others raised questions about the way the NAP received its money: the party considered making a contribution to the campaign a sign of maturity. "The more you give, the more you grow," as Fulani told those gathered at a fund-raiser, according to the *Nation*. "Take it out of your rent. It feels very, very good." Many patients, knowing where their money would go, handed over fees to their therapists, who transferred some of the payments to Fulani's campaign. Furthermore, critics pointed out that neither Newman nor any of the other therapists working at the social-therapy centers were licensed.

The NAP also drew criticism for its organizing of the Rainbow Movement (also referred to in various sources as the Rainbow Alliance and Rainbow Lobby), essentially identical in aim to Jesse Jackson's Rainbow Coalition and with a name similar enough to suggest that it was run by the same people. Critics pointed out that the NAP had used similar strategies many times. It was also noted that party members had infiltrated or tried to destroy other progressive organizations, such as the New York chapter of the New Jewish Agenda. In 1990 the party had attempted to block the ballot petitions for the All-African Unity Party in New York state elections, citing an insufficient number of signatures. Other such actions included infiltrating a mostly black mental-health center in Philadelphia and converting part of the program into a social therapy practice, and taking over the Peace and Freedom Party's San Francisco chapter and putting it at odds with the rest of the party. It was reported that U.S. gay and lesbian groups came together in 1989 to ask the International Lesbian and Gay Association to reject the NAP's attempt for membership, because of the group's supposed homophobia and its taking over of gay rallies for Fulani's campaign speeches. Chip Berlet, the author of a study of the NAP, stated in the 1992 article for *Ms.*, "They talk about democracy, fighting sexism and racism, but their style across the country has been to disrupt community-based groups that are fighting on these issues. . . . This is a group on the left that has gone bad." "The NAP and Fulani," Bruce Shapiro wrote for the *Nation*, "offer the false but alluring appearance of a symbolically charged and emotionally outraged response to the feelings of exclusion from the political process many Americans harbor." The criticism had virtually no effect on the campaign's success, as Fulani was on the ballot in 45 states. "There is no difference between the Democratic and Republican parties," Fulani claimed in *Emerge* (October 1992). "They are both tied to corporate America. They've ripped the black community in a way that is an outrage." Fulani received 217,000 votes on Election Day.

In 1994 Fulani succeeded in getting enough signatures—60,477—to run in the Democratic primary for governor of New York against the incumbent governor, Mario Cuomo. Questioning her commitment to the Democratic Party, Cuomo refused to debate Fulani. In a strong showing, Fulani received 142,000 votes, or 21 percent of the ballots cast. In the meantime, the NAP sought to align itself with the backers of H. Ross Perot, the independent candidate who had won approximately 20 percent of the vote in the 1992 presidential election. Perot supporters in Virginia were forming the precursor to the Reform Party in the state. Many were surprised when the convention was besieged by Fulani and her supporters, who ended up accounting for half of those present. A number of the leading independents who were there walked out, and Fulani placed herself and several supporters among the executive committee of what became the Patriot Party. In the general election for governor, other New York independents asked Fulani to promise not to run, in exchange for increased influence within the state's new, Perot-affiliated party. Fulani thus appeared on the ballot as a candidate for lieutenant governor, not governor. However, when the party began setting up its system a few months later and shunned Fulani's input, she took the party to court and attempted—without success—to get a ruling from the U.S. Justice Department to the effect that the party was discriminating against minority voters. Meanwhile, the New Alliance Party dissolved. In 1995 Fulani and Newman were influential in getting Perot on the ballot in all 50 states for the following year's presidential election.

In 1998 Fulani again fought a losing war for the lieutenant governorship of New York. That same year a federal appeals court ruled that the NAP had to repay over $117,000 in federal matching funds from Fulani's 1992 presidential campaign that had been used illegally. (The party had used the money to support companies owned by its members.) Meanwhile, reports began to surface that delegates in New York were being disqualified from the Reform Party convention, while strangers were showing up at county and state meetings, pressing their candidates for delegates. "It's like a hostile takeover," a Reform Party member was quoted as saying in the *New Republic* article. "They move their members around, they shadow me at events, they try to intimidate me. I've asked them to stay out of our county, and they won't." These actions were traced by Jack Essenberg, the head of the Reform Party's New York affiliate, to an organization called the Committee for a Unified Independent Party (CUIP). It was soon discovered that CUIP was run by Fulani and her followers. However, "no one knows what the hell it even is," Essenberg said. As an unincorporated entity, the CUIP is not required to disclose information about itself. Reports soon surfaced of infiltrations by Fulani's followers in the Connecticut and New Jersey branches of the Reform Party. In the spring of 1999, Essenberg was kicked out of the New York Reform Party, thanks to charges from Fulani's growing forces that he was corrupt. "I'm watching a Marxist takeover," he said for the *New Republic* piece, "and we don't have the means to stop it." The same article reported that Fulani and Newman had control of as many delegates as Perot and Jesse Ventura, the Reform Party candidate who had won the governorship of Minnesota.

Despite her growing influence within the Reform Party, Fulani's 1999 endorsement of her political opposite, Pat Buchanan, surprised many members of the media. The alliance prompted much derision in the press. Bruce Shapiro, in a separate article for the *Nation* (November 1, 1999) in which he analyzed their reasons for joining ranks, concluded, "This is the Buchanan-Fulani project: an authoritarian, bigoted populism in which resentment matters more than overt content. It is a tradition, going at least as far back as the anti-Catholic Know-Nothings of the 19th century, that has repeatedly scapegoated immigrants, the poor, intellectuals, and the left. Buchanan and Fulani propose a phony populist coalition in which the only 'leftists' to gain a foothold will be those willing to sell out all the gains of feminism, gay liberation, and civil rights in return for a narrow economic nationalism. This is the meaning of the new Buchanan-Fulani alliance—an axis that can only divide, not unite, America's disaffected and disempowered constituencies." Other analysts compared the partnership to European systems in which diametrically opposed parties come together to serve their respective interests. It was pointed out that Buchanan now had access to one of the tightest organizations on the American political landscape and also had control of one-third of the delegates to the Reform Party convention. Meanwhile, Fulani and her organization had access to the Reform Party's prestige and bankroll.

The Buchanan-Fulani alliance did not last long. After increasing tension between the two factions, Fulani resigned from her position as co-chair of the Buchanan campaign, contending that Buchanan's campaign was divisive and was not bringing the Reform Party together and that the former Republican was interested only in fostering his right-wing social agenda. As evidence for the latter accusation, Fulani cited the fact that he would not support her bid for national party chairwoman. Soon afterward, Fulani threw her support behind John Hagelin, the Natural Law Party candidate, who was also vying for the Reform Party nomination. "I've endorsed John Hagelin because he wants to keep the party as it was originally engineered by Ross Perot and others—a populist party that is inclusive, non-ideological and pro-reform," Fulani announced, as quoted by Anthony York on *Salon.com* (June 30, 2000). "Some in political circles have said that Mr. Hagelin's greatest virtue as a candidate is that he is not Pat Buchanan. I disagree."

At the Reform Party convention, held in August 2000 in Long Beach, California, those behind Hagelin walked out, charging the Buchanan forces with corrupt electioneering and balloting processes. When Fulani and her New York delegation attempted to enter the convention after the walkout, they were denied seats by a floor vote. "We have two candidates running," Fulani said, as quoted by Jake Tapper on *Salon.com* (August 11, 2000). "There is no requirement that you have to come attached to one or the other candidate." Hagelin was nominated as the Reform Party candidate by his supporters in a nearby building. Since then, Hagelin's name has appeared on the ballot as the Reform Party nominee in several states, thanks to official coin-tosses in some cases, and in others, as a result of the decisions of state Reform Party leaders, among them Fulani.

Fulani has two children, Ainka and Amani, whom she once described as "supportive and politicized." Fulani was divorced from their father in about 1979. "Obviously I'm articulate and I'm good and the Democrats would love to have me as one of their black success stories," Fulani once declared, as reported in the *New York Times* (September 11, 1994), "and they would do with me as they do with the rest of them, which is use me to tout them as the best way to our liberation. But I'm not interested in politics as a career." Fulani is currently the host of *Fulani!*, which is carried by various TV stations countrywide. She writes a weekly column for *WorldnetDaily.com* and another column that appears in several African-American newspapers. She is the author of two books, *The Politics of Race and Gender in Therapy* (1988) and *The Making of a Fringe Candidate 1992* (1993), and the editor of another, *The Psychopathology of Everyday Racism and Sexism* (1988). — G.O.

Suggested Reading: CUIP (on-line); *Emerge* p59 Oct. 1992; *Fulani Online*; London *Observer* p43 July 26, 1987; *Ms.* May/June 1992; *Nation* p585+ May 4, 1992, p21+ Nov. 1, 1999; *New Republic* p20+ Dec. 13, 1999; *New York Times* A p23 Oct. 26, 1988, I p56 Sep. 11, 1994; *Wall Street Journal* A p16 Nov. 4, 1988

Selected Books: as author—*The Politics of Race and Gender in Therapy*, 1988; *The Making of a Fringe Candidate 1992*, 1993; as editor—*The Psychopathology of Everyday Racism and Sexism*, 1988

Fuller, Bonnie

Sep. 8, 1956– Editor of Glamour *magazine.*
Address: Glamour, *350 Madison Ave., New York, NY 10017*

In the fall of 1998, when Condé Nast Publications announced that Ruth Whitney, who had edited *Glamour* magazine for 31 years, was losing her job to Bonnie Fuller, "the news created such a fuss among media critics you would have thought that Jerry Springer had just replaced Dan Rather," Esther Davidowitz reported for the *Columbia Journalism Review* (May/June 1999). The critics' fears—that after the change in the masthead, *Glamour* would offer, as Davidowitz put it, "more visuals and fewer words, more celebrities and fewer serious articles, more sex and less substance"—turned out to be well-founded. On the other hand, as Davidowitz pointed out, the first issue that came out under Fuller's stewardship, in 1999, sold more copies than any other issue of *Glamour* in more than two years and was "the best-selling January issue in a decade." Clare McHugh, a former colleague of Fuller's who became the deputy editor of *Sports Illustrated for Women*, told Davidowitz that Fuller "understands better than anyone else what women want." Fuller's previous job change—from the editorship of the American edition of *Marie Claire* to that of *Cosmopolitan*—also made a big splash in the world of magazine publishing. Earlier in her career she boosted sales of the Canadian magazine *Flare* and then breathed new life into *Young Miss*, which she renamed *YM*. "Change is not a dirty word," Fuller told Cathy Hainer for *USA Today* (February 7, 1997, on-line). "Every business has to evolve in order to stay on top of the changing world."

The first of the three children of Stanley and Tanya Hurowitz, Fuller was born Bonnie Hurowitz in Canada on September 8, 1956 and grew up in Rosedale, a wealthy suburb of Toronto. Her mother did not work while raising the children. "My mother tells me now she was bored silly," Fuller told Janny Scott for the *New York Times* (May 22, 1997). Her father, a successful lawyer, hoped that she would take over his practice one day, but during her teens she decided to become a reporter, af-

John Spellman/Retna Ltd.

Bonnie Fuller

ter taking a summer job at a local suburban paper. In an effort to please her father, she enrolled at a law school after her college graduation, but she left a year later (with the approval of her parents), after hearing about an opening for a fashion writer at the *Toronto Star*. She had never had much interest in fashion, but she reasoned that the job would be a step on the path to more serious reporting. Much to her surprise, she found covering the fashion scene exciting; she especially enjoyed couture shows in Milan and Paris.

Fuller's assignments often took her to New York, and she decided to seek a job there. Using what was to become her trademark strategy, she bombarded the city's fashion publications with calls and letters. Her persistence paid off: the influential trade paper *Women's Wear Daily* hired her as a sportswear editor. The relentless pace and charged atmosphere at *Women's Wear Daily* suited her perfectly. Meanwhile, Fuller continued to file occasional freelance pieces for other publications, among them the Canadian magazine *Flare*. When Keitha McLean, *Flare*'s editor, left, in 1982, Fuller lobbied strongly to succeed her; she charmed *Flare*'s publisher, Donna Scott, with her creativity and drive and got the job.

Although Fuller and Scott often clashed, *Flare* became one of Canada's premier fashion magazines during Fuller's six years as its editor. Fuller developed a column called "*Flare* Was There," which showcased photos of Fuller socializing with designers and celebrities. She attended every important Canadian fashion event, handing out issues of the magazine and shaking hands. In her mid-20s when she took the job, she was in charge of a $1 million editorial budget and a staff of 15, some of whom greatly resented her aggressiveness and management style, which has been described as controlling.

Fuller exhibited her penchant for control in her personal life as well. While at *Flare* she began going out with Michael Fuller, an architect, and during their third date, she gave him an ultimatum. "I told him, 'You know, if you're not interested in being open to marriage after we've been seeing each other for six months, that's it,'" she related to Marci McDonald for *Macleans* (February 17,1997). "I just laid it on the line. . . . I wanted the engagement. I wanted the ring." He proposed on schedule, six months later, and the couple were married in June 1983.

Marriage and the births of the couple's three children did not distract Fuller from her career goals. *Flare's* managing editor, Dianne Rinehart, has recalled being in a meeting with her in 1987, when Fuller was pregnant with her first child. "She kept looking at her watch," Rinehart told Sarah Hampson for *Saturday Night* (May 1997). "I said, 'Bonnie, what are you doing?' And she said calmly, 'I'm timing my contractions. They're five minutes apart.'" After giving birth to her son, Fuller concluded the meeting from her hospital bed the next morning.

After six years at *Flare*, Fuller became restless. Having made it her practice to mail copies of the magazine, along with personal notes, to influential editors all over the world, she now began relentlessly sending them story ideas and proposals for improving their publications. Again her persistence paid off: she was hired by Gruner & Jahr to revitalize their moribund teen magazine *Young Miss*. She rechristened it *YM*, which stood for "young and modern," and within five years increased its circulation from 750,000 to almost 2,000,000, with a blend of beauty and fashion features, celebrity coverage, advice on dealing with boys, and a column in which teens were invited to reveal their most embarrassing moments.

Fuller's success with *YM* attracted the attention of the Hearst Corp., and in 1994 Hearst executives recruited her to edit the soon-to-be launched North American version of the company's French magazine *Marie Claire*. Industry insiders warned that there was no room in the already-glutted market for another beauty-and-fashion magazine, and Fuller took note of their concerns. Instead of concentrating solely on beauty and fashion, *Marie Claire* also offered information on careers and health and an occasional serious feature, such as a report on women in war-torn Bosnia. Under Fuller's guidance, *Marie Claire*'s circulation reached 600,000 within 18 months—a remarkable feat for a start-up publication and one that inspired *Advertising Age* to name the magazine the "Launch of the Year."

In January 1996 Hearst announced that the company had selected Fuller to succeed *Cosmopolitan*'s longtime editor Helen Gurley Brown. In a press release posted on Hearst's Web site, Brown is quoted as saying, "I've had my eye on Bonnie

Fuller for most of the last decade. . . . I wrote her so many notes of praise when she was editing *YM* that it was almost embarrassing. She thoroughly understands the Cosmo girl, and her success at *YM* and in the launch of *Marie Claire* have certainly prepared her to succeed to the editorship of *Cosmopolitan.*" Fuller, in turn, is quoted as saying, "I am thrilled! It is every editor's dream to edit *Cosmopolitan.* Under Helen Gurley Brown, *Cosmopolitan* is one of the publishing industry's greatest success stories. Succeeding to the editorship will be a great responsibility. As I work under Helen's tutelage over the next months, I hope to steep myself in every nuance of the Cosmo girl's life: her worries, her aspirations, and her ambitions."

In reality, according to various sources, acrimony and dissension had surrounded Hearst's choice of Fuller. Brown, who had edited *Cosmopolitan* for three decades and was closely identified with it, had been loath to turn over the reins to anyone else. From her office, famously decorated in shades of pink and leopard-skin patterns, she had overseen the transformation of *Cosmopolitan* from a failing general-interest magazine to one that at its height had sold almost 3,000,000 copies a month and was commonly referred to as the crown jewel of the Hearst empire. Brown had pioneered provocative cover lines—"The way to improved orgasms," for example, or "How to drive a man wild in bed"—which became a permanent fixture of the publication. Such cover lines, along with images of cleavage-revealing models, made *Cosmopolitan* instantly recognizable on the newsstand. The journalist and feminist Gloria Steinem has frequently been quoted as calling the magazine "the unliberated woman's survival kit," but Brown believed that being sexually attractive to men was just as important to her readers as having a fulfilling career, and that the two goals were not mutually exclusive. Her creative innovations and ability to charm advertisers had made her a legend, not only in the publishing world, but among the general public as well. Rather than retire, Brown accepted a position in which she would oversee *Cosmopolitan*'s more than two dozen foreign editions, even though she knew she would be serving largely as a figurehead.

Some industry analysts theorized that since *Cosmopolitan*'s revenues in the U.S. had been falling slightly, Hearst hoped that a new editor would boost the numbers. Others thought that Brown had simply not responded sufficiently to the changing times, and that her frothy, man-pleasing attitude had become downright anachronistic. Hearst officials would say only that the 73-year-old Brown would obviously be unable to work much longer and that they wanted the transition to a new editor to be as smooth as possible. Fuller was to serve as deputy editor under Brown for 18 months before being put in charge.

Reports of creative tension and professional jealousy between Fuller and Brown during the next year and a half circulated among members of the media, but when Fuller's first independently edited issue came out, in March 1997, right after the birth of her third child, it turned out to be very similar to Brown's product. The scantily clad model and racy cover lines remained. Fuller expanded fashion, beauty, and fitness coverage and eliminated recipe and travel columns that she felt were no longer relevant. She planned more celebrity news and greater coverage of the AIDS epidemic, which Brown had been criticized for ignoring. The biggest change was in the look of the magazine, which now featured more photos, larger expanses of white space, and fewer dense blocks of type. Other changes were evident in *Cosmopolitan*'s Midtown Manhattan offices: several staffers either had been fired by Fuller, earning her the sobriquet "the Fuller brush-off girl," or had left out of loyalty to Brown. Readers, apparently, felt no such loyalty. Newsstand sales, subscriptions, and ad revenues all increased, and *Advertising Age* named Fuller the 1998 "Editor of the Year."

Janny Scott interviewed Fuller for the *New York Times* 23 days after the March 1997 issue of *Cosmopolitan* came out and 19 days after Fuller had given birth. In an article that is cited by Fuller's supporters as proof that she is a modern-day superwoman and by her detractors as a portrait of a blindly ambitious automaton, Scott reported that Fuller was planning the next issue of *Cosmopolitan*, breast-feeding her baby, supervising the renovations on her 87-year-old house, and organizing a party—all at the same time.

Eighteen months after assuming leadership at *Cosmopolitan*, Fuller announced that she was leaving to edit Condé Nast's rival magazine, *Glamour*, which had developed a reputation for combining beauty and fashion features with plenty of serious news. Among the many in the publishing industry who were surprised by the announcement was Ruth Whitney, who, as *Glamour*'s editor since 1967, had been almost as closely identified with the magazine as Brown had been with *Cosmopolitan.* Angry about being forced to retire sooner than she had planned, Whitney was also distressed by Condé Nast's choice of Fuller to take her place. "*Glamour* has worked very hard to develop a strong journalistic reputation," she explained to Richard Turner and Yahlin Chang for *Newsweek* (August 24, 1998). "We've won four National Magazine Awards. I'm worried that [Fuller] won't keep that reputation. It has nothing to do with her as a person. In any magazine that she's been in, there is no track record of serious journalism." Fuller discounted the criticism, pointing to the AIDS coverage in *Cosmopolitan* as proof of her journalistic credentials.

Nevertheless, in one of her first changes after her arrival at *Glamour*, Fuller eliminated a column about women in the nation's capital that Whitney had initiated and replaced it with a horoscope column. (A cover line announced the new offering: "You asked for it! Psychic details you need for your love, lust, and work life.") In response, the National Council of Women's Organizations, a Washington, D.C.–based coalition, sent the chairman of Condé Nast a letter expressing concern about the editorial direction of the magazine. Whitney's fears—and those of the women's groups—seemed to be warranted. The January 1999 issue, Fuller's first, included the cover line "Doing It! 100 Women's Sexual Agendas—Who Wants What, How Bad and How Often." An inside headline trumpeted, "Go Ahead, Play Nooky Hooky." That month's issue was the biggest seller since 1996, thus cementing Fuller's reputation as the consummate mass-audience editor. And although critics have charged that *Glamour* is becoming increasingly a clone of *Cosmopolitan*, with eye-catching headlines and graphics but little substance, its sales continue to be good.

On May 24, 1999 Alex Kuczynski reported in the *New York Times* that less than a month after the death of Liz Tilberis, the editor of *Harper's Bazaar*, in April 1999, Cathleen P. Black, the president of Hearst Magazines, *Harper's Bazaar*'s parent company, had approached Fuller about succeeding Tilberis. Furious at the prospect that Fuller would jump ship, S. I. Newhouse Jr., the chairman of Condé Nast Publications—who had lured Fuller from *Cosmopolitan* to *Glamour*—and other Condé Nast executives threatened Fuller with legal action if she left Condé Nast before her three-year contract expired. At a subsequent meeting with her staff, Kuczynski reported, Fuller "compared the Hearst dalliance to a high school flirtation with a handsome classmate." "We convinced her to stay," James Truman, Condé Nast's editorial director, declared, according to Kuczynski.

In 2000 Amnesty International USA cited *Glamour* as a "human rights champion," by presenting the magazine with a Media Spotlight Award in the category of periodical journalism. As reported on the Amnesty International USA Web site, the organization credited *Glamour* with "focusing on issues affecting women's human rights"—in particular, for publishing, in July 1999, the article "Kosovo's Women: Running for Their Lives," and for honoring Mavis Leno (the wife of Jay Leno, the host of *The Tonight Show*), in its March 2000 issue, for her work on behalf of women in Afghanistan.

Fuller and her husband—who was "the family's primary caregiver" in 1997, when Janny Scott interviewed the couple—live in a six-bedroom house in Hastings-on-Hudson, New York, with their son, Noah, and two daughters, Sofia and Leilah. Fuller told Scott that she no longer felt what Scott referred to as "working-mother guilt." "You can't beat yourself up about it because it's not going to help," she said. "I think at a certain point, you have to give up on the guilt." "In my marriage, we've made realistic compromises and taken a practical approach to child-rearing responsibilities," she told Cathy Hainer. "I make sure I'm there for the important things, like concerts and meetings with teachers. And we worship our nanny." — M.R.

Suggested Reading: *Columbia Journalism Review* (on-line) May/June 1999; Hearst Corp. Web site; *Macleans* p60+ Feb. 17, 1997, with photos; *New York Times* C p1+ May 22, 1997, with photos; *Newsweek* p50+ Aug. 24, 1998, with photos; *Saturday Night* p38+ May 1997, with photos

---

Gandolfini, James

Sep. 18, 1961– Actor. Address: c/o Writers and Artists Agency, 8383 Wilshire Blvd., Suite 550, Beverly Hills, CA 90211

Possessing sleepy eyes, a voice that sounds perpetually congested, and an ursine build, James Gandolfini is perhaps the most unlikely heartthrob on television. Speaking of his role as one of the title characters in HBO's runaway hit drama series *The Sopranos*, he told *Entertainment Weekly* (June 25, 1999), "I thought they'd hire someone much more suave. Suave is not something that comes to mind when you think of me." Gandolfini's modesty notwithstanding, his nuanced portrayal of the ruthless but confused mobster Tony Soprano has helped make *The Sopranos* one of the most acclaimed programs on television. And his thoroughly human characterization of Tony—by turns addled son, tender father, conflicted husband, and merciless killer—has transformed Gandolfini into a sex symbol and one of the entertainment world's most promising leading men.

A shy, unassuming person who guards his privacy fiercely, Gandolfini has revealed few details about his personal life in interviews. He told Sophfronia Scott Gregory and Sue Miller for *People* (September 13, 1999), for example, "Just say I came from a nice Italian family from New Jersey." James Gandolfini was born on September 18, 1961 and raised in the suburban New Jersey town of Westwood, not far from Englewood, John Travolta's hometown. "My father used to buy tires from his father," he noted to Frank DeCaro for *TV Guide* (February 6, 1999). According to an unofficial Gandolfini Web site, his sister Johanna is "a prominent official with the New Jersey Family Court system." By his own admission, as a child Gandolfini was a troublemaker and a source of worry for his parents. "By the time I was 21," he joked to DeCaro, "anything I could do that was legal, they were happy."

Gandolfini graduated from Rutgers, the state university of New Jersey, in 1983, with a bachelor's degree in communications. He worked as a bouncer before becoming the manager of a New York City nightclub. When he was 25 a friend of his brought

Archive Photos

James Gandolfini

him to an acting class, where he participated in focusing exercises, which require slipping in and out of the personas of several characters. "Getting up in front of people was frightening, and it made me angry that I was frightened," he told the *People* interviewers. "So I stayed." "I'd also never been around actors before," he told Ginia Bellafante for *Time* (March 22, 1999), "and I said to myself, 'These people are nuts; this is kind of interesting.'"

While supporting himself by driving a delivery truck for Gimme Seltzer, Gandolfini immersed himself in acting. In one of his first professional roles, he appeared in a production of Tennessee Williams's drama *A Streetcar Named Desire* that toured Scandinavia, and he won a part in the 1992 Broadway revival of the play, which starred Alec Baldwin and Jessica Lange. According to the unofficial Gandolfini Web page, his stage credits also include parts in the plays *One Day Wonder*, an Actors Studio production; *On the Waterfront*; *Summer Winds*; and *Tarantulas Dancing*.

Also beginning in the early 1990s, Gandolfini found himself in increasing demand for small film roles. He was cast as Tony Baldessari in the director Sidney Lumet's *A Stranger Among Us* (1992); Virgil in the cult classic *True Romance* (1993), starring Christian Slater and Patricia Arquette; Mike in Anthony Minghella's *Mr. Wonderful* (1993); Billy Coyle in *Money for Nothing* (1993), with John Cusack; Ben Pinkwater in the action-thriller *Terminal Velocity* (1994); and Vinnie, the title character's plumber boyfriend, in *Angie* (1994), starring Geena Davis. Gandolfini's credits for the silver screen also include the role of Will in the French film *Le Nouveau Monde* (1995); Kiefer in *She's So Lovely*, Joey Allegretto in *Night Falls on Manhattan*, and Dumas in *Perdita Durango*, all in 1997; Kenny Kane in *The Mighty*, Lou in *Fallen*, and Al Love, the father of a cancer victim, in *A Civil Action*, all in 1998; and Eddie Poole, the owner of a pornographic-film company, in *8MM* (1999). He also played juror number six in a made-for-TV remake of the 1957 film *12 Angry Men* (which itself was an adaptation, by Reginald Rose, of his same-titled teleplay).

Thanks to his supporting roles in several hit films—that of Bear in *Get Shorty* (1995), Lieutenant Bobby Dougherty in *Crimson Tide* (1995), and Eddie in *The Juror* (1996)—Gandolfini impressed the television writer David Chase as the right man to play Tony Soprano in the mob-based drama series that Chase had been trying to sell to one of the major television networks. After a series of rejections, Chase (the executive producer of the TV series *Northern Exposure* and *I'll Fly Away* and occasional writer and director for the latter) found a home for his concept at the HBO cable network. The FCC imposes fewer regulations concerning profanity and nudity on pay cable channels than it does on over-the-air networks, and HBO was experimenting with a number of edgier comedy and drama series that it planned to run head-to-head with its rivals' offerings. Chase's idea, HBO executives felt, fit in well with their long-term programming plans.

After the publication of Mario Puzo's novel *The Godfather* (1969) and the movies it inspired, books, films, and television shows that portray some aspect of organized crime became commonplace. Adding a fresh spin to the shopworn genre, David Chase has attempted to depict a mid-level mob boss not only as an icy executioner but also as a middle-class family man and friend. Suffering from what he views as a midlife crisis, Tony Soprano attends weekly psychotherapy sessions, during which he tries to work through the conflicts inherent in his way of life. The therapist, played by Lorraine Bracco, is the vehicle through which Chase reveals Tony's motivations and past experiences.

"College," an episode from *The Sopranos*' first season, illustrates the series' thrust. In that installment Tony takes his daughter, Meadow, to visit small, prestigious liberal-arts colleges in New England. (Meadow's name is an example of her parents' yearning to fit into the middle-class American ethos while maintaining a darker existence on the periphery of mainstream society.) During the trip Tony stumbles upon a mob informant who had disappeared through the witness protection program. After depositing Meadow at Colby College for her interview, Tony finds and kills the informant—by strangling him—and then returns for his daughter. During the ride home, Gandolfini characterizes a man at war with himself: still flush from the kill, Soprano struggles to hide from his daughter what he has done, to protect her from knowledge of his criminal activities. "As Tony, Gandolfini is masterly at conveying the simmering rage beneath his character's humanity,"

Ginia Bellafante wrote. "He brings all the right sweaty fidgetiness to a man whose life demands that he take his daughter to a college interview and kill a Mob informant in the same afternoon." "James is very likeable as a father and a leading man, but then when he turns brutal, he's so real," Chase told Frank DeCaro. "He really showed me that dichotomy about the character, even more than I knew when I wrote it."

Because critics and reviewers responded so positively to *The Sopranos* from the very outset, HBO rewarded the show with a contract for renewal after only two episodes had aired. In 1999 the Emmy committee recognized the series as one of the best on television, by nominating the show, its cast, and crew—including Gandolfini—for awards in 16 categories, a greater number than the total for any other program, broadcast or cable. In addition, *The Sopranos* became the first-ever cable series to be nominated for best drama, and went on to win four Emmys. In 2000 the series garnered 18 Emmy nominations, and Gandolfini took the award for best actor in a drama series.

James Gandolfini reportedly feels bewildered by his newfound fame. Edie Falco, who won an Emmy for her portrayal of Carmela, Tony Soprano's wife, told Ginia Bellafante, "You go into these TV things always worrying about the kind of egos you're going to encounter, but he just doesn't have one." "I do a job," Gandolfini told Sophfronia Scott Gregory and Sue Miller. "A carpenter does a job. He doesn't have to do an interview about the job he did."

Satisfying a wish to try his hand at a romantic comedy, Gandolfini took a minor role alongside Jim Carrey in *Me, Myself and Irene* (2000), written and directed by Bobby and Peter Farrelly. Unlike many actors, Gandolfini has expressed no desire to move behind the camera into the director's chair. Although he has said that he does not want to take any more mobster roles, he will play a sensitive hit man opposite Julia Roberts and Brad Pitt in the director Gore Verbinski's *The Mexican*, a film that *Reel.com* characterized as "a violent comedy with a dry, weird sense of humor." *The Mexican* was scheduled for release in early 2001. According to the unofficial Gandolfini Web page, the actor married Marcy Wudarski in March 1999. — T.J.F.

Suggested Reading: *International Movie Database* (on-line); *Interview* p108+ Mar. 1999, with photo; *People* p58+ Sep. 13, 1999, with photo; *Time* p106 Mar. 22, 1999, with photos; *TV Guide* p38+ Feb. 6, 1999, with photo

Selected Films: *A Stranger Among Us*, 1992; *True Romance*, 1993; *Mr. Wonderful*, 1993; *Money for Nothing*, 1993; *Angie*, 1994; *Get Shorty*, 1995; *Crimson Tide*, 1995; *The Juror*, 1996; *8MM*, 1999; *A Civil Action*, 1999

Selected Television Shows: *The Sopranos*, 1998–

Michael Sofronski

Garbus, Martin

Aug. 8, 1934– Lawyer. Address: Frankfurt, Garbus, Klein, & Selz, 488 Madison Ave., New York, NY 10022

"I chose this life so that I could forever remain a student," the attorney Martin Garbus told Jeff Howe for the *Village Voice* (May 3–9, 2000, online). A staunch defender of First Amendment rights, Garbus has served as counsel to most of the country's major book publishers and movie studios as well as individuals including the comedian Lenny Bruce, the drug guru Timothy Leary, the Soviet dissidents Andrei Sakharov and Anatoly Shcharansky (now known as Natan Sharansky), and the South African civil rights leader and former president Nelson Mandela. An expert in both copyright and civil rights law, Garbus has also worked for entertainment celebrities, among them Spike Lee, Richard Gere, Robert Redford, and Al Pacino; represented the publishers of books by such controversial writers as Salman Rushdie and Henry Miller; and helped to secure copyright protections for the work of the writers Samuel Beckett and John Cheever. He is the author of three books chronicling his experiences: *Ready for the Defense* (1971), *Traitors and Heroes: A Lawyer's Memoir* (1987), and *Tough Talk: How I Fought for Writers, Comics, Bigots, and the American Way* (1998). Garbus is a frequent contributor to the *New York Times*, the *Nation*, and the *Los Angeles Times*, among other publications, and is regularly invited to provide commentary on legal issues for television news programs such as *Rivera Live*.

Martin Garbus was born in the New York City borough of Brooklyn on August 8, 1934, to Jewish parents who had come originally from Poland. When he was three years old, his mother died in a fire, and he was raised by relatives for several years, until his father remarried. Garbus worked for many years in his father's candy store in the borough of the Bronx, often putting in 10- and 12-hour days. Although he attended the prestigious Bronx High School of Science, his father fully expected him to continue to work for the family business upon graduation. "My father was a terrified immigrant, an illegal one at that, who came here from Cuba running from the pogroms in Poland," Garbus told Michael Brennan for the *Guardian* (April 16, 1992). "He thought that the way to be safe was to have a stall. He thought college was inappropriate for me and was not in favour of me going to it."

Garbus nevertheless entered Hunter College (now part of the City University of New York), where he studied economics; he also continued to work in the candy store, still expecting to follow in his father's footsteps. At Hunter Garbus developed "an identification with people who were the victims of unjust laws," as he told Michael Brennan. He was also deeply affected by tales concerning members of his father's family, 10 of whom had perished in Nazi death camps in Poland. "I was just a kid during the second world war," he told Brennan, "but I sensed the helplessness of that immigrant group which saw its people killed and could do nothing to prevent it." Garbus graduated from Hunter in 1955. After a semester at Columbia University, he was drafted into the army, where he soon discovered that his views of American politics and history did not sit well with his superiors. In a class he taught on the dissemination of news and information, Garbus criticized the government's actions in the case of Nicola Sacco and Bartolomeo Vanzetti (Italian anarchists who had been accused of murdering both the guard and the paymaster of a shoe factory in South Braintree, Massachusetts; despite an international campaign on their behalf, the two men, who maintained their innocence, were executed by the United States government, in 1927). When his superiors expressed their displeasure with the subjects he had taught, Garbus decided that the theme of his next lecture would be the First Amendment. Although he was threatened with disciplinary action, he next delivered a lecture that was critical of the Communist witch hunt conducted by Senator Joseph McCarthy; the army initiated court-martial proceedings against Garbus that were later dismissed.

Frustrated by the military's attempts to restrict his constitutional rights and wanting to protect himself against such treatment in the future, Garbus began taking night classes at New York University Law School. He was fortunate enough to land a job as an assistant to Emile Zola Berman (who later became known for representing Sirhan Sirhan, who assassinated the U.S. senator and presidential candidate Robert F. Kennedy, in 1968). Although the position was not glamorous, Garbus and Berman spent almost every day for many months in court, and Garbus gained a wealth of legal experience rather quickly. By the time he graduated from law school, in 1959, Garbus had "logged hundreds of court days, which is an extraordinary experience," he told Michael Brennan. "The day I graduated law school I started trying cases." In 1964 he married Ruth Streifer, with whom he had two daughters, Cassandra and Elizabeth.

Garbus's earliest assignments were mostly personal-injury and criminal cases, but he quickly turned his attention to the widespread violation of human rights. He accepted many cases involving free speech, as well as many lawsuits in opposition to capital punishment. In 1967 he became the director-counsel for the Roger Baldwin Foundation, a branch of the American Civil Liberties Union; the following year he became the director of Columbia University's Center for Social and Welfare Policy. Garbus represented Henrietta White, an African-American who was brutalized by a Mississippi sheriff when she tried to register to vote and who was even committed to a psychiatric hospital. Although both he and his client knew that they would lose the court case against the sheriff and other officials involved, Garbus felt that it was important enough to demonstrate that in such cases, "a black woman will bring suit, and . . . a lawyer will represent her," as he told Jack K. Robbins for the *New York Post* (July 23, 1971). "They [people such as the sheriff] will have to be more careful. That suit may have made some people's lives easier." Garbus counseled Sylvester Smith, in a landmark case in Alabama that overturned that state's policy of denying aid to poor women and their children because the women lived with men who were not their husbands. In the 1960s Garbus also lent his talents to the farm workers championed by Cesar Chavez and to the National Welfare Rights Organization.

It was during this time that Garbus began to recognize what he saw as the folly of placing one's hope for progress with the nation's highest court. "The Supreme Court is not going to move forward and I think the responsibility of lawyers like myself is not to take cases up there," he told Jack K. Robbins. "You'll get good law reversed and bad law made. In the '60s we would try to get the Justice Dept. to come into cases because they'd come in on the side of the angels. Now they come in on the side of the devil." Garbus took a hiatus of a year and a half from his duties to write his first book; *Ready for the Defense* described some of his earliest high-profile cases, such as the obscenity trial of the comedian Lenny Bruce.

Garbus has often placed himself at risk to further the cause of justice. In 1970, when the journalist Daniel Ellsberg took from the Pentagon secret documents that outlined the government's deception concerning its involvement in the Vietnam War, Garbus hid the documents in his home. (What came to be called the Pentagon Papers were initially published in the *New York Times*; in 1971 the government received an injunction against the further publication of the documents, which was later overturned by the Supreme Court. Ellsberg's indictment on charges of espionage, theft, and conspiracy was later dismissed in federal court. Garbus was not named in the case.) In 1977 Garbus traveled to South Africa as an international observer of the persecution of apartheid opponents. Soon afterward, a representative of the South African government petitioned the New York Bar Association in an attempt to have Garbus disbarred. The charge lingered for three years before being dismissed. In 1979 Garbus traveled to Prague, Czechoslovakia, to defend Vaclav Havel, who was charged with subversion; 10 years later, when Havel was elected president of that nation, he asked Garbus to supervise the drafting of the human rights clause of the country's new constitution. Garbus also smuggled a letter from Russian dissident Andrei Sakharov to U.S. president Jimmy Carter. The letter caused such a stir among the media that President Carter, under pressure, sent a reply.

In 1992 Garbus successfully defended Britain's Channel 4, producers of the documentary *Damned in the USA*, along with the film's distributors, against a suit by the American Family Association (AFA), a right-wing organization that sought to ban the film. The suit was initiated by the Reverend Donald Wildmon, the president of the AFA, who was displeased with the film's portrayal of his organization's attempts to censor ideas that they found objectionable. Two years later, to the surprise of many, Garbus represented the plaintiff in a libel suit against the New York *Daily News* writer Mike McAlary, who had concluded that a young woman's story of being raped in Brooklyn's Prospect Park was false. The attorney quickly became a pariah in the First Amendment community, receiving plenty of bad press for what some saw as his ironic and ethically suspicious position. The judge ruled in favor of McAlary; Garbus's client decided not to appeal the decision.

Most recently, Garbus served as counsel to the on-line journalist Eric Corley, who was being sued by the Motion Picture Association of America (MPAA). Corley publishes *2600*, sometimes referred to as the "hacker bible," under the pseudonym Emmanuel Goldstein. The MPAA sought to punish Corley for posting on his Web site in the fall of 1999 a program known as DeCSS; using that software, people are able to crack the digital information encoded on a DVD, bypassing the content-scrambling system designed to prevent illicit viewing of the films. The potential for DVD piracy through this technology is slim; a normal hard drive would be disabled for weeks if an entire movie was downloaded in this fashion. Additionally, most computers would not be able to store more than four feature-length films. Garbus argued that the program in question is protected under the First Amendment. The plaintiffs also attempted to curtail the posting of links to other Web sites that contain the software, a practice with far-reaching implications, especially for the news media. Although Corley is not himself a hacker, Garbus believed that the suit was aimed at curbing the activities of hackers, who are feared and despised by the entertainment industry. "There is little question in my mind this persecution of hackers is, in many respects, analogous to the Communist red-baiting of yore," he told Jeff Howe. "They are being unfairly maligned, and stigmatized, without due cause." In August 2000, the court decided in favor of the MPAA.

In addition to *Ready for the Defense*, Garbus is the author of *Traitors and Heroes: A Lawyer's Memoir*, which describes his defense of the poet Breyten Breytenbach and members of the African National Congress and warned of the consequences to civil liberties that might result from President Ronald Reagan's appointment of Judge William Rehnquist to the United States Supreme Court. *Tough Talk: How I Fought for Writers, Comics, Bigots, and the American Way*, co-authored with Stanley Cohen, describes many of Garbus's most famous cases, including his defense of the members of the American Nazi Party who sought permission to march in Skokie, Illinois. Garbus has served as a professor at both the Yale University Law School, in New Haven, Connecticut, and the Columbia University Law School, in New York. He is the founder of the firm Frankfurt, Garbus, Klein, & Selz, where he handles commercial, intellectual-property, estate, and criminal cases. He lives in New York City. — C.L.

Suggested Reading: *Columbia Journalism Review* (on-line) Nov./Dec. 1991; (London) *Guardian* p27 Apr. 16, 1992, with photo; New York *Daily News* C p37 July 23, 1971, with photo; *New York Times Magazine* p28+ Aug. 25, 1968, with photos; *Village Voice* (on-line) May 3–9, 2000, with photos; Charlotte, Susan, Tom Ferguson, and Bruce Felton. *Creativity: Conversations with 28 Who Excel*, 1993

Selected Books: *Ready for the Defense*, 1971; *Traitors and Heroes: A Lawyer's Memoir*, 1987; *Tough Talk: How I Fought for Writers, Comics, Bigots, and the American Way* (with Stanley Cohen), 1998

Ray Stubblebine/Archive Photos

Garciaparra, Nomar

July 23, 1973– Baseball player. Address: Boston Red Sox Baseball Club, 4 Yawkey Way, Boston, MA 02215-3496

After only four full seasons, Nomar Garciaparra, the young Boston Red Sox shortstop, has been compared to such baseball greats as Ted Williams and Joe DiMaggio. As one of the top offensive and defensive players at his position, Garciaparra has been named to two All-Star squads and won the Rookie of the Year Award, among several other honors. Johnny Pesky, who played shortstop for Boston in the 1940s, noted for the official Nomar Garciaparra Web page that the young athlete is "the best-looking shortstop we've ever had around here. . . . He can run. He has good baseball instincts. I'm telling you, if he'd come along in my era, I'd be sitting on the pine. You could almost classify him as the perfect player." In 1997 Garciaparra became the first Red Sox player since Jackie Jensen in 1956 to post two-digit figures in doubles, triples, home runs, and stolen bases in one season. Darren Bragg, a former Red Sox player, noted for Garciaparra's Web page, "I think by the time he's done he could probably be one of the best who has ever played, not just for the Red Sox, for all of baseball." Despite the awards and the accolades, Garciaparra remains modest. "I enjoy the game every day, and that's all that is important to me," he has said. "I take it for all it's worth. At the same time, I understand it could be all gone tomorrow. Why look at the numbers if I'm not playing tomorrow?"

The shortstop was born Anthony Nomar Garciaparra on July 23, 1973 in Whittier, California, the oldest of the four children of Ramon and Sylvia Garciaparra. His mother, a fan of University of Southern California (USC) sports teams, liked the sound of the name Anthony as spoken by USC announcers when they referred to the star running back Anthony Davis. "Nomar" is Ramon Garciaparra's first name spelled backwards. Although he was called Anthony at first, Garciaparra decided that he wanted to be known as Nomar after his kindergarten teacher called his name and several other children answered. As a boy he was close to his mother's younger brother, Victor, who was only four years older than Nomar. Garciaparra, who started playing baseball at age five, had to practice extra hard to be able to compete with Victor and Victor's friends. Despite his constant effort, the older kids would often tease Garciaparra, accepting him as one of their own only when—after a flying bat opened a gash in his head that required nine stitches—Nomar returned to the field the same afternoon, ready to play. He soon developed the nickname "No Nonsense Nomar" for his strong baseball work ethic, practicing long after the other kids were off having fun elsewhere. "I never had a baseball hero or anything like that," Garciaparra told *Sports Illustrated* (September 1, 1997). "I loved the game just for the sake of playing it. I'd tell my dad from the time I was five or six, 'Teach me that. Don't tell me about who plays the game in the majors. Tell me *how* to play it.' I wanted to learn as much as I could about every position."

Garciaparra attended St. John Bosco High School, in Bellflower, California, where he excelled in baseball, football, and soccer. In ninth grade he received the Most Inspirational Player Award for his athletic achievements. At the time, Garciaparra was only five feet three inches tall; he would pray at night that he would grow to be as tall as baseball pro Mike Gallego, who is five-eight. Meanwhile, Garciaparra was working hard at academics. During high school he maintained a grade-point average of 4.02 (exceeding 4.0 because he received an A in an advanced class) and received awards in math, Spanish, and science. "My parents always said you have to do your homework first before you can play," he was quoted as saying on his home page. "School was a priority. I had to do well in school so I could keep playing, so I was very big on education."

After playing several other baseball positions, Garciaparra was finally made a shortstop in his junior year, during which he hit .536, scoring 36 runs. In the following year he was named captain of his team and hit .494, striking out only four times in 79 at bats and being named co-MVP (most valuable player) of the Angelus League, of which his team was a part. He was also named southeastern California's player of the year and St. John Bosco athlete of the year. "He had all the tools," his coach, Tim Ellis, declared, according to the official Nomar Garciaparra home page. "He could run. He had a cannon for an arm. He could hit the ball with power or bunt the ball for a hit. I could have played him anywhere in the field. He'd be a heckuva center fielder." Although Nomar was selected to play on several high school all-star teams, he characteristically declined them all. "I always thought I was an all-star, not because of myself, but because of my teammates," he said for his home page. "I always felt bad that they picked me over another guy. I just shunned away from all-star teams and games. I always felt I was successful because of my teammates [because] baseball is a team sport." Meanwhile, as a soccer player, he was named most valuable player in his Del Ray League and also made the All-CIF (California Interscholastic Federation) Soccer Team. In his junior year he scored 17 goals in a very competitive league. Although some of his coaches thought he was better at soccer than baseball, Garciaparra had his heart set on pursuing the latter, and he honed his baseball skills through soccer. "Fielding at shortstop is with your feet, not with your hands," he was quoted as saying on his home page. "Soccer helped me with my coordination and that carried over to the baseball field." In football, he was considered one of the best high-school kickers in his region and also played as wide receiver, making the Long Beach Press "Dream Team."

After graduating from high school, Garciaparra was picked by the Milwaukee Brewers baseball team in the fifth round of the amateur draft. Choosing instead to focus on his education, he enrolled at Georgia Tech, in Atlanta. There, in spite of a case of homesickness, he continued to excel at baseball: he was named the Atlantic Coast Conference (ACC) rookie of the year in 1992 and became a two-time All-American. In three seasons with the school's Yellow Jackets, Garciaparra hit .372 with 23 home runs and 166 runs batted in (RBIs). He was named to *Baseball America*'s freshman All-American first team and set a university record for most stolen-base attempts in a season without being caught (25). Thanks to his incredible numbers, he was chosen as a member of the 1992 U.S. Olympic baseball team. In 20 at bats during the competition, Garciaparra hit .200. "It was a great thrill and a time of pride to represent an entire country," he said in an on-line chat. "To put on a USA jersey and look at the flag. I'll never forget when they lit the torch with a bow and arrow in the Opening Ceremonies." Going back to college after that event was tough for Garciaparra. "All the guys in the Olympics were preparing to get drafted or were about to be drafted," his home page quotes him as saying. "I was the only guy going back to school. It was difficult to deal with that."

In 1994 Garciaparra batted .427 with 16 home runs and set two school records, becoming the first player to get both 100 hits and the greatest number of successful consecutive steal attempts (35) in one season. That year, in the National Collegiate Athletic Association (NCAA) play-offs, Garciaparra had perhaps his most memorable baseball experience up to that point. Scheduled to play two games in one day in temperatures that rose above 100 degrees, Garciaparra became dehydrated in the first game and had to be taken to the hospital. Immediately after being treated, he returned to the ballpark and, insisting that he was ready to play, stepped into the second game as a pinch hitter. Danny Hall, the team's coach, recalled for the Garciaparra home page, "He hits the first pitch he sees out of the park. I was coaching third base, and the home plate umpire looks at me and says, 'I can't believe what I'm seeing.'"

Meanwhile, Garciaparra, who had been named to the ACC academic honor roll three years in a row, had made the difficult decision to leave college, where he had majored in business management, and participate in the amateur draft. At the time, he said, as quoted on his home page, "If I'm drafted high and I get the right offer, I think I'm ready. I'm on course to graduate, so I will always have the incentive to finish. . . . I think I'm ready now." Chosen 12th in the draft by the Boston Red Sox, he signed an $895,000 contract with the team. That summer, he was sent to the organization's class A farm club, in Sarasota, Florida, where he hit .295 with one home run and 16 RBIs. Wanting to work on his skills further, Garciaparra also played in the fall league in Scottsdale, Arizona, where he hit .328.

In the following year Garciaparra moved up to class AA in Trenton, New Jersey, where he hit .267, with eight home runs and 47 RBIs. He led his team with runs (77), at bats (513), and triples (eight) and set a team record for steals (35); as a result he was named an Eastern League All-Star. His number with the club, 5, has since been retired. Although he started the next season on the disabled list, with a sore ankle, he roared back with an impressive season at class AAA in Pawtucket, Rhode Island, where he hit .343, with 16 home runs and 46 RBIs. He was called up to Boston at the end of the season, making his major-league debut on August 31, 1996. The next day he had his first hit, which was, dramatically, a home run. Over the next month, in 24 games, he hit .241 with four home runs and 16 RBIs.

During the next year's spring training, a battle erupted between Garciaparra and veteran John Valentin over the shortstop position. Garciaparra played so well at the position that, despite Valentin's fierce protests, he became the team's starting shortstop, while Valentin was moved from that spot to second base. In his first full season in the majors, Garciaparra exploded, hitting .306 with 30 home runs and 98 RBIs for an otherwise mediocre team. He was also chosen for the All-Star team. "I really wasn't paying much attention to the All-Star Game," he wrote in an article for *Baseball Weekly* (August 14, 1997), "until everyone began talking about me having a chance and asking what I thought about it. Since we still had games going on, I was more worried about that. . . . What was really exciting was knowing that my father would be able to come out here and watch, because I hadn't seen him since we opened in Anaheim. . . . It doesn't make me feel any different to be in the clubhouse with all these guys. The way I look at it, I'm facing All-Stars day in and day out, and playing alongside All-Stars, regardless of whether they get picked or not. When you get to the major league level, you're an All-Star. It's not an easy level to reach." Before playing in the All-Star game, Garciaparra won Major League Baseball's annual home-run contest. "Even though I won," he wrote, "I'm sure there was still some laughter. When I took the picture with all the veteran contestants, fans probably thought I was the bat boy compared to the rest of those guys. If no one else was laughing, I know I was." Among his other achievements that season, Garciaparra led the American League in at bats and in triples (11) while being voted American League Player of the week for August 4–10, setting the record for most home runs by a rookie shortstop, and getting base hits in 30 games in a row (also an American League rookie record). That winter, Garciaparra won the American League Rookie of the Year Award by a unanimous vote as well as the Silver Slugger Award. "It's definitely a great honor to be selected Rookie of the Year," Garciaparra said, as quoted on the official Red Sox home page. "I never thought about winning the award during the season, but to get this honor means a lot. You only get a chance at it one time. You're only a rookie once." Former teammate Mo Vaughn stated, as quoted on the Garciaparra home page, "He's very mature in his work ethic, which gives him consistency. That gives him a chance to be one of the best in the game. More important, he's definitely a solid kid—humble, always open for help. He knows his role and has done very well."

In March 1998 Garciaparra signed a five-year contract with the Red Sox worth $23.25 million. That season he improved on his rookie numbers, hitting .323 with 35 home runs and 122 RBIs; only twice did he play two consecutive games without a hit. Despite these numbers, Garciaparra was overlooked for that year's All-Star Game. Meanwhile, the Red Sox finished second in the American League East, with a strong enough record to make the wild-card slot for the postseason, thus bringing hope to a city that had not seen a World Series victory since 1918. "That's why I enjoy playing here so much," he told *Sport* (September 1998). "I can't think of a better place to win." Although the team did not make it past the first series, against Cleveland, Garciaparra played in the first postseason game the Red Sox had won in 12 years. His efforts landed him second in the MVP balloting, behind Juan Gonzalez. "I don't see how you can even pick an MVP in a team sport," he said, according to his home page. "I can't drive in 100 runs if no one is on base ahead of me. . . . I'm not thinking about awards. My only goal is to win." In November Garciaparra joined a crew of major-league baseball players who toured Japan.

The 1999 season started slowly for Garciaparra, who experienced minor injuries—including tendinitis and a pulled hamstring—that kept him out of the game for much of the first three weeks. But in May he suddenly caught fire, hitting three home runs (two of them grand slams) in one game. He was once again chosen for the All-Star team, which played that year in Boston, and over the course of the season managed to put up impressive numbers, hitting 27 home runs and knocking in 104 RBIs. His .356 average was the highest in the American League. Finishing second to the New York Yankees after a tight division race, the Red Sox again made the play-offs as the wild-card team. They faced Cleveland in the first round; while Garciaparra, who was injured, missed game four, the Sox rallied after being down two games to none to win the series, three games to two. They then took on their arch-rivals, the Yankees, for the American League pennant, but fell in five games. "I could go out there and have a great year, but if I don't get a World Championship ring on my finger it doesn't mean much," Garciaparra said, as reported on the Red Sox home page. "You have to go out there and work hard and contribute day in and day out to try and win."

The Red Sox had high hopes coming into the 2000 season, but injuries and sub-par performances by several of their players contributed to a mediocre, 85–77 record, and they finished in second place, two and a half games behind the Yankees. Although Garciaparra started the season slowly for the second year in a row, he soon put up towering numbers: he hit above .400 well into July, an astounding hitting achievement. While he dipped below that number later, he completed the season with a remarkable .372 average, which earned him his second consecutive batting title, and he hit 21 home runs with 96 RBIs.

Garciaparra is six feet tall and weights 185 pounds. During the off-season he makes his home in Las Vegas, Nevada. While he likes hip-hop, rap, and dance music, his favorite band is the eclectic French group the Gypsy Kings, whose repertoire includes pop flamenco tunes. His favorite books are *The Celestine Prophecy*, by James Redfield, and *Animal Farm*, by George Orwell, and his favorite films are those in the *Rocky* series, starring Sylvester Stallone. As a ballplayer he is highly superstitious; every time he prepares to face a pitch, he pulls up his batting gloves several times, and he never changes his cap during the season. In addition, he always rocks on his toes while waiting for a pitch, places his backup glove in the same place under the bench, and puts both feet on each step when going down staircases. Former roommate and current teammate Scott Hatteberg was quoted on the Nomar Garciaparra home page as saying, "What you see on the field with his routine and superstitions really spills over into his daily life. It doesn't rule him, but he's very routine oriented. We take the same routes to the ballpark. He listens to the same exact songs on the way to the ballpark. He gets up and eats the same thing for breakfast. He's got these waffles he usually eats. For lunch, he's got a couple sandwich joints around there that know him pretty well. They make him sandwiches he likes." For relaxation, Garciaparra spends time at the beach and plays soccer. "When I'm not with my family and friends or at the beach," he has said, "I try to visit schools around the LA area. I love to talk to kids. During the season, I try to do the same in Boston by visiting schools or neighborhood centers." In Boston he helps run the Nomar Garciaparra Baseball Camp. He enjoys being in Boston and has signed there through 2002; contract extensions (called "club options") make it possible for the Red Sox to keep him on for one or two years after that. "I wish I could tell you something really exciting about him," his high-school friend and teammate Jim Frausto has said, "but he's just a good, down-to-earth guy, nothing extravagant. He's gotten this far—and he deserves every bit of it—because of his work ethic. I watch him on the field sometimes and I wonder what's going through his mind. I wonder when he puts on that cape and mask." — G.O.

Suggested Reading: *Nomar Garciaparra Online*; *Sport* p88+ Sep. 1998; *Sports Illustrated* p28+ Sep. 1, 1997

Courtesy of the FAA

Garvey, Jane F.

Feb. 2, 1944– Director of the Federal Aviation Administration. Address: Federal Aviation Administration, 800 Independence Ave. S.W., Washington, DC 20591

Jane F. Garvey is the first woman to head the Federal Aviation Administration (FAA), a division of the U.S. Department of Transportation whose mission is to ensure the safety of civilian aviation. Chosen by President Bill Clinton, who acted on the recommendation of Rodney Slater, the U.S. secretary of transportation, Garvey was sworn in as the FAA's director on August 4, 1997. A former high-school English teacher, Garvey successively managed the Massachusetts Department of Public Works, directed Logan International Airport, in Boston, and served as acting head of the Federal Highway Administration before arriving at the FAA. She has gained a reputation as an innovative manager and is noted for her poise, political savvy, strong sense of fairness, highly developed diplomatic skills, ability to build a consensus, and willingness to laugh at herself. Now in the fourth year of a five-year term, Garvey has introduced several programs aimed at lowering the accident rate, and her efforts to modernize the air-traffic-control system have, unlike those of her immediate predecessors, led to agreement among representatives of both government and industry about how to proceed. She has also made major strides in imposing financial accountability at the FAA. As the head of the FAA, which employs some 49,000 people, Garvey makes decisions that affect the hundreds of millions of people who travel by air in the U.S. In 1998 alone, as Garvey stated at a symposium held in May 1999, U.S. commercial airlines "carried 615 million passengers on some 14 million flights." Those numbers are expected to double within the next two decades.

Little has been reported about Garvey's early life. A native of Massachusetts, she was born on February 2, 1944. She spent her undergraduate years at Mount St. Mary College, in Newburgh, New York, from which she graduated in about 1966, and earned a master's degree in education from Mount Holyoke College, in South Hadley, Massachusetts, in 1968; like many other women of her generation, she regarded education as one of the few fields open to her. She settled in Amherst, Massachusetts, married Robert J. Garvey, a county sheriff, and became the mother of two children. At some point she took a job teaching English at a parochial high school, where she became popular for her kindness and integrity as well as her lively teaching style. Mary Fifield, a former student of hers who later became a press secretary for Massachusetts governor Michael Dukakis, told Matthew Brelis for the *Boston Globe* (June 11, 1997, on-line), "A forming incident for me was when word got out about a classmate becoming pregnant. This was [about] 30 years ago, and there was a fair amount of corridor talk. Jane got us into the classroom and laced into us . . . explaining why [such gossip] was not acceptable. It is an enduring memory."

In 1982 Garvey, a Democrat, volunteered as a campaign organizer for Michael Dukakis, during his successful run for a second term as governor of Massachusetts. After his inauguration, Dukakis named Garvey an assistant commissioner in the state's Department of Public Works. In that unglamorous position, which was traditionally held by a male engineer, she oversaw maintenance and construction work. Garvey excelled at the job, winning the respect of maintenance workers with her willingness to work hard and listen to their concerns. "People in maintenance were treated like second-class citizens, and she went to bat for them and they just loved her," Fred Salvucci, a former Massachusetts secretary of transportation, told Matthew Brelis for his 1997 *Boston Globe* article. In the *Boston Globe Magazine* (September 6, 1998), Brelis wrote, "She got down and dirty with people who fix roads."

In 1988 Garvey was chosen to replace the head of the department, who had retired. As commissioner, she dealt with projects costing billions of dollars. Prominent among them was the Central Artery/Third Harbor Tunnel Project, which was launched to improve mobility in Boston, where traffic congestion is notoriously troublesome, and to reconnect neighborhoods that had been virtually severed from the rest of the city as a result of construction of the Central Artery, an elevated highway, in the 1950s. The largest and most complicated highway project ever undertaken in a U.S. metropolis, the "Big Dig," as it is known, involved the construction of an underground expressway, a 1.6-mile-long tunnel, and two bridges, all in the heart of a bustling urban area. Begun in 1992 and budgeted at $2.4 billion, the project became ever more costly; by 1997 the price tag had climbed to $7.7 billion (currently, it has reached more than $11 billion, with building only two-thirds completed). According to Garvey, congressionally mandated changes, some related to the environment, as well as inflation accounted for the increases.

In 1991 Garvey left the Department of Public Works to join the Massachusetts Port Authority as the director of Logan International Airport, in East Boston. New England's largest transportation center, Logan Airport has five passenger terminals and five runways, and it caters to some 25 million travelers annually. As its director, Garvey oversaw a $20 million campaign to improve the airport's fire department, which entailed hiring more staff and building a modern facility filled with the best available equipment.

In 1993 Garvey moved to Washington, D.C., to become deputy administrator of the Federal Highway Administration (FHA), under Rodney Slater. An agency of the U.S. Department of Transportation, the FHA oversees approximately 42,500 miles of national interstate and defense highways and 800,000 miles of other federally administered roads; it also provides technical expertise regarding highway safety and the design, construction, and maintenance of roads and bridges. Among other responsibilities, Garvey chaired the Innovative Financing Initiative, which sought nontraditional ways to supplement the agency's funding. In *Traffic World* (June 23, 1997), David Barnes wrote that Garvey's "biggest accomplishment" while at the FHA was her development of the State Infrastructure Bank program; approved by Congress in 1995, the program enables states to "leverage and combine both public and private funds to construct transportation projects," in Barnes's words. Thanks to the efforts of Garvey and others after the devastating 1994 California earthquake, the rebuilding of damaged Los Angeles freeways was completed ahead of schedule.

On February 14, 1997 Rodney Slater was sworn in as the U.S. secretary of transportation, and Garvey was named the FHA's acting administrator. Four months later President Clinton nominated Garvey to the top post at the Federal Aviation Administration, to replace David Hinson, who had resigned as head of the FAA in November 1996. Clinton had acted on the advice of Slater; later, in a 1998 conversation with Matthew Brelis for the *Boston Globe Magazine*, Slater explained that he had recommended Garvey to the president because he believed she had precisely the skills needed for the job: "With reform and structural changes at the FAA needed, I wanted a person who is good with people, task-oriented, result-oriented," he said. "I needed someone I have the greatest respect for and trust in."

Others, though, felt misgivings about the appointment. Unlike the previous heads of the agency (all of them male), the doubters pointed out, Garvey had no hands-on aviation or military experience. Indeed, all but two of her predecessors were licensed pilots; of the unlicensed pair, one had risen to the rank of general in the air force and the other had served as secretary of the air force. In addition, during her confirmation hearings before the Senate Commerce Committee, which were held in June 1997, members of the committee expressed concern about the Big Dig's huge cost overruns under Garvey. The FAA's finances were notoriously out of control—as David Barnes reported in *Traffic World* (July 7, 1997), the General Accounting Office, the inspector general of the Department of Transportation, and an independent auditor had all failed to determine exactly how the agency had spent the $8 billion allocated to it in a recent year—and the senators hoped that the next FAA head would correct that problem. The senators' reservations notwithstanding, the committee recommended Garvey's confirmation; the full Senate approved her appointment in July, and she took the oath of office on August 4, 1997. While previous FAA directors had served at the discretion of the country's chief executive, Garvey was sworn in for a five-year term, signaling the Clinton administration's determination to develop stability in the management of the FAA.

The FAA's main job is to regulate civil aviation so as to make air travel as safe as possible. Toward that end, the agency sets standards for and regulates the manufacture, operation, and maintenance of airplanes; it also oversees the certification of pilots and airports, the operation of airport control towers, the use of airspace, and the shipment by air of hazardous materials. Among its other activities are aeronautical research—aimed, for example, at the improvement of air-traffic-control systems—and monitoring the environmental effects of civil aviation, including the noise created by airplanes during landing and takeoff.

When Garvey took the helm, public and political dissatisfaction with the FAA was running high, particularly with regard to its procedures for monitoring airline safety. The issue had stirred intense discussion following the crash, on May 11, 1996, of a ValuJet DC-9 in the Florida Everglades. All 110 people aboard had perished in the crash, the cause of which was determined to be the explosion of oxygen canisters stored (against federal regulations) in the plane's cargo hold. Investigators also discovered that in the 18 months before the accident, the FAA had cited ValuJet for a number of serious safety-related shortcomings. Fears about airline safety increased in July 1996, after TWA Flight 800 blew up off the coast of New York State, killing the 230 passengers and crew. While investigators eventually concluded that the explosion of one of the fuel tanks had led to the crash, to date they have not figured out why the tank exploded.

In one of her first moves as FAA director, Garvey launched what has been dubbed the Flight Operations Quality Assurance (FOQA) Program, which called for the installation of additional flight recorders—commonly called "black boxes"—separate from and with greater information-gathering capacity than those used in accident investigations, to help identify and correct problems before they lead to crashes. Garvey asked that all airlines share the data collected from such recorders. By the end of 1997, nearly three dozen foreign and four U.S. airlines had begun participating in the FOQA program. In one example of the program's benefits, Robert Davis reported in *USA Today* (October 29, 1997), United Airlines, after analyzing internal tire temperatures of landing planes, installed different tires on aircraft that touch down and take off in airports where the weather is often hot, so as to avoid blowouts. Edmond Soliday, vice president of safety and security at United, told Davis that the new monitoring system "has the potential to be the best safety tool of the 21st century."

In April 1998 Garvey, Secretary of Transportation Slater, and Vice President Al Gore (who had headed the White House Commission on Aviation Safety and Security, formed in August 1996) announced a new air-safety program. Called the Safer Skies Initiative, the program called for more-intensive engine inspections by airlines and the use of seatbelts by all passengers at all times; it also required the installation of advanced ground-warning systems, which audibly alert pilots about upcoming obstacles, such as mountains. The next month Garvey announced the FAA's new approach to inspecting planes and overseeing airlines. Called the Air Transportation Oversight System (ATOS), the program focused on 10 major air carriers, which accounted for 90 percent of domestic passenger travel. (Additional carriers have since been added.) Under ATOS, each carrier is provided with a safety and risk-analysis team and is subject to rigorous inspection procedures customized to their aircraft. On another front, Garvey has been directing efforts to modernize air-traffic-control facilities, which include the installation of state-of-the-art equipment to track flights and communicate with pilots.

Garvey subjected the Boeing Co., a manufacturer of some of the most widely used planes in the country, to particular scrutiny in the aftermath of a series of accidents involving Boeing 737 aircraft. Under her direction, in May 1998 the FAA grounded all older Boeing 737s to check for exposed wiring in the fuel tanks, thought to be the cause of the accidents. While some applauded Garvey's swiftness and decisiveness in making that unusual move, others—such as the Air Travelers Association, a passenger lobbying group—criticized the FAA for merely reacting to a crisis, as they saw it, rather than actively seeking to prevent it. For the most part, though, Garvey was winning over skeptics who had doubted her ability to run the FAA effectively. Later in 1998, her establishment of a board to investigate allegations of sexual harassment and misconduct within the FAA was noted as evidence of her commitment to employee satisfaction—an area largely neglected under previous chiefs. Another feather in Garvey's cap was the safety record of U.S. airlines in 1998: only one fatality occurred that year among some 615 million air travelers. By comparison, in 1998, 41,480 deaths were recorded on the nation's highways; 431 people were killed at railroad crossings; 831 people died in other railroad-connected accidents; and recreational boating, commercial fishing, and marine cargo transport claimed the lives of 908 people.

Garvey's reputation within the aviation industry and with the public was further bolstered by the success of the FAA's provisions for the arrival of the year 2000; thanks to the agency's careful preparations, air-traffic computer systems correctly recognized the digits "00" as 2000 rather than 1900, and no problems arose. To ensure continuous operation of its infrastructure, the FAA had checked 23 million lines of code written in 50 computer languages in more than 650 computer systems. Garvey herself was airborne—flying coach on American Airlines planes—as the old year greeted the new in each of the four time zones of the continental United States. At the end of her flight she sent a message to President Clinton, in which she incorporated the text of a telegram sent on December 17, 1903 by the aviation pioneer Orville Wright after he completed the world's first sustained, human-controlled flight in a motor-powered aircraft, at Kitty Hawk, North Carolina: "Success. Stop. Inform press. Stop."

Despite that success and others, at least sometimes Garvey has had reservations about taking on the huge responsibilities required of her as FAA director. In her 1998 interview with Brelis, for example, she joked, "There is not a day when I don't say,

'Why, God, why?' I told my daughter the other day that fulfillment [that is, feeling fulfilled by one's career] is highly overrated." — M.R.

Suggested Reading: *Boston Globe* (on-line) June 11, 1997; *Boston Globe Magazine* (on-line) Sep. 6, 1998; *Government Computer News* (on-line) Jan. 10, 2000; *New York Times* A p19 May 2, 1997, A p15 June 25, 1997; Women in Aviation Web site

---

Richard Heeps, courtesy of Hazard Chase Artist Management

Gavrilov, Andrei

Sep. 21, 1955– Pianist. Address: c/o Hazard Chase Artist Management, Richmond House, 16-20 Regent St., Cambridge, England CB2 1DB

When the Russian-born pianist Andrei Gavrilov made his United States debut, in 1976, a music critic for the *Christian Science Monitor* (August 4, 1976) declared that his playing revealed him to be "in an exalted class all his own." "With a prodigious keyboard technique, and a tasteful innate interpretative sense, he immediately established himself as one of the pianistic wonders of the day," the reviewer, Louis Snyder, wrote. "His facility is breathtaking, his touch a blend of lightness and power, his skill in projecting a miracle of tonal empathy." Gavrilov, who was then 20 years old, had already made a name for himself in his native land, by winning first prize in the piano division of the 1974 International Tchaikovsky Competition, held in Moscow. After his triumphal appearance in Austria later that year, he began building an impressive international reputation, through recordings and concerts on three continents. His career was abruptly cut short in 1979, as a result of the freezing of cultural exchanges between the USSR and the West following the Soviet Union's invasion of Afghanistan. He began performing in public again in 1984, thanks to the intervention of the new Soviet leader, Mikhail Gorbachev. Renowned for his dazzling technical skills and performances that combine headstrong passion and explosive energy with delicacy, lyricism, and sensitivity, he is ranked among the greatest pianists of his time.

Andrei Gavrilov was born on September 21, 1955 in Moscow, in what was then the Soviet Union. His father, Vladimir Gavrilov, was a well-known painter; like many other Soviet artists, he was subjected to relentless governmental pressure to conform to official standards of artistic correctness. (Andrei Gavrilov believes that his father's resulting stress contributed to his early death, at age 47, when Andrei was in his teens.) Andrei's mother, Assanetta Yegiserian, was a pianist and music teacher who had studied at the famed Moscow Conservatory. The family lived in a two-room apartment, and Gavrilov has recalled pretending to sleep in one room while his parents hosted impromptu concerts of classical music in the other. When his mother gave his older brother piano lessons, he would listen attentively, and it became routine for him to learn by ear the pieces his brother practiced; by the age of two and a half, he could play all of them as perfectly as his small hands would permit. After his third birthday his mother began training him formally, and he practiced diligently. Once, having injured his right hand while roughhousing with a friend, he hoped for a reprieve, but his mother simply ordered him to work on his left-hand technique. At six, Gavrilov was admitted to the Central Music School in Moscow, which had produced many of the Soviet Union's most gifted musicians. His mother continued to play a major role in his musical education, however, and her influence, combined with that of his teacher at the music school, Tatiana Kestner, "did me a lot of good," as John Gillespie and Anna Gillespie quoted him as saying in their book *Notable Twentieth-Century Pianists* (1995). Whereas his mother emphasized "emotional richness" in music, as the Gillespies wrote, Kestner favored a more intellectual approach to the piano repertoire. Gavrilov's daily practicing, which sometimes lasted up to six hours, included an hour and a half of scales and technical exercises, developed by such masters of the genre as Carl Czerny.

When he was about 14 and a half, Gavrilov began studying with Lev Naumov, whom the pianist Van Cliburn, on the Web site of the 1997 Van Cliburn International Piano Competition, described as "one of Russia's most important piano pedagogues" and as "represent[ing] the great Russian school of pianism." When he first worked with Naumov, Gavrilov told Mark Zilberquit, the author of *Russia's Great Modern Pianists* (1983), his "ungovernable temperament" usually held sway; "I was simply raging at the instrument and was already playing super-difficult compositions, but on the other hand there was no profound understanding of music." With Naumov's help, he gained "a new understanding of the essence of music, a new attitude . . . to the psychology of performance. . . . One can work with [Naumov] at a piece forever and discover something new."

Gavrilov completed his studies at the Central Music School when he was 17. As was traditional, after the school's graduation ceremony, he and other students performed a skit for those in attendance, who that day included representatives of the Soviet Ministry of Culture. The sketch, which Gavrilov had written, was sharply critical of the national system of education and other aspects of Soviet life, and it caused a minor scandal. Only the personal intervention of Ekaterina A. Furtseva, the minister of culture, who had become fond of Gavrilov, prevented him from being drafted immediately into the Russian army. Instead, he was admitted to the Moscow Conservatory, which, in a rare departure from school policy, did not require him to take the entrance exams. His teachers at the conservatory included Naumov.

As a student at the conservatory, Gavrilov served as the captain of the soccer team. One day while he was out on the soccer field, the Gillespies reported, school administrators summoned him to inform him that he was expected to enter the upcoming International Tchaikovsky Competition; held every four years in Moscow, the contest was then considered highly prestigious. Displaying what Bryce Morrison, in *Gramophone* (June 1992), described as his "flame-throwing technique" in a performance of Tchaikovsky's Piano Concerto no. 1, the 18-year-old Gavrilov won the gold medal in the piano part of the competition, which took place in mid-1974. He was the youngest first-prize winner in the contest up to that time. Later that same year he made his international debut, at the Salzburg Festival, in Austria, having been invited there by festival officials to replace the great Russian pianist Sviatoslav Richter, who had fallen ill. The audience, unhappy about this substitution of someone unknown to them, greeted Gavrilov with boos. Feeling both angered and excited by their behavior, he recalled to Hilary Finch for the London *Times* (September 24, 1985), Gavrilov completed the scheduled program "and then just went on and played more and more and more. . . . It was childish and I wouldn't do it now, but it worked. At the end they went crazy and the police had to help me escape, like a pop star." In 1975 Gavrilov won the 1975 International UNESCO Competition, in Bratislava, Czechoslovakia (now Slovakia).

Meanwhile, Gavrilov and Richter had become friends, with the older man acting as a mentor as well. Richter made it possible for him to perform at the 1976 Touraine Festival, in France, where, according to a critic for the London *Sunday Times* (July 11, 1976), he played with "a wild abandonment . . . that one would have called reckless if it had not had a precision and control seemingly and miraculously beyond the possibility of error. . . . It was the poetry of his performance that stirred one the most. Liszt's 'La Campanella' had a poise, a delicate and luminous clarity, that you would have thought quite impossible for such a rapid tempo." Later that year he thrilled an audience with his rendition of the Rachmaninoff Piano Concerto no. 3 at the Helsinki Festival, in Finland, where he was accompanied by the Bournemouth Symphony Orchestra under Paavo Berglund. He made his U.S. debut in July 1976, at the Newport Music Festival, in Rhode Island, and his London debut the following November, at the Royal Festival Hall, again with the Bournemouth Symphony Orchestra, playing Sergei Prokofiev's Piano Concerto no. 1 and Maurice Ravel's Concerto for the Left Hand (written for a pianist who had lost an arm during World War I). In 1977 he gave some 30 performances in what was then West Germany, and in 1979 he was the featured artist at a dozen concerts in Japan. Also during the 1970s Gavrilov made recordings on the Melodia label, of, among other compositions, seven Bach concertos, accompanied by the Moscow Chamber Orchestra; the Rachmaninoff Piano Concerto no. 3, with the Moscow State Orchestra; the Brahms Trio for Cello, Clarinet, and Piano; and Karl Maria von Weber's Grande Duo Concertante for Piano and Clarinet.

By all accounts, Gavrilov's prolonged absences from his native land displeased Soviet government officials, who feared that, like the dancer Rudolf Nureyev, the pianist Vladimir Ashkenazy, and other people in the arts, he might defect. In early December 1979, just before a concert that Gavrilov was scheduled to give in West Germany with the Berlin Philharmonic under Herbert von Karajan, Soviet officials stripped him of his passport and cut off his phone service. (Unaware of what had happened, von Karajan waited in vain for Gavrilov to show up at a rehearsal and then canceled the concert.) Five years would pass before the pianist appeared before a Western audience again. His absence was a consequence of the Soviet Union's invasion of Afghanistan, in late December 1979, and its subsequent occupation of that nation; Western governments' strong condemnation of those actions led to the nearly total ending of cultural exchanges between the USSR and the West. Gavrilov knew that he was far from alone among Soviet artists in being grounded; nevertheless, he has expressed the belief that the government's curtailment of his career was the means that Leonid I. Brezhnev and Yuri Andropov, who then headed the Soviet government, had chosen to punish him for criticizing the Soviet regime during interviews with journalists. Government officials allowed him to practice the piano but denied him the right to record or concertize, except in factories, where he entertained the workers. Deprived of a living wage, he resorted to selling some of his belongings. Moreover, he experienced intense loneliness, because his friends feared associating with him. (Some sources reported that the government warned his friends against contacting him.) According to a biography that appeared on an official Gavrilov Web site in January 2000, the KGB (the Soviet secret police) even threatened to commit him to one of the USSR's so-called psychiatric facilities—virtual prisons in which many dissidents had been confined—and he even received threats on his life. The tension he was under became so severe that for some time he suffered from an hysterical paralysis, a condition in which, for no detectable physical reason, he could barely move his limbs.

In March 1984, following the death of Andropov (Brezhnev had died in 1982), Gavrilov successfully petitioned Mikhail Gorbachev, who by then was recognized as the de facto leader of the Soviet Union, for permission to resume concertizing abroad. Later that month, in what various sources referred to as his "triumphal return," he gave a recital in London, playing works by Scriabin and Rachmaninoff; a reviewer for the London *Times* (August 20, 1984) declared that the performance would "surely be remembered as one of the great musical events of the year." In March 1985 he performed Rachmaninoff's Piano Concerto no. 2 with the London Philharmonic Orchestra under James Conlon, in a rendition "full of bounding energy" and "a torrent of feeling and virtuosity," as a critic for the London *Daily Telegraph* (March 22, 1985) put it. Meanwhile, two weeks earlier, Gorbachev had been elected general secretary of the Soviet Union's Communist Party. Gavrilov, who was married by then, now requested permission from Gorbachev to prolong his stay abroad, as a means of rebuilding his health. Gorbachev agreed, on the condition that Gavrilov return periodically to Russia to prove to the KGB that he did not intend to defect.

With freedom to travel at will, Gavrilov launched a tour of North America. He made his New York City debut at Carnegie Hall in April 1985, with an all-Chopin program. In a review of the concert for the *Christian Science Monitor* (May 1, 1985), Thor Eckert Jr. wrote, "Gavrilov is a large-scale pianist who tends to reach out and embrace his audience rather than bring them into a contained musical vision. He deals in a wide dynamic range, and yet the introspective moments have a beauty, a simplicity, and a communicative thrust that set him apart from just about anybody in his age group today. . . . Yes, there are a few rough edges in his playing. But Mr. Gavrilov is not yet 30. He is willing to take risks. Sometimes they don't pay off. Other times they are refreshingly startling. On occasion the tone gets harsh, but usually even the climaxes ring out with a richness and fullness of tone. And that quiet playing is incomparably beautiful, and moving."

At the end of 1987, Gavrilov returned to the Soviet Union. Then, in 1989, reportedly eager to escape the political turbulence rocking his native land, he moved to a small town near Frankfurt, Germany, where he still lives with his family; he has taken German citizenship. In the last dozen years, he has performed with major orchestras in the United States, Europe, and Asia, with the conductors Seiji Ozawa, Riccardo Muti, Bernard Haitink, Claudio Abbado, Sir Colin Davis, Simon Rattle, and Yevgenie Svetlanov, among others. His orchestral recordings for EMI include, with the Philadelphia Orchestra under Muti, his renditions of Rachmaninoff's Rhapsody on a Theme of Paganini and Piano Concertos nos. 2 and 3, and Tchaikovsky's Piano Concerto no. 1; Bach piano concertos and French Suite no. 5, with Neville Marriner conducting the Academy of St. Martin-in-the-Fields; and Prokofiev's Piano Concerto no. 1 and Balakirev's notoriously difficult *Islamey*—one of Gavrilov's signature pieces—with the Philharmonia Orchestra under Muti. Also for EMI, he recorded Handel keyboard suites for two pianos, with Sviatoslav Richter, and various solo albums, on which he played Mozart sonatas, Schumann's *Carnival* and *Papillons*, Scriabin preludes, and Chopin ballades. After he signed an exclusive five-year contract with Deutsche Grammophon, in 1990, his discography grew to include Bach's *Goldberg Variations*, the Schubert impromptus, Grieg's *Lyric Pieces*, Prokofiev's *Romeo and Juliet*, and Ravel's *Gaspard de la Nuit*. Gavrilov was one of 80 artists chosen for inclusion in *Great Pianists of the 20th Century* (1999), a 200-CD set compiled by Philips in collaboration with many other record producers and the Steinway piano company. In August 2000 Gavrilov's Web site biography reported that since 1995, he "has been working independently, in more contemporary mediums."

Gavrilov's honors include a 1979 *Gramophone* magazine award; the Deutscher Schallplattenpreis (1981); the Grand Prix du Disque de l'Academie Charles Cros (1985 and 1986); the International Record Critics Award (1985); and the Premio Internazionale Accademia Musicale Chigiana, in Siena, Italy (1989).

In his leisure time, Gavrilov likes doing manual work, especially welding and woodworking; he also enjoys theater, film, literature, and fine art. His charitable activities have included helping to stage concerts to raise funds for victims of the 1986 Chernobyl nuclear disaster and those hurt by the 1988 earthquake in Armenia. He has cited among his greatest achievements his success in paving the way for other Soviet artists to travel and perform wherever they choose. — M.R.

Suggested Reading: *Carnegie Hall Stagebill* p29+ Feb. 1994, with photo; *Christian Science Monitor* p22 Aug. 4, 1976, with photo, p29 May 1, 1985, with photo; *Guardian* p10 July 14, 1979, with photo; Hazard Chase Artist Management Web site; Gillespie, John and Anna Gillespie. *Notable Twentieth-Century Pianists*, 1995

Selected Recordings: *Bach: Goldberg Variations*, 1993; *The Tchaikovsky Box*, 1993; *Bach: 6 French Suites*, 1995; *Handel: Keyboard Suites Volume I*, 1996; *Great Pianists of the 20th Century—Andrei Gavrilov*, 1999; *Bach: Keyboard Concertos, French Suite no. 3*, 2000

Courtesy of Bantam Doubleday Dell

George, Elizabeth

Feb. 26, 1949– Mystery writer. Address: c/o Random House, 1540 Broadway, New York, NY 10036

"It's important for a writer to write about what she loves and is interested in," Elizabeth George told Anita Manning for *USA Today* (December 2, 1999, on-line). "For me, that means writing about British culture, with British characters and stories set in England." George is the author of 10 mystery novels, all of which offer detailed accounts of British life, highly atmospheric descriptions of British locales, and dialogue peppered with British slang. They present those details with such accuracy that many of her readers have mistakenly assumed that she is a native of Great Britain. But the American-born George, who has spent most of her life in California, is simply a passionate Anglophile. "England really works for me artistically," she told Lynn Carey for the *Contra Costa Times* (August 7, 1997, on-line). "The topography is emotionally charged for me and suggests elements of plot." In the *Writer* (January 1994), George reported that her books "are sometimes called literary mysteries, sometimes novels of psychological suspense, sometimes detective stories, sometimes police procedurals, sometimes British novels." But, she added, they "are always—at least to my way of thinking—'real novels' from start to finish."

George's mysteries feature Detective Inspector Thomas Lynley of New Scotland Yard, his sidekick, Sergeant Barbara Havers, and his best friend, the forensic specialist Simon St. James, and the stories describe not only the criminal investigations that occupy this trio but their emotional ups and downs as well. "To write a mystery-suspense [story] that is a 'real novel' is to write largely about character," George observed in the *Writer*. "In these novels, the characters and the circumstances engendered by those characters drive the story forward, and not vice versa. . . . Mystery-suspense novels that are 'real novels' end where they begin: with an examination of the human heart—in conflict, in despair, in peace, in anguish, in love, in happiness, in fear. When a writer decides to create a novel of character within this genre of mystery-suspense, she challenges herself to move beyond the simple mechanics of plotting, to drive from her mind the temptation to adhere to a formula, and to take a risk. She decides to begin with character and to use character as the foundation for the hundreds of pages and thousands of words that will follow that character's creation. This is what I have attempted to do with my novels." George's last three books—*In the Presence of the Enemy*, *Deception on His Mind*, and *In Pursuit of the Proper Sinner*—have all been best-sellers.

The writer was born Susan Elizabeth George on February 26, 1949 in Warren, Ohio. Her father, Robert Edwin George, was a salesman for a conveyor company; her mother, the former Anne Rivelle, was a nurse. "We weren't a family that had a lot of money," George told Marjorie Rosen for *People* (August 23, 1993). "We turned to the world of imagination." When Elizabeth's older brother, Rob, suffered an eye injury at age six and had to have his eyes bandaged, her parents "spent hours reading to him, and I listened," George recalled to Rosen. When Elizabeth was seven her mother gave her a used, 1930s manual typewriter, and throughout her elementary-school years, she composed short stories. Her favorite books included the Nancy Drew mystery series.

George continued to write for pleasure while attending Holy Cross High School in Mountain View, California. As a junior or senior, she visited England for the first time. "I was very interested in English history, English literature, England's contribution to the creative arts as well," she told Anita Manning. After her graduation from high school, she enrolled at Foothill Community College, in Los Altos Hills, California, where she earned an A.A. degree, in 1969. She then transferred to the University of California at Riverside, from which she received a B.A. degree, in 1970. The following year she married Ira J. Toibin, a business manager and, later, school superintendent. During the 1974–75 academic year, George taught English at Mater Dei High School, a Catholic school in Santa Ana, California. She was fired from that position for "union agitation," as she put it in an interview with Lisa See for *Publishers Weekly* (March 11, 1996). She spent the following dozen years teaching English at El Toro High School, in Orange County. "I called my remedial students scholars," she told Rosen. "At first they thought I was making fun of them, but it was a rare student who didn't rise to my expectations." In 1981 the Orange County Department of Education named her teacher of the year. Two years earlier she had gotten an M.S. degree in counseling and psychology from California State University.

All the while, George told See, "I knew I wanted to write, but I didn't have a lot of confidence." When, in 1983, her husband bought a computer, she said to herself, "This is put up or shut up time," as she recalled to See. That semester she was teaching a course that focused on mystery novels, and she decided to produce one herself. Almost immediately after she started to write it—on June 28, 1983—she felt moved to set her story in England. "The English tradition offers the great tapestry novel," she explained to See, "where you have the emotional aspect of a detective's personal life, the circumstances of the crime and, most important, the atmosphere of the English countryside that functions as another character." Completed within three months, George's first novel was a basic drawing-room mystery written in a style associated with Agatha Christie. It marked the debut—though not in public, since it was never published—of George's regular stable of characters: Inspector Thomas Lynley of New Scotland Yard, who is also the wealthy eighth earl of Asherton; Lynley's partner, the unattractive, aggressively plebeian Detective Sergeant Barbara Havers, who simmers with resentment against the aristocracy; Lynley's best friend, the independent forensic scientist Simon St. James; St. James's wife, Deborah, a one-time love interest of Lynley's; and Lady Helen Clyde, the inspector's most-recent flame. "The characters are strictly from my imagination, though each possesses a quality that I have," George told Linda Carey. "I am intellectual as St. James is; I am sort of ironic, casual, and slob-oriented like Barbara Havers. I am hesitant and melancholy the way Deborah is. I think I have Lynley's tendency to hot passion; he's the kind of person who's going to say something and then regret it." When she created Havers, George told Anita Manning, she tried to make her Lynley's "antithesis, because [Lynley] was a character who might be somewhat unbelievable—a detective inspector with a title in the family for 250 years, a belted earl, handsome, rich. He sounded pretty unreal. When you create a character who is unrealistic or has too much going for him, the tendency is for the reader to not like him." To nip the reader's antipathy in the bud, George had Havers describe Lynley in highly unfavorable terms before the inspector made his first appearance, so that, as George explained to Manning, "when we meet Lynley, we see he's really not so bad."

Of the various publishers to whom George sent a sample chapter of her book, only one responded—Scribner, whose representative, Suzanne Kirk, rejected it, on the ground that novels written in the "drawing-room style" were no longer commercially viable. But Kirk encouraged George to continue writing. Having decided to seek, in her words, a "buffer against rejection" from publishers, George obtained a list of agents from the organization Mystery Writers of America and sent samples of her work to 10 agents at a time; eventually, she secured the services of Kathe Trelingator. Meanwhile, during her vacations, she traveled in England and worked on two new novels, *A Great Deliverance* and *A Suitable Vengeance*. A series of rejections greeted them, and Trelingator severed her ties with George.

In September 1986 George acquired a new agent, Deborah Schneider, who sent George's two novels to Kate Miciak at Bantam Books. Bantam turned down *A Suitable Vengeance* but bought *A Great Deliverance* and agreed to take George's next novel. Published in 1988, *A Great Deliverance* follows George's sleuths as they investigate the decapitation of a rich man and his daughter's questionable confession to the murder. Enthusiastically praised by most critics, *A Great Deliverance* won an Anthony Award (named for Anthony Boucher, the pseudonym of a well-known writer, critic, and fan of the mystery genre) and an Agatha Award (named for Agatha Christie). In addition, it was nominated for a Macavity Award (named for the mystery cat from T. S. Eliot's *Old Possum's Book of Practical Cats*) and an Edgar (named for Edgar Allan Poe, who has been called the father of the modern detective story), the most prestigious prize bestowed by the Mystery Writers of America. In France, *A Great Deliverance* won Le Grande Prix de Littérature Policière.

Payment in Blood (1989), George's second published work, is about the gory murder of a controversial playwright. Most reviewers found fault with the book but also much to admire. Rex E. Klett, for example, who critiqued it for *Library Journal* (July 1989), complained that it was "a bit mechanical in places, and slow-moving in others, but steadily absorbing and masterful overall"; he also described it as "literate, vastly detailed, and intricately characterized." In the *New York Times* (November 12, 1989), Josh Rubins, put off by what he called the novel's "foolishness and excess," rated it "unequal" to its predecessor; nevertheless, he wrote, "the crisp, literate narration firmly draws us in," and he noted that the book's "page-by-page satisfactions—dry humor, juicy dialogue, smartly paced shifts from one viewpoint to another—are considerable."

In the next five years, Bantam published five other books by George, including *A Suitable Vengeance*, in 1991. The others were *Well Schooled Murder* (1990), *For the Sake of Elena* (1992), *Missing Joseph* (1993), and *Playing for the Ashes* (1994). George's eighth Lynley mystery, *In the Presence of the Enemy* (1996), earned decidedly mixed reviews, with James Hynes, in the *Washington Post* (February 29, 1996), dismissing it as "the longest, slowest, dullest book I have ever read," while Mark Harris, in *Entertainment Weekly* (March 15, 1996), considered it "superb." Despite such negative assessments, *In the Presence of the Enemy* became the first of George's books to reach the best-seller list, where it remained for eight weeks. Inspired by the kidnapping and murder of 12-year-old Californian Polly Klass, in 1993, the novel chronicled the abduction of the illegitimate daughter of a member of Parliament. "It was the easiest one to write," George told Carey. "I only had two bad days on it. That's not to say I didn't groan and moan, but I never had that sense of, 'Oh, this is too big for me, I must be out of my mind.' I felt the story was solid, but I never thought it would take off the way it did."

In her ninth book, *Deception on His Mind* (1997), George dispensed with Lynley and St. James, and focused solely on Barbara Havers. The story is about Havers's investigation of the murder of a Pakistani immigrant. The idea for the plot came to George after she met Kay, a young Anglo-Pakistani woman, during the writer's research into Muslim culture. The product of a dysfunctional family, Kay had been victimized by an abusive husband. "Kay is 90 per cent of the reason the book exists, though it's not her life story," George told Syrie Johnson for *london.com* (on-line). "The first time we met we talked for four hours in which she did nothing but tell the story of her life and of the arranged marriage which she had agreed to and from which she then fled." "George doesn't disappoint with her latest mystery, which offers more than 600 pages in which fans may luxuriate," a reviewer for *Booklist* (May 15, 1997) declared. *Deception on His Mind* became George's second best-seller.

In *newsday.com* (October 24, 1999, on-line), Matthew Flamm reported that a postcard George found discarded on a London street, offering the services of a "hot stunning Thai girl," triggered the idea for her 10th mystery, *In Pursuit of the Proper Sinner* (1999). In devising the plot, the writer, who is childless, also had in mind the saying "A thankless child is sharper than a serpent's tooth." Like its predecessors, the novel offers an intricately woven plot, this time centering on a brutal double murder that has taken place at the site of an ancient circle of stones known as a henge. Complicating the investigation is the identity of one of the victims—she was the daughter of a former Scotland Yard colleague and mentor of Lynley's—and Lynley's increasingly troubled relationship with Sergeant Havers, who has been demoted for behavior that the inspector belatedly discovers was justifiable. "Lynley makes mistakes," George told Matthew Flamm. "He has such difficulty seeing the shades of gray in life. I never wanted to have the detective as Godhead. That's obnoxious to me." She also said, "Self-doubt is the great leveler. If I can reveal a character's self-doubt and weakness, then I'm immediately creating a bond between the reader and the character." In a review of *In Pursuit of the Proper Sinner* for *BookBrowser.com* (July 13, 1999, on-line), Harriet Klausner wrote, "Once again . . . Elizabeth George creates a fantastic police procedural that will satisfy her legions of fans. . . . The who-done-it is superbly set up and well executed by linking two separate incidents that appear to have nothing in common. . . . The strained relationship between Barbara and Thomas provides insight into both characters as well as an understanding about police partnering." *In Pursuit of the Proper Sinner* debuted at number seven on the September 19 *New York Times* best-seller list and remained on the list for several weeks.

George has traveled extensively in the United States on book tours. Her most recent writing projects are a collection of short stories and another novel, to be called *A Traitor of Memory*. The British writer, critic, and American-studies specialist Malcolm Bradbury has been commissioned to write scripts for *A Great Deliverance* and *A Suitable Vengeance* for BBC television.

George told Matthew Flamm that she considers three weeks of research sufficient preparation for each of her novels. In planning each book, she first chooses a killer, a victim, and the motive, and she decides how the story will end. She writes an outline and then a first draft. Next, she composes a second outline, adding new ideas, if any have occurred to her. She starts writing each day at 9:00 a.m. and sets a quota for herself of at least five pages a day. Since her divorce, in 1995, she told See, "I've built a family amongst my friends. Divorce has allowed me to enrich my friendships by becoming vulnerable and allowing my friends to give me support." George lives most of the year in Huntington Beach, California; within the past few years she has acquired a residence in England as well. "When the plane comes down in England," she told Valerie Takahama for the *Albany Times Union* (April 9, 1996, on-line), "I feel as if I'm coming home." — J.K.B.

Suggested Reading: *Contra Costa Times* (on-line) Aug. 7, 1997; *Entertainment Weekly* p56+ Mar. 15, 1996, with photo; *New York Times* E p1+ Dec. 14, 1999, with photo; *People* p59+ Aug. 23, 1993, with photos; *Publishers Weekly* p38+ Mar. 11, 1996, with photos; *USA Today* (on-line), Dec. 2, 1999

Selected Books: *A Great Deliverance*, 1988; *Payment in Blood*, 1989; *Well-Schooled in Murder*, 1990; *A Suitable Vengeance*, 1991; *For the Sake of Elena*, 1992; *Missing Joseph*, 1993; *Playing for the Ashes*, 1994; *In the Presence of the Enemy*, 1996; *Deception on His Mind*, 1997; *In Pursuit of the Proper Sinner*, 1999

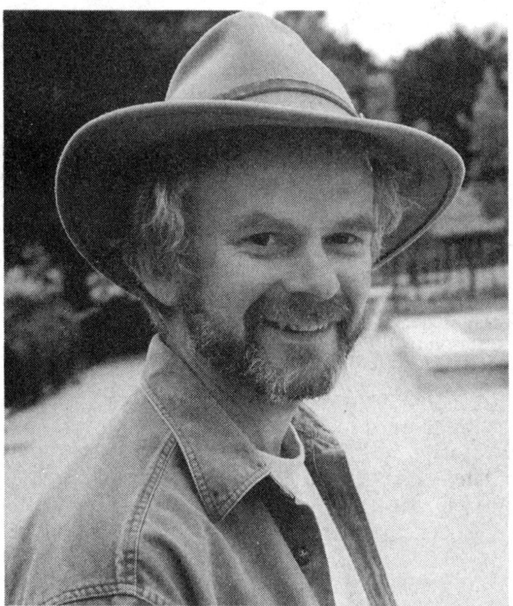

Courtesy of Andy Goldsworthy

Goldsworthy, Andy

1956– Sculptor; photographer. Address: c/o Haines Gallery, 49 Geary St., Fifth Fl., San Francisco, CA 94108

Working exclusively with common natural materials—snow, leaves, branches, stones, seeds, and sand—whose quality and availability are determined by local conditions of climate and season, the British sculptor Andy Goldsworthy assembles and photographs sculptures that seek, according to his book *Stone* (1994), not to mimic nature but rather "to draw on the energy that drives it so that it drives my work also." In doing so, he has produced, as the London-based art critic Lynn MacRitchie put it in *Art in America* (April 1995), "one of the most original and coherent bodies of work in British art."

Andy Goldsworthy was born in Cheshire, England, in 1956 and grew up outside Leeds, in Yorkshire; his father was a professor of mathematics at nearby Manchester University. Goldsworthy first began to take note of the shapes and patterns of natural materials as a teenager, while working as a farmhand outside Leeds. As quoted by Kenneth Baker in *Smithsonian* (February 1997), the artist has recalled that "what I did on the farm is where the origins of my art came from and was as important to me as art college as a formative experience." Indeed, an affinity with agriculture remains central to Goldsworthy's work; as he pointed out to Justine Picardie for the London *Daily Telegraph* (May 29, 1999, on-line), "farming itself is a sculptural process. Fields are ploughed, bales of hay are stacked, walls are built. The day is spent shaping and re-creating what is around you."

Upon completing his secondary education, in 1974, Goldsworthy enrolled at the Bradford College of Art, in West Yorkshire. One year later he transferred to Preston Polytechnic, an art college in Lancaster, where he remained through 1978. In an interview printed in his 1991 book, *Hand to Earth*, Goldsworthy characterized his work at the time as tentative and inauthentic: "I felt an increasing concern for environmental issues, and a disillusionment with the kind of art I was then producing. I had to discover my own nature, and then a work process that would use my nature like a tool. Up until that time (my first year at art college) I had gone against my own grain. My art was literary and symbolic—a dumping-ground for half-understood ideas." Recalling his time at art school in his interview with Kenneth Baker, Goldsworthy, in a manner reminiscent of William Wordsworth—the English Romantic poet who lived and worked in the same region as Goldsworthy—downplayed the importance of his academic education: "I think I've benefited from having no great teacher. I had good teachers, but no great one. I went to a good art school but not a great art school . . ." Rather, he implied, his true teacher is the landscape and its relation to the human community.

Since he graduated from art college, in 1978, Goldsworthy has produced a substantial body of work that includes gallery installations, small pieces constructed and photographed in relative isolation, and large-scale, long-term projects that require both outside funding and help from assistants. Goldsworthy has worked on the small pieces from the outset of his career; since most of these works incorporate mutable materials such as ice, water, and organic matter, they don't remain long in any particular form, and the only way to memorialize them is through photography. The photographs, in turn, are displayed in galleries or collected and published as books; Goldsworthy often captions the photos, providing short, haiku-like commentaries that review the creation of a particular piece. One is worded as follows: "Iris blades pinned together with thorns / filled in five sections with rowan berries / fish attacking from below / difficult to keep all the berries in / nibbled at by ducks." Among the best-known of Goldsworthy's books are *Stone* (1994), *Wood* (1996), and *Arch* (1999). As for examples of works Goldsworthy has created specifically to be viewed in galleries, in 1993 he covered large river stones with clay for a show at Japan's Tochigi Prefectural Museum of Fine Arts. Over time the clay dried and cracked, eventually sloughing off in large chunks to reveal the stones beneath. In 1994 he built a "herd of arches" out of red stone slabs in an empty commercial space on London's Bond Street. As he has become more widely known, Goldsworthy has tended to create more gallery-centered pieces.

More recently Goldsworthy has accepted several commissions to work on large-scale projects. The most significant of these is undoubtedly the Sheepfolds project, a publicly funded effort to rebuild a number of stone corrals, or sheepfolds, in Cumbria, a district in northwestern England whose inhabitants have long relied on sheep-herding for their livelihood. While the reconstructed stone walls are intended to be fully functional as sheepfolds, they will also incorporate such quirky touches as protruding boulders, seemingly aimless swerves, and stone cairns. Other commissions have taken Goldsworthy to such places as Japan, the Australian outback, the Sierra Nevada of the western United States, and even the North Pole; in all these places, Goldsworthy has fashioned sculptures out of local materials, seeking to understand and convey the idiosyncracies of each place.

Unlike the efforts of many other contemporary artists, Goldsworthy's work appeals to an audience that extends far beyond the confines of the art establishment. This is attributable in part to simple curiosity on the part of the public: while constructing sculptures of ice, leaves, and branches for a 1985 project in London's Hampstead Heath, for example, Goldsworthy piqued the interest of local residents and passersby. Many who had seen the artist at work on the heath—including a number of people who had never ventured inside an art gallery—were subsequently drawn to an exhibition of Goldsworthy's at the London Ecology Centre. Similarly, the Sheepfolds project, simply by virtue of its grand scale, has brought the artist into contact with a wide variety of farmers, landowners, county officials, and local politicians. Curiosity aside, however, Goldsworthy's photographs and images possess an undeniable aesthetic appeal, perhaps because they are simultaneously simple and mysterious; they are thus, on at least one level, accessible. As a result, people who might be put off by the willfully esoteric aspect of much modernist art—or indeed, those who may not particularly care for art in the first place—often feel they can relate to Goldsworthy's work, as a glance through some of the enthusiastic reviews at Amazon.com will demonstrate. As one admirer wrote of the book *Andy Goldsworthy: A Collaboration with Nature* (1990), "Many of Goldsworthy's pictures are actually beautiful. The state of the arts being what it is [these] days, this makes the man a public treasure."

Of course, widespread recognition doesn't necessarily equal popularity: the Sheepfolds project, for example, has encountered opposition from some locals, and London tabloids such as the *Sun*, the *Mirror*, and the *Mail* briefly roused public ire with the disclosure that the project had been awarded a grant of £342,000 (about $550,000) from the coffers of the national lottery. Goldsworthy, in his talk with Kenneth Baker, acknowledged the outcry with equanimity: "It's very humbling to work here where some people don't want me. But it's good for an artist to do that, instead of just working on private commissions where people really want you and do everything for you. I'm astonished at the level of enthusiasm, but also at the level of attack, especially when it's stimulated by the *Sun*, the *Mirror* or the *Mail*." For the most part, though, Goldsworthy seems to have successfully negotiated the pitfalls of public relations, and his work is well-received in Britain and abroad.

In spite of his broad appeal, Goldsworthy is by no means a pariah in the art establishment. Two criticisms, however, are frequently leveled against him. The first is that his work is closely allied with craft and therefore cannot rightly be considered under the rubric of art. Lynn MacRitchie, writing for *Art in America* (April 1995), cited one detractor as stating that Goldsworthy "was not an artist at all," and that his work amounted to nothing more than "fiddling about with nature." Hauteur aside, the comment is a perceptive one, since the boundary between art and nature—categories viewed as mutually exclusive by many in the West—is not at all easy to distinguish in Goldsworthy's work. Consequently, it is not clear precisely which aspects of his work constitute art and which are something else entirely—craft, or agriculture, or stonemasonry. Steven Adams, addressing this issue in an essay included in Goldsworthy's *Hand to Earth*, views Goldsworthy's work in terms of the Romantic search for "some kind of transparent signification in which nature is able to speak directly and more authentically without the intercession of art." While this may sound complicated, it is in fact fairly simple. Traditionally, in Western art, the phenomena of nature have been associated with human attributes. In the ancient world, these human qualities were represented as gods and goddesses—Zeus, for example, was the god of storms, and Neptune was the god of the sea. At other times, the natural world might be used to represent subjective moods and feelings. Thus a storm might represent passion or anger, or a cloudy sky might suggest sadness. According to one common (if not undisputed) interpretation, the Romantics strove to apprehend nature directly, without the mediation of symbolism. Goldsworthy, according to Steven Adams, is trying to do something similar, if often in a more subtle or more complex way.

Indeed, it can be useful to approach Goldsworthy's work by trying to distinguish the "natural" from the "artificial." Many of his works, for example, incorporate geometric forms such as circles, spheres, cones, and straight lines—forms that suggest a human presence by virtue of their artificiality. In the tradition of Western landscape painting—a tradition to which Goldsworthy acknowledges his debt—geometric structures have often been used to organize scenes by imposing human meanings upon them. Goldsworthy is aware of this tendency, but he also suggests, in *Hand to Earth*, that the presence of geometry need not signify an anthropocentric, or human-centered, subjugation of nature: "I used to think it [geometry] an arrogance imposed upon nature, and still do. But I've also realised that it is arrogance to think man invented geometry. As regards my own work, I'd like to think geometry has appeared in it to the same degree that I have found it in nature." Thus Goldsworthy is attempting to use geometry in such a way as to straddle the categories of art and nature. In a similar manner, the artist's photographs of his sculptures also blur the distinction between art and nature. In some photographs, for example, a sculpture will appear prominently situated in the foreground, thus emphasizing its character as an art object; in other photographs, the same sculpture will be captured from a distance, often with the result that it is difficult to distinguish from the surrounding landscape. The implication is that the distinction between art and nature is a trick of perspective, rather than an iron dictate of metaphysics.

A second, weightier criticism is that Goldsworthy has failed to consider adequately the wider social and political implications of his work—in particular, those works that are publicly funded, publicly displayed, or both. In fact, as an artist (as opposed to as a public citizen), Goldsworthy has consistently declined to embrace any particular political issue, including environmentalism, with which he is personally sympathetic and with which his work would appear to be compatible. He explained his stance to Kenneth Baker: "I'm instinctively very cautious about being motivated by concerns other than what I can see and feel to be right, for myself, with the land. And I think to be motivated in any way on a political basis would undermine that." In keeping with that argument, the ephemeral outdoor pieces that he often constructs and photographs in isolation—and that he considers to constitute the core of his work—do not seem especially political in nature.

Goldsworthy has himself raised some of the larger social issues involved in those large-scale works that require the use of assistants and public monies. In *Hand to Earth*, for example, he wrote, "My largest works have come from commissions. They remain close to my basic feelings towards nature, but the way of making opens new ground. Obviously the people who commission me have to be taken into account as well as materials and place. In these larger works I usually have four or five people helping me." More recently, he has addressed some of the issues involved in working with the local wallers with whom he is collaborating on the Sheepfolds project. In light of this, it would seem unfair to equate Goldsworthy's lack of an overt political stance with a disregard for the social and political implications of his work.

Goldsworthy lives with his wife and four children in Penpont, a small town in Dumfriesshire, Scotland, just over the English border. While he devotes the greater portion of his time to his work, and spends from four to seven months each year away from home, he also enjoys fishing, which, according to Kenneth Baker, "is about the only purely recreational diversion Goldsworthy permits himself." While on the road for various commissioned projects, however, he must content himself with videos about fishing. For one week out of every year, he vacations with his family on the Scottish coast. "During my holiday," he told Baker, "I work on the beach. A lot of the most recent work on the beach has been made in anticipation of its inevitable collapse when the sea comes in. That's become a fascination of mine. So that's always very dramatic and the kids just love to watch things collapse as the tide comes in." — P.K.

Suggested Reading: *Art in America* p90+ Apr. 1995; *ArtNews* p131 Nov. 1996; *Smithsonian* p94+ Feb. 1997

Selected Works: *Maze*, Leadgate, County Durham, England, 1989; *Touching North*, Dumfriesshire, Scotland, 1990; *Seven Holes*, London, England, 1991; *Stone Gathering*, Northumberland, England, 1993; *Rockfold*, Northumberland, England, 1993; *Herd of Arches*, Sussex, England, 1994; *Cone*, New York, 1995; *Boulder Wall*, Bedford Corners, New York, 1995; *100 Sheepfolds*, Cumbria, England, 1997; *A Wall that Went for a Walk*, Storm King Art Center, Mountainville, New York, 1997; *Arch*, Montreal, Canada, 1998; *Cone*, Waterside, West Drayton, England, 1998

Selected Books: *Stone*, 1994; *Sheepfolds*, 1996; *Wood*, 1996; *Arch*, 1999

Gordon, Jeff

Aug. 4, 1971– Professional stock-car racer. Address: c/o NASCAR, P.O. Box 2875, Daytona Beach, FL 32120-2875

The stock-car racer Jeff Gordon is one of the youngest and most successful drivers on the NASCAR circuit. (NASCAR is the National Association for Stock Car Auto Racing.) A competitive racer since the age of five, Gordon won two of stock-car racing's biggest events—the Coca Cola 600, in Charlotte, California, and the inaugural Brickyard 400, in Indianapolis, Indiana—before his 23d birthday, and he is a three-time Winston Cup champion. Gordon's career has grown in tandem with a surging popularity in the once regional sport of stock-car racing. The only driver represented by the William Morris talent agency, he has made regular appearances on the *Late Show with David Letterman*; his endorsements include Pepsi, Ray Ban, Edy's Ice Cream, and Quaker State motor oil. In *TV Guide* (February 13, 1999), Juliet Macur ranked Gordon among the "perennial front runners, the drivers who simply refuse to lose," including in that group Dale Jarrett, Rusty Wallace, and Mark Martin. Gordon's former crew chief, Ray Evernham, has compared the young racer to such acclaimed drivers as A. J. Foyt, Mario Andretti, and Richard Petty. "Every so often someone comes along and he's special," Evernham told Robert Markus for the *Chicago Tribune* (August 3, 1995). "Jeff is just one of those guys."

Winston Luzier/Archive Photos

Jeff Gordon

Gordon's popularity among racing fans is rivaled only by that of the veteran driver Dale Earnhardt. But along with fame has come a backlash; indeed, several anti-Gordon sites have appeared on the Internet. Many of his detractors—both older drivers who are apparently jealous of his success and fans who seem to resent him because of his good looks, California background, and near-perfect driving record—have accused him of not paying his dues. Responding to such criticism, Gordon declared to Robert Markus, "How many guys have been racing since they were five years old and racing professionally since they were 13 or 14 and winning on ESPN when they were 17 and 18?"

Jeff Gordon was born on August 4, 1971 in Vallejo, California. When he was 20 months old, his mother, Carol, remarried; her new husband, John Bickford Sr., was the owner of a company that manufactured specialized auto parts. Bickford already had one son, whom his ex-wife was raising, and within a few years, he cast his stepson, Jeff, in a special role in his life. "I always wanted to race," Bickford told *Biography Today* (April 1999), "but I couldn't afford it. I was living my dreams through Jeff. His being small made it obvious he'd never be a football player. So I taught him the only thing I knew, how to race." Gordon's training began when he was four, with a series of bicycle motorcross races (in which riders compete on bicycles designed to enable them to perform stunts), but his mother felt that the dirt tracks were too dangerous; instead, after he turned five, Jeff raced quarter-midgets—six-foot-long cars with single-cylinder, low-power engines, which provided more protection than the bikes. Before his first quarter-midget race, his stepfather made him complete several thousand laps on a homemade course. The grueling practice schedule left young Jeff little time to play with other kids. Indeed, Bickford did not allow the boy to talk to other juvenile drivers, for fear that such interactions would damage the racing strategy he had devised for him. His relationship with Jeff, he admitted to David Handelman for *Details* (September 1997), was businesslike rather than paternal. "Decisions weren't based on emotion," he said. "They were all based on logic. I have a cold personality. I'm not a hugger. I'm a guy who looks at it, attacks it, tries to succeed." He also told Handelman, "I approached [Jeff's development as a racer] from a professional standpoint. This wasn't about having fun. If we want to have fun, we'll go to Disney World."

Gordon raced every weekend, and in his first two years of competition, he won 36 contests. "We had eight or nine cars. We practiced two or three times a week," Bickford told Ed Hinton for *Sports Illustrated* (April 24, 1995). "We were the Roger Penske of quarter-midgets," he added, in a reference to a celebrated racing champion. When Gordon was eight he won all 25 races he entered. He went on to become the national quarter-midget champion in 1979. Soon he graduated from quarter-midgets to 10-horsepower go-karts, and at the age of nine, he was skilled enough to beat drivers as much as eight years his senior, as well as many adults. In 1982 he won his second national quarter-midget championship.

In early 1986 Bickford sold his business and moved his family, which included Jeff's older sister, to Pittsboro, Indiana, so that Gordon could enter sprint-car races, which did not have the same age restrictions as other competitions. Gordon, at 14, was too young to get an Indiana driver's license, so his mother chauffeured him to all events. Driving 650-horsepower sprint cars (lightweight, open-wheel vehicles) worth $25,000, he often competed against people two to three times his age. He was a regular winner on ESPN's *Thursday Night Thunder* program; it was at one of those events that Ray Evernham first saw him drive. In 1990 Gordon joined the United States Auto Club and won the national championship in the club's full-midget division. Meanwhile, he was also attending Tri-West High School, completing class assignments in advance when he had to travel. He was so busy that he had to make an extra effort to form friendships—and he succeeded, becoming popular enough to be voted king of his senior prom.

After Gordon graduated from high school, his stepfather enrolled him in the school run by the stock-car racing legend Buck Baker, in Rockingham, North Carolina. Gordon fell in love with stock cars immediately. "That first day, the first time I got in a [stock] car, I said, 'This is it. This is what I want to do,'" he recalled to Ed Hinton. "The car was different from anything I was used to. It was so big and heavy. It felt very fast but very smooth." In 1991 he joined NASCAR's Busch Grand Nationals, a racing circuit one rung below the Winston Cup. During a test session he worked for the first time with Evernham, a former NASCAR driver whose racing career had ended prematurely as the result of a head injury. Evernham recalled to Robert Markus, "I wanted to see if he was for real or just a lot of media hype. The Busch car was not competitive and he went out and was second fastest for the day." After becoming Gordon's crew chief, Evernham assembled an award-winning pit crew, called the Rainbow Warriors, a name inspired by the brightly colored designs painted on Gordon's vehicle. Evernham told Juliet Macur that the communication among the Rainbow Warriors was so strong that "we beat with one heart."

The sport of stock-car racing began as recreation among moonshiners in the South, who souped up their Fords and Chevys in an attempt to evade government agents. NASCAR was founded in 1948. The NASCAR season, which runs from February through November, consists of 31 races, most of which are either 500 or 600 miles long. Each driver collects points based on his final position in a particular race; bonus points are awarded to the drivers who lead individual laps as well as those who complete the most laps in one race. At the end of the season, the points are totaled, and the top 25 drivers receive cash awards. As a spectator sport, racing has greatly increased in popularity in recent years; between 1990 and 1995, attendance at racing events jumped 60 percent.

In the early 1990s Gordon raced Ford vehicles, but Rick Hendrick, the owner of one of the richest and most successful Winston Cup racing teams, lured him to Chevrolets. Hendrick had seen him beat Dale Earnhardt and another veteran racer, Harry Gant, in March 1992, and the way Gordon had performed had impressed him greatly. "I was almost in a daze," Hendrick told Ed Hinton. "Jeff had it all. It was just scary. He's good-looking, and I couldn't believe how well he handled himself at age 20. . . . What I found was a mature young guy who was kind of humble—a little bashful. A sponsor's dream." When Hendrick learned that Gordon was not under contract, he immediately made the young racer an offer, and Gordon accepted. As a member of Hendrick's team, Gordon won three races and 11 pole positions (starting positions based on fastest qualifying time) in 1992, racing so successfully in the Busch Grand Nationals that he was named Rookie of the Year.

The Winston Cup circuit includes 19 tracks, each with its own distinct features. Gordon's first Winston Cup appearance took place at the last race of the 1992 season, held that year in Atlanta, Georgia. Starting out in 21st place, he failed to complete the 500-mile race after hitting the wall. In 1993 he began his first full Winston Cup season at the Daytona 500, after passing the veteran driver Bill Elliott to win the first of two qualifying races. In the first regular meet, eager to be respectful, Gordon drove cautiously, taking care not to pull out to pass veteran drivers and waiting patiently as others fell behind; he finished fifth. Gordon's first Winston Cup victory took place on May 29, 1993 at the Coca Cola 600 at Charlotte Motor Speedway, the longest race on the circuit. By the end of the 1993 racing season, he had compiled 11 top-10 finishes in 30 races, for which he was named Winston's Rookie of the Year.

Meanwhile, Gordon had become romantically involved with Brooke Sealey, who was Miss Winston in 1993. Because Winston Cup rules forbade drivers to consort with a Miss Winston, he and Sealey kept their relationship secret for a long time. In 1994 Sealey's reign as Miss Winston ended, and in November of that year, she and Gordon wed. Afterward Gordon informed his mother and stepfather, much to their dismay, that he no longer wanted them to handle his business affairs. "I was growing up, I'd met a woman I was just head over heels with, and I wanted to be a man," Gordon told Steve Lopez for *Time* (May 31, 1999). "I wanted to show her that I could be a husband. That I could take care of myself and take care of her, and I felt like I was almost being treated like a little boy." Gordon's decision caused a strain in his relationship with his stepfather that has not yet healed. "You meet every goal, and then walk into a board meeting one day, and with the words of one young person it's all gone," Bickford told Roy S. Johnson for *Fortune* (April 12, 1999). "It's very, very difficult, I don't think I'll ever get over it."

In August 1994 approximately 315,000 fans witnessed Gordon's victory in the inaugural Brickyard 400, at Indianapolis Motor Speedway, 15 miles from Pittsboro. For much of the race, Geoff Bodine was the only driver who kept up with Gordon. Bodine's race ended when Brett Bodine, his younger brother, with the aim of settling a personal dispute on the track, bumped Geoff's vehicle, causing it to hit the concrete wall. After bouncing off the wall, Geoff's car crashed into Dale Jarrett's car, thus eliminating Jarrett from the race. "I saw [Geoff Bodine] have his misfortune and I thought, 'Well, all I got to do is be nice and smooth and ride it out from here,'" Gordon told Mike Harris for the *Washington Post* (August 7, 1994). For much of the final 30 laps of the race, the crowd stood and cheered as Gordon battled Ernie Irvan for first place. A flat tire eliminated Irvan, and Gordon finished four car lengths (and approximately half a second) ahead of Brett Bodine to win a cash prize of $613,000. Afterward, Gordon angered some residents of Pittsboro by skipping a parade planned in his honor, choosing instead to make an appearance at Disney World at a sponsor's request. "I definitely have learned from that incident," he told Robert Markus. "I've realized you're not going to make everyone happy, but it doesn't mean I won't try."

Gordon was forced to drop out of five races in 1994 because of accidents. At the beginning of 1995, Evernham and Gordon agreed that he had not yet become consistent enough to handle the challenge presented by the 31 races scheduled each season. "We've had our good tracks and our bad tracks," Gordon told Joseph Siano for the *New York Times* (March 26, 1995). "It could be me getting impatient at some of those tracks or could be an engine failure or a bad pit stop. I think it's taken two years for me now to get used to the 500-mile races and the long season." Speaking with Siano, Evernham said that Gordon was beginning to learn the importance of patience. "He doesn't use the car up. He knows how to save it. But sometimes he puts the car in a position it shouldn't be in."

Racing aficionados agree that the efforts of Evernham were crucial to Gordon's early successes. During a race, Evernham was in constant radio contact with Gordon. One of his main tasks was to keep the driver focused. "I just tell him . . . 'Keep all four wheels on that thing, keep the fenders straight and we'll get it in for you,'" Evernham told Joseph Siano. "Very often that settles him down . . . and he winds up going faster." Gordon is an aggressive driver prone to taking risks; he is known for his ability to maneuver his car when it is "loose" and the back end is sliding. "If I feel we're losing ground, I get very excited and want to know what's going on," Gordon told Siano. "Sometimes [Evernham will] know we're in trouble, but he'll never tell me. He'll fib a little bit."

In February 1995 Gordon beat Dale Earnhardt in the Goodwrench 500, in Rockingham, North Carolina. A few weeks later, at age 24, he became the second-youngest driver ever to win the Daytona 500. (Bill Rexford was 23 when he won the race in 1950.) The team worked hard to win as many races as possible early in the season, to avoid having to catch up later. As Gordon began to take the lead, Earnhardt referred to him sarcastically as "Wonder Boy," but after Gordon won his fifth race of the season, in July, sports announcers began using the term as a compliment. The press began to speculate about Gordon's chances of winning the championship, but Evernham believed that the team was too young to expect the prize to come so easily. Gordon, however, was more confident; he told Robert Markus, "We're still too young to be thinking about it. But we might not be too young to do it." By the end of the season, Gordon was so far ahead that, in spite of finishing 32d in the Napa 500, he won the $1.3 million Winston Cup, thereby spoiling Earnhardt's chances at a record-breaking eighth championship. By the season's finish, Gordon had racked up eight wins and won more than $4 million—a record amount.

In 1996 Gordon finished first in 11 races and earned more than $3.4 million, but the Winston Cup title went to his teammate and mentor Terry Labonte. In 1997 Gordon won his second Daytona 500, dedicating the race to Rick Hendrick, who was suffering from leukemia; Labonte and another of Gordon's teammates, Ricky Craven, finished in the second and third spots, respectively. He also captured the Winston Cup championship, and he did so again in 1998, after he won races 14 through 17 and the last two events of the season as well. By the end of 1998 he had won 13 races, tying Richard Petty's record for victories in a single season.

The following year Gordon began driving a 3,400-pound, 700-horsepower Monte Carlo, and that February he won the Daytona 500. In September, after his eighth season with Gordon, Evernham left to form his own team; five other key members of the Rainbow Warriors also left, to work for Robert Yates Racing. Evernham's successor was Robbie Loomis, who ended a nine-year relationship with Richard Petty to work with Gordon. In November 1999 Gordon's engine blew at the NAPA 500, causing him to fail to score his 50th win, and for the first time in his career he finished outside the top five. Although he won two races following Evernham's departure, he did not finish higher than 10th place in the five remaining races. He ended the season with seven wins, 18 top-five wins, and $5 million. Apparently still suffering from the loss of Evernham, Gordon began the 2000 NASCAR season with a 13-race losing streak.

Currently, Gordon drives one of several custom-made Monte Carlos, each designed for different driving conditions. Each vehicle's ignition is activated by a toggle switch, and none of the cars has a speedometer. "Knowing my speed is a distraction; it just breaks my concentration," Gordon told David Handelman for *Details* (September 1997). "I know when I'm running good or not, just by feel."

In 1995 and 1999 Gordon received the Jerry Titus Memorial Trophy, awarded by the American Auto Racing Writers and Broadcasters Association, the largest group of motor-sports journalists in the U.S. In 1999 he signed a lifetime agreement with Hendrick Motorsports, becoming an equity partner responsible for negotiating licensing and sponsoring for the organization. Outside of sports, Gordon has participated in activities aimed at raising funds for leukemia research and promoting the National Bone Marrow Registry. (In addition to Hendrick, Ray Evernham's son is a victim of leukemia.)

Gordon doesn't smoke, drink, or curse, and he has refused to appear in beer commercials. "I like country music but I don't wear a cowboy hat," he told Kevin Sack for the *New York Times* (October 16, 1997). "I didn't grow up chewing tobacco. That's just not what I'm about. . . . I think it's a stereotype that is really being put off to the side because there are a lot more drivers coming in here that give more of a clean-cut image." At his wife's request, Gordon was baptized a Christian; before each race, he tapes to his steering wheel a passage from the Bible that his wife has typed for him. His faith has "helped me put things in perspective," he told Stephanie Mansfield for *USA Weekend* (June 13–15, 1997, on-line). "God comes first, family second, and racing third. I try to keep things in line with the way I live my life." He and his wife, Brooke, live near Charlotte, North Carolina. In his spare time he enjoys skiing, racquetball, and video games. — C.L.

Suggested Reading: *Biography Today* p61+ Apr. 1999, with photos; *Chicago Tribune* H p1+ Aug. 3, 1995, with photos, IV p10 Aug. 4, 1995, with photo; *Details* p232+ Sep. 1997, with photos; *New York Times* VIII p10 Mar. 26, 1995, VIII p2 July 16, 1995, with photo, I p33 Feb. 17, 1997, with photos, G p6 Oct. 16, 1997, with photos; *Sports Illustrated* p46+ Apr. 24, 1995, with photos, p64+ Feb. 22, 1999; *Time* p70+ May 31, 1999, with photos; *Washington Post* D p1+ Aug. 7, 1994, with photos

---

Len Irish/Outline Press

Gore, Tipper

Aug. 19, 1948– Social activist; writer; photographer; mental-health adviser to President Bill Clinton. Address: Old Executive Office Bldg., Rm. 200, Washington, DC 20501

BULLETIN: At press time, the results of the presidential race between Al Gore and George W. Bush had not been determined.

"People never quite know how to introduce me," Tipper Gore, the wife of Vice President Al Gore, wrote in her 1996 book of photographs, *Picture This: A Visual Diary*, as excerpted on the White House Web site. "Sometimes they call me the Second Lady. Once I was even introduced as the Second Lady of Vice. Maybe no one has ever given the wife of the Vice President of the United States a title because the position is so poorly defined. There's no job description, no pay, no career path—and limited opportunities for promotion. The way I see it, this post is an opportunity to further the causes I believe in." Gore has dedicated herself to such causes as the eradication of homelessness and has served as President Bill Clinton's adviser on mental-health issues. Her crusade against explicit lyrics in rock music has led some to call her an enemy of the music industry. Gore is the founder of Tennessee Voices for the Children, and she and the vice president host a conference on families each year in Tennessee.

Gore described herself to Ann Gerhart for the *Washington Post* (July 11, 2000, on-line) as a "social worker at heart." Her down-to-earth approach to projects and bubbly personality render her more approachable than many Washington figures, and she has a reputation for initiating one-on-one encounters. "She breaks down barriers and makes people feel at ease," the *National Geographic* photographer Jodi Cobb, a close friend of Gore's, told Jennet Conant for *Redbook* (March 1994). "Tipper is one of the warmest people I know. She makes every minute count, whether it's with her family, her friends, or a cause." The vice president has praised his wife's intuitive understanding of areas where work needs to be done. "For her, nurturing goes beyond making sure that people are comfortable and happy; it goes to the spiritual needs," he told Ann Gerhart. "She knows when you need something that you don't even know that you need."

Tipper Gore was born Mary Elizabeth Aitcheson on August 19, 1948 in Washington, D.C. Her parents divorced when she was 14 months old, and she was raised by her mother and grandmother. The nickname "Tipper" derived from a bedtime nursery rhyme. While she had a tough time at St. Agnes, a private Episcopal school in Alexandria, Virginia—where, as in many other schools during the 1950s, children of divorced parents were ostracized—she found an escape of sorts in athletics; she played basketball, softball, and field hockey. When she was 14 she received a drum set and soon formed an all-girl band called the Wildcats; that activity, too, helped her to cope with the emotional turmoil of her adolescence. "Sometimes it is better for people to divorce," Gore told Gail McKnight for the *Saturday Evening Post* (March 1993). "It was a motivating factor for me. I learned that it takes a lot of hard work to make a relationship work. Fortunately, I found a man early on whom I fell in love with at first sight and am still in love with today. Our marriage represents a lot of loving work on both sides." She met Al Gore Jr., the son of Senator Albert Gore of Tennessee, at a high-school dance. Although both had arrived with dates, they felt an instant connection and soon became inseparable. "He was sexy, serious, smart, and funny," Tipper Gore told Jennet Conant.

Following Al Gore to Massachusetts, where he attended Harvard University, Tipper Aitcheson enrolled in Garland Junior College. She later transferred to Boston College, where she majored in psychology. After graduating from Harvard, in 1969, at the height of the Vietnam War, Al Gore was drafted into the army. Although he opposed the war and considered avoiding active duty by some means, he decided to serve, because, as Tipper Gore explained at the 2000 Democratic Convention, he knew that if he avoided military service, someone else from his home town would have to go to Vietnam in his stead. His father was also against the war, and when the senator ran for a fourth term, in 1970, his antiwar stance—despite Al Gore Jr.'s military service—cost him the election. Al Jr. and Tipper were married in May 1970, following her graduation from Boston College. Late in 1971 Al Gore left for Vietnam, where he served as a journalist for the armed forces; meanwhile, Tipper protested the war and marched in support of civil rights. When Al returned from Vietnam, six months later, the couple moved to Carthage, Tennessee. During this period, although Al Gore Jr. was "very proud of his father . . . he was very disillusioned with politics," Tipper told Jennet Conant. Al Gore attended Vanderbilt University, first as a student in the Graduate School of Religion and then as a law student, and worked as a reporter for the *Tennessean*. The couple's first child, Karenna, was born in 1973. Tipper later landed a job as a freelance photographer for the *Tennessean*. "I'd do photo essays," she told Barbara Bucholz for the *Chicago Tribune* (August 21, 1994). "A favorite was 'Ground Hog' man, who was 84 and lived in a shack. He hunted and skinned ground hogs." She took care of her daughter while studying at George Peabody College in Nashville, graduating with a master's degree in psychology in 1975.

Tipper Gore's plan to become a child psychologist was preempted by her husband's decision to enter politics. Assured by the newspaper that she could return to her position as a photographer at any time, Tipper Gore decided to accompany her husband on the campaign trail. Al Gore entered Congress in 1976 and went on to serve four terms in the House of Representatives and eight years in the Senate, dividing his time between their home in Arlington, Virginia, and a farm near his family's home in Carthage. Tipper stayed at home to raise their children: Karenna; Kristin, born in 1977; Sarah, born in 1979; and Albert Gore III, born in 1980. "I don't think you can have it all," Tipper Gore told Jennet Conant, adding that "everything in life is about choices and balances and compromise." Gore had always wanted a big family and did not resent her role as a homemaker. "If I'd wanted to have my own career and get somebody to take care of the children, I would have done that," she told Sandra McElwaine for *Good Housekeeping* (March 1993). "I truly did not wish to. I wanted to spend a lot of time with our kids. I'm having an impact in a different way."

Gore was not prepared for the sense of letdown she felt after her husband was first elected to public office. "Campaigns are for two of you, an equal partnership, but then you wake up, and he's been elected to office," she told Barbara Bucholz. "I realized I had to make myself something of a different career." In 1978 she established the Congressional Wives Task Force, a group that sought to bring attention to issues including nutrition and the effect of television violence on children. She also returned to photography, publishing photos in the *Washington Post* and the *Washington Star*. In 1984, inspired by her children's reaction of concern when they saw a homeless woman, Gore founded Families for the Homeless, a nonpartisan coalition of families dedicated to raising public awareness of issues affecting the homeless. "I have a memory of [Gore] literally sitting on the ground talking to a guy who was lying in the middle of the park," Patricia Letke-Alexander, an advocate for the homeless, told Deb Riechmann for the *Topeka Capital-Journal* (March 4, 2000, on-line). "These are people that other people don't even want to make eye contact with."

In 1985 Gore founded the Parents Music Resource Center (PMRC), a group consisting primarily of wives of Washington politicians who were concerned about violent, sexual, and occult imagery in popular music. Although the campaign was inspired by Gore's discovery of a line on Prince's 1984 album *Purple Rain* that referred to masturbation (her then–11-year-old daughter Karenna owned a copy of the record), ultimately most of the albums targeted by the group were those recorded by heavy-metal artists. The PMRC called for labels to be placed on albums that included what they saw as offensive content: "V" imprinted on the label meant the record contained violent imagery; "X"—lyrics about sex; "D/A"—references to drugs and alcohol; and "O"—"occult" material. In response to charges that her group was trampling on the rights of artists to express themselves, Gore maintained that she was merely exercising her own freedom of speech. "I am free to call it as I see it," she told David Astor for *Editor & Publisher, the Fourth Estate* (October 28, 1995). "I can say trash is trash, violence is violence, and that treating women as objects to be exploited, humiliated, raped, murdered, and forgotten is degrading beyond all moral measure. It degrades the society that permits such degradation to persist without protest."

In September 1985 Gore testified on the issue at a hearing of the Senate Commerce, Science, and Transportation Committee. Of the examples provided by Gore of music she found offensive, many were songs by obscure bands; in some cases PMRC's members had misunderstood lyrics or attributed imagery to the wrong sources. One such misinterpretation was pointed out by Dee Snider, the lead singer of Twisted Sister, who explained at the hearing that "Under the Blade," a song Gore had criticized for its sadomasochistic content, was actually about the fear of surgery. Perhaps the harshest testimony came from the composer Frank Zappa, who referred to Gore as a "cultural terrorist" and pointed out the conflict of interest inherent in the fact that the husbands of several members of the PMRC sat on the committee. Zappa characterized the PMRC's list of demands as "an instruction manual for some sinister kind of toilet training program to housebreak all composers and performers because of the lyrics of a few," according to a transcript of the proceedings, reprinted on *deesnider.com*. "The PMRC proposal is an ill-conceived piece of nonsense which fails to deliver any real benefits to children, infringes the civil liberties of people who are not children, and promises to keep the courts busy for years, dealing with the interpretational and enforcemental problems inherent in the proposal's design."

As a result of the PMRC's activities, record companies agreed to place on certain albums stickers that read "Parental Advisory: Explicit Lyrics." Emboldened by that victory, the organization put pressure on the cable music network MTV to play so-called "violent" videos only at night. In response, MTV decreased but did not end its daytime broadcasting of such videos. Gore was criticized by both the music industry and the press for her stance. Rock critic and anticensorship activist Dave Marsh told Anne Gowen for *Rolling Stone* (April 15, 1993) that barring an apology, Gore would remain "the enemy of every person who loves rock and roll." Gore steadfastly denied that her organization sought legislation that amounted to censorship—rather, she said, they favored voluntary labeling—and she pointed to her love of the band the Grateful Dead and her drumming as proof that she did not simply hate rock music. But for some this claim rang false, in light of what took place almost immediately after the hearings: many record stores refused to carry labeled records, and several states initiated legislation that made it nearly impossible for record stores to stock such albums. Today Kmart and Wal-Mart, two of the nation's largest record-selling chains, refuse to carry albums with explicit lyrics. Some record labels, bowing to pressure, now release two versions of some albums, one of which has been sanitized. "I have always felt good about my involvement in that effort," Gore told Sandra McElwaine. "I think what we did got a lot of people thinking about the way we treat children in this country."

In 1987 Gore embarked on a tour to promote her book *Raising PG Kids in an X-Rated Society*. (Ironically, the book's cover featured a warning about explicit content, in reference to the song lyrics reprinted in the text.) The following year the Gores met with MCA Records chairman Irving Azoff, TV producer Norman Lear, and Don Henley, of the music group the Eagles. *Variety* published transcripts of the meeting, in which Al and Tipper Gore were reported to have said that the hearings had been a mistake. (Both later denied having made those statements.) Some speculated that Tipper Gore's crusade had alienated many voters, contributing to her husband's departure from the 1988 presidential race. Inundated with questions about censorship during the campaign, she later helped to defeat several bills, introduced in state legislatures, whose passage would have blocked sales of records with explicit contents. Record executive Danny Goldberg, once one of Gore's most vocal opponents, was impressed with her actions. "It really helped to be able to go in and say, 'Even Tipper Gore is against this,'" he told Barbara Matusow for the *Washingtonian* (October 1994).

In 1989, as the Gore family was on the way home from a Baltimore Orioles baseball game, Albert Gore III was struck by a car. "I watched in horror as he flew through the air, scraped along the pavement, and then lay still," Tipper Gore wrote in *Picture This: A Visual Diary*. "He had so many broken bones and internal injuries that for days it was not clear whether he'd survive." For a month the Gores sat at their son's bedside at Johns Hopkins Children's Center in Baltimore. When the boy returned home in a full-body cast, the entire family contributed to his care, and he made a full recovery within a year. The accident led the Gores to reconsider their priorities. "When I looked at what I had to cancel the weeks following the accident, it was incredible," Tipper told Jennet Conant. "I realized I had let it [my appointment schedule] build up slowly and it had taken over." Al Gore postponed his second run for the presidency so that he could spend more time with the family. "I maybe gave up some career opportunities with the child psychology and photography, but I did it for my family and to support my husband," Tipper told Jennet Conant. "And years later, here's a guy who stuck with his family instead of hitting the campaign trail. He showed a real commitment in a different way at a crucial time. But the import of it was the same, they were both gifts we gave to each other."

When Arkansas governor Bill Clinton asked Al Gore to be his running mate in the 1992 presidential election, Tipper Gore's conservative stance on music helped the Democratic Party to wrest the "family values" mantle away from the Republicans. Gore told Sandra McElwaine that her husband accepted the position because he wanted to be a "voice for change, to offer leadership toward a whole range of domestic goals we thought had been ignored." In spite of rumors to the contrary, she formed a close bond with Clinton's wife, Hillary, while on the campaign trail. "I would describe [Hillary Clinton] as . . . having an analytical mind, and I would describe myself as a bit more emotional," Gore told Joel Achenbach. "Hillary and Al are very similar, and Bill and I are very similar. We joke about it when we're together as couples."

Less than two months after Al Gore was sworn in as vice president, Tipper resigned from the PMRC. The following year she joined Hillary Clinton in her efforts to bring about health-care reform. In addition, President Clinton named her the White House mental-health adviser, and she served as a member of the Interagency Council on the Homeless. She hoped to remove the stigma associated with mental illness and to combat the marginalization of those who suffer from the disease. In July 1999 Gore organized the first White House Conference on Mental Health, which took place at Howard University, in Washington, D.C. She also revealed for the first time that she had undergone treatment for depression following her son's accident. Gore was successful in altering the demeaning questions regarding mental health included in government job applications, and she worked hard for the passage of the Children's Health Initiative, which provided coverage for up to five million uninsured children, as well as more money for mental-health benefits. She also helped pass the Mental Health Parity Act, which provided those suffering from mental disorders with medical coverage comparable to the benefits available to others.

Gore has always taken an active role in her husband's affairs, and the 2000 presidential election campaign has been no exception. "She's my closest adviser and my most effective campaigner, myself included," Al Gore, the 2000 Democratic presidential nominee, told Susan Page for *USA Today* (January 19, 2000, on-line). Tipper Gore persuaded her husband to cultivate a more casual public image. She also suggested that he hire Tony Coelho to run his campaign and later recommended Coelho's replacement, William M. Daley, who resigned as secretary of commerce to take on the job. The prospect of a right-wing Supreme Court—a distinct possibility, should Al Gore's opponent, Texas governor George W. Bush, win the White House—seems to have inspired a change of heart in some: the Gore campaign has received support from two of the late Frank Zappa's children as well as from members of the recording industry. At a recent fund-raiser for her husband, Tipper Gore was accompanied by surviving members of the Grateful Dead. Gore is apparently not worried about the many changes that come with being the First Lady. "I can change and adapt," she told Ann Gerhart. "Frankly, I do that very well. To have a larger forum to advocate for issues I feel deeply about is something I hope I have the opportunity to do, but I don't see that as inconsistent with being able to continue being the individual I am and to live life the way that is important to me."

Gore received the Distinguished Alumna Award from Vanderbilt University's George Peabody College in 1997. Two years later the Arizona Foundation for Women acknowledged the significance of Gore's contributions to society by presenting her with the Sandra Day O'Connor Award. Devoted to maintaining a healthy lifestyle, she jogs daily and adheres to a strict diet and exercise regimen. For three decades she and her husband have maintained a loving marriage and often show affection toward one another in public. "He's more reserved on the surface. I'm more outgoing," Tipper Gore told Barbara Bucholz. "We had something very much in common, our shared idealism, compassion, spirituality." Gore is well known as a dedicated mother; when the children were young, she and her husband often attended their children's sports events, and she tried to work no more than three days a week, so that she could spend time with the children. "A stable family is an ethic to work toward and gift to be valued," she told Gail McKnight. "Loyalty, solidarity, flexibility, and accountability are what makes a family work." Gore believes that children "need homes where there's parental involvement of the right kind, education and guidance, not the wrong kind, like beatings," she told Bucholz. "Parents need to discuss issues, tell their children that they don't need certain things. You don't expect children to be perfect, but we need to tell them our standards and why." —C.L.

Suggested Reading: *Family Circle* p46+ Sep. 21, 1993, with photos; *Good Housekeeping* p154+ Mar. 1993, with photos; *New York Times Magazine* p28+ Oct. 1, 2000, with photo; *New Yorker* p54+ Mar. 6, 2000, with photos; *Redbook* p80+ Mar. 1994, with photos; *Saturday Evening Post* p38+ Mar. 1993, with photos; *Washington Post* F p1 May 16, 1993, with photo; *Washington Post* (on-line) July 11, 2000, with photo; *Washingtonian* p76+ Oct. 1994, with photos

Selected Books: *Raising PG Kids in an X-Rated Society*, 1987; *Picture This: A Visual Diary*, 1996

Stephane Sednaoui/Sony Music

Gray, Macy

1970(?)– Singer. Address: c/o Epic Records, 550 Madison Ave., New York, NY 10022

"People *say* they want to hear something fresh and new," singer Macy Gray told Rob Brunner for *Entertainment Weekly* (July 30, 1999), "but when it actually comes around most people kind of freak." The words "fresh" and "new" barely begin to describe Gray's unusual voice, and music journalists and critics have been scrambling to come up with more accurate terms since her debut album, *On How Life Is*, was released, in mid-1999. Gray has said that the meanest description she has heard is "a cat with laryngitis," but she has also been called "Chaka Khan meets Betty Boop," "Tina Turner on helium," "equal parts Mae West and Donald Duck," and a myriad of similarly inventive phrases. Her breathy, soulful singing has invited comparisons to Billie Holiday, Eartha Kitt, and Erykah Badu, among others, but despite their tendency to note resemblances, most journalists agree that Gray's voice makes her a one-of-a-kind talent.

Gray was born Natalie McIntyre in about 1970 in a working-class African-American section of Canton, Ohio, one of the four children of a retired steelworker and a junior-high-school math teacher. (She took the stage name Macy Gray when she began performing, in tribute to a favorite elderly neighbor.) Even when she was a child, Gray's voice was unusual, and her classmates often mocked its high-pitched, raspy sound. The teasing was so persistent that at one point she decided simply to keep quiet. "All kids are goofy. But I was extra goofy," she told Donna Freydkin for CNN (August 10, 1999, on-line). "Really tall, big feet, big ears. And I had a funny voice. When you're growing up, it's all about fitting in. I just wanted to have friends, so I didn't talk much." Gray found solace in listening to her parents' R&B and soul records for hours at a time. The extensive collection included albums by Al Green, Sly Stone, Stevie Wonder, and Marvin Gaye, among others—all artists whom Gray credits with influencing her later style. Hip-hop was in its rudimentary stages then, and she cites Parliament-Funkadelic as another early influence.

When Gray was 14 years old, her parents sent her to a mostly white boarding school, where she was exposed to little music besides rock—for which she eventually developed a taste. Although she studied classical piano for seven years, she did not initially envision a musical career for herself, concentrating instead on writing. "I've been writing since I was a little kid, little stories and so on," she explained to Rob Hoerburger for the *New York Times Magazine* (February 13, 2000). "In high school I would write other kids' term papers to make money on the side. Every kid gets this blessing, knack, whether it's drawing, writing, running. I could always come up with something on paper."

Gray enrolled in the screen-writing program at the University of Southern California, where her first student effort was an 8-mm film about a straitjacketed patient who is tormented by a fly that has landed on his nose. In her junior year she was approached by a friend who reasoned that if she could write screenplays, she could also come up with song lyrics for a tune that he had written. She did so, with widely reported results. In one version of events, her friend—needing to submit a demo tape to a publisher the next day—asked Gray to take the place of a vocalist he had hired, who had failed to show up. In a second version, Gray simply provided the guide vocals on the tape, and although another singer recorded over most of them, Gray's voice was left intact in one place. According to both accounts, the publisher found Gray's voice unlike anything he had ever heard, and word of his discovery spread in California's underground music scene. Gray was invited to sing old standards with a jazz band that played the Los Angeles hotel circuit. Although she still had little faith in her singing ability, the offer of $100 moved her to take the gig.

After leaving school, just eight credits short of her bachelor's degree, Gray took temporary work as a production assistant at MTV and later at Warner Bros., writing songs in her spare time. At that point she still considered the activity to be a hobby and had no plans to pursue a career in music. Gradually, though, she had a change of heart. "The whole time it just kind of grew on me," she told Gary Graff for the Wall of Sound Web site. "I don't know how to explain it; I got more and more attached to it and eventually fell in love with it." She became the unofficial hostess of what she called the We Ours, ensemble performances that took place in a Hollywood coffee shop. From 1:00 a.m. to 5:00 a.m. on weekends, the We Ours featured live music by Gray and her friends, open-mike performances, and guest disc jockeys. The space held only about 100 people, and well-known local acts, such as the Roots and Tricky, came to hang out and sometimes jam. In the mid-1990s, Atlantic Records executives heard Gray and signed her to a recording deal. The album she made for them, titled *A Thing of Beauty*, was never released, however, and she was dropped from the label, perhaps due to what one source called a "housecleaning" at the company. She stayed in Los Angeles for another year, trying to get another recording deal, before becoming discouraged and returning to Ohio, where she started a typing service that catered to students.

But tapes of her singing were still being circulated. When Jeff Blue, an executive at Zomba Music, heard one, he traced her to her parents' home, signed her to a recording deal, and persuaded her to return to Los Angeles to give her music career another try. He also sent a tape to Rose Noone, then at Island Music. Noone told Kent Zimmerman for *Gavin* (January 17, 2000, on-line), "[Blue's] message said, 'When you hear this voice, you're going to die.'" By the time Noone got the tape, she and her husband, James Dowdall, had moved to Epic Records. "We put it on and we were immediately mesmerized by her voice," Noone recalled. "I wasn't even focusing on the songs. After later listens, we felt the songs were great, but it's her voice that knocks you over first." Epic president Polly Anthony felt the same way and ordered Noone and Dowdall to sign Gray immediately. A bidding war ensued with Interscope, Universal, and, ironically, Atlantic, the label that had dropped Gray earlier. She signed with Epic in April 1998 and began a year of recording sessions with producer Andrew Slater, respected in the industry for his work with Fiona Apple and the Wallflowers—artists whose unusual sounds were, like Gray's, difficult to classify.

The resulting album, titled *On How Life Is*, was a combination of traditional R&B, rock, funk, jazz, and pop. The songs, each written by Gray herself, were largely autobiographical. "I think the lyrics are really relatable," she told David Furnish for *Interview* (October 1999). "Everybody's been through most of the stuff I write about: There are songs about a death in the family, about being in an abusive relationship, and about being in love. There's also a song about just sitting down and reflecting on life and trying to figure stuff out." Epic launched a seven-month promotional campaign before the album was released, sending sample cuts to select disc jockeys and club promoters. Gray continued to play weekly at the We Ours, as well as at the Viper Room, a trendy Los Angeles nightspot. She also played at a high-profile party at the Statue of Liberty, to celebrate the launch of *Talk* magazine, and began to be mentioned in such widely circulated publications as *Vibe*, *Newsweek*, and *People*. During one of her promotional appearances, Gray was heard by an employee of the popular clothing retailer the Gap, who brought her to the attention of Gap advertising executives. As a result, Gray was featured singing off-camera in one of the company's holiday television ads, which aired in November 1998.

Despite Epic's publicity drive, *On How Life Is* was not an immediate best-seller, which some industry insiders have attributed to its resistance to pigeonholing. "One characteristic of pop culture's approach to unclassifiable black artists is that there's often only room for one of them in the spotlight at any given time," Ken Tucker wrote for *Entertainment Weekly* (October 10, 1999, on-line). "It may be that Gray's eclecticism will work against her. She won't be hip-hop enough for rap programmers and fans, and she'll be too hardcore for the pop division." Nonetheless, the album's first single, "Do Something," an impassioned call for people to make productive use of their lives, was played in heavy rotation on MTV and won her new fans. Gray told a reporter for the Sonicnet Web site (August 5, 1999) that one day, while browsing the fan postings on her official Web site, she came across a letter that greatly touched her. "One guy said that he was crippled and that when he heard 'Do Something,' it inspired him to focus on his therapy so he can start dancin' again," she said. "When you hear stuff like that, it's just really a trip. That's the best." The next single, "I Try," had an infectious beat and got wide play on Top 40 radio stations across the country. Gray won two Brit Awards, the English equivalent of the Grammys, in the categories of best international newcomer of 2000 and best international female performer of 2000. Gray was named the most fashionable female artist at the 2000 VH1/Vogue Fashion Awards, and her video for "I Try," a song from *On How Life Is*, earned her recognition as best new artist at the 2000 MTV Video Music Awards. In addition, she was nominated for a Soul Train Music Award and two Grammys. Although she didn't win those, the nominations boosted record sales to more than three million worldwide, and *On How Life Is* made it onto the *Billboard* Top 10 for the first time since its release.

Gray's marriage, about which she has spoken little, broke up during the making of the album, leaving her the single mother of three children under five years of age. Since she tours heavily, the children live with her mother, and Gray visits them as often as she can. Although her 11-piece touring band is composed mainly of old friends and music veterans from her We Ours days, she feels that a tour bus is no place for a young child. At 30, Gray is older than many of the artists appearing on the charts with her; it has been noted that most of her rivals for the best-new-artist Grammy were under 20. She has maintained, however, that being a late bloomer on the music scene has been an advantage for her. "For myself I'm just on time," she told Rob Hoerburger. "If I had got here when I was a teenager, I can't imagine what I would have talked about. You have more stories to tell, relative to a 16 year old." — M.R.

Suggested Reading: CNN (on-line) Aug. 10, 1999; *Entertainment Weekly* p72 July 31, 1999, with photo; *Gavin* (on-line) Jan. 17, 2000; *Interview* p325+ Oct. 1999; *New York Times Magazine* p19 Feb. 13, 2000, with photo; Wall of Sound Web site

Selected Recordings: *On How Life Is*, 1999

Green, Tim

Dec. 13, 1963– Writer; former professional football player. Address: c/o Warner Books, 1271 Ave. of the Americas, Ninth Fl., New York, NY 10020-1300; Fox Sports Net, 1440 S. Sepulveda Blvd., Los Angeles, CA 90025-3458

Professional football player, lawyer, television sports commentator, best-selling author: a person who is identified by any one of these descriptors would generally be thought of as a success. In the case of Tim Green, all four apply. Adopted in infancy, Green spent years overcoming feelings of abandonment and a seemingly boundless need for approval caused by his biological parents' decision not to raise him. Yet, by his own admission, such feelings drove him to succeed. Following a stellar collegiate career, during which he excelled in both the classroom and on the football field, Green was drafted by the Atlanta Falcons of the National Football League (NFL) and played with them for eight seasons. Meanwhile, contrary to the stereotype of the meat-headed jock, he prepared for careers in law and writing that would ensure his success long

Maggie Smith/Courtesy of Warner Books

Tim Green

after his playing days were over. He has since produced two works of nonfiction and five legal thrillers, with a sixth due in bookstores in September 2000, and has become a veteran game-day broadcaster for the Fox Sports Net's NFL coverage.

Timothy Green was born on December 13, 1963 to a woman who immediately put him up for adoption. Dick and Judy Green of Syracuse, New York, legally adopted the infant soon afterward. Early on the Greens engendered in their son a love for the two things for which he would become most famous: football and books. "I have this vivid childhood memory of Sundays, playing football with the neighborhood kids in the yard and then coming inside to watch the NFL games with all our dads," he told Kate Meyers for *Entertainment Weekly* (November 4, 1994). "I also remember going to the library every Monday night with my parents and getting our books for the week." Throughout his childhood, Green was a quintessential overachiever. He was a successful Boy Scout, a straight-A student, and a gifted athlete who played varsity football in his freshman year of high school and won a state championship in wrestling. Green believes that his yearning to please his biological mother motivated him to excel. "My whole quest for praise and achievement was an attempt to make myself desirable to a woman who gave me away," he explained to Nick Charles for *People* (January 12, 1998). Despite, or perhaps because of, his success in nearly everything he attempted, Green's peers often shunned him. His high-school classmates voted him "class suck-up" and booed him at graduation.

Green's athletic prowess and fine grades earned him a scholarship to Syracuse University, where he chose English literature as his major and played big-time college football as a member of the Orangemen. While at Syracuse, he told Bob Summer for *Publishers Weekly* (January 1, 1996), he attended several "incredibly intellectual" parties. At such gatherings he met prominent scientists and such literary luminaries as Tobias Wolff and Raymond Carver. He explained to Summer, "I was struck by the fascination these people had with the world I lived in—the world of football—and I began to realize that this world is actually a visceral and passionate place."

Green maintained a cumulative grade-point average of 3.83 while he gained a national reputation as a defensive lineman. Despite his relatively diminutive size for a defensive end—six feet, two inches tall and 245 pounds—he set Syracuse University records for most sacks in a single season, at 15; most career sacks, at 45.5; and most tackles in a career by a down lineman, at 341. By the time he had completed his final season with the Orangemen, in 1985, he had been selected twice each as an All-American and Academic All-American, had been named a National Football Foundation and College Football Hall of Fame Scholar-Athlete, and had been a finalist for the 1985 Vince Lombardi Award, which is given annually to the nation's best lineman or linebacker. Green was named covaledictorian of his graduating class.

In 1986 Green was picked in the first round of the NFL draft, 17th overall, by the Atlanta Falcons. Being drafted by an NFL team, which had long been a dream of his, was bittersweet, however, because shortly before the draft, Green had learned that he had been turned down for a Rhodes scholarship. The reason that the scholarship committee rejected him, he suspected, was his candor regarding his career choice. "I made no qualms about the fact that I was going to play professional football, and I don't think that that was very much appreciated," Green told Vic Carucci for the *Sporting News* (April 21, 1986). "I wasn't going to deny the fact that football was my life, that it was the most important thing to me. I thought the best thing to do was be very honest and very frank about it." Green was also distracted at the time by thoughts of his birth parents, about whom he often dreamt as well. After signing a four-year deal with the Falcons worth $1.45 million, Green made an unusual request of his agent: instead of asking the agent to seek lucrative product-endorsement contracts, as most rookies do, Green asked for the name of a good private investigator, in the hope that he might find out something about his biological parents.

Although the records to Green's adoption were closed, the detective ascertained that Green's maternal grandfather had been a policeman and a professional baseball player, that his father was an army officer, and that his birth mother had worked her way through college. He was unable to discover any of their names, though. The investigation took a turn for the better in 1988, when Green used information from his birth certificate (which was presumably found by the detective) to locate the town where he was born. He struck up a friendship with a nurse in the town's one hospital, and she obtained for him a copy of his records. (A week later a fire destroyed the room in which they had been stored.) In February 1989 Green placed a phone call to Joanne Heathslide (now Burgen), the woman who had given birth to him. Not long afterward, the two met face to face. "Just looking at her face is like my face—I can't explain it," he told Nick Charles. "We both hugged each other, and we both cried." Green's book *A Man and His Mother: An Adopted Son's Search* (1997) is a heartfelt chronicle of his efforts to locate his birth mother.

Green spent eight years as an Atlanta Falcon defensive end. Initially, his size, which was better suited for a linebacker than for a down lineman, was a matter of concern even more than it had been in college; if he played as a defensive end, he would regularly face offensive linemen who would outweigh him by approximately 60 pounds. The Falcons' coaching staff tried him at several spots on defense, including all four linebacking positions, before settling him into its defensive-end rotation. Despite his relative smallness, and despite the injuries that plagued him for a few years, Green became a stalwart on the otherwise unremarkable team. He recorded 69 consecutive games between 1988 and 1992, during which he led the team in sacks and was among its leaders in tackles, and he was the only Atlanta lineman to start every game in the 1990 and 1991 seasons. Toward the end of the 1992 season, Green broke his right elbow, and though he rehabilitated quickly, a serious knee injury the following season hastened his retirement from football, in 1993. He is remembered above all for a spirited approach to the game that belied his smallish frame. "Green's 245 pounds are all in his heart," the former Atlanta coach Jerry Glanville told Ira Berkow for the *New York Times* (December 25, 1993).

Green offered an insider's observations of the world of professional football in *The Dark Side of the Game* (1996). Perhaps his best-known and most highly acclaimed book, *The Dark Side of the Game* discusses the best and worst cities to compete in from a player's point of view and offers Green's insights into serious problems that plague the NFL, including racism and steroid abuse. It also sheds light on the difficulties that face many athletes after their football careers end. "What I have seen is that players have such a drastic change in life style, in self-image, that when they leave football, it is like a death," he explained to Ira Berkow. "Some can't handle it. Some can never handle it."

While still with the NFL, Green worked on a novel for four years, writing as he traveled between games during the football season; in the off-season, he attended law school at Syracuse. "Writing enabled me to appreciate the experience of playing football more than most guys," he told Kate Meyers. "It forced me to examine it and it preserved it for me." Published in the fall of 1993, *Ruffians* is the story of a young football player whose coach pressures him to take anabolic steroids. Although there appear to be many autobiographical elements to the book, Green has insisted that the story was not drawn entirely from personal experience. "No one ever tried to force me to take drugs, and I didn't take them. . . . I know some coaches have insisted on it, overtly or subtly, and some players do it on their own," he told Ira Berkow. "They'll do anything to get or keep the life style. . . . Because winning is everything, there's a lot of pressure to compromise yourself. A lot of it reflects the values of our society. We want to be bigger, stronger, the best." Ruffians drew favorable critical comparisons to *North Dallas Forty*, Peter Gent's 1973 fictional exposé of the NFL, and sold moderately well.

In 1994 Green completed his law degree, with honors. In the same year he was hired by the Fox television network as an NFL game announcer and published his second novel, *Titans*. In that book Green presented a fictional scenario in which the Mafia controlled the outcome of pro football games and reaped profits through gambling. The plot centers on Hunter Logan, a quarterback for a championship team, whose side bets placed through a friend are traced back to him by the mob. The mob then uses that information to blackmail Logan into shaving points from the score of games in which he plays. Green's inspiration for the book came from the gambling seminars that all NFL players must attend before the start of each season; the players are addressed by FBI agents who warn them about the potential dangers of gambling. "I guess the thing that struck me was how adamant they were that the gamblers and the mob are out there," he told Don Pierson for the *Chicago Tribune* (November 20, 1994). "After hearing this message for eight years, that's really what prompted me to write *Titans* and say, 'Hey, what if what they're talking about really happened?' And if it did happen, I just think it would happen exactly the way it did in *Titans*." By this point, Green's gridiron tales were gaining popularity, and not just among the public, he told Pierson. "Last year, it was especially funny when offensive linemen I was playing against would come up after a game and say, 'Hey man, I read your book,'" he recalled. Shortly after the publication of his second novel, Green passed the New York State bar exam. His legal training has enabled him to serve as his own literary agent.

In Green's next three novels, professional football did not take center stage. *Outlaws* (1996), the first of the three, is about a football player who unwittingly finds himself snared in a black-market arms deal. In *Outlaws* Green introduced the defense lawyer Madison McCall. "I'm going to continue with her over my next several novels," he told Bob Summer around the time that *Outlaws* was published. "She's positioned now so that there's almost nothing she can't get involved in. She can go further into football, maybe as an agent, or into the world of crime." McCall returned in *The Red Zone* (1998), in which she represents a professional linebacker who is suspected of murder, and then in *Double Reverse* (1999), which finds her defending a running back with sadistic and misogynistic tendencies who is accused of killing a Hollywood starlet. Green's latest novel, *The Letter of the Law* (2000), is a departure for the writer, in that it is not connected to professional football and does not feature the character Madison McCall. Instead, the story focuses on the ambitious lawyer Casey Jordan as she defends one of her former law professors in a murder case.

Tim Green lives in Skaneateles, a hamlet in upstate New York, with his wife, Illyssa, whom he married in 1989; the couple have four children. Green remains close to both his adoptive mother and his birth mother, each of whom his children call "Grandma." He continues to work as an NFL analyst and color commentator for Fox Sports Net and is a frequent contributor to *USA Today* and National Public Radio. — J.K.B.

Suggested Reading: *Chicago Tribune* III p15 Nov. 20, 1994, with photo; *Entertainment Weekly* p68 Nov. 4, 1994, with photos; *New York Times* I p41 Dec. 25, 1993, with photo; *People* p93+ Jan. 12, 1998, with photos; *Publishers Weekly* p35 Jan. 1, 1996, with photos

Selected Works: *Ruffians*, 1993; *Titans*, 1994; *Outlaws*, 1996; *The Dark Side of the Game*, 1996; *A Man and His Mother*, 1997; *The Red Zone*, 1998; *Double Reverse*, 1999; *The Letter of the Law*, 2000

New York Times

Greenberg, Maurice R.

May 4, 1925– Chairman and CEO of American International Group Inc. Address: American International Group Inc., 70 Pine St., New York, NY 10270

As chairman and chief executive officer of American International Group (AIG), Maurice R. Greenberg heads a company that, according to *Fortune* (on-line), is the leading U.S–based international insurance firm and the number-one underwriter of commercial and industrial insurance in the nation. AIG operates in 130 countries and manages more than 300 insurance subsidiaries; its market value, as of March 2000, was almost $133 billion. Moreover, during the 33 years in which Greenberg has guided AIG, the company's earnings have grown by an average of 19 percent per year, a rate that *Fortune* called "sensational." The firm rose from 26th on the Fortune 500 list (which arranges American companies in order of revenue) in 1998, to 22d in 1999, to 17th, as of September 2000, when it also ranked 60th on the Global 500 list, Fortune's guide to the world's top concerns in terms of earnings. What makes this growth all the more impressive is that it has occurred in the insurance industry, which Carol J. Loomis, writing for *Fortune* (April 27, 1998), described as "bruisingly competitive, stingy with profits, and of late particularly hazardous for AIG's breed, the 'multilines'"—firms that sell property and casualty insurance as well as life insurance. Many industry analysts are at a loss to account for Greenberg's results, and he has become something of a financial guru on Wall Street. According to Loomis, "In the world of bigtime financial services, he is widely and enthusiastically admired for his management abilities and for his long-term consistency in pulling outstanding performance out of AIG."

Widely referred to by his nickname, Hank, Greenberg is an amalgam of astute corporate executive, entrepreneurial innovator, self-appointed statesman, and drill sergeant for those who aspire to join the business elite. He is widely characterized as hard-driving and domineering—Loomis labeled him a "predator" and a "martinet"—and his speech is direct and forceful. At the same time, he is known to give AIG staffers free rein so long as they respect the bottom line. "Part of our culture [at AIG] is that you build people with independence, who are thinking people intellectually, and who don't need to have their hands held day-to-day in order to make decisions," he told Barbara Bowers for *Best's Review* (August 1998). He also told Bowers, "We build from within a group of people with a common goal, common objectives that's almost self-cleansing. It's not for everybody." Greenberg's demand for tough-minded self-reliance seems to appeal to many aspiring executives, who regard a stint at AIG as the ultimate hands-on corporate education. "It is, in many ways, a finishing school for CEO's," Robert J. O'Connell, a former AIG executive, said in an interview with Leslie Werstein Hann for *Best's Review* (September 1999). David Walsh, another former AIG executive, elaborated: "Everyone can say philosophically that there are things I'm good at and things I'm not good at," he told Hann. "AIG will put both of those types of traits in stark relief, and you'd better get better at the stuff you're good at and good at the things you're not." Greenberg is a member of the President's Advisory Committee on Trade Policy and Negotiations, and since 1995 he has chaired the board of the Asia Society, which encourages communication between Americans and the peoples of Asia and the Pacific.

Maurice Raymond Greenberg was born in New York City on May 4, 1925, the son of Jacob and Ada (Rheingold) Greenberg. There is virtually no other public information regarding his early years. During World War II, while still in his teens, he served in the U.S. Army and took part in the invasion of Normandy, France, in 1944. In 1948 he acquired a pre-law certificate from the University of Miami, in Florida, and in 1950 he received an LL.B. degree from New York Law School (which is not affiliated with a university). Before gaining admission to the New York State bar, in 1953, he again served in the army, this time in the Korean War, rising to the rank of captain. During his first or second tour of duty in the military, he earned a Bronze Star, which is awarded for heroic or meritorious service. For eight years (1952–60) he worked for the Continental Casualty Co. In 1960 he joined AIG, where he quickly climbed the corporate ladder: he became president of its subsidiary American Home Assurance Co. in 1962, and in 1967 he was named president and CEO of AIG itself. Since 1989 his title has been chairman and CEO.

Greenberg's leadership of AIG has been characterized by two long-term business strategies. The first is his insistence on the profitability of AIG's underwriting operations, in which the company assumes liability for specified losses covered by insurance policies it has issued. AIG realizes profits by ensuring that its customers' premiums exceed the amount for which AIG would be liable in the event of a claim. That practice is rather unusual in the insurance industry, where most firms count on making money by investing the payments they collect and long ago stopped trying to reap profits from underwriting, viewing as acceptable the losses that accrue from it.

Second, Greenberg has always viewed AIG as an international company. "He saw the potential of having truly global facilities," the economist Richard Stewart has said, as quoted by Gavin Souter for *Business Insurance* (October 5, 1998). "So wherever big corporations were going, you would be able to serve them and be with them from the ground up." But AIG was always international: operations in Germany and Japan, for example, contributed greatly to the company's growth after World War II, and the firm has always been a presence in Southeast Asia. What Greenberg did was to greatly emphasize AIG's international activities. Operations in Southeast Asia and Japan expanded significantly, and in 1979 AIG became the first Western insurance company to set up joint ventures in Hungary, Poland, and Romania, all of which were under Communist rule at that time. In recent years AIG has been active in Russia, the former Soviet republics, and Eastern Europe, and it currently plans to enter emerging markets in India and Vietnam. Most important, perhaps, have been AIG's endeavors in China, which date from 1980, when the firm established a joint venture with the Chinese People's Insurance Co. In recent years AIG has been operating independently in several Chinese cities.

In a way, AIG's presence in China represents a return to the firm's roots. The company was founded in Shanghai, a city on China's east coast, in 1919 by Cornelius Vander Starr, an American; it is the largest American concern to have started overseas. Toward the end of World War I, Starr had left his home in California to travel the Orient. According to company legend, he established AIG with the paltry sum of 330 Japanese yen, all that he had left when he arrived in Shanghai. Within a few years Starr had opened offices in Hong Kong; Jakarta, Indonesia; Saigon, Vietnam (which was then part of Indochina); and Manila, the Philippines. The business grew rapidly. In 1939 Starr moved the company's headquarters to the Wall Street section of New York City. AIG abandoned China completely in 1949, as the Communist People's Liberation Army, led by Mao Zedong, advanced on Shanghai.

When AIG was granted a license to set up shop independently in China, in 1992, it became the first foreign insurance company to get such permission in 40 years. This corporate triumph followed years of efforts by Greenberg to cultivate ties with Chinese government officials. Since 1975 he had made dozens of trips to Beijing and Shanghai. AIG had provided substantial funding for the Shanghai Centre, an office, residential, and entertainment complex in the city's downtown, which was completed in 1990. Moreover, in 1992 the company had bought from a European collector the windows stolen from the Bronze Pavilion at Beijing's Summer Palace and presented them to the Chinese government as a gift. In 1990 Greenberg helped establish a council that offered business advice to Zhu Rongji, who was then the mayor of Shanghai. One year later Zhu was promoted to deputy prime minister. According to Cao Hengchen, the deputy manager of the Shanghai office of People's Insurance, Greenberg's relationship with Zhu proved valuable for AIG. "Zhu is the one who gave final approval for American International to come here," Hengchen told Seth Faison for the *New York Times* (April 5, 1995). "This Greenberg really knows how to operate," he added.

Industry insiders believe that a crucial ingredient of Greenberg's success overseas has been his skill in adapting AIG to local environments. As one former AIG executive, speaking on condition of anonymity, told Ed Paisley for *Institutional Investor* (July 1997), "His genius is that his firm is never considered a foreign company. He and his local executives broke the code decades ago." That adaptability manifests itself in a variety of business practices. One is AIG's unusual willingness to tailor its policies to local conditions. In Uzbekistan, a politically unstable former Soviet republic, for example, AIG recently began selling "political-risk" insurance to foreign joint ventures. Elsewhere, the company offers coverage for such regional hazards as kidnapping, product tampering, and the incurring of disgrace by a corporate spokesperson. Such seemingly exotic policies constitute a substantial source of revenue for AIG. In contrast, most insurance firms do the bulk of their property and casualty business in such traditional lines as auto and fire insurance. ("Property and casualty" is the catch-all industry term for policies other than those for life insurance.)

AIG's overseas success has also been traced to Greenberg's practice of investing in projects aimed at building up local infrastructures. In 1993 the company pledged $100 million to a fund that helped finance toll roads, power plants, telephone networks, industrial complexes, and other such undertakings in Asia. Greenberg was instrumental in establishing the fund, and with the crucial assistance of his friend and associate Moeen Qureshi, a former World Bank official, he secured over $1 billion in investments before ending their campaign for funds, in June 1994. Speaking with a *U.S. News & World Report* (January 9, 1995) interviewer, Qureshi pointed out that in many developing nations, "the roads are clogged, the ports are choked, there are brownouts. This has become the major bottleneck to sustained growth." Some of AIG's corporate rivals and even former AIG executives have hinted that in supporting the Asian infrastructure fund and in making other such investments, AIG hoped to ingratiate itself with regional governments and thereby protect its assets. Greenberg, however, has denied that charge. "We have not raised these funds or made these investments to 'protect' our insurance operations," he told Ed Paisley. "This [allegation] can only come from a jealous competitor or someone with a desire to denigrate AIG's motives." He described the company's investment strategy in his talk with Paisley as "building relationships" and added that "properly structured, infrastructure investments can be attractive to the private sector, and this is what we are attempting to do, quite successfully, I might add, with our infrastructure funds. It's absurd to contend that we are doing this to generate 'goodwill' locally."

Also contributing to the company's success abroad is its practice of hiring local people and giving them responsibility for regional operations. According to Leslie Werstein Hann, Greenberg "abides religiously to the view of AIG as a collection of villages with chiefs who have the authority to run things as they choose—as long as they're successful." Thus, while insurance agents in China, for example, use the same door-to-door strategy that works for AIG elsewhere, they have also adapted their sales approach to the idiosyncracies of the Chinese market. They have discovered that visiting offices is an effective sales technique, since underemployed workers seem glad for a distraction; that it is best to sell to the boss first, thereby signaling to employees that it is advisable to buy; and that parents, many of whom are quite protective as a result of China's sporadically enforced policy of one child per family, are often eager to purchase a life-insurance policy.

Thanks to AIG's extensive overseas interests, Greenberg has become an outspoken advocate of free trade. After Congress declined to renew President Clinton's so-called fast-track authority in trade negotiations, in 1997, Greenberg sought to rally his fellow insurance executives in support of such measures. (Essentially, the fast-track legislation would have abolished Congress's power to modify trade treaties negotiated by the president prior to ratification; thus, the law would have substantially augmented the president's ability to shape trade policies.) In an interview with Sam Friedman for *National Underwriter* (December 8, 1997), Greenberg insisted that "insurance CEOs have got to be more involved" in political debates dealing with free trade. "You can't just send your lobbyists [to Washington, D.C.]," he continued. "[Elected officials] see them [on Capitol Hill] all the time. It won't accomplish anything. If you want to get the attention of a U.S. Senator or Congressman, go yourself."

Taking his own advice, in February 2000 Greenberg testified before the Ways and Means Committee of the U.S. House of Representatives, urging Congress to support China's entry into the World Trade Organization and to grant normal trade relations to China permanently. (Congress had granted China normal trade relations [NTR], which eliminates many legal barriers to free trade, each year since 1980, but the country's status was subject to annual review.) A failure to do so, Greenberg argued, as reported on the Web site of the organization New York for U.S.–China Trade, would hobble AIG and other American companies that do business in China, rendering them unable to compete with their European and Japanese rivals. Ultimately, he warned, that situation would harm the U.S. economy as a whole. Permanent NTR status, on the other hand, he said, would bring about "a win-win result for both countries." Responding to the argument that by denying China NTR status, the U.S. puts pressure on the Chinese government to improve its human-rights policies, Greenberg maintained that "China and the U.S. have different values and different political systems"; whereas the U.S. places considerable value on the protection of human rights, China, as a result of "hundreds of years of internal turmoil, famine and bloodshed," is primarily concerned with "feeding and clothing . . . [its] massive population." Further, because, historically, a solid tradition of protecting civil liberties depends upon the existence of a strong middle class, "the expansion of trade will lessen our differences over time," because such trade will foster the growth of the middle class in China. In closing, Greenberg said, "This is not to suggest that the U.S. should refrain from discussing differences we have with China over human liberties, their form of government, freedom of speech, assembly and the press. But, we should do so in other, more appropriate fora."

Greenberg is a member of the Business Roundtable, an association of chief executive officers of leading U.S. corporations that advocates public policy favorable to business. He is the chairman of the U.S-China business council, a member of the board of governors of New York Hospital, and a former director of the Federal Reserve Bank of New York. He has received honorary degrees from two universities—Brown and Pace; two colleges—Bryant and Middlebury; and the New England School of Law.

Greenberg and his wife, the former Corinne Phyllis Zuckerman, have four children: Jeffrey, Evan, Scott, and Cathleen. (Evan, who worked at AIG for 25 years and was considered his father's probable successor, left the company in mid-September 2000.) An avid skier who watches his diet and works out regularly, Greenberg, who turned 75 in 2000, appears to be in robust health. "I feel good," he said to Carol Loomis when she asked him about his retirement plans. "I like what I do, and I haven't had another job offer." As of late September 2000, Greenberg owned more than 16 million shares, or about $2 billion worth, of AIG stock. — P.K.

Suggested Reading: *Best's Review* p48+ Aug. 1998, with photos, p40+ Sep. 1999, with photo; *Fortune* p106+ Apr. 27, 1998, with photo; *Institutional Investor* p129+ July 1997, with photo; *New York Times* III p1+ July 23, 2000, with photos; *Who's Who in America, 2000*

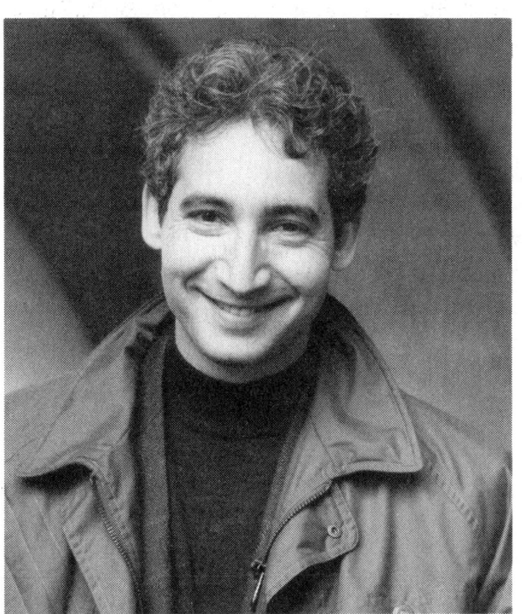

Courtesy of Brian Greene

Greene, Brian

Feb. 9, 1963– Physicist. Address: Columbia University, Physics Dept., Rm. 910 Pupin Hall, 538 W. 120th St., New York, NY 10027

Since Albert Einstein proposed the idea, physicists have been trying to come up with a "theory of everything." In Einstein's view, such a theory would be "a single master framework that would describe physics out to the farthest reaches of the cosmos and down to the smallest speck of matter," as the physicist Brian Greene put it in *Natural History* (February 2000). Greene and other contemporary physicists think about such a theory in terms of the four fundamental forces that exist in the universe: gravity, electromagnetism, and the two forces that are at work within atoms—the weak nuclear force, which causes radioactivity, and the strong nuclear force, which binds protons and neutrons. Thus, according to modern-day physicists, the so-called unified theory would, in Greene's words, "show all four forces to be distinct manifestations of a single underlying force" and, in addition, would "establish a rationale for the presence of the particular species of apparently fundamental particles"—quarks and leptons and their antiparticles, which make up the more than 100 subatomic particles that have been identified so far. The "theory of everything," many physicists have proposed, will eventually be constructed by means of string theory. At its most basic level, string theory postulates that both atoms and the four fundamental forces are made up of small looplike entities—dubbed strings—which vibrate at different frequencies, and that the differences in frequencies distinguish subatomic particles from one another.

Brian Greene is one of the world's leading string theorists. He has also helped explain the complex world of string theory to laypeople, by means of genial lectures and a best-selling book, *The Elegant Universe* (1999), which was a finalist for the Pulitzer Prize in nonfiction. "The ideas that we're currently investigating in cutting-edge physics have deep implications for questions that people have struggled with for thousands of years," Greene told an interviewer for *Columbia* (Fall 1999). "Questions that are really at the heart of the human condition, such as, What is time? What is space? What is the universe made of? It may well be that we are taking the final step to getting the deepest scientific answers to some of these questions. And it is imperative, I think, that everyone be able to share in this journey."

The son of Alan and Rita Greene, Brian Greene was born on February 9, 1963 in New York City. His father, a one-time vaudeville performer, later worked as a voice coach and composer. The family lived on the Upper West Side of Manhattan, near the American Museum of Natural History and the Hayden Planetarium (now part of the museum's Rose Center for Earth and Space). Unlike many children, as Greene recalled to Alden M. Hayashi for *Scientific American* (April 2000), he "never really [felt] excited" by the museum's dinosaur exhibits, but he was fascinated by what he saw in the planetarium. "Ever since I can remember," Greene told Hayashi, "I was always questioning what the universe was made of and how it got to be the way it got to be." At a very young age, Brian showed a talent for arithmetic. When he was five, he would multiply 30-digit numbers that his father would write out for him, doing the calculations on big sheets of construction paper that he and his father had joined with tape. "It's a weird thing, mathematics," Greene told Shira J. Boss for *Columbia College Today* (September 1999). "Even as a six-year-old you can learn a few rules and then play around with it. You can't do that with literature, where you need years of experience to say anything interesting."

When Greene was in sixth grade, at Intermediate School 44, in Manhattan, his math teacher, knowing that he had exhausted the school's math resources, suggested that he go to Columbia University to find a tutor. Going from door to door in the computer-science department with his older sister, he had no luck until he ran into Neil Bellinson, a graduate student in mathematics, who agreed to tutor him for free. Greene was still getting instruction from Bellinson when he entered Stuyvesant High School, an elite New York City public school that accepts students on the basis of an exam. While at Stuyvesant he wrestled on the school varsity team, won citywide math competitions four years in a row, and was a finalist in the prestigious, nationwide Westinghouse Science Talent Search contest. Meanwhile, he had become deeply interested in mathematics as a tool for learning more about the universe. In an interview for the *Official String Theory Web Site*, Greene said, "I think as an adolescent I had many of the questions and concerns that many adolescents do . . . , what's it all about, why are we here, what are we meant to be doing with our time and so forth. And it just occurred to me that many people much smarter than I had thought of these questions through the ages and come up with various solutions, none of which I guess were completely satisfying, and it didn't seem to me that I was going to come up with a solution to those particular problems. But it seemed to me that if one could gain a deep familiarity with the questions, a real profound understanding of the questions themselves—that is, why is there space, why is there time, why is there a Universe—then at least that would be the first step towards coming to answers."

In 1980 Greene entered Harvard University, in Cambridge, Massachusetts, where he majored in physics. At Harvard he became aware of one of the great mysteries of modern physics, which is that the two major theories that describe the physical universe—the theory of relativity, which explains astronomical phenomena, and quantum mechanics, which describes the atomic and subatomic worlds—are mutually incompatible. "Quantum mechanics is based on the idea that things can flutter, things fluctuate," Greene Greene told Kai Wu, Justin Vazquez-Poritz, and Mike Wisz for the Cornell University campus publication *Science and Technology* (Winter 1996, on-line). "Even if they are in the lowest possible state of energy, even if they're resting on the table, they're still vibrating. And, if you try to combine that with general relativity, you run into big problems, because general relativity wants to model the universe as this very smooth, placid, varying space-time geometrical shape, and that's at odds with the frenetic flutter and jitter of quantum mechanics."

After earning a bachelor's degree, Greene enrolled at Oxford University, in England, as a Rhodes scholar. In 1985 he attended a lecture at Oxford about the "theory of everything." The focus was string theory, which purportedly reconciles the theory of relativity with quantum mechanics. Soon, Greene and fellow graduate students were learning as much as they could about the theory, sharing what they found out on their own. According to string theory, the universe is composed of tiny strings, or energy loops, which vibrate at different frequencies, thus creating electrons, photons, and other particles. "String theory comes along and says, do not think about elementary particles as being little points," Greene told the *Science and Technology* interviewers. "Think about them as being little loops. And when you do that, it turns out that you get exact meshing of gravity and quantum mechanics." However, string theory postulates that the universe has more than three spatial dimensions. Specifically, string theorists maintain that there are seven additional dimensions of space. These extra dimensions, according to one approach, are too small to be observed, as they are "curled up" very tightly. For that reason, string theory remains purely hypothetical. "We've been struggling for many years now to understand how it's possible that this theory that predicts 10 dimensions can still be describing our world," Greene told the *Science and Technology* interviewers. Completely engrossed by string theory,

Greene chose as the subject of his doctoral thesis, as Hayashi explained in *Scientific American*, "a possible way to coax experimentally testable predictions from string theory." He received a Ph.D. degree from Oxford in 1987.

Greene returned to Harvard for postdoctorate work before accepting a job teaching at Cornell University, in Ithaca, New York, where his research focused on quantum geometry, the study of the mathematical properties and physical implications of the extra seven spatial dimensions. In the early 1990s, working with colleagues, Greene made two important discoveries. With physicist Ronen Plesser, he discovered, as Jennifer Senior reported in *New York* (February 1, 1999), "that for every possible shape of the cosmos there is a 'mirror shape' that generates an alternate universe with exactly the same properties." Then, in 1992, while on a sabbatical leave from the university, Greene demonstrated, along with Paul S. Aspinwall and David R. Morrison of Duke University, that if string theory is correct, the spacial "fabric" can tear and repair itself, and thus the universe can reshape itself. This conclusion, though purely theoretical, was important nevertheless, because the theory of general relativity prohibits ruptures in space-time. Greene and his fellow string theorists are eagerly awaiting the construction of the Large Hadron Collider, in Geneva, Switzerland, which will smash protons with unprecedented power; the creation, by that method, of particles whose existence is predicted by string theory would go far toward proving the validity of the theory. "What has drawn me to science is the thrill of discovery," Greene told Hayashi. "There's nothing like that moment of realizing that you've discovered something that has not yet been previously known."

In 1996 Greene left Cornell for Columbia University, in New York City, where he started a string-theory program while teaching as a professor of physics and mathematics. "He has this great reputation," Greg Langmead, a graduate student, told Jennifer Senior. "Even among students who haven't taken anything with him. He's a great communicator, he's charismatic. He's clearly top-of-the-heap intellectually. So the fact that he has gobs of raw physical appeal on top of that—it gives him a really serious mystique." In February 1999, after two years of work, Greene's book, *The Elegant Universe: Superstrings, Hidden Dimensions, and the Quest for the Ultimate Theory*, was published; it has spent more than four months on the *New York Times* best-seller list, while briefly becoming Amazon.com's highest-selling book. In a review of *The Elegant Universe* for *Washington Post Book World* (March 7, 1999), the science journalist Marcia Bartusiak wrote, "Greene does an admirable job of translating a wholly mathematical endeavor into visual terms. Throughout his work, he writes with poetic eloquence and style." She also warned that Greene's "desire to reach the general reader may be overly ambitious. His discussions of gauge symmetries and Calabi-Yau geometries will be best appreciated by the science-minded who seek an insider's perspective on the cutting edge of physics." In addition to being a finalist for the Pulitzer Prize, in June 2000 *The Elegant Universe* won the Aventis Prize, England's top honor for a science book. Greene went on a nationwide book tour to publicize *The Elegant Universe*. During the tour he lectured at the Guggenheim Museum, in New York City, to the accompaniment of the Emerson String Quartet, in an event that was called "Strings and Strings." The lecture/performance proved so popular that it was repeated, and another performance is being planned at Lincoln Center. In the fall of 1999, Greene was featured in a segment of *Nightline in Primetime: Brave New World*, on ABC-TV. Currently he is working on a three-part series on unified theories for PBS's *Nova*.

Greene has continued to investigate questions of time and space from the perspective of quantum mechanics. According to string theory, time and space may be manifestations of more complex entities. He and other physicists hope to discover why movement in space can be forward or backward, but movement in time appears to be possible only in one direction. Working in a different sphere, Greene helped the actor John Lithgow with scientific dialogue for Lithgow's role on the NBC-TV series *Third Rock from the Sun*, and he had a cameo role in the feature film *Frequency* (2000). Earlier, Greene had appeared in musicals while at Harvard, and while at Cornell, he had a part in Harold Pinter's play *Betrayal* at a community theater. "It's a release, a way to enter a new world," Greene told Boss about his sporadic ventures into acting. "The things you think about are totally different from what you think of in a normal research day. Issues of human character and genuine human response are at the other end of the universe from trying to figure out why this string vibrates this way or that." Greene is interested in psychology and issues of human consciousness, and at one time he competed in judo. He was the director of the Theoretical Advanced Study Institute, at the University of Colorado at Boulder, in 1996, and is on the editorial boards of major publications in theoretical physics. When he was 30, Greene won a Young Investigator's Award from the National Science Foundation. The next year he won an Alfred P. Sloan Foundation fellowship. Recently, he and several colleagues received $2.5 million from the National Science Foundation to restructure high-level courses at Columbia. — G.O.

Suggested Reading: *Columbia* p8 Fall 1999; *Columbia College Today* p12+ Sep. 1999; *New York* p33+ Feb. 1, 1999, with photo; *Scientific American* p36+ Apr. 2000, with photo; *Time* p83+ Dec. 31, 1999, with photo

Selected Books: as author—*The Elegant Universe: Superstrings, Hidden Dimensions, and the Quest for the Ultimate Theory*, 1999; as co-editor—*Mirror Symmetry II*, 1997

Courtesy of Metropolitan Talent Agency

Guillaume, Robert

(gee-YOME)

Nov. 30, 1927– Film and television actor.
Address: c/o Metropolitan Talent Agency, 4526 Wilshire Blvd., Los Angeles, CA 90010-3801

"I have always wondered where I got my inner drive," Robert Guillaume told Ellen Hawkes during an interview for *Parade* (May 24, 1992). "Still, I'm sure that part of it came from my anger at a system that wanted me to believe I was inferior. . . . Looking back on my own life, I'd say that the secret is not to be without anger but to focus it and generate creative energy from it." A classically trained tenor with an impressive list of stage, film, and television credits spanning three decades, Guillaume is probably best known for his portrayal of the character Benson DuBois, first on the television series *Soap* (1977–79) and then on *Soap*'s spin-off, *Benson* (1979–86). For his work on *Soap*, he won a 1979 Emmy Award as best supporting actor; he earned his second Emmy, as best actor in a comedy, in 1985, during his last season on *Benson*. Most recently, he impressed audiences with his portrayal of Isaac Jaffee, the dapper executive producer of the cable sports program that served as the setting of *Sports Night*, a sitcom that ran from 1998 to 2000 on ABC-TV.

Robert Guillaume was born Robert Peter Williams on November 30, 1927 in St. Louis, Missouri. (He changed his surname to Guillaume—"William" in French—when he was in his early 20s, because he thought it sounded prettier and more distinctive.) After his father abandoned the family, when Robert was about two years old, his mother sent him and three of his siblings—a brother and two sisters—to live with their maternal grandmother. Thereafter, he told Bob Lardine for the New York *Daily News* (September 9, 1979), his mother, an alcoholic, "drifted in and out" of their lives but never lived with them. Guillaume's grandmother raised the children with both strictness and love, and she provided for them on the meager wages she earned by doing laundry at a Catholic rectory and cleaning houses. "She was a rare breed," Guillaume told Elizabeth Kastor for the *Washington Post* (September 24, 1985). "She saw a need; she rose to the occasion and took us in. She was not wealthy—she was poor—but she wanted to keep us together, so she did what she could to do that." Through his grandmother's example he learned valuable lessons, Guillaume told Fred Rothenberg for *Newsday* (August 5, 1981). For instance, his grandmother "worked for a lady who had no space and could have cleaned her one room herself, but she was too lazy. It was inherent in this lady's personality that she considered herself better than people working for her. My grandmother was working in a respectable job to put us through school. Now who was really better?" Guillaume's mother later revealed to him her feelings of guilt about her failings as a parent. Observing that "guilt is something which you can't do anything about," Guillaume told Rothenberg that he "never mention[s] anything" about the past when he chats with his mother. Speaking of his childhood years, he told Jacqueline Trescott for the *Washington Post* (September 13, 1979), "I don't remember them as rough times. In retrospect I know they must have been rough, but I had a tremendous ability to cover them over."

At the Catholic primary school he attended, his teachers praised Guillaume for his talent at singing, which he put to use in the glee club. But as he approached adolescence, he told Ellen Hawkes, he became increasingly aware of what he described as "the subliminal negative message every poor black child receives: 'You're inferior, you're dumb, you'll never amount to anything.' That got me angry, because I had ample evidence that I was smart, and I couldn't figure out how color had anything to do with it. But my anger at the message kept my confidence alive." His anger also led to verbal outbursts in the classroom, behavior that led school authorities to expel him when he was in ninth grade.

Guillaume's outspokenness got him into trouble again after he joined the army, in 1945. "I have a big mouth," he explained to *US* magazine (August 1983), "and I had a Southern captain who hated my guts. One day he called me into his office and announced, 'This army ain't big enough for the both of us.'" Guillaume took the hint and, after just 15 months of service, left the military. "My discharge was honorable, but barely," he told Sue Reilly for *People* (January 23, 1978).

After returning to St. Louis, Guillaume finished high school and then worked at a series of jobs, among them salesclerk, dishwasher, postal clerk, and streetcar driver. Heeding his grandmother's advice, he enrolled in night classes at St. Louis University, with the intention of majoring in business administration. But the idea of singing professionally became increasingly appealing to him, so he transferred to the music school at Washington University, also in St. Louis. The opera singer Leslie Chabay, who was on the faculty then, gave him encouragement. "Chabay was the first person to say I had potential to sing the classics," Guillaume told Jacqueline Trescott. With Chabay's help, he won a scholarship to attend the 1957 Aspen Music Festival, in Colorado, and his performances there led to an apprenticeship at the venerable Karamu Performing Arts Theatre, in Cleveland, Ohio. At the Karamu, which is among the oldest interracial theaters in the U.S., Guillaume appeared in musical comedies and operas.

Guillaume next moved to New York, where he took voice lessons and, at his teachers' urging, began to audition for parts in Broadway and Off-Broadway shows. According to Aldore Collier in *Ebony* (November 1983), he "was able to find steady work," in plays, musicals, and revues, among them *Free and Easy, Fly Blackbird, Golden Boy*, and *Porgy and Bess.* In 1970 he gave what Jacqueline Trescott, in the *Washington Post* (May 6, 1976), described as a "mighty interpretation" of Johnny Williams in a production of Charles Gordone's "black black comedy" *No Place to Be Somebody.* In 1972 he won the lead role, that of a resourceful preacher, in a revival of the musical *Purlie*, Ossie Davis's adaptation of his 1961 satirical comedy *Purlie Victorious.* Also during this period he appeared in close to 800 performances of the musical revue *Jacques Brel Is Alive and Well and Living in Paris.*

By his own account, Guillaume also lost potential parts, because of his race. "I realized that a lot of times I wasn't hired because I was black," he explained to Ellen Hawkes. "Sure, I was angry—but at the system, not at individuals. But when I adopted the attitude 'I don't care what you think,' I began to make my mark. That was the challenge: 'You don't want blacks? Then I'm going to change your mind and make you hire some.'" In describing the problem to Robert Lindsey for the *New York Times* (December 18, 1977), he said, "I have trouble handling the whole idea that it's tough to get a job because you're black. White actors have problems, too; if you're black it's just one more problem that you have to solve. I just don't like the premise that, if you're black, you can't get a job, although that may well be the case."

For two years in the 1970s, Guillaume apparently could not find work in theater: "The bottom fell out, nothing happened," he told Sue Reilly. His fortunes soared again in 1976, when he won a plum role in an all-black revival of the Frank Loesser–Abe Burrows musical *Guys and Dolls*—that of Nathan Detroit, the proprietor of "the oldest established permanent floating crap game in New York." The show, which opened at the National Theater, in Washington, D.C., and moved to New York two months later, was a hit, and it brought Guillaume a 1977 Tony Award nomination.

In the early 1970s Guillaume secured jobs on episodes of various TV shows, among them *All in the Family, Sanford and Son, Good Times*, and *The Jeffersons.* In 1977 ABC offered him his first major television role—that of Benson, butler to the Tate family, in *Soap*, a sitcom that satirized daytime soap operas. Habitually refusing to comply with the Tates' requests, the cantankerous, acid-tongued, cynical Benson made it plain that though he was an employee, he was nobody's servant. While church groups and some parents criticized *Soap* for its frank handling of sexual issues, others complained that—despite his audacity—Benson was little more than a stereotype of African-American domestic workers. That charge emerged again about the title character of *Benson*, a spin-off of *Soap*, which premiered in 1979. In *Benson*, Guillaume's character had left the Tates to work for James Gatling, the widowed, dim-witted governor of an unnamed state. In the sitcom's first and second seasons, Benson headed the governor's household staff; later, he became a government official himself. Benson was still responsible only for household tasks when Tom Shales, in the *Washington Post* (September 13, 1979), condemned the show for resurrecting the message that "blacks could harbor no nobler aspiration than to serve, comfort, and mollycoddle whites." Benson, Shales declared, was a "male mammy."

Addressing such criticism, Guillaume said, as paraphrased by Robert Lindsey, that the Benson of *Soap* was "not a typical servant but rather a voice of reason in an otherwise crazy household." In his 1979 conversation with Trescott, Guillaume said, "Through my own feisty personality I think I avoided a demeaning stature on *Soap.*" He also contended that "Benson upgrades the image of the ordinary black working man. He's a character with wit and intelligence, no great ambition, no great philosophy. . . . We have not had an opportunity as actors to be ordinary." A half-year later he said to Jerry Parker for *Newsday* (March 16, 1980), "The significance of Benson is that he is a break from the stereotype. He tells people: 'I work for you, but you do not own me. You are not better than me because I work for you.'" A few months after Benson was elected lieutenant governor of his state, in 1984, Guillaume told Michael E. Hill for the *Washington Post* (March 10, 1985), "Part of my social conscience led me to want to play a character in which a lot of things were possible. Society puts labels on people. . . . Benson was labeled as butler. But if you watch the show you know that doesn't describe totally what he is. I wanted a character who was upwardly mobile." The show, he added, "says that in America all things are possible." During the series' last season, Benson attempts to unseat Governor Gatling; the final episode, on August 30, 1986, ended on Election Day, without revealing the name of the winner.

In December 1986 Guillaume starred in *John Grin's Christmas*, a retelling of *A Christmas Carol* with an all-black cast. The made-for-television film marked his directorial debut. "For a long time, I wouldn't consider directing because I'm very volatile," he told Morgan Gendel for the *Los Angeles Times* (December 5, 1986). "My tendency is to get impatient with people who don't do what I want."

Guillaume returned to the world of the TV sitcom in April 1989, with *The Robert Guillaume Show*, in which he played a divorced marriage counselor named Edward Sawyer. In a rarity for the medium, the half-hour program featured an interracial romance between Sawyer and his secretary (played by Wendy Phillips). Although the series was praised, the ABC network canceled it after just four months.

In 1990 Guillaume appeared in the title role in a Los Angeles production of Andrew Lloyd Webber's musical *The Phantom of the Opera*. His casting had aroused skepticism among those who believed that nobody—certainly not an African-American—could fill the shoes of Michael Crawford, who had previously played the role. But Guillaume believed that "being black brought another dimension to the drama," as he explained to Ellen Hawkes. "What had been figurative in the Phantom's character—what he describes as his darkness, his banishment—became the literal isolation and anger of a black man in society." Guillaume's interpretation of the role impressed Daryl H. Miller, a reviewer for the *Chicago Tribune* (May 9, 1990), who wrote, "Guillaume conveys a sense of tortured humanity, whereas his popular predecessor seemed threateningly spectral. . . . Guillaume reveals aspects of the character that weren't always evident in Crawford's portrayal. Audiences can sympathize with Guillaume's Phantom because they sense that he has been made desperate by the circumstances of his life."

Later in the 1990s Guillaume appeared in *The Meteor Man* (1993), starring Robert Townsend (who also wrote and directed the film) and provided the voice of the wise baboon Rafiki in Disney's blockbuster *The Lion King* (1994) and its sequel, *The Lion King II: Simba's Pride* (1998). His silver-screen credits also include the parody *Spy Hard* and the family comedy *First Kid*, both in 1996. On television, he appeard in the miniseries *Children of the Dust* (1995), which featured Sidney Poitier; the HBO animated family-musical series *Happily Ever After: Fairy Tales for Every Child* (1995), which Guillaume narrated and which his wife, Donna Brown Guillaume, co-produced; the Showtime movie *Run for the Dream: The Gail Devers Story* (1996), and the NBC miniseries *Pandora's Clock* (1996). On Broadway, he succeeded Bill van Dijk in the title role of a Dutch production of *Cyrano: The Musical*, mounted at the Neil Simon Theatre in 1994. In two concerts given in April 1998, he sang selections from *Phantom of the Opera* and a medley of other popular songs with the Dallas Symphony Orchestra, as part of the 1997–98 JCPenney SuperPops Series.

In 1998 Guillaume won the part of executive producer Isaac Jaffee on the new ABC series *Sports Night*—"one of the best characters I've ever had," as he told Mike Duffy for the *Detroit Free Press* (May 3, 1999, on-line). Described by Matt Roush in *TV Guide* (November 7–13, 1998) as "a cross but never clichéd father figure," Jaffee is "an intelligent man," according to Guillaume. "See, I prefer intelligence to dignity," the actor told Mike Duffy. "Dignity is very boring. But intelligence can be exciting. And Isaac's intelligence is very exciting. His relationship with his employees flows from that." Written by Aaron Sorkin, directed by Thomas Schlamme, and inspired by ESPN's *SportsCenter*, *Sports Night* was hailed by critics for its successful blend of comedy and drama, its "rigorous intelligence, intensity, and realism," in Matt Roush's words, and the outstanding acting of Guillaume and the other members of its ensemble cast.

On January 14, 1999 Guillaume suffered a stroke in his *Sports Night* dressing room. Unable to work for more than two months, he underwent an arduous course of physical, occupational, and speech therapy. When Mike Duffy interviewed him, nearly four months after the stroke, Guillaume was walking with the aid of a cane. "You quickly realize all the things you can't do," Guillaume told him. "When the phone rings now, I'm on my way to answer it at the first ring. But sometimes I don't get there before it stops." When, on March 30, 1999, Guillaume returned to the set of *Sports Night* to film a scene for the season's finale, the cast and crew greeted him with cheers and applause. At the suggestion of Guillaume's wife, Aaron Sorkin worked the stroke into the story line, by making Isaac a stroke victim, too, so the actor felt "relieved . . . of much of the anxiety of trying to appear normal," as he told Jefferson Graham for *USA Today* (April 13, 1999, on-line). He told an interviewer for *Entertainment Tonight* (March 18, 1999, on-line) that it gives him a "great thrill" to have the opportunity, as Isaac, "to say something about a stroke and that there is life after a stroke." In 1999 Guillaume's work in *Sports Night* earned him an Image Award nomination for outstanding lead actor in a comedy series. (Image Awards are bestowed by the National Association for the Advancement of Colored People [NAACP] to people in the arts who present positive depictions of African-Americans.) At the end of the 1999–2000 television season, *Sports Night* was canceled. HBO considered buying the series, but talks with ABC came to naught.

In 1992 Guillaume and his third wife, Donna, who have been married since 1985, founded the Confetti Co., which publishes "read-along" books and audio cassettes of fairy tales presented from a multiethnic perspective. For his narration of *The Lion King Read-Along*, he won a 1994 Grammy Award in the "children's spoken word" category.

Guillaume and his first wife, Marlene, who married in 1955, separated in the late 1950s, when their two sons, Kevin and Jacques, were very young. Kevin is a songwriter and musician;

Jacques died of AIDS in 1990, at the age of 33. Guillaume's grief over Jacques's death was compounded by the guilt he felt about his absence in his sons' lives when they were growing up and Jacques's failure to build a satisfying career. "I felt guilty because what I call the 'long arm of the ghetto,' where [Jacques] spent his childhood, had gotten to him and programmed him for defeat," Guillaume told Ellen Hawkes. "But I think he interpreted my urging him to put his brains and talents to use as snobbishness and disapproval. He didn't seem to understand that, at the same time I loved him without qualification and accepted his homosexuality, I still hoped he'd find direction for his life."

Guillaume's second marriage, to the actress Fay Hauser, in 1978, ended in divorce. From relationships outside of marriage, Guillaume has two daughters—Patricia, born in about 1950, and Melissa, born in about 1981. When Rachel, his daughter from his current marriage, was born, in about 1992, he "felt so blessed, almost like a sense of renewal," he told Hawkes. "I'm a different kind of father now, more attentive and patient." In 1999 Guillaume was inducted into the St. Louis Walk of Fame, which honors people born or raised in St. Louis who have left their marks on the cultural heritage of the U.S. — J.K.B.

Suggested Reading: *Ebony* p133+ Nov. 1983, with photos; *Newsday* p3+ Mar. 16, 1980, with photos; *Parade* p12+ May 24, 1992, with photos; *People* p51+ Jan. 23, 1978, with photos; *TV Guide* p35+ Oct. 6, 1984, with photo; *USA Today* D p3 Apr. 13, 1999, with photo; *1999 International Television and Video Almanac*

Selected Films: *Lean on Me*, 1989; *Death Warrant*, 1990; *The Lion King*, 1994; *Spy Hard*, 1996; *The Lion King II: Simba's Pride*, 1998

Selected Television Shows: *Soap*, 1977–79; *Benson*, 1979–86; *John Grin's Christmas*, 1986; *The Robert Guillaume Show*, 1989; *Happily Ever After: Fairy Tales for Every Child*, 1995; *Sports Night*, 1998–2000

Associated Press

Guy, Buddy

July 30, 1936– Blues musician; guitarist. Address: Buddy Guy's Legends, 754 S. Wabash, Chicago, IL 60605

Buddy Guy is one of the most influential blues musicians in the world. Born in Louisiana in the midst of the Great Depression, Guy, at the age of 20, packed his bags and his guitar and moved to Chicago, then the nation's blues capital. There, he was mentored by such greats as Muddy Waters, B.B. King, and Willie Dixon. Once a victim of stage fright, Guy conquered his fear of performing live and put together one of the most dynamic acts in all of blues. "I just feel so good when [audiences] like what I do . . . ," Guy told Scott Spencer for *Rolling Stone* (November 28, 1991). "It gives me goose bumps to see so many people smiling. There is so much hatred in the world, and music can bring so much love. This is my goal in the world. I'm a very religious Baptist and my parents brought me up to love everybody." Guy, who has always had a strong fan base in Europe, has for decades played teacher to some of rock-and-roll's most esteemed guitarists, among them Eric Clapton, Keith Richards, and Mark Knopfler. Now in his seventh decade, Buddy Guy—with well over two dozen albums in print and several Grammy Awards under his belt—is considered an elder statesman of the blues.

Buddy Guy was born on July 30, 1936 in Lettsworth, Louisiana. His family worked as sharecroppers in Lettsworth, where, in the summertime, young Buddy would help out in the cotton fields during the day. When his work was through, he would hurry home to play a pick-up game of baseball with his brothers, using a misshapen tin can as a ball. From an early age Buddy loved music; he would often clutch a broomstick and pretend to play guitar. "My mom used to get a book from a store called Altons, or something like that," Guy told Scott Spencer. "They would mail these catalogs to all the people out in the country and that's where my mother would order all our little blue jeans and they'd come COD. I would see these guitars in the book and try to make one. I'd take a paint can and put a stick in there and then tear a little piece of wire off the screen in my window and make strings. Every time I stretched one it would break, but I'd keep banging away. Until one year, my dad had a good year, raised a lot of cotton and about broke even. So he found this old guy with a beat-up acoustic and my dad gave the guy two dollars for it."

With his used guitar, which rarely had a full set of strings, Guy imitated the music he heard on the radio. "No one ever taught me anything on guitar," he told Spencer. "I was alone, out there in the country. . . . But one day I heard John Lee Hooker on the radio, and it just kept going through my head. I looked all over the guitar for that sound. My sisters and brothers would run me out of the house, it was so boring to them, me learning how to play. So I was out on the woodpile, kind of dozing off while I played, and all of a sudden I heard myself hitting the notes, that John Lee sound. And I woke up and where I had my fingers placed, you didn't have to move, all you had to do was work the last three fingers, from the first to the last. I played that thing for two or three hours because I thought if I turned it loose, I never would find it again. My hand was frozen, frozen, man, in that spot." His ability to play despite his lack of formal training led him to believe that his skill was a gift from God.

As a young adult Guy left home and headed for Baton Rouge, a cultural center of Louisiana, where he stayed with his sister. He worked as a handyman at Louisiana State University (LSU) while continuing to practice on his instrument. In Baton Rouge Guy had the opportunity to see such blues greats as Little Walter, Luther Allison, Bobby Bland, and Guitar Slim play at local venues. Before long his uncle, Mitchell Young, who also lived there, recognized his deep love for the music and bought him a new guitar.

His first musical break came when "Big Poppa" John Tilley, a musician who was well known in the area, invited Guy to play harmony to Tilley's lead guitar at Sitman's Tavern, a local pub. Guy jumped at the opportunity. During the performance, however, he was stricken with stage fright and played the entire gig with his back to the audience. Tilley fired him at the end of the set. But the bandleader's need for a guitarist apparently outweighed other concerns, and he gave Guy another chance the next evening. This time Guy used a time-honored stage-fright remedy suggested to him by a friend: a few shots of liquor. The strategy appears to have worked; Guy aficionados point to that evening's performance as the genesis of his now-famous stage act, featuring his elaborate posturing, animated facial expressions, and generally extroverted showmanship.

After a short time Guy left Tilley's group to play with another local musician, Raful Neal, but this alliance lasted only a short time, as Buddy decided in 1957 to move to what was then the biggest blues town in the country—Chicago. His first months there were not auspicious, as he watched his funds dwindle while trying, unsuccessfully, to get a recording deal with Chess Records, the home of such blues stars as Muddy Waters. Guy came close to returning to Louisiana. "I was going on my third day with no food and didn't nobody know who I was," Guy told Spencer. "And a stranger saw me walking around with my guitar. You know, hungry as I was, I would never pawn my own guitar, not after all I'd been through getting one in the first place. So this guy walks up to me, sees how lost I am and sees the guitar, and he asks me, 'Can you play the blues on that damn thing?' And I say to him, 'Yeah, I play some blues.' He said he'd buy me a drink if I played him some blues, and I said, 'Buy me a hamburger and I'll play all night.'"

For the stranger, who turned out to be Muddy Waters, Guy played a blues standard originally penned by bluesman Guitar Slim, "That Thing That You Used to Do." Impressed by the rendition, Waters took Guy to his home. "He told his wife, 'Get dressed. We're going out. I got a little nigger here who can wear that guitar *out*,'" Guy recalled to Spencer. Waters and his wife took Guy to the famous 708 Club, one of the many blues clubs that once lined 47th Street on Chicago's West Side. There, the blues guitarist Otis Rush was performing when Waters approached him and announced, "I got a black son of a bitch here that'll run you off the stage." "And I went up there and played and then I saw this white couple, a husband and wife," Guy recounted to Spencer. "The man was the club's owner and he'd just come in to pick up his receipts. I saw him looking at me and then he was gone. When I got off the stage, the manager asked me how I was feeling. Hungry, was what I told him. And he looked at me and said, 'You know you just got hired. The owner told me, right before he left. You play Tuesday, Wednesday, and Thursday, 25 dollars a night.' At LSU, that was what I made in a week."

His gig at 708 enabled Guy to meet his childhood idols B.B. King and Willie Dixon, as the established bluesmen would often visit the club to watch the up-and-coming guitarist play. A buzz soon developed around Guy, and recording contracts began coming to him. Guy was still hoping for a contract with Chess Records, but Dixon, who had recently had a falling-out with the label, offered the young bluesman a limited contract with his fledgling record company, Cobra. Otis Rush took Guy to the garage from which Cobra cut its records, and there Guy recorded the singles "I Sit Here and Cry and Sing the Blues," "This Is the End," "Try to Quit You Baby," and "You Sure Can't Do," which became modest hits. When Cobra folded, a few years later, Chess—to Guy's surprise—offered him a contract, and he soon recorded "First Time I Met the Blues" and "Broken Hearted Blues." As Spencer wrote, Chess was "the Motown of the Fifties and early Sixties, a kind of family operation in which musicians, writers, and producers were in a continual process of cross-fertilization." Indeed, artists including the rock-and-roll legends Chuck Berry and Bo Diddley, blues masters Howlin' Wolf, Muddy Waters, Willie Dixon, and Little Walter, and a host of backup players were featured on the label.

Guy became a supporting member of Chess's ensemble of already famous names, playing backup to nearly every bluesman on the label. Allowed to take center stage only occasionally in his early days with Chess, in live performances Guy developed a reputation as a musician with a galvanizing stage presence. From 1960 to 1967, on the discs for which he was the featured performer, he recorded some of his best music, such as the classic singles "Let Me Love You Baby," "Ten Years Ago," "Stone Crazy," "My Time After Awhile," "Leave My Girl," and perhaps his most famous single, "No Lie."

Guy's fellow bluesmen, including Wolf and Waters, "did not go to bed, man," Buddy told Spencer in recalling the period. "If you had a guitar, somewhere, they were there, having fun, drinking. We had so much fun in those days. Now the world has changed. People loved the music, and folks had more money and was circulating it. More people were working and every day was like Saturday night to me." Guy left Chess in 1967 to join Vanguard, where he recorded the LP *A Man and the Blues* (1968), which contains his now legendary rendition of "Mary Had a Little Lamb." He followed with the live album *This Is Buddy Guy* (1968) and the studio effort *Coming at You* (1968).

In the 1960s, even as Guy and other blues artists were recording some of their most important work, the demand for the music began to wane, as rock moved to the center of American pop culture. Soon, however, the more prominent (mostly white) rock musicians—Eric Clapton, Keith Richards, and Jimmy Page—were claiming blues as a major influence on their music, and Guy, Waters, and Wolf began touring as opening acts for the most successful rock bands of the era, such as Cream, the Rolling Stones, and the Yardbirds. (As Spencer explained, "There was a reluctance on the part of many white artists . . . to altogether duplicate the shameful history of pop music in the Fifties, which saw white versions of black music making huge amounts of money, while the black artists whose music was being watered down were often barely making a living.") During this period, seeing that he had more of an audience abroad than at home, Guy moved to London. "I was completely unrecognized in the U.S.—even my neighbors didn't know who I was," he told Spencer. With numerous middle-class British youths wanting to learn the American style of music, Guy mentored the likes of Jeff Beck and teamed up with guitarist Junior Wells to tour Europe. The duo made a now legendary live record in Switzerland, which also features the work of the Rolling Stones' bassist Bill Wyman. Among other albums Guy and Wells recorded are *Buddy and the Juniors* (1970) and *Buddy Guy and Junior Wells Play the Blues* (1972). Unable to get large enough venues to support them both, Guy and Wells were forced to break up their act.

Guy recorded for several labels in the 1970s, among them Rhino, Evidence, Blues Ball, JSP, and Harvest. His 1977 live recording, *Live in Montreux*, was a modest commercial success and is considered one of his finest records. By the 1980s most of the blues bars on Chicago's West Side were gone, and very few blues musicians could make a living at their craft, but Guy stayed afloat, by touring small venues domestically and playing at many festivals in Europe. In 1981 he moved to Alligator Records, for which he put together *Stone Crazy!* The record sold fairly well abroad, but his other albums of the decade—among them *Buddy Guy* (1983), *Ten Blue Fingers* (1985), and *Breakin' Out* (1988)—did not see domestic release. In the early 1990s Guy's backup band consisted mainly of young white musicians. "They're not the best in the world," Guy told Spencer. "But they're trying their best."

The 1990s brought a shift in the bluesman's fortunes. In February 1990 Guy played a dual headline with Eric Clapton at London's Royal Albert Hall. Guy performed material that was unknown to the audience, and the shows, enlivened by his vibrant stage presence, created a tremendous buzz in international blues circles. Partly as a result, Guy returned to the studio, where, with the help of the British producer John Porter, he recorded *Damn Right I Got the Blues*. The record—released on the Silvertone label with guest appearances by such rock legends as Clapton and Knopfler—earned Guy a Grammy Award. Guy found himself back in favor with American audiences throughout the remaining years of the 1990s. His records *Feels Like Rain* (1993), *Slippin' In* (1994), and *Heavy Love* (1998) have sold well, and several compilations of his earlier material have been released in recent years. He has also played bigger venues and appeared on television, on *The Tonight Show with Jay Leno* and *The Late Show with David Letterman*, for example. Thanks to his newfound domestic success, Guy was able to launch Buddy Guy's Blues Legends, a club on the West End of Chicago that is considered one of the nation's finest blues venues.

Guy, who is now a grandfather, lives in a Chicago suburb. "I haven't been the dumbest musician who ever played," he told Spencer. "I try to keep my family in pretty good shape so I won't be embarrassed if something happens. . . . [When not touring,] I . . . get me a cup of coffee and a newspaper. I love reading. And I fix a decent meal for me and my wife. She tells me I cook better than I play. All my kids love my cooking, too." — M.B.

Suggested Reading: *Down Beat* p17+ Feb. 1995, with photos; *Guitar Player* p88+ June 1993, with photos; *House of Blues* (on-line); *Rolling Stone* p72+ Nov. 28, 1991, with photos; *Rolling Stone Blues Today* p1 May 28, 1998, with photos

Selected Recordings: *Crazy Music*, 1965; *With the Blues*, 1965; *I Left My Blues in San Francisco*, 1967; *Blues Today*, 1968; *A Man and*

His Blues, 1968; *This Is Buddy Guy*, 1968; *Coming at You*, 1968; *Buddy and the Juniors*, 1970; *Buddy Guy and Junior Wells Play the Blues*, 1972; *Hold That Plane*, 1972; *I Was Walkin' Through the Woods*, 1974; *Live in Montreux*, 1977; *Stone Crazy!*, 1981; *Buddy Guy*, 1983; *Ten Blue Fingers*, 1985; *Breakin' Out*, 1988; *Damn Right I've Got the Blues*, 1991; *Feels Like Rain*, 1993; *Slippin' In*, 1994; *Live! The Real Deal*, 1996; *Heavy Love*, 1998

Courtesy of the *Washington Post*

Guzy, Carol
(GOOZ-ee)

1957(?)– Photojournalist. Address: Washington Post, *1150 15th St. N.W., Washington, DC 20071*

"Lately new technology has grabbed everyone's attention," the photojournalist Carol Guzy wrote in an on-line essay for the Poynter Institute Web site. "Digital cameras. Faster computers. But remember, they are merely tools. It's eyes and minds and hearts, passion, and commitment that make the most compelling images. It's the people in the pictures and those who view them that are the important ones." Guzy, who has been on the staff of the *Washington Post* since 1988, has become well known for her moving, sometimes heart-wrenching portraits of victims of natural disaster, war, famine, and illness. She has covered such subjects as civil war in Somalia; ethnic conflict in the Balkans; the funeral of Mother Teresa, in India; the activities of a nine-year-old autistic American boy; and the home life of the former boxing great Muhammad Ali at his Michigan farm, where he was coping with the effects of Parkinson's disease. Guzy has won two Pulitzer Prizes and many other prestigious awards for her work. "Photographers spend a lot of time looking for the right light," she wrote in her Poynter Institute essay. "But the most important thing we glimpse and attempt to capture is the radiance within every being."

A native of Pennsylvania, Guzy was born in about 1957. After she graduated from the nursing school at Northampton County Area Community College, in 1978, she realized that she preferred taking pictures to taking care of patients. Thankful that she had a practical degree to fall back on if the need arose, she enrolled at the Art Institute of Fort Lauderdale, in Florida, where she took only photography courses for two years. "I just wanted to take a chance," she told Debra Gersh for *Editor & Publisher* (April 24, 1993). "I always felt a little bit adventuresome. I wanted to see the world, and I thought, well, this was an opportunity. It had at least the potential for traveling." Ed Williams, the head of the institute's Department of Photography, told *Current Biography* that right from the start, Guzy's work—particularly her portraits—was outstanding. She graduated from the institute in 1980, with an associate degree in applied science. In her first job in her new field, she was hired as a staff photographer at the *Miami Herald*, which, according to Ed Williams, has rarely employed new graduates as photographers. Walter Michel, another photographer at the newspaper, became her mentor. In 1982 she won the award for best portfolio at the Atlanta Photojournalism Seminar, which, according to its home page on the World Wide Web, seeks "to promote the highest standards of photojournalism." She won the same award at the seminar in 1985. Shortly before, on November 13, 1985, the Nevado del Ruiz volcano in Colombia erupted, killing an estimated 23,000 people, and Guzy was sent to cover the devastation. She won a 1986 Pulitzer Prize for spot news photography for her photos, which graphically and poignantly depicted the suffering of the survivors.

Guzy, who prefers black-and-white photography to color, has always insisted on printing all her own pictures, and while in the *Miami Herald* photo lab one day, she met the United Press International photographer Jonathan Utz. She and Utz married, and when Utz was transferred to Washington, D.C., in 1988, Guzy accepted the position of staff photographer at the *Washington Post*. In 1990 she became the first woman to be named photographer of the year by the National Press Photographers Association (NPPA) and the University of Missouri–Columbia School of Journalism, in a competition that has taken place annually since 1944. She earned the same honor, which is judged on the basis of a portfolio submitted by the photographer, in 1993 and 1997 as well. She has also garnered an impressive set of awards from the White House News Photographers Association (WHNPA), which was founded in 1921, when Warren G. Harding was president, to help news photographers, who until then had not been allowed access to the White House press room. For six decades the group has sponsored an annual competition to reward excellence in picture taking. Guzy has won the WHNPA's Photographer of the Year Award six times since 1991. In 1997 she won not only the NPPA and WHNPA awards but also a Robert F. Kennedy Memorial Prize and a John Faber Award from the Overseas Press Club of America, the last two for her photos of Rwandan refugees. "I'm a pretty insecure person by nature," she told Debra Gersh in reference to her honors. "I never feel like the pictures are good enough, or I didn't do this right or that right—so it's kind of nice once [in] a while for someone else to say, 'Hey, you did OK.'"

In 1995 Guzy won her second Pulitzer Prize, this time for her coverage of life in Haiti, which had long endured political turmoil and widespread poverty. "I've had a lot of deep feelings for Haiti for a long time," Guzy told Howard Kurtz, a fellow staffer at the *Washington Post* (April 19, 1995). "I've seen a lot of suffering there. While [the Pulitzer] is a fine honor for me, it also recognizes the plight of a people too long forgotten. Haiti breaks my heart." The *Washington Post* printed along with its announcement about the Pulitzer Prize Guzy's photo of a Haitian woman who had been badly injured during a food riot in Port-au-Prince, Haiti's capital. The picture showed the pain in the woman's face and grains of rice, spilled from a broken sack, still clinging to her skin. In her essay for the Poynter Institute Web site, Guzy wrote, "I hear people say, 'Oh, no. Not another story on Haiti! We've seen enough of refugees. Cliché; been there, done that.' But it's hard to tell that desperate woman holding her starving child she's a cliché. These people can't turn the page when they don't like the story. They can't change channels. They remain mired in reality long after the headlines fade away." While she understands that seeing too many images of misery and death may upset or numb some readers, she rejects the argument that the media should refrain from reproducing potentially disturbing photos. "It's easier to criticize a photographer or editor than to address the root of the problem," she wrote in her Poynter essay. "But there is a great danger in censuring reality." Guzy has said that she tries to detach herself to some degree from an unsettling situation before she attempts to photograph it. "A lot of the things you see are pretty emotional," she told Gersh. "But I think at the time when you're trying to do a job, you can't let your emotions get in the way of what you're there to do, which is take the picture."

Her efforts at disengagement notwithstanding, her empathy with her subjects—conveyed in her photos—has become Guzy's trademark. She was particularly affected while covering a famine in Ethiopia in the early 1990s. "Ethiopia really got to me the first time I went there," she told Gersh. "[It was] the first time I was really confronted with something of that magnitude. . . . I came back and I was pretty bad for a while, really depressed. I was just sort of overwhelmed." Photographing in Somalia during that country's civil war in 1993—an assignment that she had specifically requested—also proved to be difficult for her, not least because she fell ill. "Physically, emotionally, everything, it was just horrible there," she explained to Gersh. "There's nothing there. It's dusty, it's dirty, it's violent. It was just a very, very hard story to cover." Although she usually liked to stay longer on location than her editors would permit, Somalia "was one place that I just wanted out," she told Gersh.

In 1992 the *Washington Post* sent Guzy to Russia to report on the end of the Cold War. After arriving in the town of Kalachevo, she wrote for the July 26 edition of the *Post*, "Suddenly we were in the middle of something splendid. It was a little village as poor as its neighbors but with a heartening affluence of spirit. The dilapidated clapboard houses were gussied up in bright pastels. Children's faces peeked at us mischievously from behind gaily embroidered curtains." Kalachevo's inhabitants welcomed Guzy and her colleagues warmly. "Everywhere our taxicab traveled, townspeople saw the Americans with the cameras and beckoned us into their homes. Everyone—even the toothless, the ragged, the bent and enfeebled—wanted his picture taken. Whenever we entered a home, however modest, however ancient or makeshift the furnishings, there always appeared a loaf of bread, some soup perhaps, a crock of tea and always a bottle of vodka. In the oppressive heat of their coal-burning stoves, toast after toast was offered to the grand new friendship between America and Russia."

In 1992, in an assignment closer to home, Guzy covered the effects of Hurricane Andrew, which had left almost 160,000 people homeless in southern Florida. She chose to focus on one family—Tommy George, Jackie Cohen, and the couple's newborn daughter—whom she met while driving through their trailer park to survey the damage. In the *Washington Post* (September 27, 1992, on-line), Guzy wrote, "Wary of looters and troublemakers, George keeps his .22-caliber rifle at hand," omitting the fact that at first he had considered Guzy a troublemaker and had consented to let her take pictures of him and his girlfriend only after the photographer had befriended Jackie. "I've done a lot of things like a follow-one-family kind of thing," Guzy told Gersh. "I don't like to be part of the pack. I really hate to be on stories where you're just elbowing your way through a million other photographers, [and] everybody's trying to get the same picture. It's really not what I do best." She has stayed in touch with some of her subjects, such as the homeless Washington, D.C., couple who were invited to one of President George Bush's inaugural balls. "Everyone donated money and clothes [to the couple] for the ball, and then they wound up getting an apartment . . . ," Guzy told Debra Gersh. "I followed them through the whole thing. . . . We got to be friends, and we still are in contact." "It's haunting to voyage into so many different souls," she wrote for the Poynter Institute Web site. "What we witness never leaves us." She also observed, "A photograph can be a powerful witness and an eloquent voice for those who have none. Pictures inform, educate, enlighten, captivate, spur governments into action. They are historical documents and poignant reminders of our human frailties. Sometimes they touch our very soul."— M.R.

Suggested Reading: *Editor & Publisher* p18+ Apr. 24, 1993, with photos; *Washington Post* B p4 Mar. 7, 1993, with photo, A p1 Apr. 19, 1995, with photos; *Washington Post* (on-line) July 26, 1992, Mar. 24, 1995, Feb. 18, 1996, May 9, 1997; *Washingtonian* p80+ Dec. 1993, with photos

---

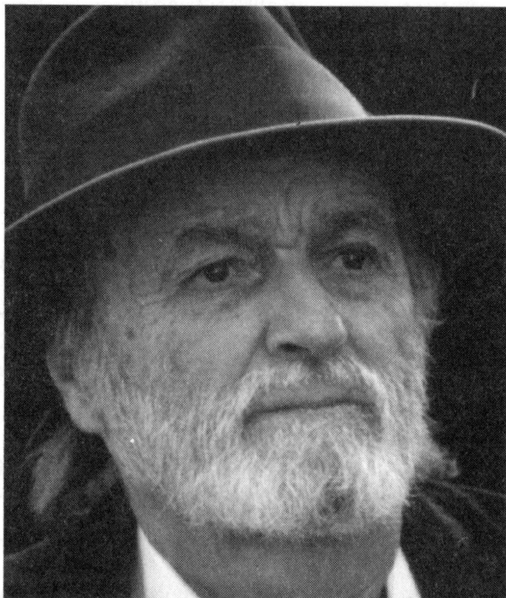

Lorey Sebastian/Courtesy of DreamWorks

Hall, Conrad L.

June 21, 1926– Cinematographer. Address: c/o American Society of Cinematographers, 1782 N. Orange Dr., Hollywood, CA 90028

"I've always imagined that cinematography is like a writer with a blank, white paper in front of him," Conrad L. Hall told Christopher Probst for *American Cinematographer* (January 1999). "Cinematographers have a blank screen that has to be filled with the story." In the same interview Hall, who is one of the most revered cinematographers in the film industry, said, "I like to equate cinema to music. I'm performing a musical composition when lighting a scene. There are crescendos, allegros, and pizzicatos. The visual language is an undulating language, and like music, it has to have its peaks and valleys. You can't just photograph everything beautifully; otherwise, how would you get the gasps if you had nothing but gasps? You can only get a gasp because the audience hasn't been paying attention to anything but the stories and the actors. Then, suddenly, there's something magical that grabs them." Hall has earned eight Academy Award nominations and two Oscars, the latter for his cinematography for *Butch Cassidy and the Sundance Kid* and *American Beauty*. His two dozen other credits include *The Wild Seed*, *Harper*, *In Cold Blood*, *Cool Hand Luke*, *Marathon Man*, *Tequila Sunrise*, *Searching for Bobby Fischer*, and *A Civil Action*, on the last two of which he worked with the writer-director Steven Zaillian. In a conversation with Christopher Probst, Zaillian said, "Conrad has the skill to make something look great in whatever way he chooses to go about it, but it's who he is as a person and his experiences in life that truly make him great."

The son of James Norman Hall and the former Sarah Winchester, Conrad L. Hall was born on June 21, 1926 in Papeete, on the South Pacific island of Tahiti, which is part of French Polynesia. (According to some film specialists, his treatment of light and shadow reflects to some degree his upbringing near the sea.) Hall's father was an adventurer and writer who became famous as the co-author, with Charles Nordhoff, of the *Mutiny on the Bounty* trilogy of seafaring tales. Every few years the family, which included Hall's sister, Nancy, would visit the United States, usually staying in California for several months.

In 1947 Hall enrolled at the University of Southern California, in Los Angeles, with the intention of becoming a professional writer. "After the first semester, I got a D+ in creative writing," he said in an interview for *Cinemad* (1999), excerpted on *premierzone.com* (on-line). "So . . . I figure there weren't any [literary] genes rattling around." Seeking another option, he began leafing through the university's liberal-arts-and-sciences catalog. "A—Astronomy, B—Biology, C—Cinema. And in '47 . . . C—Cinema? Wow! You mean you can go to school for that? Like being a mechanic? That stopped me right away for all the wrong reasons. I thought I'd rub elbows with the stars, get to travel all over the world and somebody else send you, you know. So I signed up and never looked back," he told the *Cinemad* interviewer. Hall studied under the Serbian-born film director Slavko Vorkapich, an expert in cinema theory, special effects, and montage. He left the university before graduating.

Hall began his professional life by shooting commercials and industrial films. "On one [shoot], it was just three of us on the whole damn production," he recalled to the *Cinemad* reporter. "Gripping, electrical, the whole thing. Climbing telephone poles and hooking onto wires, stealing electricity and stuff like that. Crazy stuff . . . " Hall also worked on some Disney nature films, among them *The Living Desert* (1953), for which he shot footage of snakes, lizards, and other creatures. He later served as a cameraman under the noted cinematographers Hal Mohr and Ernest Haller. Also during the 1950s he formed a production company with Haskell Wexler, who later made his mark as the cinematographer for such highly praised movies as *In the Heat of the Night, Who's Afraid of Virginia Woolf?*, and *One Flew Over the Cuckoo's Nest*. For several years he and Wexler directed and shot commercial spots. Without Wexler, Hall assisted with the filming of the second adaptation for the screen of *Mutiny on the Bounty* (1962), which starred Marlon Brando. During the shooting he and Brando hobnobbed off the set. According to an undated article from *Take One* (on-line), at around this time Hall, who had been unable to join the established Hollywood camera operators' union, helped to form the Association of Film Craftsmen Union, which became affiliated with the National Association of Broadcast Employees and Technicians and thereby eased the way for newcomers.

Hall's career began an upward swing in 1963, when he got a job on the popular science-fiction TV series *The Outer Limits*, produced by Leslie Stevens. Stevens recruited Hall to serve as his cinematographer for the feature film *Incubus* (1965), a movie notable mostly because its dialogue was entirely in Esperanto, a language invented in 1887. (After its release the *Incubus* prints and negatives were accidentally destroyed, but in 1997 a print with French subtitles was found in an archive and re-released, with English subtitles.) Hall's next project was *The Wild Seed* (1965), one of whose producers was Marlon Brando Sr. Thanks in part to his connections to the Brandos, he landed the job of cinematographer for *Morituri* (1965), directed by Bernhard Wicki. A drama set on a German freighter during World War II, the picture co-starred Brando and Yul Brynner and brought Hall his first Academy Award nomination, for black-and-white cinematography. Hall received a second nomination—for color cinematography—in 1966, for his work on Richard Brooks's *The Professionals*, about the rescue of an American businessman's wife by soldiers of fortune along the Mexico-U.S. border. (Films released in 1966 were the last for which separate Oscars were given for color and black-and-white cinematography.)

Hall garnered a third Academy Award nomination for the documentary-like feature film *In Cold Blood* (1967). Written and directed by Richard Brooks, and based on Truman Capote's widely publicized, best-selling, same-named 1966 "nonfiction novel," as Capote described it, the picture focuses on the brutal 1959 murder of a Kansas farm family by a pair of emotionally stunted drifters. Brooks chose to photograph "the actual Middle Western scenes" in which the events took place, Archer Winsten wrote for the *New York Post* (December 15, 1967), "a bus, a street entering a town, a store, a rundown farm, a landscape of the great flatlands, and in every instance that black-and-white camera of Conrad Hall hits you with its absolute rightness." In a scene that has been cited as an example of Hall's virtuosity, the shadows of raindrops on a prison window are visible on the face of one of the convicted killers (played by Robert Blake) as he talks dispassionately about his troubled childhood. Hall talked about the shooting of that footage in *Visions of Light: The Art of Cinematography* (1992), a documentary directed by the film scholar Stuart Samuels, the film editor Arnold Glassman, and the film critic Todd McCarthy. That film also included interviews with other master cinematographers, among them Ernest Dickerson, William Fraken, Sven Nykvist, Vittorio Storaro, and Vilmos Zsigmond.

Also in 1967 Hall filmed *Cool Hand Luke*, a chain-gang drama directed by Stuart Rosenberg and starring Paul Newman. To "bring a visual interest" and avoid presenting merely repetitive images of "a bunch of people walking and talking," as Hall explained to Steve Daily for *Entertainment Weekly* (October 8, 1999), he and his assistants "did all kinds of high jinks. . . . Lots of quick cuts. We had the camera sort of rocking back and forth like a swing when Luke is doing knee bends." In a review for *Life* (November 3, 1967), Richard Schickel wrote, "What one remembers best" about *Cool Hand Luke* is "its vision of the American landscape, a vision compounded of a sensitivity to the ways its face and mood change from month to month, even from hour to hour, and of an intensity of realization (thanks largely to Conrad Hall's color photography) that makes the dews of dawn and the heat of noon and the cool of twilight palpable on your flesh." But Schickel also found fault with the film's "sheer physical beauty," which, in his view, "keeps suggesting the notion that prison camp is really a rest camp, . . . and that despite the occasional unpleasantries of the guards there are worse ways of paying one's debt to society." The *Cinemad* writer observed that "with *Cool Hand Luke*, Hall began breaking established Hollywood rules," by using, for example, lens flares and muted colors—techniques that eventually became widespread. "A rule is to be used appropriately," Hall explained to the *Cinemad* interviewer. "If you find something about that rule that you can change, make it new and interesting, do it. . . . If it works for the film, hey, it's the thing to do."

Hall won his first Oscar for his work on *Butch Cassidy and the Sundance Kid* (1969), for which he shot many scenes through branches, smoke, or steam, creating a hazy, soft look. During the filming Hall became romantically involved with Katharine Ross, one of the co-stars; after he allowed her to operate a camera one day, George Roy Harris, who directed the picture, banned her from the set except during her own scenes. Hall shot John Huston's *Fat City* (1972) and two additional pictures before teaming with the director John Schlesinger to film *The Day of the Locust* (1975), an adaptation of Nathanael West's 1939 novel about losers on Hollywood's social periphery; that movie brought him his fifth Academy Award nomination. The next year he collaborated with Schlesinger again, to direct the cinematography for *Marathon Man*, starring Dustin Hoffman and Laurence Olivier. In one of the film's most talked-about sequences, Olivier, who plays a sadistic ex-Nazi, drills Hoffman's teeth without the benefit of anesthesia. Hall told Steve Daly for *Entertainment Weekly* (October 8, 1999), "I kept [the scene] very stark, sort of one light over Dustin Hoffman, one behind him, creating a kind of adversarial look to Laurence. Like an interrogation chamber."

Hall's sixth Oscar nomination was for *Tequila Sunrise* (1988), for which he also earned an Outstanding Achievement Award from the American Society of Cinematographers (ASC); a "neo-noir" thriller written and directed by Robert Towne, it features Mel Gibson, Kurt Russell, and Michelle Pfeiffer. "You don't have to do much to make these actors look good," Hall commented to Daly. A seventh nomination—and a second ASC award—followed, for *Searching for Bobby Fischer* (1993), which marked the directing debut of Steven Zaillian. A scriptwriter whose credits include *Awakenings* and *Schindler's List*, Zaillian wrote the screenplay for *Searching for Bobby Fischer*, based on the same-named book by Fred Waitzkin, which is subtitled *The World of Chess, Observed by the Father of a Child Prodigy* (1988). Hall told Daly, "I added tension by leaving the players' eyes close to the top of the frame; it gives you a sense of unease that they might move out of the image any second. What else was there to look at? A bunch of out-of-focus chess pieces is not interesting. I came to the idea that chess could be like basketball—a rhythm of fast break, then slam dunk." Speaking of Hall's modus operandi, Zaillian told Christopher Probst, "Conrad always finds a place to sit to watch a rehearsal, and no matter where he's sitting, his stock line is, 'Well, it looks great from here!' Basically, that means I can shoot the scene from any side of the room I want—he'll make it look great from that point, or make it look great from the other side if I change my mind. In that way, we work almost like a documentary team. We basically let the event take place—which in this case is a rehearsal of a scripted scene—but we don't impose some preset idea onto it. That was a great lesson for me."

Hall joined the actor-director Warren Beatty to shoot *Love Affair* (1994), a poorly received remake of a 1957 Cary Grant–Deborah Kerr vehicle (*An Affair to Remember*) that was itself a remake of the 1939 film (*Love Affair*), starring Charles Boyer and Irene Dunne. Hall told Daly that, succumbing to Beatty's entreaties, he reluctantly agreed to serve as cinematographer for the film, which, in addition to Beatty, stars Annette Bening and Katharine Hepburn. "I figured, hey, Warren directed *Reds*, how bad could this be? I do love him, and we're friends now, but we had fights like you can't imagine. I've never gone so ballistic on a picture in my life. Warren would drag me through relighting him over and over again." Hepburn, by contrast, he told Daly, sent him "a wonderful little note" complimenting him on having photographed her to her best advantage.

In 1998 Hall worked with Steven Zaillian to shoot *A Civil Action*, a legal thriller adapted by Zaillian from Jonathan Harr's complex, highly detailed nonfiction best-seller. The subject is a class-action suit brought by a flashy Boston personal-injury lawyer on behalf of eight families in the Boston suburb of Woburn, who charged that water polluted by two industrial giants in the 1960s and 1970s had caused an outbreak of leukemia among their relatives. Hall gave the film a stark, moody look, by shooting, for example, "bare trees and water reflecting white, stark, skies," as he explained to Christopher Probst. *A Civil Action*, which stars John Travolta and Robert Duvall, earned Hall his eighth Academy Award nomination.

After reading a film script, Hall told the cinematographer Caleb Deschanel for *American Cinematographer* (September 1998), "I usually try to think of some aspect of the story which represents its 'soul,' so to speak—something I can hang my hat on." For a film like *A Civil Action*, he explained, that "something" was "about 'truth' and how lawyers will get together to divert people from knowing what it really is. How can I help represent that visually? I also use references—books, magazines, or even philosophical ideas that come to me." He also said, "I work somewhat organically and try not to make decisions in advance. This begins with facing the material of the day, which often changes. Then I want to see how the actors are dealing with the material and what the location brings to the scene. But because schedules change so often, I try not to pin things down so much. . . . What I try to do is understand the material, and then understand how the director sees it as well."

Also in 1998 Hall served as the cinematographer for Robert Towne's well-received biopic *Without Limits*, about the intensely competitive track star Steve Prefontaine, who was killed in a car accident in 1975, at the age of 24. In his conversation with Deschanel, Hall described his working relationship with Towne: "Bob writes with words and I write with pictures, so the two of us make a complementary storytelling team for film. He has his own ideas about visualization, but after rehearsing the actors, he lets me choose how to visualize his words. I'll then set out a plan of attack for a scene and we'll go through it together, adding and subtracting things until we have a final plan."

Hall's next job came about because of a fortuitous set of circumstances: the British theatrical director Sam Mendes was working on the Broadway production of *The Blue Room*, starring Nicole Kidman, whose husband is the actor Tom Cruise; Cruise, who had produced *Without Limits* and was thus familiar with Hall's work, reportedly advised Mendes to hire Hall as director of photography for Mendes's debut motion picture, the dark comedy *American Beauty* (1999). During postproduction, Mendes—to Hall's dismay—cut some of the scenes that Hall had so meticulously crafted. "It was like somebody had taken a sword and drawn it through my gut," the cinematographer said to Daly. "I felt like, what the hell *happened*?" According to Daly, Mendes smoothed the situation "by running the movie for [Hall] two more times in quick succession." "The final time, I showed it to Conrad on film instead of video, and he started to get excited," Mendes recalled to Daly. "He started giving me ideas about 'what if we printed this or that a little darker,' and that's what I wanted. The process of perfecting prints is gobbledygook to me. Conrad is magnificently skilled at it." *American Beauty* won the Oscar for best film of 1999 and brought Hall his second Academy Award.

Later in 1999, filling in for a cinematographer who had to take a temporary leave of absence, Hall shot footage for the movie *Sleepy Hollow* (1999), directed by Tim Burton and starring Johnny Depp and Chrstine Ricci. "I'm not really sure why they thought they needed more footage," Hall remarked to Steve Daly for *Entertainment Weekly* (November 5, 1999). "The picture looked terrific as it was, just beautiful."

Hall—whose son, Conrad Hall Jr., followed him into the business and has operated the camera on many of his father's productions—shows no sign of slowing down. His age (he is now 74) may actually be an advantage to him in some ways, judging from remarks he made to *American Cinematographer*, as quoted on the Kodak Web site in 1999: "Being a visualist, I often absorb the environment around me and make mental notes," he said. "I don't even do it consciously, but I am always noting how someone looks in a certain scenario. That impression gets stored away in my mental computer. When you're working on a film, all of your past comes with you, with all of the observations you've stored away; you bring forth the observations that apply to the particular story at hand."

In 1993 Hall received a Lifetime Achievement Award from the American Society of Cinematographers. Membership in the organization, which was founded in Los Angeles in 1919, is by invitation only. "It took me a while to realize my peers believe I've made an impact on the history of cinema," Hall, a longtime ASC member, was quoted as saying on the Kodak Web site. "Billions of people have seen and been influenced by movies. My peers say I've made a difference. That means a lot to me." — M.R.

Suggested Reading: *American Cinematographer* p48+ Jan. 1999, with photos; *Entertainment Weekly* p36+ Oct. 8, 1999, with photos; Kodak Web site; *premierzone.com*

Selected Films: *Incubus*, 1965; *Morituri*, 1965; *In Cold Blood*, 1967; *Cool Hand Luke*, 1967; *Butch Cassidy and the Sundance Kid*, 1969; *The Day of the Locust*, 1975; *Marathon Man*, 1976; *Searching for Bobby Fischer*, 1993; *A Civil Action*, 1998; *American Beauty*, 1999

Gene Martin/Retna Ltd.

Hargrove, Roy

Oct. 16, 1969– Jazz trumpeter. Address: c/o PolyGram Records, 555 W. 57th St., New York, NY 10019

One of the so-called Young Lions who embraced the neotraditionalist movement in jazz in the 1980s and 1990s, Roy Hargrove is among the most talented and respected trumpet players to appear on the jazz scene in recent years. When he was in high school, his talent was discovered by the trumpeter Wynton Marsalis, and as a result he began performing and touring with big-name musicians while he was still in his teens. When he decided, in 1989, at the age of 20, to head his own quintet, many jazz critics and enthusiasts felt that he was simply too young for the job. During the following years, however, he demonstrated on albums and in live performances an increasingly mature sound, and upon the release of *With the Tenors of Our Time*, in 1993, most agreed that he was an important new force in jazz. His best-received album to date, *Habana* (1997), was the result of a conscious break with tradition in favor of an experimentation with Afro-Cuban jazz—similar in some respects to that made decades earlier by trumpeter and bebop pioneer Dizzy Gillespie. "I'm flattered when people say good things, but that's not what motivates me," Hargrove told Steve Jones for *USA Today* (June 2, 1997). "I get my motivation from the kind of musical experience I get when I play with other cats, and they tell me, 'You're doing this wrong. Try this.' And it comes from the appreciation I get from the audience when I perform."

Roy Hargrove was born on October 16, 1969 in Waco, Texas. When he was very young, he and his family moved to Dallas, where he spent most of his childhood. He learned to play the cornet at the age of nine. Beginning when he was in fourth grade, he played with a local middle-school band during the summers, "to keep out of trouble," as he told Peter Watrous for the *New York Times* (June 16, 1991). "My director at that time, Dean Hill [who toured with the singer Roberta Flack in the 1970s], he had a thing about how to improvise. He'd take you in his office and show you a phrase, a riff or lick, and he'd teach you how to play it with emotion. We were little kids taking our little solos and he'd be up there urging us on. That inspired us." Hill motivated Hargrove to continue his musical training. When it came time for the young musician to attend high school, Hill urged Hargrove to pursue music studies at Booker T. Washington High School for the Visual and Performing Arts, in Dallas. "There, I really learned a lot about culture and the different ways you go into music," he told Mark Felton in an on-line interview for *visionx.com*. "That was the first time I learned about that cat John Cage, the composer. His theory was that everything is music, even silence. One of the pieces he did was called 'Five Minutes of Silence,' where he'd sit down at the piano and just turn pages! . . . And then there were pieces that we would play as ensembles where he would have us doing things like blow air through the mouthpiece or clap our hands or stomp our feet a certain way, or make a buzzing sound through the mouthpiece. And he would notate that. So this opened my eyes to different concepts of music."

Published sources offer conflicting accounts of how Hargrove met Wynton Marsalis, the trumpeter who spearheaded a revival of traditional jazz in the early 1980s. According to one source, Hargrove was performing in a Fort Worth nightclub in 1986 when Marsalis showed up, having heard about the young horn player while visiting a local high school. Hargrove himself has offered another version of events. "In 1987 Wynton came to our high school to play with the band," he told Peter Watrous. "There was a break for the solos, and my director pointed at me, and Wynton started playing, too, but he stopped, and turned around and said, 'Damn!' So we talked, and he pointed me in some directions." Prior to meeting him, Hargrove had not known who Marsalis was; the jazz Hargrove had heard was primarily fusion rather than the "straight-ahead" style that Marsalis championed—and that Hargrove would embrace. Still, "as much credit as [Marsalis] deserves" for influencing Hargrove and others, "all this music was bound to happen anyway," Hargrove told Watrous. "There were young people like me, who were 16 or 17 and we didn't know anything about [Marsalis]. We were all trying to find out as much as we could about jazz, which was hard. Texas was cut off. I did a lot of things by trial and error, and I used my imagination. I played what I felt, even if it was something wrong."

With the connections he made through Marsalis, Hargrove toured Europe and Japan before his 17th birthday and played with such giants of jazz as Herbie Hancock and Dizzy Gillespie. His reputation as an up-and-comer led *Down Beat* magazine to give him a year's scholarship to the Berklee School of Music, in Boston. He also attended the New School for Social Research (now the New School University), in New York City. "I learned something from being at both those places," he told Mark Felton. "Most of what I learned from that involved being in a very competitive atmosphere. There was always somebody behind you, ready. There was always a group of people sort of in league with each other, yet in competition with each other. This gives you perspective, keeps you on your toes, and keeps you always practicing. There's always a cat behind you, so you better keep it moving!"

Concurrent with his studies, Hargrove developed his chops by performing with such established jazz artists as Frank Morgan, James Williams, Ralph Moore, Kenny Barron, Harold Mabern, John Hicks, and Larry Willis. He also played on some of their albums, most notably Ricky Ford's *Hard Groovin'* (1989), Moore's *Furthermore* (1990), and Morgan's *Jazz Round Midnight* (1989) and *Lonesome Thing* (1990). In 1989 Hargrove—at the extremely young age of 20—headed into the studio to record his debut solo record. Many jazz critics and aficionados were skeptical about the project, feeling that Hargrove was not ready to take on such an endeavor. Rumors began to circulate that his record label, Novus, had pushed him into the project to capitalize on his novelty status. But the record, *Diamond in the Rough*, silenced naysayers. "Trumpeter Roy Hargrove's debut as a leader found him occasionally recalling Freddie Hubbard but already sounding fairly original in the hard bop genre . . . ," Scott Yanow wrote for the *All Music Guide* (on-line). "The one fault in the CD is that the performances and solos are often a little too brief, with all but 'Whisper Not' in the 4–6 minute range. But for a debut, Roy Hargrove can still be proud of *Diamond in the Rough*."

Over the next two years, Hargrove and his group recorded three more studio albums for Novus: *Public Eye* (1990), which received only mediocre reviews and, many critics suspected, was put together too quickly; *Beauty and the Beast* (1992), a record that found Hargrove and respected alto saxophonist Antonio Hart playing Disney tunes; and the earlier *Tokyo Sessions* (1991), on which he was co-billed with Hart. Taken from various performances in Tokyo in 1991, that album, which featured reworkings of jazz, pop, and American standards, received rave reviews. "Hargrove's fierce trumpet solos and Hart's bluesy, equally energetic and accomplished answering alto statements fueled nine excellent reworkings of standards and jazz repertory," Ron Wynn wrote for the *All Music Guide* (on-line). Wynn's one complaint was that "it would still be nice to hear Hart and Hargrove doing their own material rather than simply putting their spin on shopworn, though wonderful, anthems." *The Vibe* (1992) was the last Hargrove record to feature Antonio Hart as part of Hargrove's group.

Nineteen ninety-two proved to be a breakthrough year for Hargrove. In the early part of the year, he won over more of his detractors by matching the legendary improvisational skills and solo ability of the tenor saxophonist Sonny Rollins during a concert at Carnegie Hall. "I was really nervous at first," Hargrove told Richard B. Woodward for the *New York Times* (September 7, 1994). "We had a rehearsal the day of the concert—just the two of us—and I felt a little more at ease. And when we got on stage, I felt this tremendous amount of energy coming from him. You don't sleep when you play with him. He's really unpredictable. When he throws it at you, you have to catch it—or you're in trouble." The word that Hargrove had played so maturely alongside Rollins greatly improved his reputation in jazz circles. In late May of that year, he played a concert at the Village Vanguard in New York City that drew praise from Peter Watrous of the *New York Times* (May 28, 1992): "The young trumpeter Roy Hargrove has often been used as an example by critics of younger jazz musicians. An extraordinary trumpet player, he has often been faulted for not having the experience needed to lead a band. Mr. Hargrove, these critics say, was pushed into the limelight by his recording label, groomed for stardom but not prepared for the responsibilities. If Mr. Hargrove's first set on Tuesday night is any example, he has been paying attention to those critics. He has fashioned a taut and precise band and constructed an exciting, carefully arranged set that led off the group's improvisations. . . . Mr. Hargrove's solos have become more logical and more audacious; he's one of jazz's finest improvisers, and he's only getting better." Later that year, while in Japan—this time playing at the Mount Fuji Festival—Hargrove, whose record contract with Novus was up at the end of 1992, found himself the object of a bidding war between that label and the noted jazz label Verve. For an undisclosed but reportedly handsome sum, Hargrove chose to sign with Verve, and the sought-after trumpeter immediately went to work in the studio.

On his next album, *With the Tenors of Our Time* (1993), Hargrove performed with several of jazz's most prominent tenor saxophonists: Johnny Griffin, Joe Henderson, Branford Marsalis, Joshua Redman, and Stanley Turrentine. The album was a commercial as well as critical success, becoming his highest seller up to that time. Many jazz writers began putting forth the idea that Hargrove was the stylistic heir to the late Lee Morgan, who is considered one of the great jazz trumpet players of the last 30 years. That same year Novus, still wanting to capitalize on its former star, released a live recording of Hargrove's entitled *Of Kindred Souls*, which featured guest appearances by alto saxophonist Gary Bartz and trombonist Andre Hayward. The album received generally positive reviews.

In 1995 the trumpeter founded Roy Hargrove's Big Band, which represented a stylistic segue from his hard-bop style into a more traditional sound reminiscent of the groups led by Count Basie and Duke Ellington. The group performed reworkings of standards in addition to original tunes by Hargrove and other bandmembers, including pianist Stephen Scott and saxophonist Ron Blake. A set at the 1995 Panasonic Village Jazz Festival, in New York, was generally praised by Jon Pareles in the *New York Times* (August 31, 1995): "Mr. Hargrove was exemplary, using fluegelhorn for melting ballad phrases and trumpet for quick be-bop runs and high-note jabs. The set also revealed one of Hargrove's lesser-known skills: he can sing. He has a high voice, almost a contralto, which was refined enough for romantic tidings and agile enough to scat sing. His vocals were the most surprising part of the group's skillful, conservative set." In the same year Hargrove also released two records: *Family*, a collection of his original compositions, with some tracks written by bassist Christian McBride, and *Parker's Mood*, a celebration of the music of sax great Charlie Parker, featuring McBride and Stephen Scott. The effort was hailed by critics. In December Hargrove accomplished the considerable feat of supplanting Wynton Marsalis as trumpeter of the year in the 1995 *Down Beat* Readers Poll.

In 1996 Hargrove satisfied the desires of many critics when he added progressive elements to his music, experimenting with Afro-Cuban rhythms. That move was inspired by his trip to Cuba in February of that year to play at the Havana Jazz Festival. There, he led an 11-piece band featuring three Americans—Gary Bartz, trombonist Frank Lacy, and guitarist Russell Malone—as well as saxophonist David Sanchez and contrabassist John Benitez of Puerto Rico, and pianist Chucho Valdes, conga drummer Miguel "Anga" Diaz, timbales player Jose Luis "Changuito" Quintana, drummer Horacio "Negro" Hernandez, and bassist Jorge Reyes of Cuba. Hargrove called the group Roy Hargrove's Crisol. "In Cuba, a crisol is a melting pot into which you put all these precious metals to make beautiful jewelry," Hargrove explained to Steve Jones. "The metaphor here is that different cultures are put together here with the result being beautiful music." So impressive were the results that Hargrove took the group on a worldwide tour.

Early in 1997 live tracks from the group's appearance at the December 1996 Umbria Winter Jazz Festival, in Italy, were released on a record entitled *Habana*. Featuring three tracks written by Hargrove—"Dream Traveler," "The Mountains," and "Ballad for the Children"—the album was a unanimous hit with critics. "At last, this highly touted, heretofore conservative Young Lion makes his move beyond neo-bop toward something new, fresh, and potentially important," Richard S. Ginell wrote for the *All Music Guide* (on-line). "Hargrove himself still seems dazzled by his new discovery, groping a bit for direction in his own solos.

But challenged by the asymmetrical rhythms, he takes more chances and jaggedly strikes some fire. . . . Chucho Valdes, an awesome pianist and progressive-minded musician, is one of the anchors of the band. . . . the tune that remains most indelibly in the memory is trombonist Frank Lacy's 'O My Seh Yeh,' which opens and closes the CD in neat, bookended fashion." The Crisol continued to tour well into 1997, playing particularly well-received sets at the Playboy Jazz Festival in June.

In 1998 Hargrove made several guest appearances on other artists' records, most notably on Sherman Irby's *Big Mama's Biscuit.* Also that year the trumpeter provided vocals for Shirley Horn's *Jazz Round Midnight.* His credits for 1999 included tracks on Danny Gatton's *Hot Rod Guitar* and on *Blue Note Plays Ellington and Strayhorn.*

Also in 1999 Hargrove released *Moment to Moment,* a collection of mostly classic love ballads, such as "You Go to My Head," arranged with strings; one song, "Natural Wonders," written by Hargrove after a visit to Big Sur, in California, also featured the trumpet player's first string arrangement. Paula Edelstein noted for *Jazz Review* (on-line), "These songs say a lot about the brilliance and contemplative side of Roy Hargrove and his brilliant trumpet playing. The registers are so relaxing and there is a lot of sophistication, class and love on this CD." Richard S. Ginell of *All Music Guide* (on-line) was less than enthusiastic. "At first," he wrote, "one's hopes are raised that this could turn out to be one of the best attempts in this field. The leadoff track, 'You Go to My Head,' is gorgeous; Hargrove plays soulfully and inwardly, and pianist Larry Willis's arrangement is emotionally satisfying without being cloying. However, the disc continues on and on in this fashion, one tune seeming to blend into another, one arrangement sounding like the next." He concluded, "Whether on flugelhorn or trumpet, Hargrove's undoubted sincerity and musicality go only a limited distance over the 68-minute span of the CD before simply repeating themselves out."

Hargrove lives in lower Manhattan, in walking distance from the major jazz clubs in downtown New York City. — M.B.

Suggested Reading: *Chicago Tribune* p2 Sep. 10, 1998, with photo; *Down Beat* p16+ June 1992, with photos, p16+ Sep. 1995, with photos, p32 Dec. 1995, with photo, p26+ Jan. 1997, with photos; *New York Times* C p5 Feb. 22, 1991, with photo, B p1 June 16, 1991, with photos, C p14 May 28, 1993, with photo, C p1 Sep. 7, 1994, with photos, C p20 Sep. 26, 1996, with photo, C p6 Apr. 4, 1997; *USA Today* D p3 June 2, 1997, with photo; *Washington Post* N p12 Dec. 26, 1997, with photo

Selected Recordings: *Diamond in the Rough,* 1989; *Public Eye,* 1990; *Tokyo Sessions,* 1991; *The Vibe,* 1992; *Beauty and the Beast,* 1992; *Of Kindred Souls;* 1993; *With the Tenors of Our Time,* 1993; *Approaching Standards,* 1994; *Family,* 1995; *Parker's Mood,* 1995; *Habana,* 1997; *Moment to Moment,* 1999

Harron, Mary

1952– Film and television director; journalist. Address: c/o Lions Gate Films, 561 Broadway, New York, NY 10012-3918

The Canadian-born filmmaker Mary Harron has written and directed two feature-length pictures: *I Shot Andy Warhol* (1996), about Valerie Solanas, who tried to assassinate the famous founder of Pop art, and *American Psycho* (2000), based on a novel by Bret Easton Ellis about a Wall Street stockbroker who is also a serial killer. Harron began her career as a music journalist, chronicling the rise of punk rock in New York and London for such publications as *New Music Express.* During four years as an employee of the British Broadcasting Corp., she did research for television documentaries and later directed, edited, or co-produced such films herself. While working on such documentaries as *The Winds of Change,* which focused on South Africa during the 1950s, she acquired many of the skills that she has used as a feature-film director. "I'm not a moralizer," Harron told Holly Millea for *Premiere* (March 2000), shortly before the debut of *American Psycho.* "I'm drawn to stories about primal fears. . . . It's good to face your fears. Meet them. I know that there's something in me that compels me to go down that dark hallway."

The daughter of the actor/comedian Don Harron and the singer Catherine McKinney, Mary Harron was born in Toronto, Canada, in 1952. She was very close to her mother, a devoted student of literature. After Harron's parents divorced, her mother married the Hungarian-born writer Stephen Vizinczey, whose novel *In Praise of Older Women* was an international best-seller. When Harron was 13 she moved to England with her mother and stepfather. After graduating from Oxford University, where she majored in English, she settled in New York, where she found herself in the middle of the city's burgeoning punk-rock scene. She became a writer, specializing in music; her articles about such bands as the Talking Heads and the Velvet Underground appeared in the *Guardian, New Music Express,* and *Punk,* the last of which she herself founded. (It was apparently short-lived.) Her interview with the British band the Sex Pistols was the first to be published in the United States. She also worked part-time as a fact checker for *American*

Rob Hann/Retna Ltd.

Mary Harron

Heritage magazine, honing her research skills at the New York public library.

Her three years in New York were "so exciting that they wiped out my college years," Harron told Alison Powell for *Interview* (April 1996). "I had been a very unhappy girl at Oxford. I felt displaced—and I never felt English. But in New York I met people who seemed more intellectually alive, more creative, and more disturbing. They were coming up with ideas and analyses and definitions of culture that were completely new to me." Harron believed that her understanding of the origins of punk resulted from her study at Oxford of "the way cultural forms shift and change when one movement reacts against another—romanticism and classicism, for example," she explained to Powell. "I'd always had a longing for the avant-garde. My father used to say, 'Mary won't go to see any [movie] unless it was made before 1910 or filmed under a wet rock.'"

After Harron returned to England, she found work as a researcher and camera operator for the British Broadcasting Corp., which offers programming on two channels—BBC-1 and BBC-2. For *The South Bank Show*, which had a variety format, she contributed to profiles of the artist Jackson Pollock, the writer Raymond Chandler, and the Velvet Underground, among others. Eventually she directed short films for *The Late Show*, a BBC-2 series about art, and co-produced a four-part series about the American electoral process entitled *Campaign!* In 1991 and 1992 Harron made six short films on popular culture for the BBC/PBS series *Edge*.

In 1992 Harron returned to New York City. Years before, she had met Andy Warhol there, through her work as a music critic and as a researcher for a documentary. She later became fascinated with the story of Valerie Solanas, an aspiring playwright who had appeared in Warhol's film *I, a Man*. Solanas was the author of *The S.C.U.M. Manifesto* (1968), a tract that advised women to reject men altogether and take control of society. S.C.U.M. was the acronym for the Society for Cutting Up Men, a radical feminist organization that counted Solanas as its founder and sole member. Desperate for attention from Warhol, Solanas began spending time at the Factory, as Warhol's loft was known, where he held lavish parties and created many of his films and works of art. She had written a play that she begged the artist to produce; when the script got misplaced, Solanas concluded that Warhol had stolen it, and she felt both rejected and exploited. On June 3, 1968 she shot Warhol three times; although he survived the attack, friends of his, Harron among them, claimed that the shooting changed him permanently. Warhol died in 1987 (of an unrelated cause); Solanas spent three years in a mental institution before moving to San Francisco, where she died, impoverished, in 1989.

Although Solanas was clearly emotionally disturbed, Harron admired her spirit and radical vision and felt sympathy for her. Speaking with Rose Troche, the director of *Go Fish*, for *Filmmaker* (Spring 1996, on-line), she said that she identified strongly with Valerie's anger about "being told what a woman was or what she could do" and about "the way that society regarded women as weak-minded and intuitive." According to Harron, Solanas was a brilliant voice struggling to be heard, and she might have fit in with the Factory crowd had she not been so serious, a trait that Warhol may have found off-putting. Although Harron maintained a deep respect for Warhol as an artist and a person and considered him "very smart," as she told Troche, she also knew that he could be "very mean to people."

Harron's research experience aided her in tracking down background information on Solanas; for example, with the help of Diane Tucker, a researcher, she was able to arrange interviews with someone who had worked with Solanas on a campus newspaper at the University of Maryland and other people who had known Solanas when she had been enrolled there. Working with Daniel Minahan, Harron co-wrote the screenplay for her debut feature film, *I Shot Andy Warhol* (1996). In what has been cited as a particularly effective device, Harron used black-and-white film when showing Solanas (portrayed by Lili Taylor) reading excerpts of *The S.C.U.M. Manifesto* aloud. (The rest of the people and film are in color.) The director told Powell that she instructed Jared Harris, who played Warhol, to eschew "maliciousness or campiness" in his depiction of Warhol and to focus instead on "Andy's physical vulnerability and the feeling that he didn't want to be touched." Harron endeavored to present three-dimensional characters, but she was also careful not to tell the story from Solanas's point of view. "I don't want to be identified with the message of killing men!" she told Bruce Kirkland in an interview for the *Toronto Sun* that was reprinted on *Jam* (May 10, 1996, on-line). "But with her analysis of how women and men behave towards each other, based on the doctrines of male supremacy, I absolutely agree."

I Shot Andy Warhol presented a complicated portrayal of a woman whose rage is matched by a hidden insecurity that leads to her "need for attention, her deep hurt and paranoia," as Harron told Hilton Als for the *New Yorker* (May 29, 1996). "She was like Andy in that they both wanted to be famous because they both wanted to be wanted." *I Shot Andy Warhol* was a hit at the 1996 Sundance Film Festival, in Utah, where it was nominated for an Independent Spirit Award; it was also shown at the Cannes Film Festival, in France. In the United States the film got mixed reviews; in *Rolling Stone* (May 16, 1996), for example, Peter Travers described it as "extremely entertaining and provocative," while Terrence Rafferty, writing for the *New Yorker* (May 13, 1996), dismissed it as "insufferably high-minded" and "flashy but conventional." Although the media treated her as if she were a first-time director, Harron, knowing that people can never completely control their public images, accepted the situation, remarking to Troche, "It is better to be underestimated than overestimated."

Earlier, in 1993, Harron had directed an episode of the NBC series *Homicide: Life on the Street* entitled "Sins of the Father"; in 1997 she directed an intallment of the HBO prison drama *Oz* entitled "Animal Farm." Turning again to the big screen, she began working on her second feature film, her adaptation of Bret Easton Ellis's controversial 1991 novel, *American Psycho*. The story concerns Patrick Bateman, a narcissistic Wall Street stockbroker and serial killer; intended as a satire of greed in the era of Presidents Ronald Reagan and George Bush, the book was attacked by some critics and feminist organizations as misogynistic, because of its graphic depictions of the torture and murder of women. Simon & Schuster and several other publishers passed on the novel before Vintage Contemporaries picked it up; currently, the book is in its 34th printing.

Edward R. Pressman, a producer of Oliver Stone's movie *Wall Street* (1988), bought the film rights to *American Psycho* in 1992. Pressman rejected scripts by Stuart Gordon (who wrote the screenplay for and directed *Re-Animator*), David Cronenberg (*Crash*), and Ellis himself (whose version ended with a musical number set to a Barry Manilow tune) before settling on Harron's screenplay, which she co-wrote with Guinevere Turner. Harron had originally found the book distasteful and had set it aside without completing it, but after picking it up again, she began to understand its appeal as a satire of consumer culture; eventually it struck her as quite funny. She viewed the text as a sociological study "about privilege and elitism and what people think they can get away with," as she told Lewis Beale for the New York *Daily News* (April 9, 2000, on-line). In an interview with a reporter for *Entertainment Weekly* (April 14, 2000), she said, "It was a shame that the violence got in the way of the book being appreciated, so part of me feels we're rescuing it from its own bad reputation."

Most independent production companies—including October, Miramax, Gramercy, Fine Line, and Fox Searchlight—expressed no interest in the film; finally, in 1997, Lions Gate Entertainment, a Canadian company whose credits include *Love and Death on Long Island, Buffalo 66,* and *Sick: The Life and Death of Bob Flanagan, Supermasochist,* agreed to finance it. Lions Gate did not agree with Harron's choice for the lead role: Christian Bale, a relatively unknown actor who had made his debut in 1988 at the age of 13 in Steven Spielberg's *Empire of the Sun* and had starred most recently in Todd Haynes's *Velvet Goldmine* (1998), a tribute to glam rock. The producers felt that casting Bale as the main character would hurt sales in the lucrative overseas market. Without consulting Harron, they sent the script to Leonardo DiCaprio, who had recently enjoyed huge success with his role in James Cameron's *Titanic*. DiCaprio loved the script, and Lions Gate offered him $21 million to star in the picture. Harron was extremely upset when she found out about the offer, after the actor had already signed the contract. Certain that his boyishness and enormous adolescent fan base made him completely wrong for the part, she refused to meet with the him. (Ellis, however, approved of Lions Gate's action. "[DiCaprio] would have turned it into something even more perverse, as a film *and* a cultural event," he told the *Entertainment Weekly* interviewer.)

Lions Gate took other actions without checking with Harron, such as enlisting the help of Oliver Stone. When Stone held a reading of the screenplay in August 1998, with actors Cameron Diaz, Reese Witherspoon, and DiCaprio in attendance, Harron began to suspect that Lions Gate had dropped her from the project in favor of having Stone direct the movie. She told Nisha Gopalan for *Film Unlimited* (March 24, 2000, on-line) that although she admired Stone's film work, "social satire is not his forte. . . . He's not well known for his well-rounded, three-dimensional female characters." As Stone began to work with her script, Harron realized that he intended to rewrite it completely. Then, after a series of creative differences arose between DiCaprio and Stone, and a disagreement emerged between Lions Gate and DiCaprio over a start date for shooting, Harron assumed more firm control of the production. After unsuccessfully pressuring her to cast Edward Norton as Bateman, the company agreed to her choice of Bale, on the condition that Harron select better-known actors for supporting roles; ultimately, Witherspoon, Jared Leto, Chloë Sevigny, and Willem Dafoe appeared in the film.

Just as production was about to begin in Toronto, the banks that had agreed to provide the settings for the first week of shooting bowed to demands from local protestors and denied access to the filmmakers. Another delay resulted after a group calling itself Canadians Concerned About Violence in Entertainment, pointing to the fact that Ellis's book had been found on the nightstand of a Canadian serial killer (Paul Bernardo), launched a fax campaign calling for the censorship of the film. An additional problem arose when executives at Calvin Klein, Stolichnaya, and Barneys—labels that figured prominently in the brand-name environment of Ellis's characters—all refused to allow their products to be used in the film.

Like Ellis, Harron saw Bateman as a vehicle with which to critique misogyny rather than glamorize it. "There's a tendency to confuse content with intention," she told Beale. "If you are writing about a misogynist serial killer, it's taken very literally. . . . It was safer for me as a woman to [make the film, because] people couldn't say I was a misogynist. I felt the only person who could make this was a woman." Guinevere Turner agreed with Harron, going so far as to characterize the book as feminist: "It's easy to believe that because the character is misogynist, the story is, too," she wrote for the official Web site of the film *American Psycho*. "But, it was obvious to me that there was something going on beneath the horror. For instance, the book shows how the excesses of the 1980s were manifested in warped relations, not only between men and women but also among men. That's where a lot of the humor lies, in poking fun at these peacocks who are so strangely preoccupied with one another. It ends up being an indictment of machismo and misogyny."

Harron regarded *American Psycho* as an opportunity to vent some of her own anger toward sexist power structures. "Clearly, this is a very anti-male film," she admitted to Holly Millea for *Premiere* (March 2000). "I went to Oxford with a group of very privileged, macho young men who had gone through that pipeline from prep school to university to banking. . . . [Still,] I don't think you can do a satire without being a little in love with what you satirize." She also recognizes the value of exploring one's fears and rejects the notion that female filmmakers cannot or should not deal with unpleasant subject matter. "I don't feel that as a woman I'm restricted from portraying violence," she told Millea. "Am I supposed to make movies about [the American artist] Georgia O'Keeffe? Affirmational portraits of women?"

Harron's adaptation omits many of the violent scenes in Ellis's book that caused such a stir. The only scene to which the Motion Picture Association of America objected involved sexual interplay between Bateman and two prostitutes. Harron told Nisha Gopalan that the scene, which includes a shot of Bateman admiring himself in a mirror, was "deliberately unerotic" and crucial to establishing the character as narcissistic and emotionally detached; nevertheless, she was forced to edit it to obtain the R rating necessary for wide distribution.

For the most part reviewers admired Harron's approach to Ellis's novel. In *Harper's Bazaar* (April 2000), Manohla Dargis wrote that Harron and Turner had "produced an unexpectedly shrewd parody of masculinity. Harron does not place meaning first and entertainment second but wants the audience to laugh at Bateman because he is ridiculous in the way all lunatics are and because she knows the best way to lose the audience is to trample them with good intentions." In the view of Anthony Lane, who assessed the film for the *New Yorker* (April 17, 2000), "Harron's adaptation of Bret Easton Ellis's *American Psycho* may be less savage than the book but, as a result, is much creepier. . . . This is a fierce and timely piece that will make the audience laugh in ways and at times that should hardly be funny at all."

Harron and Turner are currently developing a film based on the life of the 1950s pin-up icon Bettie Page, whose image appeared on dozens of magazine covers and, in addition, in "photo sets and film loops that often featured fetish gear, spankings, kidnapping scenarios, and other trappings of sadomasochistic sex," as Bunny Yeager wrote for *Interview* (July 1993). Harron and her husband, the director John Walsh (*Ed's Next Move* [1996]), have two young children. — C.L.

Suggested Reading: *Entertainment Weekly* p36+ Apr. 14, 2000, with photos; *Filmmaker* (on-line) Spring 1996; *Interview* p120+ Apr. 1996, with photos; New York *Daily News* (on-line) Apr. 9, 2000, with photos; *New Yorker* p33+ May 29, 1995, with illustration; *Newsweek* (on-line) Jan. 24, 2000, with photo; *Premiere* p51+ Mar. 2000, with photos

Selected Films: *I Shot Andy Warhol*, 1996; *American Psycho*, 2000

Hawass, Zahi

(HAH-wass, ZA-hee)

May 28, 1947– Archaeologist; Egypt's undersecretary of state for the Giza Monuments; director of the Pyramids. Address: 42 Aden St., Mohandessin, Giza, Cairo, Egypt

"This work is a constant inspiration to me," the archaeologist Zahi Hawass told Elizabeth Kaye McCall for an article reprinted on his Web site. After working for 30 years on the Giza Plateau, in Egypt, and excavating some of the most famous monuments in the world, among them the Great Pyramid and the Sphinx, Hawass has distinguished himself as the world's premier expert in Egyptology. His discoveries at every major archaeological site in Egypt, from Alexandria to Abu Sim-

Leila Gorchev/Associated Press

Zahi Hawass

beland, have helped to give the lie to many of the fanciful tales that abound about the Pyramids. One of his expeditions, for example, uncovered irrefutable evidence that the Pyramids were constructed by Egyptians rather than extraterrestrials or inhabitants of a lost civilization, as many people have believed, and by free men and women, not slaves. Hawass has also spearheaded the movement to preserve and protect the monuments of Egypt for future generations. During his campaigns for financial assistance and other help to conserve these ancient structures, Hawass has made a strong impression on scholars, scientists, and representatives of cultural organizations around the globe. "There's something about him. He's a unique phenomenon," Antonio Loprieno, chairman of the Department of Near Eastern Languages and Cultures at the University of California at Los Angeles, observed to McCall. "In many ways," Loprieno added, "he's probably the first media-conscious Egyptologist."

Zahi A. Hawass was born on May 28, 1947 in Damietta, Egypt, to a couple who owned a prosperous farm. He left home, at the age of 16, to study law at the University of Alexandria but soon discovered that law was not for him. Casting about for another major, he settled on archaeology, which was then a newly established discipline in Egypt. (Although archaeological expeditions were not uncommon in Egypt, the projects had always been led by foreigners.) Hawass didn't like his second choice any better than his first, but he stuck with it long enough to earn a degree, in 1967, in Greek and Roman archaeology.

After an unsuccessful attempt to get a job in the diplomatic corps, Hawass fell back on his academic credentials, and in 1968 he got his first taste of archeological fieldwork, as the associate director of excavations at the Ashmuneim dig in Middle Egypt. His feelings about his profession changed in 1970, when he began investigating a site known as Kom Abou Bellou. "When I started excavating—you know when you see someone and fall in love right away?—that is when I found my love," he told Siona Jenkins for *Discovering Archaeology* (July/August 1999, on-line). "And when I did that, archaeology became everything in my life. This is why I tell every young person in Egypt and outside Egypt that they have to look and wait until they find their real love." He spent the next seven years living in the desert, "in a tent, around snakes and scorpions," he told McCall, "and ate garlic, onion, and bread every day. Adventure during the day—you excavate statues, tombs, temples, artifacts, gold. I found more than 500 pieces of gold at [Kom Abou Bellou]. And in the evening you live in the dark with the noise of the birds. It was the most peaceful seven years of my life." From 1974 to 1980 he also served as an inspector of antiquities at the Giza Plateau—which hosts three Pyramids (including the Great Pyramid, which is the only one of the seven ancient wonders of the world to remain substantially intact); the Sphinx; and several smaller, supporting Pyramids and structures. During that time he earned two promotions.

Having decided that he needed additional formal training, Hawass earned a diploma in Egyptology from Cairo University, in 1980. He then journeyed to the United States on a Fulbright scholarship for graduate studies at the University of Pennsylvania (UPenn), in Philadelphia. He received a master's degree in Egyptology and Syro-Palestinian archaeology at UPenn, in 1983, and a Ph.D. in Egyptology, in 1987.

Upon returning to Egypt, Hawass became the general director of the Giza Pyramids. At the age of 40, he was the youngest person ever to attain this position, and while he was pleased with the recognition of his abilities, he viewed it more as an opportunity to better focus his energies on excavation and restoration. "I never looked for a title," he told McCall. "I always looked for excavations, for the secrets under the sand. I wanted to reveal evidence about the building of the pyramids, about the workmen. Those really were my goals, and the title came later." For centuries the monuments at the Giza Plateau have been subjected to countless ravages: they have been defaced with graffiti, filled with litter, and damaged by the elements, and people have even used burial chambers as lavatories. "The Pyramids really have magic and mystery," Hawass told Hillary Mayell for *National Geographic* (on-line). "But when you go to visit the Pyramids now, you don't really feel this magic and the mystery. You find the horse driver, saying 'Would you like to ride the horse?' or someone asking if you want to buy the postcard, Coca-Cola, Pepsi. You cannot do this at the only site in the world that has one of the seven wonders of the world that still exists. And this is really what we're trying to show the people. We're trying to make it so that when you visit the Pyramid site, you can enjoy the mystery."

Hawass's top priority was to halt unrestricted access to the monuments. First, he installed a gate at the entrance to the plateau (presumably, there is no other entryway), and made everyone who entered pay a fee. He then began plans for "a ring road around the plateau," as he remarked during an interview published on *Nova Online*. "All cars will have to use this; none will be permitted around the Pyramids themselves. We're building a new stable for camels and horses in the desert to the south of the Pyramids. And we're demolishing all unnecessary buildings on the plateau, including guard houses, rest houses, and even my office. Only then can we have the plateau as a sacred, divine place, where visitors can have private time to enjoy the magic and the mystery." The ring road and a new visitors' center in the desert outside the plateau opened in January 2000. An electric shuttle takes tourists to the monuments.

As work progressed on the cleanup of the plateau, Hawass turned his attention to the restoration of the three Pyramids and the Sphinx. "There is an ancient Egyptian saying that 'Man fears time, and time fears the Pyramids,' but this is no longer true," Hawass told Douglas Jehl for the *New York Times* (August 10, 1997). "The Pyramids must fear time, too." One by one, Hawass closed each of the Pyramids for a year so as to perform extensive conservation work both inside and out. He and his team replaced worn-out sections with limestone and constructed a ventilation system. Hawass would like to close the interiors of the Pyramids to visitors entirely someday, because human sweat, skin oils, and moist, salty breath are slowly eroding the delicate stone. "Why do you want to visit a tomb?" Hawass demanded of an interviewer for the *Chicago Tribune* (November 15, 1998). "The magic is from the outside, not from the inside." Currently, the Pyramids are open to the public on a rotating basis.

The restoration of the Sphinx required much more work than that of the Pyramids, and it became one of the defining projects of Hawass's career. Built in the shape of a beast with a lion's body and a human face, the Sphinx guards the Pyramids on the Giza Plateau. Rising 66 feet from the desert's surface and extending more than 240 feet in length, the Sphinx has long been a source of mystery and awe for architects and scholars. In 1926 the French archaeologist Emile Baraize, beginning what turned into an 11-year project to clear sand from around the Sphinx and repair it, "found that the mother rock had completely deteriorated," as Hawass told a reporter for the documentary TV series *Nova*. "This is why I say the Sphinx has cancer." In the late 1980s most of one shoulder crumbled away. Hawass's team began by refinishing parts of the south side of the monument with limestone. Then they moved to the north side, which proved to be a bigger challenge because the crumbled limestone had been covered over with cement, which did not allow the limestone to "breathe" and thus caused further deterioration. Hawass's team replaced the cement with limestone. The entire restoration took a full decade.

With plans for the conservation of the monuments in place, Hawass began planning the excavation of the chambers beneath the Sphinx. In 1939 the psychic Edgar Allen Cayce had alluded to a "Hall of Records," hidden beneath the Sphinx, that contained the secrets of Atlantis as well as the history of a lost civilization. Hawass has stated time and again that, throughout his extensive research on the Giza Plateau, neither he nor anyone on his team has found anything that would indicate a civilization that existed in Egypt prior to 3,200 B.C., nor have they found the Hall of Records. Nevertheless, a small group of critics have accused Hawass of conducting secret projects and hiding valuable research. Hawass's policy of restricting access to the Sphinx's chambers to scholars from a recognized university or museum has led to additional criticism. "Anyone is free to believe anything he wants—that the Pyramids and Sphinx were built in space, by aliens, by whatever," Hawass told Douglas Jehl for the *New York Times* (May 24, 1997). "And you can work here if you are a scholar. But when it comes to amateurs, we say no, no, and no." While the criticism has dismayed Hawass, it has not deterred him from his work. "Yes, it is unfortunate the things they are saying," he told Andrew Bayuck of *Guardian's Egypt* (March 25, 1997, on-line). "For example, Hancock and Bauval [two of Hawass's most vocal critics] are asking people to sign petitions to stop secretive work at Giza. But there is no secret work at Giza! Of course for Hancock and Bauval to suggest some kind of conspiracy at Giza helps them sell books. Thus they profit from the pyramids while in Egypt we struggle to conserve these treasures. While they turn out one profitable book after another about lost civilizations and attack us for conspiring to conceal the truth, the truth is that we are in a struggle to save these world heritage monuments, and do not have time to deal with all their theories."

Hawass's next excavation project, which drew less controversy, provided an answer to a question that had long plagued Egyptologists: who built the Pyramids? On April 14, 1990 the chief of the Pyramid guards, Mohammed Adel Razek, reported to Hawass that an American tourist's horse had stumbled over a previously unknown brick wall (and thrown its rider). The following month Hawass and his team began excavating the wall, which turned out to be part of a tomb with a long, vaulted chamber. Hieroglyphics on the wall identified the tomb as that of Ptah-shepesu and his wife. Further excavations uncovered pieces of granite, basalt, and diorite, the types of stone used to build the Pyramids, leading Hawass to conclude that the tomb held the remains of builders of the Pyramids. Offering further proof, he told a reporter for *Nova*, "All the skeletons of the men and women show signs of stress in their backs, because people were involved in moving heavy stuff. We determined through X-rays that someone had syphilis, and we found evidence of brain surgery on a workman, who lived for two years afterwards. The ancients even had emergency treatment for workers on site, because we discovered that they were fixing broken bones and even amputating legs that had been crushed by a falling stone." Hawass also noted that the discovery helped to dispel many myths that had long surrounded the construction of the Pyramids. "First of all, it proved that the Egyptians were the pyramid builders," he told McCall. In addition, he noted, the nearness of the burial places of the workers to the Pyramids proves that they were peasants who were conscripted on a rotating basis rather than slaves. "This discovery shows how 80 percent of Egyptian[s] lived," he continued. "They worked on the Pyramids from sunrise to sunset, subsisted on beer and bread, and died at the age of 30–35."

Surpassing in importance the discovery of the Pyramid builders' tombs was that of a subterranean cemetery found in the Bahariya Oasis in 1996, when a security guard's donkey plunged a hoof into the roof of one of the sand-covered tombs. Inside the tomb was the largest collection of mummies ever seen in a single enclosure. "The glare of golden ornaments was almost blinding," Hawass told Jonah Blank for *U.S. News & World Report* (September 6, 1999), after he had taken control of the site. Excavation of the tomb revealed that the mummies—placed there more than 1,300 years after the reign of King Tutankhamen, at a time when much of Egypt was dominated by the Roman Empire—had remained undisturbed for at least 2,000 years. To protect the site from potential grave robbers, Hawass kept its existence secret until 1999. Archaeologists have since hailed it as perhaps the greatest discovery in the history of Egyptology and compared its relevance to the 1922 discovery of King Tut's tomb, which had been plundered (though not very much was taken) before archaeologists discovered it. The untouched tombs at the Bahariya Oasis will undoubtedly reveal a great deal about life in a provincial Egyptian town under Roman rule. To date, only four tombs have been excavated, yielding a total of 105 mummies. Hawass has estimated that the cemetery covers several square miles and may contain as many as 10,000 mummies. He also believes that the area currently being excavated was designated for middle-class residents of the Bahariya Oasis, an area devoted to wine making at the time of the tombs' construction, and that the burial places of wealthier people probably have yet to be uncovered.

In 1998 the Egyptian government appointed Hawass undersecretary of state for the Giza Monuments, a position he holds concurrently with that of director of the Pyramids. One of three undersecretaries who work with Gaballa Ali Gaballa, the secretary general of Egypt's Supreme Council of Antiquities, Hawass oversees the antiquities housed in Cairo and Giza. In the year of his promotion, he began plans for a two-part millennial celebration at the Giza Plateau. During the first part, held on December 31, 1999, a gold-encased, triangular capstone was set atop the Great Pyramid to replace its long-missing apex. "You know [the Great Pyramid] was built in the third millennium B.C.," Hawass told a reporter for the *Chicago Tribune* (November 15, 1998). "We are celebrating the third millennium A.D. Therefore, we should have something important to mark the occasion." After the performance of a 12-hour opera written for the event, the capstone was removed. It was reported that Hawass also planned to send a robot into the Great Pyramid to peer behind a never-before-opened door, but as of early November 2000, the results of that excursion had not been published on his Web site, *guardians.net/hawass*. In February 2000 Hawass excavated the tomb of Osiris, an Egyptian ruler who was murdered and, according to Egyptian mythology, returned to life as ruler of the underworld. The shaft in which the tomb was found had been submerged in water, keeping the tomb hidden for over 3,000 years.

Although his career has been marked by adventure and astounding discoveries, Hawass feels that his primary roles as an archeologist are those of teacher and guardian of history. "I believe that Egyptologists have a mission to teach interested young people about working in the past," he told a reporter for *Nova*. "Archaeology, after all, is not Indiana Jones. I encourage young people to study and prepare for the field." Hawass has written many articles and several books, and he has served as a consultant for documentaries and other media projects. "Archaeology is a mystery world. It's a world of magic," he declared to McCall. "That's the reward that makes this my paradise." — J.K.B.

Suggested Reading: *Chicago Tribune* p6+ Nov. 15, 1998; *Discovering Archaeology* (on-line) July/Aug. 1999, with photo; *New York Times* I p4+ May 24, 1997, with photos, V p3+ Aug. 10, 1997, with photos; *U.S. News & World Report* p62 Sep. 6, 1999, with photos

Selected Books: *Pyramids of Ancient Egypt*, 1990; *Secrets of the Sphinx: Restoration Past and Present*, 1998; *Valley of the Golden Mummies*, 2000; *Silent Images: Women in Pharaonic Egypt*, 2000

Mike Blake/Archive Photos

Hawk, Tony

Apr. 12, 1968– Skateboarder; CEO of Hawk Designs and Birdhouse Productions. Address: Birdhouse Productions, 670 Broadway, Suite 504, New York, NY 10012

Commentators on the cable-television sports channel ESPN often refer to Tony Hawk as "the Michael Jordan of skateboarding." The creator of many of the most technically challenging tricks in skateboarding, Hawk has performed stunts for commercials and feature films, among them *Police Academy* (1984), *Thrashin'* (1986), *Police Academy 4: Citizens on Patrol* (1987), and *Gleaming the Cube* (1989). Although he is about 10 years older than most of the other professionals in his sport, Hawk remains at the top of his game. An entrepreneur as well, he has developed a line of skateboarding clothes and accessories for kids, called Hawk Designs, and he manages Birdhouse Productions, a multimillion-dollar skateboard manufacturing company that sponsors a team of professional skateboarders. Although some fans have criticized him for endorsing a large number of products, all agree that he must be ranked with the most talented skateboarders in the world. Hawk bears little resemblance to the stereotypical skateboarder conjured by the media—an unsavory-looking character with an outlaw mentality. Rather, he is a family man and a role model and inspiration for many young people. "The image of Tony Hawk is not so hard-core," Kevin Imamura, the editor of *Warp*, a "skate snow style sound" magazine, said to Mark Levine for the *New Yorker* (July 26, 1999). "But that guy, his level of skating is so ridiculous."

The youngest of the two sons and two daughters of Frank Hawk, a salesman, and his wife, Nancy, Tony Hawk was born in San Diego, California, on April 12, 1968. As a boy he idolized the daredevil stunt motorcyclist Evel Knievel. He first showed an interest in skateboarding at the age of nine, when his brother, Steve, allowed him to try out his board. At 11 he stopped playing basketball and quit his Little League baseball team in favor of skateboarding. "I just liked being freer, not having to submit to some practice schedule of repetitive passing and shooting, not having to rely on all the other players in order to do well," he told Mark Levine. "There's a lot of practice and repetition in skateboarding, but it's at your own pace. It's not someone telling you what to do. That was the bottom line. I just didn't want to be ordered around." Although Hawk's father was the president of the local Little League at the time, he supported his son's decision; Frank Hawk later organized the California Amateur Skateboard League and helped to develop the National Skateboard Association.

Hawk's mother told Levine that Tony was "a very intense child, difficult and stubborn and hard to handle," and she and her husband were pleased that in skateboarding, he had found an outlet for his excess energy. At age 12 Hawk began winning local contests, and by the time he was 14, he had turned professional, with sponsorship by Powell-Peralta Skateboards. He soon became the top-ranked skateboarder in the United States, and he retained the number-one position for the next 11 years. Aside from music, during his teens nothing but skateboarding interested him. In high school, he told Levine, he "didn't relate to anyone" and "never went to a single school function—sporting events, dances, prom." He spent every afternoon at a local skate park. "I never imagined any future for myself outside skateboarding," he said. The awakening of Hawk's interest in skateboarding, in the late 1970s, coincided with a period of renewal for the sport, during which many innovative skating techniques were developed. Nevertheless, skate parks began to close, because the municipalities that maintained them could not afford the liability insurance. Their demise sparked an underground movement of street skating, which influenced the sport significantly. "It really opened up a whole new door, as far as what you could do with your board and what you could do on ramps, which is my forte," Hawk told Brion O'Connor for *ZineZone* (on-line). "You can take the tricks that these guys were doing on the street and really adapt them to the ramp skating. They really fed off each other."

According to Michael Brooke, the author of *The Concrete Wave: The History of Skateboarding* (1999), the sport came into being in the early 1900s, "when kids banged roller-skate wheels onto two-by-fours," as he explained to Mark Levine. "Sometimes kids attached orange crates with handles to the two-by-fours, for steering. Sometimes kids broke the T-bar handles off scooters. This kind of thing continued through the Depression and the

Second World War." For years, police officers harassed skaters, but Hawk believes that this problem is beginning to fade. "I think the outlaw image just stemmed from the lack of a place to skate," he told Brion O'Connor. "Not too long ago, when just trying to find a place to skate, [young people would] end up skating on public and private property. . . . Now there's a lot of cities making public parks . . . and there's just a lot more support." Hawk has never been arrested for skateboarding in public, but he has received many tickets.

Many of the top skateboarders are friends; they attend competitions to socialize with others who share their passion for the sport and to share new tricks. The person who creates a new stunt has the privilege of naming it, and Hawk himself has christened some 50 to 60 maneuvers. One of the most basic tricks is the Ollie; others are the loop, the drifter, and the Frigidaire. Because of the complexity of recently invented skating tricks, they require longer names that are comprehensible only to those who know the sport well. To successfully execute the Kickflip McTwist, the skater must spin 540 degrees in the air as the board is flipped. (Since the circumference of a circle contains 360 degrees, the Kickflip McTwist entails a revolution of one and a half circles.) Hawk mastered the 720-degree twist (two full circles) "when I was trying a 540 degree twist and went too far," he told Daniel B. Wood for the *Christian Science Monitor* (December 30, 1986). Like many other professionals, Hawk practices for two to three hours a day, five days a week. "To [skateboard] requires a lot of endurance, leg strength, balance, coordination, and a sixth sense for [the] location of the board," he told Sal Ruibal for *USA Today* (June 22, 1998). "The hardest tricks are the subtle ones. The 540s look hard, but they're really the easiest." Hawk performs many of his stunts in a so-called half pipe, which resembles a 12-foot vertical pipe, half of which has been cut away lengthwise. When skating he often looks as if he is about to "bail," or crash, until the very last moment. "The guys whose styles are appreciated are the ones who look like they're almost out of control," he explained to Mark Levine. "They look like they're on the edge the whole time, and then they bring it together." He also told Levine, "I have dreams about skating all the time—anxiety dreams. Dreams in which I'm riding a board with a sawed-off tail, or in which the ramp is made of carpet. And dreams that I can't skate."

Skateboarding gained further legitimacy when the X Games (a showcase for so-called extreme sports, such as snowboarding and sky surfing) were first broadcast on ESPN, in 1995. At the 1999 X Games, Hawk became the first person to execute a 900-degree twist. "ESPN announcers quickly declared Hawk's feat to be a historic moment in alternative sports," Mark Levine reported. Hawk himself said at the time of his achievement, "This is the best day of my life."

Hawk was one of the first athletes to make a living from skateboarding. As an 18-year-old he earned an annual income of nearly $70,000 from competitions and endorsements. By the late 1980s he was collecting monthly royalty checks of $20,000. He has received numerous endorsements, from such companies as Walt Disney, Swatch watches, 55DSL clothing, Arnette sunglasses, Fury, and Club Med. He has appeared in a Gap commercial and lent his likeness to Activision for the popular video game called "Tony Hawk's Pro Skater." In 1998, after being sponsored for 12 years by Airwalk shoes, he signed a deal with Airwalk's competitor Adio. His memoir, *Hawk: Occupation: Skateboarder*, co-written with Sean Mortimer, was published by HarperCollins in mid-2000. According to a HarperCollins blurb, the book provides a behind-the-scenes look at the skateboarder's life and discusses, among other subjects, Hawk's difficulty in dealing with the death of his father.

Hawk is the founder of two companies: Hawk Designs, which manufactures skate clothing and accessories for kids, and Birdhouse Productions, a maker of skateboards, which has 40 employees. Birdhouse's team of skateboarders promotes interest in the sport by skating with youngsters at skate parks. In March 2000 Hawk Designs was bought by Quiksilver Inc., which will also sponsor Hawk as a skateboarder. Criticism of Hawk for "selling out" does not bother him. "There are skaters out there who don't want anyone to penetrate their world," he told Mark Levine. "But if my role is to be skateboarding's link to the mainstream, I'm willing to accept it. My business card for Birdhouse gives my title as 'Media Whore.'"

Hawk lives in Carlsbad, California, with his wife, Erin (a former ice-skater), their son, Spencer, and Hawk's son, Riley, from his first marriage. Aware of parents' concerns about their children's safety, he works hard to represent his sport in constructive ways. He told Brion O'Connor, "I really feel like skating is one of the most positive things a kid can get into these days." — C.L.

Suggested Reading: *Christian Science Monitor* p1+ Dec. 30, 1986, with photos; *New Yorker* p68+ July 26, 1999, with photo; *USA Today* C p16 June 22, 1998; *ZineZone* (on-line) 1999; Carbone, Ken and others. *The Virtuoso: Face to Face with 40 Extraordinary Talents*, 1999; Hawk, Tony, and Sean Mortimer. *Hawk: Occupation: Skateboarder*, 2000

Jon Ferrey/Allsport

Heinrichs, April

(HINE-ricks)

Feb. 27, 1964– Soccer player; coach. Address: c/o U.S. Soccer House, 1801–1811 S. Prairie Ave., Chicago, IL 60616

In January 2000 April Heinrichs was named head coach of the U.S. Women's National Soccer Team. Nineteen months earlier she had become the first female soccer player to be inducted into the National Soccer Hall of Fame, an honor that reflected more than 15 years of spectacular achievements in the sport. As a player for the University of North Carolina Tar Heels, from 1982 to 1986, she racked up stellar personal statistics while contributing to the team's dominance in women's college soccer. She joined the U.S. National Team in the mid-1980s, serving as the squad's captain during its 1991 victory at the World Cup. Her appointment as the National Team head coach caps a career that includes successful coaching stints with the University of Maryland, the University of Virginia, and the U.S. Olympic women's soccer team. Although Heinrich's U. S. team lost the gold to Norway in the 2000 Olympics, the members of the team captured their fellow Americans' hearts with their drive and their passion for their sport.

April Heinrichs was born on February 27, 1964 in Denver, Colorado, to Melvin Heinrichs, a firefighter, and Patricia Heinrichs, a clerk. She grew up with her four sisters in Littleton, Colorado. A highly energetic little girl, she took up soccer when she was six years old; her family, she told *Current Biography*, enjoyed having "peace in the house" when she was outside playing. As a youngster she also played competitive basketball and softball, and she ran track. After she graduated from Heritage High School, in Littleton, in 1982, she enrolled at Mesa College, in Grand Junction, Colorado, where she played on the women's basketball team. The next year she transferred to the University of North Carolina at Chapel Hill, where she joined the women's soccer team and quickly distinguished herself. She won a spot on the All-America team in each of her years there, making the first team as a sophomore, junior, and senior. At the time of her graduation, she was the National Collegiate Athletic Association (NCAA) all-time leading scorer, with 81 goals and 57 assists, and had led the Tar Heels to three NCAA titles, in 1983, 1984, and 1986. She was also the first women's soccer player in the school's history to have her jersey—number 2—retired. Speaking of Heinrichs, her coach at North Carolina, Anson Dorrance, told David Horgan for the University of Virginia's campus paper, the *Cavalier Daily* (July 3, 1996, online), "I've never trained anyone more psychologically powerful than her." Heinrichs earned a B.A. degree in radio, television, and film in 1986.

That same year Heinrichs joined the U.S. Women's National Team. She scored 37 goals in her 47-game career, and in her final season, in 1991, she was the team's captain, leading the way to the U.S.'s first Women's World Cup title. In that tournament, as part of what was dubbed the "triple-edged sword"—along with her teammates Michelle Akers and Carin Gabarra—she made an outstanding four goals in five games, and her team beat Norway 2–1 in the final. Anson Dorrance, who coached the U.S. Team, told David Horgan, "I attribute my 1991 World Cup to her leadership." In 1986 and 1989 Heinrichs was named U.S. Soccer Female Athlete of the Year, and *Soccer America* magazine voted her female player of the 1980s.

Meanwhile, Heinrichs had signed on as an assistant coach at the College of William and Mary, in Williamsburg, Virginia, in 1987. "Playing came to me very easily; as a coach I'm much more a student of the game," she told Horgan. Her coaching, she added, is "based on hard work . . . a commitment to train as hard as you play." After two years at William and Mary, she took a year off from coaching before accepting a position as head coach at Princeton University, in Princeton, New Jersey, in 1990. After one year there she was offered a position at Stanford University, in California, whose team was then second in the nation to North Carolina's. She turned the offer down. "Going to Stanford, I might have been in the final four every year, but it wouldn't have been my program," she told Jon DeNunzio for the *Washington Post* (November 22, 1995). Instead of taking the helm of a team that was already among the most successful, she wished to help a group of players fulfill their potential.

With that in mind, in 1991 Heinrichs went to the University of Maryland to coach the Terrapins. She brought the team "from oblivion," as David Horgan put it, to an 18–6 record and to the number-six ranking in the final *Soccer America* poll in her last season with the Terrapins, in 1995. "The easiest thing in the world is to spot a winner, and it was evident immediately that April was one," Gothard Lane, a Maryland assistant athletic director who helped hire Heinrichs, told DeNunzio. "The personality of a team usually reflects the personality of the coach." Commenting on her success, Heinrichs told DeNunzio, "Maryland is my program, and we've brought it to the point where it is now. I felt good about it. To me, that was more important than being in the final four every year." In 1995 Heinrichs's Terrapins set the school record for single-season victories, and that year she won the Atlantic Coast Conference (ACC) Coach of the Year Award.

Discussing her training of recruits, Heinrichs told Horgan, "The transition from high school to college soccer is very demanding, not just on the field but off the field. Our philosophy is that we recruit players that we feel can step in and replace seniors, not just break into lineups. At the same time, some kids may take a semester, a year, or even two years before they will be ready. Until they get here, we only see them on paper, but once the ball gets rolling, then we'll have a better idea how quickly they will impact the program."

Before the 1996 season Heinrichs signed on as head coach of the University of Virginia Cavaliers. In an interview published by the Official Athletic Site of the University of Virginia (on-line), she was asked what she looks for in a player, and she responded, "I don't think soccer is like track or swimming where it's very objective—what's your time in the 100m? What's your height in the high jump? Soccer is more subjective. We have to look at the qualities of their psychological dimension. Being quick doesn't mean success, necessarily, on the soccer field. So . . . we look for something special about the person. . . . Either they're the best header of the ball defensively, or the hardest defender or perhaps they are a goal scorer. . . . One special quality is what we're looking for." She told her interviewer, Julia Howell, that at Virginia she was "careful . . . not to set long term goals. I personally have long term goals set in my mind and I don't openly state those. . . . The danger of that is you forget the day to day. . . . It's very easy to lose focus when you look more than a game ahead." That strategy apparently paid off: beginning with the 1996 season, Heinrichs led the Cavaliers to four play-off spots.

Concurrent with her coaching at Maryland and Virginia, Heinrichs had served as a coach with the U.S. Women's National Team. She took the job of full-time assistant coach for the organization in January 1995 and served on the staff of that year's Women's World Cup squad. In addition, she had a hand in coaching the 1996 Olympic team, which won the U.S. its first gold medal for women's soccer. After that, she resigned from the Olympic team, and in 1997 she became the head coach of the U.S. Under-16 National Team.

On January 18, 2000 Heinrichs was appointed head coach of the U.S. Women's National Team, becoming the fourth person to take the job in the organization's 15-year history and the first woman to hold the position. Heinrichs signed a four-year contract, though one had never been offered to her predecessor, Tony DiCicco, who coached the women's team to victory at the 1999 World Cup. In a press release, the U.S. Soccer president, S. Robert Contiguglia, discussed the innovation, saying, "It is important that an individual has a chance to express themselves over time. We are talking about building a program and not an event. It involves success on the field, but it's more than that. We're building a program and sport." About Heinrichs herself, Contiguglia said, "Her vibrant and charismatic personality style mixed with a passion and unprecedented dedication to the sport of soccer makes me proud to name April as the new U.S. Women's National Team head coach." Upon being appointed, Heinrichs declared, as quoted in the press release, "It is exciting for me . . . to accept this position. Without Title Nine [the 1972 civil rights law barring gender discrimination in education] I wouldn't [have] had the opportunity to play college sports. Without Anson Dorrance . . . I wouldn't [have] had that opportunity to play college soccer and without U.S. Soccer I wouldn't [have] had the opportunity to compete at the international level. I have great pride and honor in this new position, and [look] forward to the opportunity."

Heinrichs's appointment came at an awkward time, with the 20 team members in the midst of a job action related to a contract dispute involving salaries. When the team boycotted the recent Australia Cup, they were replaced by a young U.S. team. The conflict ended when the U.S. Soccer Federation and the original players agreed to a new contract that, according to *SoccerAmerica* (February 1, 2000, on-line), "continu[es] to make the U.S. women's national team the highest paid women's soccer team in the world" and "guarantees continued payroll parity with the U.S. men's national team." On March 18, 2000 the team won its first Algarve Cup by beating Norway 1–0. The prestigious competition was held in Loule, Portugal.

At the 2000 Olympics, in Sydney, Australia, all eyes were on the U. S. women's team to defend its gold medal. In a draw for the semifinals, it had to compete against Norway and China, the world's other top teams. On September 14 the United States blanked Norway (the only team in the world that, in contests with the U.S. team, has won more games than it has lost), by a score of 2–0. In the next match, against China, Heinrichs made what proved to be a controversial decision, when, with the U.S. leading 1–0 and with 28 minutes to play, she removed a defensive player and placed an offensive one on the field. The game ended in a tie. The Chinese players "were really running at us with confidence," Heinrichs recalled, as quoted on *Slam Sports* (on-line), "and I thought [the offensive player] was certainly worthy of getting some considerable minutes with this team. If [she] had scored it would have been the greatest decision since the invention of sliced bread. That's the nature of the business I'm in, I guess." The U.S. team next faced the very physical Nigerian team, whom they beat 3–1, thereby making the semifinals. After another, 1–0 victory over Brazil, the Americans met Norway once again. The two teams moved into sudden-death overtime with the score tied, 2–2. In what is considered one of the greatest soccer games ever played, the U.S. team lost, in the 12th minute of sudden death, and the American players—in tears—came away with the silver medal. "Norway did what they had to do," Heinrichs said later, as quoted in a U.S. Soccer news release (on-line). "They kept their game plan very simple and they never gave up. We may have won the silver medal but their game was golden tonight. I'm incredibly proud of each one [of the players on the U.S. team] and incredibly proud of their achievements. . . . We couldn't have started better and it was a coach's dream to push the ball around the way we did and have as much possession as we did." After the Olympics the team returned to the U.S. for the three-game, three-city "Glory Tour," held in November and December.

On June 2, 1998, in her first year of eligibility, Heinrichs was inducted into the National Soccer Hall of Fame, in Oneonta, New York. (Athletes become eligible for induction after four years of retirement from active play.) She was also the inaugural recipient of the National Soccer Coaches Association of America Women's Committee Award of Excellence for long-term service and the advancement of women's soccer in the United States. — V.K.

Suggested Reading: *Soccer Times* (on-line) Jan. 19, 2000; University of Virginia *Cavalier Daily* (on-line) Jan. 18, 1996, June 11, 1998; U.S. Women's National Team press releases (on-line)

Vincent LaForet/Allsport

Hernandez, Orlando

Oct. 11, 1965– Baseball player. Address: New York Yankees, Yankee Stadium, 161st St. and River Ave., Bronx, NY 10451

Taking the mound at Yankee Stadium on June 3, 1998, Orlando Hernandez ended a difficult period in his life, which had begun when he defected from Cuba the previous December. Known in the Communist country for being the best and smartest pitcher on the mound, he was nonetheless banned from the game in 1996, after his half-brother defected to play baseball in the U.S.; that action inspired Hernandez's own decision to leave his homeland. After capturing the attention of the sports world with his escape from Cuba, the tall, lean right-hander with the spectacular delivery signed on with the New York Yankees. Although many baseball scouts questioned his potential as a major-league pitcher, El Duque, as he is affectionately called, became an anchor of the Yankee pitching staff shortly after leaving the minors. Confounding batters with his mastery of several different types of pitches, Hernandez is recognized today as one of the premier pitchers in the game. In his three major-league seasons, he has won 43 games, struck out 429 batters, and helped his Yankees to win three world championships, in 1998, 1999, and 2000.

Although Hernandez claimed after he left his native land that he was born on October 11, 1969 in Villa Clara, Cuba, others have maintained that he was born earlier. *New York* magazine seemed to put the issue to rest when it revealed in 1999 that court documents filed by Hernandez, for his divorce two years earlier, clearly state that he was born in 1965. Hernandez has since acknowledged the legitimacy of the documents. While details about his early life are few, it is known that his father, Arnaldo Hernandez, was a pitcher and shortstop for a Cuban baseball team and acquired the nickname "El Duque" (pronounced "DOO-kay"), which means "the duke."

Following in his father's footsteps, Hernandez became the nation's best pitcher and took his father's nickname as well. Traveling around the world in baseball tournaments, Hernandez was noted for his strong arsenal of pitches and lightning delivery. Although his fastball clocks in at more than 90 miles per hour, he has won the most attention for his breaking ball, the precision of his pitches, and his knack for knowing which pitch to throw in a given moment. In the 1992 World Junior Championships, Hernandez won two games, allowing no earned runs and only one hit and striking out 19 batters in 12 innings. Regarded with immense pride by Cubans, he compiled a 129–47 career record in his native country, and his winning percentage there (.722) is the highest of any pitcher in the history of the Cuban League. Despite being a star athlete, Hernandez never owned a car in Cuba, riding a bicycle to work instead, a practice promoted by the government to save gasoline. Hernandez was also identified as an electrician's assistant, as part of a Cuban program that pays athletes to work at nonexistent jobs.

As word of El Duque's talent spread, several attempts were made to get him to defect to the U.S. Joe Cubas, a Miami-based sports agent, was prominent in these efforts, but Hernandez always refused. "Joe told me I could make $5 million over three years," Hernandez told Brook Larmer for *Newsweek* (January 12, 1998). "But I told him I would rather have five million Cuban fans cheering me on." In 1995 Hernandez's younger half-brother, Livan, defected during a team trip to Mexico, eventually signing a three-year contract with the Florida Marlins. The following year, Orlando Hernandez was banned from Cuban baseball and the Olympic team after accusations that he had had dealings with Cubas, who had arranged his brother's defection. "It was a shock [to be banned]," Orlando told Brook Larmer. "Would I like to play in the major leagues? Of course, but I never wanted to desert my country." The ban proved difficult for Hernandez to bear; he had already been disgruntled with the lack of reward he was receiving for his hard work. "I was working very hard [touring the world], and I wasn't taking a lot of money back to Cuba with me," he told Tom Weir for *USA Today* (September 9, 1997). "I wasn't very happy with the way things were. I was tired of it." In order to make a living following his forced retirement from baseball, Hernandez worked at a psychiatric hospital as a rehabilitation therapist, earning about $10 per month. Meanwhile, he was living with his wife and two daughters in a one-room apartment. To make matters even worse, Hernandez was ostracized by his former teammates and harassed by others who considered him a traitor to his country. In order to continue playing baseball and keep in shape, Hernandez would participate in sandlot pick-up games with friends, who would never make him the pitcher—a position in which he was overpowering—but would put him in the infield. Hernandez also ran six miles a day and practiced yoga. While he continued to submit applications to pitch for Cuba again, all were turned down. Right before Christmas 1997, Cuban officials visited Hernandez, warning him with threats of imprisonment not to take any actions—such as defection—that would be embarrassing to the country, particularly since the Pope would soon be visiting Cuba and the nation would be put under intense media scrutiny. The officials also told Hernandez that he would never again pitch in Cuba.

Ironically, it was the Cuban government's paranoia that Hernandez would defect—and their resulting actions—that eventually led him to do so. Hernandez, his wife, and six others fled Cuba on December 26, 1997. As Hernandez would later tell the story, the group boarded a rickety ship that began to take on water soon after they left Cuba. The refugees were forced to start rowing during a storm on the rough seas, and at one point, according to Hernandez, the craft was even surrounded by sharks. The truth appears to be far less dramatic. According to several of the other refugees, including the captain, the "ship" was a 20-foot fishing boat with a sound, Russian-built engine. The boat never took on water, the weather was calm, and there were no sharks. The captain even reported that Hernandez, rather than rowing, had sat inside for the duration of the trip. Landing on the deserted island of Anguilla Cay, the group waited for a boat, run by a friend of an uncle of Hernandez's, that was supposed to take them to Miami. The boat never came, however, as it had taken on water and been rescued by the United States Coast Guard five miles from its destination. The group spent the next four days on the island with barely any provisions, frying sea conchs in pans left by former refugees. Eventually spotted by a helicopter, the group was picked up by a U.S. Coast Guard ship returning to Havana to drop off three other refugees. Terrified that they would be seen by the Cubans in Havana waters, Hernandez's group was transferred to another ship, which was sailing to Bimini, in the Bahamas. (The fact that they had not been processed saved them from being taken back to Cuba.) Due to bad weather this passage was indeed rough, and the ship was forced to dock at Freeport. From there, the Cuban refugees were taken to Nassau, also in the Bahamas.

After being held a few days by officials in the Bahamas, Hernandez, his common-law wife, Noris Bosch, and his fellow refugee ballplayer Alberto Hernandez were allowed United States visas, but El Duque turned down his visa to stick with the other refugees. Bosch pleaded with Hernandez to accept the visas, but as she was quoted as saying in *Sports Illustrated* (November 30, 1998), "For him, friendship is the most important thing. When he has a friend, he will stay with them until death divides them." In the end Joe Cubas, now representing the Cuban pitcher, was able to get El Duque and his six friends visas for Costa Rica, while Hernandez's wife remained in the United States. In going to another country, Hernandez also escaped eligibility for the amateur draft, which would have meant having to sign with whichever team drafted him. Instead, he became a free agent and was thus able to sign for more money. Hernandez maintained, however, that his decision to go to Costa Rica was based less on the issue of his free agency than on his concern for his fellow refugees. "There was no reason to leave five people behind," he said to Tom Weir for *USA Today* (January 9, 1998). "We have to stay together. We're all going to be enjoying the same freedoms together." In Costa Rica Hernandez trained in front of scouts from several organizations who were impressed with what they saw of his pitching and with his enthusiasm. Meanwhile, he was having a wonderful time. "I've been enjoying democracy and freedom," he said. "Here no one can tell me what to say. It has changed my life already."

In January 1998 the United States government granted Hernandez asylum, which led to some controversy, because of the appearance that a ballplayer was able to get what other refugees were refused. In March Hernandez joined his half-brother at an emotional reunion in Miami. In the time that the two brothers had been separated, Livan had gone on to become the 1997 World Series MVP for the Florida Marlins and had set a National League record for most strikeouts—15 in a single game. On March 17, 1998 Hernandez signed a four-year, $6.6 million contract with the New York Yankees. "Since a young boy, I've always dreamed about the New York Yankees," El Duque revealed to Phil Rogers for the *Chicago Tribune* (March 22, 1998). "I left Cuba in search of freedom, and with that freedom comes a chance to be a member of the New York Yankees. . . . For me to be able to wear this uniform, for me it's the maximum."

Hernandez worked out with the team for the first time on March 21, and a physical examination showed that he was in excellent shape. He endeared himself to teammates during training with his enthusiasm and his genuine surprise at all the equipment and food available to American baseball players. In fact, he soon put on a substantial amount of weight, zooming from 180 pounds to 220. "I had just arrived from Cuba," Hernandez would later explain. "There was a lot of food, and I wanted to eat it." The Yankees started Hernandez off as a single-A pitcher, then moved him up to their triple-A club in Columbus, Ohio, one step away from the majors. However, after a slow start that left Hernandez with a 2–4 record and a dismal 5.14 earned-run average (ERA), he was sent down to the double-A club in Portland, Maine. There, he compiled a 9–2 record. Carlos Tosa, the Cuban-born manager of the Portland team, later reflected to Tom Weir on how his and Hernandez's shared heritage may have helped the pitcher's performance. "Perhaps he felt a little more comfortable. I could communicate with him in his own language. I could understand him. I think in his mind I was one of his countrymen, someone who knew his culture and had been to his homeland."

Hernandez was called up to the Yankees in June, when starting pitcher David Wells complained of illness, but was denied the opportunity to pitch when Wells recuperated by game time. Just when he was about to be sent back down to the minors, however, Hernandez was asked to pitch the next day, after it was learned that the scheduled starter—David Cone—had been bitten on his index finger by his mother's dog. Hernandez's first major-league game was against the Tampa Bay Devil Rays at Yankee Stadium on June 3, 1998. In the half-filled arena, where many supporters held Cuban flags and shouted "El Duque," Hernandez met all expectations. In seven innings he gave up one run on five hits and struck out seven batters, including the first he faced. When manager Joe Torre wanted to put in a relief pitcher, Hernandez, filled with emotion, gave up the ball only after being physically forced to do so. "In Cuba," Hernandez explained to Tom Verducci for *Sports Illustrated* (August 17, 1998), "you pitch until you die. When you can't pitch with your arm, you go with your heart." The Yankees won the game, 7–1. Over the course of the season, Hernandez more than lived up to his nickname, compiling a 12–4 record with 131 strikeouts in 141 innings while walking only 52; his ERA was a fine 3.13, especially noticeable in a year of high ERAs and strong batter statistics. Pitcher David Cone told Tom Verducci about Hernandez, "He's invigorated me. Just watching how creative he is on the mound has rubbed off on me, without question." Meanwhile, the Yankees went on to one of the greatest seasons in the history of major-league baseball, winning 114 games in their march to the American League East division title.

After blowing past Texas in three games in the first round of that year's play-offs, the Yankees faced tougher opponents in the Cleveland Indians, their rivals for the league championship. Hernandez pitched game four against Cleveland, the loss of which would have put the Yankees within one game of elimination. Despite not having pitched in 15 days, Hernandez was overpowering, allowing no runs and three hits in seven-plus innings, and the Yankees won the game, 4–0. In a later contest they clinched the play-offs. In the World Series, Hernandez and his teammates' fortunes continued, as the Yankees swept the San Diego Padres in four games. For his part, Hernandez allowed only one run and six hits in his outing, striking out seven in as many innings. Right before the Yankees' victory parade, Hernandez was reunited with his mother, his ex-wife, Norma Alvira, and two daughters, whom he had not seen since his defection from Cuba. The four were granted a brief stay in the United States by the Cuban government with the help of John Cardinal O'Connor, whom Hernandez had asked to help reunite the family. "I'm very happy, I'm proud of my son," Hernandez's mother, Maria Julia Pedrosa Cruz, said, as quoted in an Associated Press article posted on *fastball.com*. "He hasn't changed, in spite of the fact that he has all that money."

With high expectations for his second season in the majors, Hernandez proved that his first was no fluke, securing a 17–9 record with 157 strikeouts in 214 and a third innings of work. The right-hander compiled a 4.12 ERA, which, although higher than the year before, was still below the

American League average of 4.52. More tellingly, Hernandez limited his opponents to a .205 batting average. Once more the Yankees won the American League East title and were sent to the postseason. Hernandez pitched the third and decisive game in the first round of the play-offs against the American League West champion Texas Rangers. In a masterful performance, he held the Rangers to two hits and no runs in eight innings. In the first game of the league championship series against the Yankees' arch-rivals, the Boston Red Sox, Hernandez pitched eight strong innings but left with the game tied at 3–3. (The Yankees would go on to win the game in 10 innings.) Once again pitching what would turn out to be the decisive game in the series, Hernandez shut down the Red Sox in game five, allowing one run in seven innings and striking out nine. The Yankees went to the World Series for the second year in a row, facing the Atlanta Braves. Hernandez was dominant in game one, striking out 10 while allowing only one run in seven innings. The Yankees swept their opponent in four games.

Favored to win the American League East title a third year in a row, in 2000 the New York Yankees struggled to an 87–74 record, which was nonetheless good enough to win the division title by two and a half games. El Duque had his troubles as well. Throughout the season he was plagued by injuries, including back trouble and a sprained right elbow that put him on the disabled list. Although he pitched some fine ball games and struck out 141 players, Hernandez's ERA rose to 4.51 while he compiled a losing record, 12–13. Nevertheless, he insisted that the injuries and his pitching problems did not faze him. "Frustration is for the weak, and I don't consider myself weak," Jack Curry quoted him as saying in the *New York Times* (August 7, 2000).

In the first round of the 2000 play-offs, the Yankees faced the Oakland Athletics; Hernandez started game three and allowed two runs on four hits in seven innings to get the win. After beating the Athletics three games to two, the Yankees faced the Seattle Mariners for the American League pennant. In a magnificent performance in game two, El Duque allowed only one run in eight innings and struck out seven men, helping his team to win, seven to one. He pitched less brilliantly in game six, allowing six runs on seven hits in seven innings. But the Yankees posted seven runs of their own, and Hernandez won his eighth straight postseason victory. The Yanks went on to win the pennant, four games to two. In the 2000 World Series, against the New York Mets, Martinez pitched seven and one-third innings of game three; although he struck out 12 batters and allowed only four runs, the Yanks lost, 4–2. It was the team's only loss in the series, which they claimed after five games.

Orlando Hernandez stands six feet two inches tall and weighs 210 pounds. He speaks mostly Spanish, managing only broken sentences in English; he gives most interviews through an interpreter, usually catcher Jorge Posada, his battery mate on the Yankee squad. In the *New York Times* (June 4, 1998), Buster Olney described Hernandez's versatility as a pitcher: "Imagine Hernandez in front of a clock: he throws with his arm angled at 11 o'clock, 10:30, 10, 9:30 and 9, and he also throws crossfire, with his body aimed in one direction and his arm moving in another in a side-arm motion." Bernie Lincicome noted in an article for the *Chicago Tribune* (October 19, 1998), "El Duque looks like he's doing all the letters of 'YMCA' before he releases the ball. His motion starts with his head tucked behind his left shoulder, his left leg lifted until it touches his left ear and the ball hidden somewhere below and behind his right thigh, and suddenly the ball will appear from any of a half-dozen places." Since he came to the U.S., Hernandez has developed an interest in cars, acquiring a Ferrari, a Mercedes, a BMW, and a Land Rover. Although he is now a millionaire, he still dresses in a low-key fashion and avoids trendy nightclubs in favor of more blue-collar hangouts. He remains popular in Cuba, where fans tune in to Yankees games to cheer on their countryman. He has been praised by most interviewers and friends for his enthusiastic demeanor, youthful energy, and easygoing, generous nature. Hernandez has, however, come under fire from Juan Carlos Romero, the captain who piloted him out of Cuba. In late 1998 Romero sued Hernandez for $800,000 for breaking a verbal agreement between them that Hernandez would help Romero get to the United States and find work. Hernandez's two children, Yahumara and Steffi, live in Cuba, with his mother and ex-wife. Regarding his separation from his family, Hernandez told Brook Larmer for *Newsweek* (August 17, 1998), "On the surface, I try not to show anything, but deep down, I am suffering a lot." As for his feelings toward the Cuban government, El Duque remarked to Tom Verducci, "I hope [Castro] watches me and is pulling the hair out of his beard." — G.O.

Suggested Reading: *Chicago Tribune* Sports p3 Mar. 22, 1998, Sports p1 Oct. 19, 1998; *New York Times* A p1+ June 4, 1998; *Newsweek* p44+ Jan. 12, 1998, p54+ Aug. 17, 1998; *Sports Illustrated* p30+ Aug. 17, 1998, p60+ Nov. 30, 1998; *USA Today* C p1 Sep. 9, 1997, C p3 Jan. 9, 1998

Roy Round/Courtesy of American Ballet Theatre

Herrera, Paloma

Dec. 21, 1975– Ballet dancer. Address: American Ballet Theatre, 890 Broadway, New York, NY 10003-1278

"To have seen 18-year-old Paloma Herrera in Balanchine's *Theme and Variations* during American Ballet Theatre's 1994 spring season at the Metropolitan Opera House was to be in the presence of a near miracle. . . . Here was a prodigy at work." John Gruen, who penned those words for *Dance Magazine* (December 1994), is among the many ballet enthusiasts who have exclaimed over Herrera's technique and artistry. A native of Argentina, Herrera has dedicated herself to ballet since the age of seven. She moved to New York City as a teenager, in 1991, to dance with American Ballet Theatre (ABT), one of the world's most prestigious troupes. Two years later ABT promoted her to soloist, and two years after that, to principal dancer. In addition to *Theme and Variations*, Herrera has performed leading roles in such standards of the ballet repertoire as *Don Quixote*, *Sleeping Beauty*, *Swan Lake*, and *Romeo and Juliet*. "My real life is on the stage," she told John Gruen in 1994. "I just love to perform. I get really sad whenever we finish a season, because performing means so much to me. It's really what I care about most. I love to make art on the stage, not just technique. That's what I always work for—to make something good happen onstage."

Paloma Herrera was born in Buenos Aires, Argentina, on December 21, 1975, about a year after her only sibling, a sister. Her father, Alberto, is a prominent lawyer; her mother, Marisa, has worked as a professor of literature at the University of Buenos Aires, an interior decorator, and a furniture designer. According to Marisa Herrera, none of their relatives had ever danced professionally, and thus she and Paloma's father regarded their younger daughter's early passion for dance as something of a mystery. Paloma herself has suggested that her interest was sparked by the classical music her parents listened to, as well as by her yearning to wear tutus and pointe shoes and look like the ballerinas she saw in photos and on television. When she was very young, she would move furniture in the living room to make space to dance. "From the beginning," her mother told John Gruen, "Paloma danced and pranced around the house. . . . Then, when she was seven, Paloma announced that she wanted to be a dancer. . . . Paloma was very determined. We had no choice but to find her a very good teacher in Buenos Aires." Herrera began studying with Olga Ferri, a highly respected instructor who had been trained in England and had held the title of principal ballerina at the Teatro Colón, in Buenos Aires, for three decades. While many young girls dream of becoming ballerinas, very few prove to have the combination of discipline, talent, and love for dancing that is necessary for that interest to persist through years of extremely rigorous training and personal sacrifices. Herrera was among that small number, and by her own account, she never had any doubts about pursuing dance above all else. "I loved my teacher and my dancing classes," she told Gruen of her early lessons. "I didn't want to miss a single day. I was so happy! You know, other little girls at seven or eight don't really know what they want. But I knew right away. From the first day I knew I wanted to be a dancer and there was no way I was going to change my mind." After her classes at a traditional primary school, she took dance lessons daily, for a total of about six hours each week. "She suffered a lot during vacations," her mother told Gruen. "She cried and cried because she didn't get to go to her dancing lessons."

After a year of studying under Ferri, the eight-year-old Herrera auditioned for the Instituto Superior de Arte, the ballet school of the Teatro Colón. She was one of only 15, out of approximately 500 applicants, who gained admission. The curriculum included morning classes five days a week in classical ballet; modern, Spanish, and folk dance; and art history. She would attend a regular school in the afternoon, and then, for about four hours ending at 10:00 p.m., she had private lessons. "It was a sacrifice, but I loved it," she told Paula Durbin for *Americas* (May/June 1999). Her instructors at the Teatro Colón included Olga Ferri, who continued to be her primary mentor throughout Herrera's studies in Argentina. At age 11, in the first of several periods of instruction abroad, Herrera trained at the Minsk Ballet School, in Russia. After returning to Argentina, she performed at the Teatro Colón in the role of Cupid in *Don Quixote*, a part assigned to an adult in many renditions of the ballet, and she was hailed as a prodigy.

During her student years at Teatro Colón, Herrera entered a series of ballet competitions. "To tell you the truth, I don't really like competitions," she told Gruen. "Competitions are better suited to something like gymnastics, not to ballet. For me, ballet is an art, and art is not something you compete over. But my teachers insisted that I compete. They felt it was important." By age 10, Herrera had won a gold medal in the Latino-American Ballet Contest, held in Lima, Peru, and first prize in a competition in Argentina sponsored by Coca-Cola. In 1990, at age 14, she was a named a finalist at the 14th International Ballet Competition held in Varna, Bulgaria, which is among the most prestigious of such events. Among the judges at Varna was Natalia Makarova, a former prima ballerina with the Kirov Ballet and then with ABT. Greatly impressed with Herrera's performance, Makarova invited the young dancer to take classes for a month with the English National Ballet, in London, where Makarova was preparing a production of *Swan Lake*. "It was incredible to watch her work and to see all those wonderful dancers," Herrera told Gruen. "I was . . . very impressionable, but the performances I saw and the classes I took with the company have really stayed with me."

Not long after her return to Argentina, Herrera participated in a major ballet competition that was held in Buenos Aires every two years. The master Argentine dance teacher and choreographer Hector Zaraspe, who has taught, since 1971, at the Juilliard School, in New York City, judged the competition, and like Makarova, he was immediately struck by Herrera's talent. He urged her to come to New York City to study at the School of American Ballet, run by the New York City Ballet. Herrera had long dreamed of going to New York, to study ballet and see performances by the world-class dance companies that are based there, and she hoped to perform there herself someday. She was eager to follow Zaraspe's advice, but her parents had reservations. "We were very hesitant to let Paloma go to New York," Marisa Herrera told Gruen. "She had just turned 15—she was too young to be alone in such a big city. But, as always, Paloma knew what she wanted, and finally my husband said, 'We must make this sacrifice. We must let her go.' And off she went!"

Herrera arrived in New York in 1991. Having little knowledge of spoken English, she moved into a residence for Spanish-speaking dancers and lived there for the duration of the six-month term at the School of American Ballet (SAB). (She has since become fluent in English.) The SAB assigned her to its most advanced class, and though her placement showed that she was already an accomplished dancer, she discovered that she had a lot to learn. "The minute I started, I was shocked to see that at [the SAB] you had a completely different way of working," she told Gruen. "I mean, all my training had been in the Russian style. I was completely confused. The teachers said to me, 'You have talent, but you have to change your style.' Well, I worked very hard to accomplish this, and it was good, because now I know exactly how New York City Ballet dancers are trained and how the ballets of Balanchine should be danced." (The repertoire of New York City Ballet focuses on the works of George Balanchine and other modern choreographers, which are generally danced in a style that differs from the style adopted for classical ballets first staged in Europe and Russia during the 19th century.) To her surprise, Herrera was selected to dance the lead role in the SAB's workshop performance of Balanchine's *Raymonda Variations*, which brought the semester to a close.

According to John Gruen, Herrera's workshop performance "would undoubtedly" have secured her a place in the New York City Ballet company. But Herrera had always aspired to join American Ballet Theatre, and two days after the workshop performance, she recalled to Gruen, "I learned that American Ballet Theatre was holding auditions. I decided I had to take it." American Ballet Theatre attracted Herrera in part because while growing up she had loved the performances she had seen on television and video by the one-time ABT dancer and artistic director Mikhail Baryshnikov, who is among the most famous ballet dancers of all time. In addition, she told Gruen, she knew that as an ABT dancer, "I would eventually do all the classical ballets. I would get to do [ballets by Anthony] Tudor. I would get to do [works by Agnes] de Mille and [Kenneth] MacMillan and many other choreographers. I would dance in so many different styles. I feel that a dancer has to be exposed to a wide variety of styles—it's the only way to grow and mature as an artist."

After the audition Jane Hermann, Baryshnikov's successor as ABT's artistic director, offered Herrera a contract to join the company's corps de ballet, and immediately, without consulting her parents, Herrera signed it. "It was the happiest day of my life," she told Gruen. She had been scheduled to fly home to Argentina the next day. When she called her parents to break the news to them, she tried to sound casual, as she recalled to Sasha Nyary for *Life* (April 1996). "I said, 'Oh, I'm staying here.' Maybe they expected it, I was going so fast. But it was harder for them than for me."

For a while after settling in New York, Herrera lived on the city's East Side with an Argentine couple who were friends of friends of her parents'. She had her own bedroom in their apartment. "It's one of those things you can never pay back," she told Janet Cawley for the *Chicago Tribune* (September 17, 1995). "It's how I learned to love New York, in a family. I felt so protected." In addition to pursuing her career, she studied at an Argentine school for children of diplomats, located in the borough of Queens; she also attended school in Argentina during her breaks from rehearsing and performing with ABT. As of 1999 she had received a diploma from the Instituto Superior de Arte but had not yet earned an academic diploma.

At about the time of her 18th birthday, Herrera got her own apartment, in a high-rise near Lincoln Center for the Performing Arts, where ABT performs its New York season each year. Interviewers have often asked her about the drawbacks and difficulties of life as a dancer. "The phone bills!" she exclaimed to a reporter for *Seventeen* (December 1993), shortly before she turned 18. "I miss my family so much, and I try to talk to them on the phone almost every night." About a year later she told Gruen, "Right now, I'm trying to make a life for myself. . . . I have made some friends. Still, I think the life of a dancer is quite hard. And a lot of dancers are really, really alone. They just have their work." Herrera attends mandatory company classes and rehearsals six days a week, from about 10:00 a.m. until 6:00 or 7:00 in the evening, which leaves her little time for a life outside the company, especially when she has performances at 8:00 p.m. as well. She told Cawley that in her free time she likes to go to museums and, although "it's scary," to attend ballets.

While she was still a member of the ABT corps de ballet, Herrera danced several prominent solo roles, including the Fairy of Benevolence in *Sleeping Beauty* and roles in *Don Quixote* and *La Bayadère*, and she began to win notice as a future star. Identifying her as a "born dancer," Tobi Tobias wrote for *New York* (May 31, 1993), "Herrera's most formidable—and appealing—qualities are her passion and her naturalness. . . . Her leaps are high and buoyant; the leg that leads her body into flight seems to arrow effortlessly through exhilarating crosscurrents of air. Where most other dancers deliver their fouettés [a traditional dance movement] with circusy bravado or fearful tension, she just whips hers out as if rhythm impelled her to turn. Their easy perfection of shape is not half so amazing as their steady pacing; it seems to respond to a drumbeat emanating from the heart of the earth." The critic added that Herrera possessed a "voracious appetite for movement" and "an intensity in performance that's like a hero's commitment to his mission. . . . Herrera's dedication reads as an emblem of joy."

In June 1993 Kevin MacKenzie, who had become ABT's artistic director in December 1992, promoted Herrera to soloist, and in March 1995, she was named principal dancer. Since then, in debuts in several leading roles, Herrera has made a splash with critics and the public alike, and many ballet aficionados believe that she is well on her way to fulfilling her artistic promise. In a review for the *New York Times* (June 12, 1994) of Herrera's performance in *Theme and Variations*, Anna Kisselgoff wrote, "Anyone who has followed the beautifully schooled Argentine prodigy . . . would not be surprised by her polished first try at this neoclassic Balanchine masterpiece. When she followed it up with an even more phenomenal and mature performance the next evening, all the promise of youth and exceptional talent seemed to be on display." Janet Cawley cited the assessment of the late Joseph Mazo, a critic for the New Jersey newspaper the *Bergen Record*, of Herrera's dancing in *Don Quixote* in 1994: "If Herrera continues as she has begun, she could become the outstanding American ballerina of her generation." After her promotion to ABT soloist, Herrera began to emerge as a bona fide ballet celebrity. In 1994 she appeared on the cover of the *New York Times Magazine*, photographed in the middle of a street in the Soho neighborhood of New York, posing on pointe in a striking arabesque. She was also featured in such glossy magazines as *Vogue*, *Harper's Bazaar*, and *Vanity Fair*, as well as in an episode of *Opening Shot*, a series on the Bravo cable network that aired in 1995.

Usually, critics have been unanimous in their praise of Herrera's classical dance technique. In a representative review for the *New York Times* (June 14, 1995), Jack Anderson wrote that in Herrera's performance as Kitri, the lead female role in *Don Quixote*, her "extensions were high, her balance awesomely secure. In the final pas de deux, she sustained poses with a sculptural elegance that made these moments of immobility as startling and as beautiful as the allegro outbursts that preceded and followed them." On the subject of Herrera's acting, however, reviewers' opinions have been less consistent. According to Anderson, who later saw her as Juliet in New York, Herrera's interpretation of that role was convincing. Assessing the performances of Herrera and her Romeo, Keith Roberts, in Kenneth MacMillan's evening-length ballet *Romeo and Juliet*, Anderson wrote for the *New York Times* (June 20, 1996), "Thanks to their ardent dancing, their characters were people it was easy to care about and weep over." Anderson continued, "Many of Herrera's touches of characterization were quite effective: for instance, the way she let simple steps backward indicate her total rejection of the suitor her family wished her to marry." A reviewer for the *Washington Post* (April 11, 1998) was less impressed by Herrera's portrayal of the dual role of Swanilda and Coppelia in the ballet *Coppelia*: "Herrera is no actress; her Swanilda in the first act was petulant and simpering instead of defiant. But impersonating the doll [Coppelia] came easily; [Herrera] could be technically sharp and expressionless too."

While maintaining technique requires a great deal of dancers' energy, Herrera aspires to create performances of great artistic depth as well. She explained to Cawley that in preparing to make her debut as Juliet (a role she had longed to portray for many years), she decided "to try to do it my own way, how I would feel it, how I would react. . . . If I do something, it has to be real." She recalled to Sasha Nyary her experience of dancing Juliet: "Three hours, three acts. In the third act you go through so much. You cry, you have your big pas de deux. When I finished, I was empty—nothing else left. I had given so much."

Since coming to ABT, Herrera has continued to refine both her technique and her artistry under the guidance of company coach Irina Kolpakova as well as Kevin McKenzie. The choreographer Twyla Tharp created a leading role in her ballet *How Near Heaven* for Herrera, which Herrera performed at its premiere in Washington, D.C., in 1994. Her other notable roles with ABT include Clara in *The Nutcracker*; Medora in *Le Corsaire*; the leading role in *Paquita*; Gamzatti in *La Bayadère*; and leading roles in *Symphonic Variations*, *Symphonie Concertante*, and *Tchaikovsky Pas de Deux*. "I want to work with different choreographers, dance in other theaters, in other countries . . . ," Herrera told Paula Durbin. "I would love to dance Giselle and [other roles] I don't have and don't want to miss. I'm full of projects and I'm always willing to try something new. I don't plan my life, but I feel I have always done what I love." — O.J.S.

Suggested Reading: *Americas* p38+ May/June 1999, with photos; *Chicago Tribune* VII p1+ Sep. 17, 1995, with photos; *Dance* p50+ Dec. 1994, with photos; *Life* p58+ Apr. 1996, with photos; *New York* p64+ May 31, 1993, with photo; *New York Times* II p21 May 30, 1993, with photos, C p15 June 14, 1995, with photo, C p16 June 20, 1996, E p4 July 7, 1998, with photo; *Seventeen* p38 Dec. 1993, with photos; *Washington Post* B p1 Apr. 11, 1998, with photo

Selected Ballets: *La Bayadère* (Gamzatti); *Coppelia* (Swanilda/Coppelia); *Le Corsaire* (Medora); *Cruel World* (featured role); *Disposition* (leading role); *Don Quixote* (Kitri); *Gala Performance* (French Ballerina); *Giselle* (peasant pas de deux); *How Near Heaven* (leading role); *The Nutcracker* (Clara, the Snow Queen, Dewdrop); *Paquita* (leading role); *Romeo and Juliet* (Juliet); *Swan Lake* (pas de trois); *Les Sylphides* (the Waltz); *Symphonic Variations* (leading role); *Symphonie Concertante* (leading role); *Tchaikovsky Pas de Deux* (leading role); *Theme and Variations* (leading role); *Voluntaries* (pas de trois)

Archive Photos

Herskovitz, Marshall

Feb. 23, 1952– Television and film producer; director. Address: Fox Television Station, 205 E. 67th St., New York, NY 10021-6089

The television producer Marshall Herskovitz has created some of the most memorable, if not longest-lasting, programs in recent memory. As the creative force—along with his partner, Ed Zwick—behind such shows as *thirtysomething*, *My So-Called Life*, *Relativity*, and the new hit series *Once and Again*, Herskovitz has offered insight into the turbulent worlds of middle-aged yuppies, astute teenagers, and young divorcees. A testament to his prowess as a producer is that, although many of his shows have been canceled early into their runs, they have continued to spawn legions of fans and imitators. "The interesting thing about the American television watching population is that they're happy to watch junk and they're happy to watch good stuff," he told Bernard Weinraub for the *New York Times* (August 1, 1999). "They'll watch both. And they'll recognize the good stuff."

Marshall Herskovitz was born on February 23, 1952 in Philadelphia, Pennsylvania. After graduating from Brandeis University, in Waltham, Massachusetts (where he wrote a screenplay of the 1,100-year-old epic poem *Beowulf* for his senior thesis), he attended the American Film Institute, in Los Angeles. There, he met fellow student Ed Zwick. As part of a course on directing, they were each asked to reminisce about an object that held special personal meaning; Herskovitz chose his grandfather's carpenter's ruler, while Zwick brought in his grandfather's pocketwatch. After class, Herskovitz and Zwick sat down and talked to each other about their grandfathers. That conversation led to a friendship and a partnership that have lasted more than 20 years.

After graduating from film school, in the mid-1970s, Herskovitz toiled as a writer on television projects including *The White Shadow* and *Seven Brides for Seven Brothers*, while occasionally working as a director on *Family*, a drama series for which Zwick was a producer. He and Zwick, hoping eventually to get involved in feature filmmaking, collaborated on the script for the made-for-TV thriller *Special Bulletin*, which told the story of a group of reporters taken hostage by militant antinuclear protestors. Airing in March 1983, *Special Bulletin* proved to be a moderate ratings success, won four Emmy Awards, and earned Herskovitz a Humanitas Prize, which he shared with Zwick.

The success of *Special Bulletin* led Herskovitz to a development deal at MGM, which obligated him to create a television series. He teamed up with Zwick to generate ideas, but nothing they came up with appealed to them—until Herskovitz said, as quoted by Terri Minsky in *Esquire* (November 1990), "We could do something about our generation." The result was *thirtysomething*, which chronicled the lives of Hope and Michael (played by Mel Harris and Ken Olin, respectively), a married couple in their 30s dealing with the ups and downs of adult life. Debuting on ABC in the fall of 1987, the show surprised critics and viewers with its realistic portrayals of everyday experiences, sometimes showing the lead characters doing little more than sitting around the kitchen table and talking. "I would say that we're the only show that takes the depiction of reality as one of our central aims," Herskovitz told a reporter for *Playboy* (June 1990). In spite of division among critics, many of whom felt that the show was bland and uninvolving, *thirtysomething* soon became a ratings success and earned 22 Emmy nominations in three years. Herskovitz himself won an Emmy in 1988 for outstanding drama series, as well as a DGA (Directors Guild of America) Award and a second Humanitas Prize.

In 1991 the show was canceled, and Herskovitz pursued a career in feature films. His first effort was as a writer and producer of the TV movie *Extreme Close Up* (1990), a drama about suicide that was directed by Peter Horton, who had played the role of Gary Shepherd on *thirtysomething*. Herskovitz then made the leap to big-screen fare, as the director of the family drama *Jack the Bear* (1993). That film starred Danny DeVito as a widowed father facing the responsibility of raising his two sons alone. Despite warm notices from critics, the film was not a hit at the box office, a fact that still troubles Herskovitz. "You spend at least two years of your life making a movie and you're creating two hours of entertainment and it's forgotten," he told Weinraub. "Even if it's not the whole story of making movies, that part of it is unbearable. It's very, very difficult."

In 1994 Herskovitz bounced back, by producing the Zwick-helmed film *Legends of the Fall* (1994), a sprawling romantic epic about a World War I–era prairie family. Co-starring Brad Pitt, Anthony Hopkins, Henry Thomas, Aidan Quinn, and Julia Ormond, the film got mixed reviews but grossed more than $60 million at the box office and earned several Oscar and Golden Globe nominations. The popularity of the picture notwithstanding, Herskovitz yearned to return to television. "We were spoiled," he told Jefferson Graham for *USA Today* (March 31, 1997). "We had a show on the air for four years that had such an influence on our culture. It's hard to walk away from that, because in many ways, it eclipses what movies can do." He and Zwick paired up again to create the teen drama series *My So-Called Life*, which premiered on ABC on August 25, 1994. Set in the fictional Pennsylvania town of Three Rivers, the show chronicled the life of 15-year-old Angela Chase, played by Claire Danes. Many felt that the show, peppered with self-awareness and angst, was a retread of *thirtysomething*, replacing middle-aged yuppies with precocious teens. Herskovitz maintained that this was not the case. "Believe me," he said to Joel Engel for the *New York Times* (October 24, 2993), "our impulse was not to take a look at another period of life." *My So-Called Life* was canceled after only 19 episodes, but audience response was fervent enough to lead the cable music station MTV to resurrect the series in reruns, an arrangement under which it ran successfully for a year. In spite of its perceived failure, *My So-Called Life* made an impact on television, giving rise to such similarly themed series as *Dawson's Creek* and *Felicity* and also boosting the careers of the young actors Danes and Jared Leto.

Undeterred by the failure of *My So-Called Life*, Herskovitz began preparing his next series, *Relativity* (1996), a drama about a man and woman in their 20s who begin a romance in Italy and continue their relationship after returning to the U.S., much to the chagrin of their families. A few months after it debuted, in the fall of 1996, *Relativity* was the lowest-rated series then being shown on any major network. It was canceled after 17 episodes. "ABC spent a lot of money and effort on the show, and I can't fault how they've gone selling the show," Herskovitz told Graham. "The bottom line is that not enough people tuned in."

In 1998 Herskovitz again turned to films, directing *Dangerous Beauty* (1998), which he co-produced with Zwick and others. Because of its subject matter, Herskovitz was initially hesitant about making *Dangerous Beauty*, a period drama inspired by the life of Veronica Franco, a 16th-century courtesan. "On the other hand," he explained to Rob Blackwelder for *Splice* (February 6, 1998, on-line), "we felt that this was such a remarkable life and that the issues in the movie, the sexual politics in the movie, were so applicable to today, that in fact it was a wonderful way to talk about the changes that still need to take place in our society, and to get people to experience our own sexual dilemmas in a different way by going into this other time, this other place, and this other circumstance." *Dangerous Beauty* opened on February 8, 1998 to much acclaim from critics. In spite of these positive notices, the film disappeared quickly from theaters.

In 1998 Bedford Falls, Herskovitz and Zwick's co-owned production company, agreed to create three new shows for ABC and one for Fox. The first of these is the hour-long drama series *Once and Again*, which premiered on ABC to strong ratings in the fall of 1999. The series focuses on Lily (played by Sela Ward), a newly divorced woman who becomes involved with Rick (Billy Campbell), a single father of two. Although Herskovitz himself is divorced, he has insisted that the series is not autobiographical. "I haven't been in a serious relationship with a woman who has children of her own, for example," he told Weinraub. "But I've certainly faced the struggle and also the sort of excitement and possibility and thinking that there is another chance of finding someone after you've been divorced." In the months since its premiere, *Once and Again* has proven to be a ratings winner, earning a following comparable to that of *thirtysomething*. In addition, critics have reacted favorably. Ken Tucker wrote for *Entertainment Weekly* (September 24, 1999), "Any adult who's had to scribble a hasty permission slip for a forgetful son or daughter just as the school bus is pulling up to the corner, or any young person who's had to endure the humiliation of watching a newly single parent reenter the hell of dating that the teen knows all too well, will find something to identify with while watching *Once and Again*, the new TV season's most intensely engrossing show." On December 20, 1999 the show received three Golden Globe Award nominations, including one for best television series; in August 2000 Sela Ward earned an Emmy for outstanding lead actress in a drama series.

In 1999 Herskovitz and Zwick co-produced *Executive Search* (1999), a film about a woman who hires an executive-search firm to find her a mate. For their TV shows, the two serve as executive producers and occasionally co-write and co-direct episodes as well.

Marshall Herskovitz lives in Los Angeles. He has two children from his 15-year marriage, which ended in 1993. In addition to his work on television, he continues to serve as a producer of feature films. He is currently producing the movie *Traffic*, a drama about drug runners and the law, slated for release in December 2000.— J.K.B.

Suggested Reading: *Entertainment Weekly* p129+ Sep. 24, 1999, with photos; *Esquire* p160+ Nov. 1990, with photos; *New York Times* II p29+ Oct. 24, 1993, with photos, II p25+ Aug. 1, 1999, with photos; *USA Today* D p3+ Mar. 31, 1997, with photos;

Selected Television Shows: *Special Bulletin*, 1983; *thirtysomething*, 1987; *Extreme Close-Up*, 1990; *My So-Called Life*, 1994; *Relativity*, 1996; *Once and Again*, 1999–

Selected Films: as producer—*Legends of the Fall*, 1994; *Traffic*, 2000; as director—*Jack the Bear*, 1993; *Dangerous Beauty*, 1998

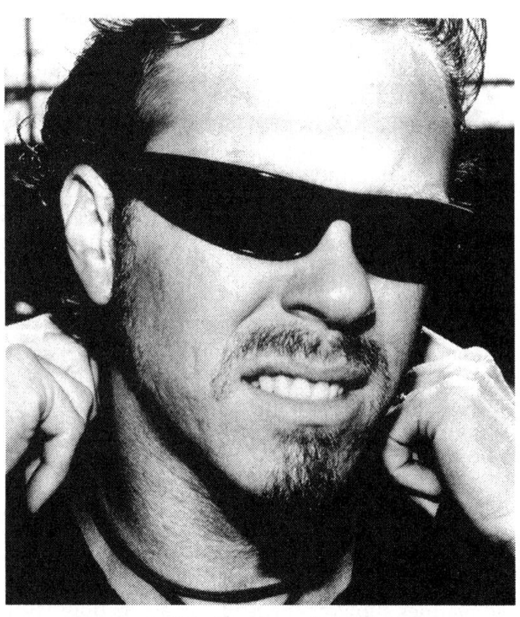

Anton Corbijn/Courtesy of Elektra Entertainment

Hetfield, James

Aug. 3, 1963– Rock singer; guitarist; songwriter. Address: c/o Elektra Entertainment, 75 Rockefeller Plaza, New York, NY 10019-6908

For over 17 years James Hetfield has been the lead singer and rhythm guitarist for Metallica, arguably the most influential heavy-metal band of its era. Combining the driving, hyper-fast sound of speed metal with the more melodic, riff-oriented hard rock of such bands as Iron Maiden and Motorhead, Metallica forged a new genre of heavy-metal music known as "thrash." In collaboration with drummer Lars Ulrich, Hetfield has written most of Metallica's songs, thus shaping the band's musical development over the years. In the 1980s the band recorded such landmark albums as *Master of Puppets* (1986) and *. . . And Justice for All* (1988). Their sound became more mainstream in the 1990s, beginning with their self-titled 1991 album and, more recently, such discs as *Load* (1996) and *ReLoad* (1997). A foursome, Metallica has included, in addition to Hetfield and Ulrich, the guitarist Kirk Hammett, since 1983, and the bass player Jason Newsted, since 1986. Discussing Metallica's longevity, Hetfield told David Fricke for *Rolling Stone* (April 15, 1993), "We keep ourselves hungry. We have high expectations for ourselves all the time, with everything—songwriting, touring. We're always trying to better ourselves. . . . As long as we wanna be together and write material together, we'll be together."

James Alan Hetfield was born on August 3, 1963 in suburban Los Angeles. His father, a trucking-company owner, and his mother, an amateur singer of light opera, were strict Christian Scientists, and they raised their son and his younger sister according to the tenets of that religion. Christian Science is based on the doctrine of divine healing and the conviction that illness is an illusion that can be overcome by the mind; believers refuse to place themselves under the care of physicians. His parents' adherence to Christian Science "alienated me from a lot of the kids at school," Hetfield recalled to David Fricke. "Like when I wanted to get involved with something like football. You needed a physical from a doctor, and I would be like, 'I don't believe in this, I have this little waiver saying I don't need this.'"

Hetfield's parents divorced when he was a child, and during the next 10 years, he never saw his father. It is only in recent years that he has become comfortable in his father's company. His mother died before he reached adulthood. Rock music, which had long appealed to him, became a refuge of sorts from his unhappiness at home. "Music wouldn't lie to me, or leave me," he told David Fricke. In his teens he began to play the guitar. During his childhood Hetfield's parents had coerced him into taking piano lessons, and although he had not particularly enjoyed playing the piano, he has said that it increased his coordination, which helped him when he later played the guitar and sang simultaneously.

In high school Hetfield listened to many hard-rock and heavy-metal bands, his favorite among them being Aerosmith. Over the years he has also cited Lynyrd Skynyrd, Tom Waits, Motorhead, Black Sabbath, and Leonard Cohen among his musical influences. Through his older stepbrother, who played drums in a local rock band, he gained a greater exposure to and appreciation for rock music. He became a part of the heavy-metal scene in about 1980, playing guitar in such California bands as Obsession, Phantom Lord, and Leather Charm. During his late teens he also held menial jobs, as a janitor and sticker-factory worker, for example.

In October 1981 Hetfield responded to a magazine ad placed by drummer Lars Ulrich, who wanted to assemble a band to record a song for the record label Metal Blade. The members of the makeshift band, consisting of Hetfield on rhythm guitar, Ulrich on drums, and Lloyd Grant, on lead guitar, christened themselves Metallica and recorded "Hit the Lights," which was released on the Metal Blade compilation album *Metal Massacre*. Later in 1981 Dave Mustaine replaced Lloyd Grant on second lead guitar and the bassist Ron McGovney came on board, and the expanded band recorded a new version of "Hit the Lights" for the Canadian release of *Metal Massacre*. Dissatisfied with several singers who had tried out with the band, Hetfield took it upon himself to both sing and play guitar. He thought that providing the vocals would be temporary, but he felt so comfortable singing that he decided to maintain his dual role. Hetfield also designed Metallica's distinctive logo.

In 1982 Hetfield, Ulrich, Mustaine, and McGovney recorded a seven-track demo entitled *No Life Till Leather*. Soon afterward McGovney left the band. In what stretched into a four-month effort, Lars Ulrich persuaded the guitarist Cliff Burton to leave the band Trauma and join Metallica. In March 1983 the members of the newly constituted Metallica signed a contract with the Megaforce label. Because Megaforce was based in New Jersey, Metallica had to move from the San Francisco Bay area and settle on the East Coast. Then, just one month into their contract, Mustaine left the band to pursue a solo career. (He would later form the successful heavy-metal band Megadeth.) Metallica recruited Kirk Hammett, a guitarist with Exodus, who had studied under the rock-guitar virtuoso Joe Satriani, as Mustaine's replacement.

Metallica's debut album, *Kill 'Em All*, was released in the summer of 1983, and it immediately spawned an enthusiastic underground following. Some critics have even declared that *Kill 'Em All* marked the birth of the thrash-metal genre. Among the tracks are the perennial Metallica favorites "The Four Horsemen" and "Seek and Destroy", the latter of which has since become an audience participation piece at most Metallica concerts. In the *Rolling Stone Album Guide* (1992), the critic J. D. Considine praised *Kill 'Em All*, noting that Metallica had "found a way to increase the music's impact and velocity without decreasing its breadth and majesty." "*Kill 'Em All* was what we knew [at the time]," Hetfield told David Fricke. "Bang your head, seek and destroy, bang your head. . . . It had a lot to do with the L.A. poser scene, where you had to look right to get into this or that club, have the poufy hair. . . . That made us angry."

Ride the Lightning (1984), Metallica's second album (and last Megaforce release), represented a huge thematic step forward for the band, in that for the first time Hetfield and Ulrich's songs dealt with social and political issues. The title song, for instance, is about a man who has been sentenced to death for a crime that he did not commit. "Fight Fire with Fire" deals with nuclear war, and "Fade to Black" addresses the problem of teen suicide. "Fade to Black" became the target of a censorship campaign organized by parents groups after the suicides of several adolescents who were believed to have been influenced by Metallica's lyrics. "These parents [were] finding their kids dead in the garage with these lyrics, sucking on an exhaust pipe," Hetfield told David Fricke. "People tried to sue [us] for *their* mistakes. But we got tons and tons of letters—we still do—that say, '"Fade to Black" saved my life.' But no one wants to read that. It's too nice, too boring."

With their new form of heavy-metal music, known as thrash, Metallica began to gain momentum. Whereas the "speed" metal that preceded it consisted solely of ultra-fast, often monotonous guitar-playing and vocals, Metallica's music incorporated the soaring guitar solos and vocal flairs that distinguish 1970s heavy metal. The result was a hybrid that allowed for individual musicianship while preserving a relentlessly loud and fast sound. In addition, the lyrics of Metallica's songs, which summed up the disillusionment and bottled-up rage that are often a part of adolescence, struck a chord among young record buyers. Hetfield has insisted, however, that he does not think of himself as someone to emulate. "I definitely don't want to tell people how to live," he said to David Fricke. "When you're a role model, you have a responsibility and you lose your creative juices. You worry about what other people think of you. Why worry about what people think?"

Ride the Lightning (1984), released by Elektra Records, sold more than half a million copies and became Metallica's first gold album. Their next effort, *Master of Puppets* (1986), which many consider Metallica's best work, includes such anthems of teen angst and rage as "Welcome Home (Sanitarium)," "Leper Messiah," and the title song, which suggests that governments consider soldiers to be expendable. According to J. D. Considine, "The music's emotional power is undeniable." By far the band's most successful album up to that point, *Master of Puppets* reached number 29 on the U.S. album chart, without any singles or videos issued. Riding a wave of popularity, Metallica was invited to perform on tour with metal icon Ozzy Osbourne. During the tour Hetfield broke his wrist while skateboarding. It was the first of a series of injuries that have incapacitated him for varying lengths of time.

On September 27, 1986, while on tour in Sweden, the Metallica tour bus ran off the road and crashed. While Hetfield, Ulrich, and Hammett escaped unscathed, Burton was killed instantly. The three survivors postponed the remainder of their overseas concerts to attend Burton's funeral. Two months later, on the eve of a U.S. tour, the band hired bassist Jason Newsted of the Arizona band Flotsam and Jetsam to replace Burton.

Metallica intended to record an album of new material in the spring of 1987. However, while skateboarding during a break at the studio, Hetfield broke his arm. By the time the arm healed, the band members had decided on a different direction for their forthcoming album: they would record a small selection of cover versions of songs by their favorite British heavy-metal bands. The result was released as an EP entitled *The $5.98 EP—Garage Days Revisited* (1987). The five-song record reached number 28 on the U.S. album chart, higher than any of Metallica's full-length albums had climbed.

In 1988 Metallica joined fellow hard-rock supergroups Van Halen and the Scorpions on a package concert tour billed as "Monsters of Rock." In September of that year, the band released its first single, "Harvester of Sorrow"; one of several works that reflect Hetfield's thoughts and feelings about Burton's death, the song fared poorly. "Harvester of Sorrow" became part of Metallica's next album, *. . . And Justice for All* (1988), which contains other songs that deal with death, among them "To Live Is to Die" and "Blackened." "One," perhaps the album's most ambitious song, was inspired by the novel *Johnny Got His Gun*, about a soldier who loses his arms, legs, sight, and hearing to a landmine in World War I and whose wish to be allowed to die goes unheeded. *. . . And Justice for All* climbed to sixth place on the U.S. album charts and soon went platinum, with more than one million copies sold. In 1989 *. . . And Justice for All* was nominated for a Grammy Award in a new category—best hard-rock or heavy-metal performance. Metallica, which performed "One" at the awards ceremony, was the clear-cut favorite before the event; nevertheless, in what was widely perceived as a snub, the band lost out to the veteran rock group Jethro Tull. Released as a single, "One" fared moderately well, rising to number 35 on the chart; it also became the first Metallica song to generate an accompanying video. Additionally, the single earned Metallica the 1990 Grammy for best metal performance, in what some observers regarded as a way to make amends for the previous year's rebuff. Metallica won a Grammy in the same category the next year as well, for their recording of the Queen song "Stone Cold Crazy," which had been included on the compilation album *Rubáiyát*, released by Elektra to celebrate the label's 40th anniversary.

Metallica began working with a new producer, Bob Rock, in 1991. The influence of Rock, who had previously worked with such less-than-hardcore metal bands as Bon Jovi and Mötley Crüe, is often cited as the source of the slicker, more mainstream style of the band's self-titled sixth album, released in June of that year. Though retaining the hard edge of earlier Hetfield-Ulrich compositions, the music could not be considered thrash or speed metal; instead, it reflected the influence of such classic metal bands as Led Zeppelin and Black Sabbath. The centerpiece of the album was the hit single "Enter Sandman." Another song, "Don't Tread on Me," which contains quotes from Revolutionary War figures, led many to believe mistakenly that Metallica had departed from the antiwar stance they had taken in "One." Other songs deal with familiar Metallica themes—suicide, drug addiction, and mental illness. *Metallica* also featured "Nothing Else Matters," the closest thing to a love song the band had ever recorded. Often referred to as the "Black Album" because of its ebony cover, *Metallica* sold over six million copies and was the band's first number-one hit. "The Unforgiven," a successful single from the album, earned Metallica the Grammy for best metal performance for the third consecutive year.

On October 12, 1991 Metallica launched their "Wherever I May Roam" tour, to publicize *Metallica*. That series of concerts extended almost two full years, cementing Metallica's reputation as the hardest-working heavy-metal band. In the summer of 1992, fellow heavy-metal giants Guns N' Roses joined Metallica's tour. "It was hard going on, dealing with [Guns N' Roses lead singer] Axl [Rose] and his attitude," Hetfield later told David Fricke. "It's not something we'd want to do again." In early August, at Olympic Stadium in Montreal, the technicians responsible for pyrotechnics installed two sets of fireworks onstage. Due to a misunderstanding, Hetfield thought there would be a single set, and during the performance he was standing directly over the other when it exploded. He was engulfed in a 12-foot column of flame that inflicted second-degree burns on his left hand and second- and third-degree burns on both his arms. He underwent daily 90-minute therapy sessions intended to help him regain the use of his damaged limbs, and although several doctors predicted that he might never again be able to play his guitar, by September he was playing limited solos and encores. By the end of the year, he was almost completely recovered. In 1994 Hetfield was injured in a hunting accident, and the 40 stitches he required to close the wound in his head made it necessary to cut his trademark long hair. Afterward he decided to keep his hair short, and the rest of the band soon followed suit, giving Metallica a whole new look.

In 1996, after a five-year hiatus from the studio, Metallica released *Load.* Entering the charts at number one, the album sold three million copies in its first three months. *Load* furthered the band's turn toward the more commercial, by incorporating more melodic elements into the band's usual hard-rock material and by toning down the roughness in Hetfield's singing. Also, Hetfield and Ulrich gave Hammett and Newsted more opportunities for creative input, which made the album more diverse stylistically. "Until It Sleeps," the album's biggest hit, is the first Metallica song composed by all four band members. *Load* also features another Metallica first: "Momma Said," an acoustic ballad. "It was a song that I wrote on the road in my hotel room that no one was supposed to hear," Hetfield confessed to James Rotondi for *Guitar Player* (October 1996). "I always envisioned it as an acoustic song. . . . I'd been thinking maybe I could sell it or collaborate with some country [music] guy. It's definitely not my style."

In contrast to the lukewarm reaction of some diehard metal fans, many music critics commended Metallica's stylistic changes. "With *Load,*" a reviewer wrote for *Rolling Stone* (July 11, 1996), "the foursome dams the bombast and chugs half-speed ahead, settling into a wholly magnetizing groove that bridges old-school biker rock and the doomier side of post-grunge '90s rock." According to Amazon.com (on-line), a *New York Times* critic declared that the band showed new and improved skills on their latest effort and noted that Hetfield had "committed himself to melodies, carrying tunes where he used to bark" and that he "no longer sound[ed] sheepish when he sings quietly." Later in 1996 Metallica headlined that year's Lollapalooza concert tour. Traditionally a showcase of alternative or "modern rock" performers, Lollapalooza had seldom featured a mainstream rock band, and Metallica's presence was cited as further evidence of the band's attempt to appeal to an audience whose tastes were shifting from heavy metal to alternative rock. Many longtime fans accused the band of "selling out" and getting too commercial. They voiced similar complaints about *ReLoad* (1997), for which Metallica made use of tracks left over from the *Load* recording sessions. Among the songs were "The Unforgiven II," a sequel to the popular track from *Metallica,* and "The Memory Remains," featuring backup vocals by Marianne Faithfull. A reviewer for *Musician* magazine (February 1998) declared that the album "captures one of rock's greatest bands at its peak."

In the fall of 1998, Metallica released the double-album *Garage Inc.* The second part is a collection of all the cover songs the band has ever recorded, including "Stone Cold Crazy" and the tracks on *Garage Days Revisited.* The first part consists of new covers, among them Metallica's remakes of songs by Bob Seger, the Misfits, Thin Lizzy, and the Blue Oyster Cult. The new tracks were recorded in just three weeks, giving them a raw, rough-edged sound quite different from that of the band's slicker recent releases. "The guitar might not be perfect, but there's a vibe of 'Let's go for it,' and I think the stuff sounds great because of that," Hetfield said in an interview for Amazon.com (on-line). In its review of *Garage Inc.*, Amazon.com described it as "a vital turning point for Metallica." In April 1999 Metallica joined the San Francisco Symphony Orchestra for two concerts, performing a selection of their hits, which had been rescored to include brasses and strings. Portions of the concerts were captured on the live album and videocassette *S&M* (1999), with the initials said to represent "San" and "Metallica."

In discussing his songwriting technique with James Rotondi, Hetfield explained, "I've got so many notes and little [things] that I write down every day. . . . Sometimes there's more than just a line and sometimes there's nothing—there's a song title and you just go, that's the beauty of it. I do have an idea of where I want to be, but I'll end up somewhere else, which is even cooler."

Currently, Metallica is at the center of a heated controversy within the music industry involving the availability of music on the Worldwide Web. Spurred by Ulrich, the group sued Napster, an online music community through which people have traded free music files. Citing copyright infringement, the group compiled a list of more than 300,000 people who had downloaded Metallica songs through Napster, a way of hearing music that until recently precluded the payment of royalties to the compositions' creators. An injunction issued in July 2000 prohibited Napster from distributing music, but it was stayed by a higher court. On October 31, 2000 Napster merged with the German media group Bertelsmann AG, in an arrangement that will guarantee royalty payment to artists. Metallica's lawsuit angered many of the group's fans, who claimed that Hetfield and his collaborators had turned their backs on their followers simply to accrue ever-greater wealth.

During Metallica's early years, Hetfield was a heavy drinker. At one point he and his bandmates were drinking a pint of schnapps every night. Such behavior soon earned the band the nickname "Alcohollica." By the early 1990s Hetfield had begun to curtail his consumption of alcohol. "I used up all my hangovers," he explained to David Fricke. "I was basically waking up, not feeling very good and not wanting to do a show. I started to feel a sense of responsibility . . . to play better."

Hetfield, who has never forgotten the disappointment he felt as a teenager at the lack of responses to fan letters he wrote, is known for his consistent graciousness with admirers; whenever possible he takes the time to chat and sign autographs. He is an avid hunter and a member of the National Rifle Association. He and his wife have a baby daughter, Cali. — B.S.

Suggested Reading: Amazon.com (on-line) Jan. 28, 1999; *Guitar Player* p49+ Oct. 1996, with photos; *People* p97+ Nov. 9, 1992, with photos; *Rolling Stone* p42+ Apr. 15, 1993, with photos; *International Who's Who in Music 1996/97*; Rees, Dafydd and Luke Crampton. *Rock Movers & Shakers*, 1991; *Rolling Stone Album Guide*, 1992; *Who's Who in America, 1998*

Selected Recordings: with Metallica—*Kill 'Em All*, 1983; *Ride the Lightning*, 1984; *Master of Puppets*, 1986; *The $5.98 EP - Garage Days Revisited* (EP), 1987; *. . . And Justice for All*, 1988; *Metallica*, 1991; *Load*, 1996; *ReLoad*, 1997; *Garage Inc.*, 1998; *S&M*, 1999

Courtesy of Dell Publishing, Inc.

Hickam, Homer H. Jr.

Feb. 19, 1943– Aerospace engineer; writer.
Address: c/o Delacorte Press, 1540 Broadway, New York, NY 10036

"I guess it's fair to say that there were two distinct phases to my life in West Virginia," the aerospace engineer Homer H. Hickam Jr. wrote in his best-selling memoir, *Rocket Boys* (1998). "Everything that happened before October 5, 1957 and everything that happened afterward." On October 4, 1957 the Soviet Union had launched *Sputnik*, the first manmade satellite to orbit Earth, thus inaugurating the age of space exploration. The next evening the 14-year-old Hickam gazed upward and watched what looked like a brilliantly lit planet glide across the night sky, and almost overnight, he and some of his friends in the small West Virginia mining town of Coalwood developed a passion for building rockets. "I wanted to be part of this great adventure, and the only way I could do that was to build my own rocket," Hickam recalled to Kyle Smith for *People* (April 19, 1999). Hickam's love of rocketry led him to a career in aerospace engineering, first with the U.S. Army Missile Command and then with the National Aeronautics and Space Administration (NASA), where his work encompassed spacecraft design, training of astronauts, and research and development in jet propulsion. *Rocket Boys: A Memoir*, a tale of a young man who longed to escape the coal mines of West Virginia in order to follow his dream of becoming a rocket scientist, delighted critics and readers alike. The feature film *October Sky* (1999) was based on Hickam's story.

The younger of the two sons of Homer H. Hickam Sr., a mine superintendent, and Elsie Lavender Hickam, a homemaker, Homer Hadley Hickam Jr. was born on February 19, 1943 in Coalwood, where the main source of employment was coal mining. In his early years he was nicknamed Sonny. Hickam's brother, Jim, was a star athlete in high school; he became a high-school teacher and football coach. After the 1957 launch of *Sputnik*, Wernher von Braun, the director of American rocket-development projects, became one of Hickam's biggest heroes, second only to Homer Sr. In a 1999 commencement address to students at West Virginia University, which was published on his Web site, Hickam said, "At night before I went to sleep, I thought about what Dr. von Braun might be doing at that very moment, and imagined that he was . . . working with a wrench on the fuel lines of one of his rockets." Hickam's parents wrote to Dr. von Braun, who sent Homer Jr. an autographed picture and some common-sense advice: "If you work hard enough, you will do anything you want."

Hickam and five of his friends from Big Creek High School established their own club, the Big Creek Missile Agency (BCMA). Using an illustration from *Life* magazine as their guide, they built their first rocket, using a flashlight casing and powder from 30 cherry bombs and firecrackers. When Hickam ignited its fuse, the rocket exploded into a ball of fire, destroying the fence around his mother's rose garden. The mishap made clear to the boys how little they knew about rocket science. "Until *Sputnik*, we had been indifferent to science and math, neither seeming to have much to do with our future," Hickam wrote for *Air & Space/Smithsonian* (February/March 1995), published by the National Air and Space Museum. Math and physics teachers at Big Creek High School soon found themselves with six very attentive students. Prominent among those teachers was Freida Riley, who demonstrated the principles of physics by using such ordinary items as balloons, wooden boats, and flatirons. "All the kids in southern West Virginia at that time were lucky to have these tough teachers," Hickam told a reporter for *Florida Today* (March 28, 1999, on-line). "I'm sure they felt we needed to be well-educated because we had a tough time in front of us."

While expanding their knowledge of mathematics, physics, and chemistry, Hickam and his BCMA friends continued with their experiments. Before long, residents in Coalwood began calling them the "Rocket Boys." Although their next 11 rockets failed, the teenagers were gradually improving their designs through trial and error. With each failure, the Rocket Boys made some important discoveries: for instance, that potassium nitrate was a more stable propellant than cherry-bomb powder; that rockets needed a strong casing to keep them from exploding; and that the diameter of the hole at the bottom of the rocket had to be cut precisely right to ensure a successful take-off. The boys bestowed the name "Auk" on each of their rockets, in honor of the flightless great auk, a seabird that was driven to extinction in the mid-1800s.

Hickam's mother often warned him against blowing himself up, but despite her worries about his safety as an amateur rocketeer, she supported what he was doing. His father, however, whose work always took precedence over his family, wanted Homer to aim for a career in mining, perhaps as a mine engineer, and he objected to his son's rocketry experiments. "I was born to lead men in the profession of mining coal. Maybe you were too," he told Homer, as quoted by Kyle Smith. Taciturn and emotionally cold, Homer Sr. rarely if ever showed affection toward or praised his younger son. Once, Hickam recalled to Smith, when his father was boasting about the exploits of his athletic older son, Hickam's mother said to her husband, "Could you please brag on Sonny once in a while?" "Dad just looked at her and said, 'About what?'" Nevertheless, Homer Jr. wrote in his memoir, he never doubted his father's love for him.

The BCMA finally enjoyed their first successful launch with the Auk XII, an aluminum tube filled with potassium nitrate and sugar that rose to an altitude of 100 feet. Following that triumph, rocket launches from a site in Coalwood became a weekly event, and the Rocket Boys started to receive "attention that had previously been lavished only on the football team," as Hickam wrote for *Air & Space/Smithsonian*. To build a rocket that would reach greater heights, Hickam realized he would have to learn more than what he had absorbed from his high-school textbooks. He found what he needed in a book written by a team of rocket scientists, *Principles of Guided Missile Design*—which Freida Riley gave the Rocket Boys as a gift. Studying from the book helped to buoy Hickam's spirits after he dropped out of school to work in the mine temporarily, after his father suffered a work-related injury. Later, with the encouragement of Riley, as a high-school senior Hickam entered the National Science Fair, where he and his fellow Rocket Boys (who did not attend the event) won first prize.

In May 1960 the BCMA fired their last rocket, the Auk XXXI, which was over five feet tall. The hundreds of people who gathered at "Cape Coalwood" that day included Homer's father, who had never before witnessed a lift-off. To honor him, Homer Jr. let his father pull the switch that triggered the firing. "The rocket flew perfectly, its smoke tracing a thin white line on the bright blue sky," Hickam wrote for *Air & Space/Smithsonian*, describing the beginning of what proved to be an ascent of nearly six miles. In *BookPage* (September 1998, on-line), Christopher Lawrence described the moment as the catalyst for what proved to be a permanent reconciliation between father and son: Homer Sr. had accepted the fact that Homer Jr. would not be following him into the coal mines.

After graduating from high school, Hickam enrolled at Virginia Polytechnic Institute (also called Virginia Tech), in Blacksburg. He graduated in 1964 with a B.S. degree in industrial engineering. (All the other Rocket Boys, too, completed college, and two became engineers.) He then enlisted in the army, where his six years of service included a tour of duty in Vietnam (1967–68), for which he had volunteered. "I felt I should go, and I had an ulterior motive: I wanted the experience," he told Christopher Lawrence. "I was young and invulnerable, and the war was something I wanted to taste—a crucible to pass through." In his West Virginia University commencement speech, Hickam said that his experience in Vietnam (where he earned the Bronze Star and the Army Commendation Medal) taught him two lessons: "Never fight a war for a people who don't care to fight it themselves, and never fight a war for the American people unless they are certain they want it fought."

After leaving the army, with the rank of captain, Hickam applied for a job with NASA but was turned down. In 1971 he began working as an engineer for the U.S. Army Aviation and Missile Command, at the Redstone Arsenal, in Huntsville, Alabama. Ten years later Hickam realized his long-held aspirations of working for NASA, when the agency hired him as an aerospace engineer. Among other assignments, he prepared astronauts for such missions as the deployment and repair of the Hubble Telescope and the first joint American-Japanese space flight. Before he retired, in 1998, Hickam served as the payload training manager for the International Space Station, a project run jointly by NASA and the European Space Agency.

Hickam has also enjoyed a second career, as a writer. In his essay "How I Came to Write the Memoir: *Rocket Boys*," published on his Web site, he said that he has "always been compelled to write." He published a neighborhood newspaper when he was in the second grade and later impressed his teachers with his short stories. While he was serving in Vietnam, his father accidentally threw out a book-length manuscript that Homer had written during junior high. Later, when he was an employee of the Army Aviation and Missile Command and NASA, Hickam wrote several freelance articles. In 1989 the Naval Institute Press published his first book, *Torpedo Junction: U-Boat War Off America's East Coast, 1942*, which chronicles American naval battles against German submarines that took place in the months after the U.S. entered World War II.

A call from Pat Trenner, an editor at *Air & Space*, in 1994 sparked the writing of *Rocket Boys*. In urgent need of a piece to fill several pages in the magazine, Trenner approached Hickam, who she had heard could write quickly. He complied by detailing his boyhood experiences in a 2,000-word article. Published in the February/March 1995 issue of *Air & Space*, "The Big Creek Missile Agency," as it was called, elicited a dramatic response. "Letters and phone calls from parents all over the country, even in England, came in a rush," Hickam recalled in "How I Came to Write the Memoir: *Rocket Boys*." One of the letter writers was a film producer, who asked if Hickam would consider selling the rights to his story. After hiring an agent, Hickam agreed to write a book about his rocket-building exploits, with the understanding that it would be made into a film. He wrote the whole book in just six months. A number-one *New York Times* best-seller, *Rocket Boys* was a finalist for the 1998 biography prize of the National Book Critics' Circle, and has been translated into eight languages. In a review of *Rocket Boys* for *Library Journal* (November 1, 1998), Gregg Sapp wrote, "Hickam's depictions and characterizations are vivid, and although his prose is a bit unpolished and overly folksy, he nevertheless tells his story with unselfconscious freshness." In an article posted on CNN's Web site (February 18, 1999), L. D. Meagher described *Rocket Boys* as "a thoroughly charming book that tells an irresistible story. The journey of Hickam and his pals from the Appalachian backwoods to the threshold of space was motivated by the same factors—pride, determination and grit—that carried Americans to the moon."

In 1999 Universal Studios released *October Sky*, which re-created the Rocket Boys' story. Directed by Joe Johnston, it starred Jake Gyllenhaal as Homer Jr., Chris Cooper as Homer Sr., and Laura Dern as Freida Riley. On the whole, the film satisfied Hickam, who had organized an unsuccessful campaign to keep *Rocket Boys* as its title and had insisted that profanity be cut from the original script. "There may have been swearing among the miners but we boys didn't talk that way," he explained, as quoted by Norman Julian in the Morgantown, West Virginia *Dominion Post* (May 9, 1999, on-line). *October Sky* made Hickam an instant celebrity. He found himself in high demand as a speaker at college graduations and on the lecture circuit. In addition, he earned praise from many West Virginia residents, who felt that the book and film portrayed them favorably.

Hickam's first novel, *Back to the Moon*, was published by Delacorte Press in 1999. The plot involves an ex-astronaut and former NASA employee who hijacks a space shuttle with the aim of landing on the moon in search of an alternative source of energy for earthlings. In a review for Amazon.com, Naomi Gesinger wrote, "Despite its high-tech premise and lunar locale *Back to the Moon* is no science fiction saga. It is, instead, a fast-paced technological thriller—filled with exceptional scientific know-how. (The author describes how spices are essential for astronauts because the normal aroma of food does not 'drift into the sinuses or caress the palate in a microgravity environment.')" Also in 1999, *Torpedo Junction* was reissued in paperback. Hickam's second memoir, *The Coalwood Way*, was published in 2000. In a review for *People* (October 23, 2000), Alex Tresniowski wrote, "Hickam's plain and tender stories of his first crush, losing his grandfather and craving his dad's love are truly beautiful and haunting." A third Hickam account of his life in Coalwood is in the pipeline.

Since he retired from NASA, Hickam has served sporadically as a consultant for the aerospace industry and has continued to write. In a scathing piece for *Space Policy Digest* (June 1999, on-line), Hickam declared that NASA "is failing the country" because it is not trying to develop a "new launch infrastructure." According to Hickam, the designs of NASA rockets are based on 40-year-old technology, and this accounts for many of the agency's well-publicized failures in recent years, such as the explosion of the Air Force's Titan-4 rocket in August 1999. "The result of all this: billions and billions of totally wasted dollars and the loss of some very important military and communications payloads," Hickam wrote. He also warned that Europe and China may surpass the United States in the development of new space technology in the next few years.

Since 1997 Homer Hickam Jr. has been married to Linda Terry, a jewelry designer and photographer. The couple live in Huntsville, Alabama, which is known as "Rocket City, USA." — D.C.

Suggested Reading: *Air & Space* (on-line) Feb./Mar. 1995; *BookPage* (on-line) Sep. 1998; *CNN* (on-line) Feb. 18, 1999; Homer Hickam Web site; *Library Journal* p96 Nov. 1, 1998; Morgantown, West Virginia *Dominion Post* (on-line) May 3, 1999; *People* p153 Apr. 19, 1999, p57 Oct. 23, 2000; Hickam, Homer H. Jr. *Rocket Boys: A Memoir*, 1998

Selected Books: *Torpedo Junction*, 1989; *Rocket Boys: A Memoir*, 1998 (reissued as *October Sky*, 1999); *Back to the Moon*, 1999; *The Coalwood Way*, 2000

Malcolm MacKinnon/Retna Ltd.

Hill, Julia "Butterfly"

Feb. 18, 1974– Environmental activist. Address: Circle of Life Foundation, P.O. Box 388, Garberville, CA 95542

In December 1997 23-year-old Julia "Butterfly" Hill climbed a tree to a spot 180 feet above the ground, in order to help defend the remaining 3 percent of the continent's original old-growth forest against destruction by a multimillion-dollar corporation. "I gave my word to this tree, the forest, and all the people that my feet would not touch the ground until I had done everything in my power to make the world aware of this problem and to stop the destruction," she said, as quoted on her Web site. Little did she know that she would spend the next two years in the tree branches, withstanding gales and a helicopter attack and in the process becoming an international figure in the environmental movement.

Julia Hill was born on February 18, 1974. Her father was an itinerant nondenominational preacher who traveled around the country with his family in a 32-foot trailer throughout Julia's childhood. She and her two brothers had a strict Christian upbringing; they were home-schooled in their early years and forbidden to use slang in the house. Julia grew up mostly in the company of adults, and her rebellion against her father's religious restrictions was limited to her dressing up in unusual outfits with her older brother. She later rejected her father's rigid religiosity, while retaining a firm belief in a "Creator," "Universal Spirit," or "Great Spirit"—terms she used when Sharon McCann interviewed her for *Ms.* (April/May 2000). According to McCann, "She speaks freely of being guided by 'visions,' and prayer is a major part of her life." Describing to McCann her father's influence on her, Hill told McCann, "His preaching was about speaking his truth and his understanding of that truth. And what I did for the last two years and what I'm continuing to do is speak my truth, and my understanding of truth."

When Hill was in her early teens, her family moved into a house in Jonesboro, Arkansas, where she went to a public high school. As a high-school student, she joined Student Activists for Earth (known by its acronym, SAFE). Its activities included planting trees and setting up and running a recycling program at the school, "which for that area was radical," as Hill told McCann.

After graduating from high school, Hill studied business and art at Arkansas State University; simultaneously, she worked three jobs, one of them as a model. After two years she dropped out of college and opened a restaurant/club with her father, who had left the ministry. As a bartender, she was beginning to put aside some money when she was involved in a serious car accident. The steering column of her car smashed into her head, putting pressure on her brain. Even after extensive surgery, she was unable to speak and had little sense of balance, and she suffered from hot flashes and fainting spells. Hill took 10 months to recuperate, and at the end of that time, she felt a need for spiritual rejuvenation. She joined some friends who were going to California; when they arrived in Humboldt County, they went to see the redwoods, and in that setting her emotions welled up—she has recalled falling on her knees and crying. It was clear to her that she needed to be in the midst of these ancient trees, and she decided to go back to Arkansas to sell her belongings and buy camping gear, and then return to her new spiritual home.

In the fall of 1997, Hill went back to California and approached the Environmental Protection Information Center (EPIC) to find out how she could contribute to the struggle to save the threatened redwoods. EPIC had been filing environmental-protection lawsuits and organizing protests against old-growth logging since the 1970s, but the struggle then going on in northern California was the fiercest yet. The EPIC staff directed Hill to the base camp of Earth First!, which had been organizing protests for more than a decade. In the 1980s Earth First! members had advocated "spiking" trees (a tactic in which people hammer a large number of nails into the trunks) to render them useless to lumber companies as well as potentially lethal to loggers. In 1988 the FBI assigned more than 50 agents to infiltrate the organization and catch members in the act of sabotage.

In 1990 Judi Bari, an Earth First! leader and former union organizer, began to insist on a policy of nonviolence and of developing an alliance with logging-industry workers. This idea challenged one of the tenets of the lumber industry: that the interests of workers and environmentalists are opposed. Far from agreeing to such an alliance, the three biggest companies, Pacific Lumber Co. (PALCO), Louisiana Pacific, and Georgia Pacific, hired Hill & Knowlton (H&K), a Washington, D.C., public relations firm, to send out false Earth First! press releases. *San Francisco Examiner* columnist Rob Morse said that a press kit he received from H&K and Pacific Lumber "read like a bad Hollywood version of what radicals talk like," according to Robert Sterling in the *Konformist* (October 1998, on-line). The fake press kit even misspelled the name of the Earth First! leader Darryl Cherney. An "Earth First Terrorism Manual" of no known origin also began turning up in the region. In April 1990 an FBI bomb expert, Frank Doyle, held an investigation training session at a Louisiana Pacific logging site, using pipe bombs to blow up cars by way of instruction. Those present at the training session may have picked up skills that went beyond self-protection. As Robert Sterling reported, on May 24, 1990 Bari and Cherney were almost killed by the explosion of a pipe bomb hidden under the driver's seat of Bari's car. Oakland police then arrested Bari and Cherney, accusing them of staging the attack. Though Bari revealed that she had received death threats for the past month, the police department refused to investigate. Instead, the department joined the FBI in a press campaign to discredit the organization.

Such was the level of the conflict Julia Hill walked into when she approached Earth First! On reaching the base camp, she found that the group's activities were being shut down for the rainy season. Someone suggested to Hill that she try to locate Earth First! activists at the annual Headwaters year-end rally, scheduled to take place in the small settlement of Stafford, 250 miles north of San Francisco.

Headwaters, which is owned by PALCO, is a 60,000-acre area that Jack Boulware, reporting for *SFWeekly* (November 11, 1998, on-line), characterized as "an environmental treasure" for the range and vigor of its habitats. PALCO is the nation's largest provider of old-growth redwood and Humboldt County's largest employer. The family-owned company, started in 1863, had for more than 100 years been considered environmentally conscientious, logging selectively and leaving behind enough trees to sustain the ecosystem. In 1986, however, Charles Hurwitz, a leveraged-buyout expert and owner of Maxxam, a Houston firm, took over the company; Hurwitz would become Hill's most lively adversary. A "corporate raider," Hurwitz had acquired the United Savings Association of Texas (USAT) for Maxxam in 1984, and his company's operation of the bank "resembled a money laundering operation," according to Robert Sterling. The junk-bond dealers Michael Milken and Ivan Boesky went to prison for their collaboration in the USAT swindle, but Hurwitz avoided that fate. Maxxam's first innovation after the acquisition of PALCO was to triple the company's rate of logging in the world's largest private ancient redwood forest. The president of PALCO, John Campbell, soon announced a commitment to cut every redwood in Headwaters by the year 2010. Environmentalists predicted that "within five years . . . Hurwitz will milk all the money he can from PALCO, then dump it and move on to another investment, leaving clear-cut hillsides and a decimated Humboldt County in his wake," as Jack Boulware wrote. Environmentalists point out that such activities lead to mudslides, pollution of streams, and the destruction of many species' habitats and people's homes. According to *Mother Jones* magazine, as Robert Sterling reported, Maxxam had already destroyed the Arizona desert water system in Pima County, and its acquisition of Kaiser Aluminum in 1988 had made it one of the top 10 producers of toxic pollution.

With their accelerated clear-cutting, Maxxam violated the Endangered Species Act, logging in an area that contained an Owl Creek observation station for the marbled murrelet (a threatened North American bird of which little is known) before a court-ordered survey was complete. The government sued Maxxam and the company had to pay a fine of $1.2 million. By 1998 Hurwitz had lost seven environmental lawsuits, but those confrontations with the law were apparently part of a larger plan "to extort funds from the federal and state government in exchange for the land they are recklessly destroying," as Robert Sterling put it: the government had to compensate Hurwitz and Maxxam for any property that it confiscated from them. Actions by both Republicans and Democrats contributed to the success of that strategy. After Hurwitz made a $20,000 campaign contribution in 1994 to California's Republican governor, Pete Wilson, the governor spearheaded efforts to get money allocated for the purchase of Headwaters. While Democratic California congressman Dan Hamburg urged a land-for-debt exchange, the state's Democratic senator, Dianne Feinstein, supported a cash buyout. That solution was seconded by President Bill Clinton, whose close friend and adviser Vernon Jordan had worked for Hurwitz as a lobbyist. (In disgust, Hamburg left the Democratic Party for the Green Party.)

In 1996 a massive rally was held against PALCO in Headwaters, and 1,000 people were arrested. But the clear-cutting continued. Then, a mudslide on New Year's Day 1997 clogged the Eel River and wiped out seven homes in Stafford, triggering lawsuits against PALCO by the homeowners. In 1997 a video showing Humboldt County Sheriff's Department deputies aiming pepper spray into the eyes of nonviolent protesters brought international media attention to Headwaters. The California Department of Forestry issued 103 citations of violations of state forest laws against the company within just three years.

When Hill arrived at Headwaters, a tree-sitting protest had been in progress for several weeks, and Earth First! activists were looking for a volunteer to sit in the biggest old-growth tree they had found. One night during a full moon, the team had constructed a six-by-eight-foot plywood platform and lashed it, 180 feet above the ground, to the branches of a tree that measured 15½ feet in diameter. When they were finished they named the tree Luna. While they estimated that Luna was 1,000 years old, PALCO put its age at approximately two centuries. Hill volunteered to sit in Luna's branches. Earth First! activists customarily adopt nicknames, to protect their identities in lawsuits, so Hill chose "Butterfly," her childhood nickname.

Hill's first "sit" lasted six days; after coming down to rest, she became ill and had to delay her next turn. On December 10, 1997 she climbed up to stay. On the first day a PALCO employee who specialized in removing protesters was sent to bring her down. Known as Climber Dan, he would climb above the sitter, cut down his or her supplies, then force the person to the ground. But this approach failed on Luna, which had lost the top of its trunk and topmost branches to lightning or a storm, and despite repeated attempts, Climber Dan could not dislodge Hill. A PALCO representative said that it would be too dangerous to remove her and assumed that the gale-force winds of winter would force her down. In fact, in the next two years heavy rains associated with El Niño arrived with 90-mile-per-hour winds. Butterfly recounted to the *San Francisco Chronicle* (December 6, 1998 on-line) that during one nighttime storm, "the wind blew me three feet sideways with every gust. I only made it because I emulated the branches that survived—by yielding to the wind. The ones that resisted broke." That winter temperatures fell to 10 degrees Fahrenheit and one foot of snow fell, but still Butterfly persisted. She felt that Luna was like "a domino": if she stood, so would other old-growth trees; if she fell, all the others would follow.

PALCO loggers working in the area argued with her. From their point of view, old-growth trees would sooner or later "just fall over and die anyway." Hill attempted to explain to them that the trees, as part of a delicate ecosystem, needed to fall naturally—and that "nature has a reason for trees falling into the soil," as Boulware wrote. When they ignored her, she began singing. The loggers then set up their chain saws to drown out her voice; when they stopped she continued the discussion. As Boulware wrote, she asked the loggers, "Do you have grandparents?" "Yeah. What of it?" one answered. "Why don't we just kill them?" yelled Hill. "They're just gonna fall over and die anyway!" "He got so angry!" Hill recalled. "And I knew it had hit home because that's really what they're saying. There's not a difference between our elder grandparents, human or in nature. They're all important." According to Hill, a few of the loggers quit their jobs after their conversations with her. "One day . . . a crew of grumpy loggers were moved sufficiently to take off their hats to her. In return she bowed to them and started crying," Boulware wrote. "It's difficult to paraphrase [Hill's] words because she speaks so much like a preacher," Boulware reported. In one of her "sermons" from the treetop, Hill said, as quoted by Robert Sterling, "I do think we can change. It happened with slavery. The idea that people could be private property was once accepted. We all have the potential to make a difference: you can be a hero or a destroyer. . . . We all have choices in life."

After six months Hill, with her Earth First! ground-crew support, broke the record for tree-sitting, and the mainstream media began to take notice. The actor Woody Harrelson visited her, and she was interviewed by cell phone from all over the country. She cited advice offered by the 1960s antiwar activist Abbie Hoffman on dealing with the media: "What he always stressed was that people need a hook. Quite simply, the mainstream media wasn't interested in the subject of forest destruction. . . . After breaking the tree sit record, surviving El Niño, being attacked by a helicopter, and harassed by Pacific Lumber security, what finally got their attention was that I had my birthday. I think that really shows the superficiality of our media. . . . I think the more important question is why I am up here, and what can others do about it." Since many journalists seemed more interested in her experiences as a tree-sitter than in why she had become one, she gave them the details of her life in Luna, explaining that she used an old margarine tub and bucket for a toilet, took sponge baths, and used candles for light and a one-burner propane stove to cook vegan meals.

But she succeeded in getting her message out. While in the tree, she served as a panelist on the U.N. Commission for Human Settlements World Gathering in Nairobi, Kenya, in May 1999; received thousands of visitors and became a regular commentator on *The Thin Green Line*, the Outdoor Life Network's environmental news show, through which she addressed eight million schoolchildren; received the Bioneers Award for Outstanding Achievement in Environmental Activism, in November 1998; was named "most admired woman" in a *Good Housekeeping* September 1998 readers' poll; was appointed a member of the board of directors of Earth Day 2000; received a Defender of the Woods Award—a painting from Native American political prisoner Leonard Peltier—in 1998; and served as keynote speaker, via cellphone, at the 1999 Environmental Law Conference on Ancient Forests. In addition, the United Steelworkers named her an honorary steelworker, New College of California awarded her an honorary doctorate in humanities, in 1998, and Local 713 of the United Brotherhood of Carpenters and Joiners presented a "care package" to her in 1999.

In the fall of 1998, at another PALCO site, David "Gypsy" Chain, an Earth First! activist, was killed by a redwood that fell in his direction after being cut during a protest. Several other demonstrators were standing within six feet of him when he died. Earth First! claimed that PALCO was violating logging restrictions, while the company claimed that Chain had been trespassing and that his death was an accident. Reacting to the increasing support that Hill was attracting to the cause, PALCO climbers cut the safety lines of other tree sitters and hogtied protesters and forced them to the ground. Repeating the action that had killed David Chain, loggers cut trees so that they would fall in the direction of activists, and they also cut trees in which people were perched. The Humboldt County police ignored PALCO's increasingly violent tactics.

Asked about the FBI's accusations that Earth First! practiced terrorism, Hill responded, according to Sterling, "The people I am in contact with from Earth First! are dedicated to peace, and [the accusations are] just an attempt to discredit those who want to save our forests. Let me ask you, Pacific Lumber wiped out seven family homes in Stafford with their logging practices: is that 'terrorist' activity? Who are the ones behaving like 'extremists'? Who are the ones who are 'radical'? They've been napalming the clearcut to destroy vegetation, dumping 40 gallons of diesel fuel per acre. You tell me who are the real terrorists." "According to the *Sonoma County Independent*," Sterling reported, "PALCO crews spread pesticides like 2-4-D and Roundup on already cut-over areas to prevent anything but commercial timber from growing in the area. To help the chemicals stick to the vegetation, the crews laced them with diesel fuel . . . [in] violation of state water quality regulations."

From the beginning of negotiations to sell Headwaters, from 1996 to 1998, the government had identified more than 250 instances of violations by Maxxam; while clear-cutting continued, Maxxam offered to sell to the government for $50,000 an acre land they had bought for $3,000 per acre. In March 1998 the federal government and government of California paid PALCO $480 million for a part of the Headwaters land that was to be turned into a public reserve. Although that land did not include Luna, publicity regarding Headwaters was having an effect. For example, Home Depot, the world's largest lumber retailer, announced that it will stop using old-growth wood by 2002, in order to protect rainforests and ecologically fragile areas.

After nine more months of negotiation, and a total of 738 days into Hill's tree-sit, PALCO finally agreed to save Luna and the surrounding area if Hill would leave the tree and pay $50,000 for the tree and land. The corporation tried to include the condition that Hill not speak about the case, but she refused. Instead, she became part of the fundraising effort to pay for the 200-foot buffer zone around Luna, as required by the so-called Preservation Agreement and Covenant. PALCO agreed to donate Hill's $50,000 payment to Humboldt State University for scientific research. Hill's fundraising efforts also led to the creation of the California-based Circle of Life Foundation, whose mission, according to its Web site, is "to develop a sustainable culture of life on Earth, rooted deeply in love and respect for the interconnectedness of all beings." Upon her descent from Luna, on December 18, 1999, Butterfly told the *San Francisco Chronicle* (December 20, 1999, on-line), "I asked God to use me as a vessel, so I guess you have to be careful what you ask for."

In 2000 Hill continued to work for environmental causes. Her book, *The Legacy of Luna: The Story of a Tree, a Woman, and the Struggle to Save the Redwoods*, was published in the spring of 2000. —V.K.

Suggested Reading: *Albion Monitor* (on-line) Oct. 1998; *Konformist* (on-line) Sep. 1999; *lunatree.com*; *Ms.* p36+ Apr./May 2000; *SFWeekly* (on-line) Nov. 11, 1998; Hill, Julia Butterfly. *The Legacy of Luna: The Story of a Tree, a Woman, and the Struggle to Save the Redwoods*, 2000

Holmgren, Mike

June 15, 1948– General manager, head coach, and executive vice president of football operations for the Seattle Seahawks. Address: Seattle Seahawks, 11220 N.E. 53d St., Kirkland, WA 98033

In 1992, after 25 years of feckless play on the gridiron, the Green Bay Packers called on Mike Holmgren to lead the team back to the glory it had known under Vince Lombardi. A legend among coaches, Lombardi had steered the Packers through their most victorious period, in the 1960s. During his regime the Packers won a string of National Football League (NFL) championships, including the first two Super Bowls, and helped tiny Green Bay, Wisconsin, justify its moniker, "Titletown." Then, in 1967, Lombardi accepted the head coaching post with the Washington Redskins. The five coaches who followed him in Green Bay failed to emerge from the long shadow he had cast; none produced even a winning record, until Mike Holmgren brought about one of the most miraculous franchise turnarounds in NFL history.

Mike Blake/Archive Photos

Mike Holmgren

With largely the same roster that had produced a 4–12 win–loss record the year before his arrival, Holmgren guided the Packers to a record of 9–7 in his rookie year as coach. During the next six seasons, Holmgren built the Packers into one of the NFL's true powerhouses and carved his own distinct place in Green Bay's football lore. He had seven consecutive winning records; made six straight play-off appearances; joined John Madden as one of only two coaches with at least one post-season victory in five successive years; and led his team to two Super Bowl appearances, including one championship, in 1996. His accomplishments made him a commodity coveted by downtrodden NFL franchises. In January 1999 he accepted a position with the Seattle Seahawks—which until he arrived owned the league's longest streak of seasons (10) without a post-season appearance—as vice president of football operations, general manager, and head coach. The deal, reportedly worth $4 million per year to Holmgren, made him the highest-paid general manager and head coach in the NFL, one with unparalleled power over all personnel decisions.

Michael George Holmgren was born on June 15, 1948 to parents of Swedish and Norwegian descent. Growing up in San Francisco, he was in many ways the paradigm of an all-American boy. He met his lifelong sweetheart, Kathy, at a summer church conference when both were 13. Shooting rapidly toward his adult height—six feet, five inches—the teenage Holmgren was popular among his peers. He was class president and the star quarterback at San Francisco's Lincoln High School and was named California's Prep Athlete of the Year in 1965, the year he graduated. After high school Holmgren attended the University of Southern California (USC), where he played quarterback from 1966 until 1969, when injuries relegated him to a backup role. Warm and outgoing, he toyed with the idea of becoming an actor, perhaps inspired by his fraternity brother and fellow USC athlete, Tom Selleck, who would later star in the television series *Magnum P.I.* His backup status notwithstanding, the St. Louis Cardinals selected Holmgren as their eighth pick in the 1970 draft. He left USC temporarily to spend time in both the Cardinals' and the New York Jets' training camps but made the cut in neither. After he earned his B.S. degree, in business finance, he got his teaching certification and married Kathy.

Holmgren began his first year of teaching at his alma mater, Lincoln High School, in 1971. A year later he transferred to nearby Sacred Heart High School to teach history, economics, and mechanical drawing. For a stipend of $300 above his salary, he helped coach the school's football team. During his tenure at Sacred Heart, from 1972 to 1974, Holmgren endured the most unsuccessful run of his coaching career—24 straight defeats. It is probable, though, that the players' poor performance was unrelated to Holmgren's coaching: among other difficulties, the team did not even have practice facilities.

From 1975 to 1980 Holmgren taught and coached at San Francisco's Oak Grove High School. To ensure that student athletes did not suffer from lack of support, Holmgren and other teachers formed a rock band, Big Bop and the Choppers, which performed to raise funds for the school's athletic programs. (Holmgren played the trombone.) On the playing field, he marshalled Oak Grove to a Central Coast sectional championship.

In 1981 Holmgren became offensive coordinator and quarterback coach for San Francisco State University. The salary for that position did little to help his home life: he and his wife, who by then had four daughters, lived in a one-room apartment, and, according to Paul Attner, the family almost qualified for a government-subsidized free-lunch program. His financial situation improved (though his workload shrank) in 1982, when Brigham Young University (BYU), in Utah, hired him as a quarterback coach. There, he served a more prestigious football program whose success was predicated on its high-octane passing offense. During his three years at BYU, Holmgren molded Steve Young into one of the college game's most dangerous passers, and in 1984 BYU captured its first national championship.

Holmgren's accomplishments at BYU attracted the attention of the legendary San Francisco 49ers coach Bill Walsh. Speaking of his decision to recruit Holmgren as a quarterback coach, in 1986, Walsh told Paul Attner, "He had limited experience. But I knew of him from his playing and coaching time in the Bay Area and he seemed the man I could personally train. He had an outstanding football mind, he had excellent communication skills, he had a natural easy-going but assertive personality, and he proved to be a hands-on guy who was an excellent teacher. The consummate coach." Under Holmgren, 49er quarterbacks and future Hall-of-Famers Joe Montana and Steve Young flourished.

In 1989 George Seifert, who had succeeded Walsh as head coach of the 49ers, promoted Holmgren to offensive coordinator; for the next three years Holmgren pulled the strings for one of the NFL's most vaunted offenses. While he served as coordinator, none of his offensive units ranked lower than third in the league. He became particularly well-regarded for his coaching efforts in 1991, when both Joe Montana and Steve Young were out with injuries. Under Holmgren's guidance, third-string quarterback Steve Bono led the 49ers to win five of their last six games of the season. Holmgren adjusted the offense to accommodate the relatively inexperienced Bono, and during that final winning streak, the 49ers outscored their opponents—including three destined for the play-offs—by an average of 16 points per game. But it was a case of too little, too late: having lost six of their first 10 games of the season, they failed to make the post-season for the first time since 1982. Nevertheless, Holmgren's display of adaptation under duress made him a hot commodity for a head-coaching position. Speaking of Holmgren, Gill Haskell, an assistant to Holmgren in Green Bay, said, as quoted on the Packers' official Web site, "My impression is that he has prepared himself to be a head coach. Many people get head coaching jobs that never expected to get them. He didn't. . . . He's been planning this for some time."

Yet it seemed doubtful that Holmgren would land in Wisconsin. For one thing, he was being courted by six other NFL teams. Furthermore, the offensive schemes he employed—the so-called "West Coast Offense"—were built around an intricately devised and executed passing game. The harsh weather conditions of Green Bay, situated on the banks of Lake Michigan in the northern reaches of Wisconsin, seemed unsuitable for a passing game. Finally, Green Bay is an NFL city unlike any other. A college town whose predominantly blue-collar residents proudly bear the collective nickname "cheeseheads," Green Bay is home to the only publicly owned franchise in professional sports. The specter of Vince Lombardi looms large over the city partly because his winning ways put Green Bay on the map, amid the big cities that dominate the rest of the league's landscape, and partly because Packer fans identified thoroughly with his system of football. Lombardi emphasized not sophistication but a workmanlike mixture of discipline, precision, and execution. His teams lined up against their opponents and in a straightforward fashion simply outplayed them. Since Lombardi's era, such a style of play has been described as "smash-mouth" football.

Perhaps because, as he put it to Paul Attner, he has always thought of himself as a "history teacher who happens to be a coach," Holmgren proved himself equal parts Lombardi-esque motivator and offensive mastermind. He proceeded by turning to his most basic tools: chalk and a blackboard. "Coach Holmgren was the first head coach I ever had that in my first meeting with him went to the drawing board and began diagraming plays and showing us what the offense meant and what he wanted," Calvin Jones, a Packer running back, told Thomas George for the *New York Times* (January 26, 1997). "It really swept me off my feet. Most head coaches are more administrators. Coach Holmgren is a man of great football knowledge. That, alone, gives him instant respect from his players." Holmgren's first goal was to establish a winning attitude and a sense of professionalism among the members of the team, which had posted only two winning seasons in the previous 19. During training camp and the football season, he demanded efficiency from his assistants and players alike. "I insist with my guys here that when we come to work, we work. We don't screw around," he explained to Paul Attner. "I mean, who wants to be here to one a.m.?" Seeking the trust of his players, he tried to be sensitive to their needs. For example, he regularly hired financial consultants to help his players manage their money and plan for retirement. "All this is a way for me to show the guys that I care about them more than just as football players," he explained to Ira Berkow for the *New York Times* (January 2, 1997). "It's a way for me to show it, rather than just say it. And I believe it helps. I'd like to think that a player will look at me a little differently, and as a football player he'll pay more attention to what I say."

In his first season in Green Bay, Holmgren showed that he was much more than simply an architect of offenses. He and his defensive coordinator, Fritz Shurmur, improved a formerly mediocre defense and placed the offense in the hands of a young, wild-armed quarterback, Bret Favre. Holmgren intuited correctly that, with direction, Favre would develop into a special player. In 1992 the Packers rolled up a record of nine wins and seven losses and placed second in the National Football Conference's (NFC) Central Division, just missing the play-offs. Nonetheless, Holmgren was named the NFL's Coach of the Year.

In 1993 Green Bay dropped to third in the NFC Central, again with nine wins in 16 games, but they clinched a berth in the NFC's wild-card play-off game against their intra-divisional rival, the Detroit Lions. The Packers defeated the Lions with a 40-yard touchdown pass from Favre to wide receiver Sterling Sharpe during the last minute of the game, but in the next round of the play-offs, they were beaten by the Dallas Cowboys. In 1994 Green Bay again made the post-season as the wild card, and again they defeated the Lions in a close game. But they were eliminated in the play-offs for the second straight year, the victims of a powerful Dallas Cowboy team. The Packers completed the 1995 regular season with an 11–5 record—the third-highest win total in team history—and in control of first place in the NFC's Central Division. Facing off against the Atlanta Falcons in the first round of the play-offs, they won by 17 points, then followed up that victory by beating the San Francisco 49ers in a notably physical game. Having earned a spot in the NFC title game, which would determine the Super Bowl entry, Green Bay again faced their nemesis, the Dallas Cowboys. Though the Packers led most of the game, Dallas mustered 14 unanswered fourth-quarter points to defeat the Packers once more.

Nearly three decades of frustration ended in 1996. The Packers capped a stellar regular season, in which they won 13 out of 16 games, by overpowering the 49ers and the Carolina Panthers in the play-offs. In their Super Bowl showdown against the New England Patriots, the overmatched Massachusetts team fell to the Packers by a score of 35–21. That year Green Bay's offense led the league with a team-record 456 points scored, while their defense allowed opponents a league-low 210 points. It was the first time since the 1972 season that the same team led the NFL in both categories; the 1996 season has since been noted as one of the few in league history dominated by a single club. In recognition of his achievement, the NFL named Holmgren Coach of the Year for the second time.

Holmgren and the Packers repeated their regular-season success in 1997, with a record of 13–3, and continued their domination of the NFC's best in the play-offs, by handily defeating the Tampa Bay Buccaneers and then the 49ers. However, the Packers failed to repeat as Super Bowl champions, instead losing to the Denver Broncos. Plagued by injuries throughout the 1998 season, the Packers failed to capture first place in the NFC Central, which they ceded to the Minnesota Vikings. That year Green Bay clinched a wild-card berth against the 49ers, and Holmgren lost his final game as chief of the Packers on a last-second touchdown pass thrown by the 49er quarterback Steve Young, his former protégé.

In the early 1990s Jimmy Johnson built a football dynasty in Dallas as both the head coach and chief talent evaluator, with the power to draft, trade, and cut players, and since then NFL organizations have come to embrace the idea of placing all control over football operations in the hands of a single visionary. Coaches, in turn, like having the power to acquire the talent they need to execute their particular strategies without having to contend with the possibly counterproductive personnel decisions of a general manager. For the players, the placement of power in one person's hands cuts bureaucracy and is the quickest way to a winning ball club. In the late 1960s and early 1970s, such legendary coaches as Bud Grant, Don Shula, Tom Landry, and Lombardi ran their own operations. The growth of football as big business in the 1970s raised the stakes and made dealing with personnel and general management on top of coaching too large for one person to handle. That precipitated the division of duties and the consequent emergence of personnel specialists, who ran intricate talent-scouting operations and negotiated player contracts with agents. With the implementation of a league-wide salary cap that limits each team's personnel expenditures, the entire process has become even more complex. Yet a number of the game's best current coaches—among them Bill Parcells, Dan Reeves, Jimmy Johnson, and Dick Vermeil—have been granted more overt authority over personnel decisions. Their number now includes Holmgren, who has become firmly ensconced in the upper echelon of NFL coaches.

In January 1999 Holmgren signed a deal with the Seattle Seahawks (owned by Microsoft co-founder Paul Allen) that made him the single most powerful football operations head in the NFL. His official titles include vice president of football operations, general manager, and head coach, and his authority extends into all facets of personnel decision-making, from the front office to the field. Furthermore, his contract, reportedly worth $4 million per year, makes him the highest-paid coach and general manager in the league; that distinction was held previously, for a short time, by George Seifert, who signed with the Panthers for $2.5 million. So far, Holmgren appears to be worth the investment: Seattle seems to be emerging from the poor talent decisions and mediocre play that have plagued the Seahawks for some 23 years. At the end of the 1999 NFL season, the team racked up a record of nine wins and seven losses, clinching the AFC West Division title and their first play-off appearance in 11 seasons. Indicative of Holmgren's influence on a team, on November 1, 1999 he and the Seahawks played a Monday night contest against the Packers in which, in front of a sold-out crowd at Green Bay's Lambeau Field and a nationally televised audience, Seattle clobbered Holmgren's former team, by a score of 27–7.

Holmgren has said that, as important as football is to him, his family will always come first; by his own account, he has strived for efficiency as a coach partly so that he can spend less time at work and more time with his family. He reportedly has lunch once a week with his mother; he also has daily coffee-break visits from his wife in his office and goes out on a "date" with her every Friday night. He makes it a point to be home for supper on Thursdays, because, as he explained to Paul Attner, "with Swedes, the dinner table is very important. Growing up with my parents and grandparents, we would use the dinner table to discuss world problems." Holmgren also uses his spare time to raise funds for local community charities, play golf, read history books, and ride his Harley-Davidson motorcycle. He and his wife have four grown daughters: Emily, Gretchen, and Calla and Jenny, who are twins.

In 1997 North Park College (Kathy, Calla, and Jenny's alma mater) gave Holmgren an honorary doctor of laws degree. That same year Green Bay renamed one of its streets Holmgren Way. Symbolic of Holmgren's place in Packer history, the street intersects Lombardi Avenue two blocks from Lambeau Field. — T.J.F.

Suggested Reading: *New York Times* B p10 Jan. 2, 1997, with photo, VIII p1 Jan. 26, 1997, with photo; *Sporting News* p12+ Jan. 27, 1997, with photos, p30+ June 22, 1998, with photo; *Sports Illustrated* p70+ Jan. 27, 1997, with photo

---

J. Bauer, courtesy of Sarah Blaffer Hrdy

Hrdy, Sarah Blaffer
(HUR-dee)

July 11, 1946– Primatologist; anthropologist
Address: Dept. of Anthropology, One Shields Ave., University of California at Davis, Davis, CA 95616

"Mother" is among the most evocative words in the English language. Beyond its explicit meaning, it often connotes a sense of comfort, warmth, and home. Yet, as the primatologist and anthropologist Sarah Blaffer Hrdy wrote for *Natural History* (December 1995), "The belief that mothers instinctively nurture their offspring—one of [Western culture's] most cherished ideals and a view widely accepted even in scientific circles—has been receiving bad press of late." Citing recent, highly publicized cases of child abandonment and infanticide as well as the 18th-century practice of wet-nursing, in which a new mother would hire a stranger to suckle her infant until the child was weaned, a number of social philosophers, psychologists, and feminist anthropologists have concluded that humans have somehow lost their maternal instincts. In *Mother Nature: A History of Mothers, Infants, and Natural Selection* (1999), the most definitive work on this topic to date, Hardy has offered a new perspective, arguing that mother love is indeed a biologically based human trait, albeit one that is hardly involuntary and predetermined. She has reasoned that because humans differ from other primates in their cooperative approach to child care, mothers have evolved to take into consideration how much social support they are likely to receive in caring for a child before they commit themselves to doing so.

With her groundbreaking studies of infanticide among langur monkeys in India in the 1970s and her comparative analyses of mothering techniques employed by primate species, which continue to this day, Hrdy has made arguably the greatest impact on the fields of primatology and anthropology since Jane Goodall lived among the chimpanzees in Gombe, Tanzania, in the 1960s. *Mother Nature,* which is the fulfillment of decades of scholarly research and technical observation, has been hailed as a lucid and thoroughly documented work and confirms Hrdy's place as one of the most provocative and influential thinkers working in the social sciences.

A fifth-generation Texan, Hrdy was born Sarah C. Blaffer on July 11, 1946 in Dallas. Her father, John H. Blaffer, was heir to an oil fortune; her mother, the former Camilla Davis, hailed from a family of well-to-do local bankers. The substantial wealth her family commanded afforded Hrdy a view of mothering from the perspective of privilege. "My mother's idea of good management was that if a child became too attached to a nanny, it was time to hire a new one, lest maternal control be diminished," she wrote in *Mother Nature.* "This meant that I was reared by a succession of governesses." Her upbringing was not unusual among "the particular tribe of elite Texans into which I was born," Hrdy pointed out, noting, "No one ever doubted that my mother loved her five children."

Although she would later credit her mother and maternal grandmother, Kate Wilson Davis—both of whom she described in *Mother Nature* as "closet bluestockings"—for engendering in her a love of books, ideas, and scholarship, Hrdy left home at the first opportunity. "I wanted out of there," she told Natalie Angier. "When I went off to [school] at 16, it was wonderful." She attended Radcliffe College (now an institute within Harvard University), in Cambridge, Massachusetts, where she first encountered anthropology and learned "that people actually studied animals to learn more about humans." Upon completing her B.A. degree, summa cum laude, in 1969, she enrolled in the filmmaking program of Stanford University, in California. Before long Hrdy concluded that she was not cut out for the movie industry, so she began taking classes in population biology, which led her to return to Cambridge to pursue a graduate degree in anthropology at Harvard. (In the *New York Times* [February 8, 2000], Natalie Angier reported that Hrdy also "considered becoming a novelist.")

Between 1971 and 1975, while working toward her Ph.D., Hrdy spent approximately 1,500 observation hours near Mount Abu, in Rajasthan, India, documenting the behavior of the region's langur monkeys. She hoped to record the effects of overcrowding, which, many scientists believed, explained the high incidence of infanticide committed by langur males. "But as I soon realised, even at very high [population] densities langur males were quite tolerant of infants—except infants that were unweaned and belonged to females the males hadn't mated with," she recalled in an interview with David Concar for *New Scientist* (December 11, 1999, on-line). With the focus of her research suddenly shifting from the social stresses of overcrowding to reproductive strategies, Hrdy looked for an explanation for the murderous behavior of the male langurs in the theories of the evolutionist Charles Darwin, who famously postulated that fertile females of a species select the best possible mates from a pool of available competing males. "Only in this instance, infanticidal males were canceling the female's last 'choice' and forcing her to choose him instead," Hrdy told Concar. "This extraordinarily destructive behaviour, I hypothesised, was actually adaptive for the perpetrator because the mother whose unweaned infant was killed would become fertile again sooner than if she had continued to nurse, increasing the new male's chances of breeding with her." Hrdy also discovered that langur females were as adaptive reproductively as the males. She observed that langur males do not kill the infants of females with whom they have mated and that the females—including those already pregnant or with infants—copulated with as many males as they could, thereby protecting their babies from harm. "What from a male view looks like promiscuous behavior is from a female's view assiduously maternal," she explained to Concar.

Perhaps because of its brutal nature and the questions it raises about parental instincts in humans, what Hrdy discovered was not widely accepted immediately. Skeptics either doubted her observations or explained away the Abu monkeys' murderous behavior as an aberration brought on by unknown stresses. Nevertheless, Hrdy's early work has weathered decades of scrutiny and analysis. Infanticidal behavior has since been observed in dozens of other animal species, and her studies on the phenomenon anchor many current theories in primatology and anthropology. "Her work on infanticide was revolutionary," Meredith Small, a Cornell University primatologist, told Natalie Angier. "Now, we've had 30 years of hypothesis-testing, and she's right. There aren't many people who can propose a paradigm shift in their lifetime and watch it unfold." As Hrdy strived to distinguish herself as a graduate student and social scientist, she took on the responsibilities of a new family and worked to define herself as a person. At the outset of her graduate work, she met and fell in love with Daniel Hrdy, a fellow anthropology doctoral candidate, whose surname means "proud" in Czech. The couple married in 1972. "It was also during those years that I first developed a feminist consciousness," Hrdy wrote in *Mother Nature.* "Often, I felt like a lonely castaway throwing message bottles from a desert island as I struggled awkwardly to become a better scholar by taking into account female as well as male perspectives. My aim was to correct biases long implicit in evolutionary thinking without simply substituting new biases of my own in the process."

After Harvard granted her a Ph.D., in 1975, Hrdy was appointed to a series of posts at the school: from 1975 to 1976 she was a lecturer in biological anthropology; from 1977 to 1978 she functioned as a research fellow; and in 1979 she served as a research associate at the university's Peabody Museum of Archaeology and Ethnology. Meanwhile, she continued to make field trips to India with her husband. Increasingly, her research focused on the roles females play in mating practices and evolution, and this work began to attract as much attention as her work on infanticide. She questioned the long-held notion that males, being the more physically aggressive gender, were more actively involved in the evolution of a species, while females played a passive role at best. Accounts of her efforts in India appear in the books *The Langurs of Abu: Female and Male Strategies of Reproduction* (1978) and *The Woman That Never Evolved* (1981). Both books brought her professional respect and recognition; *The Woman That Never Evolved*, in which Hrdy argued that the behavior of females determines primate social organization, struck a chord with the strengthening feminist movement and thus garnered her popular fame as well.

The Hrdys stopped making field trips to India in 1979, primarily because the political climate on the subcontinent at the time made their research more difficult. In part because "there was a lot of suspicion of American researchers working in India," as she explained to David Concar, and also because Hindus regard langur monkeys as sacred, she and her husband were prevented from trapping the monkeys to collect the blood samples that their work now required. Furthermore, the couple had just become parents for the first time, and field work in the jungle was not conducive to raising a child. "The decision works like a Rorschach test on journalists writing about my work," Hrdy quipped to Concar. "Some seem unable to look beyond the fact that I made this compromise. All they see is that 'she gave up her career for her family.'" In reality, Hrdy did not give up her career; rather, she adapted it to her new situation by relocating from the field to the classroom and embarking on the two books that would make her famous. Her new path, however, presented her with a basic conflict:

the needs of a newborn and the demands of scholarship both required abiding concentrated attention. "Not the least of the emotions that bubbled up was a whirring resentment—the kind I identify with the most primitive portions of my brain—toward my daughter's father, by then a medical doctor and infectious-disease researcher who could go off and spend hours in a lab while I tried to eke out of the daily interruptions enough time to write," she acknowledged in the preface to *Mother Nature*.

Being a person who has "never been content to agonize when I could analyze instead," as she has described herself, Hrdy was driven to investigate her conflicting impulses, and their wider ramifications, in the anthropological and evolutionary terms she knows best. The result of her nearly two decades of inquiry is *Mother Nature*. The book, which relies on documented research of the animal kingdom and relates it to various personal and objective observations about human parenting, presents a theory of motherhood that combines Darwin's postulates on natural selection with feminist principles. The portrait of a mother she paints is vastly different from the prevailing nurturing and passive image first depicted by "moralists" and "Victorian evolutionists." To Hrdy, all female primates—including human females—are the sum total of environmental stresses, inherited traits, and individual ambitions that converge to determine whether or not they will raise a child, abandon it to another's care, or even kill it. In the light of her research and insights, a mother's bond with her child becomes more complex than previously thought, and such phenomena as infanticide and child abandonment become more understandable, if no less disturbing. Further complicating the notion of motherhood from a human perspective, argued Hrdy, are such medical and technological advances as ultrasound and amniocentesis, which "enable women to spend decades in a career and still look forward to bearing a healthy infant," and birth control, which allows women to prevent or—in the case of so-called "morning-after" pills and abortion—terminate unwanted pregnancies.

"Often confessional, rarely dispassionate, [Hrdy] marshals facts and anecdotes in support of her case," Anne Magurran wrote in her critique of *Mother Nature* for the *New York Times Book Review* (January 23, 2000). "Despite its academic leanings the book is a compelling, if sometimes harrowing, read." More pointedly, Susan Caba concluded in a review for *Salon* (December 9, 1999, on-line), "Hrdy's book is an exhaustive—and sometimes exhausting—weaving of the scientific literature on innate and learned maternal behaviors, liberally spiked with explorations into the social history of human motherhood. . . . Her use of Darwinism with a twist of feminism will no doubt raise the hackles of critics who believe that Hrdy has chosen flat and overly convenient tools for her probe. But even her detractors will have a hard time denying the volume of her research."

Hrdy described the central message of *Mother Nature* to David Concar as "motherhood means trade-offs." "And that human mothers need a lot more help rearing offspring than other apes. This is the first book to really come out and say that humans must have evolved as cooperative breeders." As evidence, Hrdy has cited the fact that human children are by and large dependent on adult support in one form or another until the age of about 18. An extended period of nurturing another human, she has argued, is not sustainable by just one mother; it requires the support of allomothers, or adults other than the child's biological parents who can provide stable relief care. Given her observations on human mothering, Hrdy has expressed concern about the rising number of cases of neglected and abandoned children, as well as the fact that many of these unwanted children are surviving to become parents themselves. "I am convinced that current child-rearing practices jeopardise the future of the species, not in the sense that the species will die out, but in the sense that we are altering the conditions under which natural selection can operate," she explained to Concar. "People who grow up without committed kin are less likely to develop along the usual path. They're more likely to be narcissistic, not so able to put themselves in another person's shoes, and in extreme cases, unable to feel any empathy at all for other people."

A professor of anthropology at the University of California at Davis since the mid-1980s, Sarah Blaffer Hrdy is herself a three-time mother. Her and Daniel Hrdy's children are their daughters Katrinka, a recent Harvard graduate, and Sasha, who will enroll at Harvard in the fall of 2000, and their son, Niko, the only one of the three, she told Natalie Angier, "who shows signs of becoming a naturalist." — T.J.F.

Suggested Reading: *New Scientist* (on-line) Dec. 11, 1999, with photo; *New York Times* F p1 Feb. 8, 2000, with photos; *Salon* (on-line) Dec. 9, 1999; *Contemporary Authors* new revision series vol. 35, 1992; Hrdy, Sarah Blaffer. *Mother Nature: A History of Mothers, Infants, and Natural Selection*, 1999

Selected Books: *The Black Man of Zinacantan: A Central American Legend*, 1972; *The Langurs of Abu: Female and Male Strategies of Reproduction*, 1980; *The Woman That Never Evolved*, 1981; *Mother Nature: A History of Mothers, Infants, and Natural Selection*, 1999

Courtesy of Radio One

Hughes, Cathy

Apr. 22, 1947– Founder and chair of Radio One network. Address: Radio One, 100 St. Paul St., Baltimore, MD 21202

"I'm considered a maverick," Cathy Hughes told an interviewer in 1998. "People who don't like me call me crazy. But I'm crazy like a fox. And I never let it bother me." Hughes is the founder and chairperson of Radio One, which, since its launching, in 1980, has grown from a single station to a network of 26 stations in nine cities, making it the nation's largest black-owned radio group. For about 14 of Radio One's first 20 years, Hughes hosted a daily talk show from a glassed-in booth on H Street, in Washington, D.C., where passersby could watch her at work. With *The Cathy Hughes Show*, as it was called, she developed a reputation as a fiery rhetorician and passionate spokesperson for African-Americans in the nation's capital and elsewhere. Charging herself with the mission of "standing up for those who don't have a voice," as she phrased it in an interview with Keith L. Alexander for *Emerge* (September 1999), she has strived to inform, educate, and entertain urban blacks via the airwaves. On its first day of public trading on the stock market, in 1999, Radio One raised more money than any other black-owned company ever had in an initial public offering. Hughes is the first African-American woman to head a publicly traded firm in the United States. "I want to be to the black community what Katharine Graham [the publisher of the *Washington Post*] has been to the white community—quality," she told Marc Fisher for the *Washington Post* (March 6, 1995). "Call me a racist. Call me a loudmouth. But don't tell me I'm not professional." "I tell the young sisters to keep their eye on the prize and accept the fact that racism and sexism are the realities in a black woman's existence," Hughes declared in a statement on a Radio One Web page. "I don't attempt to change the world of radio, but I attempt to create my own world where racism and sexism do not prevail and to do that you must be the owner." Currently, 90 percent of Radio One's 700 employees are African-American.

The first of four siblings, Cathy Hughes was born Catherine Elizabeth Woods on April 22, 1947 in Omaha, Nebraska. Her father, William A. Woods, was the first African-American to earn an accounting degree from Creighton University, in Omaha. Her mother, Helen E. Jones-Woods, was a nurse; before her marriage she played trombone in the International Sweethearts of Rhythm, an all-female orchestra founded in about 1937 as a fund-raising group for a black orphanage. As teenagers Helen and some of her bandmates dropped out of school—the Piney Woods Country Life School, in Mississippi—"so they could be free to play swing music instead of gospel," as Charisse Jones reported for *Essence* (October 1998). The Piney Woods Country Life School was founded by Helen's father, Laurence C. Jones, in 1909; still operating, it is one of the country's last predominantly black, private boarding schools for grades seven through 12.

Cathy Hughes grew up in an Omaha public housing project. Her mother told C. Fraser Smith for the *Baltimore Sun* (August 30, 1999) that as a youngster, Cathy "didn't mind sticking her neck out if she thought it was for the better." From an early age Hughes loved radio. When she was nine her parents bought her a transistor radio; at night she would tuck it under her pillow and listen to the Everly Brothers and the Platters. A good student, she was the first African-American to attend the Duchesne Academy of the Sacred Heart, an elite Roman Catholic girls' school in Omaha, where the students wore white gloves and stockings and curtsied when nuns walked by. Her difference from the other students was driven home to her when it was suggested that she have a white priest, rather than her father, accompany her to the school's father-daughter banquet. The priest, however, saw to it that Hughes attended with her father. In addition, Hughes told Marc Fisher, the priest showed up at the affair with "a whole mess of black guys—street people—he had gone out and recruited from a mission."

When she was 16, Hughes became pregnant. Her discovery of her condition shocked her, she told Charisse Jones, "because I knew I had my whole future ahead of me. I refused to admit to myself that I was pregnant. I gained 82 pounds; I was so depressed." She dropped out of school and married the baby's father, Alfred Liggins. The baby, named Alfred Charles Liggins III, "became my motivation and my inspiration," Hughes told Charisse Jones. Her son was just a toddler when her marriage dissolved; afterward, Hughes raised him alone. Despite that responsibility, she finished high school, and between 1966 and 1969 she was enrolled at Creighton University, where she took courses in business administration and helped out at the campus radio station. During the next two years, she took classes at the University of Nebraska in Omaha. (She did not earn a bachelor's degree.) At about this time, according to a Radio One on-line biography of her, she invested in KOWH, a black-owned Omaha radio station. "After nine to 12 months," the bio reported, "spending as much as 60–70 hours a week with her 'investment,' she knew radio inside and out and had worked every job at the station."

In 1971 Hughes came to the attention of Tony Brown, the dean of the School of Communications at Howard University, in Washington, D.C.; Brown hired her as a lecturer. Her creativity, efforts to improve the curriculum, and strong work ethic impressed him, and in 1973 he appointed her sales manager at WHUR-FM, the university radio station. In 1975 she was promoted to general manager, a first for a woman in radio in the Washington, D.C., area. "It's really a story of Cathy outworking most people and out-thinking most people," Brown told Jones. "It all goes back to Cathy having a vision of what she wants to do and implementing her vision, which may be a simple statement, but that's not a simple thing to do in life."

During her approximately three years as WHUR's general manager, Hughes created a nightly program designed to appeal to single women who lived alone. Called *The Quiet Storm*, it consisted of a mix of smooth love songs spun by a sultry-voiced disc jockey. The format, now considered standard in radio, was an innovation when Hughes proposed it. *The Quiet Storm* proved to be a ratings gold mine, and it helped boost the station's advertising revenues from $300,000 to $3.5 million. Nevertheless, according to Charisse Jones, Howard University turned down Hughes's request to seek a license for the *Quiet Storm* format, claiming that it wasn't commercially viable. In 1978 Hughes resigned from her job and went to work as general manager at WYCB-AM, in Washington. She left that job, too, before the end of the year, and, having vowed that she would never again relinquish her creative freedom, she decided to strike out on her own.

In 1979 Hughes and her second husband, the television producer Dewey Hughes, began taking steps to buy the small AM radio station WOL. The target of a federal graft investigation, WOL was up for sale at a price of $950,000. The Hugheses put up $100,000 of their own money and $450,000 from investors, including $300,000 from Syndicated Communications, a powerful force in black broadcasting. After rejections from more than 30 banks, they secured the balance of the money, and in 1980 they made the purchase. They set up a company, called Radio One, with the slogan "Where information is power"; for some time Radio One was synonymous with WOL. Eager to create a platform to address the concerns of the black community, Hughes instituted an all-news-and-talk format. "We did a format search, which showed that the one area no one was addressing [for black audiences] was news and information," she told Phyllis Stark for *Billboard* (January 14, 1998).

As general manager, Hughes soon moved Radio One's headquarters from the upscale Georgetown section of the District of Columbia to a former drug den in the heart of a mostly black Washington neighborhood. Used needles still lay on the floor, and she swept them up herself. The site was only a few blocks from where a young woman named Catherine Fuller had been brutally murdered a few weeks earlier by a street gang known as the Eighth and H Street Crew. The killing reinforced Hughes's determination to reach out to the community. "Here was a woman with my name, killed by young people in the community I wanted to serve," she told Courtland Milloy for the *Washington Post* (December 16, 1986). "But instead of shunning them, or being afraid of them, I set out to embrace them." Hughes met with neighborhood gangs in a peacemaking effort. Then she built a glass booth, known as a "radiovision room," so that members of the public could watch broadcasts in progress. In 1981 she launched her own daily afternoon talk show, *The Cathy Hughes Show*; she remained its host until 1995.

Although the station began to gain listeners, for a long time it lost money. Hughes and her husband began falling behind on loan payments, and the station slipped further and further into the red. Thinking they had no chance of success, Dewey pleaded with Cathy to move with him to California, where he hoped to break into the music industry, but she balked. Finally, he threatened to end their eight-year marriage. "He gave me a deadline," Cathy Hughes told Fisher: "Move to him or we get a divorce. I don't know if that was a bluff. I filed for divorce. We are still friends, we talk all the time. . . . It was strictly my refusal to fail. Never would I choose a business over a family, but that's what happened in my life." She bought out Dewey's interest in the station and, to cut expenses, gave up her apartment. After one of her investors found her asleep at her console, he arranged for her to be tutored in budgeting and management.

In response to the demands of her bankers that she abandon the talk format and return to playing soul music, Hughes agreed only to a partial change; she insisted on keeping the talk component for the so-called morning-drive time slot. "They said they would not approve [an additional] salary for that slot," she told Phyllis Stark, "so I became a [morning] talk-show host." (A few years later she returned WOL to all talk.) Working in her glassed-in studio, she would wave to people on the street and say hello to them on the air, sometimes interrupting an exchange with a caller to do so. She would also take cigarette breaks outside and then tell her listeners about the people she had just met. Her audience, and support for the station, steadily grew. Some people took to writing "I listen to WOL" on checks and dollar bills in hopes of impressing station advertisers. In 1986 Radio One recorded a profit for the first time.

That year, despite what she considered an exorbitant price, Hughes bought WMMJ-FM, another Washington, D.C., station. She did so partly on the advice of Alfred Liggins, her son, who told her, as she recalled to Jones, "We've got to get the signal." Liggins meant the coveted FM signal, without which Radio One had little chance of surviving. Soon after the purchase, the bankers who had financed it told her that the station would become a viable commodity only if it were tailored for a white audience. They demanded that she install a computer program called Evergreen, which offered music by such artists as Barbra Streisand, Barry Manilow, and Neil Diamond. "Asking me to do Evergreen was like asking [the black activist] Angela Davis to sell memberships in the Klan," she told Marc Fisher. Nevertheless, she complied—and the station's ratings plummeted. After 18 months Hughes dispensed with Evergreen, and after that the station's listenership once again climbed. Its ratings ultimately surpassed those of such major FM contenders as WHUR and WKYS.

Meanwhile, Hughes had periodically agitated for various causes by means of her talk show. In 1986, for example, she led a protest against the *Washington Post* after the newspaper printed on the cover of its Sunday magazine a picture of a black rap artist accused of murder. In 1990 she took to the air to rally support for Washington's mayor, Marion Barry, who had been imprisoned after police, in a sting operation, caught him smoking crack cocaine. According to Marc Fisher, her campaign for Barry generated enough money from listeners to defray "nearly the entire amount Barry was charged to cover the cost of his imprisonment." (She also held a tea that raised $25,000 for the mayor's wife, to help her move out of D.C.) Her enthusiasm for Barry evaporated when he spoke from prison with an interviewer not associated with her station. In 1994 Hughes came under fire from the Hispanic community after scolding African-Americans for allowing Hispanics to move into historic black Washington, D.C., neighborhoods and to take jobs away from blacks. Hughes claimed that her intent had been to compliment Hispanics for their initiative and point up the need for greater cooperation within the black community. "Black folks run black folks out of business, yet they do business with anybody else in the community," she told Keith Alexander.

In another incident, which took place in 1998, three years after she had given up her talk show, Hughes returned a $500,000 loan Radio One had received from the state of Maryland. Denouncing the loan on the air as "blood money," she acted to protest the Maryland legislature's expulsion of Larry Young, a black state senator, for alleged ethics violations. "I couldn't be comfortable taking money from a group I felt had just lynched a brother before my very eyes," she explained to Jones. Soon afterward she hired Young as a talk-show host on WOLB, in Baltimore. "I am a nationalist," she told Jones. "And it's been hard for me to get even Black folks to understand that to love yourself and your peoplehood first doesn't mean you disrespect other cultures and other people. It just means you like being Black."

In 1992 Hughes bought radio station WWIN from the black Philadelphia broadcaster Ragan Henry. "It brought me great joy because we bought [it] from an African American, which meant we were keeping it in the family," she told Stark. In 1994, in one of the nation's biggest transactions between minority-owned broadcast companies, Radio One bought WKYS for $34 million, bringing its stable of stations to seven. Between March 1998 and December 1999, Hughes purchased 18 stations, increasing the network's total to 26, in Atlanta, Baltimore, Boston, Cleveland, Detroit, St. Louis, and Richmond, Virginia, as well as Washington, D.C., and Philadelphia. Her strategy, according to Katy Bachman in *Mediaweek* (August 23, 1999) and Chandrani Ghosh in *Forbes* (September 20, 1999), is to acquire "underperforming" stations in some of the cities with the greatest numbers of African-American consumers and then attract listeners by means of programming changes; she also expands the advertising sales force at each station. Ghosh reported that in 1998, Radio One earned a profit of $841,000 on revenues of $46 million. In its August 30, 1999 issue, *Broadcasting & Cable* estimated the market value of Radio One to be $924 million.

Earlier, Alfred Liggins had told Elizabeth A. Rathbun for *Broadcasting & Cable* (March 22, 1999) that the proceeds from the company's initial public offering (IPO) would be used to buy new equipment, pay off debts, enable Radio One to negotiate future loans at lower interest rates, and acquire additional radio stations. The IPO, held on May 6, 1999, raised $172 million.

Much of the day-to-day business of running Radio One is handled by Liggins, who began working at the company in 1985, as a salesman, and became its president in 1989. (He also serves as chief executive officer.) "It was kind of hard to put your faith and your future in someone whose diapers you used to change, who wouldn't clean their room or who used to lose their house keys," Hughes told Keith Alexander. Liggins, who graduated from the executive MBA program at the Wharton School, at the University of Pennsylvania, in 1995, told Alexander that he and his mother are cut from slightly different cloth. "My mother is the type of person who thinks it's important to sit at the switchboard and talk to listeners," he said. "You would never see me at a switchboard. That would take me away from a telephone call I would make to buy another station."

Cathy Hughes's honors include an honorary doctoral degree from Sojourner-Douglas College, in Maryland; the Trumpet Award, given by the Turner Broadcasting System to honor the achievements of African-Americans; and the 1988 People's Champion Award of the National Black Media Coalition. She reportedly works 12 hours a day and exercises by walking several miles daily. She is also a heavy smoker. According to Jones, Hughes "spouts Scripture one minute and talks like a homegirl from southeast D.C. the next. She has been called a demanding boss, yet some of her employees hug her when she walks by." Since about 1990 her "significant other," as she has identified him, has been Jeff Majors, a harpist who also composes and arranges music.

"I don't allow critics to push me into self-pity, because all of us make mistakes," Hughes told Jones. "Now I just try and correct them and do better. Sometimes the criticisms are not all wrong. Sometimes they're outright lies. And sometimes they're communiques from a higher source, telling me I need to check myself." — J.K.B.

Suggested Reading: *Billboard* p61 Jan. 14, 1995, with photo; *Black Enterprise* p22 May 1995, with photo, p130+ June 2000, with photo; *Broadcasting & Cable* p14+ Aug. 30, 1999, with photos; *Ebony* p100+ May 2000, with photo; *Emerge* p44+ Sep. 1999, with photos; *Essence* p133+ Oct. 1998, with photos; *Forbes* p86+ Sep. 20, 1999, with photo; *Mediaweek* p16+ Aug. 23, 1999, with photos; *Washington Post* B p3 Dec. 6, 1986, with photo, D p2+ Mar. 6, 1995, with photos; *Working Woman* p60 June 1999, with photo

---

Courtesy of 3 Arts Entertainment

Hughley, D.L.

(HEW-glee)

Mar. 6, 1965– Comedian; actor. Address: c/o Capital Cities, ABC Inc., 77 W. 66th St., New York, NY 10023

ABC's sitcom *The Hughleys* has won praise from critics and earned high ratings from audiences. Focusing on an African-American family who move from the inner city to an affluent suburban neighborhood, the show tackles weighty issues such as race relations and cleverly balances them with the ordinary concerns shared by all families—such as car-pooling and coping with in-laws. *The Hughleys* was the highest-rated new sitcom of the 1998–99 season. The show's creator and star, D.L. Hughley, who based the program on his own life experiences, says that its success can be attributed to its roots in real life. He has also admitted that the show's popularity is a double-edged sword. "I'll tell you what," he has said, according to the WTNH-TV Web site, "in the middle of conversations I'm having with people, they'll go 'Hey man, this ain't goin' in the show, is it? OK, now I'll tell you.' Everybody's really aware of it."

If life experience is the foundation of *The Hughleys*' success, the show should have a long run. In his 35 years D.L. Hughley has already had several lives. He was born Darryl Lynn Hughley in California on March 6, 1965, the third of the four children of Charles, a maintenance worker for Delta Airlines, and Audrey, a homemaker. Growing up in the gritty South Central section of Los Angeles, Hughley lived in an insular world, an experience he would later channel into both his stand-up routines and *The Hughleys*. "I didn't know that white people lived in L.A. until I was 19," he told Virginia Rohan for the *Chicago Tribune* (October 24, 1998). "I would see them on *The Price Is Right* and they'd go, 'I live in L.A.,' and I'd think, 'I've never seen you. Where are you at?' Then, one day when I was 19, I went to Westwood, where UCLA is, and I went, 'Oh, this is where they hang out.' It was an eye-opening experience."

Hughley found motivation scarce in his household. "There was never talk of what we would do after—college or in the future," he told Jeremy Helligar for *People* (November 9, 1998). As a result, Hughley became apathetic about schoolwork; by the time he got to high school, he had earned a reputation as the class clown, which was a cover for his fear of appearing ignorant. "I felt intimidated and didn't know the answers," he told Joy Bennett

Kinnon for *Ebony* (September 1999). In 10th grade Hughley was kicked out of school for fighting. He then joined the Bloods, a notorious L.A. street gang. "I watched people do a great deal of physical harm to each other," Hughley told Jeremy Helligar. "You know it's wrong, but you don't have the courage to be different." Hughley stayed with the Bloods until a cousin of his was killed in a gang-related incident and the body was dumped on Hughley's aunt's doorstep. "It was a terrible thing," Hughley, who was 18 at the time of the murder, told Eugene Bowen for the *Michigan Daily* (January 31, 1997, on-line). "And what was even worse was that he was in a rival gang, the Crips. So I couldn't even go to his funeral, or I might've been shot." Hughley took the tragedy as a sign that he should get out of gang life for good.

In 1982 Hughley applied for a telemarketer position at the *Los Angeles Times* and set about the task of assimilating into the larger world. Knowing that it would be difficult to get the job without a college degree, Hughley figured out a way to circumvent the system. "I paid a guy I knew at Cal State Long Beach $100 to tell personnel that I was just a few credits short of graduating from college," he explained to Allison Samuels and Rick Marin for *Newsweek* (October 26, 1998). The ruse worked, and Hughley was hired, eventually working his way up to sales manager. "I worked there for 10 years," he recalled to Samuels and Marin, "had all my kids there, bought my house there and used all their medical insurance until I left to do this. Most people had odd jobs trying to make it. I had a real job."

While working at the *Times*, Hughley met a woman named LaDonna, who was immediately drawn to Hughley's sense of humor. "I'd sit by him, and he'd always make me laugh," she told Jeremy Helligar. The pair were married in 1986 and shortly thereafter they had their first child, their daughter Ryan. His wife was not the only person who thought Hughley was funny; after several years of continual prodding from friends, Hughley decided to try his hand at stand-up comedy, participating in a local comedy showdown. "I picked up the microphone," he told Jeremy Helligar, "and I knew this is what I was supposed to do." After a string of local appearances, he left his day job to pursue comedy full-time. Before long he was offered a shot at hosting *Comic View* on Black Entertainment Television (BET). This was followed by several appearances on HBO's *Def Comedy Jam*. While he found his experiences there very positive, Hughley has since expressed a reluctance to return to the often raunchy atmosphere of those venues. "For me, *Def Comedy Jam* and BET's *Comic View* . . . were simultaneously the best and worst things to happen to black comedy," he explained to David Handelman for *TV Guide* (January 9, 1999). "The best because it exposed some really talented people who wouldn't otherwise get a chance. But the worst because a lot of people think that's all we're capable of doing."

The comedy industry quickly began to take notice of Hughley, and he was offered his own HBO special. That show gave him the chance to give depth to his material, which he was unable to do as host of *Comic View*. The show became the highest-rated special in HBO's history and was nominated for a CableAce Award; its success gave rise to an offer from CBS to star in the sitcom *Double Rush*, created by the producers of *Murphy Brown*. Hughley was hesitant, fearing that a commitment to a television schedule would limit his time on stage. He eventually agreed, but the show, which debuted on January 4, 1995, was poorly received by both critics and audiences and was not picked up for the next season. Hughley soldiered on, however, honing his stand-up routine in clubs around the country. He soon attracted the attention of Chris Rock, a wildly successful comedian in his own right, who began to champion him. "I always loved D.L. and would rave to my manager about him, like, 'This guy's the guy, I don't know why you're chasing these other wack guys,'" Rock told David Handelman.

In early 1998 Hughley began formulating the idea of using his own life as the basis for a sitcom. Rock supported the concept, and *The Hughleys* was born. Debuting in the fall of 1998, the show was a success, immediately making the list of TV's 20 highest-rated prime-time programs. Supporters of the show attribute its success not only to the reality-based situations but to Hughley's generally funny nature. "He's like a young Redd Foxx," Rock said to Jeremy Helligar. "D.L. can generate funny even when it's not on the page."

Ironically, while the show's foundation in reality may be the key to its success, Hughley's real family has had to adjust to the sitcom's demands on its star. Discussing his wife's reaction to the show, Hughley said to Virginia Rohan, "The [sitcom] house looks like the house we live in. The bedroom looks a lot like our bedroom. They even have our wedding pictures in the bedroom. And if you tell another woman that you love her—that would take some getting used to, even if you were well-indoctrinated, and she's not. She can't even look at us do the show live. She has to look at the television monitor." Also, Hughley's schedule has afforded him less time to spend in his Los Angeles home with his wife and children—his son, Kyle, and daughters, Ryan and Tyler.

The Hughleys was renewed for the 1999–2000 season, airing at 9:30 p.m. on Friday nights. "It's the first time a black show has led off the night since *The Cosby Show*," Hughley observed to Joy Bennett Kinnon. In the fall of 2000 the show moved from ABC to the United Paramount Network. Hughley is featured in the Spike Lee concert film *The Original Kings of Comedy* (2000). Shot in February 2000 at the Charlotte Coliseum, in North Carolina, one stop in an extensive, enormously successful national tour, the movie also presents stand-up comedy performances by Cedric the Entertainer, Bernie Mac, and Steve Harvey. Enthusiastic critics included David Denby, who wrote for the *New Yorker* (September 4, 2000) that the picture "offers a stunning reproof to the endless media racket in which commercialized 'rage' is packaged in CDs and on TV for the suburbs." *The Original Kings of Comedy* turned a respectable profit at the box office.

"I'm truly blessed," Hughley told Eugene Bowen. "I love what I do. I've been all over the world, and I've even performed before Bill Clinton. How can I not like what I do? There's nothing better." —J.K.B.

Suggested Reading: *Ebony* p158+ Sep. 1999, with photos; *TV Guide* p36+ Jan. 9 1999, with photos; *People* p117+ Nov. 9 1999, with photos; *Newsweek* p73 Oct. 26, 1998

Selected Television Shows: *The Hughleys*, 1998–

Selected Films: *The Original Kings of Comedy*, 2000

Courtesy of Australia Zoo

Irwin, Steve

Feb. 22, 1962– Herpetologist; wildlife conservationist. Address: Australia Zoo, Glass House Mountain Tourist Route, Beerwah, Queensland 4519, Australia

Bounding through the Australian outback like an amphetamine-fueled kangaroo, pouncing on crocodiles with leonine grace, and punctuating his sentences with buzzwords like "Crikey!," "Gorgeous!," and the cautionary exclamation "Danger! Danger! Danger!," Steve Irwin at times appears more like a real-life version of Atari's Pitfall Harry than a trained wildlife professional. "The man is like Tarzan, George of the Jungle, [and] Indiana Jones all wrapped up in one," his wife, Terri Irwin, told *Current Biography*. As the host of the hit cable-TV show *The Crocodile Hunter* and its new spin-off, *Croc Files*, Irwin draws viewers in more than 100 countries, who respond to his enthusiasm for wildlife conservation as much as his penchant for courting danger. "I take great pride in having never been maimed by a shark, snake, or croc," he told Richard Huff for the New York *Daily News* (May 30, 1998). "I have had some encounters, what I would call mistakes. I try very, very hard to avoid making those mistakes." Despite his reputation for being a daredevil, Irwin's primary aim is not thrill-seeking, but educating others on the subject of wildlife conservation. When he is not hosting his highly rated program, Irwin and his wife serve as directors of the Australia Zoo, which boasts more than 550 animals on 16 acres of land. In addition, he works with government groups and other wildlife professionals, teaching them the proper methods of handling animals. "Our whole reason to be on this planet is to educate people about wildlife," he told Huff. "I will die doing that. I have a gift."

Stephen Robert Irwin was born on February 22, 1962 in Victoria, Australia. "On my sixth birthday I was given a gift from my dad and my mum that was to be the start of our animal collection fauna park," Irwin wrote in his book, *The Crocodile Hunter: The Birthday Present Was a Python and Other Adventures* (1997), which was co-written by his wife, Terri. "I was totally excited to receive a 3.6-metre scrub python, although the difference in our sizes meant that I couldn't play with it, or I might have become its next meal!" Although his parents, Bob and Lyn Irwin, worked as a plumber and housewife, respectively, their real passion was wildlife, particularly reptiles. Eventually, Terri Irwin explained to *Current Biography*, Irwin's father said to himself, "I'm not going to be able to do what I want to do with reptiles in Victoria. It's too cold a climate, and there isn't the same reptile population as there is in the Northern States of Australia." In November 1970 Bob Irwin took the family on a holiday on the country's Sunshine Coast, in Queensland; there, they came across four acres of available land, which they purchased in the same year and established as the Queensland Reptile and Fauna Park. Steve Irwin thus spent his childhood immersed in the study of reptiles.

Since the Irwins funded the park on their own, they were responsible for procuring the animal collection as well. The resulting excursions into the Australian wilds planted the seeds of Irwin's career path. "In those early days, Dad and I shared the most marvelous adventures," Irwin wrote in *The Birthday Present Was a Python*. "We'd travel the Aussie outback for weeks at a time, catching crocs, snakes and lizards for the park. I'd help Mum raise orphan joey kangaroos and wallabies and spend endless nights rehabilitating injured birds and other animals." The park officially opened its doors in 1973, charging 40 cents for adults and 20 cents for children.

Meanwhile, when Irwin was nine years old, his father became involved in the East Coast Crocodile Management project, a government-run program that sought to end the slaughter of crocodiles by fearful locals. "My family felt that our participation in the croc management programme was the best way to protect the crocs from humans," Irwin wrote in *The Birthday Present Was a Python*. "Our aim was to catch and relocate them before they made the mistake of showing themselves around populated areas." Irwin began assisting his father in catching the crocodiles and moving them to safer territory. It was during this operation that Irwin got his first experiences with "jumping" (or catching) crocodiles. While scanning the water one night, Irwin and his father came upon a three-foot crocodile just in front of their boat. "Steve's dad said, 'OK, you give it a go, son,'" Terri Irwin told *Current Biography*. "He was so excited to have the opportunity that he dove off the boat and grabbed it perfectly. . . . And then he realized he was in a little bit of trouble. In the deep, murky water, he couldn't get to the surface, the croc was too powerful, and was taking Steve down to the bottom of the river. All of a sudden, Steve felt his dad's arm come down, fish around, grab him and the crocodile and plunk them both in the boat." As Irwin put it in *The Birthday Present Was a Python*, "That was the start of my croc-jumping career. By the age of 12 I'd become quite skilled at spearing myself out of the front of a boat."

After graduating from high school, Irwin spent time traveling, surfing, and camping out in the Australian wildnerness. In addition, he studied part-time at the Darling Downs Institute of Advanced Education. (He apparently did not earn a certificate or a degree.) By the time he was in his 20s, Irwin had begun working with the Crocodile Management Program in earnest. For months at a stretch, he searched for crocodiles in the bush. Directed to catch the largest and most dangerous of the reptiles, in time he became the top croc-catcher in Australia. Irwin's success with the program was a result of his natural ability to work with and understand animals, as Terri Irwin explained to *Current Biography*. "Nobody was able to catch crocs like Steve because he lived with them, and would see things that nobody has ever documented about wildlife," she said. In 1985 Irwin spent seven weeks living in the trees of the rainforests on the Cape York Peninsula and studying live goannas. "Living like a possum, I'd occasionally come down out of the trees for a feed," he wrote in *The Birthday Present Was a Python*. "Fortunately, God blessed me with orangutan arms. To study arboreal animals, you've got to become one: I could climb anything."

In 1991 Irwin's father turned the reins of the Queensland Reptile and Fauna Park over to him. That same year he met Terri Raines, a conservationist from Oregon. Raines, when not running her family's construction business, was head of Cougar Country, an organization that worked toward the preservation of predatory mammals. Raines was in Australia on vacation when she decided on a whim to visit Irwin's park. Watching Irwin perform a demonstration with the crocodiles, Raines was mesmerized. "His enthusiastic love for these animals was contagious," she wrote in *The Birthday Present Was a Python*. "It became impossible to see freshwater crocodiles as snappy little monsters. As he continued his talk I found my focus shifting from these most impressive crocodiles to the man who was speaking so passionately about them." She was further impressed after speaking with Irwin. "It sounds funny, but I have met men in the United States who I swear just worked with wildlife to get chicks," she told Richard Huff. "After the demonstration, I figured he was taken, I asked him a few wildlife questions and he was really on the mark." Irwin and Raines were married in June 1992.

Also in 1992, Irwin began filming *The Crocodile Hunter*, a 10-hour documentary covering his exploits in the outback. The idea for the project had come about in 1990, when the television producer John Stainton approached Irwin about recording some of his adventures on film. At one point Irwin showed Stainton a tape from his archives, which showed him catching crocodiles for the relocation program. Stainton was so taken with what he saw that he showed the tape to a network executive at Australia's Channel 10, suggesting that the documentary become a regular series. "He sat there quiet for a few minutes, then asked if the whole thing was like this," Stainton told Christopher Noxon for the *New York Times* (June 6, 1999). "I told him, 'Yeah,' and he said he wanted the first episode on the air in two weeks."

The Crocodile Hunter, which first aired in 1992, was an immediate success, earning strong ratings throughout Australia. The show was soon syndicated to other countries, among them England, New Zealand, and Sweden. In 1996 it was picked up in the United States by the cable channel Animal Planet, an offshoot of the Discovery Channel. Since its debut in the States, it has become the channel's highest-rated show and has earned a Daytime Emmy Award nomination for outstanding children's series. Viewers respond to Irwin's run-and-gun shooting style as well as to his hyperactive narration. "Most wildlife shows are shot from a distance with a telephoto lens, but I can't hang back like that," he told Noxon. "I've got to get right up there, right up in the face of these animals." (Irwin does a lot of his own camera work. At other times the action is photographed by a crew from the Discovery Channel.) Much of Irwin's fame is due to the efforts of his wife. "Steve and I are a really great combination," she told White. "He's got great instincts for animals, and I'm very good at promotion." In the last few years, Irwin has been seen on *The Tonight Show* and *The Rosie O'Donnell Show*, and his adventures have been parodied on the comedy shows *South Park* and *Mad TV*. Irwin has also been seen on American television as a spokesman for Pentax cameras, demonstrating the camera's resilience while he leaps from the jaws of crocodiles. In the fall of 2000, a line of *Crocodile Hunter*–themed toys will hit the shelves. In addition, an animated series is currently being planned, and talks are underway to make a feature-length documentary on *The Crocodile Hunter* in 2001. The show has even spawned a drinking game, in which participants consume alcohol according to the catchphrases Irwin uses.

Steve and Terri Irwin live with their young daughter, Bindi Sue, on the grounds of the Australia Zoo. The Irwins also own 1,600 acres, which they use as a wildlife preserve, where they study and document the activities of various animals. Within the next few years, the Irwins hope to purchase more land for similar uses. "We're developing plans now, along with the acreage we bought, we're looking at land with rattlesnake dens on them in the Western United States, and we're looking at property in Tasmania," Terri Irwin told *Current Biography*. "When we're not doing wildlife as a profession, we're doing wildlife for fun." When he is not filming *The Crocodile Hunter*, Irwin works ceaselessly toward educating people about wildlife conservation. "Every single day of our lives involves wildlife education," he wrote in *The Birthday Present Was a Python*. "We must teach, spread the word, the wildlife gospel. Crocodiles and sharks are only dangerous to those who make the mistake of breaking the ecosystem's rules." In an interview with Linda Brookover for *OneWorld* (on-line), he further explained his mission by saying, "Our biggest concern right now is preserving the habitat of our reptiles in order to protect them as species. Conservation of habitat, along with educating and convincing people that it is possible to live alongside so-called dangerous animals, is our goal." — J.K.B.

Suggested Reading: New York *Daily News* p31+ May 30, 1998, with photos; *New York Times* XIII p59 June 6, 1999, with photos; *Outside* (on-line) Nov. 1997; Irwin, Steve, and Terri Irwin. *The Crocodile Hunter: The Birthday Present Was a Python and Other Adventures*, 1997

Ivins, Molly

Aug. 30, 1944– Journalist; political commentator. Address: Fort Worth Star-Telegram, *1005 Congress Ave., Suite 920, Austin, TX 78701-2415*

Fort Worth Star-Telegram

"I feel my mission in life is to cheer people up," the political humorist Molly Ivins was quoted as saying by Clyde Noel for the *Los Altos Town Crier* (February 26, 1997). "To start with, things could be worse. You could live in Texas. Texas is the national laboratory for bad government." Molly Ivins's sassy Texan wit has graced the pages of more than 100 newspapers and magazines, among them the *Progressive*, the *Nation*, *Mother Jones*, the *New York Times*, *Esquire*, *Ms.*, *Playboy*, and the *Fort Worth Star-Telegram*. She has presented her astute and often hilarious observations on National Public Radio as well as on such high-profile television programs as the *Newshour with Jim Lehrer* and *60 Minutes*. Several collections of her columns have been published, including *Molly Ivins Can't Say That, Can She?* (1991), *Nothin' but Good Times Ahead* (1993), *You Got to Dance with Them What Brung You* (1998), and *Shrub: The Short but Happy Political Life of George W. Bush* (2000). Her writing is known for being honest, forthright, and amusing. Although the great majority of her targets have been Republicans, with former vice president Dan Quayle and former House Speaker Newt Gingrich high on the list, her perpetual indignation at the corruption and ineptitude of United States politicians is not inhibited by partisan biases.

Mary Tyler Ivins was born in Monterey, California, on August 30, 1944, the daughter of Jim and Margo Ivins. She was raised in Houston, Texas, where her support for civil rights as well as equal rights for women set her apart from most of her neighbors. "I was also a reader when I was a kid and I must say that in the context of Texas culture, it was not an activity that ranks anywhere close to football or the important things in life," Ivins told Linda Lehrer for the *Chicago Tribune* (October 27, 1991). Encouraged by her high-school English teacher, Bob Moore, to explore her interest in writing and literature, Ivins traveled north to Smith College, in Massachusetts, where she received a B.A. degree in history in 1965.

On summer breaks from college, Ivins worked in the complaint department of the *Houston Chronicle*. "I then worked my way up to Sewer Editor and wrote gripping articles about street closings," she told Lehrer. In an interview with Marina Malikoff for *Arts & Ideas* (Winter 1999, on-line), she recalled, "The *Chronicle* was still in those days, as a lot of papers were, that sort of raunchy old front page style of journalism, with city rooms full of spitoons and pictures of naked ladies, and the good old boys sitting around drinking Cutty Sark out of coffee cups with their hats on the backs of their heads. It really wasn't a respectable thing to do. Of course, that made it very attractive to me."

After receiving a master's degree in journalism from Columbia University, in New York City, in 1967, she studied at the Institute for Political Science in Paris, France, for one year. She soon became the first female reporter to write for the *Minneapolis Tribune*, where she was eventually given a column entitled "Movements for Social Change." From that platform she commented on the growing unrest among Americans, who were divided over the struggle for civil rights and the Vietnam War.

In 1970 Ivins moved to Austin, Texas, to accept a position as co-editor (with Ronnie Duger) of a small liberal magazine, the *Texas Observer*. Her assignment was to report on the Texas state legislature, whose members' colorful language and "good ol' boy" antics supplied her with a seemingly endless stream of comic anecdotes for her articles. "What the *Observer* gave me was a chance to make my own mistakes and develop a real style," Ivins told Marina Malikoff. "And that was actually when I fell in love with Texas politics. Basically, I have been a political writer ever since." "Molly is the epitome of what a Texas iconoclast should be," former Texas agricultural commissioner Jim Hightower commented to Giselle Benatar for a profile of Ivins in *Entertainment Weekly* (September 27, 1991). "'Institution' is far too stuffy a word to describe her, though. Molly is far too bodacious for that."

After six years at the *Texas Observer*, Ivins, feeling that she had become jaded by her work there, moved to New York City, where she was hired to report on City Hall for the *New York Times*. The newspaper later transferred her, first to Albany (the state's capital) and then to Denver, Colorado, where she served as the Rocky Mountain bureau chief from 1976 until 1982. Although Ivins has expressed her deep respect for the *New York Times*, she has also remarked that she felt stifled during her tenure there. "They hired me because I could write and then they wouldn't let me do it," she told Lehrer. "I always felt like a horse penned up in a small stall. I was kicking to get loose and every now and then some editor would stick his head in the door and say, 'We hear you in there kicking and we're not going to let you out until you learn to stop kicking!'"

Ivins found herself in Texas once again in February 1982, when the *Dallas Times-Herald* offered her a column in which she would have absolute freedom to express her opinion. "I can't get material like this anywhere else," she told Benatar, in reference to her lifelong relationship with Texas politics. "I have never lost a political contest. . . . Just on the grounds that my legislature is nuttier than yours." She stayed with the publication until 1992, when she began writing for the *Fort Worth Star-Telegram*.

Although Ivins is invariably labeled a liberal, she described herself to Lehrer as "a democrat, with a small 'd.'" She has always been pleased with the fact that her articles appear in a range of publications that represent many different ideologies. "One month my byline appeared simultaneously in *Playboy*, the *Progressive*, and *Reader's Digest*," she told Lehrer. "I was so proud."

Ivins uses humor to get to the heart of serious issues, including defense spending, abortion, the shortage of health care in the United States, and the failing education system. This approach enables her to both convey her "pathological optimism," as she phrased it to Scott Pendleton for the *Christian Science Monitor* (November 2, 1992), and give readers gentle reminders that in a democracy, citizens have a responsibility to be informed about and involved in the country's affairs. Her success as a columnist is a direct result of her refusal to remove the imprint of her personality from her articles. "Journalists make a terrible mistake writing about politics in so-called objective fashion," she commented to Benatar. "It just takes all the joy and juice and the humanity and rage and nobility and crassness out of human affairs. You can't put dehydrated cowpie on people's doorsteps in the morning and expect them to be interested in what's going on in the world. Politics ought to be covered the way sports is, as a celebration of heroes and villains. It is . . . the world's most fascinatin' poker game."

In Ivins's view, the influence on the rest of the media of tabloid-style reportage has led to a diminishment in the quality of political journalism. She is also alarmed by what she feels is the sameness of the coverage of political figures by the press. Ivins believes that the press continually presents issues as two-sided for no better reason than that this approach makes them easier to cover. She was especially disappointed in the behavior of the news media during the administration of President Ronald Reagan—in particular, for the way that a number of potentially scandalous events were under-scrutinized. "We missed Iran-Contra, missed the S&Ls [savings and loan crisis], missed the HUD

[Department of Housing and Urban Development] scandal," she told Lehrer. "But, boy, we covered [then-vice president] George Bush's dislike of broccoli. Every nuance!" Ivins told Malikoff that one significant aspect of the problem is that journalists must now answer to "giant infotainment empires. What you see happening is the psychology of the entertainment industry dominating news." According to Ivins, the news media—seduced by the entertainment industry's obsession with blockbusters—currently spend too much time on sensationalistic fare, such as the O. J. Simpson murder trial, at the expense of many important stories that more directly affect the lives of working people.

Although Ivins makes her living skewering political figures such as President Bill Clinton and Texas governor and presidential hopeful George W. Bush, she takes issue with those commentators who use their platforms to attack those who are less equipped to defend themselves. "When I listen to the radio and hear all of these little [Rush] 'Limbaughlings' making fun of people who are handicapped, homeless, or completely innocent, I think it is not only a question of decency, but I think it's just plain cruel," she told Keesia Wirt for the *Iowa State Daily* (October 9, 1995). Ivins sees humor as an important tool that can be easily misused. "Satire is traditionally the weapon of the powerless against the powerful," she explained to Michelle Green and Anne Maier for *People* (December 9, 1991). "I only aim it at the powerful. When satire is aimed at the powerless, it is not only cruel—it's vulgar."

Ivins also takes exception to the disdain and condescension with which elite politicians and journalists regard their constituents. "When you dumb down public discourse on the theory that people are just a bunch of boobs who don't know anything, you do real harm to people," she told Alden Mudge for *Book Page* (March 1998, on-line). "There are two mistakes made in politics. Usually [politicians and journalists] take a very complex subject and oversimplify it. Every now and again, they take something really simple and make it sound complicated. I don't do that. Part of what I do is try to prove that this is fascinating stuff. It's hilariously funny, full of high drama—and low drama—and it affects your life."

According to Ivins, Americans ignore at their peril the deliberate redistribution of wealth into the hands of an increasingly small group of their compatriots. "We won't have anything until we get the money out of politics," she told Noel. "There is a deep corruption in government and nothing will work until it is removed." Ivins's ongoing discussion of the widening gap between the rich and the poor distinguishes her work from that of the majority of political commentators. "Money was always a part of politics," she told Alden Mudge. "It's just that in the last decade or so the amount has become staggering. I'm convinced this is the root of the rot in American politics. The quality . . . of legislation we're seeing reflects increasingly how indebted politicians are to the people with money. It's really fouled up democracy." In her columns, Ivins has repeatedly pointed out the hypocrisy and moral bankruptcy that have infected American politics. "The people who have money and power constantly use it to bend the rules so they can get more money and more power," she told Lehrer. "Which gives everybody less and less of a chance to make it. And I think that that is what our political debate needs to focus on."

Ivins has served on the boards of many reputable news organizations, including the National News Council, Amnesty International's Journalism Network, and the Reporters Committee for Freedom of the Press. She has also written about First Amendment issues for the American Civil Liberties Union. In 1976 the Columbia School of Journalism named Ivins one of their outstanding alumni. The American Political Association presented Ivins with the Carey McWilliams Award in 1991, and in 1994 she received the Journalism Medal from the School of Journalism at the University of Missouri. Her work has made her a finalist for the Pulitzer Prize in journalism three times. But according to her profile in the *Texas Monthly* (2000, on-line), Ivins has said that she considers her two greatest honors to be "that the Minneapolis police force named its mascot pig after her and that she was once banned from the campus of Texas A&M University." Opinion polls regularly find her at the top of the lists of both the most-liked and most-hated political columnists.

Ivins believes that it is each person's responsibility to fight to maintain the principles of democracy upon which the United States of America was founded. "No matter what you do in life—beggars, poets, doctors, or plumbers—you will always have a second job to do as a citizen of this country," she told Wirt. "You must make sure the legacy that rules this country will live on forever. That is your job." — C.L.

Suggested Reading: *Arts & Ideas Magazine* (on-line) Winter 1999; *Book Page* (on-line) Mar. 1998, with photo; *Chicago Tribune* VI p3 Oct. 27, 1991, with photos; *Christian Science Monitor* p13 Nov. 2, 1992, with photo; *Entertainment Weekly* p34+ Sep. 27, 1991, with photo; *Iowa State Daily* (on-line) Oct. 9, 1995; *Los Altos Town Crier* (on-line) Feb. 26, 1997, with photo; *People* p99+ Dec. 9, 1991, with photos

Selected Books: *Molly Ivins Can't Say That, Can She?*, 1991; *Nothin' but Good Times Ahead*, 1993; *You Got to Dance with Them What Brung You*, 1998; *Shrub: The Short But Happy Political Life of George W. Bush*, 2000

Outline Press

John Paul II

May 18, 1920– Supreme Pontiff of the Roman Catholic Church; Sovereign of the State of Vatican City. Address: Vatican City

NOTE: An earlier article about Pope John Paul II appeared in *Current Biography* in 1979.

Pope John Paul II has in many ways redefined the papacy. He is the most traveled pontiff in history, having celebrated Mass on six continents and having become the first Pope to visit England, Ireland, and Spain, among dozens of other nations. He has played a large role in helping to reawaken the identity of the Polish people, who had suffered Nazi occupation followed by decades of Communist rule, and he has been credited as the impetus behind the Polish Solidarity movement. At the same time, Pope John Paul II has been criticized for not bringing the theology of the Roman Catholic Church into the modern era. His conservative stances on issues such as women's ordination, liberation theology, and contraception have placed him under heavy fire from left-leaning Roman Catholics and others. He has looked upon modern times with great sadness, referring to a "culture of death" in which abortion, euthanasia, war, and famine run rampant, superpowers ignore the poor and destitute, and large numbers of people embrace atheism. A poet, intellectual, and mystic, the Pope devoutly follows in all aspects of his life what he deems to be the word of the Lord. As his friend Monsignor Albacete has said, "John Paul II is not a man with faith. His identity *is* faith."

The youngest of three children, one of whom died in infancy, Pope John Paul II was born Karol Jozef Wojtyla in Wadowice, Poland, on May 18, 1920. His mother, Emilia Kaczorowska, encouraged Karol—who served as an altar boy at the Church of Our Lady in Wadowice—to pursue a vocation in the priesthood. Upon her death, when Karol was eight, his father, Karol Sr., a pensioned army sergeant who originally trained as a tailor, took the boy for solace to the shrine of the Virgin at Kalwaria, where Karol developed a deep devotion to Mary.

After his mother's death, the young Wojtyla grew increasingly close to his father, who instilled in his son the basic tenets of religious faith. As the Pope would later recall, as documented on a PBS program about him, "After my mother's death, [my father's] life became one of constant prayer. Sometimes I would wake up during the night and find my father on his knees, just as I would always see him kneeling in the parish church. We never spoke about a vocation to the priesthood, but his example was in a way my first seminary." People who knew him then have described Wojtyla as an optimistic and pious youth who was active in such sports as skiing and soccer. The death of his brother, Edmund, in 1932 from scarlet fever took a heavy emotional toll on him. The Pope would later state that his brother's sudden death cut "perhaps even deeper than my mother's."

As a young man Wojtyla was active in the theater, becoming passionately involved in a type of Polish drama known as the "Living Word," which was defined by its focus on language and monologues as opposed to sets and action. He met and was taught by Mieczyslaw Kotlarczyzk, who ran the Amateur University Theatre in Wadowice and was also a participant in Living Word theater. In addition, Wojtyla began writing plays and poetry. Upon graduation from high school, in 1938, he moved with his father to Kraków, and he and Kotlarcyzk continued their friendship through correspondence.

With the Nazi invasion of Poland, in September 1939, and the subsequent occupation, Jagiellonian University in Kraków, which Wojtyla was attending, was shut down, and many of his professors were deported and/or killed. Among the many new laws implemented by the Nazis to break Polish spirit were those that restricted the use of the Polish language and decreed that only Germans could take part in or attend cultural events. In 1941 Kotlarcyzk arrived in Kraków, where he and Wojtyla formed the underground theater group Rhapsodic Theatre, risking their lives for their love of Polish drama. During that period Wojtyla also worked in a quarry. Meanwhile, he was reflecting more on his faith. He befriended an eccentric tailor and mystic, Jan Tyranowski, who would be important in developing Wojtyla's spirituality and urging him toward the priesthood. Later, as recorded on the PBS documentary, Wojtyla recalled, "Tyranowski was truly one of those unknown saints, hidden among others like a marvelous light at the bottom of life at a depth where night usually reigns. He disclosed to me the riches of his inner life, of his mystical life. In his words, in his spirituality, and in the example of a life given to God alone, he represented a new world that I did not yet know. I saw the beauty of a soul opened up by grace."

The sudden death of his father, on February 18, 1941, was a crushing blow for Wojtyla, who, with no immediate family left, became deeply depressed. In the PBS documentary, Eamon Duffy, a Vatican historian at Cambridge University, in England, said, "Suffering is crucial for understanding John Paul. . . . His own personal life is one of enormous personal deprivation. . . . So he was a very austere man, from whom all human support has been stripped away. And that's made him the very strong, self-reliant, and very lonely person he is."

Wojtyla, who had grown up with Jewish friends and neighbors, watched as several of them were taken away and executed during the Holocaust. Although he was not a member of any underground resistance movement, he was quite protective of his Jewish friends and in a couple of instances saved their lives. Many of Wojtyla's friends at the Rhapsodic Theatre were rounded up, and some were sent to Auschwitz and executed. Wojtyla himself was arrested in 1942 but was released when it was discovered that he had the job at the quarry—work considered vital for the war effort. The incident did not stop Wojtyla's activity in the theater. He played the title role in a home production of *Samuel Zborowski* in 1943. Later in the war, Wojtyla was assigned to the Solvay Chemical Plant. As the Nazis continued their attempts to eradicate any semblance of Polish culture or pride, he joined the secret seminary of Archbishop Sapieha, in 1944. After the war, on October 1, 1946, he was ordained.

Following his ordination, Wojtyla did pastoral work with French working-class youth as well as with Polish refugees in France. He then engaged in further study at the Pontifical Angelicum University, in Rome. There, he came under the tutelage of the eminent French Dominican Reginald Garrigou-Lagrange, an uncompromising traditionalist. Wojtyla's doctoral dissertation, in theology, was about the 16th-century Spanish poet and mystic St. John of the Cross, and his postdoctoral thesis in philosophy (required for university status in Poland) connected the phenomenological thought of Max Scheler to the treatment of ethics in the works of St. Thomas Aquinas.

In the late 1940s Wojtyla held positions as parish priest at both Niegowic and Kraków. He became a professor of ethics at the Catholic University of Lublin, in 1956, and two years later he was consecrated auxiliary bishop of Kraków, under Archbishop Eugeniusz Baziak. In the early 1960s, after the death of Archbishop Baziak, he was named vicar capitular, in charge of the Archdiocese of Kraków, and he became archbishop in name as well as in fact in 1964. He gained recognition from Pope Paul VI for his views on sexuality, which he elaborated in his book *Love and Responsibility* (1962). In that book he promoted the idea that while human sexuality should be valued, the sexual act itself must be undertaken only for procreation. At the time Paul VI was working on his encyclical *Humanae Vitae*, which explored similar themes, and the Pope opened a correspondence with Wojtyla, who would help to draft the encyclical. Pope Paul VI elevated him to the cardinalate on May 29, 1967.

Wojtyla addressed Vatican Council II (1962–65) several times, most memorably on the subject of religious liberty—which, he pointed out, the Church could not claim for itself without conceding it to others. He worked tirelessly to add to the doctrine developed by the council the declaration disputing the centuries-old notion that Jews as a group were responsible for Christ's crucifixion. As a cardinal, Wojtyla made several international journeys, including trips to the United States in 1969 and 1976.

When he was elevated to the cardinalate, Wojtyla was regarded by the Communist regime in Poland as "moderately reformist" and as "tough but flexible," in contrast to the Primate of Poland, Cardinal Wyszynski, who was considered a hard-line anti-Communist. Many, however, knew Wojtyla to be a resilient enemy of communism, a champion of human rights, a powerful preacher, and a sophisticated intellectual. Among the themes of his cardinalate were those that Wojtyla would elaborate on in his pontificate: the value of suffering, the dangers of a secular world, a conservative view of the social understanding of the Bible, and a pessimistic view of modern society. In a 1976 lecture in Rome, Wojtyla spoke of his vision of the world "as a burial ground . . . a vast planet of tombs."

The Communist authorities feared Wojtyla for his wit but respected him for his statesmanship, as George Blazynski noted in *Pope John Paul II* (1979): "Wojtyla recognized the importance of giving expression to Polish national feeling—of which the Church is the most important embodiment—without allowing it to take an explosive form that would provoke a brutal reaction by forces within and perhaps without the country." Blazynski went on to say that Wojtyla, like Wyszynski, became for Poles a symbol of the Church as an alternative universal doctrine, one based on Christian rather than Marxist values. "Cardinal Wojtyla is identified in Poland as the chief advocate of still greater concessions by the State toward the Church and the people. The main issue is that of respect for all human rights, but in particular he has been concerned about education, access to the mass media, the elimination of censorship, the abandonment of atheistic propaganda and pressure, the building of churches, and freedom of religious instruction."

On October 15, 1978, following the deaths of Pope Paul VI, in August 1978, and Pope John Paul I, in September 1978, the College of Cardinals met in a secret conclave in the Vatican to elect the 263d (or 262d, according to some historians) successor to St. Peter as Bishop of Rome. In the eighth round of voting, on October 16, the cardinals chose Wojtyla, who accepted their decision with tears in his eyes and chose the name John Paul, becoming the first non-Italian Pope since the 16th century. Shortly after his election was announced, the new Pope appeared on a balcony overlooking St. Peter's Square and addressed the crowd in Italian. In his powerful voice he said, "I was afraid to receive this nomination but I did it in the spirit of obedience to Our Lord and in the total confidence in his mother, the most holy Madonna." Like John Paul I, he declined coronation and was simply installed as Pope during a pontifical Mass in St. Peter's Square, on October 22, 1978.

The new Pope produced an electrifying impact on the populace of Rome, duplicated—indeed exceeded—time and again as he traveled beyond the borders of Italy. For his first trip abroad, in January 1979, he chose Latin America, home of almost half of the world's 720 million Roman Catholics. Between one and three million people greeted John Paul in the Dominican Republic and later in Mexico. In his speeches, he struck a careful balance between a concern for the poor and oppressed and a repudiation of liberation theology, which holds that the fundamental mission of the church is to bring social change, even to the extent of fostering revolution. John Paul II told a conference of Latin American bishops in Puebla, Mexico, on January 28 that while "the Church must work in favor of a more just and equitable distribution of goods, not only within each nation but also in the world in general," it cannot accept "this idea of Christ as a political figure, a revolutionary." The Pope elaborated: "If the Church makes herself present in the defense of or in the advancement of man, she does so in line with her mission [which] is religious and not social or political. . . . The Church wishes to stay free with regard to the competing [political] systems."

John Paul's return to his native Poland for nine days in June 1979 gave new hope to the subject peoples of Eastern Europe. The thunderous outpouring of religious and patriotic affection he elicited throughout the officially atheistic country came at a time when the government was already embarrassed over goods shortages because of an unexpected failure of its most recent agricultural plan. "But it was the Pope's appeal to the young that frightened the Communist party the most," Paul Martin wrote in a dispatch to *Newsweek* (August 2, 1979). According to journalist Neal Ascherson, the Pope's visits to Poland "helped to bring about such profound, irreversible changes that Poland then became a country which was clearly ceasing to be a Communist country." The Pope has been credited with inspiring the Solidarity movement, which would eventually lead Poland to abandon communism and establish an identity outside the influence of the Soviet Union.

Over the course of his first year as pontiff, the Pope traveled nonstop around the globe. For several African nations, John Paul's was the first visit by a Pope. Also, John Paul became the first Pope to visit Ireland, celebrating Mass for 1.2 million people in Dublin and calling for peace in Northern Ireland. A six-day tour of the U.S. prompted an incredible turnout, with the Pope warning members of the "consumer" society to beware the dangers of secularism, materialism, and selfishness and admonishing them to accept a lowering of their living standards to help the less fortunate in their own country and in the Third World. On several occasions he pointed out that human life is a "precious gift of God" and called on Catholics to "stand up every time life is threatened" by abortion or the limiting of family size for the sake of material comfort. By the end of the year, the Pope had traveled to more than 100 countries; his travels included his first visit to a non-Christian nation, Turkey, as part of his attempt to begin a reunification with the Orthodox Church, which broke with Rome in 1054. (Although Turkey is predominantly Muslim, Istanbul [formerly Constantinople], one of its major cities, is a center of Eastern Orthodox Christianity.) Also in 1979, he wrote his first papal encyclical, *Redemptor Hominis* (*The Redeemer of Man*). Expounding the Pope's conservative views and for the most part reflecting the theology of Pope Paul VI, the paper criticized the arms race and both Marxism and capitalism, calling for a global redistribution of financial resources to help end poverty and hunger.

On May 13, 1981 the Pope was shot twice in St. Peter's Square by Mehmet Ali Agca, a 23-year-old Turk who had escaped from prison. Seriously wounded, the Pope was hospitalized for two and half months, during which parts of his intestines were removed; he later recovered fully. On December 27, 1983 John Paul went to meet his would-be assassin (who was serving a life sentence) in prison and forgave him, saying afterwards, "I spoke to him as I would speak to a brother whom I have forgiven and who enjoys my confidence." (To guard against any future attempts on his life, a car known as the Popemobile was constructed; it allows the Pope to stand and wave to adoring crowds from behind a protective covering.)

Later in 1981, in a symbolic and historic move, the Vatican established full diplomatic relations with the United Kingdom, more than four centuries after King Henry VIII of England broke with Roman Catholicism, in 1532. In June John Paul became the first Pope ever to visit England; he took a six-day tour of the island nation, during which he called for reconciliation between the main bodies of the church, stating that "restoration of unity among Christians is one of the main concerns of the church in the last part of the 20th century." In the first-ever visit of a Pope to Spain, he decried the decline in morals and the increased secularism of the modern world. He also denounced the violence in El Salvador, condemning army and rebel violence while criticizing the roles that the U.S. and the Soviet Union played in the conflict. In Portugal the Pope experienced another assassination attempt when a rebel priest, Juan Fernandez Krohn, ran toward him with a bayonet. Fernandez was apprehended before he could harm the pontiff.

In January 1984 the Pope approved the first revision in Catholic canon law since its establishment in 1917. The revisions were designed to make the church more accessible, by increasing the power of bishops, widening the role of lay people, and expanding the role of women in the church. In a major reorganization of the Vatican and its duties, a February 1984 concordat ended the privileged status of the Catholic Church in Italy, while the Pope turned over most of his temporal duties to his secretary of state. Later in the year the Pope published an essay in which he decried Marxist leanings by Latin American clergy. While praising efforts to help the poor and weak, the Pope stated that "theological reflection on liberation" must "be purified of elements that might adulterate it." A paper released by the Vatican in April 1986 stated that service to the poor and needy was a duty of all Christians and even supported armed struggle in those extreme cases when it was necessary to overthrow repressive regimes. At the same time the report denounced "the myth of revolution" and reaffirmed that the church's main duty was "evangelization and salvation." The Pope's appointment of conservative bishops in Latin American nations and his denouncing of liberation theology all but ended the movement, the final nail in the coffin being a 1988 encyclical stating that change could come about only through moral and spiritual contemplation.

During the last years of the 1980s, the Pope continued to travel and write extensively and to attack both capitalism and Marxism, stating, "Each of the two blocks harbors in its own way a tendency toward imperialism." Weathering the first Roman Catholic schism in over a century, in June 1988 he excommunicated Archbishop Marcel Lefebvre of France, who had been critical of the Roman Catholic Church since Vatican II and had refused to accept most of the changes brought about by that council. The Pope acted after Lefebvre consecrated four bishops—an act that John Paul had specifically cited as grounds for expulsion from the Church. On the opposite end of the spectrum, liberals within the Church attacked the Pope for alleged authoritarianism. A group of eminent Catholic priests stated that he was neglecting church laity and that his conservative views on the use of contraceptives were outdated. "The concept of New Testament truth and Jesus' teaching about salvation are enlisted by the pope to represent a specific teaching that cannot be justified either in Holy Scripture or in the traditions of the church," their statement declared.

The Pope's health has been a focus of great media attention since the early 1990s. In 1992 the 72-year-old pontiff entered the hospital for removal of an intestinal tumor that proved to be benign. Several mishaps created brief scares; he tripped and fell on his robe at the Vatican on November 11, 1993, fracturing and dislocating his right shoulder, then suffered another injury the next year, when, getting out of his bath at his home in the Vatican, he fell and broke his right leg. Such accidents have not slowed his pace, however; he has continued to travel widely and to write prolifically. In July 1993 he agreed with Israel to form a commission aimed at establishing full diplomatic relations between that nation and the Vatican. His papal encyclical *Veritatis Splendor* (*The Splendor of Truth*), issued in 1993, stated that certain acts were intrinsically evil regardless of motivation or outcome. An encyclical that the Pope had reportedly worked on for 12 years, *Fides et Ratio* (*Faith and Reason*), argued that faith and reason were not incompatible and that, indeed, the rational was necessary for faith to exist. The encyclical promoted the idea that both faith and reason are ways of approaching God. Reversing the previous Vatican position that capital punishment is valid, he has said that only in the rarest situations, if ever, should the measure be considered. In June 1999 the Pope incorporated many of the Vatican's teachings, such as the opposition to women's ordination, euthanasia, and sex outside marriage, into canon law, stating that those who disobeyed such teachings would be open to "just punishment," including excommunication.

In one of his most important encyclicals, *Evangelium Vitae*, put forth in March 1995 and published in the Toronto *Globe and Mail* (March 31, 1995), the Pope spoke of the modern world as a "culture of death," as seen in "violence against women, children, the poor, the weak, and the sick; the worsening situation of poverty; murder, suicide, genocide, torture, concentration camps; disgraceful living conditions; contempt for human suffering; the killing of rivals and elimination of adversaries; contraception; abortion; euthanasia; deliberate famines, experiments on mind and body, and attempts to coerce the will." Elsewhere, the Pope referred to the modern world as "a civilization of affluence and pleasure [that] lives as though sin did not exist, and as if God did not exist." He had already compared abortion to the Holocaust, stating in a 1991 speech, "The cemetery of the victims of human cruelty in our century is extended to include yet another vast cemetery, that of the unborn child, of the defenseless whose faces even their own mothers had not seen before accepting, or being pressured into accepting, that their lives be taken away from them before their birth." The Pope's pessimism regarding modern culture extends to his homeland as well. After the fall of communism, the Pope has watched Poland embrace a capitalist market and seen a rise in abortion and alcoholism there. In visits to Poland since 1989, he has forcefully urged his people to turn away from such vices and practices.

Earlier, in March 1998, the Vatican issued a report entitled "We Remember: A Reflection on the Shoah," which apologized for the church's past positions regarding Jews yet did not condemn Pope Pius XII for remaining silent in the face of the Holocaust; the report even praised him for his actions. Although it disappointed some Jews, who hoped that Pius XII would be condemned, others saw it as a step in the right direction in the relationship between Jews and the Vatican. In 1984 John Paul had become the first Pope to visit a synagogue, but he later garnered criticism for failing to repudiate—and later knighting—U.N. secretary-general Kurt Waldheim, who served in the German military during the Nazi era.

In January 1998 John Paul shocked many observers by visiting Cuba. He criticized the Cuban leader Fidel Castro's human-rights record and education system while calling on Cubans to reject the capitalism of the West and calling on the U.S. to end its embargo of Cuba. During a tour of the U.S. in early 1999, he condemned the lack of morality apparent among Americans and appealed to the nation not to forget the poor and oppressed.

In recent years the Pope has tried hard to bring together the Christian churches of the world. He became the first Pope ever to visit a predominantly Orthodox nation (Romania, in 1999), and he has continued his efforts to reunite the Roman Catholic and Eastern Orthodox churches. In 1998 the Catholic Church signed an historic accord with the Lutheran World Federation concerning "justification," or how humans achieve salvation.

The pope regarded the jubilee year 2000, a so-called Holy Year, as a time for overtures of reconciliation with people of other faiths. With the Christmas Mass on December 25, 1999, the Pope ushered in the new year. "At this hour, the word 'today' rings out with a unique sound," he said, as quoted by Alessandra Stanley in the *New York Times* (December 26, 1999). "It is not only the commemoration of the birth of the Redeemer, it is the solemn beginning of the Great Jubilee." Earlier, the pope had announced that indulgences, which are meant to shorten a person's time in purgatory, were to be given out as a reward for attending certain Jubilee services, performing charitable works, or abstaining from vice. The decision to give out indulgences, a practice that helped to trigger the Protestants' split from the Roman Catholic Church in the 16th century, dismayed many modern-day Protestants and pointed up a contradiction in the character of the Pope—a man more eager than many others to participate in interfaith dialogue, yet determined to keep alive the traditions of his church that have made reconciliation difficult. The year's fourth, and final, Jubilee service, in January 2000, was nonetheless an historic one, in that the Pope prayed with the archbishop of Canterbury and Metropolitan Athanasios of the Eastern Orthodox Church. At a Mass in March 2000, John Paul made another plea for forgiveness and harmony, when he offered an apology for all the wrongs the Roman Catholic Church had perpetrated over the past 2,000 years. "We cannot not recognize the betrayal of the Gospel committed by some of our brothers, especially in the second millennium. Recognizing the deviations of the past serves to reawaken our consciences to the compromises of the present," he said, as quoted by Alessandra Stanley in the *New York Times* (March 13, 2000). At the same time he also asked forgiveness for those who had persecuted Roman Catholics over the centuries.

During 2000 the Pope, visibly frail yet full of resolve, embarked on a trip to the Holy Land, where he visited various Christian holy sites, among them the places traditionally held to be the birthplace of Jesus and the site of the Last Supper, respectively, as well as two locations that were each said to be the scene of Jesus's baptism. The Pope's visit was also intended as an attempt to bring Jews, Christians, and Muslims together in Israel. Although the majority of Palestinians and Israelis welcomed the Pope's visit, people from both groups declared that his presence supported their particular vision regarding the region's future. In Israel he visited important Jewish sites, such as the Holocaust Museum and the Wailing Wall. At the Holocaust Museum he said, as quoted by Alessandra Stanley in the *New York Times* (March 24, 2000), "I assure the Jewish people that the Catholic Church, motivated by the Gospel law of truth and love and by no political considerations, is deeply saddened by the hatred, acts of persecution and displays of anti-Semitism directed against the Jews by Christians at any time, and in any place." Meanwhile, his visit to Palestinian-controlled areas and his meeting with Yasir Arafat were seen by many Palestinians as renewed evidence of papal support for an independent Palestine. "He is unsteady on his feet, and he appears weak, but this has probably been the strongest moment of his pontificate," Adam Joseph Maida, the cardinal of Detroit, declared, as quoted in the *New York Times* (March 27, 2000). In addition to his visit to the Holy Land, John Paul celebrated the first papal Mass ever held in Egypt. On that occasion he urged reconciliation between the Vatican and the Egyptian Coptic Church, which split with Rome in the fifth century A.D.

Formerly burly and vigorous, Pope John Paul has become bent and frail; he trembles and sometimes slurs his words—signs, some believe, of the onset of Parkinson's disease. Nevertheless, he has kept up a hectic touring schedule. He rises each morning at six to say Mass in his private chapel and works far into the night. The Pope speaks fluent Latin in addition to his native Polish, and he can switch from English to French, German, or Spanish with relative ease. He no longer writes verse but still enjoys the works of the Polish poets Slowacki and Mickiewicz. As Pope he has written one book, *Crossing the Threshold of Hope* (1994), which reiterates the themes of his papacy. A recent CD, *Abba Pater* (1999), combines archival recordings of the Pope's speeches with original music. The album and the book became best-sellers immediately after publication.

Hailed as a visionary and attacked as a relic of an outdated time, the Pope has held virtually the same opinions since his youth. He has invoked the doctrine of papal infallibility in opposing the ordination of women and has never supported the use of contraceptive devices; he has also apologized for the role the Roman Catholic Church has played in oppressing women and has remarked on the beauty of sexual relations. In his appointments of more than three-quarters of the membership of the College of Cardinals, he has attempted to ensure that his successor will share his outlook on the world. Echoing many arguments over the merits of his philosophy, the journalist Roberto Suro told an interviewer for the PBS documentary, "At the end of the day, when you look at this extraordinary life and you see all that he's accomplished . . . you're left with one very disturbing and difficult question. On the one hand, the Pope can seem this lonely, pessimistic figure . . . a man obsessed with the evils of the 20th century, a man convinced that humankind has lost its way. . . . A man so dark, so despairing, that he loses his audiences. That would make him a tragic figure, certainly. On the other hand, you have to ask, is he a prophet? Did he come here with a message? Did he see something that many of us are missing? In that case, the tragedy is ours." — G.O.

Suggested Reading: *John Paul II: The Millennium Pope* (on-line); *Observer Review* p3 Dec. 31, 1995; Toronto *Globe and Mail* A p1+ Mar. 31, 1995, A p8 Sep. 26, 1995; *Washington Post* A p1 Oct. 8, 1995; Blazynski, George. *Pope John Paul II*, 1979

Rich Freeda, courtesy of WWF

Johnson, Dwayne "The Rock"

May 2, 1972– Professional wrestler. Address: c/o WWF Entertainment, P.O. Box 3857, Stamford, CT 06902

Called by many journalists (as well as himself) "the most electrifying man in sports entertainment," Dwayne Johnson—better known as The Rock—has risen in three short years to the top of the heap in the World Wrestling Federation, becoming the youngest champion in WWF history. The professional wrestler as reimagined by P. T. Barnum, he has dazzled fans and humbled opponents with his trademark mix of bravado and sheer power. Each night on the syndicated cable show *Raw Is War* and on *WWF Smackdown*, run on the United Paramount Network (UPN), The Rock struts the ring like a Brahma bull, taunting opponents with such creative and derogatory terms as "jabroni," cocking the infamous "People's Eyebrow" in a sign of supreme confidence, and peppering his dialogue with slogans like "Know your role!" and "Do you smell what The Rock is cooking?" But Johnson, the man behind The Rock's persona and a third-generation wrestler, wants it known that "I'm the Rock inside the ring, but outside the ring I'm strictly Dwayne Johnson," as he explained to Gabrielle L. Gabrielle for *Vibe* (January 18, 1999). "The Rock couldn't give two pieces of monkey crap about anybody but himself. He's the guy everyone loves to hate. Dwayne Johnson's a good guy. Likes to hang out at home and play video games and listen to music with his wife."

"Half-Black and half-Samoan," as he described himself to Gabrielle, The Rock was born Dwayne Johnson on May 2, 1972 in the small town of Hayward, California, and spent most of his childhood in Hawaii. When he was growing up, wrestling was always a part of his life. His father was the legendary wrestler Rocky Johnson, and his maternal grandfather, the Samoan High Chief Peter Maivia, was the U.S. Tag Team Champion. "My earliest memories are of wrestling, going to shows with my mom, watching my dad fly off the top rope, practicing my dropkicks in the living room when no one was watching," he stated in his autobiography, *The Rock Says . . . The Most Electrifying Man In Sports Entertainment* (2000), written with Joe Layden. "I was always kept extremely close to the business by my parents. They never tried to shield me from it, never pretended that it was something it wasn't."

A rambunctious and mischievous child, Johnson emulated his father's wrestling moves at every opportunity, sometimes practicing them on his fellow classmates. When he was a sophomore in high school, the family moved to Bethlehem, Pennsylvania, where Johnson enrolled in Freedom High School. He arrived too late in the year to join the school's football team, so he gravitated to the wrestling squad. Shortly after starting his first practice, Johnson realized that amateur wrestling was not the same as the kind he had known all his life. "Compared to the shows I had been raised on, it just wasn't much fun," he wrote in *The Rock Says* . . . . "And after two hours of practice—two hours of calisthenics, one-on-one drilling, basic fundamentals, all endured without so much as a smile or a shout—my opinion had been hardened. Wrestling was, well . . . *boring.*"

Beginning in his junior year, Johnson excelled at football; he was named All-American and ranked the eighth-best player in the state of Pennsylvania. During his senior year he was approached by such high-profile schools as Florida State University, Clemson, and the University of Pittsburgh, all of which courted him with promises of money and other enticements—while making no mention of academics. Finding those tactics distasteful, Johnson became interested in the University of Miami. Notwithstanding Miami's previous reputation for the same sorts of recruiting practices, the defensive line coach there, Bob Karmelowics, merely told Johnson that he would have a chance to play for the Hurricanes and get an education if he enrolled at the university. "That struck a chord with me," Johnson wrote in *The Rock Says* . . . . "I found it admirable that he was laying it out that way."

In the fall of 1990, Johnson arrived at the University of Miami, where he played defensive tackle for the Hurricanes. Ten days before the season opener, he tore the ligaments in his shoulder, which kept him out of play for much of the season. This was a crushing blow to him, and he lapsed into self-pity. In addition, the injury diminished his already short fuse, and he became prone to fits of rage. In one such episode, at his uncle's wedding, he placed his hands around the throat of a woman who had used profanity while speaking to his mother. "There are few incidents in my life that have filled me with more shame and regret than [that] one," he wrote in *The Rock Says* . . . .

Eventually, Johnson returned to his team, playing in nine games during his freshman year, including a victory in the Orange Bowl. Johnson's temper was still an issue—most notably in an incident that found him literally trying to pull out a teammate's tongue—but his aggression served him well on the playing field. It also served as the catalyst for a bone-crunching brawl at San Diego State. Johnson and his teammates, as well as the San Diego players, were given to trading insults, which resulted in a bench-clearing free-for-all on the 50-yard line; that, in turn, led to the creation of a National Collegiate Athletic Association (NCAA) rule forbidding players on the bench from becoming involved in altercations on the field. The highlight of the melee was Johnson's mad pursuit of the San Diego mascot, a clip of which aired on national news broadcasts. Traces of the college football "trash-talking" culture are evident in Johnson's wrestling persona. "Oh yeah, there is a big [University of Miami] influence on The Rock," he told Peter Whoriskey for the *Miami Herald* (February 11, 2000). "Believe me, when I was there, I talked all I could."

Johnson graduated from the University of Miami in 1995 with a degree in criminology. Although he had counted on being drafted into the National Football League and beginning a career as a pro football player, he was passed over for the draft, receiving only an offer from the Canadian Football League's Calgary Stampeders. On a salary of $250 per week, Johnson soon found himself sleeping on a mattress he had fished out of a Dumpster. In addition, when he arrived in Canada, he discovered that he would be relegated to the practice team. "I never saw the Stampeders play a game, not in person, anyway," he wrote in *The Rock Says* . . . . "If they were on the road, I'd watch the game on television. Those of us on the practice team received four tickets apiece for home games, but I never used mine. The Stampeders were pretty popular in those days, so I'd usually just walk across the street to McMahon Stadium and scalp my tickets."

At the end of the 1996 season, Johnson received the word that he was being let go from the team. While he was partly disappointed, he was also happy that he would now have the chance to pursue a career as a professional wrestler, a path that had been piquing his interest more and more. Returning to Miami, Johnson moved back in with his parents and began trying to break into wrestling. "My father was skeptical," he wrote in *The Rock Says* . . . . "He had spent the better part of his life in the wrestling business, and he knew what a hard world it could be." Nonetheless, Johnson was determined to wrestle, and he eventually persuaded his father to help train him.

Johnson began training in a gym in Tampa with his father and former wrestler Ron Slinker. Before long, he was creating "spots" (or signature moves) and coming up with ideas for his ring persona. "The one thing I knew was that I did not want to try and cash in on my family's reputation," he wrote in *The Rock Says* . . . . "I didn't want to be known as Rocky Johnson Jr. or the grandson of Peter Maivia." Johnson attracted the attention of promoter Pat Patterson, who came to Tampa to watch him wrestle. Impressed with what he saw, Patterson introduced Johnson to the famed World Wrestling Federation owner Vince McMahon, who invited him to participate in a match in Corpus Christi, Texas. There, Johnson wrestled Steve Lombardi (a.k.a. The Brooklyn Brawler) and Chris Candido, defeating the former but losing to the latter. McMahon, struck by the versatility and adaptability Johnson displayed in the ring, offered him a WWF contract for $150 per night. "A door had been opened and I had been invited inside," the wrestler wrote in *The Rock Says* . . . . "The rest was up to me."

In early 1996 Johnson headed to the home of the United States Wrestling Alliance (USWA), in Memphis, Tennessee, which served as a training ground for WWF wrestlers. Driving to Memphis, Johnson began thinking up his name. Up to that point, he had been wrestling as Dwayne Johnson. However, he knew that as a member of the WWF, he would need a name with a little more panache. He decided on Flex Kavana—the last name is a Hawaiian word, and the first name, he thought, sounded heroic.

"Being in Memphis was a lot like being a triple-A baseball player," he noted in *The Rock Says* . . . . "You worked as hard as you could, did your job, and tried to laugh at some of the craziness you saw." Earning only $40 per night (the $150 salary was reserved for wrestlers in the WWF), Johnson wrestled at venues ranging from fairgrounds to car-dealership lots to barns where the patrons would sit on bales of hay. After several months in the USWA, Johnson was offered a second WWF audition, in Columbus, Ohio, with Owen Hart. Johnson lost the match to Hart but impressed the WWF brass enough to earn an invitation to Connecticut, where the WWF is headquartered and where its main training facility is located.

Johnson's first match after leaving Memphis was on November 16, 1996, when he wrestled Goldust to a victory in the WWF's Survivor Series. For this match, Johnson had retired the moniker Flex Kavana and, at the suggestion of the WWF office, adopted Rocky Maivia. Although the match captivated the audience, Johnson was still far from creating the persona of The Rock. "The character of Rocky Maivia didn't have a lot of depth back then," he recalled in *The Rock Says* . . . . He was a babyface, a technically proficient wrestler who smiled a lot and communicated almost nothing; he didn't get a lot of time on the microphone." Ultimately, Rocky Maivia provoked a vitriolic reaction from fans, who did not like his "nice-guy" image, particularly in the wake of such beer-swilling, rudely gesturing antiheroes as Stone Cold Steve Austin. Audience members would routinely chant anti-Maivia slogans and hold up signs reading "Die, Rocky, Die!" at Johnson's matches. At first, Johnson was unfazed by the abuse, but as time wore on, he began to see the need for a change of character.

In the summer of 1997, Johnson was approached with the notion of becoming a villain, or "turning heel," as it is known in the wrestling world. Eager to dispose of the smiling, winsome persona of Rocky Maivia, he jumped at the chance. Shortly afterward Johnson made his first appearance as a "black hat," stepping into the ring ostensibly to assist Chainz, a "babyface," in his match against Faarooq, the leader of a militant wrestling faction known as The Nation. Instead, Johnson helped to defeat Chainz and embraced Faarooq. The move shocked fans, a reaction that delighted Johnson, who began cultivating his newfound evil image. As he noted in *The Rock Says* . . . , "Rocky Maivia became 'The Rock,' an outrageously arrogant, self-centered, but undeniably talented wrestler who couldn't care less what other people thought, and who always—ALWAYS—spoke in the third person. . . . I saw The Rock as an extension of my own personality. He was bombastic, funny, cocky . . . but, at his core, he was an athlete with sound technical skills. He loved wrestling. He loved sports-entertainment."

Once his persona was fully realized, Johnson took the wrestling world by storm. In December 1997 he became the Intercontinental Champion when Stone Cold Steve Austin relinquished the title. A month later Johnson successfully defended the title in a furious match with Ken Shamrock. At the end of 1998, Johnson became the youngest WWF champion in history, when he defeated Mankind for the championship.

By now, The Rock's popularity was skyrocketing. Fans adored his arrogant and insulting manner, cheering even when he referred to them as "trailer park trash." Calling himself "The People's Champion," Johnson began fleshing out his character further, creating "The People's Eyebrow," "The People's Elbow" (a dressed-version of the basic flying-elbow technique), and his signature move, "The Rock Bottom," in which he would stand side by side with his opponent, hook the other man's head and neck, and bring him crashing to the mat. Johnson was winning followers with his prowess in the ring, as well. One of his most notorious bouts occurred on January 24, 1999 against Mankind; The Rock handcuffed his opponent and clubbed him 12 times with a steel chair during the match, which he won. The pair would square off again on February 14, 1999 in a vicious brawl that saw the two men knock each other unconscious, thereby ending the match.

Wrestling fans became enthralled by the rivalry between The Rock and Austin. The two men were portrayed as polar opposites (The Rock as vain, arrogant, and fond of fine clothes and jewelry, Austin, as a "man of the people" who favored jeans, T-shirts, and beer), each one repulsed by the other. The competition reached epic proportions during an event called the Royal Rumble, when Austin defeated The Rock, robbing him of his chance to face Shawn Michaels for the WWF title in *Wrestlemania XIV*, in 1998. (*Wrestlemania* is the "world series" of professional wrestling; the event pairs the most popular wrestlers.) A year later The Rock defeated Mankind for the title, but had it taken from him in a subsequent match, when Austin knocked him out with a steel chair, allowing Mankind to pin him. On March 29, 1999, during *Wrestlemania XV*, in a bone-crushing showdown that lasted for more than 30 minutes, Austin pinned The Rock for the WWF championship. While fans of The Rock were outraged at this turn of events, Johnson reveled in Austin's victory, recognizing the drama the pair had created. "As I walked back up the aisle, I could hear Steve's music playing," he recalled in *The Rock Says* . . . . "I knew he was celebrating in the ring, popping cans of Budweiser and spraying the audience, toasting a victory as only he can. I was so happy for him, and for us, and for what we had accomplished."

On April 30, 2000 The Rock regained the title, in an event against Triple H titled *Backlash.* (Austin had lost the title in August 1999.) A month later Johnson lost it to Triple H at *Judgment Day.* On June 25, 2000 he took part in a six-man tag-team match at *King of Ring* in Boston, Massachusetts, in which he, Undertaker, and Kane faced Triple H, Vince McMahon, and Shane McMahon; The Rock pinned Vince McMahon for the title. On October 22, 2000 he lost it once again, this time to the 1996 Olympic Gold Medalist Kurt Angle, at *No Mercy* in Albany, New York.

In just three years, the success of The Rock has propelled Johnson into the realm of superstardom. He has appeared on the TV shows *Martha Stewart Living* and *Star Trek: Voyager*, and he even played his father on the Fox sitcom *That 70s Show.* His appearance on *Saturday Night Live*, on March 18, 2000, garnered the highest ratings the show had received so far that season. In addition, Johnson will make his feature-film debut, in *The Mummy Returns* (2001), a sequel to the 1999 blockbuster *The Mummy*, playing the villainous Scorpion King, who stalks patrons of the British Museum alongside the title character. Advance word is that his performance is so strong that the producers are considering a third film in the *Mummy* series built around his character.

While he was attending the University of Miami, Johnson met Dany Garcia, who was a senior majoring in international finance and marketing. Right away, Johnson knew he was going to marry her. "Here I am, 18 years old, right out of high school, trying to convince a 22-year-old woman, 'Hey, believe me, I'm the one for you,'" he told a reporter for *TV Guide* (March 27, 1999). "I had a hell of a time doing that. But once she knew that she got a guy with his stuff together, that was it." Garcia, for her part, "thought he was great, but he looked so arrogant," as she recalled for *People* (November 15, 1999). That first impression notwithstanding, the two were married on May 3, 1997. Johnson has often cited Garcia as his primary motivation, and even wrote *God & Dany* on his left hand (and *Mom & Dad* on his right) during football games as a reminder of what was most important to him. Garcia, who works as an associate vice president at Merrill Lynch, also speaks very highly of her husband. "He is the kind of guy who'll sing to me when I'm not feeling well," she told *People.* "He notices that you've changed your hair."

The couple live in Davie, Florida, in a quiet, gated community. Johnson, who spends about 225 days each year on the road, has said that he treasures his time at home more than anything. "I'm quieter than The Rock," he admitted to Peter Whoriskey. "I'm laid back." Johnson is an ardent music fan who cites Sam Cooke and Willie Nelson as being among his favorite performers. Unlike many other stars of his caliber, he has claimed that he is never too busy to sign an autograph or shake a fan's hand. "I love interacting with the fans," he explained in *The Rock Says . . . .* "I know they are the backbone of our industry and that without them I would not have a job. I still find it flattering when someone comes up to me and asks for my autograph, just sticks out a scrap of paper and asks me to sign it. . . . Knowing that someone might take it home and frame it or put it in a special box on top of their dresser . . . . To me that's just a very humbling experience." — J.K.B.

Suggested Reading: *Miami Herald* (on-line), Feb. 11, 2000, with photos; *TV Guide* p32+ Mar. 27, 1999, with photos; *Vibe* p171+ Jan. 18, 1999, with photos; Johnson, Dwayne, with Joe Layden. *The Rock Says . . . The Most Electrifying Man In Sports Entertainment*, 2000

Allen Fredrickson/Archive Photos

Johnson, Randy

Sep. 10, 1963– Pitcher for the Arizona Diamondbacks. Address: Arizona Diamondbacks, P.O. Box 2095, Phoenix, AZ 85001

Standing just two inches shy of seven feet, and equipped with an arm capable of firing fastballs in excess of 100 miles an hour, pitcher Randy Johnson lives up to his nickname, "The Big Unit." "He has become what [the 1950s and 1960s Dodger pitcher] Sandy Koufax was," Texas Rangers general manager Doug Melvin told Tom Verducci for *Sports Illustrated* (July 7, 1997). "Whenever Koufax pitched, you knew if your pitcher gave up more than two runs, chances that you'd lose were pretty good. Randy's the same way." "I can be a little intimidating when I pitch because I'm so much taller than everybody and I throw hard," Johnson told Tyler Young for *Sports Illustrated for Kids* (September, 1996). "Hitters say it looks like I'm releasing the ball right on top of them." Indeed, Johnson's pitches often bear down on batters, as San Francisco Giant first baseman J. T. Snow can attest; his eye socket was fractured by a wayward Johnson pitch in 1997. Speaking of his fierce pitching style, Johnson explained to Claire Smith for the *New York Times* (March 31, 1996), "I'm always trying to work on my control and get ahead of hitters. That's pretty important for any pitcher, just being in control of the game more, dictating what's happening. I think I have a firm grasp on a majority of that, but there's always room for improvement." In 1999, his first year with the Arizona Diamondbacks, he won his second Cy Young Award. "Quite honestly, I feel . . . this was the best year I had in my career," he told a reporter for the Web site *channel6000.com* (November 16, 1999). "It almost sounds ridiculous to say that you could be surprised by a Randy Johnson," Joe Garagiola Jr., the Diamondbacks' general manager, told the *channel6000* reporter. "But those of you who watched him take the ball every five days, as good as we all thought he was, you couldn't be prepared for this level of consistent excellence."

One of six children, Randall David Johnson was born on September 10, 1963 in Walnut Creek, California. His father, Bud, whom Johnson long considered his best friend, was a police officer. "I wanted to be like my dad," Randy Johnson told Young. "I wanted to be a police officer because they help and protect people. But the more I played baseball, the more I enjoyed it. That's when I started working really hard at baseball." When he was eight years old, Johnson began to practice pitching by trying to emulate the style of a fellow lefty, Vida Blue of the Oakland A's. "I'd get in the street and do my windup, and after I threw the tennis ball at the garage door 70 or 80 times, the nails would start coming loose," he told Nick Charles for *People* (October 6, 1997). "My dad would have to hammer them back in."

A rambunctious child, Johnson often found himself in trouble at school. "I was in the principal's office a lot because I was kind of loud in the classroom," he admitted to Young. "The teacher would say, 'You have to go to the principal's office because you're disrupting the class.' Maybe I didn't learn as much as I would have liked in school, but that was my fault." He began to settle down in the seventh grade, in part because of his height: always tall for his age, he was more than six feet tall when he entered his teens, and reached six feet, nine inches in 12th grade. "I used to be a real outgoing person when I was younger," he told Hank Hersh for *Sports Illustrated* (March 20, 1989). "But then I started getting noticed a lot because of my height. I felt like I was in a three-ring circus and didn't know how to handle it."

As a member of the Livermore High School basketball team, Johnson used his height to advantage: he led the league in scoring. He was also a skilled baseball player, pitching a perfect game for the school team in his senior year. After he graduated Johnson enrolled at the University of Southern California (USC), in Los Angeles, with a baseball and basketball scholarship. At USC he played baseball alongside the future home-run king Mark McGuire. "Mark was made for success, and you could see that early on," he told Selena Roberts for the *New York Times* (September 23, 1998). "I was like 6-foot-10 and 180 pounds. I threw hard, but I'd usually hit the backstop about every other pitch."

In June 1985 Johnson was selected by the Montreal Expos in the second round of the Major League Baseball draft. By all accounts, his teammates found him moody, temperamental, and self-conscious about his height. Furthermore, his pitching, while powerful, tended to be wild. In 1988 the Expos assigned him to Montreal's Double-A team, in Jacksonville, Florida, and Triple-A club, in Indianapolis, Indiana, and he worked with the pitching instructor Joe Berrigan. On June 14, 1988, during a game in Indianapolis, a line drive hit Johnson's left wrist, and he was forced to leave the mound. Club executives witnessed the accident, having come to see him pitch with the hope that they would move him up to the majors. Angry, and fearful that his major-league career was over before it had begun, Johnson stormed into the dugout and smashed his right hand into the bat rack. "Something had to give," he recalled to Hersh, "and the bat rack was plywood three inches thick." Although his pitching hand turned out to be merely bruised, the fifth metacarpal in his right hand was fractured, and he could not play for six weeks. His action led to the establishment of the so-called Randy Johnson Rule, according to which any player who willfully hurts himself out of anger may be fined.

While with the Double-A and Triple-A teams, Johnson posted an 8–7 win–loss record, with a 3.26 earned-run average (ERA). In the fall of 1988 he started for the Expos. He began his first season in the big leagues with seven losses and a 6.67 ERA. Shortly thereafter he was traded to the Seattle Mariners. Playing his first game as a Mariner on May 30, 1989 at Yankee Stadium, he guided his new team to a 3–2 win over the New York Yankees. The velocity of his pitches, which approached 100 miles per hour, began to attract attention. Making his presence felt on the mound, during the next two seasons he hurled Seattle's first-ever no-hitter (on June 2, 1990) and became the first southpaw to strike out the celebrated Red Sox batsman Wade Boggs three times in one game.

These achievements notwithstanding, Johnson was having trouble coordinating his pitching motions. Consequently, he would walk as many hitters as he struck out. "I had a million dollar arm, but I wasn't thinking enough about how to be a pitcher," he told Nick Charles. His control deteriorated to such a degree that he considered quitting baseball. His outlook brightened after he met the strikeout artist Nolan Ryan, in August 1992, and got help with his "mechanics," as he put it. "Nolan said he saw a lot of himself in me—an unproven pitcher who had shined sporadically," he told Tim Kurkjian for *Sports Illustrated* (April 19, 1993). "Nolan walked a lot of guys in his career, and he told me how he dealt with it. It was really beneficial." Thanks in part to the advice he got from Ryan, Johnson gained more confidence on the mound.

On Christmas Day in 1992, while Johnson was en route to California to spend the holiday with his family, his father suffered an aortic aneurysm. By the time Randy arrived at the hospital, Bud Johnson had died. In the wake of that loss, Randy Johnson became a born-again Christian; he began to donate 10 percent of his salary to charity and inscribed his glove with a cross and the word "Dad." In the 1993 season, Johnson finished first in the major leagues in strikeouts, retiring 308 batters, and tied for second in the American League for most wins and shutouts. He also pitched his 1,000th career strikeout. "I had so much success and was so dominant last year because I kept reflecting on the pain my father went through," he told Rick Weinberg for *Sport* (June 1994). "What I go through on the mound is nothing compared to looking up at a team of doctors who are about to open your chest. He had so much toughness, and since he's gone, I've taken that toughness to the mound every time out." Earlier in the 1993 season, the Mariners had contemplated trading Johnson to the Toronto Blue Jays. "We didn't think we'd have the money available to sign him, and we felt we could get a great young player or two for him," Lou Piniella, the Mariners' manager, told Weinberg. But thanks to Johnson's stellar performance, the team decided to keep him. "What can I say?" Pinella told Weinberg. "We were fortunate the trade didn't happen. We got lucky. RJ wound up becoming the best pitcher in baseball in the second half of the season."

Over the next two seasons, Johnson emerged as one of baseball's elite. He became the Mariners' all-time leader in victories in 1994. The following season he set an American League record for best winning percentage in a season, breaking Ron Guidry's 1978 mark, and led Seattle to the team's first playoffs. In 1995 Johnson also became the Mariners' first Cy Young Award winner. "My teammates now come up and ask when I'm pitching, instead of asking when I'm throwing," he told a reporter for the *Chicago Tribune* (November 15, 1995). "I think there's a big difference between someone who tries to go in there and strike everybody out instead of being a pitcher and thinking about the entire game."

The 1996 season proved difficult for Johnson. Early that year he was placed on the disabled list because of an irritated nerve in his lower back. Although he appeared in games sporadically later on that season, he was wracked with pain. By early August he could no longer play; "just trying to move and roll over was painful," he told Nick Charles. Later that month he underwent micro endoscopic discectomy to correct a herniated disc. He recovered fully, and in 1997 he returned to active play. That season he led the American League in strikeouts per nine innings, became the Mariners' first-ever 20-game winner, and was the runner-up, behind Roger Clemens (who was then with the Toronto Blue Jays), for the Cy Young Award. In 1998 he was traded to the Houston Astros, where he remained a commanding presence, winning his first six consecutive starts. Before the 1999 season opened, Johnson was offered trade options to a series of teams, including the Los Angeles Dodgers and the Anaheim Angels, eager to have him in their rotations. He ultimately chose the Arizona Diamondbacks, whom he led to their first play-offs that year. He also became the first pitcher since Nolan Ryan (in 1987) to lead the National League in both strikeouts and ERA. When he won the 1999 Cy Young Award, he became only the third pitcher to have earned that honor in both leagues.

Johnson continued his outstanding performance in 2000, with a season total of 19 wins and a final ERA of 2.64—the best in the game that year. In fact, Johnson's stats for 1999 and 2000 were so impressive that, according to Ronald Blum for the Associated Press (October 31, 2000, on-line), the Elias Sports Bureau, the firm that processes sports statistics for Major League Baseball, pronounced him not only the top pitcher in baseball, but the all-around top player as well.

Besides baseball, Johnson enjoys photography. He takes pictures in every city he visits, and his work has been displayed around the country. An avid drummer, he has played with some of his heroes, including bassist Geddy Lee of Rush and members of Queensryche. He and his wife, Lisa, whom he married in 1993, live in Glendale, Arizona. They have two children—a daughter, Samantha, and a son, Tyler. Johnson had the family's house designed to accommodate his height. "All the doorways are eight feet high, and the countertops around waist level instead of at my knees," he told Charles. — J.K.B.

Suggested Reading: *New York Times* VIII p8+ Mar. 31, 1996, with photos, D p2+ Sep. 23, 1998, with photos; *People* p123+ Oct. 6, 1997, with photos; *Sport* p43+ Jun. 1994, with photos; *Sports Illustrated* p42+ Mar. 20, 1989, with photos, p46+ May 4, 1992, with photos, p58+ June 26, 1995, with photos

Armando Gallo/Retna Ltd.

Jolie, Angelina

June 4, 1975– Actress. Address: c/o Industry Entertainment, 955 S. Carrillo Dr., Suite 300, Los Angeles, CA 90048

The actress Angelina Jolie has gained wide attention for giving over her identity completely to her roles and portraying her characters with exposed-nerve intensity. "There's a truth in acting, and there is a very real part of me that can understand that or can believe in that or can see the beauty of that or see the ugliness in that and the statement that needs to be made," she told Christine James for *Boxoffice* (November 1998, on-line). "So it's all kind of me." Elaborating on the visceral connection she makes with the characters she portrays on film, Jolie explained to Tom Roston for *Premiere* (January 1999), "I don't have a lot to keep to myself. I desperately need to communicate with people through films. It's why I'm alive." Her dynamic performances in the made-for-cable biopics *George Wallace* (1997), as the wife of the controversial governor, and *Gia* (1998), in which she portrayed the ill-fated supermodel Gia Carangi, garnered her two Golden Globes and cachet in Hollywood as an up-and-comer; her Oscar-winning depiction of a disturbed young woman in a mental institution in *Girl, Interrupted* (1999) confirmed her star status. Yet although her acting has generated considerable press, newspapers and magazines have devoted just as much space to her preternatural good looks and reputation for wildness. "I read things I've said and don't realize I'm being a 'bad' girl," she told Andrew Essex for *Entertainment Weekly* (November 5, 1998). "I do like being sexual, I do collect knives, I do like tattoos. I like dark things. But there's a side of me that's soft. I love my family; I want to be a mother."

Angelina Jolie was born Angelina Jolie Voight on June 4, 1975 in Los Angeles, the second child of the acclaimed film star Jon Voight and the French actress and model Marcheline Bertrand. Voight and Bertrand gave their children middle names that could serve well as last names, in case their son and daughter became involved in acting and wanted to drop their famous father's surname. When Jolie was about two, her parents divorced, and she and her older brother were raised by their mother in Palisades, New York. Jolie recalled for Mim Udovitch for *Rolling Stone* (August 19, 1999) that she was an unusually affectionate child in kindergarten. "We would chase the boys around and kiss them a lot and they would scream, and there were a few boys who stopped," she said. "I had two good friends who became my boyfriends, and I think the school called my parents because we were in front of the school grabbing each other, and obviously that was disturbing to the parents and the people driving by." A few years later her mother took her to a Renaissance fair, where Jolie developed her oft-cited fascination with sharp instruments; her collection now includes an antique European battle ax and a spear from Africa. At 11 she moved back to Los Angeles with her mother and brother. Her extroversion during adolescence served her well as a student of acting technique at the Lee Strasberg Theater Institute and member of the MET Theater Ensemble. Jolie had already acquired considerable experience as a performer by the time she returned to New York as a teenager to attend New York University's drama school. Most notably she had appeared at age seven in the role of Tosh in Hal Ashby's *Lookin' to Get Out* (1982), co-written and co-produced by her father, who also starred in the film.

Jolie worked as a fashion model and appeared in several rock videos before landing her first starring role, as a cyborg named Cassandra Reese in the 1993 film *Cyborg 2*; upon seeing the final cut, Jolie reportedly vomited because she felt so distressed by what struck her as the film's dreadful quality. In 1995, after a two-year hiatus from film, she appeared in Gill Dennis's thriller *Without Evidence*, a mystery based on an actual unsolved murder, and Iain Softley's *Hackers*. In *Hackers*, which opened to more fanfare than *Without Evidence*, Jolie starred as Acid Burn, a computer hacker and the romantic interest of the male lead, played by British actor Jonny Lee Miller. During the course of the film, the characters played by Jolie and Miller, along with several of their hacker friends, try to thwart a criminal hacker from unleashing a dangerous computer virus. Although the movie received mixed reviews at best and failed at the box office, Jolie and Miller earned praise for their portrayals; Roger Ebert, for example, in his review for the *Chicago Sun-Times* (September 15, 1995, on-line), wrote that the two actors "bring a particular quality to their performances that is convincing and engaging." Meanwhile, an off-screen romance between Jolie and Miller kindled, and the two married soon after, in 1996. Jolie received a great deal of publicity for dressing for their small civil ceremony in a black outfit and a white T-shirt on which her betrothed's name was spelled out in her own blood. Also in 1996 Jolie appeared in two small films, *Mojave Moon* and *Love Is All There Is*, neither of which attracted critical or commercial attention. More notably, she played Margaret "Legs" Sadovsky in Annette Haywood-Carter's *Foxfire*. An adaptation of a novel by Joyce Carol Oates, *Foxfire* is about five teenage girls who form an unusual friendship after they assault a teacher who had sexually harassed them. Her search for new roles after *Foxfire* left her feeling frustrated. "There was a time when I was really going to give up on acting, right after *Foxfire*," she told James Ryan for *GQ* (December 1998). "I was trying to find characters with a certain strength and things going on, but I was always disappointed."

Jolie reached a turning point in her career in 1997. She began that year with a role in the television miniseries *True Women*, then co-starred in the TNT cable network's *George Wallace* as Cornelia Wallace, a characterization that brought her her first Golden Globe Award. On the silver screen she played the girlfriend of a big-time smuggler and counterfeiter in Andy Wilson's *Playing God* (1997). The film received mostly bad reviews, but once again, Jolie's work was looked upon favorably. "Angelina Jolie finds a certain warmth in a kind of role that is usually hard and aggressive," Roger Ebert wrote for the *Chicago Sun-Times* (October 10, 1997, on-line); "she seems too nice to be [the bad guy's] girlfriend. And maybe she is."

In the most demanding role of her career to that point, Jolie portrayed the model Gia Carangi in the HBO cable movie *Gia* (1998). Carangi dominated the world of fashion in the late 1970s and early 1980s. The product of a broken home, the troubled Carangi battled drug addiction and negative reactions to her lesbianism before she succumbed to AIDS at the age of 26. Through that role, Jolie told James Ryan, "I confronted a lot of terrible things and a lot of my personal fears. It was my therapy to cry and scream." She continued, "Deep inside [Gia] needed to be loved and understood. Like her, I go around denying that. There's an energy we share. You can never settle and be satisfied. If you don't have an outlet for it, it's a dangerous place to live." Her performance in *Gia* earned her a second Golden Globe. After the intense filming of *Gia*, Jolie took a break from acting. "I'm never satisfied," she told Tom Roston. "I don't think I was ever more depressed in my life than the time I realized I was working in the business that I'd always wanted to be in; I was in love; I had money; and I wasn't struggling. I thought, 'Well, I have everything I'd always thought would make me really happy, and I don't feel okay.'" She spent a few months living in New York by herself and reassessed her situation before returning to her craft.

In 1998 Jolie was part of the ensemble cast of Willard Carroll's *Playing by Heart*, which also features Gillian Anderson, Sean Connery, Gena Rowlands, Dennis Quaid, and Ellen Burstyn. The movie presents the parallel stories of 11 people in Los Angeles who have various romantic dilemmas. "For all its artificiality, *Playing by Heart* percolates with an earnest charm," Stephen Holden wrote for the *New York Times* (January 22, 1999, on-line). "Much of that sweetness emanates from Ms. Jolie, who conveys the vulnerability beneath the hard-shell glamour of a restless leonine beauty prowling the L.A. singles scene." Willard Carroll raved to Tom Roston that Jolie "is so vivid and alive. The main challenge was in not letting it go too far. As an actress, she's not timid, which is a rare thing. She will just go for it." Jolie also starred that year in *Hell's Kitchen*, playing Gloria McNeary, the former girlfriend of the sole survivor of a robbery gone awry, who wants her current boyfriend to kill her ex-flame. Between her movie roles Jolie also found time to appear in the video for the Rolling Stones' song "Has Anyone Seen My Baby?"

Next for Jolie was the role of Mary Bell in the film *Pushing Tin* (1999), which also stars John Cusack, Billy Bob Thornton, and Cate Blanchett. "Jolie brandishes her bangs, her crooked bee-stung pout, and her tawny ripe body with seductive abandon," Owen Gleiberman wrote about her performance for *Entertainment Weekly* (April 23, 1999), "yet she also makes Mary a wounded, insidious basket case." In her first appearance in a major studio release, Jolie took the part of a police officer in Phillip Noyce's *Bone Collector* (1999). The film's producers were unwilling to cast Jolie at first, since she was still not a proven Hollywood commodity at the time, but she persuaded them to consider her seriously for the role. "I had to basically wait and wait and wait and beg and not take another job," she told Andrew Essex. "But I don't blame them—I'd certainly never had a money-making film. They took a big risk." To prepare herself for her role, Jolie visited forensic labs and tacked pictures of crime scenes above her desk to approximate a homicide cop's environment. Although most reviewers described *Bone Collector* as contrived, the movie legitimized Jolie's status as a box-office draw, grossing over $66 million in the United States.

On the heels of her first true commercial success, Jolie scored what is to date her finest critical success, in *Girl, Interrupted*, which is based on the best-selling, same-titled 1993 memoir by Susanna Kaysen, about the two years Kaysen spent in a psychiatric institution in the 1960s. Jolie played Lisa, a clinical sociopath who befriends the film's protagonist, played by Winona Ryder. Jolie, who had read Kaysen's book, connected with the part of Lisa. "One of the passages in the book that introduces Lisa," she told Trish Deitch Rohrer for *Premiere* (October 1999), "is about her 'wild eyes that had seen freedom.' And there's this tattoo I got that's a Tennessee Williams quote. 'A prayer for the wild at heart kept in cages.' That's Lisa, and that's what I loved." Critics responded to the abandon with which Jolie portrayed Lisa. "Jolie's ferocious, white-hot performance captures the scary allure of this daredevil and brutal truth teller," Stephen Holden wrote for the *New York Times* (December 21, 1999, on-line). Roger Ebert, in a review for the *Chicago Sun-Times* (January 11, 2000, online), expressed a similar view: "Jolie is emerging as one of the great wild spirits of current movies, a loose cannon who somehow has deadly aim." For her role in *Girl, Interrupted*, Jolie won her third Golden Globe and secured an Academy Award, for best supporting actress. "I've never actually held an Oscar before," Jolie said on the night she received the statuette, as quoted by Rick Lyman in the *New York Times* (March 27, 2000). "It's quite amazing. My dad's mother had his in a goldfish bowl way up on a mantelpiece, and I've never held it." (Jon Voight won the Academy Award for best actor in 1978, for his portrayal of a paraplegic Vietnam War veteran in *Coming Home*.)

Jolie's next major film, Dominic Sena's *Gone in 60 Seconds* (2000), in which she co-starred with Nicolas Cage, is about a band of car thieves; a remake of a 1970s B movie, the picture got thumbs-down reviews. The actress's current projects include *Dancing in the Dark*; starring Antonio Banderas as a Cuban tycoon, it is scheduled for release before the end of 2000. Jolie is also slated to play a lead role in a 2001 film based on the popular video game Tomb Raider.

In August 1999, nearly two years after they separated, Jolie and Miller divorced. Currently managed by her mother, Jolie until recently was living in New York with her brother, with whom she is very close. "My brother's been my best friend," Jolie told Andy Jones for *Rough Cut* (on-line). "He's been there my whole life and we've been through a lot together. He's been unbelievably supportive of me being a sibling and he wants to be an actor." On May 5, 2000, after a brief courtship, Jolie married Billy Bob Thornton, who is 20 years her senior and a four-time divorcé. As for her relationship with her father, Jolie has said that the two have become closer over the years. "I think we speak to each other a lot through our work," she told Mim Udovitch. "You don't really know your parents in a certain way, and they don't really know you. Like, you know, he met my husband and we'd go to dinner, but he still had his opinion of me as his daughter. So he can kind of watch a film and see how I am as a woman, the way I am dealing with a husband who's been injured or the way I am crying alone. And it's the same for me: I can watch films of his and just see who he is. But not growing up in the same house and feeling that he really did belong to the world . . . as I've gotten older I learned to communicate with him as a person."

Jolie, whose body is decorated with tattoos, enjoys playing drums. Long a darling of critics, Jolie often stands as her own toughest judge. Speaking about her abilities as an actress, she observed during a conversation with her father for *Interview* (June 1997), "I have a certain energy . . . and it's either needed or it's definitely not needed. I know that I can stick out like a sore thumb, and there are some women I'm not ready to play." — G.O.

Suggested Reading: *Entertainment Weekly* p40+ Nov. 5, 1998; *Interview* p78 June 1997; *Premiere* p86+ Jan. 1999; *Rolling Stone* p60+ Aug. 19, 1999

Selected Films: *Cyborg 2: Glass Shadow*, 1993; *Hackers*, 1995; *Without Evidence*, 1995; *Foxfire*, 1996; *Love Is All There Is*, 1996; *Mojave Moon*, 1996; *George Wallace*, 1997; *Gia*, 1998; *Playing by Heart*, 1998; *Pushing Tin*, 1999; *The Bone Collector*, 1999; *Girl, Interrupted*, 1999; *Gone in 60 Seconds*, 2000

Associated Press

Jospin, Lionel Robert

(zhoss-PAN, lee-oh-NEL roh-BAIR)

July 12, 1937– Prime Minister of France.
Address: Hôtel de Matignon, 57 rue de Varenne, 75700 Paris, France

The Socialist Lionel Jospin, who became the prime minister of France in 1997, has gone far toward his announced goal of reviving the French economy through the creation of jobs. Jospin began his career as a high-ranking civil servant before turning to academia in the early 1970s. At around the same time, he became active in the Socialist Party, and with the election of François Mitterrand as president, in 1981—which ended 23 years of conservative rule—Jospin ascended within the government hierarchy. After Mitterrand completed his second term, in 1995, Jospin made a bid for the presidency, losing to Jacques Chirac. He emerged from the elections of two years later as prime minister. He has since won the respect of political allies and opponents alike with his economic initiatives and has lived up to his liberal credentials—for example, by granting legal status to immigrants and gay couples.

The second of four children, Lionel Robert Jospin was born on July 12, 1937. He spent most of his childhood in the Paris suburb of Meudon, in the Hauts de Seine region, with holidays at Tarn-et-Garonne, the birthplace of his mother, Mireille (Dandieu) Jospin. His father, Robert Jospin, an activist in the SFIO, the French section of the International Workers Party, was a candidate in a general election in the geographic district of Indre, in central France. After World War II Robert Jospin became the federal secretary of the SFIO in Seine-et-Marne, where he settled the family. Jospin's mother worked first as a midwife and then as a nurse and school social worker.

After attending high school in Sèvres, Paris, and Meaux, Jospin studied liberal arts for a year in Paris before deciding in 1956 to take up political science at the Paris Institut d'Études Politiques. On winning a scholarship, he moved to the Antony student residence hall, where he began to be politically active. He joined the student union, which opposed the war in Algeria, a French colony, where the French military was embroiled in an ultimately unsuccessful attempt to put an end to the Algerians' struggle for independence.

In 1958, stunned by the Soviet Union's 1956 invasion of Budapest, which crushed the Hungarians' demands for democracy, and in conflict with the policy of the SFIO, Jospin became a member of the Union de la Gauche Socialiste (UGS), a Socialist group. The UGS became a founding section of the United Socialist Party, which he joined in 1960. During these years he spent summers as a camp counselor, working with troubled teenagers. He was also good at basketball and played in college tournaments.

Meanwhile, Jospin studied for the competitive entrance exams for the National School of Administration (ENA), the alma mater of many top French government leaders. Once he had secured a place there, he set about performing his mandatory military service. After training in Trier, Germany, and at the reserve officers' school in Saumur, France, he joined the tank corps in Germany as a second lieutenant—just as the war in Algeria ended. In July 1963 Jospin began studying at the ENA. He stayed at the elite school until 1965; he has said that the most memorable part of that period was the time he spent mining coal in northern France. After completing his studies he worked for five years at the Ministry of Foreign Affairs. Soon he was appointed to the economic-affairs directorate, where he organized important conferences.

During his years of study at ENA, military service, and ministry work, political activism was not part of Jospin's life. He was jogged from his relatively placid existence by the events of May 1968, when a University of Paris student protest against imperialism triggered nationwide demonstrations by farmers and other workers as well as students against police brutality and in favor of changes in French society that ranged from modest to radical. Specifically, there were demands for a boost in the minimum wage and automatic cost-of-living increases; a decrease in the average workweek from 48 to 40 hours; greater latitude for union organizers; government price supports for beef, wine, and dairy products; and improvements in the system of education. In response, President Charles de Gaulle dissolved the National Assembly (the French Parliament), and in elections held in June 1968, the Gaullists won by a landslide, gaining an absolute majority of seats. His credibility reinforced, de Gaulle promised that there would be opportunities for all workers and students to "participate" in the nation's governance.

Surrounded by such tumult, Jospin began thinking about the direction his life had taken, and in 1969 he decided on a career change. In October 1970 he went to teach at the Paris XI University. Later, at the Paris-Sceaux University of Technology, where he was on the faculty for 11 years, he directed the business department and taught economics, ultimately with the rank of professor.

In 1971, with the re-creation of the Socialist Party and his sponsorship in it by Pierre Joxe, a Socialist heavyweight, Jospin returned to his earlier activism. He worked for the party, which was seeking to unify leftists, as a rank-and-file organizer in the 15th arrondissement of Paris. He quickly moved up the ranks to join the group of experts in East–West relations under the party's then-first secretary, François Mitterrand. In June 1973 he was accepted into the executive bureau of the Socialist Party and became national secretary for training. Two years later he was named national secretary for Third World affairs.

Once, in Mitterrand's absence, Jospin chaired the Socialist Party's national secretariat and executive bureau. After 1975 he had the delicate responsibility of monitoring relations between the Socialist and Communist Parties. In 1977 he ran successfully as a councillor for the 18th arrondissement of Paris, and in 1979 he was appointed national secretary for international relations. During this period he worked with Mitterrand to craft party strategy. On January 24, 1981 Mitterrand was chosen as the Socialist Party's presidential candidate, while Jospin was elected unanimously by the steering committee as the party's leader, with the title of first secretary. He ran for the National Assembly from his arrondissement and was elected as a Paris deputy that June, when Mitterrand became president of France. Jospin headed the Socialist list in the European elections of 1984 and was elected a member of the European Parliament.

In the general election of March 1986, Jospin was elected with seven other Socialist deputies. The following September, at the request of the party, he ran for a seat in the National Assembly from Haute Garonne, in the south of France. Upon winning, he gave up his seat as a Paris deputy and councillor. He was repeatedly elected to the Haute-Garonne General Council until 1993.

On May 12, 1988, during his second term as president, Mitterrand appointed Jospin minister of national education, youth, and sport. In his four years in the post, Jospin pursued an ambitious agenda of reform. In what was called the Université 2000 project, the government built seven universities and hundreds of new classrooms throughout the country for the equivalent of $6 billion in U.S. currency. Jospin supported policies decentralizing the academic system and giving more power to individual school councils; the reform of teacher training; and an improvement in the professional conditions for teachers. He implemented a reform of nursery, primary, and secondary schools and curriculum improvements. He also introduced foreign languages at the primary level and apprenticeships in secondary schools. In 1989 he was attacked for not upholding the separation of church and state after he ruled that Muslim girls would be allowed to wear chador veils in public schools.

Meanwhile, the Socialist Party had become plagued by internal conflicts and scandals. Jospin "gradually distanced himself from the internal life of the Socialist Party," according to the French government's Web site. He left the Ministry of Education in 1992 and, as required by government regulations, returned to the Ministry of Foreign Affairs, where he was a minister plenipotentiary, attached to the central administration without portfolio. On April 3, 1993 he resigned from the party's steering committee and from the executive bureau.

Jospin's return to party meetings took the form of his participation in the Conference for Social Change, in which left-wing and ecological activists discussed problems facing France. In 1994 he issued a paper evaluating the achievements of the Socialist government and offered proposals for future reform. On January 4, 1995 he declared to the Socialist Party's national bureau his intention to run in the presidential election. A month later he was chosen as the Socialist candidate. The party also chose him, almost unanimously, as first secretary. According to the *New York Times* (April 8, 1995), his "reputation for moral rectitude helped win the nomination of a party racked with scandal."

Jospin's major opponents in the election were the conservative Paris mayor and former prime minister Jacques Chirac, then-Prime Minister Edouard Balladur, also a conservative, and Jean-Marie Le Pen of the ultra-right-wing National Front party. In the campaign the candidates focused more on domestic economic issues than on matters of defense and foreign policy. Chirac, twice defeated for the presidency, ran on the slogan "France for All," promising to reduce unemployment by granting financial incentives to companies to hire the unemployed. Prime Minister Balladur, in office since 1993, adopted the slogan "Believing in France" and vowed to create jobs through tax incentives to businesses. For his part, Jean-Marie Le Pen promised to resolve economic problems by deporting most of the three to five million, predominantly North African, immigrants then living in France.

Jospin's campaign platform included a vast public-works program to rebuild deteriorated housing and a reduction of the workweek from 39 to 37 hours as a means of creating 400,000 jobs for young people in two years. He said that to stimulate hiring he would relieve employers of the obligation to pay health-insurance contributions to employees earning less than $1,000 per month—but that he would raise contributions for those with higher salaries. Jospin pledged to protect the achievements of Mitterrand's 14-year rule—such as the national standard of five weeks' paid holiday and the abolition of the death penalty—while ridding France of corruption and unemployment. He also planned to strengthen French influence in the European Union and to support commercial competition with the United States. During his campaign he touched on the perennial concern over the effects of free trade on France's cultural integrity. "As a student in the 1950s and 1960s, I was extremely affected by American literature and American movies," he was quoted as saying by Craig R. Whitney in the *New York Times* (April 25, 1995). But he expressed his desire that Europe not be "overwhelmed" by American pop culture. "If what 'threatened' us were the most elevated forms of American culture and creativity, it wouldn't be worth talking about," he said, according to Whitney. "But since it's something more mediocre that's the problem, Americans should understand that. . . . It's not cultural chauvinism or protectionism, it's a question of identity and economics."

Jospin made a good showing in the first round of balloting. The mere possibility that a Socialist might be elected president had triggered a flight of capital from France after Mitterrand's success in the first ballot of 1981, forcing the suspension of trade on all markets. But the Socialists had become "the orthodox keepers of the capitalist gospel," as Daniel Singer put it in the *Nation* (May 29, 1995), the proof being the fact that Jospin's first-round win "did not produce a ripple." One Swiss banker even said, according to Singer, "We did some of our best business under the Socialists." One result of the election was that Jean-Marie Le Pen and Philippe de Villiers, candidates of the extreme right, together polled an unprecedented 20 percent of the vote, their support extending from southern port cities to northern and eastern industrial suburbs struggling with unemployment. In the second round Jospin's support faltered, and the Gaullist Chirac won the presidency, reappointing Balladur as prime minister.

In 1997, two years after his failed bid for the presidency, Jospin revived his platform to campaign for the French National Assembly, saying he would not be bound by commitments to austerity made by conservative leaders in 1992 as part of the Maastricht Treaty. Among other things, the treaty required the countries of the European Community to hold their budget deficits to a limit of 3 percent of gross domestic product in order to join the European Union and to adopt the euro as common currency. Such a policy prevented the government from stimulating economic growth with investments and from giving aid to the poor. Jospin instead proposed a "solidarity and growth pact," part of which called for the workweek to be reduced from 39 hours to 35 rather than 37 and for 700,000 jobs to be created rather than the 400,000 he had promised in 1995. French voters, at least in part because they were unhappy that the economy had remained stalled under the conservatives Balladur and then-Prime Minister Alain Juppé, elected a Socialist plurality to the National Assembly in 1997. The Socialists immediately entered into negotiations with the French Communist Party, the Green Party, and the Citizens' Movement (each of which had secured between seven and 38 assembly seats in the election), and the resulting coalition formed a Socialist-led legislative majority. Consequently, on June 2, 1997, President Chirac appointed the leader of the Socialist Party—Lionel Jospin—prime minister.

That October, with an abrupt rise in interest rates threatening to slow down the economy even more, Jospin kept his campaign promise, submitting a bill to increase employment by cutting the workweek from 39 to 35 hours by the year 2002. He also managed to implement successful deficit-cutting measures—among them raising taxes on large corporations while shifting the personal tax to some degree from earned income (wages) to unearned income (interest and dividends)—while continuing his rhetoric of jobs as the first priority. By December of that year, both French conservatives and foreign observers had come to acknowledge Jospin's skill as a statesman. The *New York Times* (December 31, 1997) quoted a conservative member of Parliament who declared angrily, "The real President these days is not Chirac, but Jospin." The *Times* reporter then explained, "The legislator was commenting on Mr. Jospin's ability to pick his way unscathed through the minefield of budget cuts, soaring unemployment, and European fiscal policy."

Jospin's popularity was not based on smoke and mirrors. His finance minister, Dominique Strauss-Kahn, at Jospin's behest, had shifted some of the burden of health insurance onto wealthier taxpayers as promised, and Jospin had rolled back draconian anti-immigration measures. The Debré law, introduced by Chirac as an attempt to please supporters of Le Pen, had "required that the French act as informers and report to the government the departure of foreign guests," according to the *Nation* (October 27, 1997). Several hundred thousand people had signed a petition saying they would disobey the law and had marched in the streets of Paris to protest it; in response, Jospin annulled the Debré law, thus legalizing the residence of 80,000 immigrants. He also granted legal status to homosexual couples. Though he attempted to restore the traditional right to citizenship of any 18-year-old born on French soil, conservatives blocked the passage of such a law.

Meanwhile, certain large companies, such as Cofinaga, a financial-services firm, had experimented with the 35-hour workweek, which had also been in the conservatives' program. Company executives reported great savings thanks to newly hired employees' acceptance of flexible work schedules that allowed the businesses to stay open longer and on weekends.

By January 1999 the French economy had reached an undeniable slowdown, but Jospin remained popular, since overall, 1998 had been the strongest year of the decade in terms of the economy. With the slogan "Yes to the free-market economy; no to the free-market society," his administration has created 150,000 public-sector jobs, with 350,000 more planned. Though not ideologically committed to privatization, he had sold more state assets in his 18 months in office than the previous, right-wing government had done in 24, thus keeping the deficit within the limits imposed by the Maastricht Treaty.

By the beginning of 2000, however, despite his successes in reducing unemployment and stimulating economic growth, Jospin's relationship with his constituency had begun to sour, and commentators on both the left and the right had begun to question his chances of upsetting Jacques Chirac in the 2002 presidential election. Explaining this change of sentiment, Dominique Moisi, a French political scientist, told the *Economist* (September 16, 2000), "Jospin appeared modest and honest, but now he seems hesitant. . . . He has maintained an exceptionally long honeymoon with the French public; but the honeymoon is now over."

The most visible sign of Jospin's difficulties was the solid resistance with which several of his proposed reforms were met. The government's efforts to implement the 35-hour workweek, for example, ignited protests by both managers and workers. On February 2, 2000, the deadline for most French companies to adopt the new workweek, subway workers, bus drivers, and truckers, angry at having to work harder during their reduced hours, staged nationwide protests that effectively paralyzed the country. Managers, for their part, complained that the reforms would be too costly and would prevent France from competing economically with the rest of Europe. The government eventually prevailed (though it made an exception for truckers, allowing them to put in more hours). It was less successful in paring down the country's civil service and failed in its attempts to reform the educational and tax-collection systems. Protests erupted over the proposed tax reforms, with the drivers of ambulances, taxis, and tractors, who felt that the government had shortchanged them by withholding oil-tax revenues, taking to the streets.

Jospin unleashed a storm of criticism during a trip to the Middle East by referring to the Hezbollah guerrillas in Southern Lebanon as "terrorists." Not only did the remark anger many French Arabs; it was also widely seen as an inappropriate attempt to upstage France's president, who is traditionally responsible for foreign policy. Jospin later retracted the remark, but the political damage had already been done.

Jospin has three children from his first marriage: Hugo, Eva, and Daniel. His current wife, Sylviane Agacinski, whom he married in 1994, is a professor of philosophy at the Institute des Hautes Études en Sciences Sociales and has written several books. The family lives in a rented apartment. Jospin told *L'Express*, as reported in the *New York Times* (April 25, 1995), "I live off my diplomat's salary and my legislative pension. I have no fortune." —V.K.

Suggested Reading: French government Web site (on-line); *Nation* p754+ May 29, 1995, p22+ Oct. 27, 1997; *New York Times* A p3 July 11, 1998

Fred Prouser/Archive Photos

Judd, Ashley

Apr. 19, 1968– Actress. Address: c/o William Morris Agency, 151 El Camino Dr., Beverly Hills, CA 90212

Although she was born into a singing family—mother Naomi and sister Wynonna comprised the Grammy-winning country duo the Judds, and Wynonna has had a successful solo career since the early 1990s—Ashley Judd chose to pursue a career in Hollywood. She had prominent roles in the TV series *Star Trek: The Next Generation* and *Sisters* before winning the title role, that of a dreamy loner, in the 1993 movie *Ruby in Paradise*, and she has since starred in several hits, including *Heat* (1995), *Kiss the Girls* (1997), and *Double Jeopardy* (1999). Critics have praised Judd for the feminine strength she conveys on-screen; writing in *Us* magazine (January 1996) about the actress, who spent much of her childhood in rural Kentucky, David Hochman observed, "Ashley Judd is the sort of character Tennessee Williams might have created had he grown up watching MTV."

Ashley Judd was born on April 19, 1968 in Los Angeles to Michael Ciminella, a marketing specialist in the horse-racing industry, and Naomi Ciminella, who would go by her maiden name—Judd—after her divorce, when Ashley was four. Following several tumultuous years of struggling to survive on their own in California, Ashley, her older sister, Wynonna, and their mother moved to Kentucky. Money was scarce in that rural environment, and the trio moved around a lot, from one run-down house to another. Often they didn't have heat or running water. By the time she was 13, Ashley Judd had attended 12 different schools, an experience, she has said, from which she learned to be adaptable. According to Chuck Arnold in *People* (October 13, 1997), Naomi, who supported her daughters by working as a nurse, would often say, "Kids, pour more water in the soup. Better days are coming." Naomi also repeatedly told the girls that they were special and were destined to achieve great things. Judd still cites her mother's confidence in her as one of the greatest gifts she has ever received.

Because few other sources of entertainment were available, music played a big part in the household. Someone gave Naomi an old guitar, and Wynonna soon showed a knack for playing it. Although Ashley enjoyed the music, she had no interest in performing, and she has joked that given the quality of her voice, the public is lucky she followed another career path. While Naomi and Wynonna practiced the act that would eventually make them stars, the youngest Judd spent her time alone, reading. When she was 15, her mother and sister landed a major recording contract and embarked on a strenuous concert schedule. When the Judds, as her mother and sister became known, were on the road, Ashley lived with her father or grandparents. Many journalists have portrayed Ashley Judd as a Cinderella figure, pointing out that she used to clean the tour bus for pocket money. Judd herself has claimed that her family's fame didn't prevent her from leading the life of an average teenager, although she told Gail Buchalter for *Parade* (August 22, 1993), "A few times, I got mad waiting for them to stop rehearsing, but that's no different from any kid whose parents work at home. I remember getting really angry when no one picked me up at cheerleading practice or student council meetings." A television miniseries about the Judds, which aired in 1995, portrayed the teenage Ashley as petulant and dependent. Although she admitted to being engrossed by the show (she even provided the narrative voice-over for it), Judd told Lawrence Grobel for *TV Guide* (May 13, 1995), "I feel I look a little whiny, and I come across as having been frequently put out by their pursuit of their dream. That wasn't the reality, though I'm sure at times my feelings were hurt or I felt excluded."

After finishing high school, Judd attended the University of Kentucky, where she majored in French and minored in four separate disciplines—anthropology, women's studies, art history, and theater. When a prominent member of the board of trustees at the school made a racist remark, Judd led a campus-wide walkout to demand his resignation. Devoted to her studies, she generally maintained a 4.0 average. She graduated in 1990, with Phi Beta Kappa honors. (She remains passionate about the school's basketball team, the Wildcats.)

After graduation Judd was accepted into the Peace Corps. Fluent in French, she volunteered to go to a French-speaking part of Africa—preferably "an extremely traditional village," as she told Buchalter, "so I could start my career as a sociocultural anthropologist." But she felt conflicted. She had been interested in acting since she had seen Jane Fonda's performance in *The Dollmaker* (1984). Worried that her age would be against her if she delayed trying her luck in Hollywood, Judd approached her family for advice. Naomi was resistant to the idea at first. "She was aghast," Judd told Buchalter. "In her plans for me, I was running the Cousteau Society. But by the end of my presentation, Mom was as excited as I was and said she'd do anything to help me."

Judd moved to Los Angeles, got a restaurant job to support herself, and began taking acting classes. She asked the Triad Agency, where she had interned during her junior year of college, to represent her, and the firm agreed to send her on one audition. At this pivotal juncture in Judd's life, her mother announced publicly that she was ill with hepatitis C and would no longer perform with Wynonna. Some journalists have theorized that the news of the family's tribulations overshadowed the actress's fledgling career, but others think that it drew additional attention to her. "When I auditioned, I didn't tell anyone who my family was," Judd told Buchalter. "I was raised to be self-sufficient, and that's paramount to any success I attain. I guess my faith and arrogance kept me thinking I could make it on my own." Judd was offered the role for which she had tried out—the female lead in the movie *Kuffs*, starring Christian Slater—but turned it down in favor of a smaller role, because the *Kuffs* part required a nude scene. "My mother worked too hard for me to take off my clothes in my first movie," she told Cynthia Sanz for *People* (October 12, 1992).

That job was quickly followed by the recurring role of Ensign Mussler on the television show *Star Trek: The Next Generation*. Not long after she landed that assignment, she joined the cast of the critically acclaimed dramatic series *Sisters*. From 1991 to 1994 she portrayed the daughter of the character played by Swoosie Kurtz. Meanwhile, eager for more film roles, in 1993 she earned the part of the title character in *Ruby in Paradise*, the tale of a dreamer from a small Tennessee town who escapes to find her identity in Panama City, Florida. The film won the Grand Jury Prize at the 1993 Sundance Film Festival, and Judd received an Independent Spirit Award, as well as unanimously favorable reviews, for her powerful portrayal. Victor Nunez, who directed the picture, explained why, after despairing of ever finding the right person to portray Ruby, he chose Judd. "It was a fluke," he told the *New York Times* (October 3, 1993, online). "Three of the actresses were very good. But they were all a little too much Tennessee Williams and not enough Tennessee. Their experience of the South was from doing Williams, not from living in the north of Florida. Not only did Ashley have an intuitive sense of who Ruby was, she also knew what it was like to weather a winter in Appalachia."

After the success of *Ruby in Paradise*, Judd was advised to make her next project a big-budget Hollywood movie. Ever independent, she opted instead to go to New York to star in a revival of William Inge's play *Picnic*, which won a Pulitzer Prize in 1953. After that she returned to Hollywood, where her next performance, in Oliver Stone's film *Natural Born Killers* (1994), ended up on the cutting-room floor. Hired to play the sole survivor of a slumber-party massacre in the movie, Judd imbued her character with chilling realism. The Ratings and Classification Board of the Motion Picture Association of America initially gave the picture an NC-17 rating, specifically citing Judd's scenes as being too emotionally harrowing, and Stone deleted them. Judd has said that she viewed his action as a testament to her acting ability.

In 1995 Judd made an appearance in the movie *Smoke*. Cast opposite veteran actors Stockard Channing and Harvey Keitel, she drew raves from the critics with her vivid turn as Channing's drug-addicted daughter. Her Hollywood profile rose even higher with her appearance in the 1995 film *Heat*. In it she played the wife of Chris Shiherlis (Val Kilmer), one of a band of audacious robbers headed by Neil McCauley (Robert De Niro) and pursued by detective Vincent Hanna (Al Pacino). Judd held her own with the heavy-hitting cast, and she was soon offered the role of Matthew McConaughey's wife in the film *A Time to Kill* (1996), based on a John Grisham novel.

Also in 1996 Judd starred in *Normal Life*, opposite Luke Perry. The story of a bank-robbing couple, the movie went straight to video after a corporate shake-up at Fine Line Features, its distributor. In the same year Judd starred in the unusual Home Box Office (HBO) movie *Norma Jean & Marilyn*. The project, which presented the life of Marilyn Monroe from the perspectives of two different aspects of her personality, starred Mira Sorvino as the glamorous side of the screen goddess and Judd as Norma Jean, the insecure orphan who would be transformed by the Hollywood studio system. Judd had never been interested in Monroe, perhaps because she was born almost six years after the actress's death, but after studying Monroe's work, she began to develop respect for her larger-than-life subject. "I have a lot of admiration for her animal brilliance, her ability to survive, to know what she needed and how to go about getting it," Judd told Hilary De Vries for *TV Guide* (May 18, 1996). So capably did Judd portray the young Monroe that she was nominated for both an Emmy and a Golden Globe Award.

By the end of 1996, Judd felt exhausted, and she sank into a deep depression. She secluded herself and began intensive therapy, through which she examined her childhood years and came to the realization that they were not "quite as sunny as she had wanted to remember," as Bernard Weinraub reported in *Redbook* (November 1997). "I was looking at old stuff," she explained to Weinraub. "And the fact is, I really encourage people to look at it, because it doesn't break you. It actually heals you."

Judd emerged from that bleak time ready to work, and her next roles cemented her screen image as a strong woman. While the 1997 movie *The Locusts* was not a hit, critics singled out for praise Judd's performance as a free-spirited midwesterner; she herself told Michael Angeli for *Esquire* (February 1997), "It's the proudest I've ever been of my work." The actress's biggest hit to date also came out that year. *Kiss the Girls* starred Judd as a feisty doctor who teams up with a detective, played by Morgan Freeman, to thwart a serial killer. The movie was a huge success at the box office, and Judd was particularly proud that she did most of her own stunt work—even learning kickboxing for the role. Discussing her casting, Gary Fleder, who directed *Kiss the Girls*, told Lucy Kaylin for *Gentlemen's Quarterly* (October 1999), "The thing that was important to me was that the character couldn't be a victim. And I thought Ashley was the perfect nonvictim. She refused to be broken."

Judd's 1998 film, *Simon Birch*, was not as well received by moviegoers, but as usual, Judd's performance—this time as the mother of the title character—was hailed by critics. Later that year Judd narrated a Family Channel special on the life of her sister. But if 1998 was a relatively low-profile year on her résumé, 1999 would prove to be anything but. Opening in September of that year, *Double Jeopardy* starred Judd as a woman wrongly imprisoned for killing her husband. While in jail, she discovers that her husband is still alive and enjoying himself with her best friend. Reasoning that you can't be tried and convicted for the same crime twice, she plots her revenge. Originally the role had been intended for Jodie Foster, but Foster dropped out of the project when she discovered that she was pregnant. A determined Judd then lobbied the director, Bruce Beresford, for the part. The movie features several scenes of Judd working out in prison in preparation for her release; critics found those sequences charmingly reminiscent of similar scenes in Sylvester Stallone's *Rocky*. In the first two weeks after its premiere, the movie, which co-starred Tommy Lee Jones, made almost $50 million and established Judd as a bona fide leading lady. (Its earnings eventually reached more than $116 million in the U.S. alone.)

Judd next starred in *The Eye of the Beholder* (2000), as a psychopathic killer who frequently changes her appearance to foil her pursuers. The film was almost universally panned, but Stephen Holden wrote for the *New York Times* (January 28, 2000), "Judd, at least, emerges from this fiasco with her dignity intact. . . . She is clearly giving her all to an unsalvageable enterprise." Judd appeared opposite Natalie Portman in *Where the Heart Is* (2000), a movie based on the Southern Gothic novel of the same name by Billie Letts, which the talk-show host Oprah Winfrey had selected for her popular book club. Although the book sold well, the movie was neither a critical nor commercial success. Judd currently has several projects in production, including a film based on the life of the artist Frida Kahlo, which is due to be released in 2001.

Unable to pigeonhole Judd, journalists have often resorted to comparing her to other actresses, and she has been described variously as having the casual beauty of Elizabeth Taylor, the icy sophistication of Grace Kelly, and the strength of Katharine Hepburn. Feature writers seem to relish the challenge of analyzing Judd—a woman who, on the one hand, has described herself as a "ball-buster" and, on the other, carries quilts and stuffed animals with her when she travels, to make her hotel rooms cozier. "True to her rural Kentucky roots," Hilary De Vries wrote, "Judd is a classic southern woman, all syrupy charm on the outside, wrought iron underneath. One minute, she is the girl next door with her well-scrubbed sexiness and down-home aphorisms, nattering on about 'Mawma' and 'granddaddy' and life on the farm. Spend enough time with her, however, and you realize Judd's cultivated farm-fresh image can yield with startling speed to that of a cool-headed careerist."

Riveted by her on-screen work, Judd's fans have shown just as much interest in the star's personal life. Judd had a widely publicized romance with Matthew McConaughey during the filming of *A Time to Kill*, and the two remain good friends. She was also linked with Robert De Niro, but although the two admitted to admiration for each other, they denied any deeper involvement. Judd laughed at the idea that she always dated her leading men. "I actually sat down and counted," she told Ned Zeman during an interview for *Harper's Bazaar* (May 1997). "In 10 professional outings, [I was involved with] exactly two of my co-stars, both of which were wonderful love affairs. Just 20 percent. Which, by the way, is well below the national average." Judd's next confirmed relationship was with the singer Michael Bolton, whom she met through her sister. Although the romance eventually ended, she credited Bolton for helping her through her depression in 1996. In May 2000 she announced that she was engaged to be married to the Scottish race-car driver Dario Franchitti.

A devoted aunt, Judd has frequently regaled listeners with tales of Wynonna's children. She is said to be intensely loyal to her friends. The actress lives in a century-old house on the property of Peaceful Valley, the Judd family's 1,000-acre Tennessee farm. She told David Hochman for *Us*, "I'm modeling it after C. S. Lewis' *Chronicles of Narnia*, with cubbyholes and secret passageways, old gun cabinets and medicine chests built of chestnut, all because it was the first book ever read to me as a child and my house needs to be a magical place." Interviewers who have seen the house confirm that it is, indeed, magical—full of overstuffed chairs and whimsically painted surfaces. — M.R.

Suggested Reading: *Cosmopolitan* p132+ Feb. 1998, with photos; *Esquire* p81+ Feb. 1997, with photos, p150+ Oct. 2000, with photos; *Gentlemen's Quarterly* p215+ Oct. 1999, with photos; *Harper's Bazaar* p184+ May 1997, with photos; *McCall's* p38+ Sep. 2000, with photos; *New York Times* (on-line) Oct. 3, 1993; *Parade* p4+ Aug. 22, 1993, with photos; *People* p113+ Oct.12, 1992, with photos; *Premiere* p62+ May 2000, with photos; *Redbook* p112+ Nov. 1997, with photos; *TV Guide* p35+ May 18, 1996, with photos

Selected Films: *Ruby in Paradise*, 1993; *Heat* 1995; *Norma Jean and Marilyn*, 1996; *Kiss the Girls*, 1997; *Simon Birch*, 1998; *Double Jeopardy*,1999; *The Eye of the Beholder*, 2000; *Where the Heart Is*, 2000

Jung, Andrea

1959(?)– President and CEO of Avon Products Inc. Address: Avon Products Inc., 1257 Ave. of the Americas, New York, NY 10020-1196

When Andrea Jung was appointed president and CEO of Avon Products Inc. in November 1999, the company became the second-largest U.S. firm to be headed by a woman. (Hewlett-Packard, which months earlier had promoted Carly Fiorina to its top post, is bigger.) Avon, which markets primarily beauty products, also became the largest U.S. concern ever to be headed by an Asian-American woman. Jung, who has held executive positions at Avon since 1994, has been credited with revitalizing the 114-year-old company's somewhat stodgy and tradition-bound reputation—or (as journalists not above making the obvious pun have expressed it) with engineering Avon's striking "makeover." As CEO, Jung oversees direct sales of Avon products in 131 countries, including the People's Republic of China, and advises 440,000 Avon sales representatives in the United States and nearly two million additional reps in other countries. "Each year," according to the firm's home page on the World Wide Web, "Avon prints over 600 million sales brochures in more than 12 languages." Thanks to Jung, consumers can now buy Avon products via the Internet as well. In 1998 *Fortune* magazine named Jung among the "50 Most Powerful Women in American Business."

Courtesy of Avon Products Inc.

Little is known about the early years of Andrea Jung, who was born in about 1959 in Toronto, Canada, the eldest child of first-generation Chinese immigrants. The family moved to Wellesley, Massachusetts, when she was 10. Jung became fluent in both Mandarin Chinese and English, and she is said to have been an exceptional student. Recalling her upbringing in what she described as "a traditional humble Asian environment," Jung told Patricia Sellers for *Fortune* (October 12, 1998), "There was focus on achievement and education, but fame was a negative." Jung attended Princeton University, in New Jersey, graduating magna cum laude with a B.A. degree in English literature. After briefly considering a career in law or music, she settled on retail marketing. She took a job at Bloomingdale's and later was hired by I. Magnin in San Francisco, where she rose to the rank of senior vice president and general merchandise manager. Next, she moved to Dallas, Texas, to accept the executive vice presidency at Neiman Marcus, where she was responsible for women's clothing, accessories, cosmetics, lingerie, and children's wear.

After more than 10 years in the upscale environments of those three exclusive department stores, Jung examined the direction of shopping trends in the United States and decided to change paths. "I had an entire career in the prestige segment, and that was exciting," she explained to Pam Weisz for *Brandweek* (November 13, 1995). "But if you look at the consumer demographics and the growth of American consumer purchasing, and where I believe it's going to come from in the next decade, I felt the experience in the mass segment was what I wanted to take on."

In June 1993 Jung became a consultant for Avon, the world's leading direct seller of mass-market beauty products. Avon was launched in 1886, after the first "Avon lady," Mrs. P.F.E. (Persus Foster Eames) Albee, started selling beauty products door-to-door. (Although, currently, approximately 1 percent of the company's sales reps are male, all are still known collectively as "Avon ladies.") During the post–World War II years, it was common to see the reps toting sample cases full of miniature lipsticks and perfume vials from house to house. As more and more women joined the workforce, fewer of them were home to answer the doorbell, and by the early 1970s, sales had fallen dramatically. In 1973 the price of the company's stock plunged, and management faced rising debt. The company's top executives thought the solution was to diversify, so Avon acquired Tiffany & Co., several perfume manufacturers, and a variety of health-care companies. The strategy failed: one of the newly purchased health-care companies drained Avon of all its available cash, and by 1988 the company's long-term debt had swelled to $1.1 billion. Thanks to its still-loyal customers—primarily rural women and women from Middle America—the firm managed to stay afloat. Savvy sales representatives serviced customers, most of whom worked outside the home, by leaving sales brochures in beauty salons, offices, and factories.

In 1989 James E. Preston, a 24-year veteran of the company, became Avon's CEO. Determined to turn the company around, he divested Avon of most of its acquisitions. In addition, he resolved to place more women in top positions, reasoning that had there been more female executives in the 1970s, Avon would have been quicker to respond to changes in door-to-door marketing. He recruited Jung from Neiman Marcus to update the product line and change the company's downscale image—an ideal assignment for her, given her intimate knowledge of more-prestigious lines of cosmetics. In January 1994, after working as a consultant for six months, Jung joined Avon full-time as president of the product marketing group for the U.S. Most Avon staffers reportedly welcomed her arrival. Her garrulous, friendly manner is said to put people at ease, and she became known as a skilled motivator. "My original mandate and continuing mandate is to reposition Avon as the preeminent and most exciting company with beauty and fashion products for the next millennium," she told Sean Mehegan for *Brandweek* (October 7, 1996).

High on Jung's agenda was changing the dowdy image of the "Avon lady." Jung understood that although the "Avon lady" stereotype was a liability, it also had tremendous potential as an advertising tool. She developed an ironic ad campaign called "Just Another Avon Lady," featuring dynamic young women—the kinds of consumers the company was hoping to woo—extolling the virtues of various Avon products. Many of the women were ordinary, albeit photogenic, sales reps; one notable exception was the Olympic athlete Jackie Joyner-Kersee, whose image in one print ad was accompanied by copy that read, "I throw a nine-pound shot put 51 feet. I bench press 155 pounds. I have red toenails." Jung helped implement Avon's sponsorship of the 1996 Olympics, by designing a special logo, licensing new products such as an Olympic skin-care line and a sports cologne, and setting up a contest in which an Avon customer could win a trip to Atlanta, Georgia, to see the 1996 Games. "We believe it was more than just an Olympic sponsorship," Jung told Mehegan. "We understand women and women's causes, and we went out on a grass roots effort to teach women and communicate winning in sports as part of self-esteem." She also promoted another Avon grassroots effort, aimed at increasing breast-cancer awareness; so far the company has raised nearly $40 million to support that program, which began in 1993. Also under Jung's direction, the company marketed a successful line of apparel, and in 1996 the Avon Barbie doll was introduced. In the most successful new-product launch in the company's history, more than $40 million worth of Avon Barbie dolls were sold that year. (One of the dolls is meant to represent P.F.E. Albee.)

At Jung's behest, almost half of Avon's fragrances were discontinued. The terminated scents hadn't been selling well, and she felt that they had become outdated. She replaced them with others, including Far Away, which generated $30 million in sales during its first year and $50 million the next, and Natori, Avon's first designer fragrance. She replaced 20 of the company's makeup lines with a slightly more expensive brand called Avon Color, which was packaged in sleek metallic containers. While the products in the new line cost a bit more than what many of Avon's longtime customers had been used to paying—for example, $5 for a lipstick rather than $4—the stylishly packaged cosmetics attracted consumers who had been using brands selling for much more. "As women become more confident and better informed, many are shying away from high-priced status brands," Jung explained to Dyan Machan for *Forbes* (December 2, 1996). "There is a blurring of prestige and mass brands, and the best product at the best price wins." Sales shot up, and Avon's stock prices increased. "They've had the best new product lineup in the last two years that I've ever seen," Salomon Brothers cosmetics analyst Diana Temple told Mehegan. "[Jung] has raised the threshold in terms of style, performance, and image." The new fragrances and the Avon Color line, along with the company's pioneering over-the-counter alphahydroxy skin-care products, sold well overseas as well as in the U.S.

In July 1996 Jung was promoted to president of global marketing. Also in 1996 *Brandweek* named her "Marketer of the Year" in the health-and-beauty category. (It was her second honor from that magazine; the year before, its editors had included Jung on their list of marketers to watch.) In March 1997 Jung was made one of the executive vice presidents of the company, and her responsibilities were expanded to encompass new business development. In that capacity she oversaw all product research and development, market surveys, strategic planning, and joint ventures and alliances, such as Avon's Discovery Toys subsidiary. Since Jung had joined the company, sales had rocketed by 30 percent, profits by more than 40 percent, and stock prices by 150 percent, and it was generally agreed within the company and by outsiders that in large part the gains had resulted directly from her marketing tactics.

The upward trajectory of her career seemed certain to continue, but in January 1998 Charles Perrin, an executive from Duracell Batteries Ltd., was appointed chief operating officer (COO)—a position many industry insiders had assumed would go to Jung or one of Avon's other top female executives. Since Preston's appointment as CEO, Avon had become one of the country's leading employers of high-ranking female executives, and by 1996 almost half of the company's senior vice presidents were women. Perrin's appointment seemed to indicate that there might be a glass ceiling at Avon after all, and observers wondered whether Jung would leave the company. Such speculation ended in July 1998, when Preston retired: Perrin moved into the CEO position, and Jung was appointed COO. Then, in November 1999, Perrin retired, to pursue philanthropic interests, according to Avon (or perhaps because of falling profits and stock prices, as other sources suggested), and Jung stepped easily into the number-one spot.

Jung's promotion made her part of a two-CEO family: her husband, Michael Gould, is the chairman and CEO of Bloomingdale's. Jung referred to their two children in a letter to the *New York Times* that she wrote in response to a *Times* (July 25, 1999) article about female chief executives. Reed Abelson wrote in the article, "Women may be shattering the glass ceiling, but most of those next in line are doing it without young children in tow." In her letter, published in the *Times*'s August 22, 1999 edition, Jung wrote that her 10-year-old daughter had noticed Jung's name in the article. "The speculation about whether or not her mother becomes one of the next chief executives was irrelevant," she declared. "I shuddered, however, at the slightest suggestion, now planted in the mind of a young girl, that she and her toddler brother could be the very reasons that her own role model might not become all that she hopes to be. I also winced at the phrase 'in tow,' praying that its negative connotation of anything like 'baggage' would be lost in a child's translation and not taint a pure and healthy idealism." She noted that "women, including mothers of young children, are breaking through every aspect of American life," and expressed the opinion that "in the near term," "everything" is not only "possible," but "probable."

In the third quarter of 2000, Avon's sales reached $1.34 billion, 7 percent greater than the figure for the previous quarter. On October 10, 2000 a one-mile strip along Fifth Avenue in New York City was painted pink to celebrate Avon's $15.3 million gift to three cancer facilities, one at New York's Columbia-Presbyterian Medical Center and the others in other cities. Mayor Rudolph Giuliani of New York proclaimed the date "Avon Breast Cancer Crusade Day."

Jung's honors include the 1997 National Outstanding Mother Award. She was on *Advertising Age* magazine's 1997 list of "25 Women to Watch," and in 1998 she was inducted into the Advertising Hall of Fame by the American Advertising Federation. Jung sits on the boards of directors of General Electric, the Fragrance Foundation, and the Zale Corp., among other firms, and she is on the board of trustees of Princeton University.

In 1998, in a highly visible display of how far Jung has gone to revamp Avon, the company's first retail showcase opened—an elegant spa and store located in the tony Trump Tower, in Midtown Manhattan. "We want people to see the spa and say, 'Wow! Avon's not what we thought,'" Jung, who masterminded that project, told Leslie Kaufman for *Newsweek* (November 16, 1998). And people in the market for Avon products no longer have to wait for an "Avon lady" to leave a sales brochure—Jung has instituted an e-commerce site on the Internet. As of early 2000, *Avon.com* was getting more than 400,000 visitors a month. — M.R.

Suggested Reading: Avon Products Inc. Web site; *Brandweek* p22 Nov. 13, 1995, with photo, p98+ Oct. 7, 1996, with photo; *Forbes* p184+ Jan. 11, 1999, with photo; *Fortune* p74+ July 21, 1997, with photos, p76+ Oct. 12, 1998, with photos; *Newsweek* p59+ Nov. 16, 1998, with photo; *USA Today* (on-line) Nov. 5, 1999

Ted Astor Photography, courtesy of Harcourt

Kahn, Roger

Oct. 31, 1927– Writer. Address: c/o Harcourt Inc., 15 E. 26th St., New York, NY 10010

The baseball writer, novelist, journalist, and historian Roger Kahn is known principally for his 1972 book, *The Boys of Summer.* That work combines the story of Kahn's youth in Brooklyn and the saga of the Brooklyn Dodgers, the legendary baseball team that he covered during their years of glory. In all, Kahn has written more than 15 books, and while his fame rests on his coverage of baseball, he has explored a variety of subjects, in such volumes as *The Passionate People: What It Means to Be a Jew in America* (1968), *The Battle for Morningside Heights: Why Students Rebel* (1970), *Joe and Marilyn: A Memory of Love* (1986), and *A Flame of Pure Fire: Jack Dempsey and the Roaring '20s* (1999).

Roger Kahn was born in Brooklyn, New York, on October 31, 1927, the son of Olga Rockow Kahn and Gordon Jacques Kahn, both of whom taught at Thomas Jefferson High School. An editor and historian, Gordon Kahn was to become one of the originators of the radio quiz show *Information Please*; he was also passionately interested in baseball and claimed to have played for City College of New York. Olga Kahn much preferred literature to baseball and for a time led the family in weekly readings from James Joyce's novel *Ulysses.*

Perhaps the defining event of Kahn's life was his birth in Brooklyn in the late 1920s; his formative years coincided with the heyday of the Dodgers, the fabled team known affectionately as "dem bums." Part of the Dodgers' mystique was the love they inspired among fans, despite the fact that they seldom won a World Series. Throughout Kahn's youth he followed the team closely, witnessing such historic events as the integration of major-league baseball, when the gifted African-American player Jackie Robinson joined the Dodgers' lineup, in 1947.

In the same year, after having attended New York University on and off, Kahn followed his interest in both writing and sports to a job with the *New York Herald Tribune.* Five years later, when he was 24, the *Tribune* made him its Dodgers reporter. By 1955 Kahn was the highest-paid sportswriter specializing in baseball in New York City; he was also the co-author of a baseball almanac. Although he was taken off the Dodgers beat in 1953, after he referred to the team's stadium—Ebbets Field—in print as a "sarcophagus" (which means "coffin"), he maintained contact with Jackie Robinson. He collaborated with the athlete, who became his close friend, on a series of articles for *Our Sports*, a magazine directed to an African-American audience. Black star players were still a new phenomenon in baseball when Kahn, now assigned to cover the New York Giants, began writing about Willie Mays—whom he would call the "most exciting player" he had ever seen. In 1956 Kahn went to work for *Newsweek* as sports editor. He also published pieces in other magazines, such as *Sports Illustrated*, the *Saturday Evening Post*, and *Esquire.* While he lived and wrote mainly in a world of sports and the hard-bitten reporters who covered them, Kahn was interested in modern poetry and symphonic music as well (although he did not write about them). In 1962 he published *Inside Big League Baseball*; intended for young people, the book was widely praised as good reading for baseball fans of all ages.

Kahn's first major book to deal with a topic other than baseball was *The Passionate People: What It Means to Be a Jew in America*, a mixture of character sketches and history. While the *Library Journal* (May 1, 1968) reviewer found the book to be "a fascinating combination of flavor and fact, entertainment and information," other critics were not so kind. Marshall Sklare, the *Commentary* (October 1968) reviewer, declared that *The Passionate People* was "replete with technical errors" and that, in its attempt to beguile readers, it offered "vulgarity and distortion." For *Christian Science Monitor* (June 27, 1968) writer Michael J. Bandler, the book "overemphasizes the vulgar and ignores many important issues."

Like his fascination with the Dodgers, Kahn's 1970 book, *The Battle for Morningside Heights: Why Students Rebel*, came about partly as a result of geography: he lived near the Morningside Heights campus of New York's Columbia University, and during the 1968 student rebellion—which constituted a protest against the Vietnam War and racial injustice as well as a demand for "participatory democracy" on campus—he was able to interview many of the participants, including students, professors, police, and neighbors, to create an overview of the events. Critics were divided over the merits of the book. A. L. Fessler, in *Library Journal* (March 15, 1970), praised Kahn's indictment of "both racism and Big Education as the *agents provocateurs* of much of the violence on our campuses," and thought that his "account of the police bust, the finest writing in the book, resonates with the vulgarity, clangor, and terror of that night." The *New York Times Book Review* (November 8, 1970) critic, Samuel McCracken, found "Kahn's weakness for the wildly irrelevant . . . obtrusive" and "his analysis . . . little more than uncritical recitation of S. D .S. [Students for a Democratic Society] verities." In the opinion of the *Time* (March 23, 1970) reviewer, Kahn demonstrated "a fine eye for the humor and irony in the midst of turmoil."

Kahn's national reputation was achieved with his 1972 work, *The Boys of Summer*, an account of his youth as a baseball fan and of the lives of those who played for the Brooklyn Dodgers in the early 1950s. Joe Black, Roy Campanella, Billy Cox, Carl Erskine, Carl Furillo, Gil Hodges, Clem Labine, Andy Pafko, Pee Wee Reese, Jackie Robinson, Preacher Roe, Duke Snider, and other members of the Dodgers captured the imaginations of Americans, and Kahn chronicled their last seasons playing in Brooklyn; their 1955 World Series win; the team's 1958 move to Los Angeles; and the players' lives after baseball. The book, which takes its title from a poem by Dylan Thomas, was widely acclaimed and has been reprinted in several editions.

In an article entitled "Dem Bums Become the Boys of Summer: From Comic Caricatures to Sacred Icons of the National Pastime," which appeared in *American Jewish History* (March 1995), Frederic M. Roberts examined what lay behind the durability of *The Boys of Summer.* "Almost all of the critics describe *The Boys of Summer* as nostalgic," he wrote. "In fact, a major reason *The Boys of Summer* is a classic is that Kahn excelled at what could be termed mature nostalgia—a fine balancing of a fond and reassuring view of the past with a realistic appraisal of its faults. . . . Mature nostalgia allows the reader to never feel that he has forgotten one of the most important and painful lessons learned during the '60s and early '70s—avoid illusions and naiveté: at almost any cost. . . . That lesson . . . is inherently reinforced by the Brooklyn Dodger 'story.' For the story's unhappy ending—Walter O'Malley's removal of the team to Los Angeles . . . is remembered by many as one of their earliest and most traumatic introductions to the facts of the 'real world.' They discovered that in America when the values of loyalty and community clash with power and greed, the latter forces almost inevitably prevail." Peter Prescott, a contemporary reviewer of *The Boys of Summer* for *Newsweek* (March 13, 1972), caught the tone of the book itself when he wrote: "Kahn's book is knowledgeable, leisurely, and anecdotal. . . . But it is more: Kahn never forgets that he is writing about men in relation to a certain discipline, a certain level of achievement, a certain process of decline, and as such his book acquires a cumulative power. It is not just another book about baseball or a boy growing up to like baseball, but a book about pain and defeat and endurance, about how men, anywhere, must live."

Kahn's next volume was a collection of articles, *How the Weather Was* (1973); *A Season in the Sun*, another nonfiction book about baseball, followed four years later. The year 1979 saw the publication of Kahn's first novel, *But Not to Keep*, a story of divorce and a custody battle over a 14-year-old boy. The protagonist of the novel is, like Kahn, a journalist who enjoys great art. A *Kirkus Reviews* (March 15, 1979) writer found fault with the book: "Kahn, embarrassingly, interrupts his narrative early to announce: 'Aside from genius and politics, talent and venality, you always rooted for the artist over the reviewer, provided only that the artist did his honest best. Bardic best. Symphonic best. Bad best. Best, any best, deserved decency. It was frightening to stand naked out there, naked and vulnerable and stained by hope.' Kahn stuffs the novel with this kind of anxious, self-dramatizing filler." Michael J. Bandler, in the *Christian Science Monitor* (July 18, 1979), took the opposite viewpoint, finding *But Not to Keep* to be a "sensitive, occasionally frustrating, yet honest and credible first novel." Bandler pointed out that in addition to condemning divorce as practiced by Americans, Kahn "confronts other beleaguered institutions, such as religion and race, and vents himself on the hypocrisy and bigotry that incessantly pollute the rarefied air of 'Society.'" Kahn returned to baseball for the subject of his 1982 novel, *The Seventh Game.* A sentimental story of an over-the-hill pitcher reminiscing about his past, the book was reviewed in such a way as to make it Kahn's last foray into the novel form to date.

Good Enough to Dream (1985) was Kahn's nonfiction account of how he became the president and part-owner of a minor-league baseball team, the Utica (New York) Blue Sox. The team, Paul Stuewe wrote in *Quill & Quire* (March 1986), was "characterized by marginal players, an explosive manager, and a patchwork playing field. How these volatile elements coalesced into a roller-coaster ride of horsehide high jinks is the engaging subject of this immensely enjoyable book."

Joe and Marilyn: A Memory of Love, Kahn's 1986 book about the romance, marriage, and lives of baseball legend Joe DiMaggio and screen icon Marilyn Monroe, was received warmly by some reviewers as a collection of fascinating anecdotes if not a penetrating analysis of its subjects' personalities. Also in 1986, Kahn received an assignment to ghost-write the autobiography of Pete Rose, the star hitter for the Cincinnati Reds, whose career was later derailed by accusations of illegal gambling. Before the book was completed, tragedy entered Kahn's life: his son Roger committed suicide, in 1987. Kahn included mention of his son's addiction to drugs and death at the age of 22 in *Pete Rose: My Story*, his 1989 book. Although written with—and about—Rose, the book is told chiefly in Kahn's voice. Elliott J. Gorn, the reviewer for the *Nation* (January 22, 1990), called *Pete Rose* "a disappointing work, nowhere near what Kahn achieved in his lyrical *The Boys of Summer*. Kahn is too taken with Rose to explain him." Nevertheless, Gorn found that just "reading about Willie Mays, Hank Aaron, and Sandy Koufax, about the Big Red Machine, the 1975 World Series and Charlie Hustle's quest for hit number 4,192 revives old passions. What is missing from *My Story*, however, is a sense of the complexity of the game." In an interview for *Publishers Weekly* (October 4, 1993), Kahn told Craig Little that he "wouldn't collaborate" with a sports figure again. "There are people who are better at that than I am," he said.

Baseball was the subject of Kahn's next two books, *Games We Used to Play: A Lover's Quarrel with the World of Sport* (1992), his second collection of articles, and *The Era: 1947–1957, When the Yankees, the New York Giants, and the Brooklyn Dodgers Ruled the World*, published in 1993. With *The Era*, Kahn, who had already created a baseball classic in *The Boys of Summer*, returned to the time before the Dodgers left Brooklyn to cover 11 seasons of New York baseball, beginning with the arrival of Jackie Robinson. Bill Ott, reviewing the volume for *Booklist* (September 1, 1993), remarked that Kahn "brings to the familiar story of the Giants, Yankees, and Dodgers not only an eyewitness perspective . . . but also a willingness to dig beneath the surface, look beyond the legends. . . . The best stories always bear retelling, and Kahn is the right man to retell the story of baseball's greatest decade." Kahn continued to mine the golden era of baseball in *Memories of Summer: When Baseball Was an Art and Writing About It a Game*, published in 1997.

Many years earlier, in 1969, Kahn's friend Jack Dempsey—the former heavyweight boxing champion of the world—had asked him to get his "story straight." Kahn did so, 16 years after Dempsey's death, with *A Flame of Pure Fire: Jack Dempsey and the Roaring '20s*, published in 1999. While the book offered detailed descriptions of Dempsey's legend-making fights with Jess Willard, Luis Firpo, and Gene Tunney, many reviewers felt that the best part of the book was Kahn's description of Dempsey's impoverished childhood, early struggle for survival, and emergence as a boxer in mining camps before he was 20. Michiko Kakutani of the *New York Times* (December 14, 1999) judged that Dempsey did not live up to Kahn's portrait of him as an iconic figure of the "roaring '20s," and that "Kahn's determination to open out Dempsey's story into something larger causes him to lard the boxer's tale with dozens of panoramic asides. . . . These asides—about everything from Sacco and Vanzetti to Warren G. Harding, from women's suffrage to Prohibition—have little to do with Dempsey, and they end up feeling irrelevant and pretentious." Kakutani added that Kahn "is at his best in this volume describing Dempsey's actual fights, capturing the thrashing, deadly violence of the boxer in the ring."

Kahn's most recent book, *The Head Game: Baseball Seen from the Pitcher's Mound* (2000), is about pitching. Kahn described how the underhand toss of baseball's early days evolved into pitching, and he covered the careers of such great pitchers as Warren Spahn and Don Drysdale. Alan Schwarz, in an assessment for the *New York Times Book Review* (September 10, 2000), found fault with *The Head Game*: "Kahn spends so much time swooning" at what the pitchers did, he complained, "that he veers away form the promise of his book, which is to explore and explain the beauty of how they did it." Schwarz also felt that Kahn focused too much on pitchers from the 1960s and before, missing such greats as Pedro Martinez and "a chance to offer a comprehensive depiction of pitching today and where it is headed."

Roger Kahn married Katharine C. Johnson, his third wife, in 1989. He has two surviving children from previous marriages. — S.Y.

Suggested Reading: *American Heritage* p87+ Oct. 1999, with photo; *American Jewish History* p51+ Mar. 1995; *Commentary* p82 Oct. 1968; *Nation* p93 Jan. 22, 1990; *New York Review of Books* p60+ Nov. 4, 1993; *New York Times Book Review* p45 Nov. 8, 1970, p32 May 5, 1972, p5+ July 3, 1977, p12 Apr. 6, 1997, p43 Sep. 10, 2000; *Newsweek* p94 Mar. 13, 1972, p82 Nov. 10, 1986; *Publishers Weekly* p49+ Oct. 4, 1993, with photo; *Quill & Quire* p78 Mar. 1986

Selected Books: *Inside Big League Baseball*, 1962; *The Passionate People: What It Means to Be a Jew in America*, 1968; *The Battle for Morningside Heights: Why Students Rebel*, 1970; *The Boys of Summer*, 1972; *How the Weather Was*, 1973; *A Season in the Sun*, 1977; *But Not to Keep*, 1979; *The Seventh Game*, 1982; *Good Enough to Dream*, 1985; *Joe and Marilyn: A Memory of Love*, 1986; *Pete Rose: My Story*, 1989; *Games We Used to Play: A Lover's Quarrel With the World of Sport*, 1992; *The Era: 1947–1957, When the Yankees, the New York Giants, and the Brooklyn Dodgers Ruled the World*, 1993; *Memories of Summer: When Baseball Was an Art and Writing About It a Game*, 1997; *A Flame of Pure Fire: Jack Dempsey and the Roaring '20s*, 1999; *The Head Game: Baseball Seen from the Pitcher's Mound*, 2000

Archive Photos

Kaminski, Janusz

(YAN-oosh)

June 27, 1959– Cinematographer; film director. Address: c/o New Line Cinema, 888 Seventh Ave., New York, NY 10106

Thanks in large part to his work with the director Steven Spielberg, Janusz Kaminski is among the most prominent cinematographers working today, with a string of film credits that includes some of the biggest critical and commercial successes of the past decade. For his work on Spielberg's *Saving Private Ryan* (1998), Kaminski brought home the Oscar for best cinematography, adding the prestigious trophy to his previous win, for the 1993 critical favorite *Schindler's List*, also directed by Spielberg. In 1997 Kaminski received a nomination from the Academy of Motion Picture Arts and Sciences for his work on the box-office disappointment *Amistad*—another Spielberg project—and joined with the director again that year for the thriller *The Lost World: Jurassic Park*. He recently directed his first film, *Lost Souls*, which starred Winona Ryder. "As a cinematographer, Janusz is not a 'one size fits all,' he's much more of a chameleon," Spielberg told *Cinematographer.com* (June 1998, on-line). "He takes the stories he does very seriously, and he marks up the scripts. He tells a cinematography story on top of the writer's or director's story, and he designs the photography according to beats and measures of the narrative. Because of that, he's going to shoot differently on *Jerry Maguire* [a 1996 hit starring Tom Cruise] than he would on *The Lost World*. Over the course of his career, Janusz has put together a collection of amazing and completely different looks from picture to picture."

The son of Marian Kaminski and Jadwiga Celner (who died when he was quite young), Janusz Zygmuni Kaminski was born on June 27, 1959 in Ziembice, Poland. He grew up in Wroclaw, Poland. As a teenager he saw on television the American cult film *Vanishing Point* (1971), which, in an interview with Rick Lyman for the *New York Times* (October 6, 2000), he cited as the movie that had the greatest impact on his creative and intellectual life. "I have this great recollection of thinking as I was watching it, 'Wow this is what America is all about; this is what freedom of expression is all about,'' he told Lyman. "Here is an individual who is willing to sacrifice, even to sacrifice his own life, for the sake of his idea of freedom and independence." Determined to move to the United States, Kaminski succeeded in leaving Poland and settling temporarily in Vienna, Austria, where he swept factory floors and streets for six months, until he received his U.S. immigration papers. In 1981 Kaminski moved to Chicago, where he attended Columbia College and earned a B.A. in film (and, at the same time, learned English). After he graduated, he was accepted into the program for cinematography at the American Film Institute, in Los Angeles. "For me, I saw America not as this country of plenty, this country of wealth, where everyone has a car and everyone has a house, but as a country of freedom, where the individual is free, the ideology is free," he told Lyman. "That is why I so much wanted to come here."

Kaminski's debut as a cinematographer came with the 1988 film *Lisa*, which won him the Line Eagel Award at the Illinois Film Festival. That success brought Kaminski to the attention of the independent horror-film distributor Concorde, and as a result he worked on the 1990 thriller *The Terror Within 2*, written and directed by Andrew Stevens. Starring a cast of mostly unknowns, the film, which went largely unnoticed at the box office, involved a man-made plague in the 21st century that forces most of the human population underground. In the same year Kaminski worked on his second Concorde project, *The Rain Killer*, which earned $1.6 million in its limited release in the United States.

In 1991, after working as cinematographer on two unremarkable films—*Pyrates*, directed by Noah Stern, and *Cool as Ice*, a shoddy vehicle for flash-in-the-pan rap star Vanilla Ice—Kaminski teamed up with Academy Award–winning actress Diane Keaton, who was directing the made-for-TV movie *Wildflower*. That love story, set in the South in the 1930s, starred Reese Witherspoon, Patricia Arquette, and Beau Bridges. *Killer Instinct* (1992), *Trouble Bound* (1992), and the children's movie *The Adventures of Huck Finn* (1993), with Elijah Wood, were the cinematographer's next three projects.

Kaminski's big break came when, as a test of his skills, Steven Spielberg asked Kaminski to shoot a television movie, *Class of '61*, for his company. Impressed by Kaminski's work, Spielberg asked him to film *Schindler's List*. The tale of German factory owner Oskar Schindler, who employed—and saved the lives of—hundreds of Jews during the height of the Holocaust, Spielberg's ambitious film called for a special visual style that would capture the era of Nazi atrocities. "Black-and-white was the right choice for that film because of the subject matter and because most of the real footage of Nazi atrocities was photographed in black-and-white," Kaminski told Christopher Probst for *American Cinematographer* (August 1998). Starring Liam Neeson, Ralph Fiennes, and Ben Kingsley, *Schindler's List* was the most celebrated film of 1993, winning several Academy Awards, including those for best picture, best director, and, in recognition of Kaminski's work, best cinematographer.

After his success with *Schindler's List*, Kaminski shot the light-hearted comedy *Little Giants* (1994), starring Ed O'Neill and Rick Moranis as brothers and rival football coaches. The family film was a moderate box-office success. *Tall Tale* (1994), a retelling of three stories embedded in American mythology—those of Pecos Bill, Paul Bunyan, and John Henry—was Kaminski's next film, soon followed by the sentimental picture *How to Make an American Quilt*, with Winona Ryder, Alfre Woodard, Anne Bancroft, and Kate Capshaw. The next big hit for the now A-list Kaminski was Cameron Crowe's *Jerry Maguire*, in which Tom Cruise portrayed a sports agent weathering personal and professional crises. The film was a critical and financial success, amassing many Academy Award nominations, including one for best picture.

Kaminski himself was nominated for an Oscar for his follow-up project, *Amistad* (1997), another film directed by Steven Spielberg. *Amistad* tells the story of the group of Africans who took control of a slave ship in 1839. Kaminski told *Cinematographer.com* (on-line) that after reading David H. Franzoni's screenplay, "I immediately knew that the story required photography that was not too pretty. I didn't want to fall into clichés of the historical genre. The movie is about a slave rebellion . . . so it would have been wrong to apply lighting that conveyed romantic notions. It's a very harsh and emotional story: these people were kidnapped; packed like cattle into a slave ship, where they spent many days before being intercepted by a Navy ship; and then sent off to a really dungeon-like prison. They were suffering from cold and starvation, and I felt that the lighting should support that storyline."

The cinematographer contributed his talents to Spielberg's *The Lost World: Jurassic Park*, the follow-up to his blockbuster film *Jurassic Park*, based on Michael Crichton's novel about a theme park with artificially engineered dinosaurs that run rampant. The most recent collaboration between Spielberg and Kaminski was *Saving Private Ryan*, a tale of a group of G.I.s in World War II who are ordered to save the life of a lost enlisted soldier. A hit at the box office and with critics, the film will perhaps be best remembered for its opening sequence, which re-creates the historic D-Day invasion of German-occupied Normandy by Allied troops. "There is a tremendous amount of documentary footage from World War II that was photographed in color. In fact, renowned director George Stevens was a combat cameraman and shot a great deal of footage in color," Kaminski told Probst. "Steven and I really didn't want to shoot *Private Ryan* in black-and-white, and I think it would have been a little pretentious to do another World War II film that way. . . . We wanted to create the illusion that there were several combat cameramen landing with the troops at Normandy. I think we succeeded in emulating the look of the footage for the invasion scenes, which we achieved with both in-camera tricks and other technological means. First off, I thought about the lenses they had back in the 1940s. Obviously, those lenses were inferior compared to what we have today, so I had Panavision strip the protective coating off a set of older Ultraspeeds. . . . What really changed was the contrast and color rendering. The contrast became much flatter." Kaminski and Spielberg each took home an Oscar for *Saving Private Ryan*.

Kaminski's directorial debut, *Lost Souls*, was released in 2000; the film, starring Winona Ryder and Ben Chaplin, concerns a former victim of demonic possession (Ryder) who comes to believe that Chaplin's character, the author of a book on serial killers, is the devil. The movie received almost universally negative reviews. Elvis Mitchell noted in his review for the *New York Times* (October 13, 2000), "Perhaps [Kaminski] wanted to try a genre piece for his initial effort. There are some particularly fine details; it's the central story that's lacking." Of his first turn as director, Kaminski told Cameron Crowe for the *New York Times Magazine* (February 20, 2000), "It felt great to control all the elements, but I never want to create any misunderstanding that I'm moving on, and never will be a cinematographer again. I'm a cinematographer who had a chance to direct a movie." Kaminski is set to do the cinematography for *A.I.* and *Memoirs of a Geisha*, both of which will premiere in 2001, and *Minority Report*, which is slated for release in 2002. He and a fellow Oscar winner, the actress Holly Hunter, have been married since May 20, 1995. Speaking of their marriage, he told Crowe, "It takes great understanding of the commitment we make to our professions. But we're very mature. We're confident with who we are."— M.B.

Suggested Reading: *American Cinematographer* p30+ Aug. 1998, with photos, p136 Mar. 1999, with photos; *Cinematographer.com* (on-line) June 1998; *New York Times E p1+ Oct. 6, 2000, with photos; New York Times Magazine* p142+ Feb. 20, 2000, with photos

Selected Films: as cinematographer—*Lisa*, 1988; *The Terror Within 2*, 1990; *The Rain Killer*, 1990; *Pyrates*, 1991; *Cool As Ice*, 1991; *Killer Instinct*, 1992; *Trouble Bound*, 1992; *The Adventures of Huck Finn*, 1993; *Schindler's List*, 1993; *Little Giants*, 1994; *Tall Tale*, 1994; *How To Make An American Quilt*, 1995; *Jerry Maguire*, 1996; *Amistad*, 1997; *The Lost World: Jurassic Park*, 1997; *Saving Private Ryan*, 1998; as director—*Lost Souls*, 2000

Courtesy of CBS Corp.

Karmazin, Mel

(KAR-muh-zin)

Aug. 24, 1943– President and CEO of CBS Corp. Address: CBS Broadcasting, 51 W. 52d St. New York, NY 10019

It is widely agreed among insiders in the entertainment world that Mel Karmazin, the president and CEO of CBS Corp., has broadcasting in his blood. Gutsy, aggressive, and known for getting square in the faces of his rivals, Karmazin has advanced from ad salesman to president of CBS on his own terms. "He is like a fighter who is always cutting the size of the ring on you," the longtime CBS television newscaster Dan Rather told Ken Auletta for the *New Yorker* (July 27, 1998). "He corners you quickly." In a conversation with Cathy Burke for the *New York Post* (on-line), Jessica Reif Cohen, a media analyst with Merrill Lynch & Co., described Karmazin as "an incredible operator. He takes action. He tells you what he's going to do and he does it." A notorious workaholic, Karmazin has maintained that he watches nothing on television other than what CBS broadcasts, "from sign-on to sign-off," as he told a reporter for *Businessweek Online* (April 5, 1999); he has no hobbies and hasn't taken a vacation longer than five days since 1976. "He has not an ounce of poetry, yet he is a beguiling figure," the radio personality Jonathan Schwartz told Auletta. "He has unusual, almost theatrical energy."

The son of a cab driver and a factory worker, Melvin Alan Karmazin was born on August 24, 1943 in New York City. (Some sources give 1944 as the year of his birth.) He grew up in a low-rise public housing project in Long Island City, in the New York City borough of Queens. "My family had zero money," he told Marc Gunther for *Fortune* (April 14, 1997). "We never had a vacation. We never had a car." Through a teacher at Haaren High School, from which he graduated, he got a job as a typist and mail clerk atan advertising firm named for its owner, Irwin Zlowe. Not long after he began working there, Zlowe counseled Karmazin to get a college education. Acting on Zlowe's advice, Karmazin enrolled at Pace College, in New York, while continuing to work part-time for Zlowe as a media buyer. "The only day I stayed awake in college was the lecture about supply and demand 101," he remarked to Alex Kuczynski for the *New York Times* (November 14, 1999). His lack of interest in his courses notwithstanding, Karmazin earned a B.A. degree in business administration from Pace, in 1965.

After college Karmazin got a job at radio station WCBS-AM as an ad salesman, at a starting salary of $17,500 a year—more than $90,000 in 1999 dollars—plus commissions. He placed cold calls (phone calls made without advance notice to the recipients) to small-business owners, and within a few years he was selling so many ads that his yearly pay had risen to $70,000—more than $350,000 in 1999 dollars. His boss, who had already cut his commission rate, told Karmazin that such a sum was too much for a young salesman to earn. "That was the dumbest thing I'd ever heard in my life," Karmazin told Gunther. "I quit." In 1970 he joined the advertising sales staff of WNEW-AM, owned by Metromedia. He succeeded in persuading the station's clients to pay higher rates for ads broadcast during New York Giants football games, even though the team was not doing well then. Karmazin soon rose to the position of general manager of another Metromedia property, the rock station WNEW-FM, which thrived under his direction.

In 1981 Karmazin moved to the Infinity Broadcasting Corp., whose founders and owners, Gerald Carrus and Michael Weiner, made him manager of six of the company's radio stations. Implementing the business strategy that would become his trademark, he paid jaw-dropping prices for two major stations—New York's all-sports WFAN-AM and the Los Angeles oldies station KRTH-FM, both of which Karmazin once referred to as "oceanfront properties." Then he made administrative cutbacks and reduced costs in other areas as well, while bolstering the stations' sales staffs so as to increase revenues. He also bought the broadcast rights to the games of the Dallas Cowboys and five professional New York teams: the Mets, Knicks, Rangers, Giants, and Jets. In addition, Karmazin filled his morning slots with such high-profile hosts as Don Imus and Howard Stern, the latter of whom had recently been fired from WNBC-AM. He then bucked radio tradition, according to which radio personalities could not succeed outside their hometowns, by syndicating Imus's and Stern's programs in markets around the country. "A lot of radio stations play the same music," he told Gunther. "We want programming that can't be replicated."

Stern's show quickly rose to number one in each of the markets to which Karmazin had introduced it, but the controversial shock jock's graphic on-air rants and ribald antics caused him to run afoul of the Federal Communications Commission (FCC), which charged him with indecency and levied heavy fines against him. Karmazin refused to pay the fines, and he accused the FCC in court of violating the free-speech provision of the First Amendment. Eventually, Karmazin paid the FCC what he termed a "voluntary contribution" of $1.7 million. While some observers criticized Karmazin for caving in on a matter of free speech, he said that he had settled with the FCC for a practical reason: Stern's run-ins with the government were impeding Infinity's ability to purchase more stations.

In 1986 Karmazin, Carrus, and Weiner took Infinity Broadcasting public. They bought it back in 1988, in a leveraged buyout, and then, in 1992, again came out with an initial public offering. This strategy proved highly profitable for themselves and Infinity's shareholders. In 1992 Infinity's stock was worth $17.50 a share; by 1995 the value of each share had skyrocketed to $170. "Wherever I've been, it was always about the shareholder, never about Mel," Karmazin told Karl Taro Greenfield for *Time* (September 20, 1999). According to the prospectus that had accompanied Infinity's 1992 offering, at that time the firm was the largest independent radio business in the U.S.—that is, the largest U.S. concern whose business was confined to owning and operating radio stations.

In 1996 Karmazin approached CBS, which had recently merged with Westinghouse, and proposed that Infinity buy CBS. He even offered to buy Westinghouse. CBS countered by offering to purchase Infinity, for $4.9 billion. Recognizing the enormous power such a merger would bring him, Karmazin agreed to the deal, and he came aboard the newly configured company as head of the radio divisions of CBS, Infinity, and Westinghouse. Commenting on those organizational changes, Don Imus told Alan Deutschman for *New York* (March 16, 1998), "It will occur to someone over there at CBS that maybe he should run everything."

Karmazin assumed his new position determined to reduce costs and consolidate the company's assets. Almost immediately, he began making his opinions felt beyond the radio division, thus impressing some people as CBS's version of Ted Turner. He played a pivotal role in persuading Westinghouse to unload its manufacturing operations and formally adopt the CBS name. Then, in May 1997, with CBS stock in a slump, Karmazin—hungry for results and intolerant of apathy, as always—took part in a boardroom coup that forced the retirement of Peter Lund, a 20-year CBS veteran who had headed the merged company's television division. Lund quit after learning that CBS's chief executive officer, Michael H. Jordan, intended to make Karmazin CEO of a new entity—the CBS Station Group—in which position Karmazin would oversee both the television and radio departments. Lund's last day coincided with CBS's public announcement of its fall television lineup, and his departure cast a pall on the occasion, at which the president of CBS Entertainment, Leslie Moonves, presided. The events heated the already brewing rivalry between Karmazin and Moonves.

Meanwhile, Karmazin had promised investors that he would improve CBS's television lineup; even CBS sitcoms featuring such high-profile stars as Bill Cosby, Ted Danson, and Tom Selleck were getting dismal ratings. "I will not stand in front of investors and give you reasons why we haven't increased our revenues," Karmazin told Martin Peers for *Variety* (June 30–July 18, 1997). "In my opinion there are no good answers." To boost earnings, Karmazin changed the advertising sales staff's pay scheme from salary plus commission to all commission; anyone who wanted to earn a salary, he told Peters, "should work at the post office." Karmazin insisted that a commissions-only arrangement was not punitive. "The purpose of it is to have them on your side, so the salespeople don't sit there and say, 'Hey I did all this work and the big guys get all the money," he told Kuczynski.

In April 1998 Karmazin was promoted to president and chief operating officer of the CBS Corp., with responsibility for sales and marketing; Moonves was made CEO of CBS Television, in charge of programming . Karmazin gave Moonves a wide berth to plan the 1998–99 television season. Then he slashed $180 million from the company's programming budget. The amount allocated to CBS News was cut by 10 percent, which resulted in company-wide layoffs, including the dismissals of several top executives. At the same time, Karmazin raised ad prices by 27 percent; to justify his action, he explained to advertisers that the average age and income of CBS's audience were above those of other stations' viewers.

In October 1998 Michael Jordan announced that he planned to retire as CBS's chairman and chief executive officer at the end of that year—a couple of years sooner than broadcasting insiders had expected. On January 1, 1999 Karmazin succeeded him in those posts. Many industry pundits noted that Karmazin's management style had clashed with Jordan's, and Jordan all but confirmed that observation: "Mel pushes," he told Auletta. "He's a guy who pushes and challenges everything. I'm more of a selective pusher. And maybe a little better listener." Karmazin maintained a diplomatic stance about Jordan's exit. "I thought this was a non-event," he told Jay Palmer for *Barron's* (November 2, 1998), adding that he had been "running the company" for months.

By August 1999 CBS had reported a 13 percent increase in revenues for the year, to almost $1.7 billion. Confident that the company was heading in the right direction, Karmazin set his sights on the Internet as the premier tool for CBS's continued growth. "Let's assume that the American consumer likes music," he told Kuczynski. "And let's say that music might be something that might be on the Internet. Take our radio stations. Take [Viacom's music properties] MTV and VH-1, and that's a pretty compelling site. You're able to drive traffic to it [that is, direct Internet users to it] because you've got all these billboards [ad banners atop an Internet page] and forms of advertising, and I think that's all pretty compelling." Acting on that vision, on September 7, 1999 Karmazin brokered a $37 million deal with Sumner Redstone, the president of Viacom, to merge CBS and Viacom into one media empire; both Redstone and Karmazin retained their titles. "He's a master salesman," Redstone told Elise Ackerman for *U.S. News & World Report* (September 20, 1999). "I was a little bit skeptical at first, but he began to turn me on." Karmazin plans to integrate MTV and VH-1 with CBS's radio, advertising, and Internet entities. In addition, the merger gives Karmazin access to Viacom's movie studios (Paramount and Nickelodeon) and cable properties. "Up until now, CBS didn't have any cable, and that was a problem," he told Kuczynski. "And now we have cable. We didn't have a major studio and now we have a studio."

Mel Karmazin resides in a Manhattan apartment just across the street from his office at CBS. He rises at 4:00 a.m., arrives at his desk by 6:30, and usually goes home well after dark. Karmazin's workaholic tendencies contributed to the dissolution of his marriage: his wife, Sharon, who recently retired after a three-decade-long career with the East Brunswick, New Jersey, public library system, complained that he had spent too many evenings and weekends at his job. Karmazin reportedly remains close to his two children. His son, Craig, owns three radio stations in Wisconsin. His daughter, Dina, worked for the cable channel E! Entertainment Television; currently, according to Cathy Burke, she manages a charitable foundation.

Karmazin is said to be respected and feared by his employees in equal measure. Famous for his intolerance of people who do not produce results, he has in his office a sign on which the word "Excuses" has a circle around it and a slash through it. Despite his wealth, he prefers pizza to glitzy $500-a-plate dinners and eschews the perks of executive life almost entirely. "You know, I'm real comfortable getting my own cup of coffee," he told Kuczynski. "I don't need a kitchen staff. I'd rather put that money on the screen or in radio, not to behind the scenes stuff that is about making my life more comfortable." — J.K.B.

Suggested Reading: *Business Week* p60+ Jan. 10, 2000, with photo; *Fortune* p110+ Apr. 14, 1997, with photos; *New York* p38+ Mar. 16, 1998, with photos; *New York Times* III p1+ Nov. 14, 1999, with photos; *New Yorker* p26+ July 27, 1998; *U.S. News & World Report* p46 Sep. 20, 1999, with photo; *Variety* p1+ Apr. 28–May 4, 1997, with photo, p25+ June 30–July 13, 1997, with photo

---

Courtesy of Ben Katchor

Katchor, Ben

Nov. 19, 1951– Comic-strip artist. Address: P.O. Box 2024, Cathedral Station, New York, NY 10025; c/o Wylie Agency, 250 W. 57th St., Suite 2114, New York, NY 10107

Self-described as "a middle man in the memory business," Ben Katchor has been an important figure in New York City's underground comic-book scene since the late 1980s, when the *New York Press* began running his strip *Julius Knipl, Real Estate Photographer.* In the *New York Times Book Review* (December 22, 1996), the celebrated satirical cartoonist and graphic designer Edward Sorel described Katchor as "the most poetic, deeply layered artist ever to draw a comic strip," and he declared that with *Julius Knipl*, Katchor had "created perhaps the most original comic strip since George Herriman introduced *Krazy Kat* more than 80 years ago." Referring to the Talmud, the vast compendium of Jewish law and tradition that contains 15 centuries' worth of commentaries, clarifications, and elaborations, a writer for the National Foundation for Jewish Culture (on-line) characterized Katchor's strips as "almost Talmudic in their richness and complexity. In a hundred words and a few pictures, Katchor can turn a discussion of long-forgotten soda flavors into a metaphysical exploration of memory, loss, and the possibility of perfection." The winner of a 1995–96 Guggenheim Fellowship, Katchor has taught at the School of Visual Arts, in New York City, since 1996, and his work has been exhibited in solo or group shows in New York, Philadelphia, and France. He has published four collections of comic strips and written the text for an opera. His current strip, *The Cardboard Valise,* is syndicated in a dozen alternative newspapers, among them the *San Francisco Weekly,* the *Miami New Times,* and the *Nashville Scene.*

The son of Meyer and Sylvia Katchor, Ben Katchor was born on November 19, 1951 in the New York City borough of Brooklyn. He spent much of his early life in Brooklyn's Crown Heights section, surrounded by the secular Yiddish culture that flourished among the working-class Jewish intellectuals with whom his father associated. A native of Warsaw, Poland, Meyer Katchor made his living as a landlord, but, like his friends, he considered himself a steadfast socialist and was active in New York City politics. In a lecture reprinted in part in *Harper's* magazine (May 1997), Katchor said that he had grown up "with the idea that everything I saw around me was, in the end, economically determined; that everything would be different if the nation's wealth were more equitably distributed. Exactly how an economic reshuffling of the world would affect the details of my childhood—how a Pepsi-Cola could taste differently, how a brisket beef sandwich could be improved upon—this [my father and his friends] didn't go into. [They] looked at the city as though they were tourists from some more rational world. To them, the rich urban culture I basked in was the product of some businessmen trying to cut corners, save a few dollars, and reduce overhead." Katchor understood Yiddish (but resisted learning to speak the language), and his father would read humor columns from Yiddish newspapers to him.

As a boy Katchor loved comic books, and by his teens he had become an expert in the form. His friends shared his passion, as he recalled to Lawrence Weschler for the *New Yorker* (August 9, 1993): "We not only knew all the artists, we knew all the *inkers*—we could tell when they changed inkers! We'd analyze every frame, every gesture." Although his friends preferred brawny superheroes, Katchor was partial to the more cerebral Spider Man, created by Stan Lee and drawn in those days by Steve Ditko. "It wasn't his adventures that excited me," he recalled to Weschler, "as much as the drawing—the stories were good enough, but they were just an excuse for the drawing, whose energy thrilled me. I used to spend hours studying Ditko's conceptualized anatomy, the way he manipulated characters through space, observing them from every angle, in every position. Somehow, I intuitively realized that this was only a few steps removed from the most serious and elevated forms of representational drawing." Katchor told *Current Biography,* "Comics were my earliest introduction to representational art."

By his own account, Katchor became "involved in publishing" during his childhood. In his teens he began printing and distributing detective stories that he wrote and drew himself. "There was a large world of zines at that time," he told Matthew Horovitz for *Jvibe* (on-line), "teenagers self-publishing their own comics, similar to what you see now with music publications. We used to publish them in mimeograph form, and I contributed to many publications, and started my own as well." He abandoned comics for a time while studying painting at Brooklyn College. He later transferred to the School of Visual Arts, in Manhattan, and then returned to Brooklyn College, where he took courses in both painting and the history of art and earned a B.A. degree.

After his graduation Katchor and a few others established a typesetting and graphics company, called Brooklyn Bridge Publications. "We did everything—pasteup and layout for real low-end magazines, fortune-telling flyers, gypsy palm cards, self-published rants," he told Lawrence Wechsler. "We typeset books on iridology . . . , the science of diagnosing disease through the patterns and lines in the irises of people's eyes. We produced stickers for cheap watches—'Fourteen carat,' that kind of thing—and takeout deli menus, fish labels for the Fulton Fish Market, come-on pamphlets for dubious wholesale enterprises. Walking along the street, we'd constantly be coming upon our stuff, discarded, in the gutters. It was gruesome. But going out to drum up that kind of business, the people who came in through the door—this is how I learned about small business."

Katchor told Matthew Horovitz that he chose to focus on cartooning rather than painting because he "liked the idea of the thing being reproduced, of everyone owning the end result. I also liked my work being in newspapers." Much of Katchor's early cartoon work remains unpublished. The rest appeared in *Heavy Metal* magazine, *Escape* magazine, and *Bad News,* among other fanzines. In 1978 he published the first issue of *Picture Story,* a cartoon journal. The journal's second (and final) issue came out in 1986. *Picture Story* featured, along with Katchor's stories, works by Jerry Moriarty, Martin Millard, Peter Blegvad, and Mark Beyer. Katchor knew that *Picture Story* would not be profitable. "Nobody wants this sort of thing . . . ," he explained to Wechsler. "There's no market. Bookstores won't stock them, and when you attempt to get comics places to carry them it's like pouring vinegar into coke and trying to sell that."

Among the first professional artists to recognize Katchor's talents was Art Spiegelman, the creator of the two-volume *Maus: A Survivor's Tale,* the first of which is subtitled *My Father Bleeds History* and the second, *And Here My Troubles Began.* (Done in comic-strip form and awarded a special

Pulitzer Prize in 1992, *Maus* is considered a classic of Holocaust literature.) After seeing a copy of *Picture Story*, Spiegelman invited Katchor to contribute to his magazine *Raw*; launched in 1980 by Spiegelman and his wife as a showcase for cutting-edge cartoonists, *Raw* came out sporadically until 1991. Katchor's work appeared in *Raw's* second issue and four subsequent issues.

At Spiegelman's suggestion, in 1988 Katchor contacted Russ Smith, who was about to begin publishing a newspaper called the *New York Press*, and Smith agreed to make room in the paper for a Katchor comic strip. Thus was born *Julius Knipl, Real Estate Photographer.* "Knipl" (the "k" as well as the "n" is pronounced) is a Yiddish word; not easily translatable, it means something like "nest egg"—"the little treasure you store away for a rainy day . . . ," Katchor explained to Wechsler. "And the strip's all about the little treasures of the city—not exactly [New York City], but almost." In addition to culling from Katchor's memories of growing up in the city, *Julius Knipl* reflects his vision of what a city could be. "I wanted to take two fields of business—photography and real estate—that had all these powerful connotations, put them together in this *pathetic* job, that had neither connotations of money nor power . . . ," Katchor said to Rob Walker for *World Art* (January 1998). "But I decided not to make it a continuing story, so you don't have to know what went on before. . . . Before, when I did longer strips, people found them very hard to read. There's an advantage to this shortness. Even if it's dense, people can take it in, in one sitting."

Katchor's cartoon city contains many wonders: public mustard fountains installed by the Department of Health; "radiator musicians" who rent apartments for the evening and offer "concerts" consisting of the sounds emanating from the radiators; the Drowned Men's Association, which provides buses to the Hotel Good Riddance, a place designed for exhausted workers to get away from it all. "It's a strip about everything I know," Katchor explained to Peter Genovese Jr. for the *Riverfront Times* (October 22–27, 1997). "I don't have to do research for it. . . . In the strip, I'm sort of mining my own knowledge of what life consists of, which means being in a city and doing various jobs. And more often, it's a speculation of what happens between jobs." He told Lawrence Wechsler, "What Knipl does is what I, as a child, thought all grownups did—you know, head out into the city, walk around all day, have these little adventures. So it's the past but at the same time not the past, it's very much the present—but maybe it's true that that way of *looking* has been dying out. Everywhere you go these days, there's still so much of the old stuff preserved, as if in a state of perpetual decay, right there, just beneath all the superficial modernizations—the buildings with their sleek new lobbies, and one flight up you're back in the 19th century. And this strip gives me a chance to catalogue all that, to work toward something like an encyclopedia of the city. My utopian city, with all its little horrible things. Or maybe not utopian—idealized, rather. The strip is the closest I can come to approximating my perfect city."

Katchor usually renders his city in black and white, and his masterful use of contrast takes full advantage of the medium of newsprint. He changes the perspective often, so that street scenes are pictured from many different angles. Describing his visual aesthetic, he explained to Lawrence Weschler, "I am deeply engaged by the conflict, the tension, between words and pictures—the way in which the image doesn't have to just illustrate the words but can range quite far afield. At first, you do it out of boredom—who wants to be slavishly illustrating words all the time? But then it gets to be a value in itself. I spend a lot of time thinking about thinking, about the different tracks that thought and perception regularly take, how they diverge and then realign, how the divergences themselves at times disguise deeper alignments. . . . In that sense, I'm not a Surrealist, as people sometimes claim—I'm a *naturalist.* This is what thinking is like, it seems to me, what remembering is like—or, in Knipl's case, what remembering remembering is like." Katchor's strip also reflects his interest in the narrative form and his careful reading of such authors as Henry James, Vladimir Nabokov, James Joyce, and Henry Mayhew, a Victorian-era sociologist who studied impoverished Londoners. "I wanted to see if I could render [comics] with all the density of a novel . . . ," he told Wechsler. "Because they exist there on a page, the reader ought to be able to go back, to step back and get a sense of the whole, to focus in on a single detail. It's not like film, where you're inexorably propelled forward. In comics, you can get lost in a single panel for half an hour—and ideally, the panel ought to be able to bear the weight of that kind of attention."

Julius Knipl, Real Estate Photographer appeared in the *New York Press* from 1988 until 1994 and in the *Village Voice* in 1994 and 1995. Three collections of the strips have been published: *Cheap Novelties, The Pleasures of Urban Decay* (1991), *Julius Knipl, Real Estate Photographer: Stories* (1996), and *Julius Knipl, Real Estate Photographer: The Beauty Supply District* (2000). In May 1994 National Public Radio (NPR) broadcast an eight-episode radio adaptation of the cartoon; NPR subsequently aired a series of 15 additional installments, featuring the actor/comedian Jerry Stiller as Julius Knipl and Katchor himself as the narrator.

When Art Spiegelman's *Maus II* ended its run in the *Forward,* a daily newspaper that has been printed in Yiddish since 1897, in English since 1990, and in Russian since 1995, Katchor was chosen as Spiegelman's successor. The result, *The Jew of New York,* ran in the *Forward* in 1992 and 1993. Katchor conceived the idea for that strip after seeing an obscure footnote about Mordechai Manuel Noah, who in 1825 bought Grand Island, in the Niagara River, in New York State, in a failed attempt to establish a Jewish homeland near Niagara Falls.

Expanding (with considerable poetic license) on that bit of information, Katchor developed several subplots to supplement the main story line, as he has in all his longer works. One subplot involves a theater company that mounts a play mocking Mordechai Noah's utopian community. The play, entitled *The Jew of New York*, is by Professor Solidus, the proud author of pamphlets saturated with anti-Semitic propaganda. Philip Gourevitch, who was then the cultural editor of the *Forward*, told Lawrence Weschler that *The Jew of New York* acquired a devoted readership. "Each week, when a new installment arrived, we'd all gather around and try to figure out what it all meant. . . . The drawing was magnificent; the plotting—well, it was complicated. But there were people who subscribed to the *Forward* for that strip alone. Others didn't have a clue to what was going on in it, and some of *those* subscribed for its sake alone."

In an assessment of the book version of *The Jew of New York* (1999) for the *New York Times Book Review* (January 10, 1999), J. Hoberman commented on Katchor's storytelling techniques: "Set only a few years before the development of photography, *The Jew of New York* mixes actual sites, like the American Hotel on Broadway, with entirely imaginary ones. However understated his graphic style, Katchor has an extravagantly assemblagist imagination. At one point he interrupts the narrative simply to catalogue the contents of [a character's] desk drawer—'assorted leather straps, a Haggadah [a text used during the ceremonial dinner commemorating the Jewish holiday of Passover] in the Iroquois language, a Masonic pin [an object worn by members of the secret brotherhood of Freemasons], a half-dozen miniature scrolls of black parchment, a series of French boudoir prints in a phylactery bag [which normally holds objects used by Jewish men during morning prayers], a wax esrog [a citrus fruit associated with Sukkot, the Jewish harvest festival], a map of Odessa [a city in Russia that was once a center of Jewish culture].' It is the mission of *The Jew of New York* to connect these dots." According to Mike Rubin, writing for the *Village Voice* (January 27–February 2, 1999), "There's a magical quality to Katchor's imagery that transports *The Jew of New York* beyond the world of our fathers into the realm of timeless fiction."

A different reaction to *The Jew of New York* came from Morris U. Schappes, an historian who is the editor of *Jewish Currents*, the journal of the Association for the Promotion of Jewish Secularism. In editorials for *Jewish Current*, Schappes lambasted Katchor for including in his "historical" account material that was inaccurate or false. Responding to Schappes in a letter to the journal, quoted in part by Wechsler, Katchor explained, "My strip is the fevered dream of an amateur historian in which the 'real' lives of New York Jews, c. 1830, are fleshed out and given the breath of poetic truth. There was a 'New World Theater' on the Bowery in New York City. I saw it in my dream. I swear."

For the opera *The Carbon Copy Building*, Katchor wrote the libretto and designed the set and David Lang, Michael Gordon, and Julia Wolfe wrote and performed the music. The title refers to two identical buildings that stand in starkly different New York City neighborhoods, and the story is based on Katchor's strips. For the set, Katchor made watercolor drawings that were projected in the front and rear of the theater. Commissioned by the Settembre Musica Festival, in Turin, Italy, *The Carbon Copy Building* premiered in 1999; it was performed at the Massachusetts Museum of Contemporary Art and in Hamburg, Germany, in 2000. Later that year it won an Obie Award for best production.

The next collection of Julius Knipl strips, subtitled *The Beauty Supply District*, was published in 2000. For William Teitler and Chris Van Allsburg's film adaptation of "The Evening Combinator," the concluding story in that collection, Katchor is serving as a consultant to Teitler, who co-produced the 1998 film *Jumanji*, and Van Allsburg, the author and illustrator of the prize-winning children's book that inspired that movie.

Katchor himself has been the subject of an 18-minute film—*Ben Katchor: The Pleasures of Urban Decay* (1999). Directed and produced by Samuel Ball with a grant from the Fund for Jewish Documentary Filmmaking, the picture premiered in 1999 at the San Francisco Jewish Film Festival, and it was shown in January 2000 at the Sundance Film Festival, among other such venues. The San Francisco filmmaker George Kuchar's 16-minute video *Urban Doodles* (1996) shows Katchor in his Manhattan studio. Katchor, who has lectured at the Cooper-Hewitt National Design Museum (a division of the Smithsonian Institution), in New York, and the National Building Museum, in Washington, D.C., among other places, put together a 40-minute color-slide presentation, *Carfare City* (1996), which focuses on "the mysterious processes involved in navigating the streets of a city" and offers a "utopian plan" for an ideal city, according to the Jewish Film Archive (on- line). Katchor's current projects include producing a monthly strip for *Metropolis* magazine.

In addition to the Guggenheim Fellowship, Katchor has earned a Caroline and Erwin Swann Foundation Award for Excellence in Cartoon, Caricature, and Comic-Strip Art, in 1990, and the Isaac Bashevis Singer Prize in Literature, in 1998. In 2000 he won a $500,000 MacArthur Foundation fellowship, commonly called the "genius award." He and his wife, Susan Taube, a former schoolteacher who has a grown daughter from a previous marriage, live in New York City. His recreational activities as well as his art reflect his fascination with the minutiae of everyday life. "Someone sent me some old Chicago phone books, from the '60s . . . ," he told Rob Walker. "For weeks that was my bedtime reading." "There's a story behind everything," Katchor has said, as quoted by the National Foundation for Jewish Culture. "We just need to figure out what it is." — C.L.

Suggested Reading: *Harper's* p28+ May 1997; *Jvibe* (on-line) 2000; National Foundation for Jewish Culture Web site; *New York Times Book Review* p6 Jan. 10, 1999; *New Yorker* p58+ Aug. 9, 1993; *Riverfront Times* p38+ Oct. 22–28, 1997; *Village Voice* (on-line) Jan. 27–Feb. 2, 1999; *World Art* p44+ Jan. 1998

Selected Books: *Cheap Novelties, The Pleasures of Urban Decay*, 1991; *Julius Knipl, Real Estate Photographer: Stories*, 1996; *The Jew of New York*, 1999; *Julius Knipl, Real Estate Photographer: The Beauty District*, 2000

Courtesy of the Office of the Secretary of the Army

Kennedy, Claudia J.

July 14, 1947– Retired three-star general in the U.S. Army; former army deputy chief of staff for intelligence. Address: c/o William Morris Agency, 151 S. El Camino Dr., Beverly Hills, CA 90212

One of only three women who have reached the rank of three-star general in the United States military, and the only one to have done so in the U.S. army, Lieutenant General Claudia J. Kennedy was appointed the army's deputy chief of staff for intelligence on March 25, 1997. She held that position until her retirement, in mid-2000. Kennedy, who served in the army for 31 years, was the first woman ever to become a lieutenant general in that branch of the military. Reflecting on her long career and what made her so successful in her field, Kennedy told Sarah Craciunoiu for the U.S. Defense Technical Information Center Web site, "I think selfless service is everything. Selflessness in the sense that you do things because they're right. You do things because it's for the good of the Army. It may not have personal benefit for you. In fact, it may work to your personal discomfort and in no way help you. But this is not the focus. The focus is what is right for the Army, what's good for the Army." "Intelligence" refers to information about enemies or potential enemies (and sometimes allies) of a country, and government intelligence units handle the collection and analysis of such information and make recommendations based on their evaluations. As the army's deputy chief of staff for intelligence, Kennedy was responsible for developing increasingly sophisticated technology, among other duties. "We're in a time in which military budgets are getting smaller and smaller," she told Sarah Craciunoiu. "We're going to have to be more efficient and innovative than ever before."

Described in an on-line bio as "the daughter of an American government employee," Claudia J. Kennedy was born on July 14, 1947 in Frankfurt, Germany. She earned a B.A. degree in philosophy from Rhodes College (formerly called Southwestern at Memphis), in Tennessee, in 1968. Shortly after she graduated from college, Kennedy joined the U.S. Women's Army Corps. The country was embroiled in the Vietnam War then, and for many months students staged demonstrations against the war on hundreds of college campuses. Kennedy's decision to opt for military service after college was unusual for a young woman at that time. But she felt strongly that it was the right thing to do. "First, to be an equal citizen, I [believe] you need to bear equal responsibility," she told Gerry J. Gilmore for *Army Link News* (on-line), "and when your country's at war, you do what you can to help."

In 1969 Kennedy was commissioned a second lieutenant in the army. She later got additional training at the Women's Army Corps Officer Basic Course, at Fort McClellan, Alabama; the Military Intelligence Officer Advanced Course, at Fort Huachuca, Arizona; the Junior Officer Cryptologic Career Program at the National Security Agency; the U.S. Army Command and General Staff College; and the Army War College. Kennedy told Craciunoiu that early on in her career she wasn't certain that she wanted to make the military her life's work. "I can remember a few points in time when I wasn't sure how long I'd stay," she said. "But then I'd stay because the next job being offered to me sounded very interesting." Her teachers and peers, too, strengthened her desire to remain. "I think people mentor others as they were mentored," she said to Craciunoiu. "I was mentored by peers, particularly in the advanced course, my first [military intelligence] course. The students were unbelievably supportive and well beyond what you'd expect. It's never a one-person show, no matter where you are."

Kennedy told Gilmore that she enjoys "being in charge with a mission, a group of soldiers and getting it all organized." Her jobs in the army have included working as an electronic-warfare staff officer and a strategic-intelligence officer in Korea and as a cryptological staff officer at the U.S. Army Intelligence and Security Command, in which position she worked at the National Security Agency at Fort George G. Meade, in Maryland. She has served as the commander of the 3d Operations Battalion at the U.S. Army Field Station in Augsburg, Germany; the San Antonio Recruiting Battalion; and the 714th Military Intelligence Battalion. "My 'big thing' when [I was] a captain was I wanted to be a battalion commander," Kennedy told Gilmore. "That was my goal, my greatest wish. . . . When I found out I was going to be a battalion commander, it was the most thrilling moment of my life. It was everything I thought it would be, and more." In her rise up the military ladder, she also served as the commander of the 703d Military Intelligence Brigade in Kunia, Hawaii. (A brigade consists of a headquarters section and three or more battalions.)

Kennedy's other positions have included staff officer in the Directorate of Training, an arm of the office of the deputy chief of staff for operations and plans, in Washington, D.C., and director of intelligence, G2, Forces command, in Fort McPherson, Georgia. In the mid-1990s Kennedy was made deputy commander of the Army Intelligence Center and assistant commandant of the Intelligence School, both of which are at Fort Huachuca. In July 1995 she was appointed assistant deputy chief of staff for intelligence in the headquarters of the Department of the Army in Washington.

In 1996 Kennedy became a member of Secretary of the Army Togo D. West's Senior Review Panel on Sexual Harassment. The panel was formed after several reports about male soldiers' sexual misconduct toward, and harassment of, female colleagues. "This is not something men are doing to women," Kennedy said to Gilmore. "This is something the powerful are doing to the powerless." "The men and women in power must not overstep the boundaries of that power," she declared. "The young person, whether it's a man or a woman, needs to protect his or her boundaries. . . . Even in a situation where they are the most powerless, that is basic training, they still have absolute jurisdiction over the limits bounded by their bodies." She also said, "Alleged sexual misconduct and harassment incidents committed by male soldiers against female troops aren't examples of hormones out of control. It's a question of the proper use of authority. Some people have used their positions of great power, of absolute power, particularly drill sergeants, to be abusive to trainees. A male drill sergeant who is abusive to a female trainee by sexually assaulting her is using sex to control her. I'm willing to bet money that he is also being physically or psychologically abusive to the men trainees. He is not, probably, limiting his abusiveness to any one particular activity. . . . What's being experienced here by the recipient and the perpetrator isn't sex. What's experienced is a control and power issue."

Kennedy was named the army's acting deputy chief of staff for intelligence in February 1997, after her predecessor in that position, Lieutenant General Paul E. Menoher, retired from active military service. In March President Bill Clinton nominated Kennedy, who then held the two-star rank of major general, for the three-star rank of lieutenant general. He also nominated her as Menoher's permanent replacement. On May 20, 1997 the Senate confirmed the nomination.

General Kennedy sparked a highly publicized investigation when, in September 1999, she filed a complaint of sexual harassment against Major General Larry G. Smith. In her complaint, she charged that in 1996, Smith (who, like Kennedy, held the rank of major general then), had made an unwanted sexual advance to her in her office, in which he had groped her and tried to kiss her—an encounter that, in her view, was "a repulsive thing," according to an unnamed army officer quoted by Steven Lee Myers in the *New York Times* (April 7, 2000). Although she did not file a formal complaint at the time, she said that soon after the incident, she had told others about Smith's actions, and that she had come forward after a lapse of almost three years because the army had announced the appointment of Major General Smith to be the army's deputy inspector general, a position in which he would investigate charges of misconduct by senior officers, including accusations of sexual harassment. The public learned of Kennedy's action in March 2000. Nine days afer the case became news, a retired army officer whose identity was not revealed accused Kennedy herself of personal misconduct during the 1980s; the Pentagon, which investigated those charges, soon dismissed them as having "no basis whatsoever," as Elizabeth Becker reported in the *New York Times* (April 15, 2000). By that time, according to Steven Lee Myers in the *New York Times* (May 23, 2000), the army had substantiated Kennedy's statements about General Smith, through interviews with friends and colleagues of hers, and had canceled Smith's new appointment.

At a ceremony honoring her for her three decades of military service, Kennedy spoke out publicly for the first time about the sexual-harassment case. She urged women in the military to report incidents of sexual harassment immediately to their superiors and friends. If they remained silent, she warned, as quoted by Steven Lee Myers in the *New York Times* (May 13, 2000), "this discrimination and misconduct will continue to harm us and others." Borrowing words from the 19th-century French writer Émile Zola, she advised women in uniform "to live out loud." "Living out loud begins by telling a friend and then later telling people in authority who care," she said. "Our army is filled with women and men who care and are in a position to change and improve the conditions in which we serve." According to Myers, in his May 13, 2000 article, and Becker, in a May 12, 2000 *New York Times* article, many women in the military refrain from reporting sexual harassment by their male counterparts because they fear being labeled as troublemakers and damaging their chances for promotion.

Kennedy ended her service as deputy chief of staff for intelligence in June 2000. Several days later she signed a contract with the William Morris Agency, with the aim of publishing a memoir about her army career. She officially retired from the army in August 2000.

General Kennedy is fluent in German and French. Her military decorations include four Legions of Merit, which are awarded for "exceptionally meritorious conduct in the performances of outstanding services and achievements"; the Defense Meritorious Service Medal; four Army Meritorious Service Medals; and four Army Commendation Medals. In 1998 she received a Living Legacy Award from the Women's International Center. Also that year, in a poll of 100,000 Americans conducted by the White House Project, which seeks to raise awareness about women who have the potential to lead the nation as president, Kennedy was among the five top vote-getters. — C.P.

Suggested Reading: Army News Service (on-line); *Inside the Pentagon* (on-line) Nov. 5, 1998, Feb. 4, 1999; U.S. Defense Technical Information Center (on-line)

Courtesy of Media Arts Group

Kinkade, Thomas

Jan. 19, 1958– Artist; entrepreneur. Address: Media Arts Group, 521 Charcot Ave., San Jose, CA 95131

"The critics may not endorse me," the artist Thomas Kinkade declared to Tessa Decarlo for the *New York Times* (November 7, 1999), "but I own the hearts of the people." Calling himself the "painter of light," Kinkade has sold thousands of copies of his oil paintings, most of which depict quaint villages, charming cottages, beatific gardens, or bucolic landscapes. In 1990, seeking to attract a greater number of potential buyers, he co-founded the Media Arts Group, which distributes limited-edition prints of his work and arranges licensing agreements for Kinkade-decorated goods, which range from mugs to La-Z-Boy furniture. As of early 2000, he had opened some 300 galleries, where the only items for sale are reproductions of his own works, and the number of people on his payroll had reached about 500. "Thank you for sharing the light," his workers usually say when they answer the phone. In 1999 his products generated $250 million in retail sales, through his Web site as well as his galleries, and he himself is said to be worth approximately $30 million. "I represent the forefront of an entirely new trend, a populist movement that takes images people understand and creates an iconography for our era," Kinkade said to Tessa Decarlo. "We are creating an avalanche of imagery that is impacting the world." In a profile of him for *People* (April 10, 2000), Russell Scott Smith described Kinkade as "a born-again Christian who calls God his 'art agent.'" So far, the appeal of Kinkade's images has not extended to art critics, virtually all of whom have dismissed his work as slick, commercial, vacuous, and aimed at the lowest common denominator of artistic taste.

A middle child, Thomas Kinkade was born on January 19, 1958 in Placerville, California, a small town in the foothills of the Sierra Nevada Mountains. His sister, Kate, is a claims adjuster; his brother, Patrick, is a sociology professor who also manages a dozen Kinkade galleries, including the largest one in the U.S. Kinkade's father left the family before the boy started school; his mother, a county clerical worker, raised him and his siblings in what Kinkade has described as the most run-down house in the neighborhood. Deeply religious, his mother instilled in him a passionate belief in Christianity. Starting at the age of four, Kinkade began making drawings and paintings, which his mother would display on the walls of their home. By the time he was a teenager, he had apprenticed himself to the California painter Glenn Wessels, who had studied with Hans Hofmann, the "dean" of the New York school of abstract expressionism. With Wessels's encouragement, Kinkade enrolled at the University of California at Berkeley. He left after two years, he told

Russell Scott Smith, because he disliked what he described as his instructors' "very self-centered approach" to art. "My professors would say, 'Art should be all about you,'" he explained. He later attended the Art Center College of Design, in Pasadena, California. While at Berkeley, Kinkade had roomed with James Gurney, who later became well known as the author and illustrator of *Dinotopia*, a fantasy for young people about a land where dinosaurs and humans coexist peacefully. After Kinkade and Gurney completed their studies, they set off on a cross-country adventure, traveling by train to small towns, where they would sketch the local scenery. They made use of their experiences in co-writing *The Artist's Guide to Sketching* (1982).

After Kinkade and Gurney returned to California, Ralph Bakshi hired both men to work on his film *Fire and Ice* (1982), a violent animated cartoon about good and evil. Kinkade painted hundreds of backgrounds for the film; overseeing the painting was the comic-book illustrator Frank Frazetta. During the one or two years that he worked on the film, Kinkade became interested in a school of painting known as luminism, whose practitioners produced paintings that look as though they are lit from within. He began to experiment with the technique in his own paintings, and after working for a few more years in Hollywood's film industry, he resolved to make a serious effort to market his own pictures. Kinkade has alluded to this period of his life as difficult. His wife, Nanette—his childhood sweetheart, whom he married in 1982—became the primary breadwinner, working as a night-shift nurse.

Kinkade had by then built a repertoire of what would become known as his trademark images—idealized depictions of lush gardens, quaint rural bungalows and chapels, or idyllic main streets, all lit with a gentle glow. They bear such titles as *Hometown Morning, Pools of Serenity, Stairway to Paradise, Garden of Prayer, Teacup Cottage, Lamplight Manor, Wind of the Spirit, A Christmas Welcome*, and *Bridge of Faith*. In promotional literature, he began referring to himself as the "painter of light." He considered his work a sort of ministry: he said to Decarlo, "My paintings provide hope to people in despair, provide a reminder of the beauty of God's creation despite the darkness surrounding our lives," and he told Smith, "I paint scenes that serve as places of refuge for battle-weary people." Lacking business experience, in 1990 he teamed up with his friend Kenneth Raasch, a former owner of a medical-billing company, and launched the Media Arts Group, to distribute and license Kinkade's images to what he envisioned would become a mass audience. Thanks to Raasch's business savvy and Kinkade's marketability, the company has grown with extraordinary rapidity; indeed, *Forbes* magazine (November 2, 1998) listed it as one of the top-10 firms to watch in 1998. It is publicly traded on the New York Stock Exchange, where Kinkade is the only artist represented thus far. The Media Arts Group oversees the 300 or so galleries that stock Kinkade's limited-edition paper or canvas lithographs.

New technology has made it possible to bond lithographs to an acrylic that can be rolled onto a surface; the resulting images replicate tiny details present in the original paintings, including, in many cases, the brush strokes. On Kinkade's prints, further details are added by a team of touch-up artists trained by Kinkade to hand-paint highlights. Although as many as 20,000 copies of a single Kinkade image may be produced in this manner, the prints are marketed as units of limited editions, and each one sells for a minimum of several hundred dollars. *Hometown Morning*, for example, comes in three sizes, each of which was reproduced in a run of 3,950 copies; in late April 2000, the smallest, which is 24 by 30 inches, was selling for $1,135, and the largest, measuring 30 by 40, for $1,995. The few prints from each run that Kinkade himself highlights are sold as "semi-originals" for at least $30,000 apiece. While critics have dismissed the pictures as little more than giant greeting cards, Kinkade has defended his method. "People say I've sold out," he told Dan Cray for *Time* (August 30, 1999). "But not reproducing my art would be like telling a writer not to publish a manuscript because it's one of a kind."

Kinkade's images are available as ordinary greeting cards as well as frameable prints. Media Arts is also responsible for brokering and maintaining the array of licensing agreements under which Kinkade's work is reproduced on many products, which include, in addition to cards, a line of chairs, made by La-Z-Boy Furniture and upholstered in Kinkade-printed fabrics; wall tapestries and pillows produced by Goodwin Weavers; collectible plates marketed by the Bradford Exchange; decorative bottles sold by Avon; and Imperial wallpaper. The Hallmark Co. intends to feature as the centerpiece of its Christmas 2000 line of cards a selection of reproductions of Kinkade's artwork. One Texas-based home builder plans to erect replicas of the gray and yellow cottage depicted in Kinkade's painting *Home Is Where the Heart Is* and possibly to construct an entire village based on Kinkade designs. In response to those who have accused Kinkade of crass commercialism—Cray, for example, described him as a "palette-to-paycheck artist"—the artist has asserted, as he put it to Monika Guttman for *USA Weekend* (February 4–6, 2000), "I'm very excited about allowing myself to become mainstream in the sense that people would have the same enjoyment of me that they do a Walt Disney movie or a Garth Brooks piece of music."

Similarly, Kinkade remains unfazed by criticism of his art as kitschy and banal. "High culture is paranoid about sentiment. But human beings are intensely sentimental," he told Decarlo. "And if art does not speak a language that's accessible to people, it relegates itself to obscurity." He has pointed out that Norman Rockwell was subject to similar charges throughout his life, but that now museums are beginning to acknowledge Rockwell's achievements; for example, the Guggenheim Museum, in New York City, plans to mount a retrospective of his work in 2001. Kinkade has expressed the hope that his work will be similarly embraced. Meanwhile, Media Arts is devoted to establishing him as his own "lifestyle brand," in the manner of Martha Stewart.

Unlike Stewart, Kinkade has identified himself as a devout Christian, and much of his work is overtly religious. Many of his paintings depict churches or chapels; others incorporate less obvious religious imagery. "Look very closely at the light within the top of the lighthouse on *Beacon of Hope*," a Web page maintained by one gallery owner advised. "It includes a cross." In his book *Lightposts for Living: The Art of Choosing a Joyful Life* (1999), which he wrote with Anne Christian Buchanan, Kinkade described his relationship with God. He is also the co-author, with Buchanan and Debra Klingsporn, of *Christ, the Light of the World: A Devotional* (1999), and, among other books, *Chasing the Horizon: Our Adventures Through the British Isles and France* (1997), in which he and his brother traced their journey with their father to visit the senior Kinkade's World War II haunts. Books that Kinkade has illustrated also include *Come Home for Christmas* (1998), by the evangelist Billy Graham. Plans are afoot for Kinkade to present a daily radio spot and to write a syndicated newspaper column, as a means of spreading his philosophy of life.

Kinkade's original gallery, in Carmel, California, is reportedly second only to the rugged coast as the town's most popular tourist attraction. As of early 2000, well over 10,000 people had paid a yearly fee of $50 to join the Thomas Kinkade Collector's Society, which entitles them to a newsletter and the chance to purchase items marketed exclusively to them. The artist's appearances on QVC, the home-shopping channel, have led to record-breaking sales: in one notable instance, in 1998, he sold more than $2 million worth of his merchandise in about an hour. He has been honored several times by the National Association of Limited Edition Dealers and the Bradford International Hall of Fame for plate artists. For various collectibles magazines, Kinkade is an important source of ad revenue.

Burly and mustachioed, Kinkade is said to live modestly; his few extravagances include the purchases of several Normal Rockwell originals. (Kinkade has never sold any of his own original paintings.) He works in a studio next to his home; called Ivy Gate Cottage and set in a garden, it was designed to resemble a Kinkade painting. He and his wife have four daughters—Merritt, Chandler, Winsor, and Everett, all of whom have the middle name Christian. His wife home-schools the girls, and he gives them weekly art lessons. "There is room for an experimental, intellectual bent in the arts, but there is also room for a populist mainstream vision," he declared to Decarlo. Then, referring to his own work, he said, "This is a new type of art, the art of everyone, and I'm on the cutting edge." — M.R.

Suggested Reading: *Art Business News* p16 June 1999, with photos; *Art Issues* p16+ Sep./Oct. 1999, with photos; *Forbes* p222 Nov. 2, 1998, with photo; Media Arts Group Web site; *New York Times* II p51 Nov. 7, 1999, with photos; *People* p200+ Apr. 10, 2000, with photos; Thomas Kinkade Web site; *Time* p62+ Aug. 30, 1999, with photo; *USA Weekend* p8+ Feb. 4–6, 2000, with photos

Selected Books: as author—*Beyond the Garden Gate*, 1997; *Romantic Hideaways*, 1997; *The Garden of Friendship: Celebrating the Blessing of Loved Ones*, 2000; as co-author—*The Artist's Guide to Sketching* (with James Gurney), 1982; *Simpler Times* (with Anne Christian Buchanan), 1996; *Chasing the Horizon; Our Adventures Through the British Isles and France* (with Patrick Kinkade), 1997; *Christ: The Light of the World: A Devotional* (with Anne Christian Buchanan and Debra Klingsporn), 1999; *The Spirit of America* (with Calvin Miller), 1998; *With Wings Like Eagles: A Devotional*, 1998 (with Calvin Miller); as illustrator—*A Family Christmas Treasury* (by Adrian Rogers), 1997; *Every Day Light: Daily Inspirations* (by Selwyn Hughes), 1998; *Come Home for Christmas* (by Billy Graham), 1998; *Do Not Lose Heart* (by Dave Dravecky and Jan Dravecky), 1998; *Father's Memories to His Child* (by Tama Fortner), 2000

Komando, Kim

July 1, 1965– Radio host; journalist. Address: Komando Corp., 2711 N. 24th St., No. 100, Phoenix, AZ 85008

Kim Komando has been widely praised for her ability to translate the complexities of information technology into understandable concepts. Her program, *The Kim Komando Show*, which debuted in 1992, is the longest-running syndicated radio show about computers and the Internet, reaching approximately 40 million people per month in the U.S., Canada, and Australia. The witty and entertaining "Digital Goddess" is also "legendary," according to Jennifer Schu in *womenconnect.com*, for never accepting "no" as an answer when it comes to reaching her goals. By combining this perseverance with her exceptional marketing, computer, and performance skills, she has built her own multimedia company, WestStar. In addition, she writes a weekly syndicated computer column and has authored several books, including *1001 Komputer Answers from Kim Komando*, which has been translated into five languages.

Courtesy of WestStar

Kim Komando

Kim Komando was born in Union City, New Jersey, on July 1, 1965 and was raised with her brother and two sisters in the New Jersey town of Watchung. (Her surname is an abbreviation of that of her Russian-Ukranian forebears, bestowed on her paternal grandparents at Ellis Island by U.S. immigration officials who were limited to transcribing seven letters per name.) Her father, Richard Komando, worked for United Airlines and as a result was able to take the family on trips all over the world. Her mother, Virginia Komando, was a systems analyst for Bell Laboratories and often brought computers home from her office, introducing Komando to the machines at an early age. By the time she was nine years old, Kim had her own computer, and she became fascinated with it in the course of playing the game "Hunt the Wampus." Her father had her begin reading the *Wall Street Journal* the next year, exposing her to the world of business. At the age of 15, she graduated from high school. Having been impressed with the buildings she had seen during her travels abroad, she planned to study architecture in college.

Since her parents had bought a home in Phoenix, Arizona, for their retirement, Komando chose that city for her studies, enrolling at Arizona State University (ASU). Beginning in her first year of college, she lived on her own, and though they phoned her every day at first, her parents had "stressed independence," as she told Schu, and trusted her to look after herself. Komando found it strange to be surrounded by people older than herself, and perhaps for that reason, she didn't do well in her introductory architecture courses. Advised by her father to consider a profession that promised high earnings, she switched her major to computer information systems. To earn money while she pursued her degree, she gave computer-hardware and -software lessons for $25 per hour. Soon she had enough students to hold classes three full days per week, so she had to take many of her own courses at night. With newfound self-confidence, she went to the Phoenix office of the computer giant IBM and offered to train employees there for $25 an hour. The company assigned her to teach their executives how to use the DOS, Lotus, and WordPerfect systems. When she graduated from ASU, in 1985, IBM, pleased with her performance, offered her a sales job.

At first, the 20-year-old sales executive sold IBM XT computers. According to Tracy Levine, writing for *Profit* magazine (March 2000), Komando has admitted that she was "shamelessly" money-driven then; having noticed that her older colleagues drove cars more expensive than her BMW 320, she asked what their jobs were, and upon learning that they were national account managers, she asked her supervisor if she could be one, too. A female colleague confided to her that IBM would appoint only men nearing 40 years of age as national account managers, while her own manager told her that she was too young for such a position. Immediately after hearing this, Komando called the company's main competitor, AT&T, and within two weeks she had a job there as an account manager for large business systems.

In 1985 Komando sold a new hardware system to the *Arizona Republic* newspaper. She then had the idea of writing a weekly computer column for the paper. Although she had no journalistic experience, she launched a barrage of telephone calls, letters, and faxes to the editor to persuade him to give her a chance. After a six-month campaign, he finally relented.

Meanwhile, Komando had moved to the Unisys Corp., where she earned more than $125,000 per year selling computer systems. Her stay at Unisys, which subscribed to traditional corporate culture, was marked by tension. Many did not appreciate her public profile, a result of her newspaper columns, and her supervisor criticized her for her "inappropriate" manner and for dressing as if for a cocktail party instead of work, as she told Levine. She was given only one account, with Honeywell—which was, unbeknownst to her, involved in a lawsuit with Unisys. For months no one at Honeywell would receive her, so she passed the time in Honeywell's cafeteria, talking to employees about what they needed. "Persistence," Schu wrote, helped her to conclude an $11 million deal with Honeywell, the largest in Unisys history and one that brought her a $300,000 commission.

A sense of humor, Komando has said, has been important to her success in the male-dominated computer industry. She told Schu that while she never thought of herself as a woman when working, she understood that her male colleagues, seeing a pretty, young blond when they looked at her, might have thought, "She's a bimbo." So she would tell them, on occasion, "I may be a blonde, but it costs me $80 a month to be blonde"—thus disarming them and, in the process, "break[ing] down . . . barriers." Male predominance is very recent in the history of computers, arising only in the last two decades, with the emergence of the microcomputer. In fact, Ada Byron King (1815–52), the daughter of the British poet Lord Byron, has been called the first computer programmer, thanks to her work in connection with a device—a kind of calculating machine—invented by her contemporary Charles Babbage; the U.S. Department of Defense honored her by naming a software language "Ada." In 1985, when Komando obtained her bachelor's degree in computer science, only about 34 percent of computer-science degrees went to women, but only 25 years earlier, women had accounted for 65 percent of the world's programmers.

In 1991, when a friend of Komando's complimented her on her speaking voice, Komando—then 26—got the idea to broadcast "computer news bites," as she told Amanda Walmac for *Working Woman* (November 1998). She approached Barry Young, the program director at the Business Radio Network, in Phoenix, about her doing radio reports on computer-related topics. Again, she was in the position of persuading someone to let her perform a high-profile job for which she had no experience, and again, she succeeded. She began a weekly show dedicated to solving computer problems and found that it "made my adrenaline go," as she told *People* (February 21, 2000).

In 1992 Komando's fiancé was killed in a plane crash. That traumatic event was "pivotal" for her, she told Schu. One of its effects on her was to underscore the fact that no one knows for certain how long he or she will live. With that in mind, she decided to do what she enjoyed and resolved that she would never again do anything "just for the money," as she explained to Chuck Thompson for *Southwest Airlines Spirit* magazine. While she was earning a substantial income at Unisys, the atmosphere there could not be called friendly, so she quit her $200,000-a-year job in early 1992 to focus on her writing and radio work, which then brought in approximately $8,400 annually. She threw herself into those projects, doing almost nothing else from 6:00 a.m. to 11:00 p.m. daily for the next year and a half.

Komando persuaded Times-Mirror to publish her book *401 Great Letters* (1993), based on form letters she had created at Unisys to deal with clients. Soon afterward she scripted and produced Computer Tutor, a series of how-to videotapes for word processing, on-line services, and other computer activities. Next she hosted an infomercial for the Computer Tutor, which helped her to sell 300,000 copies of the training videotapes at $80 apiece. That in turn led to her own special area of America Online—"The Kim Komando Komputer Klinic"—and a line of training CD-ROMs. Her products were so well received, she told Levine, because she "used lots of analogies to . . . demystify the technology and make it less scary" and always made the products entertaining.

With the 15 percent royalties she received from the sales of Computer Tutor, she founded the Komando Corp., to handle her non-broadcast work, which included a CD-ROM series of more form letters; a contract with America Online; book deals; and a column in the magazine *Popular Mechanics*. She e-mailed and phoned the features department of the *Los Angeles Times* weekly for two years to persuade them to syndicate her column; finally they agreed. She has said that she pursues everything else that she wants with the same intensity.

Next Komando proposed to the ABC and CBS radio networks that they syndicate her radio show. One station's representatives said that her show was "too specialized . . . and the other said computers were just a fad," she told Walmac. Taking her father's advice to "do it with the biggest, or do it yourself," she returned to Barry Young and told him that if he would build a studio, they could start their own syndication network. Together they founded the WestStar radio syndicate. Young handled programming and technical issues, while Komando handled the budget, marketing, and sales. They made a barter arrangement with radio stations: the stations would get the show for free, while WestStar would receive six minutes of free commercial time in each hour of programming and would keep all the revenue from sales. Komando and Young worked out their first deal, with a station in Augusta, Georgia, three weeks before the show was scheduled to begin, in November 1995; according to Komando, the arrangement took place only because Young knew the program manager there. Gradually they made deals with other small stations, until they were taken on by their first big customer, a station in Seattle, the nation's 13th-largest market.

Before long, Komando's radio career took off, in part because news-talk listeners on the whole use computers and the Internet more than those who listen to other kinds of radio shows, as industry research has shown. Komando has reported that her weekly broadcasts draw 50,000 calls per hour as well as many e-mails. Soon Komando and Young were in a position to deal with the largest station in each city. By 1998 WestStar was a focal point for the "convergence of broadcasting, the internet and computers," as one of her press releases puts it, having entered 260 markets, including Chicago and Los Angeles. Advertising revenues had grown from $10,000 to $50,000 per month, and new stations were signing up weekly. Komando created "The Kim Komando Komputer Minute," to be played on Top 40 pop and country-music stations, which further raised the program's visibility. In 1998 the corporation was worth $2.5 million and had 11 employees, and Komando paid herself a salary of $120,000 plus a $100,000 bonus. By then the show had been bought by 350 stations in the U.S., Canada, and Australia.

In 1998 and 1999 Komando was named one of the "Top 100 Most Important and Most Influential Radio Talk Show Hosts in America" by *Talkers* magazine, a radio-industry publication. She has syndicated her computer column in almost 100 newspapers throughout the country. Her books now include *Cyberbuck$: Making Money Online* (1996), written with John Kaufeld, and *Dummies 101: Creating Web Pages* (1997), which were best-sellers. She is developing two more programs for her network and is planning to expand into Internet broadcasting. Eventually she hopes to sell WestStar to finance her retirement and to concentrate more on the Komando Corp. She was voted the most successful graduate of her class at Arizona State University and in 1999 received the School of Engineering's National Engineering Leadership Award.

So that she can relax after work, Komando has no computer in her home, but she keeps three pinball machines there. She wants to allow herself more time to indulge in leisure activities, such as improving her golf game. She has said that she feels that her most important accomplishment is her close relationship with her family. — V.K.

Suggested Reading: *Profit* p63+ Mar. 2000, with photos; *womenconnect* (on-line), with photo; *Working Woman* p41+ Nov. 1998, with photo

Selected Radio Programs: *The Kim Komando Show*, 1992–

Selected Books: *401 Great Letters*, 1993; *1001 Komputer Answers from Kim Komando*, 1995; *Cyberbuck$: Making Money Online* (with John Kaufeld), 1996; *Dummies 101: Creating Web Pages*, 1997

Remy Steinegger/Archive Photos

Koogle, Tim

1951(?)– President and CEO of Yahoo! Address: Yahoo!, 3420 Central Expressway, Santa Clara, CA 95953

Tim Koogle, the president and CEO of Yahoo!, one of the Internet's most popular and profitable search engines, has often been referred to as his company's grownup: since the median age of Yahoo! employees is 29, the 50ish Koogle, who has a dramatic mane of gray hair, stands out. He is also exceptional at Yahoo! because, while other senior members of the staff refer to themselves as Chief Yahoos and even identify themselves with that title on their business cards, Koogle has never called himself Chief Chief Yahoo, as his colleagues have asked him to do. And unlike an unknown number of the company's employees, he has refused to have the purple-and-yellow Yahoo! logo tattooed on his posterior.

Yahoo! was the brainchild of David Filo and Jerry Yang, who, as electrical-engineering students at Stanford University, in California, habitually spent more time surfing the World Wide Web than working on their dissertations in computer science. Launched in 1994 with the name "Jerry's Guide to the World Wide Web," it was designed to help Filo and Yang's friends navigate the Internet. At first the pair simply listed their favorite sites; then, as the guide grew, they organized the listings into categories. Company lore holds that Yahoo!, as they rechristened the site, is an acronym for "Yet Another Hierarchical Officious Oracle," but Filo and Yang maintain that the name simply acknowledged their low social status. (The word "yahoo" was coined by the 17th–18th-century British writer Jonathan Swift to identify a race of boorish humanoids in his satire *Gulliver's Travels*.) By developing new software to help them locate, identify, and edit material from the Internet, Filo and Yang transformed Yahoo! into a customized database for the rapidly increasing numbers of Web surfers. For a while the software was stored in Stanford University computers. By early 1995, network traffic having swelled to burdensome levels, Filo and Yang moved the operation off-campus, to the larger computers at Netscape Communications, an Internet company based in Mountain View, California, with which they are still associated.

In the mid-1990s computer culture was free-spirited and youth-oriented, but Filo and Yang realized that to ensure Yahoo!'s growth, they needed to recruit a more experienced management team. A headhunting firm found Tim Koogle for them, and after his appointment, in August 1995, Yahoo! began its evolution into a full-service Internet media company, providing maps, news, stock quotes, free E-mail, chat rooms, and more. As of late 1999, approximately 80 million people were clicking onto Yahoo! each month.

Tim Koogle was born in about 1951 and grew up in Alexandria, Virginia. He credits much of his success to his father, a navy machinist and fireman. "He said nobody owes you anything, so go out and earn what you want," Koogle told Saul Hansell for the *New York Times* (August 23, 1999), "so I've been making money since I was seven years old." He worked all through high school, repairing machines at a local McDonald's and fixing cars along with his father, who taught him how to rebuild engines from scratch. Koogle attended the University of Virginia's School of Engineering and Applied Science, from which he earned a bachelor's degree in mechanical engineering, in 1973. According to an on-line engineering-school bulletin, he gained membership in Omicron Delta Kappa, a national leadership honor society, and when he graduated, in 1973, with a bachelor's degree in mechanical engineering, he was at the top of his class.

Koogle had paid for part of his college tuition by repairing cars in his spare time, and he earned even more money that way while studying for his advanced degrees, at Stanford University. After he moved off-campus, he started another business, making controllers for electronics manufacturers. By the time he earned his Ph.D., he had saved enough money to buy his first house. His doctoral thesis focused on kinematics, a branch of dynamics that deals with factors (other than mass and force) that affect motion.

In 1983 Koogle joined Motorola, a large electronics firm that specializes in communications equipment. He held several management positions in the company's operating and venture-capital divisions, and he has credited his experience in the latter, where he was responsible for committing millions of dollars of Motorola's funds to promising business plans, with teaching him to feel comfortable about taking risks. In the luxurious marble-floored space assigned to him in the company's office tower, the unpretentious Koogle felt out of place. In 1992 he left Motorola to work at Intermec, then a less-than-successful subsidiary of Raytheon, which manufactures defense and other highly technical equipment. Based in Seattle, Intermec produces automated data-collection and data-communications equipment, such as bar-coding machines. First hired as chief engineer, Koogle was soon named president of the company. During his three years with Intermec, he increased annual sales by 50 percent. He also served as vice president of Intermec's (and Raytheon's) parent company, Western Atlas, a global information-services and technology firm with annual revenues of over $2 billion.

When Koogle was approached by the headhunter working for Yahoo!, the Internet was still largely uncharted territory in the corporate world. Koogle was intrigued by the challenge of building a business almost from scratch—a process he likened to building a car engine. "It's full circle for me," he told Linda Himelstein for *Business Week* (September 7, 1998). "The whole process of taking raw parts and building something that runs is something that appeals to me." In addition, he was impressed by what Filo and Yang had accomplished. "When I first met Jerry and David," he explained, according to Stanford University's School of Engineering Web site, "what struck me immediately was that they had filled a fundamental need and they had done it intuitively. That's what you look for in starting a business." Despite widespread skepticism, he was convinced from the beginning that an Internet business could be profitable. "I still have conversations with people asking, 'Why do you bother with profits?'" he told Saul Hansell. "But I've had enough experience to know at a gut level that if you don't build a company from the start to be profitable, you're never going to get profitable later."

Unlike most Internet start-ups, Yahoo! began to record profits relatively quickly. The company went public early in 1996, earning $35 million on the initial public offering, and reported its first profitable quarter in September 1997. Its financial success has been attributed in large part to Koogle's insistence that Yahoo! remain a free service supported by advertising. Although this is common today, in 1995 other search sites were charging a fee for searches or for their software. Koogle's approach made Filo and Yang uneasy: they felt not only that users would resent the commercialization of the site but that the ads would pose possible technical difficulties for them. But Koogle's instincts were right: the technical problems Filo and Yang anticipated did not materialize, and, perhaps because Yahoo! was careful to keep the ads unobtrusive and interesting, there was little consumer backlash. Yahoo! policy also dictated that any advertising material be plainly marked as such to avoid confusion with other content. By the time of the IPO, more than 90 percent of the company's net revenues—approximately $1.4 million—were coming from ad sales. By September 1997 Yahoo!'s net revenues, still derived principally from advertising, had climbed to almost $70 million. In 1999 the company sold $500 million worth of advertising to several hundred firms, among them Visa and Hallmark, and were guaranteeing them a certain number of viewers per ad. More recently, Yahoo! has faced a problem as struggling dot-com companies scale back on their advertising. In the *New York Times* (October 11, 2000), Matt Richtel reported that in the second quarter of 2000, the number of advertisers on Yahoo! decreased by more than 200. Still, the firm reported revenues of almost $300 million for the third quarter of the year, as well as an increase of 30 million in the number of registered users.

Koogle has insisted that Yahoo! remain independent. He has rebuffed all offers from sponsors eager to be the exclusive provider of a particular commodity on the site, and while many other search engines have formed partnerships with large corporations (Infoseek with Walt Disney and Lycos with USA Networks, for example), he has turned down several large conglomerates interested in merging Yahoo! with their publishing or broadcasting concerns. "I'm a big fan of the long term and a big fan of discipline," he told Saul Hansell. "If you are short term in your thinking, people will wave checks at you and you will take them. We've seen our competition do that. Our users value us because we are a trusted, independent, comprehensive source."

Shepherding Yahoo! from Web directory to full-service site was high on Koogle's agenda from the beginning. He implemented demographically and geographically based programs, so that users in, say, New York or Los Angeles could get local information, such as weather, news, and traffic reports. For young viewers, he launched a version of Yahoo! called Yahooligans! He also focused on making Yahoo!'s name recognizable worldwide, by establishing versions of the site throughout Europe and Asia. Such sites, presented in the appropriate languages and with indigenous advertisers, have been cited for their sensitivity to local cultures and sensibilities. They constitute a rapidly growing segment of Yahoo!'s business: each day approximately a third of Yahoo!'s users are outside the United States. "From the beginning, our intent has been to create the only place in the world that anyone would have to go to find, and get connected to, anything or anybody," Koogle said in a prepared press release, as quoted on the *ZDNet* Web site. As Yahoo! expanded its offerings, the media gradually realized that terms such as "directory" or "search engine" were inadequate and coined the now widely used word "portal" to indicate the company's function as a gateway to the Web.

Despite Yahoo!'s success, its corporate culture is said to remain friendly and low-key, and Koogle reportedly comes across as affable and serene despite his focused determination. He governs by consensus, engaging in enthusiastic debates with Filo, Yang, and chief operating officer Jeffrey Mallett. In the high-stakes Internet business, the group's camaraderie is considered rare. According to Yahoo!'s official company history, the *San Jose Mercury News* compared their work to that of Linnaeus, the 18th-century Swedish botanist who developed a system to classify animals and plants; more often, though, journalists have compared it to high-speed auto racing, an activity that Koogle loves. (On weekends he often hobnobs with pit crews at a local raceway.) The company itself has been likened to a well-tuned vehicle with Koogle at the wheel, outpacing all of its competitors. Using Koogle's nickname, Jerry Yang explained to Saul Hansell, "T.K. has ingrained in all of us that whatever we do, it should speed us up, not slow us down."

Although he is worth roughly $200 million, Koogle, who is divorced, lives in a modest home in Saratoga, California; sometimes he stays at his second home, on Lake Washington in Seattle, to see his friends from the Northwest. Besides auto racing, his hobbies include collecting and playing vintage guitars. — M.R.

Suggested Reading: *Business Week* (on-line), p74+ Sep. 7, 1998, with photo; *Forbes* (on-line); *New York Times* C p1, Aug. 23, 1999, with photos; Stanford University School of Engineering Web site; *TechWeb* (on-line); *ZDNet* (on-line)

Courtesy of Metropolitan Architecture

Koolhaas, Rem

Nov. 17, 1944– Architect. Address: c/o Monacelli Press, 10 E. 92d St., New York, NY 10128

Rem Koolhaas might best be described as an "anti-architect." Though the iconoclastic designs of the Dutch-born Koolhaas have long won critical praise, for years few of them advanced beyond the model phase. Unlike the work of the American celebrity architect Frank Gehry (best known for the curvaceous, titanium-clad Guggenheim Museum Bilboa, in Spain), Koolhaas's buildings are not immediately recognizable as his, even though many of them are conceptually radical. He is fascinated by architecture that is to some degree generic, or anonymous, and concerned with the question of how to build with minimal impact on the surrounding environment. Perhaps for that reason, he balked when he was asked to construct a planned city in an undeveloped area outside Paris. The area was "too beautiful to imagine a new city there with innocence and impunity," he said, wondering aloud if it were possible "to abstain from architecture," as quoted by Mildred Schmertz in *Architecture* (January 1995). Koolhaas's Zen-like approach is unusual in a field that has been associated with hubris—as depicted in the biblical story of the Tower of Babel, whose builders hoped to erect a structure that reached the heavens. Koolhaas himself has said that "architecture is a dangerous profession because it is a poisonous mixture of impotence and omnipotence," as quoted by Ian Buruma in the *New York Review of Books* (November 28, 1996). That is because an architect's often fantastic dreams are contingent upon the needs of a client and the people who will, in the end, have to live in the buildings created for them. In the 21st-century context of globalism and a world population that has exceeded six billion, Koolhaas sees his role as less that of an architect and more that of an urbanist: someone who has a clear-eyed view of how contemporary cities actually work, and a sense of how to build within them. At a time when critics are proclaiming a golden age of architecture, Koolhaas is being given opportunities to test his ideas. His current commissions include a planned city in France, a concert hall in Portugal, the main building of the Seattle Public Library, the new headquarters for Universal Studios in Los Angeles, and an airport on a manmade island in the Netherlands.

Rem Koolhaas was born on November 17, 1944 in wartime Holland. His father, Anton Koolhaas, was a well-known writer and the editor of a leftist newspaper that supported the Indonesian struggle for independence from Holland. When that cause prevailed, in 1952, Anton moved with his wife and three sons to Indonesia, where the family stayed for four years before returning to the Netherlands. Indonesia's capital city, Jakarta, which at the time displayed both remnants of its colonial past and signs of its burgeoning independence, made a lasting impression on the adolescent Rem. "It was a strange coexistence between very ordered sections and disordered sections," Koolhaas told Arthur Lubow for the *New York Times Magazine* (July 9, 2000). "That is the source of a kind of fundamental division of loyalties or stretch of extremes in my work." In his early 20s Koolhaas worked as a reporter for an Amsterdam weekly and wrote experimental screenplays. His wife, the artist Madelon Vriesendorp, views her husband's architectural work as a version of filmmaking. "It's very scripted, the way people move and the possibilities he leaves for people in his buildings," she told Lubow. "He sees a space and he sees what could happen—a scene in a space."

Following the example of his architect grandmother, when he was 24 Koolhaas enrolled at the Architectural Association School in London, England. As a student he became interested in the kinds of architecture that most people reject as ugly or, as one critic put it, "superficially unlovely." Koolhaas researched the Berlin Wall (which from 1961 to 1989 divided the city into the Communist eastern section and the democratic west), arguing that it was of architectural interest not because of its design but because of the human dramas it spawned and the diversity of the urban streets and pristine fields through which it passed. In 1972 he and some of his future professional partners published "Exodus, or the Voluntary Prisoners of Architecture," a proposal for surrounding portions of London with walls and forcing residents to decide whether they wanted to live inside or outside a particular enclosed space. This obsession with how structures shape our lives was also evident in Koolhaas's plan for a library in Paris, for which he created floors that warped and curved toward the ceilings, creating odd, constricted spaces. In another design, Koolhaas proposed an enormous glass block in which various oval rooms were suspended, like blobs in a lava lamp. In the cases of both the library and the glass block, Koolhaas asked fundamental questions about what comprises a wall, a floor, or a boundary. As Lubow observed, "Architecture was the right profession for Koolhaas. Because it is fundamentally concerned with stability, the discipline gave him something to push against—hard."

In 1975 Koolhaas, his wife, and another couple founded the Office for Metropolitan Architecture (OMA, or "grandmother" in Dutch); it has now grown to a team of 90. While most architects build models out of wood, OMA architects use plastic that is more easily cut than wood, thus allowing them to discard one approach and try another quickly. "Here you have this earthquake factor, everything can change at the last minute," a young OMA architect told Lubow, referring to the fact that the parameters of a project can suddenly shift, since Koolhaas prefers to keep even groundwork design tentative. Koolhaas prides himself on his ability to collaborate with other architects and with his clients as well. In 1988 a client who had recently become paralyzed as the result of a car accident asked Koolhaas to design a house that would be wheelchair accessible yet architecturally interesting. Koolhaas's solution was a "sandwich" design: three horizontal layers of concrete encased in glass. In the center of the middle layer, Koolhaas built an office on a circular platform that could be moved hydraulically up and down. "It is simple and brilliantly effective, not just as a mobility tool, but as a key to unlock different spatial combinations," Colin Davies wrote about the platform design for *Architecture* (December 1998). "From the main living room, for instance, it is possible to look up into the master bedroom, or down into the kitchen, or both, depending on the position of the platform." With the platform, Koolhaas—the movie-writer turned architect—created movable "scenes," and then "scripted" them by measuring the heights that occupants would reach as they stood, sat, or lay in bed, and creating porthole windows at the precise locations that would meet their gazes. (In this example, the "scene" is "scripted" by the architect cum director in that the occupant would be able to look out of a particular window only if he or she were sitting, say, so that the height of the window necessitates a certain bodily position if the person wants to see out of the window.)

In 1978, with only a thin résumé of completed projects to this name, Koolhaas published *Delirious New York*, "a retroactive manifesto," as he called it, for Manhattan architecture that challenged conventional thinking about urban design. Whereas the architect Frank Lloyd Wright had championed the "centrifugal city," dispersed across a horizontal landscape in which highways and cars figured prominently, Koolhaas admired the Manhattan model, which features vertical development, extreme population density, and mixed use of space. Exemplifying this architecture is Madison Square Garden (as built in 1925; that edifice was demolished in 1968), in which a tower topped exhibition halls that rose above a train station. Manhattan has undergone repeated transformations—in architectural lingo, the island has repeatedly been reinvented—but always within the limits imposed by the geometric pattern of its grid, which includes the streets and the rectangular bases assigned for buildings. Koolhaas suggested that Manhattan's "culture of congestion" makes it a kind of crucible for creativity, in which each building "strives to be a City within a City . . . all potentially at war with each other," as Ian Buruma quoted him as writing. Moreover, according to Koolhaas, the spirit of the Coney Island amusement-park architects, who used the latest technologies to construct fantasy worlds, still inhabits Manhattan, which he described as "a permanent conspiracy against the realities of the world." *Delirious New York* became a cult classic in the 1970s and launched Koolhaas's reputation as a respected critic and theorist of architecture.

In 1988 Koolhaas was given a chance to build on the urban scale that had long captivated his imagination. OMA won the commission to create the master plan for Euralille, an area in northern France that was to become a hub for the new high-speed trains that travel through the tunnel (known as the Chunnel) that connects England and France under the English Channel. At a short distance from the decaying industrial city of Lille, Koolhaas designed the self-contained "city" of Euralille, with shopping centers, restaurants, hotels, and office complexes (but no homes), all planned around a network of train tracks, expressway interchanges, and roads. A 15-year, $300 billion project, Euralille is a laboratory for Koolhaas's theories about cities as combinations of structure and chaos, bigness and beauty. "The different, autonomous parts [of Euralille]," Buruma wrote, "are so intertwined that the whole looks magnificent in the vast, webbed, human way of a Gothic cathedral." Perhaps even more surprising, Buruma observed, is that old Lille has now become a "thriving area of fine, renovated houses, excellent restaurants, attractive, well-stocked shops, and also of squares and streets teeming with life. A bold, big, modern architectural development has revitalized a dying old city," he wrote.

Although he made his reputation as a conceptual thinker, Koolhaas has also been praised as a creator of elegant designs. His buildings have been called "haunting" and "lyrical," and many of them have surrealist touches, such as tree trunks that serve as indoor support pillars or a "river" made with stones. Rejecting the flashy, mirrored façades of many new buildings, Koolhaas instead uses less expensive, industrial-grade materials, such as corrugated glass, linoleum, steel, and concrete. At one location he constructed a permanent border with the orange rubber fencing used on construction sites.

With his office in Rotterdam, his wife and college-age children in London, and projects all over the world, Koolhaas spends a great deal of time in hotels, jets, and trains. As Mariuccia Casadio wrote for *Interview* (January 3, 1992), he "is not simply an architect. He is a nomad." Koolhaas's second book, the 1,344-page *S, M, L, XL* (1996), is both a record of his projects and a travel journal, containing his observations of such places as Lagos, Nigeria; Fukuoka, Japan; Atlanta, Georgia; and Singapore. Working with the Canadian graphic designer Bruce Mau, Koolhaas included in *S, M, L, XL* film stills, architectural drawings, diary jottings, favorite quotes, and even cartoons. "Its loose, improvisatory framework suggests a model for thinking about the design of cities," Herbert Muschamp wrote for the *New York Times* (March 3, 1996). In the book, Koolhaas developed an argument about what he termed "Bigness." According to Koolhaas, in the 1970s, in the wake of modernist architects such as the Swiss-born Le Corbusier, whose massive post-war blocks of dwellings were criticized as sterile and antihuman, urban planning on a large scale was considered passé. Yet contemporary civic planners were once again beginning to look to architects to reinvigorate their cities and were commissioning such big projects as convention centers, hotel complexes, sports stadiums, and office campuses—all of which are manifestations of "Bigness." Therefore, Koolhaas argued, architects must come up with ideas about how to use large-scale projects to shape the contemporary urban stage. Rather than planning for some utopia, architects must learn to work within the urban spheres as they find them—chaotic and teeming with human activity, much of which is fueled by ambition, competition, desire, and hope.

In 1995 Koolhaas accepted a teaching position at Harvard University, in Cambridge, Massachusetts, on the condition that he be permitted to teach one graduate seminar a year on a subject he himself wanted to research. In one such seminar Koolhaas and his students investigated the Pearl River Delta in China, which encompasses Hong Kong and its northern environs—a region undergoing urbanization so rapidly that, in the next 20 years, its population is expected to triple, to 36 million people. The area is an example of what Koolhaas has termed the "Generic City," one which accommodates mass migrations from country to city and the resulting explosion in population, and which in the process gets built up with little planning. Koolhaas pointed out to Lubow that compared with a European architect, "the Chinese architect is 10 times as rare, 10 times more badly paid, and produces 10 times as much." According to *New Perspectives Quarterly* (Summer 1996), by the year 2050 or so, there will be 50 megacities in Asia, each with more than 20 million residents. But rather than condemn the Pearl River Delta and similar places as soulless, uninviting, and not worthy of discussion—as he believes the architectural establishment does—Koolhaas regards the "Generic City" as part of a trend to watch and study. "I have, as opposed to a love for architecture, an unconditional love for the city," he told Lubow.

Another of Koolhaas's Harvard seminars examined an even more unconventional subject: shopping, which, according to Koolhaas, has "infiltrated every category of building—churchgoing, education, transport." The research of Koolhaas and his students revealed that the gift shop at the Museum of Modern Art in New York City was doing far better business than similar stores in malls, "probably because [in the museum] shopping has been redefined as cultural entertainment," as Lubow observed. Koolhaas recently designed Prada's new flagship store in SoHo, a former industrial and cultural area of New York City that has become an upscale shopping district. Capitalizing on the insight that people tend to spend more money in places that don't seem purely commercial, Koolhaas designed the store so that it can be converted to a theater for live performances. Garments for sale will be displayed in movable towers that can be pushed aside to make room for a stage.

While much of mainstream architecture is invested in the past, through postmodern buildings that reference earlier styles, and many urban planners work to preserve the historical character of neighborhoods, Koolhaas implores the public to imagine the architecture of the future—"another world, another city, another way of being happy," as he put it to an interviewer for *New Perspectives Quarterly*. Koolhaas told Lubow, "There is an extremely new domain being constructed, which partly undermines architecture or eliminates the reason for being of architecture—the electronic domain. Now is an existential moment for a discipline that will decide whether it will be a dinosaur or whether it will be reinvented." — M.A.H.

Suggested Reading: *Architecture* p72+ Dec. 1998, with photos; *Harper's Bazaar* p256+ Nov. 1996, with photo; *New Perspectives Quarterly* p4+ Summer 1996; *New York Review of Books* p42+ Nov. 28, 1996, with photos; *New York Times* H p45, Sep. 11, 1994, with photos, C p1+ Nov. 4, 1994, with photo; *New York Times Magazine* p30+ July 9, 2000, with photos

Selected Books: *Delirious New York: A Retroactive Manifesto for Manhattan*, 1978; *S, M, L, XL: The Office for Metropolitan Architecture*, 1996; *Rem Koolhaas: Conversations with Students*, 1996

Chris Sanders/Outline Press

Kors, Michael

1960(?)– Fashion designer. Address: c/o Michael Kors Inc., 550 Seventh Ave., New York, NY 10018-3203

"Women want a lot out of their clothes. They want them to be provocative but strong, luxurious but practical, feminine but comfortable." The fashion designer Michael Kors, who made that observation to Nina Darnton for *Newsweek* (December 3, 1990), has remained unusually attuned to his customers' tastes and whims since starting out in his field more than two decades ago. "I listen to what women love, what they hate, what they can't find anywhere. Then I know what to do," he told Darnton. Kors's simple, contemporary designs have brought him resounding critical and popular success, and in 1999 the Council of Fashion Designers of America named him women's-wear designer of the year.

Described as a quintessentially American designer, Kors believes that his mission is to make clothing that women like to wear. "If I can genuinely make a woman look better and feel better, then I'm doing my job," he told Annemarie Iverson for *Harper's Bazaar* (March 1997). "Yes, it's divine to send five-foot-11 [British supermodel] Stella Tennant down the runway to do a quick turn looking gorgeous in a dress. But the reality of that dress—to pack it, travel in it, or hang a handbag off it so that it still works and so that my five-foot-one customer is happy—that's what really matters." In 1997 the French luxury-goods conglomerate LVMH Moët Hennessy Louis Vuitton hired Kors to design the Céline women's-wear collection. According to Anne-Marie Schiro in the *New York Times* (April 6, 1999), "Now that LVMH . . . has bought one-third of his business and infused the company with money and opportunities for expansion, Michael Kors is poised to become a global brand name."

Michael Kors was born Karl Anderson Jr. in about 1960 in Merrick, a town on Long Island, New York. His father, Karl Anderson, was a college student at the time of Kors's birth. When Kors was a toddler, his parents divorced. His mother, Joan, who is Jewish, was a model, and at the age of four, Kors, too, began modeling, appearing in television commercials for Lucky Charms breakfast cereal and Charmin toilet paper. His modeling career, and that of his mother, ended when he entered first grade. When he was five his mother married Bill Kors, an entrepreneur. By that time Kors had become adept at drawing clothing. "I have all the sketches he did of [my] wedding," Joan Kors told Anne-Marie Schiro. When Bill Kors adopted him, his mother said to him, "'You're getting a new last name, so why don't you pick a new first name?'" Kors recalled to Elizabeth Sporkin for *People* (April 8, 1991). "Michael and David were her favorites. I chose Michael as my first name and David as my middle name."

Partly because he was an only child and partly because his mother had been involved in fashion, young Michael owned a lot of clothing, and even when he was a child, he loved to shop for clothes. In his early teens he regularly shopped in New York City, where he took acting classes. Although his parents would give him money for cabs and dinner, "you would walk and not eat and then after a few weeks you'd have enough money saved up and you'd be able to pop into [the upscale department store Henri] Bendel's and buy a little something," he told Michael Gross for *New York* (March 9, 1992). Kors showed promise as an actor, but he decided against acting as a career, because, as he told Elizabeth Sporkin, "I figured I'd have better luck as a designer. Besides, an out-of-work actor usually waits tables, but an out-of-work designer can work in a store." While in high school Kors earned money by making caricatures at children's birthday parties, working as a telephone salesperson, and serving as a clothing buyer for the local tennis club's pro shop. "Every penny went on my back," he told Gross. "It couldn't go on my back fast enough." His friends were similarly obsessed with clothes.

Kors told Gross that during this period in his life, he had what he identified as "Long Island middle-class Jewish taste"—which, he came to realize, "is not very different from what you find on Milan's Via Monte Napoleone"—a reference to the most exclusive shopping street in Milan, Italy. "If there was a color, it would be taupe." Kors also remembers liking the "turquoise beaded shells" that some of his aunts wore. Coming up with designs to please people with relatively sedate tastes as well as those with a yen for the dazzling has become one of his major goals as a designer. "It's a hard thing to temper the two," he noted to Gross. "How do you do something that's low key but still has punch and glamour?"

After completing high school Kors attended the Fashion Institute of Technology, in New York City, for two semesters. "I was very impatient as a student," he told Sporkin. "I knew what clothes I liked, and I was ready to see them." He got a job at Lothar's, a boutique that specialized in tight-fitting women's jeans made by French designers. Such celebrities as Cher, Diana Ross, Farrah Fawcett, Shirley MacLaine, Barbra Streisand, and Jacqueline Kennedy Onassis patronized the shop. "I thought it was truly heaven on earth," Kors told Sporkin. The designer said that learning to "shmooze" with customers at Lothar's proved to be invaluable to him later, in the 1980s and 1990s, when a lot of his business involved "trunk shows," in which a designer makes a guest appearance at a store and displays his collection. (The name of such events refers to the trunks in which the clothing is transported.) Such showings afford customers the opportunity to meet a designer in person and to purchase items that the store's buyers may have chosen not to carry. The gregarious Kors reportedly had a rare talent for remembering repeat customers and anticipating what styles they would like; according to Rachel Urquhart in *Vogue* (August 1990), he was among "the trunk-show circuit's most popular performers." "He really seems to care about the ladies," the owner of an exclusive Dallas, Texas, retail shop told Urquhart. "His customers here just love him."

After he had been working at Lothar's for about a year, the store set up a workshop where Kors would create experimental items of clothing that the boutique would then offer for sale. His designs were a hit, not only with the women who shopped at Lothar's but with fashion editors and department-store buyers as well. "They all sort of pushed me and I put a little sample line together," Kors told Gross. With contributions from relatives, friends, and a few backers, Kors raised $75,000 and established his own business, Michael Kors Inc. His first collection, Bernadine Morris reported in the *New York Times Magazine* (August 24, 1986), consisted of "15 separates all in black and brown," in which Kors had "eliminated what he called 'nonessentials'—linings, zippers, and buttons." Kors explained to Morris that the simplicity of that collection was "a form of protest. . . . I grew up in the 60's and 70's when clothes were trendy and people rushed out to buy the newest style. I've also played around with kooky fashions, but I'm happier when styles and shapes are clean. People don't have time for disposable clothes anymore. They just want to get dressed in the morning and get on with their lives. Besides, clothes are so expensive, nobody can afford to buy crazy outfits they only wear once."

In spite of his knack for innovation, Kors was "overshadowed by more famous designers" in the early 1980s, according to Gross, because of the "label mania" that was then at its height in the U.S. For several years, Sporkin reported, he "worked at a deliberate pace in unglamorous, garment-district digs, gradually expanding his collection from 15 to 350 pieces." A number of celebrity customers—among them Belinda Carlisle, Demi Moore, Julia Roberts, and Christy Turlington—helped draw attention to his clothing. By 1985, Kors told Gross, his business had "started to get serious."

While the silhouettes, colors, and other aspects may change in Kors's collections, the clothing is always simple and contemporary, with lots of interchangeable separates made of high-quality fabrics. As Amy M. Spindler wrote for the *New York Times* (April 3, 1996), "Michael Kors is a designer with so much integrity in his work that it is wonderful when fashion comes back to the sort of simple beautiful clothes he does so well. If his is seldom a show with surprises, the nicest of the nonsurprises is that it is consistently strong. It would be a pleasure, sometimes, to see him stretch his wings and try something so daring that it fails. But he doesn't do that, and there is no failure in his collections. The clothes are all just perfect." A few signature pieces that recur in almost every Kors collection, albeit in varying proportions, shapes, and fabrics, are the strapless black dress, the white shirt, and the turtleneck top. "The turtleneck thing you have to blame on my mother," the designer told Schiro. "She's turtleneck obsessed, even living in Los Angeles." Kors has been credited with repopularizing camel as a fashion color, and he is one of several designers who, in the early 1980s, abandoned the fashion dogma that there must be a single skirt length each season. Kors has included skirts and pants of different lengths in each of his collections.

By 1990 annual sales from the Michael Kors women's-wear collection had reached $8 million. The following year Kors signed a contract with the manufacturing division of Compagnia Internazionale Abbigliamento, an Italian concern, to create a "bridge" collection, to be called Kors, that would be significantly less expensive than his original line. "I saw a lot of people who loved what I do but just couldn't afford to buy," Kors told Genevieve Buck for the *Chicago Tribune* (March 6, 1991). Buck described the first Kors collection as being "urban-looking, with plenty of things that can be dressed up to go to work or out at night. Jackets are a little more crisply tailored than [those of Donna Karan's bridge collection] DKNY, and both the workmanship (everything is made in Italy) and the quality of the fabrics appear to be quite good." The items in Kors's bridge collection sold for between $50 and $400—less than half the cost of clothing in the Michael Kors signature collection. Within a year of its debut, the new collection had raised overall sales of Kors's designs to $38 million.

This huge increase in sales allowed Kors to expand his business in several directions during the early 1990s. For the first time, he began to take risks with his signature collection. Reviewing his spring 1992 show in the *New York Times* (November 7, 1991), Bernadette Morris described the collection as containing unconventional designs such as "a short, full skirt made of three ripply tiers of gray wool, a long black and white overskirt fastened over a matching playsuit—he calls it a romper—and a skinny short green skirt embroidered in raffia lace." While the collection also featured the more sedate navy and black blazers, slacks, and skirts that had come to be expected of Kors, this time the suits were paired with lacy bodysuits. Some of the dressier outfits were made of plaid fabrics adorned with shiny navy, green, or white beads. Also for the first time, Kors launched an expensive advertising campaign, with pictures shot by the top-flight fashion photographer Steven Meisel and featuring the supermodel Christy Turlington.

At about the same time, Kors began designing men's clothing. Explaining what had inspired him to do so, he told T. J. Howard for the *Chicago Tribune* (September 30, 1992), "Women's lives have changed tremendously in recent years and their wardrobes have adjusted accordingly. Men's lives have also changed, but their clothing hasn't. . . . Women's clothes are provocative by nature, while men's clothing is all about practicality." Howard wrote that Kors had made his first men's collection interesting by "inject[ing] sexuality" into it, by using fabrics, such as cashmere and chamois, that look and feel more sensuous than the materials traditionally used for menswear.

In 1993, having decided to curtail its business in the U.S., the Compagnia Internazionale Abbigliamento stopped producing the Kors bridge collection. Because the less pricey collection had constituted the bulk of sales of Kors's designs, the announcement strongly affected Michael Kors Inc. The bridge line had proved to be "a cruelly double-edged sword," Constance C. R. White wrote for the *New York Times* (February 7, 1995). "While [the] Kors [collection] . . . raised his profile and sold out in stores around the country, it also cannibalized his signature line. The bridge styles mimicked his clean, sophisticated designs all too well." Kors has also pointed out that in the early 1990s, many stores, "especially small boutiques," went out of business; among them, he told Amy M. Spindler for the *New York Times* (July 13, 1993), were "a good 15 to 20 stores nationwide" that had bought his designs, and with their disappearance he lost another big chunk of his earnings. Convinced that he should restructure his company, Kors declared bankruptcy. "The message, as if anyone needed it underlined, is that it is extremely difficult to make money from designer fashion these days," Amy M. Spindler noted in her July 13, 1993 article for the *New York Times*. By the time collections for the next season were ready to be shown, however, Kors had "reached an agreement with [his] creditors that [brought him] out of Chapter 11," Bernadine Morris quoted him as saying in the *New York Times* (November 9, 1993), and his collection was shown as scheduled. Many of the lower-priced items that previously would have been part of the Kors bridge collection were incorporated into the Michael Kors collection for that season. T-shirts made of stretchable cotton, for instance, were worn under elegantly cut 1940s-inspired suits. While there were a few floral dresses, somber grays, browns, white, and navy predominated.

In 1995 the Japanese fashion conglomerate Onward Kashiyama hired Kors to create its ICB collection, and Kors entered the bridge-collection market for a second time. The following year Onward Kashiyama financed the reincarnation of the designer's own bridge collection. In 1997 Kors ended his association with ICB and began working for LVMH Moët Hennessy Louis Vuitton as the artistic director of the prestigious but somewhat conservative Céline line of women's clothing and accessories. "What I'd like to do is take the quality . . . the luxury Céline is known for, and push the fashion envelope further," Kors told Constance C. R. White for the *New York Times* (November 25, 1997) after his appointment. "I've always been a designer who's interested in clothes women want to wear." Reviewing one recent Céline show for the *New York Times* (March 16, 1999), Cathy Horyn wrote, "Besides being impeccably styled with a casual elegance that fulfills some people's idea of modern taste, Kors's collection was invariably practical. No space-age hokum or divinely trashy rocker gear for him. He avoided all the high-tech futuristic business by sticking to the classic fabrics he knows best."

While some fashion critics speculated that Céline would outshine Kors's own designs, Robin Givhan, writing for the *Washington Post* (February 18, 1999), called a recent Michael Kors collection "flawless." "Other designers presenting their fall collections this week searched for a way to express a sense of luxury and ease and to give voice to the nebulous concept of what it means to be an American designer entering the 21st century," she wrote. "Kors accomplished it all, effortlessly. His success was no less impressive than witnessing a perfect baseball game, riding in an expertly engineered automobile, or listening to a soloist with flawless pitch." Kors said that the collection, called "Sundance Chic," had been inspired by the colors and textures of the American West. It included jean-styled pants in a cashmere-wool blend, a variety of suede items, and rubberized-cotton ponchos. At about the time of this show, Kors announced that LVMH would buy a 33 percent stake in his company, thus enabling him to plan his first advertising campaign in several years and to explore new licensing opportunities. "At long last there was news of an American designer on the upswing rather than a tale of the most recent catastrophe," Givhan wrote. Later in 1999 Kors won the prestigious Women's Wear Designer of the Year Award from the Council of Fashion Designers of America. As of October 2000 he was designing three lines—Michael Kors, Kors (which remains under the Onward Kashiyama umbrella), and Céline. He introduced his company's first fragrance, Michael, in September 2000. For women who sew their own clothing, Vogue Patterns (a division of the Butterick Co.) now offers a line of Kors designs.

During his conversation with Anne-Marie Schiro at a trunk show held at the high-class New York department store Bergdorf Goodman in March 1999, Kors said, "I think I've been consistent. I've stuck to my guns. Fashion to a certain degree is a roller coaster, and I've held a steady course. If you sum up this time in fashion, it's casual luxe. It's what we've always done, which was for a cult and is now more mainstream, for more people. It's not just the press and retailers, but a broader group of customers who are saying, that's the way to dress right now." Regarding the attitude, prevalent in France, that the design of sportswear and casual clothing is not true fashion, Kors told Schiro, "Two of the most legendary names in French fashion—Chanel and Yves Saint Laurent—both had a sportswear attitude. And I think the two greatest garments designed in the world are the T-shirt and jeans. They're ageless and sexless and they came from America." Sales of Michael Kors clothing have reached $30 million per year and are expected to increase. Kors told Schiro that he would eventually like to have his own stores. "Everyone's biggest fear is 'Michael loves stores so much he'll be in the store all the time,'" he joked.

Annemarie Iverson described Kors as having "dizzyingly fast speech, aerobic body-language, and rapid-fire dressing advice." The blue-eyed Kors, who currently wears his blond hair very short, spends a lot of time in Paris and maintains a sparsely furnished apartment in the Greenwich Village section of New York City. "My apartment looks like no one lives in it," he told Elizabeth Sporkin. — C.P.

Suggested Reading: *Chicago Tribune* VII p18 Mar. 6, 1991, VII p14 Sep. 30, 1992, with photo; *Harper's Bazaar* p370+ Mar. 1997, with photos; *New York* p20+ Mar. 9, 1992, with photos; *New York Times* B p8 July 13, 1993, B p11 Nov. 9, 1993, with photos, B p7 Nov. 25, 1997, with photos, B p9 Apr. 6, 1999, with photo; *New York Times Magazine* p142+ Aug. 24, 1986, with photos; *Newsweek* p62 Dec. 3, 1990, with photos; *People* p69+ Apr. 8, 1991, with photos; *Vogue* p314+ Aug. 1990, with photos, p358+ Sep. 2000, with photos; *Washington Post* C p1 Feb. 18, 1999, with photo

---

Bill Davila/Retna Ltd.

Krall, Diana

1964(?)– Jazz pianist and vocalist. Address: c/o GRP Records Inc., 555 W. 57th St., 10th Fl., New York, NY 10019-2925

In an age when most jazz artists are either embraced by fans of mainstream music but derided by critics, or vice versa, Diana Krall has managed to please both camps. A talented pianist and vocalist, Krall has been compared to such jazz luminaries as Lena Horne and Nat King Cole. Meanwhile, her Grammy-nominated albums sell in numbers not usually associated with the jazz market. Geoffrey Himes noted in the *Washington Post* (March 20, 1996) that Krall "doesn't possess an overpowering voice or dazzling dexterity at the keyboard, but she's able to link her singing to her playing in closely sympathetic ways and to project tremendous feeling through both." Krall credits her skill in this area in part to wisdom she gleaned from conversations with the pop great Tony Bennett. "[He] taught me how important emotional directness is in music," Krall was quoted as saying on the Canadian Web site of Universal Music. "It's all about how you communicate. You tell a story, but you leave it open to personal interpretation." Stephen Holden noted in the *New York Times* (June 30, 1998) that "Krall is about the farthest thing from a jazz diva you could expect to find in a world where loud, pyrotechnic vocal display is confused with musical insight and emotional depth." Although five acclaimed albums have brought her enormous success at home and abroad, many journalists continue to focus on Krall's attractive looks or the fact that she is a white blond performing music traditionally associated with African-American culture. Duke Dubois, senior director of jazz at Krall's label, GRP, commented on such coverage, telling *Billboard* (June 29, 1996), "They may take that first look because she's a good-looking young lady, but when she sits down and plays, good looks can't get you through. When Diana comes on, it's the talent that she delivers first of all. Her renditions of those [Nat King Cole songs] and her throatiness and sensuality all add up to success. She plays and sings well and interprets music emotionally."

Diana Krall was born in about 1964 in Nanaimo, British Columbia, the first child of James Krall, an accountant, and Adella Krall, an elementary-school teacher and librarian. The Kralls were a musical family; both parents played piano, and her father, a stride piano player, had assembled a large collection of jazz records. "I think Dad has every recording Fats Waller ever made," Krall was quoted as saying in the *All Music Guide* (on-line), "and I tried to learn them all." She began classical piano lessons at the age of four, and on Sundays she and her family would make music at the house of her grandmother, a singer. Although at age nine she was rejected for a local youth choir because her voice was too low, Krall was able to sing in the choir of her Lutheran church. Meanwhile, she had ideas for her future that were not connected with music. "I used to build rockets with my next-door neighbor," Krall told Chuck Taylor for *Billboard* (March 21, 1996). "I wanted to be an astronaut. My parents said, 'Do whatever you want; if you want to build rockets, great.'"

Despite that early ambition—and in spite of her avid interests in a number of other activities, such as swimming and skiing—Krall continued to pursue music. Throughout her high-school years, she performed three nights a week at various restaurants, making her debut at age 15. Some of the songs she played in those early days, such as the pop standards "Ghost of a Chance" and "You're Getting to Be a Habit with Me," are still in her repertoire. In addition to playing music on her own, Krall was the pianist in her high-school jazz band, in which she drew inspiration from her teacher, Bryan Stovell. "Four bars into her first solo," Stovell told Erick Thompson for *Maclean's* (February 24, 1997), "I knew she was destined to be at least an excellent jazz player." When Krall was 16, Stovell introduced her to Don Thompson, a jazz pianist from Toronto, who came to hear her perform. "I think with giant talent like that you can be forgiven if you go the extra mile," Stovell said. "She was interested in the whole gamut." At about the same time, Krall befriended Louise Rose, a local musician who gave her piano lessons and encouraged her singing. Despite high praise from Rose, Krall's mother was not enthusiastic about Krall's becoming a professional musician. "I just smiled and thought, well, that's nice of her to say but Diana's going to university," she told David Hayes for *Chatelaine* (September 1997). "I didn't want her playing in bars. I didn't have much regard for music as a career."

After graduating from high school, Krall attended the Berklee College of Music, in Boston, Massachusetts, on a Vancouver Jazz Festival scholarship. Leaving Berklee after a year and a half, she returned to Nanaimo, where, playing at Tio's nightclub, she was heard by renowned jazz bassist Ray Brown. At his suggestion, Krall went to Los Angeles to study with jazz pianist Jimmy Rowles under a Canadian Arts Council grant. In addition to helping her to hone her technique, Rowles persuaded a reluctant Krall to sing more. "There was an instant connection made with Jimmy," Krall told a *Down Beat* (May 1995) interviewer. "Having worked with Billie Holiday, Sarah Vaughn, Carmen McRae, Ella Fitzgerald, Peggy Lee, and the like, he's the ideal person for a singer to hang out with. He taught me about the beauty of the music." After studying with Rowles for three years, Krall went to Toronto, where she became a student of Don Thompson's. In 1990 she moved to New York and began singing and playing piano in a trio. During those years, she told Erick Thompson, "I was working seven hours a night, three hours as a soloist and four with a trio. It really gave me a chance to practice, to stretch, to work on the material."

In 1993 Krall released her debut album, *Steppin' Out*, on Justin Time Records. That work featured her renditions of such classic pop tunes as "Body and Soul" and "42nd Street" as well as one of her own songs, "Jimmie." Scott Yanow noted in the *All Music Guide* (on-line) that the album "was a good start for the singer/pianist although at that point she did not stand out from the crowd." After her successful 1994 follow-up, *Only Trust Your Heart*, Krall began touring the United States and Canada as well as playing assorted dates in Europe and Japan.

Krall returned in 1996 with *All for You*, which was released on GRP's prestigious Impulse! label. A tribute to the Nat King Cole Trio, *All for You* was the record that really launched Krall's career, becoming a runaway best-seller and spending 76 weeks on the *Billboard* Top 10 traditional jazz charts; it went on to sell, worldwide, more than 18 times the number of copies moved by the average jazz album. Although comparisons to Cole were in abundance, Krall told Diane Turbide for *Maclean's* (February 24, 1997), "We're not trying to re-create the Nat Cole Trio. It's more about the beauty of the music, the joy in it, and the simplicity, which is the hardest and most complex thing to achieve." For the album, Krall was nominated for a Grammy Award for best jazz vocalist.

In May 1997, not long after the awards ceremony, Krall's mother was diagnosed with multiple myeloma. (The illness was successfully treated with a bone-marrow transplant.) "So, despite the Grammy nomination and everything else," the jazz singer told Turbide, "it was a very mixed year. When terrible things like that happen, it shows you what's *really* important. And it taught me a lot about hope and strength and kindness, things I saw while my family went through this."

In a sign of her rising popularity, Krall was ranked ahead of Ella Fitzgerald in a 1996 *Down Beat* poll of jazz vocalists. Krall was dismissive of the honor. "That's so ridiculous," she told Diane Turbide. "You don't *beat* Ella Fitzgerald; it's not about competition. It's just a sign that you're somebody's favorite right now." In 1997 Krall released the heavily promoted *Love Scenes*, on which she concentrated on the ballads that she and Impulse! president and producer Tommy LiPuma chose for the record. "I admired Tommy's work long before I ever had the opportunity to work with him," Krall said, as quoted on the Canadian Web Site of Universal Music. "He is completely involved in the studio . . . with the musicians, not in the sound booth. He's right there with us, listening, feeling the passion and beauty of the music. I especially appreciate his talent for bringing out the best in his artists. Tommy pushes you . . . makes you better." Also featured on the album were bassist Christian McBride and guitarist Russell Malone. "Russell and Christian both shared their love of the joy and beauty of the music with me as we made this recording together," Krall said. "We have a very telepathic musical relationship." She also remarked, in the same interview, that the mood created by *Love Scenes* reminded her of her hometown. "It was subtle—and I didn't even notice it until the recording was completed, but Vancouver Island is surrounded by mountains. It's a very rainy, green place, and a lot of the tunes refer to the ocean or to rain. *Love Scenes* is a look back at home, at what's important to me, of the strength of all kinds of love—familial, friendship, romantic. Love is funny, naughty, sad, joyful . . . all those things."

Although the album did well commercially, critical reaction was generally more muted than that for *All for You*. Mike Joyce noted in the *Washington Post* (November 12, 1997) that *Love Scenes* was "marred by vocals that never fully express the emotions that lie at the heart of the songs. . . . The album's greatest pleasures, in fact, derive not from her balladry or piano playing, but from the inspired pairing of guitarist Russell Malone and bassist Christian McBride." Still, *Love Scenes* was nominated for a Grammy and won an award for best jazz album at the Soul Train Lady of Soul Awards ceremony. It was also the first jazz album to go platinum in Canada. A single from *Love Scenes*, a cover of the 1926 song "Peel Me a Grape," was the number-one song on "smooth" jazz radio in the U.S. in early 1997. Impulse! also began pushing the song on adult contemporary and New Age stations. "I had an issue being played on smooth jazz at the beginning," Krall told Chuck Taylor. "A lot of people think if you're there, you're not a serious artist anymore. Now I realize that whether I'm being played on adult contemporary, smooth jazz, or college stations, it's all jazz. If I'm played on the polka hour, as long as it's honest and people like it, I'm happy. Never underestimate your audience." Also in 1997, Krall's crossover appeal was evident when she made an appearance on the hit Fox drama *Melrose Place*, playing "Peel Me a Grape." In the following year she performed at the Ottawa concert of the Lilith Fair, the traveling music festival made up entirely of female artists.

Krall's latest album, aside from the holiday EP *Have Yourself a Merry Little Christmas*, is *When I Look in Your Eyes* (1999). There were critics who felt that the record's string arrangements, by producer Tommy LiPuma, made for an overly slick and pop-oriented sound. "Some might call this fluff or mush," Michael G. Nastos stated in the *All Music Guide*, "and it depends solely on your personal taste." One important arbiter, the National Academy of Recording Arts and Sciences (also known as the Recording Academy), made its taste known, awarding Krall the 2000 Grammy for best jazz vocal performance—remarkable for a woman who has said that she did not feel confident about her singing until 1997.

Diana Krall is slender and blond and has green eyes. She is said to be very down-to-earth and to have a good sense of humor. Always a lover of jazz and classic pop, she has become a fan of modern R&B and of such contemporary artists as Sting. "I've played pop stuff in piano bars," she told Michael Bourne for an interview in *Down Beat* (July 1996), "and I wouldn't mind singing on a pop record or a commercial. I'm game, but playing the music I *want* to play is the most important thing. I grew up with eclectic tastes at home musically, but my heart is in the *groove*. I just want to play piano and sing. The bottom line is the music, the music, the *music*! And that's *fun*!" Krall has lived in New York since 1992 and makes her home in the city's Chelsea section. In the little time she has to relax, she likes to read cookbooks; she has grown fond of Japanese food. Speaking of her future, she has said that she is open to new styles and influences, although, as she told Will Hermes for *Gentlemen's Quarterly* (May 1998), she studies the standards "the way you might study Chekhov or Shakespeare: [George] Gershwin, [Cole] Porter, Sammy Kahn, Irving Berlin. I know I still have a lot to learn. I'm not ready to go out and write, direct, and star in my own show yet. But that's not to say I won't." — G.O.

Suggested Reading: *Billboard* p1+ Mar. 26, 1996; *Down Beat* p28+ Nov. 1997, with photos; *Gentlemen's Quarterly* p117+ May 1998; *Maclean's* p57+ Feb. 24, 1997; *New York* p34+ May 31, 1999, with photo; *New York Times Magazine* p32+ Feb. 20, 2000, with photo; *Newsweek* p66 Oct. 20, 1997, with photo, p68 June 14, 1999, with photos; *Saturday Night* p12+ Oct. 1999, with photo

Selected Recordings: *Steppin' Out*, 1993; *Only Trust Your Heart*, 1994; *All for You*, 1996; *Love Scenes*, 1997; *When I Look in Your Eyes*, 1999

Lang, David

Aug. 1, 1957– Composer. Address: c/o Red Poppy Music, 66 Greene St., Fifth Fl., New York, NY 10012; c/o G. Schirmer Promotion Dept., 257 Park Ave. S., 20th Fl., New York, NY 10010

"There is no name yet for this kind of music," Mark Swed, a specialist in contemporary classical music, once wrote about the works of the American composer David Lang. Lang's compositions include the distinctively titled *Bonehead*, *Eating Living Monkeys*, *International Business Machine*, and other pieces for full orchestra; such music for chamber groups as *My Very Empty Mouth*, *My Evil Twin*, *Hunk of Burnin' Love*, and *I Fought the Law*; three operas, the most recent of which—*The Carbon Copy Building*—is a "a comic-book opera in one act" that uses art by the cartoonist Ben Katchor; and music for solo instruments, such as the percussion piece *The Anvil Chorus*. ("To me, the worst thing is to write a good piece with a bad title, like 'Scientific Problem Number Seventeen,' which is what the Sixties were like," Lang commented to Peter Goodman for *New York Newsday* [January 21, 1991].) "Lang writes music that can be experimental in form yet conveyed in direct, propulsive, powerful language that picks up some of its energy from rock and minimalism but is also open to a wide variety of other stylistic expressions," Mark Swed wrote for *Opera News* (June 1995).

In an interview with K. Robert Schwarz for the *New York Times* (January 20, 1991), Lang declared that "want[ing] to fit in" with the "glorious European musical tradition" is wrong, because then, one would be "worshiping at a shrine" rather than "writing a piece of music." "You're not doing something that adds to history; you're doing something that proves you belong to history," he explained. "That's a wonderful idea, but it's a paralyzing idea, and ultimately it's one that American composers have no business believing. An American composer has a responsibility to say, 'What is it that is different about my background?'" Lang, who earned a doctorate in composition from the School of Music at Yale University, is a co-

Courtesy of G. Schirmer, Inc.

David Lang

founder of Bang on a Can, a new-music festival that debuted in New York City in 1987 and has become recognized as one of the premier events of its kind in the United States. Speaking of the genesis of Bang on a Can, Lang said to Frank J. Oteri for *newmusicbox* (May 1999, on-line), "It's easy to identify lots of things that need to get changed [in the world] in order to make sure that . . . interesting music always gets played, and the right audience knows about it, [and] that music actually can mean something large in society."

Born on August 1, 1957 in Los Angeles, David Lang became interested in music early on. In high school and college, he was particularly taken by the work of Dmitry Shostakovich, a 20th-century Russian composer of classical music. Lang told K. Robert Schwarz that in his view, Shostakovich's music is "in tremendous bad taste, and I always thought that was great, because it's the bad taste that makes you think the good taste is authentic." In the 1970s Lang wrote long compositions that he has described as beautiful but dreamy and uneventful. His style changed after he discovered punk rock. "I got my first record of the Clash in 1978," he recalled to Schwarz. "The effect was incredible. When I heard this really aggressive rock-and-roll, I started thinking there was a vitality that was missing from what I had been doing. And I haven't written a quiet piece since then." He also told Schwarz, "I wouldn't trust any young composer who grew up in America who didn't have a background in pop music, who didn't listen to that music as his first music. In America, that's your first impulse."

According to a brief biography of him on the G. Schirmer Web site, Lang has degrees from Stanford University, in California; the University of Iowa; and Yale University, in New Haven, Connecticut. At the Yale School of Music, from which he earned a Ph.D. in composition, in 1989, he studied under the Pulitzer Prize–winning composer Jacob Druckman and Martin Bresnick, the latter of whom coordinated the school's composition department. (He later studied with the German operatic composer Hans Werner Henze at Tanglewood, in Lenox, Massachusetts.) His dissertation focused on "approaches to the overtone system, the sounds made by harmonic overtones," as Peter Goodman reported in *New York Newsday* (May 1, 1988). In the mid-1980s he won a Guggenheim Fellowship and served as a junior composer-in-residence at Horizons, a new-music festival run for several summers by the New York Philharmonic. Among his works from the 1980s are *Illumination Rounds* (1982), for violin and piano; *Frag* (1985), for flute, oboe, and cello; *Spud* (1986), for flute, oboe, clarinet, horn, timpani, violin, viola, cello, and double bass; and *Are You Experienced?* (1987–88), for a dozen instruments and a narrator, which, at 23 minutes, is among his longer pieces. His compositions were presented at concerts given by the Cleveland Orchestra and the St. Paul Chamber Orchestra, among other mainstream groups.

Lang was living in a loft in Midtown Manhattan, in New York City, when, in 1987, he launched Bang on a Can, in collaboration with the composers Michael Gordon and Julia Wolfe, whom he had met at Yale. Their goal was to expand the audience for new music; the name they chose for the festival, Lang told Goodman, "seemed like the right thing . . . to attract attention." A venue for never-before-performed and seldom-heard contemporary works as well as classics of the modern repertoire, Bang on a Can began as a one-day event at the RAPP Arts Center, on Manhattan's Lower East Side. Some two dozen works were offered, in a marathon that lasted about 12 hours. At the second festival, also held at RAPP, there were 30 pieces on the program, which began at 2:00 p.m. on Sunday, May 7, 1988 and ended at 2:00 a.m. the next morning. Gordon explained to Goodman that Lang and his fellow organizers hoped that the audience would "have a really good time with new music, which is usually seen as such a serious affair. People should feel relaxed; it's very informal, the composers talk to the audience."

During the mid-1990s the Bang on a Can festival was held at Lincoln Center. By that time the performances were no longer given by "new music ensembles of all stripes," as Allan Kozinn put it in the *New York Times* (March 16, 1995), but by the Bang on a Can All-Stars: Robert Black, Mark Stewart, Maya Beiser, Evan Ziporyn, Lisa Moore, and Steve Schick. Those six modern-music specialists play clarinet, saxophone, electric guitar, cello, bass, keyboards, and percussion among them. Described as "part classical ensemble, part rock band, [and] part jazz band," the Bang on a Can All-Stars have recorded numerous albums, including *Cheating, Lying, Stealing* (1996), *Brian Eno: Music for Airports* (1998), and *Renegade Heaven* (2000). In 1999 the All-Stars concertized in several states and a dozen European countries. The five-day 1999 Bang on a Can Festival, which included a 23-hour marathon concert, was held at the Henry Street Settlement Abrons Arts Center, in New York City.

On the Bang on a Can Web site, Lang described his inspiration for *Cheating, Lying, Stealing*, a 15-minute piece for six instruments that he composed in 1993: "A couple of years ago, I started thinking about how so often when classical composers write a piece of music, they are trying to tell you something that they are proud of and like about themselves. Here's this big gushing melody, see how emotional I am. Or, here's this abstract hard-to-figure-out piece, see how complicated I am, see my really big brain. I am more noble, more sensitive, I am so happy. The composer really believes he or she is exemplary in this or that area. It's interesting, but it's not very humble. So I thought, what would it be like if composers based pieces on what they thought was wrong with them? Like, here's a piece that shows you how miserable I am. Or, here's a piece that shows what a liar I am, what a cheater I am. I wanted to make a piece that was about something disreputable. It's a hard line to cross. You have to work against all your training. You are not taught to find the dirty seams in music. You are not taught to be low-down, clumsy, sly, and underhanded. In *Cheating, Lying, Stealing*, although phrased in a comic way, I am trying to look at something dark. There is a swagger, but it is not trustworthy. In fact, the instruction on the score for how to play it says: Ominous funk."

Several musical organizations, among them the American Composers Orchestra, the BBC Singers, the Boston Symphony Orchestra, the Cleveland Orchestra, and the St. Paul Chamber Orchestra, have commissioned Lang to compose for them. On a commission from the Santa Fe Opera, he wrote the score for *Modern Painters* (1994), an opera based on the life of the British art critic and social reformer John Ruskin (1819–1900), who conceived of art as a "public good." Containing a libretto by the Pulitzer Prize–winning *Wall Street Journal* cultural critic Manuela Hoelterhoff, *Modern Painters* takes its name from the title of a five-volume work by Ruskin that Mark Swed, in *Opera News*, labeled "a vast treatise on the universality of art, morality, and national integrity." Ruskin, who exercised dictatorial powers as a tastemaker in art in his native land and wrote essays that have widely been described as brilliant, is now known mainly for his failure to consummate his six-year marriage and for the insanity that marked the last years of his life. His inability to deal with the many "unstructured, dirty, and messy" aspects of daily life, as Lang has put it, inspired the composer to write, in Swed's words, "highly structured" music for the "scenes in which Ruskin is in control." "The most interesting thing about the piece for me," Lang told Swed, "is the way his wife actually becomes the central character. When she is under his thumb, after they are married, her music is ordered, following the same rules his music follows, and she struggles to break out of them. The course of the opera is really her music breaking free of his rules." *Modern Painters* debuted at the Santa Fe Opera in August 1995, in a production directed by Francesca Zambello. In a review of the work for *Vogue* (August 1995), Michael Kimmelman described Lang's score as "a blend that lies somewhere between Philip Glass and Benjamin Britten."

Lang wrote both the words and music to his first opera, *Judith and Holofernes* (1989), a 35-minute work for eight instruments, which uses puppets to portray how the biblical heroine Judith saved her people by entrapping and then beheading the Assyrian general Holofernes. The score of his third opera, *The Carbon Copy Building* (1999), for four singers (who play dozens of characters) and four instrumentalists, was written by Lang in collaboration with Michael Gordon and Julia Wolfe. The text, by Ben Katchor, is based on Katchor's comic strips, which focus on "the disturbed underside" of city dwellers' everyday lives, as an on-line G. Schirmer, Inc. publicity piece put it. An hour and 15 minutes long, the opera uses illustrations by Katchor, which are projected onto screens and "[serve] multiple functions: story, set, guide, translator, omniscient and/or reliable narrator." *The Carbon Copy Building*, the title of which refers to two identical buildings that stand in starkly different New York City neighborhoods, was commissioned by the Settembre Musica Festival, held in Turin, Italy, after the Bang on a Can All-Stars performed there in the mid-1990s. "We understood that what [the festival organizers] liked about our work was its sense of spontaneity and irreverence," Julia Wolfe told Alisa Solomon for the *Village Voice* (September 29–October 5, 1999, online). "In Europe history weighs on them, but they think of America as not having a history, so they look to us for fresh vision. So we wanted to make an opera that was quintessentially America, quintessentially New York. So we thought of comics." *The Carbon Copy Building* had its world premiere in Turin's Teatro Carignano on September 9, 1999. It was performed again at the Kitchen, a New York City venue, in October 1999.

During the Sydney Olympics, in September 2000 in Australia, the Bang on a Can musicians played at the Sydney Olympics Arts Festival. The 2000 Bang on a Can marathon concert was scheduled to take place on December 10 at the Brooklyn Academy of Music. As of January 2001 the Bang on a Can All-Stars will begin recording for a new label, Cantaloupe Music. Also in 2001, Lang and his associates will be taking part in *Lost Objects*, a collaborative piece, commissioned by the Dresden Music Festival, that will also involve the Concerto Cologne (a German baroque chamber orchestra), Ries Kammerchor (a German chamber choir), and

La Fura del Baos (a theater troupe from Barcelona, Spain).

As of mid-1999 Lang and his wife had three children, the oldest of whom was four. In addition to the Guggenheim Foundation grant, Lang has won grants from the New York Foundation for the Arts and the National Endowment for the Arts. His other honors include the Rome Prize, a fellowship for study in Italy that is awarded by the American Academy in Rome; the BMW Prize for best composition, awarded at the Munich (Germany) Biennale for New Music Theater; and a Friedheim Award, from the Kennedy Center, in Washington, D.C. "I've been lucky," Lang commented to Peter Goodman in 1991. "I'm about as weird as the Establishment can take. I feel I am writing this sort of uncompromisingly bizarre music, but also I'm somehow not thrown out of the Establishment."

During his 1991 conversation with K. Robert Schwarz, Lang talked about the increasing multiculturalism in music in the United States. "I think that chaos is incredibly provocative," he said. "All of my friends who are composers grew up playing in rock bands, but that's not the only world—there's the effect of the Pacific cultures on the West coast, the effect of the new black music that's coming from the inner cities. These musics don't meet yet—it's like the fault lines lining up, and you're just waiting for the big earthquake. But when all those musics hit someplace, when all those cultures speak the same language, I think the earth will shift one degree off its axis." — M.R.

Suggested Reading: *bangonacan.org* (on-line); *New York Newsday* II p19+ May 1, 1988, with photo; *New York Times* II p25 Jan. 20, 1991, with photo; *newmusicbox.org* (on-line) May 1999, with photo; *Opera News* p18+ June 1995, with photo; *schirmer.com* (on-line)

Selected Recordings: *Are You Experienced?*, 1991; as contributor—*Bang on a Can Live*, Vol. 1, 1991; *Bang on a Can Live*, Vol. 2, 1993; *Industry*, 1995; *Cheating, Lying, Stealing*, 1996; *Brian Eno: Music for Airports*, 1998

Courtesy of Liz Lerman Dance Exchange

Lerman, Liz

Dec. 25, 1947– Dancer; choreographer; founder and artistic director of the Liz Lerman Dance Exchange. Address: Liz Lerman Dance Exchange, 7117 Maple Ave., Takoma Park, MD 20910

"What kind of stories could I tell if all my dancers were between 18 and 25, skinny, white, with their hair pulled back?" Liz Lerman asked Sarah Kaufman for the *Washington Post* (October 12, 1997), referring to the profile of a typical dancer in a conventional troupe. "What kind of drama is there?" While the Liz Lerman Dance Exchange, the troupe that she founded in 1976, includes some dancers who meet that rather narrow description, it has also included performers who are black, Asian, gay, HIV positive, pregnant, or older than 70. Some are professionally trained artists; others never danced before they met Lerman. "Although the beautifully developed ability of the professional dancer makes for a spectacular display of human potential," Lerman explained to Alan Kriegsman for the *Washington Post* (April 26, 1987), "it is also true that the inherent characteristics and benefits of dance belong to everyone. . . . All people should have access to [dance] no matter what their age, ability or body type." Her work, she told Cathryn Harding for *Dance Magazine* (January 1996), "is really about people dancing, not dancers dancing." "Art belongs to everyone," she told Chris Westberg for *High Performance* (Winter 1992, online), "and dancing is a birthright."

Liz Lerman was born on December 25, 1947 in southern California. Family lore has it that her parents fell in love at the opera, and music—as well as art and theater—remained important to the couple. Lerman and her brothers, David and Richard (the latter of whom became a composer), were often taken to live performances. Lerman was an active child, and almost as far back as she can remember, she wanted to dance. During downpours, she would run outside and fling herself about, splashing through the puddles that invariably covered the backyard when it rained heavily. "There was always a sense in the household that I would dance," she told Cathryn Harding. "It was like, of course, Liz's dancing is really important. There was a feeling of incredible support."

When Lerman was five years old, the family moved to Washington, D.C., where her father headed the Anti-Defamation League, an organization that fights anti-Semitism, racism, and organized bigotry. Speaking of her father, Lerman told Ken Adelman for the *Washingtonian* (July 2000), "He taught me everything I know about respecting people, having a social awareness, and making my art connect to the larger [social] fabric." Her mother, she told Adelman, often said to her, "Liz, you have to be unique in this world and find your own path." In Washington, young Lerman began taking lessons with Ethel Butler, a disciple of the modern-dance pioneer Martha Graham. Lerman kept a poster of the ballerina Maria Tallchief on her bedroom wall and dreamed of being like that regal dancer, who had inspired the choreographer George Balanchine (and was married to him briefly). When Lerman was eight, the family relocated again, this time in Milwaukee, Wisconsin, where her father worked first in a family-owned tire store and later as the head of the state Department of Labor. She took dance classes with Florence West, who, like Butler, had studied with Martha Graham. "She was the great teacher of my life," Lerman told Alan Kriegsman. West insisted that her students study both modern dance and ballet; she also ran workshops in which they would paint or read poetry for inspiration. For several seasons, as a result of West's encouragement, Lerman attended the Interlochen arts camp, a summer program for artistically gifted children located in Michigan. (The August 1962 edition of *Life* magazine featured a photo of Lerman in a tulle dress and toe shoes, dancing on the White House lawn with other Interlochen participants.)

By her mid-teens, however, Lerman had begun to lose interest in classical ballet. Fond of the camaraderie in West's classes, she now found the intense competition at Interlochen ugly and mean-spirited. She was also suffering, as most classically trained dancers do, from painful, often bloodied feet. "To this day I don't understand how ballerinas do it," she commented to Kriegsman. In addition, she could not shake the feeling that the established dance world did not suit her. Part of a politically active, socially committed family, Lerman had participated in boycotts of the Milwaukee public schools, called to protest their de facto segregation, and she had always been taught to stand by her convictions. The strictures of classical ballet, so firmly entrenched in European tradition, now seemed distasteful to her. Florence West's move to New York City was the last straw for her, and she quit dancing for a short period—the first of many times she would do so.

After her high-school graduation, Lerman enrolled at Bennington College, in Vermont, which had a well-established and prestigious dance program, and resumed dancing. During this time—the mid-1960s—the academic dance world was concerned mainly with "pure movement," a form of dance that focused on technique rather than on content or meaning. Lerman found pure movement as arid and irrelevant as she had classical ballet. "I couldn't even articulate what I was looking for, but I wasn't finding it there," she told Kriegsman. "I wanted dancing to be a major part of my life, reflecting my primary concerns. I wanted it to be . . . a humane experience." She switched her major to history, and while she found the course of study enlightening, history too proved unsatisfying to her. "That's when I figured out that the problem was institutions," she told Rose Solari in an interview on the now-defunct *Common Boundary* Web site. "My father used to say to me, 'Don't confuse Judaism with the temples,' and that's when his words finally made sense to me. What happens to the soul of what you love when you attempt to codify it, make sense of it, teach it and organize it is often, over time, disastrous. I came to see that it was the way we practiced dance that was the problem—not dancing—and that the root of movement and what mattered to me about art were essential and true."

Lerman transferred to Brandeis University, in Waltham, Massachusetts, and remained there for a year. In this period of her life, she didn't dance, performing instead what she calls "guerrilla theater" on the streets of nearby Boston. A performance by the modern dancer Merce Cunningham, during which he was accompanied by an oral reading, reignited her interest in what was going on in the dance world. By then she had married, and when her husband got a job with a division of the National Institutes of Health, the couple moved to Washington, D.C. (The marriage ended soon afterward.) Lerman resumed her dance studies at the University of Maryland, where she experimented with choreography. Her first job after earning a bachelor's degree was at a small, nontraditional, private high school in Maryland, where she taught history and started a dance curriculum. The dance program proved so popular that after three months she abandoned her history classes to concentrate on dance. When she left the school, in 1973, after three years, there were 80 dance majors there, and two instructors had to be hired to replace her. Lerman remembers the time fondly. "Everybody would be in the [school] shows," she told Solari, "the headmaster, the dogs. I taught the boys on the lacrosse field after practice. . . . That's when I began to really come into my own."

Lerman next moved to New York City to try her luck. She envisioned joining a dance troupe there, but realizing that dream proved impossible. "I lived in a sixth-floor walk-up on the same Lower East Side block with the Hell's Angel's," she reminisced to Kriegsman. "When the money I saved ran out after six months, I walked instead of taking the subway, I pinched pennies. I rented a studio where I could work by myself at 5 in the morning. I was lonely, unhappy and restless, moving from one teacher to another." Finally, to make ends meet, Lerman resorted to dancing in New Jersey go-go bars. (*New York City Winter*, a dance that she choreographed at the time, based on her experiences as a go-go-dancer, remained in her repertory for years.) She quickly tired of that work, and, having come to realize that leaving New York was not a mark of failure, applied for and won a graduate fellowship at George Washington University, in Washington, D.C. She intended to study how dance could be brought to diverse members of different communities—the very thing she had accomplished while teaching at the Maryland high school.

While Lerman was at the university, her mother died of cancer. "Her death was *the* catalyst in my life," she told Solari, "the beginning of discovering my personal story and its relationship to bigger questions—that you don't have to talk about all cancer; you can talk about *your particular* experience, and it will talk to the larger group. I figured there probably were many, many people whose mothers were dying of cancer. So, if I could get *really* specific about my experience, maybe it would touch a universal chord." Lerman choreographed a dance called *Woman of the Clear Vision* to honor her mother. The work called for several older dancers, who would represent ancestors welcoming her mother to another world. To build a source of prospective performers, Lerman Lerman received permission to run a dance class once a week at the Roosevelt Home for Senior Citizens in downtown Washington. The director of the facility "thought I was crazy, but she needed entertainment on Thursday nights," Lerman told Solari. Although Lerman had never worked with senior citizens before, the classes were a success, and after about six months, six of her students volunteered to dance in a public performance of *Woman of the Clear Vision*.

The dance, which premiered in 1975, featured students from George Washington University and professional dancers from the Washington area as well as the six residents of the Roosevelt Home. The experience of combining young performers with old, and professional performers with nonprofessionals, exhilarated Lerman, and the audience's response gratified her. She began to rehearse in earnest with the senior citizens, and they formed a small troupe called the Dancers of the Third Age. Lerman felt that seeing older dancers was invaluable for an audience. "If dance means physical virtuosity of an extreme nature, then dance can be hard to take," she told Margaret Regan in a 1997 interview posted on the *Tucson Weekly* Web site. "Old people [performing on stage] force people to say, 'Dance is more than raising a leg this high.'"

In 1976 Lerman opened the Dance Exchange. In part, the Dance Exchange was a school that offered classes in different dance styles at all age and skill levels. The exchange also ran a program in which a group of dancers carried out the same kind of community-based work that Lerman had done at the Roosevelt Home. These artists taught dance classes in hospitals, elementary schools, and prisons. By the end of the 1970s, Lerman had also put together a touring company, composed of about a dozen professional dancers, which would often perform with the Dancers of the Third Age. The pressures of managing two troupes and a school proved to be too difficult, so Lerman eventually closed the school. (It reopened in 1998, in a new studio in Takoma Park, Maryland.) In 1993 the touring company and the community-based troupe joined forces as the Liz Lerman Dance Exchange, with a multiethnic roster of dancers whose ages ranged from 20 to 70.

Throughout the evolution of the Dance Exchange, Lerman has emphasized community involvement, often choreographing parts for members of the public in her dances. She considers *Still Crossing*, a work commissioned for the centennial of the Statue of Liberty, in 1986, to be a breakthrough piece in that regard. While Lerman's trained dancers performed the more technically challenging parts of the dance, which deals with immigration, other parts were performed by Russian immigrants from the Brighton Beach section of New York City whom Lerman had recruited and coached. In 1996 the company spent about three months in Portsmouth, New Hampshire, the site of a navy shipyard threatened with closure. The dancers worked with crane operators, welders, officers' wives, students, and others connected with the shipyard, conducting workshops and exploring what the facility meant to the community. The project culminated in a dance staged on battleships harbored at the yard. Discussing the fact that she works with a wide range of people, Lerman told Alan M. Kriegsman for the *Washington Post* (June 7, 1995), "What I find so often in going out to meet people in diverse communities is that they feel distant from art, from dance. They feel it doesn't belong to them, it has nothing to do with them. When people realize it can be their own, that their own lives and experiences are aesthetic, it's like setting off an explosion."

Lerman feels that whenever members of the Dance Exchange tour, they must be ready not only to perform but to work with the community and train professionals as well (perhaps by showing a non-Lerman pro how to work with senior citizens or conducting a storytelling workshop). She insists that art consists of more than just virtuoso performances—it must have spiritual and healing dimensions, too. "We organize our society by separating," Lerman wrote for *Ms.* (January/February 1995): "therapists in one camp, spiritual leaders in another, and artistic leaders in yet another. We end up not allowing porousness between spirituality, healing, and art, when in fact those things blend all the time." While some critics and others have argued that Dance Exchange performances suffer from an overemphasis on community work, those detractors are in the minority. When the company performed at the Dance Arts Moving Arts (DAMA)

Theater, in the nation's capital, to celebrate the Dance Exchange's 10th anniversary, Alan Kriegsman wrote for the *Washington Post* (May 2, 1987), "No modern dance choreographer in Washington has created a more imposing or durable body of work over the last 10 years than Lerman." Ten years later, after seeing a performance of *Shehechianu*, based on a Hebrew prayer of thanksgiving, which the Dance Exchange premiered for its 20th anniversary, Cathryn Harding, writing for *Dance Magazine* (October 1997), described what she had experienced as unusual both intellectually and emotionally: "Rare are the occasions when you can leave a dance concert with new questions about who you are and how you got that way. Rarer still are the times when an idea and its expression can move you so fiercely." The word "shehechianu" literally means "that gives us breath," and the prayer is said in thanks to the one "that gives us breath, sustains us, and brings us to this day." Lerman has expressed fondness for the prayer, which is repeated during Jewish ceremonies, and relates it to her feelings of wonder about and thankfulness for her dancers.

Lerman's latest endeavor, the Hallelujah project, also has something of the sacred about it. A series of performances combining dance with music and storytelling, the project is scheduled to take place at many sites around the country through 2002. Lerman intends to celebrate in each community that she visits whatever its residents find meaningful (or, as she puts it, "what they are in praise of"). The series opened on New Year's Day 2000 in Eastport, Maine, where performances took place on the harbor as the sun rose. The project has also traveled to Arizona, where a multicultural chorus joined the dancers in a desert setting, and North Carolina, where artists, veterinarians, and other community members celebrated the bonds between humans and animals.

Lerman has received an American Choreographer Award as well as several fellowships from the National Endowment for the Arts. In 1997 the Dance Exchange was one of five modern-dance companies to win grants of $500,000 from the Lila Wallace-Reader's Digest Fund. Lincoln Center, the American Dance Festival, and the Kennedy Center have each commissioned works by Lerman. The choreographer told Chris Westberg, however, that culture should not be viewed in terms of "a hierarchy with the Kennedy Center on the top and nursing homes on the bottom." Lerman and her husband, the storyteller and actor Jon Spelman, have one daughter, Anna Clare, who was born in 1988. — M.R.

Suggested Reading: *Dance Magazine* p78+ Jan. 1996, with photos; *High Performance* (on-line) Winter 1992; Liz Lerman Dance Exchange Web Site; *Washington Post* G p1+ Apr. 26, 1987, with photos, C p1+ June7, 1995, with photos, G p1+ Oct. 12, 1997, with photos

Selected Dances: *New York City Winter*; *Woman of the Clear Vision*; *Still Crossing*; *Shehechianu*

Lil' Kim

July 11, 1975– Rap singer; CEO of Queen Bee Records. Address: Queen Bee Records, 127 W. 22d St., New York, NY 10011

Lil' Kim exploded onto the rap scene in 1995, as a member of the Junior M.A.F.I.A., a group formed by Christopher Wallace, also known as the Notorious B.I.G. or Biggie Smalls. Since the release of her platinum solo debut, *Hardcore* (1996), Kim has received much attention for her explicit lyrics, increasingly outrageous outfits, and general, unapologetic raunchiness. Also known as the Queen Bee, Lil' Kim has performed on recordings by Jay-Z, Missy "Misdemeanor" Elliot, Mobb Deep, Funkmaster Flex, Black Rob, and Tommy Lee's Masters of Mayhem. In addition, she has embarked on a career as an actress, with roles in the television series *V.I.P.* and the films *She's All That* (1999) and *Scary Movie* (2000). Lil' Kim's label, Queen Bee Records, had its first release in 1999; entitled *The Wonderful World of Cease A Lo*, the recording was the debut for Junior M.A.F.I.A.'s Lil' Cease.

In a review of *Hardcore* for the *Village Voice* (December 24, 1996), Robert Marriott described Lil' Kim as being "able to mime dynamic, funky self-possession while being wholly possessed by the men around her. Kim has that alchemical edge—the capacity to transform her vulnerability into that which sustains her. The anger at men manifest in her nasty little mouth comes from her complicity in the pimp/ho' dynamic she speaks so much of. But what remains when Kim steps out from under Biggie's formidable shadow is her candor and her willingness to get vulgar. When mixed with honest emotion, her storytelling is at its most persuasive." In Kim's view, the recent successes of women such as Lauryn Hill and Missy Elliott have demonstrated the power of women in hip-hop: "We're going to be taking over for the next five to 10 years," she told Missy Elliott for *Interview* (May 2000). "It's been a male-dominated industry for so many years that it's time to give the women a chance. We're just getting stronger." Her 2000 release is *Notorious K.I.M.*

Lil' Kim was born Kimberly Denise Jones on July 11, 1975 in the Bedford-Stuyvesant section of the New York City borough of Brooklyn. At a very young age, she displayed a desire to perform.

Guy Aroch/Corbis Outline

Lil' Kim

"When Kim was two," her mother told Peter Castro for *People* (July 14, 1997), "she would get into my high heels, put on lipstick and sing in front of a mirror. Her father would call me concerned and say, 'This girl's crazy. She has a problem.'" When she was nine, her father, Linwood, an army reservist and bus driver, and her mother, Ruby Mae, a homemaker, separated; after her parents' divorce, Kim and her brother, Christopher, stayed with their father. Unable to get along with him, she spent a lot of time away from home, and for that reason, at the age of 12, she became involved with drug dealers. "I never sold on the streets," she told Peter Castro. "I used to help the guys cut it up"—that is, dilute the drugs so as to expand their volume. "I'm surprised it didn't wreck my life." When Kim was 15 her father kicked her out of the house, but she always found somewhere to stay, surrounded as she was by men who sought to take advantage of her inexperience. Occasionally she roomed with an aunt who lived in a housing project in Brooklyn's Fort Greene section. "She lived right on top of the project's recreation room, and they would have talent shows down there," Kim told Ethan Brown for *New York* (September 13, 1999). "So I would rhyme and even try to DJ."

Kim and Christopher Wallace lived on the same block in Brooklyn; they became friends, and in 1992 she persuaded him to give up his life as a crack dealer and try his hand at rap. "I always thought he was cute," she told Anita Sarko, "and when I first started talking to him, I felt like I'd known him for years." In 1994, under the name Notorious B.I.G., Wallace released his debut album, *Ready to Die*, a hit that established the artist as one of the genre's premier lyricists. Although it took some time for Kim to convince Wallace that she too could rap, he finally took her under his wing, recruiting her for the group Junior M.A.F.I.A. "Biggie thought I was just going to be this little female in the back, this girl he'd put in the group because he loved me," Kim told Sarko. To his surprise, two songs featuring Kim, "Get Money" and "Player's Anthem," were hits for the group. Kim became close friends with the singer Mary J. Blige when Wallace invited Junior M.A.F.I.A. to accompany him on tour; Blige encouraged Kim to assert herself, especially when dealing with powerful men. Junior M.A.F.I.A.'s album *Conspiracy* (1995) reached number two on the *Billboard* chart and eventually went platinum. Kim also performed on recordings by Skin Deep, the Isley Brothers, Mona Lisa, and Total. Her solo album, *Hardcore*, rose to number 11 on the *Billboard* 200 chart within a week of its release, making it the most successful debut ever by a female hip-hop artist. Described by Robert Marriott as "burlesque on wax," *Hardcore* featured members of Junior M.A.F.I.A. and was produced by Sean "Puffy" Combs, Jermaine Dupri, Prestige, and High Class. The album's first single, "No Time," spent nine weeks in the number-one spot on *Billboard*'s rap chart and went on to become a gold record.

Kim suffered an emotional blow when Wallace married the R&B singer Faith Evans, in 1994. By the time the couple separated, a few years later, Kim and Wallace had become romantically involved. In March 1997 Biggie was shot to death while leaving a *Vibe* magazine party (celebrating the Soul Train Awards) that took place at the Petersen Automotive Museum, in Los Angeles. (Wallace's murder occurred only six months after the shooting death of rapper Tupac Shakur. The two killings led some to speculate that the much-publicized feud between rap artists from the East Coast, such as Wu-Tang Clan and Mobb Deep, and those of the West Coast, such as Dr. Dre and Snoop Doggy Dogg, over which group had created gangsta rap, had become too heated to remain metaphorical and was now being fought on the streets.)

After Wallace's death, Kim moved into the artist's condominium in Teaneck, New Jersey. She denied suggestions that the gangster lifestyle portrayed by the music of Wallace and others inspired actual violence, arguing that such lyrics merely reflected the reality of many people's lives. "That's what our fans wanted to hear," she told Peter Castro. "It's hard to rap about something other than people being murdered and crime. We don't *want* those things to happen . . . we're just telling it like it is. It may take time before we all start rapping about flowers."

Because she was mourning Wallace's death, Kim found it difficult to begin work on her second album. After shooting her scenes for the movie *She's All That* (in which she was billed as Kimberly Jones), Kim went to the Bahamas to prepare herself for the work that lay ahead. *Notorious K.I.M.* (2000) was produced by Sean "Puffy" Combs; the recording was delayed by Combs's legal trouble (he had been accused of involvement in a shooting in a New York nightclub) as well as the premature circulation of the songs by bootleggers. In an attempt to thwart the piracy of her work, Kim returned to the studio to record 11 new songs. At first even Combs assumed that Kim needed artistic guidance. "Puffy didn't understand what kind of artist I was," she told Tonya Pendleton for *BET.com* (2000). "He felt like Biggie had a lot of influence and he didn't know what I could do and that I could be creative by myself. In the beginning, he was picking all these tracks I did not like. But then he came around and understood, 'Oh, she's a real artist.'"

Notorious K.I.M. features guest appearances by Junior M.A.F.I.A. (on "Do What You Like"), Grace Jones and Lil' Cease (on "Revolution"), and Sisqó (on "How Many Licks"). The title track attacks Foxy Brown, Kim's biggest rival in the sex-rap game (Brown's debut, *Ill Na Na*, was released at around the same time as *Hardcore*). "The real me is on this album—there's a little bit of everything here and that's truer to who I am," she told Ethan Brown. On *Notorious K.I.M.* Lil' Kim also paid tribute to Wallace in a duet with Mary J. Blige entitled "Hold On." Her sophomore effort contains fewer sexual references than her debut album because "on this one I wanted people to see me for who I am, and I'm *not* just a walking sex doll," as she told Missy Elliott. "I did that last time around, and . . . I don't wear the same outfit twice. I'm trying to become an icon."

Lil' Kim has graced the covers of many music publications as well as *Vogue* and other fashion magazines, and she is often seen in public wearing clothes given to her by such designers as Gucci, Donatella Versace, Tommy Hilfiger, and Dolce & Gabbana. "I love to be looked at; I love to get male attention," she told Sia Michel for *Vogue* (December 1999). "But sometimes it freaks me out, 'cause I know if they saw pictures of me when I was in the projects, they'd be like, 'Why is everybody making a big deal out of *her*?'"Although today she is seen as a sex symbol, Kim has suffered from a poor self-image, and she spent years trying to heal from the emotional abuse she suffered from her father as well as a number of boyfriends. "All my life men have told me I wasn't pretty enough—even the men I was dating," she told Allison Samuels for *Newsweek* (June 26, 2000). "And I'd be like, 'Well, why are you with me, then?' It's always been men putting me down just like my dad. To this day when someone says I'm cute, I can't see it. I don't see it no matter what *anybody* says." In addition to following a strict diet and exercise regimen, Kim has attempted to improve her looks through plastic surgery. Some women criticized her for her decision to have breast-implant surgery, and later some African-Americans were angered when she adopted a blond wig and contact lenses that rendered her eyes blue. "I have low self-esteem and I always have," she explained to Samuels. "Guys always cheated on me with women who were European-looking. You know, the long-hair type. Really beautiful women that left me thinking, 'How can I compete with that?' Being a regular black girl wasn't good enough."

In 1997 Lil' Kim received a Soul Train Lady of Soul Award for the song "Not Tonight (Ladies Night)," which also featured Angie Martinez, TLC's Left Eye, Da Brat, and Missy Elliott. Her endorsements include MAC cosmetics, Candie's shoes, and Iceberg jeans. Lil' Kim and Mary J. Blige are spokespersons for Viva Glam II, a lipstick created to benefit the MAC AIDS Fund; all proceeds will go to the organization, which has been raising money through the sale of lipstick since 1994.

Kim has emphasized the profound impact that Wallace had on the lives and music of those around him. "I believe Biggie jumped into everyone he knew," she told Missy Elliott. "I believe he's made me write better, he's made me think better, he's made me a stronger person, and he's made me more businesswise." Although she has not dismissed the possibility of entering into another relationship, Kim told Anita Sarko that Wallace is "the only person I will ever love and have ever loved. Whoever I marry will have to know that when I get to heaven, I will be with Biggie." — C.L.

Suggested Reading: *Interview* p122+ Nov. 1999, with photos, p158+ May 2000, with photos; *New York* 72+ Sep. 13, 1999, with photo; *Newsweek* p56+ June 26, 2000, with photos; *People* p98+July 14, 1997, with photos; *Village Voice* p63 Dec. 24, 1996, with photo; *Vogue* p304+ Dec. 1999, with photos

Selected Recordings: *Hardcore*, 1996; *The Notorious K.I.M.*, 2000; *Conspiracy* (with Junior M.A.F.I.A.), 1995

Lou, Liza

(LOO, LYE-zuh)

Apr. 16, 1969– Artist. Address: Box 366, Topanga, CA 90290

"I am going to bead the world," the artist Liza Lou has said, as quoted on the Santa Monica Museum of Art Web site. In choosing the bead as her medium, Lou explained, she is keeping "the tradition of ancient beadworkers who enshrined that which was sacred to their culture(s)": "I enshrine objects and environments in order to describe the American dream." Lou's major works—*Kitchen* (1991–95), whose floor covers 168 square feet, and *Back Yard* (1995–97), which measures 22 feet by 24 feet—are life-size representations of a 1950s American kitchen and a contemporary American backyard, respectively, complete with walls and major appliances (in *Kitchen*), a picnic table, patio, lawn, and lawn mower (in *Back Yard*), and such

Adam Friedberg

Liza Lou

items as dishes, sandwiches, and tablecloths, all surfaces of which are completely covered with glittering glass beads—10 million beads, for *Kitchen*, and 30 million, for *Back Yard*.

"Seeing *Kitchen* and *Back Yard* for the first time is like plummeting headlong into the visual and spatial adventures of a modern-day Alice in Wonderland," Marcia Tucker, the founder and, until recently, director of the New Museum of Contemporary Art, in New York City, wrote in "Adventures in Liza Land," an essay reprinted in *Liza Lou* (1998). "It's virtually impossible not to be astounded and captivated by the magical transformation of familiar environments and objects she's presented. Grounded in the ordinary, Liza Lou's beaded world is spectacular and delightful, full of wondrous and unexpected juxtapositions and ripe with deliciously subversive details." "As staggering as the logistics of Lou's installations are, they are not the most intriguing aspect," Dorothy Rompalske observed in *Biography* (January 1999). "The artist uses all those shiny beads to accomplish a very difficult trick: She lures us into looking at the most banal objects and places with fresh eyes." "What amazed me about Liza is the merging of both fine art and craft," Thomas Rhoads, the executive director of the Santa Monica Museum of Art, which helped finance the creation of *Back Yard*, told Anita Amirrezvani for the *New York Times* (June 30, 1998). "Her work is accessible to the kinds of individuals who would go to the state fair to see craft projects, and yet it has a real conceptual grounding in feminist art. It's the bringing together of these two worlds that makes it so appealing and successful." Discussing *Back Yard* with Susan Dominus for the *New York Times Magazine* (July 11, 1999), Lou said she hoped that "when [people] look at this they say: 'Why would someone spend this much time on a back yard? What does that mean?' I want my work to ask: What is labor? What is thankless labor? What is acknowledged labor?"

Born in New York City on April 16, 1969, Liza Lou spent her early years in a suburb of Minneapolis, Minnesota. Her parents divorced in 1974. Lou has said that her mother, Marie Jordan, who writes poetry, "taught me to be brave and do hard things." When Liza was in her early teens, she moved with her mother and her sister, Christa, to a tract house on the outskirts of San Diego, California. In a poem called "Bead Here Now" in the *Utne Reader* (January/February 1997), Lou wrote, "Most of my life has been spent in the suburbs."

In early 1988, at age 18, Lou spent several months in Florence, Italy, studying art. Famous for its medieval and Renaissance churches, cathedrals, and palaces, which contain artwork by such masters as Michelangelo, Leonardo da Vinci, and Raphael, and celebrated for the ceramics, mosaics, and other objects produced there by contemporary artisans, Florence impressed Lou as utterly unlike the parts of the United States with which she had grown familiar. "Saw astonishing feats of physical labor, / Testaments to the human spirit. / Monuments that required years and years to create," she wrote in "Bead Here Now."

Late in 1988 Lou enrolled at the San Francisco Art Institute, in California, where she studied painting on a full scholarship. While in San Francisco she happened upon a store that carried a large stock of beads. "My eyeballs boinged out of my head," she recalled to Susan Dominus. "The color, the luminosity—I ran back to my studio and began to put them on my paintings." When she showed some of these paintings and her first completely beaded work—a replica of a Campbell's soup can that she made in homage to the pop artist Andy Warhol—to others at the art institute, her work was roundly criticized. "It didn't look like art to anyone," Lou told Anita Amirrezvani. "I had artist friends asking me, 'How's the life of a jeweler?' People made the most unbelievable comments. It was horrible, but it also encouraged me in a lot of ways because I thought it must be something new." By "new," Lou meant that beading was novel as a medium in contemporary Western fine art; in the West and elsewhere, people have used beads to adorn their bodies, their apparel, and other objects for thousands of years.

In 1989, after she was told that "in order to remain as a student [at the San Francisco Art Institute] she'd have to stop using beads," as Marcia Tucker reported, Lou dropped out of the school and moved to Los Angeles, where she continued developing her own beading techniques. In creating her large installations, Lou first makes many sketches and architectural plans and molds a clay model, all of which she uses as guides. Next, she constructs each object, using lumber for such large forms as walls and tables and making papier-mâché sculptures for small items. (For *Kitchen* she also bought a real refrigerator and stove.) Then she slips beads onto wires and glues the beaded wires to all surfaces. Lou prefers Czechoslovakian-made seed-shaped beads and bugle beads, which are tubular and about the size of a grain of rice. Installations must be capable of being dismantled into portable parts, so that the whole can be transported to exhibit sites.

By her own account, Lou came up with the idea for *Kitchen* while visiting her mother's house. At the start of her project, in 1991, she told Dominus, she was "in denial" about how much labor *Kitchen* would require and estimated that she would finish it in six months. In actuality, five years elapsed before its completion. The first three years were "total frustration and hell," she told Dominus. "I was constantly hitting my head against the wall, and I was complaining constantly." She worked on *Kitchen* at night; to support herself she took daytime jobs, among them waitressing and selling dresses. "I would always feel kind of like the tortured starving artist," she told Dominus. "I've got other friends who in six months could mount a show; I would maybe make one section of something. I had to realize I wasn't going to have an art career for some time." What kept her going, she told Dominus, was her "desire to see what [*Kitchen*] was going to look like." "It wasn't about making money," she said; "it wasn't about getting some outside reward. . . . I would dream about it at night. I would walk around and see it perfectly in my head. I used to work 12-, 15-hour days. At a certain point making the piece, I gave in to the fact that this was going to take a long time. I learned from the work. I changed. I wasn't a patient person originally, but the work made me bend. I had to bow to the vision, I guess." After one of her friends, a Zen Buddhist, remarked to her that she seemed to be meditating as she worked, she realized, she told Dominus, "that the process of my work was prayer. Your head is bowed, your eyes aren't closed or you'll make a mess, but you're attending to the smallest, smallest thing. It's a way of blessing everything you're touching. It really transformed things for me. You have to stop looking at the clock and stop thinking in a linear way. The nature of this work can give you a nervous breakdown—or teach you how to take life by the smallest detail and do it well."

In Lou's multicolored, multipatterned, totally beaded *Kitchen*, which has walls on three sides, a pie rests on a shelf of the open oven, a batter-filled bowl, hand mixer, and open cookbook stand on the countertop, bacon and eggs lie in a pan on the stove, and the table, covered with a checked cloth, is set with boxes of breakfast cereal, buttered toast, flatware, a cup of coffee, and a newspaper whose headlines read, "Housewife Beads the World!" and "Plus! Frogman Reveals the Secrets of Tough Love!" (The latter headline, according to Peter Schjeldahl in "Splendor in the Grass: Liza Lou and the Cultivation of Beauty," the essay he wrote for *Liza Lou*, is a reference to one of Lou's San Francisco Art Academy teachers "who denigrated the *Kitchen* in its early stages.") Plates, a teacup, and a bowl float in the double sink, where the swirling blue water looks like a Van Gogh sky and sparkling strands of water cascade from the faucet; containers of Joy dish detergent and Comet scouring powder stand next to the sink, and a box of Tide sits on the floor, next to a broom and a dustpan filled with glittering dustballs.

In what various observers have interpreted as a commentary on the roles of women and attitudes toward women in American society, Lou incorporated in *Kitchen* images of leggy pinup girls on the walls of the oven and two pieces of poetry. One, an excerpt from a poem by Emily Dickinson (1830–86) that Lou placed on one side of the stove, reads, "She rose to his Requirement, / dropped the playthings of her life / To take the honorable work / of Woman and of Wife." The other, set on a side of the refrigerator, is the first stanza of "Against Idleness and Mischief," a poem by the British theologian Isaac Watts (1674–1748): "How doth the little busy Bee / Improve each shining Hour, / And gather Honey all the day / From every opening Flower!" Speaking of the Watts poem, Lou said to Leah Ollman for *Art in America* (June 1998), "It's so condescending, and yet I have that work ethic, that hands-to-work, heart-to-God work ethic. Isn't that really what I'm doing—improving each shining hour? Every moment that I'm putting beads on something, things are being improved upon." In a review for the *New York Times* (February 9, 1996) of the show "A Labor of Love" at the New Museum of Contemporary Art, Roberta Smith praised *Kitchen* as "a radiant piece [that] effortlessly annihilates any barrier between art and craft. It proves unequivocally that . . . quality is where you find it and that it won't be denied." In 1996 *Kitchen* became the property of the software tycoon and art patron Peter Norton and his wife, Eileen. Thanks to their purchase, Lou was able to quit her daytime job, and she has devoted herself full-time to her art ever since.

Lou's first fully beaded installation, *Most Desired Disorder* (1995), debuted at the New York City gallery Franklin Furnace. Made up of about 80 bead-covered bras, panties, socks, shoes, and other personal items, it "literally flung the dirty laundry of a ruined domestic relationship into public view," according to Leah Ollman. Lou's next and most celebrated work, *Back Yard*, was two years in the making. Its creation was partly funded by the Santa Monica Museum of Art, where it was first displayed. *Back Yard* contains a cloth-covered picnic table with a bench on either side, a grill on wheels, a basket with laundry, a partially filled clothesline, a watering can, a lawn mower, and two flamingos—replicas of the plastic birds seen on many lawns. A bowl of salad, sandwiches, a plateful of corn on the cob, cans of beer, and cutlery await the picnickers. One beer can has overturned, spilling its contents on the tablecloth, and another lies, partially crushed, on the lawn. Springing up from the base of *Back Yard* are some 250,000 individual blades of grass and a tree in full leaf, and bordering the lawn on three sides is a garden with hundreds of sturdy, ramrod-straight flowers—"apparitions of no known species," in Schjeldahl's words—and several bumblebee visitors.

Soon after Lou began working on *Back Yard*, an acquaintance of hers calculated that working by herself eight hours a day, Lou would be 40 years older by the time she finished this project. To speed up the process, and to avoid a recurrence of the severe tendonitis she had suffered in her arms and hands while working on *Kitchen*, Lou held "lawn parties" at her studio, a local shopping mall, and elsewhere, at which volunteers strung beads onto wires to create the grass, each blade tipped with a round bead. Eventually, more than 300 people participated; ranging from children to octogenarians, they included Lou's mother, Peter and Eileen Norton, and the actor and director Leonard Nimoy and his wife, Susan Bay Nimoy. In *Liza Lou* (1998), a short documentary video produced by the Nimoy Family Foundation, Lou's helpers expressed great enthusiasm for the project and pleasure about making a hands-on contribution to a work of art.

For various critics and other visitors to the installation, *Back Yard* triggered thoughts about the backyard as one culmination of the American dream for people at all economic levels and as "the foremost American ideal of leisure," in Schjeldahl's words. In the video *Liza Lou*, Lou noted the irony inherent in the act of gazing at her impeccable, artificial re-creation of the outdoors or, to move back a step, in the creation of an artificial outdoors—which is what most backyards are—as opposed to enjoying the experience of being in a natural woods or other wild place.

"The *Back Yard* is a steady-state hallucination," Peter Schjeldahl wrote. "It is about peak consciousness, when awareness dilates to its maximum degree—in religious practice, in beauty, or with drugs, no matter. . . . Lou's inspired choice of a ubiquitous, humble subject for the magnificent, frozen hosanna of this work fulfills [the 19th-century French poet] Charles Baudelaire's definition of beauty as a fusion of the eternal and the fleeting, the exalted and the everyday, heaven and hell, the sacred and the profane, reason and squalor." In a reference to the often-expressed idea that Lou's astoundingly labor-intensive works provide evidence of the artist's "obsessiveness," Schjeldahl continued, "Its effect is the opposite of obsession: liberation from closed circuits of the self, prying us open to pure wonder. It brings about a high holy day of the mind, when things always obscurely true stand revealed, clothed only in the lucid radiance of the self-evident. I have many feelings about Lou's achievement. The main one is gratitude."

Another of Lou's works is *American Presidents* (1996), for which the artist painted and then beaded, in black, white, and gray, a portrait of each of the 42 presidents of the United States. Leah Ollman wrote that *American Presidents* "tweaks the power imbalance between genders by filtering the masculine political icons through the lens of the feminine and decorative." "I think it's humorous to see men in beads," Lou told Ollman. "Herbert Hoover is not someone you associate with glitter." In 1997 the toy company Mattel commissioned Lou to create two human-size Barbie figures—Business Barbie and Bridal Barbie; Lou added a third figure, named Supersister, which Guy Trebay, in the *Village Voice* (July 6, 1999), described as bearing "an uncanny resemblance to [the female impersonator] RuPaul in his early Pam Grier phase." For a commission from an art-collecting husband and wife, Lou used bottles of cleaning fluids, a can of roach spray, paintbrushes, and other objects from the couple's utility closet to create *Closet* (1998). The three female figures, *Closet*, and *Back Yard* were exhibited at Grand Central Terminal, in New York City, in the summer of 1999.

In 1999 the Academy of Motion Picture Arts and Sciences asked Lou to create a beaded entrance to the soon-to-be-built Academy Awards Theater. Envisioned as a history of film, "it's a dream project," Lou told Rompalske. Others among her future projects are a film noir–inspired black-and-white beaded hotel room and a life-size beaded chapel. Lou did research for her chapel project in 1998 during a several-month residency in Italy, as a visiting artist/scholar at the American Academy in Rome. *Chapel* is scheduled to open at Deitch Projects, in New York City, at the end of 2001. "All my pieces are, in a way, a kind of chapel," Lou told Amirrezvani. "So it makes sense to get right to the source."

Although "she makes art that is zany, polemical, and extroverted," Peter Schjeldahl wrote, "in person" Liza Lou is "serious, apolitical, and shy." Lou lives in the Topanga Canyon section of Los Angeles, California. — C.P.

Suggested Reading: *Art in America* p98+ June 1998, with photos; *Art Issues* p41+ Sep./Oct. 1998, with photos; *Art Papers* p22+ July/Aug. 1999, with photos; *Biography* p110+ Jan. 1999, with photos; *New York Times* E p2 June 30, 1998, with photo; *New York Times Magazine* p15 July 11, 1999, with photo; *San Diego Union Tribune* E p1+ Apr. 21, 1996, with photos; *Village Voice* p36 July 6, 1999, with photo; *Liza Lou* (essays by Peter Schjeldahl and Marcia Tucker), 1998

Selected Works: *Most Desired Disorder*, 1995; *Kitchen*, 1991–95; *American Presidents*, 1995; *Back Yard*, 1995–97; *Closet*, 1998; *Business Barbie, Bridal Barbie, and Supersister*, 1998

Armando Gallo/Retna Ltd.

Lowe, Rob

Mar. 17, 1964– Actor. Address: c/o Brillstein-Grey, 9150 Wilshire Blvd., Suite 350, Beverly Hills, CA 90212

The one-time teen heartthrob Rob Lowe has surmounted a widely publicized sex scandal, a reputation as a reckless carouser, and dismissal as little more than a pretty face to build a career as a serious actor. "To have that amount of excess and success and come out with two feet on the ground, a self-deprecatory attitude, and an eagerness to become a really good actor is a remarkable achievement," the actress Natasha Richardson, who starred with Lowe in a television production of the Tennessee Williams drama *Suddenly Last Summer*, told Jan Hoffman for the *New York Times* (January 3, 1993). Lowe's film credits include *The Outsiders*, *The Hotel New Hampshire*, *St. Elmo's Fire*, *Bad Influence*, *Wayne's World*, *Contact*, and *Austin Powers: The Spy Who Shagged Me*. Currently, he is co-starring in *The West Wing*, the critically acclaimed hour-long NBC television series about an eclectic group of White House staffers.

Rob Lowe was born on March 17, 1964 in Charlottesville, Virginia. Soon afterward his father, Chuck Lowe, a lawyer, and mother, Barbara, moved with their son to Dayton, Ohio. His parents were divorced when he was four, not long after the birth of his brother Chad, who is also an actor. Young Rob showed an early aptitude for performing. When he was eight he began to appear in regional theater productions and on local television. "There wasn't a lot of competition for roles," he told Jay Holden for the New York *Daily News Magazine* (July 6, 1986). "No boy in my neighborhood wanted to be an actor. It wasn't cool to be an actor—and I took a lot of flak from the kids out playing baseball and soccer." Meanwhile, his mother's second marriage, to a Dayton city planner, had ended in divorce. When Lowe was 12 years old, she married a third time; Lowe's second stepfather was Steve Wilson, a psychiatrist. The next year the family, which included Lowe's half-brother, Micah, moved to Malibu, California. Six months later Lowe registered with an agent and made the first of many two-hour bus rides into Los Angeles for auditions. Despite the fiercer competition he now faced, his perseverance soon paid off: he landed a role in a Coca-Cola commercial. That was followed by his being cast, at age 15, in the short-lived sitcom *A New Kind of Family*, as the son of the character played by Eileen Brennan. He also starred in a few of ABC's popular after-school specials. After he turned 17, jobs became more scarce. His agent counseled him to be patient and told him—correctly, as it turned out—that his luck would turn. At 18 Lowe won a role in Francis Ford Coppola's film *The Outsiders* (1983), an adaptation of S. E. Hinton's classic young-adult novel about teenage angst. His depiction of Soda Pop, a boy from the wrong side of the tracks, got a generally positive reception from critics and raves from teenage girls.

Lowe had been attending Santa Monica High School, where his classmates included the budding actors Emilio Estevez and Sean Penn. In his senior year he gained acceptance to the University of California at Los Angeles (UCLA), where he intended to major in film. But after being offered a role in another feature film—that of the preppy son of Jacqueline Bissett's character in Michael Kinberg's *Class* (1983)—he decided against enrolling at UCLA. "School is such a state of mind," he told a reporter for the *New York Post* (July 28, 1983). "If you're not ready to devote yourself to it college becomes a holding tank before going out into the real world. Too many things are happening to me right now to go to school."

At about the same time, Lowe complained to Arthur Lubow for *People* (August 15, 1983) that whenever he tried out for a role, "they say the same thing: 'We think he's too good looking.'" When Lowe made that statement, he was actually working on another film—*The Hotel New Hampshire* (1984), in which he was cast as one of the sons in an eccentric New England family. The film also co-starred Jodie Foster, Nastassia Kinski, and Beau Bridges; directed by Tony Richardson from his own script, which closely followed John Irving's same-named novel, the picture was widely panned. Still, the publicity that attended *The Hotel New Hampshire* led to a cover story about Lowe for *Interview* magazine. By the time he appeared in his next film, Robert Boris's *Oxford Blues* (1984)—a "teen rendition of the international romance," as Gene Siskel put it in the *Chicago Tribune* (August 24, 1984)—Lowe had already become a recognized teen heartthrob. In a review of *Oxford Blues* for the

New York Post (August 24, 1984), a critic gave the film a score of two out of 10 for plot predictability, a minus one for plausibility, and an eight "for the good looks of Rob Lowe." Articles about the actor appeared in both the February and July 1984 issues of *Teen* magazine.

A few months after the second anniversary of his debut on the silver screen, Lowe appeared in his fifth feature film, *St. Elmo's Fire (*1985). Co-written and directed by Joel Schumacher, *St. Elmo's Fire* concerns a group of seven self-absorbed recent college graduates who are struggling with the sober realities of life. In the opinion of various critics, the movie amounted to little more than a lackluster imitation of Lawrence Kasdan's 1983 ensemble hit *The Big Chill* and largely squandered the talents of its youthful cast. The film co-starred, in addition to Lowe, Emilio Estevez, Andrew McCarthy, Demi Moore, Mare Winningham, Judd Nelson, and Ally Sheedy. Those performers, along with fellow actors Anthony Michael Hall, Matt Dillon, and Molly Ringwald, were dubbed the "Brat Pack" in a *New York* magazine article published around that time. (Thus was *St. Elmo's Fire* referred to as the quintessential brat-pack film.) The name was an allusion to the Rat Pack, the hard-drinking, womanizing group of singer-actors from an earlier era, which had included Dean Martin, Sammy Davis Jr., and Frank Sinatra. Like their predecessors, Lowe and his cohorts provided frequent fodder for gossip columnists; they were sighted in trendy Hollywood clubs and became entangled in short-lived, tumultuous romances. Lowe was linked at the time to the actress Melissa Gilbert (now Melissa Anderson), known mainly for her role on the long-running television series *Little House on the Prairie.* In late 1986 journalists reported that Lowe was dating Princess Stephanie of Monaco. After his relationship with the princess fizzled, Lowe returned to Gilbert, to whom he was briefly engaged.

Having learned that prior commitments had forced Emilio Estevez to pass up a role in the picture *Square Dance* (1987), Lowe lobbied for the part, that of a mentally disabled 24-year-old man. To prepare for the audition, he read books about mental retardation and worked with a voice coach to develop a halting stammer. After he won the role, he spent many hours observing students at a California school for retarded adults. *Square Dance* also stars Jane Alexander, as the mother of a 13-year-old girl (played by Winona Ryder) who befriends the Lowe character. In one of the few reviews of the film that appeared in the mainstream media, Vincent Canby wrote for the *New York Times* (February 20, 1987) that of all the performances, Lowe's was "the most arresting." "The audience's attention is grabbed, if only to see whether he's going to go too far, which he doesn't. He's good," Canby declared. Lowe told Kathy O'Malley for the *Chicago Tribune* (March 5, 1987), "I did [this movie] for myself—to see if I could do it, to say that I did it, and to show people that I could do it."

On July 16, 1988 Lowe flew to Atlanta, Georgia, to attend the Democratic National Convention, along with a contingent from Hollywood that included Ally Sheedy, Judd Nelson, and Alec Baldwin. The next evening he returned to his hotel room with two young women he had just met at a popular night spot. One of them was a 16-year-old who had gained entrance to the club with a false ID. While in the room, the trio engaged in sexual activities, which Lowe videotaped. Later, while he was in the bathroom, the two young women removed the tape from his camera and then departed. Afterward they made copies of the tape, which also contained earlier footage showing the actor cavorting with an unidentified woman. One of the copies came into the possession of the 16-year-old's mother, who in May 1989 filed a personal-injury suit against Lowe. The suit charged him, according to a *People* (March 19, 1990) cover story, of using "his celebrity status as an inducement to females to engage in sexual intercourse, sodomy, and multiple-partner sexual activity for his immediate sexual gratification, and for the purposes of making pornographic films of these activities." The legal action soon became public knowledge, thanks to a news report on CNN, and tabloid reporters immediately besieged Lowe. His friends and family rallied around him and pleaded with him to defend himself publicly, but he rejected that advice, believing that such a course of action would merely fuel the media frenzy. Lowe's situation became a staple of late-night comedy bits. The matter worsened when the pornographer Al Goldstein got access to the "Rob Lowe Sex Tape," as it had become known, and began marketing a portion of it that featured close-ups of Lowe fully aroused.

Eventually, the 16-year-old and her father settled with Lowe out of court, and the district attorney who had been investigating the charges against Lowe ruled against prosecution; instead, he ordered the actor to perform 20 hours of community service. Lowe complied by giving talks at correctional facilities and detention centers in Dayton. "The basic thing I said [to them] is: Just because people will say you have [messed] up does not mean you *are* [messed] up," he told Albert Watson for *Interview* (March 1990). "And whether you're a movie star or doing time in a correctional institute, everybody can have bad judgment, and it's something you have to address. You learn to go on from it. It shouldn't stand in your way. You shouldn't let people continue to throw it in your face. Everybody makes mistakes." While taking full responsibility for his actions, he expressed his belief that very few people, and certainly not some of the talk-show hosts and comedians who had mocked him, would emerge untarnished from intense scrutiny into their personal lives.

Meanwhile, four months before news of the videotape had begun circulating, Lowe had been cast in the film *Bad Influence* (1990), and during shooting, news reporters and photographers constantly stalked the set, hoping to provoke a reaction from him. In an ironic coincidence, the movie—directed by Curtis Hanson, written by David Koepp, and co-starring James Spader—contained a scene in which Lowe's character, a charismatic yuppie Mephistopheles, as he was widely described, videotapes a sexual encounter. Concerned that the segment would appear to exploit Lowe's misadventure, the filmmakers had the crew wear T-shirts imprinted with the words "The video scene has always been in the script." Some critics referred to that fact about the script in their reviews of *Bad Influence*, while also noting the similarity of real and cinematic events. In *Maclean's* (March 26, 1990), for example, Brian D. Johnson's assessment was entitled, "Video villain: Art imitates life in Rob Lowe's new movie." Both the film and Lowe's performance drew mixed reviews. In *Entertainment Weekly* (March 16, 1990), Owen Gleiberman wrote, "The very qualities that once made [Lowe] so unexciting as a leading man—his teenybop prettiness, his smiling, liquid-eyed passivity—can now seem threateningly vague and ambiguous when he's cast as a charming psychopath." Brian Johnson, by contrast, wrote, "Playing the devil requires wit, intelligence, and style. Jack Nicholson is very good at it; Rob Lowe is not." In an interview with Glenn Collins for the *New York Times* (January 20, 1992), Lowe referred to *Bad Influence* as "a real opportunity to establish my credibility again." By all accounts, the film helped him in that regard, as did his appearance on March 17, 1990 as the host of the television show *Saturday Night Live*, on which he poked fun at himself and also "played Satan to Dana Carvey's Church Lady, who ultimately spanked him with a large paddle," as Glenn Collins reported.

In 1991 Lowe married Sheryl Berkoff, a Hollywood makeup artist. Some time before that, he acknowledged to Collins, he had stopped drinking alcohol and otherwise strived to "get [his] personal life together." "Sobriety was the greatest gift I ever gave myself. . . ," he told Ingrid Sischy for *Interview* (February 2000). "It enabled me to really connect with another human being—my wife, Sheryl—which I was never able to do before." In a conversation with Bart Mills for the New York *Daily News* (May 30, 1999, on-line), he said, "I'd been so busy on my career, I hadn't spent time on myself, to become the kind of person that someone would actually want to live with. I needed to change, and I did."

In 1992 Lowe played the part of a virginal philosophy student in a Broadway revival of the Georges Feydeau and Maurice Desvalliers farce *A Little Hotel on the Side*, mounted by Tony Randall's National Actors Theatre. Also that year Lowe appeared as a greedy television executive in the phenomenally successful *Wayne's World*, which was eventually dubbed into 16 languages. Co-starring Mike Myers and Dana Carvey, directed by Penelope Spheeris, and based on one of Carvey and Myers's *Saturday Night Live* sketches, the film goofily satirizes the media.

In January 1993 Lowe co-starred, with Maggie Smith and Natasha Richardson, in a made-for-television production of *Suddenly Last Summer*, a psycho-drama by Tennessee Williams. *Suddenly Last Summer* aired on the PBS series *Great Performances* and, in the opinion of John Leonard, the reviewer for *New York* (January 11, 1993), was "better in every respect than the 1959 Hollywood version" of the tale, in which Montgomery Clift played opposite Katharine Hepburn and Elizabeth Taylor. Lowe was not always successful at winning roles that he wanted, however; he griped to Jan Hoffman for the *New York Times* (January 3, 1993), "There have been times when my looks stood in my way." "Men hire," he explained. "And most men prefer to hire nonthreatening men. . . . Hey, if I'm 50 years old, running a studio, having to be on the treadmill five hours a day, give me Michelle Pfeiffer and Joe Shluh-moly. That's why you get much more the boy next door, someone who looks more like Everyman. And I'm a lot of things, but I'm not the boy next door and I never will be. If you have a more nondescript face, you can play all kinds of roles."

Later in the 1990s Lowe appeared in the four-part ABC-TV miniseries *The Stand* (1994), an Armageddon story by Stephen King. On the silver screen, he was seen in the historical Western *Frank and Jesse* (1995), the science-fiction epic *Contact* (1997), and the sequel—*Austin Powers: the Spy Who Shagged Me* (1999)—to Mike Myers's first spy spoof. Lowe performed his own stunts for the NBC miniseries *Atomic Train* (1999), in which he played a member of the National Transportation Safety Board who tries to stop a train hauling an atomic bomb. That role "allowed me to fulfilll a part of who I am that people haven't seen—a physical, rough-and-tumble guy's guy," he said to Jeannie Williams for *USA Today* (May 28, 1999). The year 1999 also marked the premiere of the NBC comedy-drama *The West Wing*, in which Lowe plays Deputy Communications Director Sam Seaborn. "I was born to play my character . . . ," he said to Ingrid Sischy. "It dovetailed with my personal interests, my being a political science junkie and having campaigned for various candidates and issues over the years. Temperamentally, Sam and I are very much alike. He's a lawyer, my father's a lawyer, and I always wanted to play one. On so many levels the role just felt right. I fell in love with it as I would a woman." According to various critics, Lowe is "extremely and subtly funny" and "surprisingly good" in the role. The show itself has received almost universal acclaim.

The success of the series notwithstanding, Lowe has continued to work in movies. One of his latest projects is *The Specials*, a comedy about a group of second-rate superheroes, released in late September 2000. He has also completed *Escape Under Pressure* (2000), a thriller about a cruise ship under siege, for U.F.O., an independent production company specializing in science-fiction and action films. In 2001 Lowe will appear in *Proximity*, a prison film currently in post-production, and *Acceptable Risk*, a made-for-television medical drama based on a novel by Robin Cook, set to premiere in March.

Lowe and his wife have two sons, John and Matthew. When an interviewer for *Entertainment Weekly* (July 2, 1999, on-line) asked him whether he considered his family when choosing roles, he answered, "Now that [the boys are] officially joining the movie-going public, it IS a little daunting. There was a time in my life when I wouldn't have thought twice about being in a movie like *Natural Born Killers*, and right now I just don't know if I could do it. Your kids only have their innocence once, and it's bizarre enough to see their dad on the big screen." — M.R.

Suggested Reading: *Interview* p88+ Mar. 1990, with photos, p110+ Feb, 2000, with photo; New York *Daily News Magazine* p15+ July 6, 1986, with photos; *New York Times* II p28 Jan. 3, 1993, with photos; *People* p37+ Aug. 15, 1983, with photos, p127+ Nov. 10, 1996, with photos; *Premiere* p113+ Apr. 1990, with photos

Selected Films: *The Outsiders*, 1983; *Hotel New Hampshire*, 1984; *St. Elmo's Fire*, 1985; *About Last Night . . .* , 1986; *Square Dance*, 1987; *Bad Influence*, 1990; *Wayne's World*, 1992; *Mulholland Falls*, 1996; *Contact*, 1997; *Austin Powers: The Spy Who Shagged Me*, 1999; *The Specials*, 2000

Selected Television Shows: *The West Wing*, 1999– ; *Escape Under Pressure*, 2000

Courtesy of Cheetah Conservation Fund

Marker, Laurie

Jan. 20, 1954– Co-founder and director of the Cheetah Conservation Fund. Address: Cheetah Conservation Fund/WILD, P.O. Box 1380, Ojai, CA 93024

Endowed with a highly flexible spine, oversized liver and heart, large lung capacity, wide nostrils, extra-long legs and tail, nonretractable claws, and a sleek, lightweight, muscular body, the cheetah is the fastest land animal on earth. It can accelerate from zero to 60 miles per hour in just three seconds—"one second faster than the fastest Ferrari road car," as Paul Raffaele pointed out in *Reader's Digest* (September 1999)—and can travel more than eight yards in a single stride. At full speed—as much as 72 miles an hour—it can run at about three and a half strides a second. Cheetahs have enchanted humans with their speed and grace for millennia. An image of a cheetah appears on an official seal produced in Sumeria 5,000 years ago; in ancient Egypt, the animal was revered as a cat-goddess, and pharoahs kept them as companions. Easily tamed and usually mild in temperament, they were used in hunts by Indian noblemen. The 16th-century Mogul emperor Akbar the Great is said to have owned more than 9,000 cheetahs.

At the close of the 19th century, the number of cheetahs in the world was estimated to be about 100,000. By the end of the 20th century, the population had dwindled to approximately 12,400, and the species is in serious danger of vanishing completely. Once common throughout Asia, Africa, and the Middle East, the cheetah is now found only in Iran, where only about 200 individuals survive, and in Africa, where, in about half the countries where they still exist, there are so few that their populations are not considered viable. "People don't realize how much there is to be done to save animals like the cheetah and how little time we have," the wildlife conservationist Laurie Marker told Ken Ringle for the *Washington Post* (August 19, 1989).

Marker is the co-founder and director of the Cheetah Conservation Fund, the main objective of which, according to its Web page, is "to secure the survival of free-ranging cheetahs in suitable African habitats." Working for the past decade from her base in Namibia, a nation in southwestern Africa—which, with 2,400 individuals, has more resident cheetahs than any other country—Marker has strived to find solutions to the species' grave problems. The main threat to this animal is competition with people over territory. As human development and activities have spread, cheetahs have been pushed out of their habitats or forced onto livestock farms or wild-game reserves. Even cheetahs in such preserves face difficulties. "Ironically," Marker told Ringle, "game preserves produce an expansion in the population of lions and hyenas and other animals competitive with the cheetah, so they tend to be crowded out there, too." Cheetah cubs are particularly vulnerable to attack by lions, leopards, and hyenas, all of which are stronger and more aggressive than both male and female cheetahs.

The species also suffers from a serious genetic shortcoming. Scientists believe that some 10,000 to 12,000 years ago, nearly all cheetahs died off, producing what is known as a genetic bottleneck: as is explained on-line by the Trade Environment Database, all subsequent cheetahs descended from a few closely related animals, so that "all living cheetah today are more closely related than identical twins, with less than 1 percent genetic diversity as compared to a human's 37 percent." Because of the lack of variation in the cheetah's gene pool, the species has severe reproductive problems. When David Wildt, the head of the Reproductive Physiology Program of the Conservation and Research Center at the National Zoo, in Washington, D.C., examined sperm samples taken from dozens of wild and captive cheetahs, he found that "compared with [that of] domestic cats, the cheetahs' sperm count was remarkably low, and 75 percent of what they produced was abnormally shaped, unable to fertilize an egg," as he explained to Raffaele. In the wild an estimated 90 percent of cubs die within three months of birth; in captivity, some 30 percent die before the age of one month. Attempts at captive breeding by natural means and artificial insemination have met with little success. Of the approximately 650 cheetahs currently living in zoos, only about half were bred in captivity. Lack of genetic variation also makes the species more vulnerable to disease and less able to adapt to environmental and ecological changes. Marker's organization supports reproductive research as well as educational programs and efforts to reintroduce captive-bred animals into wild habitats. "Releasing a cheetah back into the wild always gives me goose bumps . . . ," Marker told Raffaele. "The world would be a lesser place without these beautiful big cats. Each one we save makes it more likely that the cheetah will be around for a long, long time."

Laurie L. Marker was born on January 20, 1954 in Detroit, Michigan, and grew up in the tiny rural town of Rolling Hills, California. She took classes at San Francisco State University (1971–72), Napa College, in California (1972–73), and Umpqua College, in Roseburg, Oregon (1979–80), before enrolling at Eastern Oregon State College, in La Grande, in 1986; she earned a B.S. degree in wildlife management there in 1990. Meanwhile, from 1973 to 1988, she co-owned the Jonicole Vineyard and Winery, in Oregon, where she practiced viticulture (the cultivation of grapes).

Concurrently, in 1974, Marker was hired by Wildlife Safari, a drive-through game park in Winston, Oregon, as a veterinary clinic assistant, and that same year she began working with cheetahs. From 1977 until 1988 she held the title of cheetah curator (as well as the titles of veterinary clinic supervisor [1976–80] and director of marketing and education [1980–88]), with responsibility for maintaining the facility's captive-breeding program for the cheetah. Earlier, in 1976, she had begun raising a female cheetah cub, whom she named Khayam. Six weeks old when Marker adopted her, Khayam lived for some time in Marker's home, where she frolicked with Marker's Labrador retriever, Sheso. "Sheso licked Khayam's fur clean and played throat-bite with her," Marker told Raffaele. Khayam was not yet mature when, in 1977, Marker decided to bring her to Namibia, with the goal of releasing her; the undertaking was to serve as a test of whether a captive-bred cheetah could adapt to the wild.

A cheetah raised in captivity must be taught how to hunt. To instruct Khayam, for about two months Marker made a practice of running after steenbok (also known as steinbok), a small, slender species of antelope, while the cub looked on. "Eventually," Marker recalled to Ringle, "she figured, 'This must be something Mom wants. Maybe I can help,' and began trying to herd a few back to me. Finally, by instinct or a sense of play, she tripped up one little steinbok. I fell on it, she jumped on me, and I forced her jaws around the windpipe and squeezed them shut. After that she got the idea." What Marker has identified in her on-line curriculum vitae as "reintroduction research of cheetah in Namibia" extended into 1978.

From 1982 to 1987 Marker served as the North American regional cheetah studbook keeper, and she has served as the international cheetah studbook keeper since 1987. A studbook keeper maintains detailed records about all captive individuals of a particular species, including data on its genealogy, progeny, and health. According to an on-line guide prepared by the Lincoln Park Zoo, in Chicago, "The studbook keeper is a resource: a knowledgeable individual with a vast amount of information about a group of animals in captivity. Moreover, the studbook keeper is a researcher, who systematically and relentlessly pursues those individual facts that together portray the true history of the population." The records for each animal include notations of transfers from one zoo to another, usually for breeding purposes: finding suitable potential mates, and thereby increasing the cheetah population, is the main purpose of building this extensive database. Thus sterile individuals must be weeded out, and very fertile animals noted. Since 1984 Marker has also served as adviser, among other roles, for the Species Survival Plan (SSP) that the American Zoo and Aquarium Association administers for the cheetah. (Separate plans exist for many other endangered species.) The aim of the SSP is to "maintain a healthy and self-sustaining captive population that is both genetically diverse and demographically stable."

In 1988 Marker married Daniel Kraus, a wildlife expert who had worked in Kenya with the conservationist and game warden George Adamson—a pioneer, along with his wife, Joy Adamson (the author of *Born Free* and *Living Free*), in reintroducing orphaned lions to the wild. She and Kraus settled in Washington, D.C., where Marker became the executive director of a division of the National Zoo known as the NOAHS Center. (NOAHS stands for New Opportunities in Animal Health Sciences.) Using as her surname Marker-Kraus, she headed research, education, and fund-raising programs.

In 1990 Marker and Kraus co-founded the Cheetah Conservation Fund (CCF), as a project of the Ojai, California–based International Wilderness Leadership (WILD) Foundation. Determined to try a more hands-on approach to preserving the cheetah, the couple accumulated $40,000 in grants and their own savings, and in April of that year, with the support of the Namibian government, they moved to a farm some 300 miles north of Windhoek, the capital of Namibia. Encompassing large deserts, savannahs, and open farmland, Namibia is well-suited for cheetahs; individual animals may range over areas as large as 600 square miles. "We're not just here to do a little research project and leave," Kraus told Susan K. Reed for *People* (June 14, 1993). "We've come to work with the people to accomplish something on a long-term basis. We want to try to make Namibia the cheetah capital of the world."

Marker and others at the CCF began by launching outreach efforts to inform Namibian farmers and ranchers about cheetah conservation. Many farmers and ranchers were killing every cheetah they happened to come upon, to prevent any of their animals from becoming cheetah prey. (In actuality, leopards, baboons, and other wild predators in addition to cheetahs are responsible for such killings.) Since nearly 95 percent of Namibia's cheetahs live close to livestock and wild-game farms, the cooperation of Namibia's farming and ranching communities is crucial in preserving the cheetah. The CCF workers urged farmers and ranchers to seek alternative livestock-protection methods, including the use of donkeys, special guard dogs, and even tougher strains of cattle to fend off hungry cheetahs. Because cheetahs are not aggressive, donkeys and guard dogs can be effective deterrents.

The farmers' and ranchers' responses to Marker and her colleagues ranged from sympathetic to antagonistic. Those who were moved to help the conservationists would trap cheetahs that had wandered onto their land and would then contact Marker, who would collect the animals and transport them elsewhere. Some continued to slaughter the intruders. Others, while not expressing outright disapproval of the conservationists' efforts, felt skeptical about the whole enterprise. Jan Oelofse, the owner of a private game preserve in Namibia, for example, told Bill Keller for the *New York Times* (May 17, 1993), "I think the farmers might talk to the Krauses politely, but deep in their hearts they wonder, what are these people doing here? In no way do they believe the cheetah is threatened in this country." In the following years, however, more Namibians came round to Marker's point of view; in 1999 she told Raffaele that, as he reported, "two out of three farmers in her area of the country no longer kill cheetahs."

In 1992 the Cheetah Conservation Fund was incorporated as a trust in Namibia. With growing support from concerned individuals, the organization soon expanded its conservation efforts, particularly the outreach programs that spread awareness of cheetah conservation to schoolchildren as well as farmers and ranchers. The CCF has also implemented research projects to collect biological data about cheetahs and has studied the movements of the animals by tagging individual cheetahs with a radio transmitter and tracking them from an airplane. Information about cheetah movements will aid in the prevention of violent interactions between cheetahs and livestock.

In 1996 Daniel Kraus left the CCF, and he and Marker divorced soon afterward. With Marker as its sole director, the CCF has continued to expand since then, with the help of expert associates, donors, and volunteers from Namibia and elsewhere. In Namibia the CCF operates out of the International Cheetah Research and Education Center, located on an 18,000-acre farm. A cheetah outreach program has been launched in South Africa; in the United States, CCF chapters have been set up in the Pacific Northwest, northern California, Chicago, and Phoenix. In Los Altos, California, in 1999, two cheetahs displayed their speed at a fund-raiser called Run for Survival; the event attracted 400 supporters and netted $150,000 (half of which came from a matching grant). Sales of T-shirts, mugs, note cards, books, and other merchandise, all of which are listed on the CCF's Web page, bring in additional funds.

In Namibia, where she makes her home, Marker is a member of the Namibian Veterinary Association, the Conservancy Association of Namibia, and the Namibian Large Carnivore Management Forum, among other groups. Her honors include the 1988 White Rose Award, which is given to Oregon's "top 10 women." In 1992 the African Safari Club, in Washington, D.C., named her conservationist of the year. — K.S.

Suggested Reading: *Cats* p26+ Oct. 1993, with photos; *cheetah.org* (on-line); *Endangered Wildlife* p3+ June 1993, with photos; *New York Times* A p4 May 17, 1993, with photo; *People* p132+ June 14, 1993, with photos; *Reader's Digest* p69+ Sep. 1999, with photos; *Washington Post* C p1+ Aug. 19, 1989, with photos

Tracy Smith/Courtesy of University of New Orleans

Marsalis, Ellis

Nov. 14, 1934– Jazz musician; educator. Address: New Orleans University, Dept. of Jazz Studies, New Orleans, LA 70148

Ellis Marsalis is often referred to as the "Father of Jazz," because of his having taught so many now-famous musicians and because of the musical success of his progeny. His son Branford, a prolific recording artist, had a high-profile stint as Jay Leno's musical director on *The Tonight Show.* Wynton, the winner of numerous Grammy Awards, is considered one of the best jazz trumpeters in the world and is credited with spearheading the renaissance of acoustic jazz. Delfeayo, a trombonist, composed and produced several of the songs on his father's *Heart of Gold* album, and Jason was already drumming professionally at the age of 14. In January 1996 the whole clan appeared in *New Orleans* magazine's list of the most influential people in that city's recent history because, as Carolyn Kolb wrote, "If New Orleans' best gift to 19th-century music was jazz, then New Orleans' best gift to 20th-century music might be the entire Marsalis family."

Ellis Marsalis denies himself the credit for the accomplishments of his offspring. "When people talk about heredity, I always say, 'Check [my wife] out,'" he told *Down Beat* (April 1992), "'cause musically, I ain't related to nobody." His wife, Dolores, on the other hand, is related to Duke Ellington's bassist Wellman Braud on her father's side and the clarinetist Alphonse Picou on her mother's. That Marsalis married into a jazz-oriented family and has sired leading jazz artists sometimes obscures the fact that he himself is considered by experts to be one of the world's premier jazz pianists. His self-effacing manner and modesty are partially responsible for this. He is happy to allow his sons to bask in the spotlight, and when asked if he is at all jealous of their success, he has been known to reply, as he did for *Down Beat,* "Are you jealous of your grandmother?"

Marsalis was born on November 14, 1934 in the uptown section of New Orleans. He played tenor saxophone in a high-school rhythm-and-blues band called the Groovy Boys and dabbled a bit with the piano while attending Dillard University, in New Orleans, from which he graduated in 1955. As he recalled for the April 1992 *Down Beat* article, he "vacillated" for a time between the saxophone and the piano. His explanation of why his focus shifted to the latter is characteristic of his humility: "I didn't really get serious about the piano until I graduated. . . . The decision had a lot to do with hearing a tenor saxophone player named Nat Perrilliat. I was sittin' in on piano at the Dew Drop Inn and this cat started to play, and I didn't know what he was doing. So I stopped playing to listen. . . . After I heard that, there was no doubt in my mind that I was going to play piano."

In the mid-1950s Marsalis joined the American Jazz Quintet, a modern-jazz group that included drummer Ed Blackwell. Marsalis has recalled driving out to Los Angeles with Blackwell in 1956 to meet legendary free-jazz innovator Ornette Coleman, a friend of Blackwell's. He told *Down Beat* of the visit, "I could appreciate what Ornette was trying to do without really understanding a lot of it." Marsalis was to return to California shortly after the visit—this time as an enlisted Marine. At the time, the Marines had a television variety show, *Dress Blues,* which aired locally on Sunday afternoons. Much of Marsalis's tour of duty was spent playing the piano in the show's band.

When he returned to New Orleans, after his military discharge, Marsalis married fellow New Orleanian Dolores Ferdinand, with whom he would eventually have six sons. He assembled a quartet, which included Perrilliat (the saxophonist whose talent had intimidated him earlier) and James Black, who would remain his drummer on and off for the next quarter-century. Marsalis's father owned a motel and gave the group a gig in its small lounge, which was called the Music Haven. (The pianist's song "Swingin' at the Haven" pays tribute to the venue.) The band recorded an album, *Monkey Puzzle,* on AFO, a musician's co-op label.

In 1960 Dolores gave birth to the first of their sons, Branford. To pay the bills Marsalis began teaching music, first in the suburbs of Jefferson Parish and later in the largely Cajun town of Breux Bridge. In 1961 the couple's second son, Wynton, was born. Also that year, a chance encounter with the manager of Al Hirt's club led to an invitation for Marsalis to join the well-known trumpeter's band. The first black musician in the group, he was to remain for three years, playing the catchy tunes that had made Hirt so popular in the mainstream.

While playing with Hirt, Marsalis continued to teach and served as an adjunct professor at Xavier University. As quoted on the ASCAP Web site (Summer 1996), he recalled, "The chairman of the department had told me then: 'If you get your master's degree, I'll put you on full time.'" So after leaving Hirt's band, Marsalis—having tired of looking for gigs on Bourbon Street—remembered the offer. "Fortunately [President] Richard Nixon made the G.I. Bill retroactive for Korean veterans," he told Erik Philbrook and Jim Steinblatt for the ASCAP site. "It was the perfect time to go to school. I had been out of school for 19 years." Marsalis thus obtained a master's of music education degree from Loyola University, in New Orleans.

Meanwhile, in 1974, New Orleans opened an arts magnet high school, the New Orleans Center for Creative Arts (NOCCA), with a $30,000 grant from the National Endowment for the Arts. Marsalis auditioned and got a job as head of the fledgling school's music department. NOCCA's alumni list reads like a who's who of modern jazz. Wynton and Branford Marsalis are both graduates, as are the singer Harry Connick Jr. and the trumpeters Terence Blanchard and Nicholas Payton. "There was no real philosophy to the program," Marsalis told Carolanne Griffith-Roberts for *Southern Living* (December 1992). "I knew that jazz was music close to me, and we developed instruction in jazz improvisation. These kids were raised in the era of Funkadelic and Earth, Wind, and Fire. They had garage bands. What I really didn't understand going into the school was that kids growing up in the city of New Orleans didn't care about jazz, didn't care about it at all." He continued, "There was this thing called a television and FM radio and AM radio dealing with popular music. It's not any different now. Ask kids what they want to do, they say, 'I want to be a rapper.' And there is enough evidence around that it pays."

Using a combination of patience and discipline, Marsalis was eventually able to explain to his students his aversion to commercial music. "I used to tell students that it reminded me of a dessert I bought at the store once," he said to Carolanne Griffith-Roberts. "I looked on the box and there were no natural ingredients in it at all. I'm sure that it tasted sweet, but if you have a chance to eat desserts that have apples and oranges, pears and bananas, it's got to be a lot better for you. In [jazz] we were still playing instruments like the saxophone, which you have to breathe into to get sounds. And the drums, which you have to strike, and the piano, which is made out of wood. There was human control over them."

Contradicting others' accounts, Marsalis has denied responsibility for the success of the school's music program. He has pointed instead to the excellence of the rest of the faculty, the dedication of the principal, the individualized attention to each student's needs, and the musical atmosphere of New Orleans itself. In 1986 he left the school, accepting an invitation to become the coordinator of jazz studies at Virginia Commonwealth University, in Richmond. Then, in 1989, he returned to his native city to accept an honorary doctorate of music from Dillard University and a position as director of the Jazz Studies Division at the University of New Orleans (UNO), where he now also holds the prestigious Coca-Cola Endowed Chair in Jazz.

The trumpeter and vocalist Jeremy Davenport, a student of Marsalis's at UNO, remembers his teacher's low-key manner and straightforwardness. In an interview with Keith Spera for *Down Beat* (September 1996), he recounted, "We were playing 'Tenderly' together. I was playing the melody. He stopped in the middle of the tune and looked at me over his glasses, in his Mr. Marsalis way, and goes, 'Do you know the lyrics to this tune?' I said no. 'You know what this song is about?' No. 'Why are you playing it?'"

Despite a heavy teaching schedule, Marsalis has taken on other responsibilities. He is chairman of the Louisiana Music Commission, a member of both the International Association of Jazz Educators and the American Federation of Musicians, and a member of the board of the National Endowment for the Arts. He has written scholarly forewords for two publications: a collection of the works of the composer R. Nathaniel Dett and *Rejoice When We Die*, an illustrated look at New Orleans jazz funerals.

Perhaps more impressively, throughout his teaching career Marsalis has also continued to tour and record extensively, sometimes as part of a trio and sometimes as a solo act. (He has commented that touring is just another form of teaching; only the audience is different.) In 1995 he released *Loved One* with his son Branford. An album of songs about unforgettable women, *Loved One* was originally conceived as a solo project for Marsalis. For *sonymusic.com*, he explained his willingness to share the project with his son: "As I played through these songs, I thought Branford would sound really good on some of them. Branford, to me, is the most imaginative and creative person playing music today." To those who questioned whether the selection of old standards would cause dissent between the younger musician and his father, Marsalis answered, "There's no culture clash between Branford and me. He's extremely eclectic. He knows these songs and the idioms from which they come." The album, with its unique interpretations of such tunes as "Maria" and "Miss Otis Regrets," was well received by both critics and the public, and the pair followed up by touring together. John Pareles of the *New York Times* (April 29, 1996, on-line) wrote of one concert, at Town Hall in New York City, "There was no Oedipal conflict on stage. [Branford] was deferential but not servile, [Ellis] affectionate without pulling rank."

On February 17, 2000 PBS aired *Ellis Marsalis: Jazz Is Spoken Here*, a one-hour documentary on his life and music, which included interviews with his children, students, and fellow musicians and footage taken at the University of New Orleans and the New Orleans Center for Contemporary Arts. Marsalis has won numerous honors, including the Three Key Award at the International Jazz Festival of Bern and installation on the Hilton Riverside Walk of Fame. He rarely speaks of those things in interviews, though, preferring instead to dwell on the accomplishments of his brood. Despite his enormous pride in them, he will not take any credit for their success. He told Laura B. Randolph for *Ebony* (February 1993), "All I did was make sure they had the best so they could be the best. They did the rest." Wynton Marsalis disagrees with that assessment. The trumpeter informed Randolph that even though he was garnering most of the glory, his father was still guiding the way. To illustrate that point, he related his experience in writing a piece for the New York City Ballet. He wanted to use elements of three songs from the early part of the century but didn't know the melodies. "I called my father and he just wrote out all of the songs," he told Randolph in amazement. "He's like a library of information I can always count on." That anecdote points up Marsalis's multiple talents and roles—devoted father, wise teacher, and master jazz musician. — M.R.

Suggested Reading: ASCAP (on-line); *Down Beat* p23+ Apr. 1992, with photos; *Ebony* p96+ Feb. 1993, with photos; *Southern Living* p78+ Dec. 1992, with photos

Selected Recordings: *Father and Sons*, 1982; *Syndrome*, 1985; *A Night at Snug Harbor, New Orleans*, 1990; *Jazz Wonderland*, 1991; *The Classic Ellis Marsalis*, 1991; *Heart of Gold*, 1992; *Whistle Stop*, 1994; *Loved Ones*, 1996

Steve Sands/Outline Press

Martin, Steve

Aug. 14, 1945– Actor; comedian; writer. Address: c/o International Creative Management, 8942 Wilshire Blvd., Beverly Hills, CA 90211

NOTE: An earlier article about Steve Martin appeared in *Current Biography* in 1978.

The comedian, actor, and writer Steve Martin has remained in the public eye for a quarter-century, in part by continually and successfully reinventing himself. He shot to fame in the mid-1970s as a stand-up comic whose jokes were riffs on a central conceit—the boorishness and stupidity of his persona, which belied Martin's intelligence and his background as a student of philosophy. His comedy albums of the late 1970s were tremendously popular with fans who ate up his self-description as "a wild and crazy guy" and such signature lines as "Well, ex*cuuuuuse ME!*" That stage of his career perhaps hit its peak when he starred in the 1979 film *The Jerk*, whose title perfectly summed up Martin's act. Just as some began to sense that his shtick had run its course, Martin left stand-up to focus mainly on movies, appearing in a string of critically praised but ill-attended comedies before hitting his stride in the late 1980s and early 1990s with the hits *Roxanne* (which he also wrote); *Planes, Trains, and Automobiles*; *Parenthood*; and *Father of the Bride*, films in which he gave subtly humorous performances that contrasted sharply with his earlier work. Also in the 1990s he turned his hand to other forms of writing, with plays such as the well-received *Picasso at the Lapin Agile* and short, funny pieces for magazines including the *New Yorker*, some of which were collected in the volume *Pure Drivel*. Most recently, while acting in such films as *The Spanish Prisoner* and *Bowfinger*, Martin has expanded his literary efforts, editing a book of writings by the humorist S. J. Perelman and penning *Shopgirl: A Novella*.

Steve Martin was born on August 14, 1945 in Waco, Texas, the son of Glenn Martin, a real-estate agent and local theater actor, and Mary (Lee) Martin. At the age of five, he moved with his parents and older sister, Melinda, from Waco to Inglewood, California. By the time of the move Martin had developed a desire to perform, as he told Tony Schwartz for a cover story in *Newsweek* (April 3, 1978): "I'd watch the skits on the Red Skelton show, memorize 'em and then go to school and perform during 'Show and Tell.'" Martin would later describe his early years as comfortable. "We were not close-knit—not a lot of hugging and kissing, not vocal or loud," he told Richard Corliss for *Time* (August 24, 1987). "We were middle class. When frozen food came in, we were right in there buying frozen food."

In 1955 the Martin family moved to Garden Grove, in southern California's Orange County, two miles from Disneyland, which had opened that summer. There, the 10-year-old Martin landed his first after-school job. Rigged out in 1890s style, with a straw hat, vest, and bow tie, he sold 25-cent amusement-park guidebooks. He worked at Disneyland over a period of eight years, in several capacities; during that time a friend of his taught him to play the banjo, a skill that would later make its way into his act. He was especially fascinated by the vaudeville comedian Wally Boag, who performed at Disneyland's Golden Horseshow Revue. Boag's show included comedy routines, songs, and bits in which he twisted balloons into outlandish shapes. At 16, after memorizing Boag's entire act, Martin was featured as "Mouth and Magic" in a Wally Boag production called "It's Vaudeville Again." He also moonlighted at local coffeehouses, appearing as the straight man in a two-person comedy act with his friend Morris Walker.

When Martin was 18 he heard a record by the bluegrass legend Earl Scruggs that led him to become fanatical about playing the banjo. After his years at Disneyland, he went to work at nearby Knott's Berry Farm, where he appeared in a melodrama at the Birdcage Theatre four or five times daily; following each show he presented a 10-minute melange of comedy, magic, and banjo-playing.

Although Martin considered school of secondary importance and was admittedly "the class clown in high school," he nevertheless graduated from Garden Grove High School and enrolled in a junior college. He has said that he was something of a loner during that period. Inspired by his girlfriend and fellow performer Stormie Sherk, who introduced him to W. Somerset Maugham's novel *The Razor's Edge* and advised him that "knowledge is the most important thing there is," he later entered Long Beach State College, in California, to major in philosophy. But when, after three years of studying "like crazy" and earning straight A's, he became aware of the British philosopher Ludwig Wittgenstein's view that all philosophical problems are merely issues of semantics, he became disillusioned and dropped out of college to return to the performing arts. "It was the only thing that had real meaning because it had no meaning," he explained to Tony Schwartz. "In art, truth comes and goes according to fashion. It can't be measured. You don't have to explain why, or justify anything. If it works, it works. . . . Non sequiturs make sense, nonsense is real."

Developing a stand-up act filled with dumb gags and goofy gestures, Martin played at any venue that would take him. At one club in San Francisco, he performed at a window facing the street, in order to attract crowds; at a gig in Las Vegas, he followed an elephant act. In 1967 he enrolled in a television-writing course at the University of California at Los Angeles (UCLA).

Martin got his first major break after he submitted material to Mason Williams, the head writer for *The Smothers Brothers Comedy Hour*, who had once seen his act. Hired for the show, Martin became one of its 10 writers to share an Emmy Award, for installments of the show that aired in March 1968. Now in demand as a writer, he went on to prepare material for such performers as Glen Campbell, Ray Stevens, Pat Paulsen, and John Denver, and after writing routines for Sonny and Cher, he was invited to appear on their show as a supporting player. Martin also helped to write an episode for Dick Van Dyke's NBC special *Van Dyke and Company*, which aired on October 30, 1975 and was nominated for an Emmy Award.

Although Martin was earning $1,500 a week at that point—a princely sum at the time—he found that writing for others did not satisfy him. "Comedy comes down to a split second and by the time it leaves the typewriter to the director to the star, it was gone," he told Dave Hirshey for the New York *Sunday News* (October 23, 1977). "That's why I left." On his slow route to stardom through performing his own material, Steve Martin endured a depressing period during which he opened for "stoned-out" rock groups in small California clubs. Unable to function as a comedian in that chaotic atmosphere, Martin left the rock scene after about two years. "There's got to be order for my comedy to work," he has explained, "because chaos in the midst of chaos is not funny, but chaos in the midst of order is funny."

In what Dave Hirshey termed his "Straight Arrow Period," Steve Martin trimmed his hair, shaved off his beard, donned a neat three-piece white suit, and hit the Las Vegas circuit, opening for such headliners as Sonny and Cher, Helen Reddy, and Ann-Margret. Martin's act failed to ignite the enthusiasm of Las Vegas audiences. He would later comment on the circuit, "It's blow-your-brains-out time. Absolutely the worst audiences in the world. You learn technique, though, you sharpen your ad lib."

Disillusioned by his failure to make a real hit with nightclub audiences, by 1975 Martin was seriously considering leaving show business. Then he decided to change his routine, turning to a more bizarre, outrageous kind of humor, and his prospects immediately improved. In an era in which much comedy was tinged with politics, Martin's act was decidedly apolitical and absurdist, involving arrows through his head and balloons. His popularity soared, and other comics began to imitate him. A turning point in his career occurred in August 1975, when he headlined a sold-out two-week engagement at San Francisco's Boarding House. Soon afterward, Martin was appearing on dozens of television programs, including *The Tonight Show*; he served as a writer and guest performer on the *John*

Denver Rocky Mountain Christmas Show in December 1975 and was a regular for four weeks in the summer of 1976 on the *Johnny Cash Show.* That fall he appeared for the first time as a guest on the comedy show *Saturday Night Live*, for which he thought up and performed in new routines, including the first of a series of skits that featured him and Dan Aykroyd as dim-witted Czech playboys. In January 1977 he made his first appearance as guest host of the *Tonight Show*, which became a regular gig for him. Later that year he went on a two-month tour of colleges and large auditoriums across the U.S.

At the peak of his popularity as a stand-up comedian, with his comedy albums *Let's Get Small*, *A Wild and Crazy Guy*, and *Comedy Is Not Pretty* selling phenomenally, Martin switched his focus to movies. He would later reflect in an interview with Elvis Mitchell for *GQ* (July 1990), "Once I got to the big arenas, I knew it was over artistically. I just couldn't change anything. It *was* like doing hit songs. Even new material was greeted with 'Yeah, yeah . . . get it over with so we can hear the other stuff.' I had taken it as far as it could possibly go." He made his movie debut as the evil Dr. Maxwell in the universally panned *Sergeant Pepper's Lonely Hearts Club Band*, starring the singing group the Bee Gees. More auspiciously, he was nominated for an Academy Award for his 1978 short *The Absent-Minded Waiter*, in which he played the title role. But it was the screwball comedy *The Jerk*, released in 1979, that would catapult Martin to movie stardom. The film revolves around Martin's character, Navin R. Johnson, a clueless, white 18-year-old who, raised by an African-American family, believes that he too is black. After discovering the truth, he leaves home and embarks on a series of bizarre adventures. *The Jerk*, which Martin wrote with Carl Gottlieb, drew mediocre reviews from most critics but earned almost $100 million, making it the third-highest-grossing movie of the year. On a personal level, Martin started dating his *Jerk* co-star, Bernadette Peters, with whom he would star in *Pennies from Heaven* (1981). Adapted from a British TV miniseries, with the story transplanted to the Depression-era U.S., *Pennies from Heaven* found Martin turning away from comedy. The film, complete with songs from the period, focuses on the tragic life of a sheet-music salesman, Arthur Parker, played by Martin, and his relationships with his wife and lover. Garnering some good reviews, *Pennies from Heaven* went on to be nominated for several Academy Awards and won the New York Film Critics Award for best screenplay. It was far from a hit with audiences, however, who had a difficult time associating Martin with a serious movie that had an unhappy ending.

Martin returned to comedy with the deadpan private-eye spoof *Dead Men Don't Wear Plaid* (1982). Directed by Carl Reiner, who had also helmed *The Jerk*, the film was peppered with clips from 1940s film noir. Again, reviews were stronger than audience reaction. After making a brief appearance in the hit film *Fast Times at Ridgemont High* (1982), Martin starred in *The Man with Two Brains* (1983), which approached the science-fiction B-movie in much the way that *Dead Men Don't Wear Plaid* had interpreted film noir.

Martin's next project was another Carl Reiner movie, *All of Me* (1984). Martin starred as a man whose right side is possessed by the soul of a dead woman (played by Lily Tomlin). The movie was far more successful at the box office than his previous three films and won Martin, who took on multiple personalities and accompanying gestures, the New York Film Critics Award for best actor as well as a nomination for best actor at the Golden Globe Awards. Martin became romantically involved with a member of the cast, the British actress Victoria Tennant; the two married in 1986.

Even with the relative commercial success of *All of Me*, Martin was gaining a reputation for making box-office bombs. The sentimental comedy *The Lonely Guy* (1984) did not change that perception; nor did the Western spoof *The Three Amigos* (1986), which Martin co-produced and co-wrote. He received a boost with his next assignment, a supporting role in the movie remake of *Little Shop of Horrors*. (The remake was based on a new Broadway version, which had opened in 1982.) Martin played a sadistic, motorcycle-riding, Elvis Presley–like dentist in the musical tale of a talking, man-eating plant. Many critics noted that Martin's scenes were among the movie's funniest.

Focusing his energies on writing *Roxanne* (1987), a modern film adaptation of Edmond Rostand's 1897 play *Cyrano de Bergerac*, Martin found it hard to receive backing, and while making the film he had his own doubts. "*Roxanne* was very frightening to make," Martin said, as quoted by Gail Buchalter in *Parade* (April 28, 1991). "It was my first solo writing effort, and I was tampering with a classic. I was going out there with a big nose on and didn't know if people would think it was incredibly stupid." Martin played fire chief C.D. Bales, who, though ashamed of his overlong nose, aspires to win the affections of the local beauty, Roxanne (Daryl Hannah). His friend on the force, Chris McDonnell, is also after Roxanne, and Bales, believing that he himself doesn't have a chance, dictates the lines with which his less-than-suave friend tries to woo her. A critical and commercial success, *Roxanne* was Martin's first hit since *The Jerk.* Richard Corliss noted, "Though the role skirts smugness—C.D. is the first Martin character to spend more time humiliating others than being humiliated by them—the performance locates frolic and pathos in a wry, romantic, slightly aloof soul." *Roxanne* earned Martin a New York and also a Los Angeles Film Critics Award, which he found satisfying, "because you can't campaign for them." He followed that up in the same year with another commercial success, *Planes, Trains, and Automobiles*, starring John Candy in a tale of unlucky and mismatched travelers. Though it received mixed reviews, the film grossed almost $50 million. Film critic Roger Ebert of the *Chicago Sun-Times* (November 25, 1987), one of the film's supporters, wrote, "This is a funny movie, but also a surprisingly warm and sweet one."

Martin appeared on Broadway in 1988 in the Samuel Beckett play *Waiting for Godot*, along with Robin Williams and F. Murray Abraham. Also that year Martin starred opposite Michael Caine in Frank Oz's film *Dirty Rotten Scoundrels*, a remake of the 1964 comedy *Bedtime Story* that found the pair playing con men who prey on wealthy women in Europe. The film grossed over $42 million at the box office, becoming one of a string of Martin's movie successes in the late 1980s and early 1990s.

Martin was nominated for a Golden Globe for his next performance, as the hard-working father Gil Buckman in *Parenthood* (1989), Ron Howard's take on suburban family life. A comedy with dramatic elements, showing both the positive and frustrating aspects of raising children, *Parenthood* was a box-office smash that won strong reviews for its insight and its pointed but warm vision of suburbia. "What I liked about the movie was it presented the incredible virtues of the average man," Martin said, as quoted in the *Parade* article. "It takes a tremendous effort to raise children and figure out what's right. It's so common to everyone, but no one realizes how magnificent it truly is."

On the heels of that success, Martin received largely poor reviews for *My Blue Heaven* (1990), in which he played a mobster in the witness-protection program. He rebounded in 1991 with *Father of the Bride*, a remake of the 1950 film of the same name. Martin, in an understated performance, was cast as George Banks, whose daughter returns from a semester in Europe accompanied by her new fiancé. The movie finds Banks dealing with wedding-related headaches and with the idea of losing his daughter to marriage. *Father of the Bride* was a solid commercial hit for Martin and returned him to the ranks of the most successful comic actors in Hollywood. His next project was *L.A. Story* (1991), a witty if sentimental comedy, written by Martin, about looking for love in the strange, yet beautiful world of Los Angeles. The movie co-starred his wife, Victoria Tennant. Martin was quoted in *Parade* as saying about the film, "The trick is to make something sentimental without crossing the line into dopiness. . . . The environment of Los Angeles lends itself to jokes. It's love that's serious." Victoria Tennant stated that *L.A. Story* was "a completely personal piece of work, and the place in it is unmistakably [Martin's]—like Barry Levinson's Baltimore or Woody Allen's New York." Martin rounded out the year with a supporting role in *Grand Canyon*, a serious, multi-character film that explored the nature of class and race separation, among other issues. Martin played a producer of violent Hollywood movies who has a temporary change of heart about his creations after he is shot during a holdup. *Grand Canyon* was given one of that year's "Ten Best" awards for film from the National Board of Review.

In the midst of a run of unremarkable movies—*Leap of Faith* (1992), *Housesitter* (1992), and *Mixed Nuts* (1994)—Martin wrote a play, *Picasso at the Lapin Agile*, which opened in 1993 in Chicago's Steppenwolf Theatre. A humorous, intellectual farce, the work offered a fictional dialogue between the artist Pablo Picasso and the physicist Albert Einstein, just before their major achievements were realized. It received sterling reviews and went on to be performed in New York and Los Angeles. Returning to movies, Martin changed his pace by writing, producing, and starring in *A Simple Twist of Fate* (1994), an updated version of George Eliot's 1861 novel *Silas Marner*. Martin played Michael McCann, a furniture maker who leaves his wife after she becomes pregnant during an affair, then comes to value his life anew when he finds an orphan child left on his doorstep. During the filming of the movie, Martin—who had separated from Victoria Tennant the previous year—started dating his co-star Anne Heche. Although some critics praised the film, it went almost unnoticed at the box office, as did *Father of the Bride, Part II* (1995), which picks up the story of George Banks as he deals not only with becoming a grandfather but with becoming a father once again. His next starring role was in *Sgt. Bilko* (1996), based on the 1950s sitcom about the wisecracking, scheming sergeant played by Phil Silvers. Around the time that that movie was released, Martin's relationship with Heche ended; Martin later wrote a one-act play, *Patter for the Floating Lady*, about what he called his and Heche's "torturous love affair."

Martin received good reviews for his straight and unusually dark role in David Mamet's 1997 thriller *The Spanish Prisoner*. He lent his voice to the 1998 animated feature *Prince of Egypt*, then wrote the screenplay for Frank Oz's *Bowfinger* (1999), in which he played a director who decides to make a low-budget movie without the knowledge of his film's star (Eddie Murphy). The film was a moderate success, earning Martin some of his best reviews for a comedy in years. (Martin's representatives denied that Heather Graham's character in *Bowfinger*, a woman who sleeps with people of both sexes to further her career, was created as a jab at Martin's former flame Anne Heche, who in 1997 had "come out" as the lover of the actress and comedian Ellen DeGeneres.) Martin played opposite Goldie Hawn in the critically panned *Out of Towners* (1999), based on Neil Simon's comic play about a midwestern couple who move to New York. Most recently Martin played the host for one segment of *Disney's Fantasia 2000* (1999) and had a small role in *Joe Gould's Secret* (2000).

Outside of film acting, Martin enjoys collecting art, holding in his possession works by Picasso, Willem de Kooning, and Georgia O'Keeffe, among others. "Collecting art is my biggest hobby . . . ," he told Richard Corliss, "because this art is so different from what I do that it's an escape for me. Paintings exist in space; show business exists in time." He has continued to appear sporadically on *Saturday Night Live*, with numerous appearances as host since the show began. As for the stand-up circuit he left behind, Martin doesn't follow the present scene, saying in the 1990 *GQ* interview, "I don't feel like I'm missing much. I just have a physical aversion to the clubs." He has written two short plays besides *Patter for the Floating Lady*, namely *The Zig-Zag Woman* and *WASP* (all were published in the 1996 book *Picasso at the Lapin Agile and Other Plays*) and has contributed humorous articles to the *New Yorker* and other publications; some of those pieces were collected in the 1998 volume *Pure Drivel*. (He published his first book, *Cruel Shoes*, in 1979.) His publishing credits for 2000 include *Most of the Most of S. J. Perelman*, which he edited, and the well-received novella *Shopgirl*.

With a longstanding reputation for being a very private person, Martin has remained an enigma to journalists and friends alike. (Martin's former house in L.A. was a one-story, L-shaped building with no front windows, which Martin called the "house that says, 'Go away.'") His former boss, Tom Smothers, was quoted in *Entertainment Weekly* (February 22, 1991) as saying, "He's a real nice guy, a deep guy, but when he stops being funny he reveals very little about himself," and the director Mike Nichols said of Martin to Peter de Jonge for the *New York Times Magazine* (May 31, 1992), "He's a warm and loving friend, but you have a sense of him coming to you across a great distance." Responding to charges of aloofness, Martin told Gail Buchalter, "I just can't be what I'm not, and that's outrageously funny. Sometimes people are offended if you're not their best friend in 30 seconds." As a compromise with those seeking his autograph, Martin has signed business cards that read, "This certifies that you have had a personal encounter with me and that you found me warm, polite, intelligent and funny."

"I realized long ago that working on acting is best done by working on yourself," Martin remarked to Prairie Miller in a recent interview transcribed for the *All Movie Guide* (on-line). "The smarter and richer you become as a person, the better actor you're going to be. Because you'll know more about people. Reading, thinking, experiencing life, having your heart broken, and observing, being observant. You never really find yourself, but I came out of it with something." Martin was given a Lifetime Achievement Award at the 1996 U.S. Comedy Arts Festival. He continues to reside in Los Angeles. — G.O.

Suggested Reading: *All Movie Guide* (on-line); *Chicago Tribune* XIII p6+ Feb. 10, 1991, with photos; *Entertainment Weekly* p12+ Feb. 22, 1991, with photos, p81 Sep. 18, 1998, with photo; *Esquire* p66+ April 1996, with photos; *GQ* p115+ July 1990, with photos; *Internet Movie Database* (on-line); New York *Daily News* p12+ Feb. 3, 1991, with photos; *New York Times* H p13+ Feb. 3, 1991, with photos; *New York Times Magazine* p29+ May 31,1992, with photos, p26+ Aug. 8, 1999, with photos; *Newsweek* p60+ Apr. 3, 1978, p59 Feb. 11, 1991, with photo; *Parade* p8+ Apr. 28, 1991with photos; *Rolling Stone* p10+ Feb. 18, 1982, with photos; *Time* p50+ Aug. 24, 1987, with photos, p90 Oct. 30, 1995; *Washington Post* D p7+ Dec. 18, 1992, with photos

Selected Films: *The Jerk*, 1979; *Pennies from Heaven*, 1981; *Dead Men Don't Wear Plaid*, 1982; *The Man with Two Brains*, 1983; *All of Me*, 1984; *The Lonely Guy*, 1984; *Three Amigos!*, 1986; *Little Shop of Horrors*, 1986; *Roxanne*, 1987; *Planes, Trains & Automobiles*, 1987; *Dirty Rotten Scoundrels*, 1988; *Parenthood*, 1989; *My Blue Heaven*, 1990; *L.A. Story*, 1991; *Grand Canyon*, 1991; *Father of the Bride*, 1991; *Leap of Faith*, 1992; *House Sitter*, 1992; *Mixed Nuts*, 1994; *Father of the Bride Part II*, 1995; *Sgt. Bilko*, 1996; *The Spanish Prisoner*, 1997; *The Out-of-Towners*, 1999; *Bowfinger*, 1999

Selected Books: *Picasso at the Lapin Agile and Other Plays*, 1996; *Pure Drivel*, 1998; *Shopgirl: A Novella*, 2000

McBride, Christian

May 31, 1972– Jazz bassist. Address: c/o Verve Records/Universal, 555 W. 57th St., 10th Fl., New York, NY 10019

Among the younger generation of jazz musicians, Christian McBride is arguably the foremost bassist on the scene today. With his five solo recordings, *Gettin' to It* (1994), *Number Two Express* (1995), *Fingerpainting: The Music of Herbie Hancock* (1997), *A Family Affair* (1998), and *Sci-Fi* (2000), as well as performances on numerous albums by other artists, he has fashioned a style that echoes the work of his forebears in hard bop as well as the music of James Brown and other masters of funk. After a short stint with saxophonist Joshua Redman's group in the early 1990s, McBride became the leader of his own groups, which have included such up-and-coming musicians as trumpeter Nicholas Payton and tenor saxophonist Tim Warfield. "The primary role of the bass is to be a support instrument," McBride told *GQ* (February 1999). "It's more satisfying when you are doing that well than when you are taking your solo. The frequency of the instrument is so low that if you're not trying to play something both simple and profound, it becomes a big muddle that people can barely hear." A one-time student at the Juilliard School, McBride has been compared by critics to such great jazz bassists as Ray Brown, Paul Chambers, Ron Carter, and Charles Mingus. "[When] I'm walking

Barron Claiborne/Outline Press

Christian McBride

the bass, and everyone's foot is tapping, and heads are nodding," McBride told GQ, "that's when I know I'm doing my job."

Christian McBride was born in Philadelphia, Pennsylvania, on May 31, 1972. His father, Lee Smith, worked successfully as a bassist throughout the 1970s with such R&B groups as the Delfonics, Major Harris, and Blue Magic. His father's example inspired Christian to pick up the electric bass at the age of eight. "I started very young, and it was just an instrument," McBride told *GQ* (February 1999). "Since I never thought of my father as being in the background, I never thought of the bass as being a background instrument." Since he was a teenager, McBride has been a big fan of soul singer James Brown, whom he credits with influencing his own work. But it took an uncle—who was himself a bassist—to spark McBride's interest in jazz, by giving him a stack of old records. Among them was a 1953 session at Massey Hall, in Toronto, Canada, featuring the bebop masters Charlie Parker, Dizzy Gillespie, Bud Powell, and Max Roach. The recording, according to McBride, changed his outlook toward music.

Before long, McBride had developed into an accomplished musician, and in 1985 he succeeded in getting a spot among the freshman class at Philadelphia's High School for Creative and Performing Arts. There he studied classical bass while taking private lessons from respected bassist Neil Courtney, who was then a member of the Philadelphia Orchestra. When McBride was 15 a stroke of luck sent him on the road to jazz stardom: his bass teacher at the time (apparently, Courtney was no longer instructing him) was friendly with the influential jazz trumpeter and composer Wynton Marsalis, and he took McBride to a workshop held by the artist. When the two were introduced, McBride told Marsalis that he was familiar with all of his music, and during the workshop Marsalis called McBride up to jam on a duet. Marsalis was so impressed with the young musician—who already knew that particular Marsalis composition by heart—that the trumpeter began periodically calling McBride while on the road, to inquire about how his instruction was progressing. Before long, McBride—still in high school—was receiving invitations from pianist Marcus Roberts, and others among Marsalis's band members, to jam with them on their solo gigs when they passed through Philadelphia.

By the time McBride graduated from high school, he had been given a scholarship to the prestigious Juilliard School, in New York City, and had generated a considerable buzz in progressive jazz circles. During the one year that he attended Juilliard, he played alongside such bandleaders as Bobby Watson, Freddie Hubbard, and Benny Green. Then he served as a sideman for Joshua Redman. "[McBride's] sense of what's appropriate is incredible," Redman would later tell Peter Watrous for the *New York Times* (March 7, 1995). "When I'd be soloing, I'd listen to what he was doing for inspiration, playing off his rhythms and his harmonies. His tone and execution are so strong that you can hear what he's doing clearly. If anybody is a musical genius, he's it." Among McBride's early studio recordings are Ray Brown's *Super Bass* (1989), Roy Hargrove's *Public Eye* (1990), and an eponymous album by Kenny Kirkland (1991). Soon, McBride, Redman, and several other innovative yet commercially minded young jazz musicians came to be known collectively as the "Young Lions." Infiltrating the genre in the late 1980s and early 1990s, these artists embraced the professional standards and respect for tradition advocated by Marsalis since the early 1980s.

After playing on Joshua Redman's debut recording, *Joshua Redman* (1993), McBride went into the studio to make a record of his own, *Gettin' to It* (1994). In addition to Redman, McBride used other up-and-coming musicians on the album: the trumpeter Roy Hargrove, drummer Lewis Nash, pianist Cyrus Chestnut, and trombonist Steve Turre. "McBride's big rock-solid tone and melodic agility give his playing the properties of a horn . . . ," Richard S. Ginell wrote for the *All-Music Guide* (on-line) of the then–22-year-old's debut effort, "yet his ideas as a leader were not yet as imaginative as his bass playing. One exception—and easily the most entertaining and musical track on the CD—is the birth on records of McBride's bass trio with mentor Ray Brown and veteran Milt Hinton in 'Splanky'; you'd never guess that three unaccompanied bassists could make such sublimely enjoyable music. Another is the title track, whose funky tune and rhythm are audibly inspired by James Brown." Although not hailed as a masterpiece, *Gettin' to It* received generally positive reviews and established the young bassist as a bandleader in his own right.

McBride hit the road in support of the album, and the tour played to large crowds and critical praise. "Jazz is an idiom in which musicians usually require years of conditioning and experience to create a mature statement," Peter Watrous wrote. "Mr. McBride, who is 22, plays with a polish and a confidence that belie his age. Yet his improvisations burst with the freshness associated with youth. His playing is perfectly edited. His intonation is beyond reproach. His logical note choices suggest somebody who has spent years absorbing music." "It's eye opening to call the shots," McBride told Watrous, discussing the experience of leading a band. "I've never been responsible for having to create a comfortable atmosphere. I've always had people making it comfortable for me. You have to check that everybody's satisfied playing the music, you have to be a leader, and crucially, you have to have the ability to pick musicians that can complement the music."

McBride's second studio effort, *Number Two Express* (1995), featured several established jazz artists, among them alto saxophonist Gary Bartz, pianist Kenny Barron, and drummer Jack DeJohnette. Another commercial success, that record fortified McBride's position as one of the most prominent bassists on the jazz scene. Still, McBride drew criticism from some corners; the saxophonist Branford Marsalis, Wynton's brother, for example, argued that McBride's critically acclaimed and crowd-pleasing renditions of standards and relatively safe newer compositions brought the young bassist dangerously close to musical stagnation. "If they [McBride, Redman, and others] don't start playing music that's more challenging, they're not going to have much of a jazz credibility . . . ," Marsalis told Joseph Hooper for the *New York Times Magazine* (June 25, 1995). When the Marsalis brothers were McBride's age, he said, "we were so cocky and arrogant, we just played what we wanted to play and gave the middle finger to anyone who tried to tell us otherwise. I think it's that kind of hubris that actually made it work. What's ironic to me is that you have a whole legion of musicians being lauded for what Wynton and I were roasted for, for being neoclassicists, and our stuff was way less mainstream than what you have now." Responding to the criticism, McBride told Hooper, "Sooner or later I'm going to have to develop my writing skills so I'll be able to write something more on the edge."

Over the next two years, McBride toured with his quartet throughout the U.S. and abroad. While his lineup occasionally changed, his focus remained the same—to build up his jazz credentials while attempting to add innovation to his tradition-based, hard-bop sound. His next effort, *Fingerpainting: The Music of Herbie Hancock*, released in 1997, featured Nicholas Payton and guitarist Mark Whitfield and garnered positive reviews from critics but did not sell as well as McBride's two previous albums. Evident on the record was the funk influence of James Brown, as Scott Yanow wrote for the *All-Music Guide* (on-line). "McBride shows throughout why he is rightfully considered a young giant. Due to the many unfamiliar themes and offbeat instrumentation (which includes a duet apiece featuring each of the three possible combinations), this is a CD that takes a few listens to fully appreciate, but it is worth the effort. An underrated gem." McBride followed up that release with *A Family Affair* (1998), which further flexed the bassist's funk muscle, as he combined traditional jazz with 1970s-style bass rhythms. The record was a tremendous critical and commercial success. "Hallelujah! Christian McBride is not one of those straitlaced, down-the-line neo-boppers after all," Richard S. Ginell wrote for the *All-Music Guide* (on-line). "Here, the prodigiously talented young standup bassist proves that he is also an astoundingly gifted electric bassist, and that '70s-vintage funk and soul is every bit as close to his heart as '50s and '60s hard bop. On electric, McBride weaves inventive countermelodies around tenor sax Tim Warfield's lead lines, taking Jaco Pastorius' technique a step further in sheer speed and the ability to play really nasty funk patterns. . . . This is a most encouraging step out of the trap of lockstep bop for McBride." *Sci-Fi*, McBride's fifth solo effort, was released on September 12, 2000. In the *All-Music Guide* (on-line), Paula Edelstein described the album as "a seminal work by seminal artists" that "should be considered one of the most essential jazz recordings of the 21st century."

When not on tour or making his own records, McBride enjoys recording on other artists' albums, most recently Joshua Redman's *Introducing Joshua Redman* (1999), Bobby Hutcherson's *Skyline* (1999), and Don Braden's *Fire Within* (1999). McBride has also appeared in two feature films—Raymond De Felitta's *Cafe Society* (1995) and Robert Altman's *Kansas City* (1996). "Someone got on me for smiling too much on stage," McBride told Hooper. "I say, get out of my face, I'm having fun. I'm not going to frown because it looks hipper in your eyes. He certainly wouldn't have said that to Dizzy Gillespie. I guess when the music got more serious and searching in the 60's, to look gleeful probably wouldn't match. But we're playing happy music, so why not look like it? I didn't watch James Brown all those years for nothing." — M.B.

Suggested Reading: *All-Music Guide* (on-line); *Down Beat* p24+ Feb. 1997, with photos; *GQ* p168+ Feb. 1999, with photos; *New York Times* C p13 Mar. 7, 1995, with photo; *New York Times Magazine* p34+ June 25, 1995, with photos

Selected Recordings: *Gettin' to It*, 1994; *Number Two Express*, 1995; *Fingerpainting: The Music of Herbie Hancock*, 1997; *A Family Affair*, 1998; *Sci-Fi*, 2000; as contributor—*Testimonial*, 1994; *So Many Stars*, 1995; *To Ella with Love*, 1996;

Fire Within, 1999; *Absolute Benson*, 2000; *Our Mister Brooks*, 2000

Craig Blankenhorn/Outline Press

McCarver, Tim

Oct. 16, 1941– Baseball commentator. Address: c/o RLR Associates, 7 W. 51st St., 4th Fl., New York, NY 10019

Few sports broadcasters command as much respect for their knowledgeable, impartial, and at times trenchant analyses as Tim McCarver. Never was this more clear than when the New York Mets, two months before the opening of the 1999 baseball season, dismissed McCarver, who had by then served for 16 years as the team's play-by-play man and color analyst. Ordinarily such a move wouldn't make many waves, since announcers regularly come and go, move from city to city, and graduate from local to national markets. But the sacking (which happened over the phone) of a nationally renowned baseball expert and local sports fixture outraged the city's sports press, many of whom view television and radio announcers as journalists who sketch first drafts of every game's history rather than as corporate spokespeople who plug a product. Although the press clamored for an explanation, the Mets offered none. "Rumors remain that it was Mets manager Bobby Valentine who pulled the trigger," Roger Angell wrote in a profile of McCarver for the *New Yorker* (September 6, 1999), "because of McCarver's persistent and terrifyingly clear presentations, over the air, of some awaiting pickle or tactical miasma that the smiling skipper might have just brought upon himself with his latest pitching or pinch-hitting move." "I always tried to give the fans the honest truth," McCarver told Richard Sandomir for the *New York Times* (February 4, 1999) right after his ouster.

McCarver, who has routinely displayed a fondness for the teams he covers, wore major-league uniforms himself from 1959 to 1980; a two-time All-Star Game catcher with a lifetime batting average of .272, he played mostly for the St. Louis Cardinals and the Philadelphia Phillies. The uproar over his dismissal, and his subsequent hiring by Fox Sports to call New York Yankee games, reminded baseball aficionados of what a valuable commodity he had become and of what sets him apart from so many others in his profession. "Tim is unapologetic about bringing an intellectual perspective to the game," Steve Hirdt, the executive vice president of the Elias Sports Bureau, which compiles statistics for the organization known as Major League Baseball, told Roger Angell. "Better than anyone, he understands that baseball has this great capacity that allows fans to play along in their minds. He has also stayed current with the players of the day, and connects his opinion about the specific play—whether to bunt or not bunt, that sort of thing—with the abilities of the batter and the infielders he's looking at. He's as well prepared as anyone I've ever dealt with."

Although McCarver has often been criticized for talking too much and, more recently, for his outspokenness, he is among baseball's most popular commentators. He has covered 10 of the last 12 World Series and has earned 10 Emmy Award nominations. McCarver has been associated with ABC Sports, CBS, and, for the last four years, Fox Sports. *Talking Sports with Tim McCarver*, which offers his editorials on sports-related issues, airs daily on radio stations throughout the U.S. and Canada. On his weekly half-hour cable-television series *The Tim McCarver Show*, he interviews athletes and others connected with the world of sports. According to a blurb on his Web site, "His humor, wit, insight, and affability bring out the best in his guests." McCarver's three books—*Oh, Baby, I Love It! Baseball Summers, Hot Pennant Races, Grand Salamis, Jellylegs, El Swervos, Dingers and Dunkers* (1987), co-written with Ray Robinson, and the two books that he co-wrote with Danny Peary, *Tim McCarver's Baseball for Brain Surgeons and Other Fans: Understanding and Interpreting the Game So You Can Watch It Like a Pro* (1998) and *The Perfect Season: Why 1998 Was Baseball's Greatest Year* (1999)—are considered important additions to the vast library of baseball literature, and they confirm McCarver's status among the game's foremost scholars.

The fourth of the five children of a police officer and his wife, James Timothy McCarver was born on October 16, 1941 in Memphis, Tennessee, where he grew up with his brothers and older sister in a working-class Irish neighborhood. According to Roger Angell, McCarver "attributes his athletic and intellectual persistence to his father." His sister, Marilyn, an outstanding athlete, helped him hone his skills at baseball. "When I was five," McCarver told William Plummer for *People* (February 10, 1992), "Marilyn, being quirky, said, 'Why don't you turn around and hit the other way?' It's the only thing I do left-handed." He and another boy spent many hours playing a game they called corkball, which involved hitting a tape-wrapped cork with a broomstick and taking turns announcing the action. They tried to emulate Harry Caray, who was then a radio sportscaster for the St. Louis Cardinals. "It didn't matter how we played, but how we announced, how much we sounded like Harry," McCarver told Angell. As a youngster he sold peanuts at games of the Memphis Chicks, a popular Class AA Southern League team. (In 1978 the Chicks named their stadium after McCarver.) He donned catcher's equipment at age 10.

McCarver attended the Roman Catholic–run Christian Brothers High School, where two of his teachers awakened in him a love for the classics. In high school he established himself as a standout in football as well as baseball. By the time he graduated, in 1959, he had become one of the most sought-after young players in the country. He turned down offers of football scholarships from both the University of Tennessee and Notre Dame University to sign a contract with the Cardinals, who had enticed him with a $75,000 bonus. In off-seasons during the next seven years, he took courses at Memphis State University and the University of Oklahoma.

As a Cardinal, McCarver immediately entered a much wider world than the environment of his upbringing, which had been largely segregated racially. In an interview with Pete Dexter for *Esquire* (April 1985), he recalled that one day during his first spring training, he took a seat in the team's bus across from the future Hall of Famer Bob Gibson. "I was a 17-year-old kid with a bottle of Nehi orange pop who'd hardly even spoken to anybody black. Gibson saw it right away, where I was from. He said, 'Hey, kid, let me have a swallow of that. . . .' I looked at his mouth and then at the lip of the bottle. I said, 'I'll save you some.'" He and Gibson later became close friends, as did he and Joe Torre, with whom he roomed when the Cardinals were on the road. According to Angell, Torre remembers McCarver reading Aleksandr Solzhenitsyn's novel *The Gulag Archipelago* and other literary works before going to sleep.

In the summer of 1959, his first season in professional baseball, McCarver played in the majors for a month, getting four hits in 24 at-bats. For the next two seasons he alternated between the minors and majors, hitting lightly in very limited playing time. Then, in 1963, the Cardinals assigned him to everyday catching duties. The following year he hit .288 during the team's successful run for the National League Pennant, and in the grueling 1964 World Series, which pitted the Cardinals against the New York Yankees, the 22-year-old began to turn heads. Emerging as a clutch batsman, he slammed the winning hit—a 10th-inning three-run homer—in game five. The blast gave St. Louis a 3–2 lead in the series, which they clinched in the seventh game. McCarver hit .478 in the series, with five RBIs.

In 1967 the Cardinals conquered the Boston Red Sox in a seven-game World Series, in which McCarver got only three hits in 24 at-bats. The following year, in another seven-game nailbiter, which St. Louis lost to the Detroit Tigers, the catcher hit .333, with a home run and four RBIs. By 1970, when he was traded to the Philadelphia Phillies, McCarver had become known as a solid contact hitter who would not provide much power but wouldn't strike out often and who could deliver a clutch hit. In recognition of that and of his defensive skills behind the plate, he was chosen to play in All-Star Games in 1966 and 1967.

In the 44 games that McCarver played during his first year in Philadelphia, he continued his solid hitting. In 1971 he took over full-time catching duties and posted good numbers—a .278 average with eight homers and 46 RBIs. This proved to be his last truly strong season. During the next five years, McCarver was shuffled from the Phillies to the Montreal Expos, back to St. Louis, over to the Red Sox in the American League, and finally back to the Phillies, where he ended his career on the field. His best season during this period was in 1973, when he saw limited playing time as the Cardinals' first baseman. The veteran catcher also served the Phillies well during his second stint with the team, when he backed up and mentored the young All-Star Bob Boone and helped to handle the Phillies' pitching staff. The Phillies won their division three times while McCarver was on the squad. He was played sparsely during the postseason in those years but contributed both as a pinch hitter and as pitching ace Steve Carlton's personal catcher during the regular season. Although McCarver retired after the 1979 season, in which he hit .241, the Phillies suited him up for six games during 1980 so that he would become the only modern-era catcher to play in four different decades—a rare feat because of the daunting physical demands of the position.

McCarver wasn't on the Phillies postseason roster in 1980, when they became world champions for the first time; however, he did don the Phillies' uniform to serve as an on-field interviewer during their successful World Series campaign. That experience marked the start of his second career, which he and Phillies officials had envisioned since the late 1970s, when they agreed that upon his retirement McCarver would join the celebrated former Phillie center-fielder Richie Ashburn and others on the franchise's crack broadcasting team. McCarver trained for three months in a local studio by calling the action for videotaped games that had been muted. In an interview with Glen Waggoner for *Esquire* (September 1986), he said that "all the Phillies announcers were extraordinarily helpful" to him. In 1981 he went on the air full-time. Two years later he began his long tenure with the Mets, moving easily between play-by-play and color responsibilities. In 1984 he began to moonlight for ABC as a reporter who roved the stands during the National League Championship Series. The following year, just days before the start of the World Series, a spot opened in the network's broadcasting team, after Howard Cosell was fired (immediately following the publication of his autobiography, which was harshly critical of his colleagues). Named as Cosell's replacement, McCarver remained with ABC until 1989, when he moved to CBS for four years. During the strike-shortened 1994 season, McCarver worked at ABC. In 1996 he moved to Fox.

"To succeed as a major leaguer, you must be able to adjust and adapt continually, and that's what I've tried to do as a broadcaster," Tim McCarver remarked in his book *Baseball for Brain Surgeons and Other Fans*. As a sports announcer, he has learned, for example, to avoid starting a lengthy story when there are two men out and to choose words and anecdotes carefully so as to avoid diminishing the audience's visceral experience of the game. In his book, he wrote that Richie Ashburn, "the minimalist among sports broadcasters," had advised him, "If you don't have anything to say, don't say it." "A simple but wise statement," McCarver observed. Far from a minimalist himself, he is known for the rhetorical flourishes that elevate his broadcasting above the banal. Once, for instance, while covering the Chicago Cubs' record-breaking 1997 losing streak, McCarver quoted from Shakespeare's play *Love's Labour Lost* as the camera panned the sullen faces in the Cubs' dugout: "Mirth cannot move a soul in agony," he intoned. Prominent among those qualities that have made McCarver a much-in-demand baseball authority is his ability to place what is basically just a game in the larger context of human experience, much as Shakespeare was able to illuminate the universal in events happening in remote times and locales. This skill is not unique to McCarver, of course; it is almost de rigueur for sportscasters to talk about the mythic aspects of baseball as an integral part of American history and culture. But McCarver is widely considered more adept than his many colleagues at illuminating the splendor of momentous occasions without sliding into bathos. He got the nod to call the game—played on September 8, 1998—in which Mark McGwire hit his record-shattering 62d home run of the season.

Among McCarver's abilities are his highly developed powers of observation and an uncanny prescience that enables him to predict correctly, and with unusual frequency, the way a particular strategic move will pan out. A weakly hit fly ball will drop in for a base hit in front of an outfielder whom McCarver has just chastised for playing too deep, for example, or a sharply hit grounder will sling by a diving first baseman whom McCarver has observed too jealously hugging the first-base line. Despite complaints sounded by skippers who bore the brunt of his critiques, by 1986 McCarver had received offers to manage the Montreal Expos and the Minnesota Twins and to serve as general manager for the St. Louis Cardinals, all of which he turned down. Recognizing McCarver's uncommon talents, CBS network executives expanded his exposure by having him cover the 1992 Winter Olympic Games, held in Albertville, France. As a supporting player in the large Olympic broadcasting team, he earned many failing grades from the media. In the *New York Times* (March 1, 1992), however, Richard Sandomir rose to his defense. "CBS didn't let McCarver be McCarver," Sandomir argued. "His duties—to read scripts off TelePrompTers, tell stories about athletes to fill time, manufacture immediate chemistry with his co-host, Paula Zahn, and work in fits and starts until 5 A.M.—conspired against McCarver's talents for wit, analysis, and spontaneity." Despite carping from media critics, McCarver described his Olympics stint to Sandomir as "the experience of a lifetime."

When *Baseball for Brain Surgeons and Other Fans* came out, in 1998, McCarver's status as a baseball savant and as the game's leading analyst was reinforced. The book covers practically every aspect of the game, from pitching to batting to fielding to managing; it includes McCarver's interpretations of baseball strategy, a description of the several-hour-long routine McCarver himself goes through prior to each telecast, and anecdotes culled from McCarver's playing career and his longtime associations and friendships with some of baseball's most colorful personalities. According to an on-line reviewer for Amazon.com, "McCarver goes into impressively thorough detail, which is his ultimate strength and occasional weakness. . . . He's an engaging storyteller, he never hides his biases, and while he's naturally strong on his perceptions into the game's most primal relationship of pitcher and catcher, he's never less than major league everywhere else around the diamond." McCarver's most recent book, *The Perfect Season* (1999), argues that the astonishing events of 1998—the Yankees' 125 wins, Mark McGwire's and Sammy Sosa's home-run race, and the perfect game that the Yankees' David Wells pitched against the Minnesota Twins, to name just a few—made that year's baseball season the best in the history of professional sports.

McCarver and the former Anne McDaniel were married in 1964. The couple have two grown daughters, Kathy and Kelly. — M.C.

Suggested Reading: *Esquire* p46+ Apr. 1985, with photo, p15 Sep. 1986; *New York Times* B p20 Oct. 2, 1987, with photo, C p1+ June 17, 1992, with photos; *New Yorker* p28+ Sep. 6, 1999; *People* p47+ Feb. 10, 1992; *TV Guide* p26+ Oct. 5, 1996, with photos;

Selected Books: as co-author—*Baseball Summers, Hot Pennant Races, Grand Salamis, Jellylegs, El Swervos, Dingers and Dunkers* (with Ray Robinson), 1987; *Tim McCarver's Baseball for Brain Surgeons and Other Fans: Understanding and Interpreting the Game So You Can Watch It Like a Pro* (with Danny Peary), 1998; *The Perfect Season: Why 1998 Was Baseball's Greatest Year* (with Danny Peary), 1999

Jason Trigg/Archive Photos

McDaniel, James

Mar. 25, 1958– Actor. Address: NYPD Blue, *Steven Bochco Productions, 20th Century Fox TV, 10201 W. Pico Blvd., Los Angeles, CA 90035*

By the time actor James McDaniel was hired, in 1993, to play Lieutenant Arthur Fancy on ABC-TV's police drama *NYPD Blue*, a role that brought him to the attention of millions of viewers every week, he had already appeared in more than 75 theatrical productions, several movies, and numerous television guest shots. But it is as the sensible and dignified police lieutenant that he is best known. The show's sole black character, Fancy commands respect with his stern but compassionate manner, as he calmly presides over the chaos of the fictitious squad room. He wisely mediates disputes among the diverse band of detectives under his command, while always maintaining his sense of decorum. McDaniel is proud that he provides one of the few strong black role models on television. "More than anything, my character is a Black man in control of a situation and I show what a Black man goes through," he said in an interview for *Jet* magazine (February 20, 1995).

McDaniel was born at Children's Hospital in Washington, D.C., on March 25, 1958. His father, James, an obstetrician, and mother, Miriam, a computer programmer, divorced when McDaniel was 12 years old, and he was sent to a series of boarding schools, earning his high-school diploma in 1976. In an attempt to combine his love of horses with a medical career that would satisfy his father, he then enrolled at the veterinary school of the University of Pennsylvania, but he was unhappy there. Along with his older sister, Nan, who eventually became a lawyer, he had harbored childhood dreams of acting. In 1980, having participated in only one high-school production, and with only $600 to his name, he moved to New York to study voice and dance. He remembers this time as unhappy, because his mother died soon after his move, and his father, angry about his decision to leave school, refused to speak to him. (They have since reconciled.)

While living at a YMCA, McDaniel soon braved his first audition—for a role as a basketball player in a cola commercial. He got the part, and the spot won a Clio Award (the advertising industry's equivalent of an Oscar). The royalties from the ad supported him while he looked for other parts, which gradually began to come his way. The producers of the Off-Broadway production *A Soldier's Play* needed someone who could play the harmonica and guitar, and McDaniel, who had been doing both since he was young, got the role. Other jobs soon followed, and he was seldom without work. He originated the role of Paul Poitier in the play *Six Degrees of Separation* (1990), by John Guare, which was later made into a movie starring Will Smith. McDaniel's portrayal of Paul, a clever young black man who cons his way into the homes of liberal whites by playing on their guilt and social insecurity, won him a coveted Clarence Derwent Award. He earned both an Obie Award and a Drama Desk Award nomination for his characterization of Wendal Bailey, a bisexual black musician who is stricken with AIDS, in the 1992 New York production of Cheryl L. West's drama *Before It Hits Home*. He won equally favorable reviews for his work in both the London and 1992 Broadway runs of *Someone Who'll Watch Over Me*, a play by Frank McGuiness about three hostages in Beirut. Critics found the performance all the more remarkable because McDaniel's character has one foot chained to the wall during the entire show, and the script called for him to do 150 push-ups in the course of each performance.

Meanwhile, McDaniel had also appeared in several motion pictures, among them Woody Allen's *Alice* (1990)—an unusual casting decision for Allen, who has rarely featured black actors in his pictures. McDaniel worked with the acclaimed director Spike Lee in 1992, when he played Brother Earl in the movie *Malcolm X*, a role for which he did extensive research into the Muslim faith and the history of the period. Meanwhile, television work was plentiful. He acted in several miniseries, including

The Old Man and the Sea (1990), *Murder in Black and White* (1990), and *Internal Affairs* (1988). He also did numerous guest shots on shows as diverse as the sitcom *Kate and Allie* and the drama *Crime Story.*

McDaniel met the producer Steven Bochco in the mid-1980s, when he appeared briefly on the popular show *Hill Street Blues.* Thus began one of the most gratifying professional relationships of McDaniel's career. Bochco cast him in the short-running experimental series *Cop Rock*, a quirky combination of traditional police drama and musical numbers. Although the show wasn't a success, Bochco immediately thought of McDaniel again when he was casting *NYPD Blue*, a more conventional police drama scheduled to debut in the fall of 1993 on ABC-TV. "I can't imagine anyone else in that role," Bochco told Mark Nollinger for *TV Guide* (August 15, 1998), explaining his choice of McDaniel for the part of Arthur Fancy. "He does so much with so little. He brings context to every moment, and that's a remarkable gift." Although Fancy is in charge of the squad room, he is generally given fewer lines than the other detectives, because while the story lines often follow the police beats and personal lives of the other main characters, viewers typically see Fancy only at the precinct. That situation has been slowly changing, and some episodes have focused on Fancy—most notably during the 1996 season, in which he confronted a subordinate officer, played by Dennis Franz, who used the word "nigger." The episode garnered wide media attention for its realistic look at racism, and McDaniel's performance was lauded for its strength and sensitivity.

McDaniel lives with his wife, Hannelore, and their two sons, Dorian and Evan, in Los Angeles. He is still fond of New York, where he recently had an unsettling experience: Two police officers slapped handcuffs on him and hustled him into their squad car for jaywalking in Midtown Manhattan. At first he felt angry; indeed, aware of several highly publicized incidents of police violence against black males in the city, McDaniel admitted that he would have been "terrified" if one of the officers had not been black. When one of his captors turned to him and asked, "So where can we take you, Lieutenant Fancy?," McDaniel realized he had been the victim of a practical joke played by overzealous fans. (*NYPD Blue's* most avid watchers include police officers.) Although the officers catered to him, by bringing him to his destination, and he gave them some promotional pins he happened to be carrying, he felt shaken by their action, because in real life McDaniel has been a frequent victim of racial slights. (Once, although he was wearing an expensive Armani suit, an elevator operator assumed he was a deliveryman.) Before he said goodbye to the officers, he gently lectured them on the foolishness of their behavior—in much the same effective way that his television character might reprimand his subordinates. —M.R.

Suggested Reading: *ABC.com* (on-line); *Jet* p63 Feb. 20, 1995, with photo; *TV Guide* p18+ Aug. 15, 1998, with photos; *Washington Post* p7 Jan. 19, 1997, with photo

Selected Films: *Alice*, 1990; *Malcolm X*, 1992; *Truth or Consequences*, 1997; *Silencing Mary*, 1998

Selected Television Shows: *NYPD Blue*, 1993; *Alex Haley's Queen*, 1993

Selected Plays: *Six Degrees of Separation*, 1990; *Someone Who'll Watch Over Me*, 1993

Courtesy of AFSCME

McEntee, Gerald W.

(MAK-en-tee)

Jan. 11, 1935– President of the American Federation of State, County, and Municipal Employees. Address: AFSCME, 1625 L St. N.W., Washington, DC 20036-5687

Gerald W. McEntee is the international president of the American Federation of State, County, and Municipal Employees (AFSCME), the second-largest union, and one of the fastest-growing, in the American Federation of Labor–Congress of Industrial Organizations (AFL-CIO), the national umbrella organization for many labor-related groups. The 1.3 million-member AFSCME represents secretaries, clerks, social workers, park and recreation workers, employment counselors, school and highway employees, health-care specialists, and other people who work (or have worked) for government agencies. AFSCME encompasses three national organizations: the 50,000-member United Nurses of America, which serves as an advocate for professional nurses and quality health care; the 100,000-member AFSCME Corrections United, lobbying for the interests of corrections officers on issues such as privatization; and the 200,000-member AFSCME Retirees, promoting issues such as public-sector pensions and retirement benefits. According to the AFSCME Web site, Nelson Mandela, the antiapartheid leader and former president of South Africa, has said that AFSCME is "unique" in that it is "the voice of working people." Joseph Califano Jr., a former secretary of the U.S. Department of Health, Education, and Welfare (now the Department of Health and Human Services), has said that AFSCME is "the nation's most powerful and effective union."

President of AFSCME since 1981, McEntee has been involved in efforts to overhaul the health-care system and is a member of the Health Care Reform Project, a coalition of consumers, businesses, labor organizations, and health-care providers dedicated to enacting comprehensive health-care reform. He is also a co-founder and chairman of the board of a Washington, D.C.–based think tank, the Economic Policy Institute.

Gerald W. McEntee was born in Philadelphia on January 11, 1935. His father, Bill McEntee, was a garbage-truck driver who organized Philadelphia's first city employees' union, in 1938, and led the strike that forced the city to acknowledge the union's power. As Laura Winter reported in the *Philadelphia Daily News* (June 23, 2000, on-line), young Gerald "ate his scrapple while his father told the family about pitched battles between city workers, the mounted police and the strike-breakers under their protection." Gerald McEntee studied economics at La Salle College and did graduate work at Temple University, both of which are in Philadelphia, and at Harvard University's Trade Union Program, in Cambridge, Massachusetts.

In 1958, after a stint in the military, McEntee—"more out of familiarity than fervor," as Julie Kosterlitz put it in *National Journal* (August 2, 1997)—became an AFSCME organizer in Philadelphia. Founded in 1936, AFSCME grew out of efforts of Wisconsin state employees to unionize as a way of preventing the state government from abolishing civil-service examinations in favor of a political patronage or "spoils" system. Its first president, Arnold Zander, served for 28 years; under his successor, Jerry Wurf, AFSCME pushed successfully for collective-bargaining laws throughout the country, thus helping to raise the living standards of its members, and its membership grew from 200,000 to more than a million. The growth of the union during the 1960s resulted in part from the successes of the civil rights movement. In one landmark victory, in 1968, African-American sanitation workers in Memphis, Tennessee, went on strike to gain recognition of their union—Local 1733 of the AFSCME. The assassination of the civil rights leader Martin Luther King Jr., who had come to Memphis to help their cause, led the city government to acquiesce to the union's demands.

During the 1960s McEntee spearheaded the drive to unionize more than 75,000 Pennsylvania state employees. He was elected executive director of AFSCME Council 13 at the founding convention, in 1973; he became international vice president of AFSCME in the following year. Over the next two decades, the union turned from militancy to politics, forming a political-action committee (PAC) to deal with state legislatures. The committee has since become one of the largest PACs in the country. Unlike many unions, AFSCME continued to grow during the 1970s, affiliating independent associations of public employees. Upon Jerry Wurf's death, in 1981, McEntee was elected president of AFSCME, becoming one of the youngest presidents of a major union and representing one million members out of 16 million municipal workers nationally.

McEntee took over AFSCME at a time when many government employees were facing hard times in terms of both job security and public image. According to Ed Townsend, in the *Christian Science Monitor* (December 21, 1981), research showed that 5,934 strikes by government workers, lasting an average of 12 days, had created a 75 percent increase in days lost from 1979 to 1980. In the midst of this volatile climate, the workers' wages were affected by a decline in city revenues and by a growing resistance to tax increases, thanks in large part to Ronald Reagan's election as president in 1980. With intense debates on the national budget and widespread calls for spending reductions, some public employees—such as traffic police and Internal Revenue Service (IRS) auditors—were portrayed as being useless or worse, and others were criticized by political candidates at all levels as overpaid and underworked. During the 1980 presidential campaign, for example, Reagan attacked "faceless bureaucrats," as Martin Tolchin recalled in the *New York Times* (April 13, 1986). Some of the sloganeering was so bombastic that some public officials worried out loud about a threat to the quality of the public work force. Congresswoman Patricia Schroeder, a Colorado Democrat, said that some of the problems in the delivery of government services, such as long lines, were caused directly by cutbacks in government employment. During this period McEntee lamented that "the public employee has been caught in the crossfire of the political rhetoric," according to Tolchin.

Under the guidance of Lane Kirkland, the AFL-CIO president, affiliated unions focused on protecting members' jobs rather than recruiting new members. Perhaps as a result, the labor movement in the U.S. continued to weaken for the next dozen years. McEntee, together with John J. Sweeney, who was then president of the Service Employees

International Union, wanted to change the direction of the AFL-CIO. Together, beginning in about 1993, they planned for two years to challenge Kirkland's presidency. Some of their colleagues resisted, not wanting to see a public fight among labor leaders. But another seven or eight union heads agreed that it was important to shift the union movement's focus to organizing. McEntee's position on Kirkland and the AFL-CIO was, "I don't think loyalty to a person is as important as loyalty to this institution," as Peter T. Kilborn reported in the *New York Times* (September 4, 1995). At a February 1995 meeting of the AFL-CIO executive council, the conflict erupted. Kirkland defended his record while attacking McEntee. "In that room, there was an aura about being president of the AFL-CIO," McEntee told Kilborn. "You were the president of the presidents, the pope of the cardinals. But after [Kirkland] spoke . . . he became one of us. He lost this aura, this distinction that he had." McEntee announced his federation's support for a challenger for the AFL-CIO presidency, and that spring Kirkland resigned, leaving Sweeney to take up the leadership of the AFL-CIO.

In 1996 AFSCME noted that the health-care industry was undergoing significant changes, driven by several factors, including the public demand for low-cost care; the rise in the number of for-profit managed-care organizations; the frequent shift from more-expensive, inpatient treatment sites, such as hospitals, to less-costly, outpatient facilities and patients' homes; interhospital competition due to an oversupply of hospital beds; and finally, because of the aging of the overall population, the changing nature of medical needs. In March 1997 President Bill Clinton appointed McEntee to the Advisory Commission on Consumer Protection and Quality in the Health Care Industry, to recommend measures that would promote "health care quality and value and protect consumers and workers in the health care system," as a commission press release (November 11, 1997) stated. The commission of 34 representatives from business, consumer, labor, health-care, and financing groups held a series of six public hearings around the country, which included testimony from dozens of expert witnesses and representatives from more than 20 national and regional organizations. The commission initially recommended that the health-care industry adopt a Consumer Bill of Rights and Responsibilities, which would support a "stronger relationship of trust among consumers, health care professionals, health care institutions, and health plans" by clarifying the sphere of responsibility of each party. In March 1998 the advisory commission concluded its work with a final report stating that while many patients were well treated, "too many patients receive substandard care." The report found that too many Americans went without needed care, while many others received unneeded services, which raise costs and—since all medical procedures present some risks—may even endanger lives. It went on to say that the quality of health-care delivery varies greatly, even within small geographic areas.

Perhaps the most notable finding was that there were too many avoidable errors made during treatment, which resulted in the deaths of up to 7,000 Americans each year. Representing the 80,000 nurses of the United Nurses Association (UNA), and thus well aware of the factors discouraging health-care workers from reporting errors and making suggestions for improvement, McEntee fought for "whistle blower" protection in the health-care workplace. "Health care workers must be encouraged to identify and report clinical errors . . . and must be protected against retaliatory action," he was quoted as saying on the AFSCME Web page. In one UNA case, the Philadelphia Children's Hospital ended its automatic discipline policy for nurses who make mistakes in chemotherapy and encouraged staff to report errors. As a result, the total number of errors in chemotherapy declined by 90 percent, the AFSCME Web site reported.

In January 2000 AFSCME released a union-generated report documenting in detail illegal activities by 35 local union officials, ranging from the forging of union checks to the use of union credit cards for personal expenses. As Steven Greenhouse pointed out in the *New York Times* (January 21, 2000), many unions never make public their discoveries of embezzlement and other illegal practices by their officials, so "it remain[ed] unclear how the amount stolen [a total of $4.6 million] compare[d] with what has happened at other unions, particularly those better known for struggling with corruption." Echoing the remarks of others interviewed by Greenhouse, Edward A. McDonald, a former director of the Organized Crime Strike Force for Eastern New York (an arm of the Criminal Division of the U.S. Attorney's Office), said, "Any time you have multiple acts of corruption in an international labor organization, it doesn't look good, but if there are 3,000, 4,000 locals and you're talking about three dozen people, it's certainly not a crime wave. . . . The corruption that's reported pales in comparison to the racketeering activities that characterized certain mob-dominated unions throughout the 70's and 80's."

Later in 2000, McEntee hailed the progress made when the House Judiciary Committee approved the Health Care Coalition Act, allowing health-care professionals to join associations for collective bargaining. McEntee said that the balance of power in health care was slanted "in the insurance industry's favor," allowing it to "strong-arm doctors into signing one-sided contracts," which adversely affect professional and ethical standards. The Health Care Coalition Act will "allow health care professionals to collectively negotiate over the quality of care provided to patients" and provide "leverage against insurers who insist upon contracts that harm patients," he continued.

McEntee has declared that "privatization is 'public enemy No.1'" of the labor movement, according to the National Center for Policy Analysis Web site (August 1998). Privatization occurs when the government enters into contracts with private businesses to provide public services and goods. Positive results, such as better management and lower costs, have been associated with privatization, but according to the AFSCME Web site, there may be negative consequences as well. Privatization may encourage corruption, as in the case of contracts used as political payoffs to campaign supporters, and may be used to dilute union representation on projects that involve civil-service workers, especially during periods leading up to negotiations with permanent government employees. The costs of privatized services often rise over time, because private companies must make profits and pay taxes. The overall economic impact of privatization is a lowering of income for government employees and, ultimately, people in the private sector as well, according to the AFSCME. While the number of private-sector jobs may increase to fill the new contracts, these tend to be lower-skilled and to offer lower pay, with benefits, insurance, and retirement pensions sacrificed to the profit margin, the Web site warned.

Under the goad of privatization, McEntee's union has been successful in 90 percent of its attempts to organize in the public sector. Its enrollment has climbed to 1.3 million members, making the AFSCME the second-largest union, after the 1.5 million-member Teamsters Union, in the 80-union AFL-CIO. AFSCME is unique in having a "Members' Bill of Rights," and it offers services "unequaled by any other union," according to the AFSCME Web site. The services are in four areas: workplace issues; legislative and political action; communications and leadership training; and union building. The union prides itself on being strongly democratic. Every local autonomously defines the issues it will address. There are 3,500 local unions and affiliates in 47 states, Puerto Rico, and the District of Columbia. Each writes its own constitution, elects its own officers, and sets the figure for its dues. Union locals may pool their resources by forming regional councils or groups based on occupation. There are 61 councils offering support in bargaining and training, as well as members-only benefits such as low-interest-rate credit cards, home mortgages, legal aid, and scholarships for members' children. Union locals organize campaigns on issues affecting members, among them taxes, health care, social security, and privatization.

McEntee and his wife, Barbara, have four children and live in Washington, D.C. — V.K.

Suggested Reading: AFSCME Web site; *BMWE Journal Online* June/July 1998; *National Journal* p1549+ Aug. 2, 1997, with photos; *New York Times* p7 Sep. 4, 1995 with photo; *Philadelphia Daily News* (on-line) June 23, 2000, with photos

Annie Liebovitz/Courtesy of American Ballet Theatre

McKenzie, Kevin

Apr. 29, 1954– Artistic director of American Ballet Theatre. Address: American Ballet Theatre, Peter T. Joseph Studios, 890 Broadway, New York, NY 10003

For 12 years "danseur noble" Kevin McKenzie gave exquisite performances in most of the important classical ballets presented by the American Ballet Theatre (ABT). McKenzie retired from ABT in 1991, but less than two years later, at a time when the company was plagued with directorial and financial problems that almost caused it to cease operating, he was named ABT's artistic director. With that title he took on the heavy responsibility of restoring ABT to its former status among the most prestigious performing arts organizations in the United States. Although he had no experience directing a company of that magnitude, ABT's dancers and staff cheered him on. "He's very smart, very articulate, and I believe he's got a vision," former ABT ballerina Cynthia Gregory told Terry Trucco for *Dance Magazine* (April 1993). "I also think he will devote himself to the company 100 percent. A lot of big names were being bandied about for the job, but the big names mentioned were not going to give a hundred percent." For his part, McKenzie felt comfortable in his new role at ABT. "Subliminally, I had thought I'd probably run a company one day," he told Trucco. "I displayed an ability to coach, and I was always into making people look better." His confidence seems to have been well placed: since his return, ABT has regained financial solvency, through acclaimed stagings of such classic ballets as *Don Quixote* as well as commissions for new and experimental works.

The youngest of Ruth and Raymond McKenzie's 11 children, Kevin McKenzie was born on April 29, 1954 in Burlington, Vermont, where his grandfather had established a successful meat-packing business. "Burlington was a great little town," McKenzie recalled to Laura Leivick for the *New York Times Magazine* (December 27, 1992). "It was like any New England town then—a little depressed, the weather's severe. But the church was beautiful, a teeny replica of a Gothic cathedral—and I was an altar boy. I completely loved the ceremony, the traipsing about, the robes, the singing; it was my introduction to the theater."

McKenzie's dance training began when he was about seven years old. "My dad's a meat packer, but in his high school days he was the terror of the dance floor," McKenzie told Alan M. Kriegsman for the *Washington Post* (August 1, 1978). "He really wanted to see me doing tap dance in the worst way. When a friend of mine . . . said 'I'm taking tap, why don't you come along,' I did." McKenzie said that in his first tap-dance lessons, he was "a total klutz." One of his sisters was taking ballet, and he began taking classes with her, "thinking maybe I'd learn to stand up long enough to get better at tap," he said. "To my dad's horror . . . I liked ballet, so I gave up the tap idea and stayed."

McKenzie's first teacher, Rosemary O'Brien, saw that both Kevin and his sister had a great deal of natural ability. When McKenzie was 12, O'Brien encouraged the siblings to audition for scholarships to a prestigious ballet school in Washington, D.C., run by Mary Day, who would later found the Washington Ballet Company. Both children won scholarships, and their mother agreed to let them board at the school, which also offered academic subjects. By that time their father, described by McKenzie as "a severe and total alcoholic," had lost interest in his son's dancing, and he never went to any of McKenzie's performances.

Mary Day was particularly enthusiastic about the prospect of teaching Kevin, who was tall, lean, and unusually flexible for a boy. "I think I finally have the makings of a prince," she said upon meeting McKenzie, according to Robert W. Larkin in *Newsday* (May 20, 1979). McKenzie thrived at Day's school, but when he was 15 years old, he became ill and was diagnosed with ulcerative colitis, a severe inflammation of the large intestine. "I was five feet eight inches and weighed 158 pounds before I got sick," he told Leivick. "Afterward, I was six feet one and weighed 124." The colitis recurred several times during McKenzie's dance career, occasionally preventing him from working to his full potential. His treatments, he told Leivick, sometimes left him "chemically depressed" and with "an adrenal system stripped to the bare bones."

In 1972, the year he was to graduate from Mary Day's school, McKenzie won a silver medal at the International Ballet Competition in Varna, Bulgaria, thus becoming one of the youngest Americans ever to capture the prize. "It wasn't until I got to the third stage of elimination—when it suddenly dawned on me that I might actually win something—that I got nervous," he told Kriegsman. "Then I got very nervous, of course. But the whole thing was a tremendous experience for me—I hadn't ever been east or west of the line between Vermont and D.C. before that."

After winning at Varna McKenzie returned to Washington and joined the now-defunct National Ballet. In 1972 he gave his first performance at the Kennedy Center, dancing the male lead role, that of the Romantic poet, in *Les Sylphides*. "It was great fun," he told Kriegsman. During his first season McKenzie was also cast as the male lead in *Swan Lake*, and during one performance he slipped during that ballet's notoriously difficult pas de deux, the ballet term for a dance performed by a ballerina and her partner, a danseur noble. "I fell flat on my face," he told Kriegsman. "I can still remember my face stinging from the floor. The thing was, I managed a very high jump [earlier] in the second variation and I could actually hear the audience responding. So I thought to myself, if you liked that just wait'll you see this, and that's when I took my flop of course. I was so frightened from the fall, I took a breath when I got up and don't think I let it out till the end of the piece." In addition to *Les Sylphides* and *Swan Lake*, McKenzie learned the choreography to many other ballets at the National Ballet; he was taught by Frederic Franklin, a British dancer turned director who was famous for his work with the Ballet Russes de Monte Carlo in the 1940s, and Ben Stevenson, a former dancer with the Royal Ballet of Great Britain. Almost immediately, McKenzie became a favorite with the National Ballet's audiences, especially for his interpretations of the more classical, princely roles, to which he was physically well suited.

By 1974 McKenzie felt ready to take on greater challenges, and he moved to New York City, hoping he would be able to get into a company there. The American Ballet Theatre, a New York–based touring company that was internationally praised for its renditions of classical ballets, was by far his first choice. After auditioning for the company, McKenzie was told that although his dancing was excellent, there were no openings at that time. Hopeful that he would be hired when the company next needed a male dancer, he bided his time. But when a spot became available, it was the Russian dancer Mikhail Baryshnikov, who had just defected to the U.S., who filled it. Disappointed, McKenzie instead joined the prestigious Joffrey Ballet, whose diverse repertoire included many modern ballets. "I do feel most at home in classical roles," the dancer told Kriegsman, "but I find myself really enjoying the more contemporary things too. . . . I think one actually learns things from such new styles of movement that have application in classical roles as well—classicism was never meant to be rigid and inelastic. If you're intelligent about keeping up your classical technique, you can only gain from exposure to other idioms." According to Leivick, after watching McKenzie dance with the Joffrey Ballet in 1977, the critic Clive Barnes wrote that McKenzie was "among the best classic virtuosos in the country."

Then, beginning in 1977, McKenzie suffered a series of physical setbacks that prevented him from performing for almost three full seasons. After recovering from a bout of colitis, he hurt his rib cage while balancing another dancer on his chest in the modern ballet *Heptagon*. Almost as soon as he recovered from that injury, he broke his foot during a rehearsal. In terms of his dancing, that accident was by far the most serious. McKenzie told Larkin that he remembers thinking, "[My foot] may always be stiff. I may never [dance] again."

While recuperating McKenzie began working with the renowned New York ballet teacher Maggie Black, who helped him not only to regain his strength but also to decide what direction he wanted his career to take. "While my foot was healing I started thinking, 'What do I need mentally, what do I really feel?'" he told Larkin. "I've wanted to do *Swan Lake* and *Giselle* . . . and it's not helping me to get there by dancing in a company that doesn't have those roles. So I resolved that once I got better I would finish up with the Joffrey, and take whatever I could get with ABT. I'd swallow my pride and just do it. *Corps de ballet* [the ensemble of a ballet company, as opposed to the soloists] or assistant to the shoe boy."

McKenzie, whose talent was such that he had performed in lead roles since the very beginning of his career, never danced with the corps de ballet at ABT. In April 1979, after he was back on his feet, ABT called on him to undertake the *Holberg* pas de deux—which he had performed frequently at Joffrey—opposite the popular ballerina Martine van Hamel, in Chicago. After that successful engagement, McKenzie was offered a soloist's contract. "I signed it thinking, 'I hope this won't get me in trouble,' because I knew, technically, I was under contract to the Joffrey until the end of the . . . season. . . . It was the first time in my life I ever made a decision to do anything that might possibly get me into trouble. But I didn't care, I wanted to join ABT so badly," he told Larkin.

In December 1979 McKenzie was promoted to the rank of principal dancer by then–company director Lucia Chase. He was the last dancer to be promoted under Chase, who was succeeded by Baryshnikov, the star Russian émigré whose presence had prevented McKenzie from being accepted by ABT a few years earlier. Baryshnikov, who is short, athletic, and bold, was the stylistic opposite of McKenzie, and according to several sources, the two clashed in other ways as well. "I had a real chip on my shoulder," McKenzie explained to Leivick. "I was miserable when he was in my life. . . . I always felt he looked at [the company] and thought, 'Pity they're not Russian.'" The bad feelings between the two dancers came to a head in 1986, when, during an interview for *Dance Magazine*, McKenzie was overtly critical of Baryshnikov's directorial style; Baryshnikov responded with a strongly worded letter to McKenzie, after which the two men talked through their differences. According to Leivick, that was the only time that McKenzie and Baryshnikov actually exchanged angry words.

Baryshnikov kept McKenzie in the company's most important classical roles throughout the 1980s. McKenzie performed lead roles in many of the classics to which he had long aspired—among them *La Bayadère, Carmen, Cinderella, Coppélia, Don Quixote, Giselle, Paquita, Raymonda, Romeo and Juliet, The Sleeping Beauty, Swan Lake, La Sylphide*, and *Les Sylphides*. He also danced lead roles in much of the company's modern repertory, including the ballets *Dim Lustre, The Garden of Villandry, Jardin aux Lilas, The Leaves Are Fading, Pillar of Fire, Requiem, Rodeo, Other Dances, Sylvia Pas de Deux*, and *Theme and Variations*. During his years as a principal dancer with ABT, McKenzie also performed as a guest artist with the London Festival Ballet, the Bolshoi Ballet in Moscow, the National Ballet of Cuba, and the Universal Ballet in Seoul, Korea. McKenzie frequently danced with the first ballerina to serve as his partner at ABT—Martine van Hamel, with whom he had begun a romantic relationship. Meanwhile, although ballet audiences adored him, and reviews of his performances were almost uniformly positive, McKenzie had developed significant self-confidence problems and suffered frequent bouts of colitis, a condition that is worsened by stress. "The only time I was all right during that period was when I was on stage," he told Leivick.

In 1989 McKenzie fell ill with a virus and was hospitalized. He lost 30 pounds and once again needed to take time off from dancing to regain lost strength. While he was recovering, Baryshnikov resigned from his position as artistic director of ABT, and Jane Hermann and Oliver Smith, who had been involved with the direction of the Metropolitan Opera for several years, took his place as co-directors. Because van Hamel couldn't reach an agreement with the new directors about the works she would perform, she resigned, and she and McKenzie moved to Washington, D.C. Van Hamel made appearances with Mary Day's new company, the Washington Ballet, and worked with her own ensemble, the New Amsterdam Ballet, which performed works by new choreographers. McKenzie became an artistic associate with the Washington Ballet, and he continued to make special appearances with ABT until 1991. He also began to choreograph. Reviewing the 1991 premiere of his *Liszt Etudes*, which the New Amsterdam Ballet performed at the Jacob's Pillow dance festival in Massachusetts, Jennifer Dunning of the *New York Times* (August 22, 1991) wrote, "A danseur noble who can act, Mr. McKenzie would never have seemed capable of the tumultuous, Lisztian excesses of *Liszt Etudes*. . . . McKenzie's new ballet sends its eight dancers hurtling headlong through cross-stage runs and slides, sleek pileups and improbable, imaginative lifts as if this were the last dance left before the cataclysm." McKenzie created a second work for the New Amsterdam Ballet, titled *Groupo Zamaria*, and for the Washington Ballet he created *Transcendental Etudes* and the story ballet *Lucy and the Count*.

In 1992, when McKenzie was offered the artistic directorship of ABT, the company was almost $6 million in debt. Dancers and staff had not been paid for several weeks, and much of the company's touring schedule had been canceled. Because he enjoyed his work with Mary Day in Washington, and because his health had been good since moving there, deciding whether to accept the offer was difficult for McKenzie. After a few days of reflection, he told ABT's board of directors that if they met two criteria—that a business manager would be hired and that the board of trustees would fund the remaining performances of the company's touring season—he would accept the position. But even after the board of directors complied with his wishes, he stated bluntly, according to Leivick, "If we don't get through the next 12 to 18 months and get through them right and get rid of the debt, the party's over."

In his first week at ABT, McKenzie fired six dancers and began planning the company's 1993 season at the Metropolitan Opera House in New York, which, for financial reasons, would consist of proven pieces from the company's existing repertoire, with the exception of one new piece—the Royal Ballet's *Manon*. McKenzie felt that *Manon* was an important ballet for the company to acquire because, as he explained to Trucco, "it's a star maker, with those great self-discovery roles, where the dancers have to play real-life, blood-rushing people as opposed to fairy-tale characters. It's theater, real theater."

Indeed, maintaining ABT's sense of theatricality has been one of McKenzie's main goals as artistic director of ABT. He told Anna Kisselgoff of the *New York Times* (May 2, 1993) that he hoped to distinguish the company from the many ballet and modern-dance companies that reflect the strong influence of the late choreographer George Balanchine. Balanchine, he said, choreographed "movement for movement's sake," while ABT's work is about "emotional expression through dance." McKenzie feels that by encouraging expression in his dancers, he will nurture the kinds of performers who will further popularize ballet. "I think we've reached a point where, if the dancers are encouraged to explore their individuality, we will have an environment where stars will emerge," he told Trucco.

Since McKenzie took the helm at ABT, ticket sales have gone up, and the company is now financially sound. McKenzie has choreographed new renditions of the classical ballets *The Nutcracker* and *Don Quixote* for the company; other productions have included *Coppelia* and Jerome Robbins's *Fancy Free* in 1997, *Le Corsaire* in 1998, and *Anastasia* in 1999. McKenzie has also commissioned several new works from such contemporary choreographers as Christian Holder and Lar Lubovitch. In addition, he has begun a second company of young dancers, through which, as he explained to Leivick, he and other choreographers who create experimental works can have the "freedom to fail" without putting ABT's reputation on the line. McKenzie told Alan M. Kriegsman that he has let his experiences as a dancer with ABT more than anything else guide his leadership of the company. "I came of age as an artist [at ABT]," he said. "I know the company inside out, the repertory, the tradition, the texture, the dancers. It's also the place where I lost my focus for a time, where I floundered and grew uncertain. But I learned a lot from the kind of support I got at the time—and didn't get."

Leivick described McKenzie as "tall, with dramatically allongé proportions, lissome and gallant, more understated than dazzling." Describing his hands-on approach to directing the company, one ABT dancer told Trucco, "It's really good to have someone who has done the roles. He'll take what I do and say, 'This is valid, but why not try it this way?'" Principal dancer Amanda McKerrow added, "You're not made to feel like you're getting scolded. He tells you things to make it better." —C.P.

Suggested Reading: *Dance Magazine* p14+ Feb. 1993, with photos, p44+ Apr. 1993, with photos, p12+ May 1993, with photos, p16 Sep. 1993, with photo; *Newsday* II p39 May 20, 1979, with photo; *New York Times* C p13 Aug. 22, 1991, with photo, C p1 Oct. 2, 1992, with photo, II p10 May 2, 1993, with photo, II p39 May 10, 1998, with photo; *New York Times Magazine* p16+ Dec. 27, 1992, with photos; *Washington Post* C p1 Aug. 1, 1978, with photos, G p3 Sep. 12, 1992, B p4 Sep. 15, 1992, G p3 Jan. 31, 1993, with photo

Selected Ballets: as dancer—*La Bayadère*; *Carmen*; *Cinderella*, *Coppélia*; *Dim Lustre*; *Don Quixote*; *The Garden of Villandry*; *Giselle*; *Jardin aux Lilas*; *The Leaves Are Fading*; *Other Dances*; *Paquita*; *Pillar of Fire*; *Raymonda*; *Requiem*; *Rodeo*; *Romeo and Juliet*; *The Sleeping Beauty*; *Swan Lake*; *La Sylphide*; *Les Sylphides*; *Sylvia Pas de Deux*; *Theme and Variations*; as artistic director—*Anastasia*; *Baroque Games*; *Coppélia*; *Le Corsaire*; *Diversion of Angels*; *Don Quixote*; *Fancy Free*; *Jabula*; *The Nutcracker*; *Prodigal Son*; *Sleeping Beauty*; *Tchaikovsky Pas de Deux*; *Theme and Variations*; *Weren't We Fools*

Courtesy of Vashti Murphy McKenzie

McKenzie, Vashti Murphy

May 30, 1947– African Methodist Episcopal bishop; writer. Address: Payne Memorial AME Church, 1714 Madison Ave., Baltimore, MD 21217-3750

"I stand on the shoulders of the unordained women who served without appointment or affirmation," Vashti Murphy McKenzie said in July 2000, upon accepting her post as the first female bishop of the 213-year-old African Methodist Episcopal (AME) Church. As pastor of Baltimore's Payne Memorial AME Church from 1990 to 2000, McKenzie—described as an "electrifying speaker" by *Jet* magazine—increased her congregation from 330 to 1,700 members. She established 15 new ministries and worked as a visiting preacher, revivalist, and seminar leader for congregations from Alaska to Bermuda, as well as in Europe. Called "a visionary in urban ministry" by the *San Francisco Bay View* (June 21, 2000, on-line), McKenzie attracted millions of dollars in state funds to establish a church-run job-training program for welfare recipients and to fund building-renovation projects in abandoned neighborhood structures, where the church now offers community programs such as senior day-care. As a bishop, McKenzie will carry out humanitarian and missionary work in Africa.

McKenzie was named Vashti Murphy when she was born, on May 30, 1947, into an established Baltimore family. Her great-grandfather John H. Murphy founded the *Afro-American* newspaper in 1892; her grandfather Carl H. Murphy was publisher and editor of the weekly, which is still published, in both Baltimore and Washington, D.C. Her grandmother Vashti Turly Murphy was a founding member of the Delta Sigma Theta sorority, a national, Christian, African-American college sorority that currently has more than 250,000 members. Her mother, Ida Murphy Smith Peters, wrote for the *Afro-American,* and her father, Edward Smith, worked for the federal government.

McKenzie told Caryle Murphy for the *Washington Post* (July 31, 2000) that she grew up as "a church child," spending Sundays at St. James Episcopal Church, singing in the junior choir, and attending Bible camps. In August 1963 her parents took her out of camp so that she could accompany them to the March on Washington, the historic civil rights demonstration in which 250,000 people participated and at which Martin Luther King Jr. delivered his famous "I Have a Dream" speech; McKenzie has recalled her gratitude at being able to take part in that event. Noting that many of King's goals have not been achieved, McKenzie told Audrey McCombs for the *Savannah Morning News* (January 7, 1999, on-line) that "human rights improvements [were] needed in America and abroad."

McKenzie attended Morgan State University, in Baltimore, where she met and fell in love with Stan McKenzie of the Baltimore Bullets basketball team. During her junior year, when Stan McKenzie was traded to the Phoenix Suns, he asked her to marry him. Although her parents wanted her to finish college, she married McKenzie and moved to Arizona with him. "Good men are hard to find," she told Caryle Murphy, "and when you find them you don't let them go and let them know they can live by themselves and get along without you!"

McKenzie went to work for the *Arizona Republic* newspaper, but was overwhelmed by the long hours and soon left to pursue modeling work. When Stan McKenzie retired from professional basketball, in 1974, the couple returned to Baltimore. Vashti McKenzie later earned a B.A. in journalism at the University of Maryland in College Park and became the mother of a baby boy, Jon-Mikael.

"I knew that I wasn't going to be a housewife," McKenzie told Caryle Murphy. "Other women do it and they love it and I'm glad for them. But it wasn't me." She began working for her family's newspaper, where she wrote a column called "The McKenzie Report," then hosted a weekend entertainment program on Baltimore television station WJZ. She worked next at WEBB Radio and as a day-time disc jockey for WYBC, a gospel radio station in Washington, D.C., where she was soon promoted to program director.

While hosting her gospel show, McKenzie often received calls from people who were suffering from various problems and needed someone to talk to, and she realized that she, like many of them, was searching for direction in life. After a period of fasting and praying, she felt that she had received the call to preach. McKenzie joined Bethel AME Church; as a volunteer there, she made commercially sold videos of sermons given at the church.

The AME denomination grew out of the Methodist Episcopal Church, which had been founded in the American colonies by Irish immigrants. In November 1787 African-American members of the Methodist Society of Philadelphia, having experienced racist treatment at the hands of their white brethren, decided to secede from the mother institution and build their own church. By 1793 they had done so, with Richard Allen (1760–1831) as their pastor, and after repeated disputes with white Methodist preachers in Philadelphia, the Pennsylvania legislature established the new church as an independent member of the Methodist Society. In 1816 Allen was consecrated as a bishop, and the AME church was formally recognized by the Methodist Society. While women make up the great majority of the 2.5 million AME members, the denomination was for two centuries governed exclusively by male clergy.

McKenzie studied for her new calling at Howard University, in Washington, D.C., where she received a master of divinity degree, and then at United Theological Seminary, in Dayton, Ohio, where she earned a doctor of ministry degree. In 1984 she was ordained as a deacon and assigned a seven-member congregation in Chesapeake City, Maryland. After a year she was ordained as a full minister and assigned as pastor of the Oak Street AME Church in Baltimore.

In 1990 McKenzie was appointed as the first female pastor of the 102-year-old Payne Memorial African Methodist Episcopal Church, in Baltimore's midtown. By that time she had given birth to two daughters, Vashti-Jasmine and Joi-Marie. She continued to advance in rank, becoming an Ordained Itinerant Elder of the AME Church, while studying and writing about female ecclesiastical leadership in four cultures and religions. The results of her research were published in 1996 in the book *Not Without Struggle*.

That same year McKenzie announced her bid to become bishop, launching her campaign with the slogan "It's time." The Delta Sigma Theta sorority, of which McKenzie is the national chaplain, donated almost $50,000 to her campaign. Her husband, Stan McKenzie, compared her campaign to a United States presidential contest. "There was that much intensity . . . travel . . . kissing the babies and shaking the hands," he told Caryle Murphy. Payne Memorial's assistant pastor, the Reverend Angelique Mason, directed the effort to get McKenzie "into the old boys' club," as she put it, and other clergywomen supported her as well. During church conferences McKenzie's supporters were "stonewalled," as Mason explained to Murphy, and felt the need to counter sexist and homophobic attitudes: "We had to be careful not to lose our femininity, because what's the first thing men say about strong women? She's gotta be gay! It's that mentality we had to deal with. We always wore our wedding rings, and when we could, we had Brother Stan [McKenzie] present, and we were always mentioning how long they have been married, their kids. . . . They didn't come out and say, 'She's gay,' but it was 'There's gotta be somethin' wrong. Why would a woman want to come and run for bishop?'"

There were 42 candidates, including another woman, for four bishoprics, each paying an annual salary of $55,000. McKenzie was elected on the second ballot of the AME General Conference in July 2000. "The stained-glass ceiling has been pierced and broken!" McKenzie told church members, as quoted by Murphy. In her first post-election sermon, McKenzie warned "against personality cults," according to the reporter. "Pastors come and pastors go," she continued, "but the church remains the same. . . . It's not me. It's all about God." Her female friends in the clergy presented her with a bishop's ring—a large, diamond-encircled amethyst. Her victory was celebrated by her whole neighborhood, and she received a congratulatory card "from your Muslim neighbors."

McKenzie's ministry is augmented by her "Vision to Victory" project, which involves various other congregations and a nonprofit community-service agency, Payne Memorial Outreach Inc. The activities of "Vision to Victory" include acquisition of property and a back-to-work campaign. The agency sponsors a summer youth camp, an after-school program, the "Science Is for Everyone" program, the Boy Scouts, the Girl Scouts, a mentoring program for young people ages nine to 16, and the church Web site. The church maintains a radio and television ministry as well.

In 1996 the church bought a five-story building that now houses the Human Economic Development Center, which provides senior daycare as well as youth and adult-education programs. Payne Outreach Inc. was awarded a $1.8 million contract in 1997 for a job-service program aimed at training and placing 1,000 clients. The success of the program has led to its imitation by other agencies. The church also took over the management and operation of a failing public school. In 1999 Payne Memorial bought a three-floor, 28,000-square-foot office building containing an auditorium with more than 500 seats and a kitchen and banquet facility for their expanding job-service program. The building will host a catering service, employing former welfare recipients; computer classes for senior citizens; and high-school job fairs. McKenzie has also worked with banks and officials from other churches to form the Collective Banking Group, to help ensure fair treatment and equal opportunity on the part of lending institutions.

All AME bishops are expected to make a four-year tour abroad, and McKenzie was scheduled to go in the fall of 2000 to the AME's 18th Episcopal District, headquartered in Lesotho, in Africa, and including Botswana, Swaziland, and Mozambique. Because AIDS is widespread in those nations, McKenzie plans to build orphanages and to establish other parental-support systems. Her husband will oversee the district's missionary and fund-raising activities, in the role historically filled by bishops' wives. In fact, the name of the Bishops' Wives Council has been changed to the Bishops' Spouses' Council.

McKenzie has been honored by many organizations, including the Richmond, Virginia, chapter of 100 Black Women; Operation PUSH; the National Alliance of Black School Educators; the Baltimore Alumni Chapter of the Delta Sigma Theta sorority; CBDC Housing; and Howard University. In 1997 *Ebony* magazine listed McKenzie among the top 15 African-American women preachers.

Caryle Murphy described Vashti Murphy McKenzie as "a tall, soft-spoken woman with striking good looks" who "favors simple, long-skirted suede suits and often detonates her hearty laugh with her own jokes." — V.K.

Suggested Reading: Payne Memorial AME Church Web site; *San Francisco Bay View* (on-line) June 21, 2000; *Washington Post* (on-line) July 31, 2000

Selected Books: *Not Without Struggle*, 1996

Courtesy of Lisa Berg

Michelman, Kate

(MY-kel-man)

Aug. 4, 1942– President of the National Abortion and Reproductive Rights Action League; psychologist. Address: NARAL, 1156 15th St. N.W., Suite 700, Washington, DC 20005

Kate Michelman is the president of the National Abortion and Reproductive Rights Action League (NARAL). Since she joined the group, as its head, in 1985, she has transformed NARAL from a small grassroots effort into a major force in the political arena, owing in large part to her ability to attract those with more moderate views who are not comfortable with the extreme rhetoric used by the opposing sides in the abortion debate. "[Those people] have to know that abortion rights isn't about radical rhetoric," Michelman told Jayne Garrison for the *San Francisco Examiner* (June 21, 1992). "It's about children and families." She continued, "You would never hear me say that abortion is a *good* thing. I think it's a fundamental right, a difficult decision. But an unintended pregnancy that needs an abortion is not something anyone wants. To say that it's a good thing is not the way people think about it. Because it's not. It's a negative act." Still, Michelman contends, the right to terminate an unwanted pregnancy is a decision belonging solely to the pregnant woman, not the government. In a 1998 speech reprinted on the official NARAL Web site, Michelman said, "The very essence of womanhood—who we are—is our freedom to choose what we believe is right. How can we women ever hope to take an equal place in America if we aren't given that respect—if we aren't trusted? Without interrogations. Without indignities. Without violence."

Kate Michelman was born on August 4, 1942 in New Jersey, where her father was a canning superintendent at a Campbell Soup Co. factory. Even as a child Michelman was bothered by injustice, and she remembers questioning the nuns at her parochial school about why some people were forced to beg. Michelman's family moved from New Jersey to Defiance, Ohio, when she was a teen, and while attending high school there, she circulated a petition to protest the ineptitude of some of the school's teachers; she received a three-day suspension for that action. She soon became involved with the plight of the Hispanic farmworkers in Defiance, whose housing was substandard and who were shunned by many of the townspeople. Michelman formed a club aimed at bringing white students and the children of the farmworkers together, and as the treasurer of her senior class, she organized a Christmas-tree sale to buy presents for members of some of those same families. Her dedication to justice was not restricted to the school environment; she also questioned her parish priest about his insistence that the Hispanic laborers sit at the back of the church. "I was constantly pricking the conscience of whatever power system was imposing on our lives," Michelman recalled to Jayne Garrison. Although raised as a Catholic, Michelman found herself increasingly at odds with the Church, mainly because she felt it had been too slow in addressing the concerns of women and minorities. In 1966 Michelman received a dual bachelor's degree, in developmental psychology and art history, from the University of Michigan, where she had participated in rallies to protest the Vietnam War and marched for civil rights. In 1969 she earned a master's degree in developmental psychology from the university.

Although she would eventually become a Quaker, when she got married Michelman was still a practicing Catholic and believed that birth control violated God's law. She gave birth to three daughters within three years; then in her early 20s, she gladly stayed home to raise them. "I wanted to play that role," she told Garrison. "Being a wife was important to me. And family was very important to me." Michelman's life was changed forever in 1970 when her husband, a graduate student in archaeology at Penn State University, revealed that he had been having an affair. He took their car and left her to care for their three girls, who were then between three and five years old. Michelman fell into a deep depression; her feelings of despair worsened four weeks later, when she learned that she was pregnant. "Having another baby would have pushed my family to a crisis of unmanageable proportions," Michelman told Mary T. Schmicl for the *Chicago Tribune* (July 23, 1989). Now that she was raising her children alone and forced to rely on public assistance, she knew that she could not afford to keep the infant. She didn't feel that she could face the prospect of putting the child up for adoption, either. She told Jayne Garrison, "I labored over this all alone, because I couldn't tell anybody. You just didn't talk about abortion, certainly not in my family, not in those days."

Michelman visited her doctor, who informed her that abortion was illegal in the state of Pennsylvania, where she then lived, except in exceptional cases. Like many women who found themselves faced with such decisions in that era, she was forced to prove that her psychological health was in danger. (At the time, it was far easier to get approval for psychiatric reasons than for physical ones.) Michelman stated her case before a panel of four male doctors, who "cross examined" her about "the most intimate and personal details" of her life, she recalled in a speech later excerpted in *U.S. News & World Report* (September 30, 1991). "It was humiliating. I was an adult woman, and yet I had to win their permission to make a decision about my family, my life, my future." Although the panel approved the abortion, moments before Michelman was scheduled to undergo the procedure, her doctors informed her that they had forgotten one important detail; according to Pennsylvania state law, she would need her husband's written permission in order to get an abortion. "I literally had to leave the hospital and find the man who had rejected me," Michelman was quoted as saying by *U.S. News & World Report*. Although she succeeded in finding her husband, who agreed to the procedure, she kept with her the number of an illegal abortionist, to whom she felt she would turn if she had to. "I was prepared to break the law and risk my life because my family's survival depended on it," she explained in the excerpted speech. Michelman had fully examined the religious and moral implications of her decision, and she told Jayne Garrison that she was confident that she had done the correct thing. "It was more moral for me to have an abortion than to bring a child into the world at that point. The children's needs and my responsibility to them was of greater moral weight than the moral weight I did feel to a developing fetus," she said. Michelman's experience led her to the realization that women's reproductive choices were completely in the hands of men. "I was saved from having a back-alley abortion, but I was not saved from the degradation and humiliation of having to put my life in the hands of others who didn't care about the outcome," she told Mary T. Schmicl. When *Roe v. Wade*, the landmark 1973 Supreme Court decision ensuring a woman's right to a safe and legal abortion, was announced, three years after Michelman's abortion, she felt vindicated. "It felt like a retroactive pardon of my decision," she wrote for *Choices*, a NARAL publication. "The ruling from the highest court in the land provided an affirmation that my decision was indeed right."

Unable to collect child support from her ex-husband, Michelman worked part-time to support her family. She has recalled being turned down for credit at a local variety store where she wanted to buy her eldest daughter school supplies for first grade. Unable to pay the mortgage, she was forced to sell her house and move into a small rental with the three girls. In 1970, convinced by her own experience that being dependent on a man was dangerous, Michelman decided to concentrate on working with single mothers and disadvantaged children. During the 1970s Michelman developed a model diagnostic treatment program for developmentally disabled preschool children and their families in rural Adams County, Pennsylvania; the program was later replicated across the country. She was named executive director of Adams County Early Childhood Services in 1978. From 1978 to 1980 she also worked in the Department of Psychiatry at Pennsylvania State University School of Medicine, in Hershey, as a clinical assistant professor, providing training in child development to medical students. After the funding for early childhood programs in Pennsylvania was cut, Michelman became the director of Tri-County Family Planning, a clinic in Harrisburg. Her own experience had shown her that the well-being of a family depended on the ability of women to control their own pregnancies. Following her introduction of prenatal care, infertility counseling, and abortions to clinic patients, the facility became an affiliate of Planned Parenthood.

In late 1985 Michelman heard that NARAL was looking for a new president. By this time she had remarried, and her husband, encouraged her to take the job even though the organization's headquarters were in the District of Columbia. Once she was hired, one of her primary goals was to expand the abortion debate to include "people who'd been sitting on the sidelines forever," Michelman told Jayne Garrison, especially those who had been "polarized by the extreme rhetoric." Within a few years of assuming the presidency, Michelman had increased NARAL's membership from 95,000 to 500,000, thanks in large part to her talent in working with the media and her ability to win over those people who disapproved of abortion but opposed even more strenuously government interference in pregnant women's decisions. Her opponents have charged that Michelman's carefully cultivated image, rather than her platform, is responsible for much of her success. "She's glamorous. She looks good. She's articulate," a member of the anti-abortion group Operation Rescue told Jayne Garrison. "She wins half the country on that alone." Michelman is also perceived as nonthreatening, an important quality for a woman whose goal is to change the minds of everyday Americans who remain undecided about the abortion issue. "She's able to convert basic people," her husband told Garrison. "Republican types, who might start out anti-choice. And she gets a lot done because of her manner."

The Supreme Court's 1989 decision in *Webster v. Reproductive Health Services*, a case involving litigants from Missouri, diminished the stability of abortion rights considerably. The justices held that life begins immediately upon conception and forbade the use of public funds in counseling women regarding the abortion option except in cases in which an individual's life was in danger. The *Webster* decision allowed the state of Missouri to ban abortions at public hospitals and clinics and opened the way for state regulation of abortion. Some commentators saw it as an initial move by the court to reverse the effects of *Roe v. Wade*. Although the outcome of the case was not altogether unexpected, Michelman was devastated. "I'd been preparing for months for this decision, but when I heard it, I felt I'd been punched in the stomach," she told Mary T. Schmicl. "My whole body went tense and I gasped." While the case was being considered by the court, Michelman spent every morning for weeks at an ABC-TV studio, ready to deliver an immediate response to the day's events. "I've got to be on TV," she explained to Jennie Nash for *New York Woman* (November 1989). "The other side has dominated, and we've suffered from that."

The day after the *Webster* decision, NARAL launched an expensive advertising campaign centered on a two-word catchphrase: "Who Decides?" "It was risky for us to spend that kind of money," Michelman told Jennie Nash, "but we reframed the debate. We took it away from 'are you for or against,' to 'who decides.'" NARAL's membership increased considerably after the "Who Decides?" campaign. The advertisements urged voters to accept or reject candidates based on their abortion-rights stance. Michelman told Chip Brown for *New York Woman* (May 1990) that the *Webster* decision made abortion "an election issue," which immediately changed the political landscape. "There is now a powerful prochoice force in this country," she said. "The sleeping giant is awake."

Although by law the political action committees of organizations can donate only a small, fixed amount directly to candidates during campaigns, the organizations can legally engage in independent activities of support, as long as those activities remain separate from the candidates' own efforts. Antiabortion activists had successfully used their political clout to elect candidates sympathetic to their cause, and Michelman's organization began to do the same. In 1990 NARAL launched successful campaigns in support of Lawton Chiles for governor of Florida and Ann Richards for governor of Texas. They also supported the reelection of Senator Tom Harkin of Iowa. Although Harkin was initially reluctant to accept NARAL's endorsement, he publicly thanked the organization after he was elected. The group has since run several such supportive campaigns, including Charles Schumer's successful Senate campaign in New York State, in 1998, and Gray Davis's 1998 gubernatorial bid in California. NARAL also helped defeat anti-choice ballot issues in Washington State and Colorado that year.

NARAL took an active role in commemorating the 25th anniversary of *Roe v. Wade*, in 1998. In a column for the *Detroit News* (January 20, 1998, online), Michelman, calling a woman's right to choose "one of the most fundamental precepts in our Constitution," wrote, "For women, Roe was the final judgment that reproductive choice is central to a woman's full emancipation and full participation in American life. It was a national promise that was ours forever." She warned, however, that "25 years after our great victory, we're still at the barricades. Fighting battles we thought were won long ago. Defending ground that had long been ours." Michelman pointed out that of the 431 representatives then in the House, only 130 were prochoice, and in the Senate, only 33. Since 1995 abortion opponents had voted more than 80 times to limit reproductive choice, and the only states that came close to fully supporting a woman's right to choose were California, Connecticut, Oregon, Vermont, and Washington, along with the District of Columbia. Michelman opposes the ban of a controversial late-term abortion procedure, which is performed only when the mother is at great risk of dying or there is a severe fetal abnormality. (Although this type of abortion is performed fewer than 500 times a year, it has become an issue of heated contention in the abortion debate, because it is sometimes performed in the third trimester of pregnancy, when the fetus is in an advanced stage of development.)

Although Michelman and her husband sometimes dream of retiring to southern France, she has no intention of abandoning her fight for reproductive freedom. She has declared that the results of the 2000 presidential election are crucial to the future of abortion rights, particularly since John Paul Stevens and Sandra Day O'Connor, both pro-choice justices of the Supreme Court, may be poised to retire, and if they are replaced by justices of a differing ideology, *Roe v. Wade* might be overturned.

Michelman rises at dawn every day to exercise, and even her opponents have expressed grudging respect for her work habits and drive. In 1994 she served as a fellow at the John F. Kennedy School of Government's Institute of Politics, at Harvard University. In October 1998 *Vanity Fair* named her one of "America's 200 Women Legends, Leaders, and Trailblazers," and she has also been named one of the "100 Most Powerful Women" by the *Washingtonian* (September 1989). — C.L.

Suggested Reading: *Chicago Tribune* V p6+ July 23, 1989; NARAL Web site; *New York Woman* p51 Nov. 1989, with photo, p92+ May 1990, with photos; *San Francisco Examiner* p6+ June 21, 1992, with photos; *U.S. News & World Report* p19 Sep. 30, 1991, with photo

---

Deidre Davidson/Archive Photos

Milchan, Arnon

(MIL-shan, AR-non)

Dec. 6, 1944– Film producer; entrepreneur. Address: New Regency Enterprises, 10201 W. Pico Blvd., Bldg. 12, Los Angeles, CA 90035

Averse to publicity and little known outside Hollywood, Arnon Milchan is the founder of New Regency Productions, an independent company whose nearly four dozen films include such box-office successes as *JFK*, *Under Siege*, *Free Willy*, *Natural Born Killers*, *L.A. Confidential*, and *Fight Club*. Known for his aggressiveness, highly developed business instincts, and uncommon charm, the Israeli-born Milchan began his professional life far from the world of cinema: at age 21 he took over his family's agricultural-supply company, and within a few years he had guided it to international prominence. He later became a go-between for American weapons manufacturers and the Israeli government, thus playing a major role in the strengthening of the Israeli military. He objects to the media's universal description of him as an arms dealer, however. "I'm their rep in Israel," he declared to Ann Louise Bardach for *Los Angeles* magazine (April 2000), referring to the American companies. "I get a fee, a commission. I'm not even the buyer. I'm an agent."

Milchan launched his career in the film industry in the 1970s, first in Israel and then in the U.S., where he produced such films as *Brazil* and *The King of Comedy*. With the conviction that "the synergy between films, music and sports" is "where the future lies," as he put it to Bardach, he has branched into network television, for which he has produced the shows *Roswell* and *Malcolm in the Middle*; sports entertainment, with deals for broadcasting women's tennis; and music, by acquiring Restless Records. Bardach quoted Steve Reuther, a former partner of his in film production, as saying that Milchan is "one of those rare people who can do the detail work and also stay focused on the big picture." He has also favorably impressed the actor Robert De Niro, who has starred in five Milchan-produced films. "Compared to some of the people out there who have nothing on them but an Armani suit, Arnon is the real thing," De Niro said to Bardach. "He's paid his dues, he's got good taste, works very hard, and he's totally committed. He spins circles around those other guys."

Arnon Milchan was born on December 6, 1944 in Rehovot, in what was then Palestine. Among the earliest Zionist settlements in Israel, Rehovot was founded in 1890 by emigrants from Russia, one of whom was Milchan's paternal grandfather. His other grandparents were natives of Palestine, as were their forebears for hundreds of years. Milchan's father owned a successful company that sold fertilizer and sprinkler systems for the vast irrigation network that enabled settlers to grow crops in the large parts of Israel that were once desert. At the age of 16, Milchan entered a boarding school in England; he was later expelled for leaving campus after hours (in the hope of meeting girls). He graduated from a London college, after which he returned home to complete his service in the Israeli army. (Universal conscription has been in force in Israel for decades.) His duties reportedly included instructing fellows soldiers in sports. Milchan himself was such a good athlete that he briefly considered becoming a professional soccer player. Instead, he enrolled at the University of Geneva, in Switzerland, where he studied chemistry and business administration. Boris Davidson, a friend of Milchan's during his youth, told Frank

Rose for *Premiere* (June 1993) that during this period, "if you didn't know Arnon, you'd think he was only a playboy. He'd have fast cars, speedboats, the good life."

That carefree life soon ended. In 1966, while still at the university, Milchan received word that his father was dying, so he returned to Israel to run the family business, called Milchan Brothers. (His father died before the end of that year.) Arnon, then 21, assumed control of the company at a difficult time: one of its important clients had gone bankrupt while owing the firm more than $500,000. While holding the company's creditors at bay, he worked with DuPont Chemical to develop a new fertilizer for nutrient-deficient citrus trees. According to Bardach, the substance made possible a fourfold increase in the yield of citrus fruit, which in turn led to a "stratospheric" jump in Milchan Brothers' sales. The company became the Israeli licensee for DuPont, and in time Milchan secured similar contracts with North American Rockwell (now Rockwell International), Rhône-Poulenc, and Ciba-Geigy. He also bought up a handful of additional firms, thus expanding his business into the areas of aerospace, chemicals, electronics, and plastics. By 1977 the combined revenues of his companies totaled approximately $200 million. In early 2000, Milchan told Bardach, Regency Enterprises, the parent company of all his businesses, was worth at least $1 billion.

At some point Milchan became a consultant to American companies that manufactured military materiel, among them Raytheon, Bell Helicopter, and Magnavox. He and some of his employees served as intermediaries between those firms and the Israeli government and thus aided the government in building the nation's weapons arsenal. According to Bardach, "Throughout the 1970s, '80s and even up until the Gulf War in 1991, Milchan was Israel's foremost weapons procurer, brokering deals for such prized superweapons as the Hawk missile and the famous Scud-foil of the Gulf War, the Patriot [missile]."

In the mid-1970s the Israeli government, then headed by Yitzhak Rabin, recruited Milchan to launder money from South Africa, by routing it through European banks. In those years the world community ostracized to some degree both Israel and South Africa, the latter because of its policy of apartheid. The money laundering was part of the two countries' plan to buy newspapers and other media in various parts of the world, with the goal of softening opposition to apartheid and thus making foreign trade with South Africa more palatable. At first Milchan supported his government's relationship with South Africa. "There were a lot of dialogues between Jewish brains and American money to prevent [South Africa's] treasures of uranium and diamonds and gold from falling into the wrong white hands—meaning Cuba, Russia," he explained to Frank Rose. "When you're called by some very important people and they tell you how strategic this is and they ask your opinion before you see through your own eyes, it's all theoretical." But a visit to South Africa aroused Milchan's conscience; after seeing a restroom sign at a zoo that read "Blacks, Asians, and dogs not allowed," he decided, as he told Rose, "A Jew cannot live with apartheid. Simple as that."

Meanwhile, in Tel Aviv, where he lived with his French-born wife and their three children, Milchan had continued his long association with the local arts community, which centered on Dizengoff Street, famous for its many outdoor restaurants. He developed a reputation for sharing his wealth with struggling artists and intellectuals. "I wanted to live in the creative community," Milchan explained to Rose. "I felt I would have been an artist if it had gone other ways. And—I don't want to use the word 'guilty'—but you feel uncomfortable doing very well in a country like Israel, where your friends are not doing well. You have this need to help without judging artistically." Early in the 1970s Milchan produced a few Israeli films and plays. When the American producer Elliott Kastner learned of his interest in cinema, he arranged for Milchan to meet with the actress Elizabeth Taylor, as a way of inducing him to invest in Kastner's films. The stratagem worked, and Milchan put a total of $8 million into three Kastner pictures. (Only one of them—*The Medusa Touch* [1978], a supernatural thriller starring Richard Burton—made a profit.)

Milchan was more directly involved in the making of the $22 million, four-part television miniseries *Masada,* about a group of first-century Jews who committed mass suicide rather than surrender to the Roman troops that were poised to overtake the Jews' mountaintop fortress. For that project, he acted as the completion bond guarantor, whose job is to insure that a film is finished on time and under budget. Renowned for his cost-consciousness, he "sat on a mountaintop counting light bulbs" during production, as he recalled to Lisa Gubernick and Julie Schlax for *Forbes* (March 4, 1991). He eventually earned $2 million from the film, which aired on ABC in 1981. Milchan next produced Martin Scorsese's *The King of Comedy* (1983), starring Jerry Lewis and Robert De Niro as a would-be stand-up comic; Sergio Leone's *Once Upon a Time in America* (1984), a saga about Jewish gangsters, featuring De Niro and James Woods, in which Milchan had a bit part; and Terry Gilliam's *Brazil* (1985), whose screenplay (by Gilliam, Tom Stoppard, and Charles McKeown), about an Orwellian future world, won an Oscar nomination. Milchan lost a fight with Gilliam and Sidney Sheinberg, the president of MCA Inc., over the ending and release of *Brazil.* Soon afterward he entered into a deal with Warner Bros. and a company called Canal + that gave him a free hand in selecting and producing films. He produced most of his next films with Warner.

Milchan's career as a Hollywood producer was gathering steam when, on May 27, 1985, both *Time* and *Newsweek* reported that an associate of his, a

North American Rockwell executive named Richard Kelly Smyth, had been indicted for illegally shipping kryptrons (devices that, among other uses, can trigger the explosion of nuclear weapons) to Israel. Milchan, while not denying his involvement in supplying arms to Israel, claimed to be unaware of the kryptron shipments. "If some American citizen got the wrong license, I can't be responsible," he declared, referring to the official approval the U.S. requires for exports of that type, as quoted by Frank Rose. "I'm not saying I'm an innocent person—but in this specific case, I knew nothing about it." His similarly awkward handling of subsequent interviews with CNN and the *New York Times* did little to assuage those who suspected him of wrongdoing. Nevertheless, Milchan was never charged in the case; Smyth vanished days before the scheduled start of his trial, and, to date, he remains in hiding. Although Milchan told Bardach that his weapons-related activities ended in 1991, after the Gulf War, he has left the door open to future endeavors of that nature. "I love Israel, and any way I can help Israel, I will," he said to her. "I'll do it again and again. If you say I'm an arms dealer, that's your problem. In Israel, there is practically no business that does not have something to do with defense."

Milchan produced Ridley Scott's *Legend* (1986), a fairy tale with Tom Cruise, and Paul Flaherty's *Who's Harry Crumb?* (1989), a farce starring John Candy, before creating a stir with Danny DeVito's *The War of the Roses* (1989), a controversial depiction of marital breakdown in which Kathleen Turner and Michael Douglas portrayed a bitterly antagonistic couple. Despite a thumbs-down critical response, Milchan's next film, Garry Marshall's romantic comedy *Pretty Woman* (1990), starring Richard Gere as a greedy corporate raider and Julia Roberts as the heart-of-gold prostitute with whom he falls in love, proved to be a huge commercial success, abroad as well as in the U.S. Earlier, Milchan had begun financing his films wholly through the sale of foreign rights prior to production, which meant that he reduced his risk of losses; but by doing so, he reduced his profits as well.

In January 1991 Milchan announced the largest international co-production deal in cinema history—a 20-film, $600 million agreement in which the French pay-television company Canal Plus, the German media group Scriba & Dehyle, and Warner Bros. International signed on to support his newly launched, independent production company, New Regency Productions. (David Matalon, with whom he has been friends since childhood, has served as the company's president and chief executive officer since 1995.) The transaction gave Milchan more control over the films his company supported; he no longer needed Warner Bros.' permission to go ahead with a project. Milchan now had the clout to take more risks, and he did so with such films as the highly controversial *JFK* (1991), directed by Oliver Stone, which ascribed the assassination of President John F. Kennedy to a conspiracy concocted by the U.S. military-industrial complex, and the largely ignored pictures *Memoirs of an Invisible Man* (1992), directed by John Carpenter, and *The Power of One* (1992), directed by John G. Avildsen. His successes more than made up for the occasional flop; *Under Siege* (1992), for example, an action film starring Steven Seagal, earned $85 million at the box office. Among New Regency's other hits are *Free Willy* (1993), about a troubled boy who bonds with a captive killer whale, and *L.A. Confidential* (1997), a critically acclaimed, hard-boiled detective story about corruption in the 1950s Los Angeles Police Department, which brought Kim Basinger an Oscar for best supporting actress.

In 1994 and 1995, respectively, Milchan formed partnerships with the Australian media mogul Kerry Packer and the South Korean company Samsung Electronics. In 1997 the Kirch Media Group, a German conglomerate that owns the worldwide rights to World Cup Soccer, invested more than $60 million in New Regency Productions. Also in that year Milchan sold 20 percent of New Regency to 20th Century Fox, a division of News Corp., which is owned by Rupert Murdoch. New Regency's relationship with Warner Bros. ended in 1998. Terry Semel, a Warner Bros. executive during Milchan's years with the firm, regarded him as "a superb producer—brilliant at putting people and things together," as he told Bardach.

When he is in Los Angeles, the peripatetic Milchan currently works out of a studio located on the lot of 20th Century Fox. In a collaborative venture with Fox Television Studios, Regency Television, another of Milchan's businesses, is producing the hit TV shows *Roswell*, which airs on the WB network, and *Malcolm in the Middle*, broadcast on Fox. *Roswell*, which premiered in September 1999, focuses on three teenage aliens who "hatched" sometime after their parents' spacecraft crashed in New Mexico in 1947. In a review for *New York* (October 11, 1999), John Leonard described *Roswell* as "a friendly merger of [the film] *E.T.* and [the novel] *The Catcher in the Rye*," and he judged it to be "well-acted" and "surprisingly moving." *Malcolm in the Middle*, a sitcom about a highly intelligent six-grader and his oddball but loving family, premiered in March 2000. It was greeted with lavish praise from critics, who lauded it for its honesty, warmth, and wit. "Few other shows so skillfully straddle the line between children-friendly slapstick and sly adult satire," Marc Peyser wrote in a review of the series for *Newsweek* (February 21, 2000).

In 1997, at a price of between $10 million and $15 million in cash plus shares of Regency stock, Milchan acquired the independent label Restless Records, which had released the soundtracks for such Regency-produced films as *L.A. Confidential*, *Dangerous Beauty* (1998), *The Negotiator* (1998), and *Simply Irresistible* (1999). As a result of the purchase, which reflected Milchan's recognition of the lucrative ties between music and film, "all proceeds from soundtrack sales . . . remain within the company rather than revenues being shared with an unrelated label," as the New Regency Web site pointed out. Milchan, an excellent and fiercely competitive tennis player, has also entered the world of professional sports. In 1998 he formed a partnership with the World Tennis Association. He also signed a deal with Eurosport, the European sports television network, to broadcast women's tennis on European television. Thanks to purchases made in the late 1990s, Milchan currently owns nearly 33 percent of Puma AG, the Germany athletic-shoe and sportswear company, and he has signed the tennis sensation Serena Williams to a multimillion-dollar deal that encompasses shoes, clothing, and movie roles. "As an entertainment company, we spend $500 million a year making movies and $300 million in advertising," Milchan told Doug Smith for *USA Today* (June 4, 1998). "When I go to networks, I say, 'You want my movies? You want *L.A. Confidential*? Do me a favor. I need more air time for women's tennis, and I want it closer to prime time.' It's a strategic move." Milchan also plans to invite movie superstars to attend tennis matches, to attract greater numbers of viewers. "If I'm paying some guy $18 million to do a part, I don't think he'll say no if I ask him to come watch some games and have some fun," he told Brad Wolverton for *Business Week* (August 17, 1998).

Ann Louise Bardach described Milchan as "young-looking" and "exceedingly fit," with "the boyish jaunt and ease of a tennis player." Indeed, Bardach wrote, Milchan plays tennis for "at least three, sometimes six hours a day." He owns homes in Malibu, California; Tel Aviv; Monaco; and Montfort l'Amaury, France, on a 50-acre estate about an hour's drive from Paris, where he lives in a former hunting lodge built in the 18th century. Milchan, who is divorced, took over parenting duties when his children were in their teens. According to Bardach, his son and two daughters "speak reverentially of their father." One daughter, Alexandra, works with him, as vice president of production in Los Angeles; the other, Elinor, is an independent film producer. His son, Yariv, is a photographer. His large circle of friends includes the former Israeli prime minister and Nobel Peace Prize winner Shimon Peres, whom he has known for three decades. "Arnon is too smart to waste life on pessimism," Peres commented to Bardach. "But he is more than an opportunist; he's an opportunity creator." — C.L.

Suggested Reading: *Business Week* p66+ Aug. 17, 1998, with photos; *Forbes* p 113+ Mar. 14, 1991, with photo; *Los Angeles* p74+ Apr. 2000, with photos; *Premiere* p91+ June 1993, with photos; *USA Today* C p7 June 4, 1998, with photos

Selected Films: *The Medusa Touch*, 1978; *The King of Comedy*, 1983; *Once Upon a Time in America*, 1984; *Brazil*, 1985; *The War of the Roses*, 1989; *Pretty Woman*, 1990; *JFK*, 1991; *The Mambo Kings*, 1992; *Memoirs of an Invisible Man*, 1992; *Power of One*, 1992; *Under Siege*, 1992; *Sommersby*, 1993; *Free Willy*, 1993; *The Client*, 1994; *Natural Born Killers*, 1994; *Heat*, 1995; *Six Degrees of Separation*, 1995; *A Time to Kill*, 1996; *Tin Cup*, 1996; *The Devil's Advocate*, 1997; *L.A. Confidential*, 1997; *Dangerous Beauty*, 1998; *City of Angels*, 1998; *Fight Club*, 1999; *William Shakespeare's A Midsummer Night's Dream*, 1999

Plinio Lepri/Associated Press

Morricone, Ennio

(mor-ih-KOHN-ee, EN-ee-oh)

1928– Film composer and arranger. Address: c/o Virgin Records American, Inc., 338 N. Foothill Rd., Beverly Hills, CA 90210-3611

Almost anyone with even a cursory knowledge of movies can instantly recognize the composer Ennio Morricone's anthem for the "spaghetti" Western *The Good, the Bad, and the Ugly*, starring Clint Eastwood. One of the most frequently played, honored, and spoofed pieces of modern music, the score has come to typify the genre. Morricone has also provided the scores for hundreds of other films, by such well-known and respected directors as Bernardo Bertolucci, Brian De Palma, Mike Nichols, and horror maven Dario Argento. Morricone believes that he succeeds as a composer when his music blends smoothly into the flow of a film. "Film music is like a very special invited guest," he told David Rooney for *Variety* (January 22–28, 1996). "To get the best possible reception, it has to enter very discreetly and leave with that same kind of discretion. It's that discretion, that modesty, that makes it essential to film."

Ennio Morricone was born in 1928 in Rome, Italy, to Libera Ridolfi and Mario Morricone, a trumpeter who played jazz and opera and lent his talents to several movie scores. Morricone grew up in Rome with his four siblings: Adriana, Aldo, Maria, and Franca. When he was six years old, Morricone began writing his own compositions. At the age of 12, he enrolled at the Santa Cecilia Conservatory, in Rome, and studied trumpet. There he met fellow classmate Sergio Leone, with whom he would become famously linked in later years. Gifted in composition, Morricone studied under some of the most prestigious professors in Rome, including Goffredo Petrassi, one of Italy's leading composers. Among the many lessons he learned from his teachers was that "one of the values of a music script is the pain that produces it," as Morricone told Jay Cocks for *Time* (March 16, 1987).

According to a summary of Sergio Miceli's book *Ennio Morricone: La musica, il cinema* that appeared in mid-2000 on the Web site *lavender.fortunecity.com*, Morricone received a diploma in instrumentation, in 1952, and a diploma in composition, in 1954. He began composing and arranging pieces for radio dramas, and in 1955 he started ghostwriting scores for films, working alongside such composers and performers as Mario Lanza, Paul Anka, Charles Aznavour, and Gianni Morandi. That same year, he left for military service, which gave him the chance to transcribe music by various composers for a military band. Shortly after joining the military, Morricone married Maria Travia, whom he had met six years earlier. In 1957 his first child, Marco, was born.

In 1960 Morricone began writing music for television shows. The following year, he penned the score for the Luciano Salce film *Il Federale* (1961). Over the next few years, Morricone lent his talents to several other films, including *La Voglia Matta* (1962), *Il Successo* (1963), and the TV series *The Virginian*. In 1964 he supplied the music for the Sergio Leone film *Per un Pugno di Dollari*, released in the U.S. as *A Fistful of Dollars*. Made for $200,000 and starring a then-unknown actor named Clint Eastwood, *A Fistful of Dollars* revived the Western genre, creating a world where even heroes had questionable morals. The film drew attention for its depiction of an amoral West, as well as for Eastwood's fear-inspiring turn as The Man with No Name. Audiences also responded to Morricone's score, which embraced a gritty aesthetic rather than copying the epic and romantic sound more commonly associated with Westerns at that time. The inspiration for this departure was "first and foremost, Leone's stories and screenplays," Morricone commented to Joe Gore for *Guitar Player* (April 1997). "The music wasn't only eerie, it was grotesque and ironic. We wanted to have that type of sound, not only from the guitar but from all the instruments in the score. There are elements of irony, taunting and meanness in those movie characters—a bit harsh, but also comical, even picaresque. Therefore I didn't take into account the kind of westerns that were being made in America at the time. I wanted to make my personal kind of music and a music that belonged to Leone's movies." Morricone's inspiration for the theme came from a lullaby he had composed years earlier. In an interview with *Cané-Telé-Revue* (May 10, 2000), reprinted in mid-2000 at *lavender.fortunecity.com*, Morricone explained, "Sergio asked me if I could imitate a Mexican military song he brought along. It reminded me of a lullaby I had composed for the Peters Sisters but was never used. I decided to make a parody of it. I only told Sergio years later. From then on, it became a hobby for him to listen for each film to what I had available in my drawers."

Morricone worked with Leone on the two sequels to *A Fistful of Dollars*: *For a Few Dollars More* (1965) and *The Good, The Bad and The Ugly* (1968). In the years since, the latter film's main theme, with its whistling piccolo and ominous drumbeat, has become one of the most memorable movie tunes in history. Many films that feature a standoff between two characters have employed the theme for dramatic or comedic effect.

Morricone continued to work with some of the more renowned European filmmakers of the period. He created music for Pier Paolo Pasolini's *Hawks and Sparrows* (1965), Elio Petri's *Investigation of a Citizen Above Suspicion* (1969), and Henri Verneuil's *The Sicilian Clan* (1969). In 1969 he reteamed with Leone for his operatic masterpiece *Once Upon a Time in the West*. Again, people responded to Morricone's use of ambient music, which deftly punctuated the sprawling saga of a widowed landowner who becomes the target of a hired assassin. The film quickly gained notoriety for its first scene, in which the gunman, played by Henry Fonda, shoots down a running child. To create the peculiar harmonica music for that sequence, Morricone and Leone employed an unusual technique. "For the key sequence with the child, we wanted a sound that expresses more pain than what we were hearing," Morricone explained to *Cané-Telé-Revue*. "So Sergio Leone ran to the musician and strangled him. With a compressed glottis, he gave exactly what we wanted. But don't worry, he is still alive!"

By this time, Morricone's music had attracted a number of Hollywood directors, and he composed the score for such high-profile pictures as the Clint Eastwood film *Two Mules for Sister Sara* (1970), directed by Don Siegel; the horror sequel *The Exorcist II: The Heretic* (1977); and the *Jaws*-inspired *Orca* (1977). In between these projects, he continued to work with noted Italian directors, penning the music for Henri Verneuil's *The Burglars*, Leone's *Duck, You Sucker* (1972), and Bernardo Bertolucci's epic *1900* (1976). In 1978, for his work on Terence Malick's moody, turn-of-the-century love saga, *Days of Heaven* (1978), Morricone earned his first Oscar nomination. Although Morricone did not win the award, the nomination served to raise his profile in the United States. Before long, he was penning music for such notable films as *La Cage Aux Folles* (1978), John Carpenter's *The Thing* (1984), and Leone's gangster saga *Once Upon a Time in America* (1984), which features Robert De Niro and James Woods as Jewish boys who grow up and become gangsters in Depression-era New York City.

Up until the mid-1980s, despite having put his name on more than 300 films, Morricone was still known only to collectors of movie soundtracks and ardent fans of film. His reputation received a boost that year, however, when he wrote and arranged the score for Roland Joffe's *The Mission*, which stars Jeremy Irons, as a Jesuit priest who builds a mission in the forests of Brazil, and Robert De Niro, as the rogue who helps him. For the film, Morricone employed traditional Brazilian instruments, children's choirs, and pieces for oboe and pan flute. "This music represents me nearly completely," he told Cocks. His longtime collaborator Leone had high praise for the film's score, telling Cocks, "It's practically like a sung mass." When composing the score, Morricone brought several factors to bear. "With regard to the music, there were many considerations," he told Jon Burlingame and Gary Crowdus for *Cineaste* (1995). "I was conditioned by the following things: the Jesuits, who were bringing their civilization and beliefs to South America, as well as the type of music they were accustomed to. The instruments they brought to teach the Indians were instruments from Western Europe. This was the first condition. Second, one of the two protagonists played the oboe. That's another condition. And the third condition was the music of the Indians themselves. Therefore, I had to take into account these facts, two of which were historical." Morricone wove together the three different sounds in a way that amplified the film's primary themes of intercultural conflict and harmony. Although not a box-office blockbuster, *The Mission* received favorable reviews and earned seven Academy Award nominations, including Morricone's second for best original score. Morricone also collected a Golden Globe and a British Academy Award.

The Mission secured a permanent place for Morricone in Hollywood. The following year he provided the score for Brian De Palma's gangland epic *The Untouchables* (1987). Utilizing many musical tools, including brass, strings, and harmonica, to evoke the struggle of Eliot Ness to bring down crime lord Al Capone in Prohibition-era Chicago, Morricone's score earned him a third Oscar nomination, a British Academy Award, and a Grammy Award. He followed his work on this film with a score for *Cinema Paradiso* (1988), directed by Giuseppe Tornatore. For his work on *Cinema Paradiso*, Morricone won another British Academy Award for best original film score.

In the ensuing years Morricone worked ceaselessly, composing scores for De Palma's *Casualties of War* (1989); Barry Levinson's *Bugsy* (1991), for which Morricone earned another Oscar nomination; the Clint Eastwood thriller *In the Line of Fire* (1993); and the Oliver Stone–directed *U-Turn* (1997). Most recently, Morricone worked on Warren Beatty's political satire *Bulworth* (1998), Tornatore's *The Legend of 1900* (1998)—for which he won a Golden Globe Award for best original score—and De Palma's space opera *Mission to Mars* (2000).

Morricone lives in Rome with his wife, Maria. The couple have four children. "Andrea is a conductor," he told *Cané-Telé-Revue*. "I tried in vain to dissuade him from it, because music is the most invading thing in life. Praising it without concessions during a complete life is the source of many sufferings as well as joy. Giovanni, my second son, is a director. My two daughters take care of the essential: my grandchildren." In addition to his passion for music, Morricone is an avid collector of art. When asked about his fervent work ethic, he told Harlan Kennedy for *American Film* (February 1991), "I don't believe that I do work hard. I don't believe that I work too much. Think of J. S. Bach, think of W. Mozart and of many others. Their music was their life. Without being as great as they, the same is true for me. I'm not tired of writing music. It's the only thing I believe I know how to do." — J.K.B.

Suggested Reading: *American Film* p39+ Feb. 1991, with photos; *Guitar Player* p57+ Apr. 1997, with photos; *Time* p83 Mar. 16, 1987, with photo; *Variety* p89+ Jan. 22–28, 1996, with photos

Selected Films: *Il Federale*, 1961; *A Fistful of Dollars*, 1964; *For a Few Dollars More*, 1965; *Hawks and Sparrows*, 1965; *A Bullet for the General*, 1966; *The Return of Ringo*, 1967; *The Good, the Bad and the Ugly*, 1968; *The Big Gundown*, 1968; *Once Upon a Time in the West*, 1969; *Investigation of a Citizen Above Suspicion*, 1969; *The Sicilian Clan*, 1969; *Two Mules for Sister Sara*, 1970; *The Cat O'Nine Tails*, 1970; *1900*, 1976; *Exorcist II: The Heretic*, 1977; *Days of Heaven*, 1978; *La Cage Aux Folles*, 1978; *La Cage Aux Folles II*, 1980; *Once Upon a Time in America*, 1984; *The Thing*, 1984; *The Mission*, 1986; *The Untouchables*, 1987; *Cinema Paradiso*, 1988; *Casualties of War*, 1989; *Bugsy*, 1991; *City of Joy*, 1992; *In the Line of Fire*, 1993; *Wolf*, 1994; *Disclosure*, 1994; *The Star Maker*, 1995; *U-Turn*, 1997; *Bulworth*, 1998; *The Legend of 1900*, 1998; *Mission to Mars*, 2000; *Vatel*, 2000

© 1999 Bachrach Photographers, courtesy of David Belenzon Management

Moschen, Michael

(MO-shun)

Apr. 23, 1955– Juggler. Address: c/o David Belenzon Management, Box 3819, La Mesa, CA 91944

When Michael Moschen performs, he juggles balls, rings, and other objects, but few people who have seen his act feel that the label "juggler" really conveys what he does. So innovative is Moschen's work that various critics have called him a "dancer-physicist," a "movement artist," an "animator of objects," and the "Nijinsky of juggling," the last a reference to one of the greatest ballet dancers of the 20th century. "Moschen is less a juggler than an artist who uses juggling as his medium," Bruce Giduz, a board member of the International Jugglers Association and a former editor of the organization's magazine, *Juggle*, told Jamie Monagan for the Connecticut edition of the *New York Times* (July 25, 1999). "Most jugglers are fascinated by their ability to throw things around, but Michael explores this skill to lengths and depths that are almost unheard of." In Moschen's signature piece, *Light*, glistening crystal balls roll gracefully around his body—apparently of their own volition, since he seems to barely touch them. In other acts, he sends a series of rubber balls careening around the inside of a 10-foot-tall triangular sculpture too rapidly for the eye to follow, or twirls long metal rods in intricate and dizzying patterns. Describing Moschen's effect on his audience, Marilyn Hunt wrote for *Dance Magazine* (February 1991), "One begins to see spinning molecules and planetary systems and the forces that shape them." "Each new piece I create is a risk, but that's the only way to discover something truly new and alive," Moschen told Jamie Monagan. "To bring something out from inside you, that sense of discovery, of giving birth to something original, when it works, the reward is worth the risk." Moschen has starred in an installment of the PBS television series *Great Performances* and has been featured at such prestigious venues as Lincoln Center, in New York City, and Jacob's Pillow, in the Berkshire Mountains of Massachusetts; he has even lectured, on "the juggler as architect, physicist, and mathematician," before hundreds of students and faculty members at the Massachusetts Institute of Technology (MIT).

According to a MacArthur Foundation spokesperson, Moschen is the only full-time juggler to have won a "genius" grant from the organization. Moschen; the actor, clown, and sporadic juggler Bill Irwin (who has also received a MacArthur fellowship); the performance-duo-cum-magicians Penn & Teller; and the acrobatic comedy troupe the Flying Karamazov Brothers have often been called "New Vaudevillians"—contemporary practitioners of the varied stage entertainment popular in the United States from about 1875 until the early 1930s. "My goal," Moschen told Pamela Sommers for the *Washington Post* (October 1, 1991), "is to find that which makes people see something they haven't seen before, feel something they haven't felt."

The youngest of four children, Michael Moschen was born on April 23, 1955. During his first decade he lived with his family in a Greenfield, Massachusetts, housing project. He felt close to his Italian-American grandfather, a stonemason who made his own wine and grew his own vegetables. His grandfather, Moschen recalled to Hunt, was "steeped in the physicality of the world. I remember the smells, the tastes, the touchings of that world that just overloaded my senses and made me feel so much more alive. It was all exotic and different and very much to be loved." Moschen's father, a stonemason and toolmaker, and his grandfather instilled in him a love of working with his hands. As a youngster he was adept at several sports; most of all he enjoyed golf, which he learned to play when he was five. With characteristic persistence and patience, he would practice hitting the ball for hours. "This taught me about rhythm. I just thought it was such a beautiful sport," he told members of the audience after a show he gave in 1998 at the Emerson Majestic Theater, in Boston, as quoted on *sceneplay.com* (on-line). The competitive aspects of athletics did not interest him; rather, he told Hunt, he was drawn by "that Zen quality of just becoming one with what you're doing." He recalled to the Emerson Majestic theatergoers that as a schoolboy, he "stayed in at recess to finish special projects and discover things," and that "every time I went into the woods I would say to myself that I would not come back out the same way I went in." "I was always trying to find different ways to do the same thing," he said.

When Michael was 11 the Moschens moved into a house, also in Greenfield, next door to the home of Penn Jillette and his family. One summer day when he was 12, Moschen, his brother Colin, and Jillette borrowed a book about juggling from the library. The boys soon began to practice juggling obsessively for hours a day. The trio called themselves the Toss-Ups, and they eventually became proficient enough to entertain at nursing homes, hospitals, and other local venues. Moschen had no interest in attending college; instead, after he graduated from high school, he worked on farms or in factories. In his spare time he read voraciously. He was also adept at carpentry and making pottery. After Colin joined the navy, Jillette and Moschen, who was then 19 years old, renamed themselves the Tumescos and landed a job at Great Adventure, a large amusement park in New Jersey, where they played six shows a day, six days a week. The two also worked up a street act, which they performed in various locations—outside New York's Madison Square Garden, during a Bob Dylan concert, for example, or at a gathering of Hell's Angels motorcyclists in Baltimore, Maryland. Between shows Moschen practiced juggling, often for as many as eight hours a day. At one point he rigged up a net that stretched from the corners of the ceiling to his clothing, so that any balls he failed to catch would roll back to him. His family was supportive of his juggling, although the idea of performing professionally was foreign to them, as were Moschen's bookishness and avid interest in philosophy.

When Penn Jillette met Teller (who does not divulge his first name), and the pair decided to form an act, they did so with Moschen's approval. "I realized there was probably more money in talking than in throwing stuff around," Jillette told Steve Kemper for *Smithsonian* (August 1995), "whereas Mike went on to be, in anybody's view, the most significant juggler of the 20th century and probably the most innovative in history." (Although Jillette still juggles a little, Penn & Teller's act relies mainly on magic and verbal comedy.) After Jillette's departure, Moschen, who had remained interested in athletics, practiced with the University of Massachusetts gymnastics team for a while, although he was not enrolled at the school. He eventually took tai chi and acrobatics classes, as well as ballet, tap, and jazz dancing. Critics have often commented on Moschen's grace and pointed out dance movements in his performances, but, despite appearing on stage in leotards, he considers himself "someone who moves," in his words, rather than a dancer. "A dancer uses his body as an expressive instrument," he explained to Pamela Sommers. "What I do is get my body to react to an object. The object is the conduit, and I am the reactor. I'll spend countless hours sitting with, say, a ball until I finally figure out how it moves." He cited Charlie Chaplin, Buster Keaton, and Fred Astaire as artists who used a similar technique. Moschen told the Emerson Majestic theatergoers that for him, "balance is more important than strength." He also said, "All my senses are wrapped up in the sense of touch."

Moschen's activities in the mid-1970s also included street performances; usually, he juggled in front of the Metropolitan Museum of Art, in New York City. In 1977 the jugglers Paul Binder and Michael Christensen founded the Big Apple Circus, a nonprofit performing group dedicated to making the one-ring circus popular once again. At Binder and Christensen's invitation, Moschen joined the circus; he stayed with it for three years, performing a three-ball routine and a fire-torch finale. He turned down an offer of a job in Reno, Nevada, that would have put him on track to perform in Las Vegas, choosing instead to work for Lotte Goslar's Pantomime Circus. The German-born Goslar, who was then in her 70s, was a highly regarded mime, clown, and dancer, and Moschen was eager to learn her techniques—in particular, how she went about choreographing her routines, which have been described as balletic.

In 1981 Moschen won a choreography fellowship from the National Endowment for the Arts. He used it to develop, along with Bob Berky and Fred Garbo, each a mime and clown, an acrobatic variety show. Called *Foolsfire* and mounted Off-Broadway, the production won a 1982–83 Obie Award in the category "special citation." After *Foolsfire* closed, Garbo took a job on the PBS children's series *Sesame Street*, and Moschen and Berky began performing together Off-Broadway as the Alchemedians—the name being a blend of the words "alchemists" and "comedians." "The basic concept of 'The Alchemedians' is that you have two people who are both outcasts of a sort attempting to transform objects into gold, although our gold is not of the 24-carat variety but ethereal and abstract," Berky explained to Stephen Holden for the *New York Times* (March 23, 1996).

Among the objects that Moschen and Berky used during their 10-year partnership were aluminum mixing bowls of various sizes and the crystal balls—actually, spheres of Lucite—that have become one of Moschen's trademarks. "When I researched the history of juggling in Berlin, I saw the amount of amazing things people had done in the field, and I was overwhelmed," Moschen told Holden. "It seemed that everything had been done before. Then, in 1975, in a window, I saw a crystal ball. I was mesmerized by the beauty of it, by the sense of its being both weightless and heavy, by the appearance of light being taken into it and also reflected off of it, and by the fact that you can never see if the surface is moving." Eager to exhibit their beauty, he decided early on never to close his hands fully around the balls.

During those years Moschen had married Danielle Mailer, a daughter of the writer Norman Mailer, and the couple were living with their child, Isabella, in a loft on the Bowery, a section of Lower Manhattan. One day when Isabella was a baby, he watched Danielle nurse her, as he idly manipulated his crystal balls. "Instead of the balls all going in one direction, one suddenly went *over* the other two," he recalled to Steve Kemper. "I immediately thought that that's what a child does to a relationship. It weaves over and around and through it, always touching it and adding another dimension of beauty and depth. It was a truthful image, and I knew it would take me months and years to explore it." Indeed, building his skill with the balls to a level that he deemed acceptable took him eight years. He worked for more than a year simply to get one ball to move from beneath a cupped palm to the top of his hand with what appeared to be buoyancy—a move that lasts only a few seconds in his show and that, when seen in slow motion, appears physically impossible. Before Moschen, jugglers manipulated objects by grasping them; by contrast, the open-handed technique he devised for the Lucite spheres makes them appear to move independently of their manipulator. Another way in which Moschen's work differs from that of most other jugglers is that while traditional jugglers try to keep as many objects as possible in the air, Moschen concentrates instead on juggling just a few to perfection.

Moschen presented his first solo show, *Michael Moschen in Motion*, in 1988 at the Next Wave Festival, an event held annually at the Brooklyn Academy of Music, in New York City. Reviewing the performance for the *New York Times* (December 11, 1988), the dance critic Anna Kisselgoff wrote, "Even the varying rhythm of the balls he bounces with increasing complexity inside a huge triangle tells us something of the human condition. Natural man, starting simply, has the Promethean spark. Form talks." Called "brilliant" and "virtuosic" by other critics, the show led to Moschen's *Great Performances* special, in 1991, as well as an engagement at the Serious Fun Festival, held at Lincoln Center.

In 1990, with the help of the $230,000 MacArthur Foundation grant, Moschen and his family moved to a house in Cornwall Bridge, Connecticut. "There's no place on earth I'd rather live," Moschen told Jamie Monagan nine years later. "The aesthetics of Cornwall, the extremes of the seasons, even the stone walls . . . all mean a lot to me. Having lived on the Bowery in New York City for 15 years, this is heaven." Situated on five acres near a pond, the house is painted in vibrant colors, unlike its more sedate neighbors. When Monagan visited, the yard was littered with such objects as barrel hoops and tomato cages, with which Moschen was experimenting. In 1997, with the proceeds from a Motorola commercial he had filmed in the Far East, Moschen added to his property a 1,000-square-foot practice studio with a 19-foot-high ceiling and unbreakable windows.

Explaining his creative approach to Monagan, Moschen said, "I'll get fascinated with something, an object, photo studies, a phenomenon, work on it for six months, put it away for two years, then go back to it again. Usually, the third or fourth time is when the piece actually gets made. When I finally commit to the technique, that's when I can't turn back. I first built the pyramid [in which he bounces a series of balls] nine years ago, but it took me five years to achieve the technical level I'm at now with it." When the Montreal-based troupe Cirque du Soleil commissioned him to create a piece based on the mythology of the sea, Moschen bent old vinyl floor tiles into S-shapes that reminded him of breaking waves and devised a way of spinning them around his body. In addition to *Light*, he has created pieces with such names as *Three Balls*, *Triangle*, *Sticks/Vectors*, *Circles*, *Oscillation*, *Curves*, and *Spark*. His collaborators have included the composer David van Tieghem, the lighting designer David Feldman, the dancer, choreographer, and singer Janis Brenner, and the sculptor and set designer John Kahn.

On television, Moschen has been featured on *L.A. Law*, *Sesame Street*, and *The David Letterman Show*. On the big screen, he appeared as a juggler in the films *Hair* (1979) and *Annie* (1982). His hands were seen in Jim Henson's 1986 fantasy film *Labyrinth*, during a scene in which a wizard, played by David Bowie, manipulates a set of crystal balls. During the filming of that sequence, Moschen crouched behind Bowie and performed the manipulation totally blind—a feat that, in a documentary about the making of *Labyrinth*, Henson called "as close to real magic as anything that I really know." Moschen was profiled in the book *The Virtuoso: Face to Face with 40 Extraordinary Talents* (1999), by Ken Carbone and others. Also in 1999 he introduced his most recent maneuver—juggling foot-high cylinders, the idea for which stemmed from his fascination with ancient clay pots. "Most jugglers want to hang on to an order that's already out there," he observed to Steve Kemper. "But when I start a new piece I want chaos, and then I want chaos to give up a *new* order."

As of mid-1999 Moschen and his wife had separated, and he was serving as the coach of his daughter's softball team. Sometimes, he would treat the team to post-practice juggling sessions. "Throwing a ball is a very sophisticated act," he said to Monagan. "It takes continuity of musculature and skeletal action to throw it correctly. I don't care about winning or losing; I'm interested in the discovery the girls go through." — M.R.

Suggested Reading: *Dance Magazine* p44+ Feb. 1991, with photos; *New York Times* Connecticut edition p1 Oct. 4, 1992, with photo, II p7+ Mar. 23, 1986, with photo, New Jersey edition p13 Apr. 11, 1999, with photo, Connecticut edition p3 July 25, 1999, with photo; *Smithsonian* p38+ Aug. 1995, with photos; *Washington Post* E p1+ Oct. 1, 1991, with photos; Carbone, Ken et al. *The Virtuoso: Face to Face with 40 Extraordinary Talents*, 1999

Selected Videos: *In Motion with Michael Moschen*, 1998

Reed Saxon/Associated Press

Murch, Walter

1943– Film editor; sound designer; director; screenwriter. Address: c/o Mirisch Agency, 1801 Century Park E., Suite 1801, Los Angeles, CA 90067

Walter Murch is one of the many unsung heroes of Hollywood. While he hasn't experienced the adoration familiar to many other people in the movie business, his contributions to film are no less significant. An editor and sound designer for more than 30 years, Murch put his signature touch on *THX 1138* (1971), the debut film of *Star Wars* director George Lucas, and on such celebrated works as *The Godfather, Part II* (1974), *Apocalypse Now* (1979), and *The English Patient* (1996). Noted for his precise editing and expert blending of sound, Murch is regarded by many film scholars (as well as ardent fans) as a master of his crafts. "Film editing is very linear: it's like lining up a complicated freight train, trying to get all the cars you need, one after the other, in the best order possible, all on one track," he explained to *Current Biography*. "With sound, there may be 160 tracks running simultaneously. The trick is to hide that fact, and make it seem like it's just happening, organically."

Walter Murch was born in 1943 in New York City. His father was an artist, working primarily with paint, and his mother was a secretary at Riverside Church, an interdenominational, interracial house of worship. During his childhood his mother instilled in him a love of reading. Among many other books, she introduced him to L. Frank Baum's *Wizard of Oz* and others in the 14-volume *Oz* series, which she had loved as a girl in her native Ceylon. Murch also became enamored of the tape recorder, a device just becoming available. "All during my early teenage years, I had a little tape recorder," he told *Current Biography*, "and I would go and record sounds and then take the recordings and cut them up and rearrange them. And without knowing it, I was doing the kind of things that I do professionally now."

After graduating from high school, Murch attended Johns Hopkins University, in Baltimore, Maryland, where he studied romance languages and art history. He spent his junior year (1963–64) studying in Europe, where he met his future wife. While in Paris he became interested in the bold new-wave films being made by such directors as François Truffaut and Jean-Luc Godard. "I probably got the film bug at that time," he told *Current Biography*. In 1965 Murch enrolled in a graduate film program at the University of Southern California (USC), in Los Angeles. "When I arrived at film school, I wasn't thinking about sound [design] at all," he told *Current Biography*. "But after a couple of weeks there, I began to get the idea, just from watching what people were doing, that films manipulated sound in exactly the way that I had done as a teenager with my tape recorder. . . . Then I saw that manipulating images was really kind of the same thing I had done with sound. So I gravitated pretty quickly to editing and sound."

While at USC Murch met the young writer and director George Lucas. The two worked on several films together, including Lucas's student film *THX 1138*, a science-fiction horror story. (Later, using a script that he co-wrote with Murch, Lucas expanded it into the same-named feature film [1971], which starred Robert Duvall and Donald Pleasence.) In 1968 Lucas introduced Murch to Francis Ford Coppola, and Coppola hired Murch as the sound designer for his film *The Rain People* (1969). "It was the first [feature] film that I did sound on," he told Tom Kenny for *Mix* (April 1998), "and I did everything—recording, transferring, cutting, mixing. It was a one-man band. Many of the lessons that I was to learn later are present in that film embryonically." Along with Lucas, Murch next shot film for the documentary *Gimme Shelter* (1970), by David and Albert Maysles, which focused on the infamous 1969 Rolling Stones concert at the Altamont Speedway, in California, where a patron was stabbed to death by a member of the Hell's Angels. "Everybody automatically assumes that I must have done the sound on that film," he told Kevin Hilton for *prostudio.com* (on-line), "but I was just a cameraman"—one among many.

After assisting with *THX 1138*, Murch worked on a major Hollywood film for the first term, as the supervising sound-effects editor on *The Godfather* (1972). Next, he served as sound designer on Lucas's *American Graffiti* (1973). Set in the early 1960s, depicting the escapades of a group of teenagers on their last night of cruising together, the film broke new ground with its soundtrack made up of continuous songs and with commercials and disc-jockey chatter emerging from the characters' car radios. A smash hit that ignited a wave of nostalgia, *American Graffiti* widened the doors for Murch in Hollywood.

Under Coppola's direction, Murch worked on sound for *The Godfather, Part II* (1974) and then as both sound designer and supervising editor on *The Conversation* (1974). The latter film is about Harry Caul (Gene Hackman), a surveillance expert who, while working on a case of marital infidelity, unwittingly becomes entangled in a murder plot. Sound played a special role in the story, since Caul's modus operandi involves recording voices. "Voices come in and out of aural focus in a superb tease" in *The Conversation*, according to the 1996 *Variety Movie Guide*, which declared that Murch's "sound collage and re-recording" were among the film's "major artistic asset[s]." "It's a film that has an intensely single point of view," Murch told Tom Kenny. "Everything in the film is seen or experienced by Harry Caul. You know he's a soundman, and the film never lets you off the hook, so after a while, you just begin to accept the fact that you, too, are a soundman."

The disappointing reactions of test audiences to *The Conversation* led Murch to innovate while editing the film. "In previous films, characters in Gene Hackman's role were conventionally portrayed as being hard-boiled . . . ," he explained to Joy Katz for *Parnassus: Poetry in Review* in 1997. "We found that test audiences were bringing the wrong expectations to the film, and it was making them impatient: The last thing they expected was Gene Hackman to anguish over somebody who might have died because of some miscalculation he made. We couldn't 'solve' the problem and make Harry Caul into something he wasn't, so we had to find a way to diffuse people's preconceived notions. . . . As a result, in the opening reels of the film . . . we dwelt an unusually long time on small things that would ordinarily have been cast aside in the interests of getting on with the story, in order to tune people's expectations back to normal, where life is precious." *The Conversation* was a critical (but not box-office) success, winning Oscar nominations for best picture, original screenplay, and sound.

In his next major project, Murch edited *Julia* (1977), directed by Fred Zinnemann. Based on Lillian Hellman's memoir *Pentimento*, the film was nominated for an Oscar for editing. "It was the first time I was working in a foreign country (England and France) and for people who I did not know [before]," he told *Current Biography*. "It was a great experience for me, . . . and taught me that I could work, and do good work . . . 'outside the nest,' so to speak." Murch traveled overseas again to collaborate on Coppola's Vietnam epic, *Apocalypse Now* (1979), which traces the journey of an army captain into the Vietnam jungle in pursuit of a rogue colonel. Inspired by Joseph Conrad's novel *Heart of Darkness*, it presented the Vietnam War as a fever dream that left its participants insane. Working with a huge quantity of footage, Murch used overlays and other techniques to convey characters' internal emotions. In the opening scene, for instance, the image of Captain Willard (played by Martin Sheen) is superimposed on a forest being ravaged by air strikes. Murch explained to Katz that the sequence "functions as an overture" to the movie. "You're looking at a character whose head is enveloped in flames, and then at slow-motion helicopter blades slicing through his body, superimposed upon a whirling ceiling fan, and strange sounds and music intermingling from different sources; you're probably aware you're watching a film, not an imitation of real life. Even dreams, despite their odd surreality, don't look quite like that. Inevitably, the superimposed images in *Apocalypse Now* betray a self-consciousness because they come at the very beginning and are intended to expose and explore Willard's inner state of mind. If there had been no resonance between that scene and the film as a whole, the opening would have been a meaningless exercise, empty virtuosity." Hailed as revolutionary, *Apocalypse Now* is regarded as one of Coppola's masterpieces, and Murch received no small measure of praise for his work on the film: he received his first Academy Award, for best sound, and was nominated for best editing.

The opportunity to direct came his way when Tom Wilhite, then Disney's head of production, proposed to Murch that he make a film about a subject that especially interested him: Oz. In 1980, with co-writer Bill Dennis, Murch began writing the script for *Return to Oz*, a blending of two L. Frank Baum tales—*The Land of Oz* and *Ozma of Oz*. Murch's story opens with Dorothy, unable to sleep because of her disturbing memories of Oz, admitted to a clinic to get electroshock treatment. She flees the facility and makes her way back to Oz, only to find Emerald City destroyed. With the help of new characters, Dorothy battles the evil Nome King and struggles to return order to the city. During production of *Return to Oz*, Murch was fired for falling behind schedule, and then rehired, thanks to George Lucas's intercession in his behalf. Extremely somber overall, the film, which did not reach theaters until mid-1985, received mixed notices—in the *Washington Post* (June 21, 1985), for example, Rita Kempley described it as "offbeat children's entertainment, a little intense, but enjoyable," while Gene Siskel declared in the *Chicago Tribune* (June 21, 1985), "Rarely has a movie been created that seems so pointed to frustrate the reasonable expectations of the audience"—and box-office receipts failed to meet expectations. Murch's only directorial effort to date, *Return to Oz* has since developed a strong following, with its champions hailing its faithfulness to Baum's vision.

Later in the 1980s Murch edited *The Unbearable Lightness of Being* (1988), a highly praised adaptation, directed and co-written by Philip Kaufman, of Milan Kundera's same-named novel, set in Czechoslovakia around the time that Russia and other Soviet-bloc countries invaded it, in 1968. Murch earned Oscar nominations for his work as editor of *Ghost* and co-editor of *The Godfather, Part III*, both of which premiered in 1990. His next 1990s credits include Michael Lessac's *House of Cards* (1993), Peter Medac's *Romeo Is Bleeding* (1993), and Jerry Zucker's *First Knight* (1995), all of which he edited. He served as both editor and, with two others, sound mixer of Anthony Minghella's *The English Patient* (1996), an adaptation of Michael Ondaatje's award-winning 1992 novel. A multi-plotted World War II–era story told in flashbacks, the film presented Murch with formidable difficulties, as he explained to *Current Biography*: "The story not only followed multiple pairings of characters within a single time frame, it had 40 transitions between pre- and postwar time frames. So the challenge was to guide the audience's focus, emotionally and intellectually, through this quite complex structure, which in the end wound up being quite different from the shooting script." A resounding critical and popular success, *The English Patient* earned nine Oscars, among them two for Murch, who also won a British Academy Award and an Eddie Award from American Cinema Editors for best editing of a feature film. Murch recently collaborated with Minghella as editor on *The Talented Mr. Ripley* (1999), which is based on a novel by Patricia Highsmith. For his work on that film, he was nominated for an Eddie Award.

Walter Murch lives in a 19th-century farmhouse in Bolinas, California, with his wife, Muriel (known as Aggie), who hosts the show *Cover to Cover* on the Berkeley radio station KPFA. The couple have two adult children and raised two others as foster children. Murch is a beekeeper, and he makes his own honey. — J.K.B.

Suggested Reading: *Chicago Tribune* II p3 June 21, 1985, with photo, XIII p6+ June 30,1985, with photos; *Entertainment Weekly* p49 June 26–July 3, 1998, with photo; *New York Times* II p1+ June 16, 1985, with photos, II p11+ Aug. 18, 1991, with photos, IIA p1+ May 2, 1999, with photos; *Washington Post* p31 June 21, 1985

Selected Films: as editor—*Julia*, 1977; *Apocalypse Now*, 1979; *The Unbearable Lightness of Being*, 1988; *Call From Space*, 1989; *Ghost*, 1990; *The Godfather: Part III*, 1990; *House of Cards*, 1993; *Romeo is Bleeding*, 1993; *I Love Trouble*, 1994; *First Knight*, 1995; *The Talented Mr. Ripley*, 1999; as sound designer—*The Rain People*, 1969; *THX 1138*, 1970; *American Graffiti*, 1973; *The Godfather: Part II*, 1974; *The Conversation*, 1974; as editor and sound designer: *The English Patient*, 1996; as sound re-recording mixer: *Dragonslayer*, 1981; *Ghost*, 1990; *The Godfather: Part III*, 1990; *Romeo Is Bleeding*, 1993; *Crumb*, 1994; *First Knight*, 1995; as writer and director: *Return to Oz*, 1985

Mutombo, Dikembe

June 25, 1966– Center for the Atlanta Hawks. Address: Atlanta Hawks, One CNN Center, Suite 405, South Tower, Atlanta, GA 30303

Peter Jones/Archive Photos

With tremendous lateral quickness and precise timing unusual for someone so gangly, the seven-foot two-inch Dikembe Mutombo has become the premier shot-blocker and rebounder in the National Basketball Association (NBA) and possibly its greatest defensive center since Bill Russell. Although Mutombo's defensive skills may not be as visible on the highlight reel as the scoring abilities of some of his fellows, they are no less capable of altering the course of a game. In the first round of the 1994 NBA play-offs, for instance, Mutombo strung together some of his finest performances to lead the Denver Nuggets to a 3–2 victory over the Seattle SuperSonics. Seattle, which had the best record in the NBA that season and was seeded first in its bracket, had gone up two games to none in the five-game series. Though Denver ended its regular season barely above .500, the Nuggets were able to counteract Seattle's highly potent fast-break style, largely on the strength of Mutombo's presence inside the paint, and turn the Sonics into ineffective, long-range shooters. The Nuggets swept the final three games of the series, thus becoming the first eighth seed to eliminate a first seed in NBA play-off history. In that series Dikembe Mutombo set a league record for the most blocks—31—in a five-game series, and he affected many other shots in ways that statistics do not record. As George Karl, who coached Seattle during the 1994 play-offs, said to Rick Telander for *Sports Illustrated* (November 7, 1994), "He got into our players' heads at the very beginning and never left."

One of the nine children of Mukamba Mutombo, a school administrator, and his wife, Biamba, Dikembe Mutombo was born on June 25, 1966 in Zaire (now known as the Democratic Republic of Congo). His full name is Dikembe Mutombo Mpolondo Mukamba Jean Jacque Wamutombo. "In Africa friends and relatives can come to the hospital and give you a name if they want," Mutombo told Telander. His father, who is also known as Samuel, named him Dikembe, which means "plantain" or "banana," because, Mutombo told Telander, "when I was little I was soft. If they sat me up, I fell this way or that." "Mpolondo" is the word for "warrior" in Tshiluba, the language that his family spoke; "Jean Jacque" is his French nickname; and "Wamutombo" means "of Mutombo."

Mutombo was raised in Kinshasa, the capital of Zaire, in a bustling middle-class household filled with his siblings and many cousins. Early on, his height made him conspicuous in his neighborhood, and he was often singled out among his peers because of it. "We have this belief in African culture that your child should not grow up and look down on your head," he told Rick Telander. "Teachers thought I had no respect because of that." Nevertheless, by his own account, Mutombo's childhood was mostly happy. His happiness was marred by the death of his older brother Kayinda, when Dikembe was seven. Though only 24 years old and seemingly in excellent health, Kayinda collapsed and died shortly after scoring the winning point in a championship handball match. The cause of his death was never determined, and for a time the family was scared away from sports. Eventually, though, Mutombo began to play soccer and volleyball and to practice karate. Because of his size, speed, intensity, and ability to focus, Mutombo became a star goalie. But despite his prowess on the soccer field, his father and brother Ilo thought that his height—by his senior year at the Institute of Boboto, a high school, he measured seven feet—made him better suited for basketball. Although he disliked the sport, Mutombo tentatively agreed with them. While on a basketball court for the first time, he slipped and fell, face-first, slicing open his chin. After refusing for some time to try basketball again, he succumbed to pressure from his father and brother and went back to it. Before long he became good enough to join Ilo as a player for Zaire's national team. He began to follow American basketball avidly, by reading the newspapers posted at the U.S. Embassy, which was six blocks from his home.

At about that time Herman Henning, a former Chicago high school basketball coach who was working in Africa for the U.S. Information Agency, saw Mutombo play and recognized his potential. Having learned that Mutombo had been scouting American colleges to attend, Henning suggested that he apply to Georgetown University, in Washington, D.C. Mutombo, who was strong in mathematics and science and was thinking about studying medicine, easily qualified for an academic scholarship to Georgetown from the Agency for International Development. Armed with a note from Henning to John Thompson, who then coached the Georgetown Hoyas' basketball program, Mutombo entered the school in 1987. That same year Ilo began playing basketball at the University of Southern Indiana, in Evansville, which had awarded him a scholarship.

Like many other residents of Kinshasa, Dikembe Mutombo was fluent in French, Spanish, Portuguese, and several African dialects when he arrived at Georgetown, but he did not know a word of English. He also lacked many of the fundamental basketball skills in which American players are drilled from grade school on. To remedy these problems, Mutombo sat out intercollegiate competition during his freshman year and got tutored in English for seven hours each day. To develop his on-court skills, he played basketball in the college's strong intramural program. In his sophomore year Mutombo joined the basketball program full-time, but he spent most of the season on the bench as second-string center to the freshman prodigy Alonzo Mourning. It was not until his junior year, when Thompson moved Mourning to power forward, that Mutombo began to accumulate appreciable numbers of minutes, and he made the most of them. He led Georgetown in field-goal percentage, averaging just over 10 points and 10 rebounds per game, while placing fourth in the nation for blocked shots, with 128. He continued to improve during his senior year, increasing his per-game averages of rebounds by two and of points by five and again ranking fourth in the nation in blocked shots. That year the Big East Conference named Mutombo defensive player of the year.

When Mutombo graduated from Georgetown, in 1991, with a bachelor's degree in linguistics and diplomacy, it was expected that he would be selected early in the first round of the NBA draft. Even though many scouts still considered him a "project," or a few years away from being a polished player, he was viewed as valuable, because big men with great athletic gifts are rare. Still, a number of team executives were concerned about Mutombo's offensive abilities. Customarily, in the weeks leading up to the draft, teams evaluate prospective draftees by reviewing tapes of them in action at college games and subjecting the athletes to a series of psychological and physical examinations, workouts, and interviews. In a conversation with Sam Goldpaper for the *New York Times* (June 26, 1991), Mutombo described a test session with the Charlotte Hornets: "The workout was all offense on my part. We played one-on-one. Mr. Bristow [Charlotte's vice president of basketball operations] was playing defense. He had me shooting jumpers, short and up to 18 feet and I really showed him. I made about 80 percent of them. I don't know why people question my offense." The primary reason for their doubts stemmed from John Thompson's system at Georgetown, which never placed the burden of scoring on only one person. Consequently, Thompson's star athletes, many of whom would go on to NBA success, never racked up gaudy numbers in college. "The point is [Mutombo is] absolutely solid, which is our goal and objective for anybody we think is going on to pro ball . . . ," Thompson told Michael Wilbon for the *Washington Post* (November 29, 1991). "The kid has been properly prepared for his future, he has money, and he is intelligent. So I don't care what anybody says as long as the kids are properly prepared for their future. And they obviously are."

To ensure that they would be properly prepared, Thompson helped his players develop one-on-one moves in practice; during the summer Patrick Ewing, a Georgetown alumnus and all-pro center, would return to Washington to run drills and scrimmage against Mourning and Mutombo to accelerate their development. Although his game tapes rarely showed it, Mutombo had developed a drop step, a spin move, and a sky hook on a par with those of most scoring NBA centers, and he still had a preternatural knack for swatting opponents' shots away at the defensive end. Moreover, his physical conditioning was tops, he adapted well to new systems and game plans, and he worked hard to cultivate his talent.

Mutombo was selected the fourth overall pick in the first round by the Denver Nuggets, and immediately after joining them, he paid the team dividends. During the early part of the 1991–92 NBA season, his per-game averages were 20 points, more than 10 rebounds, and nearly four blocked shots, thanks to which he became the only rookie selected to play in that season's All-Star game. Paul Westhead, Mutombo's first coach in Denver, attributed his center's stellar play in part to his relative lack of experience in the game as a youth. "He has no bad habits, so he doesn't have to unlearn anything. He never played on the playground as a 14-year-old and never took those crazy, wild shots," Westhead told a reporter for the *New York Times* (December 13, 1991). "Pretty much all he knows he was taught in college—he was taught well there—and what we've tried to teach him."

Mutombo severely injured his hand toward the end of his rookie season and had to sit out the final 11 games. Although his absence may have cost him the NBA rookie-of-the-year honor (it went to Larry Johnson), he had undoubtedly made a major impact on Denver, the perennial doormat of its division. Before his second season, Mutombo returned to Georgetown to train with Thompson, Ewing, and Mourning. His rigorous off-season regimen proved fruitful: he shattered the Nuggets' single-season rebounding and shot-blocking records, with 1,070 and 287, respectively. The following year he did better yet, blocking an astounding total of 336 shots during the season, and he led the Nuggets into their first play-offs in four years. After stunning the Seattle SuperSonics, the Nuggets nearly pulled off the same feat against the Utah Jazz. Similarly, Denver fell into a 3–0 hole before running off three straight victories to tie things up in the best-of-seven series. Despite a league-record 38 blocks by Mutombo, Denver lost to the Jazz in game seven.

Mutombo's next two seasons were marked more by personal achievement than team success. In the 1994–95 season the NBA named him defensive player of the year; the Nuggets, meanwhile, were swept from the play-offs by the San Antonio Spurs in the first round. In the next season Mutombo led the league in blocked shots for the third year in a row, becoming the first-ever player in NBA history to do so, and he was selected to play in his third All-Star game. His scoring average, however, which had been slipping steadily since his rookie season, fell to a career-low 11 points per game. Injuries and internal dissension doomed Denver to a losing season and removed the team from play-off contention.

Following his fifth season with the Nuggets, Mutombo became eligible for free agency. In July 1996 he signed a five-year contract worth $56 million with the Atlanta Hawks. As he had in Denver, Mutombo effected a tremendous turnaround in Atlanta. The Hawks' win record in Mutombo's first season with them, for example, was 10 games better than that of the previous year. Mutombo's presence allowed Christian Laettner to move to the power-forward spot, where he became an All-Star and anchored a once-soft Atlanta defense. Mutombo finished the season ranked second in the league in both blocked shots and rebounds and won his second NBA defensive-player-of-the-year award. He earned that honor for an unprecedented third time in the 1997–98 season and also received his fifth invitation to the All-Star game. He ranked second in the NBA again that season, averaging more than three blocked shots per game, and his 11.4 rebounds per game placed him fourth in the league in that category. During the lockout-shortened 1998–99 season, Mutombo saw his per-game productivity fall, yet as they had the previous three seasons, the Hawks made it into the play-offs, where they were ousted in the second round by the eventual runners-up, the New York Knicks. Although the Hawks failed to make the play-offs in 1999–2000, Mutombo finished another outstanding season on defense: he led the league in rebounds (with an average of 14.1 per game) and ranked second in shots blocked (with an average of 3.28).

Since entering the NBA, Mutombo has developed a reputation for generosity that is at least as impressive as his seven-and-a-half-foot arm span.

Although most professional athletes contribute to charity, few are as giving as Mutombo. "My job helps me get things done that I wouldn't be able to do if I was a regular guy—like raising money for refugees with just one phone call," he told Thomas Heath for the *Washington Post* (April 6, 1995). Mutombo has served as a nonpaid spokesperson for the international relief organization CARE and as an active volunteer with organizations that provide aid to troubled children. He helped underwrite Zaire's national women's basketball team, so that they could compete in the 1996 Olympics, in Atlanta. He started a telephone company and a bus company in Kinshasa to improve communication and transportation in that overcrowded city. Recently, he contributed $20 million toward the construction of a $44 million state-of-the-art medical complex in Kinshasa, where poor health conditions led indirectly to the death of his mother, in 1998. He has also set up the Dikembe Mutombo Foundation, with the aim of helping to improve health, education, and living standards in his native land. In addition, he helps to support several relatives who are not in his immediate family, including four nieces and nephews whom he adopted after their parents died. "In Central Africa, there is an old proverb," Mutombo explained to an Associated Press reporter, as reprinted in the *New York Times* (April 6, 2000). "'When you take the elevator up to reach the top, please don't forget to send the elevator back down so that someone else can take it to the top.' This is my way of sending the elevator down." In 2000 he won the Henry P. Iba Citizen Athlete Award, given by the Rotary Club of Tulsa, Oklahoma, to honor athletes "who have excelled in their sport and have shown by their actions a desire to help others," as the club's Web site explained.

In addition to his four adopted children, Dikembe Mutombo and his wife, Rose, who married in 1996, have one daughter, Carrie Biamba. Mutombo has expressed an interest in working for the United Nations or the International Monetary Fund after his playing days are over, and according to many who know him, his personality is well suited for diplomacy. "He has an infectious smile," the former Sacramento Kings coach Garry St. Jean told Rick Telander. "He brings everyone into the conversation, has something to say to everyone. He has a knack for dealing with people. I was on a cruise with him, and when people went up to talk to him, they went away so happy." — T.J.F.

Suggested Reading: *Christian Science Monitor* p14 Nov. 13, 1992, with photo; *Sport* p74+ Apr. 1998, with photos, p70+ Nov. 1998, with photos; *Sporting News* p40+ Mar. 25, 1996, with photos; *Sports Illustrated* p86+ Dec. 9, 1991, with photos, p150+ Nov. 7, 1994, with photos; *Washington Post* B p1 Apr. 6, 1995, with photos

---

'N Sync

Pop-music group

Bass, Lance
May 4, 1979–

Chasez, JC
Aug. 8, 1976–

Fatone, Joey
Jan. 28, 1977–

Kirkpatrick, Chris
Oct. 17, 1971–

Timberlake, Justin
Jan. 31, 1981–

Address: c/o Jive Records, 137-139 W. 25th St., New York, NY 10001

"Two and a half years ago, we were at the tail end of the grunge era, and everyone doubted that a pure pop act could get on the radio. People forgot that most of the kids in America aren't particularly unhappy and would relate to music that said life can be good," the record executive Steven Greenberg told David Wild for *Rolling Stone* (November 12, 1998), explaining the current dominance of catchy, youth-oriented tunes on the music charts. At the time, he continued, "everyone was aiming at an audience college age and above and hoping that the music would trickle *down*. The younger audience had no choice but to listen to music that was created for a much older audience, while today there's music being created *for* a younger audience." According to Wild, there are approximately 31 million teenagers in the United States, with a combined disposable income of more than $120 billion. They currently spend almost $3 billion a year of that money on CDs and cassettes, fueling a massive demand for what some have called "bubble-gum" music. A large chunk of that $3 billion figure is being spent on albums from Jive Records, a company best known for signing young, untried talent. Almost half of their artists, including Britney Spears and the Backstreet Boys, have achieved gold or platinum sales figures.

Although used to seeing astronomical sales figures, even the executives at Jive were unprepared for the level of success of one of their newest bands, 'N Sync. The group's album *No Strings Attached* sold an unprecedented 2.4 million copies in the first week of its release, in March 2000; the previous record had been held by the Backstreet Boys, whose CD *Millennium* had sold 1.1 million copies in its first week of release. Like the Back-

Fritz Reiss/AP Photo
'N Sync (l. to r.): Lance Bass, JC Chasez, Joey Fatone, Chris Kirkpatrick, Justin Timberlake

street Boys, 'N Sync is made up of five young men, each with a particular attribute calculated to appeal to their preadolescent and adolescent fans. Justin Timberlake, who was born on January 31, 1981 in Memphis, Tennessee, is the acknowledged heartthrob of the group. Distinguished by his curly blond hair and soulful eyes, he has often been linked romantically to fellow Jive artist Britney Spears by the press. Chris Kirkpatrick, born on October 17, 1971 in Clarion, Pennsylvania, is the eldest of the five. He has at times sported braided hair and a goatee, and is known for his vaguely rebellious persona. Lance Bass was born on May 4, 1979 in Laurel, Mississippi, and is known among fans for his courtly southern charm. Joey Fatone, a Brooklyn native, born on January 28, 1977, maintains a streetwise New York image: he often wears a diamond-and-ruby Superman insignia around his neck. The final member of the quintet is Joshua Chasez, always referred to by fans and the media as JC. Born in Washington, D.C., on August 8, 1976, he is considered the most serious musician in the group and has begun composing some of the band's songs.

Timberlake, who had been singing in the choir of his Baptist church since he was eight years old, had just lost to another young male vocalist on the televised talent show *Star Search* when, at age 12, he auditioned for a part on the Disney Channel's *Mickey Mouse Club.* He first met Chasez then, when both were hired as cast members on the show. (By coincidence, their fellow Mouseketeers included Britney Spears and another singer-to-be, Christina Aguilera.) They performed together on the show for three years. When the Disney program was canceled, the pair headed to Nashville, in Timberlake's native Tennessee, to cut demo tapes and pursue solo careers. They shared a vocal coach and took dance lessons from a choreographer who had previously worked with the pop phenomenon Michael Jackson. On a return trip to Florida—where they had worked on the *Mickey Mouse Club*—they met Fatone, a casual acquaintance, at a local club. Fatone had moved with his family from New York to Orlando several years earlier, when he was 13. Intensely interested in drama while in school, Fatone had won a bit part in the 1993 film *Matinee* and was also working in live shows at the Disney and Universal theme parks. "I was a little too short to play Tigger and a little too tall to play Pluto," he recalled to David Wild.

Kirkpatrick, at the time a college student in Orlando, wanted to form an all-male vocal group. He had already met with Lou Pearlman, head of Trans Continental, an Orlando-based conglomerate that owned, among other businesses, a travel agency, charter planes, and the Chippendale dancers. Earlier, Pearlman had successfully bankrolled the formation of the Backstreet Boys, and he hoped to find a similar singing group that would be equally popular. With Pearlman's backing, Kirkpatrick recruited Timberlake, Chasez, and Fatone, and the quartet began practicing a capella harmonies together. They quickly realized that they needed someone to sing bass, and through the Nashville vocal coach, they recruited Lance Bass, then president of his Mississippi high-school class. Bass, grateful for the opportunity, immediately flew with his mother to Orlando and stayed with the other members of the group. Referring to an MTV show in which a group of young strangers share an apartment, he told Wild, "It was like *The Real World*, except we all got along." (The five have reportedly maintained that level of camaraderie, and there are seldom any media accounts of dissension within the group.)

The quintet signed manager Johnny Wright, who had formerly managed the pop group New Kids on the Block and was also involved, with Pearlman, in the careers of the Backstreet Boys. In 1997 'N Sync landed a contract with RCA Records and, using a tactic that had previously proven successful with Wright's other young acts, began to tour Europe extensively. European audiences were known to be fond of pop acts, and international markets had long been considered easier to break into than their U.S. counterparts. The group was particularly successful in Germany and the Netherlands, singing a mixture of catchy pop tunes and light ballads. They released a self-titled debut album overseas that sold well, and by the spring of 1998, Wright decided that the five young men, having proven themselves in Europe, were ready to take on American audiences. In early fall of that year, 'N Sync was offered a chance to film a Disney Channel concert special, which featured them singing, dancing, and cavorting around Disney World—an assignment that the already well-known Backstreet Boys had declined. RCA then released the European album in the United States, and despite widespread dismissal from critics, it eventually sold 10 million copies and yielded four number-one singles: "I Want You Back," "Tearing Up My Heart," "God Must Have Spent a Little More Time with You," and "Drive Myself Crazy." Wright defended the tunes to David Wild, saying, "'I Want You Back' and 'Tearing Up My Heart' are quality records. If Aerosmith or someone was singing those songs, they would get a lot more credibility." At the end of 1998, the group released *Home for Christmas,* which included their versions of "O Holy Night" and "The Christmas Song (Chestnuts Roasting on an Open Fire)," and spent the following months performing more than 300 concert dates, always to hordes of screaming, predominately female fans.

Although they rarely argued among themselves, and put forth a wholesome, even religious image (they were often seen wearing matching bracelets engraved with the acronym "WWJD," which stands for "What Would Jesus Do?"), the group was soon plagued by trouble. The band members began to feel that Pearlman and Trans Continental had failed to live up to their contractual obligations, and their fears were confirmed by Chasez's uncle, a lawyer, who reviewed the contract at the band's request. In 1996 Pearlman had promised the five an American record contract, but it was revealed that their initial contract was not with RCA itself, but rather with Ariola, the company's German subsidiary. As a result, the group's royalties were being paid in deutsche marks, a form of currency subject to unstable exchange rates. The royalties were also paid at a much slower rate than would have been the case with a U.S. company. Accusations mounted, with the five charging that Pearlman had taken advantage of their early trust to wrest undue control of the group from them. Pearlman countered that he had acted as a father figure, initially paying all the group's living expenses out of his own pocket, as well as coming up with the band's name. From his point of view, the complaints were merely a symptom of his protégés' disloyalty.

'N Sync next announced their intention to sign with Jive Records, a move that set off several lawsuits. BMG Entertainment, RCA's parent company, filed a $150 million suit to stop the band from using the name 'N Sync, and the Backstreet Boys, already signed with Jive and wearying of the endless comparisons of the two acts by the press, threatened to leave the label if 'N Sync joined. The Backstreet Boys eventually agreed to remain with Jive, and in November 1999 a judge ruled that 'N Sync could continue to perform and record using its current name. A mediated, closed-door meeting took place after that decision, and the parties involved reached an undisclosed settlement. In January 2000 Jive Records released the first single, "Bye, Bye, Bye," from the band's second album, *No Strings Attached.* The video for the song showed the five portrayed as marionettes being manipulated by a young woman. Although promotional literature for the group explains that the song is an anthem calling for young women to treat their boyfriends well or risk having them leave, some observers felt that the song functioned as a warning to avaricious record executives.

The entire album was released that March and immediately began to break sales records. As of May 2000, it had sold almost eight million copies, and sales showed no signs of stopping. The press seemed to devote as much space to describing the Backstreet Boys' reaction to having their popularity challenged and their sales figures beaten as to actual reviews of *No Strings Attached.* In a representative observation, David Browne wrote for *Entertainment Weekly* (March 24, 2000), "On the positive tip . . . ['N Sync] made a livelier, more groove-friendly record than have any of their male peers. On the less than positive tip, they do so by adapting a high school locker's worth of hammy, agonizingly contrived African-American vocal mannerisms."

The group made several television appearances following the album's release, including one at the 72nd Annual Academy Awards. (They had been nominated for the song "Music of My Heart," from the movie of the same name, which they had recorded with Gloria Estefan, but did not win an award. They were, however, given a Special Achievement Award at the 2000 American Latino Media Arts Awards ceremony for the video version of the song.) 'N Sync continued to tour extensively, fueling further album sales. They pursued independent projects as well: Bass made an acting appearance on the television drama *7th Heaven* and has formed his own entertainment management company, which represents several country-and-western acts; Fatone has contributed to an acting handbook written by his former drama teacher; and Kirkpatrick has started a clothing, visual arts, and music company called FuMan Skeeto. Timberlake has appeared in a Disney television movie called *Model Behavior* and started a nonprofit foundation to promote music education. Chasez, in addition to composing and co-producing some of the tracks on *No Strings Attached,* has been doing the same for various other artists.

The group has adamantly denied any rivalry with their fellow Jive Records artists and has said that any acrimony between them and members of the Backstreet Boys has been fabricated by the press. (The Backstreet Boys have accused them publicly of riding their coattails.) There is little dispute that the unprecedented success of 'N Sync puts added pressure on other young pop acts. "The yardstick is definitely extended . . . ," a Jive executive told Richard Skanse for *Rolling Stone* (March 31, 2000, on-line). "We know now what the possibilities are. We're not going to compare a Britney Spears record to 'N Sync, or Backstreet Boys. However, 'N Sync has shown us what can be done." —M.R.

Suggested Reading: *Entertainment Weekly* p20+ Mar. 5, 1999, with photos, p99+ Mar. 24, 2000, with photo, p20+ May 19, 2000, with photos; Jive Records Web site; *Rolling Stone* p58+ Nov. 12, 1998, with photos; *Rolling Stone* (on-line) Mar. 31, 2000; *USA Today* D p1+ Mar. 21, 2000, with photos

Selected Recordings: *'N Sync*, 1998; *Home for Christmas*, 1998; *No Strings Attached*, 2000

Shamil Zhumatov/Archive Photos

Nazarbayev, Nursultan

July 6, 1940– President of Kazakhstan. Address: c/o Embassy of the Republic of Kazakhstan, 1401 16th St. N.W., Washington, DC 20036

Nursultan Nazarbayev, the powerful and, to all appearances, popular president of Kazakhstan, has set economic development at the top of the national agenda. Implicitly comparing Kazakhstan to such East Asian "tigers" as Malaysia and Singapore, so-called for the impressive economic gains they posted in the mid-1990s, Nazarbayev has predicted a strong economic performance for his country in the first decades of the 21st century. "I am convinced that by 2030 Kazakstan will become a Central Asian Snow Leopard and will serve as an example for other developing states . . . ," he wrote in a supplement to the October 11, 1997 edition of the Russian-language newspaper *Kazakstanskaia pravda*, as translated by Kirill Nourzhanov for *Russian and Euro-Asian Bulletin* (April 1998, on-line). "This will be a Kazakstani Leopard, characteristically elitist, independent, clever, manly and noble, brave and shrewd." Buried in his seemingly innocuous, if optimistic, vision is his take on the thorny debate over the relative merits of democracy for developing economies. In the mid-1990s a number of Asian leaders argued that both local exigencies and distinctive "Asian" values required them to sacrifice democratic principles for national prosperity and security. By likening Kazakhstan to the Asian "tigers," Nazarbayev seems to have agreed with such a proposition. Although the so-called "tigers" were ravaged by the Asian economic crisis of 1998, during which Asian stock markets and currencies fell to their lowest global values in decades, indications are that Nazarbayev continues to view the Asian economic model as the most appropriate one for Kazakhstan. While he has repeatedly stated that democracy remains a long-term goal for Kazakhstan, Nazarbayev continues to keep his government in tight rein; in the interim, economic development and internal security have taken precedence.

The Republic of Kazakhstan, almost twice the size of the state of Alaska, is geographically the second-largest republic of the former Soviet Union, which dissolved in 1991. Because of its strategically important location—bordering Russia, China, and the Caspian Sea—Kazakhstan has often been seen as a Eurasian bridge, or a country at the crossroads of Europe and Asia. The president of Kazakhstan is thus faced with the task of juggling the sometimes conflicting demands of the country's two powerful neighbors, while cultivating amicable relations with the United States and such regional powers as Iran. Adding to Kazakhstan's political and economic heft is a wealth of natural resources. Beyond its extensive deposits of coal and iron ore, Kazakhstan also possesses considerable oil reserves. The Tengiz Oil Field, at the northeastern tip of the Caspian Sea, is among the world's 10 largest, and preliminary studies indicate that the recently discovered Kashagan Oil Field, in the northern section of the Caspian, may be even larger.

The population of Kazakhstan comprises more than 120 ethnic groups. The largest is the Kazakhs (from whom the country gets its name), a Turkic-speaking, predominantly Muslim people who were still mostly nomadic at the beginning of the 20th century. Kazakhs constitute some 46 percent of the population, which in mid-2000 was nearly 17 million. Also numerous are ethnic Russians (35 percent), who tend to be Russian Orthodox Christians; Ukrainians (5 percent); Germans (3 percent); Uzbeks (2 percent); and Tartars (2 percent). While Kazakhstan has largely been spared the ethnic conflict that has plagued other countries in the region, there have been signs of unrest. In December 1986, for example, the forced resignation of a high official, coupled with internal tensions among various ethnic groups, led to rioting and civil unrest in the capital. More recently, the proclamation of a breakaway state in the north of the country, the Autonomous South Siberian Cossack Republic, was barely averted in 1997.

An ethic Kazakh, Nursultan Abishevich Nazarbayev was born into a family of mountain shepherds on July 6, 1940 in the Kazakhstani village of Chemolgan. Little is known of Nazarbayev before 1960, the year he began working at the Karaganda Metallurgical Combine. He remained at the combine for several years, and while working as an iron founder, a dispatcher, and a blast-furnace attendant, Nazarbayev studied metallurgical engineering at the technical college annexed to the foundry. It was there that he met his wife, Sara Alpysovna Nazarbayeva, who studied at the same technical institute and is now an economist. In 1967 Nazarbayev completed his course of study. Shortly thereafter, in about 1969, he began to emerge as a presence on the local political scene. While he had been a member of the Communist Party as early as 1962, his active participation in politics appears to date from the late 1960s. Nazarbayev's political fortunes rose steadily: from 1969 through 1973 he was a member of Komsomol, a youth organization of the Russian Communist Party; in 1973 he became secretary of the Party Committee at the Karaganda Metallurgical Combine; by 1977 he had risen to second secretary of the Karaganda Regional Party Committee; and two years later, in 1979, he was nominated secretary of the Central Committee of the Communist Party of Kazakhstan. What is most remarkable about the trajectory of Nazarbayev's political career is that he was an ethnic Kazakh in a field dominated by ethnic Russians, who tended to have more clout with the central government in Moscow and thus usually received the most influential appointments.

Throughout the 1980s Nazarbayev continued his political climb. In 1984 he was appointed chairman of the Council of Ministers, and in 1989 he was elected first secretary of the Central Committee of the Communist Party of Kazakhstan. In April 1990 he became president of the Soviet Socialist Republic of Kazakhstan, at which time the Soviet Union was undergoing fundamental changes. Mikhail Gorbachev's policies of *perestroika* ("restructuring") and *glasnost* ("openness"), which had been in place since 1986, together with a moribund national economy, were leading up to the eventual collapse of the Soviet Communist system, which dated back to 1922. Throughout 1991, while Gorbachev and Boris Yeltsin fought to determine the future of the crumbling empire—Gorbachev struggling to maintain the last vestiges of centralized authority and Yeltsin calling for the Soviet leader's resignation—Nazarbayev struck a middle way, appealing to both party bureaucrats and democratic reformers. Although he criticized the Kremlin, he tended to do so quietly, and he quit the Communist Party only after its failed coup attempt in August 1991. Yeltsin, by way of contrast, had withdrawn his party membership in July 1990.

With the demise of the old Soviet system, Nazarbayev found himself at the helm of a newly independent state, the Republic of Kazakhstan. His position was officially confirmed in a December 1991 election in which Nazarbayev, the only candidate, received 98.7 percent of the vote. Among his first political successes was the incorporation of Kazakhstan into the Commonwealth of Independent States (CIS), a loose confederation of former Soviet republics. As originally conceived, the commonwealth would have comprised only three predominantly Slavic republics: Russia, Ukraine, and Belarus. Shortly after the leaders of these states had declared their plans to form the CIS, Nazarbayev announced his intention to bring Kazakhstan into the fold and succeeded in securing co-founder status for his country. The remaining Central Asian republics—Tajikistan, Kyrgyzstan, Uzbekistan, and Turkmenistan—quickly followed the example of their larger neighbor. By bringing Kazakhstan into the CIS, Nazarbayev reaffirmed his country's historic ties with Russia, thus reassuring the country's population of ethnic Russians, many of whom were concerned about their place in the newly independent state.

In the succeeding years Nazarbayev initiated a transformation and privatization of the Kazakh economy. From 1991 through 1996, over $2 billion in foreign investments flowed into Kazakhstan, and Western companies received permission to conduct business in Kazakhstan and to extract fossil fuels from the country's abundant reserves. Nazarbayev also presided over the denuclearization of Kazakhstan, which had suddenly found itself in possession of 1,400 nuclear warheads and 104 multi-warhead intercontinental missiles after the collapse of the Soviet Union. Working with American and Russian officials, Nazarbayev agreed to remove all nuclear arms from Kazakh soil in return for substantial foreign aid.

The first serious challenge to Nazarbayev's presidency came in early 1995, when the Constitutional Court, Kazakhstan's highest court, declared the 1994 parliamentary elections invalid. (The elections had been favorable to Nazarbayev's party, which won a plurality of 33 of the 177 seats.) Nazarbayev responded by calling for a referendum to authorize a postponement of free presidential elections, which had been scheduled for 1996, until 2000. According to official government results, 91 percent of eligible voters turned out for the referendum; of those, 95 percent supported the postponement, thus extending Nazarbayev's term by four years. Later in 1995 Nazarbayev called for another referendum, to ratify a new constitution. Again, government figures argued a groundswell of public support: 90 percent of all eligible voters turned out for the referendum, 89 percent of them supporting the new constitution. While the new constitution explicitly proclaimed Kazakhstan a presidential republic with a bicameral Parliament and provided for rights and freedoms in line with democratic principles, it also called for a significant expansion of executive power. The augmented powers of the presidency made many uneasy; critics questioned whether democratic values were served by placing more control in the hands of a single office. One report in the *Christian Science Monitor*, for instance, referred to Nazarbayev's reign as a "soft dictatorship." In response to accusations that he was subverting democratic principles, Nazarbayev argued that total democracy, while still a long-term goal, was not yet a viable method of governance for his country. "Kazakhstan is less than a century from feudalism, and only yesterday did we escape totalitarianism. How can we measure our democracy in the same way as the United States or Europe?" he said, according to Geoffrey York in the Toronto *Globe and Mail* (May 1, 1995). "Western models don't work in our Eurasian space." In the meantime, other goals—economic development and political stability chief among them—would take precedence.

Few expected the Central Asian republics to become democracies overnight; the political legacy of about 70 years of Soviet rule, struggling economies, and the potential for ethnic conflict all seemed to point against trying to accomplish too much too soon. But by the late 1990s, democratic reformers seemed to be growing impatient with Nazarbayev. In October 1998 the Parliament of Kazakhstan unexpectedly moved to hold presidential elections in January 1999, a year earlier than previously scheduled by the first 1995 referendum. Against the formal protestations of Nazarbayev, the motion carried in Parliament by a vote of 62 to one. Anvar Batalov, a member of the lower house of Parliament, explained that legislators wanted to avoid having their elections eclipsed by Russia's, also slated for 2000. "But above all," he added, as reported in the *Economist* (October 17, 1998), "we want to decide political questions in this century." Critics of Nazarbayev, however, suspected that the president in fact provided the impetus to move elections up a year. The new timetable required all presidential contenders to collect 170,000 signatures and to pay a $30,000 registration fee by the end of November 1998, a little more than a month before the elections. The new deadline thus gave the incumbent a considerable jump on his rivals. Moreover, the legislative branch of government is relatively weak in Kazakhstan, since the president has the authority to dissolve Parliament if it approves a no-confidence vote in the government or twice rejects his nominee for prime minister. For Nazarbayev's detractors, such an imbalance of power offered further evidence that the Parliament's resolution was a sham staged by the president.

While rescheduling the election elicited grumbles in the Western media, other events caused greater damage to Nazarbayev's reputation as a nascent democrat. Despite the new tight deadline, several challengers successfully registered for the election. Chief among them was Akezhen Kazhegeldin, a former prime minister whom Nazarbayev had forcibly removed from office in 1997. In early November, two months before the election, a Kazakhstani court excluded Kazhegeldin from the race on a technicality: Kazhegeldin, it appears, had attended a meeting of an unregistered political group, the Movement for Fair Elections. Several weeks later, on November 24, the Constitutional Council, Kazakhstan's highest legal body (with the ratification of the 1995 constitution, the Constitutional Council had replaced the Constitutional Court), upheld the lower court's decision. Again, Nazarbayev formally objected to a curtailment of democratic process; again, critics charged that his protestations were a pretense, that the judiciary was simply doing his bidding. A *New York Times* (November 9, 1998) editorial, for example, charged that "Nazarbayev is a thinly disguised dictator who stages elections he has no chance of losing." The Organization for Security and Cooperation in Europe, as reported by Steve LeVine for the *New York Times* (December 6, 1998), voiced "serious doubts that the principles for democratic elections" would be fulfilled, and State Department spokesman James Rubin detected a "pattern of harassment" directed at the opposition. Indeed, with Kazhegeldin out of the way, Nazarbayev was a shoo-in: among the remaining contenders—Kazakh Communist Party head Serikbolsyn Abdildin, parliamentarian and amateur meteorologist Engels Gabbasov, and head of the State Customs Committee Gani Kasymov, whose sensationalist campaign included a film of the candidate crushing a glass with his bare hands—no single candidate had a realistic chance of defeating the incumbent.

As expected, Nazarbayev won in January 1999 by a landslide, taking more than 78 percent of the ballots cast in an election that had an official voter turnout of 86 percent. The remainder of the vote was divided among the three contenders, the strongest of which, the Communist Abdildin, came away with a mere 13.5 percent. As reported by David Hoffman in the *Washington Post* (January 12, 1999), Nazarbayev trumpeted the result as "a serious step toward greater democracy," pointing out that it had been the first freely contested election in the nation's history. "You remember the times when turnout was 99.9 percent and the vote in favor 99.9 percent?" Hoffman quoted him as saying. "Well, you could say that we have allowed democracy to progress by 20 percent." Critics, however, remained unimpressed. Human Rights Watch, a U.S.-based nongovernmental organization, judged the campaign to have been characterized by "coercion, threats, and the repression of opposition activists," and the Organization for Security and Cooperation in Europe said that it would not recognize the results of the election.

Nazarbayev stood his ground against such detractors, invoking what he described as a uniquely Asian system of values with which, he claimed, his critics were not conversant. As Nazarbayev argued in an interview with the *Washington Times* (December 20, 1999, on-line), the specter of ethnic conflict has made political stability the paramount concern in the region. "It also should be taken into account that we are surrounded by unstable countries—the events in the Caucasus, in Western China, conflicts in Afghanistan and Tajikistan. There's also problems in Chechnya," he said. "So our primary problem is the stability of the country. It's very hard to keep this stability when you have more than 120 nationalities living together in Kazakhstan. One of the crucial issues for our people is to survive." Undoubtedly, civil strife is a concrete danger in the region, and one that Nazarbayev has thus far managed to keep at bay. The crucial question is how to best foster stability, given the current political climate in Kazakhstan: through a strong executive effectively empowered to rule by decree, or through the democratization of the polity.

In the summer of 2000, Nazarbayev reiterated his commitment to regional security after clashes between rebels and government troops intensified in Uzbekistan and Kyrgyzstan. In late July and early August, Kazakhstan provided military aid to the two countries; later, on August 20, Nazarbayev issued a joint statement with the presidents of Kyrgyzstan, Tajikistan, and Uzbekistan, pledging that, as quoted by Douglas Frantz in the *New York Times* (September 6, 2000), "terrorist actions will be crushed using the most decisive measures." Soon afterward the Kazakhstani president requested a broadening of his executive power to check religious extremism in his own country. Human-rights groups voiced the suspicion that Nazarbayev had used religious extremism as an excuse to expand his authority.

Nursultan Nazarbayev and his wife, Sara, have three children and three grandchildren. His eldest daughter, Dariga, is an historian; she is also in charge of the national television network. Dinara, his second daughter, is a graduate of the A. V. Lunacharsky Institute of Theater Arts, in Moscow. His youngest daughter, Aliya, is currently a student at a U.S. university. In 1992 Nazarbayev successfully defended a doctoral thesis in economics at the Russian Academy of Management, in Moscow. His hobbies include tennis, hunting, and horseback riding. He is also an avid reader; among his favorite subjects are history, philosophy, and economics. According to his official Web site, a star—Perseus RA 3h 23v Osd 40° 43—has been named in his honor. — P.K.

Suggested Reading: *Bulletin of the Atomic Scientists* p24+ Oct. 1993, with photos; *New York Times* A p24 Nov. 9, 1998, I p11 Dec. 6, 1998, IV p5 Jan. 3, 1999; *Time* p19+ Dec. 23, 1991, with photos; *Washington Post* A p10 July 30 1991, A p17 Feb. 14, 1994, A p12 Jan. 12, 1999

Norton, Edward

Aug. 18, 1969– Actor; director; screenwriter. Address: c/o Endeavor, 9701 Wilshire Blvd., 10th Fl., Beverly Hills, CA 90212

Armando Gallo/Retna Ltd.

Nearly every actor has faced moments when he or she must decide whether or not to keep reaching for the brass ring. Edward Norton confronted one such moment in the early 1990s. He had auditioned for Georgianne Walken, a theater casting director (and the spouse of actor Christopher Walken), in the hope of securing a role in a New York Shakespeare Festival production. Rather than offer him a part, Walken counseled him to quit acting. "Those moments can be very important, because if they make you doubt yourself, you oughta get out," Norton told Peter Biskind for *Vanity Fair* (August 1999). "But if you walk out pissed off and convinced that they're wrong, then you're probably in the right business. I walked out pissed off, thinking she was an idiot, and I was going to show her." A few years later he landed a major supporting role opposite Richard Gere in the film *Primal Fear* (1996). Unknown beyond the insular world of Off-Broadway theater, Norton stunned audiences and critics alike with his portrayal of Aaron Stampler, a soft-spoken altar boy charged with the murder of Chicago's archbishop. Norton's outstanding performance earned him an Academy Award nomination and a Golden Globe Award for best supporting actor. Since his stellar debut Norton has been featured in a range of offbeat roles, has garnered a second Oscar nomination, and has drawn comparisons to such thespians as Dustin Hoffman and Robert De Niro.

The eldest of three children, Edward Norton was born on August 18, 1969 in Boston, Massachusetts, and raised in Columbia, Maryland, between Baltimore and Washington, D.C. Columbia was designed and founded in the late 1960s by Norton's maternal grandfather, the famed real-estate developer James Rouse, who headed such successful urban revitalization projects as Boston's Faneuil Hall Marketplace, Baltimore's Harborplace, and New York City's South Street Seaport. Since its inception, the municipality has been a model of racial and economic integration and diversity, largely thanks to Rouse's careful planning. Norton's father, Edward Norton Sr., an attorney, was a federal prosecutor during President Jimmy Carter's administration; later he served as director of public policy for the National Trust for Historic Preservation. The actor's mother, Robin, taught high school English before becoming director of educational grants at the Abell Foundation. Norton's childhood was pleasant, if unremarkable, and for some time he regarded his serene suburban origins as a hindrance professionally. "I used to envy people who were driven by the textures of their history," he acknowledged to Catherine Hyde for *Horizon* (November 1, 1997, on-line). "I believed that unique art was produced by intense needs to break out of some kind of confinement. I didn't think defining and iconic art could come out of a sheltered life."

Norton has traced his discovery of acting to a serendipitous relationship with another budding performer. "I started studying acting when I was about six," he told Drew Barrymore for *Interview* (April 1996). "I had a babysitter [Betsy True] who subsequently went on to play Cosette in *Les Misérables* on Broadway. At the time, she was in a musical version of Cinderella, called *If I Were a Princess*, at the local drama school. There were a lot of little kids my age playing Cinderella's mice, and I really wanted to be a mouse. I had a notion that if my babysitter got me down to the school quick enough, I could actually get to be a mouse before the production closed. She did take me down the day after I saw the play and I signed up for classes." Although Norton arrived too late to join the corps of mice, he began several years of training at the Columbia School for Theatrical Arts, under Toby Orenstein. The young actor's precocity and focus were evident almost immediately. Orenstein recalled to Phoebe Hoban for the *New York Times* (January 19, 1997), "He played Little Jake in *Annie Get Your Gun*, and he had to sit in a boat through most of the production. The first thing he asked me was, 'What's my objective?' He had tremendous analytical ability that most kids don't have."

At Wilde Lake High School, in Columbia, Norton got good grades, played varsity baseball, and argued for the debate team in defense of First Amendment rights and affirmative action. Because his peers did not consider acting a "cool" activity, he drifted from that pursuit after entering high school. He realized how much he missed it when, at age 16, on a class trip to Washington, D.C., he saw the British actor Ian McKellen's one-man performance in *Acting Shakespeare*. "It blew my mind," Norton told Peter Biskind. "I remember riding on the school bus back. I sort of sat by myself, away from my friends, and I was thinking, You have to reconsider this whole thing. You have to take this very, very seriously because what [McKellen] was doing was a serious thing you could do for life. And so I started taking acting classes again and I did a lot of it in college."

Norton gained entrance to Yale University, in New Haven, Connecticut. At first he declared himself an astronomy major; troubled by the difficulty of his physics courses, he switched his major to history. As an extracurricular activity, he appeared in productions of the school's acclaimed student theater companies. He also studied Japanese, eventually becoming fluent in the language. He put this new skill to use during the summer he spent in Osaka, Japan, working for the Enterprise Foundation, which his grandparents had founded with the goal of reviving decaying urban areas in Japan and elsewhere. (Sources differ as to whether he was still in college then.)

Following his graduation from Yale, in 1991, Norton hesitated to pursue a career in acting because of the fear of financial instability. He turned to his grandfather for advice. "He told me 'Don't, don't, don't go into a job just for money or because you think that's what you have to do,'" Norton told Catherine Hyde. (Later, after *Primal Fear* was released, he said, his grandfather "was tickled to see his advice pay off. He was glad he hadn't set me up for disappointment.") For the next four years, while living in New York City, Norton supported himself with the sorts of jobs often associated with aspiring actors: waiting tables, proofreading documents for a court-reporting service, and assisting a casting director. He even applied for a license to drive a taxi but was too young to qualify. Meanwhile, he studied acting with the theatrical director and noted drama teacher Terry Schreiber and auditioned for numerous stage and film roles, coming close several times to being cast in such films as *With Honors*, *Sabrina*, *Hackers*, and *Up Close & Personal*.

Norton's first break came in 1994, when he auditioned with the Signature Theatre Company for a role in Edward Albee's play *Finding the Sun*. He did not get the part, but he impressed Albee and the Signature's artistic director sufficiently that they cast him in the company's production of another Albee play, *Fragments*. "He is one of the two young actors that I've seen in the last few years who really knocked me out," Albee declared to Phoebe Hoban. "Every once in a while you see a special kind of talent, that makes you say, 'Wow!,' and Edward is one of those." Shortly after his appearance in the Albee play, Norton was alerted to an open casting call for a major motion picture, *Primal Fear*, in which the marquee idol Richard Gere had agreed to star. Leonardo DiCaprio had been slated to take the supporting role but had backed out, leaving Paramount Studios—and in particular Deborah Aquila, head of features casting for Paramount—scrambling to find a replacement. About 2,100 actors were auditioned for the part of Aaron Stampler, whose schizophrenic persona demanded tremendous range from an actor. The search for a supporting actor lasted so long that Gere threatened to back out of the project.

In preparing for his audition, Norton practiced speaking with an eastern Kentucky twang. "I knew the accent because my grandparents were from that area," he told David Handelman for *Vogue* (January 1997). "But I certainly don't have it, so I prepared by watching *Coal Miner's Daughter*." In addition to the accent, he gave Stampler a stutter. In his audition, Norton moved seamlessly from innocence to rage; his convincing portrayal led Aquila to ask Gregory Hoblit, the film's director, to fly to New York to be present for Norton's second audition. Hoblit, too, was impressed by the young actor; Paramount, however, was unwilling to take a chance on an unknown. Positive that Norton was right for the role, Aquila and Hoblit flew him to Los Angeles to film a screen test for studio executives. He did so well that he won the part.

The tapes of his screen test were passed around Hollywood, and before *Primal Fear* even opened in theaters, Norton was contacted by the directors Woody Allen and Milos Forman, both of whom offered him choice roles. In Allen's musical comedy *Everyone Says I Love You* (1996), Norton portrayed a crooning, preppie lawyer who vies for the affections of a character played by Drew Barrymore. He was cast as a First Amendment lawyer opposite Woody Harrelson in *The People vs. Larry Flynt* (1996), Forman's acclaimed biopic about the famed publisher of *Hustler* magazine. Meanwhile, the early and highly laudatory notices from his work in *Primal Fear* were starting to appear.

Thanks to his impressive feature debut, for which he won a Golden Globe Award, and his sudden popularity among high-profile directors, Norton began to attract the attention of the entertainment media. "By definition, you're sharing something publicly [when you act in a film], and I like that," Norton told Deanna Kizis for *Cosmopolitan* (December 1998). "I feel very content with the work I do—it's intended to be enjoyed by people. And to the degree that that makes me known, I'm absolutely fine. After all, it's what I set out to do." The flurry of notice coming Norton's way coincided with a series of personal losses. In March 1997, within a year of the deaths of two of his grandparents, his mother died, shortly after surgery to remove a brain tumor. "People come up to me and say, 'You must be flying!' But my experience of the last year and a half has not simply been about working on *Primal Fear*, *The People vs. Larry Flynt*, and *Everyone Says I Love You*," Norton explained to Graham Fuller for a piece in *Interview* (January 1997) that appeared not long before his mother's death. "It's been a period of downtime, personal unhappiness, and traumas that distract you from your work and the good things that are happening, as they would anybody." Norton organized a preview screening of *Everyone Says I Love You* in Baltimore and donated the proceeds to the medical research team at the Johns Hopkins Medical Center that cared for his mother.

Refusing to play the conventional roles expected of a young star, Edward Norton has since starred in the offbeat productions *Rounders* (1998), in which he was cast as a cardsharp opposite Matt Damon; *American History X* (1998), as a hatemongering neo-Nazi who undergoes a transformation; and *Fight Club* (1999), as a disaffected professional involved with an underground group of like-minded young affluents who find bare-knuckle fighting therapeutic. For his work in *American History X*, he received his second Oscar nomination.

Norton's most recent project is *Keeping the Faith* (2000), a romantic comedy that marked his debut as a director and co-writer (with Stuart Blumberg, a friend from Yale). In a conversation with Richard Corliss for *Time* (April 17, 2000), Norton said that in deciding to venture into other areas of cinema, he had followed the advice of the actor/director Warren Beatty. Unbidden, Beatty had phoned and told him, "I've been watching the stuff you're doing, and I think you're a lot like me. You're gonna be frustrated like I was, 'cause you're gonna want to do it yourself. I wanted to tell you, don't wait. 'Cause I waited too long. If you're gonna write and direct, just do it." Speaking with Corliss, Milos Forman expressed confidence in Norton's then-undemonstrated directorial abilities: "He's very bright and analytical, but that doesn't close the door to his instincts. I'm sure he analyzed the directors he worked with as thoroughly as he analyzes his parts as an actor. So now, when he says 'Action,' everything is there as planned—plus a few privileged moments, which come from his talent."

Released in April 2000, *Keeping the Faith* is about a love triangle involving a priest (played by Norton), a rabbi (Ben Stiller), and a corporate executive (Jenna Elfman) who entranced both men when all three were adolescents and who does so again some 20 years later. In an enthusiastic review of the film for the *New Yorker* (April 24–May 1, 2000), David Denby wrote, "The plot is movieish, obvious, a bit of a gimmick. . . . But it's gimmicky only in outline. Scene by scene, *Keeping the Faith* plays well, sometimes extremely well, with lots of goofy and charming detail. . . . I was impressed by Norton's acumen as an entertainer and as a storyteller: *Keeping the Faith* skirts about a dozen potential traps and embarrassments and grows in emotional force, and by the end I had to brush away a tear or two." Elvis Mitchell, on the other hand, reviewing *Keeping the Faith* for the *New York Times* (April 14, 2000), concluded that the film might have gotten more mileage out of its subject: "It is competent, but it seems driven to clear up complications as quickly as acne is dispatched in an infomercial."

Speaking of Norton to Corliss, Stuart Blumberg said, "He hasn't mastered the art of being a fake celebrity. But to his friends, Edward's the quintessentially normal guy. He's funniest when he's just being a nerdy goofball." While accepting the realities of celebrity, Norton has tried to establish parameters for the publicizing of his life. Though reportedly an open and engaging person, he has been reluctant to discuss his personal affairs with the press. He has stated his belief that prior knowledge of an actor's personal life impedes audiences' suspension of disbelief, because if viewers know too much about an actor, their perception of his or her performance becomes cluttered by questions of personality or fame. Norton wants his performances to speak for themselves. "I did almost no publicity for *Primal Fear* and that was a calculated strategy," he explained in a conversation with Graham Fuller. "No one was going to see that movie because of me, and the most I had to offer it was anonymity. The potency of the revelation about who my character really was in that film was in part reliant on the fact that people had *absolutely* no prior knowledge of me. They had no reason to expect a different voice or anything different from what they were initially presented with."

Norton observed to Richard Corliss that "in the absence of collective gods, we've created a poor man's Olympus in our entertainers. We've taken the clowns and elevated them to minor deities. We revere our clowns a little too much. But strip away all the nonsense that surrounds the movie business and, at its core, our kind of storytelling fills a real social, almost metaphysical need. People need and want the experience of getting together to watch stories. Films are our most potent cultural mythology. It's how you feel connected, not alone." —T.J.F.

Suggested Reading: *Interview* p86+ Apr. 1996, with photos, p82+ Jan. 1997, with photos; *New York Times* II p17+ Jan. 19, 1997, with photos; *Time* p76+ Apr. 17, 2000, with photo; *Vanity Fair* p128+ Aug. 1999, with photos

Selected Films: *Primal Fear*, 1996; *The People vs. Larry Flynt*, 1996; *Everyone Says I Love You*, 1996; *American History X*, 1998; *Rounders*, 1998; *Fight Club*, 1999; *Keeping the Faith*, 2000

Obst, Lynda

(OHbst)

Apr. 14, 1950– Film producer; writer. Address: Lynda Obst Productions, 5555 Melrose Ave., Bldg. 210, Hollywood, CA 90036; c/o Lavin Agency, 77 Peter St., Suite 400, Toronto, Canada M5V 2G4

According to the Hollywood producer Lynda Obst, women who wield power in the entertainment industry "have to be as tough" as their male counterparts—which makes them appear tougher, as she observed to Andrea Darvi Plate for *New York Newsday* (September 25, 1989). "But they also have an advantage: I call it the Powerful Mommy Syndrome. To be a good producer, you have to be the best mommy in the world. You have to give strength and encouragement and inspire confidence in everybody on the set. That kind of nurturing comes naturally to women." Obst began her career in Tinseltown in 1979, with a job in film development. She served as an associate producer for *Flashdance* (1983) and has produced or executive produced 10 other films, among them *Adventures in Babysitting*, *The Fisher King*, *This Is My Life*, *Sleepless in Seattle*, *One Fine Day*, *Contact*, and *The Siege*. Her book *Hello, He Lied: And Other Truths from the Hollywood Trenches* (1996), which describes some of her experiences in cinema and offers advice for aspiring female producers, became a best-seller in Los Angeles.

Rick Morton, courtesy of Broadway Books

Obst was named Lynda Rosen when she was born, on April 14, 1950. She grew up in the town of Harrison, New York, a suburb of New York City, with her younger brothers, Michael (who is now an ABC News bureau chief) and Rick (who cofounded the talent agency Endeavor). Her mother, a schoolteacher, emphasized to Lynda and her brothers the importance of education, while her father, who worked in the garment business, "had this profound belief that if you do, you accomplish," as Obst told Jason Cohen for *Texas Monthly* (July 1997).

Obst earned a B.A. degree in philosophy at Pomona College, in Claremont, California, and then pursued a graduate degree in the same subject at Columbia University, in New York City. Eager to enter the New York literary scene—"the most interesting world I'd ever been in in my life," as she described it to Cohen—she left Columbia before finishing the program. She had become immersed in that world thanks to her friendship with, and then marriage to, David Obst, a literary agent. At that time David Obst's clients included the prize-winning *Washington Post* journalists Bob Woodward and Carl Bernstein, whose book about their reporting of the Watergate scandal, *All the President's Men* (1974), became a best-seller (and later, a popular film). With Jann Wenner, the publisher of *Rolling Stone*, David Obst launched a publishing venture called Rolling Stone Press. Among its first titles was *The Sixties: The Decade Remembered Now, by the People Who Lived It Then* (1977), a compilation of *Rolling Stone* articles and photos, which Lynda Obst (under the name Lynda Rosen Obst) edited. She also contributed her own commentaries to the book, which is often referred to (erroneously) as the "Rolling Stone History of the Sixties."

Soon after the book came out, Obst got a job as an editor with the *New York Times Magazine*. According to Jason Cohen, "In some ways, it remains the credit she is most proud of." She quit after her husband made what Cohen described as a "near-unilateral decision" to move to Hollywood with the aim of advancing his own career into the area of film. Lynda Obst, who by then had a baby son, has told interviewers that she felt she had no choice but to follow her husband to California. Had he not relocated, she told Cohen, "I never would have left [the *New York Times* job]—never."

In 1979 Peter Guber, the chairman of Casablanca Records and Filmworks and a principal of Polygram Pictures, hired Lynda Obst to work in film development. The first picture to which she was assigned was Adrian Lyne's *Flashdance* (1983), an MTV-style romance about a young woman (portrayed by Jennifer Beals) who works as a welder by day and a dancer by night. While critics panned the movie, youthful audiences greeted it with enormous enthusiasm, and the film inspired countless preteen and teen girls to add torn sweatshirts and legwarmers to their wardrobes. Obst was greatly impressed by the "influence [of *Flashdance*] on popular culture," as she told Alison Rogers for *Women's Wire* (on-line) in the mid-1990s, and the movie's success led her to view a career in filmmaking in a far more positive light than she had previously.

In 1982 Obst joined the Geffen Film Co., headed by David Geffen, where she worked on such films as Paul Brickman's *Risky Business* (1983), starring Tom Cruise and Rebecca De Mornay; Martin Scorsese's *After Hours* (1985), with Griffin Dunne and Rosanna Arquette; Albert Brooks's *Lost in America* (1985), with Brooks and Julie Hagerty; and Tim Burton's *Beetlejuice* (1988), featuring Alec Baldwin and Geena Davis. Meanwhile, in 1985 she had left Geffen to co-found Hill/Obst Productions, with Debra Hill, a one-time scriptwriter. Their debut film, which also marked the directing debut of Chris Columbus, was *Adventures in Babysitting* (1987), a comedy starring Elizabeth Shue that attracted little notice. The same fate befell their second production, *Heartbreak Hotel* (1988), another Chris Columbus–directed comedy.

Obst's next film, *The Fisher King* (1991), was the product of her own company, Obst Productions, which she had launched in 1989. Co-produced by Debra Hill, directed by Terry Gilliam, and written by Richard LaGravanese, *The Fisher King* is a modern retelling of the medieval legend involving the knight Parsifal (also known as Percivale), King Arthur, and the Holy Grail. The movie, which starred Robin Williams, Jeff Bridges, Mercedes Ruehl, and Amanda Plummer and was distributed by Columbia Pictures, earned four Academy Award nominations despite its highly mixed reviews. Next, for 20th Century Fox, Obst produced *This Is My Life* (1992), directed by Nora Ephron and written by Ephron and her sister Delia Ephron from the same-titled novel by Meg Wolitzer. Starring Julie Kavner as a single mother whose attempts to become a stand-up comedian upset her two young daughters (Gaby Hoffman and Samantha Mathis), *This Is My Life* drew a lukewarm critical response. Obst served as executive producer of *Sleepless in Seattle* (1993), which Ephron both directed and co-wrote and which was released by TriStar Pictures. Reminiscent of the 1957 Carey Grant/Deborah Kerr tearjerker *An Affair to Remember*, *Sleepless in Seattle* featured Tom Hanks as a recently widowed West Coast father and Meg Ryan as an East Coast reporter who falls in love with him after hearing him talk about his late wife on a radio show. Although many reviewers found serious faults with the film, audiences flocked to see it.

Under the terms of a multi-picture contract she had secured in 1993 with 20th Century Fox, Obst produced Michael Hoffman's light romantic comedy *One Fine Day* (1996), starring Michelle Pfeiffer and George Clooney as two single parents who fall in love; Forest Whitaker's *Hope Floats* (1998), featuring Sandra Bullock as a former prom queen who returns to her hometown in Texas after discovering that her husband has been cheating on her; and Edward Zwick's *The Siege* (1998), with Denzel Washington, Annette Bening, and Bruce Willis, about the bombings of a crowded Brooklyn bus and a packed Manhattan theater by Arab Muslim terrorists. When the film was 10 weeks into production, the Council on American-Islamic Relations and the American-Arab Anti-Discrimination Committee, fearful that *The Siege* might stir up anti-Arab and anti-Muslim sentiment, wrote a long memo to

Zwick, Obst, and Fox, expressing their objections to many facets of the movie. The memo detailed 60 specific objections and suggested that the terrorists be represented as a home-grown militia. In their response, Obst and Zwick agreed to some changes but insisted that the bombers would remain foreign Muslim terrorists. Later, the Fox studio declared in a press release, "Within the framework of an action-adventure, the film deals seriously and sensitively with timely and important themes, such as prejudice and persecution, the price of our personal freedoms, and the protection of those freedoms—for all Americans."

While working for Fox, Obst also executive produced, along with Joan Bradshaw, *Contact* (1997), a $90 million adaptation for cinema of the 1985 novel by the famous astronomer and popularizer of science Carl Sagan. The film, which was released in the year following Sagan's death, focuses on the successful search for extraterrestrial life by a determined astronomer (played by Jodie Foster) and on how she ultimately prevails over the opposition of skeptical colleagues and military men. Directed by Robert Zemeckis, *Contact* garnered praise for its scientific accuracy and its extraordinary special effects; critics expressed far less enthusiasm for its earnest but—in the view of most of them—unsuccessful attempts to confront boldly and realistically "the tension between science and religion" and between "intellect and faith," as Bernard Weinraub wrote for the *New York Times* (July 6, 1997).

In 1999 Obst served as executive producer for NBC's *The '60s*, a two-part miniseries that presented such aspects of the 1960s as the civil rights movement; the Vietnam War and the student protests it sparked; the assassinations of President John F. Kennedy, Senator Robert F. Kennedy, and the Reverend Martin Luther King Jr.; and the burgeoning sexual revolution. On an NBC Web page, Obst described the 1960s as "the time in my life I felt most alive" and joked that she had "been waiting for the '60s to come back since December 31, 1969." Using actors, the docudrama re-created events of the decade from the perspective of a white family from Chicago and a black family from Greenwood, Mississippi. To avoid excessive nostalgia, Obst told Graham Fuller for *Interview* (February 1999), she presented what she described as "straight stuff." For example, she explained to Fuller, "to show kids waking up to social awareness—as one of our characters . . . does when he sees [on TV] 'Bull' Connor's police hosing black children in Birmingham in 1963—without comment, without grotesque underscoring, without reading ideology into it, feels powerful and poetic to me." On the NBC Web site, Obst wrote that the message of the production was that "cynicism is more dangerous than mistakes." She invested so much of herself in the production, she disclosed in the same article, that after completing it she experienced "work-induced postpartum depression" for the first time in her professional life.

With the screenwriter Carol Wolper, Obst co-wrote the novel *Dirty Dreams*, which was published in 1990. Her book *Hello, He Lied: And Other Truths from the Hollywood Trenches* (1996), is "a post-feminist, post-P.C. [politically correct] survival guide for women in Hollywood, a book that confronts and then breaks through female and male stereotypes into a knowing report on how real people work together in the hurly-burly world of movie making," according to David McClintick, writing for the *New York Times Book Review* (October 13, 1996). "The laughs in *Hello, He Lied* are somewhat deceptive," McClintick noted, "for the book is quite serious. In the end, Ms. Obst is not optimistic about change in the fundamental power dynamics of Hollywood, which has always been an oligarchy of white men."

Among other projects, Obst is currently involved with the film version of Laura Zigman's novel *Animal Husbandry* (1998), which is slated to star Ashley Judd and Hugh Jackman. The movie is due to be released in 2001, as are two other Obst projects: *How to Lose a Guy in 10 Days* and *The Wishbones*. When asked how she chooses projects, Obst told Marjorie Baumgarten for the *Austin Chronicle* (Vol. 17, Issue 5, 1997, on-line), "There are two things that I look for. One, basically, is visceral pieces that move me. They make me laugh, they make me cry, they somehow express what we're going through next. Either it moves me emotionally, it moves me philosophically, or it moves me culturally. . . . It just sort of has to knock my socks off in that way. And I use my internal gut. And then there's the occasional premise I buy because I believe it's an incredibly cool premise. . . . And I'm also very attracted to . . . things that reflect American culture."

Obst, who maintains one home near Austin, Texas, and another near Hollywood, has one son, Oliver. — V.K.

Suggested Reading: *Advancing Women* (on-line); *Austin Chronicle* (on-line) Vol. 17, Issue 5, 1997, with photo; *New York Newsday* p51 Sep. 25, 1989, with photo; *New York Times* C p15 Oct. 28, 1996, with photo; *Texas Monthly* p84+ July 1997, with photo, p118+ May 1998, with photo; *Women in Film* (on-line)

Selected Films: *Flashdance*, 1983; *The Fisher King*, 1991; *Sleepless in Seattle*, 1993; *Contact*, 1997; *Hope Floats*, 1998; *The Siege*, 1998

Selected Books: *Dirty Dreams*, 1990; *Hello, He Lied, and Other Truths from the Hollywood Trenches*, 1996

Deidre Davidson/Archive Photos

Palin, Michael

(PAY-lin)

May 5, 1943– Writer; actor; founding member of Monty Python's Flying Circus. *Address: Python Pictures Ltd., 68A Delancey St., London NW1 7RY, England*

"Michael Palin is not just one of Britain's foremost comedy character actors, whose inventive genius and astonishing versatility were vividly demonstrated in his widely acclaimed *Ripping Yarns* [television] series; he also talks a lot. Yap yap yap he goes, all day long and through the night, 23 to the dozen, the ground littered with the hind legs of donkeys, till you believe it is *not* possible, simply *not* possible for him to go on any longer, but he *does*." That description came from the actor John Cleese, Palin's friend and co-founding member of Monty Python, the famed British six-man comic writing and acting team that produced *Monty Python's Flying Circus*, one of BBC-TV's most enduring exports. Three decades after the show premiered, in 1969, it remains a powerful influence over British and American comedy. Independently of Monty Python, Palin has distinguished himself as a screenwriter, actor, children's writer, novelist, and travel documentarian. Writing in the *Washington Post* (June 22, 1998), Gary Krist asked rhetorically, "Is there anything that Michael Palin can't do?"

The son of Edward and Mary Palin, Michael Edward Palin was born on May 5, 1943 and raised in the industrial town of Sheffield, in northern England. His father was an organist until the Great Depression forced him to give up music as a profession, and he became a sales manager for an engineering firm. Eager for Michael to enjoy financial stability when he grew up, Edward Palin hoped that his son would attend Cambridge University and go into business. "He saw acting as a way to total moral compromise and financial despair," Michael Palin told Steven Drachman for the *Washington Post* (April 12, 1993). "Within his particular circle acting wasn't the right thing to do. He didn't see it as a man's job."

As a child Michael exhibited little skill for performance. "I had a very traumatic experience in the [Birkdale Preparatory School] music class, where we used to sing stirring songs like 'Men of Herlech,'" Palin recalled to a reporter for the *London Independent* (October 16, 1997, on-line). "The master said, 'Someone's not singing in tune!' I was denounced and forced to go up to the front to sing scales next to the piano. My voice shook. I was banished to a table in the same room called 'Non-singers' and I've been embarrassed about my singing ever since." Soon afterward, at age nine, Palin was cast as Martha Cratchit, the mother of Tiny Tim, in his school's production of *A Christmas Carol*, and during the Christmas dinner scene, he fell off the stage.

As a teenager at the Shrewsbury School, Palin displayed a talent for mimicry and a heightened sense of the absurd, but he did not take part in any organized performances. In 1962 he enrolled at Brasenose College, a division of Oxford University, in England, where his major was modern history. At Brasenose, he told Chris Chase for the *New York Times* (November 12, 1982), "there were people writing scripts for little college revues and setting up groups to go around doing cabaret. I spent as much time as possible doing that." In his first year he was coaxed into performing a cabaret act for Oxford's psychology society Christmas party. In his second and third years, the Oxford Revue chose him to travel to Scotland and perform at the 1964 and 1965 Edinburgh Festivals. He earned a B.A. degree with second-class honors from Brasenose after three years there.

While at college Palin had befriended Terry Jones, another revue member, and in 1966 the two began collaborating on scripts, which they peddled to BBC-TV shows. "If we managed to get a script on the *David Frost Show*—even half a minute would be enough—we'd open a bottle of brown ale and celebrate," Palin told Chris Chase. Over the next three years, the BBC bought enough of their scripts to provide them with a living wage. Moreover, through their work for such network programs as *Do Not Adjust Your Set* and *How to Irritate People* as well as David Frost's show, Palin and Jones met the American cartoonist Terry Gilliam and the young television writers Eric Idle, Graham Chapman, and John Cleese. The six men pooled their talents to produce a total of 45 half-hour episodes of *Monty Python's Flying Circus*.

Driven by silliness and irreverence and punctuated by the bizarre, often grotesque animation of Gilliam, *Monty Python's Flying Circus* lampooned sacred cows and cultural icons. Loony, uninhibited, and often pointless, Python skits were distinguished by their cartoonish exaggerations, illogic, incongruities, air of chaos, and abrupt endings; many lacked punch lines and failed to build to a climax. In the *Oxford English Dictionary*, "Pythonesque," an adjective, is defined as "pertaining to or characteristic of *Monty Python's Flying Circus*," and its use is said to date from 1975.

Michael Palin's favorite Python sketch is "The Cheese Shop," in which he played the owner of the National Cheese Emporium ("Finest in the district!" he exclaims). A verbose customer, played by John Cleese, enters the shop and asks for red Leicester. The proprietor says the store is "fresh out" of that cheese. The customer next asks for Tilsit; again, the Palin character responds that it is out of stock. After another 41 such exchanges, the customer asks if the shop has any cheese at all, to which the shopkeeper replies, "No, sir. Not a scrap. I was deliberately wasting your time, sir." The skit ends with the customer taking out a gun and shooting the owner. Frequently, skits segued directly into a completely unrelated sketch or to a shot of Cleese, dressed in the conservative style of a news anchor, seated behind a desk, announcing, "And now for something completely different."

In Great Britain, where the weekly show began airing in 1969, some 10 million people became loyal *Monty Python* viewers. A compilation of episodes, called *And Now for Something Completely Different* (1970), was shown in American theaters in 1972. The TV series came to the U.S. in 1974, the year that Palin and his colleagues decided to cease creating new episodes. American audiences quickly succumbed to "Pythonmania." According to some sources, the 45 episodes have been broadcast continuously on American television for the past 30 years. The series has been credited as a major influence on such American sketch-comedy shows as *Saturday Night Live*, and it has spawned successful books (*Monty Python's Big Red Book* [1970]; *Monty Python's Brand New Book* [1973]), records, and feature films. The motion pictures are *Monty Python and the Holy Grail* (1975), a spoof of the King Arthur legend; *Monty Python's Life of Brian* (1979), which the *Variety Movie Guide* described as an "utterly irreverent tale of a reluctant messiah whose impact proved something less pervasive than that of his contemporary Jesus Christ"; and *Monty Python's The Meaning of Life*, which won a Special Jury Prize at the 1983 Cannes Film Festival.

Seen as "the nice Python," Michael Palin has attributed a large part of *Monty Python*'s success to class distinctions, which are still important in British society. "Python is a pretty middle-class phenomenon, really," he explained to Larry Kart for the *Chicago Tribune* (October 10, 1982). "I should think we [the members of the Python troupe] all have similar sorts of education, and I think our parents were earning about the same amounts of money doing similar jobs. Graham's father was a policeman, and mine was an export manager, middle-management level. Very middle. Terribly middle. *Awfully* middle." From the middle, Palin said, it was easy to lampoon the extreme rungs of the social ladder and thus reach a wide audience. He has also attributed *Python*'s success to its creators' masterful use of silliness. Palin considers silliness "a very strong" weapon whose powers of subversion are even greater than those of its more sophisticated relative, satire.

After ending their *Monty Python* work, Palin and Terry Jones collaborated to create another critically acclaimed BBC-TV series, *Ripping Yarns*, which was broadcast in Great Britain from 1976 to 1980. A series of folktales set in Edwardian England, *Ripping Yarns* won the 1977 award for best comedy show from the British press critics and the 1979 BAFTA (British Academy of Film and Television Arts) Award for best light-entertainment program. Also for television, Palin acted in the BBC presentations of *Three Men in a Boat* (1975), an adaptation of a Jerome K. Jerome story, and *East of Ipswich* (1987).

For the silver screen, Palin co-wrote, with Terry Gilliam, and acted in the Gilliam-directed *Time Bandits* (1980), a fantasy about the origins of the universe that was aimed at young moviegoers as well as their parents. In the *Washington Post* (November 6, 1981), Gary Arnold called *Time Bandits* "a marvelous cinematic tonic, a sumptuous new classic in the tradition of time-travel and fairy-tale adventure"; Vincent Canby, who reviewed the movie for the *New York Times* (November 6, 1981), called it "a cheerfully irreverent lark—part fairy tale, part science fiction, and part comedy." *Time Bandits* was one of the highest-grossing movies of 1981.

Palin wrote, co-produced, and played the title character in *The Missionary* (1982), a film about an Anglican reverend who opens a mission for prostitutes in London's East End in 1906. In the cult classic *Brazil* (1984), an Orwellian fable that Gilliam directed, Palin played Jack Lint, an interrogator at the Ministry of Information Retrieval. Palin's best-received film performance to date was his portrayal of a stuttering animal-lover and crook named Ken in the hit comedy *A Fish Called Wanda* (1988), which earned him the 1988 BAFTA Award for best actor in a supporting role. (The film also starred Monty Python alumnus John Cleese.) Palin's characterization of Ken brewed a minor controversy, because some people thought that he was making fun of stutterers. This criticism was misdirected, however; Palin based his character on his father, a lifelong stutterer, and he has devoted much energy to studying and understanding this speech disorder. To David Denby, the reviewer for *New York* (July 18, 1988), Palin's performance was inspired: "The great rubber-faced British clown Michael Palin does something in *A Fish Called Wanda* that no American actor could get away with," Denby declared. "Palin turns a physical infirmity—stuttering—into a series of comic riffs so excruciatingly funny that stuttering no longer seems like a handicap: For the moment, at least, it seems an explosion of fantasy, an actor's poetry. At the climax of this wild, profane gangster comedy, Palin, aided by John Cleese, mimes the flight through the air of words he cannot speak, and the sustained moment is so close to tragic that I nearly laughed and wept at the same time. A comic performance this inventive transcends cruelty."

In 1980 Palin contributed to BBC-TV's *Great Railway Journeys of the World* series, and since then he has made his mark as the host of popular television travelogues. A train lover since childhood, he combined his affability, charm, and wit with his penchant for travel to produce three of the BBC's most successful miniseries ever. His first travelogue, *Around the World in Eighty Days* (1990), was inspired by Jules Verne's 19th-century novel of the same name. Verne's adventurer, Phileas Fogg, wagers another gentleman that he can circumnavigate the globe within 80 days. Opening the seven-part series with a wager against himself, Palin retraced Fogg's fictional steps through 17 countries, using only the preflight modes of travel available when the novel was written. Described in the media as a megahit, the series was imported by the A&E (Arts & Entertainment) cable network to the U.S., where it enjoyed similar success. At the invitation of the BBC, Palin next served as a guide in *Pole to Pole* (1992), for which he journeyed on land and sea along 30 degrees east longitude from the North Pole to the South Pole. The 141-day trip, condensed into eight hour-long episodes for television, took Palin through some of the most extreme meteorological climates—and volatile political climates—on Earth: the cold of the Arctic region and Antarctica, the heat of African wadis, and the turmoil of Russia in August 1991, only 24 hours before a failed coup in which Communist hard-liners attempted to oust Soviet president Mikhail Gorbachev. "The journey was as uncomfortable and dangerous as any journey I've ever taken in my life," Palin told Ken Clark for the *Chicago Tribune* (January 10, 1993). "But on the other hand, I got a chance to stand on both poles, cross the Nubian desert, and see Victoria Falls and the Nile and Istanbul, all in one journey. That's quite something; that keeps you reasonably cheerful."

For his most ambitious travel documentary, *Full Circle* (1997), in 1995 and 1996 Palin circumnavigated the Pacific Ocean, covering 50,000 miles and 18 countries. Though he has described this trip as his most taxing, it was also his favorite, because of "the sharply defined difference between all the [Pacific] Rim countries . . . ," as he explained to Don George for *Salon* (November 18, 1997, online). "It is what you want out of travel: to cross a border and find that border means something." Like its two predecessors, *Full Circle* was an unqualified hit in England and the U.S., where it aired on the Public Broadcasting System. Furthermore, each of the three televised travelogues spawned companion books (*Around the World in Eighty Days* [1989], *Pole to Pole* [1992], and *Full Circle* [1997]), with texts from Palin's travel diaries, and each became a best-seller in England and North America. In 1993 the British Book Awards committee named Palin travel writer of the year, for *Pole to Pole*.

Palin has also written books for children, among them *Small Harry and the Toothache Pills* (1981), *Cyril in the House of Commons* (1986), *Cyril and the Dinner Party* (1986), and *The Mirrorstone* (1986), co-written by Richard Seymour, about a British boy named Paul who falls through a mirror into another world, where he meets a wizard who wants him to recover a lost mirror from the ocean. Writing for the *Times Literary Supplement* (December 26, 1986), Lachlan Mackinnon called *The Mirrorstone* "gripping and imaginatively expansive." In *Hemingway's Chair* (1995), his only novel for adults, Palin wrote about an eccentric, bookish British postal clerk named Martin who is obsessed with the life and work of Ernest Hemingway. When Martin's Luddite work life is threatened by a new, technophilic postmaster, he slowly loses his mental moorings and takes on the masculine, take-charge personage of his hero. Though the material sounds like fertile ground for the madcap comedy of a Python, Palin used more understated humor, which Bruce Weber characterized in the *New York Times Book Review* (May 24, 1998) as owing "a lot more to Kingsley Amis than to John Cleese"; in the *Washington Post*, Gary Krist called *Hemingway's Chair* "an engaging and accomplished first novel."

Palin's next project, *Michael Palin's Hemingway's Adventure* (1999), a series of BBC documentaries on Hemingway's extensive travels, further explored the life of the American writer, who Palin described to Marjorie Miller for the *Los Angeles Times* (May 2, 2000) as "a fantastic, compulsive, competitive bully in many ways, but also someone who managed to change modern writing." In an online chat hosted by *Time*'s Web site, Palin characterized the series as "a homage from one traveler to another, and an attempt to drink as many strange alcoholic beverages in one series as possible. And maybe catch the odd 900-pound marlin." Like Palin's previous television travelogues, this one generated an eponymous book. For the most part, the critical response to the book was tepid. Karen Karbo, in a representative assessment for the *New York Times Book Review* (June 4, 2000), wrote, "Palin seems to make only two sorts of discoveries as he moves from location to location: reaffirming that yes, Hemingway did in fact drink there, or revealing that no, despite the myth, Hemingway did not drink there." David F. Turnbull, on the other hand, who reviewed the television series for the *New York Times* (May 3, 2000), praised Palin for his "wry" and "often delightful"observations.

Michael Palin lives in North London with his wife, Helen Gibbons, whom he married in 1966. The couple have three grown children: Thomas, William, and Rachel. For *Who's Who 1999*, Palin listed his recreational interests as "reading, running, railways—preferably all three in a foreign country." — T.J.F.

Suggested Reading: *Chicago Tribune* VI p18+ Oct. 10, 1982, with photos; *Salon* (on-line) Nov. 18, 1997; *Contemporary Authors* new revision series vol. 35, 1992; *Who's Who 1999*

Selected Television Shows: *Monty Python's Flying Circus*, 1969–74; *Three Men in a Boat*, 1975; *Ripping Yarns*, 1976–80); *East of Ipswich*, 1987; *Around the World in Eighty Days*, 1990; *Pole to Pole*, 1992; *Full Circle*, 1997; *Michael Palin's Hemingway Adventure*, 1999

Selected Films: *And Now for Something Completely Different*, 1970; *Monty Python and the Holy Grail*, 1975; *Monty Python's Life of Brian*, 1979; *Time Bandits*, 1980; *The Missionary*, 1982; *Brazil*, 1984; *Monty Python's The Meaning of Life*, 1983; *A Fish Called Wanda*, 1988

Selected Books: *Small Harry and the Toothache Pills*, 1981; *Cyril in the House of Commons*, 1986; *Cyril and the Dinner Party*, 1986; *The Mirrorstone*, 1986; *Around the World in Eighty Days*, 1989; *Pole to Pole*, 1992; *Hemingway's Chair*, 1995; *Full Circle*, 1997; *Michael Palin's Hemingway Adventure*, 2000

Patterson, Francine

1947– Zoologist; animal-rights activist. Address: Gorilla Foundation, Box 620530, Woodside, CA 94062

"I hate to tell you this, but we are all great apes," the zoologist Francine Patterson told Jane Meredith Adams for *Biography* (May 1999, on-line). "We're all in the same family, but some people don't like to think about it that way." For over a quarter-century, Patterson has been working ceaselessly to bridge the gap between people and apes through the use of sign language. In the 1970s, working with Koko, a gorilla she acquired from the San Francisco Zoo, Patterson spearheaded the longest-running interspecies communication study in the world. Over the years Koko has mastered a vocabulary of more than 1,000 words and has learned to respond to spoken English as well. Of paramount importance to Patterson is to erase from the public consciousness the image of gorillas as fear-inducing, savage beasts. Through her work, she hopes to make people aware that "one cannot really understand the mental workings of animals or bring them to the limits of their abilities unless one first has true rapport with them," as she wrote in her book *The Education of Koko* (1981). "Even the critics admit this possibility. What they fail to see is that the problem really is a misunderstanding of the purpose of language. Once that misunderstanding is straightened out and we accept language as a communicative behavior, the evidence of Koko's abilities is compelling for those who want to see it."

Known as Penny, Francine Patterson was born in Chicago in 1947 and grew up in Edina, Minnesota. She was an animal lover from the start. "I'd come home with baby rabbits that had been abandoned, a bat that was incapacitated," she recalled to Jane Meredith Adams. "I had everything: cats, turtles, fish, gerbils, mice, hamsters, lizards." When Patteron was young, her mother, Frances, died of breast cancer, and she was forced to assume almost total care for her five younger siblings.

After high school, Patterson entered the University of Illinois, where her father had once been a professor of educational psychology. She graduated in 1970 with a degree in psychology and went on to graduate school at Stanford University, in California. There, she attended a lecture by Allan and Beatrice Gardner, who were teaching a chimpanzee named Washoe to communicate using human sign language. Patterson was fascinated by the talk, which included film footage of the Gardners' efforts. "This lecture gave focus to my lifelong interest in animals," Patterson wrote in *The Education of Koko*. Inspired to pursue the Gardners' line of work, she enrolled in a class in American Sign Language (as it is officially known). A few weeks later, while at the San Francisco Zoo, Patterson came across a three-month-old female lowland gorilla named Hanabi-Ko, or Koko for short. She decided to teach a gorilla sign language as her doctoral project, and persuaded the zoo's directors to allow her to use Koko as a subject for her research.

Patterson spent days on end in Koko's glass cage, in full view of zoo patrons, trying to teach the animal to communicate. Dubbing her efforts "Project Koko," Patterson would repeatedly show Koko a slice of apple while positioning the gorilla's hand into the sign for "food." After two weeks, with no prompting, Koko signed food when Patterson held up a slice. Using constant repetition, as human parents do with their babies, Patterson continued teaching Koko various signs. In time Koko was able to respond to whole sentences using sign language. Patterson's success spurred her on, and she worked with Koko constantly. "I never took a vacation—I did not feel the need," she told Adams. "All my staffers needed it desperately, and I couldn't relate." Some skeptics have charged that Koko's achievements amount to little more than imitation and that she doesn't really comprehend how words are put together. They have also noted that Patterson has not published her findings in scientific journals.

In 1976 Patterson was embroiled in a number of conflicts with zoo officials. As a result, she and her partner, the biologist Ronald H. Cohn, left the zoo and founded the Gorilla Foundation, a nonprofit organization devoted to the study of primates. After acquiring Koko, and also Michael, a male gorilla, she and Cohn moved the foundation to the forested hills of Woodland, California. There, Patterson and Cohn, along with a former zoo employee, Barbara Hiller, began working on their project in earnest. In 1977 the project was temporarily derailed when the zoo requested that Koko be returned and Patterson found herself short of the $12,500 needed to buy her. Patterson applied for a Rolex Award for Enterprise, a cash prize given by the watch company to pioneers in various fields. She won the award, becoming the first woman to be so honored. "Rolex provided support when it was most needed," she commented on the Rolex Awards Web site. "In 1978 the Gorilla Foundation was still a new organisation with few sources of financial support."

After she won the award, Patterson's profile was raised considerably. In 1981 she joined two other gorilla activists, the primatologists Jane Goodall (who has worked for decades with chimpanzees) and Dian Fossey (who worked with mountain gorillas for 18 years before her murder, in 1985, in the African nation of Rwanda) in an international symposium designed to increase the visibility of ape research as well as to promote awareness regarding gorillas' endangerment. "Current zoo gorilla population levels are barely large enough to sustain the species," she wrote for the Rolex Awards Web site. "Gorillas are more psychologically delicate than other great ape species. Environmental stresses often negatively impact gorilla reproductive potential." A prime example of the last problem is Koko's refusal to mate. Although she had been with Michael for 25 years before his death, from heart failure, in April 2000, the two had never mated. Patterson then pinned her hopes on Ndume, a male gorilla she purchased after Michael's death. Koko became excited upon seeing Ndume's image on a videotape, but the romance progressed no further. To date, Patterson has had no success in this area.

In 1983 Patterson began planning to move the Gorilla Foundation to a new location. "Koko, Michael and Ndume have made it clear they have an aversion to cold, damp weather which occurs often in the mountains of Northern California," she remarked in *Gorilla* (the twice-yearly publication of the Gorilla Foundation), as quoted on the Rolex Awards Web site. "They refuse to go outside and seem to exhibit lethargy and depression during these periods." After an extensive search, the foundation members settled on a 70-acre preserve on the island of Maui, in Hawaii. Patterson felt that the new preserve would make a fitting environment for the three gorillas as well as provide sanctuary for gorillas that were either troubled by zoo life or threatened by human encroachment in their natural habitats. Patterson had noted on several occasions that the gorillas under the care of the foundation became frightened and distraught when strangers came to visit. In addition, she learned that mountain gorillas were being wiped out as a result of the civil unrest in Rwanda. As of mid-2000 there were fewer than 650 left in the wild.

By the early 1990s Patterson and the Gorilla Foundation had made progress with the Maui project. Through the generosity of Mary Cameron Stanford, the owner of the property, the foundation signed a 65-year lease at the rate of one dollar a year. In addition, in April 1993 the Gorilla Foundation was formally recognized by the Hawaiian House of Representatives, thus ensuring that the Maui Preserve, as it was to be called, would have the support of the Hawaiian state government. At around the same time, Patterson began designing the preserve, with input from Koko and Michael. "Through sign language, they make their desires known to their human care-givers," she wrote on her official Web site, *gorilla.org*. "The gorillas' preferences and opinions were taken into consideration during the planning stages." Currently, the budget and expenses for the Maui preserve are being evaluated with an eye toward moving the foundation closer to the lowland gorilla's natural habitats within the next few years.

Patterson has written three books for young people: *Koko's Kitten* (1985), *Koko's Story* (1987), and *Koko-Love! Conversations with a Signing Gorilla* (1999), all of which include photos by Ronald H. Cohn. She currently makes her home in Woodside, California. For over two decades she lived in a cottage that was within walking distance of Koko's trailer and got up during the night whenever the gorilla needed her. In 1993 she was forced to scale back her availability somewhat, after she suffered broken bones as a result of osteoporosis. "I can actually go a weekend without calling the foundation or getting faxes and e-mails," she told Adams. "It hasn't happened recently, but I've done it before, so I can do it again." On April 27, 1998 Koko made history when she participated in the first "interspecies" chat on America Online. For 45 minutes she answered questions from on-line users all over the world. Patterson has noted on her Web site that since Michael's passing, Ndume has begun to assume the dominant role that Michael once filled. She is hopeful that this may eventually lead to his mating with Koko.

Patterson has eschewed having a family of her own, preferring instead to concentrate her efforts on raising her gorillas. Her reasons for this stem not only from her love of the animals, but also from her experiences as a child, when she raised her siblings almost single-handedly. "I've already done the human-family thing," she explained to Adams. "Maybe that's why I opted not to do it again in this lifetime." — J.K.B.

Suggested Reading: *Biography* p72+ May, 1999, with photos; *E Magazine* p16+ May/June 1995, with photos; *U.S. News & World Report* p72 July 22, 1985; Patterson, Francine, and Eugene Linden. *The Education of Koko*, 1981; Young, Lisa. *A to Z of Women in Science and Math*, 1999

Selected Books: *Koko's Kitten*, 1985; *Koko's Story*, 1986; *Koko-Love!: Conversations with a Signing Gorilla*, 1999; with Eugene Linden—*The Education of Koko*, 1981

Frank Capri/Archive Photos

Penn Jillette (left) and Teller

Penn & Teller

Performance duo

Jillette, Penn
Mar. 5, 1955–

Teller
Feb. 14, 1948–

Address: c/o Mofo, 4132 S. Rainbow Blvd., Suite 377, Las Vegas, NV 89103

Penn Jillette, at six feet six inches, is almost always referred to as the large, talkative member of the performing duo Penn & Teller. Teller, who refuses to divulge his first name (according to some sources, it is Raymond), is known as the small, silent one—an apt description, since the five-foot-nine-inch showman is dwarfed by his partner and never speaks during performances, instead projecting a hapless Harpo Marx–like persona. Harder to describe than their physical attributes is their act, and most who have attempted to do so have settled for calling it comedic magic, magical comedy, or some other variation on that theme. When the pair won a special Obie Award, in 1985, for their Off-Broadway show, the awards committee announced that the prize was for "whatever it is that they do."

To call Penn & Teller simply comedians would be to ignore the amazing and sometimes death-defying tricks that they pull off. Yet much of their act revolves around making fun of and debunking more traditional magic shows, which they have derided as being performed by "old guys in greasy tuxes with lots of birds." They are equally scornful of the current crop of Las Vegas–based acts, in which elaborately costumed magicians perform flashy tricks over a soundtrack of ersatz Motown tunes. The pair's chief complaint about performers of this ilk is the dishonesty and condescension with which they generally treat their audiences. Jillette has often quoted the comedian Jerry Seinfeld's description of a typical magic act: "Here's a quarter, now it's gone. You're an idiot. Now it's back. You're a jerk. Show's over." He told Terri Gross during the April 1, 1994 edition of her radio show *Fresh Air*, as transcribed on Penn & Teller's Sin City Web site, "There's a philosophy in magic, that is in really all of magic, there's a level of condescension, the I can do something you can't. And the problem with that theory is that when you're doing the show you have people in your audience that can do heart surgery and fix motorcycles. I mean—program computers. And I think in no other form of performance do people come out and have that kind of chip on their shoulder." He has publicly lampooned David Copperfield, Lance Burton, and the late Doug Henning, practitioners of the flamboyant, self-congratulatory style that Jillette finds so distasteful. "Do I feel a sense of wonder when someone makes a DC-3 disappear onstage?" he asked Merrill Shindler rhetorically for the *Chicago Tribune* (April 23, 1989). "That's not where wonder comes from. Wonder does not come from a box or a trick. That's the wonder of an uneducated age. It's a whiny sort of unsophisticated reaction. Wonder is the feeling that physicists have looking into the atom, and finding out how particle physics works."

Setting themselves apart from those they criticize, Penn & Teller have often demonstrated the mechanics of tricks to audiences. In one now-famous bit, they use transparent cups in the classic ball-and-cup routine so that viewers can follow the path of the "disappearing" ball. Most people are so amazed at the manual dexterity required to perform the trick that knowing how it's done does nothing to lessen their enjoyment. Penn & Teller's willingness to reveal their secrets (or "tip the gaffe," in the parlance of magicians) has not endeared them to many amateur illusionists who take their hobby seriously. The pair would like the public to believe that their fellow professionals hold them in similar contempt, and they have gone to great lengths to perpetrate that myth in the media—even vociferously denying the fact that their peers named them Magicians of the Year in 1996. Despite that honor, the duo have little in common with the other members of the Magic Castle, the organization that presented them with the award. When they make a rabbit disappear, as they did during a recent tour, it is with the help of a mulch-spreading machine. When they shuffled a deck of cards during that same tour, they manipulated the cards—enormous and made of metal—with a pair of forklifts. Like many magicians, they also perform a card trick using a standard cardboard deck, but in their version of it, Teller impales Jillette's hand on a knife. They have often referred to themselves as "two eccentric guys who have learned how to do a few cool things," which may be as appropriate a description as any. According to their fellow skeptic and magician James Randi, Penn & Teller are "the most refreshing catastrophe to befall the art of magic."

Teller was born to Joe and Irene Teller, both commercial artists, on February 14, 1948 in Philadelphia, Pennsylvania. In the mid-1950s Irene bought her son a magic kit that had been advertised on the television program *The Howdy Doody Show*. From then on, as Joe told Pamela Miller in an interview transcribed for the Sin City Web site, "handkerchiefs were always flying around. It was a damn nuisance." The family lived in a row home within walking distance of a branch of the Philadelphia public library, where Teller spent a lot of time happily perusing books on magic and theater.

Jillette, who was born on March 5, 1955 in Greenfield, Massachusetts, remembers his first encounter with a do-it-yourself kit less fondly. Passionately interested in anything even remotely related to science, at age 12 he persuaded his parents to buy a kit that the popular mentalist Kreskin was hawking on television. Its contents would purportedly aid in the development of the user's extrasensory perception, a phenomenon that, Kreskin maintained, should be classified as a science. Although young Jillette followed all the directions precisely, the process failed to work, and the boy was very disappointed.

Teller attended Central High School, an academically elite public school in Philadelphia. Shy and studious, he found a mentor in David Rosenbaum, an English teacher who ran the school's drama society and performed a magic act as a sideline. The two had long conversations about theater and magic and about how to combine those pursuits. Teller's goal was to follow the same path as Rosenbaum, teaching for a living and moonlighting as a magician. After graduating from Amherst College, in Massachusetts, he took a job as a Latin instructor at a New Jersey high school, and, also like his mentor, he performed a magic act on weekends, often for rowdy groups of fraternity boys. During these gigs he learned that if he performed in studied silence rather than trying to compete with the noisemakers, he garnered greater attention from his sometimes drunken audiences, so he developed a voiceless stage persona and has affected it ever since. (It is, however, just a persona. By all accounts, Teller is talkative and articulate offstage.)

In contrast to his partner, Jillette was far from shy or studious. Awkward and ungainly, he was taller than many of his teachers by the time he finished elementary school. He prided himself on being an outsider and eschewing activities like organized sports in favor of more unconventional interests. In Greenfield, the Jillette family lived next door to a family named Moschen, which included two boys, Colin and Michael. Jillette and the Moschen brothers often practiced juggling together (a pastime that he has described to outsiders as evidence that he had no social life), and the trio occasionally juggled at a school assembly or local nursing home. Michael Moschen is now widely considered the world's greatest juggler; in the press he is often referred to as an artist or "sculptor in motion." (He has even been awarded a MacArthur Foundation "genius" grant for his work.) While honing his juggling skills, Jillette cultivated a rebellious image, sometimes wearing makeup, odd clothing, or strange hairdos and hanging out with a hard-drinking crowd. Despite the image, he never drank or took drugs himself—a policy to which he strictly adheres as an adult—and was rarely in any real trouble. After graduating from high school, Jillette briefly attended Ringling Brothers and Barnum & Bailey Clown College.

Penn and Jillette met in 1974, when a mutual friend, Wier Chrisemer, introduced them. Chrisemer had gotten to know Teller while majoring in music at Amherst, and Jillette while working in a stereo store. He persuaded the pair to help him put on a comic tribute to an obscure, untalented Swiss composer named Othmar Schoeck. Staged by Teller, the tribute featured Chrisemer playing such "instruments" as a nose flute, a trash-can lid, and a slide whistle, and the bushy-haired Jillette riding a unicycle and juggling. Sometimes Teller, dressed as a blind beggar, would sell pencils from a cup during intermission. In 1975 the trio formed a troupe, which they called the Asparagus Valley Cultural Society. Their act combined Teller's magic skills, Jillette's juggling, and Chrisemer's musical arrangements, with the first performance taking place on August 19 of that year, during the Minnesota Renaissance Festival. Over the next few years, they appeared at numerous festivals and colleges. Jillette and Teller were then performing street acts individually as well. Jillette found that he could make as much as $1,000 in a single weekend with his 12-minute act, one portion of which involved juggling knives. As he passed the hat at the end of each performance, he would advise the audience to remember that he was larger than any of them and had several sharp knives in his possession. Teller's most popular bit remains his signature today: he would swallow 100 sewing needles, a few at a time, followed by a six-foot length of thread. When he would regurgitate the items (with appropriate grimacing and gagging), the needles would emerge from his mouth strung onto the thread. In 1981, after the Asparagas Valley Cultural Society's three-year run in San Francisco, Chrisemer left the group. The devout son of a Lutheran minister, he had frequently clashed with Jillette and Teller, both of whom are outspoken atheists.

Without Chrisemer, the duo began performing under the name Penn & Teller, and by the mid-1980s, they were appearing on daytime variety programs, such as the popular *Merv Griffin Show*. In January 1985 their first television special, *Penn & Teller Go Public*, aired on PBS; it went on to win two Emmy Awards. That was just the first of many triumphs that year. In April they took their act to the Westside Arts Theater, an Off-Broadway venue in New York City, where they played until 1987, much of that time to sold-out audiences. By then the pair had adopted the stage uniforms they still wear—matching gray business suits and red ties. They liked the comical look of two such physically different people wearing identical clothing; they also reasoned that the traditional magician's stage garb—top hat and tails—was a throwback to the previous century, when male audience members actually dressed that way. By that time they had also adopted their respective roles of speaker and mute. The reviews of their show were consistently positive, and in May 1985 Penn & Teller received their Obie.

The next month they were seen on *Late Night with David Letterman*, in the first of what would be many appearances over the course of the next several years. On that show, which was then considered to be on television's cutting edge, they performed the trick in which Teller stabs Jillette in the hand in the process of finding a particular playing card, and the pair became an instant favorite with Letterman, who invited them back a few months later. This time they unleashed hundreds of cockroaches onto his desk. In November 1985 they made their first appearance on *Saturday Night Live*, performing a variation of Harry Houdini's water-escape act. In that stunt, which still receives wide press attention when it is performed, Penn remains indifferent while Teller appears to drown in a failed attempt to escape from the tank. They made several follow-up appearances on the show, once cutting a live snake in half and another time performing the celebrated routine in which Teller, suspended in a straitjacket over a bed of nails, must free himself before Jillette finishes a recitation of the poem "Casey at the Bat" and stands up to take a bow—thereby releasing the pulley that is keeping Teller aloft.

Penn & Teller proved so popular with late-night television audiences that producers of other shows soon took notice. They now appear frequently in guest roles on prime-time programs, including *Sabrina, the Teenage Witch*, in which they play minions of Satan, and *The Drew Carey Show*, in which they play a pair of crooked lawyers named Fenn & Geller. They have also had parts on *Friends*, *Dharma & Greg*, *Babylon 5*, and (in animated form) *The Simpsons*. In 1998 their own variety show made its debut on the FX channel. Taped in Las Vegas, where they both live, *Penn & Teller's Sin City Spectacular* features acts by well-known stars, as well as offerings by quirky performers reminiscent of those on the long-defunct *Ed Sullivan Show*.

Despite the availability of television work, Penn & Teller have continued to tour extensively. After their show at the Westside closed, in 1987, it reopened later that year at the Ritz on Broadway, where it played until the middle of 1988. At the Ritz, Penn abandoned juggling in favor of fire eating, an art with which he had long been fascinated. During the fire-eating part of the show, he explained the exact process to the audience, emphasizing that there was no "trick" involved: The fire was real, and it did indeed inflict minor burns as the lighter fluid evaporated. Imparting some of the sideshow lore that he loves, he would ask patrons to consider the carnival workers who, in the course of performing up to 50 shows a day, would gradually ingest enough lighter fluid to damage their livers. When the Broadway run was over, Penn & Teller embarked on several cross-country tours, performing at a wide variety of venues, ranging from small colleges in Vermont to venerable old playhouses in Boston and glitzy theaters in Las Vegas—an itinerary that they still maintain. The two are legendary among fans for staying after live performances to sign autographs, pose for photos, or simply chat.

Jillette is an avid movie fan, seeing several films a day when his schedule permits, so it seemed natural for the pair to become involved in filmmaking. In 1989 *Penn & Teller Get Killed*, in which they play performers stalked by a homicidal admirer, was released. A failure at the box office, it became available on home video shortly after it closed in theaters. Their books have been much more successful, critically and financially. Together, they have written three. *Penn & Teller's Cruel Tricks for Dear Friends* came out in 1989; a practical guide to playing harmless pranks, it was also available in a video version. In 1992 *Penn & Teller's How to Play with Your Food* was published. Along with the book, the purchaser received a set of props for performing the described gags, including fake fortunes to insert in fortune cookies and a sugar packet made of a material that couldn't be torn open and was meant to be slipped into a sugar bowl to frustrate an unsuspecting victim. (The book caused a minor scandal in the publishing industry when it was discovered that, due to a manufacturing defect, the packet could be opened after all, and that the chemical contents were harmful if ingested. Villard, the book's publisher, quickly recalled the defective packets and provided replacements, and no injuries were reported.) *Penn & Teller's How to Play in Traffic*, a witty guide to tormenting fellow travelers on planes, buses, and other public conveyances, appeared in 1997.

Both men also write extensively for magazines. Teller, a serious scholar of the history of magic, has published thought pieces on the subject in the *New Yorker* and the *New York Times Magazine*, among other periodicals. Jillette, who is greatly enamored of computer technology, writes a back-page column for *PC Computing*. The columns rarely contain technical advice; one frequently cited piece advised readers to paint flames or nude women on their computers, in the style of motorcycle art. Another advocated leaving a message about an impending bomb explosion on the screen, to bait airport security officers who insist that passengers turn on their laptops for examination before boarding. In an April Fool's gag that is now infamous among computer aficionados, Jillette once used the bottom half of the back page to print a realistic-looking advertisement for a $20,000 computer system that was being sold for $1,278. More than 12,000 credulous readers called the printed toll-free number to order the system, only to be answered by a message recorded by Jillette, berating them for their gullibility. Jillette mentions the actress Uma Thurman in every column as proof of his devotion to her—even when the reference makes no sense at all in the context of the piece. Thanks to his column, he has become so popular in computing circles that *Wired* magazine once featured him on its cover. Jillette is also an avid music fan and especially likes the band Velvet Underground. He performs with his own band, called Captain Howdy, and has even released an album, *Tattoo of Blood*, which has enjoyed modest cult success. (The title was inspired by his experience at a bikers' convention at which he got a tattoo, sans the permanent ink, simply to learn how much pain was involved.)

Both men have built their dream homes in the Las Vegas area. Jillette's, which is called "the Slammer," looks very much like an armed fortress. Teller's is just as distinctive: he reportedly asked his architect to design a cross between the Hoover Dam and Disneyland's Pirates of the Caribbean ride. Penn and Jillette are both outspoken in their political views, which tend to be conservative; Jillette, in particular, has pilloried the administration of President Bill Clinton in the media. They are wary of any form of censorship and have vigorously protested what they see as Attorney General Janet Reno's attacks on First Amendment rights. They hope that encouraging people to be more skeptical about stage illusions will lead to less public gullibility about fallacies perpetrated by politicians. Despite their agreement about many issues, each views the other as a partner rather than a friend, and they credit the longevity of their union to mutual respect and trust. They rarely socialize when not working.

Penn & Teller's most recent projects include an interactive CD-ROM by Steven Spielberg, on which they play a pair of evil magicians named Paine and Terrore. They also appear in the Disney animated film *Fantasia 2000*. The two were recently named visiting scholars at the Massachusetts Institute of Technology (MIT). — M.R.

Suggested Reading: *Chicago Tribune* p14+ Apr. 23, 1989; Juggler's World Web site; New England Skeptical Society Web site; *New Haven Advocate* Web site; *New Yorker* p58+ May 15, 1989; Sin City Web site

Selected Books: *Penn & Teller's Cruel Tricks for Dear Friends*, 1989; *Penn & Teller's How to Play With Your Food*, 1992; *Penn & Teller's How to Play in Traffic*, 1997

Selected Films: *Penn & Teller Get Killed*, 1989

Pittman, Robert

1954(?)– President and COO of America Online. Address: America Online, 22000 AOL Way, Dulles, VA 20166

Robert Pittman is perhaps best known for creating MTV, the cable-television channel that plays three-to-five-minute music videos almost 24 hours a day. Sometimes denounced by critics—who charge that the frequent cuts and frenetic pace of most of the clips have shortened the attention span of the

Courtesy of AOL-Online Inc.

Robert Pittman

channel's predominantly youthful audience—MTV is generally credited with having changed the nature of television programming, and with proving that a television show doesn't have to follow a traditional, linear format to be widely watched. "The key to MTV, from day one, was our logo," Pittman told Ron Powers for *Gentlemen's Quarterly* (March 1989). "We had a logo that changed colors and shapes and positions. That goes against the grain of what logos are supposed to do. But what we wanted it to do was tell our audience that MTV was change."

Pittman has always been known as someone dedicated to inciting change—in whatever medium he happens to be concentrating on at the time. While still in his 20s, he built a reputation as one of the most successful radio programmers in broadcasting history, revitalizing failing stations across the country. Currently, as president and chief operating officer of America Online (AOL), the world's leading Internet provider, he is helping to make that company's blend of interactive services, e-commerce, and computer technology as much a part of daily life as television and radio.

Born in about 1954 in Mississippi, Pittman grew up in the small town of Brookhaven, about 60 miles outside of Jackson. His father was a relatively progressive Methodist minister who encouraged Pittman and his older brother, Tom, to question the racial intolerance and discrimination that were common in their conservative southern town. When he was six years old, Pittman, who was spending Thanksgiving weekend at his grandparents' farm, was thrown from a horse and lost his right eye as a result. He got a glass eye that, although barely distinguishable from a normal eye, caused him to feel different from his peers. He turned the situation to his advantage, however, by becoming a class clown—horrifying unsuspecting teachers and entertaining classmates by jabbing pins at the fake eye. He cultivated several hobbies in his early teens, among them skeet shooting and fly fishing, but much of Pittman's youth was also spent watching television. "We grew up with *cable* TV," he told Powers. "Gosh, we had that in elementary school. That's because we were so rural. In Hattiesburg, they erected a huge antenna to pick up distant signals. You know, later, when HBO started, it got tested simultaneously in two places—West Palm Beach and Jackson, Mississippi. So Mississippi has always been in the forefront of cable TV." He has theorized that television has even more of an impact in small towns, where entertainment options are limited, than in other places, and explained to Powers, "Television prob'ly showed me more of the world than my parents did. I can't get enough of television. I accept it."

When Pittman was 15, he became interested in flying and decided to find a job in order to finance lessons. By then, he was sporting slightly longer hair than was the norm in Brookhaven and was considered to be the town rebel. Rejected when he applied for work at the local haberdashery, Pittman found a part-time job spinning records at WCHJ-FM, a nearby radio station. Other radio jobs followed; he was only 17 when he began programming music for a Detroit station, and 18 when he landed in Pittsburgh, where he was hired by Charles Warner, then manager of a failing station, with whom he continued to work for several years. "[Pittman] is just brilliant," Warner told Les Brown for the *New York Times* (August 19, 1977). "The kid is analytical and totally research oriented. Unlike other program managers, he's very objective in his interpretation of research and doesn't let his own tastes or desires interfere with his judgment." Under Pittman's program direction, the Pittsburgh station became one of the most popular with teens in the metropolitan area.

Warner and Pittman moved as a team to WMAQ, an NBC affiliate in Chicago, in 1974. The station, which played popular urban music, ranked a dismal number 22 in Chicago at the time. In what has been called one of the most remarkable turnarounds in broadcasting history, Pittman changed the format to country-western music—although he himself had always disliked the style—after his market research indicated that more listeners would tune in to that type of programming. The station shot to number three within a single ratings period, thanks in part to the change in format and in part to heavily advertised cash giveaways that Pittman developed. These promotional contests were so popular that callers sometimes made it impossible to dial into the area's telephone exchange. Pittman also did programming for an NBC rock station, and during his time in Chicago he won two *Billboard* Program Director of the Year awards, one for country and one for rock. He had also begun appearing in television ads for the stations, as well as producing and hosting a show for NBC-TV called *Album Tracks*, making him a minor local celebrity.

In 1977 Warner and Pittman were summoned by NBC to New York to help revitalize WNBC-AM, the flagship station of NBC Radio. At the time, the station ranked the lowest of all the major, 50,000-watt stations in New York City. Pittman began by firing most of the disc jockeys then on staff, including the popular morning shock-jock Don Imus, and replacing them with his own selection of talent from across the country; making hours of the station's airtime commercial free; and instituting promotional contests similar to those he had used successfully in Chicago. By the end of 1979, the station was posting the largest advertising sales that it had ever had, listenership was up substantially, and industry insiders were crediting Pittman with another triumph. In 1979—at age 25—Pittman had reached what for many would be considered the pinnacle of a career in radio, even though he had never graduated from college. (He had attended occasionally, for brief periods; he would complete a summer course at the Harvard Business School, in 1985, and later be awarded an honorary degree from the Bank Street School of Education.)

By then a well-recognized figure at NBC headquarters, for his long hair and casual dress as well as his programming prowess, Pittman had been in the radio industry for more than a decade, and was tiring of the life. He turned his attention to television, the medium that had been such an important part of his youth, joining Warner Amex Satellite Entertainment, a joint venture between Warner Communications and American Express. The company was launching the Movie Channel to compete against the popular pay channels Showtime (with which it later merged) and HBO; Pittman was hired as program director of the fledgling channel. He was still interested in music, however, and he knew from his work on *Album Tracks* in Chicago that bands often produced promotional video clips of their performances that could be sent to a TV station for no charge. Pittman hypothesized that the clips might provide a new way to combine contemporary music and television. "John Lack [an executive at Warner Amex] had already had the idea of a cable channel devoted entirely to music," Pittman explained to Powers. "But even though John is a brilliant guy, he was thinking in conventional-television terms. He envisioned a whole series of *programs*." Pittman reasoned that young people no longer thought in a rigid, linear manner, and that television programming didn't have to provide conventional plots with beginnings, middles, and ends. He told Christian Williams for the *Washington Post* (September 16, 1982), "When I was a kid, my parents read the *New Yorker*. But I grew up listening to the radio, doing my homework, and watching TV all at once. I could jump from one to the other, but they were always saying turn off the TV. They can't have two people talking at the same time, they have to go A, B, C, D." He concluded, "My attention span is too short; I just get bored. I don't think one way was better than the other—I think they're just different ways of processing information." He persuaded Lack to try airing the video clips one after another, interspersed with occasional appearances by "video jockeys," who would banter, deliver a piece of music news or trivia, and introduce the next set of clips. Despite skepticism on the part of network executives and advertisers, who could not imagine anyone's wanting to watch a string of music videos, MTV—as the new enterprise was dubbed—debuted on August 1, 1981, with the pertinently named clip "Video Killed the Radio Star," by a band called the Buggles. The record companies saw immediate results. Little-known groups such as the Buggles and the Psychedelic Furs, who had never played in certain parts of the country, began to sell significant numbers of albums in those areas virtually overnight. Savvy companies began to produce even more videos, which quickly became the primary marketing tool in the record industry.

Pittman, drawing on his experience in radio, developed innovative contests to attract viewers. People could win the opportunity to accompany the singer Bruce Springsteen on the road for a week or spend a weekend with the group Van Halen. To promote "Little Pink Houses," a song by Indiana rocker John Cougar Mellencamp, the station gave away a pink house on an acre of land in Bloomington, along with a pink Jeep and 500 cases of Hawaiian Punch fruit drink. Pittman recruited high-magnitude rock stars, such as Mick Jagger and David Bowie, to film commercials for the station. "I want my MTV," Pittman's chosen advertising slogan, became a catchphrase all over the country. After seeing the ratings the station was getting, advertisers gradually began to take notice; major soft-drink companies and automotive manufacturers, hoping to appear trendy to young consumers, began to buy ad time. "At MTV, we don't shoot for the 14-year-olds—we own them," Pittman proudly told Christian Williams. "We will reach 90 percent of them in any given household. You'd have to be a social outcast not to watch it. And about 10 or 20 percent of our audience is over 35." Although the station lost money in its first two years of operation, in the first half of 1984 alone, it made more than $8 million, and its initial public offering (IPO), which Pittman orchestrated, raised nearly $80 million.

MTV's frantic, special-effects-driven style began to be reflected in other areas of pop culture. Movies and television shows began to exhibit the fast pans and abrupt cuts of the video clips. Commercials featured exploding snack foods and flying cars in imitation of the eye-catching devices used by many of the video producers, and fashion designers started to make clothes inspired by the now instantly recognizable style of popular rock stars. Even politicians jumped on the bandwagon: when Indiana governor Robert Orr aired a music-video political commercial in 1984, he broadened his appeal among young voters and won the election with 53 percent of the vote. (His jealous opponent sent him a Boy George [the sexually ambiguous pop star] costume and suggested he wear it during his next campaign.)

Pittman, who had by then trimmed his hair and begun favoring conservative suits, had been made chief operating officer of MTV in 1983. Two years later executives at Viacom, an entertainment conglomerate that had recently purchased the company, made him chief executive officer of MTV Networks, which operated not only MTV but VH1, a more mellow music-video channel he had created for those 25 to 54 years of age; Nickelodeon, a children's channel; and Nick at Nite, which showcased reruns of popular shows from previous decades. Pittman was leery of being branded forever as simply the man who created MTV, and shortly after the network was purchased by Viacom, he began announcing his intention to leave, despite his promotion to CEO. When he did so, in the fall of 1986, he had stock options worth more than $2 million dollars.

In the late 1980s, with the backing of entertainment conglomerate MCA Inc., Pittman founded Quantum Media Inc. He planned to purchase and build companies in every medium of the entertainment industry, including records, TV programs, home videos, and movies. Quantum, according to industry observers, was perhaps the only project of Pittman's that could not be deemed an unqualified success. Its first product, a home video of the Sugar Ray Leonard/Marvelous Marvin Hagler boxing match, was released in April 1987, soon after the fight actually took place. The video was a moderate success, selling 50,000 units, and within a year Pittman had also developed two television shows for national syndication. *The Morton Downey Jr. Show* featured a former Chicago talk-radio host, known for his brash on-air persona. Downey transplanted that image successfully to television—chain smoking, posturing, and berating guests. While some critics considered the show a new low in broadcasting—Downey once appeared on the news with a swastika painted on his face, claiming to have been the victim of neo-Nazi persecution—he did inspire a loyal, if small, following. The second show, *The Street*, a police drama with unusually graphic language, was considered by some critics to be a bold experiment in true-to-life programming, but it went off the air after 40 episodes because of a writers' strike. Quantum's record division released only one album, from a little-known Memphis band, and Pittman was having trouble acquiring the capital he needed to expand.

In 1990 Pittman sold the business to Time Warner and was hired by that massive conglomerate to head Time Warner Enterprises, its division for strategic development and entrepreneurial ventures. In that capacity he helped Steven Brill launch the Court TV cable network. In 1991, when Time Warner acquired Six Flags Entertainment, a regional theme-park company, Pittman was named Six Flag's chairman and CEO. The company managed seven parks across the country, none of which was widely profitable. Of all the country's amusement-park chains, Six Flags was, in fact, the least profitable, earning about $400 million in yearly revenues to Disney's almost $3 billion, and posting a lower pre-tax profit margin than other competitors, such as Busch Gardens and Cedar Fair. Pittman attributed this not only to the ever-changing ownership the chain had seen since its opening in 1966, but to its unfocused marketing efforts and forgettable advertising.

Some questioned Pittman's decision to accept a position in the less-than-glamorous world of amusement parks. In an interview with Kate Fitzgerald for *Advertising Age* (June 1, 1992), he defended the move: "Entertainment and marketing are merging," he explained. "Physical entertainment is a new theme, and there's no better place to pull those concepts together than in a theme park. People come into a theme park in the best possible mood, ready to have the time of their lives. It's an ideal environment for advertising and consumers to meet." Pittman instituted an aggressive ad campaign that touted the parks' proximity to most people's homes, citing the fact that more than 80 percent of the country's population had a Six Flags park within a day's drive. He also boasted about the parks' size, since six of them were, in fact, larger than the 80-acre Disneyland, in California. Pittman himself starred in many of the television ads, which often showed shots of the chain's newest features based on Time Warner properties—such as a Yosemite Sam ride, inspired by the Looney Tunes cartoon character, and a Batman-based attraction in which riders were conveyed through an atmospheric Gotham City. Attendance at the parks increased by close to 25 percent almost immediately, cash flow nearly doubled, and the chain's reputation as a distant second-best to the Disney parks began to change.

In 1995, however, Time Warner announced plans to sell Six Flags, hoping to use the $800 million purchase price to reduce debt it had accrued from a previous leveraged takeover. When a company called Boston Ventures purchased the parks, its executives expressed hope that Pittman would remain in the same capacity. They balked at his salary demands, however, when he asked for not only a reported $2 million to $3 million a year, but also an equity interest in the parks that could have been worth more than $100 million after five years. Pittman decided to leave Six Flags, but denied that the issue of money was the pivotal factor, saying instead that he was not prepared to make the five-year commitment that Boston Ventures had requested of him. Some sources speculated that Pittman had simply lost interest in the prosaic world of theme parks and missed the hipper circles in which he had once traveled.

Pittman's next step shocked those who foresaw a move back into television or music for him. In 1995 he became a managing partner and CEO of Century 21, a large real-estate organization. Although most consumers saw the company's focus as simply the purchase and sale of homes, Pittman saw an untapped marketing opportunity. He envisioned Century 21 agents selling home insurance, mortgages, cable service—anything a new homeowner might need—all via computer. He started brokering deals with mortgage lenders, insurance companies, and home-product retailers, to ensure their participation in Century 21's revitalization. To the surprise of no one familiar with his usual tactics, Pittman also started a massive promotional push, arranging, for example, consumer credit cards co-branded with the Century 21 logo and a series of how-to books with the Century 21 imprimatur. Although he stayed with the company for only 15 months, during his tenure he saw many of his plans put into effect and earnings increase dramatically.

Part of Pittman's campaign for the newly revamped company had been to place innovative ads on-line, and as a result Century 21 had purchased $1 million worth of ad space from America Online Inc., a large Internet services provider. In the process Pittman met Steve Case, the CEO of AOL, who was impressed enough by Pittman's marketing skills to woo him away from the real-estate business. Case invited Pittman to join AOL as president and CEO of its AOL networks unit, which operates core on-line services, in October 1996. Pittman saw the Internet as a new frontier and compared its emergence to the early days of cable TV, when the idea of a music-video channel seemed revolutionary. He began to envision AOL as a brand that would rival not merely other Internet providers, such as Yahoo! or Compuserve (which it would later buy to cut down on competition), but television itself. While his generation had been formed by TV, Pittman saw a future generation being just as influenced by the computer.

Pittman began his tenure during a turbulent time in AOL's history. Shortly after Pittman was hired, Case instituted an affordable monthly service charge for unlimited usage, rather than the hourly rate that had been in place previously. Subscribers logged on in record numbers to take advantage of the deal, and phone lines were frequently jammed, making AOL virtually impossible to access. Class-action suits were filed by angry consumers, and the company became the butt of jokes by late-night talk-show hosts and computer-magazine columnists. Stock prices dropped precipitously. The AOL name now seemed a liability rather than the selling point that Pittman had predicted. He realized that the company had to be repositioned in a way that would focus attention on future possibilities rather than past problems. He therefore began approaching analysts and investors he had known while involved in television, inviting them to tour the company's Virginia-based headquarters and find out more about his plans for AOL. Thanks to Pittman's seeming genius for selling his own vision to others (he was sometimes referred to as Bob "Pitchman" by other executives at AOL), the strategy worked; Wall Street reporters began talking about AOL and other service providers in television terms—how many viewers could they deliver to advertisers?—rather than in computer lingo. By 1999 AOL stocks were trading at more than 500 times the 1992 IPO price, for brief occasional periods even surpassing the market value of Coca-Cola, a longtime Wall Street giant.

After technical problems had been resolved, making it possible to log onto the service again, viewers did so in droves; currently AOL boasts more than 22 million subscribers, with an estimated 600,000 logged on simultaneously at certain hours. Some advanced computer users deride AOL and other Internet portals as being only for novices, since new viewers tend to concentrate on company-provided content—chat, entertainment, and news, for example—rather than using the services as a gateway to the broader, more challenging World Wide Web. But Pittman concentrated on making AOL's content attractive and diverse enough to be appealing to all but the most hard-core Internet users. He has said that his amusement-park experience is very helpful in this area, since, like the Internet, the parks are interactive and cater to many different tastes simultaneously. Once Pittman had wooed viewers (or "eyeballs," as they are known in the industry), advertisers followed. Companies such as 1-800-Flowers, Preview Travel, and Tel-Save long-distance service have currently paid between $4 million and $40 million for multiyear contracts to advertise exclusively on AOL.

Pittman was appointed president and COO of AOL in February 1998, second in command only to Case himself. He has seen AOL grow into the instantly recognizable brand that he envisioned at the start of his tenure with the company. AOL now has more than 10 times the number of subscribers of any other Internet provider. The company operates Netscape Netcenter, the second-most-visited portal in the workplace, Spinner.com, the first and largest Internet music service, and many other concerns. In January 2000 AOL announced a merger with Time Warner to form AOL Time Warner Inc., with combined revenues of more than $30 billion. Billed as the world's first Internet Age media and communications company, AOL Time Warner's brands include Warner Bros., Warner Music Group, *Time*, CNN, *Sports Illustrated*, *Fortune*, *Entertainment Weekly*, Looney Tunes, and a host of others. The company aims to bring Warner's properties into the digital environment while providing AOL with content of proven mass appeal. There now seems to be little danger that Pittman will be remembered solely for MTV, given his mission, already well under way, to position AOL as a global medium central to people's lives.

Pittman's list of honors includes induction into the Broadcasting and Cable Hall of Fame in 1999. He was named one of *Advertising Age*'s "50 Pioneers and Visionaries of TV" and was on *Business Week*'s list of "25 Top Executives of 1998." *Life* magazine named him one of "Five Original Thinkers of the '80s," as well as one of the "50 Most Influential Boomers." He was a runner-up for *Time*'s 1984 Man of the Year, and he has received *CableVision Magazine*'s 20/20 Vision Award for being one of the 20 people who have had the greatest impact on cable broadcasting. Pittman serves on the boards of the New York University School of Medicine, the Robin Hood Foundation, and the New York Shakespeare Festival, among other institutions. He married the former Sandy Hill in 1979; the couple have one son. The family lives on the Upper East Side of New York City, where they are active in philanthropic and social circles. They also have a country home in Connecticut. Pittman, a visionary in almost every other respect, has said that he never quite envisioned such a privileged life, and he has described himself as the "luckiest S.O.B. ever walked out of Mississippi." — M.R.

Suggested Reading: *Advertising Age* p47 June 1, 1992, with photos; America Online Web Site; *Esquire* p380+ Dec. 1985, with photos; *Forbes* p232+ May 25, 1992, with photos; *Gentlemen's Quarterly* p324 + Mar. 1989, with photos; *IQ* p22+ Sep. 21, 1998, with photos; *New York* p20+ Jul. 30, 1990, with photos; *New York Times* C p21 Aug. 19, 1977, with photo; *Washington Post* E p1+ Sep. 16, 1982, with photos

---

Archive Photos

Poitier, Sidney

Feb. 20, 1927– Actor; director. Address: c/o Creative Artists Agency, 9830 Wilshire Blvd,, Beverly Hills, CA 90212

NOTE: An earlier article about Sidney Poitier appeared in *Current Biography* in 1959.

In his long and distinguished career, Sidney Poitier has broken down every barrier placed in his path. Until his arrival in Hollywood, most black actors had been relegated to demeaning roles that favored stereotype over substance; with his fierce good looks and quiet, measured eloquence, Poitier swiftly rose above those conventions to become the most prominent black American actor of his and possibly any generation. Audiences' embrace of Poitier served to open doors for other black actors in Hollywood, allowing them to shine in roles previously available only to white actors.

As impressive as Poitier's defiance of stereotypes is his box-office clout. In 1967, at the height of his prominence, he starred in the three highest-grossing films of the year, *In the Heat of the Night*, *Guess Who's Coming to Dinner*, and *To Sir, with Love*, and to this date, he remains the only black performer to be honored with an Academy Award for best actor, which he received for his work in *Lilies of the Field* (1963). In the 1970s he turned his hand to directing, and in more recent years, he has been seen in a number of film and television projects, including the made-for-TV movies *Separate but Equal*, in which he portrayed Supreme Court justice Thurgood Marshall, and *Mandela and DeKlerk*, for which he took on the role of South African president Nelson Mandela. Poitier has dedicated his life and his work to bringing honor not only to himself but to his family as well. "That's how I always looked at it: that my work is who I am," he wrote in his recent memoir, *The Measure of a Man* (2000). "I decided way back in the beginning, back when I was still washing dishes in a barbecue joint in Harlem, that the work I did would never bring dishonor to my father's name."

Beginning life as an American citizen by chance, Sidney Poitier was born on February 20, 1927, while his parents, Evelyn and Reginald Poitier, residents of the Bahamas, were visiting Miami, Florida, to sell tomatoes at the Produce Exchange. At birth Poitier weighed only three pounds, and, having lost previous children to stillbirth and disease, his father feared that he would not live. He even purchased a shoebox from a local undertaker, to use if necessary as a coffin for his infant son. Poitier's mother, however, was hopeful. She visited a local soothsayer, who told her, as quoted by Poitier in *The Measure of a Man*, "Don't worry about your son. He will survive and he will not be a sickly child. He will . . . travel to most of the corners of the earth. He will walk with kings. He will be rich and famous. Your name will be carried all over the world. You must not worry about that child."

One of seven children, Poitier grew up on Cat Island, a three-mile-wide strip of land in the Bahamas. There, as he wrote in *The Measure of a Man*, "life was indeed very simple, and decidedly preindustrial. Our cultural 'authenticity' extended to having neither plumbing nor electricity, and we didn't have much in the way of schooling or jobs, either. In a word, we were poor, but poverty there was very different from poverty in a modern place characterized by concrete. It's not romanticizing the past to state that poverty on Cat Island didn't preclude gorgeous beaches and a climate like heaven, cocoa plum trees and sea grapes and cassavas growing in the forest, and bananas growing wild." While such an idyllic setting may have lessened the burden of poverty, life was not always easy for Poitier and his family. "My mother literally made my clothes from flour sacks," he told Gene Siskel for the *Chicago Tribune* (January 31, 1988). "She would unravel the thread and weave an outfit. I remember being so ashamed of the label being on my bottom. But my mother told me that the clothes one wore didn't matter. 'The only disgrace,' she said, 'is if your clothes are not clean.'"

Although he had six siblings, Poitier spent many hours alone as a child. "Cat Island was not that big a place," he told Tom Seligson for *Parade* (February 28, 1988), and since there were no movie theaters or other places where children traditionally congregate, Poitier spent much time "just roaming around. I had a relationship with the elements, the birds and the trees, and I used to walk the beaches and imagine what was beyond the point where the sea and the sky met." Cat Island was so isolated that he had little or no knowledge of what lay beyond it. "I never knew what a city looked like," he told Seligson, "but I could create one in my mind and place myself in it. I had dreams about all these distant places and what life would be like there."

When he was 10, the Poitiers moved to Nassau, the capital city of the Bahamas, because an agricultural blight had ruined most of the family farm. As Poitier described it in *The Measure of a Man*, "I ran smack into Urban. Modern. Cars. Movies. Hotels. Restaurants. Night Clubs. Bars. Dance Halls. And that transition from childhood idyll to Urban launched me straight into manhood. By the age of 14, I was no longer a child."

As a teenager Poitier was briefly jailed for stealing some corn, after which his father sent him to live with Sidney's brother Cyril, in Miami. There he encountered a world that contrasted starkly with the life he had known in the Bahamas. "Miami shared a climate and lifestyle with the Caribbean," he wrote in *The Measure of a Man*, "but its culture and mores were of the American South, 1940s Jim Crow style, and nothing had prepared me to surrender my pride and self-regard sufficiently to accept those humiliations." Poitier found work as a delivery boy and soon got his first taste of racial prejudice. One day, he delivered a package to a woman in a wealthy section of the city, only to have the woman became irate at his bringing it to the front door. Puzzled at her behavior, he set the parcel down on the front stoop and promptly left. A few nights later, he arrived at home to discover that members of the Ku Klux Klan had been by the house looking for him. Not long after this incident, he was picked up by police while walking home. "They really had their fun with me," he recalled to Josh Greenfeld for *Good Housekeeping* (May 1968). "They put a pistol right to my forehead. Right here. And for 10 minutes they just joked about whether to shoot me in the right eye or left eye."

Deciding that Miami was no place for him, the 16-year-old Poitier hopped a bus to New York and arrived in Harlem with three dollars in his pocket. He landed a job as a dishwasher but had nowhere to live. In an interview with Lois Armstrong for *People* (August 4, 1980), he said of those early days in New York, "I was sleeping on the roof of the Brill Building and using the *New York Times* for a blanket. I had nothing but summer clothes that winter and I froze. I got arrested for vagrancy for sleeping in Penn Station one night . . ." In order "to have something to eat and a place to sleep," Poitier lied about his age and joined the army. He was no happier in the military, however, than he had been on the streets of Manhattan. "Which is why," he explained in *The Measure of a Man*, "in 1944, I was in custody of the U.S. Army military police, charged with assaulting a senior officer." In the hope of being discharged on grounds of insanity, Poitier had flung a chair at the officer's head, barely missing him and destroying a bay window behind him. Thrown out of the army, he again found himself on the streets of New York, where he scrounged for nickels so he could sleep in pay toilets. At one point he wrote a letter to then–president Franklin D. Roosevelt, asking him for $100 to get back to Nassau. He received no reply, which angered him at the time. Years later, however, he came to see it as a stroke of good luck. "If I had succeeded in that effort," he wrote in *The Measure of a Man*, "I probably would have spent my life at some low-level job taking care of tourists, spending Sundays sitting on a rock outside Nassau trying to catch me a big fish. So even in my lack of luck, once again I was very lucky."

Resigned to living in New York, Poitier scoured the "help wanted" section of the *Amsterdam News*, a black newspaper published in Harlem. Once, happening to glance at the theater section, he saw the words "actors wanted." Deciding that he "might as well give this a go," he went to an audition at Harlem's American Negro Theater, only to discover that his lilting Bahamian accent was not welcome. After he had gotten through only a few lines—speaking each word slowly and sounding much like a young child reading aloud—the director physically ejected him from the theater, saying as he did so, "Why don't you get yourself a job as a dishwasher?" "I have to tell you that his comments stung worse than any wasp on any sapodilla tree back in my childhood," Poitier wrote in *The Measure of a Man*. "His assessment was like a death sentence for my soul. I had never mentioned to him that I was a dishwasher. How did he know? If he *didn't* know, what was it about me that implied to this stranger that dishwashing would accurately sum up my whole life's worth?"

Following that episode, Poitier became determined to rid himself of his accent. After landing another job as a dishwasher, he bought a radio for $13 and "repeated back everything I heard until I got rid of my Bahamian singsong," as he told Armstrong. Meanwhile, with the help of an older man who worked as a waiter at the restaurant, he set about improving his reading skills. After six months he tried his luck at the theater again, and this time the management took him on as a regular member of the company. Still, his lack of education made it difficult for him to meet the demands placed on him as an actor. Desperate to stay, he made a last-ditch effort to remain at the theater. "I made a deal with them," he told Seligson. "I became their janitor."

After a few months of cleaning the building, Poitier got his break. One of the actors, a fellow unknown named Harry Belafonte, was unable to make a performance, and Poitier was asked to go on in his place. At the end of the performance, the director, impressed with Poitier's skills, gave him a role in an upcoming Broadway production of *Lysistrata*. On opening night, however, Poitier was so nervous that he flubbed most of his lines, inspiring raucous laughter from the crowd. Although critics panned the play, they praised Poitier for his apparent gift for comedy. While serving as an understudy in a road production of *Anna Lucasta*, Poitier heard about an upcoming film called *No Way Out* (1950). He auditioned for the movie and landed the role of Luther Brooks, a doctor who becomes the target of a racist criminal after the man's brother dies while Brooks is operating on him. The film was a success and paved the way for Poitier's next role, that of Reverend Msimangu in the drama *Cry, the Beloved Country* (1951), which examined the racial division in South Africa.

Soon after completing that film, Poitier returned to Harlem, where he again found himself out of work. During this period, he married Juanita Marie Hardy and opened a restaurant called Ribs in the Ruff. Not long afterward he received a call from Marty Baum, a Hollywood agent who was interested in representing him. Baum helped Poitier get a role in *Blackboard Jungle* (1955), a drama in which Poitier played a student at a high school overrun with toughs, who terrorize a teacher played by Glenn Ford. That film too was a success, though for Poitier it was followed by another spell of unemployment, during which he closed his restaurant. Next, he was cast in *Edge of the City* (1957), a film about corruption on the New York City waterfront. He then appeared in a quick succession of movies, including *Band of Angels* (1957) and *Virgin Island* (1958). In 1959 he co-starred in Stanley Kramer's *The Defiant Ones*, a thriller in which he and Tony Curtis played chained-together escaped convicts who must put aside their differences in order to evade the law. "Stanley Kramer. That's all I need to say about that one," Poitier told Michael Bandler for *Cable Guide* (April 1989), about his decision to act in the film. "He spoke his mind and made the kind of pictures most other filmmakers were afraid to touch. It still has the visceral gutsiness that it had originally." *The Defiant Ones* was a box-office success and earned Poitier an Academy Award nomination for best actor, making him the first black actor to be so honored.

After *The Defiant Ones*, Poitier appeared in *Porgy and Bess* (1958), a cinematic adaptation of the George Gershwin musical about a crippled beggar who falls in love with a prostitute, played in the film by Dorothy Dandridge. (The musical was inspired by DuBose Heyward's 1925 novel, *Porgy*.) While he was working on this film Poitier became romantically involved with Diahann Carroll, one of his co-stars. "She was confident, inviting, sensuous—and she moved with a rhythm that absolutely tantalized me," he told Armstrong. "I invited her to dinner, telling her that since we were both married we would talk about our absent loved ones. And we did. I acted very, very gentlemanly for weeks, but halfway through the picture we fell in love." Although Poitier was honest with his wife about his feelings for Carroll, the two did not immediately separate. "To a large degree I felt trapped by my four daughters," he explained to Armstrong. "They were young and I loved them. And my father had thoroughly indoctrinated me when I was young that, as a law of life, a parent should take care of his children even if it means not putting food in his own mouth." Several years later Poitier and his wife were divorced. Shortly thereafter, his relationship with Carroll also dissolved.

While his personal life was in turmoil, Poitier's career was proceeding smoothly. He had appeared in a string of well-received films, including *All the Young Men* (1960) and *A Raisin in the Sun* (1961). In the latter he appeared as Walter Lee Younger, a part he had also played on stage. In 1963 he took on the role of Homer Smith, a construction worker who helps a group of German-speaking nuns build a church in the desert, in the film *Lilies of the Field*. For his performance in that picture, Poitier was honored with an Academy Award for best actor. To date, he is the only black actor to have earned the Oscar in that category.

Over the next few years, Poitier appeared in a variety of movies, some more successful than others. A high point in the actor's career came in 1967, when he starred in three celebrated movies. He took the part of Mark Thackeray, an engineer turned schoolteacher who wins over a class of unruly English students, in James Clavell's *To Sir, with Love*. He followed this with a turn as Detective Virgil Tibbs in the racially charged crime drama *In the Heat of the Night*, directed by Norman Jewison. The film was a smash hit, winning five Oscars and spawning two sequels as well as a hit television series. While many scenes from that film are memorable, it was Poitier who provided its defining moment. Questioning an elderly white southern man about his activities on the night of a murder, Poitier's character is answered with a slap to the face. Without hesitating, he responds in kind. "In the original script I looked at him with great disdain and, wrapped in my strong ideals, walked out," he wrote in *The Measure of a Man*. "That could have happened with another actor playing that part, but it couldn't happen with me. I could too easily remember that Miami night with the gun pointed at my forehead, that 50-block march with those guffawing cops in the patrol car behind me. I told the director that the script needed to be changed." Poitier next appeared in Stanley Kramer's *Guess Who's Coming to Dinner*, in which he played a successful doctor who meets the parents of his fiancée, a young white woman. That landmark film earned several Academy Awards and high praise for Poitier and the rest of the cast, which included Katharine Hepburn and Spencer Tracy.

Writing of that period in his 1980 autobiography, *This Life*, Poitier recalled, "I was convinced that the brick-by-brick growth of my career was complete—it had peaked, and there was no place to go but down." His pessimism was brought on by a 1969 *New York Times* article by Clifford Mason, entitled "Why Do White Folks Love Sidney Poitier So?" The article implied that Poitier was an "Uncle Tom," a black man who catered to the tastes and styles of white people, and that in choosing roles he aimed solely to curry favor with the white community. "It was the most devastating and unfair piece of journalism I had ever seen," he wrote in *This Life*. "When I read it, I said to myself: This definitely signals a bad period for me." Around this time, the so-called "black-exploitation" films began to arrive in theaters. Paralleling the shift in the late 1960s from the pacifism of the civil rights era to the overt fury of the Black Power movement, films such as *Shaft* (1971), *Super Fly* (1972), and *Black Caesar* (1973) depicted angry black men who settled their conflicts with fists and fury, a far cry from the measured eloquence of Poitier's performances. These films had little room for Poitier, but he appreciated them nonetheless. "I, too, enjoyed seeing the black guys beating up on the white guys for a change," he wrote in *This Life*. "It was delicious. And not only did I like watching the revenge syndrome at work, I also liked watching my fellow actors at work." The rise of these films convinced Poitier that, he told Armstrong, "a shift in the tide had taken place, so I bought a boat and a lot of books and just went down to the Caribbean and cooled it for about a year."

All the while Poitier kept abreast of developments in Hollywood, and during the next few years he made a handful of films, including *They Call Me MISTER Tibbs!* (1970), *Buck and the Preacher* (1972), his directorial debut, and *A Warm December* (1973). In 1974 he directed and starred in the film that was regarded by many as his "comeback" effort, the urban comedy *Uptown Saturday Night* (1974), in which Poitier and Bill Cosby played two friends who embark on a series of bizarre adventures while attempting to recover a winning lottery ticket. The film featured a stellar cast of black performers, including Harry Belafonte, Flip Wilson, and Richard Pryor. *Uptown Saturday Night* did well at the box office, proving to Poitier "that black people wanted to laugh at themselves and have fun," as he wrote in *This Life*. "They were weary of being represented on the local movie screen by pimps, hustlers, prostitutes, private detectives, violence, macho men, and dirty words. They wanted to have good, clean, family-type fun, and my recognition of that hunger committed me to a try at fulfilling the need." Poitier and Cosby re-teamed the following year for a follow-up to *Uptown Saturday Night*. The plot of *Let's Do It Again* (1975) found the actors' characters from the earlier film attempting to raise money for their lodge, by hypnotizing a scrawny boxer (Jimmie Walker) into believing he is unbeatable—and then betting on him. *Let's Do It Again* proved to be twice as successful as its predecessor, and it spawned a third film, *A Piece of the Action* (1977). After the completion of that movie, Poitier took another sabbatical from acting. During this time he concentrated on writing *This Life* and married the actress Joanna Shimkus (with whom he has two daughters, Anika and Sydney). He also continued directing movies, such as the very popular *Stir Crazy* (1980), which starred Richard Pryor and Gene Wilder, *Hanky Panky* (1982), and the dance-themed *Fast Forward* (1985).

In 1983 Poitier's name had appeared in the newspapers for other reasons, after a 19-year-old con artist, David Hampton, pleaded guilty to attempted burglary, having insinuated himself into a prominent New York family by claiming to be Poitier's son. The incident inspired John Guare's play *Six Degrees of Separation*. Poitier attended a performance of the play, mostly out of curiosity. "Oh, I wish [Hamptom] had used another celebrity, and he did at times," he told Jacqueline Trescott in the *Washington Post* (April 7, 1991). "But the play was well written and very well performed. . . . It is sort of disconcerting that your name is being used on stage [without your input]."

In 1988 Poitier returned to acting, appearing in two films released within months of each other. The first was *Shoot to Kill*, an action-thriller in which he played an FBI agent pursuing a killer through the mountains of the Pacific Northwest. Fairly well-received by critics, the film was a modest financial success. He portrayed an FBI agent again in *Little Nikita*, in which his character befriends a teenager whose parents are KGB agents.

He was next seen playing the Supreme Court justice Thurgood Marshall in the made-for-TV drama *Separate but Equal* (1991). Of his performance in that film, Trescott wrote, "After a few minutes . . . the viewer forgets it is Poitier on the screen. It really is Thurgood Marshall."

Over the next few years, Poitier appeared in a wide variety of films, including the espionage thriller *Sneakers* (1992), *A Good Day to Die* (1995), and *The Jackal* (1997), a remake of *Day of the Jackal* that starred Bruce Willis and Richard Gere. In 1996 he reprised the role of Mark Thackeray in *To Sir, with Love 2*, a made-for-TV sequel. Speaking of the film, he told David Richards for the *Washington Post* (December 3, 1995), "It was my idea. I felt [that] this character, had he stayed at the game, would have matured into quite an impressive individual. I thought it might make an interesting piece of material to have him face the seemingly intractable problems of getting through the calcification that has taken hold in too many of our inner-city schools today." In 1996 he starred with Michael Caine in the television film *Mandela and DeKlerk*, playing the political prisoner and later South African president Nelson Mandela.

The six-foot three-inch, 200-pound Sidney Poitier makes his home in Beverly Hills, California. He continues to work steadily, most recently appearing in the title role in the made-for-TV movie *The Simple Life of Noah Dearborn* (1999) and penning *The Measure of a Man*, which is subtitled "A Spiritual Autobiography." Over the years, Poitier has received a number of honors for his accomplishments, including a Lifetime Achievement Award from the American Film Institute and a knighthood from Queen Elizabeth II. In 1997 he was appointed the Bahamian ambassador to Japan. His sophisticated screen image notwithstanding, Poitier told Brent Staples for the *New York Times Magazine* (April 16, 2000) that his "biggest job" is controlling his temper, which he described as "seismic." While Poitier enjoys his success and has expressed thankfulness for the opportunities he has been given, he told Richards that celebrity has its drawbacks. "I am sorry that I can no longer sit in a bar or restaurant and observe people, as I did 40-odd years ago," he explained. "I love to listen to snatches of conversation. It's amazing. When there isn't a camera in our faces, when we're just speaking in life, we put the emphasis on the right word. We make our pauses with expert precision. Any actor who comes close to that is doing his job very well indeed." — J.K.B.

Suggested Reading: *American Film* p18+ Sep. 1991, with photos; *Cable Guide* p45+ Apr. 1987, with photos; *Chicago Tribune* XIII p4+ Jan. 31, 1988; *Ebony* p33+ Nov. 1977, with photos; *Parade* p4+ Feb. 28, 1998, with photos; *People* p68+ Aug. 4, 1980; *Washington Post* G p1+ Apr. 7, 1991, with photo, G p1+ Dec. 3, 1995, with photos; Poitier, Sidney. *This Life*, 1980, *The Measure of a Man*, 2000

Selected Films: *No Way Out*, 1950; *Cry, The Beloved Country*, 1951; *Blackboard Jungle*, 1955; *The Defiant Ones*, 1958; *Porgy and Bess*, 1959; *A Raisin in the Sun*, 1961; *Lilies of the Field*, 1963; *To Sir, with Love*, 1967; *In the Heat of the Night*, 1967; *Guess Who's Coming to Dinner*, 1967; *They Call Me MISTER Tibbs!*, 1970; *Buck and the Preacher*, 1972; *Uptown Saturday Night*, 1974; *Let's Do It Again*, 1975; *A Piece of the Action*, 1977; *Shoot to Kill*, 1988; *Little Nikita*, 1988; *Sneakers*, 1992; *The Jackal*, 1997

Selected Television Shows: *Separate But Equal*, 1991; *A Good Day to Die*, 1995; *To Sir, with Love 2*, 1996; *Mandela and de Klerk*, 1997; *David and Lisa*, 1998; *Free of Eden*, 1998; *The Simple Life of Noah Dearborn*, 1999

David Davidson/Archive Photos

Powell, Sandy

1960– Costume designer. Address: c/o Neil Jordan, 2 Martello Terrace, Bray, County Wiclow, Ireland

"There's a beauty in dirt," the costume designer Sandy Powell said to Lynn Hirschberg for the *New York Times Magazine* (December 20, 1998). "When I go to the movies, I think, 'Why is that dress so clean? The boat is going down and they look perfect.' You want to have beauty in a film, but if something looks a bit worn, a bit soiled, it usually has more depth." With more than 25 pictures to her credit, as well as an Oscar for her work on the romance *Shakespeare in Love* (1999), the 40-ish Powell is arguably the most celebrated costume designer currently working in film. "Sandy comes with strong responses to the material," John Madden, the director of *Shakespeare in Love*, said to Ginia Bellafante for *Time* (February 22, 1999). "She comes armed with instinct." While many costumers strive first and foremost to represent accurately the period in which a film is set, Powell has produced designs that not only serve the films in which they appear but also stand on their own as artistic creations. She commented in *Premiere: Women in Hollywood* (1998), "I'm more interested in fashion as an art form, in the collaborative aspect of working on a film."

Born in London, England, in 1960, Sandy Powell recalled in an interview with Brian Sibley for the BBC Web site (September 2, 1999) that as a youngster she was drawn to films with opulent costumes. "I suppose one of the earliest ones I remember being impressed by was *Death in Venice*," she said. "I must have been about 13 when I saw that at school, and it was one of those films where me and all my school friends went back time and time again to see it. And then there were the Derek Jarman films, . . . *Jubilee* [1977] and *The Tempest* [1979]. They inspired me to give him a call, rather naively! I thought, 'That's the person I want to work with. I'll give him a call.'"

Powell attended London's Central School of Art, where she studied theater design. In 1981 she abandoned her studies and sought out Jarman. "I called him at a time when I had quite a visual show on at the ICA [Institute of Contemporary Arts, in London], a theatre piece called *Rococco*," she told Sibley, "which was by a fringe theatre company called Rational Theatre. There were some big frocks in it which I'd made myself, like you had to in those days, as well as build the set, and I thought he might like to come and see it. He did and he was very generous and very sweet afterwards, and invited me to tea. I basically said I want to work in films." Powell first worked with Jarman on the homoerotic drama *Caravaggio* (1986) and then on *The Last of England* (1987), which took a gloomy view of that nation under the leadership of Prime Minister Margaret Thatcher.

Later in the 1980s, Powell worked on such movies as *Stormy Monday* (1988), directed by Mike Figgis; *Killing Dad* (1989), written and directed by Michael Austin; and *For Queen and Country* (1989), starring Denzel Washington. In these films, each set in a different period, Powell displayed her ability to create provocative costumes whatever the milieu, a talent that has defined her as a designer. "Sandy's great gift is her ability to make historical costumes look contemporary," Harvey Weinstein, the head of Miramax, which produced *Shakespeare in Love*, told Lynn Hirschberg. "She manages to be both true to the period and modern." Powell's costumes reflect her method of drawing inspiration from a period rather than attempting the precise re-creation of its styles. "Unless of course the film requires it, I'm not interested in an exact replica of the period," she told Bellafante. "I look at the period, how it should be, how it could be, and then I do my own version."

Powell put her signature touch on the romance *Shadow of China* (1991) and the controversially titled comedy *The Pope Must Die* (1991). In 1992 she worked on Neil Jordan's *The Crying Game*. That film was her second collaboration with the Irish director, the first being *The Miracle* (1991). A drama with an audience-grabbing twist, *The Crying Game* proved to be the sleeper hit of 1992, and it both raised Powell's visibility in Hollywood and cemented her professional relationship with Jordan.

Powell reunited with Jarman in 1993, to design the costumes for *Wittgenstein*, an avant-garde examination of the life and thoughts of the Viennese-born philosopher Ludwig Wittgenstein. She then worked on two films whose plots each spanned several centuries. The first was *Being Human* (1993), a humorous look at the lives of five average men (all played by Robin Williams) born in vastly different eras over the course of 10,000 years. For *Being Human* Powell produced garb associated with prehistoric times, ancient Rome, the Middle Ages, the Age of Exploration, and contemporary society. The other project was an adaptation of *Orlando*, a novel by Virginia Woolf that chronicles 400 years in the life of the ageless, gender-switching protagonist. For her efforts on that film, Powell received her first Oscar nomination for best costume design.

In 1994 Powell again worked with Jordan, on the gothic epic *Interview with the Vampire*, which stars Tom Cruise and Brad Pitt. Based on Anne Rice's best-selling novel, the film follows the lives of a pair of immortal vampires in such settings as 18th-century Louisiana and modern-day San Francisco. *Interview with the Vampire* is one of the few high-profile Hollywood films for which Powell has designed costumes. "It was different," she told Hirschberg. "Tom Cruise was lovely to me, but there were many discussions about his height in relation to Brad Pitt's. There are always vanity concerns." The following year she undertook the costume design for the historical drama *Rob Roy* (1995), the story of the famed Scottish patriot Rob Roy MacGregor. To avoid sparking controversy over the accuracy of MacGregor's tartan, she came up with her own design. "It was very difficult to find an original tartan dating back to the period that the director liked the looks of," she explained to Kathryn Shattuck for the *New York Times* (May 21, 1995), "and it was easier to make one up so it wouldn't be wrong. In that day and age, tartans didn't exist as we know them. The tartans were earthy and designs were simple."

During the next two years, Powell again worked with Jordan, on *Michael Collins* (1996) and *The Butcher Boy* (1997), before collaborating with director Iain Softley on *The Wings of the Dove* (1997). Based on a Henry James novel that takes place in 1902, the film is about a well-to-do young woman whose love for a working-class man threatens her aspirations for greater wealth and position. After signing on for the project, Powell persuaded Softley to change the time to 1910, because, as she explained to Hirschberg, that year was more "bohemian" and "uninhibited" than 1902. "And besides, every Merchant-Ivory film is set in 1902, and I wanted the costumes to look different," she added, referring to the producer Ismail Merchant and the director James Ivory, whose films popularized costume dramas in the 1980s. Powell's instincts paid off; *The Wings of the Dove* brought her a second Oscar nomination for best costume design.

Powell's next film, *Velvet Goldmine* (1998), was an exploration of the glam-rock scene of 1970s London, which gave rise to such artists as T. Rex, Mott the Hoople, and David Bowie. The dazzling array of costumes and adornments worn by the stars of *Velvet Goldmine* drew a lot of attention and reflects Powell's love for the styles of that time and place. "It was part of my development," she told John Calhoun for *Entertainment Design* (February 1999). "I'm 38 now, so I was 10 to 15 in the years that we cover [in the film]. I was really into the music and the fashion, so I was quite keen to do this." For her costumes for *Velvet Goldmine*, Powell was recognized with a third Oscar nomination.

Powell worked on Anand Tucker's movie *Hilary and Jackie* (1998), about the celebrated cellist Jacqueline du Pre and her sister, before signing on as costume designer for *Shakespeare in Love* (1998), a fiction in which the bard falls in love with a woman who inspires him to write *Romeo and Juliet*, thereby curing his writer's block. The project was an especially challenging one for Powell, because she had to design costumes ranging from the grimy tatters of street urchins to the opulent royal garb of Queen Elizabeth I. "On the one hand, we'd be sewing more jewels on Elizabeth's gown," Powell told Hirschberg. "And on the other, we'd be painting and spraying garments to make things look more worn." *Shakespeare in Love* was an unqualified hit, earning more than $100 million at the box office and the Academy Award for best picture of 1998. In addition, Powell won the Oscar for costume design.

In 1999 Powell collaborated with Jordan on the 1940s-era romance *The End of the Affair*, which is based on a novel by Graham Greene and stars Ralph Fiennes, Julianne Moore, and Stephen Rea. She designed constumes for Mike Figgis's *Miss Julie* (1999), an adaptation for the screen of the Swedish playwright August Strindberg's same-named drama. In 2001 actors in two major feature films will wear costumes of Powell's design. The first movie, *The Queen of the Damned*, is the sequal to *Interview with the Vampire* (1994), based on Anne Rice's popular series of *Vampire* novels. The second, *Gangs of New York*, is Martin Scorsese's epic about Italian immigration to New York during the late 19th century.

Although Powell, who lives in London, has put her touch on films ranging widely in genre and period, she has described herself as choosy about her projects. "I couldn't do a project if it was all just fantastic costumes and a rubbish script," she told Bellafante. "I couldn't be bothered to give it my time." — J.K.B.

Suggested Reading: *Entertainment Design* p22+ Feb. 22, 1999, with photos; *New York Times* II p11+ May 21, 1995, with photos; *New York Times Magazine* p60+ Dec. 20, 1998, with photos; *Premiere: Women in Hollywood* p38 1998, with photos; *Time* p82+ Feb. 22, 1999

Associated Press

Putin, Vladimir

(POO-tin, VLAH-dih-meer)

Oct. 7, 1952– President of Russia. Address: Office of the President, 103073 The Kremlin, Moscow, Russia

After December 31, 1999, when he became acting president of Russia, Vladimir Putin saw his public image undergo a slight transformation. Initially, the poker-faced official was best known for how little was known about him, other than the fact that he had spent nearly 17 years as a member of the KGB—the Soviet Union's elite intelligence organization—followed by less than 10 years in politics, which had led to his appointment as prime minister in August 1999. But when he emerged as President Boris Yeltsin's heir apparent, his public-relations team saw the need to demystify him for the voting public, in time for the 2000 presidential election. Putin thus began to reveal himself as "a man of simple tastes," as Bernard Gwertzman described him in the *New York Times Book Review* (May 14, 2000)—a family man who had been inspired to join the KGB by a movie he saw as a teenager.

What has not changed is Putin's reputation as a capable leader. Since he was elected president, by an overwhelming margin, in March 2000, he has taken steps to increase Russia's control over its many provinces, to strengthen its military, to fight corruption, and to ensure the continued improvement of its once-ailing economy. While some have worried that Putin's firm hold on power comes at the cost of liberty within the country, many perceive him as the strong figure Russia needs at its helm.

The only child of a factory foreman and his wife, Vladimir Vladimirovich Putin was born on October 7, 1952 in Leningrad (renamed St. Petersburg after the collapse of the Soviet Union, in the early 1990s). Putin grew up in a communal apartment shared by three families, but he enjoyed a comfortable upbringing. His parents enrolled him in martial-arts classes, and by the age of 16, he ranked as an expert in sambo, a combination of wrestling and judo. He became Leningrad's judo champion in 1974, while he was attending university, and he instructed students in karate while he was with the KGB.

Putin has often been described as driven and ambitious, traits that he exhibited even as a teenager. At age 16 he entered a college-preparatory secondary school that had a reputation for academic rigor. The school emphasized debate-oriented classes over traditional lectures, and it accepted only the brightest students, who were thereby guaranteed spots at St. Petersburg's most prestigious technical university. Although Putin intended to study chemistry, he soon switched his focus to the humanities and such "soft" sciences as biology, letting his grades in math and chemistry slip. "I spoke to his father about this," his biology teacher told Michael Wines. "He said his son was so goal-oriented that he already knows what he wants—and between us, why should he be expending so much energy on chemistry and math when he is going to do something else?" Putin also played handball and was a deejay for the school radio station, playing Western rock music for his fellow students.

Putin has revealed that the 1968 movie *The Sword and the Shield*, whose main character is a Soviet double agent in Nazi Germany, led to his desire to join the KGB. According to *Komsomolskaya Pravda* (February 17, 2000, as reprinted on-line by *Russia Today*), Russia's largest newspaper in terms of circulation, Putin approached the KGB when he graduated from high school and asked to be admitted into the service; KGB officials advised him to get a degree in law. In 1970 Putin enrolled at Leningrad State University to study civil law, and by all accounts, he conducted himself quietly and seriously. He graduated five years later, with honors, and was recruited by the extremely selective KGB.

Reports about Putin's time with the intelligence organization are sketchy and contain half-statements and misinformation. It appears that the KGB trained him in Moscow and that he then spent some time in St. Petersburg. Igor Antonov, a former KGB co-worker of Putin's, told Michael Wines that the KGB would not station an unmarried agent outside the country; in the early 1980s Putin married, and in 1985 he was sent to East Germany, considered one of the most important foreign posts. The nature of his work abroad remains unknown. Some reports claim that he did nothing more than push papers. The Stratfor Intelligence Service, a private think tank based in Austin, Texas, suggested that he acted as an "economic spy," stealing Western technology. Still other sources maintained that he kept tabs on East Germans and recruited agents for the KGB. In 1989 the Berlin Wall, which separated Communist East Germany from democratic West Germany, fell, and the two nations united under democratic rule. Putin returned to Russia, which was undergoing major reforms instituted by President Mikhail Gorbachev with the goal of pushing the Soviet Union toward democracy, economic privatization, and rapprochement with the West. According to some sources, Putin's stint with the KGB ended at this point, but most observers agree that he continued to work as a KGB mole at his new job in the international relations department at Leningrad State University, where he monitored reaction to Gorbachev's new policies.

In the early 1990s Putin accepted a position in the St. Petersburg government. The mayor, Anatoly Sobchak, had taught Putin law at the university, and they had become reacquainted when Putin returned to Russia. "[Putin] worked under the cover of the University International Department and participated in meetings of the external economic politics," Antonov told a reporter for *Komsomolskaya Pravda*. "Sobchak noticed him because Putin gave him advice several times. If Sobchak hadn't needed him badly, how could he take a person from the KGB to work as his closest aide at a time when all special services were marred with criticism?" Putin worked behind-the-scenes for Sobchak's administration, earning the sobriquet "gray cardinal" because of his colorless yet powerful presence. Under Sobchak, Putin oversaw St. Petersburg's businesses and exports and persuaded foreign financiers to invest in the city. "In outside appearance, he is a calm, inconspicuous, quiet man," Sergei Stepashin, a former prime minister of Russia, told Michael Wines for the *New York Times* (January 1, 2000). "But his grip, which was felt by all the financiers in St. Petersburg, was amazing." In 1994 Putin became the first deputy mayor of St. Petersburg. His stint in city administration ended two years later, when Sobchak failed to win reelection and fled the city amid charges of corruption.

Shortly after Sobchak's departure Putin was invited to Moscow to work for the Kremlin. He started in the office of the property manager, which oversees the Kremlin and all its outlying properties, including government buildings and homes for officials. In March 1997 he became the head of the Main Control (or Oversight) Department, responsible for carrying out President Boris Yeltsin's decrees, and a year later he was appointed to oversee the Kremlin's relations with Russia's many regions. (The Stratfor Intelligence Service maintained that he was awarded the title of first deputy chief of staff at this juncture.) In July 1998 Putin became the head of the Federal Security Service (FSB), one of the two sections into which the KGB had been divided after the Soviet Union disbanded. In March 1999 he took on the duties of secretary of the presidential Security Council. Then, on August 9, 1999, Yeltsin sacked his fourth prime minister in 17 months, Sergei Stepashin, and appointed Putin to the post.

Putin's incredibly quick succession of promotions has been attributed to his unswerving loyalty to Yeltsin, who fired prime ministers when their public approval ratings rose to a point that he considered unacceptably high. Reporters and political analysts speculated that the upcoming presidential elections, scheduled to be held less than a year later, spurred Yeltsin to appoint a successor who would follow his decrees and protect his interests—someone who would be, in effect, a puppet. (Yeltsin was finishing his second term in office and was thus disqualified from running again.) Putin had always remained faithful to his bosses; in 1996, for example, when Sobchak lost the election for mayor of St. Petersburg, Putin was the only top aide to resign, saying, "Better to be hanged for loyalty than rewarded for treason." He had proven his loyalty to Yeltsin in 1999, when chief prosecutor Yuri Skuratov ran a corruption-finding campaign against a close Yeltsin associate. Videotapes depicting Skuratov cavorting with two prostitutes aired on Russian television, and Putin, as head of the FSB, verified their authenticity. Rumors circulated that Stepashin had failed the loyalty test because he did not stop Yuri Luzhkov, the mayor of Moscow and a strong opponent of Yeltsin's, from forming a coalition with other competitors for the presidency. One of Putin's first actions as prime minister was to weaken Luzhkov's regional and Moscow-based support, which he accomplished, many claimed, with the help of knowledge he had acquired through the FSB.

When Yeltsin appointed Putin prime minister, he also declared that his new right-hand man was his choice for the next president of Russia, despite Putin's lack of experience in any elective office. Neither reporters nor citizens knew anything about the new prime minister, and Putin began his new job with an approval rating of just 2 percent. By November, however, his rating had climbed to 29 percent, an unprecedented level in Russia, where a rating of 18 percent is considered extremely favorable. The turnaround came as a result of the renewed war against Chechnya, an independent, primarily Muslim region within Russia. Chechnya's declaration of independence in 1994 had precipitated a war with Russia, which did not want the region to secede. The war continued into 1996, until Chechen guerrillas routed the Russian soldiers, some of whom had already captured Chechnya's capital. After the ignominious Russian defeat, Chechnya secured an agreement that granted the region the right to govern itself independently and the chance to discuss its official status at meetings to be held in 2001. In August 1999, however, Chechen militants launched several incursions into the neighboring Russian region of Dagestan, which has a substantial Muslim population. Under Putin's leadership, the Russian army rebuffed the rebels and set up watch posts along the Chechnya border. The majority of Russian citizens, still feeling the sting of the humiliating loss of three years before, approved Putin's actions, and the prime minister promised to eradicate the rebels. Then, in September, several bombs tore through apartment buildings in Volgodonsk and Moscow, killing many civilians. The Russian government claimed that the bombs were set by Chechen terrorists, and though the charges have never been proven, the Russian army once again entered Chechnya. Its advances and victories buoyed Putin's reputation, and the Russian press hailed him as a strong leader, one strikingly different from the ailing and sometimes incoherent Yeltsin. Reactions outside Russia, however, were not favorable: the brutality of the second Chechen campaign provoked criticism from the U.S. and other Western powers dismayed about the killing of Chechen civilians trapped in the conflict.

In December 1999 elections were held for the Duma, the lower house of the legislature, which was dominated by the Communist Party. Although the Communists held onto their majority, the Unity Party, which had formed only a couple of months prior to the election and had made its support of Putin the sole item on its platform, won a significant number of seats, thus diminishing the Communists' base. Two weeks later, assured of Putin's loyalty as well as of his popular support, Yeltsin resigned as president of Russia. On December 31, 1999 Putin became both prime minister and acting president of Russia.

As one of his first acts as president, Putin granted Yeltsin and his family lifetime immunity from prosecution for corruption (charges of which were already being aired) and allotted them a salary and secret-service protection. For his part Yeltsin had done his best to ensure Putin's succession to the presidency by moving the election up from June to March 2000, thereby reducing the preparation time of any rivals.

Before the election, under Putin's guidance, First Deputy Prime Minister Mikhail Kasyanov negotiated with London-based investors a new repayment schedule for Soviet debts. Putin expressed the hope that the West, with renewed confidence in Russia's ability to control its finances, will invest more money in the economy, which has been boosted by recent increases in the price of oil, one of Russia's major exports. Putin also started investigations into political corruption, which more than anything else has been responsible for weakening Russia's economy and government. Charges of corruption had been leveled against Putin himself in the past, particularly during his St. Petersburg years and during his tenure as FSB chief, but none has ever stuck.

In elections held on March 26, 2000, in a field of 11 candidates, Putin commanded just over 50 percent of the vote; he was sworn in as president on May 7. Since the election, he has maintained his high level of popularity, by taking steps that have bolstered his image as a strong leader. While he stressed the need to modernize the country's nuclear arsenal, he won the Russian Parliament's approval for the Start II nuclear arms reduction agreement with the United States, which calls for both nations to cut the number of such weapons by half. Over the summer, he succeeded in pushing through Parliament his plan to organize Russia into seven large districts—each to be headed by a figure in the Kremlin—with the aim of stripping provincial governors of much of their power and increasing central control over the country. Along with Putin's high approval ratings came concern from some corners that his firm hand was maintained at the expense of freedom within Russia. Fueling these worries was an incident in May, in which federal agents raided the offices of Media-Most, the country's largest independent media conglomerate, whose television network had been critical of Putin; Media-Most's head, Vladimir A. Gusinsky, was arrested and charged with financial wrongdoing. Gusinsky was released after four days and the charges dropped, and Putin himself publicly criticized the arrest. Gusinsky, however, accused the president of having been behind the agents' actions.

More damaging to Putin's reputation were missteps in the wake of a military disaster. Shortly before midnight on August 12, 2000, the Russian nuclear submarine *Kursk* sank in the Barents Sea after explosions on board, which instantly killed most of the 118 crew members. (The 23 men left alive after the blasts later perished.) In the days that followed, the government was slow to request foreign help in rescuing the surviving crew members and seemed reluctant to share details with the public; Putin himself remained for days at the Black Sea resort where he had been vacationing. Later, however—in what some viewed as a sign of a new openness on the part of the Russian government—Putin admitted to feelings of "responsibility and guilt" over the tragedy, and he promised that for the next 10 years, each of the families of the dead crew members would receive payments equal to an officer's salary.

Putin's wife, Lyudmila, is a specialist in foreign languages; their two teenage daughters, Katya and Maria, study at home. Putin has boasted that his children's knowledge of German surpasses his own facility with that language, which is good enough to enable him to imitate regional dialects. He is fond of literature and music, and he has acknowledged that he is a practicing Orthodox Christian. "When I was a few months old," he recalled to a Reuters reporter, as quoted in *Russia Today* (February 13, 2000, on-line), "my mum and her neighbor in the communal apartment where we lived took me to church without telling my father, he was a Communist Party member, and baptized me." Such personal disclosures have apparently not damaged his reputation as a no-nonsense leader. "A lot about him is a mystery," the Russian actor and singer Mikhail Boyarsky said to a reporter for *People* (February 28, 2000). "When I once asked him about his great workload, all he answered was, 'I am a soldier and I must work.'" — K.S.

Suggested Reading: *Maclean's* p46+ Jan. 17, 2000, with photo; *Nation* p3+ Jan. 24, 2000; *New York Times* A p11 Jan. 1, 2000, with photo, A p4 Jan. 10, 2000, with photo, p1+ Feb. 20, 2000, with photos; *Russia Today* Web site; Stratfor Intelligence Service Web site; *Time* p90+ Jan. 1, 2000; Putin, Vladimir, with Nataliya Gevorkyan, Natalya Timakova, and Andrei Kolesnikov. *First Person: An Astonishingly Frank Self-Portrait by Russia's President Vladimir Putin*, 2000

Raines, Franklin D.

Jan. 14, 1949– Chairman and CEO of the Federal National Mortgage Association. Address: Federal National Mortgage Association, 3900 Wisconsin Ave. N.W., Washington, DC 20016-2892

In 1996 Franklin Raines chose to resign as vice chairman of the Federal National Mortgage Association (better known as Fannie Mae), a post reportedly worth $2.25 million a year in salary plus benefits, in favor of an appointment from President Bill Clinton to head the White House Office of Management and Budget (OMB), which carried an annual salary of about $150,000. His decision undoubtedly raised some eyebrows, but Raines had a ready explanation. "My view is that when the President of the United States says he needs your help, you have to have a very good reason to say no," he told Joyce Jones for *Black Enterprise* (August 1996). "And money is not one of them." Raines guided the OMB for two years, becoming the first director in a generation to balance the federal budget. Few blamed him, however, when he left the OMB, in 1998, to accept the reins of Fannie Mae from James A. Johnson, the outgoing chairman of the company. Although Raines was a likely candidate to become White House chief of staff or even U.S. secretary of the treasury had he stayed in government, the lure of heading Fannie Mae—the nation's largest provider of home-mortgage financing and, at

Courtesy of Fannie Mae

Franklin D. Raines

the time, the 33d largest company in America—proved compelling. "This was a once-in-a-lifetime opportunity," he told John Broder for the *New York Times* (April 15, 1998). "I wanted to stay in government for the Social Security debate, but my real life's ambition is to run a major company, and you only get asked a very few times to run a company like this one." On January 1, 1999, after a transition period during which he worked alongside Johnson, Raines took over as chairman and CEO of Fannie Mae, becoming the first African-American ever to head a Fortune 500 firm. Under Raines, Fannie Mae has become the 26th largest company in the U.S.

Franklin Delano Raines was born on January 14, 1949 in Seattle, Washington, the fourth of the six children of Ida and Delno Raines. Although Raines's parents intended his middle name to be the same as his father's first name, hospital personnel added an "a" to the name in his birth records, assuming he was being named after President Franklin Delano Roosevelt. His parents had relocated to the Pacific Northwest from the Deep South after World War II, attracted by the burgeoning aircraft industry. Ida Raines cleaned offices and bathrooms at the aircraft manufacturer Boeing, a job that Raines proudly noted when he accepted a position on that company's board of directors, in 1995. Delno Raines, who had built the family's home himself using materials scavenged from a structure that was being razed, worked as a mechanic, also at Boeing, but severe bouts of depression landed him in the hospital and caused him to lose his job. The family, which included a nephew whom Raines's parents had agreed to raise, was forced to accept Aid to Families with Dependent Children, as welfare is officially known. Between the ages of eight and 14, young Franklin contributed to the family's income by working at a local grocery store. His father eventually regained his health, but he never attained his previous level of economic stability. Raines has said that his family's plight made him more sensitive to the financial hardship of others. His early memories include those of Sunday afternoon drives through Seattle's more prosperous neighborhood, during which his parents would point out to their children the rewards of staying in school and working hard.

In high school Raines served as student-body president, member of the school's championship debating team, and—although skinny and nearsighted—captain of the football team. When he graduated, in 1967, with perfect grades, he was awarded a four-year scholarship to Harvard University, in Cambridge, Massachusetts, which arranged for his parents to contribute $400 a year (worth about $1,750 in 1999), payable in installments. Like most campuses across the country during the late 1960s and early 1970s, Harvard's was the site of numerous protests and rallies. Raines, a moderate who had joined both the Young Republicans and the Young Democrats clubs, took part in the politically charged atmosphere in a nonextremist fashion. For example, during a 1969 campus rally against the Reserve Officers Training Corps (ROTC, a program established at many U.S. colleges to train undergraduates to become military officers) at Harvard, he grabbed the microphone to argue against a hostile protest and in favor of a peaceful strike. He angered the student demonstrators, who had been planning to take over a university building, as well as the administration, which had already called in 400 police officers to quell the protest. Raines later explained to Karen Tumulty for *Time* (February 10, 1997), "Unless someone took the initiative, this was going to turn into a confrontation between the administration and the radicals and we would see the institution torn apart." His performance impressed a future senator from New York, Daniel Patrick Moynihan, who was then a Harvard professor known for his moderate views and who soon became the only Democrat to serve in the White House during the administration of President Richard Nixon. At Moynihan's invitation, in the summer of 1969 Raines worked in Washington, D.C., as an intern in the office of Moynihan, who was then a White House assistant for urban affairs. Raines was assigned to track the source of campus protests and, before he returned to Harvard in the fall, to brief Nixon's Cabinet on his findings. Raines reported to the Cabinet members that, despite their fears, there seemed to be no clandestine central organization fomenting the unrest. According to Raines, they didn't believe him, which seems consistent with the paranoia often associated with the Nixon administration.

After earning his B.A., magna cum laude, in government studies, in 1971, Raines traveled to England on a Rhodes scholarship to attend Magdalen

College, at Oxford University. Relating the news, his hometown paper, the *Seattle Times*, referred to Raines as a "super black," a sobriquet that reportedly rankled him at the time. Following his studies abroad (he did not earn a degree), he returned to Cambridge to attend the Harvard Law School; he earned a law degree in 1976. He then resettled in Seattle to practice law at a private firm. When a congressional seat opened the following year, Steve Pruzin, a former high-school classmate and debate partner of his, encouraged Raines to run for the office and began organizing a campaign for him. Raines, however, accepted an offer—extended at the recommendation of his fellow Harvard Law School graduate Stuart Eizenstat, who was then an aide to President Jimmy Carter—to join the White House domestic-policy staff. Raines worked on welfare reform, Social Security, and the federal food-stamp program, and was quickly promoted to an associate directorship of the OMB. When Carter lost the 1980 presidential election to Ronald Reagan, Raines returned to the private sector. He took a position at Lazard Frères & Co., a New York–based investment bank, where he was made general partner in 1985. Specializing in municipal finance, Raines helped state and local governments organize their budgets and raise operating capital. The several days a week of travel that the job required led Raines, who by then was living with his wife and children in Washington, D.C., to quit Lazard, in 1991. "I didn't know what I was going to do," Raines told Clay Chandler for the *Washington Post* (November 17, 1996). "But I had two young daughters I wanted to spend more time with, and I was sick of all that flying."

A few months later, Fannie Mae's then–CEO, James A. Johnson, asked Raines to join the company. Established in 1938 by the federal government, Fannie Mae is the country's largest mortgage underwriter, mandated to encourage low- and moderate-income families to purchase homes. While the firm does not lend money to home buyers directly, it ensures that mortgage funds are available on a regular and affordable basis by purchasing existing mortgages from the lending institutions themselves, thereby freeing up money that can then be lent to additional home buyers. Since Fannie Mae is protected by a government guarantee on its own debts, its stock does consistently well on Wall Street, and the firm has little competition except for the Federal Home Loan Mortgage Corp. (Freddie Mac)—a company with similar charters, congressional mandates, and regulatory structures established by Congress in 1970 specifically to maintain free-market competition for Fannie Mae. While Fannie Mae is sometimes criticized for being the "800-pound gorilla" of the mortgage industry, because of its federal backing and massive profits, Raines defends the company, pointing out that those profits fund the company's efforts to promote affordable home ownership to those who otherwise could not qualify for it.

Raines was excited to join Fannie Mae as a vice chairman: the company paid a generous performance-based salary, and its corporate offices were close to his home. During this stint at Fannie Mae, Raines streamlined the mortgage-processing paperwork, established mortgage standards that are still in use, and was instrumental in creating both an electronic underwriting program and an electronic system called the Desk Top Home Counselor, which helped prospective homeowners get their finances in order. He also forged partnerships between lenders and the U.S. Department of Housing and Urban Development (HUD) across the country and led an aggressive effort to reduce the cost of each Fannie Mae mortgage by about $1,000.

In 1993 Vice President Al Gore, whom Raines had met through his extensive Harvard alumni work, and the lobbyist Vernon Jordan arranged for Raines to join President Bill Clinton's economic transition team. Clinton called on him again in April 1996, when he was seeking a new director of the OMB to replace Alice M. Rivlin, who was leaving to vice chair the Federal Reserve. Referring to the massive pay cut that Raines would take if he accepted the job, Clinton joked that Raines could help the middle class through the OMB and then benefit as a member of it. While some observers cited Raines's past experience in the OMB as justification for Clinton's interest, others pointed out that the Clinton administration had few black staffers and that Raines would help fill that gap. Still others felt that the appointment had been orchestrated behind the scenes by Fannie Mae executives reportedly anxious to protect the firm's line of U.S. Treasury credit and exemption from local income taxes. Such speculation angered Raines, who assumed the OMB post in September 1996, after Senate confirmation, yet he ignored his critics and set out to win bipartisan support for his budgetary plans. Though recognized on Wall Street from his turns at Fannie Mae and Lazard Frères, he was relatively unknown in fiscal-policy circles. Ironically, his status as a Washington outsider, and his desire to remain so, helped him in his new post. In his conversation with Clay Chandler, James A. Johnson characterized Raines as "not a backslapper." "He's not a politico, he's not a part of that world. He has come at his current job almost entirely from the public policy side," Johnson added. Raines's low-key manner and professional demeanor won him the broad support of Democrats and Republicans alike. Republican House Majority Leader Dick Armey, who is known as intensely antagonistic toward most Democrats, told Karen Tumulty for *Time* (February 10, 1997) that Raines is "a serious guy who understands what needs to be done and is going to do his level best to do it. He is a man who strikes me as not having a lot of guile." Another Republican, Pete Domenici, chairman of the Senate Budget Committee, said, "It's obvious he tries very hard to understand our side."

While some staunch Democrats reportedly felt slighted by Raines's courtship of their opposition, most felt he was simply exhibiting his intuitive sense of diplomacy. Raines devoted himself to helping District of Columbia officials solve the area's financial woes and to representing the Clinton administration on various Sunday morning news programs, where his calmness and polished delivery reportedly impressed viewers. His major contribution to the administration was his role in drafting the $1.69 trillion budget plan that Clinton presented to Congress in February 1997 for the 1998 fiscal year. The plan called for a $51 billion increase in spending on education and a $21 billion increase in welfare over a five-year period, but substantial decreases in other areas, such as Medicaid. The plan also called for the federal budget to be balanced by 2002. In previous years the Republican response to Clinton's budget proposals had been to reject them out of hand, but they were willing to consider this one, thanks in part to Raines's sensitivity to their concerns. Raines was the key negotiator during the ensuing talks that led Congress to give final approval to the Balanced Budget Act of 1997. The House passed the resolution 327–97, and the Senate ratified it 76–22. Although some skeptics thought Raines's projection overly optimistic and doubted that the act would actually achieve a balanced budget by 2002, almost all prognosticators agreed that winning bipartisan approval put him on the fast track within the Clinton White House.

Raines himself expected to remain in the administration at least until Clinton's term had ended, hoping to be a pivotal figure in an upcoming debate about Social Security policy. But when James Johnson contacted him in 1998 about returning to Fannie Mae—this time as CEO—speculation about his future in government became moot. Explaining his decision to lure his one-time vice chairman back to the company, Johnson explained to Hamil Harris for *Black Enterprise* (August 1998), "Frank's integrity and business acumen make him the ideal leader of Fannie Mae as it enters its fourth decade as a privately managed, shareholder-owned corporation." Although Fannie Mae's stock has been publicly traded since 1970 and its nearly $400 billion in annual revenue ranks it in the upper echelon of Fortune 500 companies, some journalists, citing its ties to the federal government, refuse to consider the company part of the private sector and refer to it as a quasi-governmental agency. Consequently, journalists of that opinion were loath to recognize Raines as the first black CEO of a Fortune 500 firm. Others saw his appointment as merely a symbolic gesture with little practical significance for the country's African-American community. Raines disagreed. "The boards of companies tend to be fairly conservative," he told Harris, "and the fact that the Fannie Mae board saw me as the best CEO, I think, will be reassuring to other boards as they seek to promote black executives." Clinton, who called Raines a "brilliant OMB director," accepted his resignation on January 1, 1999. Following a nine-month period as Fannie Mae CEO-designate under Johnson, Raines took over the company's head office. One of his first acts as CEO was to reduce the amount of mortgage insurance home buyers were required to purchase—a move projected to save consumers more than $16 million a year.

Raines serves on the boards of several companies besides Boeing, among them America Online and Pfizer Inc. He is a fellow of the American Academy of Arts and Sciences and a member of the Council on Foreign Relations, the National Academy of Social Insurance, the Trilateral Commission, and the Business Council. He chairs the Visiting Committee of Harvard's Kennedy School of Government and is a past president of the university's board of overseers. Raines, who reportedly earns close to $7 million a year at Fannie Mae, lives in Washington, D.C., with his wife, Wendy, and their daughters, Laura, Andrea, and Sarah. — M.R.

Suggested Reading: *Black Enterprise* p15 Aug. 1996, with photo, p103+ Aug. 1998, with photos; *Business Week* p88+ Oct. 21, 1999, with photo; *New Republic* p20+ Dec. 15, 1997; *New York Times* I p8 Apr. 13, 1996, with photo, III p1 May 17, 1998, with photos; *Time* p34+ Feb. 10, 1997, with photos; *Washington Post* H p1 Nov. 17, 1996, with photo

---

Redgrave, Steven

Mar. 23, 1962– Rower. Address: c/o Leander Club, Henley-on-Thames RG9 2LP, England

After crossing the finish line in first place at the 1996 Summer Olympics, in Atlanta, Georgia, Steve Redgrave and his crew mate, Matthew Pinsent, acted very differently: Pinsent, 10 years Redgrave's junior, pumped his fist in a display of triumph and youthful exuberance, while Redgrave slumped exhaustedly over his oar. "I've had enough," he was quoted as saying following their victory. "This is it for me. If anyone sees me near a boat they can shoot me." Then 34, Redgrave had devoted the previous 20 years to practicing the relatively low-profile sport of rowing. The winner, at that point, of gold medals in four consecutive Olympics, as well as an Olympic bronze, three Commonwealth Games titles, and many world rowing championships, he could have retired secure in the knowledge that he was England's, and perhaps the world's, greatest oarsman ever. But within six months of the Summer Games, Redgrave had resolved to return to rowing, to compete in the 2000 Olympic Games, in Sydney, Australia—where he achieved the first-ever feat of winning five consecutive gold medals in an endurance event.

Pascal Rondeau/Allsport

Steven Redgrave

In the final leg of his preparations for the 2000 Olympics, Redgrave was often reminded of his request to be shot. "Not a day goes by when someone doesn't quote that back to me," he told Sophie Davies for *Balance*, the on-line publication of the British Diabetic Association. Although Redgrave was diagnosed with diabetes in 1997, he continued to train intensively. "I can't say that I want to win the next Olympics because I've got diabetes—I want to win it anyway," he explained to Davies. "The diabetes is just something that needs to be coped with if I'm to achieve, something I won't let hamper me." In viewing the disorder as little more than an obstacle along the path to victory or as simply another opponent, Redgrave displayed the focus and persistence that have kept him at the pinnacle of his sport for so long. "I don't row for pleasure," he explained to John Seabrook for the *New Yorker* (July 22, 1996), "I row to win gold medals." "Other competitors ask what Steve Redgrave has got that they haven't," Hillary Gates, a physiologist with the British Olympic Association, said to John Goodbody for the London *Times* (July 15, 1996, online). "The answer is that he has something that you cannot analyse."

The son of a laborer and his wife, Steven Redgrave was born on March 23, 1962 in Marlow, England, an historic riverside town on the banks of the Thames. Hindered by dyslexia, he was not a good student, but he had athletic potential, as he learned from his school's rowing coach. "The coach said he liked the looks of my hands and feet," Redgrave told Brad Wetzler for *Outside* (July 1997, on-line). "They were awfully big for the rest of my body. I was quite clumsy then, you know." (Like veterinarians, who calculate from the size of a puppy's paws how large the dog will be when fully mature, the coach predicted that Redgrave would grow to be unusually large, and he was right: Redgrave is six feet, five inches tall and weighs 225 pounds.) The gangly 13-year-old began to concentrate his energies on rowing. By the time he was 16, he had dropped out of school and was training full-time. He has been a professional oarsman ever since, training six hours a day, seven days a week and garnering a living from sponsorships, promotional endorsements, and speaking engagements that have come his way as a result of his celebrity. His wife, Ann Redgrave, a British national rowing-team physician and former international rower, has hypothesized that Redgrave's intense competitive drive can be traced to his struggle with dyslexia; his learning disability made his academic life difficult, while rowing enabled him to shine. Redgrave, however, has rejected this theory.

Rowing is generally considered the consummate team sport, because the speed of a boat depends so heavily on all its rowers' moving in unison. When a crew achieves synchronicity—all the athletes moving as one, so that the whole becomes greater than the sum of its parts—the team is said to have "swing," and swing usually translates into velocity. Because rowers typically defer to their crew's collective identity, few oarsman have attained celebrity as individuals. The main exceptions are single scullers, who race alone and, as athletes, are answerable only to themselves.

As a young oarsman with a strong streak of independence, Redgrave aimed to become a single sculler. He debuted on the international racing circuit at the 1979 junior world championships in a single (one person, two oars). At the next year's event, he paired with another junior sculler, and their double (two people using two oars each) won a silver medal. In 1981 Redgrave was promoted from junior to senior status by the British national team, and he was selected to represent England at the world championships in the quadruple scull. Though his quad rowed strongly together for two consecutive years, it never placed higher than sixth in major international competitions, and Redgrave returned to single sculling. After failing to make the finals of the 1983 world championships in a single, Redgrave abandoned sculling and began to train for the 1984 Summer Olympics as a sweep oarsman (keeping both hands on a single, larger oar). He was selected to stroke for England in the coxed-four event—that is, a race in which there are four rowers and a coxswain in each shell (a narrow, lightweight racing boat). The coxswain, a non-rower, steers the shell and directs the oarsmen, adjusting racing tactics to take into account weather conditions and other variables, and tries to motivate the crew as well. As the four's stroke—the rower who sits in the fourth seat—Redgrave set the pace and interacted with the coxswain. In 1984, on Lake Casitas in Los Angeles, Redgrave won his first Olympic gold medal.

Despite his success in the four, Redgrave felt dissatisfied. Posing a rhetorical question during a conversation with John Seabrook for the *New Yorker* (July 22, 1996), he said, "The eight is a country's blue-ribbon event, but can you name the people who were in the gold-medal–winning eight in the last Olympics? Whereas you would at least stand a chance of naming the winning single sculler." Redgrave returned to single sculling in the mid-1980s, a time when single sculling had become unusually competitive and was dominated by both Pertti Karpinnen of Finland, who would win three Olympic championships in his single, and Peter-Michael Kolbe of West Germany. During the 1985 world championships single event, Redgrave fell far behind, and he stopped rowing before reaching the finish line. Whether or not he had been injured, as he later contended, his action became the subject of an oft-repeated tale among elite oarsmen, because, one rower told Seabrook, it provided "the only proof we have that Redgrave is mortal."

Redgrave became convinced that his future lay with sweep team boats. His solo mentality led him to settle on the boat with the fewest team members: the pair (one oar each for two people). He formed a partnership with Andy Holmes, one of his crewmates from the 1984 four, and he and Holmes captured back-to-back gold in the pair-without-coxswain event at the 1986 and 1987 world championships and a silver in the coxed pair in 1987. Buoyed by their success, the two entered both events in the 1988 Summer Olympics, held in Seoul, South Korea. They handily won gold in the coxless event and took bronze in the pair with coxswain.

Following their achievement at the 1988 Olympics, Holmes retired from rowing, and Redgrave considered competing as a bobsledder. Then, after reaching the final trials for the British national bobsled team, he decided to return to rowing. Paired with Simon Berrisford, he competed in the 1989 world championships, where the duo earned silver in the coxless pair and fifth place in the coxed. The following season Berrisford suffered a serious back injury that ended his rowing career. Acting on short notice, the then–19-year-old Matthew Pinsent took his place.

The son of a country vicar, Pinsent attended Eton, a prestigious British secondary school, and Oxford University, a similarly renowned institution. (John Seabrook reported that Pinsent sometimes helps Redgrave, who still struggles with dyslexia, write inscriptions to fans who ask for his autograph.) Matching Redgrave in size and brawn, Pinsent has been described as carrying himself a little more erectly than Redgrave and thus acquiring an air that harkens back to the era when rowing was a sport of the upper class. Despite their differences, Redgrave and Pinsent have made a formidable team. Within their first year of training together, they won a bronze medal at the 1990 world championships; the following year they won the gold.

Less than a year before the start of the 1992 Olympics, Redgrave suffered an attack of colitis, and the disorder threatened his chances of returning to his third consecutive Games. But his symptoms subsided in time for him to recover his form. He and Pinsent won the Olympic title that year in the coxless pair. The 1992 Olympics was the first in a six-year streak of wins for Redgrave and Pinsent. In that span the duo competed together in 74 races, in both pair and four-without-coxswain competitions, and they did not lose once. Their streak included three world championships and the defense of their Olympic title in the coxless pair at the 1996 Games in Atlanta. The only other athletes who have won four or more consecutive Olympic gold medals are the American discus thrower Al Oerter (1956 through 1968), the Danish yachtsman Paul Elvstroem (1948 through 1960), and the Hungarian fencer Aladar Gerevich, who dominated Olympic team sabre fencing from 1932 through 1960.

Months before the 1996 Games began, Redgrave publicly revealed that he was thinking of retiring from rowing. "Whatever I do, it won't be a nine-to-five job," he told John Seabrook. "I've been my own boss for 20 years and I'm not going to work for someone else." Ann Redgrave, however, was certain that her husband's retirement would be brief. "He has lived with the job so long now he doesn't know any other way," she explained to Seabrook. "My training as a doctor tells me people just can't switch off like that." She was right; within months of his announcement to retire, Steve Redgrave had retracted his statement. "My heart lies with the competition," Redgrave was quoted as saying in *Outside* (December 2, 1996, on-line). "If I had to put it down to anything it was the desire to go to another Olympics. I still feel I am young enough to carry on." For their assault on the 2000 Summer Games, in Sydney, Redgrave and Pinsent decided to compete in the coxless-four event with Tim Foster, who won a gold medal with Pinsent at the 1988 junior championships in the coxless pair, and James Cracknell.

The newly formed quartet became the crew to beat almost from its inception. Undefeated through the 1997 international season, the team captured the gold medal at the 1997 world championships. Shortly after that win, Redgrave discovered that he had developed type-two diabetes, a relatively mild form of the disease that is usually controllable through diet or low doses of medication. Because of the extreme demands his training regimen places on his body, however, Redgrave must treat his diabetes more aggressively. "I have to take insulin because it's the easiest way to control it," he explained to Davies. "Tablets give a steady release of insulin which doesn't suit training at all. Training brings blood glucose levels down loads anyway, so if I've got too much insulin in my body when I'm training hard, my levels of blood glucose will plummet and I may go too low. It really is a juggling act." Redgrave's insulin regimen has been developed by trial and error. He tests his blood sugar levels often, and he always carries precise amounts of insulin and sugared drinks with him. He has even come to view his lifestyle as helpful in his effort to regulate his diabetes. Being an athlete, he told Davies, "is definitely an advantage. You have to be very disciplined about your whole lifestyle. Diabetes is just another part of the equation. It's not difficult—it's a pain in the neck, but that's all really."

At a May 1998 competition in Munich, Germany, an injury to Foster's hand forced the crew to replace him with Luka Gurbor, and the makeshift team came in fourth. They reasserted their dominance—with Foster back in play—at the 1998 world championships, with a decisive win over their chief rivals, the Italian and French coxless fours. For Redgrave it was a record eighth world-championship gold. "It's not the thrill my first title was but this one is a statement for me," Redgrave said, as reported on *CNN/SI* (September 12, 1998, on-line). "I came close to chucking it in this year, it was just so difficult. After coming down with diabetes it took so long to get it back."

At the 2000 Olympics, in Sydney, Redgrave and his teammates scraped by a strong Italian crew to win the gold medal in the coxless-four by 0.38 seconds. "It was desperate and fraught at the end," Redgrave told a reporter for *BBC Sport Online* (September 23, 2000), "but we never doubted we would win." With his fifth consecutive Olympic gold medal, Redgrave was one consecutive gold shy of the record, held by the fencer Gerevich. Redgrave became the first, however, to win five consecutive golds in an endurance event.

On October 31, 2000 Redgrave announced that he would retire from rowing for good. While he admitted that he had considered shooting for a sixth gold medal, at the 2004 Olympics, in Athens, he said, as quoted on *BBC Sport Online* (October 31, 2000), "Then I thought of the long winter training and the full commitment you have to put into it." As for his plans, Redgrave added, "I don't think I'll go into coaching. The coaches have the same time commitment as the athletes so if I was going to do that I might as well keep on rowing. But maybe in the future I will once I've had a break from the sport. I still want to be involved in the sport."

Steven Redgrave lives in Marlow Bottom, England, with his wife, Ann, and their two daughters. His recreational interests include golf. Great Britain's Olympic Committee chose him to carry the Union Jack at two Olympic opening ceremonies, in 1992 and 1996; he is the only athlete to be so honored twice. In 1996 the Sports Writers Association of Great Britain named Redgrave and Pinsent the sports team of the year. — T.J.F.

Suggested Reading: (London) *Times* (on-line) July 15, 1996, with photo; *New Yorker* p32+ July 22, 1996, with photo; *Outside* (on-line) July 1997

Regan, Judith

(REE-gan)

Aug. 17, 1953– President of ReganBooks; editor; television host. Address: ReganBooks, 1211 Ave. of the Americas, New York, NY 10036

Courtesy of Fox

Judith Regan seems to thrive on contradictions. As a book editor at Simon & Schuster, she published work by the raunchy and anarchic "shock jock" Howard Stern, as well as by the archconservative radio and television commentator Rush Limbaugh and the similarly conservative educator and judge Robert H. Bork. She holds a degree in English literature and wrote her thesis on Shakespeare; she is also a self-proclaimed pop-culture addict who once wrote for the *National Enquirer.* As one of the most powerful figures in New York's publishing and entertainment scene, she has a reputation as a hard-nosed and powerful player in an industry often dominated by men. The decor of her suite of offices, however, is unabashedly feminine, with dried roses, gaudy floral lamps, and dainty antiques, and she cites as her greatest achievement her being a mother. According to Susan Shapiro, writing for the *New York Times Magazine* (July 17, 1994), Regan's detractors have called her "pop vulture," "demolition woman," "a guerrilla publisher," "a tabloid-trained carpetbagger," and "the demise of Western civilization." Clearly, she has managed to rock some boats while pursuing her vision of publishing books not as literary objects but as commercial and entertainment products, with ties to television, film, and the Internet. In so doing, Regan has arguably become the most successful editor in the book business, and she now has her own imprint, ReganBooks. She has also broken into the worlds of television and film. Regan has put a distinctive spin on culture, bringing new, sometimes brash, often scandalous voices into the public eye. "If you want to be in television, film, and publishing you have to know what's going on," she said to Cynthia Daddona for *womenswire.com* (February 5, 1998). "I read a zillion newspapers, a zillion magazines, and watch a lot of television. You have to pay attention and keep your eyes and ears open. Then you've got to listen to your friends and family—what people are saying and not just what is being reported. Basically, you have to work your tail off."

Born on August 17, 1953, Regan is the daughter of two teachers. She spent the first years of her childhood on a farm in Massachusetts that belonged to her Sicilian immigrant grandparents, and lived in a house with no television. She has attributed her fortitude to the example of her grandmother, who was, she told Marilyn Stasio for *Cosmopolitan* (October 1994), "a secure and strong woman." When she was 10, her family moved to Bay Shore, a Long Island suburb of New York City. The middle child of five competitive siblings, she understood early on that she had to fight for her mother's attention and approval. "My mother was very strong," Regan told Shapiro. "She wouldn't give me money. If I wanted something I earned it. . . . If I got A's, she said, 'Why not A+'s.' If I got A+'s, it was, 'It's not a hard school.' My mother's responsible for my drive. I've always had drive." Despite the atmosphere of rebellion that influenced many young people during the 1960s, Regan remembers practicing the viola and working at the local Carvel ice-cream store more than chafing against her parents' values. She attended Vassar College, in Poughkeepsie, New York, where she studied English literature and voice. After a brief stint in New York City, where she studied voice with a teacher from the Juilliard School in the hope of becoming a professional singer, she moved to Boston and decided to look for a job.

With that goal in mind, she visited the career-planning office at Harvard University, in Cambridge, Massachusetts, on a day when the *National Enquirer* happened to be recruiting young talent. After an impromptu interview, she was flown to the paper's Florida headquarters, and, within days, she had landed what she described to Marilyn Stasio as the "best job I ever had." As a young reporter, Regan wrote about Elizabeth Taylor and Siamese twins, went undercover dressed as a man, and, at a youthful-looking age 26, disguised herself as a 16-year-old in order to write an exposé on the nation's high schools. Once, eager to interview Mia Farrow after her divorce from André Previn, she discovered Farrow's Martha's Vineyard hideout by ordering dozens of flowers for Farrow from a local florist and then following the delivery van. "I had a natural desire to ask people about their lives in dramatic ways," Regan told Rebecca Mead for *New York* (October 25, 1993). "I was interested in the human aspects of people's lives, which is more tabloid, I suppose. I used to say to people, 'Everything is going to become the *National Enquirer*,' and it did. Everything became the *National Enquirer*, including what I do now." Her education in pop culture continued with stints as a producer on the television programs *Geraldo!*, the talk show hosted by Geraldo Rivera, for which she organized an installment on married men who cruise male prostitutes, and *Entertainment Tonight*, for which she covered celebrity weddings.

In 1987 Regan approached editors at Simon & Schuster with a proposal for a book that would examine American families in relation to various role models, such as the television characters Ozzie and Harriet. The editors were so impressed with her proposal that they offered her a job as a consultant to Pocket Books, a Simon & Schuster subsidiary. There, she soon became editor of several successful, "tell-all" books, among them Drew Barrymore's *Little Girl Lost* (1991), Richard Marcinko's *Rogue Warrior* (1992), Kathie Lee Gifford's *I Can't Believe I Said That* (1993), Georgette Mosbacher's *Feminine Force* (1994), and Dawn Steel's *They Can Kill You . . . But They Can't Eat You* (1993). Rejecting the usual route of wooing agents to access high-profile potential authors, Regan often went directly to subjects whom she found compelling and book-worthy. In that way she eventually coaxed books out of Rush Limbaugh, who wrote *The Way Things Ought to Be* (1992) and *See, I Told You So* (1993), and Howard Stern, whose autobiographical book *Private Parts* (1993) was made into a film in 1997. Both new authors sold millions of books and contributed to the phenomenon of the book as part of the celebrity and entertainment package. When asked by Shapiro about her secret for picking best-sellers, Regan cited her pragmatic business sensibility. "I'm an average American with a two-minute attention span. . . . I don't pay attention to what critics say about most of my books. Celebrity and personality books are not review-driven. Who reads book reviews anyway? Small numbers. I look at big numbers."

In certain circles in the publishing world, Regan is more infamous than famous. Her sales-oriented approach has offended many of those in the literary establishment who see a book as a unique entity that should not be judged strictly on commercial grounds. "Publishers today are manufacturers," one prominent editor told Shapiro. "They're dangerous. The bad tends to chase out the good. . . . Books [such as those Regan publishes] appeal to the worst instincts of the mass mind." Roger Straus, of the respected literary publisher Farrar Straus & Giroux, said to Mead, "The public, rightly or wrongly, has an appetite for looking through keyholes. . . . My partner, Giroux, calls [celebrity books] 'ooks,' because they're not quite books."

Regan expresses frustration with such sentiments, which she views as both elitist and misinformed. "In a business in which it is increasingly difficult to stay alive, we have to publish a wide range of books," she told *Current Biography*. "I publish everything from the highly commercial to the highly esoteric." Regan complained that much of her editing career has been unfairly characterized by journalists who, as she told *Current Biography*, "only want to hear the noise about high-profile authors, and ignore the rest." Regan's commercial success has allowed her to try her hand at editing literary fiction, such as *She's Come Undone* (1993), a first novel by Wally Lamb, a New England high-school teacher, about a young woman's nervous breakdown and self-discovery. *She's Come Undone* has sold remarkably well, in addition to enjoying critical success.

After five years at Simon & Schuster, where she was sometimes snubbed by her fellow editors, Regan met someone who shared her views—the media mogul Rupert Murdoch, owner of the News Corp. and chairman of Twentieth Century Fox Productions. After a friendly lunch and a period of negotiations, Murdoch made her an expansive offer—a five-year, multimillion-dollar deal that would encompass her own imprint at HarperCollins (a division of the News Corp.), the option to develop television programs and movies, and her own show on the Fox News Channel. The deal was announced to the public as "the first of its kind in the history of the media industry," according to a reporter for the *New York Times* (May 25, 1994). Her imprint was named ReganBooks.

The move to Fox allowed Regan to test her ideas about synergy in the publishing world. A business concept that first gained currency in the early 1990s, synergy is the idea that one property—be it a book, a music group, or a personality—can be developed in many different media. Martha Stewart is the reigning queen of synergy, with her empire of entertainment, information, and products that are spread across many media, including her own magazine, books, and television show. "My goal is to find properties that can be developed in a number of areas, including television and film," Regan told Susan Hornik for *Variety* (September 26, 1994). "Disney just made a deal with the Boys Choir of Harlem to do a movie, and they're talking about a theater show and a tour. It's synergistic." One of Regan's first "polymedia" projects (as she terms them) for Fox was Douglas Coupland's *Microserfs*, a book about the young technical wizards who work at Microsoft, which she published in 1996 and is now producing as a movie for Universal. She has also developed a book and a CBS television miniseries about the deadly standoff between federal agents and right-wing survivalists at Ruby Ridge, Idaho, in 1992. Regan published Gregory Maguire's *Confessions of an Ugly Stepsister* (1999), an imaginative retelling of the Cinderella story that has been widely praised; the movie version of the book, which she is producing, will debut on ABC in the fall of 2000. Not all of her books result in such projects, though many have been best-sellers. She published *Quivers: A Life* (1995), the autobiography of Robin Quivers, Howard Stern's sidekick, and Stern's latest book, *Miss America*, which was Barnes & Noble's fastest-selling book when it was published, in November 1995. Only two years into her tenure at Fox, *Entertainment Weekly* named Regan one of the most powerful people in entertainment, and during its first three years, her company's revenues were approximately $100 million, according to Cynthia Daddona.

Regan's pursuit of Christopher Darden, who was co-prosecutor alongside Marcia Clark in the O. J. Simpson murder trial, provides an example of her aggressive working strategy, carried over from her days as a tabloid news hound. "I called [Darden] the day after the Simpson verdict. At that point, everybody was chasing Marcia Clark for a book deal, so I knew the competition for Christopher wouldn't be stiff," she told Laura Ziv for *Cosmopolitan* (May 1997). "Had I waited it would have been much tougher. I immediately flew out to Los Angeles to meet him. I was the first." Regan also offered Darden a big financial incentive—a $1.3 million advance. "You can't do it unless you pay, and it takes guts to sign the big checks," she told Ziv. As of mid-2000, more than a million copies of Darden's *In Contempt* (1997) were in print.

As part of her deal with Murdoch, Regan hosts her own program on the Fox News Channel. *Judith Regan Tonight* is a one-hour talk show on which she conducts roundtable discussions and one-on-one interviews with celebrities and newsmakers from Hollywood, the music industry, the business world, and the political arena. Here, too, her style is forthright and loose. According to Jefferson Graham for *USA Today* (February 4, 1997), she once opened an interview with former political consultant Ed Rollins, who is known to have said nasty things about his former clients Ross Perot and Nancy Reagan, with the question, "Why hasn't someone killed you yet?"

As a packager of books and other media, Regan has also learned how to package her own public image. She first made headlines in the late 1970s in Utah, where, after making an illegal left turn, she was arrested and strip-searched. Furious, she secured the representation of the American Civil Liberties Union in a suit against the state of Utah and won. She again proved herself a fighter in Manhattan in 1990, when police pulled her cab over and began harassing the driver, who was black. After attempting to intervene, she was arrested for disorderly conduct, obstruction of government administration, and resisting arrest; the charges were eventually dropped, and the incident helped to revive dormant rules about the legal rights of bystanders to criticize arrests, as D. T. Max reported for the *New York Observer* (September 20, 1993).

Regan is known among journalists to be unusually accessible and extremely candid about her personal life. In a profile of her for *Esquire* (August 1994), Dominick Dunne wrote, "By the end of lunch, I knew all about her divorce, her kids, her custody battle." Shapiro called her subject a "dream interview," because Regan is so loquacious and opinionated. In a conversation with Stasio, Regan alluded to her troubled and often abusive relationships with men. During her second pregnancy, late-term complications led to the death of the fetus and nearly cost her her own life. While she recovered in the hospital, the baby's father "decided he needed a vacation. So he took off to the Caribbean with two women," she told Stasio. Jobless at the time, she was left alone to care for their one-year-old child, Patrick, and then lost all her possessions when a fire destroyed her apartment and a truck plowed into her parked car during a snowstorm. From this bizarre and devastating series of events, Regan learned some life lessons. "I wasn't always strong," she told Stasio. "I wasn't always this capable or knowledgeable. . . . You have to take the bad with the good and understand that both are equally important in the total fabric of your life. . . . If people can understand this concept, they can cope with anything." In 1987, she married for the first time, at age 34; with her husband, Robert Kleinschmidt, a New York financial analyst, she had a daughter, Lara, in 1990. The couple separated a year later. After bruising legal battles, Regan won custody of Lara. Her son, Patrick, is now a college student.

One of Regan's causes célèbres is women's empowerment. "I want to teach women . . . to use their will to develop strengths and courage," she told Shapiro. "Women often don't know how to play the game. They think they can bond with each other and fix the world. I don't see myself as a victim; I only see myself as victorious." In the early 1990s Regan began work on a book based on her own experiences and store of survival tips, to be called "The Art of War for Women." The title was inspired by the Chinese classic treatise *Art of War*; written more than 2,500 years ago, that book has become a kind of spiritual guide for contemporary politicians and executives, as well as for Regan, who plans to remain on the front lines of today's turbulent media, entertainment, and information battlefields. — M.A.H.

Suggested Reading: *Cosmopolitan* p80+ Oct. 1994, with photo, p150+ May 1997, with photos; *Esquire* p52 May 1996 with photo; *New York* p60+ Oct. 25, 1993, with photos, p18+ Apr. 5, 1999, with photo; *New York Times Magazine* p22+ July 17, 1994, with photo

---

Ribbs, Willy T.

Jan. 3, 1956– Race-car driver. Address: c/o Victoria Motor Sports, P.O. Box 8343, Victoria, B.C., Canada V8W 3R9

Courtesy of Victoria Motor Sports

Willy T. Ribbs is one of the few African-American drivers to ascend the ranks of auto racing in the United States. After his brief but successful training period in England in the late 1970s, Ribbs established himself as the top racer of pony cars—factory-built sports cars that have been modified for road racing—in the 1980s, with 17 wins and 28 top-three finishes in 50 starts; in 1991 he became the first black driver to compete in the premier auto-racing event in the U.S., the Indianapolis 500. His skill notwithstanding, Ribbs, who has been outspoken about the absence of minorities in auto racing, has lacked throughout his career the significant corporate sponsorship necessary to operate a high-performance racing team—one of the most expensive endeavors in professional sports. Following a hiatus in the late 1990s, he returned to pony-car racing on the professional Trans-Am Series of the Sports Car Club of America (SCCA), the oldest ongoing road-race series in the nation.

Born on January 3, 1956 in San Jose, California, William Theodore Ribbs Jr. was practically raised on a racetrack. His father was a successful amateur racer who had first tasted competition on local motorcycle dirt tracks. By the late 1950s he had graduated to sports cars and was a regular presence at the winner's circle on the West Coast amateur circuit. Willy, known to his parents as Bill, was so enamored of his father's exploits that when he was eight years old, he hid in the family car to accompany his parents to a race in Phoenix, Arizona. William Sr.'s successful plumbing business, which he inherited from his own father, Henry, afforded the family a comfortable middle-class lifestyle and gave Willy the opportunity to earn enough money to go to Europe to study racing. In 1976 he received a racing license from the world's first institute of its kind, the Jim Russell School of Racing, in England.

At the time, England was a proving ground for Europe's best up-and-coming driving talent, thanks in large part to what Peter McAlevey described for the *New York Times Magazine* (October 9, 1988) as "a sophisticated set of racing series using inexpensive, lightweight cars to ferret out skilled drivers." Ribbs rented one such vehicle for $500 a weekend and entered the Star of Tomorrow racing series. With little more than his racing license and raw ability, he took first in six of the series' 11 races and the overall series title from, in McAlevey's words, "a horde of England's most promising young race drivers," including Nigel Mansell, who has since won Formula One and Indy car championships. While abroad, Ribbs also got the opportunity to meet his hero, Muhammad Ali. According to Jim Myers in *USA Today* (April 17, 1990), Ribbs waited all night outside Ali's hotel in London, where the boxer was staying during a promotional tour, in the hope that he could join the legendary athlete on his morning run. They struck up a friendship, and Ali advised him to undertake a boxer's training regimen, so as to keep in top racing condition. To this day, Ribbs has done as Ali suggested.

In 1978, on the heels of his triumphant European debut, Ribbs returned to the U.S. and was almost immediately signed by the organizers of the Long Beach Grand Prix to compete in a warmup race for young drivers. He placed a respectable 10th among a talented field and was subsequently invited by the National Association for Stock Car Auto Racing (NASCAR) to drive a preliminary test to qualify for the World 600 race in Charlotte, North Carolina. Ribbs's flamboyant off-track behavior gained as much notice as his skill behind the wheel. Jerry Garrett wrote for *Car and Driver* (February 2000) that Ribbs had Ali's "swagger," "good looks," and "mouth," a combination that, in Ali's case, had already caused a commotion in the world of sports. The caretakers of an expensive sport that is corporate-friendly and controversy-shy, the auto-racing establishment was offended by Ribbs's boastful nature—most famously manifested by the victory dances he would perform on the hood of his car. To make matters worse, Ribbs was ticketed in Charlotte for driving in the wrong direction on a one-way street, which indirectly led NASCAR to pull his entry. "As a newcomer, I didn't know how the racing fraternity expected me to carry myself," he explained to Peter McAlevey. "I was, in effect, blacklisted." Ribbs did not compete in another race until 1981, nearly three years later. "I had no money, no sponsor," he said of that time to Jim Myers. "I was sending proposals out. A lot of people knew who I was. I just didn't get backing."

Ribbs was back working for his father when a friend suggested that Ribbs accompany him to Monterey, California, to see a race. Reluctantly, Ribbs agreed. In Monterey he met Jim Trueman, the late owner of a midwestern motel chain and an auto-racing sponsor. Trueman had remembered Ribbs's success three years earlier and agreed to provide the young driver with a car to race in Long Beach. Ribbs earned the pole position as the fastest qualifier and led for most of the race before blowing his engine. Regardless, his performance was enough to persuade Neil DeAtley, who ran a high-tech, two-car Trans-Am team, to ask Ribbs to drive for him in the 1983 series. The SCCA's Trans-Am series is among America's premier road-racing circuits. Begun more than three decades ago, the circuit is the country's oldest continuous auto-racing series and features factory-built street cars that have been modified for competition. Although its prize purses are smaller than those of NASCAR and the Indy car circuits, which has made Trans-Am known as the "minor leagues" of racing, it has proven to be a very lucrative circuit for successful drivers and still attracts major corporate sponsorship.

What Ribbs didn't know at the time he signed with DeAtley was that his team's biggest sponsor, Anheuser-Busch, the maker of Budweiser beer, was facing a boycott of its products by African-Americans organized by Jesse Jackson. Jackson felt that the company took for granted its black customers, who accounted for a significant portion of Budweiser sales, and accused the company of returning little support to the black community. DeAtley hoped that signing a black driver to his racing team would be advantageous to Anheuser-Busch in its fight against the boycott. Ribbs, oblivious to the sponsor's situation, went on to win five out of 12 races in the 1983 series, place second in the overall series championship, behind his teammate David Hobbs, and earn rookie-of-the-year honors. It wasn't until the season ended that Ribbs discovered that he had been hired in part because of the Budweiser boycott, and he grew disgruntled. Prior to the first race of the 1984 season, he got into an altercation with another driver, who, Ribbs claimed, had tried to push him off the course during warmups. As a result, DeAtley fired Ribbs. Jack Roush's Ford-sponsored team immediately signed Ribbs to drive for them, and over the ensuing two seasons, 1984 and 1985, Ribbs won 11 races in 27 starts; again placed second in the overall driver championship to his teammate, this time Wally Dallenbach Jr.; and helped secure the manufacturer's title for Lincoln-Mercury.

Following his successful 1985 Trans-Am campaign, Ribbs sought to move up to Indy car racing, specifically the Indianapolis 500. He hired the controversial boxing promoter Don King to manage his quest and secure corporate sponsorship. By the time King succeeded in attracting funds, the faster cars had been taken by better-prepared teams, and Ribbs was saddled with a less-competitive racer. In 1985, 33 drivers qualified for the Indianapolis 500, the preliminary tests for which require speeds averaging over 200 miles per hour. (Cars on the Trans-Am circuit reach speeds of only about 150 miles per hour.) Ribbs couldn't push his car beyond 172 miles per hour in his practice runs, and he was forced to withdraw.

In 1986 Ribbs was approached by the DiGard racing team to drive for them in the NASCAR Winston Cup series. Although the team had just lost their major sponsor from the year before, they supposedly had other prospects lined up. No sponsor materialized, however, and the team folded after three races in the series. "The team didn't have any finances at all," Ribbs told Jerry Garrett. "It all came to an end at Watkins Glen [International Speedway, in New York State] when five engines blew, all within 35 laps." He finished the 1986 racing season on the International Motor Sports Association (IMSA) GTO circuit—a pony-car series similar to Trans-Am—registering two wins and absorbing the largest fine ever levied on a driver by IMSA: $2,000 for what series officials termed "reckless driving." (GTO is the acronym for Gran Tourismo Omologato and refers to specific technical standards for cars.) Around that time, Dan Gurney, a former Formula One and Indy car driver whom William Ribbs Sr. knew, was managing his own Toyota-sponsored team on the IMSA GTO circuit, and he hired Ribbs Jr. to drive for them during the 1987 and 1988 seasons. With the hard-driving Ribbs behind the wheel, the turbo-charged, four-cylinder Toyota engines blew more frequently than those of the typical American pony car, which is usually powered by a much larger and more rugged V8 motor. Nevertheless, Ribbs managed to record seven wins in 24 starts on the GTO circuit under Gurney. Most memorably, he touched wheels with another car early in the final race of the 1987 season. After stopping to change the damaged tire, which left him in last place, Ribbs "maneuver[ed] with brilliant abandon," as Peter McAlevey reported, to finish third, thus securing a manufacturers' title for Toyota and driver-of-the-year honors for himself.

In June 1988 Ribbs received a call from the comedian Bill Cosby. "I thought it was a prank; it was incredible," Ribbs told Jim Myers. "He said he'd followed my career a bit and asked what my objectives were. I said Indy cars were the top of the mountain." They agreed to meet in Las Vegas, where Ribbs explained the financial demands of auto racing in greater detail to Cosby. Despite the prohibitive costs involved, the entertainer offered Ribbs seed money for a run at an Indy-car series. According to Jerry Garrett, Cosby set only one condition: "Just don't tell my wife." Cosby's commitment laid the foundation for the Raynor/Cosby Indy car-racing team. Meanwhile, under the auspices of Dan Gurney's Toyota team, Ribbs moved up in class to the more competitive and prestigious IMSA GTP series for the 1989 season.

Despite Cosby's substantial support, the Raynor/Cosby team remained underfunded for the 1990 season, thus keeping Ribbs from making another run at the Indianapolis 500. Instead, the team focused on eight races in the Championship Auto Racing Teams (CART) series. Ribbs's highest finish among the eight races was 10th place at a September 1990 CART event in Vancouver, Canada. During that race, a fatal accident occurred: after a car driven by one of Ribbs's competitors stalled behind a blind curve, track officials raised the cautionary yellow flag, which signals to the other drivers that there has been an accident and diverts them from it. While coming around the turn, Ribbs ran over three track workers who were trying to push the disabled vehicle from the track. One of the three died later in a nearby hospital. Ribbs claimed at the time that he was not directed away from the vicinity of the stalled car; a later inquiry cleared him of responsibility. June Cioppettini, a spokesperson for Victoria Motorsports, the racing team with which Ribbs has been affiliated since February 2000, told *Current Biography* that to her knowledge, Ribbs has never spoken of the tragedy.

Ribbs introduced Bill Cosby to Derrick Walker, former manager of the defunct Porsche Indy car syndicate, and they struck a deal to form Derrick Walker Racing in 1991. That season, armed with Walker's expertise and Cosby's cash, Ribbs completed nine races and finished 17th in CART's overall driver point standings. (Points are awarded to each driver in each race based on his or her finish: the higher a driver places, the more points he or she receives. Bonus points are assigned for the number of individual laps led and the highest number of laps completed. The drivers with the top 25 point totals at the end of the season are awarded proportionate cash prizes above those earned in each race.) Ribbs had performed well, considering that Walker Racing's budget, only $2.3 million, was not enough to be consistently competitive. It was enough to allow a serious run at the 1991 Indianapolis 500, however. Ribbs became the first African-American ever to qualify for the preeminent event of American racing; but only five laps into the race, his engine failed, and he placed 32d.

A general paucity of funds over the next three seasons produced similar results for Ribbs on the CART circuit. He raced only once for the Walker team in 1992. Buoyed by an injection of $7 million in sponsorship from Service Merchandise Co., a discount retail chain, he started in 13 of the 16 races in the series the following year; after qualifying again for the Indianapolis 500, he finished that race in 21st place. In 1994 Ribbs logged his most successful Indy car season: he crossed the finish line five times in the top 10 and was presented with the Sports Image Award.

Regardless, he decided to drop out of racing for a while to take care of his family. Two years earlier his marriage had dissolved, and he had become a full-time single father to his son, William Theodore III, and his daughter, Sasha. "I had never changed a diaper, never cooked. I had always been on the road traveling," Ribbs told Jerry Garrett. "But when I decided I was going to have children, I knew that was a responsibility I was not going to run from, despite whatever hardship I was going to have to endure in my career." Save for a NASCAR event in September 1998, in which he drove very well until a blown engine undermined his performance, Ribbs made his living mostly from speaking engagements and personal appearances.

Returning to racing in 1999, Ribbs qualified for the Vegas.com 500, becoming the first African-American driver to compete in an Indy Racing League (IRL) event. (The IRL competes directly with CART.) He drove well, and team owner Dennis McCormack signed him for a two-race deal, with Cole Bros. Natural Spring Mineral Water as his sponsor. But the first race ended with a crash into the third turn wall, leaving the team's only car completely disabled and incapable of completing the season. McCormack and Cole Bros. promised Ribbs backing for the 2000 IRL season, but no such deal ever materialized. Instead, Ribbs signed for the 2000 racing season with Victoria Motorsports to race once again in the Trans-Am series. They secured a lead sponsor, Simple Green, which runs a line of environmentally safe cleaning products; nevertheless, the team remains relatively underfunded. As of September 2000 Ribbs is 12th in the drivers' championship point total, with one second- and one third-place finish in seven starts. Before the eighth race of the 12-race series, during a practice run, Ribbs's Camaro caught fire, and he was unable to start.

Ribbs was featured in a March 1999 segment of the HBO cable network's program *Real Sports with Bryant Gumbel*, where he displayed his outspokenness about the limited opportunities available to minorities in the traditionally all-white sport of auto racing. Expanding on the comments he made during the show, he told Jerry Garrett, "Racing's gotta look like America. Like America today. Not like America in the 1930s." Yet Ribbs's criticism of the sport falls shy of accusations of bigotry. "I'm never gonna say I dealt with a sport that was racist. . . . The reason is, it's not true. Because some of my greatest mentors, and biggest supporters, were white men," he said to Garrett. He continued, "When you slide down into the cockpit and get strapped in, you'd better believe in the people around you. You'd better be colorblind. And how could you not be? It's about human beings, and what you feel about them, and the respect you have for them."

In his leisure hours Ribbs enjoys trap and skeet shooting; he has said that if he weren't a car racer, he would be a jazz musician. Ribbs was deeply affected by the death of the pro basketball player Bobby Phills, who was killed in a car accident while illegally racing a teammate on the streets of Charlotte, North Carolina, in January 2000. Recognizing that many professional athletes own sports cars yet are not trained to drive them properly, Ribbs teamed up with the Derek Daly Driving Academy in Las Vegas to establish a driving and safety program specifically for them. — V.K.

Suggested Reading: *Car and Driver* p123+ Feb. 2000; *New York Times Magazine* p26+ Oct. 9, 1988; *Sports Illustrated* p83+ Oct. 17, 1983, with photos; *USA Today* C p1+ Apr. 17, 1990, with photo; *Village Voice* p126 Sep. 2, 1986; Caines, Bruce. *Our Common Ground: Portraits of Blacks Changing the Face of America*, 1994; Porter, David L. *African-American Sports Greats*, 1995

Courtesy of Mayor Riordan's office

Riordan, Richard

1930– Mayor of Los Angeles. Address: City Hall, 200 N. Spring St., Los Angeles, CA 90012

When the founders of Los Angeles drew up the city's original charter, in 1925, they wanted to avoid the abuses of power that plagued older cities in the East. Their solution was to give more power to a multimember city council rather than to a mayor, who might be more easily susceptible to corruption. That plan has often proved to be counterproductive, as the mayor of Los Angeles has historically had little power to effect needed changes, and constituents have been forced to hire sometimes less-than-scrupulous lobbyists in their attempts to influence the bureaucratic city council. When

Richard Riordan, a conservative former businessman and lawyer, decided to run for mayor of Los Angeles in 1993, he believed that he could change that imbalance of power by using skills he had learned in the private sector. Riordan envisioned a problem-solving, nonpartisan government, based on models of successful businesses with which he had been involved. He vowed to privatize many of the city-run services, such as garbage collection, which were being managed by inefficient civil servants, and he promised widespread reforms in education, an area with which he was already familiar because of his extensive philanthropic efforts. He also announced a plan to raise funds by leasing Los Angeles International Airport to private operators, and to use the income to hire more police officers. His pragmatic, goal-oriented approach appealed primarily to white middle-class voters, and in part because turnout at the polls was poor that year among minority groups, Riordan was elected by an 8 percent margin over his opponent, Michael Woo.

The first Republican mayor to have been elected in the city in 20 years, Riordan began immediately to put his business acumen to work. During his first term he set up a marketing department, with the aim of drawing new business to the city. He began publishing a detailed version of the annual budget, using corporate annual reports as a model, and simplified the process by which businesses apply for licenses. In addition, he increased the police force by over 30 percent, and when the police department needed new computers, he raised $16 million from his friends in order to provide them. Actions like that one led his opponents to charge Riordan with running an elitist "shadow government" composed of the wealthy white men who make up his social circle; he has been accused of giving too much power to backroom movers and shakers who have no official accountability. But despite such criticism, the people of Los Angeles—including, this time, a substantial number of minority voters—were pleased enough with Riordan's accomplishments to elect him in 1997 to a second term. Crime and unemployment were down, and a majority of the respondents to a *Los Angeles Times* poll reported feeling safer and better off than previously. Voters seemed not to care that some of Riordan's most effective plans were hatched with the help of his cronies and without the input of the contentious city council.

Richard Riordan was born in 1930 in the New York City borough of Queens and raised in Westchester County, adjacent to the city. He was the youngest of eight children of a devout Catholic family. His father, an Irish immigrant, rose through the ranks of Stern's department store, eventually becoming president; in his will he left his last child an inheritance of $80,000. Riordan attended Princeton University, in New Jersey, graduating in 1952 with a bachelor's degree in philosophy. After serving as a field artillery lieutenant in the U.S. Army during the Korean War, he earned a law degree at the University of Michigan and then founded the law firm of Riordan & McKinzie. Riordan eventually moved to Los Angeles and began dabbling in investments, mainly venture-capital schemes and technology stocks, using his inheritance. He was one of the original investors in Convergent Technologies, a California-based computer manufacturer involved in building one of the first widely used workstations. By the time he sold his stock in the company, in the late 1980s, it was worth $40 million. He had made other successful investments as well, quietly buying property in downtown Los Angeles for years until he had acquired an entire block. When he sold the property, in 1983, he made a profit of almost $20 million. Also in 1983, he founded a leveraged-buyout firm that earned him $35 million before he dismantled it, sensing that the heyday of large leveraged buyouts would soon be over. "All of sudden, I was asked to join lots of boards and civic groups," he told John H. Taylor for *Forbes* (October 1, 1990). "I was happy to do it, but what I found out was that my skills as a problem solver and my contacts in the business community enabled me to get a lot done that others might not have been able to."

When Archbishop Roger Mahoney's financial director died unexpectedly, in 1985, Mahoney asked Riordan to help assess the archdiocese's financial situation. Riordan responded by forming a diocesan finance council and setting up the Diocesan Education Foundation, which has thus far raised $100 million for Catholic schools. (Some maintain that this is the main reason Riordan has remained in the Church's good graces, despite his well-publicized pro-choice stance and other positions and actions that seem to clash with Catholic ideology.) Besides aiding parochial schools, he took an interest in public schools. Riordan traced his interest in education back to a study he read in the early 1980s, which stated that children who did not learn to read by the age of nine stood little chance of ever doing so. Having been involved in the technology industry, he felt that computers could help foster literacy, and in the late 1980s he donated more than 4,500 computers to schools in cities all over the country. He hired a staff of five to oversee the donations, making sure that the computers were being used properly and that the teachers were receiving proper training in their use. Closer to home, Riordan tried to form a coalition to force Los Angeles's monolithic school district to allow individual schools more autonomy in improving their operations. He also founded a grassroots group, LA's Better Educated Students for Tomorrow (LA's BEST), to provide after-school recreation and other services to some of the city's poorest children. When the educational establishment in Los Angeles—predictably—expressed resentment at being told by a businessman how to run their schools, Riordan's response was that the bureaucrats had made such a mess of things that outside agitation was needed. While education was Riordan's priority, he also took an interest in California's legal system, leading a successful campaign to oust the liberal chief justice of the state Supreme Court, Rose E. Bird, in a so-called judicial retention election in 1986.

Despite his activism, Riordan claimed to have no interest in political office, telling Taylor, "I'm just trying to get the politicians to get off their asses." By the end of 1992, he had changed his mind. That year, Los Angeles had been plagued by some of the worst riots in modern American history, following the acquittal, on April 29, of four white police officers charged with beating Rodney King, a black man they had apprehended after a high-speed automobile chase. During three days of rioting, about 50 people had been killed, according to the city coroner's office, and more than 2,000 injured, and 10,000 businesses had been looted or burned. Amid the devastation, Mayor Tom Bradley, a black liberal Democrat who had held the post for 20 years, decided not to seek a sixth term. Riordan had been one of Bradley's biggest campaign contributors, a fact perplexing to those who sought to pigeonhole him as a right-wing Republican. Some had even labeled Riordan the city's unofficial co-mayor, for his success in buying up the needed rights-of-way for a commuter rail system and in renovating the Los Angeles Coliseum to keep the Raiders football team from leaving town. In the wake of Bradley's decision, Riordan began to consider entering the mayoral race. It was clear, he told John Taylor for the August 2, 1993 issue of *Forbes*, that "the internal workings of Los Angeles government were getting worse day by day. I felt it would take someone from the outside to turn it around."

Riordan's opponent was Michael Woo, a city councilman and one-time Berkeley activist who had applied for conscientious-objector status during the Vietnam War. Woo, who was calling for tens of millions of dollars in new social spending, was being positioned as the perfect representative of the city's rich ethnic and cultural variety. A liberal Democrat in a predominantly liberal Democratic city, Woo was considered the clear front-runner. Still, he engaged in a vicious campaign, dredging up events from his opponent's personal life: Riordan had by then been divorced twice and convicted on more than one occasion of drunk driving. Woo also questioned Riordan's use of $3 million of his own money to finance his campaign. Riordan's supporters countered that Riordan had little choice but to use his own money to oppose the city's two-to-one Democratic majority—and that his personal life would have little effect on his efficiency as mayor. A controversy erupted over Riordan's campaign claim to have helped save the financially ailing California toy company Mattel from insolvency. Woo supporters charged that Mattel's restructuring, which Riordan had helped to engineer, had led to the closing of the company's last factory in Los Angeles, costing 250 jobs.

On Election Day, June 8, 1993, fewer than one-third of all registered voters showed up at the polls. Riordan received 54 percent of the ballots cast, with his strongest support coming from the mostly white San Fernando Valley. Most sources credit his election to poor minority turnout; of those minority members who did vote, however, 40 percent of the Latinos, 20 percent of the African-Americans, and more than 30 percent of the Asians voted for Riordan, higher numbers than had been predicted. "Bradley's liberal, biracial coalition of suburban whites and inner-city blacks has been replaced by a surprisingly multiethnic conservative coalition," Jordan Bonfante observed in *Time* (June 21, 1993). Bonfante quoted Riordan as saying, "The meaning of my election is that people not only in L.A. but throughout the country are saying, 'We don't want any more business as usual.'" According to Bonfante, the mayor-elect also pledged to form an administration of "doers and implementers," while acknowledging, "I am not such an amateur that I'm going to ignore the political side, because if you try to implement things over the dead body of the politicians, they're going to eat you alive." Many observers, particularly blacks, worried that the "doers and implementers" to whom Riordan referred would be too homogeneous a group. "This signals the end of the Bradley-era Jewish/Black coalition and a regurgitation of the white, Valley, and business coalition that ruled before Bradley," H. Erik Schockman, the director of a multiethnic study group, told Daniel B. Wood for the *Christian Science Monitor* (June 10, 1993). Riordan tried to dispel that impression. "My administration will be made up of Democrats, Republicans, and independents, people of every race, creed, colour, and sexual orientation," he told Louise Kehoe for the London *Financial Times* (June 12, 1993). The two weeks between the election and his swearing-in on July 1, 1993 were busy ones for Riordan. He traveled to Indianapolis to study that city's privatization of public services, a system he wanted to introduce in Los Angeles; to Philadelphia to listen to the advice of Mayor Ed Rendell, known for his ability to solve problems and to delegate responsibility; and to Washington, D.C., to jog with President Bill Clinton and to meet the members of Congress who would be responsible for providing federal funds to Los Angeles.

After taking office, Riordan announced that unlike Tom Bradley, he would not be living in Getty House, the official mayoral residence. Rather, he would continue to live in his own, admittedly luxurious home and would open Getty House to the public for free tours. He also declined to take the usual mayoral salary, agreeing instead to live on his private income and accept one dollar a year from the city—an arrangement that saved Los Angeles more than $100,000 annually. These were not the only signs that the new mayor intended to function in an iconoclastic fashion. A typical anecdote from early in his first term has it that when garment-industry workers came to him, complaining that their businesses were suffering because customers' cars were constantly being towed away, Riordan asked a deputy mayor how to rid the area of tow-away signs. A month later the deputy produced a 25-page report outlining a bureaucratic process that would take several years. Angered, Riordan ordered him to find a simpler way, and the deputy complied, going out one night and removing the signs himself, much to Riordan's satisfaction.

That episode notwithstanding, Riordan knew that to effect any real change, he would have to alter the city charter. He therefore made it one of his priorities to convince voters that the unwieldy civil-service system was severely hampering his efficiency. In 1995 voters approved a charter amendment that would allow the mayor to fire any of the city's 26 general managers who proved incompetent or corrupt. Commentators saw the amendment's passage as a vote of confidence for Riordan, who was proving that he was far from the right-wing zealot his opponents had feared. During his first term, as he had promised, he added 3,000 new officers to the police force (following that move, crime decreased by 25 percent); created a new city department devoted solely to children's issues; and created 42,000 new jobs, many in either the entertainment industry or the city's newly expanded port area. He proposed a popular five-year freeze on business taxes for companies that agreed to relocate to or stay in economically depressed parts of the city. He was less successful in his drive to allocate airport-generated revenue to fund social programs, as a new federal law prohibited using those funds for non–aviation-related purposes.

In 1997 Riordan ran for a second term, against state senator Tom Hayden, best known for his stance against the Vietnam War and his environmental activism (and as a former husband of the actress Jane Fonda). Using the same tactics that Michael Woo had tried, Hayden attempted to portray Riordan as a right-wing Republican in the pocket of big business. He questioned the sources of Riordan's campaign financing and disparaged many of the accomplishments for which Riordan was taking credit—pointing out, for example, that the majority of the city's newly created jobs were low-wage service positions. Despite Hayden's rhetoric, on April 8, 1997 Riordan was elected to a second term, with 61 percent of the vote. He had won the support not only of whites but of Hispanics, who were, at that point, the city's fastest-growing minority group. Despite Hayden's well-publicized support of migrant workers, who are championed by the United Farm Workers, Riordan even won the support of the AFL-CIO.

Election Day was not an unqualified success for Riordan, however. Voter turnout had fallen to a record low, and Riordan was distressed to have still failed to win the approval of most black voters. Also, while his proposal to create a citizens' committee to draft changes to the city charter easily passed in the same balloting, his candidates for the commission were rejected in favor of council- or union-backed candidates. Moving ahead despite these disappointments, Riordan vowed to make education a top priority in his second term and to continue pushing charter reform. He has made notable progress on both fronts: in April 1999 four Riordan-supported school-board candidates were elected. These four made up the majority of the new board and were ideally situated to push Riordan's agenda of fiscal and facility restructuring as well as individual accountability on the part of teachers and principals. Then, in June of that year, a new city charter, giving him even greater power, passed, with 60 percent voter approval.

In September 1999 a police scandal broke in Los Angeles after a rogue officer began confessing illegal activities to prosecutors in an attempt to lighten his sentence on charges of stealing drugs from an evidence locker. He implicated more than 20 of his fellow officers in an antigang unit in instances of evidence planting, perjury, and brutality. More than 40 convictions were overturned in light of his allegations, and the city seemed certain to face millions of dollars of damages from lawsuits. Riordan responded quickly, proposing that Los Angeles issue a $90 million bond, covered by the city's share of a pending settlement with four tobacco companies, to pay plaintiffs.

Some observers found the police scandal paradoxical: Riordan's commitment to public safety had been a major part of his appeal to the public, certain segments of which now seemed less safe because of the police. Observers have found much that is paradoxical in Riordan himself. While he likes to be regarded as a champion of law and order, for example, he has readily admitted to his drunk-driving convictions. A devout Roman Catholic, he is twice divorced. He takes a pro-choice stance in public but privately contributes to antiabortion groups.

Riordan is married to the former Nancy Daley, who is active in several children's-rights groups. He has three grown daughters from a previous marriage. He is said to own more than 40,000 books, many of them works of philosophy or theology. Although he is known as a consummate backroom politician and smooth operator, Riordan's public persona is that of an unsophisticated stumbler. He has admitted that he is not much of a public speaker but has suggested that his lack of polish is part of his appeal to the electorate. (He has often told friends that he wishes there were two mayors—one for ceremonial duties, such as press presentations and ribbon cuttings, and one to actually run the city.) Term limits (which took effect on the day of his first inauguration) will require Riordan to step down in 2001, and he has not yet revealed what he plans to do when that time comes. — M.R.

Suggested Reading: *Christian Science Monitor* p1+ June 10, 1993; *Forbes* p104+ Oct. 1, 1990, with photos, p16 Aug. 2, 1993, with photo; (London) *Financial Times* p10 June 12, 1993;

New York Times I p25 Feb. 9, 1997, I p20 Mar. 9, 1997, D p4 Feb. 23, 1998, A p8 Aug. 12, 2000, with photo; *Time* p32 June 21, 1993, with photo

---

Frank DiMeo/Courtesy of Cornell University

Rodriguez, Eloy

(rod-REE-ges, ee-LOY)

Jan. 7, 1947– Plant chemist and biologist; educator. Address: 259 Biotechnology Bldg., Bailey Hortorium, Cornell University, Ithaca, NY 14853

Eloy Rodriguez has overcome both poverty and negative racial stereotyping to become one of the nation's top scientists. Trained as a plant biologist and organic chemist, Rodriguez is perhaps best known as a founding father of zoopharmacognosy (pronounced "ZOH-uh-far-ma-KOG-no-see"), the study of how animals medicate themselves. Under-the-weather wild chimpanzees, for example, ingest leaves so bitter that the animals grimace while eating them; they swallow such unpleasant-tasting greenery, Rodriguez believes, to rid themselves of intestinal bugs. Among many other naturally occurring compounds, Rodriguez has studied substances that protect plants from predatory animals. Some of them are now used as drugs in human medicine, and many more are potential cures for human illnesses. The homely, desert-dwelling creosote bush, for instance—the focus of one of Rodriguez's long-term projects—contains more than 500 secondary chemicals (compounds whose molecular weight is relatively small), any number of which may prove to be beneficial to people.

Rodriguez, who has worked in the field in South America, Africa, and Asia as well as in university laboratories for nearly three decades, has purposely diversified his research. "It is very enriching to be able to meet different kinds of scientists," he said during an interview with Neil Campbell for the *American Biology Teacher* (May 1996). "Never in a lifetime would I have stumbled across the idea of zoopharmacognosy if I had just been stuck within an isolated field of organic chemistry. You can't separate the chemistry from the biology. I say this so students realize that an interdisciplinary approach is the way things are going." In an effort to make science attractive to young members of minority groups, Rodriguez founded a program called KIDS—Kids Investigating and Discovering Science. In the past decade KIDS has introduced hundreds of elementary- and junior-high-school students to wonders of the natural world. "Never let yourself be discouraged by negative and mean-spirited people," Rodriguez advised young people in an on-line autobiographical sketch for the Society for Advancement of Chicanos and Native Americans in Science (SACNAS). "Education will get you what you want in life, but you must work at it."

Of Mexican ancestry, Eloy Rodriguez was born on January 7, 1947 in Edinburg, at the southern tip of Texas. He has one younger brother and two younger sisters. His father was a laborer and short-order cook; his mother cleaned houses. His father's schooling ended with first grade, and his mother left school during the seventh grade; the schooling of the other adults in his large extended family (all of whom lived within a five-block radius of his home) was similarly limited. But his parents and other relatives held education in very high regard. Eloy's mother made sure that he went to school every day, and she kept him supplied with reading material given to her by her employers. Eloy ended up with a perfect attendance record from elementary school through high school. (His siblings and the offspring of his aunts and uncles did well, too: of the 67 Rodriguez cousins, 64 graduated from college, and 11 earned master's degrees or Ph.D.s.) "There was a high emphasis on honesty, fairness, cooperation, and compassion" in his family, Rodriguez wrote in his essay for the SACNAS Web site. "Family members encouraged us to be 'vivo,' which means to think on your feet and use common sense. We didn't have television while I was growing up, and I think that had a positive effect on how I saw myself and the world around me."

Rodriguez's early memories include those of visits to his grandfather's farm in Mexico. "He would always take me out and show me animals and plants," he told Neil Campbell. "I was intrigued with them, and I think it just stayed with me." He also recalled that when he was ill, he was given medicinal herbs, some of which came from an aunt's garden. As a youngster he learned Spanish as well as English; his fluency in Spanish, he told Campbell, has been invaluable to him as a researcher in South America, where Spanish is the main language in every country except Brazil.

Rodriguez shone in school despite overt prejudice directed against him. His primary-school teachers, for example, "hit me on my hands and made me write on the blackboard, 'I will not speak Spanish,'" he told Virginia Morell for the *New York Times Magazine* (December 18, 1994). "They had this idea that your brain didn't have the capacity to handle two languages." Moreover, white children taunted him mercilessly about the Mexican foods he brought for lunch; he has recalled "begging his mother to give him peanut-butter-and-jelly sandwiches instead," Morell reported. In high school, although he ranked in the top 5 percent of his senior class and clearly displayed enthusiasm for learning, a counselor told him that he should go to a technical school. "At that time, a technical school was a place to learn how to fix air conditioners," he told Campbell. "I didn't even know what the engine of a car was! I was shocked! Fortunately, I didn't pay attention to her." Instead, Rodriguez enrolled at the University of Texas at Edinburg (now called University of Texas–Pan American), where he intended to study accounting. "As an undergraduate I felt very lonely," he recalled to Campbell. "I was one of a very small number of minority students. There were no programs for minority students. We were kind of abandoned. It was like shopping at a 7-11 store, you know—just get your stuff and get out."

While he was studying at the Edinburg campus, a herpetologist on staff rekindled his interest in science. Rodriguez subsequently transferred to the University of Texas at Austin, where he changed his major to zoology; he also studied botany and organic chemistry. Through a work-study program, he got a job as a janitor in a research laboratory. One of the postdoctoral researchers assigned to the lab—"kind of a lazy guy," as Rodriguez described him to Campbell—enlisted him to do chemical separations (procedures for isolating specific substances) and other work for him. "I was really good at it . . . ," Rodriguez told Campbell. "One day the professor in charge of the lab came in and asked, 'What's going on?' That is how I got my first publication." The professor was Tom J. Mabry, who became his mentor. By the time Rodriguez earned his B.A. degree, in 1969, he was helping to manage Mabry's lab. "The research bug got to me, the passion, the excitement of science," he said to Campbell. "Once it gets you, you can't let go of it." According to Mabry, Rodriguez wrote a paper even though he knew that the postdoctoral student's name rather than his own would appear as a co-author, simply because "he wanted to know how to do it," as Mabry explained to Morell. Rodriguez earned a Ph.D. degree in phytochemistry (plant chemistry) and plant biology from the University of Texas, in 1975.

In 1975–76 Rodriguez held the position of medical postdoctoral fellow in the botany and dermatology departments at the University of British Columbia, in Vancouver, Canada. From there he joined the faculty of the University of California at Irvine (UCI), with a joint appointment as assistant professor in both the Department of Developmental and Cell Biology and the Department of Ecology and Evolutionary Biology. In 1983 he began working, concurrently, as a professor in the Environmental Toxicology Program of the Department of Community and Environmental Medicine at UCI's College of Medicine. For his first eight years at UCI, Rodriguez worked 18 hours a day, often sleeping in his lab; he turned out a steady stream of papers, because he "knew" that his colleagues "were waiting for me to slip up," for no other reason than that he was Hispanic, he told Morell. Because of his single-minded devotion to his career, he postponed getting married until he was 36; after his marriage he reduced his workday to 14 hours.

In 1984 the Harvard University primatologist Richard Wrangham enlisted Rodriguez for a collaborative project because of Rodriguez's expertise in a family of plants known as Compositae, which includes sunflowers, dandelions, ragweeds, and a species called aspilia. Wrangham had been observing the feeding behavior of apes and monkeys in the Kibale Forest (now part of Kibale National Park), in the east-central African nation of Uganda. "Richard told me he'd seen these sick chimpanzees swallowing Aspilia leaves whole," Rodriguez told Morell. "But these are very bitter plants, and so they were making faces like they were tasting something as nasty as cod-liver oil. And as soon as I heard that, I said, 'This is exciting.'" Wrangham theorized that the animals wanted to add roughage to their diets, but Rodriguez thought, "It's got to be more than that," as he recalled to Campbell. During a trip to Kibale with Wrangham, Rodriguez observed the chimps' behavior for himself. Back in his laboratory, he analyzed the leaves the chimpanzees had swallowed (after rolling them around in their mouths but not chewing them) and discovered that they contained thiarubrine, a chemical that is toxic to some fungi and viruses. "We calculated that [the chimps] were getting more or less a set dosage of the drug or drugs in the leaf," he explained to Campbell. A paper describing that finding, and listing Rodriguez, Wrangham, and six others as co-authors, appeared in the journal *Experientia* in 1985. One outcome of Rodriguez's work with aspilia has been the production of a potent antibiotic called thiarubrine-A.

Rodriguez and Wrangham hypothesized that the chimps were suffering from intestinal parasites and were, in effect, medicating themselves. In 1989 the two scientists coined the term "zoopharmacognosy" to label this new field of study. Since then he and others have watched obviously ill mountain gorillas in the wild displaying similar self-medicating behavior. "Of the 15 plant species that we have looked at while studying apes, we have figured out the chemistry of five of them," Rodriguez told Campbell. "It is really exciting because it is almost like breaking the Mayan code. When you figure out a chemical structure, you are breaking a code of nature. That code gives you a considerable amount of information. It says, 'Look at me, look at my triple bonds. Do you know what I can do with these triple bonds?'" Rodriguez added, "It is fascinating what a new discipline can do! It cracks the door open to very creative, young graduate students who are looking for new things to do." Rodriguez and Wrangham's article "Zoopharmacognosy: The Use of Medicinal Plants by Animals" appears in *Recent Advances in Phytochemistry*, Volume 27: *Phytochemical Potential of Tropical Plants* (1993), edited by K. R. Downum and others.

Other subjects of Rodriguez's investigations include flavonoids (aromatic compounds used in perfume production); biochemical interactions among higher plants and invertebrate animals known as arthropods; the biology and chemistry of a so-called problem weed in India; plant components that cause allergic reactions in humans; desert plants potentially useful as energy sources; Amazonian natives' use of psychoactive drugs to cure themselves of parasitic worms and other afflictions; properties of guayule, a shrub that produces rubber; natural insecticides; and the biochemistry of chilies. In a 1992 article for *California Agriculture*, Rodriguez and three colleagues demonstrated that when goats eat poison oak, as they do in areas to which they are brought specifically to eradicate the plant, the poison oak's toxic oil does not transfer to the female goats' milk.

In 1994 Rodriguez left UCI for Cornell University, in Ithaca, New York. At Cornell he has taught courses in the biology and chemistry of natural products, environmental toxicology, and the chemistry of biomedicines and nutraceuticals (botanical products that may be beneficial to health). His laboratory is in Cornell's renowned biotechnology complex. "My coming to Cornell is like paradise in terms of my scientific research," he told Julie L. Nicklin for the *Chronicle of Higher Education* (July 7, 1995). Rodriguez also does a great deal of fieldwork. "When I do chemistry," he explained to Campbell, "I don't just do it for the sake of chemistry. It's exciting to look at new chemical structures . . . , but I have always wanted to understand the reason for their existence. To do that you have to get out in the field. You have to learn to observe the natural world, 'see' the interactions, and ask the question, 'What is the function of these chemicals?' . . . I always tell [students] that a lot of research starts from going out in the field and observing."

Rodriguez is the James A. Perkins Endowed Professor of Environmental Studies at Cornell. He is believed to be the first U.S.-born Hispanic to hold an endowed position in the sciences at an American university. The births of his children, Pilar and Francesco, in the 1980s and his dismay about the high drop-out rate among Hispanic high-school students inspired him to develop a program to increase black and Hispanic youngsters' interest in science. The program, called KIDS—Kids Investigating and Discovering Science—was launched in 1990; it is a three-week summer program at UCI for students in kindergarten through eighth grade who are from very poor families, have limited proficiency in English, and are considered at high risk for failure in school. While conducting various experiments, participants wear child-size lab coats provided by KIDS. "The whole idea is self-esteem, motivation, and passion," Rodriguez explained to Campbell. "How can you develop these things early in the game? How do you get kids . . . to become critical thinkers? You can flood them with science. But they are not going to get it unless you take a plant and show them trichomes and ask, 'Hey, what is the function of these trichomes?' They come up with 50 reasons. That's what scientists do, by and large—try to figure out the function of things. This program has been extremely successful." Manuel N. Gomez, UCI's vice chancellor, told Virginia Morell that with KIDS, Rodriguez had "essentially created a pipeline of future minority scientists."

In working with undergraduates, Rodriguez has tried to increase students' awareness of threats to biological diversity—particularly in Earth's rain forests, where the diversity of species is greater than anywhere else. Each summer he brings several students with him to do research in the South American rain forest; they return to the U.S. "with a passion [for preserving the natural world] like you have never seen before!" Rodriguez exclaimed to Campbell. And because "students are very good communicators," he added, "they will spread the word" about the importance of conservation.

According to Virginia Morell, "Rodriguez's brain is so crammed with ideas and projects that he sometimes sounds like a barker at a science fair." Rodriguez has written or co-written more than 150 scientific articles and has given dozens of talks as an invited lecturer at universities and research facilities worldwide. His many honors include the Martin De La Cruz silver medallion for outstanding research in traditional herbal medicine, which he earned in Mexico in 1992, and a 1994 National Science Foundation Educator Achievement Award. He and his wife, the novelist and short-story writer Helena Maria Viramontes, have been married since 1983. Rodriguez maintains lengthy professional and personal home pages on the World Wide Web. —J.R.

Suggested Reading: *American Biology Teacher*, p282+ May 1996, with photo; *Black Issues in Higher Education* p27+ Dec. 15, 1994, with photo; *Chicago Tribune* VII p3 July 5, 1995; *Chronicle of Higher Education* pA5 July 7, 1995, with photo; *New York Times Magazine*, p50+ Dec. 18, 1994, with photos; SACNAS Web site; *American Men & Women of Science, 1998*

Courtesy of U.S. House of Representatives

Ros-Lehtinen, Ileana

(ross-LAY-tih-nen, il-ee-AHN-ah)

July 15, 1952– U.S. Representative from Florida. Address: 2240 Rayburn House Office Bldg., Washington, DC 20515; 9210 S.W. 72d St., Suite 100, Miami, FL 33173

Ileana Ros-Lehtinen, who has represented Florida's 18th Congressional District since she won a special election in 1989, has accomplished several firsts in her political career. Among others, she is the first Hispanic woman and first Cuban-American ever elected to the United States Congress. She is also the first Republican member of the Congressional Hispanic Caucus. Proudly showcased by Republicans to refute charges that their party is not as inclusive as that of the Democrats, Ros-Lehtinen has followed her party's line in working to pass conservative legislation on abortion, government spending, and relations with Cuba; ending the four-decade-long regime of the Cuban dictator Fidel Castro and bringing democracy to her native land are among her primary goals as a member of the House of Representatives. However, she has broken with her Republican colleagues on several other issues, most notably to fight for immigrant rights. Widely loved by Hispanics in her district, she believes that Latinos—particularly Hispanic women—will play a large role in the future of the U.S. "Now more than ever," she wrote for *Vista* (February 4, 1992), as quoted in *Notable Hispanic American Women* (1993), "we Hispanic women must re-energize and refocus our efforts to realize the vast potential that lies within our grasp."

Known to friends and family as Lily, the congresswoman was born Ileana Carmen Ros on July 15, 1952 in Havana, Cuba, to Armanda Adato Ros and Enrique Emilio Ros, both of whom were prominent educators in that country. Along with thousands of others among their compatriots, the Ros family—which included Ileana's brother—left their nation for Miami in 1960, after the revolutionary leader Fidel Castro started to move his country toward communism. "One of my sharpest memories about being a 'Cuban refugee,'" Ros-Lehtinen recalled in an article she wrote for the *Wall Street Journal* (July 3, 1990), "was standing in line in downtown Miami's Freedom Tower with my family and hundreds of other newly arrived Cubans waiting to receive U.S. government-issued boxes of powdered milk, cheese, and processed meat." Although at first the Ros family was involved in efforts to overthrow Castro's regime, they resigned themselves to living in the United States after the failure of the Bay of Pigs invasion, in 1961. As Armanda Adato Ros recalled to Chris Black, a commentator for the *Boston Globe* (August 31, 1989), Ileana's father maintained that "you cannot educate two kids without a flag and a country. This is going to be their country and they have to love it."

Ros-Lehtinen attended Southwest Miami High School, from which she graduated in 1970. She spent the next two years at Miami-Dade Community College, graduating in 1972 with an Associate in Arts degree. In 1975 she earned a bachelor of arts degree in English, with honors, from Florida International University, also in Miami. (Years later, in 1986, she earned from that school a master of science degree, again with honors, and she has since taken courses toward a doctorate in educational administration at the University of Miami.) In 1978 Ros-Lehtinen founded the Eastern Academy, a private elementary school in South Hialeah, Florida, where she taught and served as principal for 10 years.

Under the influence of her father, who was active with groups that hoped to bring democracy to Cuba, Ros-Lehtinen developed a strong interest in politics. In 1982 she ran successfully for the first of two terms in the Florida House of Representatives. In the following year she married a fellow Florida state representative, Dexter W. Lehtinen, a Democrat. The two were noted for being the only legislative couple in the United States at that time. In 1986 Ros-Lehtinen became the youngest person and the first Hispanic to be elected to the Florida State Senate. As a state legislator she was known as a staunch conservative. Although early on she involved herself in matters that reached far beyond her constituency, eventually, according to Chris Black, she came to focus "almost exclusively on the most parochial of issues" and the specific needs of individuals and businesses in her district. Among her accomplishments, Ros-Lehtinen introduced and helped get passed an amendment to the state constitution that created a victims' bill of rights. She was also instrumental in the passage of the Florida Prepaid College Tuition Program, which helps lower-income families pay the costs of a college education; the School-Area Drug Law; and the Missing Children Identification Act.

Ros-Lehtinen leaped into the national political arena in 1989, after the sudden death of the liberal Democrat Claude Pepper, the longtime representative of Florida's 18th Congressional District, on May 31 of that year. With a special election scheduled for that August, Ros-Lehtinen resigned her Florida Senate seat and joined three other Republicans in vying for their party's nomination. After defeating her opponents, she hired Jeb Bush, the son of then–president George Bush (and currently the governor of Florida), as her campaign manager. In the general election Ros-Lehtinen faced the Democratic nominee, Gerald F. Richman, a former president of the Florida Bar Association, who is Jewish. Although Ros-Lehtinen ran on a conservative platform and Richman a liberal one, the heated campaign focused less on issues than on ethnicity. Lee Atwater, the national chairman of the Republican Party at the time, announced that since the 18th District was 50 percent Hispanic, it was essential that a Cuban-American win the seat. According to *Time* (September 11, 1989), Richman responded by asserting, "This is an American seat." Although his supporters interpreted the remark to mean that the position should be open to all citizens, Ros-Lehtinen criticized Richman's words as racist, contending that they implied that Hispanics were not Americans. Spanish radio stations soon began broadcasting the warning that a vote for Richman was a vote for Castro. When Richman offered to debate Ros-Lehtinen, she refused. The Republican Party's eagerness to win the district was indicated by President George Bush's trip to Miami to give Ros-Lehtinen a personal endorsement. On August 29, 1989, the day of the election, Ros-Lehtinen won 53 percent of the vote, including 90 percent of the ballots cast by Hispanics. "I think it's been a terribly divisive and ethnically divisive campaign," Adela Gooch and Dan Balz quoted her as saying in the *Washington Post* (August 31, 1989). "But now it's time for healing; now we have to reach out to all those sections." In the 1990 election, in which the industrialist Bernard Anscher ran on the Democratic ticket, she won 60 percent of the vote; two years later, in an election that pitted her against Magda Montiel Davis, a lawyer, 67 percent of the people who went to the polls in her district cast their ballots for her. Since then she has run unopposed in her district, which comprises parts of Miami—including much of the downtown and the inner-city section known as Little Havana, whose residents tend to vote Republican—and other, nearby portions of Dade County, such as the upper-middle-class suburbs of Key Biscayne and Kendall. The population of the district, which was redrawn during the 1990s, is now two-thirds Hispanic.

At her first swearing-in ceremony at the Capitol, on September 6, 1989, Ros-Lehtinen became the first Republican in 26 years to represent Florida's 18th District. She soon established herself as an outspoken voice in Congress, especially on international issues. She criticized visits of Nelson Mandela, then head of the African National Congress and later president of South Africa, to the United Sates because of his friendliness toward Yasir Arafat, the head of the Palestine Liberation Organization, and Fidel Castro. She also expressed opposition to the 1991 Pan American Games, which were held in Cuba.

Although on such issues as abortion, taxes, and so-called big government, Ros-Lehtinen has voted along Republican Party lines, she has broken with her party on education issues and by supporting family and medical leave, a raise in the minimum wage, voter registration through motor-vehicle offices, and gun-control measures. In 1994—the year in which Republicans regained control of both the House and the Senate for the first time in 40 years—she did not join the more than 300 Republican congressional incumbents and other candidates who signed the Contract with America, a Republican campaign manifesto that called for, among other measures, a balanced-budget amendment to the Constitution, an overhaul of welfare programs, tax cuts, curbs on death-penalty appeals and product-liability claims, and an increase in defense spending. In particular, she objected to proposed legislation that would have denied to most legal immigrants benefits provided under Title XX of the Social Security Act, such as cash assistance and food.

Indeed, Ros-Lehtinen's greatest differences with the Republican Party leadership have been in the areas of welfare and immigration. In 1996 she was one of only two Republicans in the House to oppose the GOP-introduced bill that radically altered the country's system of welfare. The previous year, during consideration of the House version of the welfare-overhaul legislation, she declared, as quoted in *Politics in America 1998*, that cuts to social services for immigrants stemmed from an "anti-immigrant sentiment" that was "growing from an unreal perception that immigrants only come to the United States to take advantage of our generous society and become a burden on the state while never integrating nor becoming productive citizens." She also opposed a Republican measure that aimed to control illegal immigration through tighter border controls and easier-to-implement deportation measures. "I don't think this bill is in the American tradition," she said, as quoted in *Politics in America 1998*. "I don't think it really stems the problems of illegal immigration, and it puts new restrictions on legal immigrants and U.S. citizens." Ros-Lehtinen left the Congressional Hispanic Caucus in January 1995, at the start of the 104th Congress, in line with the desire of Newt Gingrich, who was then the Speaker of the House, and some of his followers to disband such organizations. Then, in March 1996, she rejoined the caucus, as a way of underlining her stance on immigration issues.

At present, Ros-Lehtinen serves as the chair of the Subcommittee on International Economic Policy and Trade and vice chair of the Subcommittee on the Western Hemisphere, both of which are offshoots of the House International Relations Committee. She has become influential in the shaping of foreign policy, notably with relation to Latin America and particularly Cuba. Since her arrival in Congress, three major pieces of legislation concerning Cuba—each of which she supported—have become law. The first is the 1992 Cuban Democracy Act, which reiterates the U.S. government's condemnation of human-rights violations in Cuba, states as a goal of the U.S. government Cuba's turn toward democracy, in the form of free and fair elections, and outlines plans for the post-Castro era. Toward those ends, the act prohibits subsidiaries of U.S. corporations from trading with Cuba. According to a U.S. Merchant Marine Academy Web site, Thomas R. Taggart Jr. reported in a speech at the 1997 Naval Academy Foreign Affairs Conference that the act "advises the President to influence other countries to restrict trade and economic assistance to Cuba. If foreign countries continue to 'provide assistance' to Cuba, Congress prohibits such countries from being eligible for aid under the Foreign Assistance Act of 1961 and the Arms Export Act." Ros-Lehtinen also favored the Cuban Liberty and Democratic Solidarity Act of 1996 (the so-called Helms-Burton Law), which tightened sanctions against the Cuban government and called for the punishment of foreign countries or individuals who have profited from investment in property that the Cuban government confiscated from American owners after Castro seized power. That law triggered protests from Canada, Mexico, and many European countries. In response to those protests, and with the goal of encouraging the continuing multilateral efforts to push Cuba toward democracy, President Bill Clinton has repeatedly suspended (as a provision in the law permits him to do every six months) the right to file suit against anyone profiting from the confiscation of another's property in Cuba.

In 2000 Ros-Lehtinen voted with the majority of the House to support a Republican-introduced measure (which was added on to an agriculture-related bill) that allowed the sale of medicine and food to Cuba. Thanks to Ros-Lehtinen and other Cuban-American members of Congress, the provisions also tightened travel restrictions for American citizens intending to go to Cuba and banned the financing of sales to Cuba by the United States government or American banks. Critics of the bill, which was approved by the Senate and signed into law by President Clinton, complained that the Cuba-related elements would be of little help to Cubans or American farmers. Castro himself criticized the bill as a publicity stunt. He organized mass protests against the new law and declared that he would buy no American products.

Earlier, Ros-Lehtinen had vehemently criticized the North American Free Trade Agreement (NAFTA), which went into effect in 1994, because of the possible loss of jobs in her district to Mexican workers. She has also opposed increases in aid to Africa, for fear that aid to Latin America would decrease as a result. In 1997 she again resigned from the Congressional Hispanic Caucus, after its chairman at that time, California congressman Xavier Becerra, visited Cuba. She has voted against the allocation of funds to international family-planning programs, on the grounds that such programs advocate abortion as a means of birth control.

On the domestic front, Ros-Lehtinen voted to impeach President Clinton in 1999. With regard to legislation, she has focused on education and other issues that affect children. She is a member of the Subcommittee on Criminal Justice, Drug Policy, and Human Resources and of the Speaker's Task Force for a Drug Free America. In 1998 she was the chief sponsor the Child Custody Protection Act, which would have outlawed transportation of minors across state lines for abortions had it passed a vote in the Senate.

In a highly publicized matter that was surrounded by bitter controversy for seven months, Ros-Lehtinen urged the United States to confer citizenship on, or grant permanent residency to, Elian Gonzalez, a six-year-old Cuban boy who was rescued from the ocean off the Florida coast on Thanksgiving Day 1999, after his mother drowned while fleeing Cuba by boat along with other would-be refugees to the U.S. Echoing the sentiments of many other anti-Castro Cuban Miamians, the congresswoman maintained that the boy's father, Juan Miguel Gonzalez, was following a script imposed on him by the Cuban government when he said that he wanted the child returned to Cuba to live with him there. She said it would be in Elian's best interest to grow up in a democracy, and that therefore the Miami relatives who were caring for the boy should be made his permanent guardians. In a dialogue with Representative Charles Rangel of New York that aired on the *NewsHour with Jim Lehrer* on January 25, 2000, she denied Rangel's charge that "this is really a case against Castro, a case for the embargo, a case for the Cuban-American Foundation . . . and not what's in the best interest of the child." At the end of June, after the Supreme Court refused to consider the case, Elian's father took the child back to Cuba.

Ileana Ros-Lehtinen and her husband, Dexter Lehtinen, who currently works as an attorney in private practice, live in Miami with their two children, Amanda and Patricia. (She also has two stepchildren, Katharine and Douglas, from Lehtinen's previous marriage.) The 60 Plus Association, a national organization for senior citizens, has awarded her the Friends of Seniors Award and the Guardian of Seniors Award. — G.O.

Suggested Reading: *Boston Globe* p3 Aug. 3, 1989; *Congressional Quarterly Weekly Report* p2267 Sep. 2, 1989; *New York Times* A p12 Jan. 10, 2000, with photos; *Washington Post* A p3 Aug. 27, 1989; Foerstal, Karen. *Biographical Dictionary of Congressional Women*, 1999; Meier, Matt S., Conchita Franco Serri, and Richard A. Garcia. *Notable Latino Americans*, 1997; *Politics in America*, various editions; Telgen, Diane, and Jim Kamp, eds. *Notable Hispanic American Women*, 1993; *Who's Who in American Politics, 1999–2000*

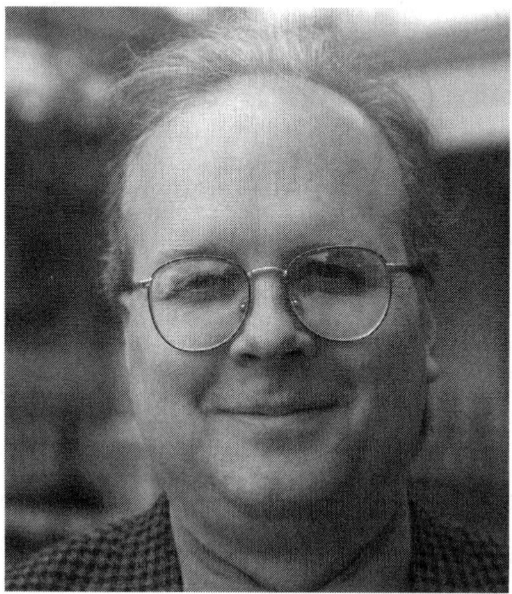

Corbis Sygma

Rove, Karl

Dec. 25, 1950– Political consultant. Address: P.O. Box 1902, Austin, TX 78767-1902

BULLETIN: At press time, the results of the presidential race between Al Gore and George W. Bush had not been determined.

One of three top aides (along with Joe Allbaugh and Karen Hughes), known collectively as the "Iron Triangle," who have been working with Republican presidential nominee George W. Bush since he ran successfully for governor of Texas in 1994, Karl Rove is acknowledged by many political insiders as a consummate strategist. "Karl plays politics like Bobby Fischer plays chess," Mark McKinnon, Bush's top media adviser, told James Carney for *Time* (August 23, 1999). "He looks at the whole board and thinks 20 moves ahead." In two decades of advising politicians in Texas, Rove has helped the Republican party gain complete control of the state's elected offices, all previously held by Democrats. "Karl's very flexible in running a pretty modern campaign, one that talks directly to the target audience," said Tony Proffitt, who served as spokesman for the Democratic former lieutenant governor of Texas, Bob Bullock. "He's not from the far right or the far left, he's from the middle and that's where America is." Although he has been accused of negative campaigning and sometimes of "dirty tricks," even his political enemies praise Rove for his intelligence and ability to guide his candidates to victory on a consistent basis. "Basically as a party election draws near, you head to Karl," Fred Meyer, the former Texas GOP chairman, told Scott Baldauf for the *Christian Science Monitor*. "He knows and understands the state, the issues and the political process. He's a genius."

Karl Rove was born on December 25, 1950 in Denver, Colorado. His mother was the manager of a gift store; his adoptive father, a geologist, often worked far from home, and Rove's mother moved the family often, from Colorado to Nevada to Utah. During his childhood Rove missed his father and had a tense relationship with his mother. By age nine he was already very interested in politics and the Republican Party. "The little girl across the street I can remember beating the hell out of me in 1960," during that year's presidential election campaign, "because I was for [Richard] Nixon and she was for [John F.] Kennedy," Rove recalled to Melinda Henneberger for the *New York Times Magazine* (May 14, 2000). "She had a couple of years and a few pounds on me, and I can remember being on the pavement." Rove attended high school in Salt Lake City, Utah. He remembers being a "strange kid" who, as he told Henneberger, grew into "a big nerd, complete with the pocket protractor, briefcase, the whole deal." He loved reading and studying history and spent much of his free time in the library, preparing for his work on the debate team. Rove also volunteered in high school for one of the campaigns of Utah's Republican senator Wallace F. Bennett.

In 1969 Rove enrolled at the University of Utah, where he planned to major in political science. During his freshman year, his father left his mother for good on Christmas Day, Rove's birthday. (A few years later, his mother committed suicide.) In order to pay for college, Rove took a job at a convenience store, where he was once robbed at gunpoint. He soon dropped out of the University of Utah and moved to the District of Columbia, to run for chairman of the College Republicans National Committee (CRNC). (Since then he has enrolled in almost a half-dozen schools but has yet to receive his bachelor's degree; he is currently close to getting his degree in political science at the University of Texas and has been provisionally accepted in the school's doctorate program in government.) He won his campaign for chairman of the CRNC against John "Terry" Dolan, later the founder of the National Conservative Political Action Committee. Lee Atwater, later chairman of the Republican National Congress (RNC) and a consultant to presidents Ronald Reagan and George Bush, was Rove's southern regional coordinator during the election campaign; Rove has said that Atwater had a significant influence on his life. For a week the two traveled throughout the South by car, trying to recruit new members for the CRNC and campaigning on a platform of inclusion over dogmatic conservatism. Soon controversy dogged the young Rove, as the *Washington Post* reported that he was teaching Watergate-style "dirty tricks" to college Republicans. The *Post* article noted that he had once posed as a Democrat in order to get his hands on campaign stationery—which he then used to send fake invitations to hippies and other of what he called "deadbeats," offering "free beer, food, and girls, and a good time" at the 1970 opening of the headquarters for a Democratic campaign in Illinois. Rove has since confessed to the act, which he terms a youthful prank he now regrets. According to a biography of Atwater by John Brady, quoted by Wayne Slater in the *Dallas Morning News* (March 21, 1999), Rove organized conferences that taught young Republicans such campaign maneuvers as "purloining the opposition party's garbage to obtain inside memos and lists of contributors." When the *Post* story broke, future president George Bush, then head of the RNC, stated that he would investigate the situation. After a month, Bush cleared Rove of charges—and then hired him.

From 1973 to 1974 Rove served as an assistant to Bush at the RNC, and in 1977 he moved to Texas to work for Bush's Political Action Committee. In Texas Rove also took part in the unsuccessful campaign of George W. Bush, Bush's son, for Congress. When the elder Bush announced his decision to run for the 1980 Republican presidential nomination, Rove was the first person hired by the campaign. In part to save his failing marriage, however, Rove soon left the Bush team and moved with his wife to Austin, Texas, where he helped steer Bill Clements's campaign for governor of Texas. Clements was successful, becoming the first Republican in over a century to become governor of the state; meanwhile, in spite of his efforts, Rove's marriage fell apart. In 1981 Rove founded a consulting business, Karl Rove & Co., in Texas. His first direct client was Bill Clements, and he also worked for conservative Democratic Representative Phil Gramm, among others. In 1984 Rove advised Gramm, by then a Republican, in his successful Senate campaign against Democrat Lloyd Doggett, while also handling direct mail for Ronald Reagan's presidential re-election campaign. (George Bush was then Reagan's vice president.) In 1986 Rove again worked with Clements, in his successful run for re-election as governor of Texas, and in 1988 Rove advised Tom Phillips in his bid for election to the Texas Supreme Court. Phillips won, becoming the first Republican ever to be elected to that position. Ten years later, Republicans held all nine seats on the Court.

Meanwhile, Rove was building a reputation as an intense and successful political adviser who specialized in aggressive and negative campaigns. Although accused of underhanded strategies and of intimidating both the press and people in the Republican Party who have spoken out against Bush, Rove denies any wrongdoing. The most infamous of the allegations against Rove surfaced in the 1986 race between Clements and Mark White for the Texas governorship. Just as the two were about to debate, Rove claimed to have found a bug in his own office. White's supporters were furious, charging that Rove had planted the bug himself in order to discredit their candidate. (An investigation into the alleged planting of the bug came up empty.) Even when he was not being accused of playing dirty pool, Rove's negative campaigns themselves often aroused the ire of his candidates' opponents. During the run against White, Rove printed up material suggesting that White had been drinking when he was in an auto accident during college. In 1990 he effectively ended the political career of progressive Texas Agricultural Commissioner Jim Hightower, when he circulated information about Hightower's alleged participation in a contribution-kickback scheme. Although Hightower was never charged, three of his aides were convicted.

Today, however, Rove disdains negative campaigning. "I think we've gone through a period in American politics from the 70s and the 80s where the negative campaign worked to where it doesn't," Rove was quoted as saying by Dan Balz in the *Washington Post* (July 23, 1999). "I think what does work in politics is the counterpunch rather than the punch." Scott Baldauf reported that Rove currently has several key rules for running a successful campaign: "Know your client and choose a format that works to his or her benefit. Develop three or four central ideas that define your campaign (jobs, education, smaller government) and stick to them. Most important: Use humor to deliver your points. Reporters may remember what you said, but the voting public will remember how you said it."

In 1993 George W. Bush announced his candidacy for governor of Texas and hired Rove as an adviser, cautioning Rove to stay positive during the campaign. With Rove's help, Bush defeated Democratic governor Ann Richards in an upset victory. In fact, all six Texas Republicans advised by Rove that year were successful. By 1999 all 29 Texas state offices, once filled across the board by Democrats, were held by Republicans, almost every one of whom had been assisted by Rove. "It's because of Karl's planting seeds years ago that Republicans have a bumper crop of candidates now," Mark McKinnon, George W. Bush's top media adviser, told Scott Baldauf. "Karl's not easily distracted. He's more focused than anyone I've known." Thanks to his unparalleled success rate since the mid-1980s, Rove has won clients from as many as 23 states and from as far away as Sweden. In 1996 Rove handled Senator Phil Gramm's brief, unsuccessful run for the Republican presidential nomination. In that same year, Texas government officials forced Rove to quit his job as a paid consultant to the Philip Morris tobacco companies, because the state government was in the midst of a lawsuit against the firms. Further controversy erupted when Tom Pauken, former chairman of the Texas Republican Party, alleged that Rove had effectively cut off contributions to the state party treasury after Pauken had publicly challenged Bush's tax proposal in 1997. "He made it very difficult for us to raise money," Pauken told Slater. "Any time something negative is said about the governor by anybody, he chews on them and makes sure they pay a price." In 1998, when George W. Bush ran for reelection as governor, Rove was again one of his top advisers. This time, Bush won 68 percent of the overall vote and over 40 percent of the ballots from the Hispanic community. "Karl knew that a dramatic victory was the best way to launch [Bush's] presidential campaign," a Bush aide told James Carney. "So he ran up the score."

In early 1999, as George W. Bush began to gear up for his presidential run in 2000, almost a quarter of his expenditures went to Rove's consulting firm. At the request of Bush, Rove later sold his firm to concentrate on running the Bush campaign. Rove initiated what became known as the "yellow rose garden" strategy, which kept Bush until mid-June 1999 in Austin, Texas, where he did not campaign or make any major speeches. Instead, Rove arranged for prominent GOP governors and members of Congress to fly to Austin to endorse the Texas governor. Although seen by many as a risky strategy, as it gave Bush only a couple of months to catch up with Republican candidates such as Steve Forbes and Elizabeth Dole before the Iowa straw poll, the strategy nonetheless paid off. On the strength of the hype created by Rove's approach, Bush swung into the straw poll and won by a convincing margin over Forbes, who placed second. In early 2000 Bush won the Iowa Caucus, as expected. After he lost primaries in New Hampshire and Michigan to Senator John McCain, some Republicans began to doubt Rove's tactics, but those doubters were silenced when Bush's convincing Super Tuesday win on March 7 all but assured him of the nomination, which he received officially in August 2000. Although Bush received a large boost in the polls after the Republican National Convention, he and the Democratic nominee, Vice President Al Gore, soon became involved in the tightest presidential race since 1960, separated in opinion polls by only a few percentage points. Meanwhile, Rove and Bush faced criticism among some Republicans that their campaign was ignoring advice and opinions from party members outside Austin. But Rove insisted to Richard S. Dunham for *Business Week* (September 18, 2000), "A campaign is consistently listening to people. We are hearing criticism and advice. I hear that each day, and it's useful. I don't recognize [the GOP panic] the newspapers are talking about." "Karl Rove is the one indispensable component in Governor Bush's team," the Democratic consultant Chuck McDonald told Wayne Slater. "You need a talented cast, but there has to be a single dominant force at the staff level—and that's clearly Karl Rove."

Rove is known for being intelligent and hardworking. He has thinning brown hair, glasses, and owl-like features. He is fascinated by history, particularly that of presidential elections in the United States. Said to have a self-deprecating sense of humor, Rove is known for being reluctant to speak in front of cameras as well as for having a short fuse behind the scenes; in particular, mistakes on the part of his staff make him angry. "I get revved. I'm a competitive guy. I like to win," he was quoted as saying by Dan Balz. In front of the press, Rove is modest about his role in the Bush campaign, claiming to be one of many advisers. Most sources say that he and George W. Bush get along well and consider each other friends, although it is known that Bush likes to make fun of him for his intellectual nature and has become irritated by the occasional suggestion in the media that Rove is the brains behind his candidacy. Now working on his first presidential campaign, Rove told Melinda Henneberger, "It's not much different [from smaller campaigns]. In some ways, it's easier, because there are more places where [voters] haven't heard the same thing" time and time again. In addition to his work as an adviser, Rove also teaches graduate students at the Lyndon B. Johnson School of Public Affairs at the University of Texas. Asked once how he could teach at a graduate school without a college degree, Rove responded, as quoted by Wayne Slater, "I'm very good at what I do."

Rove lives with his wife, Darby, whom he married in 1986, and their son, Andrew, in a house in the hills overlooking Austin. Darby is a graphic artist who worked for Rove's direct-mail business before the two were married. The family is currently renovating an old lodge on the Guadalupe River, to the southwest of Austin, where Rove can pursue one of his favorite pastimes, hunting quail. Talking to Melinda Henneberger, Darby Rove called her husband "a combination of in-your-face and sensitive." Rove is known as a devoted father. According to his wife, the intensity he is famous for in the political world sometimes gets the better of him in other settings. "He's learned to lay back a little bit when he and Andrew play chess," Darby told Henneberger, "but even in croquet he'd be hitting my ball so far I was crying on vacation." — G.O.

Suggested Reading: *Dallas Morning News* (online) Mar. 21, 1999; *New York Times Magazine* p52+ May 14, 2000; *Washington Post* C p1 July 23, 1999

Courtesy of Scholastic, Inc.

Rowling, J. K.

(ROLE-ing)

July 31, 1966– Children's writer. Address: c/o Scholastic, 555 Broadway, New York, NY 10012

Unicorns, dragons, flying broomsticks, a talking hat, a gentle giant, pictures that come to life, a cloak that makes the wearer invisible—magic is everywhere in the "Harry Potter" books, the series by the British writer J. K. Rowling, which features the young apprentice wizard Harry and his cohorts at Hogwarts School of Witchcraft and Wizardry. "Magical" seems an appropriate term to describe the series' success in the marketplace as well: as of October 2000 the first four books—*Harry Potter and the Sorcerer's Stone*, *Harry Potter and the Chamber of Secrets*, *Harry Potter and the Prisoner of Azkaban*, and *Harry Potter and the Goblet of Fire*—had sold more than 43 million copies in the United States alone. Indeed, in the U.S. Harry has become a true celebrity: his portrait appeared on the cover of *Time* magazine's September 20, 1999 issue.

Described by various reviewers as "fabulously entertaining," "entrancing," "superbly constructed," "brilliantly imagined and beautifully written," and "full of wonderful, sly humor," Rowling's stories have been translated into at least 28 languages and are being distributed in some 130 countries. Although children's books rarely show up on the *New York Times* best-seller list (a notable exception being E. B. White's classic *Charlotte's Web*, which appeared for three weeks in 1952), on November 28, 1999 the third book in the series, *Harry Potter and the Prisoner of Azkaban*, *Chamber of Secrets*, and *Sorcerer's Stone* occupied the first, second, and third spots on the list, respectively. As of that date *Sorcerer's Stone* had been on the list for 49 weeks; *Chamber*, for 24 weeks; and *Prisoner*, for 10. Indeed, adults as well as children have become "Harry Potter" enthusiasts. In Great Britain, Rowling's publisher, Bloomsbury, has even gone so far as to produce different, more dignified dust jackets for the books, so grownups will not feel self-conscious reading a children's book in public.

On July 23, 2000 the editors of the *New York Times Book Review* introduced a separate best-seller list for children's books, in response to complaints that the "Harry Potter" books were crowding many deserving "adult" books off the list. When the new list debuted, *Harry Potter and the Goblet of Fire*, which had been published amid much fanfare two weeks earlier, appeared in first place, followed closely by the other three Rowling volumes. If, as expected, sales continue at the current rate, on December 17, 2000 *Harry Potter and the Sorcerer's Stone* will have spent two years on the *New York Times*'s best-seller list.

The "Harry Potter" craze in Great Britain resembles the recent rage for Beanie Babies in the United States. For example, before *Harry Potter and the Prisoner of Azkaban* became available to readers in England, on July 9, 1999, Bloomsbury asked that no sales be made before 3:45 p.m., ostensibly to keep youngsters from playing hooky. As the designated minute approached, children in school uniforms crowded into bookshops all over the country. After a jubilant countdown, the stores became carpeted with kids who began reading the moment they owned the book. Within three days approximately 68,000 copies of *Azkaban* had been sold; by contrast, sales of its closest competitor that week, *Hannibal*, a horror story by Thomas Harris, reached only 13,000 copies in the previous seven days. In the United States, many fans unwilling to wait for *Azkaban* to come to bookstores ordered the British edition of the story via the Internet. (Those numerous Internet sales led some publishing insiders to speculate that the "Harry Potter" phenomenon will lead to a change in traditional copyright law, such that the rights to popular books will be sold by language rather than by country.) A similar frenzy greeted the arrival of *Goblet of Fire*. The book's title had been kept a secret until July 8, 2000 at 12:01 a.m., when bookstore employees were allowed to open their shipments and begin selling. (Many stores in the U.S. remained open into the early hours of the day to accommodate the thousands of people who had waited in line to buy the book.) The book's initial printing of 3.8 million copies was among the largest in publishing history. Rowling helped publicize her latest volume by undertaking a book tour through England on a chartered train, dubbed the *Hogwart's Express*.

The world created by J. K. Rowling, Elizabeth Gleick wrote for *Time* (April 12, 1999), is "every bit as fantabulous and vividly original as those created by C. S. Lewis, Roald Dahl or, for that matter, George Lucas." The hero of the series, the skinny, bespectacled Harry Potter, is an orphan; he lives with his hateful aunt and uncle, Petunia and Vernon Dursley, who force him to sleep in a cupboard under the stairs and never acknowledge his birthdays, while they shower attention and gifts on their insufferable son, Dudley. Having long believed that his parents were killed in an auto accident when he was an infant, 11-year-old Harry is amazed to learn that they were actually powerful wizards and were killed by the dreaded Lord Voldemort, an evil wizard who is trying to take over the world. Harry also finds out that he himself is quite famous in the wizard world. Harry is invited to study at Hogwarts School of Witchcraft and Wizardry, which is housed in a 1,000-year-old castle and is charmingly reminiscent of a British boarding school—complete with a beloved headmaster, strict instructors, arrogant head boys, and rivalrous residence houses. At school he becomes best friends with Hermione Granger, who is studious, very smart, and a bit of a know-it-all, and Ron Weasley, the youngest in a family of six wizard brothers. Aided by the devoted groundskeeper, Hagrid, and the wise headmaster, Professor Dumbledore, Harry battles Lord Voldemort and becomes wiser and more mature in the process. Each of the books chronicles one year in the life of the hero at Hogwarts. In a letter to *Hadassah Magazine* (December 1999), Rahel Musleah and Shira Klayman, both 12-year-olds, noted that the series "comes alive with biblical echoes" and praiseworthy values, among the latter "hospitality, care for all living creatures, study, respect for the poor, visiting the sick, freeing the captive, pursuing justice, saving a life, and doing the right thing." But there has also been a minor outcry by a small number of parents and evangelical ministers who have complained that the books glorify witchcraft and should be banned from school libraries. Though they have gotten little support from educators, such dissenters have filed lawsuits in at least eight states in an attempt to remove the books from library shelves.

Rowling has said that there will be seven books in the series, because the Hogwarts curriculum takes seven years to complete. She has also warned that the next books will be "darker," to use her word. "Harry's going to have quite a bit to deal with as he gets older," she said during an on-line interview for the UK Office for Library and Information Networking (UKOLN), at the University of Bath, in England. Children who have contacted Rowling consistently petition for the safety and continued appearance of their favorite characters. Nevertheless, in *Goblet of Fire*, one character dies.

As the publisher of R. L. Stine's "Goosebumps" series and Ann M. Martin's "Baby-Sitters Club" books, Scholastic, the American publisher of the "Harry Potter" books, has had first-hand experience with blockbusters in children's literature. But Scholastic executives have expressed wonderment at the magnitude of the "Harry Potter" series' popularity. "You could say that Harry is a great character or that Joanne Rowling is a really promotable author," Michael Jacobs, a senior vice president at Scholastic, told a *Newsweek* interviewer (August 23, 1999), "but there are no models, no rules for children's books or adult publishing that explains this." As is evident from the contents of the many "Harry Potter" Web sites and numerous "Harry Potter" fan clubs that have sprung up, thousands of children are following Harry's adventures with a rare passion. Many youngsters reportedly have read each of the first three books in the series half a dozen times or more—a significant achievement, in light of the fact that each is more than 300 pages long. One boy whom Rowling met at a British school "recited the first page of the first book to me from memory," the author told Elizabeth Gleick. "When he stopped, he said, 'I can go on.' He continued reciting the first five pages of the book. That was unbelievable."

"Rowling's secret is as simple and mysterious as her uncanny ability to nourish the human hunger for enchantment: she knows how to feed the desire not just to hear or read a story but to live it as well," Paul Gray wrote for *Time* (September 20, 1999). Rowling herself has suggested that a major part of the appeal of her books rests with Harry: "Harry is smart and good at sports and a lot of things that other children would like to be, but children feel for him because he's lost his parents. If an author makes a character an orphan, few children will want to be an orphan, too. But it is a freeing thing, because the weight of parental expectation is lifted." In *School Library Journal* (October 1998), Eva Mitnick described Harry as "the perfect confused and unassuming hero," and she noted the "delight" to be derived from Rowling's "juxtaposition of the world of Muggles (ordinary humans) with the world of magic." The writer's skillful blending of magic and mundane pleased Michael Winerip, too: "Rowling has a gift for keeping the emotions, fears, and triumphs of her characters on a human scale, even while the supernatural is popping out all over," he wrote for the *New York Times* (February 14, 1999). Winerip revealed that he identified closely with Harry: "As Harry worries that first day [at school] about whether he can compete with the privileged children of Hogwarts alums, I found myself thinking back 30 years to my first days at Harvard, wondering how, coming from a blue-collar shipyard town and a public high school, I could ever compete with preppies from Exeter and Andover." In *Booklist* (September 15, 1998), Michael Cart offered another clue to the books' appeal to adults as well as children: "Rowling's wonderful ability to put a fantastic spin on sports, student rivalry, and eccentric faculty contributes to the humor, charm, and, well, delight of her utterly captivating story."

Rowling's books have won numerous awards. *Sorcerer's Stone* earned the Nestlé Smarties Book Prize gold medal; the Federation of Children's

Book Groups' Book Award, in two categories (longer novel and overall); the Birmingham Cable Children's Book Award; the Young Telegraph Paperback of the Year; the British Book Awards' Children's Book of the Year; and the Sheffield Children's Book Award. In addition, it was shortlisted for the Guardian Fiction Award and the Carnegie Medal. *Chamber of Secrets* garnered the Smarties Prize and the British Book Awards Children's Book of the Year, and it was shortlisted for several others.

Joanne Rowling—called Jo by friends and relatives—was born on July 31, 1966 in Chipping Sodbury, near Bristol, in southwestern England. Until about 1975 her family lived in suburbs of Bristol—first Yate, then Winterbourne, where her friends included a brother and sister whose surname was Potter. From almost as far back as she can remember, Rowling liked to tell stories. In her essay "The Not Especially Fascinating Life So Far of J. K. Rowling," reproduced on the Web site of the British booksellers okukbooks, she wrote that her sister, Di, who is two years younger, "was the person who suffered my first efforts at story-telling. (I was much bigger than her and could hold her down.) Rabbits loomed large in our early story-telling sessions; we badly wanted a rabbit. Di can still remember me telling her a story in which she fell down a rabbit hole and was fed strawberries by the rabbit family inside it. Certainly the first story I ever wrote down (when I was five or six) was about a rabbit called Rabbit. He got the measles and was visited by his friends, including a giant bee called Miss Bee. And ever since Rabbit and Miss Bee, I have wanted to be a writer, although I rarely told anyone so. I was afraid they'd tell me I didn't have a hope."

When Rowling was nine years old, her family moved to Tutshill, in a rural area called the Forest of Dean. She and her sister spent much of their free time playing along the banks of the River Wye and in neighboring fields. "The only fly in the ointment was that I hated my new school," Rowling recalled for the okukbooks Web site. "It was a very small, very old-fashioned place where the roll-top desks still had ink-wells. My new teacher, Mrs. Morgan, scared the life out of me. She gave me an arithmetic test on the very first morning and after a huge effort I managed to get zero out of 10—I had never done fractions before. So she sat me in the row of desks on her far right. It took me a few days to realize I was in the 'stupid' row. Mrs. Morgan positioned everyone in the class according to how clever she thought they were; the brightest sat on her left, and everyone she thought was dim sat on the right. I was as far right as you could get without sitting in the playground." Eventually, the teacher moved her to a seat on the left—"but at a cost," as Rowling explained: "Mrs. Morgan made me swap seats with my best friend, so that in one short walk across the room I became clever but unpopular."

After leaving the Tutshill Primary School, Rowling entered the state-run Wyedean Comprehensive School, where she became friendly with quiet, studious girls like herself. She often entertained them at lunchtime with connected tales in which all of them performed "heroic and daring deeds we certainly wouldn't have done in real life," as she noted in her essay. Her favorite subject "by far" was English, she wrote, "but I quite liked languages too." By her own account, she had no talent whatsoever for sports. In her senior year she was made head girl, an honor that, in her case, was mostly symbolic. During much of her spare time, she wrote stories, few of which she showed to her friends "except for funny stories that again featured us all in thinly disguised characters," she recalled in her essay. As a youngster she particularly enjoyed such books as *Manxmouse*, by Paul Gallico, about a creature with a mouse's body, a rabbit's ears, and a monkey's paws; stories by Noel Streatfeild, whose best-known writings include the "Shoes" series; and *The Lion, the Witch, and the Wardrobe* and the other books in C. S. Lewis's series "The Chronicles of Narnia."

After her graduation from Wyedean, Rowling entered Exeter University, where she studied French on the advice of her parents; fluency in a foreign language, they had told her, would provide her with job security, since bilingual secretaries were in great demand. But pursuing a career as a secretary proved to be "a big mistake," according to Rowling; in the succession of jobs that she held after earning her degree, she discovered that she had neither interest in nor aptitude for office work. Many times, for example, when she was supposed to be taking the minutes of a meeting, she would find herself scribbling names of potential characters in the margins of her notepad instead of paying attention to whatever was being said. "All I ever liked about working in offices was being able to type up stories on the computer when no-one was looking," she has confessed.

At the age of 26, Rowling abandoned office work (according to one source, she was fired from her last job) and moved to Portugal, where she taught English as a foreign language. She loved that work, and her schedule allowed her ample free time to write. Earlier, in 1990, during a four-hour train trip in England, she had daydreamed about a boy—Harry—who attends a school that teaches the arts of wizardry. "Harry just strolled into my head fully formed," she told Elizabeth Gleick. On the Scholastic Web site, she is quoted as saying, "The idea that we could have a child who escapes from the confines of the adult world and goes somewhere where he has power, both literally and metaphorically, really appealed to me." By the time her train ride ended, she recalled for UKOLN, "many of the characters in the books had already been invented." She told the UKOLN interviewer that some of the characters are based on real people: "Hermione Granger is a little bit like I was at my age, though I was neither as clever or as annoying (I hope!). Ron is a little bit like my oldest friend, and Professor Snape is a lot like one of my old teachers." When asked how she came up with the names of people and things in the stories, she said, "I collect unusual names from all sorts of different places. 'Dumbledore' is an Old English word meaning bumblebee, and 'Hedwig' [the name of Harry's pet owl] is a medieval saint." She also uses such sources as street names; other names she makes up.

While in Portugal Rowling began fleshing out her story, and by the time she returned to Great Britain, in about 1993, the manuscript filled half a suitcase. Rowling had become a mother by then (she was married briefly to a journalist during her sojourn in Portugal), and with her infant daughter, Jessica, she settled in Edinburgh, Scotland. Before taking another teaching job, she decided, she would attempt to finish her novel. Her apartment was unheated, so, to keep warm, she would sit in a local café, and while Jessie napped in her carriage, she would write. "I wasn't really aware that it was a children's book," she told a *Newsweek* (August 23, 1999) reporter. "I really wrote it for me, about what I found funny, what I liked." For almost a year, before she resumed teaching French, she was supported by the dole, the British equivalent of welfare. She also won a grant from the Scottish Arts Council. Eventually, Rowling secured an agent by means of a writers' directory, and in 1995, after she had received rejections from several publishers, Bloomsbury gave her a small advance—an amount equal to about $4,000. A few months later Scholastic Press bought the American rights to the book, and Rowling give up teaching to write full-time. (Thanks to the "Harry Potter" books, the value of Bloomsbury stock has soared.)

Rowling has joked that she should have the words "penniless single mother" tattooed on her forehead, since virtually no story about her in print or on the air has failed to mention her reliance on public funds during her year of unemployment. Ignoring her middle-class upbringing and her university education, the media have portrayed her as a welfare mom who got lucky, and some journalists have pointed to her success to suggest that other poor single women follow in her footsteps. "That's absolute rubbish," Rowling declared to a reporter for *Time* (September 20, 1999). "This is not vanity or arrogance, but if you look at the facts, very, very few people manage to write anything that might be a best seller. Therefore, I'm lucky by anyone's standards, let alone single mothers' standards. The crucial thing is, I had a talent you need no money to pursue."

Rowling enjoys traveling on book tours, and she has described her fans' devotion as gratifying. "My very favorite [comment] was from a 12-year-old Scottish girl who came to hear me read at the Edinburgh book festival," she was quoted as saying on the Scholastic Web site. "The event was sold out and the queue for signing at the end was very long. When the girl in question finally reached me she said, 'I didn't WANT there to be so many people here, because this is MY book!' That's exactly how I feel about my favorite books. . . . Nobody else has a right to know them, let alone like them!"

Warner Bros. has optioned the rights to the "Harry Potter" series and has hired the writer-director Steve Kloves, whose credits include the films *The Fabulous Baker Boys* (1989) and *Flesh and Bone* (1993), to write the script of a live-action film about Harry; Chris Columbus, who helmed *Home Alone* (1990) and *Mrs. Doubtfire* (1993), has been tapped to direct the picture, which is scheduled to be released in 2001. The toy-manufacturing giant Hasbro has won the right to produce "Harry Potter" trading cards, games, and candy. Recently, an anonymous bidder paid $15,000 in an Internet auction for an inscribed copy of Rowling's first book, from Bloomsbury's small initial printing.

In July 2000 Queen Elizabeth II named Rowling an officer of the Order of the British Empire. Her sudden wealth notwithstanding, the red-haired Rowling still lives modestly in Edinburgh with her daughter. Her favorite writer "of all time," she told UKOLN, is Jane Austen. Not long ago, fulfilling another of her childhood dreams, she became the owner of a pet rabbit. "She is large and black and scratches me ferociously every time I try and pick her up," she told the okukbooks interviewer. "Some things are best left in the imagination." —M.R.

Suggested Reading: *Business Week* p54 Aug. 9, 1999; *National Review* p60+ Oct. 11, 1999; *Newsweek* p58+ Aug. 23, 1999, with photos; *New York Times* (on-line) Feb. 14, 1999; okukbooks.com (on-line); *People* p85+ July 12, 1999, with photos; scholastic.com (on-line); *Time* p72 July 26, 1999, p66+ Sep. 20, 1999, with photos

Selected Books: *Harry Potter and the Sorcerer's Stone*, 1998; *Harry Potter and the Chamber of Secrets*, 1999; *Harry Potter and the Prisoner of Azkaban*, 1999; *Harry Potter and the Goblet of Fire*, 2000

Rule, Ann

Oct. 22, 1935– True-crime writer. Address: P.O. Box 98846, Seattle, WA 98198; c/o Foley Agency, 34 E. 38th St., New York, NY 10016

Sometimes called the "queen of true-crime writers," Ann Rule is the author of 17 books, all but two of which were best-sellers. The most popular of her works include *The Stranger Beside Me, A Rage to Kill: And Other True Cases, Bitter Harvest*, and two—*Small Sacrifices* and *Dead by Sunset*—that were made into television miniseries. In a review of *Dead by Sunset*, Walter Walker wrote for the *New York Times* (October 22, 1995) that Rule

Courtesy of Simon & Schuster

Ann Rule

"brings to her work the passion, the prodigious research and the narrative skill to create suspense from a situation in which the outcome is a matter of fact, known to many readers before they open the book." Regarded as an expert on serial killers, Rule has testified at congressional hearings and lectured before behavioral scientists receiving instruction at the Federal Bureau of Investigation's training academy. She served as a member of the United States Justice Department task force that instituted the FBI's Violent Crime Apprehension Program (VI-CAP), which uses a computerized system to help the police discover patterns in what may appear to be unconnected crimes. In an interview with Cheryl Bartky for *Writer's Digest* (December 1992), Rule said, "I think I have a God-given instinct for people—for knowing what makes them tick and for making them come alive on the page."

Rule was born Ann Stackhouse on October 22, 1935 in Lowell, Michigan, to Chester Stackhouse and Sophie Hansen Stackhouse. Both of her parents worked at schools—her father as a football, basketball, and track coach, and her mother as a teacher for the mentally disabled. Her father changed jobs several times, forcing the family to move periodically; during her childhood they lived in Pennsylvania, Oregon, California, and New York. For 11 summers from the time she was seven, Rule stayed in Stanton, Michigan, with her maternal grandparents—who, like others among her relatives, held jobs in law enforcement. Her grandfather, Chris Hansen, was Stanton's sheriff; he and his wife lived in part of the same building that housed the town jail. In an interview with Montgomery Brower for *People* (September 14, 1987), Rule recalled that watching her grandfather in the process of solving crimes fascinated her. Her grandmother cooked meals for the prisoners, and young Ann would help by passing trays of food to them. The inmates almost always treated her well, and she often wondered what they had done to land them behind bars. "I grew up wanting to know: Why do nice, little kids grow up to be criminals?" she recalled to Angie Cannon for *women-connect.com* (May 5, 2000). By the age of eight, she knew that she wanted to be a police officer.

Rule still harbored that ambition when she enrolled at the University of Washington. Knowing that she would get good grades in writing courses, she majored in English and took classes in psychology, criminology, and penology as well. After graduating she joined Seattle's police force, where she soon learned that her male co-workers did not regard female officers as equally qualified to do the job. Speaking of herself and her female colleagues, Rule told Marie Arana for the *Washington Post* (October 17, 1999), "We were glorified caseworkers. We didn't wear uniforms. . . . If things got dangerous, we were told to call for male back-up." Nevertheless, she told Angie Cannon, "I loved that job"—"the excitement of it, . . . never knowing what was going to happen," and "being able to help people." But after a little over a year at the job, she was forced to leave, because, although she got high marks on all her written and performance tests, her extreme nearsightedness prevented her from passing the eye examination. Rule later worked as a caseworker for the Washington State Department of Public Assistance.

By the 1960s she had married Bill Rule, a high-school English teacher and former classmate of hers, with whom she had four children. After her husband took a break from his job to further his education, she began writing to support her family. By 1969 she had become a full-time writer as well as a homemaker. Having chosen to focus on real crimes, she increased her expertise by talking with officers in the homicide and arson divisions of her local police department. She gradually widened her contacts to law-enforcement personnel throughout the Northwest and slowly gained their trust. (Later, when they learned that she had become her children's sole source of support, they helped her by giving her information that they might otherwise have withheld from her.) Her work appeared in newspapers and national magazines, among them *Cosmopolitan*, *Redbook*, and *Ladies Home Journal*. She has cited the acclaimed investigative reporter and true-crime writer Thomas Thompson, whose books include *Blood and Money* and *Serpentine*, and Truman Capote, the celebrated author of *In Cold Blood*, as influential in her development as a writer.

In the early 1970s Rule volunteered during the late shift at a Seattle crisis center, answering a telephone hotline whose callers included people who felt suicidal. There she befriended one of her co-workers, a good-looking, charming 24-year-old law student named Ted Bundy, who loved gourmet food and the music of Mozart. Bundy reminded her of her younger brother, Don, who had committed suicide, and she trusted him enough to confide in him. She revealed to him that she had decided to end her marriage but that she felt guilty about doing so, because her husband had been diagnosed with a potentially fatal form of skin cancer. "On the surface at least, it seemed that I had more problems than Ted did," Rule told Deb Price for the *Detroit News* (May 6, 1996, on-line). "He was one of those rare people who listen with full attention, who evince a genuine caring by their very stance. You could tell him things you might never tell anyone else." Rule divorced her husband in 1972, and from then on she raised her children alone. (Her ex-husband died when the children were between the ages of eight and 15.) To make ends meet, she shopped at a Goodwill store and sewed clothing for her children herself. She also took night classes, in such subjects as crime-scene investigation and photography; police administration; and arrest, search and seizure, first at Highline Community College, in Des Moines, Washington, and then at the University of Washington, where she eventually received an M.A. degree in criminal psychology. For 13 years she wrote two 10,000-word pieces each week for *True Detective*, which paid her $250 per article. At the insistence of the magazine's editors, who "thought nobody would want to read a crime story written by a female," as she told Robert Lindsey for the *New York Times* (February 21, 1984), she used the pseudonym Andy Stack.

In May 1975 Rule signed a contract to write a book about a series of unsolved murders in the Seattle area. The next year Ted Bundy was linked to those murders and others, after one of his former fiancées told Utah police about the bag filled with women's clothing, plaster of Paris, and instruments of torture she had seen in his room; he was subsequently arrested on charges of killing more than 30 women in five states. Bundy, who had graduated from college with honors in psychology, was serving as a mental-health counselor and as the assistant director of the Seattle Crime Prevention Advisory Commission; he had also written a popular pamphlet on rape prevention. In addition, he had been so successful in local Republican politics that some expected him to run for the governorship of Washington State someday. Expert at masking his true personality, he had manipulated many women—including Rule—into trusting him, often tricking them by wearing a fake cast on his arm and asking for their help.

For a long time Rule could not believe that the man who had always walked her to her car at 2:00 a.m. on her crisis-center nights was capable of the savage crimes he was accused of committing. She had found him to be "young, idealistic, clean, sure, and empathetic," she told Peter Gorner for the *Chicago Tribune* (September 17, 1980). "He seemed to ask nothing but friendship." Rule's perception of him changed when Bundy was tried for beating a woman to death in a Florida State University sorority house. During the trial, which ended in 1979, prosecutors displayed photographic proof that the teeth marks found on the buttocks of the dead woman exactly matched the configurations of Bundy's teeth. "Every single one of his teeth, every little broken spot, the shape, size, everything fit perfectly," Rule recalled to Deb Price. "There was no explaining that away. It made me physically ill. I had to run down the hall and throw up."

The Stranger Beside Me (1980), which she completed after 90 days of nearly nonstop writing, chronicles Rule's friendship with Bundy as well as his trials for murder. A best-seller, the book describes the physical resemblance between each of Bundy's victims and the first of his fiancées, who had rejected him and caused him to feel humiliated. "He got her back . . . ," Rule told Deb Price. "He was in effect killing her [when he killed other women], and each time he killed her image, he felt worse instead of better. . . . He just became more and more addicted to getting rid of this empty place inside him." In the *New York Times Book Review* (August 24, 1980), Thomas Thompson described *The Stranger Beside Me* as "dramatic and occasionally as chilling as a bedroom window shattering at midnight"; in the *Saturday Review* (August 1980), Arthur Spiegelman characterized the book as "serious, balanced, and absorbing."

Rule's next book, a novel called *Possession* (1983), apparently attracted little notice. She also published three true-crime books under her pseudonym, Andy Stack: *Lust Killer* (1983), *Want-Ad Killer* (1983), and *The I-Five Killer* (1984), all of which are about serial killers and have since been reissued. Her real name appears on the cover of the highly successful *Small Sacrifices: A True Story of Passion and Murder* (1987). That book focuses on Diane Downs, who was found guilty of shooting each of her three children—killing one and seriously injuring the others. Downs had claimed that the perpetrator was a "bushy-haired stranger," but according to the prosecutors, she had been driven to murder by her fear of losing her married lover, who did not want children. The television adaptation of *Small Sacrifices*, written by Joyce Eliason and directed by David Greene, starred Farrah Fawcett and Ryan O'Neal. The miniseries won a 1989 George Foster Peabody Award, which recognizes outstanding achievement in radio and television.

In 1989 Simon & Schuster paid Rule $3.2 million for her next two books. The first, *If You Really Loved Me: A True Story of Desire and Murder* (1991), describes how David Brown, a millionaire computer expert, murdered his fifth wife, so that he could collect more than $800,000 in insurance and marry his teenage sister-in-law; he pinned the blame on his 14-year-old daughter from an earlier marriage, who spent several years in a juvenile-detention facility before Brown's guilt was discovered. *If You Really Loved Me* was followed by *Everything She Ever Wanted: A True Story of Obsessive Love, Murder, and Betrayal* (1992), about Patricia Allanson, a sociopath who attempted to poison her husband's grandparents and later trapped her spouse into unwittingly killing his mother and father, while she maintained the façade of a "modern-day southern belle." Rule's most recent books are *Dead by Sunset: Perfect Husband, Perfect Killer?* (1995), about Brad Cunningham, who for seven years escaped prosecution for the murder of his fourth wife; *Bitter Harvest: A Woman's Fury, a Mother's Sacrifice* (1998), about a Kansas physician who tried to poison her husband and set a fire that claimed the lives of two of her children; and *And Never Let Her Go: Thomas Capano, the Deadly Seducer* (1999), about a successful lawyer who was sentenced to death for the murder of his former lover Anne Marie Fahey, a secretary to the governor of Delaware.

Before deciding on the subject of a book, Rule considers as many as 500 possible cases, many of which are suggested by readers—including, in some instances, the relatives of crime victims. "When I get over three dozen messages, e-mail, letters, or phone calls [about a single case], I pay attention," she told Angie Cannon. "My readers know what I'm looking for." She has no interest in writing about high-profile cases, such as the O. J. Simpson trial. Her research includes reading newspaper accounts, interviewing both the lead detective and the prosecutor, and visiting the scene of the crime. She also attends the trial, where she makes contact with witnesses. She does not approach the accused until he or she is found guilty, because, as she told Angie Cannon, "I don't want to mess up the prosecutor's case." She explained to Cannon, "A lot of [criminals] are anxious to talk to me after they've been convicted. . . . Most of the people I write about are antisocial personalities, and they are so convinced that they're smarter than anyone else that all they have to do is just explain to a reporter or a jury what really happened." She has learned to be a good listener and to hide her feelings and opinions when interviewing a subject.

To discover as much as possible about the roots of a killer's behavior, Rule thoroughly investigates each suspect's childhood and family history. Although it is, in her words, "almost impossible" to feel sorry for the vicious criminals she meets, she told Cannon that she does "feel empathy and sympathy for the children that they were." Rule also tries to portray the victims accurately, although she sometimes omits personal details or changes people's names at the request of their families. Her books often detail the strenuous efforts of particular law enforcement officials or prosecutors who were determined to solve a case or put a murderer behind bars. "When you are dealing with the blackest side of the human soul," Rule told Cheryl Bartky, "you have to have someone who has performed heroically to balance that out." She tries to keep gore and sensationalism out of her books. "I try to be as sensitive as I can," she explained to Bartky, "and I try to think, 'Now if someone was writing about my family, . . . what would I want the writer to say?' I try to stick within those guidelines."

After writing several books about serial killers, Rule began to document the circumstances surrounding acts of violence perpetrated by women, whose motives, she realized, often differ from those of their male counterparts. "Women kill for two reasons, broadly defined: for love—and you've got to include jealousy, revenge, sex—or for money," Rule told Angie Cannon. "Women also tend to kill people they know, people who trust them, people they are very close to—their children, mother, their series of husbands. Women are willing to delay gratification for a long time. They plan their murders very, very carefully and coldly." Although the motives of sociopaths may differ, Rule learned that such people have certain characteristics in common. "These are people who have no conscience, no empathy," she told Deb Price. "They can lie with the clearest eyes and the nicest smiles. These people wear a mask that is so perfect. Where unless they choose to lift just a little piece of it, we never know that there's a monster behind."

Rule told Cannon that being a true-crime writer requires courage. "The hardest thing for me to do is to approach people who have been through so much stress and tragedy and then have the temerity to ask them to talk to me . . . ," she said. "Every time I'm amazed that people will talk to me. You have to have a compassionate heart." For many years Rule felt guilty about benefitting from the misfortunes of others, but over time she began to realize that her books had helped many people, and in some cases may have saved lives. Many of her readers are women, and some have thanked her for helping them to avoid potentially violent relationships. "I want to warn readers of the dangers—the ruses, devices, and techniques that sociopaths use to ensnare people," she told Cheryl Bartky. Rule regards her contributions to the development of the FBI's Violent Crime Apprehension Program (VI-CAP), in the early 1980s, as one "vindication for profiting from other people's tragedies," as she told Robert Lindsey.

Rule has received the Washington State Governor's Award and two Anthony Awards (named in honor of the mystery writer Anthony Boucher and bestowed at the annual World Mystery Convention), and she is a two-time nominee for the Mystery Writers of America's Edgar Award. She assists with programs that aid the victims of violent crimes and their families and also helps support groups for women and children who have been abused. She has often done book signings jointly with her best friend, the suspense writer Donna Anders, author of *Flower Man* and *Dead Silence*. A resident of Washington State, Rule lives with her two dogs and five cats. She enjoys gardening and collecting such objects as antique bottles, cobalt-blue glass, police memorabilia, wind chimes, and teddy bears. Rule's daughter Leslie has written two mysteries, *Whispers from the Grave* and *Kill Me*

Again, both of which deal with supernatural phenomena. Her other daughter, Laura, works with the elderly and with children of battered women. Her son Mike serves as her office manager and conducts interviews for the Blind Radio Network; her son Andy works in the field of consumer research. According to her official Web page, she has a third son, Bruce Sherles, whose job is in the cookie industry. Rule also has three grandchildren. — C.L.

Suggested Reading: *Chicago Tribune* I p15 Sep. 17, 1980; *Detroit News* (on-line) May 6, 1996, with photo; *New York Times* B p9 Feb. 21, 1984, with photo, VII p38 Oct. 22, 1995; *Washington Post* X p8 Oct. 17, 1999; *Writer's Digest* p27+ Dec., 1992, with photos

Selected Books: *The Stranger Beside Me*, 1980; *Possession: A Novel*, 1983; *Small Sacrifices: A True Story of Passion and Murder*, 1987; *If You Really Loved Me*, 1991; *Everything She Ever Wanted*, 1992; *Dead By Sunset*, 1995; *Bitter Harvest*, 1997; *And Never Let Her Go: Thomas Capano: The Deadly Seducer*, 1999

Andrew Eccles/Courtesy of AAADT

Rushing, Matthew

Aug. 5, 1973– Dancer with the Alvin Ailey American Dance Theater. Address: Alvin Ailey American Dance Theater, 211 W. 61st St., Third Fl., New York, NY 10023

Matthew Rushing, a member of the New York–based Alvin Ailey American Dance Theater, has often been described as one of the greatest dancers of our time. The dance specialist Joan Acocella succinctly summed up his talents when she wrote for the *New Yorker* (December 27–January 3, 2000), "There seems to be nothing Rushing can't do." In the *New York Times* (November 30, 1997), the dance critic Jennifer Dunning declared, "[He is] a superb technician whose whizzing turns and catapulting leaps have the surging excitement of modern dance and the fine-scaled classicism of ballet." Commenting on the blend of grace and athleticism for which Rushing is renowned, Robert Gottlieb wrote for the *New York Observer* (December 20, 1999), "He's both a jumper and a balancer. The dynamic and precise articulation and thrust of every gesture are riveting, and yet he's supple and lyrical. He's dapper and he's smoldering. Most important, every moment is totally focused and filled, though he never demands attention by selling himself."

Matthew Rushing was born into a deeply spiritual family on August 5, 1973 in Inglewood, California, in the Los Angeles metropolitan area. His parents were both ordained ministers, and his mother, to whom he gives much of the credit for his success, also developed Christian games and toys. Eager to keep her son off the city streets, she enrolled him in a recreational program at a local park. The program offered music, drama, and dance, the last with the All That Dance Company, directed by Ruth Ashton Black. After joining the group, Rushing told his mother, "'I really like this dance thing,'" as he recalled to Susan Elia for *Dance Magazine* (November 1999), "and, well, she knew all the stereotypes out there and all the obstacles I would have to go through, and she wanted to make sure this was what I really wanted to do. So she took me to my first performance, the Ailey Company at the Wilshire Theater."

Launched in 1958, the Alvin Ailey American Dance Theater (AAADT) is named for its founder; born in rural Texas in 1931, the dancer and choreographer Ailey studied under the modern-dance pioneer Lester Horton before forming his own troupe. Widely recognized as the most popular modern-dance repertory company on the international touring circuit, AAADT is best known for works that, drawing upon the African-American experience and musical idioms as well as classical ballet, celebrate the richness of black history and culture and American modern-dance tradition. According to alvinailey.org (on-line), AAADT operates under the auspices of the Dance Theater Foundation, which also oversees its junior company, Ailey II (formerly the Alvin Ailey Repertory Ensemble); the Ailey School, which offers a B.F.A. (bachelor of fine arts) degree program in association with Fordham University, in New York City; and a program called Arts-in-Education, in which young Ailey dancers share their expertise with schoolchildren. Matthew Rushing was 12 or 13 when he first saw members of Alvin Ailey perform. He was close enough to hear the dancers breathe, and the dancing "mesmerized" him, as he put it to

Elia. "I remember leaving and thinking, 'If that's possible for me to do, I want to do that,'" he told Marc Shulgold for the *Denver Rocky Mountain News* (March 31, 2000). "Being in Ailey was my goal. There was no question."

Rushing attended the Los Angeles County High School for the Performing Arts, a two-hour commute from his home. Located on a campus of California State University, the school was among the first of its caliber in the Los Angeles area. At Arts High, as it is familiarly known, Rushing studied choreography and many forms of dance. He continued to dream of working with Alvin Ailey, and he was devastated when Ailey died, in 1989. "I was really hurt, even not knowing him," he said to Elizabeth Zimmer for the *Village Voice* (December 10, 1997). "My grades started to fall. One of my teachers choreographed a solo for me to vent all the hurt; I can honestly say it did the job." Rushing told Susan Elia, "I can't describe to you how [Ailey] affected my life. I remember, in high school I was so overwhelmed by his talent, by his vision, by his company that I actually memorized all the dancers' bios in the program and memorized a hundred names of dancers, past and present, with the Ailey company. My teachers were really supportive of my dance career; if I finished my schoolwork early, they would let me go to the chalkboard and write all the one hundred names. That's just an example of how much I loved this man."

While in the 11th grade, Rushing flew to Berkeley, California, to audition for a place at the Ailey School, which is headed by Denise Jefferson. He won not only a full scholarship but also membership in Ailey's junior company, directed by the former Ailey dancer Sylvia Waters. In 1991 Rushing received the highest honor awarded by the president of the United States to students graduating from high school: he was named a Presidential Scholar—specifically, a Presidential Scholar in the Arts. He also earned the Spotlight Award from the Los Angeles Music Center. Just before his high-school graduation ceremony that year, he flew to New York to begin studying at the Ailey School. "I knew no one and I was on my way to pursuing my dream," he said to Elia. "It was exciting, but it was really scary." Most dancers remain in Ailey II for two to four years, but Rushing's talent was so apparent that he left in 1992, after only one year. He was not yet 20 when Judith Jamison, a renowned Ailey dancer who had taken over the artistic directorship of AAADT after Ailey's death, elevated him to the senior company. Speaking of his move, Rushing told Marc Shulgold, "I had a lot of doubts at the beginning. I wondered, 'How can I fit in?' Plus I had a great lack of experience. But [Jamison] and the dancers accepted me with open arms. Miss Jamison really helped direct my career."

In a statement sent to *Current Biography* in June 2000, Jamison described Rushing as "a remarkable young man." "He possesses a sense of humility that mirrors his artistry," Jamison wrote. "To be so young and so committed to one's craft is a special gift. Matthew generously shares his unique talents with both his colleagues and audiences around the world. He has accomplished so much at such an early age and has received many wonderful accolades from those who are lucky enough to see him perform. It is a genuine pleasure to work with Matthew and I am so pleased he continues to share his journey through life with the Alvin Ailey American Dance Theater."

In 1995 Jamison assigned him his first solo, in Garth Fagan's piece *Jukebox for Alvin* (which the company had premiered in 1993)—a performance that Rushing regards as pivotal in his career. Another pivotal experience came in 1996, when the troupe toured South Africa. "There are certain times when things come together—the energy from the audience, the energy from everyone else on the stage—and a magical and spiritual thing happens," Rushing observed to Elia. "And that happened in South Africa—not just for me, but for a lot of the dancers. This is where our ancestors came from."

One of the pieces in which Rushing performed in South Africa was *Revelations*, arguably Ailey's best-known and best-loved work. Created in 1960, the multi-part dance is choreographed to a rousing selection of gospel songs and spirituals, among them "Fix Me, Jesus," "Wade in the Water," and "Rocka My Soul." *Revelations*, which rarely fails to receive a thunderous reception from audiences, was one of the pieces that the Ailey dancers had performed when Rushing first saw them. In 1999 Jamison assigned Rushing the lead male role in the "Wade in the Water" section of *Revelations*. "Since I first saw the company, I've always wanted to do that part," he told Elia. "For eight years, I waited. I would actually pray at night to do that role! . . . My identity is in *Revelations*, just as it's in the Ailey company. I'm a very spiritual person; it's a huge part of me. So when I finally danced it, it was so innate it needed no explanation. I learned the steps, and the steps and the music told the story. Whenever I dance it, it's like the ultimate form of self-expression." Although the company's program frequently includes *Revelations*, since it is an audience favorite, Rushing told Elia, "I'll never get tired of doing *Revelations*, no matter how many times I do it. And I'll be honest: Sometimes you're really tired—your body and mind and your spirit are fatigued. But once you hear that music, it's so uplifting and inspirational that it sets you up and you have all this energy and you're ready to go out there and just explode."

Each year Rushing tours with AAADT both internationally and domestically; the U.S. performances include a December season at City Center, in New York. Despite occasional fatigue, Rushing considers it his professional responsibility to give his all every time he performs. "For me to go onstage only halfway prepared, and for me to not commit myself 100 percent—I would feel like I was cheating myself and I'm cheating the audience," he explained to Elia. "And sometimes you really just don't feel like it, because you're tired or you have your own problems, but the audience doesn't care if your hamstring is pulled; they don't care if you just had an argument. The only thing they see is you out there onstage. So how could you cheat them or yourself?" Given the rigors of professional dancing and the injuries that dancers frequently sustain, many dancers—and many aficionados of the art—believe that they are underpaid. In the *Village Voice* (December 10, 1996), Guy Trebay pointed out that at that time, the salary of the basketball player Dennis Rodman was about 180 times more than Rushing's. "I can't explain to you how hard it is to do this job," Rushing said to Elizabeth Zimmer. "It's amazing to watch basketball and football, and know the players' salaries—apart from all the endorsements of Wheaties and tennis shoes—and know my own. And we have to buy foot tape, our own practice clothes, massages, pay gym fees. We're fighting for more money, but it's a slow process." Still, Rushing encourages young people to dance and has acted as mentor to several students in his capacity as teacher at the Ailey School. With the goal of preparing them for possible full-fledged membership in the troupe, he has choreographed works for the young dancers, pushing them to try steps and movements that they might not have otherwise. But Rushing has noted that it takes more than technical ability to become an Ailey dancer. He told Marc Shulgold, "Alvin always choreographed ballets about real people. And his work needs to be danced by real people."

While many critics persist in describing Rushing and his talent in almost superhuman terms, he has consistently deflected such praise, preferring to view himself simply as someone who has been blessed with a supportive family and helpful colleagues. He considers his talent, too, a blessing. "I guess I'm OK with all the attention," he told Shulgold. "But what I do is not just me. It's a gift from God. Give God the glory." — M.R.

Suggested Reading: *Dance Magazine* p62+ Nov. 1999, with photos; *New Yorker* p138+ Dec. 27–Jan. 3, 2000, with photo; *New York Times* II p32 Nov. 30, 1997, with photo; *Village Voice* p97 Dec. 10, 1996, with photo

---

Courtesy of NBC

Sassa, Scott

1959– Television executive. Address: NBC, 3000 W. Alameda Ave., Burbank, CA 91523; NBC, 30 Rockefeller Plaza, New York, NY 10112

In 1999, the year he turned 40, Scott Sassa was named president of NBC West Coast, the highest-ranking position within the NBC television network. Sassa came to NBC in 1997 to head NBC Television Stations, and a little more than a year later, he was named president of the network's entertainment division. Early in his career in the television industry, which began when he was in his early 20s, Sassa helped start up the Fox network. Celebrated as a "cable-programming prodigy," he worked for the Turner Broadcasting System for nine years, during which time he launched seven networks in as many years. "Scott is one of the hardest working, most talented people in the business," the longtime NBC executive Don Ohlmeyer, who became Sassa's mentor, said to John Dempsey for *Variety* (January 7, 1991). "He makes things happen." As president of NBC West Coast, Sassa serves in effect as the network's top programmer.

A third-generation Japanese-American, Scott Michael Sassa was born in 1959 in California. He grew up in Torrance, an industrial city in Los Angeles County. In high school he was caught smoking marijuana and was suspended. He later enrolled at the University of Southern California, in Los Angeles, where he was the "yell leader" for the cheering squad. In *Fortune* (February 1, 1999), Patricia Sellers reported that he left college "a few credits short of a degree." After quitting school he worked briefly for Rogers & Cowan, a public-relations agency. Then, in 1982, he became the director of sales promotion at Turner Broadcasting Systems (TBS). Just over a year later, he became vice president/general manager of TBS's ill-fated Cable Music Channel. After the music channel folded, he was hired by the Playboy Channel. Thanks to a string of minor successes that he compiled at Playboy, industry insiders began to take notice of his abilities, and in 1985 he won his first full-fledged executive position, at the upstart Fox

Network. Sassa, whom an NBC bio describes as "the first person hired by Fox," helped the network launch its operations, in 1986. "The Fox Network wouldn't have come off the way it did if it wasn't for Scott," Jamie Kellner, a former Fox executive, told John Dempsey. "He's young, aggressive, driven, and not locked into the old-fashioned way of doing things."

Although Sassa is credited with formulating what amounted to the Fox Network's financial blueprint in its first years and handled its advertising, promotions, operations, and administration, Barry Diller, who then headed Fox, eventually fired him. "He was in over his head," according to Diller, as paraphrased by Sellers. His dismissal devastated Sassa. "I just got killed," he told Richard Turner for *Newsweek* (November 9, 1998, online). "I was too young to go through that." Diller later regretted his action. "Firing Scott was one of my supreme mistakes," he told Sellers. In any event, Sassa quickly bounced back: he got a job with Don Ohlmeyer, who, at the time, ran his own business, Ohlmeyer Communications. Ohlmeyer had gotten to know Sassa after Fox had commissioned his company to produce the Emmy Awards telecast, and the two had become close. Sassa served as Ohlmeyer Communications' vice president of new business development.

In about 1988 Sassa left Ohlmeyer to return to Turner Broadcasting, but he and Ohlmeyer maintained their relationship. Indeed, Ohlmeyer aided Sassa in his first big assignment at Turner, namely, building Turner Network Television (TNT), where he held the title of executive vice president, into a force within the cable industry. In what some observers described as a risky creative endeavor, Sassa guided the production of high-quality made-for-television films, among them *Cold Sassy Tree*, starring Faye Dunaway and Richard Widmark and produced by Ohlmeyer. To lure advertisers and viewers, Sassa used other big-name stars as well, among them Val Kilmer, Farrah Fawcett, and Ben Kingsley, and a logo that read "The Best Movie Studio on Television." Within a few years TNT began getting higher ratings than had been thought possible for a cable-television station. The venture eventually spurred TNT competitors—notably Home Box Office (HBO) and NBC—to undertake in-house movie-production projects themselves.

Earlier, in the late 1970s, Ted Turner had begun to amass an archive of cartoons. The archive grew considerably in 1991, when he purchased Hanna-Barbera's cartoon library, which consisted of such classics as *The Jetsons*, *The Flintstones*, *Yogi Bear*, and *Scooby-Doo, Where Are You?* The next year he launched the Cartoon Network, the first 24-hour all-cartoon channel. In addition, in 1985 he had purchased MGM's prized library of 3,300 films, most of which were made in the 1930s, 1940s, and 1950s and which included such classics as *Gone with the Wind*, *Casablanca*, and *Citizen Kane*; in 1994 he launched Turner Classic Movies. Sassa's success with TNT led Turner to appoint him to prominent positions with both the Cartoon Network and Turner Classic Movies. Contrary to the predictions by many industry insiders that the two networks would fail, as of 1999 both were running at a profit. Sassa also helped Turner to expand into major motion-picture production. Although Turner Pictures' first full-length movie, *Michael* (1996), starring John Travolta, was a critical disappointment and did poorly at the box office, it earned a respectable sum through video sales and rentals. Sassa was also in charge of other Turner subdivisions, among them Turner Home Video, Turner Publishing, Turner New Media, and Turner Licensing and Merchandising. In addition, he was responsible for operations and programming for Turner's international entertainment networks in Europe, Asia, and Latin America. He became a major decision-maker at Turner, and for the most part, he answered only to Ted Turner himself.

In mid-1996 Turner agreed to merge TBS with Time Warner. As a member of a seven-person steering committee, Sassa assisted with the nuts and bolts of the consolidation, and according to Sellers, he lobbied vigorously to be named Turner's second-in-command. "Scott is good at self-promoting, and there's nothing wrong with that," Turner said to Sellers. "He wants to get to the top. I wanted to get to the top too." But Turner chose Terence F. McGuirk, TBS's executive vice president, for the position, and in response, Sassa resigned. Commenting on his departure, Jessica Reif (now Jessica Reif Cohen), an entertainment-industry analyst at Merrill Lynch, told Bill Carter for the *New York Times* (September 17, 1996), "I think it's a very significant loss for Turner. [Sassa is] one of the brightest executives in the entertainment business. He has a ton of operating experience, a great track record, and he's very young. You don't want to lose young executives like that."

In October 1996, only weeks after he left Turner, Sassa was named chairman and CEO of the comic-book giant Marvel and appointed to the newly created positions of president and chief operating officer of Marvel's parent company, the MacAndrews Group, a unit of MacAndrews & Forbes Holding. Marvel had brought him on board to strengthen its entertainment, publishing, and toy businesses and had identified one of his missions as the development of feature-length films based on Marvel's comic-book characters—among them Spider Man, the Hulk, and Captain America—ventures that in the past had not been profitable. But these projects never got off the ground, because Sassa arrived in the midst of a fierce battle for control of Marvel. The combatants were two powerful financiers—Ronald O. Perelman, who owned 80 percent of Marvel stock, and Carl C. Icahn, who owned 25 percent of the company's bonds and had become the leader of a group of dissident Marvel bondholders. In late December 1996 Marvel declared bankruptcy, and in June 1997, after a court ruling in favor of the bondholders, Icahn and his allies booted Perelman from the board of directors. Sassa, meanwhile, had found himself devoting his time to matters connected with the bankruptcy proceedings and the Perelman-Icahn imbroglio. "Scott was a champ," Perelman said to Sellers. "He could have quit, but he stuck with it and proved himself a real standup guy."

In late August or early September 1997, Sassa did quit. Although, as various media reporters pointed out, he had no experience in operating a television station, General Electric, which owns NBC, hired him as the president of NBC Television Stations, which was then a group of 11 local "owned-and-operated stations," as they are known in the trade, that accounted for an estimated $500 million in annual revenue. After Sassa took over, two more stations were added. Little more than a year later, in October 1998, Sassa was promoted to president of NBC Entertainment, with the understanding, as the network announced publicly, that he would move to an even higher position—that of chief of West Coast operations—by the end of 1999, when Don Ohlmeyer, the occupant of that post, was expected to leave. Commenting on his promotion, Sassa told Bill Carter for the *New York Times* (October 27, 1998), "I've developed animated shows, I've developed television movies. I've developed theatrical motion pictures. I've even developed a comic book. But I've never developed a network series. I'm curious to learn the process." Robert C. "Bob" Wright, the president and CEO of NBC, reportedly regarded Sassa's inexperience in that facet of the television industry as an asset. "We have to break away from the traditional network-type show," Wright declared to Sellers. "We need breadth." John F. "Jack" Welch Jr., the chairman of General Electric, told Sellers that to become more successful, NBC would have to develop "more complicated business relationships." "Scott can do that," he said. "He has a lot of runway to do a lot of things."

When Sassa took the reins as head of NBC Entertainment, the network was "healthy overall," Patricia Sellers reported; moreover, as she pointed out, it was "the only network earning a profit." Nevertheless, NBC had suffered some serious blows. In 1997, thanks to such highly popular programs as *Seinfeld*, *ER*, and *Friends*, NBC had made a handsome profit. But in 1998 NBC's earnings had begun to drop substantially, largely because of Jerry Seinfeld's decision to conclude his series at the end of 1998. More damage stemmed from the loss of broadcasting rights to National Football League games, hefty increases in the licensing fees for *ER*, *Mad About You*, and National Basketball Association games, and the continuing flight of viewers to cable channels. In *Forbes* (March 8, 1999), Robert La Franco reported that NBC's prime-time viewership had dropped 17 percent in the previous 12 months. In light of all that bad news, Tom Wolzien, an analyst for the investment firm Sanford C. Bernstein, expressed the view that Sassa had accepted "a thankless job." Wolzien remarked to Sellers that, in effect, NBC had told Sassa, "Here, the network is tanking. Have a nice day."

In January 1999, speaking during a Television Critics Association press tour, Sassa admitted that, in its current crop of sitcoms, NBC had failed to reach out sufficiently to "traditional families" and to minority groups; moreover, it had placed too much emphasis on sex and had relied too heavily on New York City settings. "We need to make sure the shows we have on the air are accurately reflecting the composition of the audience we're serving," he said, as reported by Jenny Hontz in *Variety* (January 18–24, 1999). "People like to see themselves on TV." He also said that, while he had no intention of reshaping NBC into a "family channel," its sitcoms "could use a few more words between 'Hello' and 'Will you sleep with me?'" Sassa guided the development and production of prime-time series for the 1999–2000 season, among them *Third Watch*, *The West Wing*, *Law & Order: Special Victims Unit*, *Freaks and Geeks*, *Stark Raving Mad*, *Cold Feet*, and *The Mike O'Malley Show*. (Although it earned critical acclaim, *Freaks and Geeks* has been canceled, as have the next three shows listed.)

In May 1999, according to his official NBC bio (other sources give different dates), Sassa succeeded Ohlmeyer as head of NBC's West Coast operations. He reports directly to Bob Wright and is responsible for overseeing all of NBC's entertainment-related businesses. In one of his first actions in his new position, he recruited Garth Ancier, who had compiled an impressive record of hit shows for teenagers at Time Warner's WB network, for the job of president of NBC Entertainment. In August Sassa made another major hire, with the addition of Ted Harbert, the former top entertainment executive at ABC, as president of NBC Studios, the network's in-house television production unit.

Shortly before, on July 29, again addressing journalists from the Television Critics Association, Sassa had acknowledged that NBC's prime-time offerings lacked racial balance, and he had urged television writers and others in the industry to strive for "meaningful" diversity. "There is diversity and there is meaningful diversity," he said. "You not only want to see someone that looks like you on TV, you want to see someone that is a role model, someone that you want to be with, someone that you want to be like. That's what we need to do: Create diversity models for people, role models that are diverse, that make people in these minority groups feel good." "I don't know that I'm qualified to tell you how African-Americans or Latinos feel about how they're portrayed or what they see on television," he continued. "But I can tell you how I feel about seeing Asian Americans portrayed on television. I've got to tell you, seeing David Carradine as a Chinese guy [on *Kung Fu*] pissed you off."

In conversations with Patricia Sellers, Ted Turner described Scott Sassa as "brilliant," Ronald Perelman called him "a networker in the best sense," Barry Diller noted his "very good instincts," and Jack Welsh—who insisted that he wasn't exaggerating—said, "I never interviewed anyone I liked more." — M.B.

Suggested Reading: *Broadcasting and Cable* p87+ Oct. 28, 1996, p10 Nov. 2, 1998, with photo; *Fortune* p30+ Feb. 1, 1999, with photo; *Mediaweek* p5 Sep. 8, 1997, with photo; *Newsweek* (on-line) Nov. 9, 1998; *New York Times* D p6 Sep. 17, 1996, D p2 Sep. 5, 1997, with photo, C p1+ Oct. 16, 1998, with photo, C p6 Oct. 27, 1998, C p1+ Nov. 2, 1998, with photo; *U.S. News & World Report* p56 Nov. 9, 1998, with photos; *Variety* p67 Jan. 7, 1991, with photo, p7+ June 16–22, 1997; *Wall Street Journal* B p7 Oct. 24, 1996, B p1+ Oct. 27, 1998; *Wired* p110+ Mar. 1995, with photo

---

Courtesy of MicroStrategy

Saylor, Michael

Feb. 4, 1965– Co-founder and CEO of MicroStrategy, Inc. Address: MicroStrategy, 8000 Towers Crescent Dr., Vienna, VA 22182-2700

"At the core of every great movement is the articulation of a grand utilitarian design," Michael Saylor told *Red Herring* (June 1, 1998, on-line). "Ours is that information flows like water, and we want to use it to purge ignorance." Saylor is the CEO and co-founder of MicroStrategy, a leading software company that aims for the eventual streamlining of all telecommunications, so that businesses and consumers can obtain instantaneous information, or "real-time" updates, on their health and financial status, among other aspects of their lives. This will be achieved, Saylor believes, through the customization of data-mining software, such as MicroStrategy's decision-support systems software. "My principal professional objective is to introduce Intelligence as the ubiquitous utility," Saylor told Harry Jaffe for the *Washingtonian* (March 2000). "I'd like to be the Thomas Edison of intelligence." Currently MicroStrategy boasts more than 900 corporate clients and sends out 200,000 real-time alerts to its customers every day.

Saylor sees a parallel between the innovations of Thomas A. Edison—the American inventor of the incandescent electric bulb, the phonograph, and many other electric-powered devices—and his own creations, which include the MS Telecaster, an instrument that transmits information directly from data warehouses to telephones. Citing the example of General Electric, which grew out of the various companies started by Edison and built the dynamos that deliver electricity to millions, Saylor hopes to "see a world where we have universal intelligence, and that will mean 10,000 intelligence dynamos," as he told Daniel Roth for *Fortune* (May 24, 1999). "There ought to be dynamos everywhere, spinning data, always delivering the right information to the right person. I want to know when . . . my boat is smacked or my equities are in trouble or the government's unstable and something has happened to my hometown. I think that people will surrender their personal information to a centralized intelligence dynamo . . . because the cost of not doing so is an early death, an accidental death, a lack of an opportunity, a lack of income, a lack of happiness." Sanju Bansal, the co-founder of MicroStrategy, told *Electronic Business* (January 1999) that Saylor is a "phenomenal synthesizer of information" with a near-photographic memory. "Mike believes at his core that people should have access to information and be able to synthesize information because he himself can do that."

Saylor's passion for ideas and innovation often manifests itself in sweeping, almost evangelical public proclamations. "I think my software is going to become so ubiquitous, so essential, that if it stops working there will be riots," Saylor told Larissa MacFarquhar for the *New Yorker* (April 3, 2000). "I'm on a mission from God, and if you don't buy from me we're all going to hell. I mean that literally. I mean that people will die this year because they didn't buy my software. . . . I feel that if I don't succeed it's an abomination in the eyes of God."

Michael Saylor was born on February 4, 1965 in Lincoln, Nebraska. His father was a noncommissioned air force officer, so Saylor grew up on a series of military bases around the world. Saylor told Harry Jaffe that his father was "the kind of guy that was absolutely, 100-percent straight. I can't remember a single time in my life where my father ever said an untruth or tried to slide by with a half effort. . . . My father taught me character. My mother taught me charisma." During high school Saylor lived on the Wright-Patterson Air Force Base in Dayton, Ohio; he was a National Merit

Scholar and graduated first in his class. A voracious reader, he enjoyed science fiction and was particularly affected by Robert Heinlein's *Have Space Suit—Will Travel,* a novel about a high-school senior who travels beyond the planet Pluto to save the human race from a monster. When the boy returns to Earth, he is rewarded with a full scholarship to the Massachusetts Institute of Technology (MIT). "So it stuck in my mind that really cool people go to MIT to build spaceships," Saylor told Jaffe.

Saylor entered MIT as a nuclear-engineering major, his tuition paid for in full by an ROTC scholarship. "I had a volatile personality, kind of incendiary," he told Harry Jaffe. "I'd walk into a group of people, and they'd all split—like nuclear fission." Saylor's intensity earned him the nickname "Nuclear." One source of the inspiration for MicroStrategy was a class on systems-dynamics theory that he attended with his roommate and fraternity brother, Sanju Bansal. Saylor and Bansal learned that social and business problems could be modeled using nonlinear math, a revelation that completely changed the way they looked at business and inspired their later work in data-mining software. Before Saylor completed his studies, he wrote a thesis for MIT's Sloan School of Management, for which he created a mathematical model of the book *Discourses*, by the Italian political philosopher Niccolò Machiavelli (1469–1527). In 1987 Saylor graduated with honors, earning dual degrees—one in aeronautics and astronautics and the other in science, technology, and society. Although he had been accepted to the air force's prestigious jet-pilot program, a routine physical exam revealed that he had a benign heart murmur, and the military grounded him. When defense cutbacks placed him in the reserves, he found himself, only two months before graduation, with no job lined up.

But this setback proved temporary. For a time after his graduation, Saylor designed computer-simulation models for a company in New York, but he left when he was asked to sign an agreement not to work for competing companies. He then offered his services to DuPont Chemical, in Wilmington, Delaware; there, he built a global computer model for the company's titanium business. After finishing the project in only 18 months, he asked DuPont to allow him to stay on as an independent contractor. The company paid him $250,000, a portion of which he and Bansal (who had earned a master's degree in computer science) used to co-found MicroStrategy, in 1989; Saylor was then 24. "We had similar views of the world," Bansal recalled to Chuck Salter for *Fast Company* (April 2000). "We realized that the information used by corporate decision makers was incredibly shallow. We believed that we had a better way: Set up a system that's continuously being fed lots of information from a company's operation, then apply rigorous mathematics to the data. To run a business successfully, you have to make better business decisions than your competitors. And you can do that by applying carefully analyzed information to the process."

A small group of employees worked long hours for comparatively little pay, investing their trust in Saylor's vision, and in 1991 MicroStrategy, based in Wilmington, introduced its first software to the market. The next year the company acquired a $10 million contract with McDonald's to track the effectiveness of the fast-food company's promotional campaigns. In 1993 Saylor coined the term Relational On-line Analytical Processing (ROLAP); this referred to the use of large relational databases in performing decision-support analysis, a method of gathering and analyzing information that enables the user to find answers to very specific questions. ROLAP paved the way for MicroStrategy's Intelligent E-Business program, a series of products aimed at rapid information processing. In 1994 Saylor and Bansal moved the company from Wilmington to Tyson's Corner, Virginia, and began hiring people to create decision-support systems (DSS) software. (For the first three months that they were in Tyson's Corner, Saylor slept on his friend's couch. Eventually he bought a house a few yards away from his partner's; because he was so busy, three years passed before he furnished it.) MicroStrategy Web was a DSS program that saved corporations money because it required no client hardware, software, or technical support. "We want to addict people to our technology like crack cocaine," Saylor told *Red Herring*. "The same thing will happen with information that happened with the telephone: people will decide they can't do without it." According to an industry publication, the *OLAP Report,* MicroStrategy was the ninth-largest maker of DSS software in 1995; four years later, it was fourth. By that time, the company had settled in Vienna, Virginia.

In June 1998 MicroStrategy went public, making Saylor a billionaire overnight. He reviewed 500 prospectuses before deciding on an unusual deal, in which MicroStrategy's 11 founding executives and employees got 10 votes for every share they owned, while new stockholders received only one vote per share. This strategy enabled Saylor to maintain control over the company, of which Bansal owned 14 percent. In less than a year, the company's stock rose from $7 a share to $333. Saylor's ownership of 44 million shares ensured that every time the stock went up one dollar, he made $44 million. "When I became a billionaire on paper, then all of a sudden my ability to get to meetings to gain influence increased by an order of magnitude," Saylor told Harry Jaffe, "whereas if I was just a millionaire or a multimillionaire—well, they're a dime a dozen."

MicroStrategy's reported annual employee turnover rate is approximately 10 percent, extremely low for a high-tech company. Many of the executives at MicroStrategy are in their mid- to late 20s; top jobs are awarded on the basis of merit. New employees must complete a six-week, six-day-a-week, 16-hour-a-day "boot camp." Every quarter Micro-

Strategy shuts down for company outings, and in the winter, Saylor takes all his employees on a cruise in the Caribbean. "Our culture is part intellectual, part military, part fraternity, part religion," he told Janet Novack for *Forbes* (September 7, 1998). Saylor's unfailing energy fuels the speeches he traditionally delivers at boot camp; one of his monologues went on for more than eight hours. "Mike gets a little excited about the company," Bansal explained to Sherri Dalphonse for the *Washingtonian* (February 1998). "Those people came out at two in the morning a bit dazed. But Mike can go two, three days with little food and an hour of sleep."

Saylor promotes the notion of "intelligence everywhere," or a consolidation of all of the telecommunications devices businesspeople and consumers rely upon every day. To realize this goal, in 1998 MicroStrategy developed MS Broadcaster, which delivers "personalized, mission-critical information directly from data warehouses to common communication devices, such as cell phone, pager, and fax," according to the company's Web site. MicroStrategy also provides a data-sifting service that analyzes enormous databases so that customers can call up very specific information in a matter of seconds. For example, MicroStrategy once assisted the women's apparel company Victoria's Secret in discovering that stores in New York sell 20 times more size-32 bras than shops in other cities. "Knowing what's selling and how fast it's going lets you plan ahead of the competition," Bansal told Chuck Salter. "The beauty of that kind of information is that it eliminates the inefficiencies of any process: You don't order products that aren't selling. You don't advertise items that are out of stock. You control your system." According to *Forbes* (September 7, 1998), the company's programs provide far more detailed analysis of databases than do larger competitors, such as Oracle and Microsoft. "Everyone's always wanted to do this, but to do it well requires that you collect 100 million to a billion pieces of information," Saylor explained to Sherri Dalphonse. "Until '93 it was prohibitively expensive to collect that data." Today MicroStrategy's list of clients includes Nike, Johnson & Johnson, Giant Food Inc., KMart, Visa, Hallmark, and AT&T.

Saylor hopes to become the information-providing intermediary between consumers and the corporations and agencies that sometimes take advantage of their trust. Of course, those consumers would be required to transfer their trust to MicroStrategy, at least enough to give the company access to highly personal records in exchange for an understanding of the options available to them. He recently called for the auctioning off of the federal government's databases, including those containing information about Medicaid and Medicare. "Information is like mineral or land rights," he told Glenn R. Simpson for the *Wall Street Journal* (January 3, 2000). "If you wanted to get a chain reaction going in medicine, you auction off rights to mine it and harness it, and sell intelligent medicine back to 100 million people." His critics argue that customers are already concerned about the privacy of their medical records and that Saylor's proposal, if implemented, would constitute a further invasion of their personal lives. The same information employed to afford customers more choices could also work against them if it fell into the wrong hands, those critics point out. Saylor believes that ignorance costs people millions of dollars every year, and that simple comparison shopping can lead them to better rates on life insurance, home mortgages, and other necessities. With his software, bank customers can monitor their accounts on a real-time basis. "When Alan Greenspan announces a rate change, there ought to be 37 million people doing something with that information," Saylor told *Business Week* (December 1, 1999, on-line). "But the reason finance people want a relationship with you is . . . whenever you're asleep, stupid, or on vacation, die accidentally, or you're ignorant or you're afraid or insecure, in all those circumstances, they make money. When you're asleep you're not thinking about how you're only getting 3% on your savings account." Saylor also envisions MicroStrategy's software being used as a form of high-tech insurance that can inform a user when his or her house is on fire, for example. "What are you afraid of?" he asked Larissa MacFarquhar. "I'm afraid of missing my plane. I'm afraid I'll be outside when there's a crime in my neighborhood. Even if you're not afraid of these things, the beauty is, with proper marketing, we can make you afraid."

Saylor sees his software as the answer to many common concerns, including highway gridlock and law enforcement. He recently met with Virginia governor Jim Gilmore to demonstrate ways in which databases could be used to predict traffic patterns. "All the arteries in our civilization are clogged," he told Larissa MacFarquhar. "We just don't know they're clogged, because they've been so bad for so long that we've stopped thinking about it. When I say 'Intelligence everywhere,' what I mean is, I want to purge every single piece of waste and inefficiency from every single industry on the planet." Saylor wants to develop a device that would whisper customized information directly into the customer's ear, a proposal that reminds Saylor's critics disturbingly of Big Brother, the omnipresent government surveillance force prophesied in George Orwell's 1949 novel *Nineteen Eighty-four*. "I can't imagine anyone who would want a chip implanted behind their ear that lets an organization track and talk to them that frequently," Joel Reidenberg, an information privacy expert and Fordham University law school professor, told Harry Jaffe. "It's an Orwellian vision come to life. It's astonishing for civilized people."

In March 2000 Saylor announced his plans to pledge $100 million of his own money to establish an on-line university that would be free to all and feature on-line lectures from accomplished professors as well as world leaders. Soon after he made this announcement, the Securities and Exchange Commission, enforcing stricter accounting scrutiny, found that MicroStrategy had overstated its revenues in order to increase its status in the market. After the company restated its financial results for the years 1997–99, its revenue dropped by 25 percent, immediately transforming $12.6 million in profit for 1999 into a loss of $40 million. In one day, Saylor's personal wealth decreased by $6 billion. The value of MicroStrategy's stock dropped 62 percent, from $226.75 to $86.75. "There's no doubt this is a bump in the road," Saylor told Adam Zagorin for *Time* (April 3, 2000), "but we signed up to change the world and never believed it was going to be easy."

As of mid-summer 2000, Saylor was worth $7 billion. Recognized as one of the technology industry's leading visionaries, he was named the Ernst & Young software entrepreneur of the year in 1997, and *Red Herring* listed him among the Top 10 Entrepreneurs of 1998. He has been profiled on many television news programs, including CBS's *60 Minutes* and PBS's *Charlie Rose.* MicroStrategy won the Data Warehousing Institute Award for best practices in data warehousing in 1998 and the next year was named one of the 12 most influential companies by the Information Technology Industry.

Saylor enjoys the study of architecture and history, counting Abraham Lincoln and Winston Churchill among his greatest influences; his thirst for knowledge drives him to read constantly. "When trying to solve a problem or think creatively, I find that the more you know, the easier it is to avoid getting stuck in a rut," he told Shannon Henry for the *Washington Post* (March 18, 1999, online). "Often I will draw from political theory, Roman history, architecture, military theory, chemistry, etc. to solve a business problem. Thus, keeping an open mind is critical."

Saylor remains single, his schedule leaving very little time for socializing. Bansal told Jeff Glasser for the *Washington Post* (July 15, 1996) that his friend and partner decided that "women are an incredible time sink. . . . Work is more enjoyable for him in that it is a growing experience. Dating's a fluff experience for him." In spite of his long hours and aggressive business practices, Saylor insists that being rich is not his primary goal. "At this point for me to actually appreciate the money, I would have to quit my job, and of course, the paradox is if I quit my job, the stock would crash," he told Harry Jaffe. "So I'm effectively on this gerbil wheel, this treadmill, and you've got to run faster and faster. . . . My obligations have escalated as fast, if not faster, than the money." — C.L.

Suggested Reading: *Business Week* (on-line) Dec. 1, 1999; *Electronic Business* p34+ Jan. 1999; *Fast Company* p190+ Apr. 2000, with photos; *Forbes* Sep. 7, 1998, with photos; *Fortune* May 24, 1999, with photos; *New Yorker* p34+ Apr. 3, 2000, with illustrations; *Time* p86 Mar. 27, 2000, p66 Apr. 3, 2000; *Wall Street Journal* Jan. 3, 2000; *Washington Post* (on-line) July 15, 1996, Mar. 18, 1999, with photos, F p10 June 7, 1999; *Washingtonian* p35+ Feb. 1998, p51+ Mar. 2000, with photos

---

Scardino, Marjorie

1947(?)– CEO of Pearson PLC. Address: Pearson PLC, 3 Burlington Gardens, London W1X 1LE, England; Pearson Inc., 1330 Ave. of the Americas, Seventh Fl., New York, NY 10019

"Pearson has set the pace for British stodginess—the prototypical furledbrolly pinstripe-and-watchchain type of firm, dominated by the same titled family that founded it in 1856," Bonnie Angelo wrote for the *Columbia Journalism Review* (May/June 1997), in describing the corporate culture of that British media-and-entertainment conglomerate. Pearson's own Web site boasts that the company's rise to prominence in the late 19th century "is a story of Britain at the height of her power and influence." When Marjorie Scardino became CEO of the venerable firm, in January 1997, she became not only the first woman ever to head Pearson, but also the first to head *any* of the top 100 firms on London's stock exchange. Her appointment was all the more remarkable since she was not a native Briton but had been born and raised in Texarkana, Texas. Before she took the helm of Pearson, Scardino had been a journalist as well as the CEO of the Pearson-affiliated Economist Newspapers Ltd.

Scardino, who was born Marjorie Morris in about 1947, has described her childhood in that east Texas town as fairly typical. The British press often identifies her as a former barrel racer, referring to her participation in a rodeo event in which a female rider negotiates a series of tight turns around a set of obstacles, but she has explained that that was a pastime of many girls growing up in Texarkana in the 1960s. After graduating from Texas High, in 1965, Scardino received a bachelor's degree from Baylor University, in Waco, Texas, and began law school at George Washington University, in Washington, D.C. She dropped out in 1970, however, to pursue a job in journalism. Hired by the Associated Press office in Charleston, West Virginia, to take dictation, she rose rapidly to the position of desk editor. There she met a young reporter named Albert Scardino. Although she reportedly disparaged his writing skills at first, the two became romantically involved. Together they

Dith Pran/New York Times

Marjorie Scardino

moved west, where they were married. Scardino completed her law degree at San Francisco University.

In 1978, the couple moved to Savannah, Georgia, Albert's native town. While there, Marjorie Scardino worked briefly on a shrimp boat off the coast of Georgia, a fact that the press mentions almost as often as it does her barrel-racing trophies. Eventually she found work at a Savannah law firm, a position she took solely to have a steady source of income; journalism remained her passion. "Desk editing! That's what God meant me to do," she told Bonnie Angelo. Pooling their savings, the Scardinos purchased a failing weekly paper, the *Georgia Gazette*, with the aim of serving the community. Scardino had learned from her grandfather, a liberal Democrat, to sympathize with the underdog, and as publisher and sometimes reporter for the *Gazette*, she began a crusade to expose government corruption. "We played a part in putting 35 public officials in jail, from the clerk of court to the state labor commissioner," she told Angelo. Although Albert's editorials won a 1984 Pulitzer Prize—the first awarded to a weekly publication since the 1960s—the financial picture at the newspaper was bleak. Circulation rarely rose above a few thousand, and the paper's editorial slant alienated many of its conservative advertisers. In 1985, just a year after being awarded the Pulitzer, the *Georgia Gazette* folded, leaving the Scardinos with $250,000 in debts that would take them a full decade to pay.

Thanks in part to the prestige of the Pulitzer, Albert was hired as an editor by the *New York Times*, and later in 1985 the couple moved to New York City. (His job at the *Times* would be followed by a high-profile stint as press secretary for New York mayor David Dinkins.) Marjorie Scardino searched for a job in the city by contacting headhunters; when any of them questioned her about the recent failure of the *Gazette*, she responded emphatically that she had learned more from that failure than from any success. She was sent by a headhunter to the offices of the *Economist*, a highbrow British financial magazine, owned in part by Pearson PLC, that focused on the free-market policies then adopted by the administration of President Ronald Reagan. Due to a misunderstanding, Scardino ended up waiting in the lobby for 20 minutes, while David Gordon, then the CEO of the Economist Newspapers Ltd., waited in his office. When the two finally met, they laughed about the mishap and immediately developed a rapport. "My view was that she had extraordinary human qualities and talent," Gordon told Laura Colby for *Fortune* (March 16, 1998). Furthermore, he considered the failure of the *Georgia Gazette* to be "one of those searing experiences that either makes or breaks you." Gordon hired Scardino as the managing director of the *Economist*'s North American division. The magazine had already started a marketing push in North America, but under Scardino's direction circulation soared from 100,000 readers to more than 230,000 by 1992, making the United States its largest market. She targeted her audience, a select group of affluent businesspeople, very carefully—devising a series of catchy slogans and plastering them wherever those businesspeople gathered: bus stops, train stations, and airports. She arranged for free copies of the magazine to be given out at shuttle terminals in Boston, New York, and Washington, D.C. The red-and-white *Economist* logo became instantly recognizable, the price of a subscription rose to $85 a year, and the magazine began selling red-leather daily planners emblazoned with the logo. These diaries quickly became status symbols, earning substantial profits for the company. Scardino used those profits to acquire other properties for the company, including *CFO* magazine; *Roll Call*, a Washington-based weekly; and the Business International publishing company.

In 1992 Gordon left the Economist Newspapers Ltd. to run Independent Television News, a British television network, and Scardino was asked to come to London to replace him as worldwide CEO, a position she kept for four years. Not all of her professional decisions during that period were profitable ones. In 1995 she purchased the *Journal of Commerce*, a daily American publication focusing on the shipping industry. When asked by Bonnie Angelo why she had bought the daily, she replied, "I couldn't afford the *Wall Street Journal*," and added that she would love to edit that New York–based publication herself. Despite her boldness, profits at the paper dropped steadily—from $5.5 million in 1996 to $3.5 million just a year later. Circulation dropped by 10 percent, and management was forced to lay off 65 workers. David

Gordon, her former boss, defended Scardino to Laura Colby, saying, "The *Economist* finds it quite difficult to make large acquisitions. It took us years to turn around Business International, and the *Journal of Commerce* clearly isn't turned around yet." Yet the *Economist* was profitable enough to make up for an occasional slow performer, and during Scardino's tenure, earnings more than doubled, while worldwide circulation of the magazine increased by more than 20 percent.

Meanwhile, for Pearson PLC, a 50 percent owner of the *Economist*, 1996 was proving to be one of the most difficult years in the company's 140-year history. There was increasing pressure from stockholders to change the company's strategy to increase earnings. In addition to the *Economist*, Pearson was part or sole owner of a host of disparate properties, including an Australian soap company, a game show, and several medical and sports-related publications. Although several of its holdings were considered prestigious—among them, the Penguin Publishing Group, Madame Tussaud's Waxworks, and the Lazard banking empire—many felt that the firm was spread too thin and needed greater focus on select industries. In recent years Pearson had divested itself of certain properties, such as Chateau Latour Wines, Royal Doulton China, and an oil-service company, and used the profits to acquire more holdings in education, information, and entertainment, which were considered strong areas for the firm; still, the company's bottom line had yet to improve. In the first half of 1996, Pearson had purchased a California-based CD-ROM firm, Mindscape, for $465 million—an investment that failed so miserably that it caused a 31 percent drop in group operating profits, despite the fact that Pearson's profits from other ventures had risen by almost 25 percent. Shareholders doubted Pearson's ability to thrive in a fast-paced global environment, in part because of the Mindscape debacle and in part because of the company's reputation for being antiquated.

In an attempt to remedy the situation, late in 1996 Pearson announced that Scardino would be made CEO of the entire $3.5 billion conglomerate, upon the retirement of then-CEO Frank Barlow, at the end of the year. The news was not greeted with universal approval. Most stockholders had been hoping for a tough-minded outsider to reshape the firm, and since Scardino had been at the *Economist* for nearly 12 years by then, she was seen as a Pearson insider. Many also doubted that she had the experience to run an operation of Pearson's magnitude. On the day of the announcement, the firm's share prices fell by 18 cents, to $10.69.

At the same time, there were those who considered Pearson a breath of fresh air. After her appointment, journalists flocked to interview her, and most of their reports concentrated on her down-to-earth style. She often appeared in public wearing a baseball cap, which, along with her rodeo and shrimp-boating experiences, was taken as proof that she was the ideal candidate to counteract Pearson's stuffiness. On her first day as CEO, on January 8, 1997, she sent all 17,000 Pearson employees an E-mail message, peppered with colorful American slang, to introduce herself. (She has continued to send similar E-mails explaining all major corporate decisions and is said to be delighted to get feedback from employees at any level.) She immediately announced—unsurprisingly, given her background—that she would be focusing on the firm's journalistic and media holdings and would continue to sell off many of the non-media properties. Her first major decision as CEO was to invest $160 million over a five-year period in the *Financial Times*, one of Pearson's most prestigious publications and one that many analysts felt had been neglected by the firm's old guard. The paper, although well respected, was selling only about 32,000 copies of each issue in the U.S. when Scardino took over, and she hoped to at least triple that figure by the end of the five years. Despite a catchy ad campaign (one current slogan reads, "There are 143 countries in the world. All of them have money"), the paper faces stiff competition from the *Wall Street Journal* and the *New York Times*, both firmly established among readers looking for global financial news.

Scardino's first large purchase as CEO was All American Communications Inc., a California-based producer of game shows and other TV programs, for which she paid $513 million. She hopes to earn royalties from television stations worldwide from the company's shows, which include *Baywatch* and *The Price Is Right*. Since her appointment Scardino has also acquired the Simon & Schuster education, reference, and business publishing divisions, an animation company, and an on-line publishing group. She has disposed of Mindscape, the Tussaud's Group (owners of the famed waxworks), and the Lazard investment group, among other concerns. The direction in which she is steering the company has been met for the most part with approval. Pearson's stock price has more than doubled since her appointment, and she has promised that the company will continue yearly double-digit growth. Referred to fondly as "our Marjorie" by the *Texarkana Gazette*, Scardino was named one of the most important Texans of 1999 by *Texas Monthly* magazine. That year she was also named the fourth most influential woman in England by *Good Housekeeping*, on a list in which Queen Elizabeth II ranked 89th. Scardino is on the board of directors of ConAgra Inc. and W. H. Smith & Sons PLC, as well as a number of charitable and advisory groups. She is an honorary fellow of the London Business School and has won awards from both the Women's Economic Roundtable and the New York City Partnership.

Scardino and her husband, who is now a writer and lecturer, have three children, Adelaide, Will, and Hal. The youngest, Hal, who was born in 1984, is an actor; he starred in the film *The Indian in the Cupboard* and appeared in *Searching for Bobby Fischer* and *Marvin's Room*. Scardino makes a point of taking her children's phone calls no matter what she's doing, and she feels that her work has not affected the quality of her relationships with them. Although she reportedly earns more than $1 million a year, much of it in performance-based bonuses, the family lives relatively simply in central London. Scardino often returns to Texas to visit her mother and recently attended a ceremony at Texas High, during which she was named distinguished alumna. Despite her apparent lack of artifice, Scardino is said to have cunningly manipulated the stereotypes that many Americans hold about Britons—for example, by promoting the "snob appeal" of the *Economist* to class-conscious U.S. businesspeople. She has just as cannily taken advantage of the preconceptions held by Britons. "I think it's a great advantage to be a women and to be a Texan," she told Lisa Bose McDermott for the *Texarkana Gazette* (September 5, 1999, on-line). "Because you know Texans have this image in everyone's minds that is bigger than what we are or really doesn't have anything to do with what we are and so they don't know quite what to think of you." — M.R.

Suggested Reading: *Columbia Journalism Review* p44+ May/June 1997, with photo; *Fortune* p102+ Mar. 16, 1998, with photos; Pearson Web site; *Texarkana Gazette* (on-line) Sep. 5, 1999; *Texas Monthly* (on-line) Sep. 1999

Tim Chapman/*Miami Herald*

Schapiro, Miriam
(shuh-PEER-oh)

Nov. 15, 1923– Artist; educator. Address: c/o Steinbaum Krauss Gallery, 3550 N. Miami Ave., Miami, FL 33127

For three decades, through her paintings, drawings, collages, and sculpture, Miriam Schapiro has created woman-centered art that often strays outside the bounds of what is generally considered to be feminist terrain. "Every woman has the right to interpret her feminism on her own," she told Barbara Delatiner for the *New York Times* (June 11, 2000). "There shouldn't be one agenda. Each woman, each artist, should work out her own agenda, just as I have." For Schapiro, that "agenda" has involved the celebration of aspects of female experience, such as child rearing and household chores and crafts, that she feels are undervalued by other feminists as well as by the larger, patriarchal society. To that end, in the 1970s she began working on feminist collages, or "femmages," in which she combines paint with such items as potholders and handkerchiefs to form homages to an unsung side of womanhood. "I just wanted to say that this is part of the female world and we don't have to be embarrassed about it," Schapiro told Dorothy Seiberling for *New York* (July 12, 1976).

Schapiro, recognized internationally as one of the originators of the feminist-art movement in the early 1970s and as a leader of the pattern-and-decoration movement, began mounting exhibitions of her expressionist paintings in the 1950s, before developing—with the artist Judy Chicago—a program in feminist art at the California Institute of the Arts in Valencia. In recent years many of her paintings and collages have alluded to Jewish themes or functioned in part as tributes to female artists of the past. One characteristic of her art "is an open kindness," as Paul Richard wrote for the *Washington Post* (May 11, 1997), discussing an exhibit of Schapiro's work at the National Museum of American Art. "[Her works] seldom wag the angry finger; when they scold they do so gently. Entering their spaces is like entering Mom's kitchen— the room, full of treats, is orderly, scented and warm. What's consistent in these paintings is their authentic generosity. Here, take some, they keep saying, feed your mind and feed your eye." Richard also observed, "You don't have to read feminist critical theory, or even be a woman, to appreciate Schapiro's art."

Miriam Schapiro was born on November 15, 1923 in Toronto, in the Canadian province of Ontario, to Theodore and Fannie S. (Cohen) Schapiro. Her father, an artist and industrial designer, initiated her training in art while she was young. Early on, Schapiro began imitating her father's practice of cutting from old magazines reproductions of the works of great artists and placing them in scrapbooks. "My father was a socialist and I was raised with a sensible attitude about humanism," Schapiro explained to Barbara Delatiner. "My feminism grew out of that humanism, a belief that men were in as much trouble as women were when it came to being victimized." Schapiro was raised in New York City, where she particularly loved studying dance with Nita and Lola Rohm. The lessons were held in an immense studio across from a branch of the Brooklyn Public Library, and Schapiro has said that she developed her sense of space by dancing across the floor of the large room. Moira Roth noted in the College Arts Web site that a love of space and dance is expressed throughout Schapiro's work.

Schapiro spent two years at Hunter College (now a division of the City University of New York) before transferring, in 1944, to the State University of Iowa to major in graphics; there, she studied with Maurizio Lasansky. She received a bachelor of arts degree from Iowa in 1945 and continued working under Lasansky as his graduate assistant. In 1946 she received a master's degree in printmaking. She began exhibiting her prints at the Brooklyn Museum, the Art Institute of Chicago, the Walker Art Center, and many colleges, while she extended her study to painting, earning a master of fine arts degree in 1949. In 1957 Schapiro was included in the New Talent Exhibition at the Museum of Modern Art, in New York City. Two years later her work was featured in the Whitney Biennial, and from 1958 to 1971 she had seven solo shows at the Andre Emmerich Gallery, in New York. Between 1953 and 1957 Schapiro created a large body of work that represented her interpretation of Abstract Expressionism, then the dominant form of painting. "For her," Thalia Gouma-Peterson wrote in *Miriam Schapiro: Shaping the Fragments of Art and Life* (1999), "painting was gesture and motion, 'substitutes for the physical act of dancing.'" Schapiro referred in the journal she kept at the time to "automatic stroking," or her method of painting in unpremeditated fashion, which "engaged her unconscious in the process of painting" in the tradition of the surrealist painters of the 1920s and the 20th-century American artist Jackson Pollock. This practice, she felt, added spontaneity and freshness to her work. Gouma-Peterson quoted Schapiro as saying that in the 1950s, the work of Pollock and the 16th-century Italian painter Jacopo Robusti Tintoretto "spoke to me. Tintoretto was the dense, many layered stage with people advancing and receding. Pollock was the chance to move across this stage at my own speed." In these early paintings by Schapiro, "there are . . . allusions to recognizable imagery, usually human figures, embedded in the abstract network of brushstrokes," as Gouma-Peterson noted. Examples are *Homage to Rubens* (1953) and *Idyll # 1* (1956).

At the same time, as Gouma-Peterson wrote, figuration—or the use of clearly defined figures and shapes—had "both overtly and covertly . . . been significant in her work" since her time as a graduate student at the University of Iowa. As the 1950s progressed, this strain in Schapiro's work became stronger. This was due in part to her eventual conviction that the style of Tintoretto and Abstract Expressionism "had completely excluded her as an an artist," according to Gouma-Peterson. "She wanted to articulate in her paintings a personally relevant content that would speak to the realities of her life." Thus by about 1958 Schapiro "was moving to simplified forms with an underlying geometric structure and a symbolic meaning. She said, 'I wanted to become stylistically clearer, to put new order in my work.'" As a result, in the 1960s she began creating hard-edged, geometrically structured, intensely colored canvases, such as *Painting City* (1966), *Byzantium* (1967), and *OX* (1967). Many have detected in her work references to Cubism, the art movement originating in Paris in 1907, which analyzed three-dimensional subjects through fragmented and redefined planes.

In 1971 Schapiro joined the staff of the California Institute of the Arts in Valencia. She told Barbara Delatiner that in California, "I had my epiphany and realized what I had to do was interpret feminism in my own way; that how you expressed yourself was based on all of your experience from the very beginning. I had the same life, the same experiences that everyone else had, and the parts of a woman's life that I love gave me satisfaction." In Valencia, along with the artist Judy Chicago, she developed a feminist art program that sought to address the self-esteem of women—which she and Chicago believed had been damaged by patriarchal culture. The two women received national attention in 1971 for *Womanhouse*, a collaborative environment designed with students in the program. *Womanhouse* is a "still-discussed whole-house installation with its breast-strewn kitchen and its 'Menstruation Bathroom,'" according to Paul Richard.

Schapiro collaborated with Sherry Brody on *Dollhouse* for the *Womanhouse* exhibit. That three-dimensional structure combines "the beauty, charm, and supposed safety and comfort of the home with the unnameable terrors existing within its walls," Schapiro told Linda Stein for *Fiberarts* (March/April 1998). Schapiro told Dorothy Seiberling that she had worked on *Dollhouse* in order to express "the woman side of my life that I had always shut out when I walked into my studio. I had excluded my role as an wife and mother—the nestmaker who tried to make things beautiful in order to de-escalate the dreariness of household maintenance."

During this time, Schapiro began to travel around the U.S., speaking on feminist art and encouraging the work of female artists. Her activities earned her the nickname "Mimi Appleseed." Arlene Raven observed in the *Women's Review of Books* (February 2000) that Schapiro "has eased the way for more female artists to assume a place in the contentious environment of the gallery system. One of the very few to be included before the

1970s, Shapiro did not guard her territory. Instead, she has been a generous mentor to women of three generations."

During her 1976 show in the spacious Andre Emmerich Gallery, in New York City—where she had returned to live the previous year—Schapiro became unhappy with how small her paintings looked on the wide walls of the gallery. She decided to create large representations of kimono robes in order to claim the space around her and to address the "question of territory," as she told Stein. Schapiro said that in the 1960s women found it difficult to claim physical space for themselves, which was symptomatic of a general lack of self-esteem. To comment on this issue further, she painted a series of fans—"a woman's object, the fan, the flirtatious little fan, which can be seen as trivial . . . and I heroicized it," Schapiro told Stein. She made each fan painting six feet by 12 feet "in those fabulous days of the 1970s, when we were just starting to think in terms of feminist art," as she told Stein. "I felt that by making a large canvas . . . I could raise a housewife's lowered consciousness," she is quoted as saying on the Albany Museum Web site.

As she gained more recognition, Schapiro continued collaborating with others. She was one of the founding members of a group of artists, including Joyce Kozloff and Valerie Jaudon, who spearheaded the pattern-and- decoration (P&D) movement, receiving critical attention in the mid- and late 1970s. Schapiro coined the term "femmage" (an amalgamation of "female" and "collage") to describe the painting and collage techniques she combines to represent women's craft traditions, such as quilting, embroidery, and sewing. In her work she elevates these crafts from routine household chores to fine art. "We saw craft as a bridge to a new democratized art of the future," Schapiro told Stein, in describing the movement. She collected pieces of fabric, doilies, potholders, or napkins from audiences when she spoke and later used them in her works. "When you look at this painting," Paul Richard quoted Schapiro as saying, "I want you to think about the ordinariness of handkerchiefs, how women used them to soak up their tears. . . . The grid is there in my painting so you can think about the form, the handkerchief so you can cry."

Since 1970 Schapiro has struggled to "erase the line between high art and craft," in Linda Stein's words. "Craft belongs to women," Schapiro explained to Stein. "That's how it's been designated. Our culture insists that ornamentation and decoration are innately female. But unfortunately, it then follows that what is female is considered inferior." As an example of an alternative to this scenario, she pointed out, "Eastern and Islamic cultures don't feminize their decorative arts. What is done here is sexist as well as racist. The binary concept of fine art being above craft is false." Schapiro also uses domestic images and symbols "to push the limits of sentimentality, to test how far I can go with it because it's such a taboo subject," she continued. Opening her new phase, she used floral decoration, geometric patterns, and an abundance of the color pink in *Garden of Paradise*, to explore how these "female" components had been trivialized.

Schapiro was excited by what she calls "geometry and flowers," or the combining of opposites, which, she has noted, the Chinese and Japanese have practiced for ages. In the future, Schapiro feels, the technology of the P&D movement, such as computer graphics and animation, will continue the trend of fusing different arts, such as music and film, as well as the different "ranks" of the creative process: craft and high art.

Schapiro has written that her art often attempts to tackle such questions as "how did women live, what did they do, what did they think about, where did their hearts lie, what kind of art did they make? . . . Meaning in my work can be about timely interests or it can be about painting qua painting . . . or it can be both: the whole enchilada," she said, according to Richard. After Judy Chicago wrote that from her perspective, feminist art is not for an audience with sophisticated tastes in art, Richard suggested that this stance might be the reason for the eventual end of the two artists' collaboration: Schapiro is not afraid of either sophistication or, at the other extreme, sentiment. For her, the paramount issue is "quality in art."

In 1987 Schapiro accepted the challenge to create art in what was, for her, a new form. *Anna and David*, her 1,200-pound, 35-foot-high aluminum sculpture, was installed in front of an office building in Roslyn, Virginia. The J. W. Kaempfer Corp. commissioned the work and arranged for it to be placed in an area of modernist high-rise buildings; the sculpture was built at Tallix Foundry, in Beacon, New York. The work's two, monumental figures dance on a flat, circular, grassy mound. The sculpture required a team of Swiss and U.S. engineers to position it on its three points. In contrast with traditional sculpture, which can be viewed in the round, *Anna and David* has two flat planes, a front and back, clearly inspired by the French artist Henri Matisse's *Dance* (1909–10). Schapiro developed it from her 1986 painting *Pas de Deux*, which J. W. Kaempfer Jr., a commercial builder and art collector, had seen and liked. *Pas de Deux* was part of "I'm Dancing As Fast As I Can," a series of paintings of dancing figures in cabaret-like contexts representing a "theater of life." In the paintings the dancing figures are deemphasized and weakened by the richly decorated surroundings, especially when compared with the figures reproduced alone for sculpture, according to Norma Broude, who reviewed the paintings and *Anna and David* in *Art in America* (February 1991). Schapiro told Broude that her goal in making sculpture was "to make a work of very high energy, charged energy, so that people walking by it, if they connect with it, would be recharged." *Anna and David* is representative of a new "user-friendly" kind of public sculpture, "sensitive to the issues of siting, scale, content and public response," according to Broude. But the sculpture is still strong, "criticiz[ing] its environment," as Broude wrote, with its vivid colors standing in contrast to the corporate buildings that surround them.

Many of Schapiro's recent paintings feature a grid with a rooflike triangle on top, suggesting a dollhouse. In some, different kinds of dolls are painted, each against a patterned or bright surface; in others, baby dolls, African statues, and Amerindian dolls are photocopied and made to fit into the grid spaces, with some of them touching one another across the grid. In a biographical work, Jewish ceremonial objects, a voter-registration-drive flyer in Yiddish and English, Nazi graffiti in several languages, and photos from the "Old Country"—Eastern Europe several generations ago—are all multilayered together. Schapiro has used Jewish references in certain pieces since 1996, to signify Jewish identity and culture rather than religious convictions, she has said.

During the 1990s Schapiro explored her relations with female artists of the past. In a series of paintings collectively called "Frida and Me," she focused on Frida Kahlo, the Mexican painter who inspired her. The collage *Portrait of Frida Kahlo* recalls the artist's habit of dressing in brightly colored, patterned, traditional Mexican clothing. Schapiro mixes her "femmage" bits of fabric and swirls of paint to evoke the arts and tropical flowers and plants of Mexico. In addition to the Frida Kahlo paintings, she has explored the work of Mary Cassatt. Another series pays tribute to revolutionary female artists of early 20th-century Russia. In 1997 Schapiro produced the painting and collage piece called *Father and Daughter*, acknowledging for the first time in her art her father's role in her development.

Schapiro has written two books: *Women and the Creative Process* (1974) and *Rondo, An Artist's Book* (1988). Her work has brought her six honorary doctoral degrees and numerous other awards, among them a National Endowment for the Arts Fellowship, a Ford Foundation Fellowship, a Guggenheim Fellowship, a Skowhegan Medal, a Rockefeller Fellowship/Bellagio, and the Women's Caucus for Art award. Schapiro's exhibit "Works on Paper—a 30-Year Retrospective" began touring in 1999. Schapiro and her husband, the painter Paul Brach, have a son, Peter. — V.K.

Suggested Reading: *Art in America* p72+ Feb. 1991 with photos; *Fiberarts* p35+ Mar./Apr. 1998 with photos; *Washington Post* G p1 May 11, 1997; Gouma-Peterson, Thalia. *Miriam Schapiro: Shaping the Fragments of Art and Life,* 1999

Selected Works: *Homage to Rubens*, 1953; *Painting City*, 1966; *Byzantium*, 1967; *OX*, 1967; *Anna and David*, 1987; *Alexandra and Me*, 1994; *In the Heat of the Winter*, 1994; *Una Furtivo Lacrima*, 1995–96; *Father and Daughter*, 1997

Selected Books: *Women and the Creative Process,* 1974; *Rondo, An Artist's Book*, 1988

Schiffrin, André

June 12, 1935– Co-founder, director, and editor in chief of the New Press. Address: New Press, 450 W. 41st St., 6th Fl., New York, NY 10036

"When you let the market determine what you're going to publish, then there are all sorts of victims; and often it's the books that at a later date will become important works. . . . Cultural conservatism and financial pressures tend to reinforce each other, and the culture is the poorer for it," the publishing icon André Schiffrin told Calvin Reid for *Publishers Weekly* (January 13, 1992). In an era when the publishing industry is largely controlled by corporations and multinational conglomerates, and self-help books and ghostwritten celebrity profiles crowd the shelves of chain booksellers and best-seller lists, Schiffrin has become recognized as a leading champion of serious publishing and a passionate advocate for maintaining the editorial independence of quality publishers. To some observers he is an anachronism, a throwback to the decades when publishing was distinguished from brazenly commercial enterprises and was dominated not by corporate managers focused solely on the bottom line but by men and women who loved books.

Schiffrin, whom David Streitfeld described in *Book World* (March 18, 1990) as "obsessed with books," was on the staff of Pantheon Books from 1962 until 1990, serving there as editor and then editor in chief before being named managing director, in 1969. His forced departure from Pantheon made headlines and triggered a protest march in which many world-renowned authors participated. In 1992 Schiffrin co-founded the New Press, which publishes books that describe and analyze existing social conditions—works that are not usually considered commercially promising but are important nevertheless, in his view. During his long and illustrious career, Schiffrin has published the works of many social theorists and other respected writers, among them Simone de Beauvoir, Noam Chomsky, Julio Cortázar, Marguerite Duras, Michel Foucault, Jean-Paul Sartre, George Kennan, R. D. Laing, Gunnar Myrdal, Ralph Nader, and Studs Terkel. In "Bottom Line or Public Interest? Serious Publishing in the Age of Conglomeracy," which appeared in 1999 in *Logos*, a periodical for

New York Times Photo

André Schiffrin

people in the book industry, Schiffrin wrote, "If we look at the books that have had important cultural, social, or political impact in the U.S. today, we find that a large number of them come from independent houses where public service is seen as part of a publisher's duty."

André Schiffrin was born on June 12, 1935 in Paris, France, to Jacques Schiffrin and Simone (Heymann) Schiffrin. The family immigrated to the United States in 1941. Jacques Schiffrin, who had founded the distinguished publishing company La Bibliothèque de la Pléiade in Paris, served from 1943 until his death, in 1950, as the editor and vice president of production at Pantheon Books, Inc., a prestigious publishing house founded in 1942 by the German émigrés Kyrill S. Schabert and Kurt and Helen Wolff. André Schiffrin grew up immersed in literature. As a teenager he held summer jobs at Pantheon, and according to David Streitfeld, he "knew about the list [of books published by Pantheon] the same way another boy would know the stock of his father's candy store." Helen Wolff told Streitfeld that she sent André a copy of every book that Pantheon published. "We always thought André would be the right person to carry on," she said. Schiffrin attended Yale University, in New Haven, Connecticut, where he received a B.A. degree in history, summa cum laude, in 1957, and was named a member of the honor society Phi Beta Kappa. He then studied at Clare College, a division of Cambridge University, in England, as a Mellon fellow (1957), with a Fulbright travel grant (1958–59), and as an honors scholar (1959). He was the first American to edit *Granta*, the school's literary journal. (In 1979 *Granta* severed its ties to Cambridge.) Schiffrin earned an M.A. degree from Cambridge, with first-class honors, in 1959.

For the next four years or so, Schiffrin worked in New York for the publishing house New American Library. In 1962 he joined the staff of Pantheon; purchased by Random House the previous year, the company was known as the American publisher of various classics of European literature, among them *The Tin Drum*, by the German writer Günter Grass, and *Doctor Zhivago*, by the Russian writer Boris Pasternak. In 1963 Schiffrin became Pantheon's editor in chief, and in 1969 he became the firm's managing director. Under his leadership the company introduced many European writers to an American audience, and it was noted for publishing serious works on social and political theory. Meanwhile, in 1965, Random House had been purchased by the RCA Corp. In 1980 the company changed hands once again; this time the buyer was Advance Publications, which is owned by the billionaire publishing magnate Samuel I. Newhouse Jr. In 1987 Random House purchased Schocken Books, which specializes in Judaica, and Schiffrin was made its head.

In late February 1990 Schiffrin was forced to resign, amid controversy concerning Pantheon's fiscal health and editorial direction. According to Madalynne Reuter in *Publishers Weekly* (March 16, 1990), in most years Pantheon, which accounted for 3 percent of Random House sales, either broke even or lost hundreds of thousands of dollars—substantially more than that in some years. Precisely what led to Schiffrin's departure, on March 15, has never been disclosed, partly because a clause in Schiffrin's contract forbade him from revealing such matters publicly. The media reported that, in a move driven by Random House's efforts to increase profits across the board, the team of professional managers brought in by Newhouse had ordered Schiffrin to reduce his staff and to cut by 60 percent the number of books Pantheon planned to publish in the upcoming season. Schiffrin refused to comply, and his conflict with Random House higher-ups proved irreconcilable. Four of Schiffrin's five senior editors left Pantheon with him to register their dismay over Random House's business tactics, and the fifth eventually followed suit.

To the chagrin of Random House executives, the circumstances surrounding Schiffrin's exit caused an uproar in publishing circles. Soon after he left, an estimated 350 to 500 writers—among them Studs Terkel, Kurt Vonnegut Jr., and E. L. Doctorow—and other protesters picketed outside Random House's headquarters. Their reaction reflected their belief that publishing had become tainted by corporate greed and the quest for ever-increasing profits; to some, Schiffrin was a martyr who represented everything that they considered worthwhile in publishing. Madalynne Reuter quoted Terkel as saying that he would no longer publish with Pantheon. "André Schiffrin is the man responsible for all my books," he declared. "His imagination, his spark, his encouragement, his inspiration, is what did it." Such world-renowned writers as Nadine Gordimer, John Hersey, William Styron, Arthur Miller, and Amy Tan signed a protest ad that ran in various publications. The board of directors of the American Booksellers Association released a statement expressing alarm about the events at Pantheon, as did 16 European publishers, who called Schiffrin "one of the most respected persons in the international publishing world" and declared, "That he will no longer be the head of Pantheon is a severe blow to the standard of American publishing." Helen Wolff told David Streitfeld, "I'm deeply sorry to see that a gifted publisher who comes from such a publishing milieu, whose father was a publisher, who has devoted his life to books, should be treated as if he were a shirt-dealer." An editorial by John F. Baker, the editor in chief of the weekly trade publication *Publishers Weekly* (March 9, 1990), described what had happened as a "sad moment in American publishing history." After noting that through the years Pantheon had built up a list of authors and books "of which any publisher could be proud"—one that did not lack humorous fare and so-called escape reading—he declared that Pantheon's "50-year publishing history" was, "unhappily, all too rare in an American book business increasingly dedicated to the superficial and transitory. Pantheon published nothing trivial or merely fashionable, nothing contemptible or money-grubbing; it was always a shining example, to those critics who complained of conglomerate publishing, of how sophisticated work could still flourish in its context. Now it seems as if perhaps those critics were right: that big-money publishing cannot tolerate important, exciting work that does not always reap instant profits."

Erroll McDonald, who was named executive editor and vice president of Pantheon under Fred Jordan, Schiffrin's successor, had a strikingly different view of the course of events. In an op-ed article for the *New York Times*, according to Roger Cohen in the *New York Times* (September 25, 1990), McDonald wrote that he considered the protest over Schiffrin's resignation evidence of the pervasive "welfare mentality" that led writers to believe that "their own cultural and political passions" should be "subsidized by philanthropy." The protesters "seemed to be saying they deserved money by virtue of their sheer brilliance regardless of their accomplishment." Moreover, he told Roger Cohen, the goal of a publishing company "is to make money by publishing books that have value—to make money for the authors and for Pantheon." According to Streitfeld, some of Schiffrin's colleagues at Pantheon accused Schiffrin of "act[ing] as though he had permission to lose money."

After leaving Pantheon, Schiffrin set his sights on creating a publishing company that would serve the public interest by printing books that might be ignored or overlooked at a larger, more commercially oriented publishing house. He envisioned it as analogous to the Public Broadcasting Service (PBS), in the realm of television, and National Public Radio (NPR), in that it would serve the public interest and thus adopt an approach qualitatively different from those of for-profit publishing houses. "Publishing in the public interest means publishing books because they are inherently important, not for financial reasons," Schiffrin told Liz McMillen for the *Chronicle of Higher Education* (June 23, 1993). "This was the case we made to foundations." In January 1992, along with Diane Wachtell, a former Pantheon editor, he co-founded the New Press, a not-for-profit publishing house, and began functioning in offices provided by the City University of New York. His venture was financed by more than a dozen foundations and philanthropic organizations, among them the John D. and Catherine T. MacArthur Foundation, the Rockefeller Brothers Fund, and the Andy Warhol Foundation for the Visual Arts. Profits that accrue to the New Press go not into the pockets of the owners but into whatever is required for publishing more books. Asked why he chose nonprofit status, Schiffrin told Jim Bencivenga for the *Christian Science Monitor* (January 9, 1992), "The structural change is essential." "With increasing conglomerate control of publishing, it seemed essential to create a new structure for publishing books with important, new ideas, books often rejected by the large houses as 'risky' or 'insufficiently profitable,'" he added.

In 1992, in its first year of operation, the New Press published *Race: How Blacks and Whites Think and Feel About the American Obsession*, by Studs Terkel; *AIDS Agenda: Emerging Issues in Civil Rights*, a compilation of writings about AIDS and civil rights edited by Nan D. Hunter and William B. Rubenstein; *Early Black Photographers 1840–1940*, a book co-published by the Schomburg Center for Research in Black Culture and edited by Deborah Willis-Thomas; *Japan at War: An Oral History*, by Haruko Taya Cook and Theodore Failor Cook; and *Slaves Without Masters: The Free Negro in the Antebellum South*, by Ira Berlin. Among its later titles are *Failed Transitions: The Eastern European Economy and Environment Since the Fall of Communism* (1993), by Roger Manser; *If I Could Write This in Fire: An Anthology of Literature from the Caribbean* (1994), edited by Pamela Maria Smorkaloff; *The Pink Glass Swan: Selected Essays on Feminist Art* (1995), by Lucy R. Lippard; *Mexican Lives* (1994), by Judith Adler Hellman; *Banishing the Beast: Sexuality and the Early Feminists* (1995), by Lucy Bland; *Try This at Home! A Do-It-Yourself Guide to Winning Lesbian and Gay Civil Rights Policy; An ACLU Guidebook* (1996), by Matthew A. Coles; *The Spears of Twilight: Life and Death in the Amazon Jungle* (1996), by Philippe Descola; *Paul Robeson* (1996), by Martin B. Duberman; and *Sensible Justice: Alternatives to Prison* (1998), by David C. Anderson. One of the New Press's steady sellers is a book and tape set of major Supreme Court hearings; among its best-selling books is *Lies My Teachers Told Me: Everything Your American History Textbook Got Wrong*

(1994), by James W. Loewen, which Schiffrin has described as "a long and detailed study comparing the 11 most widely used American history high school textbooks."

In his own writings for the public, which have appeared in various periodicals, Schiffrin has railed against the increasing monopolistic trends in the publishing industry and the resulting decrease in diversity in published books. He has cited the merger in 1998 of Random House and Bertelsmann, a global multimedia and entertainment firm, as an example. In its latest incarnation, Random House accounts for about 30 percent of trade books that are published in the U.S.; in 1998, Schiffrin reported in *Logos* (vol. 10, no. 1, 1999), "more than 40 percent of all bestsellers in 1998 came from houses now under the Bertelsmann-Random House conglomerate umbrella." In the same article he wrote, "Publishers bought by media conglomerates with vast holdings in newspapers, magazines, television, and cable are no longer evaluated against the norms of book publishing, but are required to bring in profits comparable with those generated by the information and entertainment media." "Book publishing in North America and Europe has changed more in the past decade than in the preceding 100 years, and not—so far—for the better," he declared. "A major cause of the decline is the number of publishing houses absorbed by conglomerates whose managements have no experience—and often little interest—in books. These conglomerates are both the embodiment and the very vehicles of the new global capitalism, whose unquestioned goal is to maximize profits throughout the world." Schiffrin has also argued that this development is ultimately poor business. In the *Nation* (July 5, 1999), he wrote, "In a few years, these conglomerates have managed two seemingly contradictory achievements. They have lost unprecedented amounts of money, and they have eliminated from their lists many of the serious and lasting books on which publishing traditionally relied. Of course, the few remaining independent presses and many of the university presses are doing their best to publish the books that have disappeared from the conglomerate lists. But as the investment of the major publishing houses, which control 80 percent of sales, continues to shift to more commercial fields, the choice of ideas presented to American readers will continue to dwindle."

In *Publishers Weekly* (April 12, 1985), Schiffrin wrote about a visit he and other publishing executives made to Cuba, where they talked with representatives of the struggling Cuban publishing industry. In 1983 and 1987, at the invitation of the Chinese Ministry of Culture, Schiffrin and cultural delegations from the United States visited the People's Republic of China; in the *Nation* (February 6, 1988), he described his meetings with Chinese publishers and filmmakers and the steps they were taking to "com[e] to grips with the imperatives of the marketplace." In an article for *Travel Holiday* (April 1991), he wrote about the charms of Santander, a town on the Atlantic coast of Spain. His article "Shaped by War and Genocide: Indochina Today" is in the May 14, 1999 issue of the *Chronicle of Higher Education*.

Schiffrin is the author of *The Business of Books: How the International Conglomerates Took Over Publishing and Changed the Way We Read* (2000). In writing the book, which is part memoir and part diatribe against the commercial publishing world, Schiffrin drew freely from his own experiences. *The Business of Books* has earned wide critical praise.

For many years Schiffrin has been a board member of the New York Civil Liberties Union and the New York Council for Humanities. He has served on the Council of the Smithsonian Institution and the New York Council on the Humanities. He has taught at Princeton University, in New Jersey, since 1978 and at the New School University (formerly called the New School for Social Research), in New York City, since 1995. Schiffrin and his wife, Maria Elena de la Iglesias, who have been married since 1961, live on the Upper West Side of Manhattan. Their daughter Anya, a journalist, has written for the Asian edition of the *Wall Street Journal*; their daughter Natalia has worked for Interight, a London-based human-rights organization. — Y.P.

Suggested Reading: *Book World* p15 Mar. 18, 1990, with photo; *Christian Science Monitor* p14 Jan. 9, 1992; *Chronicle of Higher Education* pA8 June 23, 1993, with photo; *Logos* p47+ vol. 10 no. 1, 1999; *New York Times* C p21 Jan. 9, 1992, with photo; *Publishers Weekly* p26+ Mar. 19, 1982, with photo, p8+ Mar. 16, 1990, with photos, p8+ Jan. 13, 1992, with photo; *Washington Post* p15 Mar. 18, 1990, with photo; *Who's Who in America, 2000*

Selected Works: *The Business of Books: How the International Conglomerates Took Over Publishing and Changed the Way We Read*, 2000

Sevigny, Chloë

(seven-EE, KLOH-ee)

Nov. 18, 1974– Actress; fashion model Address: c/o William Morris Agency, 1325 Ave. of the Americas, 15th Fl., New York, NY 10019-6026

The actress Chloë Sevigny first won widespread attention with her performance in the jarring independent film *Kids* (1995), in which she played a teenager struggling with the consequences of a sexual encounter. With devastating honesty, in almost documentary-like fashion, *Kids* portrayed a culture of drug use, sexual promiscuity, and general aimlessness among modern urban teens. The film,

Archive Photos

Chloë Sevigny

while controversial, was lauded in many quarters, and Sevigny's work in it received particular praise. Sevigny has continued to act in small independent films, including *Trees Lounge* (1996), *Gummo* (1997), and *julien donkey-boy* (1999), and has also moved into the world of larger-budgeted movies, such as the noir thriller *Palmetto* (1998), co-starring Woody Harrelson and Elizabeth Shue, and *The Last Days of Disco* (1998). More recently she received an Academy Award nomination for best supporting actress for her role in *Boys Don't Cry* (1999), based on the true story of a woman who lived for a time as a man. Sevigny played the love interest of the main character, with what *Newsweek* (October 11, 1999) called a "slow, lazy sexuality [that] makes this blowsy small-town girl oddly valiant."

Chloë Sevigny was born on November 18, 1974 in Darien, Connecticut, a place she has often referred to in interviews as "Aryan Darien" because of its mostly white population. She grew up in a modest ranch house near Long Island Sound. Her father, who died of cancer in 1996, worked in the insurance field, "until his company was sold, and then he started painting trompe-l'oeil," as Sevigny told Jay McInerney for a profile of the actress in the *New Yorker* (November 4, 1994). "He started with our kitchen, and then he did it for other people. . . . We never had as much money as everyone else." Largely for that reason, when she was growing up Sevigny did not feel that she fit in with the kids around her. "It seemed like everyone had BMWs and Jeeps and nice cars and a lot of money, and I just thought it was really obnoxious," she told Ingrid Sischy for *Interview* (August 1995). "Maybe I wasn't fair. But I didn't want to be involved with all that." She instead preferred to watch her older brother and his friends skateboard in the family's backyard. As soon as she was old enough to travel on her own, she tried to get out of Darien as often as possible—first visiting Boston and Vermont and later traveling all over New England. But she always had her eye on New York, having become fascinated with the city through her father, who had taken her there once a month to go shopping. By her late teens she was traveling to New York frequently, staying at friends' houses for the weekend and hanging out with skateboarders in Washington Square Park, in the city's Greenwich Village neighborhood. She also got involved with the "rave" scene, which involved all-night, drug-fueled teenage parties.

During one of her trips to New York, Sevigny was spotted by the photographer Nina Schultz—who saw Sevigny through her car window and was entranced by her look, particularly her blond hair, which at that time hung past her waist. Schultz later photographed her for a magazine. Similarly, Andrea Lee Linett of *Sassy*, a since-defunct publication for teenage girls, first put Sevigny in a commercial, then asked her to do a shoot for the magazine, after spotting her at a newsstand in Greenwich Village, wearing baggy tan corduroy overalls. Not long afterward, while Sevigny was sitting in a friend's car at Washington Square, another woman approached her about appearing in the British music and fashion magazine *I-D*. When asked by Riley John-Donnel for *Surface* (Autumn 1997, on-line) why she thought people found her look so interesting, Sevigny remarked, "I think I look very average. Very, you know, *plain jane*. Very all-American. So I think I try and play it off by looking like a crazy Eastern European girl! . . . By wearing an insane outfit I don't look so boring and normal."

In the summer of 1992, between her junior and senior years of high school, Sevigny landed an internship at *Sassy* as the fashion editor's assistant. Though the job involved such mundane tasks as stamping envelopes and running errands, it gave her first-hand experience in the world of fashion, leading her to dream of working in that field. She was not to do so in a behind-the-scenes capacity. Through *Sassy*, she met Daisy von Furth, who was working on a video for the rock group Sonic Youth—and who, with the group's bass player, Kim Gordon, had designed a line of clothing called X-Girl. Taken with her look and fashion sense, von Furth and Gordon put Sevigny in the video and had her model for the New York launch of the X-Girl line. A short time later she appeared in a fashion spread in *Paper* and in the Lemonheads' "Big Gay Heart" video. Through her video work, modeling assignments, trend-setting taste in clothing, and escapades among the young and hip in New York, Sevigny came to personify the "down-low" scene. In his *New Yorker* profile, in which he famously pronounced Sevigny to be the "It Girl," Jay McInerney explained, "'Down low' is a cherished concept: secret, alternative, not commercial—

everything one wants to be. Except one also sort of wants to be famous, and here is the contradiction at the heart of Chloe's world, the dilemma of subcultures that ostensibly define themselves in opposition to the prevailing commercial order, the dilemma of all the boys and girls who want to be in *Paper* and *Details*: What do you do if [the more mainstream] *Harper's Bazaar*, or Calvin Klein, comes calling? In Chloe's case, so far, you sort of blow them off."

Indeed, even though photographers were clamoring to shoot Sevigny, she did not appear overly excited by her burgeoning fame. She took a part-time job at Liquid Sky, a clothes and record shop in Greenwich Village, where large numbers of club-going kids hung out. She continued to spend time in Washington Square Park with skateboarders, go to raves nightly, and crash on friends' couches. During one of her weekend visits to Washington Square Park, she became acquainted with the photographer Larry Clark, who was in the park shooting the skaters. Clark, interested in making a film about that crowd, eventually persuaded one of them, Harmony Korine, to write a screenplay based on their experiences. In the meantime, Clark had gotten backing for the project from the writer and filmmaker Gus Van Sant. Korine worked for three weeks on the screenplay, which formed the basis for the film *Kids*. He wrote the part of Jennie, the female lead, with Sevigny in mind, but Clark cast a professional actress in that role. Later, however, Clarke and Korine agreed that the actress stuck out among the real-life members of the skateboard crowd who were playing the other parts in the movie, and they replaced her with Sevigny, who had been given a minor role.

Though fictional, *Kids* was shot in a documentary style and was based on the real lives of aimless urban teenagers who spend much of their time using drugs, skateboarding, and bragging about their sexual conquests. The film's action focuses on Telly, who believes that he can avoid venereal disease if he sleeps only with virgins. Sevigny, playing one of Telly's conquests, discovers that she has caught the HIV virus from him and tries to prevent him from spreading it to other girls. The film's straightforward approach to sex and drug use among teens made *Kids* extremely controversial. In the United States it was released without a rating; in the United Kingdom it was edited to tone down some of the more disturbing scenes. Sevigny was lauded for her realistic portrayal of Jennie, a role that, while limited in terms of dialogue, allowed her to show a range of emotions through her expressions.

Though Sevigny was sent a number of scripts after her performance in *Kids*, she decided to hold out for the right role. By all accounts, she found it in *Trees Lounge* (1996), the directorial debut of the independent-film actor Steve Buscemi. The movie is Buscemi's downbeat view of what his own life might have become had he not succeeded in cinema. In it he played an unemployed mechanic turned ice-cream-truck driver who spends most of his off-hours in the local bar of the title. Sevigny appeared as Debbie, the 17-year-old with whom Buscemi's character, against his better judgment, becomes romantically involved. In an interview for *Dazed and Confused* (May 1996, on-line), Buscemi described the experience of working with her: "There was something very real in her approach, and it throws you off initially, because you're so used to having actors going for the result"—that is, obviously acting. "I think she has a lot of talent and is the type of actress that can do anything. She's also the kind of actress who delivers once the cameras are rolling."

Her next film, *Gummo* (1997), reteamed her with Harmony Korine, her then-boyfriend. *Gummo* was set in a poor, white suburb of Nashville, Tennessee, and shot on location. The film consists of interwoven stories about Sevigny's teenage character; the character's sisters, who are obsessed with cats; and the bored teenage boys who kill the animals for fun. *Gummo* was Korine's directorial debut, for which he also wrote the screenplay, with help from Sevigny. In an interview for the *Mail and Guardian* (February 27, 1997), Sevigny discussed the movie, then about to be released: "In *Kids*, [Korine's] female roles are really weak. Now you'll see how strong they are, they're the focal point of the film—that's my influence." Sevigny also designed the costumes for the film.

Gummo annoyed many American critics, including Leonard Maltin, who in his *Movie and Video Guide* (1998) called the film a "plotless, clueless, mind-numbingly awful" work that attempts "to be shocking and outrageous . . . but succeeds only in being trite, with scenes pointlessly dragging on . . . and on . . . and on." Sevigny expressed exasperation with the film's dismal reception in the U.S., calling *Gummo* "an amazing, funny and hilarious movie" and pointing out that it had won several awards at European film festivals.

The next year Sevigny began appearing in films that were more mainstream. She was first seen in *Palmetto* (1998), starring Woody Harrelson and Elizabeth Shue, as a scheming young woman who stages her own kidnapping in order to get money from her rich father. "I wasn't really aware at the time I was hired for it that it was going to turn into such a commercial thing, with Elizabeth Shue and Woody Harrelson," Sevigny stated in an interview for *Surface* (Autumn 1997). "And then [the actress] Gina Gershon was hired also—halfway through shooting. So [the Hollywood hype] sort of happened after I was already involved with the project."

Sevigny was unable to make that claim with her next film, *The Last Days of Disco* (1998), a major release that was directed by Whit Stillman and brought Sevigny her first starring role. The story takes place in the early 1980s, during the waning days of the disco phenomenon, and centers on the lives of rich young Harvard graduates. Sevigny's character, Alice Kinnon, is among the characters who pursue excitement and romance at Studio 54, then one of New York's most popular discos. Though the film received mixed reviews, it boosted Sevigny's profile and allowed her to stretch into different types of roles. For *Interview* (November 1999), she remarked, "Part of the reason I did *Last Days of Disco* is because I'm always pigeonholed as a white-trash girl, which I'm not. I'm from Darien, Connecticut, and I have the preppiest background ever."

Sevigny's most celebrated performance to date was in the first-time film director Kimberly Pierce's *Boys Don't Cry* (1999). The film is based on the real-life story of Teena Brandon, a woman who left her native Lincoln, Nebraska—as well as her female identity—behind, in order to live as Brandon Teena in Falls City, Nebraska. Brandon was played by Hilary Swank, who won the Academy Award for best actress for her work in the film. Sevigny played Lana, the girl who falls for Brandon; she was nominated for the Oscar for best supporting actress. A writer for *Entertainment Weekly* (March 2000) declared that Sevigny "has a splendor all her own. She puts a fresh, seductive spin on a character type we've seen before: Her Lana is at once tough yet vulnerable, determined yet delicate." Kimberly Pierce found that Sevigny's performance helped to make the film accessible: "For a lot of people for whom Brandon might be odd, [Lana was] the way in."

Chloë Sevigny also recently starred in *julien donkey-boy* (1999), the latest film by Harmony Korine, and *A Map of the World* (1999). In addition, she was featured in the HBO film *If These Walls Could Talk 2* (2000), which looks at the lives of lesbians in three different decades. She can also be seen in the film adaptation of Bret Eaton Ellis's 1991 novel, *American Psycho* (2000). — C.M.

Suggested Reading: *Entertainment Weekly* p34 Jan. 14, 2000, with photo; *Interview* p62+ Aug. 1995, with photos, p66+ Nov. 1999, with photos; *Mail and Guardian* (on-line) Feb. 27, 1997, with photo; *New York Times* p39+ Feb. 20, 2000, E p2 Feb. 21, 2000, with photo; *New Yorker* p182+ Nov. 7, 1994; *Newsweek* p85 Oct. 11, 1999; *Surface* (on-line) Autumn 1997; *Vogue* p166 June 1999, with photo

Selected Films: *Kids*, 1995; *Trees Lounge*, 1996; *Gummo*, 1997; *Palmetto*, 1998; *The Last Days of Disco*, 1998; *Boys Don't Cry*, 1999; *julien donkey-boy*, 1999; *A Map of the World*, 1999; *If These Walls Could Talk 2*, 2000; *American Psycho*, 2000

Shipley, Jenny

Feb. 4, 1952– Former prime minister of New Zealand; leader of the National Party. Address: c/o Parliament House, Wellington, New Zealand

Archive Photos

"I would rather do what's right than what's popular," Jenny Shipley declared to Simon Robinson for the South Pacific edition of *Time* (December 15, 1997). The leader of New Zealand's right-wing National Party (NP), Shipley became the first female prime minister of New Zealand on December 8, 1997, after engineering the ejection of her predecessor, Jim Bolger, from the NP's top post. A farmer's wife and woman of action in her community, she served on a county council before entering national politics, in 1987, when she was elected to Parliament for the first time. During Bolger's seven years as prime minister, she worked for three years as minister of both social affairs and women's affairs; subsequently she headed the ministry of health and, later, five other ministries. Her successful efforts to slash welfare and other social-service expenditures led demonstrators to burn her in effigy in 1991. Renowned for her toughness and formidable powers of persuasion, she has been likened in the media to a steamroller and an armored personnel carrier. "Jenny has three wonderful attributes," George E. J. Hutton, a deputy chairman of the county council during Shipley's tenure there, told Robinson. "She's a listener, she's a worker, and she's a bloody fox terrier. When she gets something in her mind that she believes is right, she does not let go." As prime minister, Shipley narrowly survived two parliamentary votes of confidence. She lost her post after the November 27,

1999 general election, in which the Labour Party won a majority of the seats in Parliament.

The second of the four daughters of Len Robson, a Presbyterian minister, and his wife, Adele, a homemaker, Jenny Shipley was born Jennifer Mary Robson on February 4, 1952 in Gore, near the southern tip of South Island, one of New Zealand's two main islands. In a conversation with Simon Robinson, Shipley recalled being "a very healthy, very plain, very sports oriented young person who thought that the world was my oyster." "It didn't occur to me that girls couldn't do everything until my early 20s, and even then I still didn't believe it," she told him. In her teens she excelled at swimming.

After graduating from Marlborough Girls' College, a private day and boarding school in Blenheim, in 1968, Shipley enrolled at Christchurch Teachers' College (having failed the university entrance exam). She earned a diploma in teaching in 1972 and that same year married Burton Shipley, a fifth-generation farmer. For the next four years, she taught at the small Greendale Primary School, near Christchurch, where she would sometimes play her 12-string guitar for her pupils and was, as one of her former supervisors told Robinson, "a stickler for the three Rs." She quit her job to raise her two children—Anna, born in about 1977, and Ben, born about a year later. In addition to helping to run the 1,200-acre family farm, she became very active in her community, initially in child-care matters. From 1979 to 1982 she served on the board of Plunket, New Zealand's primary provider of child-health services, and from 1980 to 1982 she was president of the parents' committee at the play center her children attended. To help raise funds for a new play-center building, she held sewing bees in her home. Judy Chamberlain, the center supervisor, remembered Shipley as "a very warm, compassionate person" who, at meetings, "certainly had an opinion," as she phrased it to Robinson. "Usually her color scheme [for portions of the new building] was the one you went with. She just had that knack of knowing what she wanted and going to get it." Shipley also volunteered in the local chapter of the 15,000-member national organization Federated Farmers as well as, for shorter periods, the Malvern Community Arts Council and the Aged Peoples Welfare Committee. From 1983 to 1987 she tutored at Lincoln College, near Christchurch, and concurrently served on the Malvern County Council. In that capacity, against all odds, she persuaded a majority of the other members, most of whom were "older, conservative farmers," "to declare the county a nuclear free zone." "It was just by the sheer power of persuasion and the arguments she put forward," Gwen Clucas, the only other councilwoman at that time, told Robinson. Shipley strengthened her considerable leadership skills in 1984, when she attended the Kellogg New Zealand Rural Leadership Program.

Meanwhile, in 1975, Shipley had joined the National Party. (Her parents had staunchly supported the NP. Simon Robinson reported that her mother's father had maintained a friendship with the National Party leader Keith Holyoake, who served as New Zealand's prime minister from 1960 to 1972.) The NP emphasizes free enterprise, personal initiative, and removal of governmental control over industry—an ideology that attracted the conservative Shipley. After she became a party member, she held various positions at the NP's lower echelons, including head of the NP's Canterbury-Westland Division Policy Committee. In 1987 she won election to what is officially called the House of Representatives and familiarly known as Parliament; it is New Zealand's sole national legislative body. Shipley represented the rural district of Ashburton (now known as Rakaia). After her election her husband sold the family farm to devote himself to child care; he also went back to school and eventually became a business development manager for a major New Zealand bank.

When Shipley took her seat in Parliament, Labour had been the majority party for more than three years. In October 1990 power shifted back to the NP, and Jim Bolger, the party's leader, became prime minister. Bolger named Shipley minister of social affairs and minister of women's affairs, titles that she held simultaneously until 1993. In line with the NP's goal of decreasing New Zealanders' dependence on government, she and Finance Minister Ruth Richardson pushed successfully for drastic reductions in welfare benefits—"The welfare state is not an unconditional right," Shipley has said—and the imposition of a six-month waiting period for people applying for unemployment benefits. Such moves made her highly unpopular, and at a widely publicized protest held in 1991, she was burned in effigy (as was Richardson).

The cuts in welfare, along with a rise in both unemployment and crime, led to a swelling in anti-government sentiment, and in the 1993 elections the NP held onto its majority by a single seat. Bolger formed a new Cabinet, and in a highly controversial move, he named Shipley both minister of women's affairs and minister of health. In the latter role, she was charged with ensuring that public-health services kept pace with innovations in modern medicine in a way that would not strain the national budget. Toward that end, she demanded that state-run hospitals and clinics, virtually all of which were financially strapped, begin to turn a profit. Many hospitals were forced to close operating rooms and to cut services in other ways as well; some placed employees on unpaid leave for three weeks and began to lease wards to the private sector. Also during her stint as minister of health, Shipley made the popular decision to distribute free birth-control materials as a way to lower the abortion rate, and in a surprisingly liberal move, she authorized sex education in the schools.

On October 12, 1996, in the first general election conducted under a new electoral system that voters had approved in the previous general election, the NP won only 44 seats—17 fewer than necessary to capture a majority in Parliament, which had expanded to 120 members under the new system. Two months later Prime Minister Bolger formed a coalition government with the three-year-old, right-wing, nationalist New Zealand First Party (NZFP), the founder and leader of which, Winston Peters, was named deputy prime minister and treasurer in the Cabinet. (A descendant of Maoris, whose ancestors are the original, Polynesian settlers of New Zealand, Peters had served as minister of Maori affairs until his ejection from an NP caucus in 1993.) Shipley, meanwhile, had reportedly requested a job change, specifically to reduce her involvement in controversy, and in response, Bolger made her head of five ministries: those of state services, state-owned enterprises, broadcasting (with responsibility for Radio New Zealand), transport, and accident rehabilitation and compensation. (Most other members of the Cabinet also held multiple portfolios.)

According to public-opinion polls, in 1997 New Zealanders grew increasingly dissatisfied with Bolger's rule; as the year progressed, reports of possible misuse of public funds and other forms of misconduct on the part of various government officials, among other complaints, caused the administration to become "sensationally unpopular," to quote the *Economist* (November 8, 1997). Shipley decided to take advantage of the dissatisfaction many of her fellow NP legislators felt toward Bolger. In October 1997, while the prime minister was attending a Commonwealth leaders' meeting in Scotland, she circulated a letter to all NP members of Parliament in which she called for the ouster of the unsuspecting Bolger as party leader, and she asked the legislators to express, in writing, their decision to switch their support to her. Thirty of the 44 NP legislators agreed to back her. Speaking after an NP caucus named her party leader, Shipley praised Bolger's accomplishments and contributions and made no mention of the party coup she had masterminded. (She later appointed Bolger ambassador to the United States.) Bolger was unwilling to face a vote of confidence, and on November 3, 1997 he announced that he would retire in December.

On December 8, 1997 Jenny Shipley was sworn in as New Zealand's first female prime minister. Later that month, as part of her plan to push the government rightward, she appointed what the *New York Times* (December 9, 1997) identified as "economic hard-liners" to head the commerce, education, health, welfare, and other ministries. Her initial proposals as prime minister included imposing a new toll to increase highway funds; making community service obligatory for welfare recipients; and narrowing eligibility requirements for disability benefits. She also announced plans to simplify the tax system.

When the 1998–99 national budget was unveiled, in June 1998, the Shipley government announced that it aimed to cut the national debt from 20 percent to 15 percent of the gross domestic product within five years and to lower expenditures by $300 million (in New Zealand dollars) during the next two fiscal years. It also disclosed plans to increase taxes on gasoline and cigarettes, with the extra funds collected to be earmarked for road construction and antismoking campaigns; to encourage competition from the private sector in the provision of accident insurance, which at that time was totally handled by the government; and to end tariffs on cars.

On August 12, 1998 New Zealand's coalition government collapsed, after four NZFP ministers left a Cabinet meeting to protest a proposal by Shipley and other NP Cabinet members to sell the government's 66 percent stake in Wellington International Airport. (The Cabinet approved the plan after the dissenters' departure.) The disintegration of the coalition led Parliament, on September 8, to conduct a vote of confidence. Thanks to the support of members of ACT New Zealand, the political arm of the right-wing Association of Consumers and Taxpayers, the vote was 62 to 58 in Shipley's favor. Only 61 members of Parliament cast their ballots for Shipley on February 23, 1999, when a second vote of confidence occurred. It was carried out at the request of the opposition Labour Party after Shipley refused to answer questions in Parliament regarding a multimillion-dollar contract awarded by the Ministry of Tourism that, according to members of the Labour Party, benefited the NP. Because of her unwillingness to respond to the lawmakers' queries, Shipley was not allowed to defend her role in the contract negotiations on the floor of the legislature; instead, in an unprecedented action, she did so outdoors, on the steps of the Parliament building. The controversy over the contract led the minister of tourism, Murray McCully, to resign his post. (He retained his two other Cabinet positions.)

Shipley campaigned vigorously before the 1999 general election, reminding voters that the budget had been balanced, new jobs had been created (though the unemployment rate had increased), and crime was down. She promised to cut personal taxes and decrease interest rates. Her opponent, Helen Clark, the leader of the Labour Party, by contrast, told voters that she intended to raise taxes, in order to make possible improvements in the health-care system and other social services. On November 27, 1999 some 90 percent of New Zealand's registered voters came to the polls and—in what *Facts on File* (December 2, 1999) identified as "a desire for change rather than a strong preference for either candidate"—voted 52 Labour candidates and only 41 NP aspirants into office. Late that night Shipley conceded defeat. In her concession speech she declared, as quoted in a New Zealand government press release (on-line), "I assure New Zealanders that National will be a loyal and highly active opposition as we seek to ensure that the gains New Zealand has made are locked in. I look forward to vigorously fulfilling the role of Leader of Opposition." Her successor, Helen Clark, is the first female elected prime minister of New Zealand, which, in 1893, became the first country in the world to allow women to vote. — M.R.

Suggested Reading: *Economist* p43 Nov. 8, 1997, with photo, p34 Aug. 22, 1998; New Zealand Government (on-line); *Time* (South Pacific edition) Dec. 15, 1997 (on-line); Victoria University of Wellington (on-line); *Political Handbook of the World, 1998*

Courtesy of Pritzker Architecture Prize

Siza, Alvaro

(SEE-zuh, AL-vah-roh)

June 25, 1933– Architect. Address: Faculdade de Arquitectura, Universidade do Porto, Rua do Gólgota 215, 4150-755 Porto, Portugal

Widely regarded as the foremost architect in Portugal, his native land, Alvaro Siza is known as a modest, humble designer whose mantra is "Architects invent nothing." Ada Louise Huxtable, writing in the *New York Review of Books* (April 6, 1995), described him as a "seemingly unspectacular man—soft-spoken, chain-smoking, politely professorial." "He is a study in brown," she reported—"brown beard, brown business suit of indeterminate cut, brown tie of indistinct pattern. . . . He is beyond fashion." Perhaps because of his low-key manner, few architects outside of Europe were familiar with his work until 1992, when he won the Pritzker Architecture Prize. Being awarded the most prestigious prize in his field served as the equivalent of a coming-out party for Siza. Since then, several books and monographs about him have been published, and he has continued to work at a rapid pace. He has designed more than 100 buildings, primarily in Portugal but also in the Netherlands, Germany, Italy, Spain, and the island of Macau, a Portuguese territory in the South China Sea.

As many commentators have pointed out, Siza as an architect is very different from the winner of the 1991 Pritzker Prize, Robert Venturi, whose buildings and book *Learning from Las Vegas* sparked and epitomize the postmodern movement in architecture. In contrast to the pastiche of historical styles that characterize postmodern architecture, Siza's buildings are rooted in the modernist vocabulary of design. Some of his more famous buildings recall the designs of Alvar Aalto, Le Corbusier, and Frank Lloyd Wright. Ada Louise Huxtable described his buildings as "a fugue of orchestrated views and events." In *Progressive Architecture* (April 1995), Abby Bussel wrote, "Siza has mined the complexities of the modern world, cultivating a language at once local and universal, while pursuing what Kenneth Frampton has called an 'ethical imperative.'"

Born Alvaro Joaquim de Meio Siza Vieira on June 25, 1933 in Matosinhos, a coastal town in northern Portugal, Siza originally wanted to become a sculptor. His parents—particularly his father, a pragmatic engineer—tried to persuade him to choose a more stable career. As it turned out, they didn't have to force their views: Siza failed to get accepted to sculpture school. Surmising that the architecture curriculum was very similar to that of sculpture, in 1946 he enrolled in the School of Architecture at the University of Porto, on Portugal's Atlantic coast, with the intention of transferring to a sculpture program at a later date. He never did switch his major. Exposure to the work of such architects as Aalto, Le Corbusier, and Walter Gropius convinced him that architecture could be as expressive as any other art. In 1954, while still in college, he opened a private architecture practice in Porto (also called Oporto), and before he graduated, in 1955, he had already started constructing four houses in Matosinhos. From 1955 to 1958 he collaborated primarily with Fernando Távora, one of his professors from the University of Porto, who was simultaneously studying the indigenous architecture of Portugal and traveling abroad to learn firsthand about the latest architectural developments. "When I began to work with Távora—I worked as a draughtsman for two months or so, and then as an architect for two or three more years—it was obviously his architecture that interested me," Siza recalled in an interview for the catalog *Alvaro Siza: Works and Projects* (1995). "The new Portuguese architecture and the influence of the investigation which Távora was then carrying out were entirely in my first works, with a recognizable difference, I think, but his was basically the model I worked with." Siza's early designs reveal his struggles to incorporate both regional architectural traditions and more modern forms. At the Boa Nova Tea House (1958–63), located on a rocky promontory along the coast of Leça da Palmeira, the stucco finish and the clay tile roof recall regional buildings, while the clean, swooping lines suggest more modernist impulses.

Gradually Siza moved toward the rationalism and simplification espoused by modernist architects. "The way of vernacular architecture, for very many different reasons, was absorbed by terrible conservatism and mechanicism in the very moment in which tourist programmes began," he recalled in *Alvaro Siza: Works and Projects*. "Popular architecture became a kind of universal prescription due to them." The most striking design dating from early in his career is almost minimalist in its economy of expression: the Ocean Swimming Pool complex, located on the coast of Leça da Palmeira (1961–66). The walls of the pools, one of which is rectangular and the other curvilinear, are integrated with natural rock formations on the beach, so that they appear partly manmade and partly like natural features of the landscape. Siza also designed the changing rooms and the walkways that lead from the street to the pools.

In such projects as the Banco Pinto & Sotto Mayor (1971–74), in Oliveira de Azeméis, and the Beires House (1973–76), in Póvoa de Varzim, Siza demonstrated his use of the modernist idiom to create more dynamic forms. Located on a corner site, the Banco Pinto is composed of three ascending curved structures. "The importance of this project stems from the fact that it anticipates an entire series of new schemes which Siza produced during the seventies and eighties," the architect José Paulo dos Santos wrote in the monograph *Alvaro Siza: Works and Projects, 1954–92* (1993). Similarly bold, the Beires House is a rectangular block with a concave wall of windows in what would normally be a corner.

Before 1974 Siza worked mostly on small private houses, for some of which he designed everything, including doors, doorknobs, keys, entry mats, lighting fixtures, chairs, tables, and cabinets; many of these items later went into mass production. Then, after a group of leftist Portuguese generals led a bloodless coup, on April 24, 1974, Siza began work on several public-housing projects. "My activity was developed in a very intense context of social change and political fight," he recalled in an essay in *Alvaro Siza: Works and Projects*. "I myself felt emotionally and rationally affected by that context." The Bouça Social Housing (1973–77), in Porto, was one of his early attempts to deal with the design requirements of mass housing. The design of Quinta da Malagueira Social Housing, built in phases in Évora since 1977, has earned much praise. One of his largest projects, it consists of 1,200 housing units, infrastructure, and commercial facilities. Siza started with a basic, two-storied, L-shaped housing unit similar to a courtyard house common to the area; he designed a concrete aqueduct reminiscent of Renaissance-style aqueducts to carry water, energy, and telephone services to these units. Quinta da Malagueira Social Housing won the Prince of Wales Prize for Urban Design from Harvard University.

With his reputation established, in the 1980s work poured into Siza's office, and his designs from that decade display a diversity of types and forms. Among his smaller buildings is the Duarte House (1981–85), in Ovar, a rectangular structure with recessed vertical incisions that mark the front and back façades; some critics have compared the design to Adolf Loos's Steiner House (1910). The two-story Figueiredo House (1985–94), in Gondomar, changes from rectangular to a half-octagon sitting atop a prow-shaped form at one extremity. The Banco Borges & Irmao (1982–86), in Vila do Conde, which is curved at two opposite corners, won the European Award for Architecture, given by the European Economic Community and the Mies van der Rohe Foundation of Barcelona. Siza has also designed several larger multi-use buildings. The Joao de Deus Kindergarten, in Penafiel (1984–91), is designed around three interior courtyards. The H-shaped Teachers' Training College, in Setúbal (1986–92), surrounds a century-old cork oak tree. The School of Architecture at the University of Porto (1986–95) is composed of two rows of buildings meeting at an angle. The northern, continuous row serves to block out noise emanating from a nearby highway; the southern row consists of four separate buildings that vary in height, shape, and window placement. Some observers have suggested that the variously articulated façades of the southern row, which resemble faces, are caricatures of Siza's architectural colleagues. In the realm of urban planning, Siza tackled the reconstruction of the Chiado District, in Lisbon, after a fire in 1988 damaged and destroyed 17 buildings. His plan calls for restoring the buildings, most in the regional Pombalino style, and opening up dynamic new public spaces.

Despite the diversity of his projects, many critics agree that one constant in Siza's work is his sensitivity in adapting each design to its setting (including landscape and surrounding buildings) and the local culture and history, no matter how fragmentary or chaotic them may seem. In an essay in *Alvaro Siza: Works and Projects, 1954–92*, the critic Kenneth Frampton called this approach an "ethical imperative" for Siza. In a reference to the 20th-century philosopher Ludwig Wittgenstein, Frampton wrote, "Looking at Siza's work, one is reminded of the Wittgensteinian aphorism, 'What is torn must remain torn.' Thus, as far as Siza is concerned the imperative task for a late modern architecture is to remain ever aware of an unstable, emerging, multi-layered history."

Starting a design, Siza has said, is almost like being at sea. In *Alvaro Siza: Works and Projects*, he was quoted as saying that he proceeds as if he is in "a kind of boat, subject to the will of the waves. . . . I study currents, whirlpools; I seek inlets before taking any risks." In another essay in the catalog, he recalled "a discussion in the School of Architecture, some years ago, in which I was criticized for not doing my duty of indicating clear ways to the students. My answer was: 'Of course not, because the ways aren't clear.' I tried to explain to [my critics] that if I showed them clearly, I would be falsifying reality, wouldn't I?"

Siza usually begins a project by making numerous sketches; he has filled at least 365 notebooks with drawings. (Some of them appear in the 1994 monograph *Alvaro Siza: City Sketches*, assembled by Wilfried Wang.) Quick drawings seem appropriate to Siza's search for a site's fleeting qualities. "Every design is a rigorous attempt at capturing a concrete moment of a transitory image in all its nuances," he was quoted as saying on the Pritzker Prize Web site. He stated in another essay on the site that his architecture "aims at re-encountering the lost spontaneity, the joy of spontaneity and of difference; the disinhibited and collective competence to find or model the place for exceptional urban episodes."

Siza has designed many buildings outside Portugal. Among his projects in Germany, he constructed the Vitra Metal Furniture Production Building (1991–94), in Weil am Rhein, and the Sclesisches Tor Housing Complex (1980–84), in Berlin. The design of the latter—a bell-shaped curve—won first prize in an International Building Exhibition competition, though due to financial considerations, the building was not built precisely according to Siza's specifications. In Macau Siza designed an urban expansion plan (1983–84). In the Hague, in the Netherlands, he has built, among other works, 106 housing units in the Schilderswijk Ward (1986–88) and two houses and shops in Van der Venne Park (1986–88). In Spain he designed the Galician Center of Contemporary Art, in Santiago de Compostela (1988–94); critics have said that movement through the museum is similar to movement through the city. Another Siza creation, the Meteorological Center (1989–92) on the shoreline of Barcelona, is a cylinder with a circular courtyard.

From 1966 to 1969 Siza taught at the University of Porto. In 1976 he became a professor of construction there. A frequent guest lecturer, he has spoken at some of the most prestigious architectural schools in the world.

When he won the Pritzker Architecture Prize, in 1992, Siza became the 15th Pritzker laureate. He has also won the Gold Medal of the Colegios de Arquitectos of Spain (1988), the Gold Medal of the Alvar Aalto Foundation (1988), the Berlage Prize (1994), the Gubbio Prize (1994), the Nara World Architecture Exhibition Gold Medal (1995), and the Imperial Prize for outstanding lifetime achievement in architecture, from the Japan Arts Association (1998).

Siza married Maria Antonia Marinho Leite in 1962; she died in 1973. They had two children together. — W.G.

Suggested Reading: *New York Review of Books* p18+ Apr. 6, 1995, with photo; *Progressive Architecture* p54+ Apr. 1995, with photos; *Washington Post* D p1 Apr. 27, 1992, with photo; de Llano, Pedro and Carlos Castanheira, eds. *Alvaro Siza: Works and Projects*, 1995; dos Santos, José Paulo, ed. *Alvaro Siza: Works and Projects, 1954–1992*, 1993; Testa, Peter. *Alvaro Siza*, 1996

Selected Buildings, Urban Plans, Renovations, and Public Monuments (in Portugal unless another country is indicated; a date followed by an en-dash with no following date indicates either that the work is still under construction or that the completion date is unknown): Four Houses, Matosinhos, 1954–1957; Parochial Center, Matosinhos, 1956–59; Carneiro de Melo House, Oporto, 1957–59; Rocha Ribeiro House, Maia, 1960–62; Ocean Swimming Pool, Lecça da Palmeira, 1961–66; Coastal Development Plan, Lecça da Palmeira, 1966–74; Cotton Warehouse, Matosinhos, 1966; Caxinas Housing, Vila do Conde, 1970–72; Pinto & Sotto Mayor Bank, Oliveira de Azémeis,1971–74; Pinto & Sotto Mayor Bank, Lamego, 1972–74; Bouça Social Housing, Oporto, 1973–77; Sao Victor District Rehabilitation, Oporto, 1974–77; Housing in Quinta da Malagueira, Évora, 1977–; Schlesisches Tor Housing, Kreuzberg, Berlin, Germany, 1980–84; Avelino Duarte House, Ovar, 1981–85; Borges & Irmao Bank, Vila do Conde, 1982–86; J. M. Teixeira Apartment, Póvoa de Varzim, 1982–85; Pombais Urban Development Plan, Guimaraes, 1982–88; Nina Boutique, Oporto, 1983; Macao Urban Expansion Plan, Island of Macau, 1983–84; Joao de Deus Kindergarten, Penafiel, 1984–91; Schilderswijk Urban Redevelopment Plan and Social Housing, The Hague, Holland, 1986–88; Teachers' Training College, Sétubal, 1986–92; Two Houses and Shops in Van der Venne Park, The Hague, Holland, 1986–88; Galician Center for Contemporary Art, Santiago de Compostela, Spain, 1988–94; Main Library, University of Aveiro, Aveiro, 1988–95; Chiado District Reconstruction, Lisbon, 1988–; Doedijnstraat Plan and Social Housing, Schilderswijk-West, The Hague, Holland, 1989–93; Meteorological Center, Barcelona, Spain, 1989–92; Boavista Mixed Use Development, Oporto, 1990–; Santo Domingo de Bonaval Gardens, Santiago de Compostela, Spain, 1990–94; Vitra Furniture Factory and Offices, Weil am Rhein, Germany, 1991–94; Grandella Department Store, Chiado, Lisbon, 1991–96; Serralves Foundation Museum of Contemporary Art, Oporto, 1991–; Chiado Subway Station, Lisbon, 1992–; Coastal Development Plan, Costa da Caparica, Lisbon, 1992–94; Alvaro Siza Studio, Oporto, 1993–; Plan Cenre Ville, Montreuil, France, 1993–; Ateliers for Artists, Montreuil, France, 1993–; Social Housing, Guarda, 1994–; Children's Farm,

Serralves Foundation, Oporto, 1994–; Granell Museum of Surrealist Art, Santiago de Compostela, Spain, 1994–; Social Housing T1 and T4, Malagueira, Évora, 1994–; Stadium and Athletic Complex, Palermo, Italy, 1994–; Pavilion of Portugal EXPO '98, Lisbon, 1995–; Primary Schools, Alcoi-Alicante, Spain, 1995–; Van Midellem-Dupont House, Oudemburg, Belgium, 1995–; Biophysics Institute, Düsseldorf, Germany, 1995–

Kris Snibbe/Courtesy of Harvard News Office

Skocpol, Theda

(SCOTCH-pole, THEE-da)

May 4, 1947– Professor; social scientist. Address: Harvard University, Dept. of Government, 470 William James Hall, Cambridge, MA 01238

Theda Skocpol is the Victor S. Thomas Professor of Government and Sociology at Harvard University, in Cambridge, Massachusetts, and one of the country's leading commentators on social policy. For over two decades she has engaged in a comparative study of the U.S. and other nations, in terms of the formation of governments, revolutions, and the development of public policy; she has provided a "voice of cautious optimism" in the debate over social policy, as Robert C. Bannister wrote for *America* (July 6–13 1996). The author of several books, Skocpol told *Current Biography* that her work was influenced by scholars and thinkers including Seymour Martin Lipset, George Homans, Albert Hirschman, and Barrington Moore Jr., the Harvard professor whose comparative historical scholarship became a model for her own research. From 1991 to 1992 she served as the president of the Politics and History Section of the American Political Science Association, and in 1996 she was president of the Social Science History Association, a scholarly society bringing together social scientists and historians. Although there are some who disagree with her opinions on subjects including the need for universal health care and welfare, she is highly respected by many for the thoroughness of her historical research.

Skocpol is a feminist social democrat who believes that more can be done to help ordinary citizens of the United States. Much of her writing debunks the myth that America as a rule has never embraced social-welfare programs. "Jobs must be available to all adults who can work, and they must have wages, benefits, and protections that are suitable for families," she and William Julius Wilson wrote for the *New York Times* (February 4, 1994). "Policies must require and enable parents to devote time and money to the care of children. These things can be done without huge amounts of new public resources." Skocpol and Wilson contended that the U.S. welfare system has been flawed in "its failure to support efforts to *combine* employment and child-rearing." One of the measures they suggested was stricter enforcement of child-support law, through the automatic deduction of child support from parents' paychecks, a measure similar to the collection of Social Security funds and one that would ensure that parents would meet their financial responsibilities to their children. In a lecture delivered to the Carl Albert Congressional Research and Studies Center and reprinted in *Extensions* (Fall 1999), Skocpol stated that throughout her career she has been "interested in the way in which politics—as a set of processes, struggles, policy outcomes, patterns of conflict and institutional changes—develops at the intersection between state and society. . . . Social science, in my view, should take up important, real-world problems and not simply engage in navel gazing discussions of purely internal theoretical or methodological issues."

The older of two daughters, Theda Ruth Barron Skocpol was born in Detroit, Michigan, on May 4, 1947 to Allan Ernest Barron, a high-school economics and business-education teacher, and Jennie Mae (Becker) Barron, a homemaker and occasional substitute teacher. She grew up in Wyandotte, an industrial city to the south of Detroit. "In school, I was always 'the brain' rather than a popular beauty, and I drowned my sorrows about this in books," Skocpol wrote in *Theory and Society* (Volume 17, 1988). Skocpol enrolled at Michigan State University (MSU), where, as an honors student, she developed self-confidence. During her years there, she met Bill Skocpol, when both participated in a teaching program in English and math in Mississippi, sponsored by a Methodist youth group at MSU. The two were married in 1967. Two years later Theda Skocpol earned her B.A. degree.

Skocpol wrote in *Theory and Society* that she benefitted from the "groundedness" of MSU professors James McKee and John and Ruth Useem, who were dedicated to studying "actual social patterns" rather than relying upon traditional European scholarship. During this period she also became familiar with the work of Barrington Moore Jr., which inspired her to study at Harvard University, where he taught. It was difficult for Skocpol to convince some of her professors "that as a married woman I should still be seriously considered for fellowships and for the best graduate departments," she recalled in *Theory and Society.* It was assumed that, because she was a married woman, childrearing and household duties would sooner or later prevent her from doing scholarly work. "Bill and I talked openly with our teachers about the incipient discrimination I was facing, and upon reflection everyone changed their outlooks," she wrote.

Skocpol acquired the necessary fellowships to continue her studies. At Harvard, where she received her M.A. degree (1972) and Ph.D. (1975) in sociology, she worked with Barrington Moore Jr., whom she described in her Gordon Gray Lecture on the Craft of Scholarly Writing (November 19, 1997) as "a transdisciplinary scholar who urged his students to define compelling questions about politics and develop answers by comparing the diverse pasts of England, France, Germany, the United States, and other countries." Both Skocpol's decision to pursue a career as an historical social scientist and her inspiration for her first book resulted from "the disconnects I saw between theories and historical patterns," she stated for the Gordon Gray Lecture. *States and Social Revolutions: A Comparative Analysis of France, Russia, and China* (1979) evolved out of Skocpol's doctoral dissertation, which examined the revolutions that had taken place in France, Russia, and China; the book came to be considered one of the most significant social-science texts of the 1970s and won the 1980 American Sociological Association Award for a Distinguished Contribution to Scholarship, the top prize in the field of sociology. "I was so pleased to have brought my early inchoate ideas into focus," Skocpol wrote for the Gordon Gray Lecture. "When the cover for *States and Social Revolutions* was designed by Cambridge University Press, I set it up next to my reading chair and stared at it with delight for hours. . . . In scholarly life, there is no feeling, ever, like the triumph of publishing that first book."

Skocpol served as a member of the sociology faculty at Harvard from 1975 until 1981, when she was denied tenure by the university's sociology department. "After I had, in my own view and the view of many others around the country, 'earned' tenure at Harvard, I was denied it with no explanation that I found credible, other than what I felt were reactions against me as an ambitious woman," Skocpol recalled in *Theory and Society.* For the next five years, she served as a tenured professor in both the Department of Sociology and the Department of Political Science at the University of Chicago while waiting to hear the results of her tenure dispute at Harvard. A Harvard faculty committee chaired by Professor Stanley Hoffman concluded that Skocpol's grievance had merit, and in 1986 she returned to the university as a tenured professor. Skocpol wrote in *Theory and Society* that she decided to "endure the hostilities of my senior colleagues" in order to live and work closer to her husband. In 1995 she became a tenured member of the Department of Government. Currently she is Harvard's Victor S. Thomas Professor of Government and Sociology. She was recently named director of the school's Center for American Political Studies in the Department of Government.

Skocpol told Michael Keating for the *Cambridge Chronicle* (November 7, 1996) that although much progress has been made by women, both institutional and unconscious sexism are still a problem. "As a woman, you can either be personally very nice and deferential, in which case people will think you don't count. Or you can really be assertive and people will think you're a pushy woman. There's a level of anxiety in men that's often not consciously sexist at all; it's just part of the larger transformation in society. It's a big change to have men and women competing for the same jobs."

Bringing the State Back In (1985), co-edited by Skocpol, Peter Evans, and Dietrich Rueschmeyer, criticized social scientists for focusing on persons or groups outside government in its examination of how public policy is formed, thus neglecting to demonstrate sufficiently the role of governmental agencies. Skocpol wrote in *Extensions* that the book was "an attempt to set up a series of debates about what it would mean to take seriously governmental institutions and administrative and military institutions as sites of independent action, of independent interest articulation, interacting with social movements and classes."

In 1992 Belknap Press published Skocpol's *Protecting Soldiers and Mothers: The Political Origins of Social Policy in the United States,* an important book that revealed a precedent for social welfare in the United States as far back as the post–Civil War period and documented the role women played in shaping policy at the turn of the 20th century. The book received five major scholarly awards, including the Woodrow Wilson Prize from the American Political Science Association and the Ralph Waldo Emerson Award of Phi Beta Kappa. According to Karen J. Winkler's review for the *Chronicle of Higher Education* (February 24, 1993), the book signaled a "shift in [Skocpol's] methodology from what she called 'state centered' to 'polity centered' history. The difference lies not in abandoning a focus on institutions, but in seeing how they interacted with individuals and social groups."

For the book, Skocpol had originally planned to concentrate on social policy in the U.S. since the 1930s, but as she conducted background research into earlier developments, a new focus emerged.

Protecting Mothers and Soldiers revealed the little-known fact that the United States government had once instituted a highly developed social-welfare system, spending over one-quarter of the federal budget in the years 1880–1910 to provide pensions for many wounded Union veterans of the Civil War as well as their families. At the turn of the century, programs were also implemented to assist women and children. "The United States during the late 19th century became for many of its citizens a kind of precocious social spending state," Skocpol commented in an adapted excerpt of the book in *Political Science Quarterly* (Spring 1993), "precocious in terms of the usual presumptions of an absence of federal involvement in social welfare before the New Deal, and precocious in terms of how the United States around 1900 compared to other Western nations."

Although *Protecting Soldiers and Mothers* was one of the first texts to acknowledge the contributions of women in the history of welfare, the book was criticized by some feminist scholars, who felt that Skocpol's focus on white middle-class women failed to reflect the more inclusive social theory to have grown out of recent developments in women's studies. Scholars including Linda Gordon, a historian at the University of Wisconsin at Madison, found Skocpol's analysis to be superficial and were disappointed that the author did not discuss the ways in which the "maternalist" policies of the early 19th century, discussed in the book, had demeaned women. (Maternalist policies were based on the belief that women were fundamentally different from men in such a way that they required more governmental assistance.) "Though Skocpol makes social policy history between 1865 and 1920 intelligible, she does so by avoiding the theoretical tensions feminism has taught us to think about and by ignoring story lines that don't easily fit with her point of view," Gwendolyn Mink wrote for *Women's Review of Books* (January 1993). "Ultimately, this allows her to generalize from middle-class women's politics to a gender solidarity and women's agenda that transcended privileges and subordinations based on race, culture, and class."

Skocpol responded to her critics by stressing that middle-class women were the ones who influenced policy aimed at women at that point in history, and that, given this reality, she admired the broad-based coalitions they were able to form with women all over the country. "I'm not saying that everything women reformers advocated was admirable," she told Karen Winkler. "But I think that some of my critics bring their present-day concerns into the way they do history. Back then, it was reasonable to think that maternalist policies were the best way to help women and children. These programs were a positive alternative to the courts' taking children away from poor women, which is what had been happening." Skocpol was quick to add that she would not be in favor of implementing maternalist measures today. Eileen McDonagh, a professor of political science at Northeastern University, in Boston, Massachusetts, defended Skocpol's work: "By continuing to articulate her institutional model to include citizens, Theda is answering her critics," McDonagh told Winkler. "She provides a valuable model of how policy is developed."

In 1994 Skocpol published a book of essays, *Social Revolutions in the Modern World*, which built upon the points she had made in *States and Social Revolutions*. According to Daniel Chirot, who reviewed *Social Revolutions in the Modern World* for *Social Forces* (March 1997), both texts concluded that "societies ruled by classes and systems unable to keep abreast of international competition and directly threatened by that lag were the ones ripe for revolution." Chirot pointed out that this argument was a far cry from the Marxist interpretations made by many sociologists in the 1970s, who had claimed that revolution was primarily a "product of internal class conflicts set off by commercialization and economic modernization."

In *Social Policy in the United States: Future Possibilities in Historical Perspective* (1995), Skocpol argued that in order for significant changes to occur in social policy, the nature of the proposals put forth by those interested in reform must be appropriate to the political climate at that point in history. "Thus, even though the US began to implement social insurance and comprehensive benefit programs in the late 19th century," N. B. Rosenthal wrote in his review of the book for *Choice* (November 1995), "limited federal authority and a concomitantly weak national bureaucracy prevented the development of a full welfare state. The lesson of this history, [Skocpol] contends, is that the only benefits proposals that have lasted and flourished in the US are universal ones—like social security—that have spread costs and visibly delivered benefits across classes and races." The book contained a series of previously published essays that trace the history of welfare policies from the New Deal to the present. Skocpol once again challenged the assumption that most Americans oppose progressive social policy, while reminding readers that in order for such policy to be implemented, its benefits must be distributed equitably. Robert A. Isaak referred to the book in *Perspectives in Political Science* (Winter 1996) as "an indispensable historical preface to social policy in the United States for professionals who desire to understand the political limits of social reforms as we end the 20th century."

Skocpol's *Boomerang: Health Reform and the Turn Against Government* (1997) chronicled the social and historical factors that led to the defeat of Democratic president Bill Clinton's health-care reform proposals in 1993, in spite of general support among U.S. citizens for universal health coverage. Skocpol suggested that the proposals had failed because the Democrats were divided on the issue and lost credibility when they could not explain to their constituents the complicated compromises they had made in order to reach an agreement; in contrast, the Republicans were unified in their opposition to the proposed reforms and had once again demonstrated their ability to organize effectively at the grass-roots level. Also, there was widespread antigovernment feeling among Americans at the time, as revealed by the 1994 elections, in which Republicans gained control of Congress for the first time in four decades. *Boomerang* recommended that academics and upper-middle-class progressives forge new relationships with their fellow Americans in an effort to bring about much-needed change in the health-care system.

Skocpol told *Mother Jones* (September/October 1996) that she believes that the Republicans' popularity soon declined because they took it for granted that the American public would support any legislation that sought to take advantage of antigovernment sentiment: "I don't believe that Americans in general are hostile to getting things from government or even doing things through government. Americans like government programs that embody broadly shared values and deliver resources to people who are perceived as behaving properly and contributing to work and community," Skocpol said. Furthermore, she believes that most of the GOP leaders at the time—academics who lived in the suburban South—were out of touch with the needs of many Americans. "That milieu has nurtured the sense that the only institutions that really matter are the individual family, the small business, and maybe a church congregation or two. If you visit some of those areas, there are not a lot of big institutions around, such as universities and hospitals. [Former Speaker of the House Newt] Gingrich targets the professionals and managers who work for those nonprofit institutions as the enemy. And a lot of the freshmen are New South, entrepreneurial types. Many have never been involved in government or in big institutions of any kind. So they've lived out a politics that flows from a certain kind of lifestyle." Skocpol also told *Mother Jones* that although the labor movement had seen a revival, the Democrats still had a long way to go to build a sustainable grass-roots presence. "Democrats are split between people who would like to sustain the major New Deal programs of the past, and a business wing that wants to scrap all that, just like the Republicans. And the racial splits in the Democratic Party remain very strong."

Although Skocpol encourages the activity of grassroots organizers, she emphasizes that this alone is not enough to bring about the changes that she feels are needed. "Organized civil society has never flourished apart from active government and inclusive democratic politics," she wrote for *American Prospect* (March/April 1996). "Civic vitality has also depended on vibrant ties across classes and localities. If we want to repair civil society, we must first and foremost revitalize political democracy. The sway of money in politics will have to be curtailed, and privileged Americans will have to join their fellow citizens in broad civic endeavors. Re-establishing local voluntary groups alone will not suffice."

Skocpol is a frequent lecturer and serves on the editorial boards of several scholarly journals, including *Studies in American Political Development* and the *American Political Science Review*, the premier journal in the field of political science. She has received research grants from both the Ford Foundation, the MacArthur Foundation, and the Russell Sage Foundation; her honors include a John Simon Guggenheim Fellowship as well as the C. Wright Mills Award. She is an elected member of both the National Academy of Social Insurance and the American Academy of Arts and Sciences.

In her spare time Skocpol enjoys collecting old ribbon-badges and reading murder mysteries. She lives with her husband, Bill, a physicist based at Boston University, and their son, Michael. Skocpol wrote in *Theory and Society* that her "excellent marriage to an egalitarian man of the sixties . . . has always been a major factor in my career achievements as well as my long-term personal happiness." During the summer she lives and writes in Mount Desert, Maine. — C.L.

Suggested Reading: *American Prospect* p20+ Mar./Apr. 1996; *Cambridge Chronicle* p10 Nov. 7, 1996; *Chronicle of Higher Education* A p7+ Feb. 24, 1993, with photo; *Extensions: A Journal of the Carl Albert Congressional Research and Studies Center* p2+ Fall 1999, with photos; *Mother Jones* p47+ Sep./Oct. 1996, with photo; *New York Times* A p21 Feb. 9, 1994; *Political Science Quarterly* p85+ Spring 1993; *Theory and Society* Vol. 17 p627+ 1988

Selected Books: *States and Social Revolutions: A Comparative Analysis of France, Russia, and China,* 1979; *Protecting Soldiers and Mothers: The Political Origins of Social Policy in the United States,* 1992; *Social Revolutions in the Modern World,* 1994; *Social Policy in the United States: Future Possibilities in Historical Perspective,* 1995; *Boomerang: Health Reform and the Turn Against Government,* 1997

Smith, Frederick W.

Aug. 11, 1944– Founder and head of FedEx Corp. Address: FedEx Corp., P.O. Box 727, Memphis, TN 38132

Every night several hundred planes bearing a purple, white, and orange design touch down at Memphis Airport, in Tennessee. Crews unload the planes' cargo of, on average, more than half a million parcels and letters, picked up from locations all over the United States earlier in the day. The packages and envelopes are rapidly sorted according to address, then loaded onto other aircraft and

Associated Press

Frederick W. Smith

flown to their destinations, to be hand delivered—many within 24 hours of leaving their senders. This sequence of events is the culmination of a dream of Frederick W. Smith, the founder, president, chief executive officer, and chairman of the board of the FedEx Corp.—known originally as Federal Express—the largest and most successful overnight delivery service in the world. Conceived when he was in college and now in its 28th year of operation, Smith's brainchild has become the standard for door-to-door package delivery. Known for his geniality as well as his business acumen, Smith is reportedly held in high regard by his competitors as well as his employees. "I always said I thought one of the most brilliant parts of Fred Smith was his ability to deal with each person individually," Tuck Morse, a former Federal Express lawyer, recalled to Vance Trimble, the author of *Overnight Success: Federal Express & Frederick Smith, Its Renegade Creator* (1993). "That is a real talent that I haven't seen much of in my business career." Indeed, 3.2 percent of the entire Memphis workforce is made up of FedEx employees, who are said to have been drawn by the company's high wages and family ethos. "The first thing people do when they move to Memphis is apply for a job at Federal Express," one FedEx worker told an interviewer for *Fortune* (August 17, 1987). "Then they go get another job until one opens up here."

Frederick Wallace Smith was born into a wealthy family on August 11, 1944 in Marks, Mississippi. He has at least two sisters. His father, also named Fred, helped to build the Greyhound bus system for the entire South; he also co-owned Toodle House, a successful chain of restaurants. After his father's death, when he was four years old, his mother, Sally Smith, often talked to the boy about her late husband. "I kept his father alive in his mind all those years," she recalled to Trimble. "I told him how much big Fred loved him, and how much he wanted him to have the best education possible. And how much he was certain his son would surpass his achievements in business."

As a child, Smith suffered from Legg-Calvé-Perthes disease, which is characterized by the interruption in the blood supply to the thighbones and the consequent improper development of one or both legs. Unable to walk normally, Smith was picked on by bullies, and he learned to defend himself by swinging at them with his crutch. Reportedly cured of the disease by the age of 10, he became a star athlete in high school, playing football, basketball, and baseball. At 15 he learned how to pilot a plane, while working with a local crop duster.

After graduating from Memphis University High School, in 1962, Smith attended Yale University, in New Haven, Connecticut, where he joined both the Delta Kappa Epsilon fraternity and the Marine Corps Reserve and enjoyed great popularity. In his senior year Smith was tapped to join the prestigious, secret campus society Skull and Bones. As an undergraduate he wrote a term paper for an economics class detailing his idea of an overnight-delivery service that relied on air transport. It was widely assumed at the time that sooner or later, airlines would replace railroads and trucks as the primary method of freight delivery. "I started off to write the paper to support . . . the conventional wisdom," Smith explained to Les Seago for the Yonkers *Herald Statesman* (September 5, 1978). "The longer I went into it. . . the more I found that whole theory . . . was erroneous. That there just wasn't any way an airplane was ever going to compete with a truck as long as they were fossil fuel based." Smith was referring to passenger airplanes that also carried freight; the system he proposed could work, he wrote in his paper, only if a certain number of flight routes were restricted to planes that carried only freight. His idea (or perhaps the way he presented it) did not impress his professor, who gave the essay a C.

After graduating from Yale, with a B.S. degree in economics, in 1966, Smith served two tours of military duty as a marine company commander during the Vietnam War. While on his first tour, in Vietnam, he survived an ambush that left most of his company dead. During the assault he became separated from his gun, but he managed to retrieve the weapon in time to bring down a Vietcong soldier who was about to attack him. "I was so frightened that I aimed at his head and hit his knee," he told Robert J. Flaherty for *Forbes* (March 1, 1977). "To this day I don't understand how he missed me because they always aim for the company commander." During his second tour Smith served as a pilot, flying more than 200 ground-support missions. By the end of his 27 months in Vietnam, he had earned the Silver Star, the Bronze Star, two Purple Hearts, and the Presidential Regiment Citation. He had also learned a valuable lesson from his sergeant, as he told Linda Grant for *Fortune* (November 10, 1997). "There's only three things you gotta remember," the sergeant had told him: "shoot, move, and communicate."

During his wartime service and the period following it, Smith told Flaherty, "I got so sick of destruction and blowing things up—on people I had nothing against—that I came back determined to do something constructive." According to *Who's Who in America, 2000*, from 1969 to 1971 he owned Ark Aviation. Meanwhile, he had resolved to make his undergraduate freight-delivery idea a reality. He envisioned a delivery service in which planes would bring packages to a central location, or "hub," and then fly them to their destinations. Thus, all parcels bound for, say, San Francisco, would travel there together from Memphis, which he chose as the hub because the weather there is rarely bad enough to delay flights. The planes would fly primarily at night, to avoid air traffic and airport congestion. Using the $11 million he had inherited from his father and an additional $60 million in venture capital that he had raised, Smith assembled a fleet of 14 French-built Falcon jets and many vans. "People thought we were bananas," he recalled to Winston Williams for the *New York Times* (January 7, 1979). "We were too ignorant to know that we weren't supposed to be able to do certain things. We wanted to fly uneconomic planes and fly everything to Memphis." On April 17, 1973 Federal Express began picking up packages in 25 cities, and the next day FedEx trucks began whisking them to their recipients.

The early days of Federal Express were marked by extreme frugality and enormous financial losses. It was not uncommon for FedEx drivers to pay for gasoline for their vans out of their own pockets, and pilots were constantly on the lookout for deputy sheriffs with writs of attachment for their airplanes. But despite such problems, Smith always showed concern for the welfare for his employees (as he has continued to do ever since). "Even when we didn't have the money, even when there weren't couches in this office and electric typewriters, we had a good medical plan for our people," he told Les Seago. After two years in operation, the company had incurred losses amounting to $26 million. In addition, Smith's sisters had brought suit against him for mishandling the family fortune. Then, thanks largely to a strike by employees of its competitor Air Express, in 1976, Federal Express began to turn a profit. Also helping to improve the firm's fortunes was the streamlining of the delivery schedule by Arthur Bass, a former pilot and airline consultant who helped to launch the company and served as its president from 1975 to 1980.

While the Falcon jets served Federal Express well, they sometimes proved inadequate to handle the tremendous volume of packages consigned to the company for delivery. So, after Federal Express climbed out of the red, Smith began a campaign to persuade Congress, Department of Transportation officials, and the Civil Aeronautics Board to lift restrictions on using larger planes for the transport of freight. In an energetic lobbying campaign, he pushed his employees to write letters urging their congressional representatives to change the law. He also distributed a brochure entitled *Free Enterprise Needs a Little Help*, and he sent top Federal Express executives to speak on the issue before civic and business organizations. On October 20, 1977 President Jimmy Carter signed into law a transportation bill that included an amendment permitting all cargo carriers to use aircraft of any size. Smith immediately put into service Boeing 727s, which were capable of carrying a 42,000-pound payload. Before long Federal Express retired its Falcons (one was displayed for a time in the Smithsonian Institution, in Washington, D.C.) and added McDonnell Douglas DC-10s and Boeing 737s to its fleet.

By 1983 the not-yet-10-year-old Federal Express had earned its first billion dollars, and its stock was selling at $47 a share. Later in the decade the company suffered a setback, stemming from Smith's idea of offering a fax-transmission service called ZapMail. Designed to compete with fax machines, which were just coming into wide use and were threatening to encroach on Federal Express's letter-delivery service, ZapMail enabled a customer to fax a letter from one Federal Express fax machine to another. By the time Smith had the service up and running, fax machines had become standard equipment in most U.S. offices. When Smith pulled the plug on ZapMail, in September 1989, the project had racked up pretax losses of $326.8 million.

By the end of the 1980s, Federal Express had suffered additional losses, in part because of stiff competition from United Parcel Service's airfreight business. Hoping to end such reversals, Smith set his sights on expanding the company's overseas operations. In December 1988 he announced Federal Express's purchase of Tiger International Inc., the world's largest heavy-cargo airline, for $880 million. Smith had been eager to gain control of Tiger's delivery routes and overseas landing rights, so that Federal Express would no longer have to depend on outside contractors to deliver to other countries. Speaking of the merger, which entailed the addition of 6,500 Tiger employees to the Federal Express payroll, Smith admitted to Dean Foust for *Business Week* (February 13, 1989), "It's a big challenge—no question." But, responding to warnings that the company was "playing big casino, with big risks," as the industry consultant Bernard J. La Londe put it to Foust, Smith declared to the same reporter, "I don't know that it's a bet-the-company move. We get a lot of hard assets with this acquisition."

Nevertheless, Federal Express ran into trouble almost immediately. With the goal of setting up a hub in Frankfurt, in what was then West Germany, the company requested that the city airport alter night-flight curfews and amend labor laws. But airport officials refused, so FedEx made Brussels, Belgium, the European center of operations, while using a separate site in Frankfurt for the storage of freight. By 1991 FedEx's international operations were showing losses hovering at around $200 million. "The operations needed to support our intra-European service have been extremely costly, and we have not generated adequate revenues to cover our costs," Smith told an unnamed reporter quoted by Trimble. "In addition, the market in Europe has not developed express traffic as quickly as we had expected it to." At the start of 1992, Smith began a retreat from Europe, closing the Brussels hub, laying off 6,600 employees, and canceling the leases on a dozen planes. In addition, FedEx struck deals with Securicor Omega Express Ltd. and TNT Express Europe N.V., turning over many of its European courier services to them in exchange for delivery of their packages in the United States. "It's important to understand what we are doing and what we are not doing," Trimble quoted Thomas R. Oliver, who in 1990 was named FedEx's senior vice president for international operations, as saying. "We will pick up a package in Rome, Georgia, and fly it to Paris, France. We still pick up a package in Paris, France, and fly it to Rome, Georgia. But we will not pick up a package in Paris, France and fly it to Rome, Italy." Before long FedEx was delivering packages within 48 hours to 210 countries. In *Forbes* (December 9, 1991), Seth Lubove wrote that Smith's "decision to buy Flying Tiger looks all the smarter now, since lack of foreign landing rights has slowed the global expansion of rival United Parcel Service, one of the few freight companies besides FedEx that own and operate their own airplanes." In 1993 FedEx's international division began showing a profit.

In 1994 Federal Express officially changed its name to FedEx. Also that year it became one of the first companies to use the Internet for customer service, by introducing a system on its Web site that enabled clients to schedule pickups, track packages, and print labels using their personal computers. "It was not acceptable in our minds," Smith told David Joachim for *Internet Week* (October 25, 1999, on-line), "that customers should be willing to take goods that were very valuable to them and just throw them into this big anonymous transportation system and hope it came out the other end."

In January 1998 FedEx acquired Caliber System, a trucking company with revenues of $2.7 billion, and formed FDX Corp., a holding company that oversees all operations of the FedEx corporation and its subsidiaries. Describing FDX to Joachim, Smith said, "We are a transportation and logistics company which has as its heart these Internet, information, and telecommunication technologies. Just as a modern air force is still an air force but at its heart are all these sophisticated IT [information technology] technologies." In early 2000 FDX changed its name to FedEx Corp. and streamlined the company's services by allowing the various divisions to operate independently. In April 2000 FedEx made headlines when federal drug officials announced that 45 of the company's drivers and couriers had been arrested for their roles in a scheme in which more than 120 tons of marijuana had been ferried from California to the East Coast over the previous two years.

Although Smith avoids the media and the trappings of public life, he is said to be a gregarious and accessible employer. He reportedly visits FedEx's Memphis site at night from time to time and addresses sorters by name, and for years he extended an offer to any courier with 10 years of service to come to Memphis for an "anniversary breakfast." His first marriage, to the former Linda Grisham, ended in divorce in 1977. He and his second wife, the former Diane Avis, live in an upscale section of Memphis; the couple have 10 children, among them two from Fred Smith's first marriage and one from Diane's. Smith is an avid tennis player and a voracious reader who is said to love giving as well as receiving books as gifts. — J.K.B.

Suggested Reading: *Business Week* p66+ Feb. 13, 1989, with photos; *Forbes* p36+ Mar. 1, 1977, with photos; *Fortune* p35+ Aug. 17, 1987, with photo; *New York Times* III p1+ Jan. 7, 1979, with photos; (Yonkers) *Herald Statesman* B p14 Sep. 5, 1978, with photo; Trimble, Vance. *Overnight Success: Federal Express & Frederick Smith, Its Renegade Creator*, 1993

Smith, Robert

Mar. 30, 1941– U.S. Senator from New Hampshire. Address: 307 Dirksen Senate Office Bldg., Washington, DC 20510

While many politicians prefer to steer clear of controversy, United States senator Bob Smith, the two-term Republican from New Hampshire, has staked a claim in the front lines of many political battles. On the floor of the Senate, he delivers impassioned speeches that champion conservative causes and leave no doubt about his opposition to legalized abortion, homosexuality, gun control, high taxes, Cuban dictator Fidel Castro, and expansion of the North Atlantic Treaty Organization (NATO). Not surprisingly, liberals dismiss Smith as a divisive, right-wing extremist. By contrast, conservatives embrace him as a hard-working legislator who has the courage to stand up for his beliefs, regardless of their popularity. In July 1999 Smith received national attention when he left the Republican Party, angrily accusing the party's leadership of abandoning its traditional, conservative principles, and announced his intention to run for president as an independent candidate. By the end of the year, however, he had withdrawn from the presidential race

Courtesy of the U.S. Senate

Robert Smith

and rejoined the Republican Party to become chairman of the influential Senate Environment and Public Works Committee. In a statement (November 1, 1999) published on his Web site, Smith explained: "My goal in public life is to make conservative policy the national policy of the United States. I want to unite those of us who believe in small government, low taxes, Second Amendment rights, a strong military, pro-life, local control of education, national sovereignty, and the restoration of Constitutional freedoms in our society. . . . I am like the pioneer scout who has returned to the wagon train—to report that the path I've explored is more dangerous. Like that scout, I am returning to the Republican Party with enthusiasm and vigor to re-energize and re-unify conservatives in this nation. . . . I speak from experience when I say that the best way to do that is through the Republican Party."

Robert Clinton Smith was born on March 30, 1941 in Trenton, New Jersey. During World War II, and shortly before Smith's fourth birthday, his father, a navy pilot, was killed in a plane crash. According to his Web site, Smith was raised on his grandparents' farm, in Allentown, New Jersey. His mother worked hard to support him and his brother.

After graduating from Lafayette College, in Easton, Pennsylvania, where he majored in political science, Smith joined the navy in 1965. The following year, he was sent to Vietnam, where he was stationed on a ship in the Gulf of Tonkin. In 1970, after leaving the military, Smith settled with his wife, Mary Jo, in New Hampshire. There, he taught high-school history and government and also coached baseball and football. He later opened a real-estate business and served on the local school board.

Smith ran for a seat in the House of Representatives in 1980 and 1982, losing both times. In 1984, on the coattails of President Ronald Reagan's landslide reelection victory, Smith was finally elected to Congress, representing New Hampshire's First District. He was easily re-elected in 1986 and 1988. A profile in *USA Today* (November 8, 1990) observed that Smith's "voting record has been one of the most conservative in the House."

In 1987 Smith joined then–House minority whip Newt Gingrich and two other Republican congressmen in sponsoring legislation to create an independent commission to investigate corruption in the House of Representatives. The four Republicans argued that the House Committee on Standards of Official Conduct had failed to properly discipline members who were charged with ethical breaches. Although the proposal was rejected by the House, its sponsors gained credibility when both House Speaker Jim Wright of Texas and majority whip Tony Coelho of California resigned from Congress in 1989, after being accused of corruption.

In 1990 New Hampshire senator Gordon Humphrey, a conservative Republican, stunned political observers when he announced his retirement. Smith promptly entered the race to replace him and won a narrow victory over former Democratic senator John Durkin in the general election. In his first year in the Senate, Smith clashed with the Democratic majority leader, George Mitchell of Maine. Smith introduced legislation that would prohibit Maine from taxing the incomes of the 4,000 New Hampshire residents who worked at the Portsmouth Naval Shipyard, which is located on an island in the Piscataqua River connected by two bridges to Kittery, Maine, which lies opposite Portsmouth, New Hampshire. Mitchell strongly opposed Smith's proposal, which would have taken money away from his home state. Although the legislation was defeated by a wide margin, Smith claimed a moral victory, having been successful in bringing the dispute to a vote.

On the morning of January 25, 1993, Smith, driving to the Capitol on Route 123 in Virginia, passed the CIA's headquarters in Langley as a gunman there began shooting at several cars, killing two people and wounding three others. "My first reaction was I was glad my sons were not in the car," Smith told D'Vera Cohn, a reporter for the *Washington Post* (January 26, 1993). In spite of that incident, he has refused to support gun-control legislation. In "Bob Smith on the Issues," which appears on his Web site, Smith explained his opposition to gun control: "It is the right of every American citizen to own a firearm to protect himself and his family. . . . I believe that [crime] is the result of moral decay, the breakdown of the family, and a revolving-door criminal justice system. The solution is to punish the guilty, not the peaceful citizen who owns a gun for defensive or sporting purposes."

Throughout his political career, Smith has championed the cause of those who believe that American military personnel are still being held as prisoners of war (POWs) in Vietnam. In 1992 he served as vice chairman of a Senate select committee that investigated the controversy, which had been fueled in recent years by a number of movies. Although Smith initially agreed with the committee's report, which found no evidence that American POWs were still alive in Vietnam, he changed his mind in 1993. In an interview with Adam Clymer for the *New York Times* (September 8, 1993), Smith noted that after visiting Vietnam in July of that year, he had discovered "compelling evidence," which he declined to discuss in detail, that American POWs were still alive. Smith also made public a letter he sent to Attorney General Janet Reno, demanding that the Department of Justice investigate 10 former government officials, who had submitted testimony to the committee, for allegedly committing perjury. "If you don't raise hell on this issue and be aggressive and really push people, you don't get any answers," Smith said to Clymer. Two of Smith's Senate colleagues, the Democrat John Kerry of Massachusetts and the Republican John McCain of Arizona—who both served in the Vietnam War—strongly criticized his actions as reckless and irresponsible. Clymer quoted McCain as saying, "I frankly don't feel it's appropriate to publicly make these charges without public substantiation." Smith backtracked, admitting that releasing the letter publicly had been a mistake. The Department of Justice declined to pursue the allegations, citing a lack of evidence.

In 1995 Smith introduced legislation to overhaul the Superfund Program, created by Congress in 1980 to clean up toxic-waste sites. Critics have argued that Superfund has been ineffective due to high costs and endless delays in cleaning up sites. The Clinton administration opposed Smith's legislation, arguing that it would absolve companies that are guilty of dumping toxic waste from financial responsibility. The senator has continued his efforts toward Superfund reform every year since then. Smith led the 1995 fight in the Senate to outlaw so-called partial-birth abortions, a medical procedure used to end pregnancies in the late stages. A significant number of pro-choice politicians, including the Democratic leaders of the House and Senate, objected to partial-birth abortions on moral grounds and also endorsed the ban. The legislation passed both houses of Congress, only to be vetoed by President Clinton; Congress lacked the votes to override the president's decision.

In 1996 Smith ran for reelection against former Democratic representative Dick Swett, whose chances were bolstered by the Democrats' aggressive campaigns to win New Hampshire's two congressional seats as well as the governorship. Another factor in Swett's favor was that in that year's presidential race, most polls showed President Clinton leading his Republican opponent, Bob Dole, by double digits in the traditionally conservative state. The race between Smith and Swett was often nasty in tone. Swett portrayed himself as a pro-choice moderate while attacking Smith as a far-right ideologue; he also criticized Smith's vote for a congressional pay raise in 1991. Smith countered by branding Swett as a liberal who had supported President Clinton's failed health-care plan in 1993. Smith also referred to the fact that Swett had voted in 1994 to outlaw assault weapons, after pledging to oppose the measure. Most experts predicted a close race. After analyzing several exit polls during its election-night coverage, CNN announced that Swett had ousted Smith. However, after all the votes were counted, Smith emerged the victor, by only three percentage points.

During his second term in the Senate, Smith has renewed his efforts to reform Superfund and pass legislation to outlaw partial-birth abortions. He supported the deployment of an antimissile defense system (but not NATO expansion); he also opposed military intervention in Kosovo and the Clinton administration's decision to return Elian Gonzalez—the young son of a woman who had died while fleeing Cuba—to his homeland. During the trial of President Clinton in the Senate, following charges that he had obstructed justice in trying to hide his relationship with the former White House intern Monica Lewinsky, Smith voted guilty on both articles of impeachment.

As early as 1997, Smith had hinted that he would run for president in 2000. He announced his candidacy on February 18, 1999. Most political commentators gave him little chance of winning the nomination or even making a strong showing. "I've been fighting day after day for the past 15 years in the United States House and the Senate for the conservative values I believe best represent New Hampshire," Smith said, as quoted by Richard Berke in the *New York Times* (February 19, 1999). "I might be a new face in this Presidential campaign, but I'm an old warrior."

Many Republicans in New Hampshire were not pleased with Smith's plans to seek the presidency, believing that his candidacy would jeopardize New Hampshire's cherished role as host of the first-in-the-nation primary, which often makes or breaks presidential bids. As Carey Goldberg, a reporter for the *New York Times* (October 5, 1997), observed, "The problem . . . is this: If Mr. Smith runs, other candidates may figure that he is a hometown boy against whom they have no chance, so they may decide to forgo a serious effort in the state."

Over the next few months, Smith campaigned energetically, making several trips to Iowa, which holds its caucus before the New Hampshire primary, and courting support from Christian conservatives. Smith's efforts were frustrated by his failure to raise sufficient campaign funds and his inability to make a strong showing in most polls, including those conducted in his home state. Meanwhile, Texas governor George W. Bush raised almost

$100 million in campaign funds for the primary, and the publisher Steve Forbes and the activist Gary Bauer also received some Republican backing.

In July 1999 Smith shocked political observers when he announced that he was officially leaving the Republican Party. "This is not a party. Maybe it is a party in the sense of wearing hats and blowing whistles, but it is not a political party that means anything," Smith said on the floor of the Senate, as quoted by Carroll J. Doherty in *Congressional Quarterly Weekly* (July 17, 1999). "The Republican platform is a meaningless document that has been put out there so suckers like me . . . can read it." He criticized the Republican leadership for abandoning the party's core principles, especially with regard to abortion. Smith also condemned the influence of professional pollsters and campaign consultants, whom he accused of urging party leaders to downplay such controversial issues as abortion and gun control for fear of alienating voters. The Senator vowed to continue his presidential campaign as an independent, though he made overtures to both the Reform Party and the conservative U.S. Taxpayers Party.

Many Republicans decried Smith's actions, not least because they feared that Smith would contribute to a Democratic victory by splitting the Republican vote. According to John DiStaso, a writer for the *Union Leader* (July 10, 1999, on-line), Jim Nicholson, the chairman of the Republican National Committee (RNC), sent a letter to Smith, warning him that leaving the Republican Party was "a serious mistake for you personally, with only a marginal political impact. . . . In other words, I hope you do not confuse the success of our shared message with your own failure as its messenger." Steve Duprey, the chairman of the Republican Party in New Hampshire, also expressed disapproval, telling DiStaso, "He was elected with a lot of help from Republicans, and quite honestly, without the financial support of the Republican national and state committees in 1996, Bob Smith wouldn't have been reelected to the Senate."

Some conservatives, however, applauded Smith. In the *Union Leader* (July 18, 1999, on-line), conservative columnist Jack Kenny wrote, "Bob Smith's bold step to political independence was a much deserved and long overdue kick in the pants to the national leadership of the Republican Party. . . . Thanks to Sen. Smith, a great many Americans . . . will know there is an alternative to the typical two-party Presidential menu, offering a choice between the truly horrible and the merely useless."

Smith decided against seeking the nomination of the U.S. Taxpayers Party after discovering that some of its members were anti-Catholic. With little money to campaign, Smith abandoned his presidential hopes in the fall and returned to the Republican Party. The *Concord Monitor* (March 16, 2000, on-line) quoted Smith as saying,"Leaving the party was a mistake. . . . I've learned the hard way, in the legislative process you have to compromise."

With the death of Republican senator John Chafee of Rhode Island, in October 1999, Smith became chairman of the Senate Environment and Public Works Committee. Many activists expressed fears that Smith would seek to weaken laws that protect the environment. "With Smith chairing the Senate Environment Committee, polluters could have a field day," Debbie Sease, the Sierra Club's legislative director, said to Margaret Kriz, a writer for the *National Journal* (January 29, 2000). Speaking with Kriz, Smith denied allegations that he was "anti-environmental" but admitted that he would set a more conservative agenda than the previous chairman of the committee. He also vowed to use his influence to push for the reform of Superfund. In the *Washington Post* (May 31, 2000), Helen Dewar wrote that Smith had taken "one action after another that surprised and pleased his erstwhile environmental critics." Dewar cited Smith's support for a $7.8 billion plan for the restoration of the Florida Everglades, the protection of the Arctic National Wildlife Refuge from oil and gas drilling, and the banning of a gasoline additive that pollutes drinking water. "It's not anti-conservative to be pro-environment," Smith told Dewar.

Bob Smith also serves on the Senate Armed Services Committee, the Judiciary Committee, and the Ethics Committee. He and his wife have three children and make their home in the New Hampshire town of Tuftonboro. Smith will be up for reelection in 2002. — D.C.

Suggested Reading: *Concord Monitor* (on-line) Mar. 16, 2000; *Congressional Quarterly Weekly* p1713 July 17, 1999, p2587 Oct. 30, 1999; *National Journal* p324+ Jan. 29, 2000; *New York Times* I p16 Sep. 8, 1993, I p36 Oct. 5, 1997, I p15 Feb. 19, 1999; Senator Bob Smith Web site; *Union Leader* (on-line) July 10, 1999, July 18, 2000; *Washington Post* I p8 Feb. 18, 1999, I p25 May 31, 2000

Smith, Zadie

Oct. 27, 1975– Writer. Address: c/o Random House Inc., 299 Park Ave., Eighth Fl., New York, NY 10171

The 25-year-old British writer Zadie Smith took readers and the literary establishment by surprise with her first novel, *White Teeth* (2000), portraying the private hopes and fears of Londoners, native and immigrant. In colloquial dialogue, with humor and wit to spare, she has displayed a profound understanding of the aspirations driving her characters, as each one struggles with the baggage of his or her cultural origins.

Roderick Field/Courtesy of Random House

Zadie Smith

Zadie Smith was born in England on October 27, 1975. Her mother had immigrated to England from Jamaica, settling in London to work as a model and later becoming a child psychoanalyst. Her father, who is British, worked as a photographer. Smith and her two younger brothers were raised in Willesden Green, a working-class suburb in northwest London, where much of her novel is set. When Smith was a child, she has recounted, the family spent holidays in the English town of Devon, where, "if you're black . . . everyone turns and looks at you. So my instinct . . . was always to over-compensate by trying to behave three times as well as every other child in the shop. . . . I think that instinct has spilled over into my writing . . . which is not something I like very much or want to continue," she told Maria Russo in an interview for *Salon* (April 28, 2000, on-line).

Smith's parents divorced when she was 12 years old, perhaps contributing to what she described to Nadya Labi for *Time* (May 8, 2000) as a "pathologically angst ridden" adolescence. For solace she turned to writing poetry and short stories as well as tap dancing, which she studied for 10 years and dreamt of pursuing as a career. She gave up that ambition after she "got too fat," as she told Nadya Labi. Similarly, she entertained hopes of being a jazz singer, but she "wasn't as good as Aretha [Franklin]."

Smith has said that she was a badly behaved teenager when she attended the local, state-run schools, but this did not prevent her from earning admittance to one of the oldest and most prestigious colleges in Britain—Cambridge University. She majored in English at the university's King's College, nicknamed "The People's Republic of King's" for the left-wing political views associated with it. While Smith discovered that there was only one other black girl at King's College, she did not feel alienated there, since she was able to find "kindred spirits," as she told Sam Wallace for *The Age* (February 5, 2000, on-line). During her years of study, she consciously pursued the prestigious Rylands Prize, awarded by King's College for student fiction and poetry. In her senior year she won the award with a collection of stories.

In 1996 Smith published the story "The Newspaper Man" in *May Anthologies*, a well-regarded annual collection of short stories and poetry by Cambridge and Oxford University students. The story brought her to the attention of the publishing house HarperCollins. It has been reported that Smith offered to write a novel for an advance of $5,000 from the publisher; a friend of hers then intervened and persuaded her to get a literary agent. As a result, Smith spent evenings in the college computer room during the exam-preparation period, writing an 80-page sample chapter to show to agents. The high-profile Andrew Wylie literary agency, whose clients include the novelist Salman Rushdie, signed her on. When the agency auctioned her novel to London publishers, a bidding war began. Smith, then only 21 years old, signed a two-book contract with Penguin Books for a figure said to be in the vicinity of $390,000.

The high level of excitement stirred by *White Teeth*, whose action begins in 1970s Britain, was partly a result of its appeal to a wide range of readers, regardless of age, gender, or politics. Two of the main characters in the sprawling novel are middle-aged men—Samad, a Bengali Muslim, and Archie, a white Englishman—navigating their wartime memories and their marriages to much younger women. The men find themselves bewildered by, and unable to conform to, late-20th-century conventions. Other prominent characters include Samad's twin sons and Archie's biracial daughter, all seeking to define themselves amid the expectations of others. In the novel Smith "exposes the hilarity of the rules we live by," as Nadya Labi put it in *Time* (May 8, 2000), her characters spending their lives in "a negotiation in disappointment." Salman Rushdie called *White Teeth* "an astonishingly assured début," according to the Random House Web site. As of November 2000 the BBC (British Broadcasting Corp.) was said to be developing *White Teeth* into a miniseries.

"I really don't think anyone should write a first novel at my age," Smith told Kevin Jackson in an interview for the *New Yorker* (October 18–25, 1999). "The question is," she said to Sam Wallace, "do you want a writer to carry on writing? If you give them a huge amount of money, that's going to help them in that they're going to have food and heating, but if you turn them into celebrities then you're killing them." In that regard, Smith looks up to J. M. Coetzee, the South African writer who is the first novelist to win the prestigious Booker Prize twice and who declined to attend the award ceremony on the second occasion. Smith called this refusal to be drawn into celebrity culture "basic writer survival technique," according to Wallace.

Smith has named E. M. Forster, John Updike, and Thomas Pynchon among the writers whose books have influenced her. Speaking of recent works by writers of the African diaspora, Smith told Labi, "A lot of black writing is this love-in, and I definitely don't write love-ins." In writing *White Teeth*, Smith sought to defy people's expectations of the subject matter she would tackle, given what Labi called her "personal demographics." "What did people think I was going to write?" Smith asked Labi. "Some kind of searing slave drama or single-girl-in-London tale?" Smith did not entirely avoid drawing from her own experiences, since the background of her character Irie—the daughter of an English man and a Jamaican woman—is similar in many ways to her own. At the same time, the novel's subject matter extends far beyond the autobiographical; her characters include Bengali Muslims, Jews, Jamaicans, teens, and octogenarians. Thanks to her remarkable ear for dialect, those characters' speaking styles emerge as distinct without lapsing into caricature.

Sam Wallace described Zadie Smith as being "tall with high cheekbones and long curly hair." Smith recently published a short story in the *New Yorker*'s millennial fiction issue. In February 2000 she began a stint as a writer-in-residence at the Institute of Contemporary Arts, in London. She is currently working on her second novel, "The Autograph Man," about a London autograph dealer who is involved with various religious sects. Smith lives in an apartment in London, five minutes away from her mother and two brothers, who still reside in Willesden Green. — V.K.

Suggested Reading: *The Age* (on line), Feb. 5, 2000, with photo; *New Yorker* p182 Oct. 18–25, 1999, with photo; *Salon* (on-line), Apr. 28, 2000; *Time* p94 May 8, 2000, with photo

Selected Books: *White Teeth*, 2000

Armando Gallo/Retna Ltd.

Sorkin, Aaron

1961– Screenwriter; playwright; television producer. Address: NBC Studios, 3000 W. Alameda Ave., Burbank, CA 91523

"My advice to young writers would be: 'Don't write two television shows at the same time,'" Aaron Sorkin stated in a piece for *Written By* (September 1999, on-line). While the creator of the critically acclaimed (but now canceled) program *Sports Night* and the ratings powerhouse *The West Wing* may be good at dispensing such advice, he is not apt to take it. During the 1999–2000 season Sorkin routinely wrote each episode of both shows while maintaining his reputation as one of the hottest screenwriters in Hollywood. He first made a name for himself in the late 1980s, when his play *A Few Good Men* was performed on Broadway. Later he pursued screenwriting, working with the director Rob Reiner on the film version of *A Few Good Men* as well as on the highly regarded movie *The American President* (1995). Most recently Sorkin has turned to political drama, a genre once considered anathema to prime-time television, to create the most watched new series of the past year, *The West Wing*. Those who have worked with Sorkin—or are eager to do so—invariably cite the quality of his writing, which brims with passion, clever language, and penetrating metaphors. "With Aaron's dialogue you're walking on the razor's edge of comedy and drama," Rob Lowe, who plays deputy communications director Sam Seaborn on *The West Wing*, told Bernard Weinraub for the *New York Times* (September 26, 1999). "When I read the [*West Wing*] script, it was as good as any movie I've read, and certainly better than any television show I've ever read."

Aaron Sorkin was born in 1961 in the Chelsea district of Manhattan, in New York City. As a child he attended the Little Red School House in Greenwich Village, a nearby section of the city, along with many students—such as a daughter of the music legend Bob Dylan—who came from colorful backgrounds. "I used to think I could never be a successful playwright because I didn't have an exotic life story," he told Ross Wetzsteon in an interview for *New York* (November 6, 1989). "No trailer-park childhood. No school in Lisbon. No broken family or Catholic guilt. I feel disqualified to write plays. Boy, have I had a white-bread life!" When Sorkin was eight his years old, his family moved to Scarsdale, a suburb of New York. During his eighth-grade year at Scarsdale Junior High School, Sorkin, who was president of his class, appeared as General Bullmoose in the school's production of *Li'l Abner*. "I still remember the wild laughter, the standing ovations," he told Wetzsteon. "That's when I first knew I wanted to be in the theater." His love of theater spilled over into his family life, particularly when, in spite of having no religious preparation, he tried to throw together a Bar Mitzvah a few months before he turned 13. "Every Saturday, I would go to a [different] friend's Bar Mitzvah. It was so theatrical," he recalled for Michael Elkin's "On the Scene" column (November 17, 1995, collected for the on-line publication *Elkin's Jewish Entertainment Home Page*). "I wanted the synagogue, the theatrics. So I called the rabbi. Here I was, 12, calling the rabbi on my own and saying to him, 'Could you teach me Torah in three months?'" In high school Sorkin joined the student drama club, appearing in such plays as *My Fair Lady* and *Pippin*.

Sorkin attended Syracuse University, in upstate New York, where he studied musical theater. "Oh, I thought I was such hot [expletive]," he told Wetzsteon. "I didn't realize that every member of the freshman class had been a star in high school. I even failed freshman acting—which I still count as one of the 10 best things that ever happened to me. Turns out I wasn't any good in musicals after all." He graduated from Syracuse in 1983 and returned to New York City, intent on breaking into the theater world. To support himself, he took a series of odd jobs—working at the TKTS half-price theater-ticket booth, tending bar, and donning a moose costume to hand out promotional items for a sport and game show, among other activities. One weekend, while living at a friend's apartment (where he slept on the floor), he spotted an old typewriter that had belonged to his friend's grandfather. With nothing else to do, he sat down and began typing random dialogue. Before long, he had produced three pages of what would be his first play, *Removing All Doubt*. "It's about seven close friends from Scarsdale who get together three years after graduation from college," he told Wetzsteon. "Okay, it's every playwright's first play, and it's a baldly yuppie play at that." Although *Removing All Doubt* was never produced, it was given a reading at the Helen Hayes Theater by Matthew Broderick and Kevin Bacon, among other actors, and the experience gave Sorkin the confidence to keep writing.

Sorkin's next effort, the military-courtroom drama *A Few Good Men*, was the work that thrust him into the limelight. Originally conceived as a movie script, *A Few Good Men* told the story of a navy lawyer defending two marines charged with accidentally killing a fellow soldier during a hazing ritual. While working on the script, Sorkin, who had no legal or military experience, sought information from various sources, including his sister, who had served as a lawyer in the navy. "I wanted to be as right as I could and to do it with a fair amount of technical expertise," he told Joseph C. Koenenn for *Newsday* (November 12, 1989). "In fact, there are some scenes that have been cut, and it's good that they're cut for the sake of the play, but I'll always miss them because there was a lot of technical dexterity in those scenes."

Sorkin's agent sent the first draft of the script to the film producer David Browne, who liked it but felt that it needed revisions. After working on it further, Sorkin proposed turning the script into a play. Browne agreed, and he helped finance a trial run on stage, although he still considered the work a feature-film project. *A Few Good Men* debuted at the Kennedy Center, in Washington, D.C., in the fall of 1989, before moving to Broadway a few months later. Veteran stage actor and Academy Award nominee Tom Hulce played the lead role, that of Lieutenant Daniel Kaffee, in both Washington and New York. While the play was generally well-received, some labeled it "old-fashioned," a term that irked Sorkin. "Underneath Kaffee's uniform beats the heart of a yuppie," he protested in an interview with Megan Rosenfeld for the *Washington Post* (October 10, 1989). Still, he added that the play is "not just a yuppie coming-of-age drama," despite the fact that Kaffee's language and humor showed him to be from Sorkin's generation.

Sorkin's play *Making Movies* arrived on Broadway in March 1990. A black comedy in the vein of David Mamet's *Speed-the-Plow*, *Making Movies* comments on the absurdities of filmmaking, taking its inspiration from Sorkin's struggle to get *A Few Good Men* made into a movie. A prime symbol of the chaos of moviemaking is a scene in which a herd of cows lumber into the frame of a key shot of marines running across a sun-drenched hill. "Ultimately," Sorkin told Judy Clain for *Elle* (February 1990) in explaining the scene, "as powerful as the movie business is, nothing is more powerful than nature. You can have all the money in the world in your budget, and you can have Cecil B. DeMille directing that film—the cows just don't care."

In December 1992 the film version of *A Few Good Men* arrived in theaters. Directed by Rob Reiner and starring Tom Cruise, Demi Moore, Jack Nicholson, and Kevin Bacon, the picture divided critics, some of whom felt that it was stiff and outmoded. Nevertheless, most championed Sorkin's writing. Richard Schickel wrote in *Time* (December 14, 1992), "Sorkin's dialogue is spit-shined, and the energy and conviction with which it is staged and played is more than a compensation; it's transformative. And hugely entertaining." In spite of some critical derision, *A Few Good Men* was a rousing success, earning over $200 million and four Academy Award nominations, including one for best picture. In addition, Sorkin received a Golden Globe Award nomination and an Edgar Allan Poe Award for his screenplay. The film also gave audiences one of the most memorable courtroom scenes in recent history. Nicholson and Cruise's fiery witness-stand exchange—in which Cruise shouts, "I want the truth!" and Nicholson thunders back, "You can't handle the truth!"—has been imitated, spoofed, and otherwise paid homage to in numerous films and television shows.

The success of *A Few Good Men* opened doors in Hollywood for Sorkin. In 1993 he received story credit for the film *Malice*, which stars Alec Baldwin and Nicole Kidman and focuses on a hotshot surgeon who worms his way into the lives of a happily married couple. Sorkin then reunited with Reiner for the romantic drama *The American President* (1995), in which Michael Douglas played a widowed president of the United States who romances a political lobbyist (Annette Bening). Once their relationship becomes known, the president's approval ratings plunge, as the public questions his moral fiber. Part of what Sorkin found intriguing about the subject was the standard to which the public holds its leaders. "A couple hundred years ago, we fought a war that we had no business winning so that we would not have to be ruled by kings, but by regular men," he told Elkin, referring to the American Revolution. "Now, we are led by regular men, but we still want them to be kings." *The American President* proved to be another feather in Sorkin's cap, winning over audiences and earning five Golden Globe nominations, including Sorkin's second for best original screenplay. The film's success boosted the demand for Sorkin as a writer, and he next worked, uncredited, on the screenplay for the smash-hit action film *The Rock* (1996), the kidnapping comedy *Excess Baggage* (1997), and the as-yet-unfilmed screenplay "Ocean of Storms," about an aging astronaut who returns to the space program. The writing of *The American President* affected Sorkin in ways that he may not have anticipated. "I sat in this hotel room for 13 months writing *The American President*," he told Keith Olbermann for *Esquire* (June 1999). "To keep me company, I would have [the ESPN sports commentary program] *SportsCenter* on. I'd watch *The Big Show* four times in a row, and I thought it was the best-written show on television. It turned me into a big-time sports fan. As soon as I was done with *The American President*, I told ABC head Jamie Tarses, 'Send me off and let me write a pilot.'"

The result of Sorkin's effort was *Sports Night*, a comedy-drama about the inner workings of a late-night cable sports show. *Sports Night* ran into trouble almost from the start. Sorkin wanted to write an innovative program that had its roots in reality, rather than reproducing the hackneyed format that characterized many sitcoms. ABC executives, however, wanted the show to include such conventions of the form as pratfalls and a live audience. Also, the network representatives felt that *Sports Night* should stay strictly within the bounds of comedy, while Sorkin envisioned a show that would combine elements of comedy and drama. "Everything untraditional was seen as fatally bad," Sorkin told Tad Friend for the *New Yorker* (September 28, 1998), "and the gist of the research seemed to be that I should consider myself extremely lucky that ABC had ordered 13 episodes, and that any further departures from the norm would end my participation in the show." Ultimately, the network won out. Each week during the filming period, one episode of *Sports Night* would be shot before a live audience; all remaining episodes to be filmed would use a laugh track. Sorkin explained his take on the situation to Friend, saying, "I decided to give in so we could win the next battles—about promotion, and about keeping us on the air when we're in 98th place."

Sports Night premiered on September 22, 1998 with an ensemble cast that included Robert Guillaume in the role of Isaac Jaffee, the show's executive producer. From the beginning, the show's main ongoing plot involved the obstacles to romance between one of the cable program's co-anchors, Casey McCall (Peter Krause), and its producer, Dana Whitaker (Felicity Huffman). What distinguished *Sports Night* from many other shows was Sorkin's clever, rapid-fire dialogue. Critics instantly warmed to the show, but the ratings were poor, and throughout its first season *Sports Night* was in constant danger of cancellation. Nonetheless, in 1999 the show won two Emmy Awards, for directing and editing, and earned Sorkin a nomination for writing. The show was brought back for a second season, during which *TV Guide* (March 11–17, 2000) ran a cover story about *Sports Night* titled "The Best Show You're Not Watching." That vote of confidence was not enough to save the show, which was finally dropped by ABC in mid-May. Sorkin attempted to find a new home for the show on the cable channel HBO, but negotiations fell through.

While the fate of *Sports Night* was still being decided, Sorkin began planning his next foray into television. "There were all these stories I wanted to tell in *The American President* about the senior staffers in the White House," he said to Weinraub, "but didn't because it was about the romance of these two people." While having lunch with John Wells, a TV producer whose credits include the acclaimed drama *ER*, Sorkin realized he had found a way to tell those stories. "I knew that he was a big deal, and the moment I sat down at lunch with John, I realized he's a busy and important guy, and he was expecting me to pitch something, to have an idea or two," he told Weinraub. "So it suddenly occurred to me: what about senior staffers at the White House? I had never really said it out loud. And that's how *West Wing* happened."

Chronicling the day-to-day lives of the White House staff—and reinvigorating the political television drama in the process—*The West Wing* provides an insider's look at the people who help keep the wheels of the presidency turning smoothly. In the months since its debut, on September 22, 1999, the show has become one of NBC's biggest ratings contenders, routinely ranking first in its time slot. *The West Wing* boasts a stellar cast, including, in addition to Rob Lowe, Martin Sheen as President Josiah "Jed" Bartlett, and it is buoyed by its crackling dialogue, almost all of which is written by Sorkin. In a rare feat for a television writer, during the 1999–2000 season Sorkin penned and executive-produced each episode of *The West Wing* while performing similar duties on *Sports Night*. While the results were usually positive, Sorkin admitted that the process of working on two shows simultaneously could be trying at times. "*The West Wing* script I'm on page six with right now was due a week ago today and I'm not kidding when I say I don't know what's going on in page seven," he told Tucker. On September 10, 2000 *The West Wing* earned a record nine Emmy Awards, including the one for best drama. Sorkin collected one award as a producer and another for outstanding writing for a drama series. The first installment of *West Wing*'s second season attracted more than 25 million viewers, thus placing the show at the top of the television ratings for that week.

Aaron Sorkin lives in Los Angeles with his wife of five years, Julia. He continues to work extensively in film, "doctoring" scripts for major producers, and is currently working on the book for a Broadway musical adaptation of the Oscar-winning 1955 film *Marty*. While some television writers dash off scripts without looking back, Sorkin feels an attachment to what he has written. "I wish I could work more on each script," he told Weinraub. "I'll often look at a completed show and think, 'Now I know how to write it.' But you can't take it back. You can only learn from that show and put it back in the next." — J.K.B.

Suggested Reading: *Elle* p58 Feb. 1990, with photo; *Entertainment Weekly* p32+ Feb. 25, 2000, with photos; *New York* p58+ Nov. 6, 1989, with photos; *New York Newsday* II p15+ Nov. 12, 1989, with photos; *New York Times* E p12+ Oct. 16, 1998, with photos, XIII p4+ Sep. 26, 1999, with photos; *Washington Post* G p1+ Oct. 1, 1989, with photo

Selected Films: as writer—*A Few Good Men*, 1992; *Malice*, 1993; *The American President*, 1995

Selected Television Shows: as writer and producer—*Sports Night*, 1998–2000; *The West Wing*, 1999–

Spears, Britney

Dec. 2, 1981– Pop singer. Address: c/o Britney Fan Club, P.O. Box 7022, Red Bank, NJ 07701

Matthew Jordan Smith/Outline Press

At the age of 18, the singer Britney Spears has won honors and accolades—and also become the target of media critics, for reasons having nothing to do with her talent. Her singles ". . . Baby One More Time" and "Sometimes," from her debut album, *. . . Baby One More Time* (1999), soared up the record charts while drawing accusations that their lyrics condoned domestic abuse and masochism, interpretations that miss the mark, according to the singer. The criticism has done little to deter Spears's fans: they have purchased almost 12 million copies of her album, and her stadium concerts typically sell out the day tickets are made available. In *Entertainment Weekly* (December 24/31, 1999), Ken Tucker wrote that Spears has "chosen her . . . influences well: a bit of Janet Jackson in her take-charge dance moves, a smidgen of Mariah [Carey]'s sultry sassiness, some Stevie Wonder in her croon, and, behind the scenes, Backstreet Boys mentor Max Martin cowriting and coproducing unshakable hits."

Britney Spears was born in the small town of Kentwood, Louisiana, on December 2, 1981 to Jamie Spears, a construction contractor, and Lynne Spears, a second-grade teacher. She has an older brother, Bryan, whom she has described as protective, and a younger sister, Jamie Lynn, who is considering a singing career. Britney Spears has always loved to sing, and she remembers standing in front of the bathroom mirror while holding a hairbrush she pretended was a microphone. "My mom would have company over when I was little, and she was so used to [me singing all the time], she didn't even realize I was doing it," Spears told an interviewer for *TV Guide* (May 8, 1999). "And the company was always like, 'Lynne, tell her to be quiet.'" Spears, who remains a devout Baptist, made her first public appearance when she was four, singing "What Child Is This" in her church. When she was eight years old, she traveled with her mother to Atlanta, Georgia, to audition for the Disney Channel's *Mickey Mouse Club*, based on the original series, which aired in the 1950s. Although the producers considered her too young for the show, they were sufficiently impressed by her singing ability to refer her to an agent in New York. There, for the next three summers, Spears studied at the Professional Performing Arts School at the Off-Broadway Dance Center. The lessons paid off: she began to win parts in commercials, and in 1991 she landed a role in the Off-Broadway production of *Ruthless*, based on the 1956 film thriller *The Bad Seed*. When she was 11, Spears auditioned again for *Mickey Mouse Club*, and this time she was invited to join the cast. She performed for two seasons alongside fellow mouseketeers Justin Timberlake, JC Chasez, Christina Aguilera, and Keri Russell, each of whom has also gone on to fame as a singer or actor.

When the show was canceled, in 1993, Spears returned to Kentwood, where she completed one year of high school. During that time she lived a normal high-school life, attending the prom and other functions, but she quickly became discontented. "I went home and it was like a year and I was just like 'Eh,'" she told John Norris during an interview for the MTV Web site. "I wanted to sing and I wanted to perform and performing for all these functions in my home town just wasn't enough. You know?" At 15 she returned to New York to try to find singing jobs. An executive at Jive Records, eager to win a share of the burgeoning teen market, heard a demo tape she had made and signed her to a development deal. Eric Foster White, a producer who had previously collaborated with the singer Whitney Houston, was assigned to work with her—an arrangement that delighted Spears, since Houston had long been an idol of hers. She also traveled to Sweden to work with the producer Max Martin, who had already teamed up with several other young performers—including the Backstreet Boys and Ace of Base—and has been credited with helping to rejuvenate pop music in the latter part of the 1990s.

In October 1998 Spears's first single, ". . . Baby One More Time," was released. To promote the song, Jive Records sent Spears on a cross-country tour of the nation's shopping malls, a strategy that had been used in the 1980s to launch the careers of Tiffany and Debbie Gibson, pop singers to whom Spears is often compared. Backed by two dancers and armed with promotional copies of the record, Spears was seen by thousands of teens, and by December of that year her single had sold 500,000 copies. Spears later toured as the opening act for 'N Sync, a band made up of five boys who were quickly becoming teen idols. This gave her even more exposure to her intended audience, and as a result her debut album, also called . . . *Baby One More Time*, quickly landed on the *Billboard* charts at number one. The title song's lyrics were criticized by some, who interpreted them as a celebration of domestic violence. The song's refrain, "Baby, hit me one more time," was taken literally by these critics, despite Spears's protests that its meaning was metaphorical; in the *Rolling Stone* interview, she said, "It means just give me a sign, basically. I think it's kind of funny that people would actually think [it meant to hit me physically]." A second single from the album, "Sometimes," caused similar concerns, when the lyrics "Sometimes I run from you / Sometimes I hide / Sometimes I'm scared of you" were thought to have masochistic overtones. Neil Strauss, a music critic for the *New York Times* (July 6, 1999), found fault with the song for other reasons. "These meanings—the hitting, the fear, the implication that when Ms. Spears says no she means yes—are not so much intentional as they are evidence of careless songwriting, glitches in the pop machine." Spears stirred still more controversy when she appeared scantily clad on the cover and inside photos of *Rolling Stone*'s April 1999 issue. Fans were apparently less offended than media critics, as . . . *Baby One More Time* went on to sell more than 11 million albums worldwide. The music industry showered her with honors. Spears won four *Billboard* awards, including female artist of the year, new pop artist of the year, Hot 100 Singles artist of the year, and female Hot 100 Singles artist of the year; several MTV awards; a Teen Choice Award; a People's Choice nomination for favorite female performer; and a 2000 Grammy nomination for best new artist. Her second album, *Oops! . . . I Did It Again*, was released in May 2000 and sold 1.3 million copies during its first week. In June the television special *Britney in Hawaii* aired on the Fox network.

Spears recently agreed to endorse Clairol's Herbal Essences line of hair-care products. Despite the trappings of celebrity, she generally comes across in interviews as a typical teenage girl. She often talks of her fondness for the actor Brad Pitt and for cookie-dough ice cream. She has named shopping as a favorite activity, and she collects dolls. (Unlike most teenage girls, she has had a Barbie-like doll made in her image.) Although she has been frequently linked with Prince William of England and Justin Timberlake of 'N Sync, Spears has claimed that her concert and recording obligations get in the way of dating. She has said that she would like to try acting once more. — M.R.

Suggested Reading: *Entertainment Weekly* p28 Dec. 24/31, 1999, with photo; *Forbes* p164+ Mar. 20, 2000, with photo; MTV Web site; *New York Times* E p1 July 6, 1999; *Newsweek* p64 Mar. 1, 1999, with photo; *Rolling Stone p46+ May 25, 1000, with photo; Rolling Stone* (on-line) Apr. 1, 1999, with photos; *TV Guide* p30+ May 8, 1999, with photos, p28+ Oct. 9–15, 1999

Selected Recordings: *. . . Baby One More Time*, 1999; *Oops! . . . I Did It Again*, 2000

Selected Videos: *Time Out with Britney Spears*, 1999

Courtesy of HarperCollins Publishers

Staples, Brent

Sep. 13, 1951– Journalist; memoirist; editor
Address: New York Times, *229 W. 43d St., New York, NY 10036*

The African-American journalist and memoirist Brent Staples entered the literary consciousness of the English-speaking world when he published *Parallel Time: Growing Up in Black and White* (1994). The autobiography describes in poetic language Staples's childhood and young manhood, focusing on his growing detachment from his family members, who were drawn into a world of drug using and dealing, early childbearing, and early death. Staples, by contrast, went on to graduate school and eventually to a position on the editorial board of the *New York Times*, where the commentaries carrying his byline often address the topic of race.

Brent Staples was born on September 13, 1951 in Chester, Pennsylvania, one of the nine surviving children of Geneva Brown Staples and Melvin Staples and the oldest of their five sons. The family was poor; although Melvin Staples made "a handsome living" as a truck driver for the Blue Line Transfer Co., "much of what he earned he drank up," as Brent Staples wrote in *Parallel Time*. "My mother lacked the skill to stretch what was left." Staples's mother was charitable to an extreme, often taking in young people who had been abandoned by their families, sometimes after they had become pregnant. The family moved frequently, usually due to imminent—or actual—eviction. At one point Staples's mother and father split up; they later reconciled, only to separate again. The family lived for a time in Roanoke, Virginia, close to the parents' hometown.

Staples was permanently marked by those moves. "As a child I was never where I was," he wrote in *Parallel Time*. "Part of me raced ahead looking for a foothold in the future. Part of me was somewhere behind rushing to catch up." (As an adult, he wrote, he lived for stretches of five years and longer in apartments that he could not bring himself to furnish: "Grown and out on my own, I was phobically wary of possessions, of anything that would trouble me when it was time to go.") One of Staples's greatest fears as a child was of losing his memories, of having no grasp on "moments I'd lived."

In high school Staples took what he described as a secretarial course of study. He also appeared in a production of Lorraine Hansberry's play *Raisin in the Sun*, emulating one of his heroes, Sidney Poitier. To try out for the play, he made up a monologue "on the spot," adopting the character of a man working in a bottling factory: "Cap on bottle. Cap on bottle. Cap on bottle," he repeated. "The monologue sprang from a primal source. The man watching the bottles go by was me. This was my failure dream, the ritual of meaningless acts that was out there, waiting to claim me." Staples exhibited political consciousness during this period, allying himself to the goals of the Black Panther Party.

Despite his family's poverty and his pessimism about his future, Staples was able to attend college with the help of a remedial-training and financial-aid program called Project Prepare, through which he participated in a kind of academic boot camp with 23 other young black men. He graduated cum laude from Penn Morton College (now Widener University), in Chester, in 1973, with a B.A. degree in behavioral science, after making the dean's list numerous times. From there he pursued graduate studies at the University of Chicago through a Danforth Fellowship, one of the nation's most prestigious academic awards.

Staples's success in his studies was coupled with an acute awareness of racism, both institutionalized and casual. One instance he wrote about involved a University of Chicago psychology professor, whom Staples approached in the hope of enrolling in her class. Disregarding, or unaware of, the fact that Staples as an undergraduate had fallen six one-hundredths of a percentage point short of graduating magna cum laude, she accepted him with the air of one making a benevolent gesture, based on the need for racial reparations. In another example in *Parallel Time*, Staples recalled learning that Robert Maynard Hutchins, developer of the "great books" program at the university, was implicated in efforts to clear people of color out of the neighborhood surrounding the campus. After Hutchins's death, these efforts continued, one result being that Staples saw his friends lose their basketball court. "A neighborhood that had once played host to [the jazz musicians] Charlie Parker, Miles Davis, and Earl (Fatha) Hines was devoid of music. By the time I arrived in Hyde Park, not a single jazz club remained. The ghetto had been beaten back, but sterility was the cost," he wrote.

Staples also noticed that his physical presence made many white strangers visibly uncomfortable. Whereas initially he tried to ease their fear—for example, by smiling at them on the street—he eventually came to resent their reactions to him. He directed his anger into a game that he called "Scatter the Pigeons." A fairly large man, he would walk toward couples, who, showing fear, would draw together; he would then position himself so that they had to separate to pass him. He would also approach white strangers and greet them loudly, delighting in their fear. Staples achieved a degree of notoriety after he wrote about how he had stalked the Nobel Prize–winning novelist Saul Bellow. While he admired the work of Bellow, who taught at the University of Chicago, Staples was disturbed by the way characters in the writer's novels viewed black men. "These passages made me angry," Staples wrote. "It was the same anger I felt when white people cowered as I passed them on the street." (Staples also revealed that he followed the novelist for other reasons: "I wanted something from him. The longing was deep. . . . I wanted to steal the essence of him, to absorb it right into my bones." He added, describing his beginnings as an essayist, that he sometimes stole from the works of Bellow, who was "the writer I knew best. I mimicked his phrasing and his body-snatching eye.")

After Staples received his Ph.D. in psychology, in 1982, having written a dissertation on the mathematics of decision making, he taught at the college level. Although he "had dreamed of becoming an Ivy League professor," no Ivy League college recruited him. He wrote that he "woke up from [his] Ivy League dream at Roosevelt University," where he came to see himself as merely one of an army of adjunct professors who had little chance of obtaining tenure-track positions and were forced to move from college to college. ("Adjuncts didn't get fired; they escaped," he wrote.)

Meanwhile, he wrote constantly, chronicling the happenings around him. He soon went into journalism, joining the staff of the *Chicago Sun-Times* as a reporter, in 1983. He remained in that post for two years, also contributing to the *Chicago Reader* and writing about jazz for *Down Beat* and *Jazz Hot–Paris*. In 1985 he began his association with the *New York Times*, serving as an editor of the paper's *Book Review* and then as assistant metropolitan editor before joining the editorial board, in 1990. In that post he continues to write about politics and culture, focusing often on race.

Meanwhile, the 1984 shooting death of Staples's younger brother Blake, a drug dealer, was a signal event in Staples's life. Both the first and last chapters of *Parallel Time* are accounts of Blake's murder, the path that led to it, and Brent Staples's attempts to remove his brother from that path. "Certain trains you can see coming," Staples told Mary Ann French, who interviewed him for the *Washington Post* (March 17, 1994). "There are some people who are standing right on the tracks. And no matter what you tell them, you find them back there on those tracks in the morning." A passage from *Parallel Time* discusses his absence from his brother's funeral: "I'd done my mourning in advance. But this was self-deception on a monstrous scale. The rituals of grief and burial bear the dead away. Cheat those rituals and you risk keeping the dead with you in forms that you mightn't like. Choose carefully the funerals you miss."

Parallel Time was praised by numerous reviewers and won the Anisfield-Wolf Book Award, which is given by the Cleveland Foundation to recognize works that address issues of racism and celebrate human diversity. In the *New York Times* (March 24, 1994), Michael Eric Dyson praised Staples's "resolutely distinct voice as he negotiates the treacherous shoals of racial identity in American culture. . . . *Parallel Time* reminds us that the best personal writing is born of the courage to confront oneself." Paul Galloway noted in the *Chicago Tribune* (March 7, 1994), "Staples writes with humor and insight about the warmth and the tyranny of family and the wondrous and frightening expedition through childhood, his serendipitous decision to attend college, and then gain a graduate fellowship at one of the nation's most prestigious universities." In a conversation with Galloway, Staples said that *Parallel Time* "is a literary work. Being black enriches my experience; it doesn't define me." David Nicholson, writing for *American Visions* (May 1994), agreed that it was "a book by a black man that does not focus on race. It is almost misleading to call *Parallel Time* a black book. The truth is that it is an *American* story, a celebration of one of the many strands of the American experience."

Placing Staples in a category with the Italian novelist, poet, memoirist, and Holocaust survivor Primo Levi, Verlyn Klinkenborg wrote for the *New York Times Book Review* (February 20, 1994) that for such writers "the sadness of memory comes from recognizing yet again what they have never really forgotten: how powerless they are to help others escape what they escaped." Staples has pointed out that his own "escape" owed much to affirmative action, which he continues to champion. Alluding to himself in an editorial for the *New York Times* (March 5, 1995), Staples wrote, "This black boy who was 'not college material' went on to earn a Ph.D. at the University of Chicago. . . . There are thousands of stories like this one. But in the Reaganaut 80's, many African-Americans who could tell those stories became converts to the gospel of Horatio Alger, suddenly claiming that success had been earned through hard work and rectitude alone. . . . The convert's role I will never play. . . . When I was 17, the society spotted me a few points on the S.A.T.'s and changed my life. I became a writer—and a middle-class taxpayer—as many other black men went on to prisons, cemeteries, and homeless shelters. Sounds like a smart investment to me. The country would be wise to keep making it."

Staples received an honorary doctorate in humane letters from Mount St. Mary College, in Newburgh, New York, in 2000. The school cited him for taking on, in his editorials, "some of today's hottest, often controversial, subjects, including racial profiling, the erosion of values and the literacy gap," and "for shining light in dark spaces." On September 16, 2000 Staples married Julie Williams Johnson, a former journalist who is currently a senior managing director at the public-relations firm Hill & Knowlton. In a *New York Times* (March 12, 2000) editorial titled "How a Black Man's Wallet Becomes a Gun" (which concerned the death of an unarmed West African immigrant at the hands of New York City police in 1999), Staples revealed that his then-fiancée has a teenage son. — S.Y.

Suggested Reading: *American Visions* p28+ May 1994, with photo; *Chicago Tribune* XIV p3 Feb. 13, 1999, V p1 Mar. 7, 1994; *New York Times* C p15 Mar. 21, 1994, IV p14 Mar. 5, 1995, ST p12 Sep. 17, 2000, with photo; *New York Times Book Review* p1+ Feb. 20, 1994, with photo; *Times Literary Supplement* p14 June 10, 1994; *Washington Post* D p1 Mar. 17, 1994

Selected Books: *Parallel Time: Growing Up in Black and White*, 1994

Archive Photos

Stern, Robert A. M.

May 23, 1939– Architect; architectural historian; dean of the Yale School of Architecture.

Address: Robert A. M. Stern, Architects, 460 W. 34th St., 18th Fl., New York, NY 10001

Since the end of World War II, the Yale School of Architecture, in New Haven, Connecticut, has been one of the most fertile grounds for the nurturing of important designers; its list of alumni from the past several decades includes a roster of some of the most innovative and successful of contemporary architects, among them Charles Gwathmey, Richard Rogers, Sir Norman Foster, Thomas Beeby, and Stanley Tigerman. The school has, moreover, enjoyed a reputation as an open-minded haven for new design and theory, a reputation based in part on the role it played as host to American architecture's paradigm shift from sober, glass-and-steel modernism to its more playful offspring, postmodernism. Yet in 1998, when the school undertook a frenetic and much-publicized search for a new dean, its many recent shortcomings came to light, most notably its failure to attract top-quality students, who were scurrying in droves to the more forward-looking School of Architecture, Planning, and Preservation at Columbia University, in New York City. It became clear that the floundering school needed an effective administrator to modernize the computer facilities, set up a more inviting financial-aid system, and work out the maintenance-related bugs in the school's 30-year-old building, at least as much as it needed a visionary designer who could spark sweeping changes in the field.

In New York–based architect Robert A. M. Stern, it arguably got both. A provocative, even divisive figure, Stern is probably better known for his controversial association with the Walt Disney Co. and his architectural history of New York City than for any of his many design innovations. So when the search committee finally chose Stern from a short list that also included a young, independent designer, a prominent historian and academic, and the first female partner at Skidmore, Owings, & Merrill, a major corporate firm, it caused a commotion within the school and among observers in the architectural world at large. And Stern's precarious stature, teetering between pariah and hero, came into focus. The newly appointed don was immediately castigated by Yale alumnus Reed Kroloff, the editor of *Architecture* magazine, who called him "a suede-loafered sultan of suburban retrotecture, a Disney party boy." One observer, quoted anonymously by Mark Alden Branch in an article for the *Yale Alumni Magazine* (March 1999), said, "Like every serious architect, I was shocked by the appointment. In my eyes [Stern is] the Martha Stewart of architecture, and represents the commercial takeover of postmodernism. But on second thought, what's clear to me about Bob is that he has succeeded at everything he's ever done. The last thing he'd want to do is fail as the dean of Yale."

Implicit in that comment is an attitude of resignation concerning Stern's power and drive, which in turn signals a deep ambivalence within the profession about the worth of one of its most famous members. Such uncertainty extends beyond university and corporate politics to include aesthetic matters; unqualified praise for Stern's buildings is rare. What is clear at this relatively early stage in the critical evaluation of Stern's career is his maturation—from a young iconoclast eager to break the shackles of modernism, to an early postmodernist whose reliance on historical pastiche sometimes became hackneyed and awkward, to an interpreter of American vernacular designs. "There is no doubt that Stern was heavy-handed as a young designer," the architectural historian Vincent Scully told Carol Vogel for the *New York Times Magazine* (January 13, 1985), "but what's happened to him is exactly the right thing. His buildings have gotten stronger and stronger." His transformation involved his developing both an appreciation for classicism—which he believes to be the foundation of Western architecture—and for nature, which has led him to design for specific environments homes that look as though they could have sprung organically from the soil. "What I try to do," Stern told Linda Mandeville for *Columbia* (December 1985), "is use the local forms, which often have very complicated histories that take you back to great monuments in Europe or to early America, and pick up on them on a regional basis. Not just today I like Taos, tomorrow it's East Hampton, next week it's white columns in Georgia. No. I'm saying these things evolved organically within the culture, and my job as an architect is to button on to them and continue them, not by copying them in a literal way, but by emulating them."

Robert Arthur Morton Stern was born in New York City on May 23, 1939. His father sold insurance. As a child Stern developed both a love for plants and flowers and a fixation on buildings; he was enamored equally of the jagged Manhattan skyline and the bucolic oasis of the Brooklyn Botanical Garden. He wiled away many hours in Brooklyn public libraries, perusing oversize art and architecture books and sketching elevations of the iconic towers that rose above the city: the Art Deco Chrysler and Empire State Buildings and the neo-Gothic Woolworth Building. After attending Brooklyn public schools and graduating from Columbia University, in 1960, he enrolled in the prestigious Yale School of Architecture, where he earned a master's degree in 1965.

During this time, modernism was still the order of the day, as it had been since the end of World War II. The mass destruction wrought in Europe and Asia by the war triggered a need for massive reconstruction and left an opening for new styles that could make efficient use of the technical improvements in the development of materials—especially glass, steel, and reinforced concrete—since the 19th century. Two of modernism's most famous practitioners, Le Corbusier and Ludwig Mies van der Rohe, both of whom emerged as consequential and controversial figures between World Wars I and II, were particularly interested in minimalist designs that emphasized light and space. They created buildings that called attention to their own structures rather than boxes that concealed structure. In the U.S., however, early modernist triumphs such as Mies and Philip Johnson's Seagram Building, in New York City, gave way to an eruption of sterile, cookie-cutter glass-and-steel structures that were often disparaged as "glass boxes" and that also fell under the heading of modernism. Ensconced as it was in the nation's finest architecture schools, modernism, now discredited to an extent by the proliferation of such uniform buildings, was in the 1960s poised to surrender its theoretical dominance, or at least to offer itself up to change. At Yale, then-Dean Paul Rudolph struggled with ways to infuse modernism with some measure of vitality. His Art and Architecture building, on the Yale campus, was a negotiation between the neo-Gothic beauty of the rest of the school—with its spires and intricate ornamentation—and his personal dedication to modern forms. "External forces dictated that this building turn the corner and relate to the modern building opposite as well as suggest that it belongs to Yale University," Rudolph explained in his 1970 book *The Architecture of Paul Rudolph*. In taking this approach, he gave voice to the thinking that would distinguish imaginative endeavors like Rudolph's, which work explicitly in the modernist tradition, from the designs of vulgar modernists, and he planted the seed for the next generation of architects, who wanted to atone for the sins of modernism: its ahistoricism, disregard for locale, and lack of respect for nature.

Speaking of this period of change, Robert Stern recalled to Linda Mandeville, "I and quite a few of my classmates had a gnawing suspicion that modern architecture was inadequate in ways that older architecture was not. We would sit in the studio and look out on the Yale campus with its Gothic spires or at the local vernacular buildings and say, 'Why can't we do buildings as interesting as those.'" Possessed of an active and progressive intellect even at a young age, Stern envisioned a future for his profession. As the editor of *Perspecta*, Yale's architectural journal, he began to realize this vision through shrewd, prescient editorial decisions, such as prominent coverage of the work of Louis Kahn and pieces on the young designers Charles Moore and Romaldo Giurgola. But most important was his bold decision to print excerpts from Robert Venturi's iconoclastic classic *Complexity and Contradiction in Architecture*, prior to the book's 1966 publication. In this work, Venturi derided modernism for its blindness to the power of ambiguity and messiness and the beauty and complexity of every locale. While embracing the central tenets of modernism, Venturi recommended changes that he felt would save the movement from its own excesses. He thus laid the groundwork for postmodernism.

After graduating from Yale, Stern served for two years as the program director for the Architectural League of New York, a post in which he exerted enormous influence by organizing impressive and provocative exhibits, such as "Women in American Architecture," and a showcase for designers under the age of 40. He then began to design houses. His early work suggests Venturi's influence; his first house was simultaneously an ode to Venturi's once-shocking shingle design and an interpretation of the W. G. Low House, a famous 1887 structure designed by the firm McKim, Mead & White. Built in Montauk, on Long Island, New York, in 1967, Stern's Wiseman shingle-style house supported a broad gable. His second prominent work, the Lang House (1973), was quite different. A flat-roofed, yellow shell that sticks out from the greenery of its Connecticut surroundings, the Lang House is composed almost entirely of right angles and features a simple white ornamentation on its façade. Though a few of Stern's early houses picked up awards from New York architectural associations, none are currently regarded as especially memorable designs, a fact well known to their creator. "Stern himself concedes that much of his early work was overly didactic," Vogel wrote. "He was so caught up in theories and in the idea of using historical references in an original way, as Venturi was doing, that his buildings were rhetorical and stiff. He combined such modern clichés as large sheets of glass and severe right angles with such traditional shapes as classical columns that were too large and awkward."

By the early 1980s the negative critical tide against Stern had begun to turn, as the architect developed a style that emphasized not postmodernist riffs on classic forms but reproductions, with twists, of those forms. By embracing this style Stern achieved a great deal of fame and wealth. He designed regularly for socialites and celebrities, making, in the words of Mark Alden Branch, "new money look like old money." "Instead of making houses that are complex and, in some cases, even slightly tortured attempts to play on the notion of the great Shingle Style architecture of the late 19th century, Mr. Stern has come much closer to merely doing the Shingle Style," Paul Goldberger wrote for the *New York Times* (April 4, 1982) in an effusive review of homes Stern had designed in East Hampton, on Long Island, and on Martha's Vineyard, off the Massachusetts coast. Goldberger further cited Stern's ability to look to the past without sentimentalizing it. "At its best," he wrote, "Stern's work suggests positive directions for post-modern architecture—a movement away from the excessively polemical earlier works and toward something less flamboyant, less desperate to thumb its nose at what has come before."

By this time, postmodernism had won wide acceptance; its earliest practitioners had survived the early slings of critics and emerged with confident and idiosyncratic work, welcomed by many after decades of unmemorable buildings. An April 1984 *Vanity Fair* feature used a then-proposed and now long-abandoned movie remake of *The Fountainhead*, based on Ayn Rand's best-selling 1943 novel, as a pretext to profile several up-and-coming designers. The book and the 1949 film told the story of Howard Roark, a talented, nonconformist architect working stoically in a hostile society. The young architects of the economically booming early 1980s—referred to in the *Vanity Fair* piece as "a new breed of Howard Roarks" that "has rekindled the sense of architecture as a creative act"—included Michael Graves, Peter Eisenman, and Stern. The most radical of the trio was Eisenman, who was notorious for his "difficult" houses.

Graves and Stern, on the other hand, would shortly become notorious for a different reason: their high-profile relationships with the Walt Disney Co., anything but an antiestablishment force. In the late 1980s Disney, under the leadership of Michael Eisner, started to court the services of prominent designers, of whom Stern and Graves were the most famous. Since then, Stern has seen his designs for a pair of hotels, an employment office, and an animation building go up on property owned by Disney. He was a lead designer of Celebration, a so-called "new town" constructed on the outskirts of Walt Disney World, in Florida. The award-winning architect Roger K. Lewis, a professor at the University of Maryland, was present in 1996 when Stern unveiled the master plan for the 4,900-acre town, meant to be an homage to the clean-cut virtues of small-town American culture; writing for the *Washington Post* (December 14, 1996), Lewis characterized Celebration as an "occasionally laughable display of architectural kitsch, presumably made legitimate in the minds of some because many of the new buildings were designed by signature architects of 'distinction,' to use Stern's words." That judgment echoed many other denunciations of the Stern-Disney connection, as Mark Alden Branch described them: "For Stern's detractors, his association with Disney—he became a member of the company's board in 1992—confirmed their assessment of him as less an architect than a scenographer, cynically mining the past for its nostalgia value instead of working to advance the cause of architecture." In the Italian architecture magazine *Abitare* (May 2000), Fulvio Irace presented a different point of view: Referring to Celebration, Disney World, in Orlando, Florida, Versailles (the site of the palaces and gardens built by the French king Louis XIV in the 17th century), the Petit Trianon, a small palace in Versailles, and Marie Antoinette, the wife of Louis XVI, who enjoyed living in Versailles, Irace wrote, "Eisner is a postmodern Louis XIV of global entertainment with the ability, thanks to the wizardry of virtual technology, to reproduce the magic of the original Disney model in mass replicas all over the world. A glance at the plan of the Walt Disney World Resort or nearby Celebration reveals the extent to which both were inspired by Versailles. In Eisner's skillfully blended cocktail, aulic and vernacular, austere and bizarre, oppose each other in a park converted into a garden. Marie Antoinette's hamlet and the Petit Trianon have been replaced by Wilderness Lodge [in Disney World] and Celebration Place Office."

Stern has yet to build a universally acclaimed structure on the order of Frank Lloyd Wright's Fallingwater, Le Corbusier's Villa Savoye, or the Seagram Building. This may be due partly to the fact that he is associated more with large-scale design than with individual buildings. In that vein he has worked not only on Disney projects but also on the revitalization of New York's Times Square, which began in the 1990s. The multimillion-dollar effort called for the restoration of the area's old theaters as well as demolition and new construction. Most recently it involved the eviction of porn theaters, though Stern was once quoted in the *New York Times* as saying that he wanted to maintain some of the site's depraved flavor. "We don't want to make it so gentrified that there is no sleaze or sensationalism," he said. "We want big signs—all those things—but not in a way that looks as if we've re-created the past."

In some cases, however, as many critics have carped, hollow recreations of the past are exactly what Stern's designs amount to. His Norman Rockwell Museum, in Stockbridge, Massachusetts, built to house the artwork and papers of the famous *Saturday Evening Post* illustrator—who was himself often accused of concealing fractious American life behind small-town, white, middle-class froth—is an example of this. In the *Village Voice* (May 4, 1993), Edward Ball connected the Rockwell Museum to the work Stern had done for Disney and accused the architect of putting too much faith in the "Rockwellian fantasy": "Stern practices architecture as special effect. His museum has the appeal of a trompe l'oeil painting. The Rockwell building is comforting, picturesque, but like the ersatz that it declines to rise above, existentially thin." Herbert Muschamp of the *New York Times* (August 21, 1994) had similar complaints about Stern's redesign for Brooklyn Law School. Made over in the surrounding Classical Revival style of downtown Brooklyn, the white stone building is also classically oriented, so much so that, in the critic's opinion, it verges on kitsch. "Perhaps Mr. Stern imagines that the law school is a polemical statement," Muschamp wrote. "Perhaps he has seized on the school's poor 1968 building as a chance to demonstrate, once again, the impoverishment of modern forms. Too bad he didn't recognize the opportunity to refresh his own outlook. . . . With so many good things in this building that owe nothing to period detail, isn't it time to face the possibility that modernists may have had a point when they divorced architecture from style?" Statements of this sort led the influential architect Philip Johnson to weigh in with this assessment: "By relying on historical references as he does, [Stern] may be playing it safe," Johnson told Vogel. "It's too early to tell."

Stern's academic career began in 1973, when he was made an assistant professor at Columbia after a few semesters as a lecturer. He earned tenure in 1982, on the strength of his acclaimed writings on architectural history, which include a series of books on the evolution of architecture in New York. The first of these was *New York 1900: Metropolitan Architecture and Urbanism, 1890–1915* (1983), written with Gregory Gilmartin and John Montague Massengale, a tour through fin de siècle Gotham that was acclaimed for its generous use of rare photos. The book has come to be considered an indispensable work of social, political, and urban history. Stern followed up this work with *New York 1930: Architecture and Urbanism Between the Two World Wars* (1987), written with Gilmartin and Thomas Mellins, an 847-page coffee-table volume that charted the erection of several important landmarks—the George Washington Bridge, the Empire State Building, the Chrysler Building, and Rockefeller Center—as well as minor projects. "The book's strengths are its inevitable weaknesses," Jane Holtz Kay wrote for the *Christian Science Monitor* (March 28, 1988). "Its encyclopedic nature makes this the central document on the city; it also makes it a chore to read. You need a crane to hoist the book into position for a leisurely read on, say, the trouble in disseminating Jazz Age designs to Americans who found them resonant of the 'underworld character of speakeasies and nightclubs.'" Kay added, however, that it is "the density of detail if not the editing of the book that makes one wish it were less laborious to read. Every city might benefit from such earnest introspection and scholarship." Stern added another weighty tome to the series with *New York 1960: Architecture and Urbanism Between the Second World War and the Bicentennial* (1995), written with Mellins and David Fishman. Covering the rise of the International

Style and city planning, this installment enjoyed a glowing critical reception. Thomas S. Hines, writing for the *New York Times Book Review* (March 19, 1995), detected in the book an antimodern bias in the form of "a Modernist overdose that is sufficiently toxic to make [readers] cry for the purgative antidote of a Post-Modernist Nirvana," specifically a deluge of photos of uniformly dull "glass boxes." Still, Hines praised the book and recommended that it "be read and pondered by all who value architecture and who understand, or wonder about, its importance in their lives." Stern's *New York 1880: Architecture and Urbanism in the Gilded Age*, written with Mellins and Fishman, was published in 1999.

In 1986 Stern hosted an eight-part television documentary, *Pride of Place: Building the American Dream*, a first-ever attempt to present a comprehensive survey of American architecture. The series was panned by many reviewers, who criticized its lack of cohesion as well as the way Stern's own attitudes colored its contents. "Stern's control of the series resulted in at least two highly apparent biases," Paul Gapp declared in the *Chicago Tribune* (March 30, 1986). "One is the way he reflects the tastes of New York's rather snobbish intellectual elite, of which he is a part. The other is his seeming distaste for almost everything Chicago architects have done in the last 50 years."

Robert Stern's appointment as dean of the Yale School of Architecture was the culmination of his academic career. In a piece for the *New York Times* (July 1, 1999), Julie V. Iovine described a "general thaw" in Stern's relationship with students, following "a rocky start" that saw 10 students walk out during his first speech as dean. (They were protesting "the unilateral process by which the dapper Mr. Stern had been selected" for the post.) Students have responded well to Stern's openmindedness, which was in evidence when he decided—based on their objections—to scrap his plan for reintroducing a grade-point system. There have been mixed reactions to his having signed up the big-name architects Philip Johnson, Peter Eisenman, Daniel Libeskind, and Frank Gehry to teach at Yale; some have dismissed the hires as publicity stunts while others have hailed them as positive developments for the program.

Stern divides his time between New York, where his firm, Robert A. M. Stern, Architects, now employs more than 150 designers, and New Haven, where he entertains students and faculty in a third-floor loft designed by his firm. He is divorced and has a son, Nick, who is a theater producer. His New York architectural history is to be completed with the forthcoming *New York 2000.* — M.C.

Suggested Reading: *Columbia* p16+ Dec. 1985, with photo; *Interior Design* (New York) p S29+ Dec. 1993, with photo; *New York* p52+ Dec. 7, 1998, with photos; *New York Times* F p1 July 1, 1999, with photos; *New York Times Magazine* p41+ Jan. 13, 1985, with photos; *New York Woman* p32+ Feb. 1988, with photo; *Vanity Fair* p41+ Apr. 1984, with photo; *Yale Alumni Magazine* (on-line), Mar. 1999

Selected Books: *New York, 1900*, 1983; *New York, 1930*, 1987; *New York, 1960*, 1995

Stewart, Alice

Oct. 4, 1906– Epidemiologist; medical researcher. Address: Medical School, University of Birmingham, Edgbaston, Birmingham B15 2TJ, England

Alice Stewart came of age as a radiation epidemiologist in the 1950s, when atomic energy was celebrated by many as the hope of the future—when nuclear weapons were expected to bring world peace and atomic power to make energy plentiful and inexpensive. Stewart's research on cancer caused by low doses of radiation brought news that powerful groups, such as the U.S. Department of Energy, did not want to hear. Dedicating most of her professional life to radiation epidemiology and the fight against scientific secrecy, Stewart won a "reputation as perhaps the Energy Department's most influential and feared scientific critic," Keith Schneider wrote for the *New York Times* (May 3, 1990).

As a consultant physician, Stewart began work in general practice in 1939, but in 1941 she responded to the wartime needs of her native Great Britain and joined the medical school at Oxford University, contracted by the government to study the effects of munitions production on workers. Stewart discovered that the suppression of the workers' ability to form blood cells correlated with their exposure to the explosive TNT. Her discovery led to changes in munitions-manufacturing procedures, and she was soon regarded as one of the best and most creative epidemiologists in Britain. In 1947 she became the first woman to be elected to both the Royal College of Physicians and the Association of Physicians.

"The strength of my work [in radiation research] lay in the fact that I wasn't taking sides," she told Amy Raphael for *Ms.* magazine (July/August 1996). "At the same time, however, I've always been willing to speak up; I'd consider myself a coward if I did otherwise." Her research on munitions producers eventually led to her findings in radiation epidemiology, which enabled many organizations to focus attention on the risks surrounding nuclear power and weapons plants.

Per Frisk, Right Livelihood Award

Alice Stewart

Alice Mary Stewart was born on October 4, 1906 in Sheffield, England, to two physicians who taught at Sheffield University. Her father, Albert Ernest Naish, an internist, was a professor of medicine; her mother, Lucy Wellburn Naish, taught anatomy. Stewart was the third of eight children; with so many siblings, she learned early on "not to mind about battles," as she was quoted as saying in Lisa Yount's book *A to Z of Women in Science and Math* (1999). Unafraid of bucking tradition—as evidenced by the fact that Lucy Naish was one of the first female doctors in Britain—Stewart's parents would always support her when she met opposition in her controversial career.

At Cambridge and London Universities, Stewart trained as a doctor (as did three of her siblings), and she qualified in 1931. The following year she married a friend from her Cambridge years who had become a schoolmaster, and with him she had two children. (Following a long war-related separation, they divorced in 1950.) Stewart spent all the years during World War II as a physician, first in London and then in Oxford. During this period her main responsibility was the teaching of clinical medicine to undergraduates, but she also completed three studies of workers exposed to particular wartime risks. These included a study of munition workers that showed that TNT can destroy the body's capacity to form blood corpuscles. The studies led Stewart eventually to end her clinical work and, in 1945, begin working with biostatisticians at Oxford University in the Department of Social Medicine—a pioneer department of epidemiology. (Epidemiology is the study of the incidence and distribution of diseases; its practitioners require both diagnostic skill and expertise in statistics.)

In 1955 a jump in the occurrence of leukemia, a cancer of the blood, was noticed in British children, especially those between ages two and four. Stewart pioneered the Oxford Survey of Childhood Cancers to find the cause, collecting information on all children who had died of cancer throughout Britain between 1953 and 1955. Those involved in the survey interviewed the children's mothers, including mothers of healthy control subjects; assembled records from prenatal clinics, hospitals, and X-ray departments; collected records of climate and population density; and noted numbers of annual live births, stillbirths, and infant deaths in more than 1,000 localities. In 1956 Stewart wrote a letter to the British medical journal the *Lancet*, sharing her observations that the mothers of the cancer victims (who had solid tumors as well as leukemia) had received twice as many prenatal X-rays as had the mothers of the control-group children, who were cancer-free. Two years later, in the *Oxford Survey of Childhood Cancers*, she published her findings that X-rays absorbed in utero could provoke cancer in children. Her report stunned the medical community, which at the time did not understand the dangers of radiation and even encouraged women pregnant for the first time to have X-rays, because doctors found them useful as guides to the fetuses' development.

Probably in part because of the controversy over her research, Stewart was not promoted at Oxford, as was standard for men of comparable accomplishment, but she remained there until her official retirement date, in 1974. "I'm afraid she was frozen out," a senior Oxford scientist told Clive Cookson for the *Financial Times* (January 19, 1995). Stewart's principal rival has always been Sir Richard Doll. Britain's most influential cancer epidemiologist for decades, Doll was a member of the Medical Research Council Committee that in 1954 failed to fund Stewart's Oxford survey. In 1992 Britain's Coordinating Committee for Cancer Research, under the chairmanship of Doll, claimed that they were the first to make a nationwide study of childhood cancers, thus, as Stewart wrote to *Current Biography*, "completely misleading people about the survey, which had begun in 1955 and discovered that there was a cancer risk at low dose levels."

The science of epidemiology was just developing during the 1950s, and even though Stewart was the leading researcher in the field, no one offered her another job. She was "the wrong sex," as she put it to Raphael. Yet Stewart has said that being a woman helped her, in a way. "Had I been a man I might have walked away from difficult situations more easily. . . . I would have had all sorts of job offers . . . which would have tempted me away from the world of research," she told Raphael. Her discoveries about prenatal radiation did not become accepted worldwide until the 1970s.

Meanwhile, the International Commission on Radiological Protection (ICRP) ignored Stewart's findings and set a limit on radiation dosages based on a cost-benefit analysis, according to which a risk ratio of one to 5,000—or one death for every 5,000 workers exposed to radiation—was acceptable. Such an approach allowed for the expansion of atomic-energy programs. The U.S. Atomic Energy Commission (AEC) urged a relaxing of even these standards when studies of survivors of the explosion of atomic bombs (dropped by the U.S. on the Japanese cities of Hiroshima and Nagasaki in 1945, just before World War II ended) did not indicate harm from low-level radiation. Medical researchers resisted the easing of the standards; Stewart hypothesized that A-Bomb Casualty Commission data masked the carcinogenic effects of low-dose radiation. She realized that when people's ages at the time of the bombings were considered, children less than 10 years old were 1,000 times more likely to die from radiation than people age 10 to 55, and those 55 or older were twice as likely to die than those in the 10–55 age group. She reasoned that young and old alike are more sensitive to radiation, because their immune systems are either developing, in the case of the young, or breaking down, as happens with the elderly. She recognized that so-called "selection effects" of the bombing—meaning the overrepresentation of certain age groups among victims—were still being seen in the death rates of survivors. As evidence, Stewart cited the fact that children and the elderly were underrepresented among the Nagasaki and Hiroshima bomb survivors.

In 1964 the AEC began a study, headed by the well-known occupational epidemiologist Thomas A. Mancuso, of workers at Hanford Nuclear Reservation, in Washington State, which had produced weapons-grade plutonium on a large scale since 1944. The study focused on 20,000 workers who had been employed and monitored for radiation by 1964. The average annual radiation dose for these Hanford workers was 2.23 rem over six or seven years, the average employment period. (A rad is a measure of radiation exposure, and a rem is the measure of the biological effects of the radiation; for gamma radiation and X-rays, one rad equals one rem.) U.S. government regulations allowed for more than twice that dose each year. Mancuso worked on the Hanford data for 12 years, finding no increase in cancers. He then invited Stewart, who had become a research fellow at the University of Birmingham in 1974, and the statistician George Kneale, a colleague of Stewart's, to assist him. Working together they found that workers exposed to less than half the federal safety limit had more cases than expected of pancreatic cancer, lung cancer, and multiple myeloma. Mancuso had not detected these increases in his earlier work because cancer often takes a long time to develop. Stewart persuaded Mancuso that they should tell AEC officials of their results before publishing them. Within months of their doing so, the AEC cut funding of the 13-year grant and confiscated the team's data.

In 1977 Mancuso, Kneale, and Stewart published in the journal *Health Physics* their mortality study of 2,184 Hanford male workers whose annual exposure to radiation measured 1.6 to 2.1 rem. The Mancuso-Kneale-Stewart team had determined that, among those subjects, 6 to 7 percent of cancer deaths could be attributed to radiation and that, usually, the onset of the disease occurred more than 10 years after exposure to radiation. The unusually low cancer death rate that Mancuso had initially come up with reflected the fact that above-average health was a requirement for employment at Hanford. The three scientists called this factor the "healthy-worker effect."

The Department of Energy (DOE), which had replaced the AEC, rejected the researchers' findings and fired Mancuso. Such swift action prompted Congress in 1978 to investigate a possible cover-up. The DOE prevailed; it denied the scientists further access to relevant data and had all related research projects shifted to DOE facilities. Also in 1978 Karl Morgan, who directed the department of medical physics at the Tennessee-based Oak Ridge National Laboratory (one of the DOE facilities to which the researchers' data had been transferred) for 29 years and who was the ex-chairman of the ICRP, acknowledged the importance of Stewart's work, but Mancuso, Kneale, and Stewart were otherwise ostracized by members of their profession throughout the 1970s. Attempts were made to seize their notebooks and other papers, and they were the subject of "character assassinations," as Matt Henry put it in the *Ecologist* (November 1999). Scientists who took Stewart's side were discredited; not only were their research funds cut, but they became victims of physical attacks as well: their "cars [were] rammed off roads and evidence was stolen and suppressed," according to Henry. DOE scientists accused Stewart of spreading misinformation yet refused to debate her findings publicly, as she requested. The DOE replaced Mancuso and Stewart with Ethel Gilbert, a senior staff scientist at Battelle-Pacific Northwest Laboratory, as chief scientist on the Hanford project. In 1979 Gilbert reported, as quoted by Len Ackland in *Technology Review* (February/March 1993), that despite the correlation found between the Hanford radiation doses and the development of cancers of the pancreas and bone marrow, the results "cannot be considered definitive." She justified that conclusion by noting that there were no cases of myeloid leukemia, which is the usual consequence of radiation, and that only a small number of deaths had occurred in the higher-exposure group.

In 1988 Stewart and Kneale studied data on Japanese atom-bomb survivors who died in the years 1950 to 1982. The information had been released by the Radiation Effects Research Foundation (RERF) a decade earlier, but no one had acted on it. Upon investigating 24,416 noncancer deaths, they discovered two opposing dose-related effects: "beneficial" selection and "harmful" immune-system damage. They concluded that the average-health population had been selected out—that is, were not representative of the group studied—because of early death caused by the bomb. A "beneficial" effect of this selection was that the lower-dose survivors were healthier than the average population, as was the case with the "healthy-worker" bias of the Hanford workers. Later, the survivors' deaths, excluding those from heart attacks and strokes, revealed damage to their immune systems from the bombs' radiation. These beneficial and harmful effects had not been detected earlier because they had balanced each other out; while the sickliest of those studied appeared to have poor constitutions, they were in fact people of above-average health, a fact obscured by the deaths of many less-healthy individuals at the time of the atomic blasts. Because of such confusion, previous researchers had not discerned the effects of low-dose radiation. This conclusion challenged the consensus that low-dose radiation had no measurable effects on people.

Stewart testified in U.S. Senate and House committee hearings in 1988 and 1989 that the DOE program for assessing radiation hazards was badly flawed, and that the organization's regulations hindered the free exchange of information. She said further that it was indefensible for the government to lock up files on the 600,000 nuclear-weapons employees, files that had been collected since 1942. That material, the best raw data on low-level radiation, was available only to researchers funded by the DOE, which controlled and profited from the energy and nuclear-weapons industries. This conflict of interest was the equivalent of "the fox guarding the chickens," Stewart said, as quoted by Christine K. Cassel in "Profiles in Responsibility" (1989, as reprinted on *familyreunion.org*, on-line). "I speak out because I think there are not a lot of other people in such a good position. I have nothing to lose. A lot of people do. This area of research can get shut down," Stewart said. Although Stewart won the support of Senator John Glenn of Ohio, the DOE continued to withhold its data.

In 1987 the Three Mile Island (TMI) Public Health Fund, a private foundation established to study radiation after the 1979 accident at the TMI nuclear plant in Pennsylvania, sued for access to the Hanford documents through the Freedom of Information Act. In the interim, data gathered after the 1986 Chernobyl disaster in Russia and other reports had also begun to show that low-level radiation was three to 10 times more dangerous than had been previously thought. In 1990 the TMI Public Health Fund won its lawsuit and gained access to Hanford data on 7,342 workers who had died before 1987. Stewart credited the decision in large part to the thaw in U.S.–Soviet relations and to increased public awareness of environmental issues; recent disclosures about releases of radioactive and toxic contaminants to the air, groundwater, and soil at various DOE plants had raised widespread concern. Energy Secretary James D. Watkins, echoing Stewart's observation that the DOE data were the most important information for studying the effects of radiation on workers, decided that the data would be shifted to the Department of Health and Human Services.

Stewart was financed with $1.4 million from the TMI Public Health Fund, which had already convened an international conference to discuss the optimal choices of population groups for definitive research on low-level radiation. All conferees agreed that the hundreds of thousands of AEC/DOE workers were the best subjects. Stewart's new Hanford research concluded that 200 workers had lost, or would lose, years of their lives due to radiation-induced cancer. Those who receive small-dose radiation are four to eight times more likely to contract cancer than previously believed, and people are much more vulnerable to radiation later in life.

Stewart and her co-workers pointed out that earlier studies of radiation workers had not noted their health histories, which are markedly better than average. This "healthy-worker effect" resulted in a lower number of casualties than would have occurred in an average population. Stewart and her colleagues found that in people between 18 and 65 years of age, the cancer risk doubles with 26 rem of exposure. But after age 58, the risk doubles at only five rem, and after 62 at less than one rem. Radiation causes cell mutation regardless of a person's age, but younger workers' stronger immune systems resist it. The researchers came up with this finding despite the fact that old people often die of other causes before a cancer has had time to develop. The results suggested that perhaps employment that involves the risk of radiation exposure should be restricted to people under 45. But, Stewart hypothesized, the sperm or eggs of young workers might be genetically damaged, thus affecting their future offspring.

Stewart and Kneale also determined that several small doses of radiation could be more harmful than a single large one. While a cell receiving a large dose dies, and may not disrupt the organism, a cell irradiated by a low dosage is more likely to survive and pass on its mutations. Again, this conclusion went against the consensus that small doses are less damaging because they leave the body time to repair itself. The debate continued. In 1991 the *Journal of the American Medical Association* published a study replicating the Mancuso-Kneale-Stewart work, finding the death rate among workers at specified nuclear plants to be 63 percent higher than otherwise would be expected among white males, one group for whom statistics were available. But Stewart and Mancuso's rival, Ethel Gilbert, responded that the study had not taken into account cancers in the population due to tobacco smoking.

Stewart has continued to struggle with an industry "equipped to buy as much advertising, good publicity, and scientists as they can get their hands on," as Henry put it. Representative of an ongoing lack of institutional support, in her seven-decade career she has never been given a staff or any teaching responsibilities and consequently has no successors with first-hand knowledge of her work. But she has been able to see the difference her work has made. The AEC had set a dose limit of 36.5 rem per year for occupational exposure, but by 1993 the international standard had been decreased to two rem annually—though the U.S. DOE has continued to observe the five-rem limit.

Stewart has four grandchildren. "I am strongly a feminist. Oh yes, yes," Stewart told Amy Raphael, "banging her fist on the desk," as Raphael reported. "The world is designed by men for men. Women do have a hard time, and unless they're constantly on the alert and trying to hold their own against the odds, the men will be ready to let everything slip back. There have been obvious difficulties for me—when I've wanted to spend more time with my children or vice versa—but I think it's possible to overcome them. The prize at the end for the child is, of course, that they will find an opening into a more interesting world."

In 1986 the Swedish Parliament presented Stewart with the Right Livelihood Award, known as the "alternative Nobel Prize," for exposing the dangers of low-level radiation. She is the subject of Gayle Greene's biography *The Woman Who Knew Too Much: Alice Stewart and the Secrets of Radiation* (1999). — V.K.

Suggested Reading: *Chicago Tribune* June 24, 1990; *Ecologist* p404+ Nov. 1999; *familyreunion.org* (on-line); *Ms.* p31+ July/Aug. 1996, with photo; Greene, Gayle. *The Woman Who Knew Too Much: Alice Stewart and the Secrets of Radiation*, 1999; Yount, Lisa. *A to Z of Women in Science and Math*, 1999

Archive Photos

Strait, George

May 18, 1952– Country-and-western singer.
Address: c/o MCA Records, 70 Universal City Plaza, Universal City, CA 91608

Known to many of his fans as "the Pope of Texas," the singer George Strait has become such a country-music icon that the Texas state legislature once stopped sessions to investigate a rumor that he had died in a plane crash. Since bursting onto the country-music scene, in 1981, Strait has virtually redefined modern country music with a string of 24 hit albums, more than 35 chart-topping singles, and numerous Country Music Awards. His blend of honky-tonk, western swing, and romantic ballads has set him apart from other contemporary singers and opened the door for a new generation of country artists. He was the first in what is now a long line of country crooners clad in starched shirts, pressed jeans, and oversized hats, and his appeal has as much to do with what he represents as it does with his considerable talent. "George is the gentleman cowboy we all used to dream about," his fellow country star Patty Loveless told a reporter for *People* (November 17, 1997).

The second of three children, George Harvey Strait was born on May 18, 1952 in Poteet, Texas. When he was a child, his mother left home with his sister, and George and his brother were raised by his father, a math teacher at the local high school. "It wasn't exactly a country music upbringing," he recalled to Bob Allen for the *Washington Post* (November 8, 1986). "My dad didn't even have a record player, and when he listened to the radio, it was usually the news or the cow market reports or something like that." A fourth-generation Texan, Strait spent his childhood roping, riding, and branding cattle on his family's 2,000-acre ranch in nearby Pearsall, while developing his interest in music. "Growing up, I pretty much listened to all kinds of music, even rock and roll. . . . I'd buy all the sheet music I could find," Strait told Marty Racine for the *Houston Chronicle* (August 7, 1983), as reprinted on the *No Place but Texas* Web site. "I just taught myself how to play the guitar and sing." As he improved musically Strait began playing in his spare time with what he described to Allen as "some of your basic high school garage bands. We'd play 'Gloria,' 'Louie Louie,' and stuff like that."

After graduating from high school, Strait attended Southwest Texas State University, in San Marcos, but before long he realized that college did not particularly interest him. He dropped out of school and eloped to Mexico with his longtime girlfriend, Norma Voss; they later repeated their vows in a church service, on December 4, 1971. Strait joined the army and was stationed in Hawaii, where his and Norma's first child, Jenifer, was born, on October 6, 1972. In 1973 he successfully auditioned to be lead singer for a country-and-western band at the Schofield Barracks. The newly formed band was soon performing at army functions, first under the name Rambling Country and later as Santee. "I always knew I wanted to be a country singer," Strait told Bob Allen. "But it wasn't until I got to Hawaii that I really got serious about it."

After his military discharge Strait reenrolled at Southwest Texas State University to study agricultural education. His announcement, placed on a campus bulletin board, that he was a singer in search of a band resulted in the formation of a group known as Ace in the Hole. Having rehearsed their rollicking country-and-western sound in a nearby run-down house, they began to take their act on the road, sometimes traveling as far as 200 miles for a gig. "We played everything back then," Strait recalled to Marty Racine. "We played weddings or any kind of function they would pay us money to do." Ace in the Hole soon gained a solid reputation.

Despite the band's success, by 1979 Strait "was just fixin' to go ahead and quit," he told Bob Allen. "I was 27 years old, I'd been playing for six or seven years, and I was beginning to think I just wasn't good enough and maybe ought to try something else." He gave his band notice and successfully applied for a job with a Uvalde, Texas, firm that designed cattle pens. At first his plan for a career change seemed sensible, but Strait's wife soon realized otherwise. "George was moping around the house so much I couldn't stand it," Norma Strait told Montgomery Brower for *People* (June 3, 1985). "I figured I didn't want to live in Uvalde with him like that, so we talked about his hopes in music. I wanted him to give it one more try."

Erv Woolsey, a Texas club owner who had formerly worked with MCA Records, arranged for Strait to perform for several of the label's higher-ups. Strait impressed them, and he signed a contract with MCA in 1980, just six months after his crucial talk with his wife. In the spring of 1981, Strait's first single, "Unwound," was released; his son, George Jr. (who is also known as "Bubba"), was born almost immediately afterward, on May 14. "Unwound" shot to number four on the charts, and the album containing the single, *Strait Country*, went certified gold. Since then the country-music charts have rarely been without at least one George Strait single or album.

In June 1982 Strait released his second album, *Strait from the Heart*, which contains some of his best-known singles, among them "Amarillo by Morning," "Marina Del Rey," and the number-one hits "Fool Hearted Memory" and "A Fire I Can't Put Out." His next two albums, *Right or Wrong* (1983) and *Does Fort Worth Ever Cross Your Mind* (1984), would prove no less successful, yielding a total of four chart-toppers and going gold and platinum, respectively. In 1984 he won the *Billboard* award for top male country artist.

To support record sales Strait toured aggressively across the country with Ace in the Hole, playing a jaw-dropping 250 dates per year. Most shows were marathons that lasted four or more hours and drew praise for their high energy. Although the daily grind of stardom was beginning to wear on Strait, he resisted easing his pace. "I'd be crazy to slow down right now; things are going too good," he explained to Brower. "I have to hit it full steam until I can't stand it any more." In short order he released three more albums, the triple-platinum *Greatest Hits* (1985), *Something Special* (1985), and *#7* (1986).

A personal tragedy forced him to reevaluate his priorities. On the night of June 25, 1986, as Strait's daughter, Jenifer, was riding in a friend's car in San Marcos, Texas, the driver lost control; Jenifer was killed instantly. (She was the only fatality in the nonalcohol-related incident.) Strait was devastated. For more than a year, he refused to grant a single interview, ignoring warnings that retreating from the press might affect his record sales. "I just decided, 'If my career suffers, it suffers,'" he told Jack Hurst for the *Chicago Tribune* (November 23, 1995). "I couldn't suffer any worse than I was already suffering, and that was just the way it was going to be. And I've been that way ever since." In an attempt to lessen his pain, Strait recorded a Christmas album, *Merry Christmas Strait to You* (1986), and embarked on another grueling concert tour.

The following year Strait bounced back, with the release of *Ocean Front Property* (1987), his first album to debut at number one on the *Billboard* charts. The album produced three number-one hits: "All My Ex's Live in Texas," "Am I Blue," and "Ocean Front Property." He continued his domination of country music with two more platinum albums, *If You Ain't Lovin' You Ain't Livin'* (1988) and *Beyond the Blue Neon* (1989), and won a Country Music Award for entertainer of the year in November 1989. He accepted the award in his characteristically self-effacing manner, shaking his head while reaching for the envelope and saying, "Let me read that again." Strait kicked off the 1990s in his trademark furious style, releasing his 13th album, *Livin' It Up* (1990), which became his fastest-seller ever. The single "Love Without End, Amen" reached number one on the country charts and stayed in the top spot for five consecutive weeks. Strait also strolled off with his second consecutive Country Music Award for entertainer of the year.

After 10 years in the limelight, the strain of his touring schedule finally caught up with him. "There were times earlier in my career when I was working like 200 or 250 dates a year the way a lot of young artists are doing today," Strait said to Jack Hurst for the *Chicago Tribune* (October 18, 1992), "and I remember getting to October and November when we started slowing down for Christmas and being burned out so bad I didn't think I could go another year. It got to the point where I would start feeling that way several times during the year. I figured out that I had to get some time away from the music business." Strait had appeared with Ace in the Hole in the James Glickenhaus film *The Soldier* (1982), and in the following years had hoped to star in a movie. Thinking that working on a film would be a good diversion from music, he read several scripts and settled on the drama *Pure Country* (1992), in which he played an overworked country star who undergoes a spiritual reawakening when he returns to Texas cattle country. In a review for the *Washington Post* (October 26, 1992), Richard Harrington called *Pure Country* "a pleasant, low-key country-and-western film." Roger Ebert of the *Chicago Sun-Times* (October 23, 1992) wrote, "Strait is not an actor in the class of [John] Mellencamp or [Willie] Nelson, but he is genuine and has a winning smile, and holds his own in a screenplay that makes few demands." While the film was a moderate hit, the soundtrack album stormed the charts—going quintuple platinum—and spawned three number-one hits. Strait's son joined him for a duet on the single "Heartland."

Strait returned to music in 1993. That year he released *Easy Come, Easy Go*, which featured a hit single of the same name. That album was followed by the platinum-selling *Lead On* (1994). His next effort, *Strait Out of the Box* (1995), went quintuple platinum and became the highest-selling boxed set in music history. The collection, spanning the first 15 years of Strait's career, featured 72 of his top-10 hits, duets with such music luminaries as Frank Sinatra and Hank Thompson, and three early songs that Strait had recorded for a small company before he signed with MCA. The set also offered a new chart-topping song, "Check Yes or No," which became his 35th number-one single and received numerous awards, including a Country Music Award for single of the year.

Strait had another excellent year in 1998. He released the studio album *One Step at a Time*, which loosened the *Titanic* soundtrack's seemingly unshakeable grip on the number-one position on the pop charts and which yielded four top-10 hits. In a review of *One Step at a Time* for the *Washington Post* (May 13, 1998), Bill Friskics-Warren wrote, "George Strait continues to outclass the spate of neo-traditionalist hat acts that he's inspired." The five Country Music Award nominations he received in 1998 pushed him past Merle Haggard's record for total career nominations, and he won one prize. That summer Strait launched the George Strait Country Music Festival, which hosted a slew of country greats. Taking a cue from the acclaimed Lollapalooza rock festival, the traveling show cultivated a carnival atmosphere through such attractions as Straitland, a midway that offered games, food, and a dance floor surrounded by bales of hay. The festival was extremely popular, outselling Sarah McLachlan's much-hyped Lilith Fair, among other such events. Its success, the country singer Jo Dee Messina observed to Edna Gunderson for *USA Today* (March 9, 1999), "says a lot about the appeal of George Strait. He could do an arena tour and command any ticket price he wants, but he enjoys giving fans this festival."

In 1999, in addition to mounting the festival again, Strait released *Always Never the Same*, his 24th album. The first single, "We Really Shouldn't Be Doing This," a lilting ballad about a man who cannot forget a past lover, garnered praise from critics and topped the charts soon after its release. The tune inspired one *Billboard* critic to predict that "We Really Shouldn't Be Doing This" "will have couples swirling around a sawdust-covered dance floor and melting with delight." On March 7, 2000 Strait released *Latest Greatest Straitest Hits*, a collection of his more recent hit singles. In addition, the album featured two new recordings, one of which, "The Best Day," a ballad about a father and son, reached number one on the country charts.

George Strait lives quietly on his ranch in San Marcos, Texas, with Norma and George Jr. To have more time to spend with his family, he has scaled down the number of shows he performs to about 75 per year. He maintains his privacy fiercely, rarely granting interviews or doing publicity. "George is George," the Dixie Chicks singer Natalie Maines said to Gundersen. "He doesn't jump around a lot. He doesn't go for the glitz, the big lights, the stage scenery. He's a humble, nice Texan who stands there and sings songs that people really feel." — J.K.B.

Suggested Reading: *Chicago Tribune* XIII p17 Jan. 13, 1985, with photo, XIII p22+ Oct. 18, 1992, with photo, V p2 Nov. 23, 1995, with photo; *USA Today* D p1+ Mar. 9, 1999; *Washington Post* D p5+ Nov. 8, 1995, with photo

Selected Recordings: *Strait Country*, 1981; *Strait from the Heart*, 1982; *Right or Wrong*, 1983; *Does Fort Worth Ever Cross Your Mind*, 1984; *Something Special*, 1985; *#7*, 1986; *Ocean Front Property*, 1987; *If You Ain't Lovin' You Ain't Livin'*, 1988; *Beyond the Blue Neon*, 1989; *Livin' It Up*, 1990; *The Chill of an Early Fall*, 1991; *Pure Country*, 1992; *Holding My Own*, 1992; *Easy Come, Easy Go*, 1993; *Lead On*, 1994; *Blue Clear Sky*, 1996; *Carrying Your Love with Me*, 1997; *One Step at a Time*, 1998; *Always Never the Same*, 1999; *Latest Greatest Straitest Hits*, 2000

Retna Ltd.

Swank, Hilary

July 30, 1974– Actress. Address: c/o Creative Artists Agency, 9830 Wilshire Blvd., Beverly Hills, CA 90212

Hilary Swank, the Oscar winner for best actress in 2000, waited nearly 10 years for recognition—only to have it come when she was nearly unrecognizable, playing a woman who poses as a man in the independent film *Boys Don't Cry* (1999). The movie is based on the true story of Teena Brandon, a 21-year-old woman who was raped and murdered in 1993 near Falls City, Nebraska, after reinventing herself as Brandon Teena and seducing several of the town's young women. For the role, Swank chopped off her hair, bound her breasts, and otherwise transformed herself into a soft-talking, cowboy-hat-wearing charmer of the opposite sex. That transformation, together with a convincing and emotional performance, has launched Swank into celebrity and earned her reams of critical praise, including—in addition to the Oscar—a 1999 Golden Globe Award for best actress in a drama and honors from the New York, Toronto, and Los Angeles film critics' associations.

Born on July 30, 1974 in Lincoln, Nebraska (as it happens, in the same hospital as Teena Brandon), Swank spent her childhood in Bellingham, Washington, a college town north of Seattle. There, her acting debut as Mowgli in *The Jungle Book*, when she was nine, sparked a love for the stage and earned her a place in the local theater scene. As Swank told Ingrid Sischy for *Interview* (March 2000), the attention she won helped to make up for the isolation she felt in her private life: "I felt lonely. We lived in a trailer park, and the kids who went to my school seemed to be more upper-class." When she was 16, Swank decided she wanted to pursue acting seriously, and her mother—who was at a crossroads in her own life—said to her, as quoted by Sischy, "Let's both go to California." In a story that has already become Hollywood legend, mother and daughter drove into Los Angeles in an Oldsmobile Cutlass Supreme, with only $75 in savings and a Mobil card to charge gas and snacks. Swank enrolled at South Pasadena High School and began auditioning for parts in television sitcoms, thanks to the cold calls her mother made to agents. Before long she was paying the rent—and developing her résumé—by making appearances on *Growing Pains*, *Harry and the Hendersons*, and *Evening Shade*.

Within a few years, Swank had been offered a regular spot on ABC's *Camp Wilder* and earned her first film credit, playing a jealous friend of the title character's in *Buffy, the Vampire Slayer* (1992). She appeared for half a season on *Beverly Hills 90210* as the single mother Carly Reynolds, who was pursued by the local heartthrob Steve Sanders (Ian Ziering). A higher-profile assignment came along when she won the lead role, that of the title character, in *The Next Karate Kid* (1994), the fourth installment of the series and the first not to star Ralph Macchio. ("There's a new Karate Kid in town," read the *Chicago Tribune* [August 9, 1994] lead story, "and it's not a he, but a she.")

The producers of *The Next Karate Kid* had narrowed a pool of 500 actresses down to Swank and five others when they decided to test her physical ability. "Basically, they put me in a room and showed me a move, like a spin kick, and then they'd say, 'Okay, now you try it,'" she told Malissa Thompson for *Seventeen* (September 1994). Having been a competitive swimmer and gymnast as a teen, Swank rose to the challenge and won the part. She then worked with trainers for up to five hours a day, building her strength and coordination, until she was able to pull off her character's karate moves convincingly. "There were pull-ups, push-ups, sit-ups, and everything you could do on a bar," Swank told Thompson. "At first I was so sore I hurt in places that I never knew I had muscles."

Swank's character, Julie Pierce, was a troubled teenager whose parents are dead and whose grandmother can no longer handle her. With the help of Mr. Miyagi (Pat Morita), Julie learns the physical skills that not only help her get back at a gang of bullies who have been bothering her at school, but also, by boosting her confidence, give her control over her own life. Although the film was not a critical success, it was a test of Swank's determination, her willingness to immerse herself in her character's reality.

Discussing her eclectic résumé, Swank told Sischy that "the life of an actor is so tumultuous, so up and down. . . . I know that all my experiences contributed to my playing Brandon Teena. Because when the role came along, I was so ready for it." Indeed, when asked to play a woman who is herself playing a man, Swank again relied on the process of immersion. "To do the movie justice—because it was so close to a lot of people's hearts—it was very important to me to actually pass as a boy, to live as a boy, which I did for six weeks," she told Jim Slotek for the *Toronto Sun* (October 22, 1999, on-line). She started with the basics: cropping her hair short, dropping weight in order to accentuate her bone structure, and deepening her voice. Her transformation was a work-in-progress; as she went out each day, she observed the ways that people responded to her, noting whether they took her to be male or female. She adjusted her walk and modified her gestures, learning that seemingly minor details—such as how she entered a room or how often she smiled at strangers—were thought to hold masculine or feminine significance. And at all times she went around "strapping and packing," as she came to call the acts of strapping her breasts in tension bandages and packing socks in her pants.

The film's director and co-writer, Kimberly Peirce, had spent four years looking for the right person to portray Brandon. Peirce had first read about Brandon's life in 1994, while a graduate student in film at Columbia University, and had shepherded the film project through production since then. It was important to her to find an actress who could move beyond the sensationalism of the story's facts and delve fully into Brandon's mindset. In an interview with *Sun*, as quoted by Laurell Haapanen on the *Mr. Showbiz* Web site, Peirce recalled, "Most girls can't suddenly be boys. I saw all these great, wonderful actresses, but they could not do the boy thing. They'd strut around, they'd wink, you know. But they couldn't bring the sexuality out." But for Pierce, Swank's audition tape stood out from the rest: "[There] it was. This beam came across the screen. She was wearing a cowboy hat and had this gorgeous jaw, great big ears, wonderful teeth, big brown eyes, an Adam's Apple. . . . She blurred the gender line," Peirce told Dave Karger for *Entertainment Weekly* (October 29, 1999). "And even more important than that, she smiled. She loved being Brandon."

This quality of joy, according to Swank, was ultimately what helped her to tap into the essence of her character. "I'm not transgender and I'm not gay, so I had to find something that I could relate to," she told an interviewer for *Roughcut.com* (February 28, 2000). "And what I could relate to was that this was a person following their dream and having the courage to be themselves. So that's what I tried to play. I tried to play how exciting it is to really live your dream." Many critics responded to the integrity of Swank's performance, her ability to bring out the loneliness as well as the charisma and seductive power of her character. Writing about Swank in the *New York Times* (February 21, 2000), Margo Jefferson noted, "Her re-creation feels like a raising from the dead. But it wouldn't be so astonishing if she didn't also remind us that every boy has to practice being a boy. Getting the walk, the shoulders, the handshake right; asking a girl to dance or roller skate without looking like a dork; impressing the guys without alienating the girls. And finally the thrill of getting it right, having that power. I'd never understood this so clearly until I saw a woman lay claim to it all." Swank was also praised by gay and lesbian groups for her willingness to take on the role even though she herself is heterosexual. Indeed, both Swank and her co-star, Chloë Sevigny, who played Brandon's girlfriend, Lana, have been lauded for their emotional honesty in portraying the love between the two characters.

For Swank, "passing" as a man entailed an emotional experience beyond the thrill of getting away with it. Peirce's first words of advice to her were blunt: "I said to her, 'Go pass as a boy for four weeks,'" Pierce recalled in an interview with Karger, "'And if you [expletive] up and people discover you, you better go back home and feel embarrassed. Feel terrified about what it means to be an imposter. Go home and look in the mirror and figure out what went wrong.'" Swank told Karger, "I don't think I was really prepared for what I went through. There were people who couldn't figure out what I was. They didn't look me in the eye. I was treated poorly by people in stores, people that I had known as Hilary. I cried for two days straight."

Yet Swank was also keenly aware of the difference between her status as an actress and Brandon's own tragically curtailed existence. "[Passing] was a lonely feeling and what was sad was I knew I could get out of it, because my role would be over. But people like Brandon Teena go through their whole life feeling that loneliness," she told Slotek.

The Academy Award nominees for best actress in 2000 were mainly established talents—Meryl Streep, Annette Bening, and Julianne Moore—and the lesser-known Janet McTeer. Though Swank, through winning the award, seems to have gained entry into Hollywood's royal court—with appearances on magazine covers and talk shows, clad in the fashions that designers are begging her to wear—she is moving ahead cautiously, recognizing the often fickle nature of celebrity. In recent years Oscar nominations for best actress have gone to performers, including Elizabeth Shue for *Leaving Las Vegas* and Mary McDonnell for *Passion Fish*, who have gotten little work since. With a new publicist and the backing of the Creative Artists Agency, one of Hollywood's most powerful firms, Swank hopes to parlay her sudden success into an enduring career.

Swank is currently filming Sam Raimi's *The Gift*, with Keanu Reeves and Cate Blanchett, and will next play Jeanne de la Motte-Valois, an 18th-century Frenchwoman, in the film *The Affair of the Necklace*. For that project she will trade in her flannel shirt and boots for period finery and play an aristocratic beauty who, while searching for her heritage, becomes enmeshed in a scandal involving Marie Antoinette, a diamond necklace, a cardinal, and a cheating husband. In her search for her parentage, her character contrives to bring down Marie Antoinette and launch the events that led to the French Revolution—another instance in which Swank's character will defy boundaries.

Swank has been married to the television and film actor Chad Lowe since 1997. — M.A.H.

Suggested Reading: *Biography* p14 Feb. 2000; *Entertainment Weekly* p23+ Oct. 29, 1999; *Harper's Bazaar* p256+ Feb. 2000, with photo; *Interview* p136+ Mar. 2000, with photos; *Mr. Showbiz* (on-line) Feb. 28, 2000; *New York Times* E p2 Feb. 21, 2000, with photo; *Roughcut.com* (on-line) Feb. 28, 2000; *Seventeen* p86+ Sep. 1994, with photo; *Time* p88 Jan. 17, 2000, with photo; *Toronto Sun* (on-line) Oct. 22, 1999

Courtesy of Log Cabin Republicans

Tafel, Richard L.

(TA-fel)

1962– Executive director of the Log Cabin Republicans. Address: Log Cabin Republicans, 1633 Q St. N.W., #210, Washington, DC 20009

To many heterosexuals and homosexuals, the term "gay Republican" is an oxymoron, because the Republican Party has long been associated with condemnations of homosexuality; the Democratic Party, by contrast, and particularly its liberal wing, has traditionally expressed tolerance for different sexual preferences. The gay Republican activist Richard L. Tafel, however, sees no contradiction between his lifestyle and his conservative political views. "Homophobia is an American problem, and not a problem of one political party or the other," he said to David Tuller for the *San Francisco Chronicle* (January 21, 1994). Tafel is a co-founder of the Log Cabin Republicans (LCR); its first president and currently its executive director and chief lobbyist, he has built the LCR into the largest gay and lesbian Republican group in the country. As of December 1999, the LCR, which is based in Washington, D.C., had 52 chapters in 30 states and more than 10,000 members. Strong challengers to the powerful religious right-wing minority within the Republican Party, the Log Cabin caucus seeks to mute intraparty debate centered on such "family-value" issues as abortion and gay rights and to focus instead on traditional Republican ideology, namely the belief in limited government, free markets, and strong national defense. By concentrating on an economic rather than a social agenda, the LCR hopes to draw more homosexuals into the party.

As a spokesperson for gays and lesbians, Tafel has raised the ire not only of members of the Republican Party but of the homosexual community as well, and his steadfastness in the face of harsh criticism has earned him admiration. "To be as open and visible and tenacious as Rich requires a great deal of courage," the gay activist David Mixner, a Democrat who helped raise millions of dollars to support Bill Clinton's first presidential campaign, told Patrick J. Kiger for *Gentlemen's Quarterly* (January 1994). "It's not like you walk into the room and people in the Republican Party slap you on the back and say, 'Good job.'" Moreover, Mike Duffy, an openly gay Massachusetts politician and friend of Tafel's, told Kiger, "I think it probably has been more difficult for Rich, and the reaction more vitriolic, within the gay community. It is an article of faith with some gay people that you are a Democrat if you are gay. It's heretical to be a Republican. The amount of emotion it incites is incredible." In an account of the fifth annual Log Cabin Republican Washington Weekend for the *Washington Blade* (May 7, 1999, on-line), Bill Roundy wrote, "Log Cabin's primary goal is quelling anti-Gay bias within the Republican party, but equally important, said members, is ending anti-Republican attitudes within the larger Gay community."

Richard L. Tafel was born in 1962. He had a conventional upbringing in a suburb of Philadelphia, where his politically conservative outlook took root. In a conversation with Jesse Monteagudo for *Gay Today* (February 2, 1998, on-line), Tafel said that he is "not crazy about the term ['conservative'] because it has so many meanings to so many people. Though I am fiscally conservative, I would say that, philosophically, I am close to libertarian." As a boy Tafel attended Bible school and sang with a church choir. Although his parents held traditional values, Tafel has said that they supported him when, at the age of 23, he revealed his sexual preference; indeed, he told Patrick Kiger, his mother and father seemed more taken aback when he asked for money to help pay for graduate school than when he had openly acknowledged his sexual orientation. But Tafel's decision to out himself cost him several links to his childhood. "Some of his soccer teammates from when he was in school won't even talk to him now," one boyhood friend of Tafel's told Kiger.

Tafel attended East Stroudsburg University, in Pennsylvania, from which he graduated with a bachelor's degree in philosophy, with honors, in 1984. A devout Baptist, he earned a master's of divinity degree from Harvard University, in Cambridge, Massachusetts, in 1987. The next year he was ordained a minister in the American Baptist Church. Also in 1988, Tafel found work at Harvard as an assistant to the minister for special projects in the university's Memorial Church. The chaplain of the church, the noted reverend Peter J. Gomes, is a politically conservative African-American who has argued against literal interpretations of the Bible, including a literal reading of passages cited as condemnations of homosexuality; a professor of Christian morals as well, he revealed in 1992 that he himself is homosexual. Reverend Gomes charged Tafel with the task of pulling the church out of debt, and Tafel succeeded, by implementing substantial cost-cutting measures and new fund-raising strategies. By the time Tafel left the job, in May 1993, Memorial Church was among Harvard's best-endowed nonacademic entities.

Meanwhile, Tafel had become increasingly involved in local Massachusetts politics. In 1990 he managed the congressional campaign of Mike Duffy, a gay Republican friend of his, and rallied a large number of gay and lesbian voters in the district, which was heavily Democratic. Although Duffy lost, Tafel's efforts were not wasted, because the newly organized homosexual electorate in Boston helped carry the Republican Massachusetts gubernatorial candidate, William Weld, to a close victory. In recognition of the boost Tafel had given his underdog campaign, Weld, who had bucked his party's platform to support gay rights, appointed him director of the adolescent-health program at the state's Department of Public Health. In that post, which he held from June 1991 to August 1993, Tafel helped to institute Weld's public health reforms.

In 1990, while campaigning in Boston for Duffy, Tafel co-founded and became the first president of the Log Cabin Federation, a group of nine gay and lesbian Republican clubs that had existed separately since the battle against the Briggs Initiative in California in 1978. The Briggs measure, also known as Proposition 6, had sought to ban homosexuals from teaching in public schools; fiercely opposed by gay activists and many other Californians, it had been defeated at the polls. In the three and a half years during which Tafel served as LCR's president, the number of LCR chapters rose to 32, and total membership climbed to 8,000. He also built a base of wealthy donors, who have contributed a total of about $100,000 each election cycle to the organization's political action committee for Republican candidates. LCR also created a nonpartisan educational foundation to further its principles in the cultural arena and business community. In 1993 LCR established its headquarters in Washington, D.C.

LCR grew despite the stiff opposition that confronted Tafel and the organization at every turn. Much of that opposition came from the religious right, which for some years maintained virtual control of the Republican Party. This control was evident during the party's 1992 national convention, during which the political commentator and presidential candidate Pat Buchanan set the tone by delivering a speech filled with antigay rhetoric. Furthermore, two of the Republican Party's most prominent members, Senate Majority Leader Trent Lott and House Majority Leader Dick Armey, had made derogatory remarks in public about homosexuals and the political issues that concern them, such as gay marriage, health-care coverage for partners in same-sex unions, job discrimination, and military service.

Many homosexuals, for their part, likened Tafel's working for the Republicans to a Jew's working for the Nazis during the 1930s and early 1940s. Gay Democratic congressman Barney Frank of Massachusetts was especially vociferous in criticizing Tafel and the LCR. "For a long time, it was easier to come out of the closet as a gay than as a Republican," Tafel observed to Jerry Roberts for the *San Francisco Chronicle* (December 11, 1994). Accentuating what his Republican and gay opponents viewed as the contradiction between his political views and his sexual orientation was Tafel's 18-month relationship with Jarrett Barrios, a leader of the Boston chapter of Queer Nation, a left-wing gay and lesbian rights organization.

In 1992 the LCR refused to endorse President George Bush in his campaign for reelection against Democratic governor Bill Clinton of Arkansas, because, the group charged, he pandered to the religious right. Instead, they channeled their efforts to such high-profile moderate Republicans as William Weld, New Jersey governor Christine Todd Whitman, New York City mayor Rudolph Giuliani, and Los Angeles mayor Richard Riordan, all of whom had strong records on gay issues. Tafel worked as a consultant for both the Riordan and Giuliani campaigns, advising them on ways to attract the substantial gay vote in their respective cities. In both cases a larger-than-anticipated portion of that vote went to the Republican candidates, and consequently, the Republican Party began to view gay Republicans more seriously as constituents.

Moreover, after his election President Clinton reneged on his 1992 campaign promises to boost funding for AIDS research and lift the military's ban on enlistment by homosexuals. Seemingly kowtowing to conservatives on Capitol Hill, the president adopted a "Don't ask, don't tell" policy toward gays serving in the military, which in effect kept them closeted or forced them to leave. Angered that the Clinton administration had apparently taken their support for granted, some homosexuals switched their allegiance to the Republican Party. Tafel believes the defining moment for his organization came in 1995, during the early months of the 1996 presidential race. Solicited for funds by several officials connected with the campaign of the eventual Republican nominee, Senator Bob Dole of Kansas, in August 1995 the LCR contributed $1,000 to his campaign. But soon after, under pressure from the religious right, campaign officials returned the check. Tafel's criticism of the Republicans' action was aired on television and reported in newspapers across the country, and the coverage triggered an outpouring of sympathy for the LCR's position and condemnation of the Republican fund-raisers. In October 1995 Dole asserted that his aides had been wrong to return the check; he apologized to the LCR, and the group later endorsed him. "You would think that you can take a group like Log Cabin and marginalize it, but that didn't work," Tafel pointed out to Scott Giordano for *Bay Windows* (June 17–23, 1999). "Bob Dole had to apologize and it was considered the biggest fiasco of his campaign. A lesson was learned: you don't treat that group that way, so you had better learn how to work with them. That was the big political lesson to learn—that even in small numbers you can impact things by being on the high moral ground." Tafel's use of the phrase "high moral ground" struck some observers as poignant, since his organization and what its members represent is diametrically opposed to the position of the so-called Moral Majority, a lobbying organization of fundamentalist Christian Republicans, which the televangelist Jerry Falwell founded in 1979 and dissolved 10 years later.

Since 1996 the Republican Party has reached out somewhat to gays and lesbians. Though most Republican politicians of note have yet to lend official support to gay causes, most appear to be taking a more inclusive approach. Their numbers include Texas governor George W. Bush, the 2000 Republican presidential candidate. Nevertheless, Bush's relationship with gays and lesbians (and with the LCR in particular) during the 2000 campaign was uneven. Toward the end of 1999, Bush publicly stated that if elected president, he would appoint homosexuals in his administration. "If someone can do a job that he's qualified for, that person ought to be allowed to do his job," Bush declared, as quoted by Katharine Seelye in the *New York Times* (August 11, 1999). As the fight for the Republican nomination intensified, however, Bush equivocated. His chief Republican adversary, on the other hand, Arizona senator John McCain, met with the LCR in November and expressed his opposition to discrimination of any kind. In September, according to an editorial in the *St. Louis [Missouri] Post-Dispatch* (November 24, 1999, on-line), Bush told a group of religious conservatives that "he would not 'knowingly' hire a gay person, but he wouldn't fire someone who was later 'discovered' to be gay," and in November he turned down an invitation to meet with the LCR.

Tensions between Bush and the gay community peaked during the South Carolina primary. Fighting McCain for the Republican nomination in a state where religious conservatives dominate the GOP, Bush distanced himself from gays and lesbians. During one debate, for example, he implicitly criticized McCain for meeting with the LCR, and in an interview on Christian radio, he appeared to backpedal on his promise to employ gays and lesbians in a Bush administration. After Bush successfully overcame McCain's challenge, however, he began to warm to homosexual Republicans once again, sending out feelers for a possible reconciliation. On March 24 a spokesman for the Bush campaign told Ronald G. Shafer for the *Wall Street Journal* (March 24, 2000) that while Bush still would not meet with the LCR (which had endorsed McCain in the primaries), the candidate was willing to confer with a "group of Republicans who support him and happen to be gay." That offer was soon taken up, and on April 14 Bush met with a group of 12 prominent gay and lesbian Republicans, among them several members of the LCR. After the meeting Bush reaffirmed his promise to appoint homosexuals to government posts should he become president, thereby securing the endorsement of the LCR. "In April of this year, Governor Bush began a dialogue with the gay and lesbian community," Robert Stears, the chairman of the Log Cabin Republicans, reported in an official statement posted on the LCR Web site. "He reached out to our organization's leadership, and made it publicly clear that he has a vision of being a President for all Americans—black, white, Latino, men, women, gay and straight. That his vision of an inclusive Republican Party includes gay and lesbian Republicans." Speaking at the Republican National Convention in Philadelphia, Tafel said, as quoted by Lois Romano in the *Washington Post* (July 31, 2000), "We believe Governor Bush's goal is to unite the party and that they are reaching out to us."

Among the political commentators who have noticed a change in attitude within the Republican Party is William Kristol, former chief of staff to Vice President Dan Quayle and now editor of the conservative political publication the *Weekly Standard*. "The Republican establishment does not want to fight the conservative culture war," Kristol said to Seelye, "partly because they think it's a losing fight but more importantly, they don't believe in it." Signaling this intraparty shift in attitude toward homosexuals was Congress's defeat of the so-called Hefley amendment in the summer of 1998. The amendment, which was attached to an unrelated bill and sponsored by Representative Joel Hefley of Colorado, Majority Whip Tom DeLay, and two other Republican lawmakers, would have overturned President Clinton's executive order banning discrimination in the federal government based on sexual preference. The assault on the proposed amendment was led by Republican representative Jim Kolbe of Arizona, who is openly gay, with the support of Tafel and the LCR. Sixty-three House Republicans voted against the amendment, and its defeat further diminished the power of the religious right within the Republican Party.

Tafel believes that his religious training is his secret weapon in his political career. "My religious background gives me the strength to persevere in what sometimes seems to be extreme odds," he said to Scott Giordano. "At a pragmatic level of debate, it's handy because [the Right] quotes scripture and nobody has ever refuted them before and they are baffled when I quote it back at them. Also, Christians often are sympathetic to my argument because I base it on Christian language they are familiar with."

A frequent contributor to political journals and op-ed pages in newspapers across the country, Tafel published his first book, *Party Crasher: A Gay Republican Challenges Politics as Usual*, in 1999. Part memoir and part political treatise, the book chronicles his path to political prominence and explains his beliefs. "The best sections of the book simply describe what it is like to be a gay Republican, which seems to be akin to standing in the middle of a field with a hurricane hitting you from one side and a tornado slamming you from the other, while you look up hopefully for blue sky," David Brooks, a senior editor at the *Weekly Standard* (June 27, 1999), wrote for the *New York Times Book Review* (June 27, 1999, on-line). "From the right comes complacent prejudice. . . . From the left comes public demonization." Tafel "makes an outstanding case that some homosexuals should call themselves libertarian and maybe sometimes vote for Republican candidates," Brooks continued. "He doesn't make a good case that homosexuals should call themselves Republicans. Because the Republican Party, for all its commitment to limited government, has never been and never will be a libertarian party. It is a conservative party, believing that government should shore up middle-class moral standards. If gay people are to become a vital fixture in the Republican coalition, somebody will have to demonstrate that being gay is not an affront to middle-class morality. . . . Tafel has a developed set of arguments to champion the cause of economic liberty, but only apologetic, half-formed instincts when it comes to the moral demands of gay life. The person who can write compellingly about liberty and traditional morality will have laid the foundation for a principled gay Republicanism, ground that will be worth defending against homophobes and amoralists alike." A reviewer of *Party Crasher* for Amazon.com wrote, "There's something in this book to upset just about everyone's preconceptions, but what comes through most is Richard Tafel's passion and commitment for social justice and genuine acceptance of everybody's differences." Tafel plans to write a second book about his spiritual philosophy. Despite his extensive involvement in the behind-the-scenes work of government, he has expressed no interest in running for office. — T.J.F.

Suggested Reading: *Bay Windows* p1+ June 17-23, 1999, with photo; *Gay Today* (on-line), Feb. 2, 1998, with photo, May 10, 1999, with photo; *Gentlemen's Quarterly* p80+ Jan. 1994, with photo; *New York Times* A p1+ Aug. 11, 1999; *San Francisco Chronicle* S p9 Dec. 11, 1994; Tafel, Richard. *Party Crasher: A Gay Republican Challenges Politics as Usual*, 1999

Office of the Deputy Secretary of State

Talbott, Strobe

Apr. 25, 1946– Deputy secretary of state; journalist. Address: U.S. Department of State, 2201 C St. N.W., Washington, DC 20520-0001

Strobe Talbott, the current deputy secretary of state, has long been involved with U.S. foreign policy, first as a diplomatic journalist for 22 years at *Time* magazine and a writer on arms control, and now as a diplomat himself, promoting the policies that the United States and, indirectly, the International Monetary Fund (IMF) pursue toward Russia. Stability with regard to Russia's nuclear arms and the pursuit of economic reform, the two principal goals of the administration's policy of "strategic engagement" of Russia, have a well-equipped representative in Talbott. With six books on U.S.–Soviet relations and arms control to his name and a scholarly background in Russian literature and translation, Talbott is an experienced observer of the Russian scene.

The government official and journalist was born Nelson Strobridge Talbott III on April 25, 1946 in Dayton, Ohio, to Nelson S. Talbott, an investment banker, manufacturer, and conservationist, and Josephine Large Talbott. He has a brother and two sisters. As a child he "was a bit of a dweeb," according to Barbara Matusow, writing in the *Washingtonian* (February 1994). Wanting to be a doctor when he grew up, he conducted experiments on rabbits and frogs, anesthetizing and performing skin grafts on them. He attended boarding school at Hotchkiss, in Lakeville, Connecticut, representing the third generation of his family to do so. At Hotchkiss he grew to love the Russian language and literature. He went on to attend Yale University, in New Haven, Connecticut, where he met his future wife, Brooke Shearer, who was the younger sister of his roommate.

It has been written that in college, where he was chairman of the *Yale Daily News*, Talbott appeared to be older and more serious than his classmates. During those years he supported the decriminalization of marijuana and "tried to figure out how to oppose the Vietnam War without being against the government," as Barbara Matusow wrote. Matusow added that the journalist James Reston, after meeting Talbott in 1967, was "so impressed that he wrote a column warning that 'if the Strobe Talbotts at Yale, serious, idealistic, patriotic, progressive . . . types,' did not support the war effort, the generals had better start worrying."

Talbott studied 19th- and early-20th-century Russian literature at Yale and graduated summa cum laude, in 1968. Then, chosen as a Rhodes Scholar, he spent three years at Oxford University, in England. There, he roomed with another Rhodes Scholar, Bill Clinton. Many of Talbott's peers were serving in the military at the time, and he later "confessed to 'a moral discomfort that bordered on guilt,' when a trick knee kept him 'out of the Mekong Delta [in Vietnam] but not off the squash courts and playing fields of Oxford,'" as Cathy Horyn quoted him as saying in the *Washington Post* (July 14, 1994). He received a master's degree in literature from Oxford in 1971 and the traditional second Oxford master's degree, with additional honors, in 1976. Also during this period, when he was in his 20s, he translated and edited two volumes of the Soviet leader Nikita S. Khrushchev's memoirs, published in 1970 and 1974, respectively.

Talbott began working at *Time* magazine as a correspondent in the Balkans in 1971. He modeled himself on Walter Lippmann, an influential columnist of the period. Like Lippmann, he combined scholarship with journalism and cultivated internationalist views, which he sought to introduce into U.S. foreign policy. As a correspondent he frequented the Council on Foreign Relations, the Stanford Center on Arms Control and Disarmament, and the Aspen Strategy Group, a bipartisan policy program of the Aspen Institute, making connections with important political figures. Discussing his journalism career, Cathy Horyn cited the journalist Charles Lane's observation that Talbott's stories were almost invariably supportive of his subjects. In a conversation with Horyn, a senior fellow at the Carnegie Endowment for International Peace spoke admiringly of Talbott but, echoing others, noted that Talbott refuses to entertain opinions different from his own: "It's a mistake to think that Strobe was a reporter in the traditional sense. He was always a pundit." For two years Talbott was *Time*'s correspondent in Eastern Europe. From 1974 to 1975, during Henry Kissinger's tenure as secretary of state, he was the magazine's State Department correspondent, and during 1975 and 1976 he covered the White House. For seven years beginning in 1977 he was a diplomatic correspondent for the magazine. He became Washington bureau chief in 1984, and his career at *Time* culminated in his becoming editor at large and foreign-affairs columnist in 1989. Talbott won the Edward Weintal Prize for foreign-affairs and diplomacy reporting in 1980 and 1985 and was cited in the Overseas Press Club Awards given to *Time* in 1982, 1987, and 1989. He specialized in showing readers how policy was made in the National Security Agency, the CIA, and the State Department. "He got his access in part because his sources thought he was one of them . . . which in truth he was," Matusow wrote, noting Talbott's skill at "convinc[ing] the principals to talk to him in the midst of the most delicate negotiations, producing fly-on-the-wall accounts of what happened."

During his 22-year journalism career Talbott also wrote six books on U.S.–Soviet relations and arms control. A reviewer of Talbott's *Deadly Gambits: The Reagan Administration and the Stalemate in Nuclear Arms Control* for *Esquire* (December 1985) wrote that it was "widely believed that [Talbott]. . . contributed to the [President Ronald] Reagan administration's profound revision of its arms-negotiation tactics" toward a less hawkish stance. In Talbott's view, the Reagan administration—unlike previous American governments—held that arms control had weakened the U.S. and that the Soviets were so untrustworthy as to render treaties useless. According to Talbott, Reagan's negotiators had the goal of stalemating the arms-control process rather than reaching an agreement. In the *Atlantic* (December 1984), James Fallows wrote that Talbott's book was "an unrelieved denunciation of the Reagan Administration, which Talbott depicts as a haven for fanatical ideas and intemperate men. . . . Talbott provides so many illustrations of [Reagan's] ignorance and his torpor as to raise uncomfortable, nonpartisan questions about who has really been in charge these past few years." According to Fallows, Talbott affirmed that nuclear policies of the time arose from symbolic, rather than military, realities. Illustrating this point, Talbott quoted an assistant secretary of state who said, speaking about Pershing missiles, "We don't care if the goddamn things work or not. . . . After all, that doesn't matter unless there's a war.

What we care about is getting them in." Sales of *Deadly Gambits* received a significant boost when Walter Mondale, the 1984 Democratic presidential nominee, read from it during a debate with then-President Reagan. Talbott's other books are: *Endgame: The Inside Story of SALT II* (1979); *Master of the Game: Paul Nitze and the Nuclear Peace* (1988); *The Russians and Reagan* (1984); *Reagan and Gorbachev* (1987), written with Michael Mandelbaum; and *At the Highest Levels: The Inside Story of the End of the Cold War* (1993), on which he collaborated with Michael R. Beschloss.

Talbott came to diplomacy soon after his former Oxford roommate, Bill Clinton, became president of the United States, in January 1993. The president's first secretary of state, Warren Christopher, hired him in April of that year as ambassador-at-large and special adviser to the secretary of state on the newly independent republics of the former Soviet Union. Talbott developed initiatives for Russia, cultivating bipartisan support in Congress for a plan to give $2.5 billion in aid to the country, which was facing economic turmoil in the wake of the Soviet Union's collapse. Due in part to this accomplishment, he was confirmed as deputy secretary of state on February 22, 1994.

Talbott's first concern upon assuming that post was that many Democrats and Republicans wanted to "turn the American eagle into an ostrich," as he put it, as quoted in a *U.S. Department of State Dispatch* (October 16, 1995)—in other words, that they wanted the U.S. to focus on its own affairs to the exclusion of important international events. The Clinton administration was being criticized for being overactive in its attempts to settle foreign entanglements—namely, for taking steps "to settle war in Bosnia, restore democracy to Haiti, negotiate peace for Somalia, end the North Korean nuclear threat, and lead Russia to peace and wealth . . . the first four goals [with] the use of U.S. combat troops," Eric Alterman wrote for *Mother Jones* (March/April 1994). Talbott dismissed such critics as "isolationists" who sought to shrink the foreign-affairs budget, and he affirmed the administration position that if the United States did not lead the world, other countries, such as Iran, Iraq, Sudan, or Libya, would fill the vacuum. These "rogue states," practicing "terrorism" and using "weapons of mass destruction," had to be kept in check, he said.

In his first year in office, Talbott tried unsuccessfully to defend the U.N. embargo against arms exports to Bosnia-Herzegovina, a former province of what was once Yugoslavia. The U.N.'s intention was to stop warfare in the province from spreading, but both Democrats and Republicans in Congress voted to lift the embargo, rejecting the idea of the U.S.'s being subject to multilateral discipline.

The idea that multilateralism and international cooperation are against U.S. interests was raised in the following year during a televised interview with Talbott on *Charlie Rose*. When Rose suggested that multilateralism was "a code word for giving up U.S. leadership in the world," Talbott's response was that multilateralism represented "an opportunity" for the United States "to put together coalitions that will address crises, and sometimes prevent crises from happening or from getting out of control."

For American isolationists, or those who want to concentrate only on matters that directly affect the U.S., the Clinton administration's attempt in 1994 to pay the backlog of membership dues to the United Nations amounted to a capitulation. Talbott backed the White House's efforts, pointing out that while almost half of all the money awarded in U.N. contracts every year goes to American companies, the U.S. is the worst delinquent in terms of paying its dues to the U.N. He specified that U.N. peacekeeping costs less than half of 1 percent of the total U.S. defense budget, and that only $7 per capita would pay for the entire U.N. system of peacekeepers, UNICEF polio vaccinations, food for the hungry through the World Food Program, and WHO smallpox vaccinations. On the general theme of the foreign-affairs budget, he pointed out that during the 1980s there had been a 40 percent decline in U.S. foreign-budget expenditure, adjusted for inflation, to only 1.3 percent of total federal spending. "We've passed from cutting fat, and are now in danger of cutting into muscle and bone and vital arteries," he said in a *U.S. Department of State Dispatch* (October 13, 1995). Now, both Democrats and Republicans want to cut U.N. membership, he said, noting that the only target more ripe for attack than "big government" is "world government," and that while the U.N. is not world government, it enables world nations to attempt concerted action.

Talbott observed approvingly that the U.N. was working on a moratorium on the export of antipersonnel land mines. In 1997, however, when the agreement was finalized by 89 countries, President Clinton refused to sign it, citing military necessity. The next year, when India tested an atomic bomb, Talbott was sent to Pakistan—India's neighbor and rival—on an unsuccessful mission to persuade officials there not to respond in kind.

In that same year, 1998, Talbott gave a speech at Stanford University about changes the Russian government had made in its plans for economic recovery in the wake of the Soviet Union's collapse. The adjustments deviated from the "shock therapy" market-privatization reforms—that is, the rapid shift to capitalism—developed by Harvard economist Jeffrey Sachs in 1991 and promoted by the Clinton administration. Those reforms had abruptly eliminated decades-old price controls and subsidies, setting off a hyperinflation that reached 2,500 percent. Perhaps recognizing the precipitous decline in the Russian standard of living during his tenure as ambassador-at-large, Talbott had called for "less shock and more therapy," as Steven Greenhouse quoted him as saying in the *New York Times* (January 25, 1994). After being roundly criticized for his stance, Talbott adopted the administration's official line regarding the issue. He lamented that the Russian government's decision to increase spending in order to pay back wages and pensions and to support agriculture and energy expenditures was bound for failure.

Talbott is considered the author of the administration's "Russia First" policy. According to this program, the new independent states of the former Soviet Union would all be helped to dismantle and reduce the number of their nuclear weapons, and they would all be paid large sums of money in return for undertaking economic privatization reforms, but Russia would have first priority. From the beginning of his tenure at the State Department, Talbott was nicknamed "the czar of all the Russias," Matusow wrote. He was praised by some for his North Atlantic Treaty Organization (NATO) Partnership for Peace plan, which offered Russia and the former Warsaw Pact nations, the one-time alliance of Communist Eastern bloc countries, the opportunity to participate in joint military exercises and training with the multinational troops of NATO, their former adversary. The "Russia First" policy also counseled delay in extending NATO membership to the Czech Republic, Poland, and Hungary, for fear of antagonizing Russia. The administration was accused of "Talbottism" by those, such as commentator George Weigel, who urged a less Russia-centered foreign policy toward the independent states of the former Soviet Union. In addition, Matusow noted, "Talbott has become a lightning rod for those who think U.S. policy under his guidance is too closely tied to the success of Boris Yeltsin," then-president of Russia. But according to Talbott, "Boris Yeltsin . . . [was] locked in mortal combat with the opponents of reform, so I think our strong support for him has been very important," as he told Matusow.

What some called his uncritical support for Russia and its president notwithstanding, it was still Talbott who ordered his plane back to Moscow on June 10, 1999, when word arrived that a Russian military unit had occupied the Pristina airport in Kosovo, in the former Yugoslavia. Control of this region—between the Danube and the Adriatic Sea—has been prized since the 1980 death of Yugoslavian dictator Josip Broz Tito, and more so since the end of the Cold War. Long a smuggling crossroads, the region suffered from decreased state control and increased illicit trade, becoming the principal pipeline of illegal arms from the demilitarized Soviet Red Army, the main conduit of heroin and morphine from the Middle East into Western Europe, and the host of extensive money-laundering operations, as Paolo Rumiz wrote in *Limes* (1993), an Italian geopolitical journal. Over the decade, gang warfare for control of the extraordinary spoils had extended to clans and then to wholesale communities, giving rise to what has been termed "ethnic cleansing." Supposedly inevitable "ancestral ethnic hostilities" were the media's explanation for the deadly competition in the region's multiethnic (Serb, Croat, and Muslim) communities, which had lived together and intermarried for generations. Indeed, as the fight for control became politicized, with such figures as Serbian president Slobodan Milosovic and war commander Ratko Mladic prominent in the struggle, violence within the region grew to be ethnically motivated.

The first province to experience widespread bloodshed was Bosnia-Herzegovina, the mountainous fortress of Tito's partisans in World War II, which guarded the choice plunder of Yugoslavia's military-industrial complex. With its nerve-gas industry at Mostar and numerous munitions factories, the province was placed under a U.N. arms embargo, occupied, and put under U.N. peacekeeping control in 1995, with Russian troops joining the multinational force under NATO command in 1996. The next province to succumb was Kosovo, and in 1999 NATO bombed Yugoslavia for 78 days to gain control of the province. Russia opposed the attack, and the United Nations withheld approval of the bombings, whose targets included civilian infrastructure. (As foreseen, the NATO action was shortly thereafter cited by Israel and Russia to justify their respective bombings of civilian targets in Lebanon and Chechnya.) After NATO had taken the province, Russian peacekeeping troops in Bosnia made a lightning lunge across the border into Kosovo and occupied the airport of Pristina, capital of the province. Russian control there raised the specter of the partitioning of Kosovo between NATO and the Russians, evoking Cold War scenarios.

Talbott met with Igor Ivanov, the Russian foreign minister, in Moscow—an encounter that "rapidly turned into a long night's eyeballing with some devious generals," the *Economist* (July 3, 1999) reported. "What teetered in the balance that week was not only the whole fabric of Russian-American relations since the cold war, but the principle of democratic control over Russia's army," the British journal concluded. The Russian foreign minister stated initially that the occupation had been a mistake but said the next day that Yeltsin had authorized the incursion without his knowledge. Now Russia wanted to occupy part of Kosovo under separate command, creating a de facto partition of the country. By the end of the negotiations, Russia agreed to share control of the airport and to integrate its troops into the command structure of a U.N. peacekeeping force.

But Talbott's extraordinary diplomatic adventure and signal success was soon overshadowed by the specter of a collapsing Russia. Republican congressman Curtis Weldon had complained, "It is Strobe Talbott who is determining what intelligence will or will not be given to Congress, what will or will not be said, what will or will not be perceived as a threat" with regard to Russia, according to Kenneth R. Timmerman in the *American Spectator* (April 1998). He was so secretive, Timmerman concluded, because he wanted to hide the disasters the administration's policy was causing. By late 1999 what had been partisan grumbling became full-scale scandal. The *Economist* (August 28, 1999) reported that immense swindles were being perpetrated due to the "collusion of the American and Russian governments to cover up failures and press the IMF [International Monetary Fund] into treating Russia with greater generosity than its economic performance would warrant." The IMF, largely under U.S. guidance, had lent Russia more than $20 billion since 1992, with lending decisions thought to be based on political rather than financial criteria, especially in 1996, when the goal had been to reelect Yeltsin. In fact, Talbott had explained in 1995 that that was his approach. "[W]e use our considerable influence in the international financial institutions to make much larger amounts of money available to the Russian economy . . . in exchange for their committing themselves to market reforms," he had told Charlie Rose.

In September 1999 the House Banking Committee focused on the U.S.'s Russia policy and Russian corruption, after it was revealed that billions of dollars of Russian capital had been laundered through the Bank of New York. Talbott defended the policy before the Senate Foreign Relations Committee, saying that the corruption was due to the transitional stage of democracy and market reform in Russia. A *New York Times* (August 19, 1999) piece stated that up to $10 billion in Russian capital may have been laundered through the Bank of New York between early 1998 and mid-1999. The Kremlin's own study of corruption, released a year earlier, had estimated a cost of between $15 billion and $20 billion every year, contributing to the Russian national budget's having fallen to $29 billion, less than that of New York City. The World Health Organization estimated that three million "excess deaths"—people who shouldn't have died, according to previous demographic patterns established in Russia—had occurred there from 1992 to 1998. "'Calm down world,' was the response of Deputy Secretary of State Strobe Talbott," Matt Bivens, the editor of the *Moscow Times*, reported in the *Nation* (October 4, 1999). For Talbott it was still best for the U.S. to exercise the "strategic patience" he had advocated in his 1998 Stanford speech. "We have been aware from the beginning that crime and corruption are a huge problem in Russia and a huge obstacle to Russian reform. It's going to take decades [and] the problem will only get worse if you isolate Russia," Bivens quoted Talbott as saying. During 2000, among other activities, Talbott participated in talks with Indian government officials on security and disarmament; met with Belarusian opposition leaders to discuss their commitment to democracy; and led a meeting of the U.S.-Baltic Partnership Commission, in Estonia, concerning regional cooperation and economic issues.

To counter the stress of high-stakes diplomacy, Talbott pursues various hobbies, including writing poetry, scuba diving, and playing classical guitar, chess, and squash. He generally rises at 5:00 a.m. to pursue personal interests; jogs at 6:15; arrives at work by 7:30; and occasionally falls asleep while making the required rounds of Washington dinner parties. He and Brooke Shearer have two sons, Devin and Adrian. — V.K.

Suggested Reading: *Commentary* p36+ Mar. 1994; *Forbes* FYI Supplement p80+ Sep. 26, 1994, with photos; *Life* p16+ July 1989; *Nation* p11+ Oct. 4, 1999; *New Republic* p10+ Mar. 7, 1994; *New York Times* A p11 June 7, 1999, with photos, A p12 Sep. 27, 1999, with photo; *Newsweek* p31+ Dec. 27, 1993, with photo; *Time* p66+ Jan. 1, 1990; *Vanity Fair* p148+ Sep. 1994, with photos; *Washington Monthly* p25+ Mar. 1985; *Washingtonian* p54+ Feb.1994, with photos

Selected Books: *Endgame: The Inside Story of SALT II*, 1979; *Deadly Gambits: The Reagan Administration and the Stalemate in Nuclear Arms Control*, 1984; *The Russians and Reagan*, 1984; *Reagan and Gorbachev: The Chances for a Breakthrough in U.S.-Soviet Relations*, 1987; *Master of the Game: Paul Nitze and the Nuclear Peace*, 1988; *At the Highest Levels: The Inside Story of the End of the Cold War*, 1993

Thomas-Graham, Pamela

June 24, 1963– CEO of CNBC.com; mystery writer. Address: CNBC.com, 2200 Fletcher Ave., Fort Lee, NJ 07024

In *A Darker Shade of Crimson* (1998), her first novel, Pamela Thomas-Graham included a list of rules that the main character, Nikki Chase, believes a black woman should keep in mind when trying to excel in a predominantly white male environment: "Laugh at their jokes. Shout when necessary. Maintain a certain distance. Dress impeccably. Know who's who. Save your money. Look them in the eye. Count to 10. Straighten your hair. Pray for strength. Plot your revenge. Have a best friend. Call home often. Keep it real. Call them out. Work the phone. Remember where you came from. And be very, very good." It's hard to imagine anyone more conversant with the rigors of succeeding in traditionally white male bastions than Thomas-Graham. She holds three Harvard degrees, and in 1995 she became the first black woman to be made a partner at McKinsey & Co., the world's largest management consulting firm. She later emerged as NBC's highest-ranking black executive, when she was appointed president and CEO of CNBC.com, the on-line companion to the network's financial cable channel, in 1999. In her scarce spare time, she writes a popular series of mystery novels, featuring Nikki Chase, a black female Harvard eco-

Buck Ennis, courtesy of Simon & Schuster

Pamela Thomas-Graham

nomics professor turned amateur sleuth. It seems safe to say that Thomas-Graham follows at least one of Chase's rules to the letter: by most accounts, she is "very, very good" at what she does.

Thomas-Graham was born in Detroit, Michigan, on June 24, 1963. "My family emphasized that it was important to achieve," she told Amy Oringel in an interview posted in the business section of the Oxygen Network (on-line). "My mother always worked and I was proud of her for that. So from a very early age, my image was of a woman who had her own very real place in the world." After attending Lutheran High School West in Detroit, she was admitted to Radcliffe College (now part of Harvard University). Although she found the prestigious school intimidating initially, she obtained her undergraduate degree in economics there, graduating magna cum laude and winning election to Phi Beta Kappa. She also earned the Captain Jonathan Fay Prize—the highest honor bestowed by Harvard-Radcliffe for the graduating female student with the greatest promise. As an undergraduate she took part in an occasional theater production but did little extracurricular or creative writing, except for a short stint on a campus arts paper.

Thomas-Graham was admitted to both the Harvard Law School and the Harvard Business School, earning both a J.D. and an M.B.A. She was an editor of the *Harvard Law Review* and spent her summers gaining a wide variety of job experience, working for Bain & Co., a management consulting firm; in the corporate-finance division of Goldman Sachs, in New York City; and at Sullivan & Worcester, a Boston law firm. In 1989, after graduating, she joined McKinsey & Co., the world's largest management consulting firm. "I found the things I liked about law I could do in consulting," she told Tonia Shakespeare for *Black Enterprise* (October 1996), explaining that the stimulating environment and corporate culture at McKinsey, a privately held concern, were similar to those at a law firm. She elaborated further on the similarities: "[Consultants] give people business advice in the same way lawyers give legal advice." But she bemoaned the fact that many young people aren't aware of the possibilities in the field, saying, "Consulting is not an industry many people understand. As a result, most do not look at it as a career opportunity. Some don't even know it exists."

Thomas-Graham routinely worked 16 hours a day at McKinsey, advising her clients, which were for the most part Fortune 500 companies. After studying a client's business practices and financial data, Thomas-Graham was often able to formulate strategies that, when implemented, would add several million dollars to the company's bottom line. In December 1995 she was made the first black female partner at McKinsey. (Of the firm's 600 partners, only 34 others were female, and only two others were black.) At the age of 32, she was also one of McKinsey's youngest partners. Although she was one of the leaders of the Media-and-Entertainment division, she was frequently mistaken for a clerical worker by clients who had never encountered a black female executive. She explained to Oringel, "As a woman of color in business, you're instantly more visible, and the reality is more people will be judging you. Several times, clients have assumed that I was the partner's secretary—not the partner. But I always try to conduct myself positively and set an example." Thomas-Graham experienced racism outside of the business world as well, telling Donna Greene for the *New York Times* (July 18, 1999), "I have been followed through stores on Madison Avenue because people assume that I as a young black woman couldn't have the income to be shopping there. I've never had a violent confrontation, but I've had many instances of feeling diminished and demeaned because of people's attitudes toward me as a black woman."

Despite the pressures of an 80-hour work week and the strain of maintaining a positive attitude in the face of both subtle and overt racism, Thomas-Graham excelled at McKinsey—and found the time to write as well. "I wanted to do something that's more creative than what I do in my day job," she told Marilyn McCraven for *Emerge* (September 1999). "I wanted to use a different part of my brain." She decided to write a mystery novel because she had always enjoyed the genre. "I particularly love reading mysteries about women written by women," she told a reporter for the Barnes & Noble Web site, in an interview also posted on the African American Literature Book Club's Web site, "so I'm a big fan of Sue Grafton, Sara Paretsky, and Valerie Wilson Wesley, and I really liked the idea of having a smart feminist detective who is an amateur living her life but gets drawn into some interesting intrigue." Her first effort, *A Darker Shade of Crimson*, was published by Simon & Schuster in 1998. Set in Cambridge, Massachusetts, the story involves the murder of the Harvard Law School's first black female dean of students. Critics often point out the similarities between Thomas-Graham and her fictional amateur detective, Nikki Chase, since both are successful, Harvard-educated black women. But while Thomas-Graham has pursued a career in the business world, Chase has remained in academia, teaching economics and sitting on university committees when she is not sleuthing. Like Thomas-Graham, Chase is often judged first by her race, rather than her accomplishments. Unlike her creator, Chase is single, and between hunting for clues, she deals with the issue of interracial dating—which, as Thomas-Graham has pointed out in interviews, is a common occurrence at Harvard, where the majority of available males are white. *A Darker Shade of Crimson* was named "Page-Turner of the Week" by *People* magazine in early April 1998. In each of the cities Thomas-Graham visited on her nine-city book tour, the Harvard alumni club hosted a reading and reception for her.

In 1997, on the strength of the manuscript for her first book, Simon & Schuster signed Thomas-Graham to a three-book contract, with each book to be set at a different Ivy League college. The second novel, *Blue Blood* (1999), brought back Nikki Chase—this time to solve the murder of a white law professor at Yale. In answer to those who say that as a black author she should write in a genre better suited to socially relevant themes, Thomas-Graham told Ronald Roach for *Black Issues in Higher Education* (May 14, 1998), "The murder mystery format, while entertaining, lends itself to one that can serve as a forum for social and political comment." She elaborated on that point in her interview with Marilyn McCraven, saying, "There are a lot of ways to promulgate a serious message. At the moment, this is my best method and it seems to be working." Thomas-Graham plans to set her third mystery, tentatively titled "Burnt Orange," at Princeton University. After she began writing she continued to work at McKinsey & Co., telling Alex Kuczynski for the *New York Times* (May 2, 1999) that she had new advice for her media clients as a result of her sideline: "I'm much more in favor of large author advances now," she joked.

Despite her continued success at McKinsey, Thomas-Graham accepted a position at CNBC.com, the Internet division of the financial television channel owned by NBC. "It was always my intention to head up a company," she explained to Amy Oringel, "and the decision was an easy one. [At NBC] I am part of a wonderful institution, but operating in an entrepreneurial environment where I can implement my own working style." Appointed president and CEO of the division in September 1999, she was charged with transforming CNBC.com from what was essentially a high-tech promotional tool for the cable channel into a full-service financial Web site, able to compete with CNNfn, Yahoo! Finance, and the host of other interactive financial sites already on the Web. In addition to financial news and commentary, the site now features fund-screening options and a portfolio tracker that can be personalized by each viewer. Plans are being developed for message boards and chat rooms in which CNBC on-air personalities will participate, and there is speculation that Thomas-Graham intends to launch an online stock-trading business as well. "What we're trying to do with this is to capture the essence of the CNBC brand, but really enrich it and make it more personal and more focused on tools and utility," she explained to Kenneth Li in a cover-story interview for *Industry Standard* (October 15, 1999).

In June 1999 Consulting Magazine listed Thomas-Graham among the top 10 consultants in the United States. Her philanthropic activities include service on the board of directors of the Harvard Alumni Association, the American Red Cross of Greater New York, the New York City Opera, and the Inner-City Scholarship Fund. Thomas-Graham is married to Lawrence Otis Graham, a Princeton-educated attorney and author who is perhaps best known for his 12th book, *Member of the Club: Reflections on Life in a Racially Polarized World*, which includes an account of what he observed while posing as a busboy at an all-white Connecticut country club. The couple live in Chappaqua, New York. Graham is running as a Democrat for a congressional seat in the 2000 election; his wife will act informally as his political adviser. The couple's first child, a son, was born in 1998. Discussing their relationship, Thomas-Graham told Donna Greene, "Lawrence was highly successful when I met him and I had achieved quite a lot before I met him. Clearly, I think that the two of us combined are even more than the two of us separate." She continued, "But the reason I married him is he is incredibly supportive of my professional goals and I of his. We draw strength from each other." Thomas-Graham has begun discussing the movie rights to her mysteries with various Hollywood figures, among them several actresses who are interested in playing the role of Nikki Chase. Thomas-Graham, however, has said—jokingly, she told *Current Biography*—that she has given some thought to adding the job of actress to her already extensive résumé, by playing Chase herself. — M.R.

Suggested Reading: African American Literature Book Club Web Site; *Black Enterprise* p60 Oct. 1996, with photo; *Black Issues in Higher Education* p12+ May 14, 1998, with photo; *Crain's New York Business* p109+ May 15–21, 2000; *Emerge* p78 Sep. 1999, with photo; *Fortune* p72+ Aug. 4, 1997; *Industry Standard* (on-line) Oct. 15, 1999; *New York Times* XIV (Westchester section) p3 July 18, 1999; Oxygen Network (on-line)

Selected Books: *A Darker Shade of Crimson*, 1998; *Blue Blood*, 1999

Robin Farquhar-Thomson/Courtesy of Knopf Publishing

Thomson, Rupert

1955– Novelist. Address: c/o Vintage Books, 201 E. 50th St, New York, NY 10022-7703

The British novelist Rupert Thomson has viewed his past, beginning with his almost Dickensian childhood, through a strange kind of looking glass to produce books that turn real experience into sometimes horrifying flights of the imagination. His novels have varied settings, including London, the American West Coast, 19th-century Mexico, and Europe, all given a fantastical gloss that turns them into a kind of dream—or nightmare—world. He has received critical acclaim on both sides of the Atlantic. "In all of Thomson's books, there is a thriller element, a search, a conspiracy, a chase. Otherwise, the characters might become becalmed in the intervals between memories and perceptions. Events remind the characters of previous events, lush worlds, full of transformation," as David Flusfeder wrote in the *Guardian* (March 14, 1998).

Rupert Thomson was born in Eastbourne, England, in 1955. He had a difficult childhood owing to family illnesses. His father had developed pneumonia while he was in the navy; the treatment he underwent required removal of ribs and major portions of his lungs. After 10 years in the hospital, he married a nurse who had taken care of him. The couple had three sons, the eldest of whom—Rupert—was eight when his mother died suddenly. Rupert had to assume responsibility for massaging his father's horribly damaged back, and he had to take care of his younger brothers as well. When Rupert was 15 his father married the family's 21-year-old Swiss au pair, with whom he had two daughters. Thomson and his brothers were sent to Christ's Hospital, a boarding school known for its high academic standards but peculiar methods of discipline.

At the age of 16, according to a thumbnail biography of him on a Borzoi Books Web page, Thomson won a scholarship to Cambridge University, where he studied political thought and medieval history. (According to another source, he concentrated in English.) Immediately after his graduation he traveled to New York and then Hollywood. He later taught English in Athens, Greece. In about 1978 he returned to Great Britain, where for the next five years or so he worked as an advertising copywriter. After leaving his last copywriting job, he moved to Tuscany, Italy, and wrote *Dreams of Leaving*, his first novel. Before its publication, in 1987, he supported himself by working as a bartender, a salesperson in a bookstore, a farmhand, and a caretaker. Since then, the on-line Borzoi biography reported, he has spent time in Los Angeles, Rome, Belfast, and other cities; he now makes his home in London.

Moses Highness, the main character in *Dreams of Leaving*, also lives in London, where he spends his time drinking in nightclubs and using drugs at parties. Like his biblical namesake, Moses was put in a basket when he was a small child and placed on a river—in his case, to enable him to escape New Egypt, a mysterious village that no one is allowed to leave and whose inhabitants are in a state of despair. Moses eventually returns to the village and finds his sad but resourceful father sickly and his mother dead. The village chief of police, Peach, plots against Moses, the only person who has ever escaped.

Reviewers generally praised *Dreams of Leaving*. Bruce Allen, in the *New York Times Book Review* (October 6, 1991), termed it an "irreverently comic first novel" in which "oddball metaphors and surrealist fantasy . . . depict an innocent youngster's escape from provincial complacency and his amazed introduction to wicked, swinging London." There was some divergence in critical opinion about whether Thomson had done a better job in rendering the strange village or swinging London. For Linda Barrett Osborne, writing in the *New York Times Book Review* (August 21, 1988), Thomson's novel "moves effortlessly from one setting to the other. His London is an atmospheric blend of humor, sleaze, and innocence, his fantasy village always true to human nature and complete to the last plausible, wonderfully surrealistic detail." By contrast, Andrew Hislop, the *Times Literary Supplement* (July 17, 1987) reviewer, found that although "Thomson in town often writes well, at times very well," the scenes in New Egypt left one "wondering whether Thomson, like Highness, in this village found himself approaching the limits of his imagination." In the *Guardian* (March 14, 1998), David Flusfeder wrote that he thought the "village scenes . . . funny and quite terrifying." For him, the "more 'realistic' London scenes don't work quite so well."

For *The Five Gates of Hell* (1991), his second novel, Thomson again drew on his memories of an often motherless family and an atmosphere heavy with illness. In this book the strange town submerged in an aura of death and dying is Moon Beach, located in an unidentified country with aspects of the southwestern United States and Mexico. The town is "a place where people went to die . . . pretending to be a beach resort." Two boys, Nathan and Jed, grow up there as "rootless young souls misshapen by family trauma and uncertain sexuality," according to Bruce Allen, writing in the *New York Times Book Review* (October 6, 1991). Nathan becomes a rescuer of others, while Jed emerges as a blackmailer. Moon Beach's economy is dominated by funeral parlors, the most important of which, the Paradise Corp., is headed by Neville Creed. As a Moon Beach cab driver remarks, "The funeral parlours, that's a business, they got to expand, but people're living longer than before, advances in medicine, right? So there's all this advertising to get people to move here. . . . You know why? They've got to feed the funeral parlours, that's why. You listen to those buildings sometime. You can almost hear them chewing, man." Nathan and Jed are eventually dragged into Creed's machinations. "In the end Creed gets what he deserves," James W. Hall wrote in his review for the *Washington Post* (September 23, 1991). "The reader does as well. . . . And the language is honed and purified as the pace quickens. But *The Five Gates of Hell* is not a conventional thriller; . . . rather, it is a pastiche of the lurid and the literary, the page burner and the leisurely, the taut and the poetic . . . beautifully written, achingly vivid, and constantly teetering on the edge of disaster."

Air & Fire (1993) is also set in the suffocating atmosphere of a small town, this one in late-19th-century Baja California, where a French engineer, who has a dream of building a prefabricated metal church designed by Alexandre-Gustave Eiffel, has brought his bored wife, Suzanne. While Valence, the engineer, is absorbed in his work, his wife gets involved with other inhabitants of the town: Pharoah Wilson, an American who is on a search for a golden treasure, and Montoya, an army captain. Terming *Air & Fire* an "exquisite tale" that celebrates "dignity in the face of disillusion," Barbara Hoffert, the reviewer for *Library Journal* (November 15, 1993), also found a larger political implication in the novel. "Suzanne's growing alienation from those around her is paralleled by native resistance to outside domination, directed as much at the Mexican government as the Europeans." Dinitia Smith, assessing the novel for *New York Newsday* (January 30, 1994), likewise discerned a version "of the New World myth," in which "a slightly crazed white man ventures into uncivilized territory, carrying with him a vision of rationality, and tries to impose it on the indigenous population—only to be defeated by the 'primitive.'" "The plot . . . is less important than the haunting atmosphere that . . . Thomson skillfully describes: heat and dust and apathy and a sense of uselessness that pervades nearly everything," David Murray wrote for the *New York Times Book Review* (March 13, 1994).

With his fourth novel, *The Insult* (1996), Thomson hit best-sellerdom. David Flusfeder accounted for this when he called the novel "a book of a significantly higher order of ambition and subtlety" than Thomson's previous books. *The Insult* takes place in a vaguely middle-European locale, resembling Czechoslovakia, where Martin Blom, the protagonist and main narrator, is shot in the head by unknown assailants. He wakes up in a hospital, blind; a titanium plate is inserted to repair the damage to his skull. Martin discovers that he is not blind in darkness, and using his night vision, he finds files that lead him to believe that he is the victim of an experiment by the neurosurgeon who has treated him. (Among other oddities, the plate in his head seems to receive television broadcasts.) He leaves his old life and moves into a cheap hotel, where he encounters various strange characters and has a torrid interlude with a lovely woman, Nina. After she disappears, he goes off to find her; in the course of his search, he encounters an old woman, Edith, whose story of incest, rape, murder, and mental aberration accounts for a large portion of the novel. Edith turns out to be Nina's grandmother.

"Edith's monstrous story, written with an occasional touch of ghastly beauty, is so coldly grotesque as to seem hallucinatory. Yet, its detail is repellently real," Richard Eder wrote in his review for *New York Newsday* (August 15, 1996). Still, Eder felt that the "contrast with the abstract torment of Blom in the first part is too violent and arbitrary." "Apart from the story's mysteries," he continued, "there is the mystery of the story's deeper meaning. . . . Blom is all spooky quandary, but as his literal and metaphysical ordeal takes him among bewilderment, paranoia, and anger, he is very little else; not so much an unknown person as a virtual person." In Thomson's native England, however, critical reactions to *The Insult* tended toward lavish praise. In the *Guardian*, Flusfeder termed the novel "weird and terrifying and comic" and the grandmother's narrative "gruesome and touching"; her story, he declared, pulled "the strands of plot" together. "It's a risky tactic, introducing a second narrative voice so far into a book, but it works: this author is in utter control of his material." *The Insult* was shortlisted for the *Guardian* fiction prize.

In *Soft!* (1998) Thomson made use of his experiences in the world of advertising. Judging from the book, his impressions of that business and the impact it has had on the modern world were not favorable. *Soft!* is about the launching of a new soft drink. Jimmy, an American marketing executive, is sent to London to get the drink off the ground, no matter what the human cost. Arriving in London at the same time is a small-time criminal, Dodds Barker, who wants to improve his life but comes under the dark shadow of a man who forces him to accept a contract on the life of a young waitress, Glade Spencer. The stories of these three people eventually converge; it turns out that a sleep experiment in which Glade participates is part of a plot to implant the desire for the new soft drink into the minds of the public. When a reporter gets wind of the story, Glade must be stopped from talking to him.

Carolyn See, who reviewed *Soft!* for the *Washington Post* (September 18, 1998), detected a political subtext in the novel: "Money is behind every facet of this venture, of course. Jimmy wants more and more of it, and that is all that the author is able to do with his character. . . . On the other hand, Glade and Barker are beautifully drawn, sorrowful originals, both isolated beyond understanding. . . . The author knows that when a whole economy fails, millions of individual families fail along with it. The England he envisions is tapped out, raped, broke, bankrupt, flat. All of his characters, Barker and his mother, Glade and her father, even the repellent Jimmy, exist in a swirling vacuum. . . . The only possessions that . . . Glade and Barker get to have are the tawdry products that corporate interests cram down their throats."

In the opinion of the *Spectator* (June 6, 1998) critic, Michael Glover, Thomson was successful in building the novel's climax. At first, "we find ourselves in the company of a whole battalion of potentially mean and violent disaffected types who are not so much living their lives as washing around in the world like soapsuds in the sink. The language is laid down like bricks in a wall, solid, unadorned, utilitarian. It tastes as savoury as metal on the tongue. . . . But then the atmosphere begins to change. The plot gets burnished—and so does the language." Michiko Kakutani, the *New York Times* (November 10, 1998) reviewer, who had disparaged *The Insult* as "a shaggy dog story," lauded *Soft!* as "a fast-paced, almost cinematic narrative that holds the reader's attention with a combination of zany comedy, sardonic social satire, and old-fashioned psychological insight."

In *The Book of Revelation* (1999), Thomson created a fictional world that belongs in the realm of dream literature. A ballet dancer is drugged and kidnapped by three women and is forced to act out their erotic fantasies; years later, after his release, he travels the world and then returns to try to determine the identity of his captors. His attempt ends in failure, Nicholas Blincoe reported in the *Guardian* (September 18, 1999), because the women "left him no clues to their identity, only a fiction of female desire." Blincoe judged the novel "cool, stylish, and . . . in total sympathy with the intelligence of its audience. . . . *The Book of Revelation* is unbelievable. It takes place in a world overstuffed with fictional motifs where all the laws of reality are suspended, and the new law aims only at suspense. Yet it works because it generates real emotion out of this suspense." The *Publishers Weekly* (November 29, 1999) reviewer wrote that the action is "conveyed in Thomson's usual fluent and riveting style" but faulted the author for the ending of *The Book of Revelation*, deeming it anticlimactic. "Despite this narrative's glittering surface . . . it is not one of his sharper efforts," the reviewer concluded. To Henry Hitchings, writing for the *New Statesman* (September 27, 1999), the subject matter of *The Book of Revelation* seemed "gratuitously lurid," but, as he wrote, "Thomson is able to make it all work . . . because his writing is so nuanced and so evocative." Anthony Bourdain, in an assessment for the *New York Times Book Review* (March 12, 2000), praised Thomson as a "hugely talented writer" whose "sentences are as clean, cool and unsparing as a surgeon's blade."

In an interview for the *Guardian* (March 5, 1998), Thomson, having been asked what book he most wished he had written, cited *The Master and Margarita*, by Mikhail Bulgakov. What he considered "most extraordinary about *The Master and Margarita* is its scale, its daring, its sheer imaginative reach. Part satire, part love story, part mystical experience, it refuses to be pigeonholed. It's a book that makes other books look safe." Thomson has attempted, in all his novels, to meet those criteria, and for the most part, critical opinion has deemed him successful. — S.Y.

Suggested Reading: *Guardian* p4 Nov. 21, 1996, p10 Sep. 18, 1999; *Library Journal* p148 Aug. 1991, p101 Nov. 15, 1993; *Los Angeles Times* p5 Aug. 22, 1996; *New York Newsday* p38 Jan. 30, 1994, B p6 Aug. 15, 1996; *New York Times Book Review* p20 Aug. 21, 1988, Oct. 6, 1991, Mar. 13, 1994; *Publishers Weekly* p47 July 6, 1998, p50 Nov. 29, 1999; *Spectator* p35 June 6, 1998; *Times Literary Supplement* p766 July. 17, 1987, p11 Mar. 15, 1991; *Washington Post* C p3 Sep. 23, 1991, C p2 Sep. 18, 1998

Selected Books: *Dreams of Leaving*, 1987; *The Five Gates of Hell*, 1991; *Air and Fire*, 1993; *The Insult*, 1996; *Soft!*, 1998; *The Book of Revelation*, 1999

Courtesy of Tom Tomorrow

Tomorrow, Tom

1961– Political cartoonist. Address: c/o Village Voice, *36 Cooper Sq., New York, NY 10003-7149; c/o St. Martin's Press Inc., 175 Fifth Ave., Fourth Fl., New York, NY 10010-7848*

Dan Perkins has been described as the best political cartoonist nobody has ever heard of—but perhaps that is because he's better known by his pen name, Tom Tomorrow. The self-syndicated creator of the progressive comic strip *This Modern World*, which appears in about 130 alternative weekly newspapers nationwide, Tomorrow has been skewering American consumerism, media lapdogs, and political foppery since 1984. Imbuing his scathing satires with surface naïvete by means of his 1950s-style illustrations, Tomorrow culls from the news and uses the quoted words of politicos, pundits, and policy wonks to expose the absurdity of their positions. The mainstream media have merely flirted with Tomorrow's strips, printing them, it would seem, only when they want to appear on the cutting edge. His fans are mainly readers of alternative weeklies, most of which are available free of charge on big-city street corners. His admirers include various leftist luminaries, among them the linguist Noam Chomsky, the cartoonists Art Spiegelman and Matt Groening, and the writer Kurt Vonnegut Jr., who has described Tomorrow as "the wry voice of American common sense, humor, and decency."

Despite the limits his views have placed on his exposure, Tomorrow has resisted watering down the content in his strips for mass consumption. "Being in the [*New York*] *Times* is a nice feather in my cap. But it's certainly not the focus of what I do," he explained to David Futrelle for *Salon* (December 2, 1996, on-line). "The thing that's important to me is to keep doing good cartoons for the alternative papers, because that's where I reach my audience. I'm not going to soften what I do so I can be in the *Times* occasionally." Indeed, Tomorrow regards his lack of extensive mainstream exposure as a kind of success in itself. "To me, the big time is running in all these little weekly papers and slowly but surely building a really steady and loyal audience," he told Danny Feingold for the *Los Angeles Times* (January 11, 1999). "I'm not coming from the top down, I'm not in whatever big-time publication everyone reads and everyone sees. I sort of seep up from the underground like a polluted water table."

Tom Tomorrow was born Dan Perkins in 1961. From as far back as he can remember, he has wanted to be a cartoonist. He has traced his left-leaning political views to influences in the small college town in Iowa where he grew up—in particular, to civil-rights and political activism in the late 1960s and early 1970s and the turmoil that surrounded the Watergate scandal and the Vietnam War. "I just assumed that everyone would have my politics," Tomorrow recalled to Danny Feingold. "I think that growing up and finding out that other people had lived through these events and come to different conclusions is what led to the cartoon. It's kind of my ongoing therapy to deal with this disillusionment."

Tomorrow launched his career as a professional cartoonist in the early 1980s, when 10 to 12 papers began carrying his strip *This Modern World*. To bring his pay up to about $12,000 a year (the equivalent of approximately $20,000 in 1999), he worked for a temp agency. "I was making a living. I was word processing," Tomorrow told Paul Bass and Joshua Mamis for the *New Haven Advocate* (on-line). "To say that you're a 'word processor' is a really telling thing, because the noun is the same for the machine as for the person operating the machine. Basically a [human] word processor is the computer chip that hasn't quite been developed yet. It paid really well, relatively speaking. It bought me my autonomy so that I could do what I wanted to do." As he acquired an increasing number of outlets for his work, he gradually weaned himself from temp work and began cartooning full-time.

A connoisseur and collector of 1940s and 1950s magazines and printed advertising, Tomorrow uses collage extensively in creating his cartoons; he also retraces images from the old material. Speaking of the print ads from his files, he told David Astor for *Editor & Publisher* (August 14, 1993), "They were so blatant. You had a woman coughing, a man recoiling in horror and the tagline, 'He won't love you if you cough.' Advertising has gotten more sophisticated, but that's still the basic message." "Dan's use of clip-art—this 1950s, nuclear family, 'Ozzie and Harriet' look—really works," Bill Griffith, the creator of the cartoon *Zip-*

py the Pinhead, told Astor. "He delivers a very strong message dressed up in a comfortable coating. It's a very successful marriage of elements." Feingold reported that "the dissonance between content and image in his work represents what the cartoonist calls a subversive attempt to lure unsuspecting viewers." "It's a black widow spider dressed up as a cute little ladybug," Tomorrow told Feingold. "It sort of sucks you in."

Juxtaposing contemporary news makers with clean-cut figures wearing theatrical facial expressions, Tomorrow has satirically examined such issues as gun control, national health care, welfare, corporate media ownership, and campaign finance reform. A cast of straight-talking characters provide unvarnished commentary; they include Sparky the Wonder Penguin, a sardonic creature sporting hip sunglasses; Wilbur the Talking Stomach; and Biff, an Everyman figure. "Most people don't care about politics," Tomorrow observed to John Fox for *CityBeat* (June 18–24, 1998, on-line). "The trick is to articulate issues in a way that makes them pay attention and figure out why they should care. I boil down and distill the essence of complex issues so people can understand them while at the same time [I am] trying not to oversimplify things." Tomorrow told Feingold that some of his fellow cartoonists think that his strip is text-heavy. "When I go to these conferences of mainstream daily political cartoonists, they all want to give me fatherly advice," he explained, "which is effectively that I use too many words in my cartoons. And it drives me nuts, because they have this really myopic view of cartooning. Comic art is a very, very wide field of endeavor, and it has a very long and varied history, and they see their own sort of banal, single-image, single-word cartoon as being the only real and true political cartoon."

Although he is in the rare position of not needing the assistance of a corporate syndicate to handle the promotion and distribution of his strips, Tomorrow would like to free himself from the business demands of self-syndication. In the early 1990s, after he gained national attention, a large cartoon syndicate offered him a contract, but he declined it when he discovered that the syndicate was planning to sell *This Modern World* to daily newspapers in the same markets where it appeared in local weeklies, some of which were among his first clients. "It just seemed like an incredibly unethical way to do business," Tomorrow told David Astor. "I didn't want to stab loyal clients in the back. There were still more than 1,500 other dailies the syndicate could have tried to sell to." Moreover, he doubts that he could maintain an association with any syndicate. "I have a deeply ambivalent relationship with mainstream 'successes,'" Tomorrow told Feingold. "They say they want something edgy, so they pluck me out and use me for a while, but then they say, 'Oh, could you not be so edgy?' and then we run into trouble and it all sort of falls apart."

That sort of situation occurred in his dealings with *Time* and *U.S. News & World Report*. In late 1997 both weekly magazines asked Tomorrow to be a regular contributor. *Time* wanted to alternate his strip with those of other cartoonists, while *U.S. News* offered him his own weekly spot. An admirer of the work of James Fallows, then editor of *U.S. News*, Tomorrow accepted that magazine's offer over *Time*'s. But after six months *U.S. News* dropped Tomorrow's cartoon, reportedly because its publisher, the real-estate magnate Mort Zuckerman, and many subscribers disagreed with the strip's politics. "The readers of *U.S. News* are the sort of people who get confused by Publisher's Clearinghouse sweepstakes letters, and they had no idea what to make of my cartoon," Tomorrow said to Feingold. "They wrote in all these letters complaining that I was biased, as if a political cartoon should be anything but one man's biases and opinions. That's the whole point of it."

In another example of his difficulties with the media, in 1998 *Brill's Content*, a new media watchdog publication launched by Steven Brill, the founder of the cable channel Court TV, approached Tomorrow with the idea of running a six-panel version of *This Modern World* that would be special to the magazine. The cartoonist's first submission attempted to awaken readers to the knowledge that the media's biases often reflect their owners' agendas rather than, as many people assume, a particular political philosophy. According to Tomorrow, Brill objected to the submission, and he dropped *This Modern World* before a single strip ever appeared in *Brill's Content*. Brill has maintained that the contents of the strip did not affect his decision. "I looked at [Tomorrow] and two or three others and just decided that at the start, we should not run cartoons," he told Feingold.

Earlier, in 1996, the *Village Voice*, the nation's oldest and most famous alternative weekly newspaper, contacted Tomorrow to fill the void left when their longtime cartoonist Jules Feiffer departed after a bitter disagreement. At first, out of respect for Feiffer and in deference to their friendship, Tomorrow declined the offer. Feiffer thanked Tomorrow for his show of allegiance but counseled the younger cartoonist to accept the offer. Tomorrow took his advice, and by early 1998 his strip had become a regular in the pages of the *Voice*.

In a display of his independence from mainstream sensibilities, in his April 9, 1998 installment of *This Modern World*, Tom Tomorrow showed things no other nationally syndicated strip ever has: frontal nudity and simulated sex. In his signature collage style, Tomorrow used an 18th-century engraving of an orgy as the background for a commentary on the sex scandal involving President Bill Clinton and the former White House intern Monica Lewinsky; he tried to make the point that by focusing so much attention on the affair, the media was obscuring truly important issues, such as possible illegal contributions to Clinton's presidential campaign. "I knew I was pushing the envelope with this particular strip, but I didn't think I broke it," Tomorrow told John Fox. "I've almost never used sexual imagery, and it's not likely to come up again. But if, as an alternative journalist, you're afraid of controversies like this, how far have you moved away from your roots?" Tomorrow told Fox that, in an effort to reduce the cartoon's incendiary aspects somewhat, he "spent a whole day cutting off penises" in the engraving. "I don't know many people who can say that," he remarked.

His amputations notwithstanding, many readers harshly objected to the cartoon, and some of his clients reacted by dropping his strip. In Oklahoma City, Bill Bleakley, a lawyer who publishes the alternative weekly the *Oklahoma Gazette*, was singled out for attack by the organization Oklahomans for Children and Families (OCF). One of Bleakley's legal clients is the school board of Moore, a town on the outskirts of Oklahoma City, and the OCF contended that by publishing Tomorrow's orgy installment, Bleakley had cast doubt on his fitness to represent schoolchildren in legal matters. Buckling under the pressure from the OCF, Bleakley dropped Tomorrow's strip. "That controversy reminds you not to reach consensus with yahoos the way the Oklahoma City publisher apparently did," Tomorrow said to Fox. "Yahoos are wrong. Don't compromise with them. Freedom of speech isn't a part-time job." In an interview for the on-line comedy publication *Fade to Black*, he declared, "We've got to get our priorities in order. When my 'orgy' cartoon ran, one woman wrote a paper to say that if this is what's going on in the modern world, it's clear Satan is having a field day. And I'm thinking: this is a country in which three white guys chain a black man to their truck and drag him to his death—and then the Klan wants to hold a rally in their town. This is a country in which teenage misfits routinely gun down their high school classmates. This is a country in which an off duty cop shoots a homeless guy for trying to squeegee his windows. And Satan is having a field day because of a cartoon with some naked people?"

Several collections of Tomorrow's strips have been published, among them *Greetings from This Modern World* (1992), *Tune in Tomorrow* (1994), *The Wrath of Sparky* (1996), *Penguin Soup for the Soul* (1998), and *When Penguins Attack!* (2000), to which the writer Dave Eggers contributed an introduction. Tomorrow has also illustrated books written by others. They include *The Heretic's Handbook of Quotations: Cutting Comments on Burning Issues* (1992), edited by Charles Bufe; *Censored: The News That Didn't Make the News—And Why: The 1995 Project Censored Yearbook* (1995), by Carl Jensen and Project Censored; *The Trouble With Dilbert: How Corporate Culture Gets the Last Laugh* (1997), by Norman Solomon and Matt Wuerker; *Censored 1996: The News That Didn't Make the News—The Year's Top 25 Censored News Stories* (1997) and its successors, *Censored 1997*, *Censored 1998*, *Censored 1999*, and *Censored 2000*, all with text by Peter Phillips; and *The Habits of Highly Deceptive Media: Decoding Spin and Lies in Mainstream News* (1999), by Norman Solomon. The latest installment of *This Modern World* is available on-line at *Salon.com*.

While trying to inspire people to reevaluate their priorities, Tomorrow has acknowledged the magnitude of the task he has set for himself. "I think it's important for any political cartoonist to want to change the world," he said to Feingold, "or else you should be in another line of work. But at the same time that you want to change the world, you have to understand that there's no way in hell that you're going to, and somehow you have to be able to balance these two completely conflicting notions." "There are many, many societies that have existed in human history where someone like me would have been hauled off to the camps very quickly," he explained to Paul Bass and Joshua Mamis, "and that's because the sword was much more powerful than the pen. On an individual level, no. On an overall historical societal level, maybe." Tomorrow's pen was mighty enough to earn him the prestigious Robert F. Kennedy Journalism Award for Cartooning in 1998. — T.J.F.

Suggested Reading: *CityBeat* (on-line) June 18-24, 1998; *Editor & Publisher* p28+ Aug. 14, 1993, with photo; *Los Angeles Times* E p1+ Jan. 11, 1999, with photo

Selected Books: *Greetings from This Modern World*, 1992; *Tune in Tomorrow*, 1994; *The Wrath of Sparky*, 1996; *Penguin Soup for the Soul*, 1998; *When Penguins Attack!*, 2000; as illustrator—*The Heretic's Handbook of Quotations: Cutting Comments on Burning Issues* (edited by Charles Bufe), 1992; *Censored: The News That Didn't Make the News—And Why: The 1995 Project Censored Yearbook* (by Carl Jensen and Project Censored), 1995; *The Trouble With Dilbert: How Corporate Culture Gets the Last Laugh* (by Norman Solomon and Matt Wuerker), 1997; *Censored 1996: The News That Didn't Make the News—The Year's Top 25 Censored News Stories* (1997) and its successors, *Censored 1997*, *Censored 1998*, *Censored 1999*, and *Censored 2000* (all with text by Peter Phillips); *20 Years of Censored News* (by Carl Jensen), 1997; *The Habits of Highly Deceptive Media: Decoding Spin and Lies in Mainstream News* (by Norman Solomon), 1999

Courtesy of Ulster Unionist Council

Trimble, David

Oct. 15, 1944– First Minister of Northern Ireland; leader of the Ulster Unionist Party. Address: Ulster Unionist Party, 3 Glengall St., Belfast, Northern Ireland BT12 5AE

David Trimble is the leader of Northern Ireland's Ulster Unionist Party, which supports continued British rule in that country. A nonpracticing barrister, he is known for his negotiating skills as well as his dedication to the cause of the loyalists, Protestant supporters of the British. In 1998 he shared the Nobel Peace Prize with the leader of Northern Ireland's Labour Party, John Hume, for their efforts in establishing a multiparty government in Northern Ireland, an important step toward peace after nearly three decades of sectarian war in the region, between Protestants and Catholics and between those who favor British rule and those who seek a united, independent Ireland. In 1998 Trimble was elected first minister of the Northern Ireland assembly, a body designed to make Northern Ireland a self-governing province of Britain. The assembly's governing authority and very existence currently hang in the balance. Disagreements over the reform of the Royal Ulster Constabulary, the British police force in Northern Ireland, and the disarmament of the Irish Republican Army (IRA), a terrorist group fighting for the reunification of Northern Ireland and its southern neighbor, the Republic of Ireland, and their independence as one island nation, constantly threaten to derail the peace process.

The son of William Trimble, a civil servant, and Ivy Trimble, whose family was involved in the building business, David Trimble was born on October 15, 1944 in Bangor, a seaside resort town east of Belfast, Northern Ireland. The Trimble family were Protestants who enjoyed a comfortable middle-class life. David Trimble attended Bangor Grammar School and later Queen's University, Belfast. He was called to the Bar of Northern Ireland in 1969, and worked as a lecturer in the school of law at Queen's University, Belfast, from 1968 until 1980.

The conflict between England and Ireland dates from the 12th century, when the British army invaded the island of Ireland. Ireland's population was almost entirely Catholic until the late 1700s, when England confiscated land in the northern part of the island, and Protestants from England and Scotland settled there. Thereafter the Irish people's continuing struggle for independence was complicated by mounting tensions in the six northern counties between Catholics and the far more numerous Protestants, who came to dominate the region politically, economically, and socially. On Easter Sunday in 1916, the British quelled a rebellion by Irish paramilitary forces and then executed its leaders—an action that served only to strengthen the revolutionary movement in Ireland. In 1920, with the British Parliament's passage of the Government of Ireland Act, the 26 counties of southern Ireland were granted dominion status as the Irish Free State (subsequently, the Irish Republic or simply Ireland). The same statute established Northern Ireland—or Ulster—as a province of Great Britain. Continuing discrimination by Northern Ireland's pro-British Protestant majority against the Catholic minority, particularly with regard to jobs and housing, led to outbreaks of violence in 1968 and 1969, following which Great Britain deployed British troops in Northern Ireland in an attempt to maintain order. But the presence of the troops, and the imprisonment by Britain, without trials, of suspected Irish terrorists fueled unrest among Catholics. On January 30, 1972—"Bloody Sunday," as it came to be called—during a protest march held in Derry, Northern Ireland, by Irish Catholics in defiance of a British ban against such demonstrations, British troops shot 13 civilian marchers. Two months later, in an attempt to halt the series of terrorist attacks that had ensued, the British government suspended the Ulster Parliament, and the British government took control of the province.

That was the situation in Northern Ireland when, during the early 1970s, Trimble joined the hard-line Vanguard Party, which supported the goal of a British-ruled, semi-independent Ireland. Although Trimble came out in favor of a 1974 strike by the loyalists, who were opposed to power-sharing, he was not in agreement with all of the group's strategies: the Vanguard Party was led by William Craig, an extremist who made statements at the time opposing civil rights for Catholics and supporting the use of violence toward those who sought a united, independent Ireland. "One of these days, if and when the politicians fail us, it may be our job to liquidate the enemy," Craig was quoted as saying by Warren Hoge in the *New York*

Times (April 20, 1998). The Vanguard Party, known for its large motorcycle rallies, attempted to bring together various factions which had broken away from the Protestant cause. Trimble was elected to the Northern Ireland Convention of South Belfast as a representative of Vanguard in 1975.

Craig created a schism within the group when he advocated a merger with a major party. Trimble sided with Craig and was subsequently named the party's deputy leader. But over time his views drifted even more toward the mainstream, and in 1978 he joined the Ulster Unionist Party (UUP), which favors British rule and wants Northern Ireland to remain part of the United Kingdom. "The Unionists have a culture distinct from, and in many ways alien to, that of the rest of Ireland," according to the *Economist* (September 20, 1997). "They have different loyalties, traditions, and heroes, and a radically different view of Irish history (to say the least). They have fought and died for Britain in two world wars. They cannot imagine feeling comfortable as a permanent minority in a unified Ireland." Soon Trimble was named honorary secretary of the UUP. He also served from 1985 to 1990 as the chairman of both the Lagan Valley Unionist Society and the Ulster Society, right-wing organizations that had fought against the Anglo-Irish Agreement of 1985, which had given the predominantly Catholic Irish Republic more representation in Northern Ireland's politics. In 1990 Trimble was elected to the British Parliament. Trimble's manner during this time was described by *Newsmakers* (Issue 1, 1999): "He was not known for his charm or compromising ways; he became known as a forthright and rather undiplomatic personality who was prone to rises in temper."

In 1993 then–prime minister John Major and then–Irish prime minister Albert Reynolds signed the Downing Street Declaration; one of its provisions allowed Sinn Féin, a group founded in 1895 with the aim of winning Irish independence from Britain, to participate in the discussion of Northern Ireland's future—on the condition that the IRA, Sinn Féin's military counterpart, would renounce violence. Soon afterward the IRA declared a cease-fire. In 1995 the UUP chose the more militant Trimble as their new leader, over favored moderate John Taylor. Some Unionists were upset because Trimble was not Anglo-Irish, the traditional background of the organization's leaders. Trimble was seen by Irish nationalists as a very bigoted anti-Catholic individual. All of his colleagues in the British Parliament, too, opposed his appointment, because they considered him an extremist.

It was perhaps Trimble's involvement in what had become known as "the siege of Drumcree" (named for the church where Protestants began large protest marches) that sealed his election. In 1995 Trimble helped to organize opposition to a ban preventing the Orange Order (a coalition of various Protestant factions) from holding its annual march through the Catholic district of Portadown, in Armagh County. The march commemorated the Protestant King William's victory over Roman Catholic James II in the region in 1690. In 1996 Trimble once again attended the march, and again the police tried, but failed, to prevent it. He was seen on television marching down Garvaghy Road as police beat Catholic protestors, an act that proved his loyalty to the UUP's cause but also made him appear to be an extremist to some observers. (Later, in July 1998, the authorities once again banned the Orange Order from marching in Portadown. But rather than march alongside them, Trimble met with the family of three young Catholic brothers from Ballymoney who had been killed when a gasoline bomb was thrown through a window of their home.) The IRA reversed its cease-fire soon thereafter. The United States then sent former senator George Mitchell (believed by some to be pro-Catholic) to Ireland to mediate peace talks. The cease-fire resumed in July 1997, and the talks began in earnest in September, in spite of the August bombing of Omagh, attributed to a splinter group called the "Real IRA." The bomb attack killed 29 people and injured more than 200 others.

The peace talks brought Trimble into contact with one of his oldest enemies, Gerry Adams, the leader of Sinn Féin. Adams, a high-school dropout, grew up in a family with a history of armed resistance to British rule. Believed to be a former leader of the IRA, he was considered an important enough member of the movement to be flown, in 1972, from prison in Northern Ireland to secret cease-fire talks in London. Adams was known for his sense of humor as well as his knowledge of the Irish language, which he had studied while in prison. In 1985, after his release, Adams took control of Sinn Féin, advocating a peaceful settlement to the conflict without denouncing the IRA's history of violence. Although elected to the British Parliament as a representative of West Belfast, he had refused to take his seat in the House of Commons, as that would have required him to swear allegiance to the British monarch.

As the historic peace talks began, Mitchell was concerned about assassination attempts against one of the leaders; he and British prime minister Tony Blair thus set a deadline of Easter (which fell in mid-April that year) for the completion of a settlement. Both Trimble and Adams were heavily guarded throughout the talks. The meetings got off to a less than auspicious start, when Trimble refused to accept Adams's assertion that Sinn Féin was not closely tied to the IRA and declined to look his adversary in the eye. Although Adams and Trimble sat in the same room, all negotiations proceeded through intermediaries; the leaders refused to communicate directly with each other and to acknowledge each other's presence. The *New York Times* (September 24, 1997) quoted Trimble's deputy, Ken Maginnis, as saying that Sinn Féin had "diminished democracy, sacrificed the freedom of the people of Northern Ireland to the terrorist and elevated an evil mafia to a status that would shame any other country in Western Europe."

A new deadline of April 9 was established, but the negotiations stretched 17 hours past that date. United States president Bill Clinton made last-minute phone calls to the leaders of both parties, and both the British prime minister, Tony Blair, and the Irish prime minister, Bertie Ahern, acted as mediators in the final hours of the talks. On April 10 (the Christian holiday of Good Friday), a landmark compromise was reached. The Good Friday agreement called for a new assembly for Northern Ireland, allowing the region to govern itself while remaining a province of Great Britain. The treaty was approved on May 22, 1998 by 94 percent of the voters from the Irish Republic and 71 percent of the voters in Northern Ireland.

At the assembly's first meeting, Trimble was named leader of Northern Ireland's new governing body. Trimble's party retained 28 seats when voting for the new assembly took place in June, but many turned against him and voted for members who were opposed to the power-sharing agreement. Although the many members of Trimble's own party who were against the Good Friday agreement labeled him a sell-out, he remained as dedicated as ever to the Unionist cause. Trimble effectively brought the treaty to a halt when he proclaimed that Sinn Féin would not be allowed to participate in the assembly until the IRA began "decommissioning" its weapons arsenal. Although Adams reiterated that his organization had little or no control over the IRA, and pointed to the cease-fire as evidence of the Catholics' commitment to nonviolence, Trimble was persistent in his demands. The result was a stalemate that would stall the peace process for more than a year.

In September 1998 Trimble agreed to meet and speak to Adams face-to-face. Although this latest attempt at establishing lasting peace gave hope to some, Trimble refused to shake hands with Adams when the meeting came to an end. "The question for you when Mr. Adams comes out is whether his dirty squalid little terrorist war is over," Trimble said, according to John Murray Brown, writing for the *Financial Times* (April 11, 1998, on-line). "When he accepts the democratic process, we'll see [about shaking hands]."

In October the Norwegian Nobel Committee, in Oslo, awarded the Nobel Peace Prize to Trimble and John Hume, the head of Northern Ireland's Roman Catholic Social Democratic and Labour Party. Hume had argued for almost 25 years for a plan very similar to the Good Friday agreement. (Adams was not considered for the prize.) It was not the first time that the Nobel panel had attempted to encourage peace in the region; in 1976 it had awarded the prize to Betty Williams and Mairead Corrigan of Northern Ireland, for their efforts in creating the International Peace Group, which later disbanded.

Meanwhile, the stalemate continued into the late months of 1998. Many Republicans, feeling that the decommissioning of the IRA's weapons arsenal would be tantamount to surrender, regarded the entire peace process with suspicion. Although the treaty gave Sinn Féin and the IRA two years to begin disarmament, Trimble would not yield in his demand that the process begin immediately. At the suggestion of Paul Doris, national chairperson of the Irish Northern Aid Committee, a letter-writing campaign was launched in the U.S., urging Prime Minister Tony Blair to intervene to find a solution to the problem. "If republicans can accept the fact that loyalists do not intend to disarm prior to setting up the Executive, the Unionists must have the backbone to accept that the IRA will decommission only when it is practical to do so," Paul Doris said in his statement, which was reprinted in the *Irish People* (November 21, 1998, on-line).

The war of words continued throughout 1999, rendering the new ruling body powerless. As the debate dragged on, violence began to increase on the streets of Northern Ireland, as members of both sides of the conflict engaged in what became known as "punishment beatings"—sudden attacks by paramilitary forces on unsuspecting civilians, to exact revenge. Trimble used these beatings as a point of argument, claiming that they violated the cease-fire and thus proved that the IRA was not interested in abiding by the Good Friday agreement.

Many Protestants were angered by the premature release (as promised by the treaty) of 277 Republican national political prisoners. On June 22 the government freed Patrick Magee, an IRA member who had organized the 1984 bombing of a Tory conference, which left five dead and many others injured and nearly took the life of then–British prime minister Margaret Thatcher; although Magee had been sentenced to 35 years in prison, his release came after he had served only 14 years.

By early summer it began to look as if the assembly might be shut down entirely. In an article for the *New York Times* that was reprinted in the *Economist* (June 26, 1999), Trimble warned that closing the assembly would put an end to the agreement: "Abandoning the Agreement at the beginning of the summer would be simply irresponsible. Worse, it will be the government resolving the decommissioning issue in favor of the terrorists." According to the Good Friday agreement, a 10-person cabinet (on which Sinn Féin was slated to hold two seats) was to be established for the Northern Ireland assembly, but Trimble delayed forming the cabinet while disarmament talks continued. In spite of its own deadline, the British government rushed amendments through Parliament that would have expedited disarmament, hoping to appease Trimble and the UUP. On July 15 Trimble and 28 other members of the UUP boycotted the meeting in which cabinet members were to be chosen. This move automatically subjected the agreement to a review by the British government, a process that was expected to last for the rest of the summer. Seamus Mallon, the deputy first prime minister of the Northern Ireland Assembly and a member of the Social Democratic and Labour Party, was infuriated by the UUP's actions and resigned, calling on Trimble to follow suit. The assembly adjourned without deciding on a date to return.

George Mitchell was called in again, and after 11 weeks of negotiating, both parties released statements that seemed to point toward a compromise. Gerry Adams declared that his party would agree to paramilitary disarmament and would appoint one of its members to the International Commission on Decommissioning. The *New York Times* (November 28, 1999) reported that "in exchange for relaxing their demand for immediate IRA weapons turnover, the unionists were gaining self-rule, the right to keep Ulster British as long as its residents wished it, the end to the 1985 Anglo-Irish Agreement that gave Dublin joint authority with Britain in some of the North's affairs, and the withdrawal of the clauses in the Constitution of the Irish Republic that make a territorial claim on Northern Ireland." Encouraged by the talks, Trimble made a surprising statement in favor of peace and equality. "For too long, much of the unrest in our community has been caused by a failure to accept the differing expressions of cultural identity," he said, according to Warren Hoge in the *New York Times* (November 17, 1999). Under the terms of the new agreement, disarmament was scheduled to begin January 31, 2000.

But in mid-February 2000, after the IRA had failed to make what the government saw as sufficient progress toward disarmament, the Northern Ireland assembly was shut down by the British government; the historic experiment had lasted a total of 72 days. Britain had acted in the hope that it could head off the resignation of Trimble, who had pledged to step down if disarmament was not achieved—and without whom the peace agreement would likely cease to exist. Soon after the new government had been suspended, the IRA released a statement indicating that it was willing to cooperate with disarmament plans. The International Commission on Decommissioning also issued a report, reprinted in part in the *New York Times* (February 13, 2000), which stated, "We find particularly significant, and view as valuable progress, the assertion made to us by the IRA representative that the IRA will consider how to put arms and explosives beyond use."

As reported on CNN (February 24, 2000, on-line), Britain's Northern Ireland secretary, Peter Mandelson, spoke to reporters at the White House about the need for continued negotiation: "We need to get people talking again. We need to get ideas back on the table so that we can get the executive and the institutions back on track." The circumstances of Trimble's recent reelection as the leader of the Ulster Unionist Party, however, may undermine his ability to negotiate in the future. In March 2000 Trimble narrowly defeated Martin Smyth, a Presbyterian minister and former leader of the Orange Order who had announced his candidacy less than a week before the vote. This surprising development seemed to indicate that Trimble's influence within his party, and on the peace process, might be waning. In May 2000 the IRA announced its willingness to allow weapons inspections, and Trimble tried to persuade members of his party to trust the offer. Ultimately, 53 percent of the 862 members of the party's ruling council voted to accept the promise, opening the door to the UUP's continued participation in the governing body established by the power-sharing agreement.

Trimble and his second wife, Daphne Orr, were married in 1978. Together they have two sons and two daughters. John Murray Brown wrote about Trimble, "A prickly character in public, he is noticeably warmer in private." In his leisure time Trimble reads and listens to opera, especially the music of Strauss, Verdi, and Wagner. — C.L.

Suggested Reading: *CNN* (on-line) Feb. 24, 2000; *Economist* p20+ Feb. 13, 1999, with photo, p65 June 26, 1999, with photo; *Facts on File* (various years); *Financial Times* (on-line) Apr. 11, 1998; *Irish People* (on-line) Nov. 21, 1998; *New York Times* A p8 Sep. 24, 1997, A p12 Mar. 31, 1998, with photos, I p6 Apr. 19, 1998, with photo, A p3 Apr. 20, 1998, with photo, I p6 June 28, 1998, A p3 Feb. 1, 1999, A p8 July 13, 1999, A p3 Nov. 17, 1999, with photos, A p13 Nov. 20, 1999, with photo, I p1 Nov. 28, 1999; *Newsday* A p27 Mar. 6, 2000; *Newsmakers* Issue 1, 1999; *Political Handbook of the World 1999*

Trinidad, Felix

Jan. 10, 1973– Boxer. Address: c/o Don King Productions, 501 Fairway Dr., Deerfield, FL 33441

On September 18, 1999 Felix Trinidad surprised the jaded world of boxing when he defeated the noticeably faster Oscar De La Hoya, in the process capturing the World Boxing Council (WBC) welterweight title. While he pulled off an upset, Trinidad has not followed the career path of James "Buster" Douglas, the heavyweight who rose from mediocrity and obscurity only to return there after beating the seemingly invincible Mike Tyson in 1990. Managed by his father, who is known as Don Felix, Trinidad had already—in 1993—won the International Boxing Federation (IBF) welterweight crown, which he has defended in a number of brutal bouts. "I will fight whoever is out there," Trinidad has said, as quoted by the *Boxing Chronicle* (on-line). "I won't back down from anyone." Trinidad's 30 knockouts (KOs) in 36 outings give him one of the highest knockout percentages in boxing history.

Felix Trinidad, often referred to by his nickname, Tito, was born on January 10, 1973 in Cupey Alto, Puerto Rico. He began boxing at the age of 12 and, within only a few years, won five amateur

Al Bello/Allsport

Felix Trinidad

Puerto Rican national championships in as many weight classes—100 pounds, 112 pounds, 119 pounds, 126 pounds, and 132 pounds. By the time he decided to turn pro, on March 10, 1990, his amateur record was an astonishing 51–6, although only 12 victories were by knockout. When he announced his intention to change his style to become a knockout artist as a professional, many predicted that he would be unable to do so. In his first 10 fights as a pro, however, he knocked out nine opponents and beat the 10th as well. The most difficult challenge Trinidad faced early in his professional career was his fight against experienced puncher Jake Rodriguez, on December 6, 1991. In the second round, Trinidad injured his right hand, but he persevered and managed to win the round. Then, in the fourth, he hurt his left hand—but he fought on, although he was in great pain. He won the 10-round fight by unanimous decision.

In round two of a match in Paris, on October 3, 1992, Alberto Cortes of Argentina became the first boxer to knock Trinidad down in a professional bout. Trinidad managed to recover and, in the third round, hit Cortes with several square jabs to face. Before the round ended, Cortes prompted the referee to stop the match. Just under a year later, Tito was given his first title bout, against two-time world champion Maurice Blocker, the holder of the IBF welterweight belt. With one minute and 59 seconds left in the second round, Trinidad landed a solid left that sent Blocker to the mat for several minutes. Trinidad was crowned IBF champion and solidified his reputation as a knockout fighter.

In quick succession Trinidad defended his title against three challengers: Luis Garcia, on August 6, 1993 in Bayamon, Puerto Rico, hit the mat four times in the first round before the match was halted; Antony Stephens, on October 23, 1993, knocked Trinidad down in the second, only to lose the fight when Trinidad matted him in the 10th; and on January 29, 1994 the ever-popular but aging former champion Hector "Macho" Camacho found himself on the losing end of a unanimous decision. Following an eight-month layoff, ordered by his father, Trinidad returned to the ring on September 17, 1994 to fight the feared Luis Ramon "Yory Boy" Campas, a Mexican fighter pundits were comparing to Julio César Chávez, pound for pound one of the greatest boxers ever to enter the ring. That match took place south of the border, during the elaborate, annual Mexican Independence Celebration. Campas, sporting a remarkable 56–0 record with 50 knockouts, sent Tito to the canvas with a quick, short left in the second round. Trinidad returned in the fourth, landing a dozen shots to his challenger's head, forcing referee Richard Steele to stop the match. Trinidad fell yet again in the second round on December 10, 1995 while fighting Oba "Motor City" Carr in Monterrey, Mexico. In his usual fashion, Trinidad bounced back with a flurry of punches over the next five rounds, flooring Carr twice in the eighth. When Carr got back up, Trinidad landed another blow to his head, and the referee ended the fight.

With his defeat of the IBF's ninth-ranked contender, Roger "Stingray" Turner, in the second round of his first fight of 1995, Trinidad managed to break his three-fight streak of being knocked down in round two. It seemed as though his boxing skills were only getting sharper as he forced Rodney Moore into submission on February 10, 1996. Moore, bloodied and exhausted, refused to come out for the fifth round, handing Trinidad a victory by technical knockout (TKO). Three months later, in his 29th professional bout and ninth title defense, Tito took on Freddie Pendleton. Trinidad cruised to victory, matting the challenger in the fifth round. In Nashville, Tennessee, in January 1997, Tito went up against Kevin Leushing, who was expected to go down with little resistance. Leushing, however, sent the champ to the floor in the second with a quick right-left combination. Trinidad roared back to down his opponent in the third, recording his 31st win and 27th KO.

On August 23, 1997 Trinidad, in a first-round TKO, defeated Troy Waters (24–7) of Sydney, Australia—the WBC's top-ranked contender in the junior-middleweight division—in the main event of a five-fight card at Madison Square Garden, in New York City. Eight months later, in front of 12,000 fans at the Coliseo de Ruben Rodriguez in Bayamon, Puerto Rico, Trinidad cruised to yet another easy victory, this one over Mahenge Zulu. Before that match Trinidad had received some negative press for statements concerning Oscar De La Hoya, the glamorous and celebrated fighter who had captured the WBC junior-welterweight belt from Julio César Chávez in 1996—and who represented an obstacle in Trinidad's career. "I have no doubts about myself," Trinidad told Jack Curry for the *New York Times* (March 31, 1998), with what Curry described as a "hint of desperation." "I know that I'm the best, pound for pound. I know this year will be my year. I want to fight Oscar De La Hoya. From there on, everybody will mention Trinidad first when they talk about the best boxers."

In the meantime, several months passed before Tito's promoter, Don King, even began the process of finding the next opponent for Trinidad, and the champion soon became frustrated with the colorful and controversial promoter. As a result, Tito's camp filed suit against King and his promotion company. In August 1998 the suit went before U.S. Federal Court judge Lawrence M. McKenna. King's camp argued that Trinidad's contract, said to have expired on June 11, 1998, carried with it an automatic two-year extension if Trinidad was still champion by the expiration date. The boxer's representatives countered by stating that the extension was valid only if the boxer had secured an *additional* belt, apart from his own IBF title, before expiration of the agreement. Two months before the case came to court, in late June, Trinidad signed a reported $30 million deal with Main Events, the promotional company run by Don Duva. McKenna's decision, however, went in favor of King, and Trinidad was forced to re-sign with the promoter, inking a humongous $49.9 million contract that carried a three-fight, four-year term. Although the contract has specific time and fight requirements, most boxing pundits agree that it assured King's place as Trinidad's promoter for the rest of the boxer's career.

King—not wanting to repeat his mistake—quickly booked Tito in a fight with veteran Pernell "Sweet Pea" Whitaker, hoping, with that upcoming match, to position Trinidad as the most obvious future opponent for De La Hoya. Whitaker, a 35-year-old, six-time champion (in four different weight classes), had lost the WBC welterweight championship to De La Hoya in a 12-round 1997 decision. Since that time, controversy had dogged Whitaker, who was suspended from boxing for 16 months following a failed drug test and a drunk-driving arrest. A few months later cocaine was found in his blood after an October 17, 1997 bout with Andrei Pestriaev, held in Connecticut at the Foxwoods Resort Casino. He was next set to fight Ike Quartey, in April 1998, but the troubled former champ tested positive for the substance yet again. Early in 1999 Whitaker was at last cleared to fight again, this time against Trinidad, on February 20. "I feel like it's 1984 and I'm going for the gold again," Whitaker, a gold medalist in the 1984 Olympic Games, told Timothy W. Smith for the *New York Times* (February 20, 1999) shortly before the fight. "I feel like I've got everything back on keel. I got my legs back. I got my eyesight. I've got my skills."

Trinidad himself was ending a 10-month respite, and in pre-fight publicity meetings reporters repeatedly asked him if he would be able to make the weight requirement for the class; less than two weeks before the fight, Tito weighed as much as 156 pounds (the limit for the welterweight class is 147), and many expressed doubt that he could shed the excess baggage. Trinidad proved his detractors wrong, not only losing the weight but defeating Whitaker—who suffered a broken jaw—in a 12-round decision at Madison Square Garden. Three months later he KOed Hugo Pineda in four rounds in San Juan, the capital of Puerto Rico.

Within only a few weeks of the Whitaker fight, King announced that he had arranged a match between Trinidad and De La Hoya. Set to fight in Las Vegas on September 18, 1999, the two 26-year-olds were guaranteed the largest paychecks of their careers. "We feel he is over-popularized," Trinidad told Smith about De La Hoya. "I'm going to put him at the level we feel he is." Fearing spies from the De La Hoya camp, Don Felix closed all of his son's workouts to spectators. During a press conference several reporters noted that, when Tito was asked questions, Don Felix would mutter the answer to his son, who in turn would respond to an interpreter in Spanish. Actions such as these spurred Don King to throw some verbal jabs at the father, telling Timothy W. Smith for the *New York Times* (September 16, 1999, on-line), "[Don Felix] is scared. Tito is his whole life and future in boxing." Trinidad, angered by such statements, responded at a press conference, according to Smith, "My father is the first one to teach me to throw my first punch, and the second and the third and every punch that I am throwing today. As my father, my manager, and my trainer, he has to be with me. After Sept. 18 we will celebrate together."

The fight proved to be the most important of Trinidad's career, as he, to many onlookers' surprise, took the belt away from De La Hoya. Timothy Smith wrote for the *New York Times* (September 19, 1999, on-line) that Trinidad resembled "the loser in a track meet" through much of the 12-round bout, as De La Hoya "tagged him and ran away." But despite De La Hoya's superior speed, by the end of the fight Trinidad was ahead on points. Only one judge, Glen Hamada of the state of Washington, scored the fight a draw, at 114–114; Bob Logist of Belgium gave Trinidad the edge (115–114), and Jerry Roth, from Nevada, scored in Tito's favor as well (115–113). As the decision was announced, Puerto Rican fans in the audience erupted with applause and cheers. The victory gave Trinidad two of the three recognized welterweight belts; the third major belt—the oldest, dating back to the 19th century—is the World Boxing Association title, currently held by Pittsburgh native James Page.

Within minutes of the Trinidad–De La Hoya decision, traffic outside the Puerto Rican capital came to a stop as hundreds of Tito's supporters leaned out their windows, waving flags and cheering. "Pedro Rossello [a gubernatorial candidate who wants Puerto Rico to become the 51st state] wants to make us Americans," a man in a San Juan pub said after the fight, according to the Associated Press (September 20, 1999). "But Tito shows we're Puerto Ricans. Trinidad won because he's Puerto Rican and Puerto Ricans are hungry."

For his next bout, against WBA superwelterweight champion Dave Reid on March 3, 2000 in Las Vegas, Trinidad jumped up a weight class. Timothy Smith, covering the fight for the *New York Times* (March 5, 2000), wrote that Trinidad looked "more comfortable with the additional weight" and "entered the ring loose and confident against Reid." Although Trinidad was knocked down in the third round, he recovered, and he went on to administer a fearsome flurry of hard shots, sending his opponent to the mat three times in the 11th round alone. "When I went down to the canvas for the first time, the first thought that came to my mind was, 'It's over for David Reid,'" Trinidad told Smith. "I have been down before, but when I get up I'm always dangerous." After winning the WBA superwelterweight title, Trinidad was given 72 hours to decide whether to defend or relinquish his IBF welterweight title, in accord with IBF regulations. He gave it up and set his sights on Fernando Vargas, the IBF junior-middleweight champion. After successfully defending his WBA superwelterweight title against France's Mamadou Thiam on July 23, Trinidad was set to challenge Vargas on December 2, 2000. — M.B.

Suggested Reading: ESPN (on-line) Sep. 18, 1999, Sep. 23, 1999; *New York Times* B p15 Aug. 20, 1997, with photo, C p2 Aug. 25, 1997, C p4 Feb. 4, 1998, C p5 Mar. 31, 1998, D p5 Feb. 18, 1999, VIII p10 Mar. 5, 2000, D p11 July 24, 2000; *New York Times* (on-line) Feb. 20, 1999, Feb. 22, 1999, with photo, Sep. 16, 1999, with photo, Sep. 19, 1999, with photo; *USA Today* C p3 May 29, 1999

Courtesy of the American Museum–Hayden Planetarium

Tyson, Neil de Grasse

Oct. 5, 1958– Director of the Hayden Planetarium; educator. Address: Hayden Planetarium, Central Park West at 79th St., New York, NY 10024

At his high school's 20-year reunion, in 1996, the astrophysicist Neil de Grasse Tyson was voted the graduate with the "coolest job." Tyson earned the title because he directs the largest, most advanced, and, perhaps, most famous planetarium in the United States: the American Museum of Natural History's Hayden Planetarium, in New York City. The youngest, and first African-American, director in the planetarium's history, Tyson guided the Hayden through its $200 million reconstruction project, which lasted from 1994 until the spring of 2000. Tyson is also a researcher, and he teaches astrophysics at Princeton University, in New Jersey. A firm believer in making astronomy and physics accessible to the public, he writes monthly general-interest science columns for *Stardate* and *Natural History* magazines and has written three books for nonspecialists on space and the universe: *Merlin's Tour of the Universe* (1989), *Universe Down to Earth* (1994), and a companion volume to *Merlin's Tour*, titled *Just Visiting This Planet* (1998). In his memoir, *The Sky Is Not the Limit* (2000), Tyson declared, "I want every generation of stargazers—whether they sit atop a tenement roof or an Appalachian mountain—to have a polished lens with which to see the universe and to reach for their own star."

Neil de Grasse Tyson was born on October 5, 1958 in New York City, the son of Sunchita (Feliciano) and Cyril de Grasse Tyson. He has an older brother, Stephen, and a younger sister, Lynn. His father, a sociologist, served as a commissioner in the city's Human Resources Administration while John Lindsay was mayor. His mother was a homemaker when her children were young; later, she earned a master's degree in gerontology and worked for the U.S. Public Health Service, evaluating federal programs for the elderly. Tyson has credited his parents with encouraging his intense "astro habit," as he has called it, by taking him to museums and helping him find books on astronomy when he was a child. His mother told *Current Biography* that she and her husband considered the city's cultural institutions and ethnic neighborhoods a "learning lab" for their children, and that they tried to instill in Tyson and his siblings "street smarts and a sense of awareness" that, particularly because they are African-Americans, "anything can happen to them on the streets no matter how educated or articulate they may be." "My sons still have problems hailing cabs in New York," she added.

Tyson discovered his passion for astronomy during a visit to the Hayden Planetarium when he was nine years old. "That was the night. The night the universe poured down from the sky and flowed into my body," he wrote in *The Sky Is Not the Limit.* "I had been called." Later, his sixth-grade teacher picked up on Tyson's growing interest in the heavens from the large number of astronomy-related book reports he submitted. As encouragement she brought him a newspaper announcement of a series of courses held at the Hayden Planetarium; while in junior high and high school, he took at least six of the classes. The youngest student in most of them, Tyson profited greatly from the instruction he received there, and he still models his lecturing style in part on that of Fred C. Hess, who taught two of his classes.

At age 12, after his father received a fellowship from Harvard University's John F. Kennedy School of Government, Tyson lived with his family for a year just outside Boston, Massachusetts. That Christmas his parents gave him his first telescope, which became, upon their return to the Bronx, a fixture on the rooftop of their building ("prophetically named," as Tyson has joked, Skytop Apartments). His presence on the roof after dark proved unsettling to people in his neighborhood: "A third of the time . . . ," he reported in his memoir, "someone would call the police." When officers showed up, he would invite them to look through his telescope. "The planet Saturn alone bailed me out a half-dozen times," he recalled. "For all I know, I would have been shot to death . . . if it were not for the majesty of the night sky."

During middle school and high school, in addition to attending the planetarium courses, Tyson participated in programs for budding scientists held elsewhere. The opportunity to do so, sometimes in places far from New York, came to him thanks to Vernon Grey, the director of education at the New York Explorers Club, whom he had met at a planetarium class. Grey was impressed by the curiosity Tyson showed in class and gave him access to whatever information the club had about scholarships and programs for aspiring researchers. At 14 Tyson secured a scholarship from the Explorers Club to sail toward the northwestern coast of Africa. Set on a Cunard luxury liner that had been converted into a floating laboratory for astrophysical investigations, the cruise was arranged to provide some 2,000 scientists and laypeople with an unimpeded view of the unusually long total solar eclipse that occurred on June 30, 1973. Later that summer Tyson spent a month at Camp Uraniborg, located in the Mojave Desert, in California. He and his fellow campers took courses in advanced mathematics and physics by day and operated the station's high-powered telescopes and computers by night. "My experience at Camp Uraniborg," Tyson wrote in his memoir, "remains one of the most enduring and influential episodes of my life." (The same may have been true for some of Tyson's fellow campers, five of whom went on to earn Ph.D.s in astrophysics.) During the next summer, having won a grant from the U.S. Department of Education, Tyson went to Scotland with a team of scientists and surveyors to study possible connections between astronomical events and the location of a group of unmapped prehistoric megaliths similar to Stonehenge (which is in Wiltshire, England).

In September 1973 Tyson entered the Bronx High School of Science, a specialized New York City public school that admits students on the basis of a rigorous exam. Through the recommendation of a friend of his family's, later that fall he was invited to present a lecture about Comet Kohoutek (which became visible in the night sky later that winter) to a class of about 50 people enrolled in the continuing education program of the City College of New York (CCNY). Only 15 at the time, Tyson spoke expertly for an hour on the topic and punctuated his lecture with astrophotographs he had taken at Camp Uraniborg. The $50 speaker's fee CCNY paid him startled Tyson; until then he had walked dogs to earn money to buy telescopic equipment, and the fee represented the monetary equivalent of 100 dog walks. Although he admitted in his memoir to having felt guilty for being "paid to share information that I just happened to have lying around in my head," he kept the check. "My fleeting feelings of financial morality were replaced with the lesson that knowledge and intelligence were no less a commodity than sweat and blood," he explained.

At Bronx Science Tyson excelled both intellectually and athletically. In his senior year he was named editor in chief of the school's prestigious *Physical Science Journal* and was appointed captain of the school wrestling team; he posted an individual match record of 10–0, pinning all but one of his opponents. After graduating from high school, in 1976, Tyson attended Harvard University, in Cambridge, Massachusetts, where he majored in physics with a specialization in astrophysics. Having trained himself to think analytically for so long, he enjoyed the challenge of Harvard's broad formal approach to education. "I broke free from a logic box that I did not know had contained me," he wrote in his autobiography. "From then onward I welcomed all manner of verbal abstractions and creative use of vocabulary into my life." Following a short stint on Harvard's rowing team, Tyson returned to wrestling, in the 190-pound weight class. In some of his free time, he volunteered as a math tutor for prisoners seeking a general equivalency diploma (GED) at Walpole State Penitentiary, in Massachusetts. He came to realize that although they had been sentenced to death or to life in prison and had virtually no chance of rejoining society, even convicted murderers could help others in the prison community. His experience led him to oppose the death penalty. Also as an undergraduate, Tyson performed jazz, ballet, and Afro-Caribbean dance with a local troupe. He earned a B.A. degree in physics from Harvard, in 1980.

In August of that year, Tyson left Cambridge to begin graduate work at the University of Texas at Austin. While there he came under the influence of Frank Bash, whose teaching methods helped Tyson refine his own; Gerard de Caucouleurs, who set for him a high standard of scientific precision and thoroughness; and John Archibald Wheeler, a former student of Albert Einstein's. Tyson supported himself at this time largely through a teaching assistantship at the university, but its stipend barely met his monthly expenses. To supplement his income, he tutored undergraduates in mathematics and physics and wrote for the popular astronomy magazine *Stardate* and, later, *Natural History*, which is published by the American Museum of Natural History.

In 1983 Tyson earned a master's degree in astronomy. He remained in Texas for four more years, earning a living through speaking engagements and the writing of scientific articles for general-interest and nonspecialist publications. In 1987 he accepted a one-year teaching post in astronomy at the University of Maryland, in College Park. When that job ended he moved back to New York City to pursue a Ph.D. in astrophysics, at Columbia University. Meanwhile, in 1988 Tyson had made the first of what would be many trips to the Cerro Tololo InterAmerican Observatory, in the Andes Mountains of Chile, in South America, where he has conducted most of his observational research ever since. His scientific investigations have focused on problems related to star-formation models of dwarf galaxies and the chemical evolution and structure of the Milky Way's galactic bulge. Galactic bulges—swellings at the center of galaxies, which are thought to control the galaxies' development—were the subject of his Ph.D. dissertation.

As an African-American who yearned to become an astrophysicist, Tyson felt that, as he wrote in his memoir, "few parts of society were prepared to accept my dreams." According to Tyson, at Bronx Science people were more accepting of his captaincy of the wrestling team than they were of his editorship of the *Physical Science Journal*. At Harvard one of his wrestling teammates questioned his decision to become a scientist, asserting that service to the black community would be a better use of his talents; and at the University of Texas "faculty and fellow students suggested alternative careers for me thinking that they were doing me a favor," he reported. He also wrote, "At no time was I perceived as a future colleague, although this privilege was enjoyed by others in graduate school." Often, when he would leave his office after working late, the police would stop him and question him. Because he was a young black male, he wrote, the police, like countless others in society, immediately pigeonholed him: "My athletic talents are genetic; I am a likely mugger-rapist; my academic failures are expected; and my academic successes are attributed to others." He was especially stung by the criticism from his Harvard teammate, an upperclassman whom he respected. He found himself beginning to doubt whether becoming an astrophysicist was socially responsible in a nation where prejudice and injustice still existed. It was not until he had entered the Ph.D. program at Columbia, and subsequently was asked by a local television news program to speak on-air as an expert in astrophysics, that he felt secure in his career choice. When he saw himself on TV, he realized that he had been approached for commentary not because of his race but because of his knowledge. "I had finally reconciled my decade of inner conflict borne of a flippant comment by my fellow wrestler," Tyson wrote in his autobiography. "It's not that the plight of the Black community cannot afford having me study astrophysics. It's that the plight of the Black community cannot afford it if I don't." He also decided, he wrote, that continuously battling racism "levies an emotional tax that constitutes a form of intellectual emasculation. . . . I eventually learned that you can be ridden only if your back is bent. And of course, that which doesn't kill you makes you stronger."

When he received his Ph.D. from Columbia, in 1991, Tyson joined only six other blacks among the approximately 4,000 astrophysicists in the U.S. at that time. Shortly thereafter he got a job as a postdoctoral research associate at Princeton University's Department of Astrophysical Sciences. In 1993 he was elected to the board of directors of the Astronauts Memorial Foundation at Cape Canaveral, Florida. He has expressed his concern that the nation's space program is driven by military goals rather than scientific curiosity and the desire to ensure the survival of Earth and the human race. In July 1994 he was promoted to research scientist at Princeton and, concurrently, granted the same title at the Hayden Planetarium. Within a year of joining the Hayden's staff, he was named acting director of the planetarium; in May 1996 his title changed to director.

Tyson's promotion came about two years into the six-year rebuilding of the planetarium. Opened to the public in February 2000, the new facility represented a collaborative effort of the architect James Stewart Polshek and the exhibition designer Ralph Applebaum. The sky theater sits in an aluminum-clad sphere, 87 feet in diameter, which is set in a 10-story glass-walled cube known as the Rose Center for Earth and Science. The planetarium's custom-built star-and-planet projector—a Zeiss Mark IX—is the most modern in the world, and the three-dimensional galactic maps generated by the center's supercomputer are equivalent to those used by the National Aeronautics and Space Administration (NASA).

From December 1997 to June 1999 Tyson served as chair of the Department of Astrophysics at the American Museum of Natural History. He has written the monthly columns "Merlin," for *Stardate*, and "Universe," for *Natural History*, since 1983 and 1985, respectively. Columns and essays from *Stardate* comprise parts of his books *Merlin's Tour of the Universe*, *Universe Down to Earth*, and *Just Visiting This Planet*. In 1996 *Crains New York Business* magazine named him one of the 40 most influential New Yorkers under the age of 40, and in 1997 York College of the City University of New York awarded him an honorary doctor of science degree. He and Alice Young, whom he met at the University of Texas when she was a doctoral candidate in mathematics, married in 1988. Their daughter, born in 1997, is named Miranda, after one of the moons of the planet Uranus. — V.K.

Suggested Reading: *New York Times* B p2 Dec. 31, 1999, with photo; *New Yorker* p72+ Jan. 17, 2000; Scholastic Network (on-line) Feb. 26, 1996

Selected Books: *Merlin's Tour of the Universe*, 1989; *Universe Down to Earth*, 1994; *Just Visiting This Planet*, 1998; *The Sky Is Not the Limit*, 2000

Courtesy of Embassy of India

Vajpayee, Atal Behari

(VAZH-paiy, AH-tal Buy-HAR-ee)

Dec. 25, 1924– Prime Minister of India. Address: 7 Racecourse Rd., New Delhi, India

After India won its freedom from British colonial rule in 1947, following a prolonged struggle led by Mohandas Gandhi, the country adopted its own parliamentary form of government, which took effect on January 26, 1950. Under India's new Constitution, the chief executive was to be the president, who would be advised and aided by a council of ministers. The council would be headed by a prime minister, and since the president was mandated to act in accordance with the council's advice, much of the actual executive power lay with the prime minster. The prime minister and his council were to be, in turn, responsive to the directives of Parliament's lower chamber, the Lok Sabha (House of the People), which comprised elected representatives from each of India's 25 states and seven union territories. (The union territories, most of which were once foreign territories or are located in outlying areas, are centrally administered by the government in New Delhi by presidentially appointed lieutenant governors.) A second chamber, called Rajya Sabha (or Council of States), was made up of members either appointed by the president, because of their specialized areas of expertise, or elected by state and territorial officials.

India's current prime minister, Atal Behari Vajpayee, has held several positions in the government over the course of his five-decade political career. He has won election on separate occasions to both the Lok Sabha and the Rajya Sabha; helped found the Bharatiya Janata Party (BJP, or Indian People's Party, currently one of the country's largest political parties) and served as its leader; and assumed the post of prime minister three times, becoming the only person since Jawaharlal Nehru to do so. Known as a moderate, Vajpayee is sometimes compared to his legendary predecessor, and he has proven generally popular with the Indian public. His reputation in the rest of the world, however, has been problematic: in 1998, during his second tenure as prime minister, India tested three nuclear devices, acts that were denounced by the United States—which threatened sanctions if other detonations took place—as well as by other nations. The irony that India, a country in which much of the population lives in abject poverty, had spent money on nuclear testing did not pass unnoticed by the U.S. media. Since then, however, relations between the two countries have warmed, and in March 2000 Bill Clinton became the first U.S. president in almost a quarter-century to visit India. The visit was viewed widely there as another sterling achievement for Vajpayee, who is also admired by his compatriots as a published poet and skilled orator.

Vajpayee was born on December 25, 1924 in Gwalior, Madhya Pradesh, a city in central India. His father, Shri Krishna Behari Vajpayee, was a Hindu scholar and secondary-school teacher, and the family belonged to the Brahmin caste, considered one of the higher of India's rigid social classes. While still in his teens, Vajpayee joined a right-wing Hindu paramilitary group called Rashtriya Swayamsevak Sangh (RSS), or the National Voluntary Service, and he was imprisoned for 24 days in 1942 for his anti-British activities with the organization. Along with fighting against colonial rule, the RSS opposed what they considered to be the peace activist Mohandas Gandhi's appeasement of the Muslims, who had been engaged in a long-running battle with the Hindus—a conflict the British did little to resolve when they partitioned the subcontinent into predominantly Hindu India and Muslim Pakistan in the mid-1940s. When Gandhi was assassinated, in January 1948, members of the RSS were charged with conspiracy in his death. (A Hindu nationalist belonging to the Mahasabha, a politico-religious group, was eventually found guilty of the murder.)

Vajpayee graduated from Victoria College, in Gwalior, and earned a master's degree from Dayanand Anglo-Vedic College (DAV), in Kanpur. Although he began studying for a law degree after that, Vajpayee left school when offered a job editing a magazine published by the RSS. In the early 1950s there were more than 100 political parties and groups vying for government seats in India, and in 1951 Vajpayee joined the Jana Sangh, a conservative, nationalistic Hindu group. He acted as private secretary to the group's president, Shyama Prasad Mukherjee, and continued to edit and write for several Hindu publications. He was employed as a social worker during this time, as well. Mukherjee died in 1953, and according to the Web site of the Indian Embassy to the United States, Vajpayee was made leader of the Jana Sangh in 1955. (Other sources list the year as 1957.) He was elected to the Lok Sabha in 1957 and served there until 1962, when he was elected to a six-year term in the Rajya Sabha. (He would serve a second term in the Rajya Sabha starting in 1986.) Vajpayee would serve as president of the Jana Sangh until 1977.

In 1975 Indira Gandhi, then prime minister, became convinced that her enemies were conspiring to force her from office. A former political opponent had charged her with election irregularities, and when a high court upheld the charges, opposition party leaders quickly launched a civil-disobedience campaign to protest her holding office. Just as quickly, Gandhi responded to the crisis by declaring a state of emergency, instituting press censorship, outlawing the RSS, and arresting nearly 700 opposition leaders, including Vajpayee. By 1977, however, there was a backlash against Gandhi. Although the economy had done well under her leadership, the arrest of the opposition leaders, her implementation of a government birth-control program, and her perceived favoritism toward her son, Sanjay Gandhi, led to her growing unpopularity. (Sanjay would later be killed in an airplane accident, clearing the way for his younger brother, Rajiv, to win the prime minister's post after their mother's assassination, in 1984.) During the 1977 elections the Janata (People's) Party, a coalition that included the Jana Sangh, was swept into power, and on March 24 of that year Vajpayee was appointed external-affairs minister under the new prime minister, Moraji Desai. He held the post until July 28, 1979, and during that time became known for his diplomacy, engaging in goodwill discussions with both China and the Soviet Union.

In 1980 Vajpayee helped to found the Bharatiya Janata (Indian People's) Party, also known as the BJP, along with other staunch Jana Sangh members who were unhappy with the Janata Party's decision to ban its officeholders from participating in RSS activities. Vajpayee was BJP president until 1986, when he was appointed to his second term in the Rajya Sabha, but during that time managed to distance himself from the right-wing reputation of the group. He carefully cultivated a moderate and intellectual image, and thanks in part to his perceived sophistication, the BJP began to appeal to a wider electorate than might have been attracted to it otherwise. By 1982 the BJP held more seats in the Lok Sabha than did the Janata Party and was considered one of the best-organized opposition parties in the country. During the next decade, the BJP's fortunes fluctuated along with India's ever-changing political climate. In December 1984 the party was reduced to holding two Lok Sabha seats, but by 1989 the number had grown to 88, much to the alarm of Muslim factions, and by 1991, as part of an electoral alliance that included the militantly pro-Hindu Shiv Sena Party, the BJP held 119 legislative seats.

Despite Vajpayee's moderating influence, the party's image suffered greatly in 1992, when a group of Hindu extremists, including BJP and Shiv Sena loyalists, destroyed an abandoned 16th-century Muslim mosque in the city of Ayodhya on December 6 of that year, despite assurances by BJP officials that the mosque would be unharmed during the Hindu gathering. (The Hindus were demonstrating for the right to build a shrine at the site, which they believed to be the birthplace of one of their deities.) The incident sparked a series of violent confrontations between Muslims and Hindus that left an estimated 1,300 to 3,000 people dead. Vajpayee intervened, persuading then–prime minister P. V. Narasimha Rao to allow party meetings to continue in halls and stadiums and to refrain from arresting party members for their association with the RSS, which had been banned in the wake of the riots.

In 1996 the BJP won 161 seats in the 545-seat Parliament. Vajpayee was made prime minister, taking the oath of office in Hindi rather than English, as had been the custom, and wearing a saffron-colored sash—considered a sacred hue for Hindus. Although a leftist alliance called the United Front held 177 seats, no one party held a majority, and then–president Shankar Dayal Sharma asked Vajpayee to form a government. There seemed little chance of the BJP's commanding a majority in the Lok Sabha, as the group would have to win support from other parties to do so. The United Front and the Congress Party, which had won 140 seats, both considered the BJP—which had vowed to make India a nuclear power, toughen policies on Pakistan, and abolish legal protection for Muslims—too extremist. Rather than face a humiliating vote of confidence without their support, Vajpayee resigned as prime minister. He had held the post for only 13 days, from May 15 to May 28. (A United Front minority government was sworn in on June 1 and received a vote of confidence from the lower house two weeks later, but by November 1997 the Congress Party had withdrawn their support and the United Front's I. K. Gujral was forced to resign as prime minister.)

India's 1998 elections left the government once more without a majority party; the BJP had garnered enough allies to lead a coalition government of 252 seats, and Vajpayee was again made prime minister. This time he won a vote of confidence in Parliament and retained the post. Having more moderate allies forced the BJP to compromise some of its more extreme doctrines, such as Hindu supremacy. Vajpayee was still determined to prove India's nuclear capabilities, however, and in May 1998, foiling the attempts of American intelligence services to monitor its activity, India conducted three underground nuclear tests. Despite almost universal condemnation from other nations, Vajpayee defended the tests as crucial to national security and steadfastly maintained that India could handle whatever economic sanctions were levied against it as a result.

Pakistan responded with nuclear tests of its own, and tensions between the two countries worsened during Vajpayee's second term as prime minister, particularly over control of Kashmir, India's only Muslim-majority state. Indian forces triumphed over Pakistani rebels in that area the month before the general elections of September 1999, helping to ensure Vajpayee's and the BJP's victory over the Congress Party and its head, Sonia Gandhi, the Italian-born daughter-in-law of Indira Gandhi and widow of Rajiv Gandhi. (Rajiv was assassinated in 1991, during a comeback election campaign for prime minister.) On October 13, 1999 Vajpayee was sworn in for his third term as prime minister, a capacity in which he would play host to United States president Bill Clinton during Clinton's March 2000 visit to the subcontinent. Although the two leaders discussed India's adherence to the Comprehensive Test Ban Treaty and possible nuclear disarmament, the visit was widely reported in the U.S. media as a public-relations exercise rather than a serious summit, with Clinton being photographed repeatedly in colorful or exotic Indian locales.

The world's press has apparently had a difficult time giving a balanced and unbiased view of Vajpayee. The *Times of India* (May 23, 2000), as quoted on the BJP's Web site, trumpeted his virtues and posed the rhetorical question, "If India merged boundaries with China, Japan, North and South Korea, Pakistan and the rest of Asia, who would head the new political confederation? Who else, but Vajpayee. . . ." According to the article, he "has been running this behemoth [India] with restraint and astuteness." Yet elsewhere he is depicted as merely the "most acceptable face" in the BJP, which was described by Emily MacFarquhar in *U.S. News & World Report* (May 27, 1996) as "heir to the killers of Mahatma [Mohandas] Gandhi in 1948, patron to the demolishers of a mosque at Ayodhya that set off anti-Muslim riots in 1992 and purveyor of a creed of Hindu ascendency in one of the world's most multicultural societies." Vajpayee himself has contributed to the confusion, by condemning Gandhi's killing as a "terrible crime" and the incident in Ayodhya as a "blunder of Himalayan proportions," in an interview with John Burns for the *New York Times* (March 20, 1998), while still staunchly supporting the khaki-clad members of the RSS. And although most sources agree that Vajpayee is a firm believer in the idea of Hindutva, the supremacy of Hindu culture, he told Burns that "discrimination is not in our blood, or in our soil. All of us, Hindus, Muslims, Buddhists, and Christians, believe that God is one, but that he can be reached in different ways."

Vajpayee has served on several parliamentary committees, most notably as chairman of the Committee of Government Assurances in 1966–67, the chairman of the Public Accounts Committee from 1967 to 1970, a member of the General Purposes Committee in 1986, a member of the Business Advisory Committee from 1988 to 1990, chairman of the Committee on Petitions in 1990–91, chairman of the Public Accounts Committee from 1991 to 1993, and chairman of the Standing Committee on External Affairs from 1993 to 1996. He has been a member of numerous goodwill missions, and in that capacity he has traveled to Africa, Australia, Japan, Switzerland, and many other nations. He has received several honors for his service to India, including the Padma Ayodhya, the country's second-highest civilian honor (1992), and an honorary Ph.D. from Kanpur University (1993). In 1994 he was named Best Parliamentarian.

During 2000 Vajpayee canceled several engagements, and reports of his poor health began to circulate in the Indian press. He appeared frail and moved slowly to the microphone before making a speech in August and had to be carried off the platform by his security men. In October 2000 he had surgery to replace his left knee joint, which had been damaged by arthritis, and since then has been undergoing intensive physical therapy. Rumors have persisted that Vajpayee is suffering from a life-threatening disease, and fears are widespread that the stability of India's coalition government would be adversely affected if he were to become seriously ill. But the prime minister, who turned 75 in 1999, has insisted that he is merely showing the effects of advanced age.

Vajpayee, a bachelor, has reportedly helped to raise the daughter of a close family friend, who sometimes acts as his official hostess. Although many Hindus shun alcohol and meat, Vajpayee has been known to indulge in both. Compilations of his speeches have been published, as have many of his traditional, reflective poems—some of which he composed while in prison. — M.R.

Suggested Reading: BJP Web Site; *Business Week* p57 Sep. 6, 1999, with photo; *Maclean's* p28+ May 27, 1996, with photos; *New York Times* A p8 May 16, 1996, A p1 Mar. 16, 1998, with photo, A p3 Mar. 20, 1998, with photos, A p1 May 12, 1998, with photos; *U.S. News & World Report* p60 May 27, 1996, with photos

---

Archive Photos

Wald, Patricia M.

Sep. 16, 1928– International War Crimes Tribunal judge; former federal court judge. Address: International War Crimes Tribunal for Yugoslavia, P.O. Box 13888, 2501 EW, The Hague, Netherlands

While job-hunting in New York City in 1951, shortly before she graduated from Yale Law School, Patricia M. Wald was interviewed by a partner at a prestigious private law firm. In an account of what transpired in the *New York Times* (July 12, 1999), Linda Greenhouse wrote that the attorney, obviously impressed by Wald's outstanding record, told her, "It's really a shame. If only you could have been here last week." In response to her puzzled expression, he said, "We hired a woman last week." As Greenhouse noted, no explanation was necessary: though the firm still had openings, Wald knew that its partners had no intention of hiring another woman, no matter how exceptional her credentials. In those years, Greenhouse reported, the legal profession was "unwelcoming if not downright hostile" to female attorneys, and in building a career in law, most women made their way in uncharted territory. In Wald's case, that journey took her from a private Washington, D.C., firm to public-interest legal organizations and then to public service, in the U.S. Department of Justice; along her route, for about 10 years beginning in the early 1950s, she put her career essentially on hold to devote herself to her five children. In 1977, having gained increasing visibility through her work with the Center on Law and Social Policy and the Mental Health Law Project, she was named assistant attorney general for legislative affairs at the Justice Department. Two years later President Jimmy Carter appointed her to the United States Court of Appeals for the District of Columbia Circuit, thus making her the first female judge to serve on a federal appellate court. During the 20 years that she sat on the District of Columbia Circuit, which is widely considered second only to the Supreme Court as the nation's most influential judicial body, she wrote opinions on more than 800 cases, and from 1986 to 1991, she served as chief judge.

By the time she took her place on the federal bench, Wald had become well known for her efforts in support of juvenile justice and the rights of women, the poor, and the mentally and physically handicapped and in the areas of bail reform and treatment of drug abuse. "Throughout her career," Linda Greenhouse wrote, "she has held fast to the liberal view of the Constitution as an engine of social progress, an idea that often seems anachronistic in today's conservative judicial climate in America but that is a fresh ideal to many in Eastern Europe." Eastern Europe has claimed much of Wald's attention since the early 1990s, when she made the first of more than a dozen trips to help formerly Communist nations build legal systems consistent with democratic ideals. In November 1999 she retired from the U.S. Court of Appeals and, at the invitation of United Nations secretary general Kofi Annan, accepted an appointment as one of 14 judges on the International War Crimes Tribunal for Yugoslavia, which meets in the Hague, in the Netherlands.

At a dinner held in her honor shortly before she ended her service on the court, Harry T. Edwards, the current chief judge of the District of Columbia Circuit, paid tribute to Wald: "She is a brilliant lawyer and jurist, she is lightning fast in her work, she has an incredible memory," he declared, as quoted by Bill Miller in the *Washington Post* (November 14, 1999). "She misses no nuance in an argument; she is an extraordinary and tenacious advocate of a position once she has analyzed competing arguments. She is fair-minded, and she is gracious on the bench."

The only child of Joseph F. McGowan and the former Margaret O'Keefe, Patricia M. Wald was born Patricia McGowan on September 16, 1928 in Torrington, Connecticut. According to Linda Greenhouse, her father did not participate in her upbringing, but she benefited from the attention of various other relatives. Many of them worked in Torrington factories and became active union members. As a teenager she herself worked in the town's brass mills during summers. Early on she realized the importance of the union to her relatives, and, as she told Greenhouse, "I knew how important the [union] lawyer was to the union."

Encouraged by people in her family, who "recognized her gifts and supported her ambitions," in Greenhouse's words, Wald attended Connecticut College for Women, in New London (the school became co-ed in 1969). She graduated first in her class, with a B.A. degree, in 1948. Three years later she earned a bachelor of laws degree from Yale Law School, in New Haven, Connecticut. In 1951 she won the coveted position of law clerk to Judge Jerome N. Frank of the United States Court of Appeals for the Second Circuit, which covers Connecticut, New York, and Vermont. She remained with Judge Frank until 1952. After getting married in the same year, she moved to Washington, D.C., to be closer to her husband, Robert Lewis Wald, a lawyer who had graduated with her from Yale and who, as a U.S. Navy reservist, was stationed aboard a ship at Norfolk, Virginia. She worked as an associate with the law firm of Arnold, Fortas, and Porter in Washington during 1952 and 1953. She then spent about 10 years as a homemaker, raising three daughters and two sons, all of whom were born within a span of seven years. In the early 1960s she devoted many nights and weekends to conducting research, much of it on questions of price discrimination, and to analyzing the rules for the collection of evidence in criminal cases; she also wrote scholarly articles based on that work.

In 1963 Wald attended the National Conference on Bail and Criminal Justice, which was cosponsored by the U.S. Department of Justice, then headed by Attorney General Robert F. Kennedy. Her presentation, which she wrote with another conference participant, her law-school classmate Daniel J. Freed (who later became a professor at Yale), was expanded into the book *Bail in the United States—1964* (1964). Wald and Freed's book challenged the concept of bail (formally known as the bail bond), a sum, set by a court, that a defendant awaiting trial must pay in order to secure release from prison; since the money is forfeited if the accused does not return to court when requested, it is used as a way of insuring that the person will appear for trial. The ideas of Wald and Freed eventually led to major reforms in the bail system, whereby pretrial release is based more often on such factors as community involvement than on ability to pay.

In 1964–65 Wald served on the Johnson Commission on Crime in the District of Columbia, and in June 1965 she participated in the National Conference on Law and Poverty. The paper she wrote for that conference formed the basis of her book *Law and Poverty, 1965* (1965). In 1967 Wald was hired as an attorney in the Justice Department's Office of Criminal Justice; although she was considered a full-time employee, she got permission to leave at 3:30 p.m. so that she could be home when her children returned from school. She served as a consultant to the National Advisory Commission on Civil Disorders in 1968. In the same year she left the Justice Department, to work for the Neighborhood Legal Services Program. Then, in 1970, she co-directed the Ford Foundation's Drug Abuse Research Project; the project's findings, compiled by Wald, were published as *Dealing with Drug Abuse* (1972). In 1971 Wald joined the Center for Law and Social Policy, a public-interest organization that concentrated on such issues as consumer rights, the environment, and health. In 1972–77 she was an attorney for the Mental Health Law Project, serving from 1975 until 1977 as the project's litigation director. During this time she was also a member of the Carnegie Council on Children.

In 1977, the year President Jimmy Carter took office, Wald was appointed assistant attorney general for legislative affairs in the Department of Justice. Two years later President Carter chose her to serve as a judge on the United States Court of Appeals for the District of Columbia Circuit (commonly referred to as the D.C. Circuit). During hearings on her nomination held by the Senate Judiciary Committee, Gordon J. Humphrey, a first-term, conservative Republican senator from New Hampshire, strenuously objected to her appointment. The basis of his opposition was a speech about children's rights that Wald had presented in 1974 to about 100 law students and social workers at a seminar in St. Paul, Minnesota. Her speech was later reprinted in *Child Welfare,* a publication of the Child Welfare League, as well as in both *Human Rights,* an American Bar Association publication, and a textbook about family law. In her talk, Wald had discussed the legal status of children. According to an editorial in the *New York Times* (July 18, 1979), she had suggested in that speech and others "that parents should consult their kids about things that concern them; that some children in disturbed families need legal help, and that some 12-year-olds could vote as wisely as some of their elders." During the Senate hearings, Laura A. Kiernan wrote for the *Washington Post* (June 25, 1979), Senator Humphrey referred to Wald's words as a "stinging rebuke" to parents, in that they implied that parents are "calculated, unconcerned slave-masters," and he and other right-wing senators, the *New York Times* editorial reported, accused Wald of being "anti-family" and "a destroyer of family discipline." According to Kiernan, the attacks constituted a preemptive strike against what Humphrey and his supporters feared were the Carter administration's plans to "pack the bench with liberal activists," in the senator's words. Their charges notwithstanding, the Senate confirmed her appointment, and Wald became the first female judge on the United States Court of Appeals.

Three-judge panels, chosen at random from the dozen or so judges on the D.C. Circuit, hear each of the cases brought before the court. Partly because of the location of the D.C. Circuit, many of these cases deal with matters of national consequence, such as civil rights, the environment, the operations of utilities, and other areas of day-to-day life that are subject to federal regulations. During Wald's tenure the judges represented a wide range of legal philosophies and political ideologies, and heated clashes often occurred during deliberations in which Wald participated. Many of the dissenting opinions that she wrote, she told Miller, swayed judges on other circuit courts and even justices of the U.S. Supreme Court. In one such case, the D.C. Circuit, then headed by Judge Robert H. Bork, banned demonstrations within a radius of 500 feet of embassies; in her 48-page dissent, Wald argued that the ban was unconstitutional because it ignored rights guaranteed by the First Amendment. The Supreme Court later upheld Wald's position.

In a speech that she gave at Yale Law School, parts of which were printed in the *New York Times* (March 18, 1988), Wald described the job of a federal appellate judge as "challenging and tedious, exhilarating and depressing, ultimately lonely." She also revealed, "I constantly watch my colleagues in an effort to discern what it takes to be a good appellate judge: alertness, sensitivity to the needs of the system and one's colleagues, raw energy, unselfishness, a healthy sense of history, some humility, a lively interest in the world outside the courthouse and what makes it tick, an ability to make hard decisions with only a little bit of post mortem regret, quickness—the ability to read fast, lucidity—a comparable ability to write well. . . . 'Brilliance,' of course, is a plus, but on a day-to-day basis, humanity counts for just as much." Wald also spoke about the imprint that judges leave on American society: "We must consider the results of our rulings, not merely their conceptual consistency. Principled decision-making does not require that we be blind to how our decisions play out in the real world. If the law is to survive and flourish, it must change and develop through experience, application to new situations, testing in new circumstances, infusion of new knowledge. Today, it seems, we shy away from that philosophy for fear it may draw the stigma of 'legal activism.' But labels are deceiving and too often intimidating. The truth is that life does change and the law must adapt to that inevitability."

In 1992 President-elect Bill Clinton told Wald that he was considering her for the position of United States attorney general. She turned down the offer, for what her husband described to Bill McAllister for the *Washington Post* (December 17, 1992) as a "combination" of reasons. Prominent among them was that if she were to leave the bench at that point, her eventual federal pension would amount to much less than it would if she remained a judge for at least two more years. In addition, friends of hers told McAllister, Wald enjoyed her work and had no desire to take on the huge administrative burdens of the nation's chief law-enforcement officer. Wald herself explained to Linda Greenhouse, "I knew the job [of attorney general], and I knew how large the political component was; it was just not the right job for me."

Wald was involved in a portion of the Justice Department's antitrust proceedings against Bill Gates's Microsoft, the world's largest computer-software company. In 1997 the United States Court of Appeals was asked to decide whether Microsoft had acted illegally by compelling computer makers who sell Windows 95 to offer Microsoft's browser (Internet Explorer) as well. Later that year the Justice Department received a preliminary injunction against Microsoft from U.S. District Court Judge Thomas Penfield Jackson, which Microsoft appealed. Microsoft claimed that a 1995 consent agreement the company had signed with the Justice Department cleared the way for Microsoft to develop "integrated products," while the Justice Department claimed that the agreement had been violated. According to Microsoft, the browser was so integrated into the Windows program that it should not be seen as a separate product. After a hearing by Judge Wald, Judge Stephen Williams (appointed by President Ronald Reagan), and Judge A. Raymond Randolph (appointed by President George Bush), the Court of Appeals ruled 2–1 in favor of Microsoft. Wald disagreed with her fellow adjudicators. According to Dan Goodin, reporting for *CNET News* (June 23, 1998, on-line), Wald wrote that the court's analysis "must also consider whether Internet Explorer is a separate product under antitrust law, that is, whether 'consumers differentiate between [Internet Explorer] and [Windows 95]' such that consumers desire to purchase—and hence that manufacturers desire to supply—a substitute for Internet Explorer from another manufacturer." In April 2000 Judge Jackson decided that Microsoft had indeed violated antitrust law. The following June the judge ruled that Microsoft must be split into two entities, with the portion handling the Windows operating system separated from the rest of the company. Microsoft is appealing the decision.

In July 1999 the International War Crimes Tribunal (IWCT) for Yugoslavia announced Wald's appointment to a two-year term as a judge on the tribunal, which was set up in 1993 by the United Nations Security Council. The mission of the IWCT is to bring to justice people accused of crimes against humanity committed during the recent fighting in Bosnia, Croatia, and Serbia. "It was something I cared about, something I wanted to do," Wald, who retired as a federal judge in November 1999, told Miller. "The timing was right. I've had 20 years [on the Court of Appeals]. I felt it was important." During the previous decade, in programs sponsored by the American Bar Association (ABA), the U.S. State Department, and the U.S. Information Agency, Wald had helped to monitor elections in Eastern European nations and had advised their governments on the drawing up of new constitutions and the establishment of judicial systems. "To get beyond the high abstractions of the rule of law has been immensely interesting," Wald told Greenhouse. "Sitting around a table with homemade vodka and writing a constitution bring a kind of intimacy to the constitutional process that we've long since left behind us here."

Patricia and Robert Wald maintain a home in Washington, D.C., where Robert Wald is a partner with the law firm Baach Robinson & Lewis; since 1991 he has also served on the board of directors of the International Human Rights Law Group, a nonprofit organization that engages in human-rights advocacy. Since 1979 Patricia Wald has been an active member of the American Law Institute, which, according to its Web site, seeks "to promote the clarification and simplification of the law and its better adaptation to social needs" and "to secure the better administration of justice"; she served as a vice president of the group from 1988 to 1998. She served on the executive board of the ABA's Central and Eastern European Law Initiative from 1994 to 1999 and on the board of editors of the *ABA Journal* from 1978 to 1986. She is a member of Phi Beta Kappa and the American Academy of Arts and Sciences. "This is the kind of person who is such a star," Judge Harry T. Edwards told Bill Miller. "She could have been standoffish, and played the Washington 'I am a star' role. Instead, she was always approachable and always cared that we got the work done." — C.L.

Suggested Reading: *CNET News* (on-line) June 23, 1998; *CNews* (on-line) Apr. 21, 1998; *New York Times* B p5 Mar. 18, 1988, A p22 July 18, 1979, A p10 July 12, 1999, with photo; *Washington Post* C p1+ June 25, 1979, with photo, A p21 Dec. 17, 1992, with photo, C p8 Feb. 24, 1992, with photo, C p1+ Nov. 14, 1999, with photos; *Who's Who in America, 2000*

Selected Books: *Bail in the United States* (with Daniel J. Freed), 1964; *Law and Poverty, 1965*, 1965

Walker, Jay

1956(?)– Founder and vice chairman of Priceline.com. Address: Priceline.com, 800 Connecticut Ave., Norwalk, CT 06854

Brad Rickerby/Archive Photos

"I never considered myself a very good gambler," Jay Walker told Randall Rothenberg during an interview for *Strategy+Business* (May 2000, on-line). Nevertheless, the achievement for which he is most famous—the founding of Priceline.com, an on-line shopping service—grew out of Walker's idea for an on-line casino business and the question of whether such a system for gambling could be patented. His inquiries along those lines led Walker to establish Walker Digital Corp., which in effect is a factory that manufactures ideas—specifically, business methods and models for the electronic marketplace that are potentially patentable. An "e-commerce powerhouse," as *Time Digital* (October 5, 1998), an offshoot of *Time*, dubbed it, Walker Digital has spawned Priceline.com Inc., which enables consumers to name the prices they are willing to pay for goods and services—cars, car rentals, airline tickets, mortgages, hotel rooms, groceries, and gasoline—and then matches the buyers to sellers who agree to accept those prices. The fruits of Walker Digital also include the Perfect YardSale, for buying and selling used household items; Digital Restaurant Solutions, which aims to benefit fast-food eateries and their customers; and, until it was disbanded, in October 2000, the WebHouse Club, which focused on products offered by supermarkets, gas stations, and other local venues. If Walker's plans become reality, his business, which he characterizes as "buyer-drive commerce," will someday extend to myriad other products and services. *Time Digital* included Walker among 50 businesspeople dubbed the "cyber elite," and *Business Week* (September 27, 1999) listed Walker among 25 Internet visionaries who have "chang[ed] the competitive landscape of almost every industry in the world."

Jay Walker was born in the New York City borough of Queens in about 1956. He has revealed little to reporters about his early years. "If you're going to trace my life, we'll be here a week," he joked to Dyan Machan for *Forbes* (May 17, 1999, on-line). "I was a Boy Scout. Okay?!" Both his father, a successful real-estate developer, and his mother, who escaped Nazi persecution in Europe when she was six years old, encouraged their young son to take risks. At age nine he printed and distributed his own newspaper; at 13 he brought a large stash of candy to his summer camp and sold it to other youngsters for less than what the camp canteen charged. Walker has credited his fierce competitiveness to the influence of his mother; a champion in both bridge and golf, she died when he was 18.

As an undergraduate at Cornell University, in Ithaca, New York, Walker routinely played Monopoly between classes, and he became highly proficient at that Parker Brothers game. "I realized Monopoly was a game of skill and, despite the dice, a skillful player always won," he told Machan. "So I wrote down the mechanism by which the Monopoly player would never lose. I called Parker Brothers and said: 'I've got good news for you. Monopoly's a game of skill and I could write a book telling everybody how to play better." Parker Brothers responded by threatening to sue Walker if he followed through on the idea. Undaunted, he and a partner published *1000 Ways to Win Monopoly Games*, which, Walker told David Noonan for the *Industry Standard* (December 28, 1998–January 4, 1999), revealed "the DNA of Monopoly"; the book reportedly sold more than 100,000 copies. (A mid-2000 search of on-line catalogs of the Library of Congress and of new or used books did not find the book listed.) Parker carried through on its threat, and the $50,000 profit Walker eventually earned from sales of *1000 Ways* was swallowed up in legal fees. Parker Brothers eventually dropped the suit. In addition, the company banned Walker from participating in Parker-sponsored Monopoly tournaments.

Walker's next ventures met with similarly dismal results. During a year's leave of absence from college, after his junior year, he launched a weekly newspaper in Ithaca. Gannett, the publishing giant, ran the paper out of business, and Walker wound up with bank debts totaling $250,000 (or perhaps as much as $1 million, according to different accounts). After he earned a B.S. degree, in industrial relations, from Cornell, he took a summer course in publishing at New York University, with the intention—apparently never realized—of producing a magazine composed solely of supermarket-type coupons. He next tried to derive profits from catalogs—for example, by selling catalogs in retail outlets, with the price of the catalog credited to the customer's first order of merchandise, and by starting a marketing company whose aim was to place paid advertising in mail-order catalogs of various businesses. Neither of those schemes succeeded. An attempt at what Randall Rothenberg called "art vending"—according to Dyan Machan, it was a business that sold sculpture made from lights—also failed.

Walker's luck changed in 1985, when, operating as Catalog Media Corp., he brokered a successful agreement between hundreds of catalog merchants and Federal Express, under which the catalogers would subsidize overnight delivery of goods to their customers. The arrangement enabled retailers to continue taking orders for Christmas merchandise until just before the actual day, thereby significantly extending the holiday selling season. Walker's next big success came in the area of magazine subscriptions. He knew that in other countries it was standard procedure for magazine publishers to renew readers' subscriptions automatically, by debiting the bank accounts of all customers who had not sent notification of their desire to cancel. Convinced that a similar system would work in the United States, he teamed with Michael Loeb, son of the financial journalist and editor Marshall Loeb, to start a business called NewSub Services. Walker devised a computer program (for which a patent was granted in 1999) that made it possible for a publisher—with the prior permission of the reader—to renew a subscription indefinitely, by automatically charging the yearly fee to a stored credit-card number. The service was advertised to consumers by means of an insert in their credit-card statements. NewSub Services began operations in 1991, with Citibank as its first customer. Thanks in part to Loeb's publishing connections, by the end of 1992, NewSub Services had sold 500,000 magazine subscriptions; seven years later, that number had increased more than 60-fold, to more than 30 million, and annual sales of Synapse Group Inc., as the company had been renamed, were approaching $300 million.

In the early 1990s, in what he described to Randall Rothenberg as a "process" rather than an epiphany, Walker realized that the Internet was a fertile environment for the creation of business-related "inventions" that could be patented. In the first step of that process, he came up with the notion of an Internet casino after reading an article about encryption technology (which can be used to protect the confidentiality of information sent over the Internet). Then, as he recalled to Rothenberg, "I began to wonder how I might benefit commercially from the idea. Since I wasn't going to open a casino, I thought maybe I could own the idea. That led me to patent law." Walker learned from attorneys that his idea could certainly be patented; indeed, whoever had "invented" what became known as credit cards and frequent-flyer programs, they told him, could have gained patents for them, if they had simply applied to the U.S. Patent and Trademark Office. "And I said, 'Does it strike any of you as odd that nobody owns those things?' And they said, 'Business does that all the time. They invent things and they don't realize they could own them.'"

Armed with this new knowledge, in 1994 Walker founded Walker Digital Corp., a so-called intellectual-property laboratory that has often been compared to the famous workshops run by the phenomenally productive inventor Thomas A. Edison (1847–1931), in which scientists worked in teams to come up with solutions to particular problems. (*Forbes* headlined its May 17, 1999 cover article on Walker "An Edison for a New Age.") In Edison's case, those solutions were electrical, mechanical, or chemical systems, devices, or substances. By contrast, the duty of Walker's technical experts (among them computer engineers, financial analysts, and cryptographers) is to invent new methods of doing business on the Internet and to develop the technology to implement those methods. "Walker Digital is about reengineering the DNA of the future of business," Walker told Machan. "What we hope is that a group of thoughtful people can together reinvent whole sectors of the global economy. And not only can we reinvent them, we can own those inventions." Walker's staff also includes attorneys experienced in patent law, whose job is to ensure ownership of any ideas or solutions that the research arm of the company develops.

On August 11, 1998 Walker Digital was granted a patent for both a "buyer-driven" method of conducting business and the associated software, which allowed prospective consumers of a commodity to transmit a binding purchase offer to a prospective seller via the Internet. The awarding of the patent came four months after Walker introduced his new Web site, Priceline.com, on April 6, 1998. He financed the start-up in part with at least $20 million that he secured by selling one-third of his stake in NewSub Services and with another $100 million invested by Microsoft co-founder Paul Allen, the financier George Soros, the computer-software executive Jim Manzi, and the cable-television executive John C. Malone. The first commodities offered at Priceline.com were airplane seats. Each visitor to the site would enter a destination, preferred travel date (but not travel time), and desired price (but not desired airline), and he or she had to seal the bid by entering a credit-card number. The participating airlines would then scan the bids and decide if they wanted to meet the traveler's conditions. Since seats unsold at flight time represent a major loss of revenue, selling tickets at a discount would benefit the carriers. Within its first three months of operation, Priceline reportedly sold 40,000 tickets, worth a total of about $10 million. (According to various sources, less than 10 percent of potential customers made successful bids during that period, but, as more airlines signed on, consumers' success rates have improved.)

"In a retail economy, all goods are always mispriced," Walker told James Surowiecki for the *New Yorker* (May 22, 2000). Fixed pricing has been traced to the department-store pioneer John Wanamaker (1838–1922), who introduced price tags so as to end the bargaining between salesperson and consumer that had long been the norm in retailing. Walker, however, believes that fixed pricing works to the detriment of both customers, some of whom refrain from buying goods that they judge to be too costly, and the sellers whose goods are therefore left on the shelves. According to the company's Web site, Priceline's system avoids those problems by "enabl[ing] consumers to use the Internet to save money on a wide range of products and services while enabling sellers to generate incremental revenue."

On March 29, 1999 Priceline launched its $115 million initial public offering. Initially $16 per share, the price soared to $85 before stabilizing at $69, thus giving the company a market value of $9.8 billion—"the highest first-day value ever gained by an Internet company," as Saul Hansell pointed out in the *New York Times* (March 31, 1999). By the end of the second day, the price of each share had climbed to $82.875, the market value had jumped to $11.8 billion, and Walker's stake had increased in worth to $5.2 billion. As of the end of August 2000, the per-share price was hovering just below $30. To date, like many other Internet start-ups, Priceline has operated in the red, but industry analysts predict that it will show a profit by 2001. Priceline's April 24, 2000 financial statement reported first-quarter revenues of more than $300 million and a total customer base of more than five million, including about a million and a half people who had visited the site for the first time in 2000.

Walker suffered a setback in October 2000, when the WebHouse Club, which enabled customers to bid on groceries or gasoline, was shut down for lack of sufficient operating funds. Its demise cost Walker's investors more than $350 million. Walker blamed the shutdown on what he termed "fickle" investors who refused to provide additional funds for the venture after making their initial outlays. Priceline.com, which was not connected to the WebHouse Club, was expected to be unaffected by its termination.

The 40-odd patents that Walker currently holds provide methods for distributing prepaid phone time, issuing postpaid traveler's checks, and selling magazine subscriptions directly from computer terminals at newsstands. By his own account, eight of his more than 300 pending U.S. and international patents will revolutionize the fast-food industry, by allowing consumers to place their orders from personal digital devices such as the Palm Pilot. Several of his patents have provoked lawsuits, filed, for example, by entrepreneurs who claim that Walker has stolen their ideas. Some observers, among them Lawrence Lessig, a Harvard University specialist in "cyber law" who has been called the "Paul Revere of the Web," have even questioned the wisdom of awarding patents for business systems, warning that such patents will "inhibit, not promote, innovation," as Randall

Rothenberg wrote. In response, Walker asserted to Rothenberg, "Intellectual property has stood the test of time in every business revolution. . . . Our society benefited massively in the Agricultural Revolution, the Industrial Revolution, in every revolution prior where underlying technology played a role in protecting inventors for limited periods, in return for them taking risk to create. There is no evidence that I can see that this time, it's different. I'm not saying that patents as existing are a universal, perfect answer. Occasionally the Patent Office makes an error. It grants an overly broad patent, and people license it instead of challenging it, as they should. However, to argue that this time it's different, and that protected intellectual property in the Internet space hinders innovation, is totally wrong, unsupported by any evidence."

Walker lives in Ridgefield, Connecticut, with his wife, Eileen, and their two children. His leisure activities include reading, photography, and collecting space memorabilia. He is a licensed pilot —M.R.

Suggested Reading: *Business Week* EB p30 Sep. 27, 1999, with photo; *Forbes* (on-line) May 17, 1999, July 9, 1999; *Fortune* p193+ Sep. 6, 1999, with photo; *Harvard Business Review* p19+ Nov./Dec. 1999; *Ladies Home Journal* p106+ July 2000, with photos; *New York Times* D p1+ Aug. 10, 1998, with photo, C p8 July 26, 1999, with photo; *New Yorker* p34 May 22, 2000; *Newsweek* p42+ Sep. 20, 1999, with photo; *PC Computing* p33 Feb. 2000; *Salon* (on-line) Aug. 27, 1999; *Strategy+Business* (on-line) May 2000

Dana L. Walker/Courtesy of Brent Sikkema, NY

Walker, Kara

1969– Artist. Address: c/o Landfall Press Inc., 329 W. 18th St., #601, Chicago, IL 60616-1120

The artist Kara Walker has received both praise and condemnation for her black paper silhouettes, with which she creates disturbing images of slavery to address the topic of race relations, past and present. "She takes a genteel parlor diversion, revels in its inherent exquisiteness, and then turns it on its head," as Karen Janovy wrote in *Sheldon Selections* (1998, on-line). In the catalog for Walker's spring 1997 exhibition at the San Francisco Museum of Modern Art, Gary Garrels, the museum's chief curator, wrote that her scenes depict a "taboo subject: the true events of history," while presenting "a narrative that is as psychologically real as it is historically impossible," according to Miles Unger in *Art News* (June/July 1998).

Walker's life-sized silhouettes are cut out of the paper used by professional photographers for backdrops; with a light coating of wax, the cutouts are then affixed to a white display surface to create gallery-sized installations. Critics have applauded her rediscovery of cut paper, a medium virtually forgotten among fine artists since its use by Henri Matisse in the late 1940s, as well as her use of caricature in the tradition of the 18th-century British painter William Hogarth, the 19th-century French artist Honoré Daumier, and the 20th-century German-born American painter George Grosz. A 1997 exhibit "caus[ed] optical illusions," Robin Updike wrote for the *Seattle Times* (September 12, 1997, on-line), with her cutouts of tree branches "literally seem[ing] to be magically suspended in mid-air. And at first blush, the installation is sweet, quaint, even funny if you don't look too closely. Walker's work is a Rorschach test for everyone who takes the time to look. . . . She is intentionally apolitical and ambiguous about shame and blame. There is no political correctness in her work. White people are cruel, stupid, and morally mangled. Black people are lascivious, dim-witted, and casually violent. Everyone has an interest in bodily functions that would've impressed even the Marquis de Sade."

Walker first became widely known in 1994, when a 50-foot installation by her debuted in a solo exhibition at the Drawing Center, a New York City gallery. By 1997 the Whitney Museum of American Art, in New York City, had included her work in its Biennial exhibition, confirming her stardom. In the same year she participated in a group show at the Musée d'Art Moderne, in Paris, and received a John D. and Catherine T. MacArthur Foundation fellowship—a so-called "genius" award. Her work is in the permanent collections of the Whitney Museum and the Walker Art Center, in Minneapolis, Minnesota, among other venues.

"I knew that if I was going to make work that had to deal with race issues, they were going to be full of contradictions," Walker said in a 1999 interview for *Conversations with Contemporary Artists* (1999, on-line), a project of the Museum of Modern Art. "Because I always felt that it's really a love affair that we've got going in this country, a love affair with the idea of it [race], with the notion of major conflict that needs to be overcome, and maybe a fear of what happens when that thing is overcome—And, of course, these issues also translate into [the] very personal: Who am I beyond this skin I'm in?"

Kara Elizabeth Walker was born in Stockton, California, in 1969. As the daughter of an art professor, she started to draw with crayons virtually at the same time that she learned to walk. "I wanted to become an artist when I was about three, primarily because my father is also an artist—he's a painter. . . . Because of him I've gained a desire to have an imagination, which was never very easy for me . . . and was epitomized by being able to fantasize about traveling in time. But I could never really fully imagine myself doing that, because there was always some bit of brutality, some little hint of reality, that prevented me from getting very far," she said in the interview for *Conversations.*

When Walker was 13 she moved with her family to Stone Mountain, Georgia, the reputed birthplace of the Ku Klux Klan, as she told Lynn Gumpert for *Art News* (January 1997). There, for the first time, she encountered overt racism and, in her words, "Southern hospitality [in which a] layer of sweetness coats everything. But scratch beneath the surface . . ." In a conversation with her cousin, James Hannaham, published in *Interview* (November 1998), she described growing up in Georgia. "Sometimes simply hanging around with whites was bad enough to incite people. . . . There are times when you're friends with somebody or you're having a relationship, and you're not thinking about race for a brief moment. Then suddenly the entire history of the whole United States of America, or the American South, or post-Reconstruction comes crashing down on you. . . . At some point in Atlanta, I was with my boyfriend in the park, thinking we were alone, but when we got back to the car there was a flyer from the Ku Klux Klan, spelling out for him all the evils of black women, describing what sort of peril he was in, and identifying stereotypes of disease and moral degradation. That was an awakening for naive me. So I guess I needed a way to question how these types of issues have been represented in art previously."

In high school, and during the summers, she took college-level art courses at Georgia State University, where her father was chairman of the art department. "I was that kind of a nerd," she told Bonnie Rothman Morris for *Scholastic Update* (May 11, 1998). At the beginning of her studies at the Atlanta College of Art, race and history were not her focus. "I really avoided making any statement about race in the work, and I think I did that because of the environment I was in, and what other black people at the Atlanta College of Art . . . were doing. There was an essentialist rhetoric in their work that I thought wasn't right for me because, for some strange reason, I didn't take it seriously enough. That approach was too righteous to question itself," she told Hannaham. She earned a bachelor of fine arts degree from the Atlanta College of Art in 1991.

"When I was coming along in Georgia," she was quoted as saying in *Conversations*, "I became black in more senses than just the kind of multicultural acceptance that I grew up with in California. Blackness became a very loaded subject, a very loaded thing to be—all about forbidden passions and desires, and all about a history that's still living, very present . . . the shame of the South and the shame of the South's past; its legacy and its contemporary troubles. Race issues are always at the heart of these matters. And then I got interested in the ways that I almost wanted to aim to please . . . and fulfill these kinds of desires, these assumptions and associations with blackness, the [kind of] blackness that's exotic, animalistic, or savage; or noble and strong and forceful—worth putting on display, of something grander than grand," she explained.

Walker first began experimenting with explicit sexual images and black silhouette technique when she attended the Rhode Island School of Design, in Providence, where she received a master of fine arts degree in 1994. She uses the Victorian-era medium of paper-cut silhouettes subversively. "Initially sitters were of high social standing and the silhouette was marked by its chaste depictions of men in tail coats and top hats, ladies in hoopskirts and poke bonnets holding flowers. . . . Many women took it up as a handicraft, like needlepoint," Julia Szabo explained in the *New York Times Magazine* (March 23, 1997). But Walker's scenes parody antebellum American history, by presenting tableaux of so-called pickaninnies and mammies and slave masters and mistresses whose behavior exaggerates the racial clichés of sadism and hypersexuality. "We are drawn to the charm and whimsy of the design, and it is only after this initial seduction that the violence is thrust upon us," Karen Janovy, of the Sheldon Memorial Art Gallery and Sculpture Garden, observed in *Sheldon Selections.* Walker explained her aim in creating the silhouettes by saying, "The Master/slave narrative is expanded and inverted to include authoritarian control over children, the landscape, and the self."

The absence of detail in silhouette is part of what draws Walker to the technique. "It reflects my personality because it's a benign, quiet little form that can conceal a lot of ickiness. It leaves out a lot of information and requires the viewer to do some work . . . ," she was quoted as saying in *Scholastic Update.* "In keeping with a tradition of explorers and artists who made concrete images of historic events without having ever participated in them, I set out to document the journey. Only problem is that I am too aware of the role of my overzealous imagination interfering in the basic facts of history, so in a way my work is about the sincere attempt to write *Incidents in the Life of a Slave Girl* and winding up with [Kyle Onstott's sensationalistic 1957 novel] *Mandingo* instead," Walker told Updike.

Her interpretation of *Mandingo* would seem to come by way of the 15th–16th-century Dutch painter Hieronymous Bosch, whose works display an abundance of grotesque and bizarre images. "[Walker's] work has from the beginning featured images like a white woman in a poke bonnet and hoop skirt with the penis of a small black child in her mouth; a nude black woman vomiting human body parts, the remains of a white man lying, tellingly, nearby; and a smiling female field hand picking cotton while engaging in intercourse with a white master in hat and boots. What begins to take shape here is a tableau of subverted slavery-era icons," Szabo observed. Lynn Gumpert reported that Walker "was inspired by contemporary pulp-fiction novels set in the antebellum South that use steamy, interracial liaisons between slaves and their white masters." Walker elaborated: "My work is intended to function like Harlequin romance novels, which veil themselves in history and encourage women to participate in stories that are not in their best interests."

Esther Grisham, writing in *Art Papers* (May/June 1997) about a 1997 exhibit at the Renaissance Society, in Chicago, described Walker's watercolors as more intimate than her silhouettes, though the subjects are the same. Discussing the publication of her print *The Means to an End . . . A Shadow Drama in Five Acts*, in 1995, Walker said, "From left to right this suite of aquatints reads like the table of contents in a romantic novel: The Beginning, The Hunt, The Chase, The Plunge, The End. The remainder of the story is couched in polite silence—the kind of silence which harbors racism, distrust, fear, and intense and obsessive love."

"This is *Gone with the Wind* gone amok . . . ," Updike wrote about Walker's 1997 show at the Henry Art Gallery in Seattle, Washington. "Cotton plants, Spanish-moss-heavy tree limbs, hoop skirts, and barefoot slaves are straight out of the antebellum South," but "the stereotypes and mythologies remain a part of today's world." Updike noted that the pedophilia, bestiality, and "lynching and casual violence is rendered all the more horrific because of its cartoon-like presentation. A . . . girl seems to be floating casually to the ground . . . lynched by the bag she has just used to pick cotton." The exhibition was mounted along with a warning that its contents might not be suitable for all patrons. Walker had insisted that the flyer produced by the gallery to publicize the show resemble an ad for a 19th-century minstrel show; she herself wrote the copy, which stated that the exhibition was "Created Entirely By a Young Negress of Unusual Ability," and that "this female artisan is wont to illustrate lascivious subjects, miscegenation key among them, therefore, it is ill-advised for ladies & children to attend this exhibition." The gallery received a letter of protest from a museum member who found the flyer to be racist.

Other critics have responded to her parody differently. "Walker softens her blows by extending the campy historicism to herself: her announcement card identifies her as a 'Free Negress of noteworthy talent.' . . . But her explanation seems as true, and sick, as any . . . that slavery corrupted the humanity of all involved," Roberta Smith wrote in the *New York Times* (April 5, 1996), in a review of her exhibit at Wooster Gardens, a gallery in the Soho district of New York City. Julia Szabo detected "a central ambivalence in [Walker's] work: she seems to question and refute Southern mythology even as she conjures it, simultaneously celebrating and dashing it to the ground."

Walker's work prompted a letter-writing campaign in which many African-American artists, led by painter Betye Saar, protested her use of racist images. Two hundred letters were sent to the MacArthur Foundation asking it to withdraw the grant awarded to the artist in 1997. In an article for the *International Review of African American Art* (Volume 15, No. 2, 1998), Walker defended her work: "Still, racist icons, like resistant new strains of bacteria inhabiting the body, linger in our collective American minds . . . clearly intact enough to warrant further investigation." Nevertheless, she appreciated the viewpoint of those who are offended by the work, saying, as quoted by Franklin Cason in *New Art Examiner* (November 1999), "I can understand it, and I can't even really talk my way out of it. I can't say, 'Well, you shouldn't be offended.' Why not? It's a valid response, it's a valid way to feel." That sympathetic response notwithstanding, in the *International Review of African American Art*, she described her project as one that "[confronts] the viewer with the contradictory desires that s/he cannot bear to acknowledge. . . . You may be seduced, you may be outraged. Therein lay the unspeakable trappings of our visual codes."

The outcry spurred administrators of Harvard University's art center (which, in collaboration with the university's W.E.B. DuBois Center, was exhibiting some of Walker's artwork) to hold a symposium in March 1998 that focused on Walker and her work. Discussing the symposium and his approval of the Saar protest letters, Kelefa Sanneh wrote for the *International Review of African American Art* that the protests raised questions for "all of us—[art] dealers, museum directors—what kind of work are we supporting and encouraging? We need to stop, look, and understand . . . : Why is the phenomenon happening? . . . What does it mean about our time? . . . Why has someone risen so quickly using derogatory imagery? What is it about our society that embraces these images?"

Placing Walker's work in historical perspective, Franklin Cason pointed out in *New Art Examiner* (November 1999) that established artists of the Harlem Renaissance, such as Richard Wright, protested Zora Neal Hurston's irony in the novel *Their Eyes Were Watching God* "as little more than a minstrel show in comparison to the harsh social protest" of his own work. Cason appreciated the ambiguity he found in Walker's work, noting that "a political arena that falls back on the authenticity of racial experience and the assumption that black women's art equals the voice of a victim, makes Walker's [work] . . . even more disturbing and unconventional."

The controversy surrounding Walker's work is not its only characteristic to call to mind the Harlem Renaissance. "In a pop culture sense . . . , [blacks] are very hot. And that's good and bad, but a lot of it is market-driven," Peggy Cooper Cafritz, a member of the President's Committee on the Arts, observed to Szabo. White collectors are Walker's most enthusiastic patrons, as they were for many prominent artists and writers of the Harlem Renaissance, Zora Neal Hurston and Langston Hughes among them. Walker discussed this phenomenon when she was the first resident artist of the Capp Street Project at the California College of Arts and Crafts, in 1998: in an interview for *ArtScope.net* (on-line), Larry Rinder asked her, "How would you respond to the accusation, . . . made recently, that when 'white' institutions present work like yours they are essentially hanging out their own racism under the convenient cover of an African American artist? Do you feel used?" Walker responded, " I don't have a clear answer. Sure, maybe it's a possibility. Maybe white America is baring its racist soul through me as I [bare] my racist soul through it. Maybe that's not that bad. Because there are black artists and black thinkers talking about this issue which gives the work another element, which might be the social change element. We start to question our relation to the institution, how does it or doesn't it have power over us and how we see ourselves. It creates a whole new dialogue. Maybe that's the best we can get to now." Discussing the same topic with Julia Szabo, Walker said, "I guess it's a little bit daunting. . . . After a while I feel a bit like . . . Stepin Fetchit. To achieve success as an African-American, one must spill out one's guts constantly—like the old sharecropper in [Ralph] Ellison's *Invisible Man*, who raped his wife and daughter and kept telling his horrible story over and over, and the white people in town gave him things. He's an embarrassment to the educated blacks, and a fascination to the whites."

Miles Unger, writing in *Art New England* (June/July 1998), presented a defense of Walker's work that had its basis in the ideals of Aestheticism, which promoted "art for art's sake," meaning that no moral, political, or other value should impede an artist from realizing his or her vision. "Objections to Walker's works demonstrate a hostility to and willful misunderstanding of the nature of art, which must be permitted the irresponsibility of the interior of life unedited by decorum or good taste. This is not 'art with a message' in the usual sense. One would think that the bizarrely fantastical nature of Walker's work would free it from the type of political vetting to which history textbooks are subject, but the work still manages to offend those literalists for whom the fictive dimension of art does not exist. . . . Walker's gothic tales of violence and perversity do not claim to mirror the realities of the black experience, though. . . . Attacks on Walker's work conform to those launched by the radical right against art they consider offensive. Both camps refuse to distinguish between the social realm in which norms of civility must apply and the delinquency of the human heart that, as Freud pointed out, brooks no such constraints. Perhaps what her critics find so disturbing in her work is a certain joyfulness that revels in the bestial instead of delivering a stern moral message. But . . . an enlightened humanism, while acknowledging the need for restraint within the social context, will permit, and in fact encourage, the expression of those urges for which no other outlet is available."

Kara Walker is married to Klaus Bürgel, a German jewelry designer. When Hannaham asked if she had been harassed for marrying a German, she responded, "People are too polite to actually do that these days. They think it. And I know they think it, but it always gets more complicated. It's such a shame. Years ago I had a friend who was looking at some of my work, and just as an aside commented to me, 'I don't think white people have souls.' Meanwhile, I'm thinking about this great new guy I just started dating." Walker and Bürgel live with their two-year-old daughter, Octavia, in Providence, Rhode Island. — V.K.

Suggested Reading: *Art New England* p29+ June/July 1998; *International Review of African American Art* vol. 15, no. 2 1998, with photos; *Interview* p114+ Nov. 1998, with photos; *New York Times Magazine* p 49+ Mar. 23, 1997, with photo; *Seattle Times* (on-line) Sep. 12, 1997

Selected Works: *The End of Uncle Tom*, 1995; *The Means to an End . . . A Shadow Drama in Five Acts*, 1995; *Letter from a Black Girl*, 1998; *Negro History Minute*, 1998

Armando Gallo/Retna Ltd.

Warren, Diane

1957(?) Songwriter. Address: Realsongs, 6363 Sunset Blvd., Eighth Fl., Hollywood, CA 90028

"I want to write songs that people crank up on their car radios," the songwriter Diane Warren told David Hinckley for *ASCAP in Action* (Spring 1991, on-line). "I want to write part of the soundtrack to their lives." In her nearly two decades in the music industry, Warren has penned chart-topping hits for such celebrated singers and groups as Elton John, Toni Braxton, Kiss, and 98 Degrees. She wrote Aerosmith's first number-one single, "I Don't Want to Miss a Thing," from the film *Armageddon* (1998), and "If I Could Turn Back Time," a Top 10 hit that helped resurrect the singing career of the actress and pop star Cher in the late 1980s. In the latter half of the 1990s, she earned Academy Awards four years in a row. Occasionally dismissed by critics as having achieved a lot commercially but little artistically, Warren has acknowledged that her music leans toward sentimentality: "Corn is a pretty good crop," she observed to William Booth for the *Washington Post* (February 26, 1997). But she has also insisted that the emotions she has tried to project in her songs are very real. "I feel about songs the way [the filmmaker Steven] Spielberg said he felt about movies," she told David Hinckley. "He said he wanted to make movies he'd want to watch. I want to write songs I'd like to hear."

Diane Warren was born in about 1957 in Van Nuys, California, a suburb of Los Angeles, and grew up in the San Fernando Valley. "My family wasn't musical,"she told Hinckley, "but there was always music in the house. . . . By the time I was seven, I was aware of the rock 'n' roll my older sisters were playing. I loved the Beatles, so naturally I loved Lennon-McCartney. . . . It was all top 40 for me back then. . . . I was a lonely kid, and the radio was my friend." When she was 10, Warren's father, an insurance salesman, gave her a guitar. "I took lessons, and the teacher told my parents I was tone deaf," she recalled to Todd Gold for *People* (July 22, 1991). "I just didn't want to do the [expletive] scales. I wanted to make up my own little songs." By the time she was 14, Warren was writing several songs daily. She later came to regard all her early efforts as worthless.

As a teenager, Warren often felt like a misfit. "In school, I was the classic underachiever," she admitted to Hinckley. "I was always getting thrown out, and they'd tell my parents things like 'She's bright but she just doesn't use her head.' I could never understand why I had to do things I didn't care about, like gym. Why should I stand around and throw a ball? What was the point?" When she was 14, her father began sending demo tapes that she had made to Los Angeles publishers. "He was always tremendously supportive," she recalled on her Web site, *realsongs.com*; "he never stopped believing in me." Time and again, company reps told her that she had tremendous potential, but they would not make her an offer. "I grew to hate the word 'potential,'" she told Booth. "The word 'potential' never had a check attached to it. 'Potential' and the words 'some day,' I hated those words." She told Deborah Evans Price for *American Songwriter* (on-line), "In the beginning, it's hard to get anyone to take you seriously, if you don't have a track record. I struggled. I called people who didn't call me back. I knocked on doors that nobody answered, but that's the way it is." Finally, in 1982, the record producer Jack White asked her to write English lyrics to a French song. The result was "Solitaire"; recorded by the pop artist Laura Branigan, it became a Top 10 hit in 1983. "Laura was my first [cut]," Warren told Price. "I had some Japanese artists do some of my songs, but Laura was the first to start cutting my songs. That's when she started doing well. So that was kind of a break for me. Up until then I wasn't really making much money [from songwriting]." Two years later Warren composed "Rhythm of the Night" for the group DeBarge. The song became an international bestseller, climbing to number three on the pop charts and to number one on the adult-contemporary charts. Used in the soundtrack to *The Last Dragon* (1985), "Rhythm of the Night" also earned Warren a Golden Globe nomination for best original song in a film. "The thing about having a hit," she told Gold, "is that people become more willing to check you out, to listen."

In 1987 Warren founded Realsongs, a publishing company that handles her entire catalog of songs. "I became my own publisher because I was in a lawsuit, and I couldn't sign anybody," she told Price. "That kind of forced me to own my own publishing company, because no one was allowed to sign me or else they would have become part of the lawsuit. So the whole publishing company started kind of by accident." At present, Realsongs offers more than 600 songs; its catalog is highly regarded by music-industry insiders.

Warren wrote "I Get Weak," a 1987 Belinda Carlisle single, and the number-one hit "Nothing's Gonna Stop Us Now"; recorded by Starship for the film *Mannequin* (1987), the latter garnered her an Academy Award nomination for best original song. Among other Warren songs for feature films are the Joe Cocker–performed "When the Night Comes," for the Tom Selleck vehicle *An Innocent Man* (1989), and the smash hit "Give a Little Love," which Ziggy Marley sang for the Emilo Estevez comedy *Men at Work* (1990).

By 1990 Warren had written or co-written 18 Top 10 hits. That year she made history, when two of her songs—Milli Vanilli's "Blame It on the Rain" and Bad English's "When I See You Smile"—were number one and number two, respectively, on the *Billboard* charts. That feat was a first for a nonperforming songwriter, as well as for a female writer. Warren wrote six of the 10 titles on Michael Bolton's popular album *Time, Love & Tenderness* (1991). Earlier, she had collaborated with Bolton on his disc *Soul Provider* (1989), which includes "When I'm Back on My Feet Again," a song Warren had written in memory of her father. "I came into my office one day, thinking about my dad," she told Gold. "I just started playing the piano, and soon the tears were running down from my eyes. The song wrote itself." Bolton first heard the song when Warren played it for him over the phone. "When I finished, there was silence. So I said, 'Oh, you hated it.' But that wasn't it. He couldn't even talk because he related it to his father, too."

Warren continued to enjoy success throughout the 1990s, composing such hits as "Set the Night to Music" for Roberta Flack and "Don't Turn Around" for Ace of Base. The American Society of Composers, Authors, and Publishers (ASCAP) named her songwriter of the year in 1990, 1991, 1993, and 1997. In 1996 she wrote "Because You Loved Me" for the singer Celine Dion; another tribute to her father, it contains the lyrics "You were my strength when I was weak, / You were my voice when I couldn't speak. . . . / I'm everything I am because you loved me." Featured in the audience-pleasing romance *Up Close and Personal* (1996), which stars Michelle Pfeiffer and Robert Redford, "Because You Loved Me" soared to number one on the *Billboard* charts and earned Warren her second Academy Award nomination for best original song as well as a 1997 Grammy Award for best song written for a motion picture or TV. She later collaborated with Dion on "Because You Asked Me To," another number-one seller. Also in 1996 Warren wrote the ballad "Un-Break My Heart"; performed by Toni Braxton, it stayed at number one for 14 weeks, making it the second-longest-running single in *Billboard*'s history. "Un-Break My Heart" netted Braxton a Grammy for female pop vocal performance.

In April 1997, at Warren's request, the then 14-year-old country singer LeAnn Rimes recorded a demo tape of a song Warren had written for the action thriller *Con Air*, which was released later that year. A ballad called "How Do I Live," the song is about a woman who fears the loss of her loved one; according to Warren, the emotions conveyed in the lyrics reflect what she felt when she tried to imagine her life without music. *Con Air*'s producers, among them Jerry Bruckheimer, felt that Rimes's rendition was inadequate, but Rimes refused to try again. Ultimately, Bruckheimer hired Trisha Yearwood to record the version that was used in the film. Meanwhile, Rimes had recorded the song as a single, as did Yearwood, and during the summer of 1997, both renditions vied for air time on pop and country-music radio stations. "How Do I Live" remained on the *Billboard* charts for 69 consecutive weeks; Rimes's interpretation spent 11 weeks at number one on *Billboard*'s adult-contemporary chart and went double platinum. Rimes and Yearwood both received Grammy and Academy of Country Music nominations for song of the year. Warren's efforts, too, gained recognition: she earned a Grammy nomination for best song written for a motion picture and netted her third Oscar nomination.

In another Warren-Bruckheimer collaboration, the songwriter penned the sweeping ballad "I Don't Want to Miss a Thing" for the producer's epic *Armageddon* (1998), a tale of a group of roughneck drillers hired to destroy an asteroid hurtling towards Earth. The Boston-based hard-rock band Aerosmith recorded the song, despite their reservations that its sentimentality did not fit their image. Thanks in part to an aggressive ad campaign that connected the song and the film, "I Don't Want to Miss a Thing" became Aerosmith's first number-one single in the group's two-decade-long career. In addition, Mark Chestnutt's version of the song claimed the number-one spot on *Billboard*'s country charts. "I Don't Want to Miss a Thing" brought Warren another Academy Award nomination and an award from ASCAP for having a record number of songs by one writer performed in motion pictures. She received her fifth Oscar nomination for "Music of My Heart," from the film *Music of the Heart* (1999), starring Meryl Streep.

Warren routinely spends 12 hours a day composing in her cluttered Hollywood office. "Ideas and titles just pop into my head," she told Gold. "I've written songs on Kotex, lyrics on the palm of my hand. If I don't have a tape recorder, I'll call home and sing into my answering machine." Discussing her private life with Alanna Nash for *Good Housekeeping* (March 1998), she said, "I don't have that many friends. There's not enough balance in my life; I'm always writing. And if I'm not writing, I'm going, 'What do humans *do*?' It's like I can't even relax, except to go shopping. A good sale will make my day." When asked by Michael Laskow for *A&R Insider* (on-line) what drives her, she responded, "Hunger. The hunger is still there.

I think there are so many more heights to reach. I just want to keep getting better. I have a long way to go." — J.K.B.

Suggested Reading: *ASCAP in Action* p14+ Spring 1999, with photos; *Billboard* p45+ May 25, 1997, with photo; *Good Housekeeping* p26 Mar. 1998, with photo; *People* p60+ July 22, 1991, with photo; *Washington Post* D p1+ Feb. 26, 1997, with photo

Selected Songs: "Solitaire," 1983; "Rhythm of the Night," 1985; "I Get Weak," 1987; "Nothing's Gonna Stop Us Now," 1987; "Give a Little Love," 1988; "Look Away," 1988; "Blame it on the Rain," 1989; "If I Could Turn Back Time," 1989; "When I See You Smile," 1989; "When the Night Comes," 1989; "Don't Turn Around," 1992; "Because You Loved Me," 1996; "Unbreak My Heart," 1996; "How Do I Live," 1997; "I Don't Want to Miss a Thing," 1998; "Music of My Heart," 1999; "Painted on My Heart," 2000

Jeff Christensen/Archive Photos

Whitman, Meg

1957– CEO of eBay. Address: eBay Inc., 2125 Hamilton Ave., San Jose, CA 95125

Judging by the stock she owns in the multibillion-dollar on-line auction house eBay, which she heads, Meg Whitman is one of the richest chief executive officers on earth. In the five years since its launching, eBay, which describes itself as "the world's largest personal online trading company," has become one of the Internet's most popular sites. In 1999, during the week after Thanksgiving—traditionally, the beginning of the Christmas shopping season in the United States—more than seven million people visited eBay: on average, more than a million people a day. (Amazon.com, by contrast, recorded an average of 800,000 visitors daily, and Toys "R" Us, 300,000.) By the third quarter of 2000, eBay had some 19 million names on its list of registered users and had overseen millions of on-line auctions. On a typical day in October 2000, there were nearly four million items for sale in nearly 4,350 categories; the merchandise ranged from clothing and jewelry to computers and collectibles, most of it priced below $300. According to its Web site, "eBay is your place to find the stuff you want, to sell the stuff you have, and to make a few friends while you're at it!" After Whitman took command of the firm, in 1998, eBay went public, and the value of its stock increased 163 percent in its first day of trading. Recently, eBay announced the addition of 23 regional eBay sites in the U.S. (there are currently 52), for auctions of items whose appeal would most likely be limited to small geographic areas, such as cars, boats, and other hard-to-ship merchandise and sporting goods associated with local athletic franchises. "People are doing business in a way they really couldn't before," Whitman told Lisa Guernsey for the *New York Times* (September 22, 1999, on-line). "Out of this has grown a community."

The youngest of three children, Margaret C. Whitman was born in 1957 and raised in the affluent town of Cold Spring Harbor, on the North Shore of Long Island, New York. Her father, a businessman, often worked long hours, and she spent far more of her time with her mother, a full-time homemaker whom she has described as an adventurous free spirit. One summer her mother and a friend took their children—eight in all—on a three-month camping trip in Canada and Alaska. On mostly deserted highways, when it was clear that the children were getting restless after many hours on the road, Whitman's mother would have them run ahead of the camper while she and her friend followed closely behind. Sometimes tractor-trailers would slow down to ask if the women needed help. "You could always hear the hiss of the air brakes," Whitman told Laura M. Holson for the *New York Times* (May 10, 1999, on-line). "We finally put a sign on the back of the camper that said, 'We're OK.'"

Whitman entered Princeton University, in New Jersey, in 1974, with plans to pursue a career in medicine. She switched her major to economics after a summer job in which she sold advertising for a campus publication. After she graduated, in 1977, she entered the Harvard Business School, in Cambridge, Massachusetts, from which she earned an M.B.A. degree in 1979. She then moved to Cincinnati, Ohio, where she began working for the Procter & Gamble Co. in the area of brand management. In 1981, after her husband, Griffith R. Harsh IV, a neurosurgeon, landed a residency position at the University of California at San Francisco, the couple moved to California. There, the San Francisco–based consulting firm Bain & Col hired Whitman, with the title of vice president, and she remained there for eight years.

In 1989 Whitman took a job with the Walt Disney Co. For a while she served as the senior vice president of marketing at Disney's Consumer Products Division, where her responsibilities included developing a strategy for the company's entrance into book publishing. Whitman played an integral role in Disney's acquisition of *Discover* magazine. In 1992, after her husband became co-director of the Brain Tumor Center at Massachusetts General Hospital, in Boston, she left Disney to become president of the children's-shoe manufacturer Stride Rite, a division of the Stride Rite Corp., which also manufactures Keds and Sperry shoes.

In 1995 Whitman quit Stride Rite to take over as chief executive of Florists' Transworld Delivery (FTD), a federation of commercial florists. At FTD she suffered a lack of cooperation among people on her staff and among member florists who had strongly opposed the group's recent transformation into a privately held company. Moreover, FTD was grappling with increasingly intense competition from such Internet services as 1-800-Flowers and Florists.com. Feeling stymied, in 1997 Whitman resigned from FTD and joined Hasbro Inc., one of the country's biggest manufacturers of toys, games, and puzzles. She served as general manager of the profitable Playskool division, which markets juvenile equipment, such as highchairs, and such popular toys as Mr. Potato Head and the Teletubbies.

Earlier, in 1995, Pierre M. Omidyar had founded eBay, to provide an on-line site where his girlfriend (she is now his wife), who collected Pez candy dispensers, could easily sell to, buy from, trade with, and converse with other Pez-dispenser collectors. (The dispensers, whose design has changed periodically, come with plastic heads that depict such popular characters as Mickey Mouse and Kermit the Frog.) EBay's success has been credited to the opportunity it gives sellers to reach a vast number of potential customers, the chance it gives buyers to learn about and view merchandise from all over the world, and the community atmosphere the site has fostered. The site enables people to communicate with others who share their interests; some have even married after meeting through eBay. "We are pioneering something that is entirely new," Whitman told Martha Mendoza for the Associated Press, as reported in the *Kansas City Star* (June 3, 1999, on-line). "What's fascinating is the impact we have had on the community"—"a new community with commerce, social interaction and teamwork," as she described it.

In 1997 eBay began a search for someone to preside over the company, which is based in California's Silicon Valley. Robert Kagle, a partner in Benchmark Capital, a major eBay investor, explained to Laura Holson that in the list of qualifications for the job, "understanding technology was not the central ingredient. You have to get the emotional component of the customer experience in your gut." When a headhunter hired by eBay contacted Whitman, she was seeking neither a new job nor a career change, and she expressed no interest in the position. But Kagle persuaded her to visit eBay's modest San Jose offices, to witness the day-to-day operations of the company. During her short stay in Silicon Valley, Whitman heard the testimonials of users who felt so enthralled by eBay that they would sneak out of business meetings "to monitor their auctions," as Holson wrote. In March 1998, after several months of reflection, Whitman accepted eBay's job offer and moved with her husband and two sons to California. "I thought something was very right here," she explained to Holson. "They had touched a consumer nerve."

For some time Omidyar had been eager to have eBay go public, and immediately after her arrival, Whitman began preparing the company for its initial public stock offering (IPO). Toward that end, she hired Brian Swette, who had directed marketing at Pepsi, to oversee eBay's fledgling marketing division. In addition, she brightened the design of eBay's Web pages and "walled off all firearm and pornography auctions in separate, age-restricted sites," as Daniel Roth reported in *Fortune* (July 5, 1999). (EBay has since banned auctions of firearms and has also prohibited sales of tobacco, drugs, alcohol, animals, and body parts [such as kidneys and other organs sought for transplantation].) On September 24, 1998 the company offered 3.5 million shares at $18 apiece; by the end of the day, the value of each share had jumped to $47.1875, an increase of 163 percent. The event made Whitman very rich. It also turned her into an exceedingly high-profile CEO. Soon, thanks to advertising and the buzz generated by the IPO, eBay's list of registered users included some three million names.

In January 1999, after a minuscule number of winning bidders complained that sellers had misrepresented their merchandise or failed to send it, eBay announced that it had taken measures to protect users from fraud. In what it labeled a "comprehensive trust and safety program," eBay arranged with the British insurance company Lloyd's of London to insure, free of charge to the customer, purchases costing up to $200. "We will cooperate very aggressively with law enforcement to help investigate, identify, prosecute, and convict people who commit fraud on eBay," Whitman told *Bloomberg News*, as reported by the *New York Times* (January 16, 1999, on-line). In addition, the company instituted a mechanism whereby, for a fee of $5, sellers could obtain what amounted to a stamp of approval from Equifax, one of the nation's largest credit bureaus.

Also in early 1999, Whitman hired Sun Microsystems to maintain eBay's network, so as to prevent recurring eBay Web-site outages, a problem that had plagued the company in January of that year. In addition, Whitman increased eBay's engineering staff by 75 percent and hired Mark Ryan, formerly an IBM network troubleshooter, as eBay's chief technology officer. She also ordered the creation of a $10 million backup system, consisting of duplicate sets of hardware and software, which would take over if the main server were to shut down. Although the number of outages has diminished markedly, problems with the company's 24-hour Internet service persist—a situation that reportedly does not surprise eBay network-support engineers, in light of the continually swelling ranks of users.

In late April 1999 Whitman announced that eBay had purchased Butterfield & Butterfield Auctioneers Corp. for $260 million. Described by Saul Hansell in the *New York Times* (April 27, 1999) as "San Francisco's largest auction house," the 134-year-old, privately held fine-arts auction house would reportedly operate as an eBay subsidiary. "We felt we could accelerate our entry into higher-end price points, which means from $500 to $5,000 or $10,000, with a well-established, real-world expert," Whitman told Tim Clark for *CNET News.com* (April 27, 1999, on-line). "We will combine our proven online expertise with their expertise in higher-priced merchandise as well as their value-added services. Things like authentication and appraisals are important for this market. Butterfield & Butterfield also brings a long history of relationships both domestically and internationally with dealers, other auction houses, and higher-end buyers and sellers that we think can jump-start our entry into this market." The acquisition of B&B was in part a response to increased competition from such Internet giants as Amazon.com and Yahoo!, both of which had recently launched their own on-line auction services. Shortly after Whitman's announcement of the B&B purchase, the price of eBay stock rose. "There are only so many Beanie Babies and old records you can sell," Sara Zeilstra, an analyst with the investment bank Warburg Dillon Read, told Sandeep Junnarkar for *CNET News.com* (April 26, 1999, on-line). "It really is a volume-driven business, and moving into higher-priced items is what is needed. . . . I think it is a step in the right direction for eBay to move into much more fine arts and higher-priced antiques."

At the end of the third fiscal quarter of 1999, eBay reported 7.7 million users, almost 40 percent more than were registered the previous quarter. Gross merchandise sales—the amount that changed hands in all sales on the site—had risen to $741 million, up from $195 million the year before, and the company was handling more than 90 percent of sales conducted in on-line auctions. "Our core group of sellers is intact and doing increasing business on eBay," Whitman told *Bloomberg News*, according to *CNET News.com* (October 27, 1999). But eBay faces ever-increasing competition; as Whitman put it to Holson, "There is a constant roar. The challenge is to reorganize your business every three months." Among eBay's newest rivals is Sothebys.Amazon.com, a joint venture of the traditional, 225-year-old British auction house Sotheby's and Amazon.com that started up in the second half of 1999.

Not surprisingly in light of the huge volume of merchandise auctioned on eBay, the company has become embroiled in controversies connected with some items, such as Nazi memorabilia. "Is it really necessary for eBay to market a Nuremberg Rally flag and other items which glorify the horrors of Nazi Germany?" Rabbi Abraham Cooper, an associate dean at the Simon Wiesenthal Center, a leading Jewish human-rights organization, said to a Reuters reporter, as quoted on *CNET News.com* (November 30, 1999, on-line). In response to Cooper's complaint, Kevin Pursglove, an eBay spokesperson, told the Reuters reporter, "We expect eBay users to adhere to the policy and guidelines of the country in which they are living. It is not our role to police compliance." Pursglove also said, "From the beginning, our community was built up around the idea of being a venue where people can trade virtually anything and sometimes that freedom allows the listing of particular items that may offend people."

In mid-November 1999 eBay announced the promotion of Brian Swette to chief operating officer, with responsibility for the main eBay site and the regional sites, user services, and customer support. "It looks like [Whitman] is relinquishing some of her responsibilities because she's out on the road all the time promoting the company and talking to people," David Zale, an analyst with the investor advisers Sands Brothers & Co., told *Bloomberg News*, as reported by *CNET News.com* (November 17, 1999, on-line).

Steve Westly, eBay's current vice president of marketing and business development, described Whitman to Martha Mendoza as "relentlessly optimistic." According to Mendoza, "Whitman takes . . . problems in stride. People who work with her say her ability to stay focused and positive sets her apart from most executives." "Virtually all of my time is dedicated to eBay and my family," Whitman told Mendoza. "It's a wonderful life." On December 15, 1999 eBay stock was selling for about $155 a share, making Whitman's worth—on paper—about $1.1 billion. At the beginning of November 2000, eBay's stock price was $54 a share, still enough to rank Whitman with the wealthiest Americans. — M.B.

Suggested Reading: *Business Week* p134+ May 31, 1999, with photo; *businessjournal.net* (on-line) July 7, 1999, with photo; *CNET News.com* (on-line); *Fortune* p81+ July 5, 1999, with photo; *Kansas City Star* (on-line) June 3, 1999; *New York Times* (on-line) Jan. 16, 1999, Feb. 19, 1999, May 10, 1999, with photos, Sep. 22, 1999, with photos; *Traffic World* p28 Apr. 26, 1999

Bob Galbraith/Associated Press

Wigand, Jeffrey
(WYE-gand)

1943(?)– Educator; organization official; former business executive. Address: c/o du Pont Manual High School, 120 W. Lee St., Louisville, KY 40208-1999

Before 1993 Jeffrey Wigand led a conventional life. He held a comfortable job as vice president of scientific research at the Brown & Williamson (B&W) tobacco company; he was married, with two daughters; and he was optimistic about achieving his dream of becoming a company CEO. But with the termination of his project at B&W and his subsequent firing, Wigand's life changed dramatically. Upon learning that his former boss had testified in a congressional hearing that nicotine was not—to their knowledge—addictive, he agreed to help the Food and Drug Administration (FDA) investigate the enhancement of nicotine's addictiveness by tobacco companies and to give a deposition in a Mississippi case against so-called Big Tobacco. "I believe the industry as a whole is flagrantly deceptive and dishonest," Wigand told Elizabeth Gleick for *Time* (March 11, 1996). "It says one thing and does another, and I think the public needs to know that." Most famously, in the fall of 1994, Wigand agreed to reveal all he knew about the tobacco industry in an interview with the long-running CBS news program *60 Minutes*. Wigand, the highest-ranking tobacco-industry executive ever to become a whistle-blower, was threatened anonymously and sued by his former employers for his actions, while his family was torn apart. Meanwhile, worried about the possibility of a lawsuit, CBS ordered *60 Minutes* not run the interview, prompting derision from all sides in the media, and Wigand became the target of a smear campaign engineered by B&W. In February 1995 the saga came to an end, when CBS finally aired Wigand's interview. Thanks in part to Wigand's whistle-blowing, the FDA was able to get information necessary for regulating tobacco; in addition, his action enabled states to successfully sue tobacco companies for medical costs incurred in treating smoking-related illnesses. In the midst of those highly publicized events, Wigand began a second career, as a teacher. He is also the founder of the organization Smoke-Free Kids.

Jeffrey Wigand was born in about 1943, probably in New York City, judging from Elizabeth Gleick's reference to his Bronx accent. He earned a bachelor's degree in chemistry and master's and Ph.D. degrees in biochemistry from the University of Buffalo, in New York. He then held jobs at several medical and pharmaceutical firms, among them Pfizer and Johnson & Johnson. He also worked at Biosonics, a manufacturer of medical devices based in Mount Laurel, New Jersey.

In January 1989 Wigand, working toward his dream of becoming a company CEO, was named vice president of scientific research at Brown & Williamson, based in Louisville, Kentucky. There, his main task was to develop a safer kind of cigarette, one that was nontoxic and fire-retardant. However, the project was dropped, and not long afterward, in March 1993, Wigand was fired. He would later claim that the company had never been serious about the project and had destroyed any evidence that it had ever existed. Upon being let go, Wigand signed a separation agreement with Brown & Williamson that gave him two years of severance pay and covered his family's health care—which was especially important for the Wigands, since their daughter Rachel had a birth defect known as spina bifida (an incomplete closure of the spinal column), which required expensive daily medical treatments. Central to the agreement was a confidentiality clause. In September 1993 B&W sued Wigand for revealing the details of his separation agreement to an employee about to leave the company. As a result, Wigand's severance pay and health benefits were suspended. In a settlement in November of that year, Wigand reluctantly signed a more restrictive confidentiality agreement.

In February 1994 Wigand was called to testify as part of a Justice Department investigation of the tobacco industry's efforts to develop fire-safe cigarettes. At the hearing, he denied that his former employers had committed any wrongdoing or falsification. Concurrently, in a Massachusetts case against the cigarette manufacturer Philip Morris, Wigand submitted an affidavit that contradicted his testimony. Eventually, the judge in the case ruled that Wigand could not testify without breaking his confidentiality agreement and would not be allowed to appear as a witness.

At about the same time, Lowell Bergman, the producer of *60 Minutes*, was working on a story regarding Philip Morris's reported development—and later abandonment—of a fire-safe cigarette. After receiving 800 to 1,000 pages of confidential Philip Morris documents, Bergman received a tip that Wigand, who was still living in Louisville, could help him better understand the material. Bergman repeatedly called Wigand, who refused to come to the telephone, perhaps out of fear of breaking his agreement with B&W. One night Bergman finally reached Wigand and told him that he would be sitting in the lobby of the Seelbach Hotel at 11 a.m. the next day, reading the *New York Times*. Wigand met Bergman and agreed to come on board for the project as a consultant. For his help, Wigand was paid $12,000.

During this time tobacco company executives, including Wigand's former boss, Thomas Sandefur, appeared before a congressional committee and swore that to their knowledge nicotine was not addictive. As a result of the testimony, which Wigand believed to be false, he agreed to help the FDA find evidence that tobacco companies were enhancing the addictive qualities of cigarettes. Thanks to Wigand's help, the FDA was able to compile thousands of pages demonstrating that cigarettes were intended primarily as nicotine delivery systems. Wigand was also called to testify in various government investigations of tobacco companies. This progress in the fight to expose misconduct came at a steep price for Wigand, who began to receive threatening phone calls. In one, Wigand reported, he was told, "Don't mess with tobacco." In another he was warned to "leave tobacco alone or else you'll find [your] kids hurt. They're pretty girls now." Wigand's family was given FBI protection, and Wigand took to traveling with security guards.

Soon, Wigand told *60 Minutes* that when his severance pay ended, in March 1995, he would be interested in publicly revealing what he knew about tobacco. Because Wigand was nervous, and his wife even more so, about being sued if Wigand appeared before the camera, CBS agreed to indemnify Wigand for libel as long as his statements on television were true. Although CBS refused to cover him in the event of a suit over the breach of his confidentiality agreement, Wigand's lawyer maintained that an airing of the proposed segment would be taken as an agreement to protect Wigand in such a situation. In August, Wigand and his wife decided in favor of recording the interview. To allay the couple's fears, Bergman promised in writing that the completed segment would not air unless they agreed to it.

In the actual interview, conducted by *60 Minutes*'s star correspondent, Mike Wallace, Wigand stated that the tobacco company bosses had perjured themselves when they testified that nicotine was nonaddictive. Furthermore, he said that the main purpose of a cigarette, in the view of tobacco companies, was to serve as a deliverer of nicotine, which would result in addiction—and greater cigarette sales. Wigand also revealed that Brown & Williamson knowingly kept an additive known as cumarin in its pipe tobacco, despite the fact that the substance is known to cause liver tumors in lab mice. He said that when he was with B&W, he had wanted such information to go "out [to the public] immediately, and I was told it would affect sales, and I was to mind my own business." Wigand added that the amount of cumarin that was used was at "a hundredfold the safety level." In regard to his former job as developer of a safer cigarette, Wigand said that his former boss, Sandefur, had told him, "If we pursue a safer cigarette, it would put us at extreme exposure with every other product. I don't want to hear about it anymore."

Following the interview, CBS executives set up a series of meetings with the *60 Minutes* staff regarding the legal ramifications of running the story. The group examined, among other things, a recent ABC exposé about Philip Morris Inc., which had cost that network $15 million in lawsuits and resulted in ABC's making an official apology. Eventually, Ellen Kaden, general counsel for CBS, and the CBS executives decided that the story involved too many legal risks and ordered *60 Minutes* not to run it, despite the strenuous objections of Bergman and Mike Wallace. "The ABC lawsuit did not chill us as journalists from doing the story," Wallace said later, as quoted in the *Columbia Journalism Review* (January/February 1996). "It did chill the lawyers, who with due diligence had to say, 'We don't want to, in effect, risk putting the company out of business.'"

The *New York Times* broke the story on November 9, 1995, stating on page one, "CBS's lawyers have ordered the news program *60 Minutes* not to broadcast a planned on-the-record interview with a former tobacco company executive who was harshly critical of the industry." Many in the press cited CBS's imminent sale to Westinghouse as a possible reason for the decision; a lawsuit might have prevented the sale, from which Eric Ober, the president of CBS News, and Kaden stood to profit handsomely. On the date when the interview with Wigand was supposed to air, CBS instead ran a segment on how tobacco companies were able to withhold information from the public. Wigand appeared on screen only briefly, unidentified and with his face obscured. At the end of the segment, Mike Wallace expressed dissatisfaction with the CBS management's handling of the episode. Soon, however, the entire interview was leaked from CBS to the New York *Daily News*. Such CBS News luminaries as Dan Rather and Andy Rooney publicly chastised the network for its action. Wallace said, as quoted in *Reason* (February 1996), "It's the first time that we really feel . . . let down by my company."

After the *Daily News* printed the article, CBS decided to cover Wigand in case of a breach-of-contract suit. The day after that decision was announced, B&W filed a complaint in the State Court of Kentucky charging Wigand with breach of contract, theft, and fraud. Wigand was given a temporary restraining order, meant to prevent him from providing any other information about B&W. However, Wigand was already scheduled to give a deposition on November 29 in a case against Mississippi tobacco manufacturers, and a Mississippi judge, maintaining that the Kentucky ruling had no bearing in Mississippi, ordered him to do so. At the deposition, Wigand was questioned on the addictive nature of nicotine and the possible falsification of tobacco records.

Meanwhile, Brown and Williamson lawyers were spending millions of dollars in an attempt to discredit Wigand. Despite the fact that Wigand had received favorable performance ratings while working there, they claimed that he was "a Jekyll and Hyde personality" and that his history revealed "a pattern of lies." Calling into question Wigand's temperament, they buttressed their case with information from Jack Paller, the CEO of Biosonics, who stated that Wigand had been fired from that company for verbally abusing other employees. Wigand's lawyers countered that Wigand had left because he felt that a Biosonics product was not being represented accurately to the FDA in terms of its efficiency and that he had blown the whistle to the FDA upon leaving. Inquiries into the situation revealed that the FDA had been called to investigate a certain product but had found nothing wrong with it. Richard O'Leary, a psychologist who had worked with Wigand in the 1980s at E. Merck Diagnostic Systems, came to his friend's defense. O'Leary told Elizabeth Gleick that while Wigand tended to speak his mind bluntly and was often impatient, O'Leary had "never known him to cross the line into abusive behavior."

Seeking to call Wigand's character into question further, B&W lawyers also revealed that in 1993 his wife had filed a spousal abuse charge against him (which was later dropped) and that he had sought counseling in order to control his anger. In addition, they contacted Wigand's ex-wife for information and attempted to find his daughter by his first marriage. The company even accused Wigand of shoplifting. Richard Scruggs, one of Wigand's lawyers, stated in *Time* (February 12, 1996), "You may notice that very few of the allegations they have made have anything to do with his work at B&W. Wigand is a regular guy with regular-guy problems in life." "I don't think anyone is as pure as the driven snow," Wigand told Elizabeth Gleick. "They've distorted the truth. It's not different from what they've done traditionally." Although most of the charges were brushed off by both Wigand's lawyers and the media as exaggerated or downright false, Wigand's testimony in 1994, in which he swore before federal investigators that Brown & Williamson was innocent of any wrongdoing, was taken more seriously. "You have to remember," Richard Scruggs pointed out in a defense of his client, as reported in the *New York Times* (February 6, 1996), "that Jeffrey was out of work and had just been sued by the company. If he committed perjury, then they obstructed justice. He was prepped by their lawyers and instructed what to say." Brown & Williamson executives denied having had such control over Wigand's deposition.

Meanwhile, the stress of the case, coupled with financial insecurity, the threats against the Wigand household, and the unrelenting media coverage of the events, caused tremendous strife in Wigand's family. Upon leaving the tobacco company, Wigand went from a $300,000-a-year job to one that paid just over $30,000: a post as a science teacher at du Pont Manual High School, a magnet school in Louisville. (The U.S. and Kentucky departments of education have cited du Pont as a "school of excellence.") Although many in the tobacco-friendly area were reluctant to support Wigand, Barbara Fendly, Wigand's supervisor at du Pont and the wife of a tobacco farmer, told Elizabeth Gleick, "Not all of us agree with what [Wigand] is doing. But we all support his right to do what he thinks is right. We're bigger than Brown & Williamson." Wigand's wife, Lucretia, began working nights at a clothing store to help supplement the family income. But the strain eventually proved too much for her, and she left her husband in late January 1996. In the resulting divorce case, she won custody of the couple's two daughters. (Their daughter Rachel's health has reportedly improved since then.)

In February 1996 CBS finally allowed the Wigand interview to air, a decision that was helped by the *Wall Street Journal*'s running their own story on Wigand's claims, thus easing CBS's liability. Ironically, CBS's original decision not to run the story had kept it in the news and brought Wigand's revelations more attention than they might have received otherwise. As filmmaker Michael Mann told *Entertainment Weekly* (November 12, 1999), "It became a bigger media event than if they had just let it air. I thought, 'These people [at CBS and at tobacco companies] have just been recast as corporate villains, and they don't know it.'"

Mann, who thought that Wigand's story would make a good film, based his project on an article on Wigand in *Vanity Fair* (May 1996). Mann cast Russell Crowe as Jeffrey Wigand and Al Pacino as Lowell Bergman. The film, *The Insider*, was released in November 1999 and became one of the most critically lauded movies of the year, nominated for seven Academy Awards, including best picture and best actor (for Crowe's performance). Although Wigand admitted that the film took several creative liberties with actual events, he approved of it overall. "I have to say," he told *Entertainment Weekly*, "[the film] goes directly to some interesting times. It's emotionally wrenching, but it gets to the tone, the tenor of the times." "I've been 100 percent vindicated," he added. "The movie is just the icing on the cake. Are there scars? . . . Yeah. Are their reflections? Yes. Do I dwell on them? No. I have to do something else. And it's time to move on."

In addition to his teaching, Wigand now runs an organization called Smoke-Free Kids. In looking back over the events of the past few years, he said, as quoted in an on-line piece for *Frontline*, "I had what I would consider some moral compass issues that I was dealing with in terms of what principle do I need . . . is my guiding principle here? And I wanted to get the truth out. I wanted to make sure it got out. I felt that the industry as a whole had defrauded the American public. And there were things that I felt needed to be said." Wigand has been honored as teacher of the year in Kentucky. "One day recently," Elizabeth Gleick wrote, "he was darting about the dingy science classroom at du Pont Manual High School in Louisville, Kentucky, like a gnome on triple espresso, questioning and wisecracking in his rapid-fire Bronx rasp as 30 ninth-grade advanced physical-science students went over results of field research." "I make a difference [teaching]," Wigand told Gleick. "I feel good at the end of the day." — G.O.

Suggested Reading: *Columbia Journalism Review* p39+ Jan./Feb. 1996; *Entertainment Weekly* p35+ Nov. 12, 1999; *New York Times* A p17 Feb. 6, 1996; *Reason* p42+ Feb. 1996; *Time* p54 Feb. 12, 1996, p54+ Mar. 11, 1996, with photos; *Vanity Fair* p196+ May 1996, with photos

---

Ed Geller/Retna Ltd.

Williamson, Kevin

Mar. 14, 1965– Film director; producer; screenwriter. Address: c/o Writers Guild of America West, 7000 W. Third St., Los Angeles, CA 90048

"Fear is the greatest motivator—not being able to pay your bills, having the phone cut off," Kevin Williamson told an interviewer for *Entertainment Weekly* (June 27, 1997). "Those were the fears that pushed me to write *Scream*." Williamson no longer has such fears: *Scream*, which premiered in 1996, was a phenomenal success. By September 1998, as Robert La Franco reported in *Forbes* (September 21, 1998), that film and his next three efforts—*I Know What You Did Last Summer* and *The Faculty*, for which he wrote the scripts, and *Scream 2*, which he both wrote and produced—had grossed more than $500 million, and Williamson had become a multimillionaire.

Funny as well as uncommonly scary, *Scream* both parodies and pays homage to *Nightmare on Elm Street*, *Friday the 13th*, *Halloween*, and other spine chillers that Williamson loved as a teen. The characters in *Scream* have watched slasher videos countless times and know every convention of the form: for example, as soon as a character leaves the house to search the backyard, the killer will enter the house; virgins usually survive, while "bad" young women don't; when a character says he'll be right back, he probably won't. *Scream* earned more than six times its production cost; indeed, it made such an impact that Williamson was credited with singlehandedly reviving the horror flick's carcass. He has affected television fare, too: thanks to his efforts as creator and executive producer during the maiden season of the series *Dawson's Creek*, he is said to have breathed new life into the genre of teen-oriented drama.

Kevin Williamson was born in New Bern, North Carolina, on March 14, 1965 and raised in Oriental, a town on the state's intercoastal waterway. He lived in "a big trailer on a creek," as he recalled on his Web site, along with his father, Wade, a shrimp-and-scallop fisherman; mother, Faye; and older brother, John. "I had wonderful parents," he told Jeffrey Epstein for the *Advocate* (August 1999, on-line), "and they always provided. I always got what I needed." During the occasional times when funds were low, Williamson and his brother would help out by mowing lawns, pumping gas, and baby-sitting.

When Williamson was about nine or 10, his mother gave him a typewriter for his birthday. The gift immediately inspired him to write. "In fifth grade I wrote the sequel to *Jaws*," he related on TNT's *Rough Cut* (on-line). "I was gonna outdo Peter Benchley [who wrote the novel *Jaws*]. I wrote it in like this 30-page spiral notebook. I would pass it around school. It got to the point where everyone was coming up to me and asking, can I check out your book? So I literally would check it out like the library." The book also got him into trouble, he said, because "there was some racy stuff. . . . I had a little sex scene." His writing caused even more of a stir later, at Pamlico County High School (near New Bern), when he wrote a story about date rape for an English assignment and read it to the class. "Date rape wasn't a real big deal at the time . . . ," he said during an interview posted on *Jam!* (on-line). "[The teacher] stopped me halfway through, ripped it up in my face and just said 'Sit down.' She almost sent me to the principal's office because she thought it was so out of line . . . and I thought it was some of my finest work. Then she said, 'You'll never be a writer. Your voice shouldn't be heard. And I don't know why you even want to try this writing thing, you're from the sticks of North Carolina, you can't speak and you're illiterate and this is proof.'" Williamson has since speculated that the teacher acted as she did because she was a frustrated writer herself; putting a positive spin on the incident, he told *Jam!*, "I [eventually] realized that all these negative messages this woman sent to me, . . . paralyzing me with crippling fear, could ultimately be a catalyst."

In a *TV Guide* interview reprinted on his Web site, Williamson recalled that in high school he "went from crowd to crowd. I hung out with the smokers. I hung out with the in-crowd. I hung out with the A students." He added, "I am really glad I did because now I have such a huge filing cabinet of information" to draw upon for stories. Friends from his high-school years remember Williamson's sense of the absurd and his off-beat humor. He spent a lot of his leisure time in front of the television—by his own admission, he was addicted to the medium—or at the movies, despite having to travel 25 miles from his home to the nearest theater. He especially loved *Jaws* and other films by Steven Spielberg, whom he came to idolize. He eagerly awaited each new installment of the adventures of *Halloween*'s Michael Myers, *Friday the 13th*'s Jason Voorhees, *Nightmare on Elm Street*'s Freddy Krueger, and other evildoers. "A scary movie is a roller coaster ride," he told a reporter for CNN (on-line). "So it sort of hits all the buttons. You get to laugh. You get to jump. You get to scream." Offering an explanation for the special appeal of such films to teens, he said, "It's about fear. You know, as teenagers, we're so afraid. And there's something very primal about a scary movie. And there's something very primal about being a teenager. And so I think there's a little connection there."

The movie that most impressed the teenage Williamson was *Halloween*, starring Jamie Lee Curtis. On his Web site Williamson recalled, "*Halloween* was my revelation. I already knew my love of movies was bordering obsessive, but I had no idea of how fixated I was until the experience of *Halloween*. The movie frightened me beyond belief. . . . There were moments when I would forget to breathe because I was so wrapped up in the moment. When Jamie Lee screamed, I screamed. When she ran, I ran. I can vividly remember pounding my feet on the floor as she raced across the street trying to escape the clutches of Michael [Myers]." Williamson returned to see the movie repeatedly. "I'd go by myself and would have to sneak in because it was R-rated. I'd pay to see some bogus movie playing on the screen next door, then jump the velvet ropes. I would sit in the middle of the crowd and just watch the participation. I watched as men and women screamed at the screen, yelling and coaxing the characters on. . . . I knew from that first screening that I wanted to affect people like that."

Following his high-school graduation, having tried unsuccessfully to win a scholarship to film school, Williamson enrolled at East Carolina University, in Greenville, North Carolina, where he studied drama and earned a bachelor's degree in theater arts. In 1987 he moved to New York City to pursue an acting career. He landed a small part on the NBC soap opera *Another World* but little other work in the field. To support himself, he took temporary jobs as a waiter or word processor. Although he liked New York, he has described this period of his life as bleak and discouraging.

In 1991 Williamson moved to Los Angeles, where a music-video director hired him as an assistant. Dissatisfied with his job, he borrowed money from a friend to take a screenwriting course at the University of California at Los Angeles (UCLA). While in the class, he wrote the script for *Killing Mrs. Tingle*, which follows several teenagers as they exact revenge on a hated teacher. Thanks to the efforts of a friend of Williamson's, a literary agent agreed, as a favor, to represent Williamson and soon sold the *Mrs. Tingle* script to Interscope. Williamson's elation turned to frustration when Interscope replaced him with its own writers; moreover, the company never filmed it. (Years later Williamson himself directed *Killing Mrs. Tingle*, using his own script. The picture arrived in theaters in August 1999 with the title *Teaching Mrs. Tingle*. Without exception, critics panned the film.)

Williamson had received payment for the rights to his *Mrs. Tingle* script, and he used a lot of it to pay off student loans and buy a new car. After the money ran out, he went on unemployment. When his benefits were exhausted, he got a loan from a friend. While house-sitting for that friend one night in 1995, Williamson watched a Barbara Walters TV special about the murders of five college students by a serial killer in Gainesville, Florida, in 1990. The story, he has recalled, as quoted on the CNN Web site, "was scary as hell and was really spooking me. The idea that this man was stalking and killing these college kids in this small, unsuspecting town was very frightening. It reminded me of *Halloween*." A sudden noise and his discovery of an open window in another room unnerved him. ("I don't do well in scary situations," he acknowledged.) "With a butcher knife in one hand and a cordless phone in the other," he continued, "I called my buddy David (who now works with me) and made him talk to me while I searched the house over." But rather than reassuring him, David "kept trying to scare me over the phone, saying things like 'Freddy's gonna get you,' and 'Michael's behind you,' and 'Kill, kill, kill, ha, ha, ha. . .' Before you know it, we were arguing over which killer was scarier and what horror movie worked best. . . . We started quizzing each other with our movie knowledge. Thus, *Scary Movie* [*Scream*'s original title] was born. . . . I went home and started outlining a movie in my head." He reportedly completed the screenplay in three days.

Williamson's agent loved the script, and within two days a bidding war had started among several major studios, including Morgan Creek, Paramount, and Miramax. Run by Bob and Harvey Weinstein, Miramax had just opened a new branch, called Dimension Films, which the Weinsteins said could begin work on the film immediately. Wanting his new screenplay to avoid the fate of *Killing Mrs. Tingle*, Williamson agreed to a deal, even though Miramax had not been the highest bidder. Wes Craven, whose credits include the first *Nightmare on Elm Street* film, was hired to direct. "Wes gave [the movie] its tone," Williamson has said. "He brought it to life with a perverse wickedness and I'm forever grateful." Co-starring Neve Campbell, Drew Barrymore, Courtney Cox, David Arquette, and Skeet Ulrich, *Scream* opened during the 1996 Christmas season, and within six months the movie, which had cost $15.3 to produce, had brought in more than $103 million in box-office receipts. One representative review, from *Entertainment Weekly* (January 10, 1997), called *Scream* "the first teen horror movie comparable to both *Psycho* and *Clueless*" and predicted that "anyone who has ever shuddered into their popcorn at the sight of a kitchen knife dripping Karo-syrup blood will have a fine time." In light of its cleverness, high fright quotient, humor, and extraordinary popularity, Williamson was credited with single-handedly resuscitating the teen horror movie. He himself has expressed reservations about that idea. "Everyone talks about how the horror movie's been revived," he said in an interview for *Rough Cut* (January 15, 1998, on-line). "But I don't know if it is or not. I was that filmgoer who was so sick . . . of those scary movies that no longer work, that were so predictable. I just think that the moviegoing audience, particularly the young audience, has gotten so smart and savvy. They don't fall for the same things they've fallen for in years past. If you look at any genre I think it's true."

In late 1996 or early 1997, in accord with an agreement with Sony Pictures, Williamson wrote a screenplay loosely based on *I Know What You Did Last Summer*, a young-adult novel by Lois Duncan. Given the same title and featuring Jennifer Love Hewitt, Sarah Michelle Gellar, Ryan Philippe, and Freddie Prinze Jr., the film is about four teenagers who try to keep secret their accidental hit-and-run killing of a pedestrian. Unbeknownst to them, someone saw them dump the body into the sea, and the next year the four find themselves pursued by a mysterious killer bent on revenge. Angered by ads in which Sony billed the film as the work of "the creator of *Scream*," Miramax sued Sony and rushed *Scream 2* into production. Williamson finished the screenplay in just three weeks and served as producer as well. Filled with as many pop-culture references as *Scream* and similarly popular, *Scream 2*, directed by Wes Craven, brought in $30 million in its opening weekend alone, in December 1997.

Williamson next wrote the screenplay for *The Faculty*, based on a story by David Wechter and Bruce Kimmel. A cross between *Invasion of the Body Snatchers* and John Hughes's movie *The Breakfast Club*, as it has been described, *The Faculty* is set in a high school whose staff is being infiltrated by extraterrestrials. Directed by Robert Rodriguez and distributed by Dimension, the film premiered in December 1998. Soon afterward the Weinstein brothers signed Williamson to a $20 million contract that encompassed both television and cinema.

By then Williamson had already made a splash in television, with his series *Dawson's Creek*. Enlisted by the producer Paul Stupin to develop a show in which he could give full play to his sensitivity to young people, Williamson had outlined a series about a group of teenagers coming of age in a New England seaside town. The semi-autobiographical *Dawson's Creek*, which Williamson and a team of staff writers created, premiered in January 1998 on the WB network; the series chronicles the adventures of Dawson (Williamson's alter ego), who hopes to go to film school one day. The characters also include Dawson's platonic female friend Joey, who is based on a real-life friend of Williamson's; Dawson's buddy Pacey, who has an affair with a teacher, as a student at Williamson's high school reportedly did; and Jen, on whom Dawson has a crush. Williamson has taken issue with charges that the show's dialogue is unrealistically adult. In his interview for *Rough Cut*, he said, "I love writing kids. I think they're smart, they're sophisticated. I think they're completely underestimated in today's marketplace. I think kids just get it, you know? . . . Have you talked to a teenager lately? It sounds like they've had 10 years of therapy. I think what makes 'em so complex is they have this self-awareness, this cynical attitude toward life. But at the same time, their behavior is that of a 15-year-old. And that makes for a very interesting character."

In early 1999, feeling overburdened by his heavy workload, Williamson gave up direct involvement in *Dawson's Creek* and decided against writing the screenplay for *Scream 3*. He poured his energies instead into *Wasteland*, a new series for ABC-TV. Set in New York City, *Wasteland* focused on a group of 20-somethings trying to come to terms with life after college. About four months after its debut, in the fall of 1999, the show was canceled.

"In person, Williamson is sweet of nature, mild of manner, and decidedly nonviolent," Michael Krantz wrote for *Time* (December 15, 1997). Greg Berlanti, a *Dawson's Creek* co-producer, told Jeffrey Epstein, "You never feel like you're working for Kevin. You feel like you're working with him." After an episode in which a *Dawson's Creek* character admitted to being gay, Williamson followed suit, in interviews for such publications as the New York *Daily News* and the *Advocate*. His family and friends had known for some time that he was homosexual, and he felt that by revealing his sexuality publicly he might help gay teens. "I don't think I'm the right person to be on the soapbox," he said to Jeffrey Epstein, "but if I, this stupid Hollywood writer-director person, can talk openly about it and it helps anybody, then my job is done." According to Epstein, Williamson hopes to raise children of his own someday. "Right now I'm trying to keep a plant alive," Williamson told Epstein. "If you can keep a plant alive, then you go and get a dog, and if the dog lives, you shoot for a kid." — M.R.

Suggested Reading: *Advocate* (on-line) Aug. 1999; *Blue* (on-line), Dec. 1999; CNN (on-line); *Entertainment Weekly* p39 Jan. 10, 1997, with photo; *Fade In* (on-line), Aug. 1999; *Rough Cut* (on-line); *Time* p105+ Dec. 15, 1997, with photo

Suggested Films: as screenwriter—*Scream*, 1996; *I Know What You Did Last Summer*, 1997; *The Faculty*, 1998; as screenwriter and producer—*Scream 2*, 1997; *Halloween H2O: Twenty Years Later*, 1998; as screenwriter and director—*Teaching Mrs. Tingle*, 1999

Suggested Television Shows: as creator and executive producer—*Dawson's Creek*, 1998–99; *Wasteland*, 1999

Courtesy of FEMA

Witt, James Lee

1944– Director of the Federal Emergency Management Agency. Address: c/o FEMA, 500 C St. S.W., Washington, DC 20472

"If there is one quiet hero in Washington these days, it's James Lee Witt, the man in charge of disaster relief," Ann McFeatters wrote for the Scripps Howard News Service (September 26, 1998, on-line). Witt is the director of the Federal Emergency Management Agency (FEMA), which was set up, in 1979, "to reduce loss of life and property and protect our nation's critical infrastructure from all types of hazards" through an "emergency management program of mitigation, preparedness, response, and recovery," as *FEMA.gov* (on-line) put it. Witt, who assumed his position in 1993, is the first FEMA director with a background in emergency management. He has won praise for his successful, herculean efforts to reorganize the agency and to shift its focus from civil defense and preparations for nuclear war to providing immediate relief for victims of major natural catastrophes and man-caused disasters, such as the bombing of the Alfred P. Murrah Federal Building, in Oklahoma City, in 1995. By the end of 1999, Witt had guided FEMA in actions connected with more than 176 disasters. "What makes me proud of our efforts at FEMA is that the assistance we deliver is a message to all of these different areas that the nation cares about what has happened to them and wants to help . . . ," Witt explained in testimony before a Senate subcommittee on July 23, 1998. "The help we deliver is making a difference in removing not just wreckage and debris, but removing doubts about a community's ability to recover and prosper in the future."

James Lee Witt was born in 1944 in Arkansas. A snowstorm was raging during his birth, and he has joked that he got his first taste of disaster on that day. Witt, who has one brother and three sisters, grew up in Dardanelle, Arkansas, on his parents' farm. According to *FEMA for Kids*, on the FEMA Web site, during his childhood "a tornado came through and lifted his house up in the air when he was asleep in bed! Fortunately, no one was hurt." While attending Dardanelle High School, Witt played halfback and guard for the school football team; his performance on the field led to his election as "All District." About four years after graduating from high school, Witt (who did not attend college) set up his own commercial and residential building company, called Witt Construction. During the next dozen years he established a reputation as a successful businessman and became known in his community for his civic activities. In 1978 he was elected county judge for Yell County. At 34, Witt was one of the youngest elected officials in Arkansas. (Bill Clinton was younger—31—when he was elected to his first term as Arkansas's governor, in 1978.) On the day Witt was sworn in, a brutal snowstorm pummeled Yell County. The job responsibilities of county judge included emergency management, and in the extensive cleanup efforts that followed the storm, Witt occasionally operated a bulldozer himself.

Witt was reelected county judge six times. He was serving his seventh term when, in 1988, Governor Clinton chose him to head the Arkansas Office of Emergency Services. During his tenure there, Witt created a statewide program of inspection of vehicles that transported hazardous materials and certification of the drivers of such vehicles. He also successfully pushed for the establishment of a statewide code to ensure that newly constructed buildings would withstand earthquakes. He dealt with some three dozen disasters, most of them so labeled by Governor Clinton and a few so designated by President George Bush.

In February 1993, less than a month after Bill Clinton's inauguration as president, Clinton nominated Witt to direct FEMA. When Witt took office, in April, the agency had long been the target of fierce criticism for what was widely perceived as its inept responses to several disasters—prominent among them Hurricane Hugo, which struck the coasts of North and South Carolina in 1989, and Hurricane Andrew, which hit southern Florida and Louisiana in 1992. In the latter case, the inadequacy and inefficiency of FEMA's actions prompted the federal government to dispatch 14,000 troops to help Andrew's victims. Among those who held a low opinion of FEMA was Democratic senator Ernest F. Hollings of South Carolina, who asserted to William Claiborne for the *Washington Post* (April 1, 1993) that FEMA's staff were "the sorriest bunch of bureaucratic jackasses I've ever worked with."

Determined to improve FEMA's performance, Witt announced that he would streamline the agency, set up an "open line of communication with the White House," and take steps to ensure that FEMA approached events proactively. "It's absolutely critical that you look at your role and mission," he explained to Alasdair Roberts for the Council for Excellence in Government in April 1997, "and redefine that role and mission to what you feel is important for that agency to be responsible for." Witt resolved to take full advantage of the provisions of the Robert T. Stafford Disaster Assistance and Emergency Relief Act, known as the Stafford Act, which allows FEMA to "pre-position" resources when a disaster is anticipated. Toward that end, he abandoned his predecessors' narrow interpretation of the legislation, according to which FEMA could not react to an actual or expected emergency until requested to do so by a state government. FEMA demonstrated its new strategy in August 1993, when it dispatched 12 tractor-trailers to the North Carolina coast before Hurricane Emily struck. This action produced such successful results that FEMA created special response units, nicknamed "red-teams," that would be dispatched to targeted sites before forecasted trouble. "We made a mistake with Hurricane Andrew by waiting for the states to tell us what they needed first," Richard Krimm, an associate director of FEMA, acknowledged to Alasdair Roberts. "Now we go to the state and say, Here are the things you need, just tell us if you want them." Witt also began to forge better relationships with state governors, by hosting "hurricane summits" before the hurricane season. "We are a resource, we're not the people who go in and take charge," Witt told Roberts. "If we have an incident in any state, I always talk to that state director [of emergency management], and ask him, Do you want me to call your governor? And I will tell that governor, We are here as a resource for you, and if there's anything you want done, we will work with your state director to make sure it happens."

Earlier, in July 1993, the Mississippi River had overflowed its banks, flooding vast areas of several midwestern states. FEMA responded quickly and decisively, providing relief for victims and helping to minimize further destruction. Witt deployed high-tech mobile communications vehicles that had originally been designated for nuclear preparedness, and he prompted Congress to divert funds from the nuclear-preparedness budget to the disaster-relief program. "What we are interested in is mitigation, in helping to prevent damage and disasters," Witt told Keith Schneider for the *New York Times* (July 20, 1993). "That means finding money to relocate homes through the Federal Flood Insurance program. It also means finding money to rebuild levees." In the days after the flooding of the Mississippi Valley, Witt demonstrated his personal-relations skills as well. "He made us feel like we were the only people in the world," Mayor John Pat Dorrian of Des Moines, Iowa, told Bill Hewitt for *People* (January 31, 1994). "That's a real talent. He never mentioned his obligations in other areas." Also on display during the summer of 1993 was Witt's frugality: after refusing to use a government jet to reach a disaster site in Wisconsin, Witt took a commercial flight. Unwilling to spend $100 of government funds on taxi fare to get from the Milwaukee airport to his destination, he boarded a Greyhound bus and made the trip at a cost of $9 to American taxpayers. His strenuous efforts earned Witt much praise. "Witt is doing a fantastic job," Senator Barbara Mikulski of Maryland, formerly a frequent critic of FEMA, told Hewitt. "The President got the right person at the right time to do the right job." In late 1993 Congress withdrew a proposed bill that would have abolished FEMA, citing Witt and the agency for their impressive recent accomplishments.

During Witt's first year in office, a series of additional emergencies arose in quick succession. "I knew I was in for a challenge when I took this job," he joked to Hewitt. "But I didn't think it would be this *big* of a challenge." The devastating California earthquake of January 1994 gave FEMA the chance to make full use of its Teleregistration program, which enables victims to request aid by calling a toll-free number. More than half a million earthquake victims used the system. The agency also employed a computerized inspection system to assess damage claims with greater speed and efficiency. "We're not the old FEMA anymore," Witt told Roberts. "It used to take us 30 days before we'd get checks out to people. Now we get those checks out in five to 10 days."

The Stafford Act's list of natural catastrophes includes hurricanes, tornadoes, high water, wind-driven water, tidal waves, tsunamis, earthquakes, volcanic eruptions, landslides, mud slides, snowstorms, drought, and "regardless of cause, any fire, flood, or explosion" whose effects warrant federal intervention. The last-named grouping encompasses such unnatural disasters as the terrorist bombing of the World Trade Center, in New York City, on February 26, 1993, an event that prompted Witt to increase FEMA's preparedness for man-caused devastation. The nerve-gas attack unleashed on Tokyo subways in March 1995 "got us all thinking even more about how we need to be prepared to be able to respond to this kind of disaster and all the other kinds of nonnatural disasters," Witt told William Claiborne for the *Washington Post* (April 23, 1995). "We got to looking to our all-hazard approach, and to ways of expanding it even more." Witt's interview with Claiborne took place in Oklahoma City three days after a device planted in a van exploded in front of the Alfred P. Murrah Federal Building, destroying one third of the structure. Of the more than 800 people in the building at that moment, 167 were killed, among them children in a day-care center, and scores were injured. Within hours of the explosion, Witt was at the site, surveying the damage and providing assistance to the wounded. Ultimately, more than 1,000 FEMA employees assisted at the scene, among them 682 people trained in urban search and rescue. FEMA also set up an office in Oklahoma City in which professionals offered psychological counseling to disaster workers; later, among other measures, it allocated $4.1 million for mental-health services for explosion victims and others who had suffered emotional trauma.

The bomb that destroyed the Murrah building was made with fertilizer and fuel oil—items easily obtainable everywhere in the country. "Any type of manmade bomb like that scares me," Witt said during his April 1995 interview with William Claiborne. "We need to be aware that in the future something like that could happen again, and we need to be prepared to be able to respond to that particular kind of disaster. It's real. It's here. It happened, and it could happen again. If we did not prepare ourselves to respond in a way that could save as many lives as possible, we would be irresponsible." In a speech that he gave on the first anniversary of the tragedy, Witt said, as transcribed on the FEMA Web site, "As director of FEMA and as a former state emergency management director, I have seen disasters and tragedy. I have seen homes washed away by floods, cities crumbled by earthquakes, and communities blown apart by hurricanes. Nothing compares to the Oklahoma City bombing—the senseless horror and the unnecessary loss of lives. It was not a random act of nature but a deliberate act of man. . . . The experience in Oklahoma City taught us that we in emergency management must strive to be prepared for even the most unthinkable type of events."

In 1998 Witt announced the launching of Project Impact, the aim of which is to stimulate Americans to try to reduce the effects of natural disasters—for example, by situating homes away from floodplains, building earthquake-resistant bridges, and enforcing effective building codes. "We've got to change the way we deal with disasters or we are doomed to pay for poor planning in lost lives and lost property, over and over and over again," Witt said on July 23, 1998 in testimony before the Subcommittee on Clean Air, Wetlands, Private Property, and Nuclear Safety of the Senate Committee on Environmental and Public Works. "We must put an end to the damage, repair, damage, repair cycle. The most effective way to break this cycle is through mitigation." Project Impact, which has been implemented in more than 50 cities, has stimulated the forging of partnerships among government officials, representatives of the business sector, and local residents, all of whom will provide funding, services, technical support, and labor in activities designed to forestall the effects of disasters. "Natural disasters cost this country too much in dollars, infrastructure loss, and in sense of emotional and community well-being," Witt has said, as quoted on the FEMA Web site. "Project Impact is changing the way America deals with disasters." Also in 1998 Witt proposed eliminating federal subsidies that lower by more than 60 percent the cost of flood insurance for people who live where the likelihood of flooding is significant. "People need to accept the responsibility and the consequences of their choice to live in high-risk areas," Witt told Bill Adair for the *St. Petersburg Times* (November 11, 1998). "We should charge people who live in high-risk areas the fair market rates for insurance instead of the lower subsidized federal flood insurance rates."

Witt and his wife, Lea, who married in about 1962, live in Alexandria, Virginia. They also own a 200-acre farm in Wild Cat Hollow, Arkansas (the population of which was 10 in 1994). The couple have two grown sons, Jimmy and Michael. In his rare moments of leisure, according to *FEMA for*

Kids (on-line), Witt enjoys hunting, fishing, and playing golf with his two grandsons, Parker and Carter. — J.K.B.

Suggested Reading: *Naples Daily News* (on-line) Sep. 26, 1998; *New York Times* A p12+ July 20, 1993, with photo; *People* p38+ Jan. 31, 1994, with photos; *St. Petersburg Times* (on-line) Nov. 11, 1998; *Time* p35 Aug. 2, 1993, with photo; *Washington Post* (on-line) A p21+ Apr. 1, 1993

Courtesy of the World Bank

Wolfensohn, James D.

Dec. 1, 1933– President of the World Bank. Address: World Bank, 1818 H St. N.W., Washington, DC 20433

More like a modern-day courtier than a staid number cruncher who made his fortune as an investment banker, James D. Wolfensohn has been called "the man with the golden Rolodex," because he is on a first-name basis with the business and cultural elite. Speaking of his charisma, Suzanna Andrews wrote for *Gentlemen's Quarterly* (May 1991), "Power fishing or power fund-raising, Wolfensohn exudes intense charm and graciousness. He can talk about the environment, music, politics. He is a man who fascinates because of the extraordinary range of his life." As a fencer he competed for Australia in the 1956 Olympics. As an amateur cellist trained by Jacqueline Du Pré, he performed at Carnegie Hall. As the founder of the small investment bank James D. Wolfensohn Inc., he startled Wall Street when many leaders of blue-chip companies chose him as their financial consigliere. Not content to let his reputation rest on those achievements, he helped drum up funds among his friends to save Carnegie Hall and the Kennedy Center for the Performing Arts, prompting Suzanna Andrews to write, "Is this what the Nineties Medici looks like?" As president of the World Bank since 1995, he has been engrossed in his most ambitious endeavor yet: fighting global poverty.

James David Wolfensohn was born on December 1, 1933 in Sydney, Australia, to polyglot Jewish parents who had emigrated from England to Australia in the 1930s. His father, Bill Wolfensohn, never finished college and struggled to attain worldly success. In England he had been a secretary to the philanthropist James de Rothschild (after whom Wolfensohn was named); in Australia he worked as a small-business consultant, but he never made more than a modest living. Still, he became an intellectual leader of the small Jewish community in Sydney, and he and his wife devoted themselves to helping Jewish refugees settle in Australia after World War II. "My parents, who had nothing, gave away everything they could," Wolfensohn told Judith Weinraub for the *Washington Post* (April 30, 1990), in explaining his own interest in philanthropy as an adult. His parents were also great admirers of classical music—his mother, a native of Belgium, played piano and sang—and Wolfensohn shared that interest, taking piano lessons as a child.

Pushed to achieve by his parents, Wolfensohn enrolled at the University of Sydney at the age of 15. As Wolfensohn's wife, Elaine Wolfensohn, later told Andrews, "Jim compensated for so much that had gone wrong with his parents' lives." He did not do well his first year in college, so he redoubled his efforts. "I felt there was a lot of pressure to complete my university education—all those things my father had been prevented from doing by the First World War. . . . So as a student, I did quite a lot. That's why I was active in sports, student government, everything," Wolfensohn told Ina Ginsburg for *Town and Country* (July 1992). In particular, he distinguished himself in fencing, a sport he took up unintentionally, after a fencing-team member had approached him in search of a fourth person to compete in national championships. He agreed to join the team and learned moves on the train trip to the competition in Melbourne. He was beaten easily, but he fell in love with the sport, and five years later, in 1956, he made the Australian Olympic team.

After he earned a bachelor's degree, Wolfensohn stayed at the University of Melbourne to acquire a degree in law. He worked briefly as a lawyer in the Australian firm Allen, Allen & Hemsley, then pursued a master's degree in business administration from Harvard University, after a colleague told him he lacked basic business knowledge. "An American lawyer I was dealing with discovered that I couldn't read a balance sheet," he told Andrea Rothman for *Business Week* (August 20, 1990). "He told me—with some sense of anger—

that I should go to Harvard business school. I was so embarrassed that I did." While at Harvard, in Cambridge, Massachusetts, he earned money by operating a laundry service with a friend. He also met Elaine Botwinick, a student at Wellesley College, whom he married. His wife later earned a graduate degree in education from Columbia University and became a teacher and education expert. The couple have three children—Sara, a concert pianist; Naomi, who has written children's books and worked with people who are disabled; and Adam, who studied physics at Princeton University.

After he graduated from Harvard, in 1959, Wolfensohn became a managing director of the investment bank Darling & Co., in Australia. In 1967 he joined J. Henry Schroder Wagg & Co. and moved to London, where Schroders PLC was based. He rose rapidly at the company, and in 1970 he moved to New York to run Schroders' operation there. In 1976, at the age of 43, he became chief deputy chairman and managing director of Schroders Ltd., in London, and he returned to Great Britain.

At the same time that he was rising in the world of investment banking, Wolfensohn cultivated his interest in the arts, especially classical music. He befriended musicians, among them the composer and conductor Leonard Bernstein, who gave him a photo of himself with the inscription, "To Jim, my newest and favorite groupie." He knew the famed cellist Jacqueline Du Pré, whom he visited shortly after she was diagnosed with multiple sclerosis, in 1973. When she expressed to him her concern about what she could do now that her illness prevented her from performing, he suggested that she teach, and when she asked who would study with her, he offered to become her pupil. For the next two years, she gave him a lesson every Sunday at 3:00 in the afternoon. The ever-ambitious Wolfensohn picked as the first work he would learn Bach's Unaccompanied Cello Suite in G, a complex piece. Swearing to Du Pré that he would one day perform in a concert hall, he fulfilled his vow 10 years later, on his 50th birthday, when he played a Haydn trio and a Schumann work in a recital at Carnegie Hall, in New York City, at which the master violinist Isaac Stern also played.

In 1977 Wolfensohn joined Salomon Brothers, then the world's largest bond-trading house. In one interview he gave that year, he said that the lower tax burden in the U.S. and the prospect of joining a dynamic business contributed to his decision to switch jobs, though others speculated that he was disappointed that Schroders had not selected him as chairman. Assigned to oversee Salomon's investment-banking operation, he was a partner at the company until 1981. In his highest-profile moment, he was the lead investment banker in the bailout and reorganization of Chrysler Corp., in the late 1970s and early 1980s. The work demanded so much time and effort that he got sick and had to give orders from his hospital bed. "I figured there had to be more to life than that," he told Judith Weinraub. "Nothing was that important."

Meanwhile, Wolfensohn had become active in a wide variety of organizations. Over the course of his career, he has been a trustee of the Brookings Institution, a managing director of the Metropolitan Opera Association, a treasurer of the American Friends of Bilderburg Inc., a board member of Rockefeller University, and a director of the Rockefeller Foundation, among other affiliations; currently, he is chairman of the board of the Institute for Advanced Study, in Princeton, New Jersey. The contacts he made through these organizations, plus the number of his everyday business acquaintances and friends in the world of classical music, have led to the references to his "golden Rolodex."

Wolfensohn's extensive social connections and his interest in music made him an ideal candidate to become chairman, in 1980, of Carnegie Hall, which was in desperate need of repairs and renovation. Passing the hat among his acquaintances, Wolfensohn raised $60 million and personally gave more than $1 million. He remained chairman for 11 years and oversaw the celebration of the institution's 100th anniversary.

In 1981, just a year after becoming an American citizen, Wolfensohn sold his partnership in Salomon Brothers. The moment was opportune: Salomon had merged with Phibro, a trading firm, and the value of Wolfensohn's stock in the company had soared. Through the sale of his shares, he earned about $12 million. He then started his own company, James D. Wolfensohn Inc., a small investment-banking firm that aimed to cultivate long-term relationships with a small group of clients and offer independent advice. "As industrial companies see these big financial houses like Merrill Lynch or Shearson or Morgan becoming either their competitor or their partner in these huge deals, getting independent assessments becomes more important," Wolfensohn told Edwin Finn for *Forbes* (December 26, 1988). Guided by that vision, Wolfensohn's firm has done extremely well, acquiring such illustrious clients as Daimler-Benz, American Express, Ford, and DuPont. In 1995, for instance, the company advised on deals worth about $8 billion to $10 billion. In addition, Wolfensohn succeeded in wooing Paul Volcker, former chairman of the board of governors of the U.S. Federal Reserve System, to become chairman and part owner of the company. "It was a small firm that was doing business in a way that was comfortable to me, a firm that emphasized working with a client to establish a relationship that could persist over time, a firm that wasn't interested in hostile transactions relating to mergers and acquisitions," Volcker told Judith Weinraub. "I think we do business in an honorable way." Echoing that sentiment, W. Michael Blumenthal, then the chairman of Unisys Corp., told Edwin Finn, "In this day and age of greedy investment bankers, Jim Wolfensohn is a man who values long-term relationships with his clients over making a quick buck. It's very important for a chief executive to have someone outside his own bureaucracy to sound out ideas with."

Wolfensohn donated about 20 percent of his company's profits to charity. He also continued to study the cello, taking lessons in his office three times a week. "Having been born with few resources, I finally felt I had met a goal of financial security," he told Edwin Finn. "I wanted to work in an environment where I could take a cello lesson in my office in the afternoon without feeling inhibited, or if I wanted to spend my time on some non-business activity, I could." In one such activity, beginning in 1990, he headed the John F. Kennedy Center for the Performing Arts, in Washington, D.C. At the time of his appointment, the institution was in severe financial straits; water leaked through the ceiling, the marble was cracked, and operating expenses exceeded income. Moreover, the center had failed to establish itself as a nationally important cultural institution. "Instead of functioning as the principal showplace of American performing arts culture, the complex was rather more known as a place for locals to see *Shear Madness* if they hadn't already, and as a stop for road show companies touring in old Broadway hits," Michael Kilian wrote for the *Chicago Tribune* (May 3, 1992).

While he continued to operate his investment bank, in New York, Wolfensohn commuted to Washington to work two days a week at the Kennedy Center. He explained to Ina Ginsburg for *Town and Country* that working part-time was not necessarily a handicap "because I have a base as a result of my business, which no one who is full time could have. I have access to corporate leaders because of my work in finance, in business, and in other relationships." Actually, in the first six months of his tenure at the Kennedy Center, he spent more than two days a week there, although he received no monetary compensation for his work. Thanks to his efforts, Congress approved an allocation of $31 million for repairs at the center. He also secured donations from his friends and his own investment firm to save specific programs. Although he caused some friction among the staff when he brought in a management study team to overhaul the center's organization, many observers agree that he put the institution on a firm financial footing.

In June 1995 President Bill Clinton chose Wolfensohn to become the ninth president of the World Bank. Wolfensohn, whose appointment was approved by a vote of the bank's 24-member board of executive directors, succeeded Lewis T. Preston, who had died of cancer in May 1995, three months after announcing his resignation. Wolfensohn reluctantly gave up his position at the Kennedy Center to concentrate on running the bank. He also left Wolfensohn Inc., which was later acquired by Banker's Trust, which in turn was acquired by Deutsche Bank.

Wolfensohn had long held an interest in the developing world and had participated in investment banking deals in developing countries. He was influenced by the ideas of the British economist and conservationist Barbara Ward (1914–81), a prolific writer who was once described as "an eloquent evangelist for the needs of the developing countries and for the interdependence of nations." He had served as a board member of the Business Council for Sustainable Development and, for 14 years starting in 1970, of the Population Council. In one of his charitable activities, he had paid for Soviet government officials to attend the Harvard Business School to learn about capitalism. He had actually been considered for the job of World Bank president in 1981, when Robert S. McNamara stepped down, but was passed over in favor of A. W. Clausen.

Founded in 1944 along with its sister organization, the International Monetary Fund (IMF), at the United Nations Monetary and Financial Conference (commonly known as the Bretton Woods Conference), the World Bank—or, as it is officially known, the World Bank Group—consists of five institutions: the International Bank for Reconstruction and Development, which raises funds through bond sales to make loans to "middle-income" countries and poorer countries with good credit; the International Development Association, which relies on contributions from wealthy countries to make loans to the poorest countries; the International Finance Corporation, which assists private-sector investments in developing countries; the Multilateral Investment Guarantee Agency, which provides guarantees to foreign investors in developing countries against losses incurred because of unexpected political developments; and the International Centre for Settlement of Investment Disputes, which settles disputes between foreign investors and their host countries. The World Bank is owned by more than 180 member countries, which are represented by both a board of governors and a board of directors. Traditionally, the president of the bank is a national of the largest shareholder—the United States—and is elected to a five-year, renewable term. At the time of Wolfensohn's appointment, there were calls from both sides of the political spectrum in the U.S. to curtail the bank's activities. Those on the left accused the bank of financing environmentally unsound projects; on the bank's 50th anniversary, in 1994, some of them had launched a campaign claiming that "50 years is enough." Tax-cutting conservatives, bolstered by the Republican takeover of Congress in 1994, criticized the bank for interfering in the global economy and demanded that U.S. funding of the bank be scaled back.

Asserting that the bank has a vitally important function in relieving global poverty, Wolfensohn has been both an energetic defender and a reformer of the institution. "After just 26 months on the job, Mr. Wolfensohn . . . has become the most activist and publicly visible president the institution has had since Robert S. McNamara stepped down in 1981," Richard Stevenson wrote for the *New York Times* (September 14, 1997). As part of a sweeping reorganization known as the Strategic Compact, approved in 1997, the bank has worked to lower its costs, speed up its decision-making processes, and improve the success rate of its projects. According to the bank, these reforms have had some success. In fiscal year 1999 the bank reported that 77 percent of its projects had satisfactory outcomes, compared with 65 to 70 percent between 1990 and 1996.

Some of the changes embraced by Wolfensohn reflect the evolution of the bank's role in development. As late as 1990 investment from development agencies like the World Bank exceeded the amount of private capital flowing to developing countries; by the time of Wolfensohn's appointment, this situation had reversed. Prefiguring this change, Wolfensohn's predecessor had started shifting the bank's investments from big infrastructure projects to smaller projects that either directly benefitted the poor or stimulated private investment in countries bypassed by foreign investors. Wolfensohn helped accelerate this metamorphosis. One of his first moves, for instance, was to cancel a loan for an $800 million hydroelectric plant in Nepal. Indeed, at the beginning of Wolfensohn's tenure, the World Bank spent one in five of its aid dollars on electrical infrastructure projects; by September 2000 that ratio was one in 50. In 1995, 18 percent of the bank's loans went toward social services such as health, education, and nutrition; by 1999 that figure had increased to 25 percent.

Other programs launched by Wolfensohn include the Heavily Indebted Poor Countries Initiative (HIPC), a debt-forgiveness program for the poorest countries whose debt burdens are stifling development. Implemented in collaboration with the IMF, the program was a departure for that organization, which has often disapproved of debt forgiveness on the ground that it encourages fiscal irresponsibility in developing countries. Wolfensohn also launched the Comprehensive Development Framework (CDF), a more holistic approach to development. Historically, the World Bank has shied away from such "noneconomic" issues as democratic reform. Increasingly, however, it has embraced the idea that markets and development cannot occur without institutions that protect civil liberties and a free press. The CDF is currently being implemented in 13 countries, which willingly participate and take "ownership" of the proposed reforms.

Though the World Bank (unlike the IMF) was never supposed to be a lender of last resort, the sheer scale of the financial crisis that swept Asia in 1997 forced it to make emergency loans. In a rare public display of discord, Wolfensohn later criticized the IMF and the U.S. Treasury Department for not doing enough to help the poorest victims of the Asian financial crisis. He thought that the IMF and the Treasury Department had concentrated too much on balancing budgets and stabilizing currencies and that the reforms they called for had actually made conditions in poor Asian nations even worse.

In September 1999, despite his jostling with the IMF and the Treasury, Wolfensohn was easily reelected to another five-year term as president of the World Bank, making him only the third person to serve a second term. He spent much of the first year of that term trying to persuade increasingly vocal critics of the World Bank that the institution is genuinely committed to fighting poverty. A number of anti-globalization critics, who accuse the bank of benefitting large corporations at the expense of the environment and the poor, gathered outside the institution's meeting site in Washington, D.C. (in April 2000) and Prague, Czechoslovakia (September 2000) to protest its policies. Specifically, these critics argued that poor countries that received assistance from the World Bank and the IMF—especially sub-Saharan African nations—became dependent on those loans and often fared worse than countries that did not accept aid. The World Bank has also been attacked by government officials from economically powerful nations and others associated with those countries. Allan Meltzer, an economist who chaired a U.S. congressional commission on international financial institution reform, for instance, told Deepak Gopinath for *Institutional Investor* (September 2000), "We came to the conclusion that there is an enormous gap between Wolfensohn's rhetoric and reality. We think poverty relief is important, but it won't be achieved by a multiheaded hydra that caters to the whims of political groups around the world." On the other hand, some representatives of governments that had received assistance from the World Bank defended Wolfensohn's policies. "Wolfensohn and [Horst] Köhler [the managing director of the IMF] have become extremely important allies for us," remarked Trevor A. Manuel, the South African finance minister, to Joseph Kahn for the *New York Times* (September 25, 2000). "Our real problem is the U.S., Britain and France. The protestors seem not to understand these things." By September 2000, even some of those anti-globalization protestors had warmed slightly to the World Bank. Ann Pettifor, the organizer of the Jubilee 2000 coalition of debt-relief groups, described Wolfensohn and Köhler to Kahn as "civil servants. We know who the bad guys are. It's the G-7"—the Group of 7, an organization of seven economic powers. Kahn wrote, "Although Mr. Wolfensohn is a former investment banker, he is proving hard to outflank on the left."

Wolfensohn has been honored by Germany, France, and Australia, and Queen Elizabeth II of England named him a Knight of the British Empire. In 1994 he received a Business Committee for the Arts Leadership Award. "I wander out here some days wondering why I'm not in Jackson Hole [the site of his vacation home, in Wyoming], fishing," he told Richard Stevenson. "But it doesn't last very long. I have a passionate belief in this organization. We can make a difference between peace and war. We can make a difference between poverty and a fair life for people." — W.G.

Suggested Reading: *Banker* p30+ Oct. 2000, with photo; *Business Week* p58+ Aug. 20, 1990, with photo; *Chicago Tribune* XIII p24 May 3, 1992, with photo; *Forbes* p86+ Dec. 26, 1988, with photos; *Gentlemen's Quarterly* p193+ May 1991, with photos; *Institutional Investor* p146+ Sep. 2000; *New York Times* III p7 Sep. 11, 1977, with photo, D p1 Mar. 13, 1995, with photo, D p4 Apr. 27, 1995, with photo, D p1 Feb. 21, 1997, with photo, III p1+ Sep. 14, 1997, with photos, A p1+ Apr. 18, 2000, with photos, A p5 Sep. 25, 2000, with photo; *Washington Post* A p15 Apr. 5, 1993, with photo, B p1+ Apr. 30, 1990, with photos; *Washingtonian* p77+ Oct. 1995, with photos

---

Jeff Christensen/Archive Photos

Yamamoto, Yohji

Oct. 3, 1943– Fashion designer. Address: Yohji Yamamoto Boutique, 103 Grand St., New York, NY 10013; 155, rue Saint Martin, 75003 Paris, France

Although his name is known mainly to a small fashion-conscious coterie in the United States, the Japanese designer Yohji Yamamoto has had a major influence on clothing styles for much of the past two decades, and he is ranked among the few people in his field whose designs often strike fashion journalists and other specialists in the field as works of art. "Yamamoto proves that there is a place for a challenging, artistic vision within the fashion industry," Robin Givhan wrote for the *Washington Post* (October 26, 1997), after viewing the spring 1998 collections of Yamamoto and other top designers in Paris. "This season, he confirmed the powerful influence that Japanese culture has had on the design houses of Europe and New York. And while another Japanese designer, [Rei] Kawakubo of Comme des Garçons, may be more of a visionary, it is Yamamoto who makes the explicit connection between art and clothes. He embraces the Western traditions of the couturier, but from an Eastern point of view. He contemplates formality, propriety and customs, yet with an underlying belief in spontaneity. He is like a jazz musician—fully versed in the rules of rhythm, melody and phrasing—exploding in a brilliant, emotional riff." Although, as the fashion industry dictates, Yamamoto produces new designs for spring/summer and fall/winter every year, his creations are considered timeless. "Even his more eccentric pieces—frayed fabrics, crêpe and gabardine trapeze-line dresses, Geisha dresses coupled with Bogart fedoras—look like they've been around forever," a writer for *fashionlive.com* (published on-line by the World Media Network) declared in a recent biographical sketch of Yamamoto.

Yamamoto began selling clothing of his own design in Tokyo in the 1970s, and the garments attracted increasing attention among his country's fashion avant-garde. Several Western critics, however, greeted his first collection, which he showed in Tokyo in 1977, with highly disparaging remarks. But by the time he unveiled his fourth collection, in Paris, in 1983, he was being hailed as a major new designer. "Some say he is the best anywhere," John Duka, who attended the 1983 Paris show, wrote for the *New York Times* (October 23, 1983). "His fans use his first name when they discuss his clothes, a sure sign that a designer has arrived. Fashion experts and retailers are often inclined to exaggerate, but Mr. Yamamoto's influence is hard to dispute." In particular, Yamamoto has been credited with introducing a softening of the female silhouette, by means of his loosely fitting, understated, unpretentious designs, and with bringing cult fashion status to the color black.

"Sometimes we make strange things as a drug, . . . to experiment," Yamamoto told Hal Rubenstein for the *New York Times Magazine* (February 2, 1992). "The fun is in seeing who else wants to take this drug." The photos that accompanied Rubenstein's 1992 article showed, among other Yamamoto-designed garments, a cotton shirt and an acrylic-and-nylon vest costing $265 and $450, respectively—prices that, for the most part, place them out of reach of the average buyer. In the early 1990s the popularity of Yamamoto's designs slumped, and his influence seemed to be waning. But in the latter half of the decade, Yohji Yamamoto, as his privately owned company is called, grew robustly, and "once again [Yamamoto's] shows became pilgrimages," as Lisa Armstrong wrote for British *Vogue* (August 11, 1998, on-line). In 1999, according to *fashionlive.com*, his company's revenues reached more than $100 million, from sales of not only clothing for both men and women but also fragrances, eyeglass frames, and fabrics. His products are sold in spacious boutiques in Tokyo, New York, Paris, and London, as well as in a few upscale department stores. Yamamoto's professional activities include designing costumes for operas and ballets. He is the only Japanese fashion designer to earn the Chevalier de l'Ordre des Arts et Lettres, France's highest artistic honor; in the United States, the Council of Fashion Designers of America presented him with the prestigious International Award in 1999.

Yohji Yamamoto was born on October 3, 1943 in wartime Tokyo. His father, Fumio Yamamoto, a restaurant worker, died when Yohji was two years old, while serving in the Japanese military; his mother, Fumi Yamamoto, a dressmaker, never remarried, deciding instead, according to her son, to dedicate herself to her only child. After becoming a single parent, she reportedly wore nothing but black garments, a common practice among Japanese widows and one that at least one source suggested led to Yamamoto's preference for black and other somber colors in his designs. ("Black represents protection, arrogance, dignity, strength, sadness," he has said, as quoted in the *New York Times* [September 19, 1993] by Suzy Menkes, who noted that black "has developed into a 20th-century motif for the outsider.") During his early years, in the disreputable Shinjuku quarter of Tokyo, Yamamoto often felt lonely. In kindergarten his closest friends were girls, while he fought with the boys. "Girls were for me mikata—a friend, an ally," he explained to Harriet Shapiro for *People* (October 11, 1982). He also told her, "Even then the most important part of me was woman." He recalled that when his mother would bring home a new shirt for him, "the first thing I wanted to do was wash it before wearing it," so as to soften it.

When Yohji was 12, his mother transferred him from a public school to the École de l'Étoile du Matin, an elite French Catholic school not far from the Imperial Palace, the home of Japan's royal family. "It was a place for rich people's children," Yamamoto told Shapiro. "I felt I was different from the other boys." He attended Keio University, in Tokyo, from which he graduated with a degree in law, in 1966. But he gave up the idea of practicing law, because he lacked the connections that he had come to recognize were a prerequisite for success in that field in Japan. Casting about for an alternative, he enrolled at the Bunka Fukuso Gakuin, a college in Tokyo that specializes in the fashion trades. "I just wanted to help my mother," he told Shapiro. "I didn't know there was a kind of business called designer." A monetary prize that he won at his graduation, in 1968, enabled him to take an "extended tour of Europe," as Lisa Armstrong wrote. While in Paris he tried in vain to find buyers for his designs in the offices of fashion magazines and stores. Those failures notwithstanding, according to Armstrong, he returned to Tokyo "convinced that designing clothes could be as creatively valid as painting."

In about 1970 his mother opened a boutique, and Yamamoto helped out by designing clothing for her. But the styles his mother favored were too feminine for his taste, he told Nina Hyde for the *Washington Post* (July 14, 1983), and "not for the working woman." The stiff lines of then-current Paris fashions did not suit the average Japanese woman either, in his opinion. Indeed, by his own account, he felt angry about the plight of many Japanese working women; like his mother, many of them had become widowed as a result of World War II and had become the sole support of their families, yet "they weren't really treated as equals," as he said to Armstrong. In about 1971 Yamamoto started designing clothing that he thought women would find more comfortable—oversized, loose-fitting garments, as opposed to styles offering the "snugger fit and formality" favored by the majority of traditional designers at that time, as John Duka wrote. Discussing his conception of sportswear, Yamamoto told Duka, "When I started designing clothes, . . . I knew there were two ways. The first is to work with formal, classical shapes. The other way is to be very casual. That's what I decided on, but I wanted a new kind of casual sportswear that could have the same status as formal clothing. So I use fabrics that are heavy-duty, like army fabrics, or just look heavy-duty, to give the kimono shape a new energy."

After about two years Yamamoto had created his own line of ready-to-wear clothing and felt prepared to begin selling it, with the "Y" label, in a studio of his own. His mother helped him get started, and she has been working with him ever since. Sales remained modest until 1977, when he showed a collection for the first time, in Bell Commons, a building in Tokyo that houses clothing boutiques and fabric shops. Members of the press and others responded to the items on display with enormous enthusiasm, and he was hailed as an important new avant-garde designer. "From then on," Yamamoto said to Shapiro, "it is a very common success story. So it is not as interesting." At around this time, reportedly at one of the parties heavily attended by people who were considered members of the Japanese avant-garde, Yamamoto met his contemporary Rei Kawakubo, whose designs, under the label Comme des Garçons, had been popular in Japan since earlier in the decade. He and Kawakubo were romantically involved for awhile; later, Kawakubo married someone else, but the two designers maintained their friendship—despite the fact, as Yamamoto told Jennet Conant for *Newsweek* (February 2, 1987), that they spoke infrequently and never talked to each other about their ideas. Nevertheless, Conant reported, "their collections share[d] many details": in 1986, for example, both dressed some of their models in ballet shoes.

Earlier, in 1981, both Kawakuba and Yamamoto showed their collections during fashion week in Paris, an event considered at that time far more prestigious than the one in Tokyo. Brenda Polan, who was fashion editor of the London *Guardian* then, recalled to Lisa Armstrong that those in attendance found the styles "utterly bewildering. There just hadn't been anything like these black, billowing, layered clothes ever before in Paris. They raised all sorts of questions about conventional beauty, elegance and sexuality. No one could understand how they had been constructed. Frankly, quite a few people couldn't understand them at all." According to *fashionlive.com*, one critic who saw the 1981 Paris show wrote that Yamamoto's garments "look[ed] like leftover scraps from an atomic blast and call[ed] to mind the end of the world." Yamamoto told Armstrong, "It was upsetting as both Rei and I thought what we were doing was so international, yet the international press labelled us as Japanese."

Yamamoto fared significantly better the next year, in New York City, when onlookers cheered at the climax of his show. "Of the new breed, Yohji is certainly the leader," Jon Weiser, whose family founded the trendy New York clothing chain Charivari (which introduced the Japanese look Stateside) said to Harriet Shapiro after attending the event. The styles Yamamoto showed in New York included clothing in black and muted shades, some fabricated from stone-washed leather or from cotton that had been "broken in" in a Japanese river. Loosely draped garments and big, floppy hats were dominant. "I think to fit tight clothes on a woman's body is for the amusement of man," Yamamoto declared, as quoted by Shapiro. "It doesn't look noble. Also it is not polite to other people to show off too much."

The menswear and women's styles that Yamamoto showed in Paris in October 1983 featured oversized, liberating garments with little detail, "often with the kimono as a starting point of design . . . ," as John Duka reported. "All this came at a time when women's clothes by most traditional designers were moving in the opposite direction, toward a snugger fit and formality." Duka also noted that many of the men's garments "would work as well on women." "More and more women are buying my men's clothes," Yamamoto observed to Duka. "It's happening everywhere, and not just with my clothes. Men's clothing is more pure in design. It's more simple and has no decoration. Women want that. When I started designing, I wanted to make men's clothes for women. But there were no buyers for it. Now there are. I always wonder who decided that there should be a difference in the clothes of men and women. Perhaps men decided this."

In a review of what she labeled "major collections" by Kawakubo and Yamamoto in Paris six years after the two had first showed there, Bernadine Morris, writing for the *New York Times* (October 16, 1987), reported that they had both "displayed continuous growth as designers. . . . While their clothes would never be confused with Western classics, they are less ferocious than they were in the beginning and are a constant stimulus to avant-garde designers here and in other fashion centers. Miss Kawakubo and Mr. Yamamoto seem fearless and inventive, rare qualities in designers anywhere. . . . What comes through in the Japanese collections is a sense of excitement, as the designers experiment with new ways to deal with clothes." The new elements she noted in Yamamoto's styles included asymmetry and such "whimsical touches" as "cartwheel hats as big as umbrellas."

In early 1988 Yamamoto opened a boutique in the SoHo section of New York City. By intent, the cavernous, 3,000-square-foot space contained exceedingly few garment racks, leading to what Suzanne Slesin, in the *New York Times* (April 21, 1988), described as "the 'where are the clothes?' reaction" among patrons. Standing on the polished wooden floors were metal furnishings, including a screen and freestanding iron racks, that had been made to order by British craftsmen and, in Slesin's view, were as much sculptural as functional. Commenting on the interior of the shop, the multimedia designer Robert Currie told Slesin, "It has finally come to that time again when art and fashion are the same thing, and the art of clothing meets the art of design."

For his 1991 ready-to-wear spring/summer collection, Yamamoto created clothing reminiscent of 1930s designs by Madeleine Vionnet and late-1940s styles by Christian Dior. The Vionnet-like styles included lightly shaped dresses with an abundance of seams and darts in the fabrics, which had been cut on the bias (that is, on the diagonal of the weave, rather than on the vertical, as is customary); the Dior-like qualities were evident in long, full skirts. For footwear to accompany both the dresses and the skirts, Yamamoto chose sneakers—"black ones for really formal evenings," as Bernadine Morris reported for the *New York Times* (October 19, 1991). The following March Yamamoto included in his upcoming collection long coats and dresses to which he had attached rag dolls and highly uncharacteristic uses of gold, mirrored shards, gold paint, and elaborate gold rings. In his January 1994 menswear collection, Yamamoto showed outfits with tall satin top hats, "long clown shoes with turned-up toes," and "formal tails worn with big polka-dot bow ties," as Amy M. Spindler wrote for the *New York Times* (February 1, 1994). In his 1998 conversation with Lisa Armstrong, in an apparent reference to designs created during his early 1990s slump, he said, "I was very unhappy for a time and I suppose I wanted to make ugly things."

According to Armstrong, one of Yamamoto's 1997 collections "sparked his renaissance." "Some people thought I was parodying the old [Coco] Chanel and Dior styles," Yamamoto said to her. "But it was a homage. . . . You know, it's terrible always feeling you have to do something completely new, which was what I used to think. It's still year zero every collection, but now I feel free to draw on elements of the past." Yamamoto's spring/summer 1998 collection impressed Marisa Fox, writing for the *Chicago Tribune Magazine* (February 1, 1998), as "close to couture while still being ready-to-wear" and as still exuding "a sense of timelessness, grace and innovation." Drawing inspiration from Chanel and another renowned French couturier, Sonia Rykiel, Fox reported, he "mixe[d] old-fashioned craftsmanship with a science-fiction sensibility" and devised "oddly proportioned, highly elaborate pieces that push the boundary" but nevertheless were "utterly feminine and always flowing." These included an $800 sweater whose sleeves ended past the fingertips and an $850 pair of pants with a long "tail" that "gets wrapped around the back like some space-age coil that then is tied around the neck like a scarf," as Fox described it. Outerwear traditional among the ethnic groups broadly referred to as Eskimo or Inuit inspired Yamamoto's fall/winter 2000 collection. Long coats, jackets, hoods, and hats in wool, leather, and fur predominated in clothing that a writer for *Elle.com* (March 2, 2000, on-line) described with such adjectives as "sublime" and "both wild and elegant." "For the finale," the reporter continued, "a bride, groom and baby showed down jackets with superb workmanship in leather. A magical moment topped with fabulous fur hats."

Yamamoto is featured in a motion picture directed by the German filmmaker Wim Wenders in 1990. The movie, which Wenders made at the request of the Pompidou Center, in Paris, arrived in the United States in 1991 with the title *Notebook on Cities and Clothes*. "A loose, journalistic exploration of its subject," as Janet Maslin wrote in a review for the *New York Times* (October 25, 1991), it offers views of Yamamoto at a Paris fashion show and in his custom-built house, in a quiet, residential part of Tokyo. Like his boutiques, his home is scantily furnished, because Yamamoto does not "want to be trapped by gorgeous things, to have an attachment to anything except maybe books," as he told Melissa Barrett Rhodes for *Harper's Bazaar* (June 1999). Moreover, the rooms are bare of artwork, because it "hurts his eyes to look at art unless it's in a museum," his creative director, Irene Silvagni, told Rhodes. The only picture on view is a black-and-white portrait of the karate master Gichin Funakoshi (1868–1957), who brought karate to Japan in the early 1920s. The house, the outside of which, according to Rhodes, resembles a "concrete fortress," contains a large karate practice room, which Yamamoto, who has a second-degree black belt in karate, makes available to karate instructors and their students. His leisure activities also include playing pool and recording his own CDs (in his in-house billiards room and music studio, respectively). An enthusiastic admirer of Bob Dylan and Leonard Cohen, Yamamoto plays harmonica and guitar; he occasionally performs in Tokyo and hosts concerts in his residence. For relaxation, he also reads and sunbathes. Yamamoto was married and divorced many years ago. He has one daughter, Rimi. — V.K.

Suggested Reading: *Harper's Bazaar* p190+ Feb. 1998, with photos, p124+ June 1999, with photos; *New York Times* p63 Oct. 23, 1983, with photos; *Newsweek* p80 Feb. 2, 1987, with photos; *People* magazine p60+ Oct. 11, 1982, with photos; *Washington Post* F p1 July 14, 1983 with photo; Worldmedia Web site; Baudot, François. *Yohji Yamamoto*, 1997

Randee St. Nicholas/Courtesy of MSO

Yoakam, Dwight

(YOKE-um)

Oct. 23, 1956– Country-and-western singer; actor; director. Address: c/o Mitch Schneider Organization, 14724 Ventura Blvd., Suite 410, Sherman Oaks, CA 91403

With his cowboy hat, cowboy boots, jeans, and guitar, Dwight Yoakam looks like the typical country-and-western singer. In fact, it was his adherence to the roots of country, in spite of efforts to move the genre closer to the mainstream, that established him as one of the recording industry's most popular and critically acclaimed performers. But his love of "pure" country has not kept him from adopting other musical elements on occasion. "I'd like to bring this music to as many people as possible; to perform the music that I love and have it be accepted by as many people as I can," he said to Sara Nelson, a writer for *USA Weekend* (September 19–21, 1986). In addition to releasing more than a dozen albums, Yoakam has reached a wider audience by acting in several films, such as *Sling Blade*, *The Newton Boys*, and *The Minus Man*. Karen Schoemer, a contributor to *Rolling Stone* (September 30, 1993), explained Yoakam's appeal: "Beyond his voice . . . it's his image that has driven him to success. Neither safe nor tame, he has adapted Elvis' devastating hip swagger, Hank Williams' crazy-ass stare and Merle Haggard's brooding solitude into one lethal package."

Dwight Yoakam was born on October 23, 1956 in Pikesville, Kentucky. When he was two years old, his family moved to Columbus, Ohio. According to a *People* profile (April 26, 1993), Yoakam taught himself to play the guitar "by strumming along to Hank Williams records" and wrote his first song by age eight. During an interview published on the Austin City Search Web site, Yoakam told Rebecca Gonzales, "Music was my first love. I played music since my earliest memories. My first heroes were guitar slingers. Every week there was a new guitar slinger, Elvis [Presley], Johnny Cash, Rick Nelson, Roy Orbison, all these guys swaggered out on stage with a guitar, much like the outlaws of the movies. I became infatuated with that and I was always seduced by music first." During high school Yoakam played with several bands. According to John Callan, writing for *People* (August 4, 1986), Yoakam began playing professionally in 1974, at age 18, performing on "the honkytonk circuit in the Ohio Valley." Yoakam also enrolled at Ohio State University and studied philosophy and history.

After dropping out of college, in 1976, Yoakam headed to Nashville, Tennessee, the country-music capital of the United States, to see if he could obtain a recording contract. His traditional sound did not impress Nashville's music executives, who were trying to modernize country-and-western music in an effort to attract a wider audience. As Yoakam explained to Callan, "They said I was 'too country' for Nashville." In 1978 he traveled to Los Angeles "because of Emmylou Harris and the country-rock scene on the West Coast," as he said to Joe Sasfy for the *Washington Post* (June 16, 1986). "I knew there was still an awareness of pure country there. Merle Haggard and Buck Owens came out of there, and country music has been big in California since Capitol Records started there in the '40s. There's a real tradition conducive to guitars and Cadillacs, a real rock 'n' roll cowboy mentality."

After spending six years performing in bars, clubs, and other small venues, Yoakam released a six-song EP, *Guitars, Cadillacs, Etc.* (1984), on a small, independent label; he was unable to get a major label to record and market his brand of music. During an interview with Cameron Randle for *Rolling Stone* (May 22, 1986), Yoakam noted, "I was able to do pure, hard country in Los Angeles, but the record companies out there wouldn't touch country music because that was Nashville's territory. And Nashville was uninterested, almost embarrassed by its historical obligation to the form." In Los Angeles and New York City, where he performed in clubs with backup musicians, Yoakam attracted an unlikely following among punk-rock fans. He explained his appeal during his conversation with Cameron Randle: "Everybody knows rhythm and blues was the black predecessor to rock & roll, but for the white side of things, hillbilly music—when it came down into the cities—*was* rock & roll. It was the ostracized form of music that attracted kids. Society's leaders have never accepted country music as anything short of uncouth and crass. These kids have picked up on that, which is why I owe them a debt for opening doors to me."

In 1986 Yoakam signed a contract with Reprise Records, a subsidiary of Warner Bros. Reprise rereleased the EP with three additional songs as *Guitars, Cadillacs, Etc., Etc.* in 1986. The album was a critical and commercial success, selling more than one million copies. Among the album's hits were the title track and a cover of Johnny Horton's "Honky Tonk Man," which climbed to number three on the country-and-western (C&W) chart. Yoakam's second album, *Hillbilly Deluxe* (1987), reached number one on the C&W chart. The album also reached number 55 on the pop chart, demonstrating Yoakam's appeal to mainstream audiences. Four songs on the album, including a cover of Elvis Presley's "Little Sister," were Top 10 hits on the C&W chart.

In 1988 Yoakam embarked on a well-publicized tour with one of his musical idols, the legendary singer Buck Owens, who had been retired from the music business since 1979. The two singers also recorded "Streets of Bakersfield," a previous hit for Owens, for Yoakam's third album, *Buenas Noches from a Lonely Room* (1988). "Streets of Bakersfield" topped the C&W chart. In his review for the *New York Times* (September 7, 1988), Peter Watrous wrote that the album was "spare, tough and streamlined" and that it "represents a rebirth of what was called the Bakersfield sound—part country, part early rockabilly—in opposition to the more formulaic, sweetened country music emanating from Nashville."

By 1988 Yoakam's hectic pace of touring and recording had begun to take its toll on him. In the New York *Daily News* (September 7, 1988), David Browne quoted Yoakam as saying that he never expected the "emotional wear and tear of touring and interviewing and talking after singing all night." He added, "I don't know if it's healthy to continue at that pace. I don't think psychologically it's the best thing for the music." Despite his exhaustion, Yoakam kept himself in the spotlight by releasing two more commercially successful albums, *Just Lookin' for a Hit* (1989) and *If There Was a Way* (1990). Another album, *La Croix D'Amour*, was released exclusively in the United Kingdom in 1992.

In 1993 Yoakam returned with *This Time.* "Yearning, misery, anger, humor—whatever the mood, Yoakam delivers an unsentimental slice of his soul, not a shrink-wrapped product off a self," Tony Scherman wrote in his review for *People* (March 29, 1993). "He chuckles evilly ('Fast as You'), moans and mumbles, croons like Sinatra ('King of Fools'), imitates mush-mouthed Buck

Owens ('This Time') and swoops skyward in Sam Cooke glissandi ('Ain't That Lonely Yet'). There's nothing this boy can't sing." The cable channel VH1 aired the video for "Ain't That Lonely Yet" frequently, introducing his music to a wider audience. The single also earned the singer the Grammy Award for best male country performance in 1994. *This Time* sold more than two million copies.

Also in 1993 Yoakam fulfilled his lifelong desire to act, by performing in the play *Southern Rapture*, which was directed by the actor Peter Fonda at the MET Theatre in Los Angeles. "I was infatuated by performances I saw on TV by guitar-playing singers and became infatuated with acting in junior high," Yoakam recalled to Lorraine Ali for *Rolling Stone* (April 3, 1997). "It was a means of stepping out of myself." In 1994 he made a brief appearance in the film *Red Rock West*, which co-starred Nicolas Cage and Lara Flynn Boyle. The same year, Yoakam had a major role in the Showtime film *Roswell*, which told the story of the alleged government cover-up of a UFO crash in New Mexico. His character owned the ranch where the UFO crashed. He followed up that film with appearances in a string of movies that received little attention: *Painted Hero* (1995), *The Little Death* (1995), and *Don't Look Back* (1996). He received critical acclaim, however, for his role in Billy Bob Thornton's 1996 film *Sling Blade*. As Yoakam told Ali, "Billy saw me perform a music show a couple years ago. He turned to the person he was with at the time and said, 'I think this guy Dwight is gonna act as a means of expression at some point.'" Thornton then offered Yoakam the role of Doyle Hargraves, an abusive drunk. Reviewing *Sling Blade* for *Entertainment Weekly* (December 6, 1996, on-line), Owen Gleiberman wrote, "Yoakam, the country singer, gives a shattering performance, lending Doyle the redneck varmint authentic shades of self-loathing and cowardice." Yoakam was honored with the Premiere Performance Award at the annual Motion Picture Club Awards in New York City.

Meanwhile, Yoakam continued his singing career, releasing two albums in 1995: *Gone* and *Dwight Live*. In his review for *Entertainment Weekly* (May 26, 1995, on-line), Tony Scherman praised *Dwight Live* as "the most satisfying country record of the half year." Although *Gone* was less successful than his previous albums, it sold 500,000 copies and was nominated for a Grammy Award for best country album.

Over the next few years, Yoakam divided his time between recording albums and making movies. In 1997 he paid tribute to his musical influences with *Under the Covers*, which contained his versions of songs by such artists and groups as the Beatles, the Rolling Stones, and Roy Orbison. Yoakam also recorded a Christmas album, *Come on Christmas*, that featured holiday standards such as "Silent Night," "Silver Bells," and "Here Comes Santa Claus." On the screen, in 1998 he played an explosives expert in *The Newton Boys*, a gangster drama set during the 1920s, and a lieutenant colonel in HBO's World War II film *When Trumpets Fade*. In the *Weeklywire* (June 8, 1998, on-line), Michael McCall observed, "With these roles, Yoakam has proven that his acting skills go far beyond the usual cardboard characterizations that most musical performers give in front of a camera." While filming *The Newton Boys*, Yoakam wrote many of the songs for his 12th album, *A Long Way Home* (1998). "With a back-to-basics sound, the album recaptures the sly, succinct brilliance of his older records," Michael McCall wrote. "In a way, the stripped-down songs take him back to the honky-tonks and the mountains that inspired his original breakthrough albums of the '80s."

Dwight Yoakam kept busy in 1999, pursuing a variety of projects. He issued a greatest-hits collection, *Last Chance for a Thousand Years*, and published a book, *A Long Way Home: Twelve Years of Words*, a collection of lyrics to 61 songs he had written or co-written. Yoakam acted in another film, *The Minus Man*, playing a detective who exists only in the dreams of a serial killer. He also won his second Grammy Award, for best country collaboration with vocals, for *Same Old Train*, which was recorded with other major country-and-western singers, including Randy Travis, Clint Black, Merle Haggard, and Emmylou Harris.

In the same year Yoakam began directing a film, *South of Heaven, West of Hell*, a Western starring himself and featuring Billy Bob Thornton, Bridget Fonda, Vince Vaughan, and Scott Wilson. Yoakam also wrote the screenplay and served as producer. Shortly after its first screening, in January 2000, the film sparked controversy. Citing an interview Yoakam had given to the *Hollywood Reporter*, an article in *Billboard* (January 12, 2000) reported that the film's production company, A Cast of Strays, had filed for bankruptcy. For reasons not made public, the film's financial backers withdrew their support right before filming began, and Yoakam was forced to use his own money to finance the film. According to the article, dozens of actors, crew members, and vendors claimed they were never paid for their work on the movie; a few of them filed complaints with unions and initiated lawsuits against Yoakam in small-claims court. "Ultimately, this was the hardest experience I've gone through in my professional life in terms of executing art. I learned many lessons—it's been a long crawl for this film, and now we're in the process of getting it off its knees," Yoakam told the *Hollywood Reporter*, as quoted by *Billboard*.

South of Heaven, West of Hell was first screened during the Slamdance Film Festival in Park City, Utah, on January 28, 2000; it was later released in Europe. In his review for *Roughcut* (February 3, 2000, on-line), Rod Hewitt described the film as a "masterpiece of flaws," adding, "Yoakam has been far too ambitious, far too misinformed as to the technique and the elements that are needed to make so complex a braid tight and strong." Yoakam is currently seeking a distributor to market the film in the United States.

Dwight Yoakam lives in the Hollywood Hills, just outside Los Angeles. He supports various charities, among them the Los Angeles Mission, which provides shelter for the homeless and food for the hungry, and animal-rescue centers. In 2000 he reworked earlier songs for a new album, *dwightyoakamacoustic.net.* He also began selling his own brand of biscuits through the Internet. — D.C.

Suggested Reading: *Billboard* (on-line) Jan. 12, 2000; *Chicago Tribune* XIII p16+ May 5, 1985, with photo; *Entertainment Weekly* (on-line) Dec. 6, 1996; *People* p45 Aug. 4, 1986; *Rolling Stone* p63+ Sep. 30, 1993, p28 Apr. 3, 1997; *USA Weekend* p6 Sep. 19, 1986; *Weeklywire* (on-line) June 8, 1998

Selected Recordings: *Guitars, Cadillacs, Etc., Etc.* (1986), *Hillbilly Deluxe* (1987), *Buenas Noches from a Lonely Room* (1988), *This Time* (1993), *Dwight Live* (1995), *Gone* (1995), *A Long Way Home* (1998), *dwightyoakamacoustic.net* (2000)

Selected Films: *Red Rock West* (1994), *Slingblade* (1996), *The Newton Boys* (1998), *The Minus Man* (1999), *South of Heaven, West of Hell* (2000)

Courtesy of dolorazajick.com

Zajick, Dolora

(ZAH-chick, duh-LORE-uh)

1954(?)– Opera singer. Address: c/o E. Crittenden, Columbia Artists Management Inc., 165 W. 57th St., New York, NY 10019

"When I began, my voice was loud and ugly," the opera singer Dolora Zajick told Anthony Tommasini for the *New York Times* (January 11, 1998). "I had no high notes and no low notes. I had to find my voice." The mezzo-soprano's search has led her to the pinnacle of her profession: according to the noted soprano Birgit Nilsson, Zajick's voice is "the only one existing today without any competition in the world"; the equally renowned mezzo-soprano Marilyn Horne, whom Tommasini also quoted, described Zajick herself as "a force of nature." "It's not just her amazing voice," Horne said; "it's what she can do with her voice because of her superb technique and dedication." Zajick is considered a foremost interpreter of mezzo-soprano roles created by the great 19th-century Italian operatic composer Giuseppe Verdi. She has performed three of the best known—Azucena in *Il Trovatore*, Amneris in *Aïda*, and Eboli in *Don Carlo*—with major companies all over the world.

Zajick has revealed little about her personal life to journalists. She was born in about 1954 in Reno, Nevada, the eldest of two sisters and three brothers in a family of Slavic descent. Of limited economic means, the family owned few records; their collection reportedly consisted merely of several pieces of orchestral music—Handel's *Water Music*, Tchaikovsky's *Nutcracker Suite*, and Rimsky-Korsakov's *Scheherazade*. Zajick often sang at home with her brothers, and in eighth grade she joined her school choir. For a short time she played the drums. "Every singer should study percussion—you'd be surprised how many don't know the difference between an eighth and a sixteenth note," she told Harvey E. Phillips for *Opera News* (July 1988).

Zajick enrolled at the University of Nevada as a premed major. When journalists express surprise about that choice, she informs them that she has always had many interests other than music. Music won out, however, after she realized that she felt much happier singing with a chorus in her spare time than she did attending her biochemistry classes. After earning a bachelor's degree in music, she began to get small roles with the Nevada Opera. By her own account, the quality of her early performances was far from satisfactory; she has recalled with amusement being referred to as "King Kong" by a young tenor with whom she was to perform in *Trovatore*. "I had the basic vocal material to work with, and an instinctive ability to mimic sound, just the way some visual artists have an almost photographic gift for copying pictures," she told Tommasini. "But I was lucky to run into a teacher who knew how to form this material." That teacher was Ted Puffer, the artistic director of the Nevada Opera, to whom she has credited much of her success. "With him," she said to Tommasini, "I took my voice apart and put it back together." Although she envisioned remaining in her home state under his tutelage, Puffer encouraged her to further her studies in New York City, where he felt she would find greater opportunities to develop her career. Able to afford only a one-way plane ticket, she arrived in the city in 1982 with $200 in cash and one small suitcase. Rejected by the Juilliard School, she was admitted to the Manhattan School of Music, where she studied part-time.

Struggling to support herself, Zajick took odd jobs at the Jewish Guild for the Blind, among other places; her desperate financial straits even drove her to peddle decorated eggs from a stand outside Macy's department store, from which the police often chased her. She shared a one-bedroom apartment with 16 other students until they were evicted for violating rental restrictions. Afterward Zajick endured a period of homelessness. Unable to turn to her cash-strapped family, she sometimes stayed with friends, doing housework in exchange for a bed. Many times she slept in the music school's lounge or on a bench in Central Park. "I could have taken a job and had a stable living, but I probably would not have had my career," she explained to Tommasini. "When the choice was giving up comfort in order to have time for singing, I gave up comfort."

Meanwhile, Zajick's musical studies were going well, and her teachers encouraged her to prepare for the prestigious Tchaikovsky International Competition, held every four years for singers and instrumentalists in Moscow, in what was then the Soviet Union. Although she had no idea how she would raise the money to get there, she followed their advice. When the members of the First Presbyterian Church in Manhattan, where she sang in the choir, learned of her problem, they took up a collection to finance the trip. In addition, a member of the Manhattan School of Music's board of directors gave her $300 to buy suitable clothing. Zajick won a bronze medal in the 1982 competition; she was the only non-Soviet citizen to win that year and the first American to place in the event in 12 years.

After her performance in Moscow, Manhattan School administrators secured a loan for Zajick, thus enabling her to rent a comfortable apartment while she completed her studies. At about this time, the voice teacher and opera director Lou Galtiero approached Elizabeth Crittenden, a manager who had a reputation for nurturing young talent, and told her, according to Walter Price in the *New York Times* (February 11, 1990), "I've got this big mama with a big voice." Crittenden agreed to represent Zajick professionally, and with her manager's help, she gained admittance into the three-year Merola Opera Program for young artists, at the San Francisco Opera. While in San Francisco, Zajick has said, she turned into a full-fledged Verdi mezzo; punning to Phillips on the word "green" and the name "Verdi," which mean the same thing, she said, "I went in green and came out Verdi." In 1986 Terence McEwen, the general director of the San Francisco Opera, decided she was ready to make her San Francisco debut, and she did so in a major Verdi role, that of the gypsy Azucena in *Il Trovatore*.

That same year Zajick won the $20,000 Richard Tucker Music Foundation Award; she also auditioned for two prestigious companies—the Chicago Lyric Opera and the Houston Opera—and for the prominent conductors Riccardo Muti and Mstislav Rostropovich. Emerging from each of the auditions with an assignment, she traveled all over the world to perform, generally to great acclaim. Critics marveled at her range: while the average mezzo has a range of two octaves, from A flat to A flat, Zajick can hit a stunning high C and then descend to a solid low G. In October 1988 she made her debut with the Metropolitan Opera in New York City, singing Azucena, a role she would also perform at her debut in Vienna, Austria, later that year. In assessing her performance in Austria for the *New York Times* (October 13, 1988), the notoriously exacting opera critic Will Crutchfield wrote, "Her assumption of Azucena was distinguished by certain details of craftsmanship that have long been rare in Verdian mezzo parts." Although he felt that Zajick lacked a sense of drama, he conceded that since this was her Met debut, judging her dramatic skills was premature. At the Met the next season, she appeared as Amneris, the spurned princess in *Aïda*, a role with which she has become as closely identified as she has with that of Azucena.

Throughout the next decade almost every major opera company sought out Zajick, but she accepted roles selectively, reasoning that her voice would remain healthy longer if she didn't accept every job that came her way. Operas in which she agreed to sing included Tchaikovsky's *Dyeva*, Rimsky-Korsakov's little-performed *Mlada*, and Sergei Prokofiev's *Alexander Nevsky*. A meticulous planner, she prepares for each role by writing in a notebook the complete text of the opera, with both a phonetic transcription using the International Phonetic Alphabet and a verbatim translation into English. Zajick has sung in Russian, French, and Italian. (Italian audiences have difficulty pronouncing her name, so she has become known simply as "La Dolora" in Italy.)

Zajick has rarely indulged in the type of dramatic or demanding behavior for which some other divas have become notorious. "A successful production is one that people get wrapped up in. That happens only when everyone works together, when nobody involved—director, conductor, or singer—is out there using 'applaud me' techniques or is on an ego trip," she explained to Phillips. "Oh, celebrities are good, and they should be encouraged, but the important thing is making the piece work, not ego." She continued, "I don't mind being in the background if it's appropriate. Singers, like jewels, work better in a good setting. Who cares about being center stage?"

In addition to avoiding discussions about her personal life, Zajick—unlike many of her colleagues in the competitive world of opera—has refused to discuss her colleagues with interviewers. She is willing to express her peeves about her profession, however. For example, she has bemoaned the trend among directors to update classic pieces—often, she feels, to their detriment—rather than to commission new works. "Opera could handle a lot of social issues with sensitivity, even AIDS. What you don't want is a *Traviata* with Violetta dying of AIDS," she told Phillips. (In Verdi's opera, Violetta dies of what is universally assumed to be consumption.) "There's a real need to do new works, and they don't have to be atonal, unvocal, or unmusical to be contemporary. . . . There are a lot of composers out there, but they're not being used. The film industry soaks up the good composers, the ones who could give us new works and thereby save us from the old ones done in a bizarre way." She has also voiced her distress about the current lack of emphasis on technical training of opera students. Zajick still studies with Puffer, who joined the faculty of the Manhattan School of Music in 1994, and believes that the greatest artists are oriented toward technique. "When you're connected technically, you empty out all the energy that is in you—that is you," she told Matthew Gurewitsch for *Opera News* (March 1996), as quoted on her Web site. "All the anguish, joy, everything. That's what people pay to see." Zajick has said that she feels a deep affinity for her audience, and despite her apparent lack of ego, she has admitted that she basks in applause. She also enjoys the feedback she receives via the Internet, which she uses extensively as a means of communication as well as a way to research her many interests.

Zajick's albums include several recordings with the Metropolitan Opera conducted by James Levine, including *Aïda* (1991); *Highlights from Aïda* (1994); *Verdi: Greatest Hits* (1994); *Verdi: Highlights of Don Carlo* (1994); and *James Levine's 25th Anniversary Metropolitan Opera Gala* (1996). Another is Jules Massenet's *Hérodiade* (1995), in a live performance by the San Francisco Opera Chorus and Orchestra, conducted by Valery Gergiev, in which Placido Domingo and Renée Fleming also sang.

In 2001 Zajick will be making many appearances in Verdi operas to mark the centennial of the composer's death, on January 27, 1901. The highlight will be a performance in Munich of the Verdi Requiem, conducted by Zubin Mehta.

Marilyn Horne told Anthony Tommasini, "Tenacity has counted for a tremendous amount in Dolora's career and her life." Matthew Gurewitsch wrote, "Willpower, cognition, study, patience: these are the tools of Zajick's craft." Gurewitsch also reported, "There is something sphinxlike about [the singer], something abstract, withheld. . . . By her own account, Zajick prefers, in her work and her life, to operate on the intellectual level." Professing to favor solitary pursuits over socializing, Zajick wrote for the *New York Opera Newsletter* (June 1997), "I never feel at a loss after a performance. If anything, I feel relieved that I can go home and let my hair down and read or sleep, because by then I am very tired. Performing takes a lot out of me." According to an unsigned note in the newsletter, "While Ms. Zajick laughingly calls herself a hermit, she is known as a unifying factor in a cast, taking time to make other singers, chorus, and stage hands feel included." At her home in Nevada, she reads extensively on such topics as medicine, anthropology, history, and psychology. She also writes poetry and paints, most often pictures of natural subjects. Samples of her poetry and painting are on her Web site. In addition, Zajick is an accomplished gardener, and her home is lavishly landscaped. A self-described expert on frogs and toads, she keeps thousands of these amphibians in a pond on her property. Although she has lost some weight since she began her career, she remains a large, majestic performer, and critics agree that her voice more than matches her physique. Gurewitsch quoted an article from *Die Welt* (May 1995) that stated, "She has a voice on which one could raise whole temple complexes." — M.R.

Suggested Reading: *Classical* p12 May 1990, with photo; Dolora Zajick Web site; Metropolitan Opera Web site; *New York Times* II p39 Jan. 11, 1998, with photos; *Opera News* p10+ July 1988, with photos

Selected Recordings: *La Forza Del Destino*, 1993; *Aida*, 1994; *Don Carlo*, 1994; *Hérodiade*, 1994; *Il Trovatore*, 1994; *James Levine's 25th Anniversary Metropolitan Opera Gala*, 1996; *The Art of the Dramatic Mezzo-Soprano*, 2000

OBITUARIES

Written by Kieran Dugan

ABRAM, MORRIS B. June 19, 1918–Mar. 16, 2000 Lawyer; educator; civil-rights advocate; White House consultant; U.S. diplomat to the United Nations; American Jewish community leader; cofounder (1993) of the World Jewish Congress; was a partner at the New York law firm of Paul, Weiss, Rifkin, Wharton & Garrison (1962–68, 1970–89); chaired a number of educational organizations and foundations, including the United Negro College Fund (1970–79); practiced law in his native Georgia from 1948 to 1962; waged a 14-year battle against Georgia's county unit rule, which gave predominantly white rural voters a 155-to-one advantage over urban voters; waged the battle up to the U.S. Supreme Court, which declared the rule unconstitutional in 1963; co-sponsored the first large-scale middle-income housing development opened to blacks in Atlanta, Georgia; in defense of civil-rights workers in Georgia, won decisions that helped overturn the state's insurrection and illegal assembly laws; began his career in public service as the first general counsel to the Peace Corps, in 1961; first worked with the U.S. delegation to the U.N. as an expert member of the subcommission for the prevention of discrimination and the protection of minorities (1963–65); served as U.S. representative to the U.N. human-rights commission (1965–68); concurrently, was national president of the American Jewish Committee (1963–69); was president of Brandeis University from 1968 to 1970, a tenure rocked by student rebellion (virtually epidemic on American college campuses at that time), which he refused to appease; served on several White House commissions; was vice chairman of the U.S. Commission on Civil Rights (1984–86); served as permanent U.S. representative to the U.N.'s European office, in Geneva, Switzerland (1989–93); in Geneva beginning in 1993, chaired U.N. Watch, an affiliate of the World Jewish Congress; wrote the autobiography *The Day Is Short* (1982); died in Geneva. See *Current Biography* (October) 1965.

Obituary *New York Times* C p19 Mar. 17, 2000

ALBERT, CARL May 10, 1908–Feb. 4, 2000 U.S. representative from Oklahoma's Third Congressional District from 1947 to 1977; lawyer; in the House of Representatives, became majority leader in 1962 and Speaker in 1971; characterized himself as a "Truman Democrat"; tried to steer a course between "doctrinaire liberals" and "reactionary conservatives" and to "face issues in terms of conditions and not in terms of someone's inborn political philosophy"; died in McAlester, Oklahoma. See *Current Biography* (June) 1957.

Obituary *New York Times* p38 Feb. 6, 2000

AMES, AMYAS June 15, 1906–Jan. 24, 2000 Investment banker; patron of the performing arts; joined the New York brokerage firm of Kidder, Peabody & Co. as a securities analyst in 1932; became a partner in the firm in 1941, a management partner in 1944, a senior partner in 1958, and vice president in 1963; accepted an appointment to the board of directors of the Philharmonic Society of New York in 1955; became vice president of the society in 1958, general chairman of the Friends of the Philharmonic, the society's fund-raising arm, in 1959, and president of the society in 1963; was appointed chairman of the executive committee of Lincoln Center for the Performing Arts, the largest cultural complex in the U.S., in 1969; the following year, became chairman of the board of the New York Philharmonic and chairman of Lincoln Center; mounted two major endowment drives that raised more than $28 million for Lincoln Center; organized Concerned Citizens for the Arts, a lobbying group that persuaded the New York state legislature to approve an appropriation of $18 million for the New York State Council on the Arts in 1970 and another appropriation of $13 million for the council in 1971; subsequently organized Partnership for the Arts to lobby the federal government; at Lincoln Center, oversaw the creation of the New York Philharmonic's free "Concerts in the Parks" and the *Live from Lincoln Center* television broadcasts and the transformation of Philharmonic Hall, originally notorious for its poor acoustics, into Avery Fisher Hall; died in Lexington, Massachusetts. See *Current Biography* (April) 1972.

Obituary *New York Times* C p29 Jan. 26, 2000

ARCINIEGAS, GERMÁN Dec. 6, 1900–Nov. 27, 1999 Colombian intellectual; left-of-center politician; polemicist; journalist; university professor; author; diplomat; wrote for the liberal Bogotá newspaper *El Tiempo* from 1918 until his death; in addition to thousands of essays, published well over threescore books on the history and culture of the Americas, a number of which were translated into English, including the college text *Latin America: A Cultural History*; after earning a doctor of laws degree at the National University in Bogotá, was a professor of sociology in the university's faculty of law and political science (1925–28); during the following two decades, served three terms as a Liberal Party member of Colombia's House of Representatives and two appointments as minister of education in Liberal governments; during the same period, accepted his first diplomatic posts and did stints as editor, editor in chief, and director of *El Tiempo*; traveled widely; beginning in 1943, was a guest lecturer on American college campuses; as an exile from his native country during "La Violencia" (1948–58), a tumultuous period marked by a succession of right-wing military dictatorships, was visiting professor of Spanish-American literature at Columbia University; later served as Colombia's ambassador to Italy, the Vatican, and Venezuela; died in Bogotá. See *Current Biography* (May) 1954.

Obituary *New York Times* p62 Dec. 5, 1999

ASSAD, HAFEZ AL- Oct. 6, 1930–June 10, 2000 President of Syria since 1971; a dictator who transformed his mineral-poor nation into a key, albeit somewhat xenophobic, Middle Eastern power, a center of Arab hostility toward Israel and the American-Israeli alliance; graduated from the Syrian military aviation college as a combat pilot in 1955; as a member of the nationalist faction of the Ba'ath Party, supported a military coup in 1966, following which he became minister of defense and commander of the air force (1966–70); instigated the 1970 coup that brought him to power, first as prime minister and the following year as president; vis-a-vis the West, suffered a worsening of relations when Syria was suspected of having ties to international terrorists in the 1980s; experienced an improvement in relations with the West following Iraq's invasion of Kuwait in 1990, when he expressed support for the U.S.-led international mobilization against Iraq; died in Damascus, Syria. See *Current Biography* (April) 1992.

Obituary *New York Times* A p1+ June 11, 2000

AURIOL, JACQUELINE Nov. 5, 1917–Feb. 12, 2000 French aviator; test pilot; received the first of her pilot's licenses in 1948; as a passenger, was in an airplane accident in which her face was mangled, in 1949; over the following three years, underwent more than a score of reconstructive plastic-surgery operations; in a 100-kilometer closed-circuit flight between Istres and Avignon on May 12, 1951, flew a Vampire jet 509.245 miles per hour, breaking the women's world speed record of 469.549 miles an hour for the same distance, set by Jacqueline Cochran of the U.S. in 1947; beat her own record for the measured 100-kilometer distance on December 21, 1952, flying a Mistral jet fighter at a speed of 534.375 miles per hour; on August 29, 1953 became the second woman (after Jacqueline Cochran) to break the sound barrier, flying the Mystère IV jet interceptor at 687.5 miles per hour; was the daughter-in-law of French president Vincent Auriol; died at her home in Paris. See *Current Biography* (September) 1953.

Obituary *New York Times* C p25 Feb. 17, 2000

BANFIELD, EDWARD C. Nov. 19, 1916–Sep. 30, 1999 Political scientist; professor emeritus of government at Harvard University; author; an urbanologist who questioned the prevailing liberal approach to urban problems that began its ascendancy with President Franklin D. Roosevelt's New Deal and was reinforced by President Lyndon B. Johnson's Great Society programs; wrote or co-wrote highly respected books on the political realities of American urban government—including *Politics, Planning and the Public Interest* (1955), *Government and Housing in Metropolitan Areas* (1958), *Political Influence* (1961), *Big City Politics* (1965), and *Boston: the Job Ahead* (1966)—before triggering an explosion of controversy with *The Heavenly City* (1970); in that book, rejected the "crisis mongering" that led to federal aid-to-inner-cities programs that were, in his view, ill conceived and often counterproductive; in his analysis of the problems of the urban poor, downplayed race and stressed economic class, culture, and psychological limitations; after working as an information specialist with the U.S. Farm Security Administration for six years, went to the University of Chicago as a protégé of Rexford G. Tugwell; as an instructor at Chicago, studied for his doctorate in political science under such champions of laissez-faire economics and politics as Milton Friedman and Leo Strauss; in 1952 received his Ph.D. degree with a dissertation that expanded his book *Government Project* (1951), a study of a federally sponsored cooperative farm; with his wife, Laura (née Fasano), wrote *The Moral Basis of a Backward Society* (1958), about the contribution of clannish "amoral familism" to the poverty-stricken state of a village in Italy; taught at the University of Chicago until 1959, when he joined the Harvard University faculty; became a leader of the Harvard University/Massachusetts Institute of Technology Joint Center for International Studies; was chairman of President Richard Nixon's preinaugural Task Force on Urban Affairs (1968–69); after Nixon's inauguration, headed the president's Model Cities Task Force; in 1972 became the first William R. Kenan Jr. professor at the University of Pennsylvania; later returned to the Harvard faculty; died in Vermont. See *Current Biography* (May) 1972.

Obituary *New York Times* C p21 Oct. 8, 1999

BASKIN, LEONARD Aug. 15, 1922–June 3, 2000 Artist; a humanist and moralist with a classical approach to art that he maintained against successive waves of nondidactic abstractionism; in his black-and-white figurative sculptures and graphic works, including drawings, was "ghoulish" (his word) in pursuing the theme of death—a pursuit that was, in the words of the art critic John Canaday, "inseparable from the theme of man's dignity in the face of his own mortality"; was formatively influenced by the Orthodox Judaism of his father, a rabbi, while arguing against that orthodoxy; during the Depression, went through a leftist political phase that contributed to the development of his social consciousness; began exhibiting his sculpture in 1939; subsequently taught himself printing; in 1942 founded the Gehenna Press, which over the following six decades published approximately 100 limited-edition books noted for their fine typography and superb illustrations; in the early 1950s turned his hand to woodcuts and etchings; during the 1950s sculpted a series of effigies of the dead in wood, bronze, and stone, including the walnut *Man with a Dead Bird* and the limestone *The Great Dead Man*; had a brilliant reputation as an illustrator of books, from *The Iliad* and other classics to the children's book *Hosie's Alphabet*, which won the Caldecott Medal in 1974; among other commissions, created a bas relief of a funeral cortège for the Franklin Delano Roosevelt Memorial in Washington, D.C., and a sorrowful, seated cast-bronze figure for the Holocaust Memorial in Ann Arbor, Michigan; in 1952 became an art teacher at the Worcester (Massachusetts) Museum; taught sculpture and printmaking at Smith College, in Northampton, Massachusetts, from 1953 to 1974; was visiting professor of art at Hampshire College, in Amherst, Massachusetts, from 1984 to 1994; died in Northampton. See *Current Biography* (May) 1964.

Obituary *New York Times* A p23 June 6, 2000

BECK, BERTRAM M. Mar. 25, 1918–Apr. 3, 2000 Social worker; educator; was a psychiatric caseworker in the U.S. Army Air Forces during World War II; in 1946 became a caseworker with the Community Service Society, an organization offering help to low-income New York City families seeking health care, affordable housing, and other necessities; as assistant director of the society's bureau of public affairs (1948–52), studied the correctional treatment and detention facilities for youthful offenders and the provisions for temporary shelter for dependent and neglected children; from 1952 to 1955 directed a society project aimed at stimulating state and local action in improving services to delinquent children; concurrently, was a consultant on juvenile delinquency with the U.S. Department of Health, Education, and Welfare (now the Department of Health and Human Services); during the first two decades of his career, published a number of reports related to his work; in 1955 became associate executive director of the National Association of Social Workers; from 1967 to 1977 was executive director of the Henry Street Settlement on Manhattan's Lower East Side; was also executive director (1965–69) of Mobilization for Youth in Manhattan; returned to the Community Service Society as general director (1977–85); joined the faculty of Fordham University as a professor of social service in 1985; was associate dean of Fordham's school of social service from 1987 until his retirement, in 1996; died in Manhattan. See *Current Biography* (May) 1961.

Obituary *New York Times* A p21 Apr. 5, 2000

BELL, DAVID E. Jan. 20, 1919–Sep. 6, 2000 Economist; educator; former U.S. government official; foundation executive; was best known as a specialist in the economic problems of underdeveloped countries; early in his career, was a teaching fellow at Harvard University and an analyst with the U.S. Bureau of the Budget; during the administration of President Harry S. Truman, alternated between the posts of executive assistant in the White House and budget examiner and other positions in the Bureau of the Budget; was administrative assistant to the president during Truman's last months in office (1952–53); returned to Harvard as a Rockefeller public-service fellow in the university's graduate school of public administration, known informally as the Littauer School (1953–54); from 1954 to 1957 headed a group of economic advisers sent by the Littauer School to assist the government of Pakistan in its fiscal policies; on his return from Pakistan, was a lecturer in Harvard's Department of Economics and a research associate at the Littauer School; became the school's chief administrative officer in 1959; was director of the Bureau of the Budget from the beginning of the administration of President John F. Kennedy in January 1961 until December 1962, when he became administrator of the Agency for International Development, the federal government's foreign-aid agency; left government in 1966; subsequently, until 1980, was a vice president and an executive vice president in charge of international activities with the Ford Foundation; died at his home in Cambridge, Massachusetts. See *Current Biography* (June) 1961.

Obituary *New York Times* B p10 Sep. 12, 2000

BIRD, ROSE E. Nov. 2, 1936–Dec. 4, 1999 Chief justice of the California Supreme Court (1977–86), to which she had been appointed by Democratic governor Edmund G. (Jerry) Brown; as a proactive judicial reformer and "a soft-on-crime liberal," as many regarded her, stirred extraordinary controversy; after earning her J.D. degree, clerked for the chief justice of the Nevada Supreme Court (1965–66); passed the California bar exam in 1966; during the following eight years was a deputy public defender in Santa Clara County; concurrently, taught a seminar in criminal defense at Stanford University's school of law; worked closely with Jerry Brown as a volunteer in his successful, 1974 gubernatorial campaign; as secretary of California's Department of Agriculture (1975–77) under Governor Brown, was the first woman in California state government history to hold a Cabinet-level post; again scored a first for women in California when Brown appointed her chief justice; on the court, led a Democratic majority in bolstering consumer rights and environmental protections; drew the fire of conservatives with such decisions as those in favor of school busing and against the tax-cutting Proposition 13; especially outraged her political enemies with her repeated decisions (61 in all) vacating death sentences; repeatedly survived campaigns for her recall; was finally removed by popular vote, in 1986; died in Palo Alto, California. See *Current Biography* (May) 1984.

Obituary *New York Times* B p18 Dec. 6, 1999

BLOUGH, ROY Aug. 21, 1901–Feb. 25, 2000 Economist; former government official; professor emeritus of banking and international finance, Columbia University; beginning in 1922, taught successively at Manchester (Indiana) College and the University of Cincinnati; became a statistician with the Wisconsin tax commission in 1927; was promoted to chief statistician in 1930; joined the U.S. Department of the Treasury as director of tax research in 1938; was assistant to the treasury secretary from 1944 to 1946; returned to academe as professor at the University of Chicago (1946–52); edited *National Tax Journal* (1947–50); was a member of President Harry Truman's council of economic advisers (1950–52); directed the department of economic affairs at the United Nations from 1952 to 1955, when he began his 15-year tenure as a professor at Columbia University; in the late 1950s participated in U.N. economic advisory missions to the governments of Peru and Chile; was a consultant to the Committee for Economic Development (1965–73); wrote or co-wrote several books in his field; died in Mitchellville, Maryland. See *Current Biography* (July) 1950.

Obituary *New York Times* C p25 Mar. 2, 2000

BOURGUIBA, HABIB BEN ALI Aug. 3, 1903–Apr. 6, 2000 First president of the republic of Tunisia, the former French protectorate that he led to independence; after studying law and political science in

France in the 1920s, practiced law in Tunisia; became active in politics and journalism; in 1933 bolted Tunisia's Destour (Constitution) Party and led a group of French-educated intellectuals in forming Neo-Destour; although espousing secular nationalism rather than Islamic traditionalism, attracted Tunisia's Muslim masses to the new party, which was outlawed by the French in 1934; spent much of the following 21-year period in prison or exile; in 1955, with the blessings of his former French jailers, returned to Tunisia to guide the country into self-rule; in 1956, when Tunisia achieved its independence, became prime minister; was chosen president by a constituent assembly in 1957; was confirmed in the presidency in general elections in 1959; was named president for life in 1974; over the span of his years as president, was generally perceived as relatively moderate, generally pro-Western, and instrumental in advancing the rights of women and nomadic and seminomadic tribespeople; survived bouts with labor unrest in 1968 and 1978, a coup attempt in 1980, and rioting in 1984; was deposed in a bloodless coup in 1987; wrote two books on the colonial phase of French-Tunisian relations. See *Current Biography* (September) 1955.

Obituary *New York Times* B p13 Apr. 7, 2000

BOWERS, FAUBION Jan. 29, 1917–Nov. 16, 1999 Writer; a multilingual surveyor of international theater and dance; while studying piano at the Juilliard School of Music, in New York City, when he was 22, became interested in Japanese and Javanese music; broadened his familiarity with Asian music, theater, and dance while teaching music at the University of Tokyo (1940–41) and lecturing at Taman Siswa in Djarkarta, Java (now Indonesia), in 1941; was drafted into the U.S. Army during World War II, commissioned an officer, and assigned to military intelligence as a Japanese interrogator and interpreter; in the postwar Allied occupation goverment in Tokyo, was aide-de-camp to the administrator, General Douglas MacArthur; in 1948, when the occupation government banned Kabuki, Japan's classical theater, resigned from the army to become civilian theater censor so as to be in a position to reinstate Kabuki, which he succeeded in doing; in 1949 left Japan and made a dance-and-drama study tour of northern China, Indochina, Thailand, Indonesia, and Bali; made study tours of 14 countries during the 1950s; in addition to books on the theater and dance of the East, including that of Japan and India, wrote *Broadway USSR* (1959) and the two-volume biography *Scriabin* (1969); died at his home in Manhattan. See *Current Biography* (September) 1959.

Obituary *New York Times* A p29 Nov. 22, 1999

BOWLES, PAUL Dec. 30, 1910–Nov. 18, 1999 Expatriate American writer; a peripatetic avant-gardist in literature and the arts since the late 1920s, when his first surrealist poems were published; turned his hand to serious music in the early 1930s; later, for two decades, gained his livelihood, and the respect of his musical peers, with his incidental music for the stage (including Broadway) and, to a lesser degree, the screen; still later, revealed a decadent romanticism in his creation of a perversely cruel form of Gothic horror fiction, a mythology, as he viewed it, in which Western vacationers and curiosity seekers make harrowing one-way trips into the primitive heart of darkness; in visiting Tangier, Morocco, in 1931, discovered, as Jay McInerney observed, "a landscape and a culture which are the objective correlative of his vision of the psyche"; beginning in 1947, made Tangier his home base, returning there from the world travels to which he was driven by wanderlust and ethnological curiosity until the early 1970s; thereafter, rarely left Tangier; achieved resounding mainstream attention with the publication in 1949 of his first novel, the existential cult classic *The Sheltering Sky*, a shocking parable, set in the Sahara, in which he allegorized the vulnerability of the civilized psyche in contact with atavistic forces; in his second novel, *Let It Come Down* (1952), told the story of a young American man who descends into hashish-fueled degradation in Tangier; according to the critic Joseph Voelker, invented "demonic pseudonyms" for himself in the quasi-autobiographical novel *The Spider's House* (1955) and offered the "clearest treatment" of "the myth of the adept as demonic author" in his fourth novel, *Up Above the World* (1966); in addition to his novels and two books of poetry, published several collections of short stories; also published 13 volumes of his translations of the oral folktales he recorded, including some from the Moghrebi language; died in Tangier. See *Current Biography* (October) 1990.

Obituary *New York Times* B p14 Nov. 19, 1999

BRESSON, ROBERT Sep. 25, 1901–Dec. 18, 1999 French filmmaker; austere and aloof, was a unique purist among auteurs; with rigorous selectivity and attention to necessary detail, made tightly constructed films (almost all in black and white) reflecting a dark Jansenist Catholic vision in which belief in predestination is relieved by hope in redemptive spiritual grace; was most acclaimed for *Le Journal d'un curé de compagne* (1950, *Diary of a Country Priest*) and *Un Condamné à mort s'est échappé* (1956, *A Man Escaped*); during the 1930s apprenticed under René Clair and other directors, chiefly collaborating on screenplays; began directing full-length feature films in the early 1940s, when, under the German occupation, export of French films was suspended; did not become known to art cinema audiences in the U.S. until the late 1940s, through the belated transatlantic release of *Les Anges du péché* (1943, *The Angels of Sin*) and *Les Dames du Bois de Boulogne* (1945, *The Women of the Bois de Boulogne*); dissatisfied with the theatricality of the performances of the professional actors in those films, thereafter employed nonprofessionals or neophytes when possible; wrote or collaborated in the writing of the dialogue for most of his films; made a total of only 13 feature pictures, including *Pickpocket* (1959), *Le Procès de Jeanne d'Arc* (1961, *The Trial of Joan of Arc*), *Au Hasard, Balthazar* (1966, *Balthazar*), *Quatre Nuits d'un rêveur* (1971, *Four Nights of a Dreamer*), *Lancelot du Lac* (1974, *Lancelot of the Lake*), *Le Diable Probablement* (1977, *The Devil, Probably*), and *L'Argent* (1983, *Money*); died at his home in Droué-sur-Druette, southwest of Paris. See *Current Biography* (January) 1971.

Obituary *New York Times* C p27 Dec. 22, 1999

BROWN, NEWELL June 19, 1917–Apr. 14, 2000 Former government official; educator; early in his career, published and edited the Franklin (New Hampshire) *Journal-Transcript*, a country weekly, for three years and was managing editor of the Dover *Strafford Star*, a daily, for a brief time; was director of the New Hampshire state division of employment security from 1950 to 1955; joined the U.S. Department of Labor as administrator of the wage and hour and public contracts division in 1955; was assistant secretary of labor for wage-hour administration from 1957 to 1961; subsequently managed labor relations for a machine-tool company in Hartford, Connecticut; in 1963 established Princeton University's career and counseling services office; directed the office until his retirement, in 1980; while at Princeton, published the nonfiction books *After College, What?* and *To Call It a Day in Good Season*; died at his home in Keene, New Hampshire. See *Current Biography* (September) 1959.

Obituary *New York Times* A p21 May 1, 2000

BUDGE, DONALD June 13, 1915–Jan. 26, 2000 Tennis player; a pioneer practitioner of power tennis, perhaps the first to use his backhand as aggressively as his forehand; as an amateur during the 1930s, won a total of 14 major titles, six in singles, four in doubles, and four in mixed doubles; in 1938 had the single most successful year of any amateur in tennis up to that time, becoming the first player ever to win all four major national titles, the Australian, French, British (Wimbledon), and U.S., a sweep thenceforth known as the Grand Slam; first won the U.S. doubles title (with Gene Mako) in 1936; became the world's number-one ranking amateur in 1937; in that year won the Wimbledon and U.S. singles and mixed-doubles titles and the U.S. doubles; also in 1937 contributed to the U.S. team's capture of the Davis Cup for the first time since 1926; in 1938, in addition to the Grand Slam, again won the Wimbledon and U.S. doubles and mixed doubles and helped the U.S. in its successful defense of the Davis Cup; in his Davis Cup career, compiled a record of 10–2 in singles and 6–2 in doubles; turned professional in 1939; defeated Bobby Riggs for the U.S. Pro title at Forest Hills in 1942; served in the U.S. Army Air Force during World War II; after the war, slumped in his tennis career because of a shoulder injury suffered in military training; reached the U.S. Pro final for the last time in 1953; was elected to the International Tennis Hall of Fame in 1964; died in Scranton, Pennsylvania. See *Current Biography* (June) 1941.

Obituary *New York Times* B p7 Jan. 27, 2000

BUFFET, BERNARD July 10, 1928–Oct. 4, 1999 Painter; an independent French Expressionist who worked in the figurative tradition of Francis Gruber, free of the varied abstractionisms of Cubism, Surrealism, and Abstract Expressionism (or Action Painting, known as *Tachisme* in France); created representations of the real world according to his view of it, which was harsh and haunting; began drawing during his childhood in Paris; subsequently carried the architecturally linear and schematic craftsmanship of his pen and pencil work over into his watercolors and oils, in which color is subdued and somber and sharply outlined with straight and angular black lines; created spiky and monochromatic landscapes, cityscapes, and still lifes in addition to gaunt, almost skeletal or stick-like human figures; despite considerable critical dissent, attained overnight success spectacularly in 1948, when his controversial artistic *misérablisme*, paralleling the philosopher Jean-Paul Sartre's existentialism, struck a chord in the postwar French generation's mood of disillusionment, nihilism, alienation, and spiritual aloneness; early in his career, as a member of the school of expressive social realism known as *Homme Témoin*, executed works ranging from *Woman with Bathtub* and *The Sitting Drinker* to such depictions of human brutality and misery as *The Horrors of War, Hanging from the Gallows, The Angel of Destruction*, and representations of concentration-camp victims; during the 1950s did series of paintings of matadors, clowns and other circus people, New York and Paris cityscapes, and the life and death of Joan of Arc, among other subjects; painted, among other monumental works, a gigantic mural of Joan of Arc; for the chapel of the Château d'Arc, in 1962, created a set of canvases devoted to the Passion of Jesus Christ; worked reclusively; lost some of his expressive energy in his more formulaic and decorative later works; in addition to his drawings, oils, and watercolors, did many lithographs; illustrated several books; designed some ballet scenery; is represented in a number of museums worldwide, including the Museum of Modern Art in New York City, which has his *Self-Portrait* (1948) and *Still Life with Fish II* (1949); died at his home in the Var department, in southeastern France. See *Current Biography* (April) 1959.

Obituary *New York Times* B p11 Oct. 5, 1999

BYRD, CHARLIE Sep. 16, 1925–Dec. 1, 1999 Guitarist; a jazzman with a solid background in the theory and techniques of classical music; according to Nat Hentoff, was "more thoroughly and convincingly at ease in both idioms" than any other jazz musician; also had a masterly familiarity with such styles as flamenco and samba; was unsurpassed in his versatility over the entire repertoire of the guitar, from Vivaldi to the blues; even in his jazz performances, played without pick or electronic amplification; from 1957 on, made the Showboat Lounge in Washington, D.C., his home base; toured England and Saudi Arabia with Woody Herman's band in 1959; with his own trio, toured Mexico, Central America, and South America in 1961; from Brazil, brought back the bossa nova, a new version of the samba that he played a major role in popularizing in the U.S.; by 1952 had recorded 22 albums, ranging from an LP including some of his own blues compositions to albums devoted to Latin rhythms and 16th-century guitar music; during the last three decades of his life, recorded 20 albums on the Concord label, many of them collaborations with other guitarists, the clarinetist Ken Peplowski, the drummer Chuck Redd, and his brother, Joe, a bassist; finished his recording career with a tribute to Louis Armstrong; died at his home in Annapolis, Maryland. See *Current Biography* (October) 1967.

Obituary *New York Times* A p15 Dec. 4, 1999

CADMUS, PAUL Dec. 17, 1904–Dec. 12, 1999 Painter; etcher; an academic realist; because of the narrative content of most of his art, considered himself a "literary painter"; was at his most tranquil in his male nude studies; in such early paintings as *Shore Leave* and *YMCA Locker Room*, established what would be a dominant theme in his work; while working under the aegis of the federal Public Works of Art Project in the 1930s, offended navy brass with his *The Fleet's In* painting and Coney Island businesspeople with *Coney Island*; in his Manhattan studio during the same period, created four bitingly sardonic scenes titled *Aspects of Suburban Life*; was represented at important group shows, including one at the Museum of Modern Art, in New York City, in 1943; was honored with a career retrospective organized by the Miami University Art Museum in Ohio in 1981; in his last years was recognized in an exhibition of his cycle of paintings titled *Seven Deadly Sins* at the Metropolitan Museum of Art (1995) and of his *Sailor* series at the Whitney Museum of American Art (1996), both in New York; in 1999 received the first annual international arts award of the homosexual Pridefest America festival in Philadelphia; died at his home in Weston, Connecticut. See *Current Biography* (July) 1942.

Obituary *New York Times* B p14 Dec. 15, 1999

CÂMARA, HELDER PESSORA Feb. 7, 1909–Aug. 27, 1999 Brazilian Roman Catholic prelate; a champion of human rights; advocate for the poor and landless; was archbishop of Recife and Olinda in the arid and impoverished northeastern corner of Brazil from 1964 to 1985, a tenure coinciding precisely with the rule of a repressive military dictatorship; was a singular voice in denouncing the wide gulf between his country's rich elite and impoverished masses, the government's cultivation of that status quo, and its use of terror and torture in suppressing dissent; was exceptional among Latin American bishops in embracing "liberation theology," a controversial admixture of the Marxist concept of class struggle with the Christian pursuit of social justice; advocated radical social and economic reform, including redistribution of land and more democratic access to education; was branded "the Red Bishop" by the government-toadying Brazilian press; criticized the international predations of Communist powers as well as those of the capitalist industrialized nations and transnational corporations; before his appointment as archbishop of Recife and Olinda, was auxiliary archbishop of Rio de Janeiro; died at his home in Olinda, a suburb of Recife. See *Current Biography* (July) 1971.

Obituary *New York Times* A p17 Aug. 30, 1999

CARTLAND, BARBARA July 9, 1901–May 21, 2000 British writer; prodigious author of best-selling romance fiction; beginning slowly in the late 1920s and at an increasing pace thereafter, wrote Regency-style genre novels in which, typically, virgins are wooed passionately but chastely by rich and raffish aristocrat types; explained that her heroines "never go to bed without a ring on their fingers; not until page 118 at least" and that her notion of a sexy man was one who was "fully clothed, preferably in uniform"; dictated her novels to several assistants, backed by tape recorders; thus, during her most productive decades, was able to create two novels a month; published a total of more than 700 romance novels (with titles such as *Virgin in Mayfair* and *Passions in the Sand*) that had printing runs totaling one billion copies in 36 languages worldwide; in addition to her fiction, wrote memoirs, biographies of her mother and her brother Ronald, and books on charm and cookery, among other works of nonfiction; in 1991 was made a dame of the British Empire; died at her home near Hatfield in Hertfordshire, England. See *Current Biography* (August) 1979.

Obituary *New York Times* B p7 May 22, 2000

CASHIN, BONNIE 1915–Feb. 3, 2000 Fashion designer; as a creative sportswear designer, fashioned distinctively American casual attire by observing contemporary life and gearing her creations to its needs; used a form-follows-function approach that combined simple lines with vibrant colors and unusual textures; unlike couturiers who sought elegance, strove for classical purity of line, an "honest cut" that allowed fabrics to hang naturally, with a minimum of darts and seams; as a theatrical costume designer early in her career, demonstrated a knack for flattering the looks of women in action; in 1937 went to work for the sportswear house Adler and Adler; from 1943 to 1949 was a costume designer for Twentieth Century Fox studios in Hollywood; in 1949 rejoined Adler and Adler in New York City; in 1952 founded Bonnie Cashin, Inc., chiefly as a base for doing freelance designing; the following year began collaborating with Philip Sills and Co., a women's sportswear manufacturer then specializing in leather; for Sills, designed annual collections of coats, dresses, vests, tunics, skirts, shorts, slacks, jumpsuits, and capes of suede or smooth leather often dyed in various colors; with Sills, later branched out beyond leather to other materials, from wool to fur, still trimmed in leather; for other manufacturers, designed rainwear, cashmere knitwear, and handbags; in 1979 founded the Innovative Design Fund Awards; died in New York City. See *Current Biography* (May) 1970.

Obituary *New York Times* C p16 Feb. 5, 2000

CASTELLI, LEO Sep. 4, 1907–Aug. 21, 1999 Trieste-born American art dealer; a multilingual cosmopolite who specialized, in his words, in picking artists not "because they seem to be good, but because they seem to be leaders of a new movement"; by promoting such groundbreaking American talent to international recognition, helped to expand the boundaries of late modern art and to define the aesthetics of the post–abstract-expressionist period; fostered the emergence of pop art (with which he was most closely identified), minimalism, conceptualism, and neoexpressionism; with René Drouin, opened his first gallery (an abortive venture) in Paris in 1939 with a surrealist group show; with his first wife, Ileana Schapira, immigrated to the U.S., in 1941; with her, after years of cautious collecting, in February 1957 opened a small gallery in uptown Manhattan featuring works of such established masters as the French cubist Fernand Léger and the American abstract expressionists Jackson Pollock and Willem de Kooning; at about that time, partly inspired by his acquaintance with the work of Robert Rauschenberg, decided to concentrate on fresh talent likely to chart a new course in contemporary art; had what he called his "first great epiphany" while viewing a painting titled *Green Target*, by a then-unknown artist of the New York School named Jasper Johns in the spring of 1957; had "another great epiphany" when he first saw paintings by Frank Stella, in 1959; in the early 1960s, with the help of Ivan Karp, added to his roster Roy Lichtenstein and Andy Warhol; later added Donald Judd, Robert Morris, Dan Flavin, Richard Serra, Bruce Nauman, Richard Artschwager, Joseph Kosuth, Robert Barry, Julian Schnabel, David Salle, Sandro Chia, and Gérard Garouste, among others; in 1971 opened the first of his gallery spaces in the downtown Manhattan neighborhood known as SoHo, which his presence helped to establish as a mecca of innovative art; after his divorce from his first wife and the death of his second (Antoinette Fraissex du Bost), married the Italian art critic Barbara Bertozzi, who survives him; died at his home in Manhattan. See *Current Biography* (August) 1984.

Obituary *New York Times* p1+ Aug. 23, 1999

CHAFEE, JOHN H. Oct. 22, 1922–Oct. 24, 1999 U.S. Republican senator from Rhode Island since 1977; a member of the liberal eastern wing of the Republican Party, noted for his bipartisanship; lawyer; began his career in elective office as a Rhode Island state representative (1957–62); was minority leader of the State Assembly's House of Representatives from 1959 to 1962; served as governor of Rhode Island from 1963 to 1969; first went to Washington as secretary of the navy in President Richard Nixon's Cabinet (1969–72); resumed the practice of law in Providence, Rhode Island (1972–76); in the U.S. Senate, was instrumental in greatly expanding Medicaid, the federal health program for the poor, and in reauthorizing the Clean Air Act; chaired the Senate committee on the environment and public works in the 104th Congress; died in Bethesda, Maryland. See *Current Biography* (1969).

Obituary *New York Times* B p10 Oct. 26, 1999

CHAMBERLAIN, WILT Aug. 21, 1936–Oct. 12, 1999 Professional basketball player; widely regarded as the dominant center of his time; was popularly nicknamed "Wilt the Stilt," an allusion to his height (seven feet one inch), and "the Big Dipper," a reference to his dunking the ball from above the rim of the basket; in 15 years in the National Basketball Association, set a career record for rebounds, with 23,924; also held the career record for points scored, with 31,419, until it was broken by Kareem Abdul-Jabbar; before turning pro, was an All-American in two years on the varsity team at the University of Kansas; played with the Harlem Globetrotters for one year while waiting to become eligible for NBA competition; continued to play with the Globetrotters for several years during the NBA off-seasons; playing with the Philadelphia Warriors in his first pro season (1959–60), led the NBA in scoring, as he would in the following six seasons, and in rebounds, as he would in 10 succeeding seasons; in 1960 was voted NBA rookie of the year and received his first of four most-valuable-player awards; set records for most rebounds in a single game (55, against Boston in November 1960), for highest rebound average per game (27.2, during the 1960–61 season), and for highest scoring average per game (50.4 points, in 1961–62); playing against the New York Knicks on March 2, 1962, set single-game records for most points scored (100) and most free throws made (28); moved with the Warriors to San Francisco in 1962; during the 1964–65 season, joined the Philadelphia 76ers, with whom he played through 1966–67; finished his career with the Los Angeles Lakers (1968–73); had career regular-season totals of 1,045 games played, 22.9 rebounds per game, and 30.1 points per game; in play-offs, scored 3,607 points and averaged 24.5 rebounds in 160 games; published an autobiography, *A View from Above* (1991); died at his home in the Bel-Air section of Los Angeles. See *Current Biography* (June) 1960.

Obituary *New York Times* p1+ Oct. 13, 1999

CHAPMAN, LEONARD F. JR. Nov. 3, 1913–Jan. 6, 2000 U.S. Marine Corps four-star general, retired; compiled a distinguished record in Pacific combat areas in World War II; later served in Japan; beginning in 1956, was commanding officer of the marine barracks in Washington, D.C.; subsequently was Marine Corps chief of staff (1964–67) and assistant commandant of the corps (1967–68); in January 1968 began a four-year term as commandant of the corps; as commandant, was credited with defusing racial tensions in the corps and in maintaining strict standards of discipline at a time when the army and the navy were relxing rules regarding such matters as grooming and alcoholic beverages in military barracks; after his retirement from the military, was U.S. commissioner of immigration and naturalization (1973–76); in that position, stepped up efforts to curb illegal immigration; died in Fairfax, Virginia. See *Current Biography* (July) 1968.

Obituary *New York Times* B p9 Jan. 11, 2000

CHRISTOPHER, GEORGE Dec. 8, 1907–Sep. 14, 2000 Greek-born Republican mayor of San Francisco (1956–64); as mayor, oversaw a building boom in San Francisco and was credited with broadening the city's business base, raising the vitality of its financial district, and enlarging its international airport; in addition, succeeded in attracting the New York Giants baseball franchise to San Francisco; thus, "set a course for the city as an international destination, a major league baseball city, and a financial center for the West," in the words of Democratic U.S. senator Dianne Feinstein, herself a former mayor of San Francisco; had previously served as a member and chairman of the San Francisco board of supervisors; outside of politics, began his career as a business accountant who sometimes invested in the businesses he served; through such investment, became the president of Christopher Dairy Farms, an enterprise he turned over to relatives when he became mayor; died in San Francisco. See *Current Biography* (February) 1958.

Obituary *New York Times* A p13 Sep. 16, 2000

CLAIBORNE, CRAIG Sep. 4, 1920–Jan. 22, 2000 Gastronomist; journalist; food editor of the *New York Times* (1957–86); introduced millions of Americans to the world of fine cuisine; helped to raise restaurant reviewing from advertising- and public relations–related pap to authentic criticism and evaluation for the benefit of consumers; was trained in table and banquet service and French cuisine in Switzerland; began career with *Gourmet* magazine; developed the recipes he offered his readers in his immense East Hampton, New York, kitchen, often in collaboration his friend Pierre Franey; wrote *The New York Times Cook Book*, first published in 1961, which has sold more than a million copies; realized another perennial best-seller in *The New York Times Guide to Dining Out in New York*, first published in 1964; also published, among other books, *The New York Times International Cook Book* (1971), *Craig Claiborne's Southern Cooking* (1987), and several written with Pierre Franey; wrote an autobiography, *A Feast Made for Laughter* (1987); died in New York City. See *Current Biography* (September) 1969.

Obituary *New York Times* A p1+ Jan. 24, 2000

COCKE, ERLE JR. May 10, 1921–Apr. 23, 2000 National commander of the American Legion (1950–51); agro-businessman; scion of a Georgia farming, food-processing, and banking family; as a highly decorated commissioned army officer in the European theater of operations in World War II, was wounded in combat three times and escaped from his German captors three times; rose to the rank of major; after the war, earned a master's degree in business administration at Harvard University; in his native Terrell County, Georgia, operated a 1,200-acre peanut and blooded cattle farm and was assistant general manager of the Cinderella Foods Co.; served stints as executive director of the Agricultural and Industrial Development Board of Georgia and as industrial agent for the Central of Georgia Railway; was president of Cocke & Phillips, a lobbying firm; in politics, was an active (and conservative) Democrat; was a Defense Department consultant under President Harry S Truman and an alternate representative under President Dwight D. Eisenhower; held a World Bank position under presidents John F. Kennedy and Lyndon B. Johnson; was a brigadier general in the Georgia National Guard; died in Chevy Chase, Maryland. See *Current Biography* (January) 1951.

Obituary *New York Times* C p25 Apr. 26, 2000

COGGAN, F. DONALD Oct. 9, 1909–May 17, 2000 British ecclesiastic; former archbishop of Canterbury and primate of all England (1974–80); was the first evangelical, or low church, Anglican in 126 years to become spiritual head of the Church of England and the worldwide Anglican communion; early in his career, was a university lecturer in Semitic languages and professor of New Testament; was principal of the London College of Divinity from 1944 to 1956; subsequently served as bishop of Bradford (1956–61) and archbishop of York (1961–74); at the Lambeth Conference of the world's Anglican churches in 1978, proposed the ordination of women, not effective in the Church of England until 1994; published 21 books on the Christian faith and ministry, including works on homiletics and collections of his own sermons; helped to coordinate the translation of *The New English Bible* from the Greek and Hebrew; wrote a short book about that project, *The English Bible* (1963); also helped in the translation of *The Revised English Bible*; in 1980 was created a life peer, with the title Lord Coggan of Canterbury and Sissinghurst; died at a nursing home in southern England. See *Current Biography* (July) 1974.

Obituary *New York Times* A p25 May 19, 2000

COHEN, ALEXANDER H. July 24, 1920–Apr. 22, 2000 Theatrical producer; a master showman whose lavish promotional schemes became legendary in the theatrical world; chiefly on Broadway, produced 101 shows, from revivals of classics starring the likes of John Gielgud, Ralph Richardson, and Louis Calhern to spectacular musicals, such as *Baker Street*, and such plays as the Tony Award winners *The Homecoming* and *La Tragedie de Carmen*; introduced Broadway audiences to such artists as Richard Burton, Maurice Chevalier, Yves Montand, and Victor Borge and the comedy teams of Mike Nichols and Elaine May, Michael Flanders and Donald Swann, and Dudley Moore and Peter Cooke; also produced a number of shows in London's West End, including *Plaza Suite* and *Harvey* (starring James Stewart); was left a substantial inheritance by his financier father, who died when Cohen was four; chose for his first theatrical investment a summer-stock company at the Red Barn Theater on Long Island, which he bought in the summer of 1941; in December 1941, became associate producer of *Angel Street*, which enjoyed a Broadway run of 1,295 performances; continued to produce plays, at a reduced pace, while working in public relations for the Bulova Watch Co. for seven years, beginning in 1943; was Bulova's vice president in charge of advertising from 1945 to 1950; between 1943 and 1958 backed 10 Broadway productions that closed after relatively short runs; during the 1950s made several imaginative innovations calculated to encourage theatergoing, including a mobile box office and unusual package deals, among them special bus, train, and air connections to New York City and summer theater sites; in his late-curtain Nine O'Clock Theater series, between 1959 and 1965 presented a successful series of entertainments, including the British revues *At the Drop of a Hat* and *Beyond the Fringe*; away from Broadway, supervised the development of the O'Keefe Center for the Performing Arts in Toronto, Canada, from 1960 to 1963; on Broadway in 1967, was represented by six productions, including *Little Murders*, *Black Comedy*, and *At the Drop of Another Hat*; with Hildy Parks, the second of his two wives, produced the first 20 years of the Tony Awards telecasts, beginning in 1967; also produced Emmy Award telecasts and a score of prime-time television specials, including three *Night of 100 Stars* fund-raisers for the Actors' Fund of America; appeared in Woody Allen's film *The Purple Rose of Cairo* (1985); Off-Broadway, wrote, produced, and starred in his own one-man show, *Star Billing*, in 1998; presented his last production, *Waiting in the Wings*, in the 1999–2000 Broadway season; died in Manhattan. See *Current Biography* (June) 1965.

Obituary *New York Times* p36 Apr. 23, 2000

COMFORT, ALEX Feb. 10, 1920–Mar. 26, 2000 British physician; biochemist; writer; social and political activist; in an era of cramped specialization, achieved the Renaissance ideal of the well-rounded man; was a leading authority on the biology of the aging process; preached a gospel of greater freedom in sexual behavior in books ranging from *Sexual Behavior in Society* (1950) to the best-selling *The Joy of Sex* (1972), an uninhibited erotic manual, profusely illustrated with line drawings; espoused an anarcho-pacifist ethic, which he propounded directly in pamphlets, tracts, and other nonfiction and indirectly in such novels as *No Such Liberty* (1941), *The Almond Tree* (1942), *The Powerhouse* (1944), *A Giant's Strength* (1952), and *The Philosophers* (1989); was a conscientious objector to military service during World War II; bitterly attacked such Allied policies as the indiscriminate bombing of nonmilitary targets; after serving for several years as resident medical officer at the Royal Waterloo Hospital for Children and Women, in London, was a lecturer in physiology at the London Hospital (1948–51); began research in the biology of senescence in the zoology department of University College, London, in 1951; directed University College's medical council research group on aging from 1963 to 1970; remained at University College as director of research in gerontology until 1973; in a long sojourn in the U.S., was for a while associated with the Center for the Study of Democratic Institutions in Santa Barbara, California; was clinical lecturer in the department of psychiatry at Stanford University (1974–83), professor in the department of pathology, Irvine Medical College, University of California (1976–78), adjunct professor in the department of psychiatry at the University of Southern California (1977–81) and adjunct professor in the Neuropsychiatric Institute at the University of California at Los Angeles (1980–91); throughout his career, took part in what he called "agitatorial activities" that promoted sociological analyses of global tensions; for example, was arrested with Bertrand Russell in a massive "ban the bomb" demonstration in London in 1962; promoted an international approach to the problems of overpopulation and food shortages; in the fields of medicine and science, wrote the textbook *First Year Physiological Technique* (1948) and books on the biology of aging and geriatric psychiatry; in *The Anxiety Makers* (1967), argued that the medical profession was largely responsible for "programmed" anxiety in contemporary society; as a belletrist, published 11 novels (including a science-fiction trilogy), a book of short stories, and seven volumes of verse; also published *Art and Social Responsibility* (1946), *The Novel and Our Time* (1948), *Authority and Delinquency in the Modern State* (1950), *More Joy* (1973), *A Good Age (1976)*, and *Writings against Power and Death* (1993), among other volumes of nonfiction, many of which were collections of essays; died in Banbury, England. See *Current Biography* (September) 1974.

Obituary *New York Times* C p27 Mar. 29, 2000

COUVE DE MURVILLE, MAURICE Jan. 24, 1907–Dec. 24, 1999 French statesman; during the 1930s, rose in the French ministry of finance to become director of external finance; in 1943, during the wartime German occupation, fled France to offer his services to the Free French administration in Algiers; joined Charles de Gaulle's provisional French government, with which he returned to France following the liberation of Paris in 1944; was French ambassador to Italy in 1945; was director-general of political affairs in the foreign office from 1945 to 1950; subsequently was ambassador to, successively, Egypt, the U.S., and the Federal Republic of Germany; after Charles de Gaulle assumed the presidency of the Fifth Republic, in 1958, served as foreign minister (1958–68), finance minister (1968), and prime minister (1968–69); was elected to the National Assembly in 1968, 1973, 1978, and 1981; became a senator in 1985. See *Current Biography* (April) 1955.

Obituary *New York Times* B p6 Dec. 25, 1999

CRAXI, BETTINO Feb. 24, 1924–Jan. 19, 2000 Former prime minister of Italy; the first Socialist to hold that post in the contemporary Italian republic; joined the Socialist Party when he was 18; won election to Parliament from Milan in 1968; retained that seat in each of the four succeeding general elections; became general secretary of the Socialist Party in 1976; immediately set out to revitalize the party; made his first concern the establishment for Italy's Socialists of an identity clearly distinct from that of the country's Communists; purged extreme leftists from the party's ranks, discarded what he considered to be outmoded Marxist ideology, and changed the party's emblem from the hammer and sickle to a red carnation; was prime minister from August 1983 to March 1987, the longest continuous period in office of any Italian prime minister since World War II; lived out his last years under a cloud of convictions for graft and corruption; in 1994 escaped a warrant for his arrest by fleeing to his summer retreat in Tunisia; died in Tunisia. See *Current Biography* (February) 1984.

Obituary *New York Times* B p14 Jan. 20, 2000

CURTIS, CARL T. Mar. 15, 1905–Jan. 24, 2000 U.S. Republican representative from Nebraska's First Congressional District (1939–55); U.S. senator from Nebraska (1955–79); lawyer; a staunch social and fiscal conservative; opposed President Franklin D. Roosevelt's New Deal agenda, with the notable exception of Social Security, which he sought to extend to as many occupations as possible; was also a champion of the agricultural parity-price-support program and other legislation helpful to farmers; during the Watergate crisis that led to the resignation of President Richard Nixon, in 1974, was unfailing in his support for Nixon; died in Lincoln, Nebraska. See *Current Biography* (September) 1954.

Obituary *New York Times* C p29 Jan. 26, 2000

DANIEL, CLIFTON Sep. 19, 1912–Feb. 21, 2000 Journalist; after two decades as a correspondent with the *New York Times*, was that newspaper's managing editor (1964–69); through his marriage to Margaret Truman, was the son-in-law of former president Harry S. Truman; began his career as co-founder and associate editor of the *Daily Bulletin* in Dunn, North Carolina (1933); from 1934 to 1937 was a reporter, political writer, and columnist with the Raleigh, North Carolina *News and Observer*; with the Associated Press (1937–44), was a correspondent in, successively, New York City, Washington, D.C., Bern, Switzerland, and wartime London, England; in February 1944 moved from the news editor's desk at the AP's London bureau to the *New York Times*'s London bureau; after covering Supreme Headquarters, Allied Expeditionary Force in London for the *Times*, followed the advance of the U.S. First Army into Belgium and Germany; after World War II, was the *Times*'s chief Middle East correspondent; in the early 1950s returned briefly to London before beginning a stint as chief of the *Times* bureau in Bonn, West Germany; reported from Moscow, USSR, in 1954 and 1955; returned to the U.S. in 1955; before becoming managing editor of the *Times*, was, in succession, assistant to the foreign news editor and assistant to the managing editor; after resigning as managing editor, supervised the New York Times News Service and directed special projects; hosted two local New York City radio shows concerned with current events; on television, was moderator of the twice-monthly *News in Perspective*, produced by National Educational Television in association with the *Times*; returning to news reporting in the 1970s, covered major events in Washington, D.C., for the *Times*; retired in 1977; died at his home in Manhattan. See *Current Biography* (March) 1966.

Obituary *New York Times* p1+ Feb. 22, 2000

DAVIS, MARTIN S. Feb. 5, 1927–Oct. 4, 1999 Corporation executive; played an important part in the merger of Paramount Pictures Corp. into the sprawling conglomerate Gulf & Western Industries Inc. and the leading role in the subsequent streamlining of Gulf & Western into a more wieldy entertainment and publishing power, renamed Paramount Communications Inc.; in 1947 began working his way up from office boy with Samuel Goldwyn Productions in New York City; in 1955 moved to Allied Artists Pictures Corp. as eastern advertising and publicity manager; three years later joined Paramount Pictures Corp. as sales and marketing director; in 1962 was promoted to vice president of a Paramount subsidiary, Paramount Film Distribution Corp.; became vice president of the parent corporation in April 1966; was instrumental in arranging the merger in which Charles Bluhdorn, the head of Gulf & Western Industries, subsumed Paramount Pictures Corp. in October 1966; following the merger, was named CEO of Gulf & Western's Paramount holdings; as senior vice president of Gulf & Western, beginning in 1969, was Bluhdorn's right-hand man; during the 1970s spent much of his time and energy defending Bluhdorn and the corporation during a prolonged investigation by the Securities and Exchange Commission for violations of securities laws; upon Bluhdorn's death, in 1983, succeeded him as chairman and CEO of Gulf & Western Industries, which by that time encompassed an enormous range of diversified operations; divesting $1.5 billion of assets, consolidated the corporation's seven divisions into three by 1984 and two by 1989; in June 1989 renamed the corporation Paramount Communications Inc., to reflect its emphasis on media; sold Paramount Communications Inc. to Viacom Inc. in 1994; died in Manhattan. See *Current Biography* (November) 1989.

Obituary *New York Times* B p14 Oct. 6, 1999

DE LIMA, SIGRID Dec. 4, 1921–Sep. 19, 1999 Novelist; was the daughter of Agnes de Lima, a writer of books on primary education and for many years the director of publicity for the New School for Social Research in New York City (now called New School University); worked in New York City as a financial writer for United Press from 1944 to 1946 and as a freelance journalist from 1946 to 1948, when she began to concentrate on the writing of fiction; while attending editor Hiram Haydn's novel-writing workshop at the New School, wrote her first novel, *Captain's Beach* (1950), about down-and-out characters in a Manhattan waterfront rooming house; in her second novel, *The Swift Cloud* (1952; published in paperback as *A Mask of Guilt*), set in a California town, told the story of a man falsely accused of murdering his mentally defective son; in her third, *Carnival by the Sea* (1954), described a Eurydice-like heroine wandering through a nightmarish seaside California amusement park; published two additional novels, *Praise a Fine Day* (1959) and *Oriane* (1968); died in Nyack, New York. See *Current Biography* (Yearbook) 1958.

Obituary *New York Times* B p7 Sep. 25, 1999

FAIRBANKS, DOUGLAS JR. Dec. 9, 1909–May 7, 2000 Actor; producer; a dashingly handsome and debonair player in a variety of motion-picture roles, including swashbucklers reminiscent of those for which his more gymnastic father (and namesake) had been famous in silent cinema; as a juvenile, in the mid-1920s, had roles in *Stephen Steps Out* and *Stella Dallas*, among other silent films; at the beginning of the talkie era, was cast in *The Barker* (1928) and *A Woman of Affairs* (1929); subsequently had roles in such pictures as *Dawn Patrol* (1930), *Outward Bound* (1930), *Little Caesar* (1931), *Union Depot* (1932), and *Morning Glory* (1933); during a sojourn in England, played Emperor Peter III of Russia in Alexander Korda's film *Catherine the Great* (1934); back in Hollywood, nearly stole the show from Ronald Coleman with his performance as the villainous Rupert of Hentzau in the costume adventure/romance *The Prisoner of Zenda* (1937); remained at the peak of his career in such comedies as *Having a Wonderful Time* (1938) and *The Young in Heart* (1938), the darkly comedic melodrama *Angels Over Broadway* (1940), and the action/adventure pictures *Gunga Din* (1939) and *The Corsican Brothers* (1941); with the outbreak of World War II in Europe, turned his attention and energy to international affairs; was prominent in efforts to change American public opinion from isolationist to interventionist, on the side of England against the Axis powers; in 1941 was sent on a special political mission to Panama and several South American countries by President Franklin D. Roosevelt, who was concerned about Axis subversion in the Western Hemisphere; after the U.S. entered the war, earned a number of decorations in his service as an American naval officer in operations in the Atlantic and Mediterranean; subsequently reached the rank of captain the Navy Reserve; in the postwar years, volunteered for such organizations and projects as CARE, the Marshall Plan, and the U.N.; returned to the screen in the title role in *Sinbad the Sailor* (1947); wrote, produced, and starred (as a young King Charles II of England fighting his way out of exile in 17th-century Holland) in *The Exile* (1947); played a military leader in the costume musical *That Woman in Ermine* (1948) and the historical epic *The Fighting O'Flynn* (1949); was absent from cinema from 1951 until 1981, when *Ghost Story* was released; acted on the stage in Los Angeles in the late 1920s, in London in the mid-1930s, and later in touring productions; in the 1950s, produced scores of short films for television; from 1953 to 1956, hosted and sometimes starred in *Douglas Fairbanks Presents*, a dramatic anthology series known in some markets by other titles, including *Rheingold Theatre*; also produced half-hour films televised in the network adventure series *Terry and the Pirates*; wrote two books of memoirs, *The Salad Days* (1988) and *A Hell of a War* (1993); was a Knight Commander of the Order of the British Empire; after his divorce from his first wife, Joan Crawford, was married two more times; maintained homes and offices in both London and Manhattan; died in Manhattan. See *Current Biography* (February) 1956.

Obituary *New York Times* B p7 May 8, 2000

FANFANI, AMINTORE Feb. 6, 1908–Nov. 20, 1999 Former prime minister of Italy; a leader of the Christian Democratic Party; professor of political economy and the history of economics; author; after receiving his doctorate from the Catholic University of Milan, in 1932, taught at that university; later was a professor at the University of Rome; was elected to the National Constituent Assembly from Italy's 16th District in 1946; was a member of Parliament for the same district from 1948 to 1968; became a senator for life in 1972; in numerous governments between 1947 and 1989, held a variety of Cabinet portfolios, including labor, interior, foreign affairs, and budget; served four terms as prime minister between 1954 and 1963; was again prime minister in 1982 and 1983; served as president of the U.N. General Assembly in 1965 and 1966; published more than a dozen books, including multivolume histories of economics and economic thought and the book, published in Italian in 1934, that was translated as *Catholicism, Capitalism, and Protestantism* (1935); died in Rome. See *Current Biography* (October) 1958.

Obituary *New York Times* p54 Nov. 21, 1999

FIGUEIREDO, JOÃO DE BAPTISTA DE OLIVEIRA Jan. 15, 1918–Dec. 24, 1999 Brazilian army general; former president of Brazil; was credited with restoring his country to democracy; during much of his early career, taught at military schools; after the 1964 coup that initiated a 21-year military dictatorship in Brazil, was appointed a section chief in the federal intelligence and counterintelligence service (SNI); when General Ernesto Geisel assumed the presidency, in 1974, was named national head of the SNI; reformed the SNI's methods of operation in accordance with Geisel's policy of *aberatura* ("opening"), a liberalization of military rule aimed at a return to civilian leadership; pursued the policy to completion during his own presidency (1979–85); died at his home in Rio de Janeiro. See *Current Biography* (January) 1980.

Obituary *New York Times* B p6 Dec. 25, 1999

FOWLER, HENRY H. Sep. 5, 1908–Jan. 3, 2000 Former federal-government official; lawyer; banking executive; was counsel to the Tennessee Valley Authority during the 1930s; during World War II was counsel to the war production board; interrupted his private practice of law to return to government service during the Korean War, as administrator of defense production and director of defense mobilization; was undersecretary of the treasury under President John F. Kennedy; as treasury secretary under President Lyndon B. Johnson, beginning in 1965, was hampered by Johnson's refusal to come to grips openly with the escalating cost of the war in Vietnam; was most proud of creating a new reserve currency (known as special drawings rights, or SDRs) managed by the International Monetary Fund, and "paper gold"; on leaving government in 1969, joined the banking firm of Goldman Sachs as a partner specializing in international operations; headed the Goldman Sachs International Corp. until 1984; remained a Goldman Sachs partner until May 1999; died in Alexandria, Virginia. See *Current Biography* (September) 1952.

Obituary *New York Times* A p19 Jan. 5, 2000

FRIEDMAN, HERBERT June 21, 1916–Sep. 9, 2000 Physicist; rocket and satellite astronomer; chief scientist emeritus, the U.S. Naval Research Laboratory's E. O. Hulburt Center for Space Research; made seminal contributions to the study of solar radiation; joined the Naval Research Laboratory in 1940; was superintendent of the laboratory's atmosphere and astrophysics division from 1958 to 1963 and of its space-science division from 1963 to 1980; developed defense-related radiation detection devices during World War II; designed an X-ray exposure meter for analyzing crystals that became standard equipment in all crystal plants; after the war, began concentrating on research and development in rocket astronomy; in 1949, obtained the first scientific proof that X rays emanate from the sun, when he directed the firing into space of a V-2 rocket carrying a detecting instrument; through rocket astronomy, subsequently produced the first ultraviolet map of celestial bodies, Lyman-alpha measurements, new discoveries supporting the theory that stars are being continuously formed, and new data on space radiation affecting Earth and on the nature of gases in space; in Project Sunflare, which he directed in 1957, discovered the presence of X-rays during solar flares, supporting the view that those solar eruptions are electromagnetic in origin; in experiments during the total solar eclipse of October 1958, directed the firing of instrument-payloaded Nice-Asp and Nike-Deacon rocket combinations to altitudes as high as 105 miles; in those projects, obtained the first proof that X-radiation comes from the sun's corona and that ultraviolet radiation comes from its chromosphere; in 1960, directed the launching into orbit of a satellite equipped to monitor solar radiation from above

Earth's atmosphere; regarded as his team's most important achievement the charting of the solar spectrum for the entire range of ultraviolet and X-ray wavelengths, completed by him and his colleagues in the early 1960s; subsequently discovered the emanation of X rays from a pulsar in the Crab Nebula; contributed to the theory of black holes as well as neutron stars. See *Current Biography* (September) 1963.

Obituary *New York Times* B p10 Sep. 13, 2000

FUCHS, VIVIAN E. Feb. 11, 1908–Nov. 11, 1999 British geologist; explorer; established his major claim to fame as the leader of the Commonwealth transantarctic expedition that completed the first land crossing of the continent of Antarctica in March 1958; participated in a Cambridge University East Greenland expedition in 1929 and a Cambridge expedition to the East African lakes between 1930 and 1932; led the Lake Rudolf Rift Valley expedition in 1933 and 1934 and the Lake Rukwa expedition in 1937 and 1938; dated his active interest in Antarctica from 1947–50, when he commanded a Falkland Islands dependencies survey; returned to Antarctica as the leader of the British Antarctic Survey (1958–73); was knighted after the 1957–58 expedition; died at his home in Cambridge, England. See *Current Biography* (October) 1958.

Obituary *New York Times* p49 Nov. 14, 1999

GASSMAN, VITTORIO Sep. 1, 1922–June 29, 2000 Italian actor; during a career spanning more than half a century, moved easily from mostly classical roles on stage (his first and enduring love) to a vast variety of portrayals on screen; made his professional stage debut in 1943 and his motion picture debut in 1946; first came to international attention in the neorealistic screen tragedy *Riso Amaro* (1948), distributed in the U.S. in 1950 under the title *Bitter Rice*; starred opposite Sylvana Mangano in that film and in *Anna* (1951), another international commercial success; with his tall physique, swarthy handsomeness, and charmingly arrogant manner, quickly became one of the Italian screen's top leading men, often typecast as an egocentric hero or antihero in adventure films or socio-romantic melodramas; following his marriage to the actress Shelley Winters (the second of his three wives), in 1952, was cast as a refugee pursued by immigration authorities in New York City in *The Glass Wall* (1953), his first American film; subsequently, under a contract with Metro-Goldwyn, made three mediocre films, including *Rhapsody* (1954); after returning to Italy, was cast in such screen roles as Mario Rossi in Robert Rossen's *Mambo* (1954) and Anatole Kuragin in King Vidor's *Guerra e pace* (*War and Peace*, 1956); co-directed himself as the great Shakespearean actor Edmund Kean in *Kean* (1957), a role he had previously played on stage; first displayed his talent for comedy in several screen roles in the late 1950s and early 1960s, beginning with that of Peppe, the leader of an incompetent gang of thieves in the caper spoof *I Soliti Ignoti* (1958), which scored a great success in the U.S. under the title *Big Deal on Madonna Street*; meanwhile, returned often to the stage; in 1960, with money he had accumulated from films, founded the Teatro Populare Italiano, a large company that toured Italy with a portable tent and equipment carried by 15 trucks; as director and actor with the troupe, presented before audiences in towns large and small throughout Italy, at nominal prices, a repertory that included works of Sophocles, Aeschylus, Shakespeare, Pirandello, and such moderns as Ennio Flaiano; realized "a role worthy of his gifts," as Brendan Gill observed, in Bruno Cortona, the immoral, destructive charmer in the tragicomic motion picture *Il Sorpasso* (*The Easy Life*, 1962); at the Cannes International Film Festival in 1975, won the best actor award for his portrayal of Captain Fausto Censolo, the blind protagonist in the comedy drama *Profumo di Donna* (1974), which inspired the 1992 English-language remake *Scent of a Woman*; won the Nastro d'argento award for best actor for his portrayal of Uncle Lucca in the film *Lo zio indegno* (1989); made a total of more than 100 motion pictures; died at his home in Rome. See *Current Biography* (October) 1964.

Obituary *New York Times* C p19 June 30, 2000

GIELGUD, JOHN Apr. 14, 1904–May 21, 2000 British actor; director; along with the late Lord Olivier and the late Sir Ralph Richardson, dominated the English stage during the last two-thirds of the 20th century; of the three actors, was generally acknowledged to be "the supreme and most sensitive Shakespearean of his day"; late in his career, broadened his appeal immeasurably through his incisive handling of character parts in motion pictures and on television; made his professional debut at 17; subsequently performed in productions of the Royal Academy of Dramatic Art; joined the Old Vic Company in 1929; in two consecutive seasons there, took on a staggering variety of Shakespearean roles; over the following four decades, welcomed virtually every opportunity—whether in the West End, at Stratford-upon -Avon, with the Royal Shakespeare Company, or back at the old Vic—to reinterpret those roles, frequently in productions that he himself directed; notably refined his interpretation of such roles as Romeo, Hamlet, Mercutio, Prospero, Richard II, Shylock, and King Lear; in addition to his Shakespearean repertoire, distinguished himself in roles in Restoration comedies and plays by Chekhov, Oscar Wilde, Noel Coward, Rodney Ackland, and Christopher Fry, among others; later ventured into newer theatrical terrain, in plays by Edward Albee, Alan Bennett, Peter Shaffer, David Storey, Harold Pinter, Charles Woods, Edward Bond, and others; in one of numerous visits to Broadway, won a special Tony Award in 1959 with his internationally acclaimed one-man show *The Ages of Man*, comprising excerpts from Shakespeare; won an Emmy Award for his television version of that production, shown on the CBS network during the 1965–66 season; for many decades, had a sporadic, sometimes lackluster film career, highlighted by some excellent Shakespearean performances; won the British Academy Award for best actor as Cassius in *Julius Caesar* (1953); knighted in 1953; in the 1960s, had more consistently lustrous screen roles, in such films as *Beckett*, *Falstaff*, and *The Charge of the Light Brigade*; won his second British Academy Award, for best supporting actor, for his role as a gentleman's gentleman in *Murder on the Orient Express* (1974); starred in Alain Resnais's experimental film *Providence* (1977); subsequently was featured in such films as *Arthur*, *Gandhi*, *Shining Through*, and *Power of One*; retired from the stage in 1988; in his last movie role, was cast as Prospero in *Prospero's Books* (1991); wrote several books, including two volumes of memoirs; died at his home near Aylesbury, northwest of London. See *Current Biography* (February) 1984.

Obituary *New York Times* A p1+ May 23, 2000

GILRUTH, ROBERT R. Oct. 8, 1913–Aug. 17, 2000 Aeronautical engineer; aerospace consultant; an early leader in the American space program; joined the staff of the National Advisory Committee for Aeronautics at Langley Field, Virginia, as a flight research engineer in 1937; was chief of the pilotless-aircraft research division of the Langley Aerospace Laboratory from 1945 to 1950, when he became assistant director of the laboratory, in charge of three divisions; was director, successively, of the National Aeronautics and Space Administration's Project Mercury (1948–61), its Manned Space Center in Houston, Texas (1961–72), and its key personnel development program (1972–73); remained a consultant to NASA following his retirement, in 1973; died in Charlottesville, Virginia. See *Current Biography* (October) 1963.

Obituary *New York Times* C p19 Aug. 18, 2000

GOLDENSON, LEONARD H. Dec. 7, 1905–Dec. 27, 1999 Entertainment-industry executive; lawyer; developed the ABC television network from a distant hopeful to a close competitor of NBC and CBS; as a young lawyer, in 1933, was recruited by Paramount Pictures to help reorganize Paramount's movie theaters in New England; within eight years, was responsible for all Paramount theaters nationwide; later became involved in Paramount movie production and distribution as well; when government antitrust pressure forced Paramount to split into separate motion-picture and theater companies, became president of United Paramount Theaters, in 1950; three years later bought the American Broadcasting Co. and became president of a new corporate entity, at first called AB-PT; in 1985 achieved the merger of ABC with Capital Cities, which brought with it many newspaper holdings; died in Sarasota, Florida. See *Current Biography* (September) 1957.

Obituary *New York Times* B p10 Dec. 28, 1999

GOREY, EDWARD Feb. 22, 1925–Apr. 15, 2000 Author; illustrator; a straight-faced master of the tongue-in-cheek macabre; produced more than 100 small volumes of eerie line drawings, generally accompanied by austere, whimsically sadistic texts that read like minuscule, mock versions of Gothic novels; also illustrated scores of works by others, including Edward Lear and Samuel Beckett; after earning a B.A. degree in French literature at Harvard University, in 1950, remained in Boston for three years, living hand to mouth; illustrated covers for the Anchor series of paperbacks published by Doubleday & Co.; in 1953 moved to New York City, where he worked for a short time in Doubleday's art department; during 1953 published his first book, *The Unstrung Harp; or, Mr. Earbrass Writes a Novel*; followed that up with *The Listing Attic* (1954), a collection of illustrated limericks, some in French, about horrible mishaps experienced by frenzied people, *The Doubtful Guest* (1957), featuring a penguin-like creature in scarf and tennis shoes who invades a morbid Edwardian household and becomes a permanent, enigmatic presence there, *The Object Lesson* (1957), a surreal book consisting of 30 disjunctive illustrations with non sequitur verse captions, and *The Hapless Child* (1961), probably his cruelest book; in *The Curious Sofa* (1961), his one unsolemn work, titillated the reader with a series of intimations of pornography, none of which are realized; was inspired by D. W. Griffith's screen cliffhangers in creating such works as *The Willowdale Handcar* (1962); published several books specifically for children, including *The Wuggly Ump* (1963); created cautionary tales in the form of rhyming alphabet books ("A is for Amy, who fell down the stairs"); populated *The Epiplectic Bicycle* (1969), alone among his works, with speaking characters, human and animal, who address themselves to an obsessive Gorey theme: the childish fears that can be laughed at but never completely laughed away; anthologized selections of his previously published small-format works in *Amphigorey* (1972) and *Amphigorey Too* (1975); in *The Raging Tide; or, The Black Doll's Imbroglio* (1987), introduced the mischievous black dot named Figbate that would later appear in the alphabet book *Figbate Acrobate* (1994); subsequently published *The Just Dessert* (1997), *The Haunted Tea-Cosy* (1997), and *The Headless Bust* (1999); saw his version of Dracula become a hit on Broadway in 1977; was involved in the adaptation of many of his works to the stage; personally directed and designed the sets for a series of revues produced for limited audiences on Cape Cod; on television, has for years been represented by the animated Gorey drawing introducing each program in the PBS Mystery series; was as eccentric in person as in his work; when living in Manhattan, regularly attended George Ballanchine's productions at the New York City Ballet wearing a raccoon coat and sneakers; moved to Cape Cod in 1986, ultimately settling in Yarmouth Port; died in nearby Hyannis, Massachusetts. See *Current Biography* (November) 1976.

Obituary *New York Times* B p8 Apr. 17, 2000

GREENE, HAROLD H. Feb. 6, 1923–Jan. 29, 2000 German-born federal judge; the judicial activist who presided over the settlement bringing to an end the long, regulated monopoly that the American Telephone and Telegraph Co. (AT&T) exercised over telephone service in the U.S.; began his 45-year career as a government lawyer and federal judge after receiving his doctorate in law (1952) and subsequently being admitted to the District of Columbia bar; was assistant U.S. attorney for D.C. from 1953 to 1957; joined the office of legal counsel in the Department of Justice in 1957; soon, was chosen to head the appeals section of the department's civil-rights division; helped to draft the Civil Rights Act of 1965; became a judge of the D.C. court of general sessions in

1965; in that position, showed a scrupulous regard for the rights of criminal defendants; to insure the best available representation for the indigent defendants who crowded his courtroom, succeeded in obtaining a more attractive fee system for court-appointed lawyers; adamantly opposed sentencing guidelines, which he viewed as unconstitutional conduits to prison; was the chief judge of the D.C. court of general sessions from 1966 to 1971; during those years, helped to restructure the D.C. criminal-court system; was chief judge of the superior court of D.C. from 1971 to 1978, when he was appointed judge of the U.S. district court for D.C.; in that position in August 1983, gave final approval to the consent decree breaking up AT&T, the largest corporation in the world; heard the case of John W. Poindexter, the national security adviser to President Ronald Reagan accused of lying to Congress about the Iran-Contra affair; died at his home in Washington, D.C. See *Current Biography* (August) 1985.

Obituary *New York Times* A p22 Jan. 31, 2000

GUINNESS, ALEC Apr. 2, 1914– Aug. 5, 2000 British actor; the consummate virtuoso character actor; a self-effacing man who, in his art, underplayed a protean gallery of stage and screen personae; in crafting his roles, preferred the use of subtle facial and physical shorthand; maintained his minimalist attitude and pared-down style even when resorting to a maximum of disguise paraphernalia; established the model for his chameleonic film career with his portrayal of eight members of an eccentric and doomed aristocratic family, the fictional d'Ascoynes, including a matron, in the high comedy *Kind Hearts and Coronets* (1949); gained wide popularity in a succession of comic screen characterizations, including the meek bank clerk turned criminal mastermind in *The Lavender Hill Mob* (1951), the polygamous Mediterranean ferryboat skipper in *The Captain's Paradise* (1953), and the buck-toothed gang leader in the macabre farce *The Ladykillers* (1956); was also masterly in such difficult dramatic portrayals as the proud, conflicted British commanding officer in a Japanese prison camp in *The Bridge on the River Kwai* (1957), which brought him an Academy Award for best actor; became known to a younger generation of moviegoers as the venerable and wise spiritual warrior Obi-Wan Kenobi in the space epic *Star Wars* (1977) and two of its sequels; among a multitude of stage roles, played the beleaguered Roman Catholic cardinal in *The Prisoner* (1954) and a would-be adulterer in the boulevard farce *Hotel Paradiso* (1956), both of which he reprised on the screen; as a student actor in London, found a patron in John Gielgud; made his professional stage debut in a walk-on part in *Libel!* in 1934; went on to numerous important roles in classical and other productions at the Old Vic and with Gielgud's own London company; in 1939 and 1940 divided his time between Old Vic roles, including his first Hamlet (in modern dress), and the commercial theater; on special leave (December 1942–January 1943) from the Royal Navy during World War II, made his Broadway debut as an RAF pilot in the wartime propaganda play *Flare Path*; in postwar London, resumed his stage career as Mitya in his own dramatization of *The Brothers Karamazov*; in the late 1940s and early 1950s, took on such roles as Richard II, Richard III, the Dauphin in George Bernard Shaw's *Saint Joan*, and his second Hamlet (in Elizabethan dress); at the Edinburgh Festival in 1949, created the role of Sir Henry Harcourt-Reilly in T. S. Eliot's *The Cocktail Party*, which he took to Broadway with great success the following year; later counted among his triumphs in London's West End and/or on Broadway the title roles in *Ross* (1960), *Exit the King* (1963), and *Dylan* (1964), a reprisal of his role in *The Cocktail Party* (1968), and the part of the pathetically lonely British foreign-office defector in *The Old Country* (1977); made his first substantial screen appearance as Herbert Pocket in David Lean's *Great Expectations* (1946), a role he had played in his own stage version of the Dickens novel; in subsequent film roles, was a controversial Fagin in Lean's *Oliver Twist* (1947), the amusingly innocent title character in *The Man in the White Suit* (1951), the charming eponymous detective in *Father Brown* (1954), the humorously obsessive mural painter Gulley Jimson in the actor's own adaptation of *The Horse's Mouth* (1958), the strict Scottish regimental commander in *Tunes of Glory* (1960), Major Jones in *The Comedians* (1967), Charles I in *Cromwell* (1970), the Nazi dictator in *Hitler: The Last Ten Days* (1976), and the blind butler in *Murder by Death* (1976); in 1980 received an honorary Academy Award for career achievement; was nominated for an Oscar for best supporting actor for his role as William Dorrit in *Little Dorrit* (1987); had a total of some 50 film credits, including the grandfather in a touching made-for-TV version of *Little Lord Fauntleroy* (1980); during the 1980s, played the spy George Smiley in two television miniseries, *Tinker, Sailor, Soldier, Spy* and *Smiley's People*; was knighted in 1959; wrote the autobiography *Blessings in Disguise* (1985); lived with his wife, Merula Salaman, in Petersfield, Hampshire; died in West Sussex, England. See *Current Biography* (March) 1981.

Obituary *New York Times* A p1+ Aug. 7, 2000

HELIKER, JOHN Jan. 17, 1909–Feb. 22, 2000 Artist; former associate professor of art at Columbia University; in abstract and semiabstract paintings, including Vermont and Italian landscapes and Maine seascapes, revealed a sense of serenity and order and a deep regard for the structural forms of nature; dropped out of high school in Yonkers, New York, to pursue a program of self-instruction; studied at the Art Students League in Manhattan for three months; in late adolescence and early manhood, produced a large number of realistic line drawings of New York cityscapes and activities on a farm to which his parents had moved in Stormville, New York; with his first one-man exhibition, in 1936, impressed New York critics, who compared his drawings and watercolors to works of Brueghel, Daumier, Klee, and Grosz; in 1938 moved to Greenwich Village, in New York City; worked with the Works Progress Administration federal art project (1939–40); during his first sojourn in Vermont (1939–40), completed 20 oil paintings, including *Vermont Farm*, which established his reputation when it won the W. A. Clark Prize and the Corcoran gold medal in 1941; in the mid-1940s also began to visit the Maine coast and paint seascapes there; after experimenting with abstract geometric and biomorphic forms and shapes in such paintings as *Scava* and *Imaginary Landscape*, returned to a representational grounding in such paintings as *Of Maine* (1953) and the semiabstract landscapes and paintings of architectural subjects he produced in Italy during a year-long visit (1949–50) and several subsequent summers; later created a number of self-portraits and many intimate and fairly realistic paintings of interiors; was on the art faculty of Columbia University for more than half a century, until 1977; died in Bar Harbor, Maine. See *Current Biography* (January) 1959.

Obituary *New York Times* A p17 Feb. 28, 2000

HELLER, JOSEPH May 1, 1923–Dec. 12, 1999 Author; a novelist with a skewed sense of humor and a concern, in his words, "with the way people use and misuse language to obscure and confuse and build barriers"; achieved wide and durable fame with his first book, *Catch-22* (1961); in that darkly surreal antiwar burlesque epic, set on a U.S. Army Air Force base in the Mediterranean during World War II, created a gallery of wildly comic characters, including the protagonist, Yossarian, whose desertion is Heller's answer to the question, "What does a sane man do in an insane society?"; gathered the technical background for *Catch 22* from his own experience as an air force bombadier during World War II; after earning an M.A. degree, taught English at Pennsylvania State University (1950–52); subsequently, wrote advertising for *Time* and *Look* magazines and was promotion manager of *McCall's*; in his second novel, *Something Happened* (1974), depicted the existential crisis of a New York corporation executive; in his third, *Good as Gold* (1979), used satirical humor to convey the ambivalence felt by an assimilating Jewish intellectual climbing into the highest echelon of American government; in *God Knows* (1984), translated the story of King David into contemporary comic shtick; updated the lives of the main characters of *Catch-22* in *Closing Time* (1994); wrote a final novel, *A Portrait of the Artist as an Old Man*, scheduled for publication in 2000; in addition to his novels, published nine uncollected short stories, three books of nonfiction, including the memoirs *No Laughing Matter* (with Speed Vogel, 1986) and *Now and Then: From Coney Island to Here* (1998), and three plays, including *We Bombed in New Haven* (1967); collaborated on several screenplays; died in East Hampton, New York. See *Current Biography* (July) 1973.

Obituary *New York Times* A p1+ Dec. 14, 1999

HENNING, DOUG 1947–Feb, 7, 2000 Canadian-born magician; with his youthful and joyful style, sparked a renewal of popular interest in stage magic; in the early 1970s formed the rock group Lighthouse, which combined rock music with illusions, including the "metamorphosis" in which Henning changed places with an electric violinist in a locked and chained trunk; at the Royal Alexandra Theatre in Toronto in the winter of 1973–74, presented the rock show *Spellbound*, featuring himself and Lighthouse; performed his illusions in the context of a rock musical in *The Magic Show*, which opened on Broadway in May 1974 and ran for more than four years; in December 1975 temporarily left the cast of *The Magic Show* to star in the NBC television special *The World of Magic*, presented live (not "live-on-tape") and in the presence of a live audience to help certify that the illusions—including his version of Houdini's "water-torture escape"—were not accomplished electronically; subsequently starred in other television specials; returned to Broadway twice, in the musical *Merlin*, in 1983, and in the solo show *Doug Henning and His World of Magic*, in 1984; in *Merlin*, created the illusion of a flying horseman disappearing into thin air; subsequently devoted himself to the transcendental meditation movement; died in Los Angeles, California. See *Current Biography* (August) 1976.

Obituary *New York Times* B p10 Feb. 9, 2000

HOEGH, LEO A. Mar. 30, 1908–July 15, 2000 Former state and federal official; lawyer; began practicing law in Iowa in 1932; in 1936 was elected to the first of three terms in the Iowa House of Representatives; as a U.S. infantry platoon leader in Europe during World War II, won battlefield promotion from first lieutenant to lieutenant colonel—and drew the attention of General Dwight D. Eisenhower; served as attorney general of Iowa (1953–54); was governor of Iowa from 1955 to 1957, when he joined President Eisenhower's administration as civil-defense administrator, then a sub-Cabinet position; when the Civil Defense Administration was merged with the office of Civil and Defense Mobilization, in 1958, became the first administrator of the new Cabinet-level agency; remained in that post until the end of the Eisenhower administration, in 1961; died in Colorado Springs, Colorado. See *Current Biography* (July) 1956.

Obituary *New York Times* B p8 July 24, 2000

HORST Aug. 14, 1906–Nov. 18, 1999 German-born photographer; a fashion and society photographer who combined sensuous romanticism and understated sexuality with classical stylizing; manipulated light to achieve aesthetic distance and transform his subjects into icons of idealized femininity and masculinity; is best known for the elegant and aristocratic black-and-white studio portraits of such celebrities as Coco Chanel, Elsa Schiaparelli, Marlene Dietrich, Noel Coward, and Gary Cooper he contributed to *Vogue* magazine in the 1930s and 1940s; originally aspired to become an architect; in 1929 moved to Paris to apprentice under the Bauhaus architect Le Corbusier, abortively; soon became apprenticed instead to George von Hoyningen-Huene, the chief photographer at French *Vogue*; through Huene, enhanced his standing in the chic expatriate community in Paris and became a photographer for *Vogue*; working for both French *Vogue* and American *Vogue* during the 1930s, became a virtual transatlantic commuter; in 1939 settled in the U.S. as a staff photographer with American *Vogue*; in the years following World War II, found that he, with his brand of glamour, was at odds with the changing aesthetic in international fashion; in the 1950s turned from fashion photography to commercial advertising assignments, including campaigns for Modess, Ford, Seagram, and Saks Fifth Avenue; with an eye for telling detail, photographed the homes of the rich and famous for *Vogue* beginning in the early 1960s; in 1977 was asked by French *Vogue* to shoot fashion collections in Paris; received similar invitations from the Spanish, British, Italian, and American editions of the magazine and from *Vanity Fair* in the following years, when there was a revival of interest in the fashion aesthetic of the 1930s; at the request of such stores as Bloomingdale's and Barneys, did advertising photographs of men's fashions in his 1930s style; died in Palm Beach Gardens, Florida. See *Current Biography* (June) 1992.

Obituary *New York Times* B p10 Nov. 19, 1999

HOVHANESS, ALAN Mar. 8, 1911–June 21, 2000 Musician; a notably accessible and prolific American composer whose vast oeuvre encompasses many genres and reflects the music of varied cultures, including that of his Armenian heritage; as a concert artist, often performed his own piano pieces; as a composer, drew upon his extensive knowledge of Eastern musical instruments as well as Western instruments; among Western composers, was a pioneer in writing for the sitar and other Indian instruments; composed easily, and with speed; professed to be "interested only in serenity of the mind"; was inspired in large measure by nature—including the mountains of New Hampshire and Washington State—and Christian as well as Hindu and Buddhist mysticism; learned to play the piano in childhood; in the mid-1930s, studied composition at the New England Conservatory of Music; was strongly influenced by Sibelian romanticism during the first phase of his career, extending to the early 1940s; became seriously interested in Armenian liturgical music as an organist at an Armenian church in Watertown, Massachusetts, beginning in 1940; arrived at a turning point in his career in 1942, when he studied at the Berkshire Music Center under Bohuslav Martinu, who approved of the direction he had been pursuing, and Aaron Copland and Leonard Bernstein, who disapproved; heeding Copland and Bernstein's criticisms, destroyed everything he had written up to that point and ventured onto a new path; not long afterward, saw and heard Uday Shankar and his company of Indian dancers and musicians perform in Boston; thereafter, regarded the study of Eastern music as his "life work"; in addition to the music of India, China, Japan, and Korea, immersed himself in the traditional music of the Arabs, Syrians, and Turko-Tartars; tried to trace in Eastern music similarities in Western music up to the time of the troubadours; conducted an intensive study of Renaissance polyphony; above all, set himself to the task of superimposing Western techniques on Eastern forms, generally without departing from conventional tonality; from 1948 to 1951 taught at the Boston Conservatory of Music; during the 1950s created the music for a series of Martha Graham ballets and wrote the scores for two NBC television documentaries on India and Southeast Asia; on Broadway, wrote the incidental music for Clifford Odets's play *The Flowering Peach* (1955); beginning in 1959, toured the world for several years, playing and conducting his works in, among other countries, India and Japan (the homeland of his wife, Hinako Fujihara), in both of which he was lionized; moved to Seattle, Washington, in 1962; after witnessing the volcanic eruption of Mount St. Helens, in 1980, composed his Symphony no. 50 (1983) in celebration of the volcano and the surrounding Cascade Mountains; among other orchestral works, wrote some 70 symphonies, including the *St. Vartan Symphony*, the *Mysterious Mountain Symphony*, and the *Ajuna Symphony*; as both composer and librettist, wrote some dozen operas, including *Pericles*; left a total catalog of more than 500 works, including such cantatas as *Fuji* and a vast selection of chamber and other instrumental pieces, among them the tone poem *And God Created Great Whales* (1970); died in Seattle. See *Current Biography* (April) 1965.

Obituary *New York Times* p21 June 23, 2000

INGALLS, JEREMY Apr. 2, 1911–Mar. 16, 2000 Writer; poet; teacher; in the wealth of allusions in her first, award-winning collection of poems, *The Metaphysical Sword* (1941), revealed the depth and variety of her erudition in classical, mythological, biblical, and Oriental sources; in her long narrative poem *Tahl* (1945), told the story of a young musician, representing the inquiring human spirit, who is able to transcend time; published the poetry collections *The Woman from the Island* (1958), *These Islands Also* (1959), and *The Stubborn Quantum* (1983); also published *A Book of Legends* (1941), a collection of short stories on legendary themes, *The Galilean Way* (1953), a study of Christianity in relation to other world religions, and *The Epic Tradition and Other Essays* (1989); taught math, general science, English, and American literature at Gloucester (Massachusetts) High School (1934–41); later, was assistant professor of English at Western College in Oxford, Ohio for two years; taught English literature, Chinese history, and creative writing at Rockford (Illinois) College (1948–60); died in Tucson, Arizona. See *Current Biography* (Yearbook) 1954.

Obituary *New York Times* B p8 Mar. 27, 2000

JAKOBOVITS, IMMANUEL Feb. 8, 1921–Oct. 31, 1999 German-born British Orthodox rabbi; chief rabbi of the United Hebrew Congregations of the British Commonwealth of Nations (1967–91); was descended from rabbis on both sides of his family; fled Hitler's Germany in 1936; in London, was educated at Yeshiva Etz Chaim, Jews' College, and London University; began his ministry at the Brondesbury Synagogue in London (1941–44); in 1944 moved to the South East London Synagogue; was rabbi of London's Great Synagogue from 1947 until he was named chief rabbi of Ireland (1949–58); was first rabbi of the Fifth Avenue Synagogue in New York City, from 1958 to 1967; to resolve a schism within Orthodox Jewry in Britain, did not accept the position of chief rabbi until it was offered unanimously by the leaders of the two rival factions in the Ashkenazi community in the United Kingdom; stirred controversy within the international Jewish community by warning against the "nurturing and breeding [of] a Holocaust mentality of morose dependency among our people" and by having what some perceived to be too much sympathy for Palestinians living under

Israeli control; raised the hackles of liberals in the United Kingdom with his forcefully propounded traditionalist positions on social issues, including opposition to abortion, homosexuality, premarital sex, marital infidelity, and turnstile divorce; in 1986 countered the Church of England's report "Faith in the City" with his own "From Doom to Hope," in which he urged new immigrants to embrace the work ethic rather than the welfare state; wrote the books *Jewish Medical Ethics* (1959), *Journal of a Rabbi* (1966), *Jewish Law Faces Modern Problems* (1966), *The Timely and the Timeless* (1977), and *If Only My People . . . : Zionism in My Life* (1985), about his work in behalf of Soviet Jews and the obstacles he encountered in both the USSR and Israel; after his retirement as Britain's chief rabbi, remained active in the House of Lords, to which he had been elevated (as a life peer with the title of Baron of Regents Park) in 1987; died at his home in London. See *Current Biography* (June) 1988.

Obituary *New York Times* C p22 Nov. 2, 1999

KAHN, MADELINE Sep. 29, 1942–Dec. 3, 1999 Actress; an offbeat comedienne with a distinctive babyish voice, an intuitive mock sexiness, and a pout that easily turned into a devilish grin; was "the clown with the face of an angel," as Rex Reed described her; is most closely identified with such screen roles as Lili von Shtupp, a devastating burlesque of the Dietrich-style femme fatale, in Mel Brooks's *Blazing Saddles* (1974), a wild spoof of movie Westerns, and Elizabeth, the fussy, primping fiancée of the title character in Brooks's *Young Frankenstein* (1974), a parody of Mary Shelley's novel; early in her career, sang opera and light opera with an upstate New York repertory company; had her first Broadway break in *New Faces of 1968*; in 1969 sang in the Off-Broadway musical *Promenade*; in the late 1960s and early 1970s was a regular performer at the Upstairs at the Downstairs club in Manhattan; during the same period, became known to a national television audience as a guest on the television shows of Johnny Carson and others; had the one-song role of Goldie in the Broadway musical *Two by Two* in 1970–71; gave a sensitive performance as Chrissy in *In the Boom Boom Room* at New York's Lincoln Center in 1973; made her feature-film debut in the supporting role of Eunice Banks in *What's Up Doc?* (1972), a parody of old slapstick comedy movies; was cast as the carnival dancer Trixie Delight in the film *Paper Moon* (1973); was "not proud" of her less-than-promised share of the script in the musical *At Long Last Love* (1975); in contrast, had one of her happiest filmmaking experiences starring (as Jenny, a music-hall singer) opposite Gene Wilder in Wilder's Baker Street spoof *The Adventure of Sherlock Holmes's Smart Brother* (1975); was reunited with Mel Brooks in *High Anxiety* (1977) and *History of the World: Part I* (1981); made more than a score of films, including *First Family* (1980), *Mixed Nuts* (1994), and *Nixon* (1995); on television, starred in two series, *Oh Madeline* (1983–84) and *Mr. President* (1989), and had a supporting role in the sitcom *Cosby* (1996–99); on Broadway, starred in a revival of *Born Yesterday* in 1989 and won a Tony Award as best actress for her performance as sister Gorgeous in *The Sisters Rosensweig* (1992); died in Manhattan. See *Current Biography* (May) 1977.

Obituary *New York Times* A p15 Dec. 4, 1999

KARP, DAVID May 5, 1922–Sep. 11, 1999 Author; wrote popular novels and television dramas, often with Orwellian themes; early in his career, wrote some half-dozen formulaic paperback novels under the pseudonyms Adam Singer and Wallace Ware; in 1953 published his first serious novel, *One*, about a college professor struggling against the obliteration of his identity by a benign totalitarian state that cannot permit nonconformity; in *The Day of the Monkey* (1955), dealt with a British colonial administration faced with nationalist rebellion and Communist agitation; in *All Honorable Men* (1956), told the story of a struggle for intellectual freedom in the midst of a McCarthyite political "witch" hunt; later wrote the novels *Leave Me Alone* (1957), *Enter Sleeping* (1960), and *The Last Believers* (1964); on television, contributed to such dramatic anthologies and series as *General Electric Theater*, *Studio One*, *The Untouchables*, *I Spy*, and *Profiles in Courage*; won a Fund for the Republic Award for his television adaptation of *One*, presented on the Kraft Television Theater in 1955, and a *Look* magazine award for his script for *The Plot to Kill Stalin* (*Playhouse 90*, 1958); in 1965 won an Emmy for *The 700 Year Old Gang*, produced on *The Defenders* series; later was nominated for Emmy Awards for *The Brotherhood of the Bell*, *Rally 'Round the Flag*, and *Hawkins on Murder*; among other projects, wrote the play *Cafe Universe* (1967) and the scenario for the feature film *Sol Madrid* (1968); died in Pittsfield, Massachusetts. See *Current Biography* (Yearbook) 1957.

Obituary *New York Times* A p15 Sep. 20, 1999

KINGMAN, DONG Mar. 31, 1911–May 12, 2000 U.S.–born Chinese-American artist; a careful, cheerful, and often whimsical craftsman of watercolors (mostly based on pen and pencil sketches), including Hong Kong, New York, and other cityscapes, many of which illustrated covers and articles for *Holiday*, *McCall's*, *Fortune*, *Time*, *Life*, and other magazines; also reached a wide audience with his children's-book illustrations and his Hollywood-related paintings, including those promoting the motion picture *The World of Suzie Wong* and the background paintings for the film *Flower Drum Song*; in childhood, moved with his parents to Hong Kong, where he attended elementary school and, in adolescence, studied drawing and painting; returned to the U.S. at 18; during the 1930s Depression, developed his talents professionally under the auspices of the federal Works Project Administration; in 1940, realized the first of several sales of his paintings to the Metropolitan Museum of Art; exhibited widely beginning in 1942; taught art at Columbia University, Mills College, Hunter College, and the Famous Artists School; is represented at New York's Museum of Modern Art and the Whitney Museum of American Art, among other venues; died in Manhattan. See *Current Biography* (October) 1962.

Obituary *New York Times* A p21 May 16, 2000

KLEINDIENST, RICHARD G. Aug. 5, 1923–Feb. 3, 2000 U.S. attorney general in the administration of President Richard Nixon; lawyer; served in the Arizona House of Representatives for one term (1953–54); practiced law as a senior partner in the Phoenix firm of Shimmel, Hill, Kleindienst & Bishop from 1958 to 1969; was national director of field operations in conservative Republican candidate Barry Goldwater's unsuccessful campaign for the presidency in 1964; worked in the same position in Richard Nixon's successful presidential campaign in 1968; went to Washington as deputy attorney general when Nixon took office, in January 1969; succeeded John Mitchell as attorney general in June 1972; resigned as attorney general in April 1973, explaining that his effectiveness was severely diminished by the implication of many of his close associates in the Watergate scandal (which would lead to Nixon's resignation, in 1974); while not himself implicated in the scandal, did plead guilty to a misdemeanor charge of having testified untruthfully on one point in his Senate confirmation hearings; returned to the practice of law in Arizona; wrote the book *The Memoirs of an Attorney General* (1985); died at his home in Prescott, Arizona. See *Current Biography* (October) 1972.

Obituary *New York Times* A p27 Feb. 4, 2000

KLEITMAN, NATHANIEL Apr. 26, 1895–Aug. 13, 1999 Physiologist; a pioneer in the mapping of sleep cycles; a discoverer of rapid eye movements (REM) during dream states; by the use of such devices as the electroencephalograph (EEG machine) to record brain waves and electrodes to record eye movements, was able to replace misconceptions about sleeping, dreaming, and wakefulness with objective information; joined the faculty of the University of Chicago in 1925; became a full professor in 1950; first reported on the sleep studies conducted by him and his colleagues in the books *Sleep Characteristics* (1937) and *Sleep and Wakefulness* (1939; revised in 1963 and 1987); subsequently conducted experiments in sleep deprivation, changing patterns of sleep in caves and submarines, and the effects of diet, temperature, sunlight, and darkness on sleep; studied sleep/wakefulness patterns in various cultures, from the U.S. to Bali and northern Norway; with Eugene Aserinsky, in 1953 published a report on their recording of rapid eye movements; later, with William Dement, used electronic recordings and other techniques to establish that dreams were longer-lasting than previously believed, usually enduring from 10 to 30 minutes and totaling some two hours per night, and that the nature of the eye movements changes with the content of the dream; retired in 1960; died in Beverly Hills, California. See *Current Biography* (October) 1957.

Obituary *New York Times* B p8 Aug. 19, 1999

KNIPLING, E. F. Mar. 20, 1909–Mar. 17, 2000 Entomologist; originated the concept of agricultural pest control through sterilization, without insecticides, and proved its efficacy in eradicating the screwworm fly, once the scourge of livestock farmers in the southern U.S. and Mexico; in 1931, when he was still a graduate student, joined the U.S. Department of Agriculture as a junior entomologist in Menard, Texas, where he began his study of the biology and control of the screwworm fly, a livestock pest causing tens of millions of dollars of damage a year in the southern U.S. alone; first conceived and proposed (to no avail) his concept of insect population control through sterilization in 1938; during World War II, headed the USDA research laboratory that developed DDT and other insecticides and repellents for use by the U.S. armed forces; became director of the USDA's entomology division in 1953, when the first field tests with sterilized male screwworm flies were conducted; with his colleagues, in 1958 launched on a mammoth scale a similar project, in which almost three billion sterilized male flies were dropped by a fleet of 20 airplanes over an infected area in Florida, with dramatic success; scored equal success with an even larger screwworm eradication program in Texas in 1962; in 1971 became science adviser to the USDA's Agricultural Research Service; after retiring from the USDA, in 1973, continued to write about insect population suppression; published hundreds of articles on the subject; died at his home in Arlington, Virginia. See *Current Biography* (May) 1975.

Obituary *New York Times* B p8 Mar. 27, 2000

KOCH, FRED JR. Sep. 15, 1911–Aug. 26, 2000 Charter chairman of the Department of Drama at the University of Miami at Coral Gables, Florida; at the university, created the Ring Theater, the first fully flexible theater in the round in the U.S., accommodating all types of staging, from arena and horseshoe to proscenium, Elizabethan, and Greek; as an undergraduate at the University of North Carolina, was a member of the campus theatrical troupe, the Carolina Playmakers, founded and directed by his father; in the mid-1930s, with his wife, Edna Bryant, toured the U.S. with their own puppet show; subsequently, earned an M.A. degree in dramatic arts at the University of North Carolina (with a thesis in the form of a play, *Smokey Mountain Road*) and taught drama in summer sessions at the University of Virginia; in the fall of 1939, was recruited by the trustees of the University of Miami to establish a drama department there; proceeded to develop a department including classroom instruction, workshops, and stage productions; in 1946, transformed the rotund tower of an old building on the university's north campus into a theater-in-the-round; later moved productions to a mammoth circular tent on the main campus; for the architects Robert M. Little and Marion I. Manley, drafted the basic plans for a new permanent structure incorporating a revolving stage and movable riser units to seat 600 people, never more than eight rows from the stage in whatever arrangement; supervised the construction of the theater, which opened in January 1952; thus provided Miami with its first legitimate theater and the southeastern U.S. with a major regional theater; welcomed participation in its productions by qualified residents of the greater Miami area; in addition to the Ring, created the Box, a smaller theater with a proscenium stage, as a showcase for aspiring playwrights; for 10 years during his tenure as chairman, helped to maintain a fiscal connection between the University of Miami and the Parkway Playhouse, a summer theater workshop in

Burnsville, North Carolina, where he spent time annually; retired in 1977. See *Curent Biography* (October) 1953.

Obituary *New York Times* C p19 Sep. 15, 2000

LANDRY, TOM Sep. 11, 1924–Feb. 12, 2000 Professional football coach; head coach of the Dallas Cowboys of the National Football League from the inception of the Dallas franchise, in 1960, through 1988; after five losing seasons in Dallas, broke even in wins and losses in 1965; subsequently had 20 consecutive winning seasons (an NFL record), 20 postseason victories (another NFL record), 18 participations in play-offs, 13 division titles, and two Super Bowl victories in five Super Bowl appearances; at the University of Texas in the 1940s, played fullback and quarterback and was co-captain of the football team; in his first professional football job, played halfback for the New York Yankees of the old American Football League in 1949; after the Yankees merged with the New York Giants of the NFL, played defensive back and punter with the Giants for six years (1950–55); was named All-Pro in 1954; as the Giants' defensive coach, beginning in 1956, changed the team's umbrella defense to the 4–3 defense, which would become standard in professional football; later, in Dallas, developed a refinement of the 4–3 defense known as the flex; in his 29 seasons with Dallas, compiled totals of 270 victories (third most in NFL history), 178 losses, and six ties; was a fundamentalist Christian who remained active in the Fellowship of Christian Athletes after his retirement as coach; was inducted into the Pro Football Hall of Fame in 1990; died in Dallas. See *Current Biography* (June) 1972.

Obituary *New York Times* B p10 Feb. 14, 2000

LAWRENCE, JACOB Sep. 7, 1917–June 9, 2000 Artist; professor of art emeritus at the University of Washington, Seattle; a figurative painter who visually recorded life in Harlem as he experienced it; was perhaps even more important for his chronicling, in narrative series after narrative series, the African-American odyssey through American history; did so in vivid primary colors and a flat and simple Cubist-like geometric style; usually working in tempora or gouache on paper, created pictures modest in size but powerful individually and in combination; was a scrupulously systematic craftsman who drew all of the pictures for a series before applying one color at a time to the whole set, a red in one stage, for example, a blue or yellow in others; thus achieved overall tonal consistency; during the Harlem Renaissance of the 1930s, found a mentor in the older black painter Charles Alston; studied on scholarship at the American Artists School; in 1938 had his first one-man exhibition at the Harlem YMCA, featuring his first Harlem street and interior scenes, viewed by some as satirical; in the same year, found employment in the easel division of the Depression-era Work Projects Administration's Federal Arts Project; in 1939 first exhibited his Toussaint L'Ouverture series of 40 paintings narrating Haiti's struggles for independence; meanwhile, completed series of 32 paintings depicting the life of Frederick Douglass (1938) and 31 recounting the life of Harriet Tubman (1939); came to national prominence with *The Migration of the Negro* (1941), comprising 60 paintings recounting the mass movement of southern blacks to the North in search of jobs after World War I; in 1942 completed a biographical series on John Brown and 31 gouaches on life in Harlem, including *Pool Parlor*; created 48 paintings about life on board the Coast Guard vessel on which he served during World War II; in the summer of 1946, taught at Black Mountain College at the invitation of Josef Albers; on a Guggenheim Fellowship, produced his *War* series (1946–47) of 14 reflective paintings about World War II (1946–47); on commission by *Fortune magazine*, created *In the Heart of the Black Belt* (1947–48), 10 paintings on opportunities for blacks in the postwar South; over the following decade, created such series as *Sanitarium*, 11 paintings inspired by his stay in a hospital, and *Struggle*, 40 paintings of figures from American history, including Patrick Henry and famous early pioneers; also returned to his earlier theme of city life, but added more intricately patterned designs; beginning in the late 1950s, turned his attention to racial desegregation in the South and other aspects of the civil rights struggle; in the late 1960s replaced racial tension with racial harmony as the dominant theme of his work; at the same time, infused gray tones into his signature primary-color palette and introduced into his narrative technique a slicker graphic element, reminiscent of the illustrator's art; in the 1970s, 1980s, and 1990s, completed a number of commissioned works, including a print of the inauguration of President Jimmy Carter, a mural for Howard University, and a 14-yard-long mosaic scheduled for installation in the major subway nexus at Times Square, in Manhattan, in 2001; beginning in 1955 taught at Pratt Institute, among other schools; joined the faculty of the University of Washington in 1970; retired in 1986; died at his home in Seattle, Washington. See *Current Biography* (September) 1988.

Obituary *New York Times* A p13 June 10, 2000

LEIGH, DOUGLAS May 24, 1907–Dec. 14, 1999 Advertising executive; the major pioneer in the spectacular commercial illumination of the Times Square–Broadway–Columbus Circle area of Manhattan; erected giant advertising displays using hundreds of thousands of light bulbs and well over 25 miles of neon tubing; migrated from his native Alabama to New York City in 1929; after working for the General Outdoor Advertising Co., launched his own company, in 1933; before the end of that year, pursuant to a contract with the A&P grocery chain, erected his first Midtown Manhattan electrical sign, a steaming coffee cup 15 feet wide and 25 feet high at the southeast corner of 47th Street and Seventh Avenue; subsequently erected in the Times Square area such eye-catching displays as a Kool cigarette ad featuring a blinking penguin, a Ballantine beer ad with clowns tossing quoits, an effervescent glass of Bromo-Seltzer, a Pepsi-Cola waterfall 125 feet high, and a Camel cigarette billboard puffing out five-foot-wide rings of smoke at the corner of 44th Street and Broadway; at Columbus Circle, was responsible for a huge Schenley whiskey sign and a Coca-Cola ad providing weather forecasts; later illuminated Manhattan skyscrapers, beginning with the Empire State Building; died in Manhattan. See *Current Biography* (May) 1940.

Obituary *New York Times* B p13 Dec. 16, 1999

LEVI, EDWARD H. June 26, 1911–March 7, 2000 Former attorney general of the U.S.; former law-school dean, provost, and president of the University of Chicago; was educated at the university from 1916, when he enrolled in the kindergarten of its laboratory schools, to 1935, when he received his J.D. degree; began teaching law at the university in 1936; on leave from the university, was special assistant to the attorney general of the U.S. from 1940 to 1945; in addition to his academic duties in Chicago, was dean of the university's law school from 1950 to 1962; stressing the university's traditional interdisciplinary approach, added an economist and a sociologist to the school's faculty; founded the school's *Journal of Law and Economics*; became provost of the university in 1962 and president in 1968; was admired by other college and university administratorss for the cool deftness with which he handled the students who occupied his office during the national epidemic of campus unrest in 1968; achieved wider renown for restoring order to and public trust in the U.S. Department of Justice and Federal Bureau of Investigation in the wake of the Watergate scandal; as U.S. attorney general (1975–77), displayed, in the words of Supreme Court justice Antonin Scalia (who worked under him at the Department of Justice), "a rare intellectuality and a level of integrity such as there could never be any doubt about his honesty, forthrightness, or truthfulness"; was especially expert in antitrust law and in law relating to the development of nuclear energy; wrote the classic, pereniably reprinted textbook *An Introduction to Legal Reasoning* (1949); retired from the University of Chicago in 1984; died at his home in Chicago. See *Current Biography* (January) 1969.

Obituary *New York Times* C p25 Mar. 8, 2000

LIBERMAN, ALEXANDER Sep. 4, 1912–Nov. 19, 1999 Russian-born editor; painter; sculptor; photographer; as art director of Condé Nast Publications from the early 1940s to 1984, brought a modernist sensibility and a glamorous artistic creativity to that publisher's line of glossy high-fashion and chic lifestyle and leisure magazines, led by *Vogue*; was an art assistant and editor with the French magazine *Vu* in the 1930s; became art director of *Vogue* after immigrating to the U.S. in 1941; gradually widened the focus of that haute couture magazine to include, for example, coverage and high-caliber criticism of contemporary art; by recruiting such photographers as Cecil Beaton and Richard Avedon, made the clothing illustrations themselves classics of fashion art; in 1943 assumed the art direction of all Condé Nast publications, which over the years would include such magazines as *Mademoiselle, Vanity Fair, House & Garden, Gourmet, Condé Nast Traveler, Bride's, Architectural Digest*, and *Glamour*; in his own paintings showed the influence of the Russian constructivist art to which he had been introduced as a child; as a painter, moved from his early realistic landscapes and portraits through a post-impressionist phase to abstraction, both geometric and expressionist; was more warmly received by critics and public as the creator of large-scale, abstract welded-metal sculptures, outdoor works that can be seen in the garden of the Museum of Modern Art in Manhattan, outside the Corcoran Gallery in Washington, D.C., and in numerous shopping malls, parks, and college campuses; published a number of volumes of his photographs, including several devoted to such specific subjects as Greece, artists of the School of Paris in their studios, and Marlene Dietrich in addition to one general retrospective collection covering half a century; after the death of his second wife, Tatiana Iacovleff du Plessix, in 1991, married Melina Pechango; died in Miami Beach, Florida. See *Current Biography* (May) 1987.

Obituary *New York Times* C p15 Nov. 20, 1999

LINDT, AUGUSTE R. Aug. 5, 1905–Apr. 15 or 16, 2000 Swiss diplomat; United Nations official; in the 1930s, traveled the globe as a foreign correspondent for leading Swiss and German newspapers; during World War II, headed the Swiss army's information section; after the war was, successively, press attaché and counselor at the Swiss legation in London; meanwhile, had begun working with the United Nations (even though Switzerland, as an international "neutral," did not belong to the U.N.) as a member of the program committee of the U.N. International Children's Emergency Fund; in 1953 became chairman of UNICEF's executive board; in the same year, became Switzerland's permanent observer at the U.N.; from 1956 to 1960 was U.N. high commissioner for refugees; subsequently served, in succession, as Swiss ambassador to the U.S., the USSR, Mongolia, India, and Nepal. See *Current Biography* (November) 1959.

Obituary *New York Times* B p8 Apr. 18, 2000

LIONNI, LEO May 5, 1910–Oct. 11, 1999 Author; illustrator; designer; an artist in varied media and combinations of media, including paint, pen, pencil, crayon, and cut paper; also sculpted in bronze; was best known as a writer and illustrator of prize-winning children's books, most of which are animal fables intended as windows onto "the soul"; as an artist, was influenced chiefly by those he called "the surrealist storytellers," including Marc Chagall and Ben Shahn; was born into a peripatetic cosmopolitan family in the Netherlands and raised and educated there and in Belgium, Switzerland, the U.S., and Italy, where he married and worked as an architectural and graphic designer; in 1938 settled into a career in commercial art and magazine design in the U.S.; over the following two decades, as an art director with the N. W. Ayer Co. or on his own, was responsible for such projects as the Container Corp. of America's "Great Ideas" series of magazine advertisements, the Museum of Modern Art's *Family of Man*, and the redesigning of the format, typography, and layout of *Fortune* magazine; from 1949 to 1959 was design director for the Olivetti Corp.; in 1955 became editor of *Print* magazine; created the first draft of his first children's book, *Little Blue and Little Yellow* (1959), as an entertainment (about "two round blobs of color . . . who, when they embraced, became green") for his grandchildren; subsequently published *Inch by Inch* (1960), *On My Beach There Are Many Pebbles* (1961), *Swimmy* (1963), *Frederick* (1967), *Alexander and the Wind-up Mouse* (1969), *Fish Is Fish* (1970), *A Flea Story* (1977), *Cornelius* (1984), *Where Have You Been?* (1987), and *Matthew's Dream* (1990); in 1997 published his autobiography, *Between Two Worlds*; with his wife, maintained an apartment in New York City in addition to their home near Radda in the Chianti region of Tuscany, Italy; died at his Tuscan home. See *Current Biography* (September) 1997.

Obituary *New York Times* p51 Oct. 17, 1999

LOGUE, EDWARD J. Feb. 7, 1921–Jan. 27, 2000 Urban planner; to a degree no one before him had succeeded in contriving, tapped federal funds for radical urban renewal projects in New Haven, Boston, and New York City; was legal secretary and staff assistant to Chester Bowles in the early 1950s, when Bowles was, successively, governor of Connecticut and ambassador to India; in 1954 became deputy to Mayor Richard C. Lee of New Haven, who soon named him urban development administrator; in that position, initiated a long-term program, costing $268,000,000, that reclaimed marshland and replaced 90 percent of New Haven's slums with 1,500 new housing units and 8,200 rehabilitated units; however, failed to rejuvenate New Haven's downtown in time to stanch the shift of shopping to suburban malls; as director of the Boston Redevelopment Authority, in the 1960s, rehabilitated about 10 percent of Boston, constructing 20,000 new housing units, replacing 13,000 substandard units, and refurbishing 37,000 more; in Boston, realized his proudest achievement in the Faneuil Hall-Quincy Market restoration; at the request of New York State governor Nelson Rockefeller, in 1968 became president of the Urban Development Corp., a virtually autonomous New York State urban-renewal agency; aided by a staff of 500 architects, engineers, and others, initiated a series of innovative programs for schools, shopping centers, community facilities, industrial complexes, and new housing projects throughout New York State; created several new residential communities, including Roosevelt Island in New York City; headed his own consulting firm, Logue Development; died in West Tisbury, Massachusetts. See *Current Biography* (June) 1977.

Obituary *New York Times* B p7 Jan. 29, 2000

LYNCH, JOHN Aug. 15, 1917–Oct. 20, 1999 Prime minister (*taoiseach*) of the Republic of Ireland (Eire) from 1966 to 1973 and again from 1977 to 1979; lawyer; before entering politics, was a star athlete in hurling and Gaelic football; running on the Fianna Fáil ticket, was first elected to the Irish Dáil in 1948; remained in the Dáil until 1981; concurrently, was an alderman in his native Cork from 1950 to 1957; in Fianna Fáil governments was parliamentary secretary and minister for lands (1951–54), minister for education (1957–59), minister for industry and commerce (1959–65), and minister for finance (1965–66); was president of Fianna Fáil from 1966 to 1979 and leader of the parliamentary opposition from 1973 to 1977; in his most crucial decision as prime minister, resisted pressure from many quarters, including his own party, to send Irish troops across the border with Northern Ireland (part of the United Kingdom) to defend Catholics in Londonderry against the Royal Ulster Constabulary and Protestant paramilitaries; put Ireland on the road to economic recovery by moving it into the European Economic Community, in 1973; was vice president of the Council of Europe in 1958 and president of the European Economic Council in 1979; died in Dublin, Ireland. See *Current Biography* (May) 1967.

Obituary *New York Times* B p15 Oct. 21, 1999

MAGGIOLO, WALTER A. June 26, 1908–Aug. 7, 2000 Labor-management negotiator; lawyer; was trial attorney for the New York State Labor Relations Board from 1939 to 1943; in 1943, became a commissioner of conciliation with the U.S. Conciliation Service, which was superseded by the Federal Mediation and Conciliation Service in 1947; was named the service's acting general counsel in 1951, general counsel in 1952, and director of mediation in 1957; in the greater New York metropolitan area in the late 1940s and early 1950s, helped to prevent a three-state milk delivery strike and mediated a Wall Street strike and maritime and newspaper disputes; during the 1950s, was instrumental in settling a national telephone strike and major steel-industry disputes, among others; in 1964, mediated the signing of a national master agreement between the trucking industry and the International Brotherhood of Teamsters; as a Roman Catholic, was guided in his work in part, he said, by papal pronouncements on social justice; retired as director of mediation with the Federal Mediation and Conciliation Service in 1972; died in Arlington, Virginia. See *Current Biography* (July) 1952

Obituary *New York Times* C p16 Aug. 12, 2000

MARCA-RELLI, CONRAD June 5, 1913–Aug. 29, 2000 Artist; a Boston-born painter and collagist loosely identified with the New York–based second wave of abstract expressionism, which flowered in the 1950s; combined a classical European sensibility and a commitment to classical themes—landscape, figure, architecture—with the boldness, spontaneity, and monumental scale of the so-called New York school; as the crtitic John Canaday observed, "was always the classicist exception among his romantic abstract impressionist colleagues and fellow experimenters"; as a collagist, worked in numerous media but is primarily known for his use of cutout shapes of painted canvas attached to a larger canvas in jigsaw or mosaic fashion with black glue, which, like the lead in a stained-glass window, served to outline the forms making up the whole composition; sometimes applied multiple layers of canvas; because his father was a journalist and news commentator with assignments abroad, spent much of his childhood in European countries as well as the U.S.; began to draw at an early age; took his first art lessons in Italy; later studied at the Cooper Union, in New York City; during the early 1930s, in the depth of the Depression, supported himself by teaching and doing illustrations for newspapers and magazines; from 1935 to 1938, was a teacher and painter in both the easel and mural divisions of the Federal Art Project; began to absorb the tenets of modernism and to break away from his early figurative style partly through his acquaintance with other painters in the project (especially Willem de Kooning), who would become his peers in the New York school; after serving with the U.S. Army in World War II, worked in a succession of surrealist veins; at his first one-man exhibit, in New York City in 1947, showed canvases, some with motifs of Italian Renaissance architecture, that were reminiscent of the dreamlike metaphysical paintings of Giorgio de Chirico; in Rome in 1949, exhibited paintings of protoplasmic and invented shapes that were ostensibly automatic products of the unconscious; later in 1949, in Manhattan, joined the Eighth Street Club, an informal group of artists exploring abstract means of expression; in 1951, exhibited a series of large and brilliantly colored abstract paintings influenced by the biomorphism of Arshile Gorky; during the following two years, traveled internationally and produced semiabstract and surreal drawings and paintings inspired by the formal order of Roman architecture and Mexican cityscapes, with their geometric adobe buildings and stark contrasts of light and shadow; began to experiment with collage when he ran out of paint in Mexico in 1953; after returning to New York, apparently influenced in part by de Kooning's experiments in his Woman series, proceeded to apply collage to faceless, anonymous conceptualizations of what he called "the architecture of the human figure"; at first, created such single-figure collages as *Seated Figure* (1954); moving on to the "the architecture of the event," created more massive and abstract collages of myriad figures in states of action, such as *The Battle* (1956); in the early 1960s, experimented with new materials, including metal and plastic, in such collages as *Pilot* and *Flight-197*; later in the 1960s, in post-painterly fashion, extended collage into three-dimensional space, first in shallow reliefs and then in freestanding sculptures; in a 1970 show, exhibited brass, slate, and marble sculptures in addition to bas reliefs and mixed-media collages; later experimented with spray paint, without sacrificing his established cosmopolitan elegance; died at his home in Parma, Italy, where he and his wife had been living since 1996. See *Current Biography* (September) 1970.

Obituary *New York Times* C p21 Aug. 31, 2000

MATTHAU, WALTER Oct. 1, 1920–July 1, 2000 Actor; a character actor—tall, with a less-than-handsome face, a slouching posture, a gruff voice, and a shambling lope—who brought to his craft an ironic wit, a mischievous bent, and a natural feel for improvisation and creation of stage business (for example, actions that establish mood); after honing his skills on the stage, became that rarity among his breed, a top Hollywood box-office attraction; did so through the magnetism of the persona he established in a succession of comedy roles—that of an endearing curmudgeon; once described his acting in drawing-room comedies as that of "a Ukrainian Cary Grant"; was described by the playwright Neil Simon as "the greatest instinctive actor I've ever seen"; made his breakthrough to stardom in 1965, in the Tony-winning role Simon created for him, that of Oscar Madison, the slovenly nemesis of the fastidious Felix Unger (Art Carney) in the hit Broadway comedy *The Odd Couple*, about two dropouts from marriage sharing a household; in the film version of *The Odd Couple* (1968), co-starred with Jack Lemmon, his frequent screen foil; learned comic timing in childhood, from older actors when he was playing juvenile bit parts in Yiddish musical comedies on lower Second Avenue in Manhattan; after working in summer stock, proceeded in 1948 to Broadway; rose from walk-on parts to more substantial roles in such productions as *Twilight Walk* (1952), *Fancy Meeting You Again* (1952), and *Will Success Spoil Rock Hunter?* (1955); in a City Center revival of *Guys and Dolls* in 1955, played Nathan Detroit with what Walter Kerr called "the confidence and energy of a trained vaudevillian"; for his portrayal of Maxwell Archer in *Once More, with Feeling* (1958), won a New York Drama Critics Award; in 1962 received the first of his two Tony Awards, for his performance as the aristocratic Paris banker Benjamin Beaurevers in the Broadway hit *A Shot in the Dark*; between stage appearances, beginning in 1955, shuttled to Hollywood, to play supporting roles, including heavies; in the Oscar-winning supporting role of the unethical lawyer Willie Gingrich, shared the screen with Jack Lemmon in the Billy Wilder comedy *The Fortune Cookie* (1966); subsequently co-starred with Lemmon in the Wilder films *The Front Page* (1974) and *Buddy Buddy* (1981) and, later, in *Grumpy Old Men* (1993) and *Grumpier Old Men* (1995); earned British Academy Awards for best actor for his portrayals of Pete (opposite Carol Burnett) in *Pete 'n' Tillie* (1972) and the title role in *Charlie Varrick* (1973); co-starred with George Burns in *The Sunshine Boys* (1975), Elaine May in *California Suite* (1978), Ossie Davis in *I'm Not Rappaport* (1996), and Diane Keaton and others in *Hanging Up* (2000); had a total of some 60 screen credits, including the sheriff in *Lonely Are the Brave* (1962), Horace in *Hello Dolly!* (1969), Jordan Winston in *Cactus Flower* (1969), three roles in *Plaza Suite* (1971), the title role in *Kotch* (1971), and (directed by his son Charles Matthau) Judge Cool in *The Grass Harp* (1995); on television, made his first appearance in a drama on the Philco Television Playhouse in 1952; played a Florida sheriff in the syndicated crime series *Tallahassee 7000* in 1961; died in Santa Monica, California. See *Current Biography* (June) 1966.

Obituary *New York Times* p26 July 2, 2000

MAURER, ION GHEORGHE Sep. 23, 1902–Feb. 8, 2000 Romanian Communist political leader; government official; lawyer; jurist; from 1961 to 1974 was chairman of the council of ministers, a position equivalent to that of prime minister; joined the Romanian Communist Party, which was then illegal, in 1936; after Romania was declared a Communist people's republic, in 1947, rose through party and government ranks as a protégé of Gheorghe Gheorghiu-Dej, secretary general of the Communist Party and president of Romania until his death, in 1965; following his election as a deputy to Romania's new legislature, the Grand National Assembly, in 1948, served briefly as deputy minister of industry and trade; was foreign minister in 1957 and 1958; as president of the presidium of the Grand National Assembly (1958–61), was titular head of state; retired from government in 1974 and from politics in 1975; died in Bucharest, Romania. See *Current Biography* (September) 1971.

Obituary *New York Times* B p9 Feb. 11, 2000

MAXWELL, WILLIAM Aug. 16, 1908–July 31, 2000 Author; editor; as a writer, was gently but powerfully evocative in creating fiction informed by an old-fashioned midwestern small-town sensibility; in 1936, two years after the publication of his first novel, *Bright Center of Heaven*, joined the staff of the *New Yorker* magazine's art department; subsequently became an editor in the *New Yorker*'s fiction department, where he would remain until 1976, working with such short-story contributors as John Cheever, John Updike, John O'Hara, Mary McCarthy, Shirley Hazzard, Vladimir Nabokov, J. D. Salinger, Eudora Welty, Harold Brodkey, Mavis Gallant, Isaac Bashevis Singer, and Frank O'Connor; with O'Connor, engaged in a correspondence published as *The Happiness of Getting It Down Right* (1966); established his own reputation as a writer with his second novel, *They Came Like Swallows* (1937), a fictional recounting of the delights and sorrows of his childhood in the semirural town of Lincoln, Illinois, including the death of his mother during the influenza epidemic of 1918–19; set his sensitive coming-of-age novel *The Folded Leaf* (1945) in Chicago, where he had moved with his father and two brothers when he was 14; returned to a remembered small-town milieu in *Time Will Darken It* (1949); in his large-scale novel *The Chateau* (1961), told, with a sense of humor and an almost Jamesian restraint, of the cultural challenges experienced by an American couple traveling in France; in his last novel, *So Long, See You Tomorrow* (1980), reworked the autobiographical grist of some of his early novels, adding facts he had researched about a murder-suicide in a neighboring tenant-farm family in Lincoln; in addition to his six novels, published *The Heavenly Tenant* (1946), a fantasy for children, the collection of fables/fairy tales *The Old Man at the Railroad Crossing* (1966), and the short-story collection *Over by the River* (1977); later published the collections of short fiction *Billy Dyer* (1992) and *All the Days and Nights* (1995); outside of fiction, published the family history *Ancestors* (1971) and the collection of essays *The Outermost Dream* (1989); died at his home in Manhattan. See *Current Biography* (Yearbook) 1949.

Obituary *New York Times* B p9 Aug. 1, 2000

McCABE, GIBSON Mar. 11, 1911–Aug. 5, 2000 Magazine executive; was publisher of *Newsweek* (1958–63) and president of Newsweek Inc. (1962–75) during a turbulent period, marked by the liberalizing influence of the Washington Post Co., which bought the magazine in 1961, and coinciding with the editorship of Osborn Elliott, who steered the publication toward the side of the counterculture and the political New Left; maintained *Newsweek*'s editorial independence in the face of pressure from readers and advertisers who differed with the magazine's left-of-center positions on the American strategy in the Vietnam War, racial matters, changes in sexual mores, and other controversial issues; joined *Newsweek* as circulation director in 1942; after abbreviated World War II service with the U.S. Navy (August 1943–December 1944), was assigned by *Newsweek* to Paris, where he supervised a stripped-down version of the magazine, without advertisements, for distribution to members of the armed forces; scooped other publications with news of the German surrender, on May 7, 1945, ending the war in Europe; with *Newsweek* after the war, became manager of its international editions in 1946, advertising manager in 1947, advertising director in 1949, general manager in 1951, and a vice president in 1954; during his tenure as publisher and president, saw *Newsweek*'s circulation rise from 1.3 million to almost 3 million and its annual revenue climb from $25 million to $60.6 million; served several terms as chairman of the Magazine Publishers of America, which honored him with its Henry Johnson Fisher Award in 1971; died in Jacksonville Beach, Florida. See *Current Biography* (February) 1963.

Obituary *New York Times* C p18 Aug. 9, 2000

MERRICK, DAVID Nov. 27, 1912–Apr, 26, 2000 Theatrical producer; a contentious and litigious loner with an instinct for potential stage hits and a talent for ballyhoo that enabled him to make end runs around unfriendly drama critics when necessary; produced nearly 90 shows; at the beginning of his career, practiced law while working as an assistant to the Broadway producer Herman Shumlin; in 1940 invested $5,000 in Shumlin's hit *The Male Animal*; barely recouped his investment in his first solo production, *Clutterbuck* (1949); fared much better (888 performances) with *Fanny* (1954); over the following eight years, registered only four flops among a score of successful plays and musicals, including *The Matchmaker, Look Back in Anger, Romanoff and Juliet, Jamaica, The World of Suzie Wong, La Plume de Ma Tante, The Good Soup, Maria Golovin, Vintage '60, A Taste of Honey, Irma La Douce, Becket, Gypsy, Take Me Along, Do Re Mi, Seidman and Sam*, and *Carnival*; in 1961, kept *Subways Are for Sleeping* afloat by finding men with the same names as the New York drama critics and running rave quotations with their bylines in a full-page ad in the New York *Herald Tribune*; when the popularity of *Hello, Dolly!* began to wane in 1967, replaced the entire cast with an all-black company headed by Pearl Bailey and Cab Calloway; had a surprise hit with *Marat/Sade*; during a sojourn in Hollywood, produced such films as *The Great Gatsby* (1974) and *Rough Cut* (1980); back on Broadway, enjoyed his last big hit, the musical *42nd Street*, which ran at the St. James Theatre from 1980 to 1989 and, concurrently, in London's West End; was left impaired in speech and movement by a stroke he suffered in 1983; thereafter, was rarely seen unaccompanied by Natalie Lloyd, who served as his spokesperson and became his sixth wife; during the 1990s was involved in endless litigation arising from his multiple marriages and his theatrical finances; was a tardy investor in his last Broadway show, a stage version of *State Fair*, which flopped in 1996; died in London. See *Current Biography* (January) 1961.

Obituary *New York Times* p1+ Apr. 27, 2000

MONTAGU, ASHLEY June 28, 1905–Nov. 26, 1999 British-born anthropologist; ethnologist; social biologist; prolific writer; educator; a talented and highly visible popularizer of science who ventured into then-sensitive areas of race, the relations between the sexes, and child rearing; courted controversy by upsetting what he called "venerable errors"; in the 1930s, earned his doctorate in anthropology at Columbia University and taught anatomy at New York University; was associate professor of anatomy at Hahnemann Medical School in Philadelphia (1938–49) and professor of anthropology and chairman of the Department of Anthropology at Rutgers University (1949–55); first attracted wide attention in the 1940s, when he argued that race, as a social issue, was a matter of perception and social contract rather than physical fact; wrote the book *Man's Most Dangerous Myth: The Fallacy of Race* (1942); at the end of that decade, helped to draw up the UNESCO "Statement on Race"; impressed an even wider public with *The Natural Superiority of Women* (1953), in which he advanced the thesis that women are biologically superior to men because they have more complete sex cells, are more resistant to disease, can better withstand certain pressures, and, as mothers, bear a greater responsibility for the human race; with the success of that book, was able to quit teaching and concentrate on his writing and public appearances; became a frequent guest on television talk shows; was in demand as a lecturer; wrote a steady stream of books, some technical and academic and others for a wider audience, on subjects including evolution and culture, anatomy, physiology, heredity, genetics, female reproductive development, prenatal influences, the behavior and development of children, anthropometry, intelligence, the meaning of love, marriage, why humans weep, why they swear, and the story of John Merrick, the Victorian "Elephant Man"; died in Princeton, New Jersey. See *Current Biography* (February) 1957.

Obituary *New York Times* A p23 Nov. 29, 1999

MOORE, GEORGE S. Apr. 1, 1905–Apr. 21, 2000 Banker; in 1927 began to work in the offices of the Farmers Loan and Trust Co., which was acquired by the First National City Bank of New York (now known as Citibank) two years later; rose up the hierarchy of First National City to become president, in 1959, and chairman of the board, in 1967; reached the bank's mandatory retirement age of 65 in 1970; in retirement, devoted more time and energy to public service and work for cultural organizations, especially the Metropolitan Opera Association, of which he had been president since 1967; was the sole trustee for Onassis family interests in the U.S.; was a financial consultant to a number of American and foreign corporations; published an autobiography, *The Banker's Life* (1986); died at his home in Sotograde, Spain. See *Current Biography* (May) 1970.

Obituary *New York Times* C p7 Apr. 22, 2000

MORITA, AKIO Jan. 26, 1921–Oct. 3, 1999 Japanese business executive; in bombed-out Tokyo after World War II, founded with Masaru Ibuka the Sony Corp. (originally named the Tokyo Telecommunications Co.); built that corporation into an innovative giant in electronics, famous for its introduction to the world market of such products as the first commercially successful transistor radio (1955), the pocket transistor radio (1957), the Trinitron color-television set with its unique Chromatron picture tube (1968), the Betamax home videocassette recorder and player (1975), the pocket Walkman stereo cassette player (1979), the compact disc and compact-disc player (1982), the 8-millimeter camcorder (1985), and Playstation, the first 32-bit video-game player (1994); meanwhile, had overseen Sony's purchase of CBS Records (1988) and Columbia Pictures Entertainment (1989), which was renamed Sony Pictures Entertainment; as vice chairman of the influential Japanese business organization Keidanren, beginning in 1986, was involved in talks about opening the Japanese market to American products; died in Tokyo. See *Current Biography* (February) 1972.

Obituary *New York Times* B p8+ Oct. 4, 1999

NEUBERGER, MAURINE B. Jan. 9, 1907–Feb. 22, 2000 Democratic U.S. senator from Oregon (1961–67); began her career as a teacher of English and physical education in public high schools in Oregon; in 1945 married Richard L. Neuberger; helped him campaign for the Oregon state senate, unsuccessfully in 1946 and successfully in 1948; two years later, waged her own successful campaign for a seat in the Oregon house of representatives; was reelected in 1952 and 1954; after serving in the Oregon house through 1955, moved to Washington, D.C., to become an unpaid assistant to her husband, who had been elected to the U.S. Senate in 1954; following his death, in March 1960, won election, in November 1960, to a full six-year term in the seat he had left vacant; in the Senate, was best known as a consumer advocate; sponsored one of the earliest bills calling for health warnings on cigarette packages; was ahead of her time in urging automobile pollution controls; did not run for reelection in 1966; after leaving the Senate, taught American government at Boston University and Radcliffe College for two years; subsequently tutored elementary-school students in Portland, Oregon, in reading and arithmetic for more than two decades; collaborated with her husband in freelance journalism, publishing articles about the Pacific Northwest, for which she also did the photography; with him, wrote the book *Adventures in Politics: We Go to the Legislature* (1954); by herself, wrote *Smoke Screen: Tobacco and the Public Welfare* (1963); died at her home in Portland, Oregon. See *Current Biography* (October) 1961.

Obituary *New York Times* B p11 Feb. 24, 2000

NICHOLS, KENNETH D. Nov. 13, 1907–Feb. 23, 2000 U.S. Army major general, retired; a military and civil engineer who supervised the construction of the first, war-related atomic-energy plants and later promoted the building of plants for the production of nuclear power for peaceful purposes; following his graduation from West Point, in 1929, continued his technical education at Cornell University and other schools in the U.S. and Germany; after receiving his Ph.D. degree in experimental hydraulics at the University of Iowa, in 1937, was an instructor at West Point; later returned briefly to West Point as a professor of mechanics; with the Manhattan (Project) Engineering District during World War II, supervised the planning and building of the city of Oak Ridge, Tennessee, including laboratories for nuclear research and plants that produced nuclear fuel for the first atomic bombs; also supervised the construction of the plutonium-production plants at Hanford, Washington; following World War II, contined to head the engineering district, which was absorbed by the Atomic Energy Commission in 1947; as chief of the Pentagon's armed-forces special-weapons project (1947–50), oversaw atomic-weapons logistics and training; in addition, was the senior army member of the military committee in liaison with the AEC; beginning in 1951, was deputy director of the guided missiles division of the Department of Defense; concurrently, was chief of army research and development (1953); retired from the military in 1953; was general manager of the AEC from 1953 to 1955; subsequently worked as a consultant to many corporations, until 1992; died in Bethesda, Maryland. See *Current Biography* (November) 1948.

Obituary *New York Times* B p8 Feb. 25, 2000

NYERERE, JULIUS K. 1923(?)–Oct. 14, 1999 First president of the United Republic of Tanzania (comprising what was formerly the British-controlled U.N. trust territory of Tanganyika along with the island territories of Zanzibar, Pemba, and Matia); an idealistic pan-African Socialist who was a force for national and international moderation and harmony; called his brand of pragmatic socialism *ujamaa* or *ujamma* (Swahili for "familyhood"), explaining, "It is opposed to capitalism, which seeks to build a happy society on the basis of the exploitation of man by man, and is equally opposed to doctrinaire socialism, which seeks to build its happy society on the philosophy of inevitable conflict between man and man"; made agricultural development Tanzania's first national priority, followed by exploration of mineral resources, expansion of light industry, and self-help programs; promulgated a leadership code obliging party and government officials to eschew perquisites and sources of income other than their salaries: himself set the example, living modestly, without pomp, within the limitations of his annual salary of $8,000; began his career as a schoolteacher; in 1954 co-founded and became head of the political party called the Tanganyika African National Union (TANU); during the same year, was elected to the Tanganyikan Legislative Council; over the following two years, pressed the case for Tanganyikan independence at the U.N.; was designated prime minister when Tanganyika gained independence, in 1961; was elected president when Tanganyika became a republic the following year; remained president when, in 1964, the Sultan of Zanzibar was deposed and Zanzibar was united with Tanganyika to form the new national entity called Tanzania; beginning in 1965 was reelected to four successive five-year terms as president; in 1985 retired to a farm in his native village of Butiama; remained chairman of Tanzania's single viable party, the Chama Cha Mapinduzi, or Revolutionary Party (the product of the merger of TANU and Zanzibar's Afro-Shirazi Party, in 1977) until 1990; expounded his political philosophy in numerous speeches and published manifestos; died in London, England, where he was receiving medical treatment for leukemia. See *Current Biography* (April) 1963.

Obituary *New York Times* B p10 Oct. 15, 1999

O'BRIAN, PATRICK 1914–Jan. 2, 2000 British-born author; internationally acclaimed for his Aubrey/Maturin novels, set during the period of the Napoleonic wars, chiefly on the sea; in those books, rises above the romanticized naval genre with his extraordinary erudition on early 19th-century life, on land as well as sea, and his attention to impeccable authentic detail; his early pseudo-curriculum vitae (which had him born Irish and Catholic) notwithstanding, was born Richard Patrick Russ in London to a British mother and a father of German descent; before embarking on the Aubrey/Maturin series, published some six novels, beginning with *Three Bear Witness* (1952), a love story with a dark ending set in Wales, and including *The Golden Ocean* (1956), intended for young readers; also published *The Walker* (1955), a collection of short stories; introduced readers to Captain Jack Aubrey of Lord Nelson's navy, and Stephen Maturin, his ship's physician, in *Master and Commander* (1969); continued the series with *H.M.S. Surprise* (1973), *The Mauritius Command* (1977), *Desolation Island* (1978), *Fortune of War* (1979), *The Surgeon's Mate* (1980), *The Ionian Mission* (1980), *Treason's Harbor* (1983), *The Far Side of the World* (1984), *The Reverse of the Medal* (1986), *The Letter of Marque* (1990), *The Thirteen-Gun Salute* (1991), *The Nutmeg of Consolation* (1991), *The Truelove* (1992), *The Wine-Dark Sea* (1993), *The Commodore* (1995), and other titles; in addition to his fiction, wrote biographies of Pablo Picasso and Joseph Banks; died in Dublin, Ireland. See *Current Biography* (June) 1995.

Obituary *New York Times* A p16 Jan. 7, 2000

O'CONNOR, JOHN J. Jan. 15, 1920–May 3, 2000 Roman Catholic prelate; archbishop of New York, the Catholic Church's most prestigious American see, since 1984; was a traditionalist after the heart of Pope John Paul II, who elevated him to the rank of cardinal in 1985; had been bishop of Scranton, Pennsylvania, for nine months before his installation in New York; was staunch in his defense of traditional Catholic doctrines, including those relating to sexuality, and his resistance to the pressure for compromise from the New York City government, pragmatic Catholic politicians, homosexual activists, and others; was most passionate in preaching the Church's unconditional pro-life message; was more liberal on issues of social justice and charity; founded the Sisters of Life, a New York–based order of women devoted to sheltering unwed mothers and ministering to the sick and infirm; following his ordination as a priest of the archdiocese of Philadelphia in 1946, earned graduate degrees in ethics, clinical psychology, and political science while working as an assistant pastor and Catholic high-school teacher; worked with retarded children and helped establish an archdiocesan center for such children in the early 1950s; developed his brisk disciplinary style during his 27 years of service as a chaplain in the U.S. Navy, beginning in 1952; was navy chief of chaplains from 1975 to 1979, when he was consecrated a bishop and assigned as auxiliary bishop of New York and military vicar, the U.S. Church's liaison with Catholic chaplains in all of the armed forces; as one of the drafters of the U.S. bishops' 1983 pastoral letter on nuclear-arms policy and strategy, added "just war" considerations to that otherwise dovish document; helped to lend some conservative balance to the bishops' generally liberal statements on other issues, including multinational capitalism and finance; wrote the books *A Chaplain Looks at Vietnam* (1968), *In Defense of Life* (1981), and, with New York mayor Edward I. Koch, *His Eminence and Hizzoner* (1989); was the subject of a biography by Nat Hentoff, *John Cardinal O'Connor* (1988); died at his residence behind St. Patrick's Cathedral in New York City; was entombed beneath the altar of the cathedral, in a crypt inscribed with his motto: "There can be no love without justice." See *Current Biography* (June) 1984.

Obituary *New York Times* p1+ May 4, 2000

OBUCHI, KEIZO June 25, 1937–May 14, 2000 Prime minister of Japan (July 1998–April 2000); a leader of the Liberal Democratic Party (LDP), Japan's current governing party; in 1963, was first elected to the seat in the lower house of the Japanese Parliament that he would hold for the rest of his life; served in a series of lower ministerial positions before being tapped in 1987 for the post of cabinet secretary by his mentor, Noboru Takeshita, who was prime minister from 1987 to 1989 and remained Japan's "shadow shogun" thereafter; through Takeshita's influence, in 1997 was named foreign minister in the cabinet of Prime Minister Ryutaro Hashimoto, who fell from public grace the following year; following Hashimoto's resignation, was elected to succeed him as prime minister by the LDP representatives, again with the backing of Takeshita, among others; had some success in stabilizing Japan's economy and divisive politics before suffering an incapacitating stroke; died in Tokyo. See *Current Biography* (May) 1999.

Obituary *New York Times* B p8 May 15, 2000

OLIPHANT, MARCUS L. Oct. 8, 1901–July 14, 2000 Australian physicist; as a designer of heavy high-voltage apparatus and an expert in the electromagnetic separation of uranium isotopes, made major contributions to the creation and harnessing of nuclear energy; regretting his contribution to the development of the atomic bombs dropped on Japan in August 1945 (which he regarded as "a moral crime"), devoted himself thereafter to the exclusively peaceful implementation of nuclear energy and the cause of an international peace involving international controls to be shared (he insisted) by the Soviets and the Chinese; after earning his Ph.D. degree at Cambridge University, England, worked under Ernest Rutherford at the university's Cavendish Laboratory, where the atom was first split by artificially accelerated particles, in 1932; participated in the research at Cavendish that resulted in the subsequent discovery of a triple-weight type of hydrogen, called tritium; in his own research, concentrated on the lithium nucleus after separating the two lithium isotopes by electromagnetic means; discovered two new light isotopes, one of hydrogen and the other of helium; in 1937, moved to the University of Birmingham, England, where he supervised the building of the Nuffield Laboratory and began construction of a cyclotron; early in World War II, helped to develop radar; was a member of the group of British scientists sent to the U.S. in 1943 to participate in the Manhattan Project, as the massive but virtually secret (because compartmentalized) atomic-bomb development project was called; served as Australian representative on the U.N. Atomic Energy Commission in 1946; between 1946 and 1950, completed the construction of the cyclotron (more precisely, a proton synchrotron) at the Nuffield Laboratory; in 1950, returned to Australia, where he directed postgraduate research in the Research School of Physical Sciences at the Australian National University in Canberra until 1963; subsequently was in charge of research on ionized gases at the school; chaired a committee that advised the Canberra government on the development of nuclear power stations; was named a Knight of the British Empire in 1959; held the ceremonial post of governor of the state of South Australia from 1971 to 1976; died in Canberra. See *Current Biography* (December) 1951.

Obituary *New York Times* B p7 July 19, 2000

OPPENHEIMER, HARRY FREDERICK Oct. 28, 1908–Aug. 19, 2000 South African entrepreneur and financier; from his father, Sir Ernest Oppenheimer (who died in 1957), inherited majority control of one of the world's largest mulitinational industrial and mining conglomerates, comprising the Anglo American Corporation, De Beers Consolidated Mines Ltd., and 150 subsidiaries and affiliates; thus, had a monopoly hold on the world's supply of diamonds and exerted extraordinary power over the supply and distribution of such strategic metals as gold, platinum, uranium, vanadium, and copper and numerous minerals; also had vast holdings in banking, real estate, pulp and paper, bricks, pipe, coal, potash, beer, and locomotives; was an opposition member of the South African Parliament from 1948 to 1957; after retiring from the chairmanship of Anglo American (in 1982) and De Beers (1984), remained active in the family enterprises; while opposing international sanctions against South Africa, was an influential opponent of the Afrikaner government's institutionalized system of racial separation, known as apartheid; died in Johannesburg. See *Current Biography* (February) 1961.

Obituary *New York Times* B p7 Aug. 21, 2000

PAIS, ABRAHAM May 19, 1918–July 28, 2000 Dutch-born theoretical physicist; historian of physics; an important contributor to nuclear theory and electrodynamics; professor emeritus at Rockefeller University since 1988; received his Ph.D. degree from the University of Amsterdam in 1941, just five days before the promulgation of a Nazi prohibition against the awarding of academic degrees to Jews in the Netherlands; developed his unusual powers of cognition while living underground in safe quarters provided by Christian families and the Dutch resistance movement; survived arrest and imprisonment

(March–April 1945); worked with Niels Bohr at the Institute for Theoretical Physics in Copenhagen, Denmark, from January to August 1946; as a fellow, worked with Albert Einstein and others at the Institute for Advanced Study at Princeton University beginning in September 1946; became a professor at the institute in 1950 at the urging of the institute's director, J. Robert Oppenheimer, who said of him: "The record of Dr. Pais's work in the past decade is almost a history of the efforts to clarify our understanding of basic atomic theory and the nature of elementary particles. Pais first proposed the compensation theories of elementary particles, and much of his work has been devoted to exploring the success and limitations of these theories, and indicating the radical character of the revisions which will be needed before they can successfully describe the subatomic world"; at Princeton until 1963, and thereafter at Rockefeller University in New York City, conducted research concentrated chiefly in pursuit of the unification of strong, weak, and electromagnetic forces; over the years, beginning in the late 1940s, wrote short accounts of the development of quantum field theory, particle physics, and quantum mechanics and of discoveries regarding invariance principles, radioactivity, and the electron; brought that work together in his book *Inward Bound: Of Matter and Forces in the Physical World* (1986), in which he traced the evolution of physics from 1895 on; had already published *Subtle Is the Lord . . .: The Science and Life of Albert Einstein* (1982); later published *Niels Bohr's Times* (1992), *Einstein Lived Here: Essays for the Layman* (1994), the autobiographical *A Tale of Two Continents* (1997), and *The Genius of Science: A Portrait Gallery of Twentieth Century Physicists* (2000); lived alternately in New York City and in Copenhagen, where his widow, the anthropologist Ida Nicolaisen, is associated with a research institute; by a previous marriage, was the father of the actor Joshua Pais; died in Copenhagen. See *Current Biography* (June) 1994.

Obituary *New York Times* B p7 July 31, 2000

PASTORE, JOHN O. Mar. 17, 1907–July 15, 2000 Rhode Island liberal Democratic politician; former governor; former U.S. senator; lawyer; after serving two terms in the Rhode Island House of Representatives and a stint as an assistant state attorney general, was elected lieutenant governor in 1944; succeeded to the governorship when Governor J. Howard McGrath resigned to become solicitor general in the administration of President Harry S. Truman, in 1945; won election to a two-year term as governor in his own right in 1946 and reelection in 1948; two years later, was elected to the U.S. Senate to fill the unexpired term of McGrath, who, after moving from the position of solicitor general to the Senate, resigned to become U. S. attorney general; in 1952, was elected to the first of his four full Senate terms; in the Senate, was most influential in his chairmanship of the joint committee on atomic energy; in 1963, played a key role in winning Senate ratification of the Kennedy administration's treaty with the Soviet Union, consisting of a mutual agreement to end atmospheric nuclear testing; resigned from the Senate in December 1976; died in North Kingston, Rhode Island. See *Current Biography* (April) 1953.

Obituary *New York Times* B p8 July 17, 2000

PATTON, FRANCES GRAY Mar. 19, 1906–Mar. 28, 2000 Author; a native North Carolinian who ranged from gentle irony to sentimentality balanced by cynicism in her finely crafted, superbly narrated fiction, often set in Durham or towns like it; was at her best in offering glimpses of social and family life, especially domestic frictions, as experienced by women and adolescents; derived her last name from her marriage to Lewis Patton, a professor of English at, successively, the University of North Carolina and Duke University, at both of which she studied; received an O. Henry Memorial Award for her first published short story, "A Piece of Bread," which originally appeared in the *Kenyon Review* in 1945, about the impact on a little southern girl of her encounter with a prison chain gang; in 1951 published her first book, *The Finer Things of Life* (1951), a collection of short stories, most of which originally appeared in the *New Yorker*; in four of the stories, wrote about a college professor's family in a small southern town; published two more collections of stories, *A Piece of Luck* (1955) and *28 Stories* (1969); wrote one novel, *Good Morning, Miss Dove* (1954), chronicling (in retrospect, from the perspective of a hospital bed) the dedicated career of an unmarried schoolteacher, "terrible" in her strictness but beloved by the several generations of students whose lives she has touched and helped to shape; saw that work translated, under the same title, to the motion-picture screen in 1955; died in Durham, North Carolina. See *Current Biography* (Yearbook) 1955.

Obituary *New York Times* p36 Apr. 2, 2000

PAYTON, WALTER July 25, 1954–Nov. 1, 1999 Professional football player; a running back who, in 13 years (1975–87) with the Chicago Bears of the National Football League, set numerous NFL records, including most touchdowns by rushing (110), most all-purpose running yards (21,893), and most rushing yards (16,726); as an All-American at Jackson (Mississippi) State College in the early 1970s, scored a National Collegiate Athletic Association record of 66 touchdowns; in his first season in Chicago, led the NFL in kickoff return yardage, with 444 yards gained in 14 returns; within three years, joined teammate Ron Harper to form the best running combination in the NFL; with Harper, in 1977 paced the Bears to their first winning season (9–5) in 10 years and their first play-offs (in which they overwhelmed the Dallas Cowboys) in 14 years; individually, set a new NFL record for most yards rushing in a single game, with 275 against Minnesota on November 30, 1977; during that season, led the league in yards gained by rushing (1,852) and in average yardage per carry (5.5); in 1977 was the NFL's consensus most valuable player; was voted MVP in the 1977 Pro Bowl; led the NFL in yards rushing for five consecutive seasons, from 1976 through 1980; in 1985 helped the Bears achieve a 15–1 season; in Super Bowl XX on January 26, 1986, rushed 22 times for 61 yards as the Bears defeated the New England Patriots to win their first NFL championship in 13 years; was inducted into the Pro Football Hall of Fame in 1993; published an autobiography, *Sweetness: The Courage and Heart of Walter Payton* (1999); died at his home in Barrington, Illinois. See *Current Biography* (November) 1985.

Obituary *New York Times* C p23 Nov. 2, 1999

PETRY, LUCILE Jan. 23, 1902–Nov. 25, 1999 Nurse; nursing administrator; early in her career, was assistant director of the University of Minnesota School of Nursing for 10 years; during World War II directed the Cadet Nurse Corps, which offered women all-expenses-paid training in nursing (plus monthly stipends and free uniforms) in exchange for their promise to participate in essential military or civilian nursing for the duration of the war; later directed the division of nursing education of the U.S. Public Health Service; after leaving government, in 1966, taught nursing and served as associate dean at Texas Women's University; retired in 1971; died in San Francisco, California. See *Current Biography* (April) 1944.

Obituary *New York Times* p62 Dec. 5, 1999

PFLIMLIN, PIERRE Feb, 5, 1907–June 27, 2000 French politician; lawyer; economist; former prime minister; held numerous other cabinet portfolios; helped to rebuild France and establish European reconciliation and integration in the years and decades following World War II; was elected municipal councillor of Strasbourg in 1945; as a member of the Mouvement Rĕpublicain Populaire (MPF), was elected a deputy from Bas-Rhin to the post-liberation French constituent assemblies of 1945 and 1946; in November 1946 won election to the first of five terms in the National Assembly; in February 1946 was appointed to his first cabinet post, undersecretary for public health and population; later in the same year, became undersecretary of state for the national economy; between 1947 and 1951 held the post of minister of agriculture in seven successive cabinets; in 1951 was minister of commerce and foreign economic relations; early in 1952, as minister of state in charge of relations with the Council of Europe, reiterated his conviction that the creation of a European agricultural community would be an important step on "the necessary road of European integration"; later in 1952, was minister for French overseas territories; was minister of finance and economic affairs in two successive cabinets (1955–56, 1957–58); on the most volatile French political issue of that time, was on the public record as favoring negotiations with the National Liberation Front in Algeria, which was proceeding with the war (launched in 1954) for the independence of that French colony; therefore, with his appointment as prime minister in May 1958, ignited a violent reaction from the more than one million French settlers in Algeria, whose cause was embraced by the French officer corps; resigned after 21 days as prime minister; under President Charles de Gaulle, was minister of state (1958–59); in the Cabinet of Prime Minister Georges Pompidou, was minister for cooperation in 1962; was president of the MPR from 1956 to 1959, mayor of Strasbourg from 1959 to 1983, and president of a preparatory assembly of the Council of Europe from 1963 to 1968; was a member of the European Parliament from 1979 to 1989 and president of that body from 1984 to 1987; wrote an autobiography, *Mémoires d'un Européen de la IViéme à la Viéme Republique* (1991); also wrote a book presenting his views on the French economy; co-wrote four additional books, on the French industrial commune of Mulhouse, on Alsace, on communitarian Europe, and on the economic structure of Germany's Third Reich; died in Strasbourg. See *Current Biography* (November) 1955.

Obituary *New York Times* C p19 June 30, 2000

PHAM VAN DONG Mar. 1, 1906-April 29, 2000 Vietnamese political and governmental leader; was prime minister of the Democratic Republic of Vietnam, or North Vietnam, for 21 years beginning in 1955 (following independence of the north from France) and of the Socialist Republic of Vietnam, or the whole of reunified Vietnam, from 1976 (after the Communist northern forces defeated the American-backed Saigon regime) to 1986; after leading a student strike and street demonstration in 1925, escaped arrest by the French colonial police by fleeing to China; with other young Vietnamese activists in exile recruited by Ho Chi Minh, was schooled in Marxism/Leninism and revolutionary techniques at a military training center at Whampoa, in southern China; in 1929, returned to Vietnam to organize covert Communist cells; was caught by French authorities and imprisoned for seven years; after his release, in 1936, resumed his underground activities in Hanoi; in 1941, with Ho Chi Minh and others, founded the Front for the Independence of Vietnam, popularly known as the Vietminh, under the banner of which they waged guerrilla warfare first against the Japanese occupation forces during World War II, then against the French (who were trying to restore their colonial rule), and finally against the non-Communist South Vietnamese and the Americans; at the end of World War II, when Ho Chi Minh proclaimed Vietnamese independence (in September 1945), was named finance minister in President Ho's provisional government; later served as foreign minister; was the chief North Vietnamese negotiatior at peace talks at Fontainbleau in 1948, Geneva in 1954, and Paris in 1968; died in Hanoi. See *Current Biography* (February) 1975.

Obituary *New York Times* C p27 May 2, 2000

PINDLING, LYNDEN OSCAR Mar. 22, 1930–Sep. 23, 2000 Former prime minister of the Bahamas; lawyer; in 1953, joined the Progressive Liberal Party, a new, black, labor-oriented challenger to the entrenched, predominantly white and British colonial-run United Bahamian Party; running on the PLP ticket in 1956, was elected to Jamaica's House of Assembly, where he would retain his seat for 41 years; became chairman of the PLP in 1963; took office as the first black prime minister of the Bahamas in 1967, three years after this tropical archipelago, 60 miles southeast of Florida, won internal self-government; led the Bahamas to independent status as a British commonwealth, in 1973; in the 1980s, was the target of unresolved allegations that he had accepted millions of dollars in protection money from Colombian and other drug traffickers using the Bahamas as a transit point for cocaine and marijuana bound for the U.S.; was voted out of office in 1992; resigned his legislative seat in 1997; died at his home in Nassau, Bahamas. See *Current Biography* (May) 1968.

Obituary *New York Times* B p6 Sep. 28, 2000

POWELL, ANTHONY Dec. 21, 1905–Mar. 28, 2000 British author; clinched his claim to consideration as a major novelist with his masterpiece, the ingeniously constructed 12-volume roman-fleuve *A Dance to the Music of Time* (1951–75), the longest novel in English and a unique kind of social tapestry; in that panoramic sequence, charted, with satirical wit and authenticity, more than half a century (beginning in 1914) of change in the insular, snobbish world of upper-middle-class England and its academic and bohemian fringes; with "subtle elaboration of manner," as Bernard Bergonzi pointed out, presented "the basic human comedy where, as in Chaucer and Rabelais and Shakespeare, folly and weakness and vice are transcended in an unending comic dance"; contributed an account of his four years as a student at Eton College to *The Old School: Essays by Divers Hands* (1934), edited by Graham Greene; at Eton and later Balliol College, Oxford University, became friends with a number of incipient literary luminaries, including Greene and Evelyn Waugh; after earning his degree at Oxford, worked in publishing, editing, and writing motion-picture scenarios for Warner Brothers of Great Britain; later was literary editor of *Punch*; before beginning his long, complex, and subtle expedition into *A Dance to the Music of Time*, visited roughly the same terrain in five more-bluntly comedic, almost flippant novels, beginning with *Afternoon Men* (1931); late in life, wrote two more novels, *O, How the Wheel Becomes It!* (1983) and *The Fisher King* (1986); in addition to his novels, wrote a biography of John Aubrey, the eccentric 17th-century antiquary, four volumes of memoirs under the title *Keep the Ball Rolling* (1976–82), two unproduced plays, and a dramatized version of *Afternoon Men*; saw *A Dance to the Music of Time* adapted for television in 1997; was named a Commander of the British Empire in 1956 and a Commander of Honor in 1988; refused a knighthood in 1973; died at his home near Frome in Somerset, England. See *Current Biography* (September) 1977.

Obituary *New York Times* B p15 Mar. 30, 2000

PUENTE, TITO Apr. 20, 1923–May 31, 2000 Orchestra leader; percussionist; arranger; composer; "El Rey" of the big-band mambo; a leader in the fusion of Latin music with jazz; was known for his rousing arrangements and irresistible rhythms; was credited with introducing the timbal solo and the vibraphone to Afro-Cuban music; in addition to the trap drums, the conga drums, the claves, and the piano, occasionally played other instruments, including the saxophone and the clarinet; was born to Puerto Rican parents in East Harlem, New York City; in 1941 dropped out of high school to become a drummer with the Afro-Cubans of Machito (Frank Grillo); served with the U.S. Navy during World War II; while studying at the Juilliard School of Music after the war, worked as a sideman and arranger with a number of Latin bands; in 1948 began performing and recording with his own band; by the early 1950s was a stellar attraction at the Palladium and other venues on New York's "Cuchifrito Circuit"; over the years, was increasingly in demand at nightclubs and ballrooms across the U.S.; among well over 200 compositions, wrote such hits as "Oye Como Va," "Para Los Rumberos," "Picadillo," and "Hong Kong Mambo"; recorded more than 90 albums, including *Puente Goes Jazz, Mamborama, Cuban Carnival, Homenaje a Beny* (a three-CD set featuring Celia Cruz and other singers) , and the perennial two-volume best-seller *Dance Mania*; won five Grammy Awards; played himself in the motion picture *The Mambo Kings* (1992); co-owned Tito Puente's, a large restaurant on City Island in the Bronx, New York City; died at New York University Medical Center in Manhattan. See *Current Biography* (November) 1977.

Obituary *New York Times* B p1+ June 2, 2000

RAMPAL, JEAN-PIERRE Jan. 7, 1922–May 20, 2000 French flutist; musicologist; in his time, was one of the four or five leading players of the flute, which had been a neglected instrument for a century and a half, until the rediscovery of the Baroque repertory at the end of World War II; more than any other individual, popularized the flute as a solo instrument; enriched the literature of the instrument as well as the range of possibilities of interpretation; as a musicologist, unearthed many forgotten masterpieces; as a musician, ranged in his repertoire from the Bach family and other giants of the Baroque through such moderns as Prokofiev, Hindemith, and Khachaturian to jazz, English folk music, and Indian music; beginning in 1945, toured throughout the world, giving concerts, participating in major festivals, and appearing as a soloist with major orchestras; was often accompanied by the harpsicordist Robert Veyron-Lacroix; played on and off with the Paris Opéra orchestra and was principal flutist with that orchestra from 1958 to 1964; became the most recorded flutist in history; taught at the Paris Conservatory; died in Paris. See *Current Biography* (March) 1970.

Obituary *New York Times* p44 May 21, 2000

RICHARD, MAURICE Aug. 4, 1931–May 27, 2000 French-Canadian ice-hockey player; high-scoring superstar of the Montreal Canadiens in the 1940s and 1950s; a left-hander who brought a devastating backhand to his right-wing position; with his electrifyingly swift skating style, was the charter bearer of the sobriquet "the Rocket," later conferred on several other athletes; joined the Canadiens in 1942; began to hit his stride in the 1943–44 season, scoring 32 goals in 46 games; at the conclusion of that season, set a new Stanley Cup play-offs scoring record (later beaten) with 12 goals; in one of the play-off games, scored five goals, a record (later tied); in 1944–45, scored 50 goals in a 50-game season, a record that would stand for 36 years; in one game that season, scored a record eight points (later broken); won the Hart Trophy as the league's most valuable player in 1947; helped Montreal to win the Stanley Cup in 1944, 1946, and 1953 and to capture an unprecedented five consecutive NHL titles between 1956 and 1960; was a perennial All-Star; became a special target in the defense strategy and tactics of opposing teams; was over-checked, often "shadowed" by two opponents and generally harassed; having a volatile temper, sometimes reacted violently and suffered penalties for so doing; for hitting a linesman in March 1955, was suspended for the final three games of the regular season and all of the play-off games—a loss of playing time just long enough to deprive him of a chance at setting a new NHL career scoring record; in 1955–56 was joined on the Montreal roster by his brother Henri, a stellar center; suffered a serious injury to his Achilles tendon in the 1957–58 season; retired, in 1960, after 18 seasons with the Canadiens, with career totals of 544 goals, 421 assists, 965 points, and 1,285 penalty minutes in 978 regular-season games and 82 goals in 133 play-off games, including a league record of six overtime goals, which still stands, along with most overtime goals (three) in one play-off series (1951); had led the NHL in goals five times; following his retirement, held public-relations positions with the Canadiens for several years; in 1972 coached the NHL's Quebec Nordiques for two games; ran a fishing-supply business out of his home; served as a goodwill ambassador for the Canadiens at special events; was inducted into the Hockey Hall of Fame in 1961; with Stan Fischler, wrote *The Flying Frenchmen* (1971), about himself and the Canadiens; is memorialized in the Maurice Richard Trophy, instituted in the 1998–99 season to honor the NHL's leading goal scorers; died in Montreal. See *Current Biography* (December) 1958.

Obituary *New York Times* B p6 May 29, 2000

RICHARDSON, ELLIOT L. July 20, 1920–Dec. 30, 1999 Lawyer; former government official; a Massachusetts brahmin with an illustrious career in state and national politics and public administration; as U.S. attorney general at the climax of the Watergate scandal, in 1973, resigned rather than obey President Richard Nixon's order that he fire Watergate special prosecutor Archibald M. Cox; at the beginning of his career, in the late 1940s, clerked for U.S. Court of Appeals Judge Learned Hand and U.S Supreme Court Justice Felix Frankfurter; subsequently, practiced law in Boston and was an assistant to U.S. Republican senator Leverett Saltonstall and counsel to Massachusetts Republican governor Christian A. Herter; was an assistant secretary of the U.S. Department of Health, Education and Welfare (HEW) from 1957 to 1959 and U.S. attorney for Massachusetts from 1959 to 1961; following a return to the private practice of law, was elected (on the Republican ticket) lieutenant governor of Massachusetts (1965–67) and attorney general of Massachusetts (1967–69); in the administration of President Nixon, was undersecretary of state (1969–70), secretary of HEW (1970–73), and secretary of defense (1973) before becoming attorney general; in later administrations, was ambassador to Britain (1975–76), secretary of commerce (1976–77), and ambassador-at-large to the international law of the sea conference (1977–80); wrote the books *The Creative Balance* (1976) and *Reflections of a Radical Moderate* (1996); died in Boston, Massachusetts. See *Current Biography* (March) 1971.

Obituary *New York Times* B p7 Jan. 1, 2000

RITTER, BRUCE Feb. 25, 1917–Oct. 7, 1999 Roman Catholic priest; founder of Covenant House, an organization of crisis centers for homeless children (an estimated 25,000 at the height of its success); began training for the priesthood in the Franciscan order in 1947; was ordained in 1956; seven years later was assigned to Manhattan College in the Bronx, New York, as chaplain and professor of theology; in 1968 received the permission of his superiors to leave his college post to "live and work among the poor"; on the blighted eastern edge of Manhattan's East Village, began renting apartments, opening them to teenaged runaways and castaways, recruiting volunteers, and raising funds for the work; in 1972 officially chartered his operation as Covenant House; in 1976 moved his headquarters to a six-story building near Times Square; in 1979 took over three more buildings in Midtown Manhattan; in the 1980s opened additional crisis centers in other cities, including Toronto, Houston, and Boston, and an orphanage in Antigua, Guatemala; in 1989 was accused by two men of having had sex with them when they were teenagers; subsequently, was additionally accused of improperly diverting some Covenant House funds to help one of the youths; denied both charges, but, in 1990, recognizing the damage done to his effectiveness as director, resigned "in the best interest of Covenant House and . . . thousands of street kids"; died at the farmhouse near Decatur, New York, where he had lived out his last years. See *Current Biography* (June) 1983.

Obituary *New York Times* B p9 Oct. 13, 1999

RUNCIE, ROBERT Oct. 2, 1921–July 11, 2000 British ecclesiastic; former archbishop of Canterbury, the prime see of the Church of England and the worldwide Anglican communion; was ordained a priest in 1951; the following year, was assigned as chaplain of Westcott House, the Anglican house of theological studies at Cambridge University; was vice principal of the house from 1954 to 1956; subsequently served as dean and assistant tutor at Trinity Hall, Cambridge (1956–60) and principal of Cuddeson College, a theological school near Oxford University (1960–70); as bishop of St. Albans, a diocese comprising Hertfordshire and Bedfordshire, from 1973 to 1980, pursued closer relationships between Anglicanism and the Orthodox churches; traveled widely in Eastern Europe and the Mideast; in his enthronement speech at Canterbury, in 1980, expressed his antipathy "against rigid thinking" and his readiness to speak out on "the great political issues of the time—race relations, unemployment, disarmament, and the proper distribution of the world's resources"; when he officiated at the wedding of Prince Charles and Lady Diana Spencer, in 1981, was reportedly already aware of the clandestine long-term intimate relationship between Charles and Camilla Parker Bowles; later described the marriage as "arranged," accused Charles of having lost his Anglican faith, and judged Princess Diana to be an "actress, a schemer"; was never forgiven "his treachery" by Diana; throughout the 1980s, was at odds with the Conservative government of Prime Minister Margaret Thatcher; accused the government of neglecting the urban poor, of treating striking miners as "scum," and of adhering to a "lunatic" nuclear arms policy; after Britain's victory in the Falklands war in 1981, asked for prayers for the families of dead Argentine soldiers as well as those of the British dead; deplored the ascendancy in Britain of what he perceived to be a self-interested and intolerant "Pharisee society"; was dismissed by the Tories as a "far left" interloper; in 1986 assumed the aegis for Terry Waite's mission to meet with terrorists in Lebanon to win the release of several Western hostages; after the kidnapping of Waite in Beirut, in 1987, prayed daily for the release of his "personal envoy," which came about in 1991: while liberal, was also pragmatic, and tried to be a stabilizing force in the Anglican church's approach to deeply divisive issues, such as ordination of women and remarriage of divorcées; for example, while ordaining homosexual priests, asked that they be celibate; was instrumental in the creation of the Church Urban Fund, a charity devoted to social projects in deprived areas; in pursuit of reconciliation with Roman Catholicism, met with Pope John Paul II at the Vatican in 1989 for four days of talks and again in 1991 and 1992; wrote several books, including *Windows unto God* (1983) and *The Unity We Seek* (1989); retired as archbishop in 1991; at that time was made a life peer, with a right to the titles "lord" and "baron"; died at his home in St. Albans, Hertfordshire. See *Current Biography* (November) 1980.

Obituary *New York Times* A p27 July 13, 2000

SARRAUTE, NATHALIE July 18, 1900–Oct. 19, 1999 Russian-born French author; a sometimes mischievously playful novelist concerned "only with the inner life which is going on every moment in each of us"; returning in her own way to the experimental path opened by Proust, Joyce, and others a generation earlier, tried to capture in her fiction not streams of consciousness but glimpses of "quick movements which pass through our minds on the border of consciousness," which "best develop when people are in contact with each other"; called those movements *tropismes*, an analogy to the spontaneous inner responses of plants and animals to external stimuli; was the first and most celebrated of the writers of the *roman nouveau*, or what Jean-Paul Sartre dubbed the "antinovel" because it represented a rejection of conventional plot and narrative techniques, delineation of protagonists and antagonists, and moral significance; believed that she "showed that it was possible to write novels where the purely fictional element is freed from conventions that encumbered it, just as the purely pictorial element in painting has freed itself from subject matter, perspective, and so on"; began her career as a lawyer; in 1939 published her first book, *Tropismes* (translated as *Tropisms*, 1964), comprising 24 short sketches; in 1948 published *Portrait d'un Inconnu* (*Portrait of a Man Unknown*, 1958), described by Sartre, perhaps approvingly, as a "stumbling, groping" novel in which "nothing ever happens"; in *Martineau* (1953; English translation by Maria Jolas, her regular translator, 1959), explored interpersonal awareness in an extended family in relation to a sickly member of that family; in 1959 published the tragicomic novel *Le Planétarium* (*The Planetarium*, 1960) and in 1963, *Les Fruits d'Or* (*The Fruits of Gold*, 1964), an abstract send-up of literary criticism; was humorously critical of her own creative process in her immediately subsequent novels, whose titles translated into English as *Between Life and Death* and *Do You Hear Them?*; in 1995 published her last novel, issued in translation in the U.S. as *Here* (1997); delineated her theory of the novel in essays collected in *L'Ere de Soupçn* (1956; *The Age of Suspicion*, 1963); in 1983 published *Enfance* (*Childhood*, 1984), a memoir of her first 12 years of life; adapted *Childhood* into a one-act play for the New York stage (1985); also wrote several radio plays that she later adapted for the stage; died at her home in Paris. See *Current Biography* (June) 1966.

Obituary *New York Times* C p25 Oct. 20, 1999

SAWHILL, JOHN C. June 12, 1936–May 18, 2000 Conservationist; university president; financial expert; professor of economics; government official; adviser on energy to presidents Nixon, Ford, and Carter and on financial policy to the New York city and state governments; held degrees in both business administration and public and international affairs; worked in underwriting and research with the investment brokerage firm of Merrill, Lynch, Pierce, Fenner & Smith from 1958 to 1960; subsequently held executive positions with the Commercial Credit Co.; was administrator of the Federal Energy Administration from 1973 to 1975; meanwhile, at New York University, his alma mater, had served as assistant professor and assistant dean of business administration in the early 1960s; became president of NYU in 1975, when the university was gravely deficit-ridden; in what was hailed as "perhaps the most dramatic rescue operation in the history of American education," initiated a wide range of cost-cutting and income-generating measures that brought about a balanced budget within two years; left NYU to serve as deputy secretary of the U.S. Department of Energy (1979–80); in 1980 was chairman of the U.S. Synthetic Fuels Corp.; from 1981 to 1990 was a director of McKinsey & Co., energy-oriented international-management consultants; during the last decade of his life, beginning in January 1990, was president of the Nature Conservancy, which is devoted to acquiring land and water on which animal and plant life will be protected from environment-depredating development; died in Richmond, Virginia. See *Current Biography* (April) 1978.

Obituary *New York Times* B p11 May 20, 2000

SCHULZ, CHARLES M. Nov. 26, 1922–Feb. 12, 2000 Cartoonist; creator of the popular newspaper comic strip *Peanuts*, which he would have preferred to call *Li'l Folks*; in that strip, featured, among other juvenile characters, Charlie Brown, Charlie's nemesis, the fussbudget Lucy Van Pelt, and Lucy's younger brother Linus, a child inseparable from his security blanket—"infantile reductions of all the neuroses of a modern citizen of the industrial civilization," as Umberto Eco observed; in addition to the human characters, created Snoopy, a dog with a Walter Mitty personality; under contract to United Feature Syndicate, published the first *Peanuts* strip on October 2, 1950 and the last on February 13, 2000; was syndicated in 2,600 newspapers, in 21 languages, and reached readers in 75 countries worldwide; in spin-offs of the comic strip, published dozens of *Peanuts* books and collaborated in a number of animated television specials, most prominently *A Charlie Brown Christmas*; also saw his comic strip adapted to stage and screen; died at his home in Santa Rosa, California. See *Current Biography* (December) 1960.

Obituary *New York Times* p1+ Feb. 14, 2000

SEGAL, GEORGE Nov. 26, 1924–June 9, 2000 Artist; a sculptor whose professed primary purpose was to deal with the "mystery" of human relationships in "the intimacy of daily life—your relationship to the food on the breakfast table and to the woman across the table"; constructed life-size three-dimensional tableaux in which human figures—plaster effigies of actual people, cast from life—were set in commonplace "assembled environments," from dining room and even conjugal bed to buses, elevators, and laundromats; for many years, left his tableaux a ghostly white, conducive to a mood of metaphysical loneliness and a shock of recognition, a feeling that one is viewing one's own quotidian reality reflected in a limbo apart; grew up in the Bronx, New York City, where his father ran a butcher shop (immortalized in his sculpture *Butcher Shop* [1965]); later moved with his parents to a farm in New Jersey, the site of the vast chicken house that would become his studio; in the first phase of his career, devoted himself to expressionist drawing, painting, and pastel work; turned to sculpture in 1958; two years later, was introduced to medical scrim; had his wife wrap him in plaster-soaked gauze, thus beginning the genesis of *Man at a Table* (1960–61), his first work cast from a living body; later made castings of relatives, friends, and patrons for such tableaux as *Woman in a Restaurant Booth* (1961–62), *The Diner* (1964), *The Dentist* (1966–67), and *Artist in His Studio* (1968); enhanced authentic detail with lighting effects, including flickering film projections, in such compositions as *Cinema* (1963), *The Truck* (1966), *The Subway* (1968), and *The Aerial View* (1970); occasionally added color to the tableax, increasingly in the 1970s; after turning to casting in bronze (usually finished in white), accepted public and outdoor commissions, including *In Memory of May 4, 1970, Kent State: Abraham and Isaac* (1980) for Princeton University and *The Holocaust* (1983) for Golden Gate Park in San Francisco; also created the public tableau *Gay Liberation* for installation in Christopher Park (formerly Sheridan Square Park), in Greenwich Village, New York City, and three tableaux for the Franklin Delano Roosevelt Memorial in Washington, D.C.; died at his home in South Brunswick, New Jersey. See *Current Biography* (January) 1972.

Obituary *New York Times* A p12, June 10, 2000

SHAPIRO, KARL Nov. 10, 1913–May 14, 2000 Poet; with financial assistance from an uncle, published his first, slim volume of verse, *Poems*, in 1935; subsequently contributed verse to *Poetry: A Magazine of Verse*, the *New Yorker*, *Harper's*, the *Nation*, and other periodicals; when a group of his poems under the title *Noun* appeared in the New Directions book *Five Young American Poets* (1941), attracted wide recognition, bolstered by *Person, Place and Thing* (1942), his first full-length collection of verse, including the first of his war poems; also in 1942, published another volume, *The Place of Love*, in Australia; with one exception, wrote all of the poems in *V-Mail and Other Poems* (1944), including "Elegy for a Dead Soldier," while serving with the U.S. Army medical corps in the southwest Pacific during World War II; for that book, received a Pulitzer Prize, in 1945; contributed to a major brouhaha in American letters in 1948, when, as one of the 14 Fellows in American Letters of the Library of Congress, he cast a dissenting vote in the awarding of the first Bollingen Prize in poetry to Ezra Pound, who had made pro-fascist broadcasts under Mussolini in Italy during the war years; "as a Jew," felt obliged to disassociate himself publicly from the award, but was not comfortable in that role; published *Poems of a Jew* in 1958; at some point, studied Catholicism, but later declared himself to be "above religion"; reflected the influence of the Beat poets in *The Bourgeois Poet* (1964), regarded by some as his finest book; later published *Collected Poems 1940–78* (1978) and *New and Selected Poems 1940–86* (1987); continued publishing poetry until 1998; in addition to collections of verse, published *Essay on Rime* (1945), *Prose Keys in Modern Poetry* (1962), *A Prosody Handbook* (1964), the novel *Edsel* (1971), and his autobiography, *Reports of My Death* (1990), among other works of prose; was associate professor of writing at Johns Hopkins University from 1948 to 1950; was editor of *Poetry* magazine from 1950 to 1956; was professor of English at the University of Nebraska from 1956 to 1966, at the University of Illinois from 1966 to 1968, and the University of California from 1968 to 1985; died in New York City. See *Current Biography* (October) 1944.

Obituary *New York Times* C p27 May 17, 2000

SHEPHERD, JEAN July 26, 1925(?)–Oct. 16, 1999 Humorist; radio raconteur; author; a fluent spinner of stories, chiefly pseudo-memoirs of his boyhood in Hammond, Indiana (fictionalized as "Hohman"); in 1949 began his career with radio station WSAI in Cincinnati, Ohio; later hosted a popular late-night comedy show on station WLW in Cincinnati; in 1956 joined New York City radio station WOR-AM as a talk-show soloist; with WOR soon settled into a daily program he called *Night People*, slotted in the late-night and predawn hours, when the station's 50,000-watt signal carried his voice to a metropolitan audience of some 66,000 and beyond, to 27 states and to Canada to the north and Bermuda to the south; especially in the Northeast, attracted a formidable and loyal cult following with his mocking jabs at American fads and foibles and in particular with the elaborate free-form monologues in which he created what Marshall McLuhan called "a nightly novel"; sustained and widened his following through syndication, recordings, personal appearances (especially on college campuses), *Wanda Hickey's Night of Golden Memories* (1972) and the other best-selling books in which he translated his episodic "novel" into print, such PBS television dramatizations of his stories as *Phantom of the Open Hearth* (1976), the PBS travelogue/monologue series *Jean Shepherd's America* (1969–71), and the feature film *A Christmas*

Story (1983), adapted from a boyhood-in-Hohman chapter in his book *In God We Trust; All Others Pay Cash* (1966) and narrated by him; died in a hospital near his home in Sanibel Island, Florida. See *Current Biography* (April) 1984.

Obituary *New York Times* A p21 Oct. 18, 1999

SHOUP, CARL Oct. 26, 1902–Mar. 23, 2000 Economist; former professor of political economy at Columbia University; originally aspired to careers in, successively, law and journalism; with a dissertation on the sales tax in France, received his doctorate in public finance at Columbia University, in 1930; had begun teaching at Columbia two years earlier; with others, assisted Robert Murray Haig, his mentor, in a sales-tax survey covering many states that resulted in the report *The Sales Tax in America* (1934); served on a New York State special tax commission from 1930 to 1935; supervised studies of the federal tax system for the Department of the Treasury in 1934 and 1937; was an assistant to the secretary of the treasury for eight months (1937–38) and a Treasury Department research consultant from 1938 to 1946 and 1962 to 1968; after World War II, traveled to Europe many times to help countries develop value-added-tax systems; similarly assisted the Canadian government; at the request of an aide to General Douglas MacArthur, then head of the Occupation government in Tokyo, went to Japan to help revamp its notoriously arbitrary tax system in 1949; as head of the "Shoup mission," made proposals (including tax breaks for companies conscientious in record keeping and tax filing) that were enacted into law by the Japanese Diet in 1950; also headed fiscal missions to other countries, including Venezuela, Liberia, and Cuba; served as a consultant to the United Nations; co-directed a New York City finance study; wrote or co-wrote more than a dozen books on such subjects as the tax or fiscal systems of various countries (including Brazil), federal estate and gift taxes, taxation in general, public finance, and the economic theory of David Ricardo; retired as McVickar professor of political economy at Columbia in 1971; died in Laconia, New Hampshire. See *Current Biography* (February) 1949.

Obituary *New York Times* A p25 Mar. 31, 2000

SIMON, WILLIAM E. Nov. 27, 1927–June 3, 2000 Financier; former U.S. secretary of the treasury; a quick, shrewd decision maker and astute administrator; in politics, was a conservative Republican; on Wall Street, managed trade in municipal bonds for the Union Securities Co. (1952–57), Weeden and Co. (as vice president, through 1963), and Salomon Brothers (beginning in January 1964); after nine months became a Salomon partner, in charge of federal bonds and securities; became a major force in directing the firm's expansion; by the late 1960s, was recognized throughout the financial world as one of its most brilliant bond experts; in 1969, was elected the first president of the newly formed Association of Primary Dealers in U.S. government securities; in 1970, was named to Salomon Brothers' seven-man management committee; in December 1972 went to Washington, D.C., as deputy to George P. Shultz, secretary of the treasury in the Nixon administration; was director of the Federal Energy Office from December 1973 to April 1974, when he became treasury secretary; after leaving government at the end of President Gerald R. Ford's administration, in January 1977, returned to Wall Street; amassed a fortune with his investments in leveraged buyouts; in 1982, in partnership with Raymond B. Chambers, bought Gibson Greetings, the card maker, with $80.5 million in mostly borrowed money; 14 months later, sold the company for $290 million; with the U.S. Olympic Committee, was treasurer from 1977 to 1980 and president from 1981 to 1984; played key roles in the U.S. boycott of the 1980 Olympic Games, in Moscow, and the planning for the 1984 Games, in Los Angeles; was instrumental in the founding of the U.S. Olympic Foundation, an important financial source for American amateur sports; in the late 1980s and early 1990s, was unsuccessful in his effort to form a Pacific Rim merchant banking empire; in his last years, devoted more of his time, energy, and money to philanthropy and charitable work; in 1996 received the Blessed Hyacinth Cormier Award for outstanding Catholic leadership; died in Santa Barbara, California. See *Current Biography* (April) 1974.

Obituary *New York Times* A p27 June 5, 2000

SKILLIN, EDWARD S. Jan. 23, 1904–Aug. 14, 2000 Publisher and former editor of the weekly lay Catholic magazine *Commonweal*, a journal of opinion—covering religion, culture, literature, the arts, politics, and public affairs—categorized by some as "liberal" and by him as "socially minded"; after majoring in modern languages at Williams College, worked with Henry Holt & Co. in sales, sales management, and minor editing; subsequently earned an M.A. degree in political science at Columbia University, where the Revrend Cornelius Clifford, a lecturer in philosophy, opened to him, as he once put it, "the priceless treasure of the Christian tradition"; joined the circulation department of *Commonweal* in 1933; with Philip Burnham, co-edited the magazine from 1937 to 1942; was editor from 1942 to 1967, when he became publisher; died in Glen Ridge, New Jersey. See *Current Biography* (May) 1949.

Obituary *New York Times* B p7 Aug. 16, 2000

SOBCHAK, ANATOLY A. 1937–Feb. 20, 2000 Russian politician; law professor; legal scholar; democratic reformer; mentor to Vladimir V. Putin, who succeeded (in an acting capacity) to the presidency of Russia upon the resignation of Boris N. Yeltsin in December 1999 and won election in 2000; taught law at the Institute of Technology in Leningrad while earning his doctorate at Leningrad University; apparently because his dissertation (on the benefits of a free-market economy) was considered too audacious, experienced a delay of eight years in receiving his doctoral degree; joined the faculty of Leningrad University as professor of economic law in 1983; subsequently became dean of the university's law school; was elected to the new Soviet Parliament in 1989; in 1991 became the first elected mayor of Leningrad, to which he soon restored its pre-Communist name, St. Petersburg; amid allegations of nepotism, was voted out of office in 1996; from 1997 to 1999 lived in voluntary exile in France, for medical reasons, according to his wife, to evade criminal charges, according to others; returned to Russia in the summer of 1999, shortly before the legal charges against him were dropped; wrote several books relating to the transition to the "new Russia"; died in Moscow. See *Current Biography* (July) 1992.

Obituary *New York Times* A p17 Feb. 21, 2000

SOKOLOW, ANNA Feb. 9, 1915–Mar. 29, 2000 Modern-dance choreographer; director; teacher; as a dancer, retired in 1954; as a choreographer, created works (to scores ranging from jazz to avant-garde electronic music) typically laden with angst and satiric social content, including messages of alienation and political indignation; is perhaps best known for *Rooms* (1955), which, in her words, "reflects the tiny, awful loneliness of people shut up in their rooms in a place like New York"; was born to Polish-Jewish immigrant parents on Manhattan's Lower East Side; was especially influenced by her mother, an early member of the International Ladies' Garment Workers Union; began studying modern dance at a neighborhood settlement house; in 1930 joined the troupe of Martha Graham, one of her early teachers; in 1933, under the auspices of the Workers Dance League, introduced her first company, the Dance Unit, with a performance of her *Anti-War Cycle*; toured the Soviet Union with the Dance Unit in 1934; during the 1930s created and danced the solo pieces *Case History* and *Slaughter of the Innocents*, which condemned the Spanish dictator Francisco Franco; also created the antifascist *Façade-Expositione Italiana* and the antiwar *War Is Beautiful*; in 1937 made her Broadway debut with the Dance Unit in a concert sponsored by the magazine *New Masses*; choreographed the WPA Federal Theater Project's *Sing for Your Supper* in 1939; later in 1939, with the Dance Unit and the composer Alex North (one of her many music collaborators), toured Mexico, which became her part-time home for some years; in Mexico, taught at the Mexico City Opera and Ballet, formed the modern-dance company La Paloma Azul, and created such works as *The Exile* and *Songs of a Semite*; first presented her *Lyric Suite* (to Alban Berg's music) in Mexico; back in New York City in the late 1940s and early 1950s, choreographed for the theater *Street Scene, Regina, Camino Real, Madam, Will You Walk?*, and *The Dybbuk*; in 1953 made the first of many working visits to Israel; in the 1950s and 1960s created and staged her dances *La Primavera, Opus 63, Night, Metamorphosis, Session 58, Dreams, Time Plus 6, Déserts*, and *Tribute* (to Martin Luther King Jr.); taught at both dance and theater schools, including the Juilliard School and the American Theater Wing; died at her home in Manhattan. See *Current Biography* (February) 1969.

Obituary *New York Times* B p14 Mar. 30, 2000

STAPP, JOHN PAUL July 11, 1910–Nov. 13, 1999 Physician; scientist; flight surgeon; U.S. Air Force officer; a pioneer in analyzing actual and possible human physical and mental problems presented by such aspects of jet flight and space travel as high altitude, high-speed accelerations and decelerations, and impact forces; often at great personal risk, conducted tests that provided criteria for air and space vehicle safety design (of ejection seats and escape capsules, for example), some of which were applicable to ground transportation as well; held advanced degrees in zoology and biophysics in addition to an M.D.; was commissioned a lieutenant in the U.S. Army during World War II, in 1944; over the following 13 years, rose through the grades in the U.S. Army Air Force and the U.S. Air Force to achieve the rank of colonel in the Air Force Medical Corps; in the postwar years, as an aeromedical-laboratory project officer at a succession of air bases, conducted research into the effects of jet-flight speeds and elevations on pilots; tested for preventive measures for high-altitude bends, chokes, gas pains, and dehydration; spent many hours at stratospheric altitudes and high speeds testing a liquid-oxygen emergency-breathing system; working with *Gee Whizz*, his first rocket-propelled sled on rails, ascertained how much deceleration shock the human body can endure; developed safety harnesses; in 1953 became chief of the aeromedical field laboratory at Hallomon Air Force Base, in Alamogordo, New Mexico; there, participated in deceleration and wind-blast experiments intended to judge the effects of ejecting at supersonic speeds; personally made the definitive tests in his rocket sled; in December 1954 set a new land-speed record of 632 miles per hour, which was equal to more than 1,000 mph at a jet's normal altitude of 35,000 feet; on that occasion, accelerated in five seconds from standstill to 632 mph and decelerated to a full stop in 1.4 seconds; subsequently headed the Aero Medical Laboratory at Wright Field in Ohio (1958–60), the aerospace-medicine division at Brooks Air Force Base, in Texas (1960–65), and the impact injuries branch of the Armed Forces Institute of Pathology; later was a staff member or consultant with the National Highway Traffic Safety Administration, the Department of Transportation, and various educational institutions and projects; was chairman of the annual Ann Stapp Car Crash Conference of the Society of Automotive Engineers; died at his home in Alamogordo, New Mexico. See *Current Biography* (December) 1959.

Obituary *New York Times* B p13 Nov. 16, 1999

STEIN, HERBERT Aug. 27, 1916–Sep. 8, 1999 Economist; U.S. government official; influential adviser to President Richard Nixon; a pragmatist who, while essentially conservative, favored flexible ad hoc approaches (including, when needed, such Keynesian devices as deficit budgets and wage and price controls) to problems of the American economy, such as unemployment and inflation; began his association with the federal government as an economist with the Federal Deposit Insurance Corporation in 1938; moved to the National Defense Advisory Commission in 1940; during World War II, headed the economic analysis section of the War Production Board (1940–44) and served with the Office of War Mobilization and Reconversion (1944–45); in 1945 left government to join the Committee for Economic Development, a private-sector research organization of which he ultimately became director of research and chief economist; after 22 years with the committee, served as a senior fellow with another private think tank, the Brookings Institution (1967–69); joined President Nixon's Council of Economic Advisers in 1969; chaired the council from 1972 to 1974; later became a professor at the University of Virginia and a member of the American Enterprise Institute; contributed to professional journals, such newspapers as the *Wall Street Journal* and the *New York Times*, and several books; wrote the book *The Fiscal Revolution in America* (1969); died in Washington, D.C. See *Current Biography* (March) 1973.

Obituary *New York Times* C p22 Sep. 9, 1999

TAKESHITA, NOBORU Feb. 26, 1924–June 19, 2000 Japanese politician; a supremely powerful political conservative, with strong rural backing; with Kakuei Tanaka, led the Liberal Democratic Party, the controlling party in the Diet, the Japanese Parliament, beginning in the mid-1960s; after serving in the Diet for three decades and holding a succession of Cabinet positions, including minister of construction and minister of finance, became prime minister in 1987; resigned under pressure in 1989, in the wake of a scandal in which many in his Cabinet were found implicated in the quid-pro-quo trading of political favors for monetary bribes, particularly gifts of stocks; by continuing to control the largest faction in the Liberal Democratic Party, remained a dominant behind-the-scenes figure in Japanese politics and government throughout the 1990s; had served as chairman of the boards of governors of the International Monetary Fund and World Bank (1984) and the Group of Ten (1985); wrote six books, including *Waga michi o yuko* ("Seeking After the Path," 1979), *Magokoro no seiji* ("Honest Politics," 1983), and *Subarashi kuni Nihon* ("Wonderful Japan," 1987); died in Tokyo. See *Current Biography* (May) 1988.

Obituary *New York Times* B p7 June 19, 2000

THOMPSON, HOMER A. Sep. 7, 1906–May 7, 2000 Canadian-born archaeologist; educator; was widely regarded as the outstanding classical archaeologist of his generation; with a dissertation titled "Transport of Grain in Graeco-Roman Egypt," took his Ph.D. degree at the University of Michigan in 1929; subsequently became a fellow of the American School of Classical Studies in Athens, which was about to begin excavating the Athenian Agora (public square), the nucleus of the ancient metropolis, including the civic buildings and the library and surrounding industrial sites; worked at those digs on and off for four decades; became director of the Agora excavations in 1947; also explored the Pynx, the ancient place of assembly on a hill near the Acropolis; taught classical archaeology at the University of Toronto from 1933 to 1946; beginning in 1947, was professor of classical archaeology at the Institute for Advanced Study at Princeton University; wrote numerous books and papers on subjects related to his work, including the Athenian Tholos and its predecessors and Athenian pottery of the third and second centuries B.C.; supervised the writing of two series of publications on the Agora, one for scholars and the other by scholars for lay readers; died at his home in Hightstown, New Jersey. See *Current Biography* (April) 1948.

Obituary *New York Times* A p14 May 13, 2000

TIMERMAN, JACOBO Jan. 6, 1923–Nov. 11, 1999 Ukrainian-born Argentine journalist; publisher; a left-of-center monitor of political injustice as he perceived it and scourge of its perpetrators as he found them, on the left or right; in his book *Prisoner Without a Name, Cell Without a Number* (1981; translated from the Spanish by Toby Talbot), eloquently recounted his torturous 29 and a half months of incarceration (1977–79) under an Argentine military dictatorship; was a dedicated Zionist and Socialist from the age of 14; in 1947 began freelance writing for literary magazines; during the 1950s was a reporter for the Buenos Aires newspaper *La Razón*; during the 1960s published in succession the weekly news magazines *Primera Plana* and *Confirmado*; later, with the help of the financier David Gravier, built a printing plant and founded a book publishing company and a newspaper in Buenos Aires; as publisher, editor, and editorial writer of the newspaper *La Opinión* from 1971 to 1977, was an outspoken human rights advocate; drew political harassment and many death threats with his attacks on governmental corruption and repression and failure to deal with terrorist groups both left and right; after a military junta seized power in March 1976, was relentless in keeping before the public eye the names of persons arrested without due process and the increasing numbers (ultimately estimated at between 10,000 and 29,000) of political victims known as *desaparecidos* ("the disappeared ones"); after his arrest in April 1977, was detained in a succession of clandestine houses and two regular prisons for a total of 29 and a half months with no formal charges filed, although the government leaked allegations that Timerman was involved in a "subversive" Zionist conspiracy that included, it was said, his partner David Gravier's laundering of ransom extortion money for the Montoneros, a left-wing terrorist group; was forced into exile upon his release in September 1979; lived first in Israel and then in the U.S. and Spain until 1983, when the military regime in Argentina was succeeded by a democratically elected government; returned to Argentina, where the government reimbursed him for the value of the newspaper and other properties that had been expropriated from him and sold to others; in addition to his well-known 1981 book, wrote *The Longest War: Israel in Lebanon* (1982) and *Chile: Death in the South* (1988); with the assistance of Carlos Gabetta, was writing his memoirs at the time of his death, at his home in Buenos Aires. See *Current Biography* (November) 1981.

Obituary *New York Times* B p11 Nov. 12, 1999

TOWNSEND, LYNN A. May 12, 1919–Aug. 17, 2000 Former chief executive officer of the Chrysler Corp. (now DaimlerChrysler A.G.); after earning a master of business administration degree, in 1941, worked with accounting firms in Detroit; as supervising accountant of Touche, Niven, Bailey & Smart, audited the books of Chrysler, the firm's major client; joined Chrysler as controller in 1957; the following year, became Chrysler's group vice president in charge of international operations; in 1960, was named executive administrative vice president and took over the corporation's day-to-day operations; became chief operating and administrative officer in 1961, when

Chrysler, the third-largest automobile manufacturing company, was seemingly in a fatal downward spiral; reversed the spiral by cutting overhead, raising efficiency and quality, and reorganizing Chrysler's dealership system; within five years, succeeded in doubling the corporation's sales and raising its net income 2,000 percent, to $5.44 a share; beginning in 1969, was challenged by a new decline in sales and profits, which worsened during the recession of the early 1970s; resigned the presidency and chairmanship of Chrysler in 1975, when the corporation was on the brink of bankruptcy (from which it would be rescued by Lee Iacocca); died in Farmington, Michigan. See *Current Biography* (September) 1966.

Obituary *New York Times* B p7 Aug. 22, 2000

TRUSSELL, RAY E. Feb. 7, 1914–Sep. 8, 1999 Physician; medical administrator; was an epidemiologist with the U.S. Army in the Pacific during World War II; after the war, worked as an epidemiologist with the New York City Department of Health; from 1950 to 1955 was simultaneously director of the Hunterdon (New Jersey) Medical Center and clinical professor of preventive medicine at the New York University–Bellevue Medical Center in New York City; wrote the book *Hunterdon Medical Center: The Story of One Approach to Rural Medical Care* (1956); while directing the Columbia University School of Public Health and Administrative Medicine (1955–61), led team studies of prepaid medical care in New York City, with pessimistic results; in 1961 became commissioner of the New York City municipal hospital system, the largest and most complex in the world; in that position, liberalized the dissemination of birth-control information, initiated a suicide-prevention service, upgraded psychiatric services for children, and improved ambulance service; forged links between municipal hospitals, voluntary hospitals, and medical schools; returned to Columbia University in 1965; three years later, became director of the Beth Israel Medical Center in Manhattan, where he established one of the largest methadone centers in the U.S.; retired in 1979; died at his home in Manhattan. See *Current Biography* (January) 1971.

Obituary *New York Times* B p7 Sep. 11, 1999

TUDJMAN, FRANJO May 14, 1922–Dec. 10, 1999 Croatian head of state; led the republic of Croatia to independence from Yugoslavia; when Nazi Germany invaded Yugoslavia (a unified monarchy, including the region of Croatia, since 1918), in 1941, refused to support the Ustase government, which cooperated with the Nazis; instead, joined the anti-Nazi partisan resistance led by Josip Broz Tito; after World War II, in a Yugoslavia reorganized by Marshal Tito into a Communist federation of six republics, including Croatia and dominated by Serbia, worked in the Ministry of National Defense in Belgrade, the capital of Yugoslavia, located in Serbia; completed his studies at the Higher Military Academy in Belgrade; rose to the rank of major general in the Yugoslav Army; after retiring from the army, in 1961, founded and directed the Institute of the History of the Workers' Movement of Croatia in Zagreb, the capital of Croatia; studied political science at the University of Zagreb; taught contemporary national history at the university; lost his dedication to the Communist regime and became a born-again Croatian nationalist; signaled his breach with the Communist regime in 1967, when he joined in the publication of a declaration demanding recognition of Croatian as a literary language in its own right, apart from Serbo-Croatian; was expelled from the Communist Party and forced to resign his university and institute posts; in crackdowns on "nationalist counterrevolution," was banned from taking part in public activities for long periods and was imprisoned in 1972–73, 1982–83, and 1984; founded the nationalist/separatist Croatian Democratic Union Party in 1989; in the first democratic elections in Croatia since World War II, was elected to the presidency of the Croatian republic in May 1990; within the same year, successfully pushed to enactment a new constitution declaring Croatia to be "the national state of the Croatian nation"; following Croatia's declaration of independence from Yugoslavia, in June 1991, led Croatians in a bitter civil war with ethnic Serbs living in Croatia (who had strong support from the Serb-dominated Yugoslav National Army); agreed to honor a U.N.-brokered ceasefire concluded early in 1992, while sporadic fighting (including that with Bosnian Muslims) continued for another three and a half years; was reelected president in November 1992; in 1997, secured Croatian control of the last enclaves held by the Serb rebels in Croatia, including Eastern Slavonia; between 1957 and 1990 published several books, including one on guerrilla warfare and others on international relations and Balkan and European history and politics; died in Zagreb. See *Current Biography* (September) 1997.

Obituary *New York Times* p1+ Dec. 11, 1999

VADIM, ROGER Jan. 26, 1928–Feb. 11, 2000 French filmmaker; opened the way for the nouvelle vague in French cinema with the explicit sensuality of his first motion picture, *Et . . . Dieu créa la femme* (1956; *And God Created Woman*), in which he transformed Brigitte Bardot (cast as a wanton French Riviera beach nymph), his first wife, into a screen sex icon, a feat he would duplicate less spectacularly, and to varying degrees, with later wives and mistresses; despite the technical craftsmanship, striking color imagery, and decorative elegance that marked his films, from thrillers to fantasies and black comedies, over the following three decades, he continued to be dismissed by some critics as a superficial voyeur in his own glossy seraglio; served his apprenticeship in filmmaking as an assistant to and scenarist for director Marc Allégret at Francoeur Studios for nine years beginning in 1947; had planned the erotic screen apotheosis of Bardot from the time he contrived to meet her, in 1949, when she was 16; subsequent to *Et . . . Dieu créa la femme*, directed Françoise Arnoul in *Sait-on jamais?* (1957; *No Sun in Venice*), Bardot in *Les Bijoutiers du clair de lune* (1958; *The Night Heaven Fell*), Annette Stroyberg, his second wife, in *Les Liaisons dangereuses* (1959) and *Et mourir de plaisis* (1960; *Blood and Roses*), Bardot in *La Bride sur le cou* (1961; *Please, Not Now!*), and Catherine Deneuve in *Le Vice et la vertu* (1963; *Vice and Virtue*); directed his third wife, Jane

Fonda, in four screen roles, most notably the title character, a sexy 41st-century space adventuress, in the science-fiction burlesque *Barbarella* (1968); made 22 feature films, including *Pretty Maids All in a Row* (1971), the first of a number of movies he directed in Hollywood, and a remake of *Et . . . Dieu créa la femme* (1987), starring Rebecca DeMornay; except for his American films, wrote or co-wrote his own scenarios; died in Paris. See *Current Biography* (January) 1984.

Obituary *New York Times* B p8 Feb. 12, 2000

WARREN, WILLIAM C. Feb. 3, 1909–Sep. 11, 2000 Lawyer; educator; federal, state, and municipal consultant; a specialist in taxation and legal accounting; dean emeritus and Kent professor emeritus, Columbia University School of Law; between 1935 and 1947, practiced corporate law with firms in New York City and Cleveland; taught law at Western Reserve (now Case Western Reserve) University from 1935 to 1942; was a tax consultant to the U.S. secretary of the treasury from 1947 to 1949; joined the faculty of the Columbia University Law School in 1946; was dean of the school from 1952 to 1970; as dean, raised more than $5.5 million for a new school building, established admissions and placement offices, and increased the proportion of women and minorities in the student body; later was a major donor to the funding for another building; taught at Columbia until 1977; was a counsel with the New York law firm of Roberts & Holland until shortly before his death; was on the boards of directors of several banking, insurance, and industrial corporations; co-wrote five textbooks on tax law. See *Current Biography* (January) 1960.

Obituary *New York Times* C p19 Sep. 15, 2000

WELLS, HERMAN B June 7, 1902–Mar. 18, 2000 Indiana University chancellor; during his undergraduate and graduate study in business administration, began his careers in teaching and banking; was field secretary of the Indiana Bankers Association from 1928 to 1931, research director of the Study Commission for Indiana Financial Institutions from 1931 to 1933, supervisor of the division of banks and trust companies and the division of research and statistics in the Indiana State Department of Financial Institutions from 1933 to 1935, and secretary of the State Commission for Financial Institutions from 1933 to 1936; meanwhile, at Indiana University rose from instructor in economics in 1931 to full professor and dean of the School of Business Administration in 1935 and temporary president in 1937; was full-fledged president from 1938 to 1962, when he was given the title of chancellor, which he retained until his death; was also appointed president of the fund-raising Indiana University Foundation; throughout his career, served prodigiously as an adviser on both educational and financial matters to the federal and local governments, the United Nations, and private organizations; died at his home in Bloomington, Indiana. See *Current Biography* (April) 1966.

Obituary *New York Times* C p31 Mar. 21, 2000

WEST, MORRIS L. Apr. 26, 1916–Oct. 9, 1999 Australian author; wrote such best-selling novels as *The Shoes of the Fisherman* (1963), a prescient story about Vatican politics, built around the imagined election of a Pope from behind the Communist Iron Curtain, and *The Ambassador* (1965), inspired by the downfall and assassination of President Ngo Dinh Diem of South Vietnam, in 1963; under the pseudonym Julian Morris, wrote his first novel, *Moon in My Pocket* (1945), based loosely on his life as an adolescent and young man in the order of Christian Brothers; was publicity director at a radio station in Melbourne (1944–45); in 1945 co-founded Australasian Radio Productions; as managing director of that company until 1954, controlled a large percentage of recorded radio dramatic shows and serials, many of which were scripted and/or produced by him; in 1956 published his second novel, *Gallows on the Sand*, about a search for treasure off the Queensland coast; after publishing *Kundu* (1957), a romance set in New Guinea, began traveling the world with his wife and children; in Naples, Italy, became involved with the work of Father Don Mario Borelli with derelict street urchins; wrote about that experience in *Children of the Sun* (1957), the book with which he began to achieve literary fame; in Austria, did research for a novel set in a postwar resort town in the Austrian Alps, *The Second Victory* (1958), which he later adapted for the screen (1986); in the late 1950s also wrote two adventure novels under pseudonyms; while working as the Vatican correspondent for the London *Daily Mail*, gathered the background material for the best-selling, award-winning theological thriller *The Devil's Advocate* (1959), which was adapted for the Broadway theater (1961) by Dore Schary and for the screen (1977) by West; wrote about a vendetta and a murder trial in a Tuscan village in the novel *Daughter of Silence* (1961), which he adapted for the New York stage (1962); withdrew his credit for writing the screenplay for *The Shoes of the Fisherman* (1969) to protest rewriting that he felt was inimical to the work's integrity; in total, wrote a score of novels, including two more set in the Vatican, *The Clowns of God* (1981) and *Lazarus* (1990); wrote the plays *The Heretic* (1970) and *The World Is Made of Glass* (1982); died in Sydney, Australia. See *Current Biography* (January) 1966.

Obituary *New York Times* B p13 Oct. 12, 1999

WILSON, MALCOLM Feb. 26, 1914–Mar. 13, 2000 Republican governor of New York (1973–75); lawyer; although generally regarded as a conservative, declared himself to be a "moderate" who was "progressive in meeting human needs and conservative in handling the people's dollars"; between 1938 and 1956, was elected to a record 10 consecutive two-year terms in the New York State Assembly, where he gained a reputation as a budget expert, a brilliant debater, and a skilled parliamentarian; in 1958 was picked by the multimillionaire Nelson A. Rockefeller, a political novice, to manage his campaign for the Republican gubernatorial nomination; with his political savvy and party connections (down to the grass-roots), played an indispensable role in Rockefeller's successful quest for the nomination; at

Rockefeller's insistence, was chosen at the Republican state convention to be the gubernatorial candidate's running mate in the subsequent general election, from which the Rockefeller/Wilson ticket emerged victorious, as it would in three consecutive subsequent elections (1962, 1966, 1970); as Governor Rockefeller's lieutenant governor for 15 years, was president of the state Senate; often differed with Rockefeller, a liberal, in private; being a pro-life Roman Catholic, disagreed with him publicly (aside from a constitutional question) on only one issue, New York State's liberalized abortion law; succeeded to the governorship in December 1973, when Rockefeller (who would become vice president of the U.S. one year later) resigned; was defeated by Hugh J. Carey, the Democratic candidate, in the gubernatorial election of November 1974; after leaving office, returned to his law practice; was chief executive officer of the Manhattan Bank for Savings from 1977 to 1986; died in New Rochelle, New York. See *Current Biography* (May) 1974.

Obituary *New York Times* C p31 Mar. 14, 2000

WILSON, ROBERT R. Mar. 4, 1914– Jan. 16, 2000 Nuclear physicist; sculptor; professor emeritus of physics, Cornell University; creator and director (1967–78) of the monumental Fermi National Accelerator Laboratory, or Fermilab, near Batavia, Illinois, housing the most powerful atomic particle smashers in the world; in designing the architecture of Fermilab, was inspired by the great European cathedrals; as a graduate student in the University of California's radiation laboratory, worked under Ernest O. Lawrence, the inventor of the cyclotron; at that time, invented the "Wilson seal," a vacuum-tight seal that increased the efficiency of the cyclotron ninefold—an improvement that led to the discoveries of carbon-14 and plutonium; also demonstrated that the energy levels of the particles the cyclotron produced could be raised simply by focusing the particle beam more intensely; upon earning his Ph.D. degree, in 1940, joined the faculty of Princeton University, where he began studying the proton as a means of explicating the "strong force" that holds atomic nuclei together; interrupted that work to help develop the atomic bomb as a member of the Manhattan Project; as one of the first nuclear physicists to arrive at the Los Alamos National Laboratory, in New Mexico, formed and led the cyclotron group there; in 1944 became the head of the division of experimental nuclear physics at Los Alamos; later, supervised the designing of the instruments that measured the intensity of the initial blast during the first test explosion of the bomb, on July 16, 1945; as associate professor of physics at Harvard University (1946–47), designed the 150 million electron volt (MeV) cyclotron that was to be constructed there; also designed a prototypical small proton accelerator for use in cancer therapy; was professor of physics and director of the Laboratory of Nuclear Studies at Cornell University from 1947 to 1967; at Cornell, guided the building of a new type of particle accelerator, a 300 MeV synchrotron—the first in a series of accelerators, each more powerful than its predecessor, that he built at Cornell and used to continue his research on the proton; in 1967 accepted the invitation to build the Fermilab; during his 11-year tenure as its director, raised energies of particles to 500 billion electron volts, making possible the detection of the bottom quark and the measurement of quark charges and thus helping to establish the theory of nuclear structure known as quantum chromodynamics; concurrently with his direction of Fermilab, was professor of physics at the University of Chicago; later, was Peter B. Ritzma Professor at that school (1978–80) and Michael Pupin Professor at Columbia University; died at his home in Ithaca, New York. See *Current Biography* (August) 1989.

Obituary *New York Times* B p7 Jan. 19, 2000

WOODWARD, C. VANN Nov. 13, 1908–Dec. 17, 1999 Historian; Sterling professor of history at Yale University from 1961 until his retirement, in 1977; a southern liberal who brought a flair for storytelling and a social conscience as well as close scholarship to books in which he tried to bridge the gap between present and past, especially the southern past; regarded the writing of history as a scholarly art form in which the "historian-detective" is engaged in an adventure of which the outcome is unknown "until he reads what he has written"; earned his doctorate at the University of North Carolina in 1937 with a dissertation eventually published as *Tom Watson: Agrarian Rebel* (1955), an early effort of his to shatter the stereotype of a "Solid South"; with that book in combination with two others, *Origins of the New South, 1877–1913* (1951) and *Reunion and Reaction* (1951), presented a trilogy that revolutionized the way that historians looked at the post-Reconstruction South; created what Martin Luther King Jr. called the "historical bible of the civil rights movement" with *The Strange Career of Jim Crow* (1955); in essays in *The Burden of Southern History* (1960), expressed regret that the humble wisdom gained by the southerner in suffering defeat and guilt was not being used to challenge unrealistic northern-based shibboleths inimical to the national good; in essays in *American Counterpoint: Slavery and Racism in the North-South Dialogue* (1971), traced his deepening pessimism about the civil-rights movement and the commitment of white Americans to racial equality; after serving as a navy intelligence officer in World War II, wrote *The Battle of Leyte Gulf* (1947); edited *Mary Chestnut's Civil War*, which won a Pulitzer Prize in 1982; taught at Johns Hopkins University from 1947 until his move to Yale in 1961; died in Hamden, Connecticut. See *Current Biography* (May) 1986.

Obituary *New York Times* p66 Dec. 19, 1999

YARMOLINSKY, ADAM Nov. 17, 1922–Jan. 5, 2000 Lawyer; regents professor of public policy at the University of Maryland since 1933; former federal government official; during the administrations of Presidents John F. Kennedy and Lyndon B. Johnson, was an important but controversial behind-the-scenes figure—a brash and abrasive member of the eastern liberal intellectual establishment who stirred the wrath of many conservative politicians—who helped to reorganize the Pentagon and to plan the war on poverty; early in his career was law clerk to U.S. Supreme Court justice Stanley E. Reed (1950–

51); during the 1950s practiced law in Washington, D.C., and worked for several foundations, including the Fund for the Republic; in 1961 joined the Kennedy administration as special assistant to Secretary of Defense Robert S. McNamara; in that position, was credited with putting modern management systems in place in the Pentagon; helped to prepare the Gesell Report (1963), calling for an end to racial discrimination in towns adjoining military bases; in the Johnson administration, was temporarily released from the Defense Department to assist R. Sargent Shriver in formulating the antipoverty program passed in 1964 by Congress; contrary to his expectation, was not named Shriver's deputy director in the new Office of Economic Opportunity, reportedly because conservative southern congressmen refused to vote for the program if he were to administer it; after his return to the Pentagon, was named principal deputy assistant secretary of defense for international affairs (1965–66); left government in 1966 to join the faculty of Harvard University as a professor of law; became a member of the Institute of Politics in the John F. Kennedy School of Politics at Harvard; in 1972 moved to the faculty of the University of Massachusetts; returned to government as counselor to the U.S. Arms Control and Disarmament Agency (1977–79); joined the faculty of the University of Maryland in 1985; was university provost from 1987 to 1993; wrote the books *Recognition of Excellence* (1960), *The Military Establishment* (1971), and *Paradoxes of Power* (1983); died in Washington, D.C. See Current Biography (March) 1969.

Obituary *New York Times* A p17 Jan. 7, 2000

YOUNG, LORETTA Jan. 9, 1913–Aug. 12, 2000 Film and television actress; a long-reigning star who demanded control of her own career, with fair success on the silver screen and greater success on television; in Hollywood in the 1930s, advanced from sweet ingenue to elegant leading lady, rosily feminine, sensual but unsullied, an image she generally projected on the motion-picture screen through the 1940s; on television from 1953 to 1961, hosted and frequently starred in the presentations of *The Loretta Young Show,* a weekly half-hour anthology of morally uplifing melodramas; reached the height of her film career with her Academy Award–winning performance as the Swedish maid turned congressional candidate in *The Farmer's Daughter* (1947); was nominated for another Oscar for her warm portrayal of a French nun trying to establish a children's dispensary in New England in the sentimental comedy *Come to the Stable* (1949); with her two sisters, made bit appearances in silent movies in early childhood; after spending six years in a Catholic convent school, returned to the screen in a supporting adolescent role in *Naughty But Nice* (1927), which led to her first major Hollywood contract and more substantial screen assignments; made a smooth transition from teenager to ingenue and from silents to talkies in such films as *The Devil to Pay* (1930) and *Platinum Blond* (1931); starred opposite such actors as James Cagney, in the sassy comedy-drama *Taxi!* (1932), Spencer Tracy, in the Depression romance *A Man's Castle* (1933), Cary Grant, in the melodrama *Born to Be Bad* (1934), Clark Gable, in the Yukon adventure story *Call of the Wild* (1935), Don Ameche, in the biographical picture *The Story of Alexander Graham Bell* (1939), and David Niven, in the romantic comedy *Eternally Yours* (1939); was cast as the innocent pioneer wife coveted by a wanderer friend of her husband's in the Western *Rachel and the Stranger* (1948); in changes of pace, was seen as a woman on the run in the thriller *The Stranger* (1946) and the frightened wife of a psychotic in the film noir *Cause for Alarm* (1951); by the time she quit Hollywood, in 1953, had made 85 pictures, including *Laugh, Clown, Laugh* (1928), *The Squall* (1929), *Ramona* (1936), *Suez* (1938), *And Now Tomorrow* (1944), *The Bishop's Wife* (1947), and *Because of You* (1952); was later cast in two made-for-television movies; won three television Emmy Awards for performances on *The Loretta Young Show* between 1954 and 1958; had her first sustained television role as Christine Massey, a recently widowed writer with seven children, in the continuing romantic comedy-drama *The New Loretta Young Show* (1962–63); made rare public appearances, usually to promote charities, many of them Catholic; stressed the influence of her religious faith in her life and work in *The Things I Had to Learn* (1961), a memoir written with Helen Ferguson. See *Current Biography* (March) 1948.

Obituary *New York Times* p39 Aug. 13, 2000

ZINN, WALTER H. Dec. 10, 1906—Feb. 14, 2000 Canadian-born physicist; pioneer designer of nuclear reactors; played key roles in both the development of the atomic bomb during World War II and the subsequent application of nuclear energy to peaceful purposes; before emigrating to the U.S., taught at Queen's University in Kingston, Ontario, and was bursar at the Research Council of Canada; was on the faculty of the City College of New York from 1932 to 1941, when he became a research associate in the cyclotron laboratory at Columbia University, where he had earned his doctoral degree; early in 1942 was enlisted as a member of the Manhattan Project team, which secretly constructed the world's first atomic reactor under the leadership of Enrico Fermi at the University of Chicago; on December 2, 1942, was the person who pulled a control rod from between bars of pure uranium and thus released the first flow of atomic energy ever sparked by human beings; after the wartime project was completed, played a supervisory role in its postwar transition, as director of the Argonne National Laboratory from 1946 to 1956; subsequently formed his own consulting firm and became vice president for the nuclear division of the company, now known as ABB Combustion Engineering; retired as vice president in 1970 but remained a director of that Swiss-owned company, based in Windsor, Connecticut, until 1986; died in Clearwater, Florida. See *Current Biography* (December) 1955.

Obituary *New York Times* B p8 Feb. 25, 2000

ZUCKERT, EUGENE M. Nov. 9, 1911–June 5, 2000 Former secretary of the U.S. Air Force (1961–65); lawyer; received a combined business/law education in a special program set up between the Yale Law School and the Harvard Graduate School of

Business Administration; taught at the latter from 1940 to 1944; in 1944, joined the navy, which assigned him to the office of the chief of naval operations in Washington, D.C.; after his discharge from the navy, in September 1945, took the post of executive assistant to W. Stuart Symington, later a U.S. senator, then in charge of a Truman administration war-surplus agency; was named Symington's special assistant when Symington was appointed assistant secretary of war for air in February 1946; after the U.S. Air Force was established as an independent branch of the armed forces and Symington became its first secretary, served as Symington's assistant secretary for management (1947–52); was a member of the Atomic Energy Commission from 1952 to 1954; was an active partner in the law firm of Zuckert, Scoutt until 1988; remained counsel to the firm of Zuckert, Scoutt & Rasenburger until his death; died in Washington, D.C. See *Current Biography* (April) 1952.

Obituary *New York Times* C p23 June 7, 2000

ZUMWALT, ELMO R. Nov. 29, 1920–Jan. 2, 2000 Admiral, U.S. Navy, retired; as chief of naval operations (1970–74), liberalized codes of conduct and tried to advance racial equity and understanding; won the earliest of his many combat decorations for his performance in the battle of Leyte Gulf in World War II and as navigator of the USS *Wisconsin* in the Korean War; during the 1950s held various positions in the Department of the Navy in Washington, D.C., and was commanding officer of the destroyer USS *Arnold J. Isbell* and the guided-missile frigate *USS Dewey*; subsequently, was senior aide to the secretary of the navy (1963–65) and commander of Cruiser-Destroyer Flotilla Seven (1965–66); set up the division of systems analysis within the office of the chief of naval operations (1966–68); went to Vietnam as chief of U.S. naval forces there in September 1968; as chief, ordered the spraying of the Mekong Delta with the defoliant Agent Orange, a carcinogenic byproduct of which was dioxin, a fact that hit home when his son Lieutenant Elmo R. Zumwalt III, a commander of one of the navy boats patrolling the Mekong River, later fathered a boy with a severe learning disability and died of cancer; became chief of naval operations in 1970, when enlistments were declining; over the following four years, issued 121 directives, called Z-Grams, calculated to make navy life freer and more attractive; relaxed rules regarding grooming, dress, shore leave, alcohol in barracks, and numerous other matters; saw enlistments increase, especially among black personnel, but was accused by many, including retired admirals, of having introduced a permissiveness detrimental to military discipline, especially after major racial incidents occurred on two aircraft carriers in 1972; retired in 1974; during his son Elmo's terminal illness, wrote with him the book *My Father, My Son* (1986), which was made into a CBS television movie with the same title (1988); lived in Arlington, Virginia; died in Durham, North Carolina. See *Current Biography* (June) 1971.

Obituary *New York Times* A p17 Jan. 3, 2000

CLASSIFICATION BY PROFESSION—2000

ADVERTISING
Cussler, Clive

AERONAUTICS
Hickam, Homer H. Jr.

ARCHAEOLOGY
Bass, George
Cussler, Clive
Hawass, Zahi

ARCHITECTURE
Ando, Tadao
Foster, Norman
Koolhaas, Rem
Siza, Alvaro
Stern, Robert A. M.

ART
Byrne, John
Driskell, David C.
Goldsworthy, Andy
Katchor, Ben
Kinkade, Thomas
Lou, Liza
Schapiro, Miriam
Tomorrow, Tom
Walker, Kara

ASTRONOMY
Bahcall, John N.
Burbidge, E. Margaret
Tyson, Neil de Grasse

BUSINESS
Brenner, Charles H.
Carmack, John
Connerly, Ward
Damadian, Raymond V.
Davis, Clive
Ellis, Ruth
Evans, Nancy
Eyler, John
Fanning, Shawn
Fiorina, Carleton
Greenberg, Maurice R.
Hawk, Tony
Hughes, Cathy
Jung, Andrea
Karmazin, Mel
Kinkade, Thomas
Komando, Kim
Koogle, Tim
Lil' Kim
McEntee, Gerald W.
Milchan, Arnon
Pittman, Robert
Raines, Franklin D.
Riordan, Richard
Sassa, Scott
Saylor, Michael
Scardino, Marjorie
Smith, Frederick W.
Thomas-Graham, Pamela
Walker, Jay
Whitman, Meg
Wigand, Jeffrey
Witt, James Lee
Wolfensohn, James D.

CONSERVATION
Hill, Julia "Butterfly"
Irwin, Steve
Marker, Laurie

DANCE
Herrera, Paloma
Lerman, Liz
McKenzie, Kevin
Rushing, Matthew

DIPLOMACY
Albright, Madeleine Korbel
Annan, Kofi
Talbott, Strobe

EDUCATION
Albright, Madeleine Korbel
Bahcall, John N.
Bancroft, Ann
Blakey, Michael L.
Brenner, Charles H.
Burbidge, E. Margaret
Clark, Helen
Driskell, David C.
Feldt, Gloria
Garbus, Martin
Greene, Brian
Holmgren, Mike
Hrdy, Sarah Blaffer
Jospin, Lionel Robert
Koolhaas, Rem
Lerman, Liz
Marsalis, Ellis
Rodriguez, Eloy
Ros-Lehtinen, Ileana
Schapiro, Miriam
Skocpol, Theda
Stern, Robert A. M.
Stewart, Alice
Trimble, David
Tyson, Neil de Grasse
Wigand, Jeffrey

ENVIRONMENTAL ACTIVISM
Hill, Julia "Butterfly"

FASHION
Kors, Michael
Powell, Sandy
Sevigny, Chloë
Yamamoto, Yohji

FILM
Apted, Michael
Barry, John
Bourne, St. Clair
Burton, LeVar
Campbell, Neve
Cho, Margaret
Clash, Kevin
Crowe, Russell
Dickerson, Ernest
Driskell, David C.
Duncan, Michael Clarke
Dutton, Charles S.
Emmerich, Roland
Estrada, Joseph
Fincher, David
Gandolfini, James
Guillaume, Robert
Hall, Conrad L.
Harron, Mary

Herskovitz, Marshall
Jolie, Angelina
Judd, Ashley
Kaminski, Janusz
Lil' Kim
Lowe, Rob
Martin, Steve
McDaniel, James
Milchan, Arnon
Morricone, Ennio
Murch, Walter
Norton, Edward
Obst, Lynda
Palin, Michael
Penn & Teller
Poitier, Sidney
Powell, Sandy
Regan, Judith
Sevigny, Chloë
Sorkin, Aaron
Swank, Hilary
Williamson, Kevin
Yoakam, Dwight

FINANCE
Riordan, Richard
Wolfensohn, James D.

GOVERNMENT AND POLITICS, FOREIGN
Chávez, Hugo
Chen Shui-bian
Clark, Helen
Estrada, Joseph
Jospin, Lionel Robert
Nazarbayev, Nursultan
Putin, Vladimir
Shipley, Jenny
Trimble, David
Vajpayee, Atal Behari

GOVERNMENT AND POLITICS, U.S.
Albright, Madeleine Korbel
Barnes, Roy
Barshefsky, Charlene
Begaye, Kelsey
Clayton, Eva McPherson
Collins, Susan
Connerly, Ward
DeLauro, Rosa
Fulani, Lenora
Garvey, Jane F.
Gore, Tipper
McEntee, Gerald W.
Raines, Franklin D.
Riordan, Richard
Ros-Lehtinen, Ileana
Rove, Karl
Smith, Robert
Talbott, Strobe
Witt, James Lee

JOURNALISM
Campbell, Bebe Moore
Dhaliwal, Daljit
Fuller, Bonnie
Guzy, Carol
Harron, Mary
Ivins, Molly
Kahn, Roger
Komando, Kim
McCarver, Tim
Scardino, Marjorie
Staples, Brent
Talbott, Strobe
Tomorrow, Tom

LABOR
Chavez-Thompson, Linda
McEntee, Gerald W.

LAW
Barnes, Roy
Barshefsky, Charlene
Chen Shui-bian
Davis, Clive
Garbus, Martin
Greenberg, Maurice R.
Raines, Franklin D.
Riordan, Richard
Thomas-Graham, Pamela
Trimble, David
Wald, Patricia M.

LITERATURE
Briscoe, Connie
Byrne, John
Campbell, Bebe Moore
Collins, Jackie
Cussler, Clive
Eggers, Dave
George, Elizabeth
Green, Tim
Hickam, Homer H. Jr.
Kahn, Roger
Katchor, Ben
Martin, Steve
Obst, Lynda
Palin, Michael
Penn & Teller
Rowling, J. K.
Smith, Zadie
Thomas-Graham, Pamela
Thomson, Rupert
Vajpayee, Atal Behari

MATHEMATICS
Brenner, Charles H.

MEDICINE
Blaese, R. Michael
Canady, Alexa
Damadian, Raymond V.
Stewart, Alice

MILITARY
Abdullah bin Hussein
Chávez, Hugo
Kennedy, Claudia J.

MUSIC
Aguilera, Christina
Backstreet Boys
Barry, John
Bell, Joshua
Braxton, Toni
Byron, Don
Davis, Clive
Dixie Chicks
Fincher, David
Franklin, Kirk
Gavrilov, Andrei
Gray, Macy
Guy, Buddy
Hargrove, Roy
Hetfield, James
Krall, Diana
Lang, David
Lil' Kim
Marsalis, Ellis
McBride, Christian
Morricone, Ennio
'N Sync
Spears, Britney
Strait, George
Warren, Diane
Yoakam, Dwight
Zajick, Dolora

NONFICTION
Albright, Madeleine Korbel
Bahcall, John N.
Bass, George
Burbidge, E. Margaret
Campbell, Bebe Moore
Carter, Rubin
Connerly, Ward
Cussler, Clive
Driskell, David C.
Fulani, Lenora
Garbus, Martin
Gore, Tipper
Green, Tim
Greene, Brian
Hickam, Homer H. Jr.
Hrdy, Sarah Blaffer
Irwin, Steve
Ivins, Molly
John Paul II
Johnson, Dwayne "The Rock"
Kahn, Roger
Kinkade, Thomas
Koolhaas, Rem
McKenzie, Vashti Murphy
Palin, Michael
Patterson, Francine
Penn & Teller
Rule, Ann
Skocpol, Theda
Staples, Brent
Stern, Robert A. M.
Talbott, Strobe
Tyson, Neil de Grasse
Wald, Patricia M.

ORGANIZATIONS
Carter, Rubin
Connerly, Ward
Feldt, Gloria
Marker, Laurie
Michelman, Kate
Patterson, Francine
Tafel, Richard L.
Wald, Patricia M.
Wolfensohn, James D.

PHOTOGRAPHY
Goldsworthy, Andy
Gore, Tipper
Guzy, Carol

PUBLISHING
Briscoe, Connie
Dennis, Felix
Eggers, Dave
Evans, Nancy
Fuller, Bonnie
Regan, Judith
Schiffrin, André

RADIO
Bell, Art
Hughes, Cathy
Ivins, Molly
Komando, Kim
McKenzie, Vashti Murphy

RELIGION
John Paul II
McKenzie, Vashti Murphy

ROYALTY
Abdullah bin Hussein

SCIENCE
Banfield, Jillian
Blaese, R. Michael
Blakey, Michael L.
Burbidge, E. Margaret
Greene, Brian
Marker, Laurie
Patterson, Francine
Rodriguez, Eloy
Stewart, Alice
Tyson, Neil de Grasse

SOCIAL ACTIVISM
Bourne, St. Clair
Carter, Rubin
Chavez-Thompson, Linda
Connerly, Ward
Ellis, Ruth
Feldt, Gloria
Garbus, Martin
Gore, Tipper
Michelman, Kate
Stewart, Alice
Tafel, Richard L.
Wald, Patricia M.

SOCIAL SCIENCE
Bass, George
Blakey, Michael L.
Hrdy, Sarah Blaffer
Skocpol, Theda

SOCIAL SERVICE
Begaye, Kelsey

SPORTS
Bagwell, Jeff
Bancroft, Ann
Camby, Marcus
Carter, Rubin
Flair, Ric
Garciaparra, Nomar
Gordon, Jeff
Green, Tim
Hawk, Tony
Heinrichs, April
Hernandez, Orlando
Holmgren, Mike
Johnson, Dwayne "The Rock"
Johnson, Randy
McCarver, Tim
Mutombo, Dikembe
Redgrave, Steven
Ribbs, Willy T.
Trinidad, Felix

TECHNOLOGY
Brenner, Charles H.
Carmack, John
Damadian, Raymond V.
Fanning, Shawn
Komando, Kim
Saylor, Michael
Whitman, Meg

TELEVISION
Apted, Michael
Bourne, St. Clair
Burton, LeVar
Campbell, Neve
Cho, Margaret
Clash, Kevin
Collins, Jackie
Dhaliwal, Daljit
Dickerson, Ernest
Driskell, David C.
Duncan, Michael Clarke
Dutton, Charles S.
Fontana, Tom
Gandolfini, James
Guillaume, Robert
Harron, Mary
Herskovitz, Marshall
Hughley, D.L.
Irwin, Steve

Ivins, Molly
Jolie, Angelina
Judd, Ashley
Karmazin, Mel
Lowe, Rob
Martin, Steve
McCarver, Tim
McDaniel, James
McKenzie, Vashti Murphy
Palin, Michael
Penn & Teller
Poitier, Sidney
Regan, Judith
Rule, Ann
Sassa, Scott
Sorkin, Aaron
Swank, Hilary
Williamson, Kevin

THEATER

Apted, Michael
Dutton, Charles S.
Fontana, Tom
Gandolfini, James
Lowe, Rob
Martin, Steve
McDaniel, James
Moschen, Michael
Palin, Michael
Penn & Teller
Poitier, Sidney
Powell, Sandy
Sorkin, Aaron

CUMULATED INDEX 1991–2000

This is the index to the January 1991–November 2000 issues. For the index to the 1940–1995 biographies, see *Current Biography: Cumulated Index 1940–1995.*

Abacha, Sani Sep 96 obit Aug 98
Abbas, Mahmoud Jun 99
Abbott, Berenice obit Feb 92
Abbott, George obit Apr 95
Abbott, Jim Sep 95
Abdul, Paula Sep 91
Abdul-Jabbar, Kareem Feb 97
Abdullah bin Hussein Jan 2000
Abé, Kobo obit Mar 93
Abiola, Moshood Kashimawa Sep 98 obit Nov 98
Abraham, F. Murray Jan 91
Abram, Morris B. obit Jul 2000
Abrams, Floyd Jul 99
Abramson, Leslie Jun 99
Abs, Hermann J. obit May 94
Abu Ammar *see* Arafat, Yasir
Abzug, Bella (Savitsky) obit Jun 98
Achebe, Chinua Jan 92
Ackerman, Diane Jun 97
Ackley, (Hugh) Gardner obit May 98
Ackroyd, Peter May 93
Acuff, Roy obit 1993
Adé, King Sunny Nov 94
Adams, Alice obit Aug 99
Adams, Diana obit Mar 93
Adams, Douglas Jul 93
Adams, Eva Bertrand obit Oct 91
Adams, Gerry Sep 94
Adams, Stanley obit Mar 94
Adler, Stella obit Feb 93
Adzhubei, Aleksei I. obit May 93
Affabee, Eric *see* STINE, R. L.
Affleck, Ben Mar 98
Agnew, Spiro T. obit Nov 96
Aguilera, Christina Aug 2000
Ahern, Bartholomew *see* Ahern, Bertie
Ahern, Bertie Jul 98
Aiello, Danny Jun 92
Aikman, Troy May 95
Akalaitis, Joanne Feb 93
Akebono Aug 99
Akihito, Emperor Of Japan Aug 91
al-Turabi, Hassan *see* Turabi, Hassan al-
Alagna, Roberto Jul 97
Alaïa, Azzedine Oct 92
Albee, Edward Apr 96
Albert, Carl obit Jun 2000
Albright, Madeleine Korbel May 95
Albright, Madeleine Korbel Apr 2000
Alcorn, Hugh Meade, Jr. obit Mar 92
Aldredge, Theoni Feb 94
Aldrin, Buzz Sep 93
Alexander, Jason Jan 98
Alexander, Lamar Jul 91
Alexander, Margaret Walker *see* Walker, Margaret
Alexie, Sherman Oct 98
Alia, Ramiz Jan 91
Alioto, Joseph L(awrence) obit Apr 98
Aliyev, Heydar Sep 99
Allen, Ethan obit Nov 93
Allen, George obit Mar 91
Allen, Mel obit Aug 96
Allen, Paul Jul 98
Allen, Peter obit Aug 92
Allen, Tim May 95
Alley, Kirstie Jul 94
Allsburg, Chris Van Sep 96
Almendros, Nestor obit May 92
Alou, Felipe Jun 99
Alou, Moises Apr 99
Alphand, Hervé obit Mar 94
Alvarez Bravo, Manuel Jan 99
Amanpour, Christiane Apr 96
Amato, Giuliano Sep 93
Ambler, Eric obit Jan 99
Ameche, Don obit Feb 94
Ames, Amyas obit Jun 2000
Ames, Bruce N. Oct 93
Ames, Louise obit Jan 97
Amichai, Yehuda Feb 98
Amis, Kingsley obit Jan 96
Amos, Tori Sep 98
Amos, Wally Jul 95
Amsterdam, Birdie obit Sep 96
Anderson, Carl D. obit Mar 91
Anderson, Frances *see* Anderson, Judith
Anderson, George Whelan obit May 92
Anderson, Ian Feb 98
Anderson, Judith obit Mar 92
Anderson, June May 91
Anderson, Lindsay obit Nov 94
Anderson, Marian obit Jun 93
Anderson, Sigurd obit Mar 91
Anderson, W. French Oct 94
Ando, Tadao Jan 2000
Andreas, Dwayne O. Mar 92
Andreessen, Marc Jun 97
Andrews, Anthony Jun 91
Andrews, Dana obit Feb 93
Andrews, Julie Apr 94
Angelou, Maya Feb 94
Angier, Natalie Aug 99
Annan, Kofi Mar 2000
Antall, József, Jr. obit Feb 94
Antonioni, Michelangelo May 93
Apple, R. W., Jr. Apr 93
Appley, Lawrence A. obit Jun 97
Apted, Michael Feb 2000
Arafat, Yasir Nov 94
Araskog, Rand V. Nov 91
Arcaro, Eddie obit Jan 98
Archer, Dennis W. Feb 97
Arciniegas, Germán obit Jun 2000
Arden, Eve obit Jan 91
Areilza, José Maria de, Count of Motrico obit May 98
Argerich, Martha Sep 99
Aristide, Jean-Bertrand May 91
Armey, Dick *see* Armey, Richard K.
Armey, Richard K. Jun 95
Armstrong, C. Michael Jun 99
Armstrong, Gillian Aug 95
Armstrong, Lance Sep 97
Arnall, Ellis obit Feb 93
Arnault, Bernard Jun 98
Arnett, Peter Nov 91
Arnon, Daniel I. obit Mar 95
Arquette, Patricia Oct 97
Arrau, Claudio obit Aug 91
Arrupe, Pedro obit Apr 91
Arthur, Jean obit Aug 91
Ash, Mary Kay May 95
Ashcroft, John Sep 99
Ashcroft, Peggy obit Aug 91
Ashdown, Paddy Oct 92
Ashe, Arthur obit Mar 93

Ashford, Nickolas Apr 97
Ashley, Maurice Sep 99
Ashmore, Harry S(cott) obit Apr 98
Ashrawi, Hanan Mar 92
Asimov, Isaac obit May 92
Aspin, Les obit Jul 95
Assad, Hafez Al- Apr 92 obit Aug 2000
Atwater, Lee obit May 91
Aubrey, James T., Jr. obit Nov 94
Auel, Jean M. Feb 91
Augér, Arleen obit Aug 93
Augustine, Norman R. Jun 98
Aulenti, Gae Sep 99
Aung San Suu Kyi Feb 92
Auriol, Jacqueline obit Jun 2000
Auster, Paul Mar 96
Autry, Gene obit Jan 99
Aykroyd, Dan Jan 92
Azikiwe, Nnamdi obit Aug 96
Azil Singh *see* Zail Singh
Aziz, Tariq May 91

Babyface Jul 98
Backstreet Boys May 2000
Bacon, Francis obit Jun 92
Bacon, Selden D. obit Feb 93
Badu, Erykah Apr 98
Bagwell, Jeff Aug 2000
Bahcall, John N. Apr 2000
Baker, Nicholson Aug 94
Baker, Richard A. *see* Baker, Rick
Baker, Rick Mar 97
Bakker, Robert T. Aug 95
Baldessari, John Jun 91
Baldwin, Alec Jul 92
Baldwin, Hanson W. obit Jan 92
Ball, George W. obit Jul 94
Ball, Joseph H. obit Feb 94
Ball, William obit Oct 91
Balladur, Edouard Feb 94
Ballantine, Ian obit May 95
Bancroft, Ann Jul 2000
Banda, Hastings (Kamuzu) obit Feb 98
Banderas, Antonio Mar 97
Banderas, José Antonio Domínguez *see* Banderas, Antonio
Banfield, Edward C. obit Feb 2000
Banfield, Jillian Feb 2000
Banks, Dennis Jun 92
Banks, Russell Jan 92
Banville, John May 92
Bao Dai obit Oct 97
Barad, Jill E. Sep 95
Barak, Ehud Aug 97
Barber, Carl Jerome *see* Barber, Jerry
Barber, Jerry obit Nov 94
Barber, Red obit Jan 93
Barbour, Haley Nov 96
Barco Vargas, Virgilio obit Aug 97
Bardeen, John obit Apr 91
Bari, Joe *see* Bennett, Tony
Barker, Bob Nov 99
Barkley, Charles Oct 91
Barnes, Roy Jan 2000
Barnhart, Clarence L. obit Jan 94
Baron Franks of Headington *see* Franks, Oliver Shewell
Baron Wilson of Rievaulx *see* Wilson, Harold
Barr, Joseph W. obit May 96
Barr, William P. Jun 92
Barrault, Jean-Louis obit Mar 94
Barrett, Craig Mar 99
Barrett, William obit Nov 92
Barry, Dave May 98
Barry, John Mar 2000
Barry, Lynda Nov 94
Barrymore, Drew Oct 98
Barshefsky, Charlene Feb 2000
Bartoli, Cecilia Jun 92
Barton, Robert B. M. obit Apr 95
Bartz, Carol Jul 99
Barzin, Leon obit Aug 99
Baskin, Leonard obit Aug 2000
Bass, George Mar 2000
Bass, Lance *see* 'N Sync
Bassett, Angela May 96
Bates, Kathy Sep 91
Baudouin I, King of Belgium obit Oct 93
Baudrillard, Jean Jun 93
Bauer, Erwin A. Feb 93
Bauer, Gary L. Jan 99
Bauer, Peggy Feb 93
Baulieu, Etienne-Emile Nov 95
Baumgartner, Leona obit Mar 91
Bayh, Birch Evan, Jr. *see* Bayh, Evan
Bayh, Evan Nov 98
Bazelon, David L. obit Apr 93
Beam, Jacob D. obit Oct 93
Bean, Louis H. obit Oct 94
Bebey, Francis Apr 94
Beck, Bertram M. obit Sep 2000
Beck, Dave obit Feb 94
Becker, Gary S. Sep 93
Becker, Ralph E. obit Oct 94
Beckett, Wendy Jan 98
Beech, Olive Ann obit Sep 93
Beers, Charlotte Jun 98
Begaye, Kelsey Jan 2000
Begin, Menachem obit Apr 92
Bell, Art Apr 2000
Bell Burnell, Jocelyn May 95
Bell, David E. obit Yrbk 2000
Bell, Derrick A. Feb 93
Bell, Joshua Jul 2000
Bell, S. J. *see* Bell Burnell, Jocelyn
Bell, T. H. obit Sep 96
Bellamy, Carol Oct 99
Bellamy, Ralph obit Jan 92
Belli, Melvin M. obit Sep 96
Belluschi, Pietro obit Apr 94
Belushi, James Jan 95
Ben and Jerry *see* Cohen, Ben
Bender, James F(rederick) obit Mar 98
Benigni, Roberto Jun 99
Bennett, H. Stanley obit Oct 92
Bennett, John C. obit Jul 95
Bennett, Richard Rodney Mar 92
Bennett, Tony Jun 95
Bennett, Wallace F. obit Feb 94
Benson, Ezra Taft obit Aug 94
Bentsen, Lloyd Apr 93
Bérégovoy, Pierre Feb 93 obit Jul 93
Berendt, John Apr 98
Beresford, Bruce Mar 93
Berg, Elizabeth Nov 99
Berger, Samuel R. "Sandy" Feb 98
Bergonzi, Carlo Nov 92
Beriosova, Svetlana obit Feb 99
Berlin, Sir Isaiah obit Jan 98
Berlosconi, Silvio Aug 94
Berman, Chris Aug 98
Bernardin, Joseph L. obit Jan 97
Bernardino, Minerva obit Nov 98
Bernays, Edward L. obit May 95
Berry, Halle May 99
Berry, Mary Frances Jun 99
Berton, Pierre Oct 91
Bessmertnykh, Aleksandr A. Jun 91
Bestor, Arthur obit Feb 95
Bettman, Gary B. Mar 99
Bettmann, Otto L(udwig) obit Jul 98
Bezos, Jeff Jun 98
Bigart, Homer obit Jul 91
Bildt, Carl Jan 93

Binchy, Maeve Nov 95
Bing, Rudolf obit Nov 97
Bird, Rose E. obit May 2000
Birnbaum, Nathan *see* Burns, George
Bishop, André Jul 99
Bishop, Hazel obit Feb 99
Black, Cathleen P. Jan 98
Black, Clint Aug 94
Black, Conrad M. Aug 92
Black, Eugene R. obit Apr 92
Blackmun, Harry A. obit May 99
Blackwell, Earl, Jr. obit May 95
Blaese, R. Michael Mar 2000
Blair, Bonnie Jul 92
Blair, Tony Aug 96
Blakey, Art obit Jan 91
Blakey, Michael L. Sep 2000
Blanchett, Cate Aug 99
Blatnik, John A. obit Feb 92
Bliss, Anthony A. obit Nov 91
Blitch, Iris F. obit Oct 93
Block, Joseph L. obit Feb 93
Bloodworth-Thomason, Linda Feb 93
Bloom, Allan David obit Nov 92
Bloomberg, Michael Jun 96
Blough, Roy obit Sep 2000
Blue, Zachary *see* STINE, R. L.
Blume, Peter obit Jan 93
Bly, Robert Mar 93
Bochco, Steven May 91
Bogarde, Dirk obit Jul 99
Bogart, Anne Feb 99
Bohrod, Aaron obit Jun 92
Bok, Sissela Jan 96
Bokassa I, Emperor *see* Bokassa, Jean-Bedel
Bokassa, Jean-Bedel obit Jan 97
Bollea, Terry Gene *see* Hogan, Hulk
Bolling, Richard Walker obit Jul 91
Bolt, Robert obit Apr 95
Bolté, Charles G. obit May 94
Bolton, Michael Aug 93
Bombeck, Erma obit Jun 96
Bonds, Barry Jun 94
Bonham Carter, Helena Jan 98
Bonnell, John Sutherland obit Apr 92
Bono Mar 93
Bono, Sonny obit Mar 98
Bonsal, Philip Wilson obit Sep 95
Boosler, Elayne May 93
Booth, Shirley obit Jan 93
Borcherds, Richard Feb 99
Borge, Victor May 93
Boris III, King of Bulgaria obit Yrbk 91
Boros, Julius obit Aug 94
Borysenko, Joan Oct 96
Botstein, Leon Aug 96
Botvinnik, Mikhail obit Jul 95
Bouchard, Lucien Apr 99
Bouchles, Olympia Jean *see* Snowe, Olympia J.
Boulding, Kenneth E. obit May 93
Bourassa, Robert obit Jan 97
Bourguiba, Habib ben Ali obit Aug 2000
Bourne, St. Clair Jun 2000
Boutros-Ghali, Boutros Apr 92
Bovet, Daniele obit Jun 92
Bowden, Bobby Nov 96
Bowe, Riddick Jun 96
Bowers, Faubion obit May 2000
Bowie, David Nov 94
Bowles, Erskine Aug 98
Bowles, Paul obit Feb 2000
Bowman, Scotty Jan 99
Boxer, Barbara Apr 94
Boyer, Ernest L. obit Feb 96
Boyle, Kay obit Feb 93
Boyle, T. Coraghessan Jan 91
Bradbury, Norris E. obit Nov 97
Bradford, Barbara Taylor Oct 91
Bradley, Pat Feb 94
Bradley, Tom Oct 92 obit Jan 99
Bradshaw, John E. Apr 93
Brady, James S. Oct 91
Brady, Sarah Oct 96
Branagh, Kenneth Apr 97
Brandt, Willy obit Nov 92
Branson, Richard Feb 95
Bravo, Ellen Aug 97
Braxton, Toni Sep 2000
Brazelton, T. Berry Oct 93
Brazzi, Rossano obit Mar 95
Brennan, Peter J. obit Jan 97
Brennan, William J. obit Oct 97
Brenner, Charles H. Oct 2000
Bresson, Robert obit Jun 2000
Breuer, Lee Oct 99
Breyer, Stephen G. Jun 96
Bridges, Jeff Mar 91
Bridges, Lloyd obit May 98
Brill, Steven Nov 97
Brinkley, Christie Feb 94
Briscoe, Connie Jan 2000
Brittan, Leon Aug 94
Broad, William Michael Albert *see* Idol, Billy
Broder, Samuel Aug 92
Brodkey, Harold obit Apr 96
Brodsky, Joseph obit Apr 96
Bronfman, Edgar M., Jr. Oct 95
Brooks, Albert Apr 97
Brooks, Dede *see* Brooks, Diana D.
Brooks, Diana D. Jun 98
Brooks, Garth Mar 92
Brooks, Jack Jun 92
Brooks, James obit May 92
Brooks, James L. Apr 98
Brosnan, Pierce Jan 97
Brown, Bobby Apr 91
Brown, Edmund G. obit Apr 96
Brown, Helen Hayes *see* Hayes, Helen
Brown, James Mar 92
Brown, Jesse Nov 93
Brown, Larry Apr 96
Brown, Lester R. Jan 93
Brown, Newell obit Sep 2000
Brown, Pat *see* Brown, Edmund G.
Brown, Ron obit Jun 96
Brown, Tony Feb 97
Brown, Trisha Apr 97
Brown, Virginia Mae obit May 91
Brown, Willie Apr 97
Browne, Coral obit Jul 91
Brownell, Herbert, Jr. obit Aug 96
Brownell, Samuel Miller obit Jan 91
Browner, Carol M. May 94
Brownlow, Kevin Mar 92
Brubeck, Dave Apr 93
Bruckheimer, Jerry Mar 99
Bruton, John Nov 96
Buatta, Mario May 91
Bubka, Sergei Jul 96
Buchanan, Edna Sep 97
Buckley, Christopher Apr 97
Budge, Donald obit Jun 2000
Buffet, Bernard obit Feb 2000
Buffett, Jimmy Mar 99
Bukowski, Charles Apr 94 obit May 94
Bullock, Sandra Aug 97
Bundy, McGeorge obit Jan 97
Bunting, Mary I(ngraham) obit Apr 98
Bunting-Smith, Mary Ingraham *see* Bunting, Mary I.
Burbidge, E. Margaret Nov 2000
Burdett, Winston obit Jul 93
Burdick, Quentin N. obit Nov 92

Burger, Warren E. obit Aug 95
Burgess, Anthony obit Jan 94
Burke, Arleigh A. obit Aug 96
Burnett, Charles Sep 95
Burnett, Hallie Southgate obit Nov 91
Burney, Leroy E(dgar) obit Oct 98
Burns, George obit Nov 96
Burns, John L. obit Aug 96
Burns, Ken May 92
Burr, Raymond obit Nov 93
Burroughs, William S. obit Nov 97
Burton, Dan Sep 98
Burton, LeVar Mar 2000
Burton, Tim Jul 91
Buscaglia, (Felice) Leo(nardo) obit Aug 98
Buscemi, Steve Apr 99
Busch, Charles Jun 95
Bush, George W. Apr 97
Bush, Jeb Feb 99
Bush, John Ellis *see* Bush, Jeb
Bush, Kate Mar 95
Butcher, Susan Jun 91
Butler, John obit Nov 93
Butler, Robert N. Jan 97
Buttenwieser, Benjamin J. obit Mar 92
Butterfield, Roger Place obit Yrbk 91
Butts, Alfred M. obit Jun 93
Butts, Calvin O. Feb 99
Byatt, A. S. Sep 91
Byrd, Charlie obit Mar 2000
Byrne, Gabriel May 99
Byrne, John Oct 2000
Byroade, Henry A. obit Mar 94
Byron, Don Sep 2000

Cabot, Thomas D. obit Aug 95
Caccia, Harold Anthony obit Jan 91
Cadmus, Paul obit Mar 2000
Cage, John obit Sep 92
Cage, Nicolas Apr 94
Cahill, William T. obit Sep 96
Cahn, Sammy obit Mar 93
Calatrava, Santiago Aug 97
Calatrava Valls, Santiago *see* Calatrava, Santiago
Calderone, Mary S. obit Jan 99
Calkins, Robert D. obit Sep 92
Callahan, Harry M. obit Jul 99
Callahan, John Sep 98
Callender, John Hancock obit Jun 95
Calloway, Cab obit Jan 95
Calvin, Melvin obit Mar 97
Câmara, Helder Pessora obit Jan 2000
Camby, Marcus Jan 2000
Cameron, James Jan 98
Campanella, Roy obit Aug 93
Campbell, Bebe Moore Apr 2000
Campbell, Ben Nighthorse Oct 94
Campbell, Bill Jul 96
Campbell, Naomi Feb 97
Campbell, Neve Jan 2000
Campion, Jane Apr 94
Canady, Alexa Aug 2000
Candy, John obit May 94
Canetti, Elias obit Oct 94
Canseco, José Nov 91
Cantinflas obit Jun 93
Capra, Frank obit Oct 91
Caputo, Philip Apr 96
Caramanlis, Constantine obit Jul 98
Caramanlis, Constantinos *see* Caramanlis, Constantine
Cardoso, Fernando Henrique Oct 96
Carey, Drew Mar 98
Carey, George Aug 91
Carey, Mariah Jul 92
Carey, Ron May 92
Carlson, William S. obit Jul 94
Carmack, John Mar 2000
Carmichael, Stokely obit Feb 99
Carnegie, Dorothy obit Jan 99
Carnovsky, Morris Jan 91
Carpenter, Mary Chapin Feb 94
Carr, William G. obit May 96
Carradine, Keith Aug 91
Carrey, Jim Feb 96
Carroll, James May 97
Carroll, Jim Oct 95
Carroll, Joseph F. obit Mar 91
Carruth, Hayden Apr 92
Carsey, Marcy Jan 97
Carson, Benjamin S., Sr. May 97
Carstens, Karl obit Aug 92
Carter, Betty obit Jan 99
Carter, James Feb 97
Carter, Nick *see* Backstreet Boys
Carter, Rubin May 2000
Carter, Stephen L. Jul 97
Cartland, Barbara obit Aug 2000
Carusi, Ugo obit Sep 94
Carvey, Dana Jun 92
Carville, James Mar 93
Case, Steve Oct 96
Casey, Bernie Jul 99
Cash, Rosanne Oct 91
Cashin, Bonnie obit Jun 2000
Cassidy, Claudia obit Oct 96
Castelli, Leo obit Jan 2000
Cates, Gilbert Mar 97
Catlett, Elizabeth May 98
Caulfield, Joan obit Aug 91
Cavaco Silva, Aníbal Mar 91
Cavalli-Sforza, Luigi Luca Aug 97
Cédras, Raoul Jul 95
Celebrezze, Anthony J. obit Jan 99
Cerf, Vinton G. Sep 98
Chadli, Bendjedid Apr 91
Chadwick, Florence obit May 95
Chafee, John H. obit Jan 2000
Chaikin, Sol C. obit Jun 91
Chailly, Riccardo Jun 91
Chalk, O. Roy obit Feb 96
Chamberlain, John Rensselaer obit Jun 95
Chamberlain, Wilt obit Jan 2000
Champion, George obit Jan 98
Chan, Jackie Nov 97
Chan, Kong Sun *see* Chan, Jackie
Chancellor, John obit Sep 96
Chandler, A. B. obit Aug 91
Chandler, Dorothy Buffum obit Sep 97
Chandrasekhar, Subrahmanyan obit Oct 95
Chaney, John Mar 99
Chang, Michael Jul 97
Channing, Stockard Apr 91
Chapman, Leonard F. Jr. obit Sep 2000
Chappell, Tom May 94
Charles, Ray Jun 92
Chasez, JC *see* 'N Sync
Chast, Roz Jul 97
Chavez, Cesar obit Jun 93
Chávez, Hugo May 2000
Chávez, Julio César Apr 99
Chavez, Linda Nov 99
Chavez-Thompson, Linda Mar 2000
Chavis, Benjamin F. Jan 94
Cheadle, Don Sep 99
Chen, Joan Sep 99
Chen Shui-bian Sep 2000
Chenault, Kenneth I. Jun 98
Cheney, Lynne V. Oct 92
Cher Jun 91
Cherkassky, Shura obit Mar 96
Cherne, Leo M. obit Mar 99
Chernomyrdin, Viktor Aug 98
Cheshire, Leonard obit Sep 92
Chiang Ch'ing obit Jan 92

Chih-Yuan Yang *see* Yang, Jerry
Chihuly, Dale Aug 95
Chiles, Lawton obit Mar 99
Chiluba, Frederick May 92
Chin, Frank Mar 99
Ch'ing, Chiang *see* Chiang Ch'ing
Chirac, Jacques Apr 93
Cho, Margaret Oct 2000
Chomsky, Noam Aug 95
Chopra, Deepak Oct 95
Chouinard, Yvon Jun 98
Chow Yun-Fat May 98
Chrebet, Wayne Feb 99
Christie, William Jan 92
Christison, Alexander Frank Philip *see* Christison, Philip
Christison, Philip obit Feb 94
Christopher, George obit Yrbk 2000
Christopher, Warren M. Nov 95
Chuan Leekpai Nov 98
Chute, Marchette Gaylord obit Jul 94
Chwast, Seymour Sep 95
Çiller, Tansu Sep 94
Cisler, Walker obit Jan 95
Claiborne, Craig obit Apr 2000
Claiborne, Loretta Jul 96
Clampitt, Amy Feb 92 obit Nov 94
Clark, Eleanor obit Apr 96
Clark, Georgia Neese obit Feb 96
Clark, Helen Nov 2000
Clark, James H. Jun 97
Clark, Mary Higgins Jan 94
Clark, Wesley K. Jul 99
Clash, Kevin Jun 2000
Clavell, James obit Nov 94
Clayton, Eva McPherson Jun 2000
Claytor, W. Graham, Jr. obit Jul 94
Cleaver, (Leroy) Eldridge obit Jul 98
Cleveland, James obit Apr 91
Clifford, Clark obit Jan 99
Clinton, Bill Nov 94
Clinton, George Jul 93
Clinton, Hillary Rodham Nov 93
Clinton, William Jefferson *see* Clinton, Bill
Coburn, James Jun 99
Cochran, Johnnie L., Jr. Jun 99
Cocke, Erle, Jr. obit Sep 2000
Cocker, Jarvis Nov 98
Coe, Sue Aug 97
Coen, Ethan Sep 94
Coen, Joel Sep 94
Coggan, F. Donald obit Sep 2000
Cohen, Abby Joseph Jun 98
Cohen, Alexander H. obit Aug 2000
Cohen, Ben Apr 94
Cohen, Howard William *see* Cosell, Howard
Cohen, William S. Jan 98
Coker, Elizabeth Boatwright obit Nov 93
Colbert, Claudette obit Oct 96
Colbert, Lester L. obit Nov 95
Colby, William E. obit Jul 96
Cole, Johnnetta B. Aug 94
Cole, Natalie Nov 91
Coleman, J. P. obit Nov 91
Coleman, James S. obit Jun 95
Collins, Cardiss Feb 97
Collins, Francis S. Jun 94
Collins, Gail Mar 99
Collins, Jackie Jul 2000
Collins, John F. obit Feb 96
Collins, Leroy obit May 91
Collins, Susan May 2000
Colvin, Shawn Mar 99
Colwell, Rita R. May 99
Combs, Bert Thomas obit Feb 92
Combs, Sean "Puffy" Apr 98
Comer, James P. Aug 91
Comfort, Alex obit Aug 2000
Commager, Henry Steele obit May 98
Condon, Richard obit Jun 96
Cone, David Feb 98
Conerly, Charles obit Apr 96
Conerly, Chuck *see* Conerly, Charles
Congdon, William (Grosvenor) obit Jul 98
Conn, Billy obit Aug 93
Connally, John B. obit Aug 93
Connerly, Ward Nov 2000
Connery, Sean Jun 93
Conroy, Pat Jan 96
Conway, Jill Ker Jun 91
Coolio Aug 98
Cooper, Cynthia Aug 98
Cooper, John Sherman obit Apr 91
Cooper, Louise Field obit Jan 93
Coover, Robert Feb 91
Copland, Aaron obit Yrbk 91
Copperfield, David Jul 92
Coppola, Francis Ford Jul 91
Coppola, Nicholas *see* Cage, Nicholas
Corella, Angel Mar 99
Cornwell, Patricia May 97
Cosell, Howard obit Jul 95
Costas, Bob Jan 93
Cotten, Joseph obit Apr 94
Cotter, Audrey *see* Meadows, Audrey
Couples, Fred Jul 93
Couric, Katie Mar 93
Cousins, Margaret obit Oct 96
Cousins, Norman obit Jan 91
Cousteau, Jacques-Yves obit Sep 97
Couve de Murville, Maurice obit Jun 2000
Covey, Stephen R. Jan 98
Cox, Bobby Feb 98
Cox, Christopher Jul 99
Craig, George N. obit Feb 93
Crandall, Robert L. Nov 92
Crane, Eva Aug 93
Crawford, Cindy Aug 93
Crawford, Frederick C. obit Feb 95
Crawford, Michael Jan 92
Craxi, Bettino obit Jun 2000
Cream, Arnola Raymond *see* Walcott, Joe
Cresson, Edith Sep 91
Crichton, Michael Nov 93
Criss, Peter
Crocetti, Dino *see* Martin, Dean
Cromer, George Rowland Stanley Baring obit May 91
Cronenberg, David May 92
Cross, Amanda *see* Heilbrun, Carolyn G.
Cross, Burton M. obit Jan 99
Crouch, Stanley Mar 94
Crow, Sheryl May 98
Crowe, Cameron Mar 96
Crowe, Russell May 2000
Crumb, R. Apr 95
Cugat, Xavier obit Jan 91
Cullberg, Birgit obit Nov 99
Cummings, Robert obit Feb 91
Cunningham, Michael Jul 99
Cunningham, Randall Mar 91
Cuomo, Andrew M. Oct 98
Currie, Lauchlin Bernard obit Mar 94
Curry, John obit Jun 94
Curtin, Jane Jan 97
Curtis, Carl T. obit Jun 2000
Curtis, Jamie Lee Nov 98
Curtis, Thomas B. obit Mar 93
Cusack, Joan Jul 98
Cusack, John Jun 96
Cussler, Clive Nov 2000
Custin, Mildred obit Jun 97

Dabney, Virginius obit Mar 96

Daley, Richard M. Aug 92
Daley, William M. Mar 98
Dalrymple, Jean obit Feb 99
Daly, Chuck Apr 91
Daly, John obit May 91
Daly, Tyne Mar 92
Damadian, Raymond V. Jan 2000
Damon, Matt Mar 98
Danforth, John C. Jan 92
Daniel, Clifton obit Jul 2000
Danilova, Alexandra obit Sep 97
Danto, Arthur C. Apr 95
Darden, Christopher A. Feb 97
Darrow, Whitney, Jr. obit Oct 99
Daschle, Tom Oct 95
D'Aubuisson, Roberto obit Apr 92
Davenport, Marcia obit Mar 96
Davey, Jocelyn *see* Raphael, Chaim
David, Larry Aug 98
Davidson, Garrison Holt obit Feb 93
Davies, Dennis Russell May 93
Davies, Robertson obit Mar 96
Davies, Ronald N. obit Jun 96
Davis, Clive Jul 2000
Davis, Geena Oct 91
Davis, Gray Jun 99
Davis, Joseph Graham Jr. *see* Davis, Gray
Davis, Judy Nov 93
Davis, Martin S. obit Jan 2000
Davis, Miles obit Nov 91
Dawkins, Richard Aug 97
Day, J. Edward obit Jan 97
Day, Pat Oct 97
Dayan, Yaël Apr 97
De Creeft, José obit Yrbk 91
De Kooning, Willem obit May 97
De La Hoya, Oscar Jan 97
De La Torre, Lillian obit Nov 93
De Lima, Sigrid obit Feb 2000
De Mille, Agnes obit Jan 94
De Niro, Robert May 93
De Vries, Peter obit Jan 94
Dean, Patrick obit Jan 95
Debre, Michel obit Oct 96
Deconcini, Dennis Feb 92
Deer, Ada E. Sep 94
Dees, Morris S., Jr. Jan 95
Deford, Frank Aug 96
Degeneres, Ellen Apr 96
Dejong, Meindert obit Sep 91
Delacorte, George T. obit Jul 91
Delany, Annie Elizabeth *see* Delany, Bessie
Delany, Bessie Nov 95 obit Jan 96
Delany, Sadie Nov 95 obit Apr 99
DeLauro, Rosa Mar 2000
Delay, Tom May 99
Dell, Michael Jun 98
Dellums, Ronald V. Sep 93
Demikhov, Vladimir P. obit Feb 99
Deming, W. Edwards Sep 93 obit Mar 94
Dench, Judi Jan 99
Deng Xiaoping Jun 94 obit Apr 97
Dennehy, Brian Jul 91
Denning, Alfred Thompson obit Jun 99
Dennis, Felix Apr 2000
Dennis, Sandy obit May 92
Denver, John obit Jan 98
DePaola, Tomie Feb 99
Depp, Johnny May 91
Dern, Laura Oct 92
Derrida, Jacques Jul 93
Derthick, Lawrence Gridley obit Mar 93
Derwinski, Edward J. Aug 91
Desai, Morarji obit Jun 95
Devers, Gail Jul 96
Dewhurst, Colleen obit Oct 91
Dhaliwal, Daljit Nov 2000
Diana, Princess of Wales obit Nov 97
DiCaprio, Leonardo Mar 97
Dichter, Ernest obit Jan 92
Dickerson, Ernest Jul 2000
Dickerson, Nancy Hanschman obit Jan 98
Dickey, James obit Mar 97
Dickey, John Sloan obit Apr 91
Diebenkorn, Richard obit May 93
Dietrich, Marlene obit Jun 92
DiFranco, Ani Aug 97
Diggs, Charles C(ole), Jr. obit Nov 98
Dimaggio, Joe obit May 99
Disney, Anthea Jun 98
Dith Pran Oct 96
Dixie Chicks Jul 2000
Dixon, Jeane obit Mar 97
Dixon, Willie obit Apr 92
Djilas, Milovan obit Jul 95
Dobson, James C. Aug 98
Dodd, Martha obit Jan 91
Doi, Takako Jul 92
Dolbier, Maurice obit Jan 94
Dolci, Danilo (Bruno Pietro) obit Mar 98
Dole, Elizabeth Hanford Jan 97
Dominguín, Luis Miguel obit Jul 96
Donegan, Horace W. B. obit Jan 92
Donoso, José obit Feb 97
Donovan, Carrie Sep 99
Doolittle, James H. obit Jan 94
Dorough, Howie *see* Backstreet Boys
Dorris, Michael Mar 95 obit Jun 97
Douglas, Emily Taft obit Mar 94
Douglas, Marjory Stoneman obit Jul 98
Douglas-Home, Alexander Frederick *see* Home, Alexander Frederick Douglas-Home, 14th Earl of
Dove, Rita May 94
Dowd, Maureen Sep 96
Downey, Robert Jr. Aug 98
Downs, Robert B. obit Apr 91
Doyle, Roddy Oct 97
Dr. Seuss *see* Geisel, Theodor Seuss
Drabinsky, Garth Oct 97
Drake, Alfred obit Sep 92
Drapeau, Jean obit Oct 99
Draper, Paul obit Jan 97
Drescher, Fran Apr 98
Drexler, Clyde Jan 96
Drexler, Millard S. Jan 93
Dreyfus, Pierre obit Mar 95
Driskell, David C. Aug 2000
Druckman, Jacob obit Aug 96
Drysdale, Don obit Sep 93
Dublin, Louis Israel obit Yrbk 91
Dubridge, L. A. obit Mar 94
Duc Tho, Le *see* Le Duc Tho
Duggan, Ervin S. Oct 98
Dukakis, Olympia Jul 91
Duke, Angier Biddle obit Jul 95
Dulles, Eleanor Lansing obit Jan 97
Duncan, Michael Clarke Aug 2000
Duncan, Tim Nov 99
Duncan, Todd obit May 98
Dunn, Jennifer Mar 99
Dunne, Dominick May 99
Dunnock, Mildred obit Sep 91
Duras, Marguerite obit May 96
Durning, Charles Sep 97
Durocher, Leo obit Nov 91

Durrell, Gerald obit Apr 95
Durrell, Lawrence obit Jan 91
Dürrenmatt, Friedrich obit Apr 91
Dutton, Charles S. Oct 2000
Dutton, Charles S. Oct 2000
Duva, Lou Nov 99
Duval, David Oct 99
Dwinell, Lane obit Jun 97
Dworkin, Andrea Oct 94
Dyer-Bennet, Richard obit Feb 92
Dylan, Bob Oct 91
Dyson, Esther Aug 97
Dyson, Michael Eric Oct 97

Eagleburger, Lawrence S. Nov 92
Earle, Stephen Fain *see* Earle, Steve
Earle, Steve Oct 98
Earle, Sylvia A. May 92
Early, Gerald May 95
Ebbers, Bernard J. Feb 98
Ebersol, Dick Jul 96
Ebert, Roger Mar 97
Eccles, David obit May 99
Eccles, John C. obit Jul 97
Eckstine, Billy obit Apr 93
Edberg, Stefan Jan 94
Eddington, Arthur Stanley obit Yrbk 91
Edel, Leon obit Nov 97
Edelman, Gerald M. Apr 95
Edelman, Marian Wright Sep 92
Edmonds, Kenneth *see* Babyface
Edmonds, Walter D. obit May 98
Edwards, Douglas obit Jan 91
Edwards, Teresa Mar 98
Edwards, Vincent obit May 96
Egeberg, Roger O. obit Nov 97
Eggers, Dave Jul 2000
Egoyan, Atom May 94
Ehrenreich, Barbara Mar 95
Ehrlichman, John D. obit Apr 99
Einem, Gottfried Von obit Sep 96
Eisenman, Peter Oct 97
Eisenstaedt, Alfred obit Oct 95
Eisner, Thomas Mar 93
Eisner, Will Oct 94
Eklund, John M. obit Mar 97
Elders, Joycelyn Mar 94
Elion, Gertrude B. Mar 95 obit May 99
Eliot, Thomas H. obit Jan 92
Elizondo, Hector Jan 92
Elkin, Stanley obit Aug 95
Ellingson, Mark obit Apr 93
Ellis, Albert Jul 94
Ellis, Bret Easton Nov 94
Ellis, John Tracy obit Jan 93
Ellis, Ruth Sep 2000
Ellison, Lawrence J. Jan 98
Ellison, Ralph Jun 93 obit Jun 94
Ellroy, James Apr 98
Ellroy, Lee Earle *see* Ellroy, James
Ellsberg, Edward obit Yrbk 91
Elson, Edward L. R. obit Nov 93
Elytis, Odysseus obit Jun 96
Emanuel, Rahm Apr 98
Emmerich, Roland Nov 2000
Endara, Guillermo Feb 91
Engelbreit, Mary Oct 99
Engle, Paul obit May 91
English, Diane Jun 93
Enrique Tarancón, Vicente Cardinal obit Feb 95
Erikson, Erik H. obit Jul 94
Esiason, Boomer Nov 95
Esiason, Norman Julius *see* Esiason, Boomer
Espy, Mike Oct 93
Estefan, Gloria Oct 95
Estes, Richard Nov 95
Estrada, Joseph Feb 2000
Eszterhas, Joe Apr 98
Etheridge, Melissa May 95
Evans, Faith Feb 99
Evans, Janet Jul 96
Evans, Nancy Mar 2000
Evans, Poncé Cruse *see* Heloise
Evers-Williams, Myrlie Aug 95
Ewbank, Weeb obit Feb 99
Ewell, Tom obit Nov 94
Ewing, Patrick May 91
Exley, Frederick obit Aug 92
Exon, James Nov 96
Eyler, John Aug 2000
Eysenck, Hans J. obit Nov 97

Fadiman, Clifton obit Sep 99
Fagan, Garth Aug 98
Fairbank, John K. obit Nov 91
Fairbanks, Douglas Jr. obit Aug 2000
Faldo, Nick Sep 92
Fallows, James Nov 96
Faludi, Susan Feb 93
Fanfani, Amintore obit Mar 2000
Fanning, Shawn Sep 2000
Farmer, James obit Sep 99
Farrakhan, Louis Apr 92
Fasanella, Ralph obit Mar 98
Fascell, Dante B. obit Feb 99
Fassbaender, Brigitte Jun 94
Fassett, Kaffe Jun 95
Fast, Howard Apr 91
Fatone, Joey *see* 'N Sync
Faubus, Orval E. obit Feb 95
Favre, Brett Nov 96
Feifel, Herman Aug 94
Feingold, Russell D. Jul 98
Feininger, Andreas obit May 99
Feinstein, Dianne Aug 95
Feinstein, John Jul 98
Feldt, Gloria Jul 2000
Fellini, Federico obit Jan 94
Fenwick, Millicent obit Nov 92
Ferber, Herbert obit Oct 91
Ferlinghetti, Lawrence Jun 91
Ferré, Gianfranco Jul 91
Ferrer, José obit Mar 92
Fiennes, Ralph Sep 96
Figueiredo, João Baptista obit May 2000
Fili-Krushel, Patricia Nov 99
Filmus, Tully obit Jun 98
Filo, David Oct 97
Finch, Robert H. obit Jan 96
Fincher, David May 2000
Finkelstein, Arthur J. Nov 99
Finkelstein, Louis obit Jan 92
Finley, Charles O. obit Apr 96
Finley, Karen Sep 98
Fiorina, Carleton Jan 2000
Fireman, Paul Mar 92
Firkušny, Rudolf obit Sep 94
Fischbacher, Siegfried *see* Siegfried
Fischer, Bobby May 94
Fish, Hamilton obit Mar 91
Fishburne, Larry *see* Fishburne, Laurence
Fishburne, Laurence Aug 96
Fisher, Carrie Feb 91
Fisher, M. F. K. obit Aug 92
Fittipaldi, Emerson Apr 92
Fitzgerald, Ella obit Aug 96
Flair, Ric Mar 2000
Flanagan, Tommy Apr 95
Flansburgh, John Nov 99
Fleck, Béla Nov 96
Fleming, Renée May 97
Flemming, Arthur S. obit Nov 96
Fletcher, James obit Feb 92
Flood, Daniel J. obit Aug 94
Flynn, Raymond Oct 93
Flynt, Larry Sep 99
Folkman, Judah May 98
Fonda, Bridget Jan 94
Fonda, Pèter Mar 98
Fontana, Tom Aug 2000
Fonteyn, Margot obit Apr 91

Foote, Shelby Apr 91
Forbes, Steve May 96
Ford, Harold E. Jr. Nov 99
Ford, Richard Sep 95
Ford, Tennessee Ernie obit Jan 92
Ford, Tom May 98
Foreman, George Aug 95
Fornos, Werner H. Jul 93
Foster, Jodie Aug 92
Foster, John *see* Furcolo, Foster
Foster, Norman Sep 2000
Fowler, Henry H. obit May 2000
Fowler, William A. obit May 95
Foxx, Redd obit Jan 92
Frager, Malcolm obit Aug 91
Frahm, Herbert *see* Brandt, Willy
Frakes, Jonathan Jul 99
Francescatti, Zino obit Nov 91
Francis, Sam obit Jan 95
Frank, Anthony M. Aug 91
Frank, Barney Apr 95
Frank, Robert L. Aug 97
Frankel, Felice Apr 98
Franken, Al Jun 99
Frankl, Viktor E. Jul 97 obit Nov 97
Franklin, Aretha May 92
Franklin, Kirk Mar 2000
Franks, Oliver Shewell obit Jan 93
Franz, Dennis Jul 95
Fraser, Brad Jul 95
Frazier, Ian Aug 96
Freed, James I. Nov 94
Freeh, Louis J. May 96
Freeman, Morgan Feb 91
Frehley, Ace
French, Marilyn Sep 92
Friedman, Herbert obit Nov 2000
Friedman, Thomas L. Oct 95
Friendly, Fred W. obit May 98
Frisch, Max obit Jun 91
Frondizi, Arturo obit Jun 95
Fry, Stephen Sep 98
Frye, Northrop obit Mar 91
Fuchs, Joseph obit May 97
Fuchs, Michael J. Feb 96
Fuchs, Vivian E. obit Jan 2000
Fudge, Ann M. Jun 98
Fukuda, Takeo obit Sep 95
Fulani, Lenora Mar 2000
Fulbright, J. William obit Apr 95
Fulghum, Robert Jul 94
Fuller, Bonnie May 2000
Fuller, Kathryn S. Jan 94
Fuller, Millard Apr 95
Fuller, Samuel Aug 92 obit Jan 98
Funston, Keith obit Jul 92
Funt, Allen obit Nov 99
Furcolo, Foster obit Sep 95
Furness, Betty obit Jun 94

G, Kenny Nov 95
Gable, Dan Aug 97
Gabor, Eva obit Sep 95
Gaddis, William obit Mar 99
Gaines, Ernest J. Mar 94
Galassi, Jonathan Sep 99
Galdikas, Biruté M. F. Mar 95
Galliano, John Oct 96
Gandhi, Rajiv obit Jul 91
Gandhi, Sonia May 98
Gandolfini, James Feb 2000
Garbus, Martin Nov 2000
Garcia, Cristina Aug 99
Garcia, Jerry obit Oct 95
Garciaparra, Nomar Jun 2000
Gardiner, John Eliot Aug 91
Gardner, Howard Oct 98
Gardner, Martin Sep 99
Garnett, Kevin Sep 98
Garrison, Lloyd K. obit Nov 91
Garson, Greer obit Jun 96
Garvey, Jane F. Sep 2000
Gary, John obit Mar 98
Gary, Raymond obit Feb 94
Garzarelli, Elaine Sep 95
Gassman, Vittorio obit Oct 2000
Gaston, Cito Apr 93
Gates, Bill May 91
Gates, Henry Louis Oct 92
Gates, Robert M. Apr 92
Gates, William H. *see* Gates, Bill
Gaultier, Jean-Paul Jan 99
Gautier, Felisa Rincón De obit Nov 94
Gaver, Mary Virginia obit Mar 92
Gavrilov, Andrei Oct 2000
Gazzaniga, Michael S. Apr 99
Gebrselassie, Haile Jul 99
Geffen, David Jan 92
Geisel, Ernesto obit Nov 96
Geisel, Theodor Seuss obit Nov 91
Geldzahler, Henry obit Oct 94
Gell-Mann, Murray Oct 98
Geller, Margaret J. Jun 97
Gellhorn, Walter obit Feb 96
Geneen, Harold S(ydney) obit Jan 98
George, Elizabeth Mar 2000
George, Zelma W. obit Sep 94
Gergen, David Feb 94
Gergiev, Valery Jan 98
Gerstacker, Carl A. obit Jul 95
Gerstner, Louis V. Jun 91
Gerulaitis, Vitas obit Nov 94
Getz, Stan obit Aug 91
Ghezali, Salima May 98
Gibbs, Joe Apr 92
Gibbs, Lois Sep 99
Giddens, Anthony Apr 98
Gielgud, John obit Aug 2000
Gifford, Francis Newton *see* Gifford, Frank
Gifford, Frank Jan 95
Gifford, Kathie Lee Nov 94
Gigli, Romeo Aug 98
Gilbert, Martin Feb 91
Gilbert, Walter Nov 92
Gilchrist, Brad
Gilchrist, Guy Jan 99
Gillespie, Dizzy Jan 93 obit Feb 93
Gillespie, John Birks *see* Gillespie, Dizzy
Gilligan, Carol May 97
Gilpatric, Roswell L. obit May 96
Gilruth, Robert R. obit Yrbk 2000
Ginsberg, Allen obit Jun 97
Ginsberg, Mitchell I. obit May 96
Ginsburg, Ruth Bader Feb 94
Ginzburg, Natalia obit Nov 91
Gish, Lillian obit Apr 93
Gjesdal, Cornelia *see* Knutson, Coya
Gleason, Thomas W. obit Mar 93
Glenn, John H., Jr. Jan 99
Glennan, T. Keith obit Jun 95
Glennie, Evelyn Jul 97
Glover, Danny Apr 92
Glover, Savion Mar 96
Gobel, George obit Apr 91
Godard, Jean-Luc Oct 93
Godden, Margaret Rumer *see* Godden, Rumer
Godden, Rumer obit Jan 99
Godunov, Alexander obit Jul 95
Godwin, Gail Oct 95
Goebbels, Joseph obit Yrbk 91
Goetz, Delia obit Sep 96
Goizueta, Roberto C. Aug 96 obit Jan 98
Goldblum, Jeff Jul 97
Goldenson, Leonard H. obit May 2000
Goldin, Daniel S. Jun 93
Golding, William obit Aug 93
Goldman, William Jan 95

Goldsmith, Sir James obit Oct 97
Goldsworthy, Andy Oct 2000
Goldwater, Barry M(orris) obit Aug 98
Gong Li May 97
Gonzales, Pancho obit Sep 95
Gonzales, Richard *see* Gonzales, Pancho
Gonzalez, Henry B. Feb 93
Goodall, Jane Nov 91
Goodman, Andrew obit Jun 93
Goodrich, Marcus obit Jan 92
Goodson, Mark obit Feb 93
Goodwin, Doris Kearns Nov 97
Gorbachev, Raisa obit Nov 99
Gordon, David Jun 94
Gordon, Jeff Aug 2000
Gore, Albert obit Feb 99
Gore, Mary Elizabeth Aitcheson *see* Gore, Tipper
Gore, Tipper Oct 2000
Górecki, Henryk May 94
Gorelick, Kenny *see* G, Kenny
Goren, Charles H. obit Jul 91
Gorey, Edward obit Aug 2000
Gorton, Slade Aug 93
Gossett, William T(homas) obit Oct 98
Gott, J. Richard III Oct 99
Gould, Laurence M. obit Aug 95
Gould, Morton obit May 96
Gould, Samuel B. obit Sep 97
Grace, J. Peter, Jr. obit Jun 95
Grade, Lew obit Mar 99
Grafton, Samuel obit Feb 98
Grafton, Sue Sep 95
Graham, Donald E. May 98
Graham, John obit Apr 91
Graham, Jorie May 97
Graham, Martha obit May 91
Graham, Virginia obit Mar 99
Graham, Wallace H. obit Mar 96
Grammer, Kelsey May 96
Granato, Cammi Apr 98
Granato, Catherine Michelle *see* Granato, Cammi
Grandin, Temple Jul 94
Grant, Hugh Sep 95
Grappelli, Stéphane obit Feb 98
Graves, Earl G. Aug 97
Graves, Nancy obit Jan 96
Gray, Frizzell *see* Mfume, Kweisi
Gray, Georgia Neese Clark *see* Clark, Georgia Neese
Gray, Macy May 2000
Gréco, Juliette Jan 92
Green, Al Feb 96
Green, Julian obit Oct 98
Green, Julien *see* Green, Julian
Green, Tim Aug 2000
Greenaway, Peter Feb 91
Greenberg, Hank *see* Greenberg, Maurice R.
Greenberg, Maurice R. Nov 2000
Greene, Balcomb obit Jan 91
Greene, Bob Jul 95
Greene, Brian Aug 2000
Greene, Graham obit May 91
Greene, Harold H. obit May 2000
Greenfield, Jerry Apr 94
Gregory, J. Dennis *see* Williams, John A.
Grès, Mme. (Alix) obit Feb 95
Greuter, Helen Wright *see* Wright, Helen
Grier, Pam Feb 98
Griffey, Ken, Jr. Aug 96
Griffith, Ernest S. obit Apr 97
Griffith Joyner, Florence obit Nov 98
Griffith, Nanci Feb 98
Grimond, Jo obit Jan 94
Grisham, John Sep 93
Griswold, Erwin N. obit Jan 95
Grizodubova, Valentina S. obit Jul 93
Grodin, Charles Nov 95
Gronouski, John A. obit Mar 96
Gross, Chaim obit Jul 91
Gross, Ernest A. obit Jul 99
Gross, Hiam *see* Gross, Chaim
Grosz, Karoly obit Mar 96
Grotowski, Jerzy obit Mar 99
Grove, Andrew S. Mar 98
Gubaidulina, Sofia Oct 99
Guccione, Bob Aug 94
Guccione, Kathy Keeton *see* Keeton, Kathy
Guillaume, Robert Apr 2000
Guinan, Matthew obit May 95
Guinness, Alec obit Oct 2000
Gulick, Luther Halsey obit Mar 93
Gumbel, Greg Sep 96
Guterson, David Nov 96
Guthrie, A. B., Jr. obit Jul 91
Guy, Buddy Feb 2000
Guzy, Carol Feb 2000
Gwynn, Tony Oct 96

Haack, Robert W. obit Aug 92
Habib, Philip Charles obit Jul 92
Habibie, B. J. *see* Habibie, Bacharuddin Jusuf
Habibie, Bacharuddin Jusuf Oct 98
Hackett, Albert obit May 95
Hadley, Jerry Nov 91
Hafstad, Lawrence R. obit Jan 94
Hahn, Emily obit Apr 97
Hair, Jay D. Nov 93
Haldeman, Bob *see* Haldeman, H. R.
Haldeman, H. R. obit Jan 94
Hale, Clara obit Feb 93
Haley, Alex obit Mar 92
Hall, Conrad L. Aug 2000
Hall, Edward T. Feb 92
Hallinan, Vincent obit Nov 92
Halsey, Margaret obit Apr 97
Hamed, Naseem *see* Hamed, Prince Naseem
Hamed, Nazeem *see* Hamed, Prince Naseem
Hamed, Nazim *see* Hamed, Prince Naseem
Hamed, Prince Naseem Oct 98
Hamer, Dean H. Jun 97
Hamill, Pete Feb 98
Hamilton, Charles obit Feb 97
Hamm, Mia Sep 99
Hammer, Armand obit Feb 91
Hammer, M. C. Apr 91
Hampson, Thomas Mar 91
Hannah, John A. obit Apr 91
Hanschman, Nancy *see* Dickerson, Nancy Hanschman
Hansen, Harry obit Yrbk 91
Hansen, James E. May 96
Hanson, Duane obit Mar 96
Harberger, John Pico *see* John, John Pico
Harbison, John Feb 93
Hardaway, Tim Jul 98
Hardy, Porter, Jr. obit Jun 95
Hare, Raymond A. obit May 94
Hargrove, Roy Apr 2000
Häring, Bernard obit Sep 98
Harkin, Tom Jan 92
Harnoncourt, Nikolaus Jan 91
Harrelson, Woody Jan 97
Harrington, David Nov 98
Harris, E. Lynn Jun 96
Harris, Emmylou Oct 94
Harris, Harwell Hamilton obit Jan 91
Harris, Judith Rich Apr 99
Harrison, Jim Jul 92
Harrison, Joan obit Oct 94
Harron, Mary Sep 2000

Harsch, Joseph C(lose) obit Aug 98
Hart, Mickey Jan 94
Hartley, Hal Aug 95
Hartwell, Lee *see* Hartwell, Leland H.
Hartwell, Leland H. Nov 99
Harvard, Beverly Sep 97
Hasek, Dominik May 98
Haseltine, William A. Nov 98
Hashimoto, Ryutaro Feb 98
Haskell, Molly Nov 98
Hassan II obit Oct 99
Hastert, Dennis Apr 99
Hastert, John Dennis *see* Hastert, Dennis
Hatcher, Harlan obit May 98
Hatta, Mohammad obit Yrbk 91
Hauser, Philip M. obit Feb 95
Havel, Václav Aug 95
Hawass, Zahi Apr 2000
Hawes, Elizabeth obit Yrbk 91
Hawk, Tony Jun 2000
Hawke, Ethan May 98
Hawkins, Erick obit Feb 95
Hawkins, Erskine obit Jan 94
Hayakawa, S. I. obit Apr 92
Haycraft, Howard obit Jan 92
Hayek, Friedrich A. Von obit May 92
Hayes, Denis Oct 97
Hayes, Helen obit May 93
Hayes, Peter Lind obit Jul 98
Hazzard, Shirley Jan 91
Healy, Bernadine P. Nov 92
Healy, Timothy S. Jan 93 obit Feb 93
Hearst, William Randolph, Jr. obit Jul 93
Heche, Anne Sep 98
Heckerling, Amy Jul 99
Heckscher, August obit Jun 97
Heilbrun, Carolyn G. Jan 93
Heinrichs, April May 2000
Heinz, John obit May 91
Helfgott, David Mar 97
Heliker, John obit Jul 2000
Heller, Joseph obit Mar 2000
Helmsley, Harry B. obit Mar 97
Heloise Jun 96
Helprin, Mark Aug 91
Hemingway, Margaux obit Sep 96
Henderson, Joe Jun 96
Henner, Marilu Feb 99
Henning, Doug obit Apr 2000
Henreid, Paul obit Jun 92
Henry, David D. obit Nov 95
Henry, Marguerite obit Feb 98
Hensel, H. Struve obit Jul 91
Hepburn, Audrey obit Mar 93
Heppner, Ben Jan 97
Herbert, Bob Oct 98
Herlihy, James Leo obit Jan 94
Herman, Alexis M. Jan 98
Hernández, Livan Mar 98
Hernandez, Orlando Apr 2000
Herrera, Carolina Mar 96
Herrera, Paloma Apr 2000
Hersey, John obit May 93
Hershey, Alfred D. obit Aug 97
Herskovitz, Marshall Sep 2000
Herzberg, Gerhard obit Jul 99
Herzog, Chaim obit Jun 97
Hetfield, James Jan 2000
Heyns, Roger W. obit Nov 95
Hiaasen, Carl Apr 97
Hickam, Homer H. Jr. Oct 2000
Hickey, Margaret A. obit Feb 95
Highsmith, Patricia obit Apr 95
Higinbotham, William A. obit Jan 95
Hilfiger, Tommy Apr 96
Hill, Anita Sep 95
Hill, Benny obit Jun 92
Hill, Julia "Butterfly" Apr 2000
Hillerman, Tony Jan 92
Hilliard, Harriet *see* Nelson, Harriet
Hillings, Patrick J. obit Sep 94
Hillis, Danny *see* Hillis W. Daniel
Hillis, Margaret (Eleanor) obit Apr 98
Hillis, W. Daniel Feb 95
Hills, Carla A. Mar 93
Hines, John Elbridge obit Oct 97
Hingson, Robert A. obit Jan 97
Hirt, Al obit Jul 99
Hiss, Alger obit Jan 97
Hitch, Charles J. obit Nov 95
Hitchens, Christopher Mar 99
Ho, David D. Jun 97
Hoad, Lew obit Sep 94
Hobby, Oveta Culp obit Oct 95
Hoch, Danny Oct 99
Hockenberry, John Oct 96
Hodgkin, Howard May 91
Hoegh, Leo A. obit Yrbk 2000
Hoffa, James P. Jul 99
Hoffman, Alice Sep 92
Hoffman, Dustin Jan 96
Hofstadter, Robert obit Jan 91
Hogan, Ben obit Oct 97
Hogan, Hulk Nov 98
Hoge, James F., Jr. Apr 98
Holbrooke, Richard C. Oct 98
Holifield, Chet obit Apr 95
Holland, Agnieszka Jan 98
Hollander, John Sep 91
Holley, Robert W. obit Apr 93
Holm, Hanya obit Jan 93
Holmgren, Mike Oct 2000
Holyfield, Evander Aug 93
Home, Alexander Frederick Douglas-Home, 14th Earl of obit Jan 96
Honecker, Erich obit Jul 94
Hooker, John Lee Nov 92
Hooks, Bell Apr 95
Hopkins, Anthony Mar 97
Horgan, Paul obit May 95
Hormel, James Oct 99
Horn, Roy Uwe Ludwig *see* Roy
Horner, James Mar 97
Horner, John R. Sep 92
Horst Jun 92 obit Mar 2000
Horton, Mildred McAfee *see* McAfee, Mildred H.
Hosokawa, Morihiro May 94
Hou Hsiao-hsien Jul 99
Houphouët-Boigny, Félix Jul 91 obit Feb 94
Hovhaness, Alan obit Oct 2000
Howard, John Mar 99
Howard, Ron Aug 95
Howe, Irving obit Jul 93
Howell, Wallace E. obit Sep 99
Howorth, Lucy Somerville obit Nov 97
Hrawi, Elias Feb 92
Hrdy, Sarah Blaffer Jun 2000
Hruska, Roman Lee obit Jul 99
Hsiao-ping, Teng *see* Deng Xiaoping
Huddleston, (Ernest Urban) Trevor obit Jul 98
Hudlin, Reginald
Hudlin, Warrington May 99
Hudson, Charles L. obit Nov 92
Hudson, Jeffery *see* Crichton, Michael
Huebner, Robert J(oseph) obit Nov 98
Huerta, Dolores Nov 97
Huffington, Arianna Stassinopoulos Jul 98
Huggins, Charles B. obit Mar 97
Hughes, Cathy Feb 2000

Hughes, Edward James *see* Hughes, Ted
Hughes, Harold E. obit Jan 97
Hughes, John Sep 91
Hughes, Richard J. obit Feb 93
Hughes, Ted obit Jan 99
Hughley, D.L. Mar 2000
Huizenga, H. Wayne Jan 95
Hull, Brett Feb 92
Humphry, Derek Mar 95
Hunt, Helen Nov 96
Hunt, James B., Jr. Jun 93
Hunt, John obit Jan 99
Hunter, Catfish obit Nov 99
Hunter, Holly Jul 94
Hunter, Jim *see* Hunter, Catfish
Hunter, Ross obit May 96
Husak, Gustav obit Jan 92
Hussein, King of Jordan obit Apr 99
Husseini, Faisal al- Jan 98
Hutchison, Kay Bailey Sep 97
Hutton, Lauren Jul 94
Hynde, Chrissie Apr 93

Ice Cube Aug 95
Ice-T Sep 94
Idei, Nobuyuki Mar 97
Idol, Billy Jan 94
Iglesias, Enrique Apr 99
Il Sung, Kim *see* Kim Il Sung
Iman Jun 95
Imus, Don Feb 96
Indigo Girls *see* Ray, Amy, and Saliers, Emily
Ingalls, Jeremy obit Jul 2000
Ingalls, Mildred Dodge Jeremy *see* Ingalls, Jeremy obit
Ionesco, Eugène obit Jun 94
Ireland, Patricia Jun 92
Irvan, Ernie Jul 98
Irwin, Margaret obit Yrbk 91
Irwin, Robert Jan 93
Irwin, Steve Aug 2000
Isaacs, Susan Oct 93
Isaak, Chris May 93
Itami, Juzo obit Mar 98
Ives, Burl obit Jun 95
Ivey, Artis *see* Coolio
Ivey, John E., Jr. obit Aug 92
Ivey, Judith Jun 93
Ivins, Molly Jun 2000
Izetbegović, Alija Aug 93

Jabbar, Kareem Abdul *see* Abdul-Jabbar, Kareem
Jack, Homer A. obit Oct 93
Jackson, Bo Jun 91
Jackson, Janet Jun 91
Jackson, Jesse L., Jr. May 98
Jackson, Joe Feb 96
Jackson, O'Shea *see* Ice Cube
Jackson, Phil Jul 92
Jackson, Samuel L. Nov 96
Jackson, Shirley Ann Jul 99
Jacobs, Amos *see* Thomas, Danny
Jacobs, Marc Feb 98
Jacobson, Leon obit Feb 93
Jaffe, Harold W. Sep 92
Jaffe, Susan Sep 97
Jagan, Cheddi obit May 97
Jagr, Jaromir Apr 97
Jakobovits, Immanuel obit Feb 2000
Jamali, Mohd F. obit Aug 97
Janeway, Eliot obit Apr 93
Jansen, Dan Sep 94
Jarreau, Al Oct 92
Järvi, Neeme Nov 93
Jay, Ricky May 94
Jayewardene, J. R. obit Jan 97
Jefferson, Margo L. Jun 99
Jemison, Mae C. Jul 93
Jenkins, Lew obit Yrbk 91
Jerusalem, Siegfried Sep 92
Jett, Joan Sep 93
Jiang Qing *see* Chiang Ch'ing
Jiang Qing obit Jan 92
Jiang Zemin May 95
Jillette, Penn *see* Penn & Teller
Jingsheng, Wei *see* Wei Jingsheng
Jobim, Antonio Carlos Jul 91 obit Feb 95
Jobs, Steven Sep 98
John, John Pico obit Sep 93
John Paul II Mar 2000
Johnson, Bernice *see* Reagon, Bernice Johnson
Johnson, Betsey Jan 94
Johnson, Beverly Sep 94
Johnson, Charles Sep 91
Johnson, Clarence L. obit Mar 91
Johnson, Davey Sep 99
Johnson, Dwayne "The Rock" Jul 2000
Johnson, Frank M. obit Oct 99
Johnson, Jimmy Jul 94
Johnson, Joseph E. obit Jan 91
Johnson, Kathie Lee *see* Gifford, Kathie Lee
Johnson, Keyshawn Oct 99
Johnson, Marguerite Annie *see* Angelou, Maya
Johnson, Michael Jul 96
Johnson, Paul Sep 94
Johnson, Philip C. Nov 91
Johnson, Randy Sep 2000
Johnson, Robert L. Apr 94
Johnson, U. Alexis obit Jun 97
Johnston, Lynn Feb 98
Jolie, Angelina Oct 2000
Jones, Bill T. Jul 93
Jones, Cherry May 98
Jones, Chuck May 96
Jones, David Robert *see* Bowie, David
Jones, George Feb 95
Jones, James Earl Nov 94
Jones, Jerry May 96
Jones, Kimberly Denise *see* Lil' Kim
Jones, Marion Oct 98
Jones, Roger W. obit Aug 93
Jones, Roy Jr. Feb 99
Jones, Sam Houston obit Yrbk 91
Jones, Tommy Lee Oct 95
Jong, Erica Apr 97
Jonsson, John Erik obit Nov 95
Jordan, Barbara C. Apr 93 obit Apr 96
Jordan, I. King Jan 91
Jordan, Michael Feb 97
Jordan, Michael H. Feb 98
Jordan, Neil Aug 93
Jordan, Vernon E., Jr. Aug 93
Joseph, Keith obit Feb 95
Joseph, Lord *see* Joseph, Keith
Jospin, Lionel Robert Jun 2000
Joxe, Louis obit Jun 91
Juan Carlos, Count of Barcelona obit Jun 93
Judd, Ashley Feb 2000
Judd, Walter H. obit Apr 94
Judd, Wynonna *see* Wynonna
Judge Judy *see* Sheindlin, Judith
Judge, Mike May 97
Julia, Raul obit Jan 95
Julia y Araelay, Raul Rafael Carlos *see* Julia, Raul
Jung, Andrea May 2000

Kabakov, Ilya Apr 98
Kadare, Ismail Feb 92
Kaganovich, Lazar M. obit Sep 91
Kahane, Meir obit Jan 91
Kahn, Madeline obit Mar 2000
Kahn, Roger Jun 2000
Kamali, Norma Nov 98
Kaminski, Janusz Mar 2000
Kamprad, Ingvar Jun 98
Kanin, Garson obit Jun 99
Kanter, Rosabeth Moss Jun 96

Kantor, Michael *see* Kantor, Mickey
Kantor, Mickey Mar 94
Kaplan, Joseph obit Nov 91
Kaplan, Justin Jul 93
Kappel, Frederick R. obit Jan 95
Kapuściński, Ryszard Sep 92
Karadžić, Radovan Oct 95
Karamanlis, Constantine *see* Caramanlis, Constantine
Karamanlis, Konstantine *see* Caramanlis, Constantine
Karmal, Babrak obit Feb 97
Karmazin, Mel May 2000
Karolyi, Bela Oct 96
Karp, David obit Feb 2000
Kasdan, Lawrence May 92
Kasem, Casey Nov 97
Kasich, John R. Aug 98
Katchor, Ben May 2000
Katsh, Abraham I(saac) obit Oct 98
Katz, Lillian Vernon *see* Vernon, Lillian
Katz, Milton obit Oct 95
Katzen, Mollie Oct 96
Katzenberg, Jeffrey May 95
Kaufman, Irving R. obit Apr 92
Kavner, Julie Oct 92
Kazin, Alfred obit Aug 98
Kearns, Doris *see* Goodwin, Doris Kearns
Keating, Paul May 92
Keaton, Diane May 96
Keaton, Michael Jun 92
Keeler, Ruby obit Apr 93
Keen, Sam Feb 95
Keenan, Mike Mar 96
Keene, Christopher obit Jan 96
Keeton, Kathy Sep 93 obit Jan 98
Keitel, Harvey Mar 94
Kell, Joseph *see* Burgess, Anthony
Keller, Kasey Nov 98
Kelley, Clarence M. obit Nov 97
Kelley, David E. May 98
Kelley, Kitty Apr 92
Kelly, Edna F(lannery) obit Feb 98
Kelly, Eugene Curran *see* Kelly, Gene
Kelly, Gene obit Apr 96
Kelly, Jim Nov 92
Kelly, Nancy obit Mar 95
Kelly, Petra obit Jan 93
Kelly, R. Jun 99
Kelly, Robert *see* Kelly, R.
Kelly, Sharon Pratt Nov 92
Kemeny, John G. obit Feb 93
Kemmis, Daniel Oct 96
Kempner, Robert M. W. obit Oct 93
Kempton, Murray obit Jul 97
Kendrew, John C. obit Nov 97
Kennedy, Claudia J. Jan 2000
Kennedy, David M. obit Jul 96
Kennedy, Jacqueline *see* Onassis, Jacqueline Bouvier Kennedy
Kennedy, John F., Jr. Jan 96 obit Sep 99
Kennedy, Nigel Jul 92
Kennedy, Paul Oct 93
Kennedy, Rose obit May 95
Kenny G *see* G, Kenny
Kerkorian, Kirk Mar 96
Kerr, Steve Oct 98
Kerr, Walter obit Jan 97
Kerrey, Bob Feb 91
Kerst, Donald William obit Oct 93
Kessler, David A. Sep 91
Kevorkian, Jack Sep 94
Khan, Chaka Jul 99
Khan, Michelle *see* Yeoh, Michelle
Khatami, Mohammad Apr 98
Khatami, Seyyed Mohammad *see* Khatami, Mohammad
Kiarostami, Abbas Jul 98
Kidman, Nicole Mar 97
Kienholz, Edward obit Aug 94
Kieślowski, Krzysztof May 95 obit May 96
Kiley, Richard obit May 99
Killanin, Michael Morris, 3d Baron obit Jul 99
Kilmer, Val Jan 96
Kim Il Sung Yrbk 94 obit Sep 94
Kim Jong Il Oct 99
Kim Sung Ju *see* Kim Il Sung
Kim Young Sam Jun 95
Kimball, Lindsley F. obit Oct 92
Kincaid, Jamaica Mar 91
King Hussein *see* Hussein, King of Jordan
King, John W. obit Nov 96
King, Mary-Claire Feb 95
Kingman, Dong obit Yrbk 2000
Kingsley, Sidney obit May 95
Kingsolver, Barbara Jul 94
Kinkade, Thomas Jun 2000
Kinsley, Michael May 95
Kintner, Earl W. obit Mar 92
Kirbo, Charles H. obit Nov 96
Kirby, George obit Jan 96
Kirby, Robert E. obit Mar 99
Kiriyenko, Sergei Aug 98
Kirk, Grayson L(ouis) obit Jan 98
Kirk, Russell obit Jun 94
Kirkland, Lane obit Oct 99
Kirkpatrick, Chris *see* 'N Sync
Kirkpatrick Miles W(ells) obit Jul 98
Kirshner, Sidney *see* Kingseley, Sydney
Kirstein, Lincoln obit Mar 96
Kirsten, Dorothy obit Jan 93
Kissin, Evgeny Nov 97
Kissin, Yevgeny *see* Kissin, Evgeny
Kistler, Darci Oct 91
Kitano, Takeshi Jul 98
Klass, Perri May 99
Klaus, Václav Nov 97
Kleiber, Carlos Jul 91
Kleindienst, Richard G. obit Jun 2000
Kleitman, Nathaniel obit Jan 2000
Klopsteg, Paul E. obit Jul 91
Kluge, John Sep 93
Knight, Frances G. obit Nov 99
Knight, Philip H. Aug 97
Knipling, E. F. obit Yrbk 2000
Knopfler, Mark Apr 95
Knudsen, Semon E(mil) obit Sep 98
Knussen, Oliver Feb 94
Knutson, Coya obit Jan 97
Koch, Bill Mar 99
Koch, Fred Jr. obit Yrbk 2000
Koch, William I. *see* Koch, Bill
Kohler, Foy D. obit Mar 91
Kollek, Teddy Mar 93
Komando, Kim Sep 2000
Komarovsky, Mirra obit Apr 99
Koogle, Tim Apr 2000
Koolhaas, Rem Nov 2000
Kopal, Zdeněk obit Aug 93
Kopple, Barbara Jul 98
Kors, Michael Jan 2000
Korth, Fred obit Jan 99
Koscow, Sophia *see* Sidney, Sylvia
Kosinski, Jerzy obit Jul 91
Kotto, Yaphet Mar 95
Kouchner, Bernard Aug 93
Kozyrev, Andrei V. Sep 92
Krainik, Ardis Nov 91 obit Mar 97
Krall, Diana Jun 2000
Kramer, Larry Mar 94
Kraus, Alfredo obit Nov 99
Krauss, Alison May 97

Kravchuk, Leonid M. Jan 93
Kravitz, Lenny Apr 96
Krenek, Ernst obit Feb 92
Krick, Irving P. obit Sep 96
Kristol, William May 97
Kroft, Steve Nov 96
Krol, John Cardinal obit May 96
Kroll, Jules B. Feb 99
Kruger, Barbara Jul 95
Krzyzewski, Mike Jan 97
Kubelik, Rafael obit Oct 96
Kubly, Herbert obit Oct 96
Kubrick, Stanley obit May 99
Kuchel, Thomas H. obit Feb 95
Kuchma, Leonid Oct 97
Kudelka, James Mar 95
Kuhn, Irene obit Mar 96
Kuhn, Maggie obit Jul 95
Kukoc, Toni Jul 97
Kumaratunga, Chandrika Bandaranaike Jan 96
Kumm, Henry W. obit Mar 91
Kunstler, William M. obit Nov 95
Kuok, Hock Nien *see* Kuok, Robert
Kuok, Robert Jun 98
Kuok, Robert Hock Nien *see* Kuok, Robert
Kuralt, Charles obit Sep 97
Kureishi, Hanif Feb 92
Kurosawa, Akira Jul 91 obit Nov 98
Kurtz, Efrem obit Sep 95
Kusch, Polykarp obit May 93
Kushner, Harold S. Apr 97

L.L. Cool J Nov 97
Lagardère, Jean-luc Aug 93
Lagasse, Emeril May 99
Lake, Anthony Oct 94
Lalanne, Jack Oct 94
Lall, Anand *see* Lall, Arthur S.
Lall, Arthur S. obit Jan 99
Lamb, Brian Feb 95
Lamont, Corliss obit Jul 95
Lamont, Norman Aug 92
Lancaster, Burt obit Jan 95
Land, Edwin H. obit May 91
Landon, Margaret obit Feb 94
Landon, Michael obit Sep 91
Landrum, Phil M. obit Jan 91
Landry, Tom obit Apr 2000
Lane, Burton obit Mar 97
Lane, Nathan Aug 96
Lang, David Feb 2000
Lang, Helmut Apr 97
Lang, K. D. Sep 92
Lange, John *see* Crichton, Michael
Lanier, Jaron Jun 97
Lansky, Aaron Jan 97
Lanting, Frans Nov 95
Lanusse, Alejandro Agustin obit Nov 96
Lapiere, Cherilyn *see* Cher
Largent, Steve Jun 99
Larson, Arthur obit May 93
Larson, Gary Feb 91
Lasch, Christopher obit Apr 94
Lasker, Mary obit May 94
Lasseter, John Jun 97
Latifah, Queen *see* Queen Latifah
Laughlin, James obit Jan 98
Lautenberg, Frank Jan 91
Lawrence, Geoffrey obit Yrbk 91
Lawrence, Jacob obit Aug 2000
Lawrence, Martin Oct 99
Laxness, Halldór (Kiljan) obit Apr 98
Laybourne, Geraldine Apr 99
Layton, Joe obit Jul 94
Lazarus, Rochelle *see* Lazarus, Shelly
Lazarus, Shelly May 97
Le Duc Tho obit Jan 91
Le Gallienne, Eva obit Aug 91
Leach, Penelope Aug 94
Leakey, Mary obit Feb 97
Leakey, Richard Oct 95
Lean, David obit Jun 91
Lear, Frances Apr 91 obit Jan 97
Leary, Timothy obit Aug 96
Lecompte, Elizabeth Aug 97
Lee, Ang Mar 97
Lee, Henry C. Aug 96
Lee, J. Bracken obit Jan 97
Lee Kuan Yew Jan 95
Lee, Martin Jul 97
Lee, Robert E. obit Jun 93
Lee, Stan Aug 93
Lee Teng-hui Mar 96
Leese, Oliver obit Yrbk 91
Lefebvre, Marcel obit May 91
Léger, Paul-Émile obit Jan 92
Leguizamo, John Apr 98
Lehmann-Haupt, Hellmut E. obit May 92
Leiber, Judith Sep 96
Leibovitz, Annie Oct 91
Leigh, Douglas obit May 2000
Leigh, Jennifer Jason Aug 92
Leigh, Mike Jun 94
Leigh, W. Colston obit Sep 92
Leighton, Robert B. obit May 97
Leinsdorf, Erich obit Nov 93
Lemon, Ralph Feb 97
L'Engle, Madeleine Jan 97
Lenroot, Katharine F. obit Yrbk 91
Leonard, Bill obit Feb 95
Leonard, William A. *see* Leonard, Bill
Leone, Lucile Petry *see* Petry, Lucile obit
Leonid Danilovich Kuchma *see* Kuchma, Leonid
Leontief, Wassily obit Apr 99
Lepage, Robert Apr 95
Lerman, Liz Nov 2000
Lerner, Gerda Feb 98
Lerner, Max obit Aug 92
Leslie, Lisa Jan 98
Lessing, Doris Jan 95
Levay, Simon Oct 96
Levertov, Denise Aug 91 obit Mar 98
Levi, Edward H. obit Jul 2000
Levin, Ira Aug 91
Levitt, William J. obit Mar 94
Lévy, Bernard-Henri Nov 93
Levy, David Mar 98
Levy, David H. Jan 95
Levy, Marv Feb 98
Lewis, Carl Yrbk 96
Lewis, Claudius *see* Lewis, Lennox
Lewis, Henry obit Apr 96
Lewis, Juliette Feb 96
Lewis, Lennox Jan 99
Lewis, Loida Nicolas Apr 97
Lewis, Ramsey Oct 96
Lewis, Richard Jul 93
Lewis, Shari obit Oct 98
Leyland, Jim Nov 98
Li, Gong *see* Gong Li
Liberman, Alexander obit Mar 2000
Lichtman, Joseph *see* Layton, Joe
Lieberman, Joseph I. Jul 94
Lieberman, Rolf obit Mar 99
Lil' Kim Oct 2000
Lillehei, C. Walton obit Nov 99
Lima, Ronaldo Luiz Nazario da *see* Ronaldo
Liman, Arthur L. obit Oct 97
Limann, Hilla obit Apr 98
Limbaugh, Rush Mar 93
Lin, Maya Apr 93
Lindfors, Viveca obit Jan 96
Lindgren, Astrid Oct 96
Lindley, Ernest K. obit Yrbk 91
Lindros, Eric Apr 98
Lindt, Auguste R. obit Yrbk 2000
Link, O. Winston Jun 95
Linnell, John Nov 99

Lionni, Leo Sep 97 obit Feb 2000
Liotta, Ray May 94
Lipinski, Tara Apr 98
Lipsky, Eleazar obit Apr 93
Lithgow, John Nov 96
Litton, Andrew Sep 98
Littrell, Brian *see* Backstreet Boys
Lively, Penelope Apr 94
Livingston, John W. obit Aug 97
Lleras Restrepo, Carlos obit Nov 94
Loach, Ken Jul 95
Lobo, Rebecca Sep 97
Loeb, James I. obit Mar 92
Loftus, Elizabeth F. Jan 99
Logan, Harlan obit Mar 95
Logue, Edward J. obit Jun 2000
Long, Richard Sep 95
Long, Tania obit Jun 99
Longbaugh, Harry *see* Goldman, William
Lopez, Barry Jul 95
Lorentz, Pare obit May 92
Lortel, Lucille obit Jul 99
Lott, Ronnie Feb 94
Lott, Trent Sep 96
Lou, Liza Jan 2000
Louchheim, Katie obit Apr 91
Louis-Dreyfus, Julia Oct 95
Lovano, Joe Mar 98
Love, Courtney Jun 96
Love, George H. obit Sep 91
Love, Susan M. Oct 94
Lovelock, James Nov 92
Lovett, Lyle Sep 97
Lovins, Amory B. Jun 97
Lowe, Jack obit Aug 96
Lowe, Rob Jul 2000
Lowey, Nita M. Sep 97
Loy, Myrna obit Feb 94
Lubic, Ruth Watson Sep 96
Lubovitch, Lar Mar 92
Lucas, Craig Sep 91
Lucas, John Oct 95
Luckman, Charles obit Apr 99
Ludwig, Daniel Keith obit Oct 92
Lukas, J. Anthony obit Aug 97
Lupino, Ida obit Oct 95
Luria, S. E. obit Apr 91
Lutoslawski, Witold Aug 91 obit Apr 94
Lutz, Robert A. Jan 94
Luzhkov, Yuri Nov 99
Lydon, John Nov 96
Lynch, John obit Feb 2000
Lynch, Peter Nov 94
Lyne, Adrian Jan 94
Lynes, Russell obit Nov 91

Maathai, Wangari Sep 93
Macapagal, Diosdado obit Jul 97
MacArthur, Douglas, 2d obit Jan 98
MacDowell, Andie Nov 99
Machel, Graça Simbine Oct 97
MacIver, Loren obit Aug 98
MacKenzie, Warren Sep 94
MacKinnon, Catharine A. Jun 94
Mackintosh, Cameron Mar 91
MacLachlan, Kyle Aug 93
MacLennan, Hugh obit Jan 91
MacMurray, Fred obit Feb 92
Maddux, Greg Feb 96
Madigan, Edward R. Nov 92 obit Feb 95
Magaziner, Ira C. Apr 95
Maggiolo, Walter A. obit Yrbk 2000
Maglie, Sal obit Feb 93
Maher, Bill Jul 97
Mahoney, John Aug 99
Maines, Natalie *see* Dixie Chicks
Major, John Apr 97
Makins, Roger obit Jan 97
Malick, Terrence Jun 99
Malle, Louis obit Feb 96
Mallory, L. D. obit Sep 94
Malone, John C. Aug 95
Malone, Karl Jan 93
Malott, Deane W. obit Nov 96
Mamet, David Mar 98
Mancini, Henry obit Aug 94
Mandela, Nelson Nov 95
Manessier, Alfred obit Oct 93
Mangione, Jerre obit Nov 98
Mankiewicz, Joseph L. obit Apr 93
Mankowitz, (Cyril) Wolf obit Aug 98
Manley, Michael obit May 97
Mann, Erica *see* Jong, Erica
Mann, Michael Jan 93
Mann, Thomas C. obit Apr 99
Manning, Ernest obit May 96
Manning, Peyton Sep 98
Manson, Marilyn May 99
Mantle, Mickey obit Oct 95
Manzù, Giacomo obit Mar 91
Marais, Jean obit Jan 99
Marble, Alice obit Mar 91
Marca-Relli, Conrad obit Nov 2000
Marchais, Georges (René Louis) obit Jan 98
Marcus, Greil Oct 99
Marcus, Jacob R. obit Jan 96
Margulis, Lynn Jul 92
Mark, Herman F. obit Jun 92
Mark, Mary Ellen Sep 99
Mark, Rebecca May 99
Marker-Kraus, Laurie *see* Marker, Laurie
Marker, Laurie Feb 2000
Markey, Edward J. Nov 97
Markovic, Ante Nov 91
Marland, Sidney P., Jr. obit Jul 92
Marriott, Alice Lee obit May 92
Marrow, Tracy *see* Ice-T
Marsalis, Branford Sep 91
Marsalis, Ellis Aug 2000
Marshak, Robert E. obit Feb 93
Marshall, Barry J. Sep 96
Marshall, David obit Feb 96
Marshall, E. G. obit Nov 98
Marshall, Garry Nov 92
Marshall, Lois obit May 97
Marshall, Penny May 92
Marshall, Susan Jul 99
Marshall, Thurgood obit Mar 93
Martin, Christy Oct 97
Martin, Dean obit Mar 96
Martin, Edmund F. obit Mar 93
Martin, Mary obit Jan 91
Martin, Paul obit Nov 92
Martin, Ricky Sep 99
Martin, Steve Nov 2000
Martin, William McChesney, Jr. obit Oct 98
Mary Alice Nov 95
Mary Kay *see* Ash, Mary Kay
Masekela, Hugh Mar 93
Masina, Guilia Anna *see* Masina, Guilietta
Masina, Giulietta obit Jun 94
Masserman, Jules H. obit Jan 95
Massey, Walter E. Jun 97
Mastroianni, Marcello obit Feb 97
Matalin, Mary Sep 96
Mathis, Johnny Feb 93
Matlin, Marlee May 92
Matola, Sharon Jun 93
Matsui, Robert T. Oct 94
Matthau, Walter obit Sep 2000
Matthews, T. S. obit Mar 91
Mature, Victor obit Oct 99
Matzinger, Polly Oct 98
Maura, Carmen Apr 92
Maurer, Ion Gheorghe obit Jul 2000
Mauriac, Claude Sep 93 obit Jun 99

Maw, Herbert B. obit Jan 91
Maxwell, Robert obit Feb 92
Maxwell, Vera obit Mar 95
Maxwell, William obit Oct 2000
May, John L. Jan 91 obit Jun 94
May, Rollo obit Jan 95
Mayer, Jean obit Feb 93
Mayle, Peter Oct 92
Maynard, Joyce Jan 99
Maynard, Robert C. obit Oct 93
Maynor, Dorothy obit May 96
Mazen, Abu *see* Abbas, Mahmoud
Mbeki, Thabo Aug 98
McAfee, Mildred H. obit Jan 95
McAlary, Michael obit Mar 99
McBride, Christian Jan 2000
McCabe, Gibson obit Yrbk 2000
McCaffrey, Barry R. Jul 97
McCarthy, Carolyn Mar 98
McCarver, Tim May 2000
McClintock, Barbara obit Nov 92
McClinton, Katharine Morrison obit Mar 93
McCone, John A. obit Apr 91
McConnell, Joseph H. obit May 97
McCormick, Edward T. obit Oct 91
McCourt, Frank Feb 98
McCoy, Charles B. obit Mar 95
McCullough, David Jan 93
McCurry, Michael D. Nov 96
McDaniel, James Feb 2000
McDermott, Alice Sep 92
McDonagh, Martin Aug 98
McDonald, Audra Apr 99
McDonald, David L(amar) obit Mar 98
McDonald, Erroll Oct 99
McDonnell, Mary May 97
McDormand, Frances Sep 97
McDowall, Roddy obit Jan 99
McEntee, Gerald W. Oct 2000
McEntire, Reba Oct 94
McEwan, Ian Jul 93
McEwen, Terence A. obit Jan 99
McFarlane, Todd Feb 99
McGee, Gale obit Jun 92
McGill, William J(ames) obit Jan 98
McGinley, Laurence J. obit Oct 92
McGrath, Earl James obit Apr 93
McGwire, Mark Jul 98
McIntyre, Natalie *see* Gray, Macy
McIntyre, Thomas J. obit Oct 92
McKenzie, Kevin Jan 2000
McKenzie, Vashti Murphy Nov 2000
McKinney, Cynthia A. Aug 96
McKissick, Floyd B. obit Jun 91
McKneally, Martin B. obit Aug 92
McLaren, Malcolm Aug 97
McLaughlin, Leo obit Nov 96
McLean, A.J. *see* Backstreet Boys
McMahon, Vince Feb 99
McMillan, Edwin M. obit Nov 91
McMillan, Terry Feb 93
McMillen, Tom Jan 93
McMurrin, Sterling M. obit Jun 96
McNair, Sylvia Nov 97
McNealy, Scott Apr 96
McNeill, Don obit Aug 96
McNichols, Stephen L. R. obit Feb 98
McPherson, James Alan Sep 96
McRae, Carmen obit Jan 95
Meadows, Audrey obit Apr 96
Mečiar, Vladimír Jul 94
Meeker, Mary Aug 99
Meisner, Sanford Apr 91 obit Apr 97
Mellon, Paul obit Apr 99
Menchú, Rigoberta Oct 93
Mendenhall, Thomas Corwin 2nd obit Sep 98
Menuhin, Yehudi obit Jun 99
Merchant, Ismail Mar 93
Mercouri, Melina obit May 94
Meredith, Burgess obit Nov 97
Meriwether, John Mar 99
Merrick, David obit Jul 2000
Merrick, Elliott obit Jul 97
Merrill, James obit Apr 95
Messiaen, Olivier obit Jun 92
Messier, Mark Jul 95
Metheny, Pat May 96
Meyer, Ron Mar 97
Mfume, Kweisi Jan 96
Michaels, Lorne Aug 99
Michelman, Kate Nov 2000
Michener, Daniel Roland obit Nov 91
Michener, James A(lbert) obit Jan 98
Middlecoff, (Emmett) Cary obit Nov 98
Midler, Bette Nov 97
Mifune, Toshiro obit Mar 98
Mikhalkov, Nikita Oct 95
Milchan, Arnon Oct 2000
Millar, Margaret obit Jun 94
Miller, Bebe Apr 99
Miller, Glenn obit Yrbk 91
Miller, Nicole Mar 95
Miller, Reggie Mar 96
Miller, Roger obit Jan 93
Miller, Shannon Jul 96
Miller, Zell Jul 96
Millett, John D. obit Jan 94
Millett, Kate Jun 95
Mills, Wilbur D. obit Jul 92
Milstein, Nathan obit Feb 93
Minor, Halsey Oct 98
Mirabella, Grace Oct 91
Mirren, Helen Jul 95
Mitchell, Joan obit Jan 93
Mitchum, Robert obit Sep 97
Mitford, Jessica obit Oct 96
Mittermeier, Russell A. Oct 92
Mitterrand, François obit Mar 96
Miyake, Issey Nov 97
Miyazawa, Kiichi Feb 92
Mizrahi, Isaac Jan 91
Mnouchkine, Ariane Mar 93
Mobutu, Joseph Désiré *see* Mobutu Sese Seko
Mobutu Sese Seko May 97
Molinari, Susan Mar 96
Mollenhoff, Clark R. obit May 91
Mondavi, Robert Apr 99
Monk, Art Apr 95
Montagu, Ashley obit Mar 2000
Montana, Claude Jan 92
Montand, Yves obit Jan 92
Montenegro, Fernanda Oct 99
Montgomery, Deane obit May 92
Montoya, Carlos obit May 93
Moon, Warren Nov 91
Moore, Archie obit Feb 99
Moore, Brian obit Mar 99
Moore, Demi 1993
Moore, Garry obit Jan 94
Moore, George S. obit Yrbk 2000
Moore, Julianne Oct 98
Moore, Michael May 97
Moore, Michael C. Aug 97
Morfit, Thomas Garrison *see* Moore, Garry
Morgan, Edward P. obit Mar 93
Morgan, Henry obit Jul 94

Morgan, Lorrie Apr 99
Morgan, Thomas E. obit Oct 95
Morini, Erica obit Jan 96
Morissette, Alanis May 97
Morita, Akio obit Feb 2000
Morley, Robert obit Aug 92
Morricone, Ennio Oct 2000
Morris, Earl obit Jul 92
Morris, Willie obit Oct 99
Morris, Wright (Marion) obit Jul 98
Morrison, Van Sep 96
Morse, David A. obit Mar 91
Morse, True D(elbert) obit Sep 98
Mortier, Gérard Jul 91
Morton, Joe Feb 99
Mosbacher, Emil, Jr. obit Nov 97
Moschen, Michael Jul 2000
Mosconi, Willie obit Nov 93
Moscoso, Teodoro obit Aug 92
Moseley-Braun, Carol Jun 94
Mosley, Walter Sep 94
Moss, Cynthia May 93
Moss, John E(merson) obit Feb 98
Motherwell, Robert obit Sep 91
Mowrer, Lilian Thomson obit Jan 91
Mudd, Emily H(artshorne) obit Jul 98
Muggeridge, Malcolm obit Jan 91
Mukherjee, Bharati Apr 92
Muldoon, Robert D. obit Sep 92
Muldowney, Shirley Oct 97
Mulligan, Gerry obit Mar 96
Mullis, Kary B. Feb 96
Murakami, Haruki Sep 97
Murch, Walter Apr 2000
Murdoch, Iris obit Apr 99
Muren, Dennis Mar 97
Murphy, Franklin D. obit Aug 94
Murphy, George obit Jul 92
Murphy, Thomas F. obit Jan 96
Murphy, W. B. obit Aug 94
Murray, Albert May 94
Murray, Arthur obit May 91
Murray, Elizabeth Apr 95
Murray, Patty Aug 94
Muskie, Edmund S. obit Jun 96
Muster, Thomas May 97
Mutombo, Dikembe Feb 2000
Mwinyi, Ali Hassan Jun 95
Myers, Dee Dee Aug 94
Myers, Margaret Jane *see* Myers, Dee Dee
Myers, Mike Aug 97
Myers, Norman May 93
Myhrvold, Nathan Sep 97

'N Sync Nov 2000
Nabrit, James M(adison), Jr. obit Mar 98
Naifeh, Steven Mar 98
Nair, Mira Nov 93
Najibullah, Mohammed obit Jan 97
Narasimha Rao, P. V. *see* Rao, P. V. Narasimha
Naylor, Gloria Apr 93
Nazarbayev, Nursultan Oct 2000
Ndour, Youssou Jan 96
Nederlander, James Morton Apr 91
Neeson, Liam Nov 94
Neiman, Leroy Jul 96
Nelson, Harriet obit Jan 95
Nelson, Mrs. Ozzie *see* Nelson, Harriet
Nemerov, Howard obit Sep 91
Netanyahu, Benjamin Jun 96
Neuberger, Maurine B. obit Jul 2000
Neumeier, John Jul 91
Neuwirth, Bebe Nov 97
Newley, Anthony obit Jul 99
Newton, Christopher Feb 95
Newton, Helmut Nov 91
Niarchos, Stavros obit Jun 96
Nichols, Kenneth D. obit Sep 2000
Nichols, Mike Jan 92
Nicholson, Jack Apr 95
Nickerson, Albert L. obit Nov 94
Niederland, William G. obit Oct 93
Nikolais, Alwin obit Jul 93
Nixon, Patricia obit Aug 93
Nixon, Richard M. Yrbk 94 obit Jun 94
Nizer, Louis obit Jan 95
Nkomo, Joshua obit Sep 99
Noël Hume, Ivor Nov 97
Noble, Adrian Aug 99
Noor al-Hussein, Queen of Jordan Apr 91
Norodom Sihanouk *see* Sihanouk, Norodom
North, Oliver L. Mar 92
Norton, Edward Jun 2000
Novello, Antonia May 92
Novotna, Jarmila obit Apr 94
Nu, Thakin obit Apr 95
Nu, U *see* Nu, Thakin
Nur el Hussein *see* Noor al-Hussein
Nureyev, Rudolf obit Feb 93
Nuridsany, Claude Jun 97
Nutting, Anthony obit May 99
Nye, Bill Jul 98
Nye, Russel B. obit Nov 93
Nyerere, Julius K. obit Jan 2000

Oaksey, Geoffrey Lawrence *see* Lawrence, Geoffrey
Oates, Joyce Carol Jun 94
Obasanjo, Olusegun Jul 99
O'Brian, Patrick Jun 95 obit Mar 2000
O'Brien, Conan May 96
O'Brien, Dan Jul 96
O'Brien, Tim Aug 95
Obst, Lynda Oct 2000
Obuchi, Keizo May 99 obit Aug 2000
Ochoa, Severo obit Jan 94
O'Connor, John J. obit Jul 2000
O'Connor, Sinéad Jun 91
O'Donnell, Rosie Aug 95
O'Dwyer, (Peter) Paul obit Sep 98
Oe, Hikari May 99
Oe, Kenzaburo May 96
Oechsner, Frederick Cable obit Jun 92
Oettinger, Katherine Brownell obit Jan 98
O'Faoláin, Séan obit Jun 91
Ogata, Sadako Oct 97
Ogilvy, David M. obit Oct 99
Ohga, Norio Jun 98
Olajuwon, Hakeem Nov 93
Olav V, King of Norway obit Mar 91
Oldman, Gary Jan 96
O'Leary, Hazel R. Jan 94
Oliphant, Marcus L. obit Oct 2000
Oliphant, Pat Jul 91
Olmos, Edward James Aug 92
Onassis, Jacqueline Bouvier Kennedy obit Jul 94
Ondaatje, Michael Oct 93
O'Neal, Frederick obit Oct 92
O'Neal, Shaquille Jul 96
O'Neil, Thomas F(rancis) obit Jun 98
O'Neill, Francis A., Jr. obit Mar 92
O'Neill, Gerard K. obit Jun 92
O'Neill, Thomas P., Jr. obit Mar 94
O'Neill, Tip *see* O'Neill, Thomas P., Jr.

Ongania, Juan Carlos obit Aug 95
Oort, Jan Hendrik obit Jan 93
Oosterbaan, Bennie obit Jan 91
Oppenheimer, Harry Frederick obit Nov 2000
Ormond, Julia Mar 99
Ornish, Dean Apr 94
Orowitz, Eugene Maurice *see* Landon, Michael
Osborn, Robert C. obit Feb 95
Osborne, John obit Feb 95
Osborne, Tom Mar 98
Osbourne, Ozzy Nov 98
Osmond, Donny Feb 98
Osterberg, James Newell *see* Pop, Iggy
Otter, Anne Sofie Von Sep 95
Ouédraogo, Idrissa May 93
Ovitz, Michael S. Oct 95
Owens, Dana *see* Queen Latifah
Oz, Frank Oct 99
Özal, Turgut obit Jun 93
Ozawa, Seiji Jul 98
Oznowicz, Frank *see* Oz, Frank

Pacciardi, Randolfo obit Jul 91
Packard, David obit Jun 96
Packard, Vance obit Feb 97
Page, Irvine H. obit Aug 91
Page, Robert Morris obit Jul 92
Page, Ruth obit Jul 91
Pagels, Elaine Hiesey Feb 96
Paglia, Camille Aug 92
Paine, Thomas Otten obit Jul 92
Pais, Abraham Jan 94 obit Oct 2000
Pak, Se Ri Jan 99
Pakula, Alan J. obit Feb 99
Palance, Jack Aug 92
Paley, William S. obit Jan 91
Palin, Michael Feb 2000
Palmieri, Eddie Jun 92
Pandit, Vijaya Lakshmi obit Feb 91
Panetta, Leon E. Jun 93
Panic, Milan Jun 93
Pantani, Marco Feb 99
Papadopoulos, George obit Sep 99
Papandreou, Andreas obit Sep 96
Papp, Joseph obit Jan 92
Parcells, Bill Apr 91
Paretsky, Sara May 92
Parizeau, Jacques Jul 93
Park, Thomas obit Jun 92
Parker, Alan Mar 94
Parker, Frank obit Oct 97
Parker, Robert B. Nov 93
Parker, Sarah Jessica Sep 98
Parker, Trey May 98
Parkinson, C. Northcote obit May 93
Parks, Bert obit Apr 92
Parks, Gordon Oct 92
Parks, Suzan-Lori Apr 99
Parnis, Mollie obit Sep 92
Parr, Albert Eide obit Sep 91
Parrish, Mrs. Wayne William *see* Knight, Frances G.
Parry, Albert obit Jul 92
Pärt, Arvo Feb 95
Pastore, John O. obit Yrbk 2000
Pastrana Borrero, Misael obit Nov 97
Pataki, George E. Apr 96
Paterson, Chat obit May 92
Paterson, Katherine Nov 97
Patinkin, Mandy Jan 99
Patten, Chris Jul 93
Patterson, Francine Nov 2000
Patterson, P. J. Feb 95
Patterson, Penny *see* Patterson, Francine
Patterson, Percival J. *see* Patterson, P. J.
Patton, Frances Gray obit Sep 2000
Pauling, Linus C. Jun 94 obit Oct 94
Payne, Roger S. Jun 95
Payton, Nicholas Sep 99
Payton, Walter obit Jan 2000
Paz, Octavio obit Jul 98
Peabody, Endicott obit Feb 98
Peale, Norman Vincent obit Feb 94
Pearl, Minnie Nov 92 obit May 96
Peck, Gregory Oct 92
Peck, M. Scott Jun 91
Peña, Federico F. Oct 93
Penn & Teller Jun 2000
Penn, Sean Jun 93
Pennel, John obit Jan 94
Penney, William George obit May 91
Peppard, George obit Jul 94
Perelman, Ronald Owen Jan 91
Pérennou, Marie Jun 97
Peres, Shimon Mar 95
Perez, Rosie Sep 95
Perkins, Anthony obit Nov 92
Perkins, Dan *see* Tomorrow, Tom
Perkins, James A(lfred) obit Nov 98
Perot, H. Ross *see* Perot, Ross
Perot, Ross Yrbk 96
Perry, Anne Aug 96
Perry, Frank obit Nov 95
Perry, Harold R. obit Sep 91
Perry, William J. Jan 95
Pesci, Joe Mar 94
Peters, Tom Oct 94
Peterson, Esther (Eggertsen) obit Mar 98
Peterson, Roger Tory obit Oct 96
Petitpierre, Max obit Jun 94
Petronio, Stephen Mar 98
Petry, Ann obit Jul 97
Petry, Lucile obit Jun 2000
Petty, Tom Nov 91
Pfeiffer, Eckhard Jun 98
Pflimlin, Pierre obit Oct 2000
Pham Van Dong obit Sep 2000
Phan Dinh Khai *see* Le Duc Tho
Philbin, Regis Oct 94
Philbrick, Herbert A. obit Oct 93
Phillips, Caryl Jul 94
Phillips, Kevin Sep 94
Piazza, Mike Jul 99
Pickens, Jane obit Apr 92
Picon, Molly obit Jun 92
Piëch, Ferdinand Sep 99
Piercy, Marge Nov 94
Pile, Frederick Alfred obit Yrbk 91
Pileggi, Nicholas Jan 99
Pinay, Antoine obit Feb 95
Pindling, Lynden Oscar obit Yrbk 2000
Pineau, Christian obit Jun 95
P'ing, Lan *see* Chiang Ch'ing
Pinker, Steven A. Sep 98
Pinsky, Robert Feb 99
Piper, John obit Aug 92
Pipher, Mary Aug 99
Pippen, Scottie Mar 94
Pitino, Rick Jan 98
Pitt, Brad Mar 96
Pittman, Robert Jul 2000
Plain, Belva Feb 99
Plant, Robert Oct 98
Plavsic, Biljana Feb 98
Pleasence, Donald obit Apr 95
Pleven, René obit Mar 93
Plotkin, Mark J. Jun 97
Plowden, David Feb 96
Pogrebin, Letty Cottin Nov 97
Poitier, Sidney Sep 2000
Pol Pot obit Jun 98
Polese, Kim Jul 97
Ponnamperuma, Cyril obit Mar 95

Pop, Iggy Jan 95
Popcorn, Faith Feb 93
Pope John Paul II *see* John Paul II
Popović, Koča obit Jan 93
Popper, Karl Raimund obit Nov 94
Porter, Eliot obit Jan 91
Porter, Richard William obit Jan 97
Porter, Sylvia obit Aug 91
Posner, Richard A. Jan 93
Potter, Dennis Jul 94 obit Aug 94
Pousette-Dart, Richard obit Jan 93
Powell, Anthony obit Aug 2000
Powell, J. Enoch obit Jun 99
Powell, Lewis F(ranklin), Jr. obit Nov 98
Powell, Mike Oct 93
Powell, Sandy Jun 2000
Powers, J. F. obit Sep 99
Praeger, Frederick A. obit Aug 94
Pratt, Jane Jun 99
Prescott, Orville obit Jul 96
Preus, Jacob A. O. obit Oct 94
Prey, Hermann obit Oct 98
Price, Don K. obit Sep 95
Price, Nick Jun 96
Price, Richard Jan 94
Price, Vincent obit Jan 94
Primakov, Yevgeny Feb 99
Primus, Pearl obit Jan 95
Pritchett, V. S. obit Jun 97
Profet, Margie Nov 98
Protess, David Oct 99
Proulx, E. Annie Apr 95
Prusiner, Stanley Jun 97
Pucci, Emilio obit Jan 93
Puck, Wolfgang Jan 98
Puente, Ernest Anthony Jr. *see* Puente, Tito
Puente, Tito obit Aug 2000
Puff Daddy *see* Combs, Sean "Puffy"
Puffy *see* Combs, Sean "Puffy"
Purcell, Edward M. obit May 97
Puryear, Martin Aug 99
Putin, Vladimir Apr 2000
Puzo, Mario obit Sep 99

Qaddafi, Muammar Al- Mar 92
Qing, Jiang *see* Chiang Ch'ing
Quadros, Janio Da Silva obit Apr 92
Quaison-Sackey, Alex obit Feb 93
Queen Latifah Feb 97
Quennell, Peter obit Jan 94
Quesada, Elwood Richard obit Apr 93
Quindlen, Anna Apr 93
Quine, W. V. Nov 99
Quine, Willard van Orman *see* Quine, W. V.
Quintero, José obit May 99

Rabin, Yitzhak Jan 95 obit Jan 96
Rackmil, Milton R. obit Jan 92
Rae, Bob Feb 91
Raedler, Dorothy obit Feb 94
Rafael, Martos *see* Raphael
Rahman, Abdul, Prince obit Mar 91
Raines, Franklin D. Oct 2000
Rainey, Froelich G. obit Jan 93
Rains, Albert McKinley obit May 91
Rainwater, Richard Apr 99
Ramaphosa, Cyril Sep 95
Ramos, Fidel Mar 94
Rampal, Jean-Pierre obit Aug 2000
Rampersad, Arnold Sep 98
Ramphele, Mamphela Jul 97
Rampling, Anne *see* Rice, Anne
Randolph, Jennings obit Jul 98
Rankin, J. Lee obit Sep 96
Rankin, Karl Lott obit Apr 91
Rao, P. V. Narasimha Jan 92
Raphael Aug 91
Raphael, Chaim obit Jan 95
Raskin, A. H. obit Feb 94
Rauh, Joseph L., Jr. obit Nov 92
Raven, Peter H. Feb 94
Rawl, Lawrence G. Feb 92
Ray, Amy Aug 98
Ray, Dixy Lee obit Mar 94
Ray, Satyajit obit Jun 92
Raye, Martha obit Jan 95
Raymond, Lee Nov 99
Reagan, Ron Feb 92
Reagon, Bernice Johnson Aug 99
Reasoner, Harry obit Oct 91
Reddy, N. Sanjiva obit Aug 96
Redgrave, Steven Jan 2000
Redman, Joshua Jan 97
Redstone, Sumner Jan 96
Reed, Margie Yvonne *see* Raye, Martha
Reed, Ralph Mar 96
Rees, Mina S(piegel) obit Jan 98
Reese, Harold *see* Reese, Pee Wee
Reese, Pee Wee obit Oct 99
Reeves, Keanu May 95
Regan, Judith Sep 2000
Reggio, Godfrey Jul 95
Reich, Robert B. Apr 93
Reichmann, Paul Jan 91
Reichstein, Tadeus obit Oct 96
Reid, Kate obit May 93
Reinhard, Johan Aug 99
Reiser, Paul Apr 96
Remick, Lee obit Sep 91
Remnick, David Oct 98
Renaud, Madeleine obit Nov 94
Rendell, Ed Apr 98
Rendell, Ruth Apr 94
Reno, Janet Sep 93
Rentzel, Delos Wilson obit Jan 92
Reshevsky, Samuel obit Jul 92
Reston, James obit Feb 96
Revelle, Roger obit Sep 91
Rey, Fernando obit May 94
Reynolds, Albert Sep 94
Reynolds, Albert Pierce *see* Reynolds, Allie
Reynolds, Allie obit Mar 95
Reza, Yasmina Sep 98
Rhone, Sylvia Jun 98
Riad, Mahmoud obit Mar 92
Ribbs, Willy T. Nov 2000
Ribicoff, Abraham A. obit May 98
Rice, Anne Jul 91
Rice, Greg obit Aug 91
Rich, Frank Apr 99
Rich, Louise Dickinson obit Jul 91
Richard, Maurice obit Yrbk 2000
Richards, Ann Feb 91
Richards, Michael Nov 97
Richardson, Bill Apr 96
Richardson, Elliot L. obit Mar 2000
Richardson, Kevin *see* Backstreet Boys
Richardson, Miranda Feb 94
Richardson, Tony obit Feb 92
Richmond, Mitch Jun 99
Richter, Sviatoslav obit Oct 97
Ridgway, Matthew B. obit Sep 93
Rifkind, Simon H. obit Jan 96
Riggio, Leonard Jun 98
Riggs, Bobby obit Jan 96

Riggs, Robert Larimore *see* Riggs, Bobby
Riley, Richard W. Oct 93
Rimes, LeAnn May 98
Rincón de Gautier, Felisa *see* Gautier, Felisa Rincón de
Ringgold, Faith Feb 96
Riordan, Richard May 2000
Ripken, Cal, Jr. Jun 92
Ripley, Alexandra Mar 92
Ritchie, Dennis Mar 99
Ritt, Martin obit Feb 91
Ritter, Bruce obit Feb 2000
Rivkin, Dorothy Carnegie *see* Carnegie, Dorothy
Rizzo, Frank L. obit Sep 91
Robbins, Harold obit Jan 98
Robbins, Jerome obit Oct 98
Robbins, Tim Jul 94
Robbins, Tom Jun 93
Roberts, Cokie May 94
Roberts, Dennis J. obit Sep 94
Roberts, Julia May 91
Roberts, Marcus Mar 94
Robeson, Eslanda Goode obit Yrbk 91
Robinson, Arthur H. Mar 96
Robinson, David Jul 93
Robinson, Kim Stanley Nov 98
Robinson, Mary Apr 91
Robinson, Randall Sep 98
Robinson, Spottswood W. obit Jan 99
Robison, Emily *see* Dixie Chicks
Roddick, Anita Sep 92
Rodin, Judith Jun 99
Rodman, Dennis Sep 96
Rodriguez, Andrés Sep 91 obit Jun 97
Rodriguez, Cecilia May 99
Rodriguez, Eloy May 2000
Rodriguez, Robert Aug 96
Roebling, Mary G. obit Jan 95
Roeg, Nicolas Jan 96
Roehm, Carolyne Feb 92
Rogers, Ginger obit Jul 95
Rogers, Lynn L. Oct 94
Rogers, Roy obit Sep 98
Rogers, Will, Jr. obit Sep 93
Rollin, Betty Aug 94
Rolvaag, Karl F. obit Mar 91
Rome, Harold obit Jan 94
Romney, George obit Oct 95
Ronaldo Aug 98
Roosa, Robert V. obit Mar 94
Roosevelt, Anna C. Jun 97
Roosevelt, Elliott obit Jan 91
Roosevelt, James obit Nov 91
Root, Oren obit Mar 95
Roquelaure, A. N. *see* Rice, Anne
Ros-Lehtinen, Ileana Aug 2000
Rose, Charlie Jan 95
Rosen, Benjamin M. Jun 97
Rosen, Harold A. Jun 97
Rosenberg, Steven A. Feb 91
Rosenfield, Harry N. obit Aug 95
Rosenman, Dorothy obit Mar 91
Ross, Leonard Q. *see* Rosten, Leo
Rosten, Leo obit Apr 97
Rosten, Norman obit May 95
Rotblat, Joseph Jul 97
Roth, Ann Mar 97
Roth, Henry obit Jan 96
Roth, Philip May 91
Rothschild, Miriam Oct 92
Rotten, Johnny *see* Lydon, John
Roudebush, Richard L. obit Apr 95
Roueché, Berton obit Jul 94
Rountree, Martha obit Nov 99
Rountree, William M. obit Jan 96
Rourke, Mickey Oct 91
Rouse, James W. obit Jun 96
Rove, Karl Oct 2000
Rowan, Chad *see* Akebono
Rowland, John G. Oct 97
Rowley, James J. obit Jan 93
Rowling, J. K. Jan 2000
Rowse, A(lfred) L(eslie) obit Jan 98
Roy Jan 98
Roy, Patrick Nov 99
Royko, Mike Jun 94 obit Jul 97
Royster, Vermont C. obit Oct 96
Rozelle, Pete obit Feb 97
Rózsa, Miklós Feb 92 obit Oct 95
Rubin, Robert E. Jul 97
Rudolph, Paul obit Nov 97
Rudolph, Wilma obit Jan 95
Rugambwa, Laurian, Cardinal obit Feb 98
Rule, Ann Sep 2000
Runcie, Robert obit Oct 2000
Rush, Kenneth obit Feb 95
Rushing, Matthew Jul 2000
Rusk, Dean obit Feb 95
Russert, Tim Oct 97
Russo, Rene Jul 97
Ryan, Meg May 99
Ryan, Thelma Catherine *see* Nixon, Patricia
Ryder, Winona Jun 94
Rysanek, Leonie obit May 98
Sabatini, Gabriela Jun 92
Sabin, Albert B. obit Apr 93
Sachar, Abram Leon obit Sep 93
Sachs, Jeffrey D. Nov 93
Sadik, Nafis Feb 96
Sagan, Carl obit Feb 97
Sager, Ruth obit Jun 97
Salam, Abdus obit Jan 97
Salant, Richard S. obit Apr 93
Sales, Nykesha Jun 99
Saliers, Emily Aug 98
Salisbury, Harrison E. obit Sep 93
Salk, Jonas obit Aug 95
Salk, Lee obit Jul 92
Saloth Sar *see* Pol Pot
Salter, Andrew obit Jan 97
Saltzman, Charles E. obit Aug 94
Samaranch, Juan Antonio Feb 94
Sammartino, Peter obit May 92
Sampras, Pete May 94
Samuel, Sealhenry *see* Seal
Samuelson, Joan Aug 96
Sanborn, David Aug 92
Sánchez, Arantxa *see* Sánchez Vicario, Arantxa
Sánchez Vicario, Arantxa Aug 98
Sandage, Allan Jan 99
Sandberg, Ryne Nov 94
Sander, Jil Oct 97
Sanders, Barry Sep 93
Sanders, Bernard Jun 91
Sanders, Deion Jan 95
Sanders, Lawrence obit May 98
Sandler, Adam May 98
Sanford, (James) Terry obit Jul 98
Sanford, John Elroy *see* Foxx, Redd
Santolalla, Irene Silva De obit Sep 92
Santos, José Edwardo Dos May 94
Saralegui, Cristina Jan 99
Sarbanes, Paul S. Jan 97
Sargent, Francis W. obit Jan 99
Sarnoff, Robert W. obit May 97
Sarraute, Nathalie obit Jan 2000
Sarton, May obit Sep 95
Sassa, Scott Jan 2000
Sasser, James R. Jul 93
Sassoon, Vidal Apr 99
Satcher, David Feb 97
Sauer, George obit Apr 94

Sauvé, Jeanne obit Mar 93
Savalas, Aristoteles *see* Savalas, Telly
Savalas, Telly obit Mar 94
Sawhill, John C. obit Yrbk 2000
Sawyer, Eddie obit Jan 98
Sawyer, John E. obit Apr 95
Sayão, Bidú obit Jun 99
Saylor, Michael Sep 2000
Scali, John obit Jan 96
Scardino, Marjorie Apr 2000
Scelba, Mario obit Feb 92
Schaefer, George (Louis) obit Jan 98
Schaefer, Vincent J. obit Sep 93
Schama, Simon Nov 91
Schapiro, Meyer obit May 96
Schapiro, Miriam Aug 2000
Scheck, Barry Mar 98
Scheele, Leonard A. obit Mar 93
Scheffer, Victor B. Apr 94
Schell, Jonathan Jul 92
Scherbo, Vitaly *see* Shcherbo, Vitaly
Schiffrin, André Jan 2000
Schiller, Karl obit Mar 95
Schlessinger, Laura Sep 97
Schlink, Frederick John obit Mar 95
Schmoke, Kurt L. Feb 95
Schneerson, Menachem M. obit Aug 94
Schneider, Alexander obit Mar 93
Schnittke, Alfred Jul 92 obit Oct 98
Schoonmaker, Thelma Mar 97
Schoonmaker-Powell, Thelma *see* Schoonmaker, Thelma
Schopf, J. William May 95
Schott, Marge Aug 99
Schottland, Charles I. obit Sep 95
Schrempp, Juergen Oct 99
Schröder, Gerhard Nov 98
Schultes, Richard Evans Mar 95
Schultz, Howard M. May 97
Schultz, Richard D. Jul 96
Schulz, Charles M. obit Apr 2000
Schuman, William obit Apr 92
Schumann, Maurice obit Apr 98
Schumer, Charles E. Jul 95
Schwartz, Felice N. May 93 obit Apr 96
Schwarzenegger, Arnold Oct 91
Schwarzkopf, H. Norman May 91
Schwarzschild, Martin obit Jun 97
Schweitzer, Pierre-Paul obit Mar 94
Schwinger, Julian obit Sep 94
Scott, George C. obit Nov 99
Scott, Hugh obit Sep 94
Scott, Raymond obit May 94
Scott, Ridley Oct 91
Scribner, Fred C., Jr. obit Apr 94
Seaborg, Glenn T. obit May 99
Seal Feb 97
Sebrell, W. H., Jr. obit Nov 92
Sedaris, David Jul 97
Segal, Bernard G. obit Aug 97
Segal, George obit Sep 2000
Seibert, Florence B. obit Oct 91
Seid, Ruth *see* Sinclair, Jo
Seidel, Martie *see* Dixie Chicks
Seinfeld, Jerry Aug 92
Selden, David (Seeley) obit Aug 98
Seldes, George obit Sep 95
Seles, Monica Nov 92
Selig, Allan H. *see* Selig, Bud
Selig, Bud Jan 99
Selzer, Richard Apr 93
Sembène, Ousmane Apr 94
Semon, Waldo Lonsbury obit Aug 99
Sen, Binay Ranjan obit Aug 93
Senghor, Léopold Sédar Jul 94
Sengstacke, John H. obit Aug 97
Sereno, Paul C. Jun 97
Serkin, Rudolf obit Jul 91
Seton, Anya obit Jan 91
Sevareid, Eric obit Aug 92
Sevigny, Chloë Aug 2000
Shah, Idries obit Feb 97
Shaham, Gil Apr 97
Shalala, Donna Mar 91
Shalikashvili, John Nov 95
Shamir, Yitzhak Yrbk 96
Shanker, Albert obit May 97
Shannon, James A. obit Jul 94
Shapiro, Karl obit Aug 2000
Shapp, Milton J. obit Feb 95
Sharif, Mian Mohammad Nawaz *see* Sharif, Mohammad Nawaz
Sharif, Mohammad Nawaz Sep 98
Sharif, Nawaz *see* Sharif, Mohammad Nawaz
Sharpton, Al, Jr. Nov 95
Shaw, Bernard Feb 95
Shaw, Robert obit Apr 99
Shcherbo, Vitaly Jul 96
Shea, William A. obit Nov 91
Sheehy, Gail Jun 93
Sheindlin, Judith Sep 98
Shelby, Carroll Nov 93
Shelepin, Aleksandr obit Jan 95
Shelton, Henry H. Aug 98
Shelton, Hugh *see* Shelton, Henry H.
Shepard, Alan B(artlett) obit Sep 98
Shepherd, Jean obit Jan 2000
Sherrod, Robert obit May 94
Shevchenko, Arkady N(ikolayevich) obit May 98
Shilts, Randy Oct 93 obit May 94
Shipley, Jenny Mar 2000
Shirer, William L. obit Feb 94
Shirley, Donna Aug 98
Shoemaker, Eugene M. obit Oct 97
Shore, Dinah obit May 94
Short, Martin Sep 92
Shorter, Wayne Apr 96
Shortz, Will Apr 96
Shoup, Carl obit Sep 2000
Shriver, Eunice Kennedy Jul 96
Shriver, Maria Nov 91
Shu-meng, Luan *see* Chiang Ch'ing
Shulman, Irving obit Jun 95
Sidney, Sylvia obit Sep 99
Siebert, Mickie *see* Siebert, Muriel
Siebert, Muriel Aug 97
Siegel, Bernie S. Jun 93
Siegfried Jan 98
Sihanouk, Norodom Aug 93
Siles Zuazo, Hernán obit Oct 96
Simkin, William E. obit May 92
Simmons, Adele Smith May 91
Simmons, Gene Apr 99
Simmons, Russell Jun 98
Simmons, Ruth J. Jan 96
Simms, Hilda obit May 94
Simms, Phil Oct 94
Simon, Claude May 92
Simon, Norton obit Aug 93
Simon, William E. obit Aug 2000
Simons, Elwyn L. Jun 94
Simpson, Adele obit Oct 95
Simpson, Alan obit Jul 98
Simpson, Carole Nov 99

Simpson, Milward L. obit Aug 93
Simpson, Mona Feb 93
Simpson, Valerie Apr 97
Sin, Jaime L. Sep 95
Sinatra, Frank obit Jul 98
Sinbad Feb 97
Sinclair, April Sep 99
Sinclair, Jo obit Jun 95
Singer, Adam *see* Karp, David obit
Singer, Isaac Bashevis obit Sep 91
Singer, Peter Mar 91
Singh, Giani Zail *see* Zail Singh
Singh, Sardar Swaran *see* Singh, Swaran
Singh, Swaran obit Jan 95
Singletary, Mike Mar 93
Singleton, John Feb 97
Sinise, Gary Apr 97
Sinopoli, Giuseppe Mar 91
Sinyavsky, Andrei D. obit May 97
Sirica, John J. obit Oct 92
Sister Wendy *see* Beckett, Wendy
Siza, Alvaro Feb 2000
Skelton, Red obit Nov 97
Skillin, Edward S. obit Yrbk 2000
Skocpol, Theda Aug 2000
Skolnick, Mark H. Jun 97
Skutt, V. J. obit Apr 93
Slater, Rodney Jan 99
Slaughter, Louise M. Apr 99
Slayton, Donald K. obit Aug 93
Sleeper, Ruth obit Feb 93
Slonimsky, Nicolas Feb 91 obit Mar 96
Smallwood, Joseph R. obit Mar 92
Smith, Anna Deavere Sep 94
Smith, Austin E. obit Jan 94
Smith, B. *see* Smith, Barbara
Smith, Barbara Jul 98
Smith, Bruce Mar 95
Smith, Carleton Sprague obit Nov 94
Smith, Cyril Stanley obit Oct 92
Smith, Dean Apr 94
Smith, Emmitt Nov 94
Smith, Frederick W. Jun 2000
Smith, Gerard C. obit Sep 94
Smith, Gregory White Mar 98
Smith, Hazel Brannon obit Jul 94
Smith, Hedrick Jun 91
Smith, James Todd *see* L.L. Cool J
Smith, Jeff Aug 91
Smith, Kevin Feb 98
Smith, Margaret Chase obit Aug 95
Smith, Mary Alice *see* Mary Alice
Smith, Mary Carter Feb 96
Smith, Mary Louise obit Nov 97
Smith, Merriman obit Nov 93
Smith, Oliver obit Mar 94
Smith, Ozzie Feb 97
Smith, Page obit Nov 95
Smith, Robert Sep 2000
Smith, Rosamund *see* Oates, Joyce Carol
Smith, Will Sep 96
Smith, William French obit Jan 91
Smith, Zadie Aug 2000
Smoot, George Apr 94
Snell, George D. obit Aug 96
Snipes, Wesley Sep 93
Snow, Clyde Collins Apr 97
Snowe, Olympia J. May 95
Snyder, Peggy Lou *see* Nelson, Harriet
Snyder, Solomon H. Apr 96
Sobchak, Anatoly Jul 92 obit Jul 2000
Soderbergh, Steven Oct 98
Soeharto Oct 92
Sokolow, Anna obit Sep 2000
Soldati, Mario obit Nov 99
Solti, Georg obit Nov 97
Somers, Jane *see* Lessing, Doris
Somes, Michael obit Feb 95
Sonnenfeld, Barry Nov 98
Sontag, Susan Feb 92
Sorel, Edward Mar 94
Sorkin, Aaron Jun 2000
Soros, George Apr 97
Sorvino, Mira Aug 98
Sosa, Sammy May 99
Soth, Lauren K(ephart) obit Jun 98
Souter, David H. Jan 91
Spacey, Kevin Apr 97
Speare, Elizabeth George obit Jan 95
Spears, Britney Apr 2000
Spencer, Lady Diana *see* Diana, Princess of Wales
Spender, Stephen obit Sep 95
Sperry, Roger W. obit Jun 94
Sperti, George Speri obit Jul 91
Spiegelman, Art Mar 94
Spielberg, Steven Feb 96
Spilhaus, Athelstan (Frederick) obit Jun 98
Spinola, Antonio De obit Nov 96
Spitzer, Lyman, Jr. obit Jun 97
Spivak, Lawrence E. obit May 94
Spivakov, Vladimir Feb 96
Spock, Benjamin (McLane) obit Jun 98
Spofford, Charles M. obit May 91
Sprague, Robert Chapman obit Nov 91
Springsteen, Bruce Aug 92
Stack, Andy *see* Rule, Ann
Stader, Maria obit Aug 99
Staggers, Harley O. obit Nov 91
Stahl, Lesley Jun 96
Stahr, Elvis J., Jr. obit Feb 99
Stallone, Michael Sylvester *see* Stallone, Sylvester
Stallone, Sylvester Feb 94
Stamos, Theodoros obit Apr 97
Stanford, Otis Binet *see* Whyte, William H. Jr.
Stanky, Eddie obit Aug 99
Stanley, Paul
Stans, Maurice H(ubert) obit Jun 98
Staples, Brent May 2000
Stapp, John Paul obit May 2000
Starr, Kenneth W. May 98
Starzl, Thomas E. Mar 93
Stassinopoulos, Arianna *see* Huffington, Arianna Stassinopoulos
Stavropoulos, George obit Feb 91
Steadman, Ralph May 99
Steber, Eleanor obit Jan 91
Steele, Shelby Feb 93
Steelman, John R. obit Nov 99
Stegner, Wallace obit Jun 93
Stein, Herbert obit Feb 2000
Steinberg, Saul obit Jul 99
Stennis, John C. obit Jul 95
Stephanopoulos, George Jan 95
Stern, Arthur Cecil obit Jul 92
Stern, David Apr 91
Stern, Howard Jan 96
Stern, Leonard Mar 91
Stern, Martha Dodd *see* Dodd, Martha
Stern, Richard Jun 94
Stern, Robert A. M. Jun 2000
Stevens, Edmund obit Jul 92
Stevens, Roger L(acey) obit Apr 98
Stevenson, Bryan Mar 96

Stevenson, McLean obit Apr 96
Stewart, Alice Jul 2000
Stewart, James obit Sep 97
Stewart, Martha Aug 93
Stewart, Patrick Aug 94
Stickney, Dorothy obit Aug 98
Stigler, George Joseph obit Feb 92
Stignani, Ebe obit Yrbk 91
Stiller, Ben Nov 99
Stine, Jovial Bob *see* STINE, R. L.
Stipe, Michael Apr 97
Stockton, John Jun 95
Stockwell, Dean Feb 91
Stoddard, Alexandra Jun 96
Stokes, Carl B. obit Jun 96
Stone, Matt May 98
Stone, Sharon Apr 96
Stoph, Willi obit Aug 99
Storms, Harrison A., Jr. obit Sep 92
Storr, Anthony Jun 94
Storr, Charles Anthony *see* Storr, Anthony
Stowe, Leland obit Mar 94
Strait, George Feb 2000
Strasberg, Susan obit Apr 99
Stratton, Julius A. obit Aug 94
Stratton, Samuel S. obit Jan 91
Strauss, Robert S. Jul 92
Streep, Meryl Mar 97
Street, Picabo Apr 98
Streeter, Ruth Cheney obit Jan 91
Strehler, Giorgio Mar 91 obit Mar 98
Streisand, Barbra Sep 92
Strossen, Nadine Oct 97
Strouse, Norman H. obit Mar 93
Stuart, Gloria Apr 98
Studer, Cheryl Apr 92
Styne, Jule obit Nov 94
Suchocka, Hanna Jan 94
Suenens, Léon Joseph, Cardinal obit Jul 96
Sui, Anna Jul 93
Suits, Chauncey Guy obit Oct 91
Sukarnoputri, Megawati Sep 97
Sullivan, Walter obit Jun 96
Sulloway, Frank J. Sep 97
Sulzberger, Arthur O., Jr. Jan 97
Sulzberger, C. L. obit Nov 93
Sumner, Jessie obit Oct 94
Sunderland, Thomas E. obit May 91
Suzuki, David T. Jul 95
Sveda, Michael obit Nov 99
Swank, Hilary Sep 2000
Swann, Donald obit May 94
Swayze, Patrick Mar 91
Sweeney, John J. Jun 96
Swidler, Joseph C. obit Jul 97
Swoopes, Sheryl Jul 96

Tafel, Richard L. Feb 2000
Taft, Robert, Jr. obit Feb 94
Tagliabue, Paul Oct 92
Tagliavini, Ferruccio obit Apr 95
Takeshi, Beat *see* Kitano, Takeshi
Takeshita, Noboru obit Nov 2000
Talbert, Billy obit Jun 99
Talbott, Strobe Jul 2000
Tamayo, Rufino obit Aug 91
Tambo, Oliver obit Jun 93
Tan, Amy Feb 92
Tanaka, Kakuei obit Feb 94
Tandy, Jessica obit Nov 94
Tannen, Deborah Jul 94
Tarantino, Quentin Oct 95
Tartikoff, Brandon obit Nov 97
Tata, J. R. D. obit Jan 94
Taubman, A. Alfred Jan 93
Taubman, Howard obit Mar 96
Tavener, John Jun 99
Taylor, Charles Sep 92
Taylor, Harold obit Apr 93
Taylor, Peter obit Jan 95
Taylor, Robert Lewis obit Jan 99
Taylor, Susan L. Feb 97
Taylor, Telford obit Aug 98
Taymor, Julie Feb 98
Telkes, Maria obit Oct 96
Teller *see* Penn & Teller
Tenet, George J. Aug 99
Teng Hsi-hsien *see* Deng Xiaoping
Teng Hsiao-ping *see* Deng Xiaoping
Teng Wen-pin *see* Deng Xiaoping
Tennstedt, Klaus obit Mar 98
Ter-Arutunian, Rouben obit Jan 93
Teresa, Mother obit Nov 97
Terra, Daniel J. obit Sep 96
Terrell, St. John obit Jan 99
Terry, Randall A. Jan 94
Tesich, Steve Aug 91 obit Sep 96
They Might Be Giants *see* Flansburgh, John
Thomas, Augusta Read Nov 99
Thomas, Clarence Apr 92
Thomas, Danny obit Apr 91
Thomas, Dave *see* Thomas, R. David
Thomas, Elizabeth Marshall Mar 96
Thomas, Frank Aug 94
Thomas-Graham, Pamela Jul 2000
Thomas, Helen Nov 93
Thomas, Jess obit Jan 94
Thomas, Lewis obit Feb 94
Thomas, Michael Tilson *see* Tilson Thomas, Michael
Thomas, R. David Mar 95
Thompson, Emma Mar 95
Thompson, Fred Aug 99
Thompson, Homer A. obit Yrbk 2000
Thompson, Kay obit Sep 98
Thompson, Kenneth
Thompson, Paul W. obit May 96
Thompson, Tommy G. Jul 95
Thomson, Rupert Feb 2000
Thorneycroft, Peter obit Aug 94
Thorp, Willard L. obit Jul 92
Thurman, Robert A. F. Sep 97
Thurman, Uma Aug 96
Thurmond, Strom Nov 92
Tilberis, Elizabeth *see* Tilberis, Liz
Tilberis, Liz Nov 98 obit Jul 99
Tillinghast, Charles C(arpenter) obit Oct 98
Tilson Thomas, Michael Jun 96
Timberlake, Justin *see* 'N Sync
Timerman, Jacobo obit Jan 2000
Timmerman, George Bell, Jr. obit Feb 95
Tinguely, Jean obit Oct 91
Tippett, Sir Michael (Kemp) obit Mar 98
Tipton, Jennifer Jul 97
Tobin, Richard L. obit Nov 95
Todd, Alexander obit Mar 97
Todd, Lord *see* Todd, Alexander
Tomba, Alberto May 93
Tomorrow, Tom Apr 2000
Tompkins, Ewell *see* Ewell, Tom
Topping, Norman (Hawkins) obit Jan 98

Tormé, Mel obit Aug 99
Torre, Joe May 97
Torrence, Gwen Jul 96
Torrey, E. Fuller Jul 98
Torvalds, Linus Jul 99
Toscani, Oliviero Sep 97
Totenberg, Nina Mar 96
Tower, John G. obit Jun 91
Townsend, Lynn A. obit Yrbk 2000
Townsend, Robert May 94
Townsend, Robert (Chase) obit Mar 98
Trampler, Walter obit Jan 98
Travell, Janet G. obit Oct 97
Travers, P. L. May 96 obit Jun 96
Travolta, John May 96
Tree, Marietta obit Oct 91
Trilling, Diana obit Jan 97
Trimble, David Jul 2000
Trinidad, Felix Feb 2000
Troyanos, Tatiana obit Oct 93
Troyat, Henri Mar 92
Trudeau, Arthur Gilbert obit Aug 91
Trueblood, D. Elton obit Mar 95
Trussell, Ray E. obit Feb 2000
Tryon, Thomas obit Nov 91
Tsongas, Paul E. obit Mar 97
Tudjman, Franjo Sep 97 obit May 2000
Tully, Alice obit Feb 94
Turabi, Hassan al- Jan 99
Ture, Kwame *see* Carmichael, Stokely
Turkle, Sherry Aug 97
Turnbull, Colin M. obit Sep 94
Turner, Donald F. obit Sep 94
Turner, Lana obit Sep 95
Turner, Robert Edward 3d *see* Turner, Ted
Turner, Ted Jun 98
Turow, Scott Aug 91
Turrell, James May 99
Turturro, John Oct 96
Tuttle, Charles E. obit Aug 93
Tuttle, Merlin D. Jun 92
Tyler, Richard May 97
Tyler, Steven Aug 96
Tyner, McCoy Aug 97
Tyson, Laura D'Andrea Sep 96
Tyson, Neil de Grasse May 2000

Uchida, Mitsuko Sep 91
Udall, Morris obit Mar 99
Ulanova, Galina (Sergeyevna) obit Jun 98
Vadim, Roger obit Aug 2000
Vajpayee, Atal Behari Aug 2000
Van Damme, Jean-Claude Mar 99
Van Duyn, Mona Jan 98
Van Fleet, James A. obit Nov 92
Van Horne, Harriet obit Mar 98
Van Peebles, Mario Nov 93
Van Sant, Gus Mar 92
Vandross, Luther Sep 91
Varmus, Harold E. Nov 96
Varnedoe, Kirk Feb 91
Vasarely, Victor obit May 97
Vega, Suzanne Aug 94
Velázquez, Nydia M. Jul 99
Venter, J. Craig Feb 95
Ventura, Jesse May 99
Verdi-Fletcher, Mary Jan 97
Vermeij, Geerat J. Jun 95
Vernon, Lillian Mar 96
Versace, Donatella Jun 98
Versace, Gianni Apr 93 obit Sep 97
Vicario, Arantxa Sánchez *see* Sánchez Vicario, Arantxa
Vieira Da Silva, Maria Helena obit 1992
Villain- Marais, Jean *see* Marais, Jean
Vincent, Fay May 91
Vine, Barbara *see* Rendell, Ruth
Viola, Bill May 98
Vogel, Paula Jul 98
Vogelstein, Bert Jan 96
Voigt, Deborah Jan 99
Voinovich, George V. May 97
Volpe, John A. obit Jan 95
Von Hayek, Friederich A. *see* Hayek, Friederich A. Von
Von Otter, Anne Sofie *see* Otter, Anne Sofie Von
Vonnegut, Kurt Mar 91
Voulkos, Peter Nov 97
Vrba, Elisabeth S. Jun 97

Wachner, Linda Nov 98
Wagner, Robert F., Jr. obit Apr 91
Waits, Tom Oct 97
Walcott, Joe obit May 94
Wald, George obit Jun 97
Wald, Patricia M. Jun 2000
Walesa, Lech May 96
Walker, Eric A. obit Apr 95
Walker, Jay Oct 2000
Walker, John obit Jan 96
Walker, Kara Mar 2000
Walker, Larry May 98
Walker, Margaret obit Jun 99
Walker, Mildred obit Aug 98
Walker, Nancy obit May 92
Wallace, George C(orley) obit Nov 98
Waller, Robert James May 94
Wallerstein, Judith S. Nov 96
Walsh, Chad obit Mar 91
Walsh, Lawrence E. Oct 91
Walsh, William B. obit Mar 97
Walton, Ernest T. S. obit Sep 95
Walton, Sam Mar 92 obit May 92
Ware, Wallace *see* Karp, David obit
Warne, William E. obit May 96
Warner, H. Ty *see* Warner, Ty
Warner, Ty Nov 98
Warren, Diane Jun 2000
Warren, Fletcher obit Mar 92
Warren, William C. obit Yrbk 2000
Washington, Alonzo May 99
Washington, Denzel Jul 92
Wasserman, Lew R. May 91
Waters, Maxine Nov 92
Watkins, Gloria *see* Hooks, Bell
Watson, Thomas J., Jr. obit Mar 94
Watts, J.C. Jr. Mar. 99
Watts, Julius Caesar *see* Watts, J. C. Jr.
Waxman, Henry A. Jul 92
Wayans, Damon Nov 99
Wayans, Keenen Ivory Feb 95
Wayne, David obit Apr 95
Weaver, Robert C. obit Oct 97
Webb, James E. obit May 92
Webb, Wellington E. Aug 99
Wedgwood, C. V. obit May 97
Wegman, William May 92
Wei Jingsheng Sep 97
Weicker, Lowell P., Jr. May 93
Weider, Joe Jan 98
Weidman, Jerome obit Jan 99
Weil, Andrew Aug 96
Weill, Sanford I. Jul 99
Weinstein, Bob Mar 97
Weinstein, Harvey Mar 97
Weiss, Ted obit Nov 92
Weld, William F. Feb 93
Welensky, Roy obit Feb 92
Welitsch, Ljuba obit Nov 96
Welk, Lawrence obit Jul 92
Wells, Herman B obit Aug 2000
Wells, Julia Elizabeth *see* Andrews, Julie
Wellstone, Paul D. May 93

Welsh, Irvine Nov 97
Welsh, Matthew E. obit Aug 95
Werblin, David A. obit Feb 92
Wertheimer, Linda Nov 95
West, Cornel Oct 93
West, Dorothy Feb 97 obit Oct 98
West, Morris L. obit Feb 2000
Weston, Brett obit Mar 93
Westwood, Vivienne Jul 97
Wexler, Nancy S. Aug 94
Wexner, Leslie Feb 94
Whelan, Wendy Oct 98
Whitaker, Forest Feb 97
White, Edmund Jan 91
White, Michael R. Mar 99
White, Reggie Nov 95
White, William S. obit Jun 94
Whitelaw, William obit Nov 99
Whitman, Christine Todd Jun 95
Whitman, Meg Feb 2000
Whittle, Christopher Feb 91
Whittle, Frank obit Oct 96
Whyte, William H. obit Mar. 99
Wickens, Aryness Joy obit Apr 91
Wideman, John Edgar Jan 91
Widnall, Sheila E. Oct 97
Wiesner, Jerome B. obit Jan 95
Wiest, Dianne Mar 97
Wigand, Jeffrey Apr 2000
Wigner, Eugene P. obit Mar 95
Wilbur, Dwight L. obit May 97
Wildmon, Donald Jan 92
Wiles, Andrew J. Mar 96
Wilkens, Lenny Jul 96
Wilkins, Dominique May 95
Wilkins, Roger Aug 94
Wilkinson, Bud *see* Wilkinson, Charles
Wilkinson, Charles obit May 94
Willes, Mark H. Mar 98
Williams, Anthony A. Oct 99
Williams, Brian Jul 98
Williams, Doug Feb 99
Williams, Errick *see* Williams, Ricky
Williams, Hank, Jr. Mar 98
Williams, Jody Mar 98
Williams, Joe obit Jun 99
Williams, John A. Oct 94
Williams, Lucinda Mar 99
Williams, Myrna *see* Loy, Myrna
Williams, Ricky Aug 99
Williams, Robin Jan 97
Williamson, Kevin Apr 2000
Williamson, Marianne Feb 93
Willis, Kelly Oct 99
Wilmut, Ian Jun 97
Wilson, A. N. Aug 93
Wilson, Angus obit Aug 91
Wilson, Cassandra Mar 98
Wilson, Don obit Yrbk 91
Wilson, Edward Foss obit May 94
Wilson, Flip obit Feb 99
Wilson, Harold obit Jul 95
Wilson, James Harold *see* Wilson, Harold
Wilson, John Burgess *see* Burgess, Anthony
Wilson, John Tuzo obit Aug 93
Wilson, Logan obit Jan 91
Wilson, Malcolm obit Aug 2000
Wilson, O. Meredith obit Feb 99
Wilson, Pete Apr 91
Wilson, Robert R. obit May 2000
Wilson, William Julius Feb 97
Wilt, Fred obit Nov 94
Winpisinger, William W(ayne) obit Feb 98
Wirth, Conrad L. obit Sep 93
Wirth, Timothy E. Mar 91
Witt, James Lee Mar 2000
Witten, Edward Jun 97
Wofford, Harris Apr 92
Wojtyla, Karol Jozef *see* John Paul II
Wolf, Naomi Nov 93
Wolfe, George C. Mar 94
Wolfensohn, James D. May 2000
Wolfert, Ira obit Feb 98
Wolff, Geoffrey Jan 97
Wolff, Tobias Jan 96
Wong Kar-Wai Apr 98
Woo, John Feb 99
Woodard, Alfre Feb 95
Woods, Eldrick *see* Woods, Tiger
Woods, Tiger Nov 97
Woodward, C. Vann obit Jun 2000
Woodward, Stanley obit Oct 92
Wörner, Manfred obit Oct 94
Worsham, Lew obit Jan 91
Worthington, Leslie B(erry) obit Oct 98
Wozniak, Stephen Jul 97
Wright, Archibald Lee *see* Moore, Archie
Wright, Helen obit Feb 98
Wright, Irving S(herwood) obit Mar 98
Wright, Jerauld obit Jul 95
Wright, Peter obit Jul 95
Wu, Chien Shiung obit Apr 97
Wu, Gordon Sep 96
Wu, Harry Feb 96
Wu, Peter Hongda *see* Wu, Harry
Wyatt, John Whitlow obit Nov 99
Wyatt, Wilson W. obit Aug 96
Wynder, Ernest L. obit Sep 99
Wynette, Tammy Jun 95 obit Jun 98
Wynonna May 96

Xenakis, Iannis Sep 94
Xiaoping, Deng *see* Deng Xiaoping

Yamaguchi, Kristi Jun 92
Yamamoto, Yohji Nov 2000
Yamanaka, Lois-Ann Jun 99
Yang, Jerry Oct 97
Yankovic, Alfred *see* Yankovic, "Weird Al"
Yankovic "Weird Al", Feb 99
Yarborough, Ralph W. obit Apr 96
Yarmolinsky, Adam obit Jun 2000
Yassin, Ahmed Jul 98
Yates, Sidney R. Aug 93
Yearwood, Patricia Lynn *see* Yearwood, Trisha
Yearwood, Trisha Jul 98
Yegorov, Boris obit Nov 94
Yeoh Chu-Kheng *see* Yeoh, Michelle
Yeoh, Michelle Jan 98
Yepes, Narciso obit Jul 97
Yerby, Frank obit Mar 92
Yergin, Daniel Nov 99
Yevtushenko, Yevgeny Mar 94
Yimou, Zhang *see* Zhang Yimou
Yoakam, Dwight Nov 2000
Yokich, Stephen P. Nov 98
Yorty, Sam(uel William) obit Aug 98
Young, Coleman (Alexander) obit Feb 98
Young, Loretta obit Nov 2000
Young, Neil Jan 98
Young, Robert obit Sep 98
Young, Steve Oct 93
Youngman, Henny obit May 98
Yount, Robin Jun 93

Youskevitch, Igor obit Aug 94
Yun-ho, Li *see* Chiang Ch'ing

Zaentz, Saul Mar 97
Zail Singh obit Mar 95
Zajick, Dolora May 2000
Zamora, Rubén Sep 91
Zappa, Frank obit Feb 94
Zedillo Ponce De León, Ernesto Apr 96
Zemeckis, Robert Sep 97
Zemin, Jiang *see* Jiang Zemin
Zhang Yimou Aug 92
Zhirinovsky, Vladimir Nov 95
Zhivkov, Todor obit Oct 98
Zim, Herbert S. obit Feb 95
Zimmerman, Robert *see* Dylan, Bob
Zinn, Howard Aug 99
Zinn, Walter H. obit Aug 2000
Zinnemann, Fred obit Jun 97
Ziskin, Laura Oct 97
Zolotow, Maurice obit May 91
Zorbaugh, Geraldine B. obit Sep 96
Zorn, John Aug 99
Zsigmond, Vilmos Oct 99
Zubrod, C. Gordon obit Jul 99
Zuckerman, Solly obit May 93
Zuckert, Eugene M. obit Yrbk 2000
Zumwalt, Bud *see* Zumwalt, Elmo R. obit
Zumwalt, Elmo R. obit Jun 2000
Zyuganov, Gennadi A. Oct 96